International Marketing

A Global Pers

Hans Mühlbacher

Lee Dahringer

Helmuth Leihs

INTERNATIONAL THOMSON BUSINESS PRESS

I(T)P® An International Thomson Publishing Company

London • Bonn • Johannesburg • Madrid • Melbourne • Mexico City • New York • Paris
Singapore • Tokyo • Toronto • Albany, NY • Belmont, CA • Cincinnati, OH • Detroit, MI

International Marketing

Copyright © 1999 International Thomson Business Press

 I **T** **P**   A division of International Thomson Publishing
The ITP logo is a trademark under licence

British Library Cataloguing-in-Publication Data
A catalogue record for this book is available from the British Library

First edition published 1991 by Addison-Wesley Publishing Company, Inc.
Second edition published 1999 by International Thomson Business Press

Typeset by J&L Composition Ltd, Filey, North Yorkshire
Cover and text design by Design Deluxe, Bath
Printed in Italy by L.E.G.O. Spa, Vincenza

ISBN 1–86152–456–0

International Thomson Business Press
Berkshire House
168–173 High Holborn
London WC1V 7AA
UK

http://www.itbp.com

CONTENTS

5 The Cultural Environment   169

6 International Marketing Intelligence   215

Each student who embarks on a course in international marketing brings with him or her a rich view of the world and marketing that was acquired within that student's particular domestic culture. Nevertheless, to be successful as an international marketing practitioner, the student must open his or her 'world view' to permit a thorough analysis of opportunities in other cultures. A major goal of the second edition of *International Marketing, A Global Perspective* is to broaden the way business students view international markets and marketing in order to encourage such an expanded view.

Most marketing managers view world markets internationally, or multinationally, as a series of discrete markets that do not share many characteristics. Yet worldwide opportunities and challenges presented by recent events – the sweeping changes in Middle and Eastern Europe, the economic integration of the European Union, the increasing liberalization and deregulation of world trade, the growth of markets as well as financial problems in the Asian Pacific area, the economic integration of Latin America, and the economic strength of the North American market – require new marketing management approaches to deal successfully with global competitors and suppliers in global markets. Most important, international marketers require a **global perspective** to compete successfully.

We do not argue that a marketer should sell the same thing, the same way, everywhere. But a company that believes it *must* overhaul its marketing mix for each separate country market errs as much as one that applies only domestic marketing solutions to international marketing problems.

International Marketing, A Global Perspective discusses the current challenges of international business and the impact of different perspectives of management on business behavior. It illustrates the driving forces of international business in the late 1990s: the limited growth in domestic markets, rapid technological change, increasing global competition, and global access to resources.

Whatever perspective management takes, the leaders of a firm have to answer four fundamental questions: (1) Should the company enter international markets and is it able to conduct international operations? (2) What markets should be served? (3) How much of the firm's resources should we spend for what purpose? (4) How to build and sustain the firm's competitive advantage? This text presents a decision oriented framework to answer those questions.

International Marketing: A Global Perspective is written for the student who is interested in international business and who has completed a principles of marketing course. Thus, some knowledge is assumed on the part of the student, as basic concepts are applied internationally.

PHILOSOPHY

The underlying assertion of this book is that *any firm – regardless of size – can compete globally*. Success is a function of perspective, opportunity, motivation, knowledge and skills. International opportunities are plentiful. The challenge for today's marketing manager is to identify those opportunities appropriate for the firm, to develop an appropriate marketing strategy, and to build and sustain competitve advantages in cooperation with other members of the firm as well as external partners.

APPROACH AND ORGANIZATION

The book's four sections, as illustrated in the Exhibit 1, make the global approach to international marketing accessible to the student.

↔ Part One deals with the factors **motivating** a marketing manager to enter international markets.

↔ Part Two looks at the process of **assessing potential markets**, then matching market potential with a company's ability to market effectively.

↔ From that assessment, Part Three takes the student through the process of taking **basic strategic decisions** that guide the application of marketing tools. Managers must develop a portfolio of markets and technologies, choose a competitive strategy, build an infrastructure of management systems, and determine intended local market positions as well as market-entry modes.

↔ Part Four then discusses the process of implementing the strategic decisions by **building and sustaining** competitive advantages through product management, distribution and sales, market communication, and price management. The book ends with a discussion of how the results of various analyses and decisions on different hierarchical levels of decision may be summarized into a business plan.

To develop and implement successfully a global marketing perspective, an international marketer must be systematic in dealing with opportunities and threats. This book presents a systematic approach to global marketing decision making. Part Two, for example, which deals with assessing potential markets, addresses the important issues in the same logical order used by a global marketer. While the marketer first examines its business mission and philosophy to determine the relevant market characteristics to be looked at, in a second step it assesses those characteristics in the economic, political and legal, and cultural environments of various country-markets. Then, local product-markets are more closely analyzed in a small group of attractive country-markets. Finally, the firm's potential is evaluated and compared to the market opportunities identified, as well as the potential of important competitors.

WHY YOU SHOULD USE THIS TEXT

The turn of the century promises to be economically, socially, and politically turbulent. Fundamental changes will continue to occur in all parts of the world. Although any textbook can become somewhat outdated through the speed of those changes, *International Marketing, A Global Perspective* will remain useful because it provides a structured approach for analyzing

Exhibit 1   A GENERAL FRAMEWORK FOR GLOBAL MARKETING

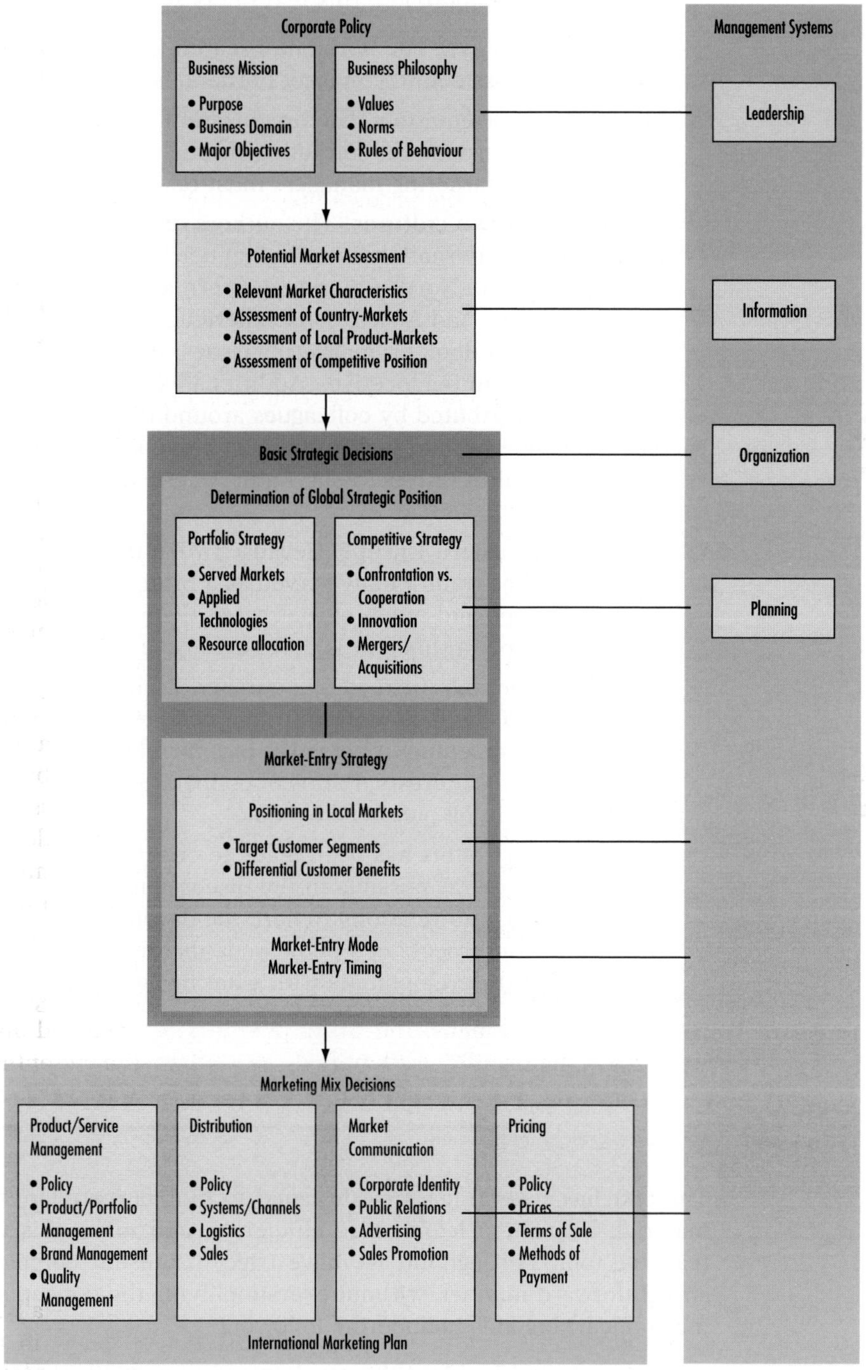

dynamic changes. The student is responsible for remaining current with world affairs. Both the analytical framework, which addresses such issues, and the global marketing perspective in this book will be valid in rapidly changing environments. Perhaps the global approach is necessary, not only to help a firm be aware of changes and their impact, but also to help it adjust successfully to such changes, which is the key to long-term survival.

To support this approach, this text offers several unique features.

↔ **Global perspective.** The horizontal search for strategically equivalent segments, across country-market borders, is a predominant theme.

↔ **Management orientation.** The organization of this book introduces students to international marketing through the decisions that international marketing managers must take.

↔ **Authors from two cultures.** The authors of the text have extensive experience in international marketing teaching, research, management, and consulting in North America, Eastern and Western Europe, Australia, India, and Africa. This experience has resulted in a truly international outlook on marketing issues, versus the more conventional U.S. or European perspective. Additionally, a host of case studies and examples contributed by colleagues around the world strengthens our global perspective and makes this text come alive to students whether they are based in Europe, Asia, Latin America, North America or Australasia.

↔ **Middle and Eastern Europe.** Because two authors are from Austria, a nation that has traditionally served as a bridge between Middle and Eastern Europe and much of the rest of the world, the coverage of Eastern Europe in this text is more extensive than in other texts.

↔ **Systemic approach.** Instead of a cursory discussion of relationship marketing, this book is written from a perspective that conceives business as happening in networks of interrelated social units with more or less different interests. Forms of cooperation as well as confrontation are discussed in all parts of the book.

↔ **Current.** Every effort has been made to ensure that the material in the text is as current as possible in the discussion of global trends, environments, and relations. Where the developments are faster than the production process of a book students are invited to update and compare latest developments with what has been said in the text.

TEACHING AND LEARNING

The text has several features designed to motivate students' interest in the material, help them learn more efficiently, and make this text an effective teaching tool. Throughout, we have tried to present complex material in a straightforward manner, without oversimplifying the concepts. Various teaching and learning aids include the following:

↔ **International Incident.** Every chapter begins with an International Incident, a factual illustration of the chapter's international marketing concepts with a global perspective.

↔ **Boxes.** Discussions in boxed material highlight global approaches to cultural, ethical, strategic, and future issues that affect marketing.

↔ **Impact on the Marketing Mix.** All chapters discussing parts of the marketing mix contain a section which encourages the student to be sensitive to how each element in the international mix affects the others, and to recognize the highly dynamic nature of marketing management.

↔ **End-of-Chapter Discussion Questions.** These questions provide a way for students to check their comprehension of the key issues discussed in the chapter. Some questions are appropriate for mini-projects, while others will stimulate class discussion. These questions also serve an excellent vehicle for review of the chapter material.

↔ **Suggested Additional Readings.** The readings suggested at the end of each chapter allow the students to go into further details concerning some points of special interest discussed in the chapter.

↔ **Cases.** Each part of the text concludes with more complex, current cases which allow for management oriented application of the material discussed in that part.

↔ **Artwork, Photos, and Maps.** Each chapter contains artwork, tables, figures, maps or photos that supplement and illustrate the chapter discussion.

↔ **Supplementary Teaching Material.** An instructors' manual, Powerpoint presentation pack and Internet resources are available to lecturers who adopt *International Marketing: A Global Perspective*. These materials are designed to provide assistance to the instructor in several ways:

 ↔ To provide valuable and time-saving support material and resources for the instructor

 ↔ To make teaching the course using this text even easier

 ↔ To help in the preparation of lectures and discussion sessions with the students

Internet resources to accompany the text can be found in the resources area of the ITBP website at www.itbp.com. The website includes continuously updated support material for lecturers and students including: overviews of each chapter in the book, links to useful international marketing sites on the world wide web and Powerpoint slides to download directly frrom the site.

ACKNOWLEDGMENTS

All textbooks are the result of a team effort. In this case, with parts written on two different continents, it is especially true. We appreciate those educational institutions that provided support and encouragement during the writing and revision of the text: Leopold-Franzens University Innsbruck, Innsbruck, Austria; Ecole Supérieure de Sciences Economiques et Commerciales (ESSEC), Cergy-Pontoise, France; College of Business, Butler University, Indianapolis, Indiana, USA.

Even more important than institutional support is the professional support, encouragement and input provided by academic colleagues around the world. The authors and the publishers would like to thank the following individuals who helped us to make this edition even bigger and better than the first edition.

Susan Bridgewater	Warwick Business School
David Gillingham	Dublin Institute of Technolgy
Harald Koerber	DATACON
Michael McDermott	University of Strathclyde
Anja Moessmer	University of Innsbruck
Charles Pahud de Mortanges	University of Maastricht
Christian Pinson	INSEAD
Milton Pressley	University of New Orleans
Stuart Rooks	Oxford Brookes University
Elyette Roux	Ecole Supérieure de Sciences Economiques et Commerciales (ESSEC)
Bodo Schlegelmilch	Vienna University of Economics & Business Administration
Jon Swift	Staffordshire University
Jeryl Whitelock	University of Salford
Hildegard Wiesehoefer-Climpson	University of Derby
Van Wood	Virginia Commonwealth University

The authors would also like to thank the various people involved in the production and design of the text, Jennifer Pegg, Acquisitions Editor; Jenny Clapham, Developmental Editor; Penny Grose, Production Editor; and Melinda and Nick Welch from Design Deluxe.

INTERNATIONAL MARKETING – MOTIVATION AND PROCESS

The history of mankind is characterized by the exchange of ideas, emotions, goods and services. Since the early days of human existence activities to ensure daily survival have been split between people. In modern times this division of labour has become increasingly structured. Different tasks are split between people in a multitude of organizations as well as between countries. The exchange of goods and services has increasingly taken place in the form of trade between businesses and other organizations from an increasing number of countries. From the early days of barter between neighbouring communities to today's large-scale international trade, the result of these exchanges has been the same: customers have been provided with more and different goods at lower prices than would have been possible if trade had not occurred.

Historically, increasing trade liberalization has contributed strongly to the growth of the wealth of nations. World trade, for example, has grown 540 times since the year 1820. In 1820 only 1 per cent of total production was exported, whereas 13.5 per cent went to other countries in the mid-1990s. Where once many national markets were difficult to enter because of natural or artificial barriers, the liberalization of world trade has opened up new markets in almost all regions of the world.

The remarkable level of world trade today has led to an economic environment in which all countries are economically interdependent. In view of this interdependency, an increasing number of countries have decided to cooperate more closely economically, which, in turn, reinforces tendencies to economic integration between countries in many regions of the world. Liberalization and economic integration not only provide new business opportunities, however. They also require all kinds of business organizations to adapt to those changes and to be managed in such a way as to master increasing international competition.

PART I

Chapter 1 discusses the current challenges of international business. In addition, it illustrates the driving forces of international business in the late 1990s: the limited growth in domestic markets, rapid technological change, increasing global competition, and global access to resources.

Confronted with the increasing globalization of trade and the driving forces of international business at the end of the twentieth century, a firm's management has to assess the company's market opportunities and threats as well as its strengths and weaknesses from a different perspective compared to strictly local business. Chapter 2 compares the impact of an ethnocentric versus polycentric, regional or geocentric perspective of management on business behaviour.

Whatever perspective management takes, the leaders of a firm have to answer four fundamental questions: (1) Should the company conduct international operations, and is it able to do so? (2) Which markets should be served? (3) How much of the firm's resources should we spend for what purpose? (4) How do we build and sustain the firm's competitive advantage? Chapter 2 discusses external and internal triggers and factors of influence which determine the way those questions are handled by top management.

One of the most important factors influencing a company's long-term market success is to ensure a steady flow of resources to and from the company. Therefore, it is critical to manage relationships with customers and other important stakeholders of the firm in a way that satisfies their expectations. Building and maintaining such relationships is the major focus of marketing. There are two basically different ways in which marketing managers can approach international business, a multinational and a global approach. Chapter 2 describes international marketing as a business perspective based on product–market orientation, the exploitation of experience curve effects, global market analysis, and the decision between standardization and adaptation of programmes and processes; and as a strategic approach to international business which relates to environmental conditions from a systems perspective and helps to answer the questions of which markets to serve, how to allocate the available resources and how to build and sustain competitive advantage.

Finally, the chapter introduces a logical sequence of analyses and decisions which lead to the development of an international marketing plan. This so-called 'International Marketing Decision Process' starts from corporate policy, and contains the assessment of potential markets, the determination of the firm's competitive advantages, the development of a global strategic position and entry strategies for the chosen markets. It leads to an international marketing plan that contains all the marketing mix decisions. This marketing decision framework represents the structure of the rest of the book.

THE CHALLENGE OF GLOBALIZATION

```
┌─────────────────────────────────────────┐
│          INTERNATIONAL INCIDENT          │
└─────────────────────────────────────────┘
```

'Europe's Competitive Position in the Second Half of the 1990s'

Peter Brabeck-Letmathe took over the position of chief executive officer of Nestlé, the world's biggest marketer of food products, in 1997. He directs a company with annual sales above USD50 billion and a multinational workforce of more than 200 000 people. In an interview he described his view of Europe's competitive position as follows:

The current growth rates in Europe cannot ensure the given standard of living. Globalization of production and communication has led to a change in worldwide economic structures to which Europe's reaction is somewhat slow.

America adapted its structures much earlier, in the typical American way. They experienced high social costs, but today America is more competitive than Europe. They have shown that employment is created through fast reaction. Who reacts first, gains business, who reacts late, loses. Speed is all-important. Following the rules of a free market economy, there must be winners and losers. The question is, how can we construct a network of social security that provides losers with opportunities to become winners again, without offering a social hammock losers find so comfortable that they do not want to leave it anymore?

Asia has never known cultural and social conditions similar to Europe. A social network in the European sense has never existed. This allows a great deal of aggressiveness in the market based on a strong competitive position. In addition, because of the highly developed communication technology, know-how transfer is accomplished very quickly today. Barriers such as existed in former times can no longer be erected.

But Asia will not march off. Europe has got some strengths to take action against it. Most important is the more deeply rooted know-how. It has grown over many decades and is based on a high general level of education. Other important resources are brands, design and culture. If Europe succeeds in combining those in new, innovative ways, it can keep its competitive position.

Source: Adapted from: 'Es ist eine Frage der Geschwindigkeit', *Der Standard*, 28 March 1996, p. 17.

GLOBALIZATION OF TRADE

Historical Development

The history of world trade is one of exotic products coming from faraway lands to customers eager to buy something new. The southern islands of the Philippines, for example, were the centre of a trading hub throughout Southeast Asia in the fourth century. Camphor from Borneo, cloves from the Moluccas and parrots from New Guinea were all traded in the area. Today, a 'typical European consumer' may wake up to an alarm clock made in Korea, drink coffee imported from Columbia, drive a Volvo from Sweden, listen to rock and roll recorded in the USA, wear shirts from Guatemala, let the kids play on a PC manufactured in Taiwan, using software produced in India, while keeping track of the time with a Swiss watch. From the early days of barter between neighbouring communities to today's large-scale international trade, the result has been the same: customers have been provided with more and different goods at lower prices than would have been possible if international trade had not occurred.

According to a study by OECD (Organization for Economic Cooperation and Development, a Paris-based organization – including 29 members (1997) representing more than two-thirds of total world production – which focuses on the planning, coordination, and intensification of economic cooperation and development (see Table 1.1)),[1] the global economy has been growing for 200 years, following a period of 300 years of stagnation. In 1820 Asia was the most important region in the world in terms of production. It contained 70 per cent of the world's population and produced 58 per cent of its total goods. With growing industrialization Europe took the lead because traditions and bureaucracy impeded the economic and social changes needed in Asia. The world wars in the first half of the twentieth century resulted in industrial dominance by the USA. Today Southeast Asia has become the most economically dynamic region of the world again. And Europe is in danger, this time, of experiencing a setback due to too large a bureaucracy and social inflexibility.

In 1820 the world population had reached one billion but rose to reach 5.4 billion in 1992. Despite this enormous growth in population, average per capita income had multiplied by eight, from USD650 in 1820 to USD5,145 in 1992. Four major driving forces have been fundamental to this development:

↔   technological change – which was led by the UK until 1913 when the USA took over the leading position followed by Germany and Japan;

↔   accumulation of capital – needed to finance the development of new products and increasd productivity in production and marketing processes;

↔   human resources – allowing faster implementation of new technologies based on increasing levels of education, specific skills and more efficient management;

↔   liberalization of trade – leading to more competition which has been a strong driver for productivity gains and improvements in the quality of products and services.

By 1994 world trade had reached a total of USD4,060 billion. Of this amount, 68 per cent was contributed by the most highly industrialized nations of Western Europe, North America and Japan. They are called the 'Triad'. With some 900 million consumers, less than one-fourth of the world's population, these 20 nations account for about 70 per cent of the world's Gross National Product (GNP) – a measure of a country's total domestic and foreign economic value added claimed by the residents of the country – which reached USD24,257 billion in 1993.[2]

In 1997 the leading countries in world trade were the same as in the previous years: the USA, Japan and Germany followed by France and the UK (Table 1.2). The next ranks were filled by the other big Western industrialized countries: Italy, Canada, the Netherlands and Belgium (together with Luxembourg). Only Hong Kong (reintegrated into China in 1997, but counted as a seperate geographical unit) had managed to squeeze in on rank

---

Table 1.1 THE ORGANIZATION FOR ECONOMIC COOPERATION AND DEVELOPMENT (OECD)

OBJECTIVES: Planning, coordination and deepening of economic cooperation and development;

MEMBERS: Australia, Austria, Belgium, Canada, Czech Republic, Denmark, Finland, France, Germany, Greece, Hungary, Ireland, Iceland, Italy, Japan, Luxembourg, Mexico, Netherlands, New Zealand, Norway, Poland, Portugal, South Korea, Spain, Sweden, Switzerland, Turkey, UK, USA;

ACTIVITIES: In all economically and socially relevant sectors, such as trade, agriculture, fishing, sea transportation, energy (IEA = International Energy Agency), capital markets and capital transfers, taxation systems, labour force, policies concerning: development, environmental protection, education, science, technology, industries, city and regional development;

PUBLICATIONS: about 250 a year, including analyses and forecasts of the economic and social status of member countries.

The members of OECD represent only 20 per cent of the world population, but they account for more than two-thirds of total world production and up to four-fifths of aid to industrially developing countries.

Source: Baratta, M. (ed.) (1995), *Der Fischer Weltalmanach '96*, Frankfurt a.M.: Fischer Taschenbuch Verlag, 859f.

Table 1.2 THE LEADING COUNTRIES IN WORLD TRADE 1997
In 1997 the USA and Germany were the leading countries in world trade.

1997	(1994)	IMPORTS IN BILLION USD	1997	(1994)	1997	(1994)	EXPORTS IN BILLION USD	1997	(1994)
1	(1)	USA	817.8	(689.1)	1	(1)	USA	622.9	(512.6)
2	(2)	Germany	445.0	(370.1)	2	(2)	Germany	513.5	(414.5)
3	(3)	Japan	349.5	(266.5)	3	(3)	Japan	411.2	(387.9)
4	(4)	UK	283.6	(220.0)	4	(4)	France	289.6	(220.7)
5	(5)	France	275.9	(217.9)	5	(5)	UK	258.3	(169.0)
6	(6)	Italy	207.0	(160.4)	6	(6)	Italy	250.7	(178.7)

Source: Adapted from Baratta, M. (ed.) (1995), *Der Fischer Weltalmanach '96*, Frankfurt a.M.: Fischer Taschenbuch Verlag and *The Wall Street Journal Europe – Putting the Euro on the Map*, 1998.

eight. The following ranks of the list impressively demonstrated the consolidated position of Southeast Asian countries in world trade. The Peoples Republic of China, Taiwan, Singapore and the Republic of South Korea had established themselves as more important in both exports and imports than other European countries like Spain, Sweden or Switzerland and big exporters of raw materials such as Mexico, Australia and Russia. They contributed the most to the 30 per cent share of world trade held by developing economies in 1997. Together with Indonesia, Malaysia and Thailand, which had also been developing rapidly economically in the last decade, they are referred to as the 'newly industrialized countries' (NICs) of Southeast Asia. Up to 1997 those countries achieved growth rates of GNP up to 10 per cent. Figure 1.1 shows the increase in trade between the Triad and the NICs from 1988 to 1994. This development was severely hit by the financial crisis of most of the NICs in 1997/98 and the following economic recession in Japan.

Only 0.3 per cent of international trade was contributed by the economically less developed countries (LDCs) of Africa and Asia. In 42 of those countries, GNP per capita decreased in the first half of the 1990s, often due to political instability and too high a national debt.

As a result of increasing international trade, buyers around the world – especially in the most economically developed markets, but also a growing number of consumers in the newly industrialized countries – have become accustomed to being able to obtain goods that have been produced in many other nations. In the past decade, soaring growth rates in the Pacific Rim, for example, have created a new class of urban, professional women with money to spend on designer goods. The rise of the Asia-Pacific market has been monitored by the Comité Colbert, a trade association for the leading names in French couture, perfume and other luxury items. Between 1984 and 1994, annual sales for Comité Colbert members in the region increased to USD2 billion from USD523 million. The market is not largely synonymous with Japan anymore, as was the case 20 years ago. Hong Kong, for example, now accounts for more than 15 per cent of sales in the region, and even developing countries such as Malaysia and Thailand are showing 'discrete but promising beginnings' as purchasers of luxury fashion and accessories.[3] The consequences of the financial crisis in 1997/98 have slowed down that development for the time being. But customers all over the world want to obtain the best products at the best possible prices. Hence, to be successful today, most businesses must be able to market to, and to satisfy, customers in a global marketplace.

Trade Liberalization

When there are barriers to trade, whether natural or artificial, customers' choices are limited and they end up paying higher prices or being forced to accept lower quality. For example, until 1993 India was a closed market for automobiles. As a consequence, the average vehicle there is 20 years old and technologically unsophisticated. Because domestically produced cars did not have to compete with imports, Indian manufacturers did not use the latest technology in styling or engineering. Maruti is the country's only well-established modern car maker, a firm owned jointly by the government and by Japan's Suzuki, which had 75 per cent of the new-car market in 1996, selling cars based on 1970s technology. Its best-selling model in 1996 was an 800cc car without any modern anti-pollution equipment. Only in 1996 did new emission standards come into force.[4] The Strategy box describes some problems of a foreign car maker trying to establish itself in the fast growing (25 per cent a year) Indian car market and how it planned to overcome them.

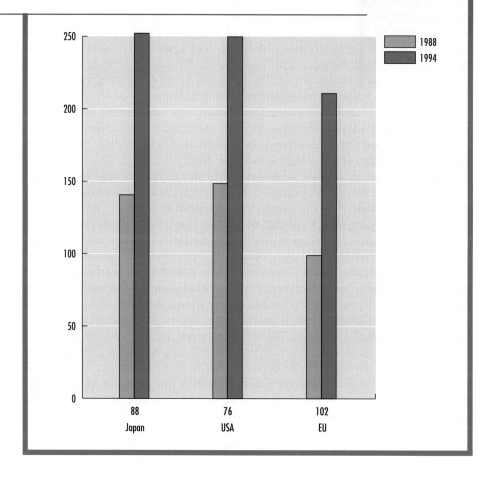

Figure 1.1 INCREASE IN TRADE BETWEEN THE TRIAD AND THE NICs (1988–1994)

Trade between the USA, Japan and Europe and the newly industrialized countries has nearly doubled in seven years between 1988 and 1994.

Source: IMF, 1995.

Barriers to trade also run counter to continual improvement of productivity. Thanks to bureaucratic dictates that have long favoured coordination over competition, Japan's telecommunications market remained dominated until 1997 by a handful of companies that only reluctantly pushed down prices. Even simple services taken for granted in other countries remained extremely expensive. A new home-telephone line, for example, cost 72,000 yen (about USD674) in 1996. Relying on legal barriers that kept long-distance and foreign companies from making international connections, Japan's three international carriers acted as expensive gatekeepers to the domestic market. A business call to the USA from Japan cost two to three times more than the same call placed from the USA. Business use of the Internet required special high-speed leased lines from NTT (Nippon Telegraph & Telephone Corp.) that cost four to five times more than they cost in the USA. The existing barriers to free trade did not do the competitiveness of Japanese telecom-equipment makers much good, since it deprived them of a thriving home market in which to hone their technology. Despite exploding global demand for telecommunications equipment, Japanese exports of such equipment have fallen since 1994, while imports have risen.[5]

STRATEGY BOX

Hyundai goes it alone

A FUTURISTIC STAND WITH DANCING GIRLS AND FLASHY sports cars helped Hyundai of South Korea to be the star of India's recent auto show. It has also upstaged its rivals by becoming the first foreign company to win the government's approval to set up a wholly foreign-owned car-making project in the country (though the government has allowed Volvo to make lorries and General Motors' Delphi division to make car parts).

Although technically not a change of policy, India's go-ahead for Hyundai and the others is being taken as a signal of the government's belief that the larger a foreign stake in a venture, the greater the prospect of large amounts of cash and new technology flowing into India. If so, it is something of a blow to India's domestic producers, some of which might anyway have found it hard to come up with their share of investment for joint ventures in the next few years.

Hyundai doubts the ability of local manufacturers to produce good quality cars, and therefore rejected their demands for a majority stake in any joint venture. It ended discussions with Bajaj Auto (which is now talking to Chrysler and Fuji Heavy Industries), the London-based Hinduja family (which controls Ashok Leyland), a lorry and bus company, and is talking to Toyota and its affiliate Daihatsu) and Eicher (which makes commercial vehicles, motor bikes and tractors, and might join up with Volkswagen).

Many outsiders suspect that joint ventures, particularly 50–50 ones such as those set up by Ford and Suzuki, are a recipe for managerial clashes and indecision. Already there are rumours that Toyota, Chrysler and Fuji might now consider going it alone.

Hyundai won over the government by promising that it would more than cover the cost of equipment imports with vehicle exports; it also said that it would buy 80 per cent of its components in India when it starts production in 1988, rising to 100 per cent by 2001 (something no other company has been brave enough to suggest). That struck a chord with a government worried about the impact of a ballooning import bill for car parts. Hyundai also says it will float off 40 per cent of the equity in its new Indian arm.

Source: 'Hyundai goes it alone', *The Economist*, 2 March 1996, p. 63.

Historically, increasing trade liberalization has contributed strongly to the growth of the wealth of nations. World trade, for example, has grown 540 times since 1820. In 1820 only 1 per cent of total production was exported, 13.5 per cent went to other countries in the mid-1990s. Western European countries had an average export share as high as 30 per cent.

Where once many national markets were difficult to enter because of natural or artificial barriers, the liberalization of world trade has opened up new markets in almost all regions of the world. The most important institution concerned with the rules of world trade has been GATT – the General Agreement on Tariffs and Trade. Its more than 130 members have agreed to respect the most favoured nation clause which stipulates that favourable tariff and trade agreements between two member countries must be applied to all other GATT members, too. Exceptions are allowed for developing countries and import restrictions on volumes in case of severe problems concerning a country's balance of payments. A milestone on the way to entirely free world trade has been the treaty signed by 128 GATT members in 1994 which brought an end to seven years of negotiations in the 'Uruguay Round' (called after the

Table 1.3 THE ECONOMIC EFFECTS OF THE URUGUAY ROUND
An econometric study of the effects to expect from the decisions taken at the Uruguay Round has provided the results given in this table.

COUNTRY	SHORT-TERM EFFECTS		LONG-TERM EFFECTS	
	IN BILLION USD (1992)	IN % OF GDP	IN BILLION USD (1992)	IN % OF GDP
Argentina	0.7	0.3	2.3	1.0
Australia	1.2	0.4	3.3	1.1
Brazil	1.4	0.3	4.3	1.1
Canada	1.3	0.2	2.6	0.5
China	1.3	0.3	2.0	0.5
EU (members 1994)	39.3	0.6	0.9	0.7
Indonesia	1.3	1.1	2.6	2.1
Japan	16.9	0.5	22.7	0.6
Malaysia	1.8	3.3	5.0	8.8
Mexico	0.2	0.0	2.3	0.7
New Zealand	0.4	1.0	1.4	3.6
Philippines	0.9	1.6	2.4	4.4
Singapore	0.9	2.1	0.7	1.7
South Korea	4.8	1.5	0.5	2.5
Taiwan	0.4	0.2	1.1	0.5
Thailand	2.5	2.1	12.6	10.9
Latin America	1.3	0.4	4.7	1.7
Africa south of Sahara	−0.3	−0.2	−0.7	-0.4
Middle East/North Africa	−0.3	−0.1	1.5	0.3
Eastern Europe	−0.2	−0.1	1.2	0.1
Developing countries	19.4	0.4	55.2	1.2
Industrialized countries	76.7	0.4	115.4	0.6
World	96.0	0.4	170.6	0.7

Source: Harrison, G., Th. Rutherford and D. Tarr (1995) 'Die Quantifizierung der Ergebnisse der Uruguay-Runde', *Finanzierung & Entwicklung*, December, pp. 36–39.

country where negotiations were started). It led to the establishment of WTO, the World Trade Organization, which replaced GATT as from 1 January 1995. WTO watches over members' compliance with the rules laid down in the treaty. The basic rules are:

↔ reciprocity – equivalency of trade policy actions between WTO members;
↔ liberalization – reduction of tariffs and non-tariff barriers;
↔ non-discrimination – in particular, realization of the most favoured nation clause.

The treaty also contained further liberalization in the trade of services as well as industrial and agricultural goods, an improvement in the protection of intellectual property rights (for example, patents) and anti-dumping rules (that is, rules prohibiting sales below cost). As a result of such changes, world trade is expected to increase by 20 per cent (USD755 billion) compared to 1992, with major beneficiaries expected to be both the highly industrialized and the newly industrialized countries (see Table 1.3).

FUTURE ISSUES
BOX

Worldwide

Free Trade

HERE IS AN IDEA WHOSE TIME IS COMING: WORLD FREE trade. It is still some way off. Most people would probably dismiss the concept as utopian, if not frightening. But it need not be either. And it is gradually creeping onto the international agenda.

On both sides of the Atlantic the global economy is often seen as a threat rather than an opportunity. Instead of dramatic new global initiatives, governments are focusing on the construction of regional free trade areas, in the Pacific, in the Americas and in and around an expanded European Union, to name but the three biggest.

A large new rock, however, has just been thrown into the pond. At the first Asia-Europe summit meeting in Bangkok, Asia challenged Europe to open its markets in step with the dismantling of trade barriers in the Asia-Pacific Economic Cooperation forum. APEC is committed to free trade among its industrial members by 2010, with developing countries following 10 years later.

That presents the Europeans with an awkward dilemma. If they fail to take up the Asian challenge, they risk seeing their goods shut out of the APEC free trade area, which will account for half of the world trade.

Assuming the APEC plan goes ahead, that could split the world into two potentially hostile blocs, one centered in Europe, the other on APEC, which includes the United States, China, Japan and most other countries of the Pacific Rim. If, however, the Europeans agree to match APEC's liberalization, they will in effect have taken a big step toward global free trade.

In the end it is quite simple. A global economy needs global rules. If half the world can commit to free trade by 2020, the other half can, too.

Source: Dale, R. (1996), 'Coming Soon: Worldwide Free Trade', *International Herald Tribune*, 8 March, p. 11.

China has not yet managed to become a member of WTO. Core areas that remain unresolved before the country may enjoy permanent most favoured nation status include subsidies to state industry, the weak dispute-resolution process in Chinese courts, product standards that discriminate against imports, and access to agricultural markets. Meanwhile, Chinese import duties remain four times as high as those of Japan. And to serve markets such as consumer electronics and automobiles, international marketers must manufacture locally and transfer key technologies. Service sectors, such as banking, media and telecommunications, are virtually off-limits.[6] The Future Issues box discusses potential future developments in world trade liberalization reaching far beyond the current state.

Critics of trade liberalization charge that it has a negative influence on employment rates in the highly industrialized countries. The move to open economic systems has initiated a process that is putting 1.2 billion workers in economically less developed countries into worldwide product and labour markets over the next generation. Most of these workers currently earn less than USD3 a day, while the approximately 250 million workers in Western Europe and the USA earn about USD85 a day. With relatively modern technology, the workforce in less industrialized countries can produce from 85 to

100 per cent of the output of their Western compatriots. Considering the major difficulties of manufacturers in highly industrialized countries brought about by the 90 million workers in Japan and the NICs in the past 30 years provides some insight into the difficulties that can be expected to take place in the West in the years ahead.

Economic Integration

Economic Interdependency. The remarkable level of world trade today has led to an economic environment in which all countries are economically interdependent. Even the USA, which represents the biggest national market of the highly industrialized countries, is far from self-sufficient. The country imports, for example, almost all VCRs, bananas and coffee. Japan, which has become famous for its export power in previous years, depends on imports for 90 per cent of its energy needs. More farmland in the USA than in Japan is used to feed the Japanese. Table 1.4 gives an overview of the interdependencies of the leading nations in world trade. The countries depend upon trade with each other to help their citizens to achieve and to ensure a high standard of living.

Table 1.4 shows that some of the economically leading countries in the world, such as the USA or the UK, tended to run trade deficits in the 1990s, whereas others like Japan, Germany or France achieved trade surpluses. Germany, for example, had trade surpluses of USD144.4 billion in 1994 and USD68.5 billion in 1997.[7] Because of its trade deficits since the late 1980s and despite its earlier role as the world's leading supplier of capital, the USA has become the world's leading debtor nation. In 1995 the US trade deficit in goods and services widened from USD106.21 billion in 1994 to USD111.04 billion as the country ran record trade gaps with both China (USD33.8 billion) and Mexico (USD15.4 billion). In goods alone, the USA ran a record deficit of USD174.47 billion. However, this imbalance was offset somewhat by a surplus in services, such as tourism and consulting fees, of USD63.4 billion in 1995. The trade deficit with Japan declined 9.7 per cent in 1995 to USD59.28 billion. While that gap was still the largest for any single country, it marked the first decline in four years and represented the first time since 1989 that US imports of Japanese cars fell.[8]

How strongly the individual economies are interdependent is also demonstrated by the global capital markets. The unification of Germany in the early 1990s led to a short boom in former West Germany's economy owing to high public investments in the infrastructure of former East Germany. Resulting high inflation rates and strongly increased deficits in public budgets led the German Bundesbank (the central bank for Germany) to set higher interest rates. They were meant to bring Germany's inflation rate down to an acceptable level and at the same time raise the attractiveness of loans in Deutschmarks to attract free capital. But higher rates also increased costs of investment in Germany and in turn, led to declining investments all over Western Europe as other national banking systems had to keep their interest rates in line to prevent speculation against their currency. Interest rates had to stay relatively high so that capital investment funds would not be shifted to Germany for a higher return. This move not only contributed to increased difficulties in national economies in Europe, but also to lower demand for goods and services in the USA and Japan. The economic upturn in the USA starting

Table 1.4 STRUCTURE OF INTERNATIONAL TRADE OF LEADING NATIONS
The table shows exports and imports of leading trading nations with their major trading partners.

USA 1993

	EXPORT USD503 BILLION	IMPORT USD669 BILLION	MAJOR TRADING PARTNERS	EXPORT	IMPORT
Machinery and transportation	45%	45%	Canada	23%	19%
Chemicals	10%	5%	Japan	11%	18%
Agricultural products	9%	–	Mexico	11%	7%
Food products and life stock	7%	4%	UK	5%	4%
Industrial raw materials	6%	3%	Germany	4%	5%
Fuel and lubricants	–	10%	PR China	–	6%
			Taiwan	–	4%

GERMANY 1994

	EXPORT DM 685.3 BILLION (1995: DM 727.6 BILLION	IMPORT DM 611.1 BILLION DM 634.2 BILLION)	MAJOR TRADING PARTNERS	EXPORT	IMPORT
Machinery and transportation	32%	16%	France	12%	11%
Electr.	13%	11%	UK	8%	6%
Chemicals	14%	9%	USA	8%	7%
Non-durables	13%	17%	Italy	8%	8%
Food	5%	6%	Netherlands	8%	8%
Agricultural products	1%	5%	Belg./Lux.	7%	6%
Raw materials	–	6%	Austria	6%	5%
			Switzerland	5%	4%
			Japan	3%	6%

UK 1993

	EXPORT GBP135 BILLION	IMPORT GBP145.7 BILLION	MAJOR TRADING PARTNERS	EXPORT	IMPORT
Machinery and transportation	41%	39%	Germany	13%	15%
Manufacturing goods	15%	16%	USA	13%	12%
Chemicals	15%	10%	France	10%	10%
Fuels	7%	5%	Netherlands	7%	8%
Food products and life stock	5%	9%	Belg./Lux.	6%	5%
			Italy	5%	–
			Japan	–	6%

(Continued)

Table 1.4 CONTINUED

JAPAN 1993

	EXPORT USD395.6 BILLION	IMPORT USD274.7 BILLION	MAJOR TRADING PARTNERS	EXPORT	IMPORT
Automotive	16%	–	USA	29%	23%
Office equipment	8%	–	Hongkong	6%	–
Chemicals	6%	8%	Taiwan	6%	4%
Optical devices	4%	–	Korea	5%	5%
Iron and steel products	4%	–	Germany	5%	4%
Generators	3%	–	PR China	5%	9%
Textiles	2%	7%	Singapore	5%	–
Fuel	–	39%	Indonesia		5%
Machinery + equipment	–	19%	Australia		5%
Food	–	16%	Arab Emirates		4%

FRANCE 1993

	EXPORT USD209.3 BILLION	IMPORT USD1201.8 BILLION	MAJOR TRADING PARTNERS	EXPORT	IMPORT
Investment goods	26%	24%	Germany	17%	18%
Semi-finished products	23%	23%	Italy	9%	10%
Non-durables	15%	17%	UK	9%	8%
Transportation	13%	11%	Belg./Lux.	8%	9%
Food products	10%	8%	USA	7%	9%
Agricultural products	7%	–	Netherlands	5%	5%
Energy	–	9%			

Source: Adapted from Baratta, M. (ed.) (1995) *Der Fischer Weltalmanach '96*, Frankfurt a.M.: Fischer Taschenbuch Verlag.

in 1993 was warmly welcomed by businesses throughout the world but was not strong enough to resolve the rather difficult situation in Europe and Japan.

The economic situation in Japan, which had already suffered from the high amount of dubious credits in the country's financial sector and the introduction of a consumption tax in 1997, was particularly hit by the financial crisis of most of the neighbouring NICs in 1997/98. In the resulting economic recession, company breakdowns rose to 17 000 a year and the unemployment rate reached a high of more than 4 per cent, unprecedented since 1945. Extremely low interest rates, intended to raise investments, resulted in a weakness of the yen which, in turn, negatively influenced the economies of the NICs. South Korea's key industries, for example, which are close competitors to some of Japan's major industrial sectors, expected a 12 per cent decrease in export revenues in 1998.[9] But the recession in Japan also had a negative influence on the most industrially developed countries. GDP growth rates in the USA and Europe were expected to diminish in the last years of the 1990s.

In reaction to the recognized interdependence of their national economies the governments of the seven industrially leading nations (Canada, France, Germany, Italy, Japan, UK, USA) have installed the 'G7' series of meetings between prime ministers, presidents and ministers of finance to cooperate closely in managing the development of the global economy, to foster stability of currency exchange rates, and to master the problems of high unemployment rates. As from 1998 onwards Russia has been accepted as a new member of G7 to make it 'G8'. However, many critics have charged that in reality, little or no positive results have been forthcoming.

International Economic Cooperation.   Economic integration is reinforced by economic cooperation among countries. Cooperation can take the form of bilateral or multilateral arrangements, ranging from simple agreements on tariff reduction to full-scale political integration (see Figure 1.2).

The simplest cooperative agreement is the **bilateral agreement**, a pact between two countries concerning trade in one or a few product groups. The purpose of the agreement is to reduce or even abolish barriers to trade. Bilateral agreements often serve as the basis for trade between countries with restrictive conditions, such as

↔   non-convertible currencies, that is, currencies which cannot be freely exchanged against each other (as in the Commonwealth of Independent States (CIS) – a group of countries including Azerbaijan, Belarus, Georgia, Kazakhstan, Moldova, Russia, Tajikistan, Turkmenistan, Ukraine and Uzbekistan – which was formed after the dissolution of the Soviet Union);

↔   centrally controlled economies, that is, economies with no or very few official free market exchanges where a central planning bureaucracy determines and controls all official flows of goods and capital (as in the Democratic Republic of Korea or in Cuba); or

↔   a lack of hard currency, that is, a national currency which is not accepted as a unit of payment by international suppliers (as in most developing countries of Africa, Asia and Latin America but also in most countries of the former Soviet Union). For example, a bilateral USD7 billion barter clearing agreement has been signed between the governments of Iran and Ukraine in which Iranian oil and gas have been exchanged for weapons, metal scrap, refined products, chemicals and machinery.

There is a tendency for industrialized nations to sign bilateral agreements among themselves. One such agreement is the Free Trade Area Treaty between the USA and Israel, which was signed in April 1985, providing for the eventual elimination of virtually all barriers to trade between the two countries. It has also been the first trade agreement ever to cover explicitly a full range of services, including transportation, travel, tourism, communications, banking, insurance, construction, accounting, education, law, management consulting, computer services, and advertising.

Another major US bilateral agreement has been the free trade accord between the USA and Canada which took effect in 1989. This agreement stated that all tariffs on bilateral trade would be eliminated within ten years, reduced non-tariff barriers, and established rules for the conduct of bilateral investment and resolution of trade disputes. In effect, it led to a 15 per cent increase in bilateral trade in goods (exports plus imports) from 1988 to 1991. Free trade helped North Carolina's furniture industry, for example, more than triple its exports to Canada to USD71.8 million in 1991. At Hart Chemical Co. in Guelph, Ontario, exports to the USA about doubled to 40 per cent of sales,

Figure 1.2 A Continuum of Different Forms of Economic Cooperation

As economic cooperative agreements move from the most basic (reduction of tariffs) towards the most complex (economic or political unions), the greater the degree of economic integration. This continuum is progressive; a common market, for example, has reduced tariffs plus movement towards removal of internal tariffs, plus harmonization of external tariffs, plus the free movement of factors of production.

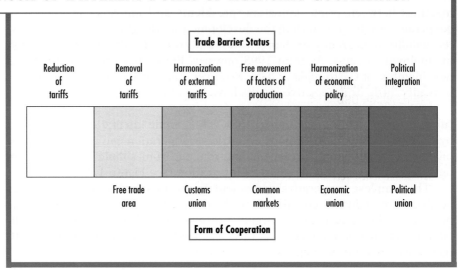

in part because of the free trade agreement. Moreover, secure access to the US market allowed Hart to justify research and development spending on its line of de-inking chemicals, used to 'wash' ink out of waste paper.

Owing to an initiative of Mexico's president, Salinas de Gortari, in 1992 the pact between Canada and the USA was enlarged to a **multilateral agreement** (regulating trade among more than two countries). Canada, Mexico and the USA agreed to build a **free trade area**, called the North American Free Trade Association (NAFTA), in 15 years. A free trade area removes all formal impediments to trade for a specified group of products. For example, the European Free Trade Association (EFTA), which in 1997 included Iceland, Liechtenstein, Norway and Switzerland, removed all tariffs on manufactured goods traded by these countries. However, the individual countries maintain independent policies with regard to non-members; a company based in a non-member country faced different barriers to entry with each EFTA member.

EFTA has lost most of its importance in Europe owing to Austria, Finland, and Sweden joining the European Community in 1996. Thus, the North American Free Trade Association (NAFTA) has become the most important free trade agreement in the world. NAFTA went into effect on 1 January 1994. It created a market of comparatively free trade with 360 million consumers (Table 1.5). NAFTA has already produced positive effects for the respective economies. Mexico, for example, received USD5.2 billion in foreign capital from January to March 1992. In the first half of 1992 its budget reached a surplus of approximately USD2.5 billion, and the number of state-owned companies was reduced from 1155 to 230. In the USA, household brand manufacturers, such as Zenith Electronics or Smith Corona, shifted production to Mexico (partly from Southeast Asia) to take advantage of low wages. Large numbers of apparel makers also moved. Wal-Mart announced a joint venture with Cifra, Mexico's largest retailer, to open wholesale clubs in Mexico City. Compaq Computer, Lotus Development Corp. and Microsoft opened subsidiaries in Mexico City. Franchises, including McDonald's, Pizza Hut, Baskin-Robbins and Athlete's Foot, are spreading fast.

Table 1.5 COMPARISON OF ECONOMIC DATA OF NAFTA MEMBERS
The USA clearly dominates NAFTA in economic terms.

	USA	CANADA	MEXICO
Population in millions (1993)	257.800	27.782	90.027
GNP in billion USD (1993)	6,387.686	574.884	343.472
Per capita income in USD (1993)	24,778	20,693	3,815
Wage of industry worker (1991) (per hour in USD)	14.77	16.02	1.80

Source: Adapted from Baratta, M. (ed.) (1995) *Der Fischer Weltalmanach '96*, Frankfurt a.M.: Fischer Taschenbuch Verlag.

But all three countries took big risks as well. While overall employment was expected to grow, and even employment lost to Southeast Asia was won back to North America (wages in important industries in Hong Kong, Singapore, Taiwan and Malaysia are up to twice as high as in Mexico), it was clear from the beginning, but not openly admitted by the US government, that workers in important industries would suffer. Under NAFTA, Mexico opened its market for corn to more efficient US farmers. That move alone has been driving a significant number of Mexican labourers off the farms. More than 60 000 low-skilled workers in the USA lost their jobs because of plant relocations or import competition involving Mexico and Canada. Therefore, opposition to NAFTA has grown. But even assuming that estimates of 300 000 jobs lost to NAFTA are correct, such a result barely registers amid the US economy's constant din of creation and destruction of jobs. In recent years, between 18 and 20 million people have experienced unemployment at some point each year. The number of 'displaced workers' – those who lose their jobs as factories close or their positions are abolished – totals 3.5 to 5.5 million every two years, and these losses stem from a wide variety of causes, such as fierce competition in the banking or retail industry. Meanwhile, the cycle of regeneration goes on: since January 1994, when NAFTA went into effect, the number of people employed in the USA has risen by an average of more than 200 000 each month.[10]

The NAFTA agreement has triggered a trade boom and spawned similar market-opening pacts throughout the hemisphere. With effect from 1 January 1995, Argentina, Brazil, Paraguay and Uruguay set up a free trade area, called Mercosur (Chile and Bolivia are associated members), with 220 million consumers which represents 60 per cent of Latin America's GNP. In 1997, around 85 per cent of all products were freely exchanged between the members in the agreement, and 90 per cent of all products imported to the Mercosur area were subject to common tariffication.[11] The Andean countries of Bolivia, Colombia, Ecuador, Peru and Venezuela signed an agreement, called the Andean Pact, to establish a free trade area which is planned to become a common market of 100 million inhabitants. They started to install a general secretariat and some other permanent organizational structures in 1996. Chile, after signing a free trade pact with Mexico in 1991, still wants a similar accord with the USA. There are even initiatives to expand NAFTA across the American continent.

As a response to NAFTA and the developments in Europe, Asian countries also started working on free trade agreements. The seven countries in the Association of Southeast Asian Nations (ASEAN), Brunei, Indonesia, Malaysia, Philippines, Singapore, Thailand and Vietnam, which have a combined annual GNP of about USD500 billion and a population of 500 million, decided to defend their economic future by creating an Asian Free Trade Area in 1993. As a first step, tariffs on 15 groups of manufactured goods were cut. Myanmar was accepted as a new member in 1997.

A really powerful Asian free trade area has to include Japan and China, however. Therefore, the Asia-Pacific Economic Cooperation forum (APEC) was founded. In November 1995 the members of APEC signed the 'Osaka Action Agenda', an agreement to abolish the barriers to trade among their countries in 15 years. The agenda contained nine principles and 100 specified actions to be completed before the next meeting. China anounced the most voluminous catalogue of trade liberalization measures. Import tariffs on 4000 goods were to be decreased by up to 30 per cent, and import restrictions were to be repealed.

Because of the big differences in the stage of economic development reached by the various members of APEC, the establishment of entirely free trade is particularly difficult. Japan's lead over its neighbours, in everything from technology to finance to living standards, is considerably greater than the edge Germany enjoys in Europe. So is the lead of countries like Singapore or South Korea compared to Vietnam. For that reason the APEC members agreed that developing countries will follow the move to free trade with a lag of ten years.

The next level of economic cooperation is the **customs union**. This type of agreement has the characteristics of a free trade area, but in addition the members establish consistent tariff policies vis-à-vis non-members. Examples of such an agreement are the Southern African Customs Union, which includes the Republic of South Africa (the dominant member), Botswana, Lesotho and Swaziland, as well as the customs union between the Economic Cooperation Organization (which brings together Iran, Pakistan and Turkey) and the three former Soviet republics of Azerbaijan, Turkmenistan and Uzbekistan. An exporter to any of these countries will receive the same tariff treatment. This has the effect of creating a larger market with a shared 'tariff wall'.

A **common market** is formed when member countries, in addition to removing tariffs between them and harmonizing their tariff policies vis-à-vis non-members, remove all barriers to the free movement of production factors among them. For example, capital can be transferred without any restrictions, workers can freely choose their jobs throughout the common market, there is free trade in services, and factories can be built in those member countries that seem best to the companies. The European Union (EU) is the most familiar example of a multilateral agreement resulting in such a common market.

Members of the European Union as of 1996 are Austria, Belgium, Denmark, Finland, France, Germany, Greece, Ireland, Italy, Luxembourg, the Netherlands, Portugal, Spain, Sweden and the United Kingdom. These nations, except for Austria, Finland and Sweden which only became members in 1996, achieved a fully integrated market by 1 January 1993. Since then the EU has been the most populous market in the industrialized world, with a total population of over 345 million, and it represents the second-largest concentration of purchasing power in the world (behind the USA).

Map 1.1   MAP OF EUROPE – THE EUROPEAN UNION

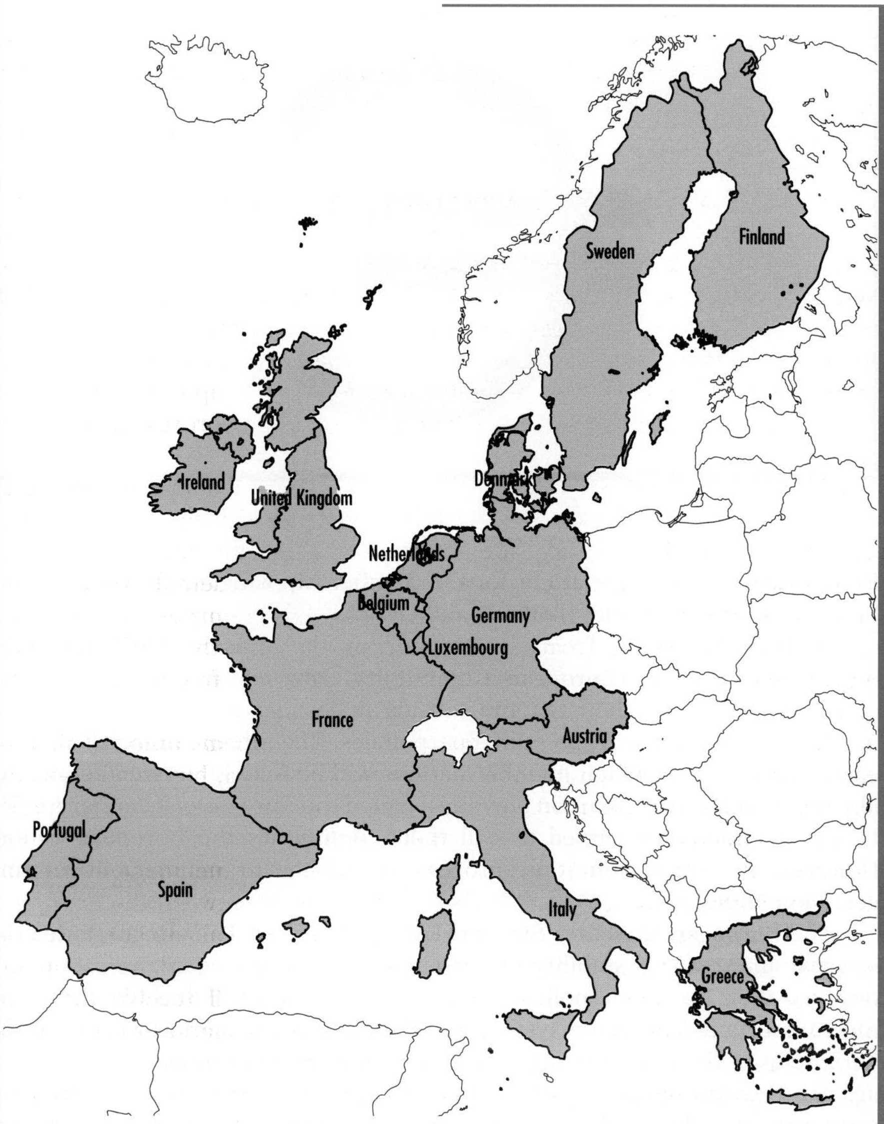

Sweden

Finland

Ireland

United Kingdom

Denmark

Netherlands

Belgium

Germany

Luxembourg

France

Austria

Portugal

Spain

Italy

Greece

Other European countries have reacted to the new situation. The remaining EFTA members, except Switzerland, have signed an agreement with the EU that creates a free trade area, called the European Economic Area (EEA), with 375 million affluent consumers, 30 per cent of world GNP and 40 per cent share of world trade. The economic situation for suppliers and customers located in the EEA is similar to that in the common market, but the political autonomy of its members is not diminished. The Czech Republic, Hungary, Poland, Slovakia, Slovenia, Malta and Turkey have gained associate status. They have also applied for membership of the EU. In 1997 the members of the

THE SYMBOL OF THE EURO

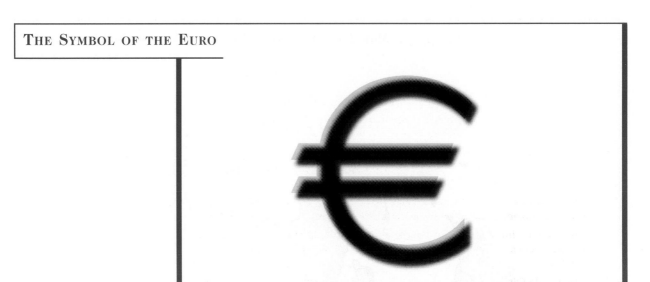

EU decided to start negotiations for EU membership with the Czech Republic, Estonia, Hungary, Poland, Slovenia and Cyprus.

In the Maastricht Treaty (and later in the Amsterdam Treaty) the members of the EC (European Community, now called European Union) agreed to harmonize their tax and subsidy policies as a precondition for the unification of their fiscal and monetary policies. The intended result will be an economic union, in which member nations will be fully integrated economically. They will have a common currency, called the Euro, as of 1 January 1999. In anticipation, they agreed to call their community the European Union. However, the implementation process is subject to major political and economic difficulties.

The European Monetary System (EMS), created in 1979 to guarantee the internal and external stability of currencies of member countries and to co-ordinate their economic policies, is a good example of such difficulties. The most important part of the system was the fixed parities (rates) between the currencies of the participating nations which were determined by their value against the European Currency Unit (ECU). The ECU was an artificial currency created to facilitate transactions. The currency exchange rates were allowed to fluctuate around the fixed levels to a predetermined percentage. If two currencies arrived at the upper and the lower end of their allowed zone of fluctuation, the national banks involved had to buy and sell the respective currencies to stabilize their exchange rates. This system was quite successful until 1992, when a downturn in the level of economic activities in some of the member countries was overlaid by high capital demand from Germany owing to its enormous investments in former East Germany. High interest rates in Germany forced other countries, such as France, Belgium and the Netherlands, to raise their interest rates, too. Because of their economic situation, the UK and Italy could not follow. To avoid enormous losses in foreign currency, they were forced to leave the EMS and to significantly devalue the pound sterling and the lira. Ireland, Portugal and Spain stayed in the EMS, but were also forced to devalue their currencies. For some time, all those countries enjoyed significant competitive advantages in trade with the

Table 1.6 MAASTRICHT CRITERIA FOR PARTICIPATION IN EU
SINGLE CURRENCY AREA

For a country to become a member of the European Monetary Union in 1999 the
following criteria had to be fulfilled by the end of 1997:

↔ The country's inflation rate does not exceed the past year's average
   inflation rate of the best three EU countries by 1.5 per cent (basis 1996,
   observation period 1997).

↔ The exchange rate of the national currency has stayed inside the
   fluctuation zone allowed by the EMS for the last two years (1996, 1997).

↔ The nominal interest rate for long-term government loans does not exceed
   the past year's average rate of the best three EU members by 2 per cent
   (1997).

↔ The net deficit of all public budgets in the country does not exceed 3 per
   cent of GDP.

↔ The total public debt of the country does not exceed 60 per cent of its
   GDP.

Source: *Internationale Wirtschaft*, No. 16, 1992.

other members of the EU, which in turn lost jobs and had to fight widespread
dissatisfaction with their political leadership.

On its way to becoming a full economic union, the European Union has
replaced the EMS by an even more restrictive system, the European Monetary
Union (EMU). Absolutely fixed exchange rates against the Euro will be determined by the European Central Bank and introduced in 1999. Starting on 1
January 2002, Euro money will be distributed and will replace the national
currencies. Such a development must be based on rather similar developments of the member states' economies (inflation rate, budget deficit, interest
rate). Therefore, the Maastricht Treaty set some economic criteria which had
to be fulfilled by the end of 1997 at the latest by countries wanting to take part
in European Monetary Union (EMU) (see Table 1.6).

In the discussion of the pros and cons of a unified European currency,
there has been a tendency to focus on lower transaction costs, because the
EMU would end currency conversion and hedging costs. For example, Hoechst
Marion Roussel, the pharmaceuticals unit of Germany's Hoechst, will save
tens of millions of German marks each year on hedging against European
currency shifts. KLM Royal Dutch Airlines will save on bank charges by closing as many as possible of the firm's bank accounts. At present, the carrier has
bank accounts in 80 different currencies, each with their separate charges. As
of January 1999, those in the currencies of countries participating in EMU will
become redundant.[12]

But these benefits, while useful, are marginal. Much more important for
companies operating internationally is the potential for a strong Euro (based
on the countries' attainment of the Maastricht criteria) contributing to a more
stable economic environment with low inflation and interest rates. If, for

example, UK long-term interest rates were to fall to German levels as a result of EMU participation, the UK government could save around USD10 billion a year in debt interest. And the cost of corporate capital would be reduced, which would encourage investment.[13]

It has been clear from the very beginning that some EU members such as Greece will not be able to participate in the EMU from the start because they are unable to fulfil the fixed criteria.

In 1997, Italy rejoined the EMS as a precondition for joining EMU. The UK, which since it left the EMS has seen economic growth rates above the average of its EU partners, does not want to participate in the European Monetary Union from its very beginning. Neither does Denmark or Sweden, despite the fact that they would be able to fulfil the criteria for participation. It may not be appropriate for those countries to go into EMU on day one. But the single currency will go ahead and, whether those countries are in or out, companies with operations in the EMU member countries, or trading with EMU partners, are likely to find many aspects of their business affected. Competitive strategy, pricing, financial systems, treasury operations, tax arrangements, terms of payment, procurement and other contractual arrange-ments will all need to be reviewed. For example, in Siemens' medical equipment division, prices for complex products like X-ray scanners will continue to vary from country to country, reflecting the high proportion of final price levels due to installation and service costs which are determined by local wage rates and other factors. Prices for smaller, more easily trans-portable products like hearing aids, by contrast, will be harmonized at a unified level. As for products like X-ray film, sales managers are expected to restructure their marketing methods around a common price base.[14]

The most advanced form of economic cooperation is **political union**, in which the agreement between the signing parties results in a new country. To a certain extent, Australia and the USA are successful historical examples of this type of agreement. A recent example may be the reunification of Germany. Today, however, most governments believe that they would have to give up too much political sovereignty if they were to enter into such an agree-ment. The difficulties with the popular vote concerning the Maastricht Treaty experienced in some of the EC member countries, such as Denmark and France, as well as the majority vote of the Swiss population against EEA mem-bership and the Norwegians' vote against the country's participation in the EU, are recent examples. Political unions, therefore, are unlikely to be formed fre-quently.

It is important to note that none of the existing arrangements falls neatly into any of the above categories. The European Union, for example, is a full customs union, a well-developed common market, a partially developed economic union, and a weak political union. Moreover, there is no automatic progression from agreements on tariff reductions to full-scale political union.

Political and Social Dimensions.　Economic integration, of course, also has political and social dimensions. For example, in 1994, cold-rolled steel was manufactured in South Korea by Pohang Iron and Steel (POSCO), the world's second-largest steel maker, after Japan's Nippon Steel, at a cost of USD489 a tonne compared with Taiwan's USD504 and Japan's USD627.[15] At this cost it can be sold in Pittsburgh at a lower price than steel manufactured in Pittsburgh. This affects employment rates in both the USA and Korea. So does the fact that more Japanese cars than cars made by Swedish manufac-

200 Million Children as Work Slaves

They work in coal mines in Brazil, on carpet looms in Pakistan and Nepal, in leather factories in India, in the fields of Senegal, and in the sex salons in Thailand. Millions of children, starting at age three, are exploited as work slaves all over the world. Following an estimate of ILO, the International Labour Organization, headquartered in Geneva, Switzerland, more than 200 million children are forced to work and many of them in dangerous activities. Only very few violations of human rights are as unanimously condemned as child labour, but nevertheless without any results.

Child labour is no side problem, but a major problem of our society, says Kenth Petterson, President of the Swedish Union of retail employees. Only a reduction of the difference in wealth between the rich and the poor countries of the world can help to resolve it. Global information campaigns can contribute to higher awareness of the problem in the highly industrialized countries. They should make governments, entrepreneurs and top managers, but also consumers, more conscious in their decisions with whom to do business and what to avoid buying.

Why should animals in the highly industrialized countries be better protected against abuses than children in the less industrially developed parts of the world? If the families there need the additional income to survive, why can't we make sure that the parents earn enough money? Is it to keep the prices of consumer products imported from those countries as low as possible? Do we want to further improve our material standard of living at the expense of child slavery?

Source: 'Weltweit 200 Millionen Kinder als Arbeitssklaven', *Der Standard*, 15–16 July 1995, p. 17.

turers are sold in Sweden. With increasing unemployment rates in Western Europe, more and more politicians accuse other countries of 'social' and 'ecological dumping', that is, selling their products at very low prices based on much lower costs due to a lack of social and ecological standards comparable to those in Western Europe. Politicians increasingly ask for internationally agreed and controlled social standards for the workforce, as well as internationally enforced norms of environmental protection. The Ethics box shows that such demands cannot easily be dismissed as long as consumers in highly industrialized countries have not become sensitive to unethical practices in less developed countries.

Films and TV programmes produced in the USA are exported throughout the world. Sales of US TV programmes to Europe alone were more than USD2 billion in 1995. Such activity is controversial, of course. Critics charge that the high pressure of the US entertainment industry not only endangers the production of films and TV programmes in other countries but also risks destroying the cultural identity of other nations in favour of a general Americanization. The global spread of fast food restaurants has been attributed to that kind of influence. The Culture box gives an impression of how strong the resistance to foreign cultural influences can be in some countries and how a firm such as Domino's Pizza can deal with such a problem.

Foreign investment also still tends to be controversial, such as the purchase of CBS Records by Sony, or foreign investment in French wine facilities,

CULTURE BOX

'Domino's Survives India's Food Fight'

IN THE CULTURE WARS OVER AMERICAN FAST FOOD coming to this land of curry, fried chicken has been taken hostage – but not pizza. In 1995, local governments shut the two Kentucky Fried Chicken restaurants in India – one in New Delhi and another in Bangalore, in the south. Court orders allowed them to reopen, but end of January 1996, anti-Western activists ransacked the Bangalore outlet in what they called an act of civil disobedience. The storming of the outlet invoked a symbol held dear in this predominantly Hindu nation – the cow. The protesters distributed a leaflet stating they wanted to 'save the country's cattle wealth'. Activists said McDonald's Corp., which has yet to open an Indian franchise, would also be a target if and when it did.

The criticism of American fast food, hurled from the political left and right, begins with nutrition but extends to anxiety about the threat to traditional lifestyles as Western products and tastes seep into a newly opened economy.

But Domino's Pizza, which opened a small restaurant in one of New Delhi's upscale neighborhoods in the end of 1995, has quietly served pizzas and Cokes to a curious stream of housewives, executives and students. 'We've not had any trouble', said Gita Agarwal, a manager at Domino's headquarters in India. 'It's an Indian company'.

The rights to open Domino's franchises in India belong to the Bhartia family of industrialists better-known for chemicals and fertilizers. Opening on New Year's Eve with almost no advertising also seems to have helped Domino's escape confrontation with fast-food critics. Domino's has respected Hindu reverence for the cow by omitting pepperoni, the beef-based topping popular with Americans, from its menu in India. Vegetarian offerings precede non-vegetarian ones on its menu, also in keeping with Indian customs.

Source: Cooper, K.J. (1996) 'Domino's Survives India's Food Fight', *International Herald Tribune*, 12 March, p. 14.

which were seen as undermining the gastronomic traditions of France. In Hungary critics complain that the boom of foreign investments (in 1997, total foreign investment reached USD17.5 billion, or 39.3 per cent of GDP) has created an industrial two-class society. The capital flow focused on those industries that promised the fastest and most profitable development: food, tobacco, alcoholic beverages and automotive as well as electrical machinery and construction. For example, foreign investors control nearly two-thirds of the capital invested in the building material production sector. Industries which would have needed new capital to survive in international competition, such as iron and steel production or chemicals, were avoided by foreign investors. Plants with foreign capital have significantly higher per capita productivity (about 80 per cent above the Hungarian average) and shares of exports above average. Added value in foreign-controlled machinery production, for example, reached 52 million forint (about USD370,000) compared to 30 million forint for locally owned firms in 1995. In 1996, 90 per cent of total profits made by manufacturing firms were made by companies with foreign capital.[16] Companies with foreign capital employed one-fifth of the Hungarian workforce, but accounted for 30 per cent of total sales and half of the country's exports. Productivity gains, however, were only partly reflected in the income of workers and employees. After having laid off up to 50 per cent of personnel, foreign-controlled companies pay salaries about 11 per cent higher than Hungarian-controlled firms.[17]

Despite all charges, foreign investment is increasing in every highly indus-trialized or fast developing country. Depending on the available skills and resources as well as their prices in a country, foreign capital is invested in dif-ferent domains. In the USA, for example, Swiss firms invested more than USD2.5 billion in research and development in 1993. This is more than 60 per cent of Swiss companies' total foreign investments in research and develop-ment. Investors from Germany, the UK, Canada and Japan have followed. As a reaction to the more liberal legislation concerning biotechnology in the USA, and taking into account the high level of specialized skills as well as the global competitiveness of the industry, the Swiss firms put their main emphasis on pharmaceutical, chemical and biotechnological research and development.

The controversy over world trade has a further dimension. Many critics charge that economically developed nations are exploiting developing ones. Criticism centres on the less developed nations' limited ability to accumulate capital needed for the production of goods to export (owing to high interest rates on loans), except for low-value-added products such as raw materials, for example coffee beans or iron ore. This means, critics say, that the value added in terms of profits and higher wages all stays (on purpose) in the more eco-nomically developed nations. Others argue that if less rich nations sell what-ever products they have, they can earn money to develop other industries which do contribute greater profit margins. This in turn would lead to their citizens becoming wealthier, and able to buy more products from their own suppliers in addition to imports from developed nations. Thus in the long run, everyone should win.

Critics counter-charge that, in effect, the rich get richer and the poor get poorer. In 1970 the industrialized countries (including the socialist countries in Eastern Europe) produced around 85 per cent of the world's GNP. Despite the very dynamic development of the countries in the Asia-Pacific Rim and the economic turmoil in most of the former socialist countries in the early 1990s, the world share of those countries had only decreased to 83 per cent of the world's GNP in 1993. Between 1970 and 1993 the GNP in the countries of Southern Africa, for example, had grown by 651 per cent to a level of USD117.3 billion (equal to USD2,124 per capita), compared to a growth of 900 per cent in Western Europe, where total GNP reached USD7,200 billion (USD17,132 per capita) in 1993.[18]

DRIVING FORCES OF
INTERNATIONAL BUSINESS

Theoretical Explanations

Economics has provided some theoretical explanations for the described evo-lution of international business. The most well known are the theory of com-parative costs and the related concept of international product life cycles or international investments.

Comparative Costs. In simple terms the theory of comparative costs suggests that each country, owing to its available resources and the efficiency of their use, has or can develop specific advantages compared with other countries. If each country specializes in products and services it can produce or perform comparatively better than others and exchanges them for products and services in which other countries have advantages, all exchange partners will profit. The standard of living will increase in all economies.

Economic reality shows, however, that resources as well as their efficient use underlie a dynamic process which leads to continual changes in comparative advantages and, as a consequence, continuing changes in production sites. For example, because of the technical expertise required, the production of TV sets first started in the USA and Europe. From there most of the production sites went to Southeast Asia, where mass production costs for labour-intensive production were much lower. But production was not lost for Western countries for ever. On the one hand, economic success led to increasing labour costs in countries such as Japan, Taiwan, Hong Kong or Singapore. On the other, the fierce cost competition from those countries led to heavy restructuring of industrial organization and processes in Europe and in the USA. As a result, some of the production came back to the highly industrialized countries, because there existed a sufficient number of highly trained workers who could ensure the expected level of high-quality output.

The passenger car industry shows a similar development. The USA, where mass production of cars started, lost an important part of its production to Japan in the 1980s. Since then, Japanese firms have opened production sites in the USA which not only serve the American home market, but surpassed Detroit in North American car exports in 1995. Honda Motor Co., America's number one car exporter, devotes 20 per cent of its North American production to exports. Toyota plans to be shipping more vehicles from US ports than it receives from Japan in 1999. More than half of Japan's American exports return to the Japanese market. But ships loaded with US-made Japanese cars are also arriving in Taiwan and South Korea (both markets closed to vehicles assembled in Japan for political and economic reasons).[19]

International Product Life Cycle. International product life cycle theory claims to explain the process of dissemination of innovations across national borders. Following this theory, an economically developed country which posesses the ability to provide a new way of satisfying customer needs, that is, a product or service innovation, will try to profit from the resulting advantages by selling the new product or service to other countries. Soon other economically developed countries will follow. They will create their own production capacities for the new product or service. Next, the less developed countries will follow when they have gained the needed production know-how in one way or another. Finally, more and more of the economically advanced countries which, in the meantime, have lost their comparative advantage to the less developed countries will start importing the product or service from their former customers.

This process can be visualized by three overlapping life cycle curves (see Figure 1.3). They show the development of the innovation in the three types of countries, the innovating country, the highly developed early followers, and the less developed late followers. Each curve is characterized by net exports when it is situated above the time axis. Below the time axis more products are imported than exported.

> ### *Figure 1.3* THE INTERNATIONAL LIFE CYCLE OF INNOVATIONS

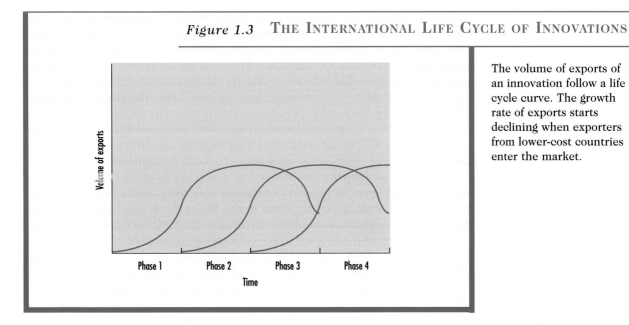

The volume of exports of an innovation follow a life cycle curve. The growth rate of exports starts declining when exporters from lower-cost countries enter the market.

Phase 1 starts with the export of the local innovation to other markets, for example when a French company which has successfully introduced an electronic telephone terminal starts exporting it to other European markets. Phase 2 is characterized by relative stability. Demand in the markets served so far continues to grow, but is increasingly satisfied by local production. In phase 3 the exports of the innovator start decreasing. Demand for the new good in the less economically developed countries is rising, but is increasingly satisfied by the production capacities installed by the early followers. Finally, in phase 4, the picture changes completely. The product or service is no longer an innovation. It has become common to an extent where companies in economically less developed countries are able to provide a, perhaps simplified, version at very low cost.

Cars, PCs, copiers, VCRs and TV sets seem to be examples of products in phase 4. An example of the entire process is the semiconductor industry. The production of semiconductors first started in the USA. Germany, France, the UK and Japan followed, before Hong Kong and Taiwan took over. Today semiconductors are produced in China, Indonesia and Malaysia.

The duration of each of the phases may vary. High tariffs or transportation costs, high production volumes needed to be cost efficient, high capital investment intensity, or patents can extend the cycles. Harley Davidson, for example, was able for some time to convince the US government of the necessity to tax Japanese motor cycles heavily. Culture-dependent innovations may not even experience the process described at all because no demand for the product or service can be created in other markets.

For individual firms in highly industrialized countries it is important to notice that the international product life cycle does not mean that firms will automatically go out of business after some time. There are at least three ways to counteract the theoretically prescribed path. First, international imitators will have a much harder time if the company does not offer an average product or service for 'everybody', but steadily improves its specific know-how for the service of defined customer segments. Differentiation potentials exist not only in the product or core service itself but concern the entire 'product' delivered to clients. Polypropylene granules for the production of plastic goods can be fairly easily imitated, for example. But it is much harder to develop the specific application know-how needed for the production of granules for re-cyclable dashboards for passenger cars. In particular, the personal relation-ships that will be built with specialists from the automotive industry, resulting in mutual trust and personal commitment, will be more difficult to 'imitate'. Internationally successful companies continuously search for opportunities to build and sustain competitive advantages through specialization.

Secondly, a company can follow the described international life cycle of innovations by moving its own production sites from one region of the world to another, depending on the phase in the life cycle. When Hewlett-Packard, for example, decided to assemble some lines of their PCs in China and to move increasing parts of production to the country, it anticipated the expected evo-lution. Finally, a firm operating internationally can use the comparative costs of different economies to optimize its own cost structure in the production of a product. Pentax, for example, had the lens of its K-1000 camera produced in Taiwan, the body of the camera came from a production site in Hong Kong, and research and development was done in Japan.

Stimuli for International Business

Searching for reasons why an increasing number of companies have decided to go international in the past decade, we find four major driving forces. One is the relative saturation of many markets in highly industrialized countries, which causes serious limits to local growth. Another is the tremendous tech-nological changes which have largely facilitated communication and transfer of knowledge among nations. Both have contributed to a significant increase in competition, locally as well as internationally, which forces companies to globalize their business perspective and to procure their resources wherever they seem to be best available.

Limited Growth in Domestic Markets. In order to remain financially healthy, most companies must grow. However, many product-markets in the industrialized nations are saturated. For many small to medium-sized firms, growth through additions to the existing product line is difficult. These firms may have limited financial resources, production capacities, or technological know-how, or they may encounter competitors offering the same products. Diversification into new areas of business as a growth alternative is always risky. The most viable way to grow may be to enter less saturated foreign mar-kets. For example, many medium-sized companies based in Western Europe, German and Austrian firms in particular, quickly grasped the opportunity to establish their own sales subsidiaries or to invest in factories in the former socialist countries of Eastern Europe.

Many foreign markets offer more opportunity for business expansion than the home market does. In the 1990s international trade has been increasing faster than domestic business in all US and European consumer sectors except services. According to a study by management consultants McKinsey in 1991, US firms depended on home sales for 70 per cent of turnover, but sales growth from the domestic market for the period 1991 to 1996 was expected to reach only 5 per cent. In contrast, sales to foreign markets were expected to grow by

10 to 20 per cent during the same period. The most important opportunities the report identified were the Pacific basin, followed by Western and Eastern Europe, Latin America and lastly, the Peoples' Republic of China.[20] Meanwhile US companies have been successful in diversifying into emerging markets in Asia and Latin America. In 1990, such markets accounted for 35 per cent of US merchandise exports, compared with 42 per cent going to Europe and Japan. But, by 1995, the emerging-market share was up 42 per cent, versus 34 per cent for Europe and Japan.[21]

International business is not only a route to growth but also a necessary means for survival. In Europe, stagnant growth, local competitive pressure and the need to reduce costs have made non-domestic business a must for many firms. Some industries, such as Germany's machinery industry, have an export rate of more than 60 per cent. European firms have reacted positively to the challenge. Austria-based Linz Textil Holding AG, one of Europe's four largest manufacturers of yarns, despite its high investments in the latest production technology, was forced to invest in joint ventures in the Czech Republic to stay internationally competitive. Carrefour SA, the French retail chain and inventor of hypermarkets, started its internationalization as early as the 1970s, when it opened its first hypermarkets in Brazil. Now it is involved in most countries of Western Europe and in the USA, but is also progressing in South Korea. Carrefour Korea Ltd has opened two hypermarkets on the outskirts of Seoul and one at Taejon. They plan to open three more stores each year. Three hypermarkets were opened in Thailand in 1996, and three more are planned by the end of 1998.[22] Owing to the low growth rates expected in the home market at the end of the 1990s and because of the legal restrictions on further expansion in France, another French retailer, St. Etienne-based Casino, a supermarket chain with reported sales of 633 million Francs (about USD126 million) in 1995, has not only started operations in the USA, but also in Taiwan, where they cooperate in a joint venture with Dairy Farm International, the largest operator of supermarkets in Asia.[23]

Critics in the USA charge that, in contrast to Europe, only a small number of companies still account for almost all exports. About one in ten small- and middle-sized companies in America, for example, export. By one estimate, there are at least 30 000 small US companies that have export potential but are not conducting business in foreign markets. Although US exports totalled USD512 billion in 1994 and merchandise exports rose by close to 15 per cent in 1995, only about 8 per cent of the country's GDP, that is, 8 per cent of the value of all goods and services produced in the country, was derived from export. Much smaller Germany had exports of over USD414 billion, some 18 per cent of its GDP. The validity of such comparison is questionable, however, because an average of about 65 per cent (from 58 per cent for the UK up to 80 per cent for Belgium and Luxemburg) of international trade of European countries is done with their EU partners. Taking into consideration that the USA consists of a considerable number of states (theoretically doing business with each other), for a better comparison only the exports of European countries to non-European (or at least non-EU) destinations should be compared to US exports. A comparison of 'corrected' export shares of GDP in the USA, the EU and Japan shows that they are very similar, 8 to 10 per cent (see Table 1.7).

Technological Change. Important drivers for international business are technological improvements and change in the areas of transportation and communication. The number of direct airline connections inside Europe, to

---

Table 1.7 Export Shares of GDP in the Triad
Export shares of GDP in the USA, the EMU and Japan are very similar.

Area	GDP 1997 billion USD	Exports 1996 billion USD	Imports 1996 billion USD	Foreign Exchange Reserves (end 1997) in billions	Total Population 1996/ in millions
USA	7,819.3	622.9	817.8	30.8	265.6
EMU*	6,303.6	540+	486+	300.1	289.8
Japan	4,223.4	411.2	349.5	207.9	125.9

* EMU = Austria, Belgium, Finland, France, Germany, Ireland, Italy, Luxembourg, The Netherlands, Portugal, Spain
+ ex EU

Source: OECD.

Asia, and from many different points in the USA to overseas destinations has dramatically increased while ticket prices have substantially decreased. Low-priced transport supports the development of international business. A small US company manufacturing air cleaners for industry and homes, for example, exports to some 25 countries. Based in Cincinnati, their task has been considerably easier since Delta Airlines began to offer direct non-stop flights to London, Paris, and Frankfurt, and one-stop service to Tokyo from Cincinnati.

Low air ticket prices have contributed strongly to increased international leisure travel. More and more consumers have physical contact with new products and services in countries they have chosen as vacation destinations. They learn about different customs and consumption patterns, and develop a demand for so far unknown products and services in their home country. Demand for Greek restaurants, French cheese, Italian pasta, Spanish wine, Mexican beer and Caribbean music, for example, was strongly supported by the vacation experiences of satisfied consumers once they had returned home.

Telecommunications have revolutionized the economic and political world, and changed the way business is conducted. A seemingly simple invention like the fax machine has permitted real-time global communication without the difficulties involved in taking time zone differences into account. A marketing manager working for Yves St. Laurent in Paris, for example, can receive a fax for information from the Tokyo office in the morning, work on it all day, respond to it in the evening, and the manager in Tokyo will find the response on his desk when he starts work in the morning of the next day (Tokyo is eight hours ahead of Paris in time zones). One small company CEO describes this technology, in terms of its impact on exporting, as 'There's only one thing greater than the airplane, and that's the fax'.

In a more advanced way, computers are increasingly hooked to each other online, around the world. An internal memo with attachments can therefore be shared by e-mail with all managers at the same time, for example. Such connections have improved the international logistics and shipment of goods. Benetton, for example, does not need to produce most of its products in advance and keep them in stock to be able to deliver to its worldwide outlets in time. Having online computer connections to their shops, they know at any time which products are bought in what numbers, sizes and colours, and are therefore able to guide their production according to the latest market response information. By getting real-time information via satellite data transmission on the location of their trucks or other transportation vehicles, shippers know at any time of the day where in the world their shipments are. Data transfer for accounting and financial systems can also be made at any time, across national boundaries. Even information bases such as disease analysis information data banks are shared by hospitals around the world.

The Internet has further revolutionized communication, providing real-time information to even very small firms and to consumers. A fast-increasing number of companies also use Internet services for advertising purposes. In November 1995, for example, General Motors Corp. signed on for advertising over a broad gamut of magazine Web sites owned by the Hachette Filipacchi publishing group, including *Car and Driver* and *Elle*. The GM deal was part of a USD 20 million advertising package for print and new media. It signalled that Web advertising had joined the mainstream, having broken out of the rarefied realm of software producers and technology companies. The auto-maker's Internet initiative is part of a broader strategy of moving into non-traditional modes of advertising where the consumers invite the message rather than having it directed at them.

Apart from the deal with the new media publisher, GM launched its own sites in North America and in Europe, where browsers can view various models from different angles, equip them with assorted options and play trivia games. Based on merely two months' experience on the Web, GM's European division decided to enlarge online advertising for its Opel line of cars beyond its original focus in Germany, Switzerland and Austria to encompass all of Europe.[24]

The next revolutionary changes in communication technology are under way. In early 1996, Intel, the world's leading producer of micro-processors which, in 1995, invested more than 20 per cent of its total sales of more than USD15 billion in research and development, announced the development of a new generation of micro-processors, the MMX, which allow users of PCs equipped with them to call others via the Internet, to see them on the screen, and to exchange data simultaneously. This is the first step to make the Internet a communication tool as simple as the phone, but with the additional benefit of real-time picture and data transmission. Compaq and IBM have signed agreements with Intel to sell PCs ready for use as video-conference terminals.[25]

Satellite TV has also changed the way business is conducted, for example advertising. Commercials broadcast in England may be seen throughout Europe, increasing the need to understand cultural differences and the effects of communication standardization. Specialized firms such as DirecTv in the USA, which delivers digital video to subscribers via a home satellite dish, have experienced tremendous growth. The company signed up 1.25 million customers in only 18 months of existence. Customers can order cable programmes, films and sporting events. In Germany, the Kirch Group, a commercial TV company, has established DF-1 GmbH, which entered the digital TV market in July 1996, a few months ahead of its main rival MMBG, formed by Deutsche Telekom AG and Bertelsmann AG, one of the largest media houses in Europe.

Perhaps more importantly, satellite television has significantly changed how quickly people receive information about significant events around the world. This in turn probably changes the way they view not only world problems, but also consumption opportunities and the solutions they think should be pursued.

Global Competition.   For many firms, the primary driving force to start international business is competition. Business today is increasingly characterized by competitors operating on an international level.   Both local and national firms are confronted with foreign competitors in their home markets. Since the mid-1980s, for example, more than 70 per cent of all goods produced in the USA have faced direct competition from non-domestic sources. For example, consumer electronics firms based in Taiwan and South Korea sell their products in the US market. Global competitors often manage to put local manufacturers under high competitive pressure or even drive them entirely out of the market.

Basically, competition can be local/national, regional or global (Figure 1.4). Competition is purely local or national when the companies serving a country market are all based in that market. Such competition is limited to countries where legal regulations erect insurmountable barriers to foreign competitors – examples are most of the European postal services which only recently started to become deregulated, or most less industrially developed countries which try to protect their vulnerable industries through barriers to foreign competition – or some local personal services markets, such as hairdressing.

Competition is regional when competitors serving a country-market come from different neighbouring countries. This was the case in most markets of highly industrialized countries until limits to growth made governments liberalize international trade and technological changes allowed competitors from all over the world to enter most of those country-markets. For example, in the European shoe market Italian manufacturers competed against German, French and local producers in the respective country-markets. In recent years, brands have stayed European, but a substantial volume of shoes is manufactured in Eastern Europe, Southeast Asia and Brazil.

Global competition exists when the companies competing for customers in a country-market come from all over the world. This is the case for an increasing number of products, such as consumer electronics, food products, cars, machinery, electrical engines and pharmaceuticals, as well as industrial engineering, bank or insurance services, especially in the highly developed industrial countries.

Industries can be domestic only, when the need they serve does not exist in other countries or when legal barriers prevent foreign competitors from entering a country-market. In that case competition will be local/national. Firms from other countries either will not have the specific skills and know-how to satisfy the local need, or will be held off by the existing barriers.

What may happen in a market which was closed to foreign competition and is suddenly opened up is well illustrated by Chile's long-distance telephone market. In 1995, all restrictions on entry into the long-distance business were removed at one stroke. More than half a dozen Chilean companies have jumped into the fray, along with three US firms: Bell South, SBC, and Bell Atlantic. As a result, the price of off-peak calls from Chile to the US fell from USD 1.50 a minute in late 1994 – just before competition began – to about 25 cents a minute – the lowest in the world for international long dis-

Figure 1.4 GLOBALIZATION OF COMPETITION AND INDUSTRIES

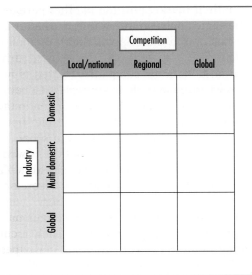

A company may be active in a purely domestic, a multidomestic or a global industry. In each of those industries a company may face local/national, regional and global competition.

tance. Callers in Chile can switch phone companies on a call-by-call basis simply by dialling a three-digit prefix. The phone companies are bombarding the country with ads touting low prices. Barely more than a year before free competition was allowed, Entel, once Chile's state-owned long-distance carrier and now private, had 100 per cent of the market. In early 1996 its share was 40 per cent.[26]

Global competition in a product or service category of a country-market does not automatically mean that the industry to which the product or service belongs is also global. It might be multidomestic. In a multidomestic industry competitors in each country can come from all over the world, but owing to differences specific to each country-market, the relative competitive position of a competitor is largely independent of its competitive position in other countries. In a multidomestic industry, which was common two decades ago and still exists today, a firm can choose to remain domestic or become multinational, applying different strategies depending on local market conditions. Mr Maucher, the former president of Nestlé, for example, followed the guiding principle that 'every business is local'. He therefore insisted on local adaptations of strategies for all brands, even globally marketed ones such as Nescafé. Other companies, such as Austria's VA Industrial Engineering, one of the three world-leading firms in metallurgical engineering, have been following a standardized strategy all over the world for the past 15 years. They are now convinced they are part of a multidomestic industry. They perceive the needs of their customers to be regionally differentiated to an extent that regionally adapted strategies seem to be justified.

In recent years a growing number of industries have become global in their competitive scope, that is, a firm's competitive position in one country is significantly influenced by its position in other countries. Examples of global industries include commercial aircraft, computers, consumer electronics and watches. In a more global industry, the firm that wants to survive must develop an integrated worldwide strategy for all of its operations. The potential success of Dell personal computers or Microsoft software in Europe, for example, depends on their market position in other parts of the world, in particular the USA. The same applies to the watch market. A brand that does not reach an important position in the USA will find it difficult to be successful in the rest of the world.

This means that large national companies (which may be small in global terms) might be forced to change their strategies. Companies like US Steel and British Leyland Motor Corporation, strong national firms that may even have been leaders in their industry at one time, find their competitive positions eroded as the industry becomes global in scope.

Most industries are somewhere between multidomestic and global. However, there is a clear trend towards increasingly global industries. The importance of different country-market strategies is decreasing in computers, pharmaceutical products, chemicals, machinery, telecommunications, transportation and industrial control systems. Similar developments are being seen in consumer and service industries such as luxury accessories, soft drinks, clothing, entertainment, tourism, insurance, shipping and banking.

The globalization of industries is characterized by take-overs, mergers and cooperation between competitors who seek to reduce their costs and build the financial and technical resources to strengthen their market position on a global level. The Swiss drug giants, Sandoz Ltd and Ciba-Geigy Ltd, for example, merged in 1996 to create Novartis, a biotechnological powerhouse with a strong presence in virtually every important area of new-drug research. With a combined 4.4 per cent global market share it is the world's second-largest pharmaceutical maker after Glaxo Wellcome of the UK and ahead of Merck & Co. of the USA.[27]

Smaller companies are not necessarily forced out of the market as their industry becomes global. Instead, they may discover opportunities in special market niches. These may be defined either by specific customer needs or tastes, or by country-market characteristics, such as legal restrictions, governmental control, or payment in products instead of money.

The menswear group Ermenegildo Zegna, an 85-year-old family-owned company based in Trevero, at the foot of the Italian Alps, is an example of successful exploitation of an international market niche. Strictly a textile company for its first 40 years, Zegna still supplies fabric to some of Europe's top fashion houses. But now it offers its own clothing line as well. It is positioned as having the highest quality and most innovative fabrics. In the USA, Zegna has been helped by the move away from boxy Ivy League suits. It offers a sleeker look in suits along with deconstructed 'casual Friday' wear. And although the total American suit market has shrunk, the upper end is still growing. Zegna's total sales in 1995 reached USD500 million, making it one of the fastest-growing fashion groups in Europe.[28]

The increased intensity of competition in domestic markets, or international market potential, should encourage entrepreneurs and managers of smaller companies to enter non-domestic markets themselves. For firms with high-quality products that have gained customer acceptance, it may actually be easier to expand into other markets than to increase their share of the domestic market. If a firm has recognized expertise in a specific area, it may be able to 'export' its know-how, thereby obtaining a considerable amount of global business.

In sum, no member of an industry, whatever its size, can continue to focus solely on domestic business. Even small firms have to consider the international business environment in order to improve their long-term chances of survival. Many decide to do so by relying on 'local charm' which means high attractiveness to local partners (customers, intermediaries, regulators, media) through better services, customer-specific differentiation (tailor-made goods), faster delivery of benefits and personal relationship building.

Access to Resources. Companies that operate internationally treat the world as a source of supply as well as demand. They obtain the resources they need wherever they can buy them at the best price. Technological know-how gained in different parts of the world is quickly applied to new products. Co-operation with firms in other nations can reduce costs and increase management knowledge, further enhancing the competitiveness of global firms relative to others.

For example, Germany's Siemens AG and French-British GEC Alsthom are fierce competitors in the European and North American markets. In 1996, GEC Alsthom had just won a contract of USD150 million for the modernization of the Washington–Boston railway line against Siemens, when the two companies decided to cooperate in marketing their high-speed trains ICE (Intercity Express) and TGV (Train à Grande Vitesse) in Asia, in particular China and Taiwan. For that purpose they founded a marketing agency, called 'Euro Train', on a joint venture basis, without placing any capital. Its purpose is to submit tailor-made offers to the Asian clients, using the best-suited parts of both train systems, and to improve their competitive position against Japanese competitors.[29]

In many industries the rate of innovation is not very dramatic. As a consequence, domestic as well as global competition for market share often boils down to a race to lower prices. Hence, opportunities to reduce costs and/or increase efficiency are welcome. Again, the firm with non-domestic business has an advantage. It has access to cheaper sources of raw material, capital and labour. For example, Fujitsu, in order to become the number two PC maker in Japan, overhauled its supply network in 1995, dumping locally made parts in favour of foreign components which were 20 to 30 per cent cheaper. Manufacturing spare parts or even entire products in low-wage countries allows global firms to engage in intensive price competition against domestic firms in many markets. Wage rates do change, however. Tandy, for example, closed a computer-component plant in Korea, due in part to Korea's industrial wage increasing 110 per cent since opening the plant.

Research and development can be conducted wherever the necessary resources in terms of brainpower, technological know-how and capital are located. Companies such as Hofman-Laroche, a Swiss pharmaceutical manufacturer, increasingly locate their research centres near to centres of intellectual excellence such as university departments specializing in their domain of research. Proximity not only furthers research cooperation but also facilitates hiring the best graduates. Other firms choose sites where companies doing research in the same field are located, such as Silicon Valley in California or Sophia Antipolis in the south of France. Most international companies procure research and development services from specialized firms or institutions in various countries. For example, in addition to purchasing business software from US vendors, American Express obtains high-quality software at a lower cost from a supplier based in India.

New developments in process technology (such as improvements in manufacturing equipment) can be identified and applied at short notice in many foreign countries. One of the biggest mistakes of US industrial policy in the 1980s was to overlook the importance of production-process technologies. A company cannot maintain a competitive advantage in industries with rapid new product development based on the latest technology when foreign competitors can produce the same products far more quickly and cheaply. US companies were slow to grasp the importance of automation and quality management control, both of which were developed in the USA but applied with much more rigour and success in other countries, including Japan, Germany, Sweden and France. In the 1990s Europe runs the risk of being too slow in restructuring its production processes to become leaner and more flexible in a much-needed reaction to changes in technological opportunities and customer needs.

To attain and maintain global competitiveness, however, it is not enough simply to keep abreast of technological developments. Serving more than one country-market allows the firm to balance resource investments in some markets against resource surpluses in others. Moreover, when a competitor attacks it in its home market, a globally competitive firm would be able to mount a counterattack in the competitor's own domain.

SUMMARY

In the past two hundred years the world economy has continually grown. Growth and accumulation of material wealth were not equally distributed across countries. Differences are mainly due to the different levels of education, skills and know-how of a country's population, the accumulation of capital for production purposes instead of consumption, the speed of technological development and its implementation in new products and processes, and the extent of liberalization of trade inside the country as well as with international partners.

Liberalization of world trade has triggered major impulses for the development of the world's economy. In recent years international trade has been growing significantly faster than most national economies. Trade liberalization has been achieved on different levels. On the one hand, deregulation of country-markets has opened up new opportunities for national and international business. On the other, international agreements on the reduction of tariffs and non-tariff barriers have become very popular in most parts of the world during the 1990s.

Such agreements do not happen by chance, however. One of the major driving forces for liberalization of international trade has been the limited growth potential in the home markets of companies based in the most highly industrialized countries. Tremendous technological changes – in particular in communication technologies – have added to that effect.

Many industries in a world with decreasing barriers to international business have changed from a multidomestic to a global state. Not only do we find the same competitors in most country-markets of the world, but their competitive position in each market also depends on their position in others. That is, in order to be successful in a world of global business, a company – of whatever size – must assess opportunities and threats on an international level, and must develop a strategy that takes into account its strengths and weaknesses compared to competitors potentially based all over the world.

ADDITIONAL READINGS

Egan, C. and P. McKiernan (1994) *Inside Fortress Europe – Strategies for the Single Market*, Wokingham: Addison-Wesley.

Hirschey, M., J.L. Pappas and D. Whigham (1995) *Managerial Economics, European Edition*, London: International Thomson Business Press.

Jeannette, J.-P. and H. D. Hennessey(1995) *Global Marketing Strategies*, 3rd. edn, Boston, MA: Houghton Mifflin.

Minc, A. (1992) *The Great European Illusion – Business in the Wider Community*, Cambridge, MA: Blackwell Publishers.

DISCUSSION QUESTIONS

1. What are the pros and cons of trade liberalization from an economic, political and social point of view? Gather some recent material from newspapers and trade magazines to substantiate your points.
2. Why is world economic integration increasing?
3. What are the major international agreements on economic cooperation? How have they been developing in the past three years? What are their most important plans for the coming five years?
4. Why is the Triad so important to marketers today?
5. Look for two examples of companies which have gone international in the past three years. What were their major reasons for doing so?
6. The importance of international or global business to large firms is real. But small firms that sell only in the domestic market do not need to be concerned.' Do you agree with this statement? Why or why not?
7. What are the latest technological changes facilitating international business? What impact do they have on how business is conducted?
8. What are the major reasons why an increasing number of industries develop from multidomestic to global?
9. Find two recent examples of companies doing business in globalizing industries. How do those companies react to globalization?
10. What kinds of resources can be advantageously procured through international business? Find examples of companies.

NOTES

[1] '200 Jahre Aufschwung', *Unternehmer*, February 1996, pp. 19–21.
[2] World Bank Atlas 1995.
[3] Tomlinson, R. (1996), 'While Asian Women Buy . . .', *International Herald Tribune*, 16–17 March, p. 22.
[4] 'Maruti's wager', *The Economist*, 2 March 1996, pp. 62f.
[5] Hamilton, D.P. (1996), 'Japan Struggles to Follow US In Telecommunications Reform', *The Wall Street Journal*, 14 February, p. A11.
[6] Magnusson, P. and J. Barnathan (1997), 'Slow Dance with the Dragon', *Business Week*, 7 April, pp. 52f.
[7] *The Wall Street Journal Europe – Putting the Euro on the Map*, May 1998.
[8] Associated Press News Service 1996.
[9] Kunz, A. (1998), 'Der asiatische Alptraum,' *Der Standard*, 17 June, p. 2.
[10] Blustein, P. (1996), 'NAFTA's Effect on Jobs: Not So Bad', *International Herald Tribune*, 9–10 March, p. 9.
[11] Abellard, A. (1997), 'Cap sur l'Amérique du Sud', *Le Monde Economie*, 11 March, I.
[12] Bray, N. (1998), 'Sign of the Times', *The Wall Street Journal Europe*, May, p. R4.
[13] Smith, P. (1997), 'Is the UK to be an EMU or an ostrich?', *Accountancy – International Edition*, March, p. 64.
[14] Bray, N. (1998), 'Sign of the Times', *The Wall Street Journal Europe*, May, p. R4.
[15] 'The war goes on', *The Economist*, 2 March, 1996, p. 62.
[16] 'Direktinvestitionen als Entwicklungsmotor', *Neue Zürcher Zeitung*, 30/31 May 1998, p. 25.
[17] Rosenkranz, C. (1996), 'Dominierendes Auslandskapital', *Der Standard*, 25 March, p. 18.
[18] 'Die Kluft zwischen Reichen und Armen wird immer größer', *Der Standard*, 18 December 1995, p. 18.
[19] Naughton, K. (1996), 'America's No.1 Car Exporter Is . . . Japan?', *Business Week*, 26 February, p. 113.
[20] Riley-Adams, R. (1993), 'Hands Across the Sea', *International Management*, July/August, pp. 23f.
[21] Koretz, G. (1996), 'US Exports Gain an Edge', *Business Week*, 4 March, p. 26.
[22] 'Carrefour en Corée du Sud et en Thailande', *Le Figaro économie*, 8 March 1996, p. VIII.

[23] 'Casino: priorité à l'international', *Le Figaro économie*, 8 March 1996, p. VIII.

[24] Covington, R. (1996), 'GM and Bass: Web Case Studies', *International Herald Tribune*, 25 March, p. 17.

[25] Gourévitch, J.-M. (1996), 'Intel: le choc de 1996', *Le Figaro économie*, 11 March, p. 9.

[26] Kupfer, A. (1996), 'Phone Competition Is Hot-Wired in Chile', *Fortune*, Vol. 133, 19 February, p. 26.

[27] Collins, G. (1996), 'Swiss Drug-Company Merger Creates Biotechnology Giant', *International Herald Tribune*, 10 March, pp. 1 and 10.

[28] Rossant, J.(1996), 'Is that a Zegna You're Wearing?', *Business Week*, 4 March, pp. 84f.

[29] Dugua, P.-Y. (1996), 'Bombardier et GEC-Alsthom remportent le projet Washington-Boston', *Le Figaro économie*, 16-17 March, p. 1; 'Siemens und GEC fahren mit ICE und TGV gemeinsam', *Der Standard*, 29 March, 1996, p. 30.

CHAPTER 2

INTERNATIONAL MARKETING STRATEGY –
THE KEY TO SUCCESS

INTERNATIONAL INCIDENT

Defend or Expand ?

On the first of January 1995 Austria, Finland and Sweden joined the European Union. From that day on, companies in the three countries had to face free international competition, whether they had been active internationally or not. Christian Sommerhuber, the owner of Sommerhuber Keramik GesmbH, a small-sized industrial producer of ceramic tiles for tiled stoves which had been largely dominating its Austrian home market, had achieved about 10 per cent market share in Germany, and had been present in neighbouring North-Italian and Swiss markets. He was confronted with the fact that the total sales volume of the industry in the entire region was shrinking. To improve their situation, competitors from Germany and Italy prepared to enter the now open Austrian market. How should he react?

One potential solution was to focus on defending the firm's position in its home market. The service to local stove makers and customers of tiled stoves could be improved by offering virtual reality computer facilities whereby potential customers would be able to see how the offered stove would look in their homes. The range of products offered to the local stove makers could be expanded by open fireplace elements or iron stoves. And the capital accumulated during the years of success could be used to strengthen the firm's position through the acquisition of distributors.

Another solution was to attack competition in their own markets head on. For that purpose a direct distribution system would have to be established in the German and Italian markets, a production site for lower-priced tiles established or acquired in the Czech Republic, and a productivity campaign launched in the Austrian factory.

Finally, as a third solution, expansion to new country-markets was considered. For that purpose the benefits the company was able to provide, the potential customers interested in such benefits, and the technologies available to the firm for providing those benefits needed to be determined. Mr Sommerhuber hired a consultant to help him assess potential markets in Northern Europe and to find out the extent of needed adaptations of his company's product range, market communication, distribution and pricing.

In summer 1996, the firm started activities to follow up on all three options.

BUSINESS RESPONSE
TO THE CHALLENGE

The saturation of many local markets and fast technological change together with the liberalization of world trade have led to increasing global competition and a need for global procurement of resources. Those major changes in the business environment require a firm to assess opportunities and threats, strengths and weaknesses from a different perspective compared to strictly local business. Basic management decisions have to include an answer to the question of whether the company should and is able to conduct international operations, and to what extent it should dedicate its resources to that purpose.

A firm does not have to be a global giant like Mitsubishi or Boeing to need to look for business opportunities and watch for potential threats outside of its local environment. Smaller firms like Waterford Wedgwood, a manufacturer of fine china based in the UK, compete successfully in Japan, the USA and Europe. Medium-sized US firms like Scientific Atlanta, a global marketer of telecommunications system, are quite successfull throughout the world against much larger corporations such as Alcatel (France) and NEC (Japan). What counts most is the managers' view of their firm's markets.

Perspectives of International Business

The critical element for success in international business is not so much the size of the company but an approach or business perspective of top management that seeks to do business where it can be done with the greatest success. As we have seen in the preceding chapter, at the end of the twentieth century, most industries are multidomestic or global. This does not mean, however, that managers must view their companies' markets in a similar way. They can approach business from various perspectives. One classification of potential views is EPRG: ethnocentric, polycentric, regional, geocentric.

Ethnocentric Perspective. An ethnocentric manager sees the domestic market as most important, reacting defensively to international markets, if at all. US car manufacturers in the 1960s, for example, held this view when they argued that imports such as the VW 'beetle', and later Toyota's cars, wouldn't sell well, since only Detroit knew what US customers wanted. The price of maintaining such a perspective in terms of sales and profit was very high, as Japanese cars have gained nearly 30 per cent of the US market.

Some small, locally operating businesses do not perceive the threat embodied in today's global business world. They feel certain that their markets are too small and too specialized to be entered by global competitors. Or they put their faith in economic, political and legal barriers to entry by foreign firms. But is any business's current success and future profit potential really independent of developments in other parts of the world? Even the owner of a pharmacy in Llandudno, Wales, needs to take a more global view. From the prices of the products sold in the store to the rate of interest on the mortgage, many elements of day-to-day business reflect the impact of decisions made in London, Tokyo or Frankfurt.

Polycentric Perspective. A polycentric manager sees international markets as a series of domestic (or national) markets. The US-based Ford Motor Company or the Netherlands-based Philips NV, for example, evolved to this orientation as evidenced by their multiple production plants and marketing organizations throughout the world. Up until recently, they by and large produced within each major domestic market, for that market, for example within the UK and within Germany. This led them to cater strongly to each individual market's tastes and preferences, and be seen as a 'UK' company, a 'German' company, and so on. But it also increased the complexity of their organization, made them less cost competitive and impeded a company-wide mutual learning process.

Regional Perspective. A manager with a regional orientation focuses on a clearly limited 'product-market', which is defined by specific benefits delivered to a group of customers by the use of certain technologies (ways to provide those benefits). National boundaries and differencies are respected, but are not of primary importance. In serving the product-market, the firm seeks opportunities for coordinating and possibly standardizing procurement, production and marketing, but usually within a geographic or perhaps culturally homogeneous region. For example, a firm like Wolford, the leading manufacturer of upscale fashionable women's tights in Europe, has focused its marketing activities on Western Europe. They concentrate production in Bregenz, Austria, communicate with their customers, intermediaries and shareholders by staging large events which attract media interest all over Europe, use the same packaging and shop displays in all countries, and distribute their products in less than 48 hours from one warehouse at their production site. Only recently has the company started to change its view to become more geocentric. It has been opening up a growing number of 'Wolford Boutiques' in the metropolitan areas of the USA, in Japan, Hong Kong and Singapore. As the Future Issues box illustrates, other companies such as global car manufacturers might be on their way back from a geocentric to a more regional perspective of international business.

Geocentric Perspective. A manager with a geocentric view is continually seeking out opportunities for procurement, production and marketing coordination and standardization in a worldwide product-market, independent of national borders. Diet Coke, for example, is produced and marketed in such a manner. The product formula, positioning and advertising are uniform across nations. The brand name varies slightly owing to various legal regulations. In some Western European countries the word diet has medical implications. So Coke Light or another name is used instead of Diet Coke. The artificial sweetener and package also differ in some countries, and promotional programmes are localized. Despite the variations, while the Coca-Cola Company is based in the USA, it earns 80 per cent its profits from international sales and clearly has a geocentric view of its markets.

Major Decisions

Confronted with the increasing globalization of trade and the driving forces of international business, entrepreneurs and top managers who have overcome an ethnocentric perspective of international business have to answer four fundamental questions:

↔ Should our firm go international or not?

↔ Which markets should be served and in what sequence?

↔ How much of our resources should we spend for what purposes?

↔ How should we build and sustain our firm's competitive advantages?

Figure 2.1 shows that the answers to these questions will depend on external and internal stimuli facing a company's decision makers, their personal motives, and the major company objectives agreed upon by the dominant management group in the firm.

FUTURE ISSUES BOX

Return to a Regional Business Perspective

CAR MAKERS SUCH AS CITROEN, HONDA, OPEL, OR Toyota increasingly try to tailor their cars to the preferences of different homogeneous customer regions.

In 1996, Toyota Motor Corp. has disclosed the first concrete details of its plan to launch a stripped-down subcompact economy car, based on its Tercel model, for fast-growing Southeast Asian nations. Asia's No.1 car maker plans to invest about 20 billion yen (USD184.6 million) to double the output of its Thai assembly plant and to expand its Thai engine plant by nearly 50 per cent, both within two years. The car will be sold in Thailand and later is expected to be sold in other Asian nations.

Toyota's aggressive expansion plan is the latest salvo in an intense battle among global car makers to woo the growing ranks of middle-class buyers in Asia with 'Asian cars,' – leaner versions of existing compact cars.

Already, Honda Motor Co. has unveiled its 'Asia Car' in April 1996, at least nine months ahead of Toyota's launch. European car manufacturers also are gearing up for the burgeoning Asian market. Citroen agreed with state-owned Malaysian car company, Proton, to produce a version of its AX compact car there. Opel is scouting out sites in the Philippines to build a Southeast Asian version of its Corsa subcompact. And Volkswagen AG, the biggest auto maker in Europe and China, with Chinese partners, is represented with the Santana compact and with cars made in Asia by its Czech Republic subsidiary, Skoda Automobilova AS.

How well these 'Asian cars' will sell remains to be seen. One key to the cars' success seems to be tailoring the models to the preferences of each country in which they are sold.

Source: Reitman, V. (1996) 'Toyota Unveils Plan to Make Leaner Car for Southeast Asia,' *The Wall Street Journal Europe*, 11 April, p. 3.

Local vs. International Business.   External and internal stimuli serve as triggers for decision-making processes concerning the first question: Should the firm expand its business internationally or not? External stimuli may include unsolicited orders from foreign customers, perceived market opportunities, competitive pressures in the home market, or government programmes to encourage exports. Honda, for example, today the leading manufacturer of motor cycles, once found competition by Yamaha so strong in its Japanese home market that it decided to enter the less competitive markets of Europe and the USA in order to grow.

Internal stimuli may include unique products, strong marketing skills or excess capacity in the areas of production, finance, marketing or management. The design of Louis Vuitton luggage, its high-quality/high-prestige image, and the attractive shape of their stores in France, for example, resulted in so many Japanese tourists buying their products that the firm decided to open their own stores in Japan. In 1996, sales to Japanese customers accounted for about 30 per cent of the company's total sales. When Apple first marketed its PC, the product had such superior graphic facilities that customers in the communication business around the world wanted to use them. Those early adopters served as the spearheads for the company's entry into the global business market.

Figure 2.1 **FACTORS INFLUENCING THE INTERNATIONALIZATION DECISIONS OF MANAGERS**

The level of a company's international involvement, the choice of markets to be served and the resources allocated to global expansion as well as the building and sustaining of appropriate competitive advantages depend on external and internal stimuli facing the company's decision makers, the personal motives of those managers, and the major company objectives agreed upon by the dominant management group in the firm.

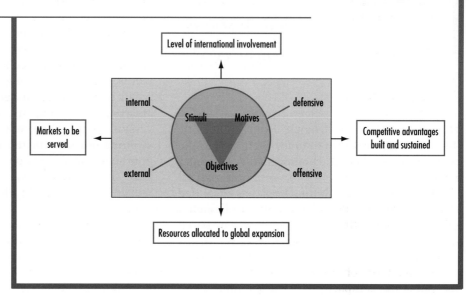

A company's top managers become aware of those stimuli. But each manager is likely to have different knowledge and skills, varying experiences and differing personal motives which make them more or less sensitive to the stimuli and lead to different reactions. Human decision making is never based on objective criteria but on subjective interpretations of information stored in memory and data gathered from the environment. Decision makers have to decide what information is needed and what information can be ignored. What managers think to be relevant in a given decision situation is determined by their cognitive frameworks, that is, their 'theories' and assumptions about the environments, the methods they use to observe and analyse those environments, and their personal involvement with the decision that needs to be taken.

Consequently, management's reactions to international business opportunities are not always governed by business strategies, profit-and-loss evaluations or capital budgeting schemes. Sometimes international sales are achieved at a very low level of marketing activities as a result of unsolicited orders from non-domestic customers. Usually they are based on psychic distance, that is, the perception of differences (psychological distance) between foreign and domestic markets. 'Going international' exposes managers to unknown environments, such as different buyer behaviour, which increases their perceived risk. Management may have heard of important differences, such as different symbolic meanings of colour. (For example, white is a symbol of death in Japan. There, products packaged in white boxes do not sell as well as they do in the USA, where white symbolizes purity.) But knowing little about such differences makes managers anxious about doing business in 'foreign' lands. They experience psychic distance. In order to reduce this tension of dealing with the 'unknown', they often choose to expand into markets which are perceived as more similar. An Irish company, for example, may respond immediately to an order from an English firm because it feels comfortable selling to a 'well-known' trading partner. Yet a potentially more profitable order from a German firm may receive no response because the Irish firm's managers feel uneasy about the large number of unfamiliar tasks and unknown risks (for example, negotiating in a foreign language, drafting contracts, hedging against changes in currency exchange, transportation overseas, financial standing of the potential customer, or keeping to the terms of payment) which might be involved.

Managers' personal involvement with the level of internationalization of their company's business largely depends on their motives. They may be classified as either defensive or offensive. Defensive motives may be, for example, to focus on protecting domestic market share from a foreign competitor or to ascertain a satisfactory level of company value added, sales or profit. When defensive motives dominate, management is reluctant to become involved in international business. Some managers will even react negatively to the idea. They may be generally reluctant to change, taking a position of 'wait and see', follow traditional lines of business, being satisfied with their local business success, or fear the additional stress of international business and the risks involved, owing to their lack of specific knowledge.

As the level of information and experience increases, perceived risk decreases and companies generally enter more dissimilar ('riskier') markets. More innovative managers appreciate the long-term growth potential that results from international business and the resulting opportunities to develop new capabilities (technologies, expertise, experience) and new products. Instead of reacting passively to stimuli from external or internal environments, more experienced, but also more entrepreneurial types of company decision makers will proactively consider non-domestic business opportunities as part of their firm's strategic decision making.

Offensive motives lead to aggressive and systematic efforts to locate or respond to global opportunities. An offensive motive would be, for example, to attack foreign competitors in their strongest market. This was done, for example, in what the Japanese called 'Compaq shokku', in 1992, when the Houston personal computer maker brought US-style competition to Japan: it started selling desktop PCs for less than half of what Japanese manufacturers had been asking. Other US PC marketers, such as Apple, caught on, and within three years, American companies drove PC prices down by 37 per cent in the Japanese market, and seized one-third of the USD12.3 billion market.[1]

Market Attractiveness.   When management has decided to internationalize the business of their firm, the question of which markets should be served arises. Because this decision will bind the company's resources for a substantial amount of time, the risk involved is high. To take a rational decision, management needs to undertake a market assessment procedure that allows them to evaluate carefully the attractiveness of different product and geographic (country) markets.

Such a market assessment procedure has its foundation in the firm's statement of corporate policy (Figure 2.2). A corporate policy includes information about the company's mission and business philosophy. The mission states the rationale for the existence of the organization. It defines its business domain, and the major objectives it hopes to achieve. The mission is the framework which guides the decisions and actions of all the members of the firm. The

Figure 2.2 THE IMPACT OF CORPORATE POLICY ON POTENTIAL MARKET ASSESSMENT

Corporate policy defines the product-market(s) to be focused upon, indicates criteria for the fast exclusion of geographic markets from further analysis, and contains major criteria for assessing the attractiveness of remaining geographic markets.

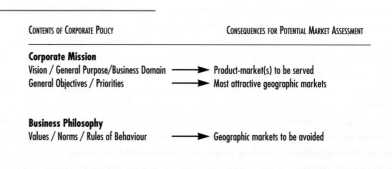

business philosophy formulates the rules of behaviour that are to be followed inside the company as well as in contacts with parties outside the company. It guides the manner in which relationships with different business partners and other groups of individuals affected by the company's activities are managed.

The mission statement begins by defining the general purpose of the company – the vision of its founders or top managers. For example, Salomon, the French marketer of sports equipment and world leader in ski sports, has formulated their corporate vision as follows: 'At Salomon everybody is passionate about sports. It is our goal to develop products for all people in the world doing sports and to provide an additional service level which together allow sportspeople to make progress and discover great new experiences.'

The mission statement then defines the business of the firm – which benefits the company will provide to which customers and which technologies (or ways to provide those benefits) it will use for that purpose. For example, Liechtenstein-based HILTI AG, one of the world's largest suppliers of all kinds of industrial fastenings, defined its business as follows: 'We satisfy market needs in the field of fastening technology for customers involved in small and industrial construction and for all other industrial purposes by offering tools, equipment, and elements in combination with pre and after-sales service from the detection of the customers' needs to their satisfaction.'

Through such a statement a firm defines its most attractive product-market(s) in general terms. In theory, a company can choose among alternatives ranging from focusing on one specific benefit for one customer segment and applying a single technology, to trying to provide an entire range of benefits to all potential customers through applying all available technologies. A restrictive business definition might be, for example, to 'serve fast food to young urban professionals through an office delivery network'. An extensive business definition would be to 'satisfy all kinds of drinking needs for all consumers, offering all varieties of available drinks'. In practice, the optimal definition of the business should depend upon the company's resources and skills, as much as on perceived market opportunities.

If management has adopted a geocentric perspective, the firm's product-markets will usually be distributed over a number of country-markets. The evaluation of which country-markets are most attractive will depend upon the firm's major objectives and their priorities as formulated in the corporate mission. Objectives may include growth versus stability, return on investment, market share, acceptable level of risk, approach to technology and innovation, image and goodwill, establishment of a specific working climate within the organization, and independence versus cooperation as a general approach to business.

For example, when Austrian Doppelmayr, the world-leading producer of ski lifts, chair lifts and cable cars, assessed Asian markets for potential investment in a production site, they had to bear in mind that their corporate mission demands the application of the latest technology in the products and production processes of the firm, a cost structure which allows lower production costs than the major competitors, a consolidated corporate real growth rate of an average 10 per cent a year, the exceptional use of foreign capital for the purpose of interim financing only, and capital flows from subsidiaries to the headquarters. Because objectives are not always consistent – a high growth rate goal may conflict with a goal restricting the use of foreign capital, for example – the mission statement indicates which priorities should be pursued. In the case of Doppelmayr the mission statement allows interim financing by foreign capital when growth cannot be exclusively financed by the firm's cash flow.

Finally, the basic values and norms – formulated in the business philosophy – a company wants its personnel to respect in their internal and external behaviour may lead management to avoid certain country-markets. For example, 93 per cent of all Fortune 1000 firms have formulated corporate ethics codes which in many cases are part of their business philosophy. Those ethics codes lead company managers to rate country-markets very low in attractiveness, for example, where bribes are needed to complete business deals. This is the case in most of the economically less developed countries of Africa, Asia and South America. The Ethics box gives an example of such a corporate ethics code.

Resource Allocation. The resources of a company, even the world's largest, are not unlimited. As there are always a greater number of attractive market opportunities around the world than can be pursued, management has to answer a third major question: How much of our resources should we spend for what purpose?

In answering this question, management has to find a balance between choosing too many markets, which inevitably leads to a lack of sufficient resources in some or each of the served markets, and deciding upon too small a number of markets, keeping the firm from efficiently exploiting its opportunities. Depending upon a number of factors such as the relative size of its home market, the competitive situation there compared to other markets, the degree of globalization of competitors, growth objectives set by corporate policy, or the kind and importance of competitive advantages, management will choose the degree of globalization for its company.

The Jefferson Smurfit Group, an international paper and packaging concern based in Ireland, for example, has decided that its Asian expansion plans will proceed in a 'phased approach'. In 1995, the company made its first direct investment in Asia with privately owned Singapore-based New Toyo to form Smurfit Toyo, which makes folding cartons. Additionally, Smurfit formed a joint venture in China where it bought a linerboard mill near Shanghai.

ETHICS BOX

Acting
with Integrity

NORTEL's CORE VALUES

"AS AN OPERATING PRINCIPLE, WE WILL CONDUCT OUR business honestly and ethically wherever we operate in the world. Acting with integrity builds credibility – that fragile, intangible asset that's so hard to gain, so easy to lose, and so difficult to regain. Ethical conduct is the way we protect our credibility as a company, establish respect for the dignity of every individual, earn the trust of our partners and customers, and define the character of our business."

CORE VALUES: A GUIDE TO ETHICAL BUSINESS PRACTICE

New ways of organizing people and work within the corporation are giving each of us more decision-making responsibility. Given the complexity and constantly changing nature of our work and our world, no book of hard-and-fast rules – however long and detailed – could ever adequately cover all the dilemmas people face. In this context, every Nortel employee is asked to take leadership in ethical decision making.

> *We create superior value for our customers.*
> *We work to provide shareholder value.*
> *Our people are our strength.*
> *We share one vision. We are one team.*
> *We have only one standard – excellence.*
> *We embrace change and reward innovation.*
> *We fulfill our commitments and act with integrity.*

PERSONAL VALUES AND CORPORATE INTEGRITY

In most situations, our personal values and honesty will guide us to the right decision. But in our capacity as employees and representatives of Nortel, we must also always consider how our actions affect the integrity and credibility of the corporation as a whole. Our business ethics must reflect the standard of conduct outlined in this document – a standard grounded in the corporation's values, and governing Nortel's relationships with all stakeholders.

Our decisions as to what is ethical business practice in a Nortel context must be guided by the seven Core Values that form the fundamental basis of our conduct as a business. From these statements stem a series of commitments that we as Nortel employees make to each other, to shareholders, customers, suppliers, and the communities in which we do business.

A SHARED RESPONSIBILITY

The final core value emphasizes our intention to fulfill our commitments and to do so with integrity. Integrity means 'wholeness' – it means that all the parts are aligned and work together. It means, for example, that each individual within the corporation is doing his or her best to live by the standard of business conduct outlined in this Code.

'Acting with integrity' also means that while we may not always be sure of every answer, we will not say one thing and then do another. We will not make promises that we have no intention of keeping or cannot be reasonably sure we will be able to keep. We will strive to the best of our ability to support all the commitments that the corporation has made to conducting business in an honest and ethical manner.

PUTTING THE VALUES TO WORK: ETHICAL COMMITMENTS

The following pages take a more in-depth look at what it means to put these values to work in our business. The section entitled *Living the Commitments: Guidelines for Ethical Decision-making* outlines your role in enabling the corporation to meet its commitments to stakeholders and maintain its ethical standards. When individuals choose to disregard the Code, we all could suffer from damage to the corporate reputation and the ensuing loss of customers community and employee goodwill, and profitability. Serious violations of the standards may result in termination of employment. Actions that are against the law may be subject to criminal prosecution.

You have a personal responsibility to make sure that all your words and actions live up to these statements. **You** have a responsibility to ask questions when you have doubts about the ethical implications of any given situation or proposed course of action. **You** have a responsibility to report any concerns about business practices within the corporation that may violate this *Code of Business Conduct*.

Source: NORTEL Northern Telecom, Code of Business Conduct.

The goal is to become familiar with these markets before making any major financial commitments.[2]

The available choices for a company which has decided to do international business range from achieving a substantial market share in a niche existing in a number of country-markets to dominating one or more global product-markets. Firms such as Japan's Matsushita, one of the world's leading marketers of consumer electronics, Stockholm- and Zurich-based ABB, the giant electrical products and engineering company, or Kodak, the US-based world leader in photographic material, have sufficient resources to master a full range of capabilities and technologies necessary to serve an extended range of product-markets (for example, different groups of consumers looking for various kinds of visual-acoustic home entertainment, or different problem solutions for various customer groups in the field of electrical installations), and to serve efficiently all country-markets in need of their products and services. Such companies strive to dominate global markets.

At the other extreme, a highly specialized company with limited resources but strong competitive advantages in its field of competency, such as Austrian RSB-Roundtech, may decide to serve a regional or global market niche. RSB-Roundtech, specializing in formwork for round constructions such as egg-shaped digesters, water towers, telecom towers, or funnels, with a personnel capacity of only 80, is active in most highly industrialized countries including Japan and the USA, but also in countries such as Cameroon, Korea, Indonesia, Malaysia and Zaire.

Building and Sustaining Competitive Advantage. The choice of new markets in internationalizing the business of a firm will only lead to success when the company possesses or can build competitive advantages in those markets. That is, it must be able to offer a benefit to potential customers that is more attractive to them than what those customers have experienced before. Additionally, competitive advantages are not available to a company forever. Management, therefore, has to answer a fourth important question: How to build and sustain the firm's competitive advantage?

To answer that question, management will need to find out the success factors, that is, the specific resources and capabilities a firm needs to be successful in a market, in the markets it plans to serve, and to compare their company's strengths and weaknesses to those of its major competitors concerning those success factors. Positive differences, that is, distinctive competencies, can be regarded as competitive advantages to be sustained by reinforcing actions. Negative differences need to be reduced to a level where they do not jeopardize market success.

When analysing the markets of Eastern Europe, John Brown, a UK industrial engineering firm, for example, found that it was not competitive on one of the major success factors: long-term relationships with decision makers or influencers. But they had other competitive advantages such as self-developed and referenced technologies. Since building the needed strength to serve the Eastern European markets seemed to take too much time, management searched for a partner interested in entering a joint venture. They finally 'married' the chemical engineering division of VAI, the Austrian metallurgical engineering firm, which was searching for a partner with the strengths of John Brown.

The discussion of the four major decisions to be taken in international business has shown that rational decision making presupposes valid information about phenomena related to those decisions. That is, the environment relevant to the decisions has to be defined, and information has to be researched, analysed and structured.

Business Environments

When taking and implementing decisions concerning the internationalization of their business, a firm's management has to be aware of the considerably higher complexity of the environment to be considered than for a strictly local firm. Figure 2.3 shows a general nested model of a firm's environments. It demonstrates that the decision makers of a company live in their firm's internal environment which is embedded in the operative environment of the company which, in turn, is surrounded by the macro environment.

Operating Environment. The operating environment of a firm contains all actors, that is individuals or people representing organizations and institutions, who have aspirations concerning the behaviour and performance of the company in doing its business. Those are customers, competitors, suppliers, intermediaries, potential and existing workforce, owners, shareholders, banks, media, trade unions, and other so-called stakeholders of the company. They can have a strong impact on the success of a firm. For example, when the management of Air France, the international air carrier of the country and one of the most important airlines in Europe which ran high deficits at that time, planned to downsize the company to improve productivity, its workforce went on strike. Not only was air traffic from and to France heavily disturbed, but the company lost millions of dollars every day of the strike. Because of the firm's high importance to the country, top French politicians finally intervened. The result: the president of Air France was changed and most of the planned measures were postponed. Management must consider the various self-interests, power, capabilities and resources of the stakeholders forming their company's operating environment. Depending on those factors, they can manage the relationships with important stakeholders to help achieve the firm's objectives.

Macro-environment. A company's macro-environment is generally defined as the political, legal, economic, ecological, social, cultural and technological dimensions of the universe in which the operating environment of the firm is

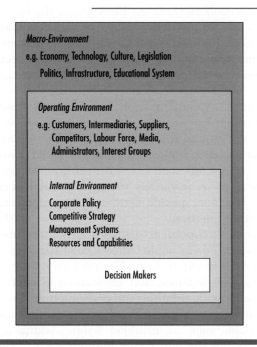

Figure 2.3 A NESTED MODEL OF A FIRM'S ENVIRONMENTS

Macro-Environment
e.g. Economy, Technology, Culture, Legislation
     Politics, Infrastructure, Educational System

Operating Environment
e.g. Customers, Intermediaries, Suppliers,
     Competitors, Labour Force, Media,
     Administrators, Interest Groups

Internal Environment
Corporate Policy
Competitive Strategy
Management Systems
Resources and Capabilities

Decision Makers

A company's decision makers live in their firm's internal environment which is embedded in the operative environment of the company which in turn is surrounded by the macro-environment.

embedded. Whereas the macro-environment of a company strongly influences the structure and state of its operating environment, individual members of the operating environment are restricted in their influence on the development of the macro-environment.

Management has to be aware of current and potential future developments in the relevant dimensions of their firm's macro-environment. For example, when Zuegg, the Verona-based leading Italian manufacturer of fruit juice and second-largest marketer of jam in the country, planned its expansion to other European markets, they had to analyse the forseeable and potential developments in a number of dimensions of the macro-environment relevant to their business. Legislation concerning food preparation, product declaration, packaging and recycling had to be studied. The potential impact of culture, in terms of consumption patterns, country-of-origin prejudices or ecological awareness, was considered. Trends in economic and demographic development, such as the unemployment rate, distribution of purchasing power, or ageing of the population, were analysed, and the effects of changes in the technological environment concerning transportation, warehousing infrastructure and media had to be considered.

The operating and macro-environments of a company are not separated from each other by objective and clear-cut boundaries. Depending on the business of a company and its resources varying parts belong to its operating and macro-environments. American Motorola Corp. and Finland's Nokia Mobira Oy, the two leading marketers of cellular phone equipment in the world, for example, have reached a level of importance in their market such that regulators will not easily pass them by without consultation when new norms and regulations have to be set. For them, parts of the regulatory environment can be personalized. The regulators with whom they have relationships belong to their operating environment. A very small, but internationally active firm such as Omicron Electronics, the leader in the global market niche of test sets for protective relays, transducers and energy meters for electrical utilities and industry, can hardly directly influence parts of the regulatory environment by building personal or organizational relationships. For them, legislation is part of the given macro-environment.

Internal Environment. Company decision makers play their role as part of an organization which has an implicit, if not explicitly stated, corporate policy that lays out the ground rules of how it wants to function. It follows a competitive strategy, a basic indication of where to do business and how, based on management systems such as the organization structure or the controlling system as well as on resources and capabilities – personnel, capital, know-how – which result in specific actions. These elements make up the internal environment of the firm.

The firm's internal environment defines the borders of its macro- and operating environments. For example, when Coca-Cola decided to serve the soft drink markets of the world, it defined its relevant operating environment to be all customers, organizations and institutions concerned with or interested in the production, distribution and consumption of soft drinks worldwide. The macro-environment was defined as all factors that influence the operating environment, such as drinking habits, commercial legislation, retailing infrastructure, or the climate in different parts of the world. When Coca-Cola went a step further to enter the alcoholic beverages market, it substantially widened the borders of its operating environment. This also broadened the ranges of macro-environment factors which had to be considered, for example social campaigns against drinking and driving. Coke's withdrawal from the alcoholic beverages market may well have been hastened by their having to play a 'different game' in that market than in their traditional market where they were much more familiar with the rules, norms and expectations of stakeholders.

The internal environment also limits the firm's potential for influence on the development of its operating environment, and its set of alternative responses to trends in the macro-environment. If a big globally operating corporation, such as Swiss Novartis, develops a new pharmaceutical substance, many smaller manufacturers of drugs will be forced to purchase that substance in order to stay competitive with their final products. If the same firm decides to concentrate its production of basic substances for antibiotics in one country, factories in other countries will go out of operation. Some stakeholders, such as trade unions or politicians, supported by local media, may try to use their power to force the firm into developing 'social plans' to decrease the impact of those shutdowns on the former workforce and the local economy. A small drug manufacturer will not be able to spend enough money in research and development to influence the worldwide use of pharmaceutical substances. But, on the other hand, it will also have fewer problems with the general public when management decides to change the location of the factory.

The internal environment of a firm has no clear-cut boundaries with its operating environment. Increasing numbers of cooperative agreements and deepening relationships between companies to fight mutual competitors in globalizing industries have contributed to management increasingly often having to consider (parts of) internal environments of partner firms when taking decisions. For example, when Mercedes Benz, the Stuttgart (Germany)-based manufacturer of high-quality vehicles, decided to develop, produce and market a small Swatch-car together with SMH, the Swiss holding group of watch-producing companies, they established a joint task force. Task force members interacted intensively. The two companies had formed an interface which partly abolished the formal boundaries between their internal environments. Mercedes managers could no longer take decisions concerning the Swatch-car project without considering the strategy, resources and capabilities of their Swiss partner.

Consequences for Internationalization. Managers have to consider all levels of environments when business decisions are to be taken. But if they want their company to become involved in international business or to raise their firm's level of international activity, they must be aware of a change in organizational focus. The relevant macro- and operating environments become increasingly complex. The internal environment will have to adapt to new demands.

The different stages and trends of economic development in various parts of the world will be important, such as the major structural changes in European economies or the fast industrialization of the Pacific Rim. So will cultural developments, such as the increase of wine consumption in the USA which has raised the attractiveness of this market to wine producers from other continents (Australia, Europe, South America), and has decreased the outlook for producers of Scotch whisky because of the decline in consumption of hard liquor.

Legal differences can have a strong impact on business decisions. For example, regulations concerning smoking in public buildings, transportation or restaurants, and the packaging of and advertising for tobacco products, are very different across countries. In the US, BAT, the UK second-largest manufacturer of cigarettes in the world, is (not unlike other tobacco companies) under siege from class-action lawsuits and government plans to regulate cigarettes as drugs. In other parts of the world there is virtually no regulation. BAT posted record profits in 1995 mainly due to its activities in Southeast Asia, the fastest-growing and most lucrative tobacco market, as well as South America and Eastern Europe. Even in China, where tobacco advertising is totally banned, BAT's Kent brand gets high exposure throughout big cities, because it sponsors the Tour of China bicycle race. When the company has finished its substantial investment in the production site in Southampton, most of the additional capacity will be dedicated to exports to those parts of the world.[3]

During internationalization of business, management will identify potential customers in different geographic areas; competitors as well as intermediaries and suppliers will be spread throughout the globe. In fact, the variety in environments may not support one single corporate policy. They may call for different competitive strategies, or at least different capabilities and resources of the firm, to deal with different environmental combinations.

The point is that management must not take decisions without a careful assessment of the environments and their interaction. It must follow a strategic approach to international business. Actions must be taken based on a long-term orientation towards resource procurement and allocation. To ensure a steady flow of resources to and from the company, it is critical to manage relationships with customers and other important stakeholders of the firm in such a way as to satisfy their expectations. Building and maintaining such relationships is the major focus of marketing.

Marketing Orientation

Marketing may be described as a bundle of management techniques, often referred to as marketing capabilities or competencies. These capabilities guide a company in searching for appropriate markets, in building and sustaining competitive advantages in those markets, and in managing the relationships with all important stakeholders belonging to those markets. On the other hand, marketing can be viewed as a basic approach to doing business; this is termed a marketing orientation. An organization that is marketing oriented focuses in a planned and systematic way on the management of its exchange relationships with stakeholders in its operating environment. A marketing orientation may be characterized by a number of basic convictions or perspectives: (1) a systems perspective, (2) an exchange perspective, and (3) a benefit perspective.

Systems Perspective. The long-term success of a company depends on a continuous influx of resources from raw materials through capital, manpower and information to regulations, which become transformed in the company into resources such as products, information, dividends or skilled labour, and flow back out to all kinds of customers or stakeholders interested in getting them. To make sure that this two-way flow of resources takes place in quantities and qualities needed for the attainment of the company's objectives, mutually satisfactory relationships with all suppliers and customers of those resources have to be established and maintained. The marketing orientation, therefore, includes a systems perspective. That is, marketing-oriented managers hold the conviction that their company's well-being depends on relationships with customers and stakeholders that fulfil certain minimum levels of expectations and do not interfere with each other. For example, a new liquid fertilizer increasing farm production may represent an attractive solution to a customer problem. But at the same time it may create living conditions near the company's production facilities difficult to accept because of air pollution, or may come close to violating government regulations, perhaps by exposing workers to dangerous fumes. In such a case, the company may be well advised not to start production of that product.

Exchange Perspective. Lasting customer and stakeholder relationships can be established and maintained only if all the partners in the relationship are willing and able to contribute to the relationship in such a way that each directly or indirectly benefits from his or her point of view. Marketing orientation, therefore, includes an exchange perspective. That is, marketing-oriented managers hold the conviction that the establishment and maintenance of relationships needed for long-term business success has to build on balanced exchange relations between two or more partners.

A Fiat Punto, for example, is exchanged between a customer and a Fiat dealer. The exchange takes place only as long as the customer believes that she will gain something (for example, reliable transport, fun driving, attractive styling, good resale value, social acceptance) at least as valuable as the value of what she brings to the exchange (for example, money, trust in the dealer and the brand, social status). The dealer will sign the contract only if he thinks that he will gain at least as much (for example, money to keep his business running, good reputation attracting more customers, follow-up business when servicing the car) as he gives away. Some of those benefits on both sides cannot be achieved from the simple dyadic exchange relationship between the customer and the car dealer. Others, such as family members enjoying the car, friends interested in its performance, or reliable service personnel working for the dealer, have to play their role in the exchange to fulfil some of the expectations (such as social acceptance or good reputation).

Benefit Perspective.   Both partners need to have a good reason to establish and maintain an exchange relationship. The best reason is when the potential partner offers a solution to an actual or potential problem (the satisfaction of a need) which is more attractive than other solutions offered. The attractiveness of a problem solution depends on the subjectively valued benefits it is able to provide. The third perspective of marketing orientation, therefore, is the benefit perspective. That is, marketing-oriented managers hold the conviction that balanced exchange relationships between a company and its customers and stakeholders cannot be established and maintained unless the company personnel involved in those relationships are aware of the actual and potential problems (needs and aspirations) of their exchange partners and offer them solutions which seem more beneficial to them than others. Thus, the first question to ask when analysing a potential relationship is not what the company can gain from the deal, but whether it can make a substantial contribution towards solving the problems faced by its exchange partner. If so, then sales and profits or other benefits for the company result.

The marketing orientation requires that the company's personnel adhere to the three perspectives on a long-term basis. One of managers' most important duties is keeping track of current relationships with customers and stakeholders, anticipating future developments, and assessing their implications for the firm. Managers must understand that while present success is a result of past efforts, it is no guarantee of success in the future. Future success can be achieved only by preparing for likely changes in the company's relationships with customers and stakeholders, that is, in the nature of the problems it will be called upon to solve and the expectations concerning the problem solutions. Repsol, a Spanish manufacturer of granules for the production of plastic wrapping materials, which has been concentrating on compound technology for special applications in the food industry, may find, for example, that consumers' growing environmental concerns will force governments to raise recycling standards in the coming years. To prepare for new specifications from customers and to preempt competitive entry in its markets, the company will broaden its focus to include the recycling potential of its material, in time.

In international business, the conditions for establishing and maintaining the relationships with customers and stakeholders which are needed to secure long-term success may be different from one country-market to another. But the ground rules of relationship management remain the same all over the world. Therefore, the marketing orientation is a universal approach to international business conduct when long-term success is a major objective.

International Marketing

International marketing is the application of marketing orientation and marketing techniques to international business. There are two basically different ways in which marketing managers can approach international business: a multinational and a global approach.

Multinational Marketing

In multidomestic industries, international marketing has traditionally concentrated on differences between product-markets in countries which, beforehand, had been assessed to be attractive business environments. For example, many managers of companies located in neighbouring countries, such as the Netherlands, Denmark or Switzerland, have found Germany to be a very attractive business environment, because of its political stability, its economic wealth, its highly developed infrastructure, and the number of potential customers compared to the domestic market. They decided that their company had to do business in Germany before they had analysed the state of the product-market they were planning to serve in that country. This did not seem to be a problem to them because they thought they knew that differences were abundant and had to be considered by developing a specific marketing strategy.

The result was a multinational approach to marketing which concentrated largely on country-markets, developing a distinct marketing strategy for each market. In the past two decades, increasing trade liberalization, economic integration and technological change have allowed competition to become global. Globally operating firms are in fierce competition with each other concerning effectiveness and efficiency, which leads to the development of global industries and forces the firms to look for synergy and learning potential across their international activities. They found that on the one hand, rising economic wealth led to individual and industrial customers having increasingly differentiated aspirations, which resulted in country-market segments becoming ever smaller. On the other hand, international differences among such narrowly defined country-market segments still exist, but in serving them, substantial parts of a marketing strategy can be kept the same across geographic market boundaries.

Beefeater Gin, for example, can be positioned as the authentic English (exclusively London distilled) gin for people of discernment worldwide. It can have the same premium quality (alcohol content) and taste, and use the same bottle, label (including the Beefeater Yeoman) and premium pricing strategy. It can be sold via wholly owned distributors, and distribution can be focused on hotels, bars and restaurants all over the world. Country-market differences still exist and have to be accounted for. For example, sales personnel in the various countries do not react to the same sales incentives. Bar-keepers in Chile were offered vouchers for children's school clothes and goods, an incentive that would be considered ridiculous in Germany. Sponsorships must embrace different kinds of sports to have the same effects. For example, in the UK, Beefeater sponsors the Oxford vs. Cambridge boat race, in Thailand deep sea fishing competitions, and in Spain American football games. But in general the focus of Beefeater's marketing management is on a specific group of customers which exists worldwide and not on local differences. The result is a global approach to international marketing.

Global Marketing

A global approach to international marketing occurs when a company's managers concentrate on product-markets, that is, groups of customers seeking shared benefits or to be served with the same technology, emphasizing their similarities regardless of the geographic areas in which they are located, rather than focus on country-markets, that is, differences due to the physical location of the customer groups. The location continues to be important, of course. Cultures still vary considerably, transportation difficulties plague successful international marketing, and laws and regulations vary. But a global approach to international marketing considers such constraints, real as they may be, after first examining what the most attractive product-market for the company is and where in the world groups of customers that fit into that product-market can be found.

For managers who adopt a global marketing approach to international business, the critical point is not whether countries are more or less similar and buyers are the same everywhere, but to what extent shared customer aspirations and similar marketing infrastructure (distribution system, logistics, media, norms and regulations) exist in different nations. If they do, the company can develop a relatively standardized marketing strategy to appeal to those needs. It serves a global product-market. For example, it can offer the same high-tech, high-quality camcorders to video 'freaks', around the world.

However, a global approach to international marketing does not ignore differences among local market segments. These differences are taken into account when implementing the marketing programme. For example, advertising is translated into different languages for different national markets. 'Coke is it', for example, is translated into 'Echt is echt' in Dutch (literally 'the real thing is the real thing'). And different distribution strategies are developed for areas with different distribution structures. Most Indian grocery stores, for example, are quite small, requiring wholesale distribution and more frequent delivery of smaller quantities than French hypermarkets which can be served directly from one central production unit.

Experience Curve Effects. The most powerful argument in favour of a global product-market orientation is the opportunity to benefit from experience curve effects. (See Figure 2.4.) This concept has two dimensions: increased efficiency due to size effects and increased effectiveness due to experience (accumulated know-how) effects. The size effects result from decreasing fixed costs per unit sold. The principle of economies of scale states that whenever the output volume of a firm increases, total costs per unit fall. Average fixed costs, such as the costs for production equipment, administration, sales subsidiaries, the information system, or the production of an advertising campaign, decrease when the total fixed costs are distributed across a bigger volume of products sold. The Strategy box gives an example of how a firm can gain efficiency effects by adding volume through acquisitions.

For an internationally operating firm, an important source of economies of scale (in addition to procurement, administration and production) is

Figure 2.4 EXPERIENCE CURVE EFFECTS

The experience curve shows the decrease of cost per unit when the cumulative production volume in units increases.

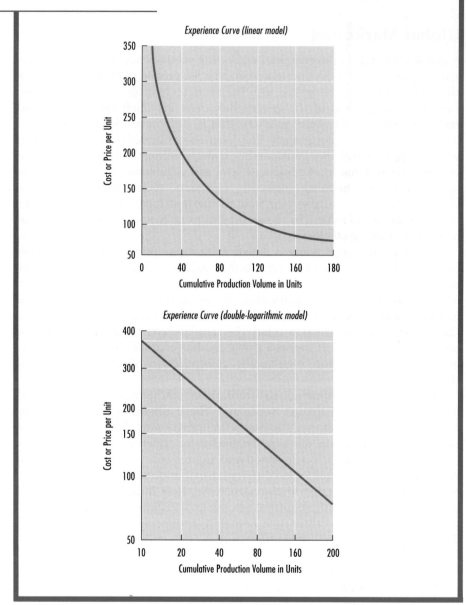

the marketing mix. When a company can use the same marketing mix in several different countries, with only a few adjustments such as translation of advertising copy, the average cost of marketing per unit declines, even if the share of advertising production costs compared to media costs is decreasing internationally. An example is the advertisement for Longines watches in the European edition of *Cosmopolitan* magazine, which used the same model and slogan (in English) for several national markets (see Figure 2.5). The company gained higher efficiency by appealing to highly educated, wealthy consumers everywhere.

STRATEGY BOX

Experience Curve

Effects through

Acquisitions

IN 1994, H.J. HEINZ CO. CHAIRMAN ANTHONY J.F. O'Reilly boasted that his then-faltering company was 'poised for a breakout' despite a stagnant food industry.

In 1996, Mr. O'Reilly has proved true to his word. After a string of quarters with good growth, Heinz can expect sales surpassing USD9 billion in the current fiscal year and USD10 billion the next year. Nearly half the increase was due to volume gains, for products such as Ore-Ida frozen potatoes and StarKist tuna, with the same amount coming from recent acquisitions.

The company combined cost-cutting with the acquisition of other firms in its drive for greater efficiency. In the field of baby foods, the purchase of Earth's Best Inc., a Boulder, Colorado, marketer of organic baby foods gave it new brands, factories bought in the Czech Republic, in the U.K., and in India added markets and volume. The 1995 acquisition of Quaker Oats Co.'s North American pet-food operations also brought established brands – such as Gravy Train and Kibbles 'n Bits – under Heinz's control and the purchase of a majority interest in an Argentinian pet-food producer added market and production volume. The company remains on the prowl for affordable businesses that either will spread its geographic reach or add to its manufacturing efficiency.

Source: Murray, M. (1996) 'Heinz Realizes O'Reilly's Growth Promise – Acquisitions Help to Boost Sales 12% in Quarter', *The Wall Street Journal Europe*, 11 April, p. 8.

Increased efficiency is more easily attained by larger than by smaller companies – if costs for increased coordination needs and substantially rising transportation costs are kept under close control (see Map 2.1) – and by serving a global rather than a local product-market. Because of their greater size, Paris-based Cartier, a marketer of high-prestige accessories, for example, can more easily profit from reduced average production, marketing or administration costs per watch or piece of jewellery sold than their competitor Poiray, also a Paris-based manufacturer of fine jewellery, which targets women in major capital cities all over the world who can afford to wear expensive contemporary jewellery. But even this smaller firm, by totally standardizing the packaging of its products, display materials, advertising visuals and catalogue layout, can profit from marketing efficiency effects.

Increased effectiveness occurs when a company 'learns by doing'. The second time a worker or manager does a job, he or she usually does it better than the first time, thereby becoming more effective. Similarly, when a company enters its second foreign market using what it learned when it entered its first such market, it should be more effective. Companies such as Marks & Spencer, the UK's internationally successful department stores, that offer their services in a product-market spread over several nations, benefit from both dimensions of the experience curve. Because of their high sales volume and the resulting purchasing power, they can procure products and capital at lower costs. They can distribute their administration overheads across a higher total turnover, and can transfer the experiences gained in one country-market to other markets.

Figure 2.5 STANDARDIZED ADVERTISING

Map 2.1 Global Product Flows – Honda

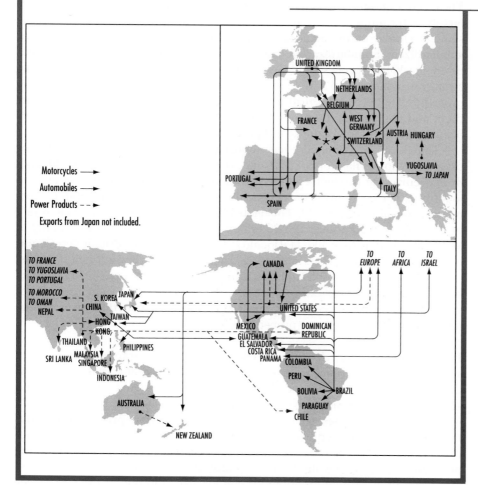

Motorcycles ——▶
Automobiles ——▶
Power Products – – ▶

Exports from Japan not included.

Another example of a globally oriented firm is Honda. Map 2.1 illustrates the flow of Honda's motorcycles, automobiles and power products. For example, its French built lawnmowers and tillers are exported throughout the European community. It also imports motorcycles from Taiwan to China and Central America and cars from the USA.

Global Market Analysis.   A second argument in favour of a global product-market approach to international marketing is the opportunity to find new and sufficiently large market niches through global market analysis. A marketer of a line of cosmetics, such as Guerlain, a member of the French Groupe LVMH which holds a number of internationally well-known luxury brands such as Christian Dior, Louis Vuitton and Moët Hennessey, for example, might not find a single country-market big enough to be served by an adequate marketing programme and provide a sufficient return on investment (except the USA). But it might be able to identify a target market consisting of high-income, fashion-conscious women above 40 years of age in several countries (for example, Argentina, Brazil, North America, Southeast Asia and Europe). This 'global' product-market is much larger than a single domestic market. A marketing mix with highly standardized product features, distribution system, pricing strategy and promotion activities emphasizing the French style of classic fashion could appeal to this target market. Thus, it offers a greater opportunity to take advantage of experience curve effects in production, administration and marketing.

Standardization vs. Adaptation

The degree of similarity among a company's international product-markets largely determines the extent to which its marketing activities can be the same or similar across country-markets, that is, to what extent they can be standardized. Standardization may occur either in marketing programmes or in marketing processes. Marketing programmes contain the marketing strategies, policies and activities of a company. Marketing processes are the procedures followed by a firm in making marketing decisions, implementing them and controlling their outcomes. The greatest experience curve effects occur when both programmes and processes are standardized.

The Coca-Cola Company has almost totally standardized the marketing programme for its flagship brand, Coke. Travellers to all parts of the world readily recognize the product's red-and-white logo, whatever language is used to identify it. The company's goal is to achieve 'one sight, one sound' brand recognition throughout the world. This global branding approach has resulted in a brand name valued at over USD25 billion dollars, second in the world only to Marlboro. Corporations like McDonald's, Benetton and BP (British Petroleum) have also standardized their marketing programmes with considerable success.

Both Procter & Gamble and Nestlé are well known for their high degree of standardization of marketing processes. Their product concept testing, advertising campaign development and evaluation of distribution investments, for example, follow stepwise procedures outlined in manuals.

Programme Standardization. The degree of marketing programme standardization can range from a standardized strategy only, that is, a general determination of how business should be done and to what effect, through a standardization of marketing policies, that is, a specification of how a bundle of marketing techniques, such as market communication, pricing or distribution, should be managed, to the standardization of particular marketing activities. The degree of standardization that exists in Coke's global marketing programme is rare owing to legal, cultural and other differences. Most standardized marketing programmes can be placed in one of the four stages illustrated in Figure 2.6.

Stage I represents a product that is essentially the same in all country-markets but is marketed through varying promotion, price and distribution activities for each market. An example is Canon's 35mm camera. It was conceived and designed as a global product. But in the United States it was promoted as a 'mistake-proof' camera, whereas in Japan it was presented as the leader in state-of-the-art photographic equipment. In other country-markets, different price, promotion and distribution activities were followed.

The gains that are achieved through standardization increase as a company moves from Stage I to Stage IV. A company in Stage IV offers the same product, promotion, price and distribution mix to all of its markets. This level of standardization is not found often, partly because pricing and distribution are very difficult to standardize. A company can adopt a standardized pricing policy, for example being the low-price provider in all markets, but the actual price charged will almost always vary in response to demand, competition and regulation. Distribution, by its nature, is a marketing activity that is performed close to the market. It frequently varies according to national differences in transportation systems, regulations, geography and tradition. But again, the distribution policy can be standardized across country-markets.

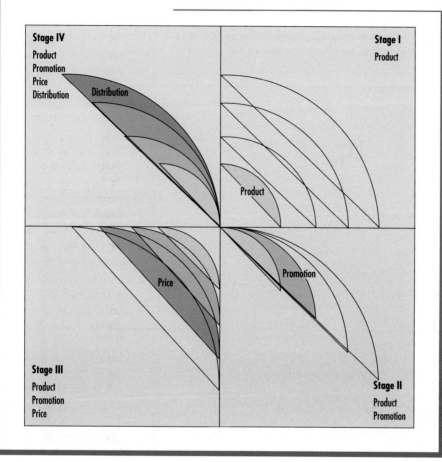

Figure 2.6 STAGES OF MARKETING MIX STANDARDIZATION

Source: Adapted from Huszagh, S.M., R.J. Fox and E. Day (1995) 'Global Marketing: An Empirical Investigation', *Columbia Journal of World Business*, Winter, Twentieth Anniversary Issue, 31–43.

Hirsch Bracelets, the Austrian market leader in leather watch straps worldwide, for example, has a standardized range of straps which is sold in all country-markets. Variations come from colours and different kinds of leather which are more or less preferred by consumers depending on the country. Prices cannot be fixed on a global basis. But Hirsch follows a standardized pricing policy all over the world. Their Hirsch branded products are highly priced compared to competitors everywhere (even if the actual consumer price in India is only a small part of the consumer price in Germany). Retailing outlets cannot be standardized either, because there are no jewellers or department stores with outlets in all the countries served by the company. But the firm's distribution policy clearly standardizes the kind of distribution system and retail outlets to be chosen. Distribution is achieved through either sales subsidiaries or exclusive distributors, and retail outlets must represent the same quality standard as jewellers and department stores compared to other outlets.

Market communication policies can also be standardized, and certain parts of communication, such as logos, visuals, jingles or layouts, can be kept the same worldwide. Benetton, for example, applies the technique of pattern advertising to its brand. In pattern advertising, the theme and components

Figure 2.7 **Factors Influencing the Standardization Potential of Marketing Programmes**

The potential for standardization of a firm's marketing programme depends on factors from the macro-environment and the market as well as on characteristics of the company's internal environment and its product.

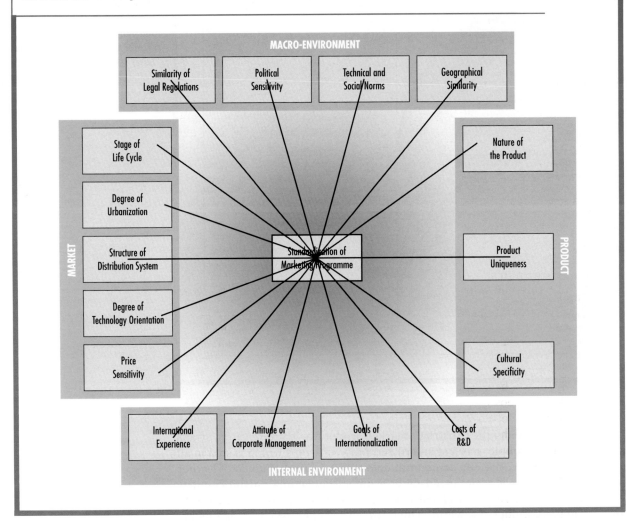

Source: Adapted from Cavusgil, S.T., S. Zou, and G.M. Naidu (1993) 'Product and Promotion Adaptation in Export Ventures: An Empirical Investigation', *Journal of International Business Studies*, 479–506.

of the advertising campaign are designed for use in several country-markets. This 'pattern' gives the campaign a uniform direction and appearance. Benetton uses the themes of modernity, liberality and fun in all country-markets, regardless of location.

When evaluating foreign markets and deciding whether to standardize the marketing programme for those markets, several factors must be taken into consideration. These factors are shown in Figure 2.7. They are (a) the macro-environment, (b) the market, (c) the product and (d) the internal environment.

(a) Macro-Environment.   A number of forces from the macro-environment affect a firm's ability to market successfully with a standardized programme. The most important of these forces are political, legal, cultural and geographic.

When a product is politically sensitive in a particular country-market, an adapted marketing campaign is called for. For example, Hollandsche Beton Maatschappij BV is a construction company in the Netherlands with projects throughout the world. It must meet the unique requirements of each host-country government regarding plant construction, the number of host-country contractors that must be hired, and the amount of training of local personnel that must accompany the project. Thus it prepares a marketing programme specifically for each market.

If legal regulations concerning taxes, patent and trademark protection, product liability, norms of hygiene, or licensing and registration prerequisites, to cite a few examples, in the country-markets served by a company are similar, marketing programme standardization is facilitated. However, in countries that do not offer mutual registration of trademarks, a company may be unable to operate under its standard brand or trade name. Different hygiene norms may make sales of standardized agricultural products impossible. US product liability regulations have forced marketers of consumer durables from other countries out of the market or to adapt their products.

One reason for using an adapted strategy may be that technical specifications are different in the target markets. Technical norms such as measurement units (centimetre vs. inch, for example) or industrial conventions, for example DIN (Deutsche Industrienorm) in Germany, can represent insurmountable obstacles to standardization. They are part of the specifications that industrial products and durable consumer products have to fulfil in order to be regarded as acceptable by potential customers. For example, US producers of manufacturing equipment are at a disadvantage against local competitors in Europe because they have to adapt every machine and tool for those markets – a costly process. Similarly, cars may have to be adapted for different markets, depending on the safety and pollution-control standards of the country in which they are sold.

Social norms involve a wide variety of patterns of living, including behaviour norms such as those regarding diet or styles of dress. They play a major role in determining what can and cannot be done in a given market. In the USA, for example, gift giving to business partners is seen as an attempt to undermine free competition and is therefore badly accepted or even banned as bribery. In many other countries all over the world, gifts are seen as a signal of good personal relationships which are needed to close a deal and to maintain business contacts (for an example, see the Culture box).

In markets with unique cultural characteristics, a standardized strategy from another culture is likely to be unsuccessful. For example, the prohibition of the consumption of alcoholic beverages in Moslem countries affects the design of hotels, as well as the services hotels offer. Where social norms concerning public behaviour are fairly similar, as is true of most European countries, a standardized marketing programme, such as that of Ibis Hotels, a French operator of an international hotel chain, might be viable.

A society's attitudes towards change or the rate of change also affect the viable degree of standardization in particular markets. Rather conservative consumers in a country-market may not accept a marketing strategy that

Culture Box

Gifts versus Bribery in the Gulf States

When doing business in the Gulf States, it is important that the distinction between gifts and bribes is clearly noted. Presents are frequently given to family, friends, business contacts and as a gesture of thanks for some service rendered. The Arabic people are by nature extremely generous. Bribes on the other hand are completely taboo: they are anathema within both the culture and the law and can, and do, incur stiff penalties.

As to the distinction between the two, and why stories should still be told of endemic bribery, the root lies in the disparity between Arabic and Western (European, USA) culture. At heart it is a question of *mens rea*, the legal concept of a guilty mind without which no crime is possible. A present given with a generous heart is a gift; if it is given to induce favor it is wrong. Payment for a service is quite different and does not come into the equation. Needless to say, it is only the conscience of the giver that can make the ultimate distinction.

When giving a present, it is important that the status of the recipient is reflected in the choice and value of the gift. A company once gave a minister signing a contract worth many hundreds of thousands of dollars the, albeit expensive, pen with which he had signed. This was regarded as an insult. In this difficult area it is necessary to think carefully before acting, and to take advice.

Source: Cole, S. (1992) *The Gulf States: a Business Handbook*, Oxford: Blackwell Publishers, pp. 86f.

---

originates in a more liberal society. Some of Benetton's billboards, for example, showing a priest and a nun kissing, an HIV-infected person, or a dead soldier from the Bosnian war, which created critical interest in Italy, their country of origin, provoked substantial consumer protests in the USA. Resistance to change can be especially difficult to deal with when the product itself represents a marked change in the way people do things.

Variations in geography, such as climate, may make it necessary to adapt either a product or its distribution or promotion for different country-markets. For example, Toyota has stripped out unnecessary items from the special version of its Tercel model destined for markets in Southeast Asia, such as heaters because the warm climate renders them unnecessary.

(b) The Market. If a standardized marketing programme is to succeed, the country-markets of interest must have certain characteristics in common, at least to some degree. For example, customers must seek similar benefits or use the product or service in a similar way, the available distribution infrastructure must be similar, or customers must be comparable in their reaction to prices.

An important factor of influence on the standardization potential of marketing programmes is the stage of product life cycle a market is in. For a standardized marketing programme to be successful, the product should be in the same stage of the life-cycle in all of the country-markets involved. When the stages of the life cycle are different, variations in the degree and type of competition, the rate of growth in sales, and the most effective form of promotion, distribution and pricing require adapted marketing programmes. If, for example, personal computers are in different stages of the product life cycle in Egypt and Sweden, companies that wish to compete in both of these markets would have to adjust their marketing mixes to take this difference into account. Although their physical products might be similar, the rest of the marketing mix would have to be adapted for each country.

The degree to which a market is urbanized is another important factor in deciding whether to standardize a marketing programme. A programme that was developed for a highly urbanized market like Hong Kong or Singapore might not be able to reach enough potential customers in countries like India, where more than half the population lives in rural areas or very small towns. In another country with a high level of urbanization, such as Australia, such a programme would be more likely to succeed.

The structure of distribution systems available in most international consumer product markets is far from being similar. The UK, Belgium, Germany, Austria and France have a high degree of concentration in food retailing, for example. A few retailing firms dominate those markets, whereas in Italy wholesalers and small retailers have kept an important role in their market. The process of concentration has just started. Under such conditions, standardization of distribution seems very difficult for a European food producer such as Jacobs-Suchard which dominates important parts of the coffee, chocolate and sweet snacks business.

The distribution of industrial products and services in most cases is more direct and relies on personal selling. Therefore, the distribution system can be more easily standardized; communication with customers, however, is based even more on individual relationship building. For example, an industrial engineering firm like Italy's Danieli which is the country's most important supplier of metallurgical plants, offers its services through participation in international tenders worldwide. To close a deal, individualized personal communication can be crucial. In bigger projects, Mrs Danieli even intervenes personally to underline the customer's importance to her firm.

When the customers in a market are mainly interested in the technology of a product because the benefit they are looking for is mainly technology driven, a higher degree of marketing programme standardization will be suitable. For example, Xerox or Canon copiers are mainly bought by customers interested in their capacity, speed, quality of printing, price per printed unit, or service intensity. Customers' expectations vary more according to their use of the copier than because of their nationality. Therefore, if the firm focuses on a particular customer group, such as universities or public administrations, which exists across country borders, it can largely standardize its marketing programme.

Whether the life cycle of a firm's product is driven by technological or cultural factors is an additional important consideration. A firm that is faced with two country-markets in which its product is in the growth stage of the life cycle might assume that a standardized marketing programme could be used in both markets. But if one market is driven by technology and the other by cultural factors, a standardized campaign is unlikely to be successful. For example, cellular phones might be in the early growth stage of the product life cycle in two markets, but in one of those markets sales may grow slowly owing to the expectation that new technology will soon be available (a technological factor), while in the other market sales may grow slowly as a result of customers' fear of loss of privacy (a cultural factor). A standardized marketing programme would not have the same results in both markets, because it would be unable to overcome the differing sources of sales resistance in the two markets.

Products or services that are purchased largely on the basis of low price, which means that potential buyers are willing to give up satisfaction of individual expectations in exchange for a (standardized) good with a lower price, can be marketed through relatively standardized programmes. For such products, global marketers are able to take advantage of large international product-markets and pass the resulting economies along to buyers in the form of lower prices. Thus, products such as BIC shavers or services such as fast-food restaurants have been marketed successfully throughout most parts of the world. In the case of products for which price plays a less important role, adaptation is more likely to succeed; luxury yachts, which are custom-built at great expense to suit specific customer tastes, and haute couture dresses are examples of this.

(c) The Product.   It is often argued that industrial products can be marketed more easily with standardized programmes than consumer goods which, in turn, allow more standardized marketing programmes than services. Such general rules are difficult to maintain, however, in business practice. As an example, McDonald's has highly standardized its range of products served, the way the customer service is delivered, the design of their restaurants, and their visual communication. Compared to that service firm, a manufacturer of industrial products, such as Sweden's Alfa Laval, one of the world leaders in ultra filtration technology, may have products which need more adaptation of their marketing programme. For example, they must treat fims from the agricultural business sector differently depending on the regulatory and market environment they live in.

Many food products, in particular those with high cultural specificity, must be marketed through adapted programmes in other countries where the cultural background is different. Tiled stoves, for example, are highly specific to the Alpine areas of Europe. Some consumers from non-Alpine countries have learned to like them during their vacations in Austria, Germany, Northern Italy or Switzerland. And some Canadians with family roots in those countries also have tiled stoves in their homes. Nevertheless, to sell ceramic tiles – a major part of those stoves – in other parts of the world needs a marketing approach very different from the one applied in the product's home area. Consumers there first have to be informed about the benefits of the product compared to what they are used to buying.

Products and services that are highly unique allow a higher level of marketing programme standardization. A show of internationally well-known illusionists from Las Vegas, the London Philharmonic Orchestra or the Chinese National Circus, and watches labelled Patek Philip, Ebel or Vacherin can be marketed relatively unchanged and using the same kind of distribution system, market communication and pricing worldwide.

(d) Internal Environment.   The amount of international experience a firm's management has accumulated will influence their attitudes. An inexperienced firm is likely to seek a close match between its current offerings and the demand of new country-markets, so that only minimal adaptation of the marketing mix is required. Internationally more experienced managers will have

a higher degree of flexibility and acceptance of change that may support more adaptation of marketing programmes. The successful management of differentiated products, multiple communication campaigns, different distribution systems and various pricing schemes requires a flexible corporate view and culture, one which accepts quick change and multiple perspectives on who the customer is, and what benefit is being sought.

It is important to note that in companies operating internationally a low tolerance for differences at local management levels might prevent the success of a standardized marketing programme. The local managers may be hesitant to accept the amount of change required to shift to a standardized approach. They tend to think in terms of their own country-markets as that is where they have their experience. It is difficult for them to think in global terms, that is, in ways that cross other country-markets.

For example, when France's Thomson Consumer Electronics purchased TV set manufacturers in Sweden, Germany, Italy, and the UK and wanted to standardize their European marketing programme, local managers protested. They claimed that customer expectations concerning product design and features, distribution outlets, pricing and after-sales service were different and did not allow common market communication. In such cases top management must help them develop a global perspective. In the case of Thomson Consumer Electronics, the general marketing manager asked the local managers to produce lists of consumers' expectations concerning TV sets in their countries. At a meeting in Paris he let them present and compare those expectations. They discovered to their great surprise that 80 per cent of the expectations listed were highly similar. The way to increased marketing programme standardization was opened.

The goals a firm's management wants to achieve through internationalization have an impact on their willingness to adapt the existing marketing programme to different needs. If the goals are operational, such as taking up excess capacity, a standardized approach to new markets will be preferred. If internationalization of business is a strategic objective, the firm will need deeper penetration of its markets and therefore be ready to adapt its marketing programme.

Finally, if research and development costs for a product are low, an individualized marketing programme may be appropriate. But if these costs are high, such as for pharmaceutical products, largely standardized marketing programmes are essential. They permit the higher development costs of new products to be amortized over their increasingly shorter lives.

Evaluating the Potential for Programme Standardization. There are several techniques that can be used to evaluate the potential for standardization of a marketing programme. One is the use–need model, which examines the way a product is used in comparison with the need it fulfils. Another is the benefit–cost approach, which analyses the balance between the customer's perceived benefits and the costs of the product in different markets.

(1) The Use–Need Model. A popular framework for making decisions on how much to standardize a product and the related market communication is the use–need model, which evaluates the market need that is met by a given product as well as how the product is used. Figure 2.8 illustrates this model. Five combinations of use and need determine the degree of product and communication standardization that is desirable and their related costs. For example,

---

Figure 2.8 THE USE–NEED MODEL

Source: Based on W.J. Keegan (1969) 'Multinational Product Planning: Strategic Alternatives', *Journal of Marketing*, January, 58–62.

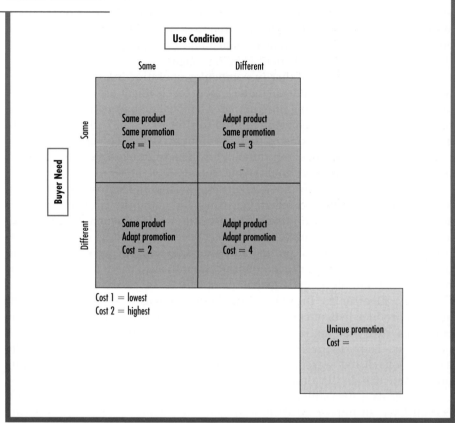

---

if a product is to be used differently in different markets but it meets the same basic need, adapting the product while standardizing its market communication would be an appropriate decision. Thus, TV sets need to be slightly re-engineered for different markets to allow for differences in broadcast standards, electrical service and quality of transmission, but the communication theme of 'best picture' could be standardized.

Only when use and need conditions are the same are fully standardized product and market communication appropriate. On the other hand, when differences between country-markets in both use and need are great, a totally adapted programme is needed. For example, an Italian bicycle manufacturer such as Bianchi which compares the need for bikes and their use in its home market to their need and use in China will find great differences in both. Italians do not need their bikes as family transport as well as for professional purposes like their Chinese counterparts. They need them for sporty outings in groups on weekends or during vacation. Their bikes have no transportation usage other than their owners'. The features of bicycles (mass-)marketed in Italy compared to China have to be entirely different, therefore, and communication has to be adapted to the use of the product.

(2) The Benefit–Cost Approach. This technique evaluates the potential for programme standardization by looking at customers' perceptions of benefits

	Table 2.1 ILLUSTRATIONS OF PERCEIVED BENEFITS AND COSTS	
TYPE	CUSTOMERS' BENEFITS	CUSTOMERS' COSTS
Sensory	Appealing appearance, feel, sound, smell or taste	Unpleasant appearance, feel, sound, smell or taste
Psychological	Positive state of mind (feeling good, generous, satisfied)	Negative state of mind (feeling bad, guilty)
Place	Attractive, convenient or comfortable	Unattractive, inconvenient or uncomfortable
Time	When desired	Time spent in obtaining information, purchasing or using product
Economic	Potential for resale, enhanced earning power, lower relative financial cost	Higher relative financial costs, high total costs

Source: Adapted from C. Lovelock and C.Weinberg (1984) *Marketing for Nonprofit Organizations,* New York: Wiley, p. 48.

(advantages) and costs (disadvantages) related to the purchase and use of a product or service. Customers buy when the 'bundle' of perceived benefits is greater than the bundle of perceived costs. Table 2.1 illustrates these benefits and costs.

A benefit associated with place, such as convenience, may lower the related monetary costs, thereby encouraging a purchase. For example, Convenient Food Mart stores in the USA offer a quick way to purchase groceries on the way home. In societies that value convenience highly, such as the USA, consumers will pay a higher price to gain convenience; in other societies, such as Pakistan, convenience may be perceived as irrelevant or of low value. A lower price might be more important.

Different perceptions of benefits as well as different perceptions of costs offered by the marketing mix, such as the gain or loss of social prestige through the use of a foreign product, suggest that the company needs to adapt the marketing mix for different consumer groups. On the other hand, if perceived benefits are similar – for example, the sensory benefits of colour and style – the company may offer a more standardized marketing mix.

A way to analyse customers' perceptions of benefits and costs related to a product or service is to assess their cognitive structures by the use of the so-called 'laddering' technique and to compare to what extent the same benefits and costs are related to the product or service by customers in different country-markets. For example, Geiger, an Austrian manufacturer of ladies' apparel, asked Austrian, German and Italian customers of their clothes to compare them with the products of major competitors. The consumers were first asked to indicate the product characteristics that made them prefer one or the other product. Then consumers were asked why they thought those characteristics were so important. The answers revealed expected consequences which in turn led to expected benefits that the consumers were looking for and the values related to those benefits. A comparison of findings in the three countries showed that Geiger could standardize its products, as well as distribution and pricing policy, but had to adapt its basic promotional message to the expected benefits in each country. Italians were more interested in fashionable styles, for example, than Germans who expected enduring quality for a satisfactory price.[4]

Process standardization. When no global or at least regional product-market can be detected which allows marketing programme standardization because local customs and needs are too different, a company with a global marketing approach can develop individualized strategies for country-markets in different parts of the world and still benefit from experience curve effects. Nestlé, for example, sells different blends of coffee in different country-markets. But it coordinates the marketing planning process for all of those markets, sometimes even using the same brand name, thereby benefiting from the sharing of ideas and more effective allocation of corporate resources.

Process standardization is the attempt to make the procedures of decision making, implementation and control as similar as possible across all organizational units belonging to a firm or under its control. Richardson-Vicks, a US manufacturer of healthcare products, for example, coordinates its product-line planning for numerous markets. When evaluating a product line in a country, marketing managers not only follow a fixed sequence of analytical steps and use pre-specified tools for each step, they also evaluate its potential in other countries. Other companies, such as Philips NV, use standardized new product testing procedures, corporate design manuals or price calculation procedures. Product designers follow the same guidelines in all the company's local units. Caterpillar sets the same standards of service for customers in all of its national markets. This policy serves to reinforce the brand's image as well as the company's image.

Companies might be able to standardize their marketing processes more easily than their marketing programmes, because they have more control over their own procedures than over their markets. In fact, standardizing processes may be considered as a form of corporate control. In the case of financial and accounting processes and systems, companies have experienced difficulty in standardizing such apparently 'objective' systems. It is even more difficult to standardize marketing processes. These have usually developed in response to, and after considerable analysis of, local markets. Foreign managers trying to impose standardized marketing processes will be frequently criticized for their 'lack of understanding' of local or national market conditions. Because marketing is often perceived as being more 'subjective' than finance, for example, managers hold highly emotional, and highly personal, opinions on how best to deal with markets.

Henkel, the Germany-based manufacturer of industrial and consumer chemical products, such as adhesives and detergents, for example, spent five years orienting its local managers to the company's new global marketing approach. It used organizational development processes – sharing personnel, training, and the reinforcement of a common corporate culture – so that its managers would work and think in the same ways. In a similar manner, the manager of the Finnish market for Reader's Digest was sent to a management development seminar at an American business school, so that he could learn American management techniques and coordinate his planning processes more closely with those at corporate headquarters.

As the Henkel example illustrates, standardizing marketing processes frequently requires significant cultural change. In such cases, if the corporate culture is too rigid and change is not managed properly, significant costs occur, and the probability of successful process standardization is low.

Evaluating the Potential for Process Standardization.   When a company's management has to decide whether to standardize marketing processes, two factors must be considered. These factors are (1) the sequence of activities and (2) the dynamics and homogeneity of the environments.

(1) Sequence of Activities.   To gain efficiency effects from process standardization, the processes need to be an uninterrupted sequence of foreseeable activities. Routines of behaviour, such as physical product quality tests or the calculation of break-even analyses for new investments in logistics facilities, can be standardized fairly easily.

If a sequence of activities is adaptive, that is, it is interrupted by purely intellectual steps (considerations) which determine the following activities, their standardization potential is low. The creative processes of research and development, for example, or processes that depend on the specifics of the business and the macro-environment of a country-market, such as the introduction of a service in a new country-market, are rather difficult to standardize. Guidelines can be given which indicate a certain sequence of steps to be followed and a number of techniques from which to choose. For example, the pre-testing of advertisements can be imposed on sales subsidiaries and a number of approved testing techniques can be determined. They provide experience curve effects because process sequences and techniques which have proven to be effective and efficient do not need to be reinvented by local managers. But on the other hand, such guidelines provide enough flexibility for situational variations.

(2) Dynamics and Homogeneity of Environments.   The standardization potential of marketing processes also depends on the dynamics and homogeneity of a firm's environments. A company which specializes in biotechnological problem solutions for their customers, for example, will have difficulties in standardizing its marketing processes because of the dynamic development of its technological environment and the low level of homogeneity in the legal regulations of potential country-markets. Where innovative behaviour is needed, process standardization is not advisable.

THE INTERNATIONAL MARKETING DECISION PROCESS

As may be gathered from the preceding discussion, a strategic approach to global business is very closely related to marketing analyses and decisions. For international marketing to be effective and efficient, analyses and decisions

Figure 2.9 THE INTERNATIONAL MARKETING DECISION PROCESS

Starting from corporate policy, the international marketing decision process follows a series of steps of analyses and decisions with increasing levels of concreteness. First potential markets and the company's ability to serve them successfully are assessed. Then basic decisions concerning the firm's global strategic position and market-entry strategy are taken. Finally, marketing-mix policies and actions have to be planned and their financial impact evaluated in an international marketing plan. To allow consistent decision making and continual implementation of those decisions, management systems appropriate for international marketing have to be developed.

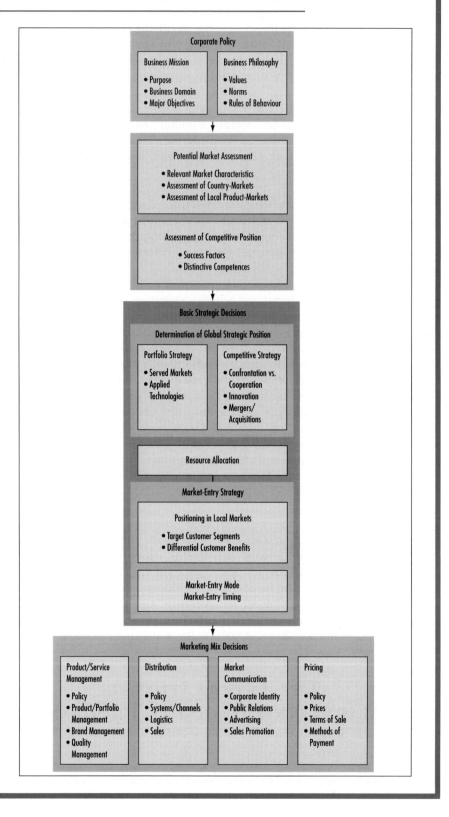

need to follow a specific sequence which is called the international marketing decision process (Figure 2.9).

Potential Market Assessment

After a corporate policy has been developed and the product-markets to be served are identified in general terms, the global marketing process starts with an assessment of potential country-markets. Their economic, cultural, political and legal environments, that is, their macro-environment, as well as the specific operating environments of the local product-markets have to be carefully analysed to determine the most attractive markets.

From this assessment, the success factors in those markets – the major capabilities and resources needed to be successful – are derived. They serve as the basis for a comparison between the firm's potential to serve the most attractive markets, and the related potential of its most important competitors. For example, an Italian furniture manufacturer may find the Scandinavian living room furniture market to be among the most attractive options. To be a successful contender there, a marketer needs to rise to Scandinavian expectations concerning design and weight, as well as do-it-yourself potential. Through an assessment of its own capabilities and resources the Italian firm may discover that it can easily meet the design and weight factors, but has no experience in the production or marketing of do-it-yourself furniture.

Basic Strategic Decisions

The comparison with major competitors will help the firm identify whether it can excel in any of the success factors; that is, whether the firm will be able to profit from a competitive advantage. Further, through such a comparison the firm can identify which, if any, success factor it is lacking which would prevent it from successfully serving a market. In the case of the Italian furniture manufacturer, the company may find that the most important Danish and Swedish competitors have an advantage in the do-it-yourself area, whereas the Italian firm has an edge in creative design.

Management will then assess existing strategic alternatives based on those distinctive competencies which can be transformed into customer benefits, that is, relying on the firm's competitive advantages. It will develop an international portfolio strategy, that is, it will choose the product- and country-markets to serve as well as select the technologies necessary to satisfy the existing and potential aspirations of customers and stakeholders in those markets. Closely related to their choice of markets, management has to select the most promising competitive strategy – the way the firm will behave in the chosen markets. Choices range from a frontal attack on any competitor to cooperative agreements that not only allow peaceful coexistence but also the exploitation of mutual strengths, achieving synergy. Microsoft, for example, frontally attacks any rival in its major product-markets, but cooperates with the most powerful marketers of PCs, such as IBM or Compaq, to increase the benefits to its customers. The competitive strategy also comprises decisions concerning the innovation behaviour of the firm as well as its policy concerning growth through mergers and acquisitions. Portfolio strategy, competitive strategy, and the subsequent resource allocation decisions define the intended global strategic position that should help ensure the survival of the company.

In addition, the company must position itself in every market it has selected. That is, it must select the customer group(s) to be served and how it wants to differentiate itself attractively from the most important competitors. HILTI's global strategic position, for example, involves offering high-quality, high-priced fastening solutions employing the latest technology to all construction businesses throughout the world. Nevertheless, positioning in individual country-markets has to be done in the light of the existing customer segments and competition.

The intended global strategic position and the intended positions in the chosen country-markets determine the ways in which markets are entered. If international marketing is conducted only to reach operational goals such as boosting the total sales volume or taking up excess capacity, and control over local marketing activities is considered less important, low-risk market-entry alternatives with a minimum of resources required, like indirect exporting or exporting via importers in each country-market, will be favoured. If internationalization of business is a strategic objective and the company wants to keep its local positions under close control, it will take bolder steps, such as direct investment. IBM, for example, often prefers to invest directly abroad in order to maximize control over marketing activities linked to its name.

Building and Sustaining the Global Position

Finally, decisions are made regarding the marketing mix: the contribution of product and services management, distribution, including logistics and sales management, market communication and pricing to building and sustaining the intended global strategic position and the intended country-market positions is determined. The chosen strategies serve as guidelines for those decisions. HILTI's headquarters, for example, developed a policy for each element of the marketing mix, such as a corporate design handbook and HILTI services guidelines. Country-market managers, however, are given enough flexibility in setting prices, establishing product characteristics and service levels, and managing market communication to adapt to local market conditions. All the analyses made and the decisions taken to reach that point are summarized in an international marketing plan. This plan also indicates what and how much resources are to be spent, and how the planned activities are to be financed.

Even if the process described is closely followed by marketing managers, objectives, resulting strategic decisions, resource allocation and marketing-mix implementation may be incompatible or even contradictory. For example, a firm may say it wishes to be the technology leader in its industry, but it may be managed as if a maximum return on investment were more important. To ensure that its international marketing is properly managed, and that its intended global strategic position is transformed into adequate actions, a company needs management systems that support global business. Such systems enable a company to plan, implement and evaluate its decisions. Organization, information, planning and leadership must be shaped in ways that make the firm's intended strategic position become reality.

The international marketing decision process, supported by the company's management systems, will be discussed in detail in the following chapters. It must make sure that all members of a company work towards attaining the set objectives.

SUMMARY

The critical element for success in international business is not so much the size of a company as an approach or business perspective of top management that seeks to do business where it can be done with the greatest success. Managers of locally operating companies who have overcome an ethnocentric perspective of international business must decide whether their firm should go international or not. Each company operating internationally has to determine which markets should be served and in what sequence. Because the resources of a company are not unlimited they have to be allocated in such a way as to maximize potential success across the product- and country-markets served. For that purpose a plan has to be developed indicating how competitive advantages should be built and sustained in those markets.

When taking and implementing decisions concerning the internationalization of their business, a firm's management has to be aware of the considerably higher complexity of the environment to be considered than for a strictly local firm. A careful assessment of macro- and operating environments and their interaction in various country-markets will show different developments to be considered. Management will identify potential customers in different geographic areas. Competitors as well as intermediaries and suppliers will be spread throughout the globe. A strategic approach to international business is needed to ensure a steady flow of resources to and from the company.

The critical aspect of such an approach is to manage relationships with customers and other important stakeholders of the firm in a way that satisfies their expectations. Building and maintaining relationships is the major focus of marketing. International marketing is the application of marketing orientation and marketing techniques to international business.

There are two basically different ways in which marketing managers can approach international business: a multinational and a global approach. A multinational marketing approach focuses largely on country-markets, developing a distinct marketing strategy for each market. A global approach to international marketing occurs when a company's managers concentrate on product-markets, emphasizing their similarities regardless of the geographic areas in which they are located. The most powerful argument in favour of a global product-market orientation is the opportunity to benefit from experience curve effects. These include increased efficiency due to size effects and increased effectiveness due to experience effects. The size effects result from decreasing fixed costs per unit sold. Increased effectiveness occurs when a company 'learns by doing'.

The greatest experience curve effects can be reached when both marketing programmes and marketing processes are standardized. The degree of potential standardization of marketing programmes depends on the similarity of the local product-markets served and their macro-environments, on product uniqueness and cultural specificity as well as the internal environment of the company. The potential extent of marketing process standardization depends on the sequence of activities constituting a process and the dynamics as well as the homogeneity of the firm's product-markets.

The described analyses and decisions needed for a strategic approach to international business constitute the international marketing decision process which will be discussed in the following chapters.

ADDITIONAL READINGS

Botschen, G. and A. Hemetsberger (1998) 'Diagnosing Means-End Structures to Determine the Degree of Potential Marketing Program Standardization', *Journal of Business Research*, 42 (2), June, 151–159.

Cavusgil, T.S. and S. Zou (1994) 'Marketing Strategy–Performance Relationship: An Investigation of the Empirical Link in Export Market Ventures', *Journal of Marketing*, 58 (January), 1–21.

Cavusgil, S.T., S. Zou and G.M. Naidu (1993) 'Product and Promotion Adaptation in Export Ventures: An Empirical Investigation', *Journal of International Business Studies*, 479–506.

Donaldson, T. and L.E. Preston (1995) 'The stakeholder theory of the corporation: concepts, evidence and implications', *Academy of Management Review*, 20, 65–91.

Foster, T.R.V. (1993) *101 Great Mission Statements*, London: Kogan Page.

Kaku, R. (1997) 'The Path of Kyosei', *Harvard Business Review*, July–August, 55–63.

Meffert, H. and J. Bolz (1995) 'Erfolgswirkungen der internationalen Marketing-standardisierung', *Marketing-ZFP*, Heft 2, 99–109.

Schlegelmilch, B.B. (1998) *Marketing Ethics: An International Perspective*, London: International Thomson Business Press.

Troiano, J. (1997) 'Brazilian teenagers go global – Sharing values and brands', *Marketing and Research Today*, August, 149–161.

DISCUSSION QUESTIONS

1. How does psychic distance influence a firm's motives for engaging in global business?
2. Suppose your company is based in Oslo, Norway, and manufactures fish-smoking equipment for the home market. A Brazilian firm inquires about your company's products. Prepare a script for a role play in which you (1) play the role of a manager having mainly defensive motives and (2) play the role of a manager having mainly offensive motives in its reaction to this inquiry.
3. What are the major decisions a company's management has to take when considering international business? Find examples from business magazines to illustrate each of the decisions.
4. Choose an example of a firm and describe the environments the decision makers of this firm have to consider in taking international business decisions. How are those environments interrelated?
5. What are the basic convictions underlying marketing orientation? Why are they important for business success?
6. What is the basic distinction between multinational and global marketing? What are the consequences of each of the two perspectives to a firm?
7. How does a company that adopts a global marketing perspective benefit from experience curve effects?
8. What factors can influence the extent of a firm's marketing programme standardization and why?
9. Using the benefit–cost approach, evaluate the potential for standardization for a toy that is designed to be played with by children between the ages of 18 and 36 months. Assume that the potential markets are your home country and the People's Republic of China.
10. How can the use–need model be helpful in evaluating the appropriateness of standardization versus individualization of product and market communication? Find a practical example to illustrate your points.
11. What are the major steps in an international marketing decision process? How do they build on each other?

NOTES

[1] Brull, St.V. and G. McWilliams, '"Fujitsu Shokku" Is Jolting American PC Makers', *Business Week*, 19 February 1996, p. 50.

[2] Marks, D., 'Smurfit Issues Cautious Outlook Despite a 32% Jump in Profit in '95', *The Wall Street Journal Europe*, 11 April 1996, p. 3.

[3] Parker-Pope, T., 'Legal Pressure in US Doesn't Cloud Outlook For B.A.T. Overseas', *The Wall Street Journal Europe*, 2 April 1996, pp. 1 and 6.

[4] Botschen, G. and A. Hemetsberger, 'Diagnosing Means-End Structures to Determine the Degree of Potential Marketing Program Standardization', *Journal of Business Research*, 42 (2), June 1998, pp. 151–159.

POTENTIAL MARKET ASSESSMENT

When a company applies a multinational or global approach to marketing, it views the entire world as made up of a variety of potential markets, country- as well as product-markets. Limited resources, however, mean that no company can serve all potential markets in the world in such a way that customers are satisfied and the firm's objectives are achieved. The company must select the most appropriate markets. It might focus on one product-market and serve it in many different geographic areas, but it might also choose to serve various product-markets in a small group of selected geographic areas. Because of the great number and diversity of markets to choose from, the task of assessing the markets' attractiveness and selecting the most interesting ones is rather complex.

This part of the book describes the process of how to determine the most attractive markets in an international environment. It discusses the factors which may be considered in the preselection of

PART II

markets to be analysed in greater detail, suggests some market characteristics which should be assessed in a detailed market analysis, gives an overview of how to gather and treat the data needed for informed decisions and describes a way to determine a company's competitive position in the most attractive markets (see Figure II.1).

To be meaningful, the assessment of potential markets must be based on detailed and continually updated information. The great number and diversity of markets prevents gathering and analysing the vast amount of information needed for a detailed simultaneous comparison of all potential markets at a reasonable cost. Further, at a given point in time, not all potential markets will be attractive to a firm. Management must, therefore, find a way to preselect the most attractive markets in a quick and low-cost manner, and gather relevant and precise information that leads to an accurate evaluation of a restricted number of potential markets.

Figure II.1 POTENTIAL MARKET ASSESSMENT

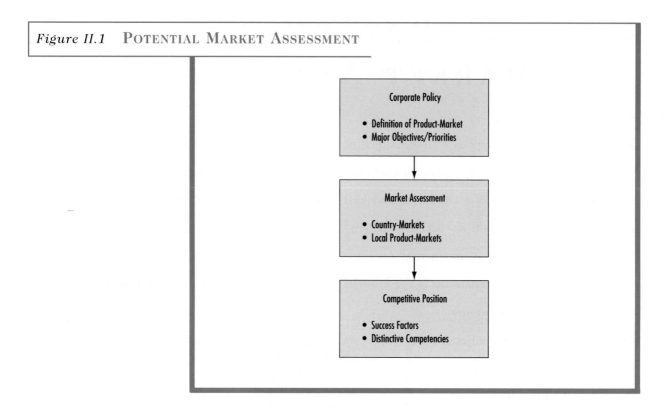

Top management has made a first choice of which markets the company should serve in the statement of corporate policy where it has determined the firm's product-market(s) in general terms through the formulation of a corporate mission and business philosophy. Depending on the intended degree of internationalization the firm will either: (1) do business on a global level; (2) try to expand a local business to a regional one and later one of global size; or (3) keep its business local.

If the firm's corporate mission contains the objective of keeping the business local, management has no need to assess the attractiveness of potential markets. It must continually screen the global business environment, however, to make sure that its local competitive advantage can be sustained. Developments in other local parts of the same product-market have to be followed in order to prevent unpleasant surprises from competitors intruding into the local home market. A US producer of kitchen furniture serving the consumers in the Carolinas, for example, has to watch for developments in similar product-markets in Europe and Southeast Asia. From there, competitors that try to enter the home market of the US firm could emerge.

If the firm's corporate mission contains the objective of internationalizing the business from a local market base, country-markets will have a prominent position in managers' minds. This will occur despite the fact that every market assessment procedure has to start from the definition of the firm's business. Characteristics relevant to the attractiveness of geographically limited product-markets have to be determined. A company that wishes to grow quickly, for example, will choose country-markets in which its product-market is large enough and has sufficient purchasing power to support a high growth rate. A company that prefers more stable development, or slower growth, may look for country-markets where its product-market is in later stages of development.

If the company has adopted a global perspective of international marketing, management will think primarily in product-market terms – serving cross-national customer segments in particular product categories. Specific characteristics of geographic submarkets will only be used for the purposes of adaptation of marketing mixes and resource allocation decisions. For example, firms such as Boeing, Compaq or Whirlpool serve certain segments of a global product-market. They use information about different technical standards for product adaptation in country-markets. Information on local customer activities or on legal restrictions of financial transfers affects decisions on how much resources to deploy in which geographic area. In any case, characteristics of the specific product-market relevant to business success have to be assessed across country-markets in order to allow a comparison of geographic submarket attractiveness.

Independent of the international marketing perspective of management – multinational or global – product-markets will usually be distributed over a larger number of country-markets. Characteristics relevant to the evaluation of those geographically defined parts of the global product-market can be found in its macro-environment. For example, legal regulations concerning the production technology applied can strongly diminish the attractiveness of a country-market for investors in the textile or pulp and paper industries. Because these industries have heavily polluted the rivers of Austria, Germany and Switzerland, their governments, pushed by strong political movements for environmental protection, have imposed such restrictive standards of pollution control that international investors have stayed away from the three countries since then. The primary parts of a firm's macro-environment are economic, political, legal and cultural. These environments will be discussed first in terms of their effects on country-market attractiveness (Chapters 3 to 5).

Other evaluation criteria are related to the firm's operating environment, for example the high intellectual level of the available labour force in India has led investors from the software industry to transfer some of their capacities to that country. Another example is Japan's Shinseido, one of the world's leading marketers of perfumes. The existing infrastructure in the area of perfume development and production as well as the image of the French perfume industry have made this company invest in a production site in France. To gather information concerning the operating environments in potential markets a company has to establish a system of international marketing intelligence. This will be discussed in Chapter 6.

Based on criteria from the macro- and operating environments, management can determine the attractiveness of potential markets. The process of market assessment can take different forms. Chapter 7 will discuss some of them and will suggest a procedure which is fast and cost effective. By using easily available data, the great number of available country-markets is reduced to a small set of highly attractive markets which have to be analysed in more detail. As a result, the company possesses a short list of country-markets ranked according to their attractiveness.

Before company management can decide which markets should be served, how, and in what sequence, it has to consider the competitive position of the firm in each of the attractive markets. Only if the company is able to satisfy the existing and potential expectations of customers and stakeholders in the preselected markets to a degree that makes it more attractive than its competitors can long-term success be ensured. Therefore, success factors have to be determined for each of the preselected markets. A comparison between the major competitors and the firm on those success factors reveals distinctive competencies of the firm which, hopefully, can be transformed into competitive advantages. Chapter 8 will describe this process, suggest some tools to be applied, and prepare the basic strategic decisions to be discussed in the third part of the book.

CHAPTER 3

THE ECONOMIC ENVIRONMENT

> # INTERNATIONAL INCIDENT

Blast From the Past

When British Ispat International Ltd., one of the world's 10 biggest steel-makers, bought Karmet, Kazakhstan's largest steel plant, for about USD1 billion in the Fall of 1995, the KGB came along with it, at no extra charge. The intelligence agency had set up shop in the Karmet steel plant in the 1940s, when Stalin built the mill as a work camp. When the plant was sold to the British firm, more than a dozen agents refused to leave their electronically sophisticated corner office.

For Ispat, ousting the KGB may be the least of its worries. The company faces a tough test on the Kazak steppes, on the edge of Siberia. Following some failed government attempts to sell the plant to its managers, Kazakstan's most important industrial asset, and the source of 10 percent of its gross domestic product was near collapse in summer of 1995. Yet while Karmet lingered near death, its managers lived like kings. Across Lenin Avenue from the plant, Karmet's former directors built a lavish guest house complete with several restaurants, a massage parlor and a disco. The company spent USD1 million on armchairs alone. Hundreds of Karmet's employees came to work drunk. (Ispat, after taking over, fired about 100 people a week for coming to work drunk and others for allegedly cheating the company by getting paid for two jobs but working only one). There were at least ten management layers (as one new manager put it: 'Everyone has got his assistant and his assistant and his assistant'); and the biggest customer was broke.

Because Ispat is the first Karmet owner in years to have any money, it was quickly viewed as a soft target. Soon after Ispat arrived, a man claiming to represent a society for the blind asked the company for donations. If Ispat would donate steel, he said, the society could resell it and raise money. After the company agreed, 68 other societies for the blind turned up.

But the worst problem is the dearth of orders. In the former Soviet Union Karmet's steel was used to make half of all tin cans produced in the country. With that demand almost gone, Ispat now sells about 90 percent of the plant's products outside the Commonwealth of Independent States. Two-thirds of them go to China. Ispat wants to ship more there, but it is thwarted because the railway gauges, which are different in China, create a bottleneck. Trains loaded with steel must stop at the border, where the load is shifted to a train that can run on Chinese track. While other markets are a possibility – Ispat already sells Karmet steel to Iran, Iraq, Turkey and Afghanistan – further geographical expansion is expensive.

Kazakstan, the last of the former Soviet republics to declare its independence, desperately needs Karmet to work. Its economy shrank 9 percent in 1995, and estimates are that foreign investments of about USD20 billion will be needed until the turn of the century if the country is to be stabilized. While it has privatized about 9,000 state enterprises, mostly small stores and state farms, other high-profile projects have faltered. Of the 126 big state enterprises targeted for privatization in 1995, only the Karmet deal was completed.

Source: Adapted from Pope, K. (1996) 'Blast From the Past, Troubled Kazak Mill Is Testing the Mettle Of British Steelmaker', *The Wall Street Journal Europe*, 2 May, pp. 1 and 6.

ASSESSING THE
ECONOMIC ENVIRONMENT

The macro-environment of a company strongly influences the structure and state of its operating environment which, together with the firm's resources and capabilities, determines its potential success. The economy of a country is a major part of each company's macro-environment. It is a complex system of interdependent local, regional and international forces. In addition, besides purely economic factors such as the economic system or the existing industrial sectors, a modern society is strongly characterized by its human, technological and natural resources. That is, the skills and flexibility of a country's population and the available infrastructure and level of technology, as well as the level of relative ecological balance, for example, constitute essential bases of a country's economic wealth.

A marketer serving international markets or planning to go international is confronted with a greater number of such economic environments. Therefore, when considering which country-markets' operating environments to analyse more closely or how much of the firm's resources to invest in which of the currently served country-markets, the international marketer first has to determine the various characteristics of the economic environment which are relevant for the company's business. For example, a producer of food products such as Very Fine Products Inc., a Littleton, Massachusetts-based juice manufacturer, may define the existing economic system, the population size and age structure, disposable houshold income, level of urbanization, climate, transportation, communication and distribution infrastructure, the currency exchange rate, and the country's level of economic development as important characteristics of the economic environment (Figure 3.1).

Having determined the relevant factors of influence from the economic environment, the marketer will need to analyse their current state in the country-markets under consideration. A full evaluation of the impact of those factors on the potential success of the firm will only be possible, however, if management also tries to anticipate the potential states of the relevant factors on the planning horizon. For example, economic factors such as four years of recession, reduced tariffs and a strong yen compared to other leading currencies helped to increase significantly Japanese purchases of imported food in the mid-1990s. Recession has fostered innovations in the traditional distribution system of the country. Discount retailing, convenience stores and direct-delivery services have grown. Such developments, helping non-Japanese food marketers to enter the market, will not be dropped when the economy starts booming again. Because of international agreements, tariffs can be expected to stay low in the coming years. The exchange rate of the yen to other currencies is more volatile, however. An international marketer who has based its success mainly on the strong yen may find itself driven out of the market when exchange rate changes occur, such as the high appreciation of the dollar in 1997/98.[1]

A comparison of the current states of the economic environments in the country-markets served or being considered, and their potential developments, allows the marketer to decide how to 'manage' those environments. That is, management will be able to find ways of specifically reacting to the expected developments. It may, for example, decide to invest in a market with

Figure 3.1 ANALYSING THE ECONOMIC ENVIRONMENT

In analysing the economic environment of the firm, the marketer first has to determine which factors are relevant to the product-market(s) the company is serving. Then the current state of international, regional and local factors of influence can be assessed and their potential states on the planning horizon anticipated. From the results of the analysis, managerial consequences concerning the further treatment of the analysed country-markets may be drawn.

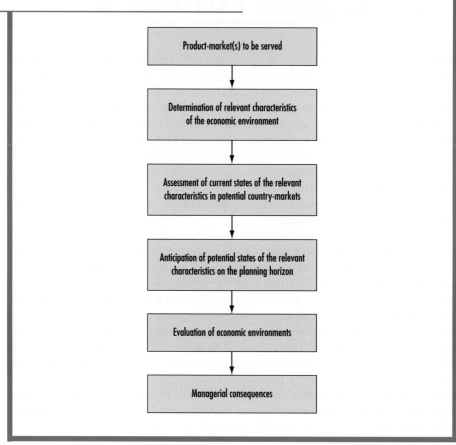

an interesting future potential which currently would not be attractive enough. For example, Russia in 1996 had an inflation rate around 35 per cent, the gross domestic product had been falling since 1991, its economic reform had remained a patchy process, and the task of making privatized factories efficient and internationally competitive had only just begun. Nevertheless, companies such as chewing-gum maker Wm. Wrigley Jr. Co. and Salomon Brothers Inc. published plans to invest directly in the country because of its expected more positive economic development.[2]

In other cases, companies may not continue to consider a potential country-market or may decide to withdraw from a market because of its unsatisfactory economic development. For example, Bulgaria saw a drying up of foreign investments when privatization was at a standstill in 1996, and the economy remained largely state-owned and dominated by clunky, Soviet-era companies with ageing facilities and products that could not compete on world markets.[3] Interested investors such as British Rover or US-based Texaco retreated when faced with a jungle of bureaucratic and financial hurdles as well as mafia-like structures up to the highest levels of government. Other international firms such as South Korea's Daewoo which bought 67 per cent of the Sheraton Balkan hotel in the centre of Sofia, or the Austrian freight forwarder Willi Betz which bought the Bulgarian transportation firm Somat, invested in Bulgaria because of the country's geographic location as a bridge between the Middle East, the Black Sea and Central Europe.[4] In 1998, the picture has changed: following a change in government after the country's economic breakdown in Winter 1996/97, Bulgaria's currency has been tied to the German mark. Macro-economic stability has helped to overcome recession, the national budget is balanced, and legal as well as economic reforms are under way.

This chapter will discuss various characteristics of the economic environment that may be relevant to the business of an internationally operating company, and provide examples of how international marketers try to accommodate the current and anticipated status of those characteristics.

BASES OF ECONOMIC WEALTH

The economic wealth of a country is based on its human, natural and technical resources. These resources affect a country's ability to produce globally competitive goods and services and to offer a viable market for such products. The human resources of a country are the most important factor of influence on its economic wealth. Factors such as the composition and distribution of the population, the degree of urbanization, and the available capabilities in a country's population which are based on the level of education, skills, flexibility and mobility of people determine how well the natural resources of a country can be used and how far the country's technical resources are developed. The presence or absence of natural resources, and geographic features such as topography and climate, are a second important basis of economic wealth. The technological resources available to a country, such as energy, transportation, communications and commercial infrastructure, also have a strong impact on its economic wealth. Finally, the skilful use and maintenance of all available resources also determines a country's level of economic development. How resources are used is largely influenced by the economic system of the country. The better this system allows the building, maintenance and use of the (existing) bases of economic wealth, the more economically attractive the country will be for an international marketer.

Population

The total population of a country, its growth rate, the distribution of age groups within the population and the degree of urbanization are of interest to many international marketers. After all, the size of a potential local product-market is a key element in its viability. The distribution of age groups in a country is closely related to the demand for certain products, and the degree of urbanization represents concentrations of potential customers.

Size and Growth. Many international marketers are interested in rapidly developing markets in China and India, which together represent some 70 per cent of Asia's population (about 2 billion consumers) and about 40 per cent of the population of the world. The higher population also helps to explain why the USA and multinational cooperative agreement areas like the European Union have so much appeal to many international marketers. Clearly, the size

Map 3.1 REGIONS WITH STRONG POPULATION GROWTH

Source: *Der Fischer Weltalmanach '96*, Frankfurt a.m.: Fischer Taschenburch Verlag, p. 1123.

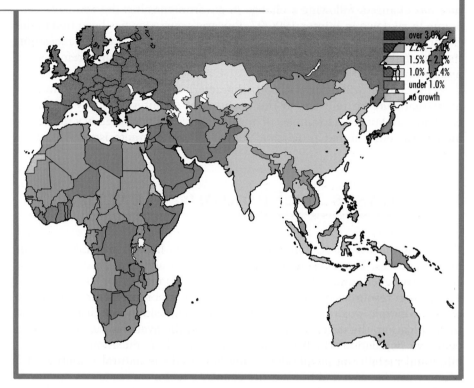

over 3.0%
2.2% – 3.0%
1.5% – 2.1%
1.0% – 1.4%
under 1.0%
no growth

of the population and its rate of growth affect a society's ability to progress economically and provide for the future.

However, population size without purchasing power is not economically meaningful. Sometimes population growth outpaces economic growth. This is a particular problem in developing countries, notably those in Africa. Even when those countries experience positive economic growth, their per capita economic growth is negative owing to the rapid rate of population growth. Developing countries with close to half of their population under the age of 15 have a major drain on their economic resources owing to the 'non-productivity' of so many young people. Brazil, as an example from Latin America, must balance the need to create more than 1 million new jobs a year to absorb the increase in population that needs to work against the need to pay the interest on its foreign debt. Many other nations with high population growth rates, including India, Mexico and Vietnam, face similar economic dilemmas. At the other extreme, political leaders in Germany or France have traditionally been concerned about those countries' insufficient population growth rate. There is the fear that too few economically active people will not be able to support the great number of retired members of the workforce in the future.

Within a society, it is often the economically poorest classes that exhibit the highest population growth rates. From the standpoint of the individual, there may be strong economic reasons for having a larger family. In Egypt, for example, there is no general social security system to help support elderly people who can no longer support themselves, and most Egyptians do not have the necessary income to pay for their retirement during their work life. Therefore, the more children one has, the greater one's chances of living relatively comfortably in old age.

Religious beliefs can also contribute to higher birth rates. For example, according to Hindu doctrine, funeral rites must be performed by the eldest son if a dead parent is to progress to the next life. Families are thus encouraged to have several sons, to ensure that the rites will be carried out properly. Regardless of the motivation, however, the results are similar: larger families reduce per capita income. Ironically for the international marketer, the markets that are growing fastest in terms of number of consumers are usually those that are increasingly unable to afford the marketer's products.

Immigration.   Population growth may be due not only to a high reproduction rate but also to immigration. Between 1980 and 1990, for example, almost 9 million immigrated into the USA, compared to just over 6 million the decade before, matching the earlier record of 1900–1910. Given the slower rate of population growth overall, this new inflow represented 39 per cent of total population growth for that decade. The large majority of the immigrants came from Asia and Latin America, changing the distribution of different races that constitute the US population. For the international marketer, this means the creation of new markets or the growth of traditionally less important niches. For example, media in Spanish have a much higher reach, or Asian food producers are faced with an increasing market potential.

Immigrants bring considerable job skills and even investment capital. Many entrepreneurs come from immigrant groups, and of the immigrants of the 1980s the percentage of male workers who are college graduates is higher than for native-born US citizens. But such high proportions of immigrants also have political consequences, as they compete for jobs as well as resources for social and medical care with those already in the country. Particularly in countries where the economy is growing slowly, if at all, considerable political backlash has occurred, particularly in Europe. There, prosperous countries such as France, Germany and Italy have tried to absorb immigrants – economic as well as political refugees fleeing because of political and economic problems in some former communist countries, such as (former) Yugoslavia, Albania or Romania, as well as in African countries like Algeria, Ruanda, Liberia or Congo.

Perhaps the most extreme example is Germany, which not only has to overcome the economic difficulties of its now integrated but former communist part, but is also the most preferred destination, after the USA, of immigrants from all over the world. Germany has spent USD600 billion on revamping the economy of the formerly communist East Germany from reunification in 1990 to the budget year 1996. That is almost ten times the amount the West has promised to Russia, though Eastern Germany has just one-tenth Russia's population. Moreover, Bonn expects the torrent of funding to continue for five to ten years more before living standards in the east reach 80 per cent of western German levels.[5]

Age Distribution.   The age composition of a population may also be of interest to international marketers. As fertility increases, new markets emerge for products for young families and children. But as Table 3.1 shows, the most fertile countries have major problems sustaining their economic wealth.

Table 3.1   The Most Fertile Countries in the 1990s

Increasing fertility in most countries means decreasing economic wealth for the individual. Exceptions are mainly due to special resources or political influences.

Country	Population in millions 1993	Fertility rate in 1993	Yearly GDP per capita growth in % (1980–93)
Côte d'Ivoire	13.3	7.3	−4.6
Niger	8.6	7.3	−4.1
Uganda	18	7.2	1.9
Malawi	10.5	7.1	−1.2
Oman	2	7.1	3.4
Benin	5	7.0	−0.4
Mali	10	7.0	−1.0
Honduras	5.3	4.8	−0.3
Bolivia	7	4.7	−0.7
Philippines	65	3.9	−0.6
Vietnam	71	3.8	4.8
India	900	3.7	3.0
Malaysia	19	3.5	3.5
Venezuela	21	3.2	−0.7
Mexico	90	3.1	−0.5
Indonesia	187	2.8	4.2
Thailand	58	2.1	6.4

Fertility rate = Births per female inhabitant capable of childbearing.
Source: Translated/adapted from Baratta, M. (ed.) (1995) *Der Fischer Weltalmanach '96*, Frankfurt a.M.: Fischer Taschenbuch Verlag, pp. 31–45.

As people become older, new markets emerge among older age groups. In the Triad markets, such changes have resulted in a variety of new market opportunities. For example, retirement villages have become popular in the USA, Australia and Spain. The need for home-care services for elderly people is growing, and both retirement funds and retirement age insurance are booming. Products and packages are redesigned to make them easier to handle and read for 'mature' consumers. The smaller number of children in those countries, combined with the increased resources of dual-career households, also means that parents have more money to spend on their fewer children. The increasing amount of pocket money those children have makes them a very interesting market for products targeted to more and more precisely defined segments of children and youth. (Table 3.2 shows population trends in the countries of the European Union.)

The maturing of the population in the economically most advanced markets not only leads to new product-markets, but also presents significant problems to their societies which should not be ignored by international marketers (see Figure 3.2). In Japan, for example, economists are worried that there will soon not be enough workers to support the retired generation – traditionally, retired people in Japan live with their families. In Hong Kong, where some 80 per cent of the companies listed on the stock exchange are controlled by a single family, 'mom-and-pop' multinationals are finding it increasingly difficult to continue to do business run by family members as leaders retire, and fewer sons and daughters are available to take their place.

Table 3.2 **POPULATION TRENDS IN THE EUROPEAN UNION**

COUNTRY	POPULATION IN TSD. 1993	POPULATION GROWTH IN % 1992/93	POPULATION BELOW 15 YEARS	
			1960	1993
Austria	7,990	1.3	22.0	17.5
Belgium	10,010	−0.3	23.5	18.2
Denmark	5,190	0.4	25.2	17.0
Germany	81,190	0.8	21.3	16.3
Finland	5,066	0.5	30.4	19.1
France	54,729	0.5	26.4	19.8
Greece	10,370	0.5	26.1	17.4
Ireland	3,560	0.4	30.5	26.8
Italy	57,070	0.4	23.4	16.5
Luxembourg	380	−2.6	21.4	17.7
Netherlands	15,300	0.8	30.0	18.3
Portugal	9,887	0.2	29.0	18.4
Sweden	8,718	0.6	22.4	18.6
Spain	39,080	0.2	27.3	17.7
UK	57,830	−0.3	23.3	19.3

In the 1990s, population growth rates in the European Union have been below reproduction level. The share of below 15-year-olds is dramatically decreasing.

Source: Adapted from Baratta, M. (ed.) (1995) *Der Fischer Weltalmanach '96*, Frankfurt a.M.: Fischer Taschenbuch Verlag, p. 47.

Figure 3.2 **COMPARISON OF THE AGE PYRAMIDS FOR THE YEARS 1985 AND 2025 IN INDUSTRIALLY DEVELOPING AND HIGHLY DEVELOPED COUNTRIES**

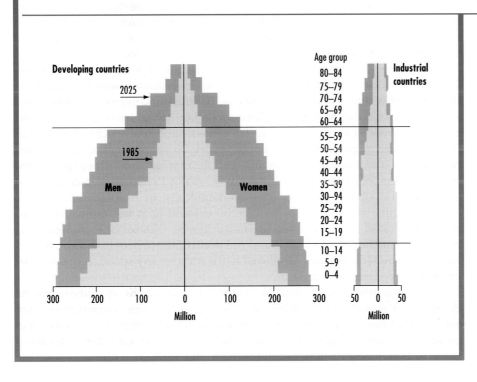

Many industrially developing countries experience high birth rates compared to industrially developed countries. While the latter have increasing difficulties in financing their retirement systems, the former need high economic growth rates to avoid substantial unemployment.

Source: Translated/adapted from United Nations Population Division, in Baratta, M. (ed.) (1995), *Der Fischer Weltalmanach '96*, Frankfurt a.M.: Fischer Taschenbuch Verlag, p. 1125.

The worry in most western European countries is who will work to generate the retirement funds needed for a longer-living population. People retire at around 60 years of age and live until around 80. That is, they want to receive retirement payments for approximately half as long as they have been active in production processes during their working life. In addition, for example, in France three people held a job for every retired person in 1970. In 1990, that ratio had fallen to 2.3, and was expected to be less than 2 to 1 in 2000. As a result, the existing social security systems simply cannot afford to continue at their present levels. Politicians, but also company managers, will need to find ways to ensure the level of individual wealth in the years to come. In other words, the future of highly industrialized countries may hold a most challenging major market for international marketers – more older people, perhaps with less money, and fewer younger people more preoccupied with financially ensuring their retirement. Certainly not only new goods and services and altered marketing campaigns will be necessary if this scenario comes true. The entire concept of pricing, credit and the viability of certain product-markets may be called into question.

Urbanization. The term urbanization refers to the proportion of a population that lives in cities. The degree of urbanization in a society is of interest to international marketers because it represents concentrations of potential customers. In addition, despite all the faults of urban agglomerations, they are centres of industrial productivity and economic growth. For example, Metro-Manila is characterized by a concentration of economic, social and political activities, as evidenced by the presence of 90 per cent of the biggest companies in the country, all of the major newspapers, all of the main television stations and 60 per cent of the country's non-agricultural labour force. The area serves as the distribution centre for exports and capital goods. It is the Philippines' centre for non-primary goods production, providing almost one-half of the total national output in manufacturing, commerce and services. In addition, about 90 per cent of internal revenue collection for the entire country is taken from Metro-Manila and almost 80 per cent of the Philippines' imports enter through the ports of the City of Manila.

As the same example shows, however, despite the cited economic performance, too rapid urbanization can lead to high unemployment, harsh living conditions and frequent episodes of political and social unrest. Other examples are Ciudad de México (Mexico City) or Al-Qahira (Cairo), the most urbanized areas of their countries. They have such high population growth rates that their population could double every 20 years. Much of this growth results from rural–urban migration – people moving away from poor rural areas in search of better opportunities. Whereas in 1970 less than 20 per cent of the world's population lived in urban complexes, in 2000 about half of all people will live in cities. Jobs cannot be created at a fast enough pace to absorb this rapid increase in the urban workforce. Ghettos of extremely poor people become larger and larger, and the percentage of people working in the informal sector (mainly self-employed work without any social, retirement or medical care security) increases.

European urban agglomerations experienced the same phenomena during the period of capitalist industrialization in the early 1800s. In contrast, Japan and the USA have histories of slow but steady urbanization. Their active and growing economies, coupled with a lower rate of urbanization, have allowed them to better absorb new urban dwellers and workers without a dramatic increase in unemployment. Nevertheless, today every big urban agglomeration is characterized by a duality: ghettos of poor unemployed people with largely low levels of education and a centre with sky-scrapers, bank offices and luxury boutiques.

It may come as a surprise to discover that Australia is the world's most urbanized country, with 86 per cent of its 15 million people living in urban areas. For the international marketer, this is of particular interest because urban and rural dwellers often have different consumption patterns. In the USA, for example, Sears Roebuck built a tremendous business by catering to the rural population through catalogue sales. But, as an increasing proportion of the population moved to the cities, Sears found it necessary to follow its customers; it changed its product offerings and placed more emphasis on stores in suburban shopping centres.

Urban dwellers in different countries are more likely to have similar consumption patterns than urban and rural consumers within the same country. For example, urban women in Argentina, Brazil, Peru, Algeria and Morocco have more similar consumption patterns with regard to cosmetics than do urban and rural women within any one of those countries. In industrially developing countries, such as India, international marketers are often unable to reach consumers outside urban agglomerations. In China this represents only 20 per cent of the population. Yet that market contains around 200 million potential customers and is increasing rapidly.

Capabilities. Besides the size of a country's population combined with the purchasing power of those potential customers which is in turn influenced by the age structure of the population and the society's degree of urbanization, the capabilities to be found in a country's population have a significant influence on its wealth. Because such capabilities are to some extent based on the available knowledge, the nature of a country's educational system is of interest to international marketers. It affects the literacy rate, that is, the proportion of the population that can read and write, the generally accepted rate of change, the level of available technology, the number of highly educated people in the workforce, and the marketing mix that will be most effective for a country.

In Sweden, for example, the literacy rate is virtually 100 per cent, and all students start English as a foreign language in the first grade, compared to Chad, where the literacy rate just about reaches 20 per cent. Swedish workers who are familiar with printed materials will not only react to print advertising campaigns, but they also have no difficulties working with machinery provided with user information in English. In Chad much knowledge is passed along through family and kinship groups. Most consumers there cannot be effectively reached through print media, and most user instructions for the workforce need to be given through visual methods. Because the educational system of the country provides less information about other cultures, the majority of customers in Chad can also be expected to have a lower tolerance for change than customers in Sweden, which in turn will influence the rate at which new products of international marketers are accepted.

The educational system also affects the level of local technological know-how an international marketer can take advantage of. For example, manufacturers of highly sophisticated software for industrial robots and control systems, such as Japan's Oki or Germany's Siemens, choose the locations of their research and development units according to the availability of advanced teaching institutions and research laboratories. But education is not the only factor influencing capabilities. Skilfulness, diligence and flexibility, as well as the mobility of people, have an impact, too. They are mostly based on the prevailing local culture and will therefore be discussed in Chapter 5.

Natural Environment

The natural environment of a country-market represents an important source of potential wealth for its population. Natural resources, such as minerals, water and water power, oil, coal or gas, and the country's climate and topography are a major determinant of the economic structures and interdependencies of a local economy. The Netherlands, for example, is rich in natural gas but has limited mineral resources. Therefore, it has had to depend on international trade to build and sustain its economy – exports and imports account for over 50 per cent of the Netherlands' GNP. Because natural resources are 'given' by nature, in most countries they have been exploited for the profit of individuals, firms or society. The fact that they are limited has largely been overlooked. Only recently have voices demanding a sustainable world economy based on a sustainable use of the natural environment become more prominent and got some attention.

Natural Resources. The oil wells of the North Sea have made a major contribution to the economic success of the UK and Norway. They might even be a major reason why the UK can afford to follow a rather independent policy inside the EU and why Norway was able to refuse EU membership without suffering any significant economic disadvantages. In addition to their oil industry, they have a long-standing tradition of other industries which profit from the countries' oil income and also substantially contribute to the countries' economic wealth.

Some countries are overly dependent on a single resource, however. Lesotho, a politically independent country surrounded by the Republic of South Africa, for instance, has traditionally supported itself by supplying labour to mines in South Africa. As a result of trade sanctions against the apartheid policy of South Africa and the unstable political situation some years ago, many of the men who worked in those mines were sent home. To broaden its economic base, Lesotho developed its export of another abundant natural resource, water, to farms and industry in South Africa. In addition, many labour-intensive construction projects have been initiated in Lesotho with funds provided by the United Nations Development Programme and the World Bank. These not only offered employment but also provided improved roads, airfields in remote areas, and increased soil conservation needed to develop tourism.

Topography. Topography affects a country's economic wealth in fundamental and enduring ways. Topographic features like rivers, waterfalls, mountain ranges and beaches constitute resources, such as natural trade routes or sources of energy, but can also be viewed as products. The Netherlands, for example, is located at the mouth of the River Rhine. Rotterdam is the busiest port in the world, and the country is crisscrossed with canals and rivers bustling with commercial traffic. Half of the exports and imports that move through the Netherlands are on their way to and from Germany, France and Switzerland (all three border on navigable parts of the Rhine). Goods can be shipped to the Netherlands for distribution throughout Europe, or for export to the rest of the world via Rotterdam.

Topography as a product is illustrated by the examples of the beautiful Maldive Islands off the southwestern coast of India which attract USD30 million worth of tourist income annually, and the coast of Thailand which – together with the cultural treasures of Bangkok – makes tourism the biggest foreign-currency earner of the country. Niagara Falls, located on the border between the USA and Canada, is a source of electric power for both countries as well as a famous tourist destination.

Topography may also be a major constraint on a country's economy as well as for international marketing. It has a major impact on the cost and ease of distributing an international marketer's products. A firm wanting to trans-port its products from the coast of Brazil westward to Peru will find that the only efficient way to do so is by air. The surface route up the River Amazon and across the Andes Mountains would take many weeks and expose both travellers and products to considerable risk. The Andes thus act as a topo-graphic constraint on both domestic and international business. Many other examples of topographic conditions as economic constraints can be given. The lack of water supplies, or the presence of rivers that flood regularly, influences the location of agricultural processing plants. Countries with no coastline, such as Zimbabwe, Nepal or Switzerland, must rely on the ports of neigh-bouring countries to export goods by sea.

Climate. Climate is a part of a country-market's natural environment that is closely linked to the country's economic development and functioning. The importance of climate as a potential source of economic wealth is illustrated by the ability of Central American countries to produce tropical fruits for export to countries where they cannot be grown, because of different climatic conditions. Economic constraints resulting from climatic conditions are illus-trated by monsoon winds and rain that hamper business in countries like Bangladesh, India or Pakistan through flooding, mudslides and washed-out railroads. And in Siberia, where natural resources are plentiful, the extremely cold climate makes it difficult to exploit them.

For the international marketer, climate has a great deal to do with market viability. Consumers living near the equator prefer different food products to those living in milder climates. Heat and humidity result in lower levels of pro-duction, and therefore income, particularly in countries with limited energy for climate control and poorly developed infrastructure systems.

Patterns of consumption and production are, of course, influenced by many other factors besides climate. For example, ownership of in-home air conditioners in Brisbane, Australia, is estimated at 8 per cent. In New Delhi, where the heat and humidity are so oppressive that they severely limit eco-nomic activity, the proportion of homes with air conditioners is even lower. Yet in Atlanta, Georgia, where the climate is far milder than that of either Brisbane or New Delhi, 80 per cent of the homes are air-conditioned. Ob-viously, cultural norms, economic resources and many other factors affect the purchase of goods such as air conditioners. Nevertheless, it remains true that the natural environment of a country-market has an important impact on the market's viability.

Impact on Country-Market Viability. How strong the influence of the natural environment, that is, present or absent natural resources, topography and climate (and how the resulting income is spent), can be on the economic development of countries and their viability for international marketers is impressively illustrated by the countries in the Middle East. The rich, oil-producing countries of the Middle East include Kuwait, Saudi Arabia and the United Arab Emirates. They have per capita income of more than USD19 000, 7000 and 21 000 respectively. Their normally stable governments are encouraging industrialization by importing high-tech industrial goods, turnkey plants for food production, packaging, plastic and metal treatment, and construction material, as well as maintenance contracts and industrial services.

Those Middle Eastern countries constitute a generally promising market for industrial goods. There are also markets for many consumer goods, provided that they are not prohibited by Islamic religious principles. However, because of small populations these markets are limited. In spite of their substantial capital resources, these countries are still developing economically. Their topographic and climatic conditions, combined with a rather uneven distribution of wealth, are not supportive of faster development. For example, attempts to increase agricultural production by using substantial underground supplies of sweet water for irrigation purposes have largely failed owing to the hot and dry climate.

Two other oil-producing countries, Iraq and Iran, would have much bigger populations and could be included in this category if the wars that they have had, combined with embargoes from the industrialized countries and political self-exclusion from international developments, had not seriously interfered with their economic development. Iran has tried hard to re-establish better relationships with highly industrialized nations. The stock exchange in Tehran was reactivated, 270 state-owned firms are now privatized, and the use of drafts and credit cards was allowed. But the religiously justified backing of terrorist activities and enduring antagonism towards the USA has strongly impeded economic development. The Iranian market is predominantly interesting to marketers of industrial goods, such as equipment for paper mills, petrochemical and iron and steel plants, power stations, or the production of vehicles and construction material. France's Total, for example, is the major partner in a multibillion-dollar project to develop Iran's offshore Sirri oil and gas field.

Yet another group of Middle Eastern countries is made up of those that are directly involved in the Arab–Israeli conflict: Lebanon, Syria, Jordan, Egypt and Israel. In addition to their large military expenditures, these nations have been investing heavily in economic and human development. Egypt, for example, has developed a large cadre of trained administrators. Along the Red Sea roads, apartments and hotels have been constructed to boost tourism income. Despite suffering from a population explosion and the declining importance of the Suez Canal, long a source of a significant portion of its foreign-currency income, Egypt's economy has been growing at about 5 per cent after inflation, which has been declining since 1991 and in 1997 was around 6 per cent a year.[6] Lebanon (especially its capital, Beirut), once the centre of commerce and banking in the Middle East, has been devastated by war, political instability and civil strife. Because of a certain stabilization of its internal situation after 1990, the country has regained some of its commercial business that had been lost to its oil-producing neighbours. But despite very similar natural resources compared to its neighbour Israel, the country is far less economically developed.

Israel is by far the most economically developed country in this group. It has strong agricultural and tourism sectors and many high-tech companies, especially in defence-related industries. The imbalance in Israel's international trade accounts, caused by its need to import many consumer goods, and its high spending on national defence are offset by large inflows of capital from Western industrial nations. Nevertheless, a high inflation rate and problems with its Palestinian population have created serious political and economic difficulties for Israel.

Jordan, another of Israel's neighbours has access neither to the Mediterranean Sea nor to oil and gas as its Arabian neighbours do, but it suffers from similar climatic and topographic conditions. Jordan's economy mainly relies on the export of mineral resources (phosphate, potassium), tourism and the import of industrial goods, food and energy. Its per capita income is only about USD1200.

Finally, Turkey offers a market that is growing in importance. Turkey has achieved relative political stability after years of turmoil and military rule, and its liberal economic policies have encouraged foreign investment. Growth rates of GDP, in recent years around 5 per cent, were mainly due to private business success in the areas of communication, tourism, textiles and transportation. Turkey's location between Europe and Asia as well as at the Bosphorus, the entrance to the Black Sea, enables it to engage easily in trade with countries on both continents. Its beautiful shores and the Mediterranean climate attract increasing numbers of tourists. After the goal of free convertibility of the Turkish lira had been reached, the country also succeeded in signing a customs union agreement with the EU (which excludes the free trade of agricultural products and the free movement of Turkish workers).

Sustainability. In using resources from the natural environment of a country-market for their business purposes, international marketers need to take care of the sustainability of their activities. That is, they must be aware that a business will only be successful over a long period if it does not destroy its own bases. For example, the 18 countries located around the Mediterranean Sea have based much of their economic development on increasing tourism. But tourists not only come to those countries because of the warm and sunny weather, or the low-priced hotels and good food, many of them want to enjoy swimming in the sea. If tourism activities pollute the Mediterranean to an extent that swimming becomes dangerous for the tourists' health, they will go somewhere else. Tourism managers, therefore, need to be concerned with organizing their businesses' activities in a way that does not destroy one of its bases.

Many international marketers are not sufficiently aware of the dangers to the natural bases of their income in what they are doing or how they do it. For example, Thai prawn farming companies, such as a business unit of Charoen Pokphand, successfully export their products all over the world, in particular to Japan and the USA. Prawn farming in Thailand takes place in the coastal mangrove forests. The problem is that the chemicals used in farming are highly polluting, as is the waste left behind. Many farms are abandoned after a few years, when the land ceases to be cultivable. Prawn farming has resulted in the clearing of about two-thirds of Thailand's 388 500 hectares of coastal mangrove forests, the breeding grounds of the prawns.[7]

Sustainable production and marketing of goods and services may increase costs, but not necessarily. In many cases it provides increased customer satisfaction and secures increasing returns on investment. For example, Costa

Rica's small-scale coffee farmers are spurning chemicals to win customers, at better prices, from the swelling ranks of organic-coffee drinkers in Europe and North America. The 20 per cent premium is not the only reason for going organic. The local coffee-growers' cooperative also worries that the modern arsenal of fertilizers, pesticides and herbicides kills the ground cover that prevents erosion. Organic methods mean a lot more work and it takes time to switch to them. But growers such as Coocafé, a consortium set up by small cooperatives in Costa Rica, is helped by 'fair trade' companies that buy the coffee at a usually guaranteed premium over world market prices and sell it without intermediaries under such brand names as CaféDirect in the UK, Equal Exchange in the USA, and Max Havelaar on the European continent. Demand for organic coffee in rich countries is expanding and far from saturation.[8]

Technological Resources

Besides the human and natural resources available in a country-market served or under consideration by an international marketer, the existing technological resources in that market may influence its attractiveness. Managers of internationally operating companies need to be attuned to differences between the technological environment of their home country and those of their various country-markets. A lack of technological resources may make it difficult to sell the marketer's product and to satisfy customers. For example, when US computer manufacturers first came to China, they were eager to close a sale. But they did not know that air conditioning was not readily available there. As a result, their computers, which at that time required a temperate environment, did not perform as expected.

Differences in technological development may also offer opportunities to market a firm's product. Thus, Austria's VA Industrial Services has been successful in marketing training programmes and management assistance in advanced steel-production methods and maintenance of steel-production plants to industrially less developed countries. There, new steel plants had been constructed and run up to full capacity use by the suppliers, but local managers and personnel lacking the needed experience were not able to sustain that production level. Many plants were running at no more than 30 per cent capacity. VAIS assisted the plant owners by training their personnel in subjects such as work organization, proper use of the machinery, and maintenance.

As the example shows, international marketers must consider not only the level of technological development in a society, which is represented by the existing infrastructure (such as the availability of a container terminal for the shipment of products or the existence of a digital phone system for communication with sales people), but must also be aware of the concept of technology that is characteristic of that society.

Infrastructure. A country's infrastructure is the transportation, energy, communication and commercial systems available to its population and industries. For international marketing to be possible, a certain infrastructure has to be in place or needs to be installed in a country-market. The level of development of a country's infrastructure affects the extent to which its natural resources can be used. Alaska's vast oil reserves could not be used until the Alaskan pipeline was built. The water that powers turbines to generate electricity in northern Canada would be economically useless if there were no electrical system to transport power to industrial sites in the south.

The level of development of a country's infrastructure also determines how well its human resources can be developed and used. Modern research and medical centres, for example, only function at the highest level if the existing infrastructure allows instant international communication. Complicated medical operations, for instance, are carried out by a team of specialists in one place, but this team may be in online visual contact with specialists in other countries who assist with their know-how and expertise when it is needed. Infrastructure also determines whether international marketers can reach their potential markets. A large target market with adequate buying power is of little value if goods and services cannot be sold to customers because of a lack of transportation infrastructure, energy shortage, faulty communications or a lack of financial institutions.

Transportation infrastructure is particularly important to international marketers. Managers from Triad markets often take for granted the availability of distribution systems made up of good roads, railways, waterways and air cargo systems. But Western Europe, Russia and China have different gauges (railway track widths), for example. To transport a load of electrical appliances from Lyon, France to Xian, China by rail, France's SEB would twice have to unload freight cars at borders and reload the cargo onto cars that fit the other gauge. Similarly, roads and dependable trucking lines are not equally available throughout the world. The freeways in the USA may have their counterparts in the 'autostrada' in Italy, but on a 'freeway' near Shanghai truck drivers encounter cyclists transporting coal for their homes and pigs from neighbouring farms crossing the road. In large parts of Eastern Europe, dirt roads connect one village to another, and these may be difficult to pass in rainy seasons, when the roads turn into mud.

Communication infrastructure has become a major factor of influence on the economic wealth of a country. For instance, Singapore, the very dynamic newly industrialized country with the second-largest per capita income in Asia behind Japan, prides itself on being ahead of the technological game. Its economic success relies on a state-of-the-art communication infrastructure. By the end of the century the government hopes to have created an 'intelligent island', with at least 95 per cent of homes cabled for services like the Internet and interactive television. In 1996, 100 000 of Singapore's 3 million inhabitants already had Internet accounts, twice as many as in China (with a population of 1.2 billion).[9] Owing to global competition between the suppliers and countries involved, the development of communication infrastructure in the highly industrialized and newly industrializing countries it extremely fast. The Future Issues box illustrates what seemed to be part of the upcoming technology in 1996.

Global networks using satellite transmission, digital telephones, fax systems, telexes and e-mail permit daily communication among far-flung business units of an internationally operating company. Many governments strongly support that development. The Australian government, for instance, released its Creative Nation statement in 1994. In this statement the government recognized the potential of the emerging multimedia industry and announced five strategic initiatives for its development. These include the creation of the Australian Multimedia Enterprise to finance development and commercialization of interactive multimedia products, and the establishment

FUTURE ISSUES BOX

Beyond Computers: A Look at the Cutting Edge

The world's computer journals are full of reports on programs and peripherals that allow PCs to display, process, store and transmit moving images, sound and data. But non-computer-based multimedia systems are now the cutting edge of technological innovation.

Take Digital Audio Broadcasting (DAB). If a group led by Daimler-Benz Aerospace (DASA) realizes its plans, six DAB satellites will broadcast multi-track TV, ultra-high-quality radio and data packets to moving automobiles, trains, trams and ships. To receive the DAB signals, these vehicles will use a technology premiered by Bosch and Deutsche Telekom. DAB piggy-backs TV and data transmission on to the 'spare' space left on broadcast radio waves.

To supply attractive entertainment consortia of software and media companies such as the AOI-Bertelsmann Online service, an alliance between Germany's Bertelsmann AG and US-based America Online has been formed. These consortia may soon find themselves and their services obsolete if the latest Web-based multi-media hit – CU-Seeme – continues its rapid ascent. Developed at Cornell University in 1993, the CU-Seeme software takes the consortia's standard products and goes them one better. Instead of e-mail, CU-Seeme offers live face-to-face video conferences. Instead of a selection of specially designed on-line entertainment, CU-Seeme users have access, via the World Wide Web, to the world's films, TV programs and video games, on demand and at local telephone rates.

Source: Swartzberg, T. (1996) 'Beyond Computers: A Look at the Cutting Edge', *International Herald Tribune*, 15 March, p. 17.

of six Cooperative Multimedia Centres across Australia which provide resources for education and training, state-of-the-art equipment, leading-edge research and development, and assistance with issues such as intellectual property and product testing.[10]

Economically less developed countries are experiencing an ever-widening gap between themselves and the industrially more developed parts of the world. In some African, Asian and Latin American countries, telephone connections with other countries are easier, faster and clearer than connections within the same country. The home office of an international marketer may be able to communicate with the local representative, but that representative may not be able to communicate easily with local customers.

The **commercial infrastructure** of a country-market relevant to an international marketer contains the existing distribution channels (which will be discussed in Chapter 14), market research (see Chapter 6) and market communication agencies (see Chapter 17), logistics service providers (see Chapter 15), and financial institutions. How important the existence of a well-functioning commercial infrastructure may be for an international marketer is illustrated by the following example. After 13 years of talks, Nestlé was finally invited into China in 1987 by the government of Heilongjiang Province to help boost milk production in the region. Capitalizing on its experience in Sri Lanka and India, Nestlé opened a powdered milk and baby cereal plant in 1990. Then it had a choice: use the severely overburdened local trains and roads to collect milk and deliver finished goods, or create its own infra-structure. The latter was a lot more costly but would ultimately be more dependable. So Nestlé began weaving a distribution network known as 'milk roads' between 27 villages in the region and the factory collection points, called chilling centres. The farmers, pushing wheelbarrows, pedalling bicycles or on foot, followed the gravel roads to the centres where their milk was weighed and analysed. Then the area managers organized a delivery system using vans dedicated to carrying Nestlé products. Nestlé hired retired teachers and government workers to serve as farm agents, bringing Swiss experts to train them in rudimentary animal health and hygiene. Once this system was in place, the business took off. In 1990 the factory produced 316 tons of powdered milk and infant formula. In 1994 it turned out 10 000 tons, and capacity was tripled.[11]

A country's financial institutions are of interest to an international mar-keter because they affect customers' purchasing power and the availability of capital. National banking systems, like the Federal Reserve System in the USA, contribute to economic stability by regulating the money supply and banking operations. If the money supply grows too quickly, the result may be inflation; if it grows too slowly, the economy may stagnate. The major task of a national banking system, therefore, is to optimally balance the money supply for the local economy. This can be done through policies that govern interest rates, the amount of money in circulation, and the lending practices of banks, savings and loan associations, and other financial institutions.

In centrally controlled economies the banking system is an entirely regu-lated monopoly in the hands of government. The central bank in former communist Eastern European countries, for example, had the monopoly for short-term credits, some special state-owned banks were responsible for long-term credits, and a bank for external trade held the monopoly for all currency issues as well as export/import financing. To transform that system into a market-oriented banking system following the example of Western industrial-ized countries was no easy task. In Russia, for example, after 1991 about 2500 banks were formed. Following the country's liquidity crisis in 1995, 300 of them lost their licences and 600 more were expected to go out of business because of bad credits, the loss of returns from currency fluctuations, inflation and treasury bonds, luxurious bank buildings, and simply inexperience. As a consequence, international marketers doing business with Russian partners are well advised to seek information about the reliability of those partners' banks before signing any contract.

Similar to the Japanese keiretsu and South Korea's chaebol, in Russia Financial Industrial Groups (FIGs) have been created. FIGs, such as Interros, a conglomerate of nickel, aluminium and steel-producing firms around Unex-imbank and ICFI bank, or Menatep, a conglomerate of metallurgical, chemical and petrochemical plants grouped around Menatep bank, are industrial groups formed by financial institutions. Banks, having earned high profits through low central bank refinancing rates, high inflation and currency speculations, bought largely undervalued shares of companies in order to control them. The Culture box gives some additional information concerning commercial infra-structure problems in Russia which result in monopoly-like industry struc-tures, protectionist measures and a lack of market transparency.[12]

In Central Europe an estimated 27 per cent of credits in Hungary, 30 per cent of credits given to companies in the Czech Republic, and 29 per cent of credits of Poland's export development bank (Bank Rozwoju Exportu) were

CULTURE BOX

Remains of the Old Business Culture

'Here's the new boss, same as the old boss', sing the British rock group The Who, and observers of privatization in Russia have exactly the same experience. Alexander Putilov, chief of oil company Rosneft, held high rank in the Soviet Ministry of Oil. Vagit Alekperov, the chairman of Lukoil, another oil producer, was acting minister of oil when the Soviet Union fell apart. Sergej Muravlenko, head of Yukos, again an oil company, led the powerful Yuganskneftegaz producing association and is still known in Siberia as 'the general'.

It is impossible to reform an entire society overnight. The old communist elites also produced talents, and when it comes to filling leading positions with highly qualified managers the political past might not be of great importance, in particular when the number of experienced managers is low. But when the same members of nomenklatura than before the fall of the communist government fill the leading positions of companies, a diversity of problems result.

Since 1991 many of the new Russian companies have been created by edict in Moscow, where officials divided up the country's resources and doled the best of them out to influential comrades. Ownership of Russian companies is still evolving, sometimes along curious lines. In the 1995 loans-for-shares auction, Moscow doled out stakes in former state-owned concerns in exchange for loans to the government. A 40 per cent interest in Surgutneftegaz, Russia's third-largest oil producer, was awarded to the company's own pension fund. Yukos, the second-largest producer, ended up being 78 per cent owned by the Moscow banking and investment group Menatep – which happened to run the Yukos auction for the government.

For all Soviet-era problems they inherited, the companies are also handicapped by their own reluctance – or inability – to shrug off the past. Capital investments are often made without a master plan, and cash flow is not well monitored. None of the big oil producing companies has yet fully adopted internationally recognized accounting standards. When Lukoil, now a partner of US-based Atlantic Richfield, issued its convertible bond prospectus in 1995, Morgan Stanley discovered that the company did not include any financial analysis – no profit and loss counts, no cash-flow statements, no balance sheets – to give potential investors clues as to whether they should buy.

Source: Adapted from Reifenberg, A. and N. Banerjee (1996) 'Crude Enigma, Despite Iffy Finances, Russian Oil Companies Draw Western Dollars', *The Wall Street Journal*, 29 March, pp. A1 and A9; Frydman, R., K. Murphy and A. Rapaczynski (1996) 'Das langsame Sterben der Nomenklatura', *Der Standard*, 15 February, p. 22.

considered difficult to recover in 1996. Nevertheless, ten large Central European banks had managed to establish themselves in the world finance markets. Half of them are located in the Czech Republic, three in Poland, one in Hungary and one in Slovakia.[13]

Some countries do not have a national banking system. In those countries the money supply is potentially unstable, a situation that can result in high inflation rates. Thus, the existence of a national banking system may be a sign of a relatively stable economy, but it is by no means a guarantee – too many other factors determine the extent to which an economy is stable over time.

Concept of Technology.   Besides the existing and developing infrastructure in a country-market, an international marketer assessing a market's attractiveness needs to consider the predominant concept of technology in the society being analysed. Concepts of technology can vary considerably from one country-market to another and may demand entirely different marketing mixes to assure long-term success. The significance of such differences can be seen in the following example. Several years ago, 200 trucks were supplied to Sudan where transportation had traditionally taken place on the back of camels (or on trains as long as the British administration looked after the maintenance of the system). Two years later, when the supplier wanted to sell more trucks, they were unsuccessful. The customer considered the quality of the trucks to be far below the expected level. No further order would be placed. When the truck manufacturer's salespeople tried to find out why the customer was so dissatisfied, they were informed that none of the trucks was any longer in service. The truck drivers, unfamiliar with the concept of preventive maintenance, had failed to change the oil or otherwise maintain the trucks. When the trucks broke down, the drivers left them where they had stopped, and returned to transportation by camels, a technology that they understood and knew how to maintain.

Economic System

The economic system of a country is its specific combination of the bases of economic wealth discussed so far. Depending on the level of industrial development, the shares of different industrial sectors of the economy will vary. So will the ownership of the means of production, depending on the market orientation of the governing political forces.

Industrial Sectors.   Industrial sectors are categories of economic activity, such as mining, manufacturing, agriculture, wholesale and retail trade, construction, transportation, and business and personal services. In general, countries with a high proportion of their GDP coming from agriculture have less per capita income than those with high proportions coming from manufacturing or service sectors. Countries in which a single industrial sector dominates the economy are referred to as a **monoculture**. Usually, monocultures rely upon a commodity such as coffee or copper (see Figure 3.3). Because prices of commodities have strong cycles, monocultures are at the mercy of the world market price for the commodity.

Chile, for example, frequently suffered economically because too much of its GNP was derived from copper mining. When the world market price of copper fluctuated, so did Chile's GNP. Moreover, when good substitutes for copper were developed, such as high-quality plastic pipes used in construction, Chile's economy faced difficulty. To resolve that problem, Chile has diversified its economy by increasing its exports of grapes, timber, fish and wine. This policy has somewhat improved the balance of Chile's economy, but nevertheless, more than one-third of the country's total exports is still copper.

In assessing the attractiveness of potential country-markets, the international marketer must consider such factors of economic instability. They may present a market opportunity, when the marketer's product or service provides a potential remedy for the country's problem. For example, a supplier of fruit juice and canning plants may find fruit monoculture markets attractive.

Figure 3.3 Commodity Dependency

Some countries strongly depend on one sector of industry and its exports. They are called monocultures. Historically, a monoculture is economically more unstable than a more balanced economy.

Source: Adapted from Baratta, M. (ed.) (1995) *Der Fischer Weltalmanach '96*, Frankfurt a.M.: Fischer Taschenbuch Verlag.

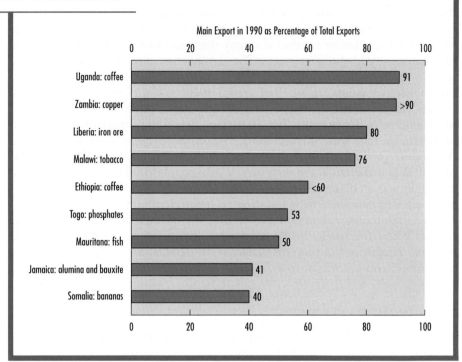

In most cases, however, strong imbalances in the industrial sectors of a country-market diminish the attractiveness of its product-markets.

Another potentially important factor for an international marketer interested in a country-market is the existence and importance of an **informal sector** of the economy. In industrially developing countries, the informal sector is characterized by a large number of small-scale production and service activities that are individually or family owned and use labour-intensive and simple technology. The usually self-employed workers in this sector have little or no formal education, are generally unskilled and lack capital resources. Moreover, workers in the informal sector do not have any job security, lack decent working conditions and have no retirement security. Their motivation is usually to obtain sufficient income for survival. As many members of the household as possible are involved in income-generating activities, including women and children, and they often work very long hours. Most inhabit shacks that generally lack electricity, water, drainage, educational and health services.[14]

To better understand the functioning of many (rapidly) developing economies, it is important to note that the informal sector is closely connected with the formal – mainly urban – sectors. Many formal sectors depend on the informal sector for low-priced inputs to their own production. The informal sector in fact subsidizes the formal sector by providing basic inputs at very low prices maintained through the formal sector's economic power (the informal sector depends on the growth of the formal sector for a substantial portion of its income and clientele) and its legitimacy granted by governments.

The informal sector not only exists in industrially developing economies, however. In Southern, Central and Eastern Europe the informal sector takes the form of an underground economy. The estimated sizes of those hidden sectors compared to the countries' official GDPs run up to 25 per cent, improving the officially available government statistics concerning the economic standing of those economies. Compared to Switzerland and Japan, the world leaders in per capita income, where the size of the informal sector does not exceed an estimated 5 per cent, an international marketer interested in serving markets with a substantial informal sector must consider its potential impact on local competition. Italy, for example, is the European champion in sales of pirated CDs. Estimates are that Italy would have no public deficit if the informal sector paid the same percentage of income and added-value taxes as the formal sector.

Economic Decision Making.   Economic systems vary considerably in their approaches to economic decision making. The economic systems associated with socialist or communist political systems traditionally rely on central decision making to allocate scarce resources, to meet industrial as well as consumer demand according to the priorities of society. In capitalist and Islamic economic systems, market forces predominantly guide economic development. The USA is generally considered to have a highly free market, yet its economic policies in effect establish production quotas for some agricultural products, limit automobile imports, and protect domestic manufacturing in such areas as textiles and shoes. Most economies lie somewhere between the two extremes of centrally planned versus free market economy. They are considered 'mixed' economies, because they are guided partly by market forces and partly by centralized decision making.

Centrally Controlled Economies.   The Republic of North Korea may have been the most centrally controlled economy in the world in 1998. All production facilities have traditionally been in the possession of government. Because of the breakdown of its international trade relationships with Eastern European countries, Cuba was forced to take some cautious steps in the direction of a somewhat more market-driven economy. Until 1995, 212 joint ventures with foreign companies were allowed. Foreign firms may establish wholly owned subsidiaries after government checking on a case-by-case basis. Cubans may possess foreign currency, and the peso became convertible as of December 1994. Since that time, farmers and craftspeople have been allowed to sell their products in private markets.[15]

The People's Republic of China calls itself a 'socialist market economy'. It is encouraging private investments and enterprise, and is actively attracting private foreign investments. Nevertheless, the ninth Five-Year Plan was fixed by the National People's Congress dominated by the Communist Party in October 1995, a Central Planning Committee is discussing and making decisions about new projects, and a large part of China's industry remains state-owned (attempts to close the state-owned firms with the highest deficits led to unemployment rates in urban areas of around 15 per cent and in rural areas of up to 25 per cent in 1997). International marketers interested in investing in more centrally controlled economies need to inform themselves carefully about the specific legal regulations of those countries.

Economies in a State of Transition.   This is also true for many of the Central and Eastern European countries which are in various states of transition from former centrally controlled economies to more or less market-driven economies.

Until 1989, all countries in Eastern Europe were centrally controlled economies (CCEs). Their foreign trade was a state monopoly. Traditionally, only official foreign trade organizations (FTOs) were authorized to make international purchases and sales for these nations. FTOs had to conform to annual and five-year plans that were developed, supervised and administered by the nation's ministry of foreign trade. FTOs received information about product requirements and specifications, even the number of items to be produced, from an office of central planning. These products were manufactured internally whenever possible. Orders were placed with outside firms only when product requirements could not be met by domestic sources. Because of such centralization of planning, it was usually difficult for a company accustomed to conducting business in market economies to enter Eastern European markets. Lack of direct information about customers created a barrier, as did the FTOs' inability to react quickly to changes. On the other hand, once a company had established a foothold in a centrally controlled economy it was likely to encounter less competition than is typically found in market economies.

Since 1989, the political as well as the economic environments in this part of the world have changed dramatically. The Council for Mutual Economic Assistance (CMEA, also called COMECON) was broken up in September 1991. Bulgaria, Hungary, Czechoslovakia, Poland and Romania started to trade on world market terms. The Soviet Union was dissolved and split into 15 sovereign states, 11 of which (Lithuania, Latvia and Estonia had left the USSR earlier, Georgia has been participating since 1993) agreed to form the Commonwealth of Independent States (CIS) in December 1991. Table 3.3 shows the membership population and GNP details for CIS countries.

The CMEA had accounted for 70 to 80 per cent of its members' exports and imports. Furthermore, owing to central planning, industrial production of many goods had been centralized at certain locations. Because of the sudden loss of their former market relationships, the economies of all these countries suffered from substantial difficulties. In 1991 Hungary, for example, lost two-thirds of its exports to its former partners in the CMEA. In early 1992 only 20 per cent of the country's exports went to Eastern Europe, whereas exports to Western nations expanded by 29 per cent in this year.

In the three central European countries (now there are four, because Czechoslovakia was split into the Czech Republic and Slovakia), production output fell by 40 per cent between 1990 and 1992, real wages plummeted, unemployment climbed, and inflation rose to hitherto unknown heights. The real income of Czechs in 1991, for example, was 24 per cent less than in 1990. Official unemployment figures in Hungary in 1992 were around 12 per cent. But from the middle of 1992 on, some indicators showed an improvement. For example, despite the worst drought for decades, Polish GDP rose slightly; the collapse in industrial output had ended. A turnaround came into sight.

Reformers had freed domestic prices and opened their countries up to foreign trade in order to provide incentives for firms to produce goods and services people wanted to buy. Many of those goods and services today come from the private sector. In Poland in the third quarter of 1992, which was the first period of recovery in the region as a whole, industrial output rose 7.7 per cent compared to the previous year. Almost all of this came from private firms.

Table 3.3 MEMBERS OF THE COMMONWEALTH OF INDEPENDENT STATES

COUNTRY	POPULATION IN MILLIONS	GNP IN BILLION USD	GNP PER CAPITA (USD)
Armenia	3.3	14.0	4,195
Azerbaijan	7.2	24.0	3,340
Belorussia	10.4	55.1	5,309
Georgia	5.5	21.7	3,921
Kazakhstan	16.8	55.8	3,313
Kyrgyzstan	4.4	11.8	2,694
Moldova	4.4	15.1	3,418
Russia	194.8	775.2	5,173
Tajikistan	5.3	10.9	2,080
Turkmenistan	3.6	10.9	3,009
Ukraine	52.5	219.7	4,184
Uzbekistan	20.4	49.9	2,448

The Commonwealth of Independent States (CIS) is an association of 12 countries which until 1991 belonged to the USSR. It is dominated by Russia which controls more than half of the economic activity.

Source: *World Development Report 1995*, New York: Oxford University Press, 1995, pp. 162-167

An example of such private initiatives is Tosca, a manufacturer of machine tools and automatic production lines in Brno, Czech Republic (see also the Strategy box). The company was founded in October 1991 by a group of five managers of a state-owned firm who did not want to wait until their bosses reacted to the changes in the environment. They invited 25 of the best technicians to join them, bought a CAD machine, hired a production hall from a state-owned enterprise, equipped an office for top management, and started business. In Spring 1992 Tosca already had 70 people employed, doubling their previous average income, and plans for an expansion to 100 employees.

After only three years, the Czech Republic, Poland and Hungary were closer to being market economies than centrally planned ones. In Poland, private firms today account for over 50 per cent of GDP and nearly 60 per cent of the labour force. In 1997, about 80 per cent of Hungary's GDP came from private enterprises. Starting in 1990, government had handed over small service companies, such as restaurants and shops, to their employees. Five per cent of industrial firms were privatized through management buy-outs. Today, about 66 000 small private firms and 180 000 one-man firms account for 50 per cent of output. Only very few companies, such as the atomic power plant Paks, the state forests and some special agricultural units, stayed in full public ownership. In some others, government has kept a 25 per cent share with veto rights.

Much privatization has been financed through joint ventures with or the purchase of equity stakes in existing companies through foreign investors. In 1996, the European Bank for Reconstruction and Development (EBRD) estimated that in the last seven years about USD50 billion of foreign direct investment had flowed into Central and Eastern Europe (see Table 3.4). With a share of 50 per cent from a stock of USD11 billion overall for Central Europe in 1992, Hungary has been most successful in attracting foreign direct investment. This may be partly due to privatization by tenders and sales to the

Private Enterprise

in Central Europe

'I have become an entrepreneur by chance', said 23-year-old Noah Steinberg in 1992. A Princeton graduate, he came to Vienna, Austria, to study at the Diplomatische Akademie in Fall 1990 and to enter local politics in New York later on. But there he met Tibor Veres, 26 years old, who had just founded Wallis International, a Budapest-based firm that traded low-priced PCs from Taiwan. Steinberg recommended a change to branded products and offered to talk to AT&T as well as Rank Xerox. Both companies were interested; Steinberg got a 10 per cent share in Wallis International.

After a year, subsidiaries had been set up in

New York, Vienna, Czechoslovakia, Bulgaria, Russia and Lithuania. Sales offices opened in Ukraine, Armenia, Kazakhstan, Latvia and Estonia. The holding company in Budapest manages ten companies, either as the owner or holding decisive shares. Steinberg and Veres took care only to invest in traditionally profitable sectors of the Hungarian economy. Wallitrade offers office technology, mainly to the 5000 joint ventures set up in Hungary since 1989. But it also imports everything from toys to agricultural products, and runs its own rental car operation. Wallimpex manages a newly aquired chain of supermarkets and restaurants in Budapest. Tricoinvest manufactures low-priced sweaters for the USA and imports fashion from Italy. Other firms handle consulting jobs in the areas of marketing research and financing, or prosper in the real estate business. Working capital in the first year was about USD25 million, profits reached 10 per cent.

Source: Translated/adapted from 'Der historischen Stunde Gunst', *Der Standard*, 3 April 1992, p. K4.

highest bidders. In August 1989, Getz, a US trading company, was the first Western company to own 100 per cent of a formerly public Hungarian company, Intercooperation. IKEA, the Swedish furniture retailer, opened its first outlet in Budapest in the spring of 1990. In 1992, five of seven former state-owned Hungarian breweries had already been sold to foreign investors. Stella Artois (Belgium), Heineken (Netherlands), Elders (Australia), Spaten-Bier (Germany) and Österreichische Brau AG (Austria) now offer their brands to Hungarian consumers. At the same time French wine marketers had bought great parts of Hungarian wineries and set about improving their quality. Forty per cent of Hungary's productive assets, including energy providers and public telecommunications, were sold through tenders. Just recently, privatizations occurred through the stock exchange. By the end of 1996 there were 32 000 firms with foreign investment out of a total of around 150 000 companies in Hungary.[16]

Foreign direct investments, mainly from Germany, the USA, France and Austria, have begun to dominate some of the sectors of Hungarian industry. The sugar, tobacco, car, lighting equipment and refrigerator industries, for example, are dominated by one or more foreign-owned companies. To avoid such foreign investors' domination, the Czech Republic and Poland have pursued their privatization process primarily through the encouragement of domestic private investors. Poland has been very slow to privatize its state-owned industries. By the end of 1997, only 4234 firms, that is, 50 per cent of

Table 3.4 FOREIGN DIRECT INVESTMENT IN CENTRAL EUROPE

	1994	1995	1996 (revised)	1997 (projection)	CUMULATIVE FDI-INFLOWS 1989–97	CUMULATIVE FDI-INFLOWS 1989–97 PER CAPITA	FDI-INFLOWS PER CAPITA IN 1997	FDI-INFLOWS AS A % OF GDP IN 1997
	(in millions of USD)				*(in millions of USD)*	*(in USD)*		*(in per cent)*
Albania	65	89	97	33	369	115	10	1.4
Bulgaria	105	82	100	575	1,000	121	69	5.6
Croatia	95	83	509	500	1,276	267	105	2.7
Czech Republic	749	2,526	1,388	1,275	7,473	726	124	2.4
Estonia	212	199	111	131	809	557	90	2.8
Hungary	1,097	4,453	1,986	2,100	15,403	1,519	207	4.7
Latvia	155	244	379	415	1,287	515	166	7.6
Lithuania[1]	31	72	152	327	612	165	88	3.6
FYR Macedonia	24	13	12	16	65	31	8	0.5
Poland[2]	542	1,134	2,741	3,044	8,442	218	79	2.3
	1,846	*3,617*	*4,445*	*6,600*	*19,250*	*497*	*171*	*4.9*
Romania	347	404	415	998	2,389	106	44	2.9
Slovak Republic	203	183	177	150	912	169	28	0.8
Slovenia	128	176	186	321	1,074	538	161	1.8
Eastern Europe and the Baltics[3]	*3,753*	*9,657*	*8,252*	*9,885*	*41,111*	*357*	*86*	*2.8*
Armenia	3	19	22	26	70	19	7	1.6
Azerbaijan	22	284	661	1,006	1,993	262	132	24.4
Belarus	10	7	75	100	267	26	10	0.7
Georgia	8	6	25	65	104	19	12	1.3
Kazakhstan	635	859	1,100	1,200	4,267	272	76	5.7
Kyrgyzstan	45	96	46	50	247	54	11	3.1
Moldova	18	73	56	71	249	58	17	3.4
Russia	584	2,021	2,040	3,900	9,743	66	26	0.8
Tajikistan	12	17	20	20	86	14	3	1.8
Turkmenistan	103	233	129	108	652	139	23	4.7
Ukraine	100	400	526	700	2,096	41	14	1.4
Uzbekistan	73	−24	50	60	216	9	3	0.4
The Commonwealth of Independent States	*1,613*	*3,991*	*4,750*	*7,306*	*19,990*	*70*	*26*	*1.2*
Eastern Europe, the Baltics and the CIS[3]	**5,366**	**13,648**	**13,002**	**17,191**	**61,100**	**153**	**43**	**1.8**

Foreign direct investment in Central Europe reached close to USD60 billion in 1996. Most of it went to Hungary, the Czech Republic and Poland. Source: European Bank for Reconstruction and Development.

Sources: IMF, central banks and EBRD estimates.

[1] FDI figures for Lithuania are only available from 1993. For 1993 and 1994, figures cover only investment in equity capital. For 1995 and 1996, equity capital and reinvested earnings are covered but inter-company debt transactions are not covered.

[2] Second series for Poland, *in italics*, supplements banking system data with information from a survey of foreign investment enterprises in Poland (as provided by PAIZ: data taken from the IMF Balance of Payments Statistical Yearbook). The difference between the two series arises, in part, from investments-in-kind and reinvested earnings.

[3] Totals are based on balance of payments series for Poland.

public companies, had been privatized. Forty per cent of those firms employed 50 to 200 people, and 30 per cent had a labour force of more than 500 people.[17] International capital started flowing in more substantially from the middle of the 1990s onwards. For example, Daewoo, the Korean conglomerate, bought 70 per cent of the state enterprise Fabryka Samochdow Osobowych for USD1.1 billion in March 1996. In addition to FSO, Daewoo has acquired a smaller truck factory in southeast Poland for USD700 million. That heavy industrial investment came on top of a USD42 million complex making televisions, washing machines and circuit boards that Daewoo began building outside Warsaw in 1993.[18] In 1996, the inflow of foreign capital to Poland exceeded that to Hungary for the first time. The Polish government's privatization programme has plans for the privatization of telecommunication, petrochemical, electrotechnical, pharmaceutical, spirits and insurance industries until 2000. A year later, energy providers, the sugar, wood, paper, furniture and construction materials industries and the banking sector are planned to be privatized.

In the Czech Republic, where at the beginning of 1993 the private sector accounted for only about 15 per cent of GDP, mass privatization began as an attempt to create a nation of shareholders. Every adult got a voucher that could be used to bid for shares in state firms at auctions. The first auctions, which ended in December 1992, transferred 2000 firms with a book value of USD7 billion to the public. The next round sold off another 1500 firms. By 1998, 5780 out of 6284 state-owned firms had been formally privatized in that way. The Czech Republic reached a level of 68.4 private companies per 1000 inhabitants, a level not only far beyond the neighbouring countries in transition, but also above the EU level. To canalize the multitude of shares, however, government encouraged the development of investment funds. Nearly three-quarters of Czech vouchers were invested by 400 such funds, many set up by publicly owned banks. Most of those funds had no industrial management experience. They did not pay attention to the needed restructuring of the companies. At the end of the century, therefore, a substantial number of the companies privatized through the voucher system are in economic difficulties.[19] (Exhibit 3.1 illustrates the difficulties that privatization through vouchers may encounter in other countries in transition.) The success of privatization – about 70 per cent of the country's GDP comes from private firms today – was based on additional auctions, tenders, management and employee buy-outs, and direct sales to foreign investors. For example, Nestlé together with French BSN, the manufacturer of Danone, bought 43 per cent of Cokoladovy, a Czech-based manufacturer of chocolates and candies. And Germany's Volkswagen AG bought Czech Skoda to produce less expensive small and middle-sized cars for Eastern Europe based on VW's technology.

In former East Germany, reunited with its western brother state, the 'Treuhandanstalt', a government agency, took over all the publicly held firms, sold the better ones to private investors, closed the worst, and tried to improve the situation of the remaining ones so that they could sell them. They finished their work in 1996, but could not help leaving the eastern part of Germany with too much concentration on the construction industry and a lack of internationally competitive firms. The radical change in economic decision making forced on former East Germany's economic system also had significant social implications. Unemployment increased drastically, since private firms, forced to compete on world markets, could not continue to support the large workforces previously employed by the publicly owned companies.

Exhibit 3.1 FOOT-DRAGGING THREATENS KIEV'S PRIVATIZATION PLAN

The Ukrainian government had prepared a mass-privatization program for 8,000 state-owned companies in1996. But public apathy and official foot-dragging threatened to derail the process which was essential for an economy that had contracted by 52 per cent over the past five years and had shown only very slow progress on economic stabilization.

Launched in January 1995, the project entitled every Ukrainian citizen to receive a privatization certificate free of charge. Under complex rules, these must be swapped at auctions for shares worth USD250 in state assets. Unlike citizens of some other post-communist countries in Central Europe that have launched similar programs, Ukrainians were prohibited from selling their vouchers for a quick cash fix. As a result, although the stock was theoretically worth about three times the average monthly wage, the process of acquiring equities was so foreign and bewildering to many ordinary Ukrainians that they were content to let the paper gather dust.

In addition to widespread public disinterest, enterprise directors – who stood to lose considerable privileges because the introduction of corporate watchdogs and accounting procedures would have made selling products out the back door more difficult – were blocking the process. These directors had numerous supporters in the communist-dominated parliament. More than 2,000 firms had yet to be corporatized in 1996, effectively removing them from the privatization program.

Source: Brzezinski, M. (1996) 'Foot-Dragging Threatens Kiev's Privatization Plan', *The Wall Street Journal Europe*, 12–13 April,p. 4.

Unemployment went up to more than 20 per cent, despite a great number of people 'employed' in retraining programmes and in part-time jobs.

Of all the countries of former Yugoslavia, Slovenia has managed the transformation process best. In 1996, one-third of all 1359 former state-owned companies were entirely privatized. For the rest, 80 per cent of privatization certificates had been subscribed by Slovenian citizens. The Slovenian tolar became convertible in 1995.[20] After USD27 billion of war damage between 1992 and 1995, in 1997 Croatia's economy was just about reaching the level of 1991. More than 50 per cent of GNP came from private enterprises, and inflation was around 4 per cent. The Republic of Yugoslavia suffered from the embargo during the war. It will need large foreign investments to recover. Macedonia first stabilized its economy in 1997. In Bosnia 95 per cent of production facilities are either destroyed or at a standstill. Unemployment reaches 75 per cent. Western industrialized countries have promised to support reconstruction with about USD5 billion, but political insecurity has barred economic recovery so far.[21]

Mixed Economies.   Most governments allow private investments in parallel with public investments. In countries with economically liberal traditions, public investments mainly focus on technical and social infrastructure projects that do not attract enough private interest to be carried out. In most countries of Western Europe and in industrially developing countries such as Indonesia, governments also tend to hold stakes in business firms which are of some public interest. For example, the government of the Netherlands, before privatizing their shares, was the owner of the Koninklijke PTT Nederland (the postal and telecommunications company), the public utilities companies and the Dutch railways. It held shares in KLM (the Dutch airline), Schiphol Airport in Amsterdam and DSM (a chemicals group).[22]

Overall, privatization of public investments has been in progress during the first half of the 1990s. This privatization process has dramatically increased the opportunities for international private investors. In Western Europe, Portugal has been the second most active privatizing country after the UK. The privatization programme for 1996 alone was projected to bring USD2.4 billion in revenue. Companies such as Portugal Telecom, the cement maker Cimpor, Electricidade de Portugal, the tobacco monopoly Tabaqueira, the petroleum group Petrogal, and the Banco Fomento & Exterior were on the list of privatizations. Those privatizations were not so much due to a change in the government's investment policy as a budgetary need to qualify for EMU, Europe's Economic and Monetary Union. The revenue from privatization mostly went towards cancelling public debt and thereby reducing the budget's debt-servicing costs.[23]

The extent to which a country-market's economy is governed by free market forces versus central planning is important to an international marketer. A centrally planned economy generally offers an international marketer fewer opportunities than an economy that is more market-led. In the former, decisions regarding what goods and services will be offered to consumers, and their prices, are made by a government agency as part of an overall economic plan. Thus, the degree of market orientation serves as a 'gatekeeper' function. It affects a firm's ability to reach target markets in other countries.

INDICATORS OF ECONOMIC WEALTH

When assessing the attractiveness of a country-market's economic environment, the international marketer needs to establish a list of evaluation criteria against which to systematically compare potential and served markets. The chosen criteria should be relevant to the product-market(s) of the company and significative of the economic standing of the country. In the following, some potential evaluation criteria are presented.

National Product

A country's level of production of goods and services may be considered an indicator of its economic wealth and attractiveness as a potential market. The level of production is traditionally expressed through the country's Gross National Product (GNP) or its Gross Domestic Product (GDP) per capita. Depending on the firm's product-market, one or the other may be a better indicator of a country-market's attractiveness. For example, steel, cement and energy producers and companies active in the public transportation sector might prefer GNP because it is more closely related to the potential of their product-markets.

Gross National Product.   In general, the higher the level of economic development, as measured by GNP, in a country-market, the more economically viable it is likely to be. As Chapter 1 has illustrated, most of the highly industrialized countries are located in Europe. They are joined by Canada, Japan and the USA. Australia, Israel, New Zealand and Singapore can also be classified as highly developed in economic terms. Large numbers of customers with sufficient economic resources make these strong potential markets.

Most of the world's poorest countries in terms of GNP are located in sub-Saharan Africa. Countries like Burkina Faso, Burundi, Chad, Ethiopia, Mozambique, Malawi, Mali, Rwanda, Sierra Leone, Somalia, Sudan and Tanzania repeatedly experience devastating droughts, as well as civil strife and enormous refugee and health problems. Today they are the largest recipients of foreign assistance. Their stagnant economies lack almost all the resources necessary for development: capital, infrastructure, trained industrial and agricultural workers, and political stability. To do business in such nations, the marketer must identify the nation's most urgent needs, develop specific solutions, assist in financing, train personnel and maintain products. For example, Peter Dyk, an Austrian producer of grain mills, discovered that farmers in Sudan have a need for small transportable mills with little energy consumption which can not only treat wheat, corn, sorgum and other local grains, but are also able to eliminate bugs and the grains of other plants during the milling process. In contrast to competitors' products, Dyk's mills can be maintained on site by technically skilled Sudanese. The sales results in this market have encouraged the firm to look for other markets in LDCs.

Even countries which produce crude oil, coffee, cacao and cotton, such as Cameroon, experience only a little economic development because of their inefficient government-related firms, high budget deficits and political instability. The example of Uganda (coffee accounts for more than 90 per cent of its export revenues) shows that economic reforms and strong fiscal policies can help in improving the situation. Its per capita income rose steadily in the first half of the 1990s.

Asia contains another group of very poor countries, including Afghanistan, Bangladesh, Bhutan, Cambodia, Myanmar, Nepal and North Korea. All have recently suffered from war, floods, overpopulation, political instability or autocratic governments. Myanmar, for example, was one of the world's primary exporters of rice until 1962, when an autocratic government took power. It is now one of the poorest countries in the world and continues to be plagued by political turmoil. In Afghanistan, differences between rival groups of Mujahadee (freedom fighters) led to ongoing civil strife after they had overthrown the former communist government. The Democratic Republic of Korea has to seek barter deals and gifts from richer countries, such as shiploads of rice from its southern neighbour South Korea, in order to nourish its population.

Even in Europe there is a country in a state of very low economic development: Albania. Because of its closed and centrally administrated economy under communist rule and its subsequent political instability, the country's GNP shrank substantially between 1980 and 1997. In the early 1990s the budget deficit reached 50 per cent of GNP. Industrial production equipment is up to 60 years old. Because of corrupt governments and civil war in 1996, things got increasingly worse. In 1997 the survival of Albania's population depended on massive aid from Western Europe. But nevertheless, the country provides interesting opportunities. It has rich mines of copper, nickel and chromium,

Map 3.2 **Sub-Saharan Africa**

Source: *The World Atlas.*

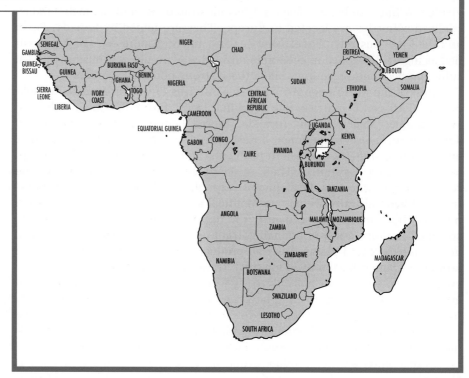

its own sources of crude oil, unused water power, and so far untouched coastlines on the Mediterranean Sea. The wage level has reached USD30 to 50 a month.

The potential for conducting profitable international business in these countries is very low. Low income, restrictive legislation and poor infrastructures present major obstacles to marketing in these countries. Why, then, should international marketers be interested in these markets at all? The answer lies in both current and future opportunities. (The Ethics box gives an example of the 'opportunities' a marketer should avoid.) Many markets in highly industrialized countries are almost, if not entirely, saturated. Developing economies with the natural and human resources to overcome periodic financial and political crises are therefore becoming interesting target markets. To be successful in these markets, companies will have to take a long-term view. They must be willing to train local residents and facilitate the transfer of technology, and they must be adept at cultivating relationships with local firms and influential individuals.

Sometimes governments attempt to attract the participation of non-domestic firms by providing financing for projects with potentially high sales volumes. Opportunities may also arise because many LDC governments want technology from more advanced economies. But technology transfers do not occur in a single step. Rather, there is a multistage flow of technology and managerial expertise between countries at different levels of economic development. Korea, India, Brazil and the Eastern European countries import significant amounts of advanced technology. At the same

ETHICS BOX

'Opportunities'
to Avoid

Mr Alhadi Tijani Aminu, following his own indication as 'special assistant' to Nigeria Central Bank's general manager, offered a deal: USD16 million were to be gained without much hassle. Heinz Roester-Schmidt of Transmedimpex in Vienna had very good reasons not to accept.

The scheme is always the same, sometimes easy to recognize, sometimes you lose money or delivered goods; in other cases there is an open invitation to launder money. In Roesler-Schmidt's case, Mr Aminu offered the following deal: the Ministry of Defence and the Central Bank of Nigeria had paid a sum of USD40 million to a foreign company, but the books so far showed it as unpaid. The Austrian firm should figure as the supplier and cash the sum without any counter-performance. Forty per cent should be the Austrian firm's profit, 55 per cent should go back to people in Nigeria, and 5 per cent was calculated as expenses.

In some cases the goals of the 'business partners' are less evident. Nigerian offers look tempting. Sidney Conn, CEO of a California-based manufacturer of fire prevention equipment received an official demand for the delivery of goods worth USD5 million. He only needed to come. Two elegant gentlemen together with an armed soldier picked him up at the airport. A visa was not needed. After arrival at the hotel, the two 'business people' with the help of the soldier started their business: to extort signatures. Conn was lucky. He was able to inform a journalist from the *International Herald Tribune* about his situation. The US embassy managed to free him after long negotiations. Another businessman, the British David Rollings, was found dead in his hotel room. He had tried personally to pick up USD3 million promised for a money laundering job.

Source: Translated/adapted from 'Es wird ernst, es geht um Tod oder Leben,' *Internationale Wirtschaft*, No. 20, 14 May 1992, p. 3.

---

time, they are playing a significant role in the transfer of technology to developing countries. For example, Indian and Czech firms have cooperated with German, Finnish and Swiss engineering firms such as Demag and Lurgi (steel plants) or Jacob Poeri (paper mills) in industrial projects throughout the developing world.

GDP Per Capita.   GDP per capita is an assessment criterion preferred by international marketers that are more interested in individuals' purchasing power in the countries under consideration, such as manufacturers of consumer products or service providers. However, when applying this criterion in the comparison of country-market attractiveness, managers should be aware of the manifold problems related to that measure.

Traditionally, for comparative purposes GDP measured in local currency has been converted into USD at currency market exchange rates. However, exchange rates are not only influenced by the economic situation of a country. Therefore, a conversion of GDP per capita at market exchange rates in general understates the true purchasing power in developing economies relative to more industrially developed countries. An international marketer wanting to make meaningful comparisons needs to use purchasing power parities for conversions. Purchasing power parities take into account the difference in price levels among countries. Because price levels in industrially developing countries are traditionally rather low, their GDP per capita in USD increases compared to conversions at currency market exchange rates. A calculation of the World Bank shows, for example, an increase in GDP per capita for Vietnam from USD170 to USD1,040 when purchasing power is taken into account.[24]

The problem for the international marketer is to determine the proper purchasing power parities. A theoretically proper approach would be to construct a basket of goods and services available in all countries under consideration, to determine the local prices for that basket, and then to calculate multipliers that equalize the prices of the identical baskets across countries. Because it is rather difficult to define a standard basket of goods and services across different country-markets, less sophisticated approaches have been proposed. One is the Big Mac basket illustrated in Figure 3.4 which gives the currency exchange rates that result in hamburgers costing the same in each country.

Other problems of GDP per capita to be aware of have already been discussed in this chapter or will be discussed in Chapter 7. They include lack of consideration of the income effects of the informal sector (which, for example, reaches an estimated 15 per cent of the official GDP in Germany) and of varying distributions of income. Bimodal distributions of income are quite common in many industrially less developed and developing countries. That is, a very small part of the population controls most of the income of the entire country, setting a trap for GDP per capita which is calculated as a (then meaningless) mean across the entire population. But income distribution may also need to be more closely considered by international marketers interested in highly developed economies, such as the USA where the middle class is shrinking.

For example, in the early years of the twentieth century, South Carolina built a formidable manufacturing base in the textile industry, which thrived by consuming Dixie's cotton crops. Red-brick mills sprang up even in remote hamlets, as owners reached out to take advantage of low-cost rural labour. But after decades of textile dominance, South Carolina began an economic transformation in the 1960s. It diversified by aggressively courting outside investments, including investment by foreign companies. The inflow of overseas capital increased in the 1980s, when the state won the symbolic capstone of the international trend: a sprawling BMW plant near Greenville, which the German company has been expanding over the years. Foreign investments have transformed the state's economy. American subsidiaries of foreign companies now employ more than 111 000 South Carolina workers, more than double the 1980 figure, and up to almost 9 per cent of South Carolina workers. The new manufacturing sector is producing Fuji film, Michelin tyres, Hoechst fibres and BMW cars for sale to Americans and for export as well. Average annual salaries in the state have risen some 38 per cent in the past decade, and the average manufacturing hourly wage has risen 33 per cent. These figures mask a costly, offsetting erosion in textiles and related businesses. Employment in the state's textile and apparel industries was down to 116 000 in 1995 from 150 000 a decade ago. About half those losses stemmed from technological advances that raised productivity; the rest related to low-priced imports. Thus, if one part of new South Carolina's population is thriving, another part is suffering.[25]

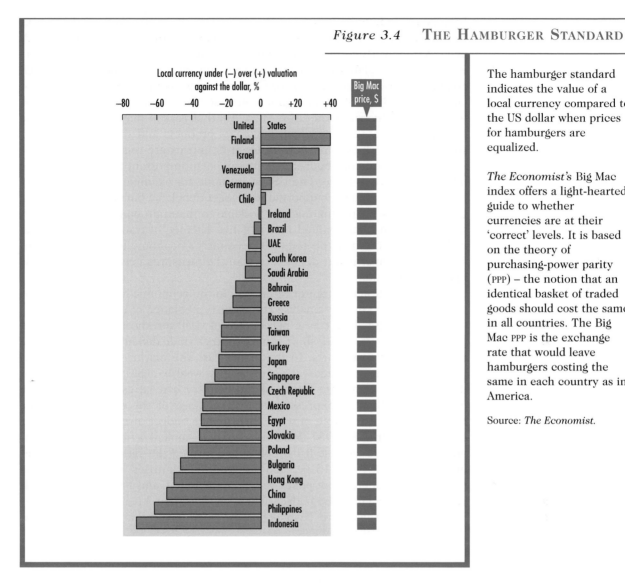

Figure 3.4 THE HAMBURGER STANDARD

The hamburger standard indicates the value of a local currency compared to the US dollar when prices for hamburgers are equalized.

The Economist's Big Mac index offers a light-hearted guide to whether currencies are at their 'correct' levels. It is based on the theory of purchasing-power parity (PPP) – the notion that an identical basket of traded goods should cost the same in all countries. The Big Mac PPP is the exchange rate that would leave hamburgers costing the same in each country as in America.

Source: *The Economist.*

Balance of Payments

Countries, like firms and individuals, need to keep track of their transactions. The account that records all the economic transactions that take place between a country and other countries over a period of time is the balance of payments. This account is divided into several categories, including one or more capital accounts (recording all financial transactions) and the current account, commonly known as the balance of trade, which keeps track of the country's exports and imports of goods and services.

By definition, the balance of payments must balance – it cannot be either a credit or a debit. But within the balance of payments account any given category, such as the balance of trade, can be either positive or negative. In the 1990s, for example, the US balance of trade has been notoriously negative, whereas during the same years the trade balances of Japan and Germany have been positive. In the short run a country may be able to offset a negative balance of trade by borrowing, using savings, selling off assets, and the like. But in the long run it is not possible for a country to sustain a negative balance of trade without jeopardizing its economic wealth.

A negative balance of trade can have many causes. One is that not enough companies engage in exporting, or the companies are not internationally competitive enough (because of high labour costs, lack of technology, high taxes, inadequate industrial structures, etc.). Another reason may be an overrating of the country's currency which makes its products and services too expensive to export, while imports from other countries are relatively low priced. Finally, a government's budget deficit may be an important factor leading to a negative balance of trade. The US government, for example, not unlike many European governments, supported its budget deficit by borrowing from other countries. This borrowing made it possible to maintain consumption at high levels which in turn resulted in a negative balance of trade. Because of the negative effects to be expected for the country's economy in the long run, in 1997 the US government decided to take the measures needed to balance its budget until 2000.

An international marketer interested in the economic outlook of a potential country-market may analyse the country's balance of trade and the government's budget deficit as a percentage of GDP for short-term effects and longer-term effects. In the short run a country's trade deficit indicates that the market is open to imports. In the longer run, the market may become less attractive because of decreasing economic wealth. The impact of budget deficits on the economic future of the country can be estimated from the country's public debt expressed as a percentage of the country's exports. Ireland is a good example of what government budget discipline may do for economic health. In 1987 Ireland's economy looked a mess. Inconsistent growth and years of loose fiscal policy had pushed the ratio of gross government debt to GDP to 115 per cent; among EU countries, only Belgium was more deeply indebted. But policy was then tightened, and 1996 was the eighth year in a row in which the budget deficit was less than 3 per cent of GDP. This has helped to make the Irish economy grow faster than the EU average throughout the 1990s.[26]

Exchange Rate

The exchange rate of a currency is its price in terms of another currency. When exchange rates of currencies fluctuate greatly, they may have a dramatic effect on the success of an international marketer and a destabilizing effect on world trade. Thus, MAN AG and Mercedes, the two most important German truck makers, were hit heavily by the devaluations of the Italian lira and Swedish kronor in the early 1990s, which favoured Iveco, a unit of the Italian automotive firm Fiat SpA, and Sweden's Scania and Volvo. Mercedes, the European truck market leader, saw its European market share drop 30 per cent between 1991 and 1996.[27]

On the other hand, when currency exchange rates are entirely fixed, currencies can only be bought or sold at specific rates that do not vary. Governments can change those rates, but compared to the minute-by-minute fluctuations of floating exchange rates, fixed exchange rates offer the advantage of predictability to business firms that need to exchange currencies. However, fixed exchange rates may prevent international business transactions. For example, if the US dollar is set at USD1 = 8.25 Indian rupees, an Indian company that wants to buy dollars to pay for imports may not be able to find anyone who is willing to sell dollars at that rate. Potential sellers of dollars may want to sell for a higher rate, but the rate fixed by government prevents the buyer from paying more. The fixed exchange rate may actually act as a barrier to international trade.

Therefore, most governments let their currencies' exchange rates fluctuate to a certain extent. When induced by market forces, exchange rate fluctuations may have short-term or longer-term causes. Short-term fluctuations stem from the very complex offer and demand structure of the international currency market. There, an individual consumer changing currency for vacation or other consumption purposes acts as a buyer or seller, as do large corporations, buying and selling foreign currency for international trading purposes, investors, trying to profit from different interest rates across country-markets, commercial banks and brokers, serving their clients, central banks, intervening to reach macroeconomic goals such as decreasing inflationary pressures, or speculators who buy and sell foreign currencies in anticipation of their changing future value. Longer-term fluctuations are the result of a country's growth and inflation rates.

Inflation is an increase in prices in an economy that results in a decline in real purchasing power for customers in that economy. Inflation increases the prices of factors of production which results in increasing costs. Increased costs are reflected in higher prices of goods and services. Their international competitiveness is reduced. Exchange-rate fluctuations are in theory supposed to offset that effect of inflation exactly. Devaluation of a currency should increase exports, because export prices will be lower.

To keep exchange rate fluctuations at a level that is manageable by international business, and to promote international monetary cooperation, the International Monetary Fund (IMF) has been established. Exhibit 3.2 describes its pupose and functioning in more detail.

Independent Floating. Independently floating currencies, such as the US dollar, the UK pound, the Japanese yen or the Swiss franc, can be bought, held and sold like any other commodity. This helps to ensure the availability of foreign currencies for conducting international transactions, but it can also result in an 'overvalued' or 'undervalued' currency (compared to the economic status of the country), because market mechanisms are strongly influenced by personal perceptions of central bank govenors, currency traders, investors and speculators.

For example, during the first half of the 1990s, the US dollar was greatly undervalued (estimates run between 30 and 60 per cent depending on the actual exchange rate). The US government and the US Federal Reserve took joint action to keep the value of the US currency down in order to decrease the country's large deficit in the balance of trade. American companies enjoyed a significant price advantage. The Big Three auto makers, for instance, were revelling in an average price advantage of USD3000 per car over Japanese models. Japanese car makers were experiencing big losses in the US as the yen rose to a mid-1995 peak near 80 yen per dollar. Exports of Toyota from Japan declined by 17 per cent. Nissan even closed a car factory in Zama, near Tokyo. At the same time, direct foreign investments in the USA were largely facilitated by the low dollar exchange rate. Jetro, the Japanese organization for the promotion of external trade, counted 1681 US companies, employing 273 156 people, controlled by Japanese interests in 1994. Since

Exhibit 3.2 The International Monetary Fund

Established in 1944 at the Bretton Woods Conference, along with the World Bank, the International Monetary Fund today is a special organization of the United Nations Organization. Its major objective is to promote international monetary cooperation through information and consultancy, to stabilize currency exchange rates, to establish and maintain a multilateral payment system for trade, to reduce barriers to foreign exchange transactions, and to support a balanced expansion of world trade (along with the World Trade Organization). The IMF acts as a lender of last resort to countries that are unable to pay the interest on their external debt by providing foreign currency loans.

For example, in April 1996 the IMF reached a USD10 billion loan accord with Russia based on a series of preconditions, including a significant reduction of the country's budget-deficit, the elimination of export tariffs, the liberalization of trade rules and boosting taxes on the oil-and-gas industry. As another example, in August 1997, Thailand agreed to privatize important state-owned companies, to reform its taxation system, and to stop paying subsidies to firms that are close to bankruptcy in exchange for a loan of USD8 billion from the IMF together with Japan's Export-Import Bank which should refill the country's foreign exchange reserves. (The country at that point in time had an external debt of around USD100 billion, and its currency, the baht, had been devalued against the US dollar by more than 20 per cent in one month, leading to problems in servicing the external debt.) In addition, the accord fixed a maximum inflation rate of 7 per cent to be reached, and a maximum budget-deficit of 7 per cent of Thailand's GDP. In exchange, the IMF offered to stabilize the baht, in relation to the US dollar, at a level not more than 15 per cent below the exchange rate before the exchange rate crisis struck.

As of August 1996 the IMF had 181 members. The regular fund of IMF is financed by quota subscriptions of those members. The major financiers are the 'Group of 10' (G-10), including 11 members: Belgium, Canada, France, Germany, Italy, Japan, The Netherlands, Sweden's Riksbank, the Swiss national bank, the UK, and the USA. In 1962, they signed a General Loan Agreement that created preferential (AAA) credit lines from which the IMF can issue Special Drawing Rights (SDRs) to member countries according to their quota. There exists also an association agreement with Saudi Arabia which offers similar credit conditions. The SDRs allow the member countries to purchase foreign currency in case of liquidity problems. Non-IMF-member countries may also receive loans from the IMF, but only along with the obligation to implement specific economic guidelines. The G-10 also agreed to lend money to the IMF if the institution's funds should not be sufficient in case of debt and payment crises. In 1996, in a new agreement including 13 additional lenders, such as Austria, Denmark, Finland and Luxembourg, the funds of the IMF were doubled to 34 billion SDRs. In addition, the IMF may take bank loans to supplement its basic fund.

Sources: Translated/adapted from IWF Nachrichten, September 1996, Washington, DC: IMF; 'Währungsfond belohnt Thailands Strukturpaket mit Milliardenkrediten,' *Der Standard*, 4 August 1997, p. 15; and White, G. (1996) 'Russian Bureaucracy Slows Reforms IMF Required for $10 Billion Loan,' *The Wall Street Journal Europe*, 12–13 April, p. 4.

then, the dollar exchange rate against the other important currencies has substantially increased, presenting trouble for the US car manufacturers. To illustrate, a move from 95 to 115 yen to the dollar translates into more than USD6 billion in additional operating income for Japanese auto makers which can be used, at least to some extent, for price reductions.[28]

Stepwise and Block Floating. Some currencies, such as the Greek Drachme, the Swedish Krona and the Danish Krone, do not fluctuate freely against each other. The currency exchange rates are allowed to fluctuate 'stepwise' around fixed exchange rates to the Euro in a predetermined percentage. If two currencies arrive at the upper and lower end of their allowed zone of fluctuation, the national banks involved must buy and sell the respective currencies to stabilize their exchange rates. As of January 1999, the currencies participating in European Monetary Union have been entirely fixed in their value relative to the Euro. The EMU currencies float as a block relative to other currencies.

Foreign Investment Ratio

In theory, foreign investment is simply capital flowing from one country to another according to the country's relative advantage. That is, in the absence of artificial barriers such as tariffs, investment funds can be expected to seek the highest real rate of return. Therefore, with increasing liberalization of global trade, foreign investment expressed as a percentage of GDP in a country under consideration becomes an increasingly valid indicator of the market's economic attractiveness.

For example, in 1995 and 1996 Singapore attracted foreign direct investments of more than USD4 billion each year. That is more than the entire sum of foreign direct investments in the European countries in a state of transition. On the other side, up to 1996, Singapore's firms had invested about USD7 billion in China, USD4.5 billion in Indonesia and USD1 billion in Vietnam.[29]

In the countries of the former Soviet empire, foreign investments decreased from 1994 to 1995. They were not economically attractive markets in the mid-1990s. Their economic reforms were much less advanced than the transformation process in the Central European countries. Because of political instability, bad economic data (GDP had declined by 50 per cent since 1991) and an insecure legal situation, Russia, for example, had only acquired USD6.7 billion of direct foreign investment by 1996.[30] Not unlike the situation in many industrially less developed countries, the economy has been split into two parts. Exporting sectors such as the oil and gas, mining and energy industries are doing relatively well and attract international investors. Sectors serving the home market, such as consumer goods (minus 80 per cent production), machinery (more than 60 per cent production decline), construction, chemicals and wood (minus 50 per cent production), are faced with a crisis of existence.[31] Privatization of retailing, consumer services, restaurants, accomodation businesses and small to middle-sized enterprises mostly active in those suffering sectors is well advanced. More than 100 000 firms, representing 80 per cent of commercial activities, have changed owners. About 1 million new small businesses have been (officially) created. But privatization of big companies has either been stopped or ended in 'shares for loans' swaps between the government (in need of funds) and a small number

Exhibit 3.3 DEVELOPMENT BANKS AND FUNDS

The richer economies of the world have established financial institutions to support the economic development of countries with a lower level of economic development.

THE WORLD BANK

The World Bank Group consists of four organizations: The International Bank for Reconstruction and Development (IBRD), the International Development Association (IDA), the International Finance Corporation (IFC), and the Multilateral Investment Guarantee Agency (MIGA), which have a common president and are organizationally integrated. Their common objective is to support the economic and social development of their less developed member countries by providing financial aid and consultancy as well as some help in getting support by third parties. IBRD and IDA, both heavily involved in fighting poverty, play a major role in the coordination of foreign aid, that is, in the coordination and financing of development programmes for individual countries.

IBRD, a special organization of the UNO, was established at the currency and finance conference of the ONU in Bretton Woods in 1944 and has been operative since June 1946. Its members are most countries of the world. The IBRD is mainly capitalized by the USA (17.7 per cent), Japan (6.7 per cent), Germany (5.1 per cent), France and the UK (4.9 per cent each). It makes loans to economically developing countries throughout the world (against interest payments or governmental guarantees) if private capital for productive investments is not available at adequate rates, provides technical assistance to aid in development across a variety of projects, including water supply, infrastructure development, population planning, industrial development and tourism, and provides loans for measures to improve a country's industrial structure. Funds are mainly generated through borrowing in international capital markets.

IDA provides long-term (35–40 years) loans at no interest to the countries with the lowest per capita GDP for projects reducing poverty, improving economic structures and protecting the environment. IFC supports private productive enterprise in industrially less developed countries through partly (usually 25 per cent) financing investment projects without government guarantees at market conditions (if sufficient private capital is not available at reasonable conditions), as well as through provision of investment capital (giving takeover guarantees), technical assistance and consultancy. MIGA has the main objective of supporting private direct investments of citizens of member countries in economically developing member states by providing guarantees for non-commercial risks such as currency transfer limitations, expropriation, war, or civil unrest. Guarantees are given for 15 years for up to 90 per cent of the investment, limited to a maximum of USD50 million per project.

INTER-AMERICAN DEVELOPMENT BANK

The Inter-American Development Bank (IaDB), established by 19 Latin American countries and the USA in 1959 (today 26 Latin and Central American members, the USA and Canada as well as 16 European countries, Israel and Japan) has the main objective of supporting the economic and social development of the less industrially developed members in this part of the world by providing project loans to governments or against governmental guarantees, supporting industrial sector adaptation programmes, and helping in foreign debt reduction programmes. The fight against poverty, the improvement of environmental protection, and modernization of the members' industries are of primary importance.

AFRICAN DEVELOPMENT BANK AND FUND/ASIAN DEVELOPMENT BANK AND FUND

Both banks focus on similar development needs in the most deserving countries of their respective regions.

ISLAMIC DEVELOPMENT BANK

The Islamic Development Bank (IsDB) was founded by the members of the Organization of Islamic Countries in 1974. It supports the economic development and social improvements of member countries and other Islamic societies conforming to sharia. Loans for 15 to 25 years are made for infratsructure projects such as education centres or irrigation projects, free of redemption for the first three to seven years. In addition the bank engages in equity financing of industrial and agricultural projects, leasing, and part payment sales in international trade.

EUROPEAN BANK FOR RECONSTRUCTION AND DEVELOPMENT

The 58 members of the European Bank for Reconstruction and Development (EBRD), including the EU and the EIB (European Investment Bank), have capitalized it with 20 billion ECU (about USD22 billion). The main purpose of EBRD is to support a balanced development of the former communist countries in Central and now mainly Eastern Europe through financing of investments in infrastructure projects as well as the restructuring of industrial sectors.

Source: Translated/adapted from Baratta, M. (1995) *Der Fischer Weltalmanach '96,* Frankfurt a.M.: Fischer Taschenbuch Verlag.

of banks such as Menatep and Onexim bank.[32] Despite all these problems, international investors, in particular from the USA, started to increase their investments after the re-election of president Boris Yeltsin in 1996 because they expected a more positive economic development.[33]

Financial Institutions.   Because the economic situation in many industrially less developed countries around the world is not promising enough to attract international direct investment, international financial institutions play an important role in funding investments needed for economic development. The most important institutions are international banks and funds, such as the World Bank, the European Bank for Reconstruction and Development, the Asian Development Bank and Fund, the Inter-American Development Bank, the African Development Bank and Fund, and the Islamic Development Bank. Exhibit 3.3 illustrates their major objectives and functioning. The international marketer should be interested in the activities of these financial institutions because they provide business opportunities in otherwise economically unattractive markets.

International Stock and Debt Markets. In the highly developed economies, private institutions, such as pension funds and insurance companies, are important capital sources, for example in the USA, the Netherlands and the UK. They operate via international stock and debt markets which present an opportunity for international companies to find the lowest interest rate for loans or the highest stock price for equity issues. For example, the Tokyo Stock Exchange has grown to be second only to the New York Stock Exchange. Since the mid-1980s, more foreign than domestic companies have been newly listed in Tokyo. In fact, the international growth of stock markets has changed the corporate financial picture considerably. More and more often, companies in industrial countries are going directly to financial markets, meaning that commercial banks are being replaced by other sources of funds.

Table 3.5 Model for an Economic Viability Profile

An international marketer may want to develop a model to comparatively evaluate the economic viability of various country-markets.

Criteria	Indicator	Weight	Target
Growth rate	Change of real GDP		≥ + 5%
Level of development	GDP per capita		≥ USD10,000
Inflation	Inflation rate	40%	≤ 0%
Investments	Investments in % of GDP		≥ 30%
Fiscal policy	Net budget deficit in % of GDP		≤ 0%
External debt	Public external debt as % of exports	30%	0%
Debt repayment	Repayment of external debt as % of exports		0%
International trade	Balance of trade in % of GDP		≥ 5%
Liquidity	Foreign exchange reserves in % of imports	30%	≥ 100%

Source: Adapted from Schicklgruber, W. (1991) 'Die Beurteilung des Länderrisikos,' *Report*, April, Wien: Länderbank, p. 6.

ECONOMIC VIABILITY PROFILES

When the international marketer has gathered the relevant data to comparatively evaluate the economic environment of various served and potential country-markets, it may find that the comparison is largely facilitated by developing profiles of economic viability. Of course, each company will construct a profile relevant to the specific product-market(s) it is targeting, but Table 3.5 shows an example of one such model.

The model suggested in Table 3.5 is rather simple. It contains data and evaluations concerning the internal economic status of a country-market, its foreign debt position, and the country's status in international trade. To gain 100 points (the best evaluation) for a criterion, specified target figures must be reached. The number of points given to a country for any criterion depends on the value that the respective indicator reaches in that country. The result of such an analysis is one figure that can be compared across countries.

To be managerially meaningful, however, such profiles and comparisons need to be established on an ongoing basis. Table 3.6 shows how the basic economic data of a country-market may change over time. The resulting conclusions of an international marketer concerning a country-market's economic viability should, therefore, be taken in the light of time series data. To better understand their meaning, they need to be further supplemented by information concerning the political and legal environments as well as the cultural specifics of the country. These will be discussed in the following chapters.

Table 3.6	Development of Selected Economic Indicators in the Czech Republic						

Indicator	1990	1991	1992	1993	1994	1995	1996(ests.)
Real growth (%)	−1.6	−14.2	−6.4	−0.9	2.6	5.2	5.4
Inflation rate (%)	10.0	57.8	11.1	20.8	10.0	9.5	8.2
Total exports (billion USD)	8.0	11.5	16.3	18.3	19.7	23.3	25.4
Total imports (billion USD)	8.9	11.2	16.4	17.7	19.9	24.7	27.9
Balance of trade (billion USD)	−0.9	0.3	−0.2	0.7	−0.1	−1.9	−2.3
External debt (billion USD)	6.4	7.2	6.8	8.7	12.8	15.0	15.8
Debt service ratio (%)	0.8	0.5	0.7	0.6	1.2	1.2	1.0
Frgn. exch. reserves (billion USD)	1.4	3.5	1.3	3.9	6.3	13.9	15.0
Gross frgn. investments (billion USD)	0.2	0.6	1.0	0.6	0.9	1.2	1.5

The development of some economic indicators in the Czech Republic over a time period of 7 years illustrates the importance of observing time series to take meaningful conclusions.

Source: Adapted from Schrick-Hildebrand, P. (1996) 'Tschechische Republik – erfolgreiche Transformation und interessanter Investitionsstandort,' *IKB-Mitteilungen*, No.1, Deutsche Industriebank, pp. 15–19.

Summary

The economy of a country is a major part of each company's macro-environment. Generally, it is the first dimension to be studied in assessing the attractiveness of any country-market. In a first step the international marketer has to decide which characteristics of the economic environment are relevant to the company's business. Having determined the relevant factors of influence, the marketer will need to analyse their current state in the country-markets under comparison and to anticipate their potential states on the planning horizon.

If a market does not contain enough customers with the purchasing power to buy the product, it is not economically viable. The degree of urbanization in a society is of interest to many international marketers because it represents concentrations of potential customers and strongly influences distribution needs. Besides the size, structure and purchasing power of a country's population, the capabilities to be found in that country's population have a significant influence on the country's wealth. The educational system and the skills and flexibility of the population may therefore be important factors to be considered.

The natural environment of a country-market, its resources, topography and climatic conditions, represents an important source of potential wealth for its population. In using resources from that natural environment for their business purposes, international marketers need to take care of the sustainability of their activities. That is, they must be aware that a business will only be successful over a longer-term period if it does not destroy its own bases.

Besides the human and natural resources available in a country-market, its existing and emerging technological resources may influence its attractiveness. For international marketing to be possible, a certain energy supply, transportation, communication and commercial infrastructure has to be in place in a country-market. In addition, an international marketer needs to consider the predominant concept of technology in each of the societies analysed. They may demand entirely different marketing mixes to ensure long-term success.

The economic system of a country is its specific combination of human, natural and technological resources. Depending on the level of industrial development, the shares of different industrial sectors of the economy will vary. So will the ownership of the means of production as well as economic decision making, depending on the market orientation of the governing political forces.

To finally assess the attractiveness of a country-market's economic environment, the international marketer needs to establish a list of evaluation criteria against which to systematically compare potential and served markets. The chosen criteria should be relevant to the product-market(s) of the company, be significative of the economic standing of the country, and applicable across all country-markets to be compared. If the economic analysis yields positive results, the international marketer may continue the evaluation process by examining the political and legal as well as the cultural environments of the country-markets.

DISCUSSION QUESTIONS

1. Explain how the structure of a country's population influences the viability of the country-market to an international marketer of your choice.
2. Discuss why the capabilities of a potential country-market's population may be of great importance to international marketers. Find examples to underline your points.
3. A country-market's natural environment influences its attractiveness to a marketer of industrial products. Discuss, based on examples from business magazines.
4. Find examples of companies that show how a sustainable method of production and marketing helps to assure their economic success. What is the difference in those companies' decisions and actions compared to their competitors?
5. Illustrate the influence of a country's infrastructure on the economic attractiveness of local product-markets by comparing a self-chosen highly industrially developed market with an economically less developed market.
6. What are the major points of attraction for international marketers interested in European countries on their way to economic reform? Explain how different methods of transition may influence the result of the assessment process.

7. Discuss what information about a country-market's attractiveness a specific international marketer can derive from the country's GNP and GDP per capita data.
8. Explain why a country's balance of trade may be of interest to an international marketer from a short-run as well as a long-run point of view.
9. Illustrate the role of international financial institutions in maintaining the economic viability of country-markets.
10. Take an example of an internationally operating company and establish a profile of relevant indicators for the assessment of its served country-markets' economic viability. Explain the reasons for choosing those indicators.

ADDITIONAL READINGS

Blasi, J., M. Kroumova and D. Kruse (1997) *Kremlin Capitalism*, Ithaca, NY: Cornell University Press.

Hirschey, M., J.L. Pappas and D. Whigham (1995) *Managerial Economics, European Edition* London: International Thomson Business Press

NOTES

[1] Glain, St. and M. Kanabayashi (1996) 'Shoppers at Japan's Grocery Stores Are Buying More American

Foods', *The Wall Street Journal Europe*, 10–11 May, p. 7.

[2] Gumbel, P. and C.A. Robbins (1996) 'Making Inroads, Has the West 'Lost' Russia? Probably Not, For Much Has Changed', *The Wall Street Journal*, 28 May, pp. A1 and A10.

[3] Beck, E. (1996) 'Dangerous Delay, Bulgarian Backlash Against Reform Shows Perils of Procrastination', *The Wall Street Journal Europe*, 20 May, pp. 1 and 7.

[4] Tietze, W. (1997) 'Undurchsichtiger Privatisierungsprozeß verprellt Investoren', *Der Standard*, 21 January, p. 17.

[5] Gumbel, P. and C.A. Robbins (1996), op.cit.

[6] Rossant, J. (1997) 'R.I.P., Gamal Abdel Nasser', *Forbes*, 21 April, p. 376.

[7] 'Turtles in the soup', *The Economist*, 16 March 1996, p. 64.

[8] 'Green, as in greenbacks', *The Economist*, 1 February 1997, p. 42.

[9] 'Not too modern, please', *The Economist*, 16 March 1996, p. 42f.

[10] Hopkins, N. (1996) 'Australia: A Fast Uptake on New Technology as Industry Develops', *International Herald Tribune*, 15 March, p. 19.

[11] Rapoport, C. (1994) 'Nestlé's Brand Building Machine', *Fortune*, 19 September, pp. 147–156.

[12] Rögl, O. (1996) 'Rußland im Zeichen der Wahlen', *Auslandsdienst der Raiffeisen Zentralbank*, April, p. 9f.

[13] Zwass, A. (1996) 'Banken aus Reformstaaten Mitteleuropas drängen vor', *Der Standard*, 1 March, p. 15.

[14] Farolan, M, (1996) 'The Philippine Informal Sector: Its Status as an Area of Scientific Research', Working Paper, Manila.

[15] 'KUBA: Vorsichtige Reformen des Systems', *Außenhandel*, Nachrichten der Raiffeisen Zentralbank für den Außenhandel, March, 1996, 1f.

[16] Hooley, G.J., T. Cox, J. Beracs *et al.* (1998) 'The Role of Foreign Direct Investment in the Transition Process in Central and Eastern Europe', in Hooley, G. R. Loveridge and D. Wilson (eds) *Internationalization: Process, Context and Markets*, London: Macmillan.

[17] Heller, E. (1998) 'Erst Halbzeit bei polnischem Strukturwandel', *Der Standard*, 23 June, p. 37.

[18] Michaels, D. (1996) 'To the East, Central Europe Enjoys A Surge in Investment From Top Asian Firms', *The Wall Street Journal Europe*, 13 June, pp. 1 and 9.

[19] Koch, R. (1998) 'Prager Privatisierungen: Tempo statt Korrektheit', *Der Standard*, 23 June, p. 37.

[20] 'Slowenien: 'Success-story' mit kleinen Schattenseiten', *CA-exclusiv*, March 1996, p. 9.

[21] 'Sieger und Verlierer', *Finanzplatz Osteuropa*, 29 August 1996, p. B4.

[22] 'The pragmatic way of privatization', *Euromoney*, November 1995, pp. 117f.

[23] 'Privatization Becomes a Top Priority', *The Wall Street Journal Europe*, 9 July 1996, p. 13.

[24] *World Bank Atlas 1995*, Washington, D.C.: World Bank, 1995, pp. 18f.

[25] Seib, G.F. and Harwood, J. (1996) 'Proving Ground – Free Trade or Tariffs? Key US Primary Tests Two Republican Visions', *The Wall Street Journal Europe*, 29 February, pp. 1 and 6.

[26] 'A Gaelic boom', *The Economist*, 27 April, 1996, p. 58.

[27] Mitchener, B. (1996) 'Europe's Truck Makers Face Challenge', *The Wall Street Journal Europe*, 8 July, p. 12.

[28] Kerwin, K.(1996) 'Detroit is Getting Sideswiped by the Yen', *Business Week*, 11 November, p. 54; and Malingre, V.(1995) 'L'appréciation du yen accélère les délocalisations chez les constructeurs nippons', *Le Monde*, 10 May, p. 26.

[29] Baburek, G. (1996) 'Singapurs neues Entwicklungskonzept heißt: "Go regional"', *Der Standard*, 9 August, p. 19.

[30] Mentré, P. (1996) 'La Russie retrouverait la croissance en 1997', *Le Figaro économie*, 14 March,p. B I.

[31] Rosenkranz, C. (1996) 'Rußlands Wirtschaft auf Dritte-Welt-Niveau', *Der Standard*, 23 May, p. 18.

[32] Mentré, P. (1996) 'Russie: les privatisations gelées', *Le Figaro économie*, 8 March, p. B XI.

[33] Kranz, P. (1997) 'The Rush to Russia', Business Week, 24 March, 48–50.

CHAPTER
4

POLITICAL AND LEGAL ENVIRONMENT

INTERNATIONAL INCIDENT

Beeg Mek and Ketoflio Fry

On 31 January, 1990, McDonald's opened the first of 20 restaurants planned for Moscow. Over 20,000 Moscovites stood in line that first day. But behind the highly successful opening were over 14 years of political negotiations.

George Cohon, president of McDonald's Canada, initiated discussions in Montreal, at the 1976 Olympics, aimed at opening a McDonald's restaurant at the 1980 Olympic games in Moscow. Discussions proceeded after that, but the Western countries' boycott of the 1980 Olympics resulted in a decision by – at that time – Soviet officials to call off the talks. Cohon was advised by Alexander Yakoulev, Soviet ambassador to Canada at that time, 'At the moment this is ideologically impossible. One day you will be able to do it.' After Mikhail Gorbachev came to power in the USSR in 1984, political relations between the USSR and western countries changed dramatically. Yakoulev became a close advisor to Gorbachev. Discussions regarding a joint venture between the city of Moscow and McDonald's became serious in 1987, after passage of a new joint venture law.

After devoting about half of his time during 1988 and 1989 to the joint venture, Cohon opened the world's largest McDonald's – with 27 serving lines and seating for over 700 people – on Pushkin Square. The BBC's report called the restaurant's signs 'garish'. But consumer response was overwhelmingly positive, despite the 5-kopeck price of a 'beeg mek and ketoflio fry' – roughly half the daily salary of the average Moscovite worker at that time. Today the Puskin Square restaurant is both the busiest McDonald's in the world – with 40,000 customers a day – and the most profitable.

Although the changed political environment allowed McDonald's to open the store in Moscow, the political system was still a major source of problems. Production decisions had traditionally been made by a central government body. New businesses like McDonald's found it difficult to obtain supplies in adequate quality and quantity. But the company established its own vertical marketing system to support the planned restaurants. Cucumber and potato seeds from the Netherlands were imported for use by – now – Russian farmers, who were taught how to grow produce to meet McDonald's exacting standards. McDonald's also helped to establish bakery and meat processing plants, improving cattle production standards – in total a USD100 million investment. In April 1996, McDonald's opened its first drive-in, the sixth McDonald's in Moscow.

Sources: Based on Uchitell, L. (1992) 'Coming Soon: The All-Russian Big Mac,' *International Herald Tribune*, 28 February p. 13; 'McDonald's in Moscow – Slow Food,' *The Economist*, 3 February 1990, pp. 74, 79; Keller, B. (1990) 'Of Famous Arches, Beeg Meks and Rubles,' *New York Times*, 31 January pp. 1, 7; and Gumbel, P. and C.A. Robbins (1996) 'Making Inroads, Has the West "Lost" Russia? Probably Not, For Much Has Changed,' *The Wall Street Journal*, 28 May, pp. A1 and A10.

ANALYSING THE POLITICAL
AND LEGAL ENVIRONMENT

The political systems of the countries served or being considered by an international marketer are an important part of the firm's macro-environment. A multitude of more or less powerful groups of stakeholders from inside but sometimes also outside a country's borders influences who governs the country, what policies the government follows and what legal regulations result from those policies. Most companies are not able to influence their political and legal environment directly but their opportunities for successful business activities largely depend on its structure and content. A marketer serving international markets or planning to do so, therefore, has to assess carefully the political and legal environments of the current or potential markets to lead to successful managerial consequences. Such consequences may be resource investments, adaptations of competitive strategy, policies and actions, or even divestments.

The first step in assessing the political and legal environments of country-markets is to determine which parts or characteristics of the political and legal environment are relevant to the product-market(s) of the company (Figure 4.1). For Airbus Industries, the UK, French and German manufacturer of Airbus jetliners headquartered in Toulouse, France, for example, the political climate between its home governments and the governments of potential customers' countries can have a determinant effect on sales. For some years after China cracked down on the democracy movement in 1989, France had taken a clear position concerning human rights in China. As a consequence, it took Airbus two years, 1994 to 1996, when China's Premier Li Peng visited Paris, to finalize a contract for 33 Airbus planes. The deal could only be struck because at the same time, the US government came close to taking sanctions against China in an attempt to make them reduce piracy of software, CDs and other products. China's government believed that Boeing, the largest US exporter and fierce competitor of Airbus Industries, could influence the US government's policy if it found out that its business interests were at stake.[1]

Having determined the relevant factors of influence from the political and legal environment, the marketer may analyse their current state in the country-markets under consideration. To fully assess the potential impact of the relevant factors on the success of the firm, their potential states of development at the planning horizon will need to be anticipated. For example, in 1995, when the USA had not yet established full diplomatic relations with Vietnam, US-based companies from capital intensive industries, such as Mobil Oil or Unisys Corp, were hurt by not having access to US Export-Import Bank financing, Private Investment Corp. guarantees, risk insurance, and other subsidized credits. From that point of view, Vietnam would have been a very unattractive market. But because the establishment of full diplomatic relations in the not too distant future was highly probable, those companies still considered the market as interesting.[2]

An evaluation of the impact of the current state and future potential development of all relevant characteristics of the political and legal environment in the country-markets under consideration will allow the international marketer to decide how to 'manage' those environments. That is, the company's management will decide how to react to the expected development. It may, for

Figure 4.1 ASSESSING THE POLITICAL AND LEGAL ENVIRONMENT

In assessing the political and legal environment of the firm the marketer first has to determine which factors are relevant to the product-market(s) the company is serving. Then the current state of international, regional and local factors of influence can be assessed and their potential states on the planning horizon anticipated. From the results of the analysis managerial consequences concerning the further treatment of the analysed country-markets may be drawn.

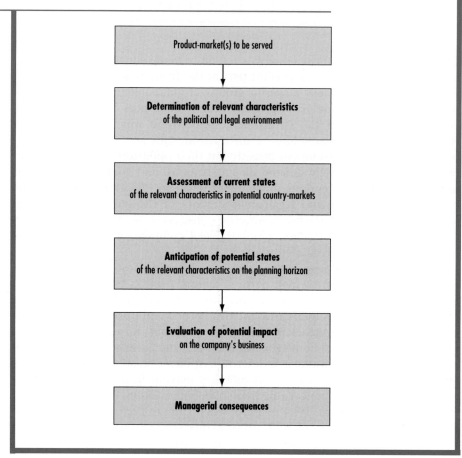

example, decide to withdraw from a market, to search for a local business partner to improve its situation, or to invest heavily in order to profit from a promising development.

For example, in 1993 France's Peugeot had considerable ambitions in China. The auto maker announced it would invest USD1 billion by the turn of the century to boost output at its joint-venture plant in Guangzhou from 20 000 units to 150 000. But the meddling of government has created major problems. In the early 1990s, when China regarded cars as a 'pillar industry' of the future, policymakers pushed to set up huge plants. But when the economy overheated, Beijing imposed tight-money policies that suppressed car demand. The result: in 1996, passenger-car sales rose by 19 per cent, to 382 000. Capacity, however, reached 700 000 and will continue to grow dramatically. Compounding the problem is that passenger-car prices are fixed by the government at between USD15 600 and USD26 000. At those levels, few manufacturers can realize profits because of their low production volume. Peugeot turned out only 2674 vehicles, and rumours are that the company is trying to sell its stake.[3]

This chapter will discuss various political and legal factors which may be relevant for the business of internationally operating companies and give examples of how they influence the decisions and actions of international marketers.

THE POLITICAL SYSTEM

When analysing the political environment of a country-market, the international marketer is mainly interested in the existing political system and its stability. The political system is characterized by the form of government which may take various forms between the two extremes of democracy and dictatorship. But for doing business successfully it is more important for the international marketer to know what political parties and interest groups exist in a specific country-market, what their goals are and how much influence they can exert on the local government. Such interest groups and their ability to influence the major political objectives of government strongly determine the stability of the political environment.

Political System Stability

For the international marketer, the most important factor of the political environment is the stability of the served country-markets' political systems. The extent of political stability can have a major impact on the economic development of a country or region because it influences the perceived risk of potential investors. Events like the change of the government in former Zaire – now the Republic of Congo, the return of Hong Kong to the People's Republic of China, or the breakdown of the communist governments in most parts of Eastern Europe produce changes in the 'rules of the business game'. Political instability, even if it is highly welcome for other reasons, makes the business environment less predictable – and predictability is a key to long-term business success.

For example, in the mid-1980s, three European metallurgical engineering firms, VAI, SMS and Mannesmann DEMAG, started to develop thin slab casting and rolling technology. All three of them had potential customers as development partners. Swiss SMS cooperated with the US steelmaker Nucor. Germany-based DEMAG had an Italian partner, the steel manufacturer Arvedi, and Austrian VAI cooperated with EKO, an East German steelmaker. A couple of months before VAI could finalize its first thin slab casting order by EKO, the Berlin Wall collapsed, and so did the investment project at East German EKO. SMS succeeded in building the first thin slab casting and rolling plant in Crawfordsville, USA and, because of that reference plant, has won world market share leadership with no less than 16 orders for such plants (as of 1996).

Form of Government.   Forms of government differ in the extent to which they permit political participation by the general population. Democracies provide opportunities for the population to take an active role in the formulation of governmental policies. Although they vary greatly in the actual forms of their political mechanisms, Denmark, Thailand, Mexico, Tunisia, Canada and Australia, for example, consider themselves as democracies. Countries such as the Netherlands, the UK and Japan are also constitutional monarchies.

Each has a royal head of government with limited and specified roles. In addition to performing important ceremonial roles, the Queen of the UK, for instance, can convene Parliament, reads the government's policy statement and may ennoble meritorious persons (following the suggestions of government). But she does not rule by holding centralized power, in contrast to the royal heads of absolute monarchies, like the King of Saudi Arabia.

Observers from Western democracies tend to attribute the extent of political stability in a country to the country's form of government. However, as a number of examples show, the form of government and political stability are not directly related. For example, when the communist regimes in Eastern Europe were replaced by more democratically constituted governments, political stability decreased in most of those countries. The centrally controlled power of the former dictatorships with rather stable civilian and military structures deeply entrenched in the local societies was replaced by the weak power of newly constituted political parties who started fighting each other. The result in some of the countries was that the old government structures were not entirely abolished but did not function as before and the newly established structures did not have the power to impose new rules. In addition, frustrated by the worsening economic situation under their newly elected governments, a majority of voters in Eastern European countries decided to return to the former rulers of the countries, now converted into 'sociodemocratic' parties. The resulting political instability strongly hurt efforts to rebuild the countries' economies following a market-oriented model.

On the other hand, the examples of China and Vietnam as well as Singapore show that dictatorships (those countries only have pseudo-elections) can provide stable environments that allow fast economic progress in the sense of a market-oriented economy. The remaining question is how far economic market development can go without changes in the political system of a country. The examples of South Korea and Taiwan seem to point in the direction of increasing pressures to introduce more democratic structures when the economic welfare of large parts of a country's population increases. In Indonesia, as another example, President Suharto's dictatorial government oversaw unprecedented growth over the past three decades. But his policies also ignited popular discontent bubbling to the surface. Rampant corruption, nepotism, economic inequality and political oppression became flashpoints for disgruntled workers, the urban unemployed, and muzzled intellectuals. Despite Jakarta's glistening office towers, American steak houses and young millionaires, factory wages in 1996, that is, even before Indonesia's currency lost a substantial part of its value, averaged USD2 per day, while the average monthly pay for civil servants was less than USD45. Fifteen per cent of Indonesia's population (about 30 million people) still live in poverty. All this led to riots which in turn resulted in Suharto's being forced to give up the presidency and the reluctance of international marketers to invest further in Indonesia.[4]

In Western-style democracies the political administration usually continues as a country's political leadership changes, lending much stability to the entire political system. Of course, sometimes administrations provide 'too much' stability. For example, when a new government in Argentina attempted to privatize state-owned businesses and reduce government intervention in the private sector in the mid-1980s, many members of the public administration, apparently feeling threatened by these changes, joined forces with trade unions to block the reforms.

In the face of radical political changes like the revolt led by Ayatollah Khomeini that occurred in Iran in the late 1970s, even the government bureaucracy may be unable to continue to operate. Sometimes when such changes take place, opportunities to conduct business increase. For example, when the apartheid system in South Africa was ended and Nelson Mandela became president, the economic sanctions on the country were lifted. The new government created a Reconstruction and Development Plan, a policy framework for ushering the black population into the economic mainstream. The plan calls for various public and private initiatives in land reform, as well as training and capital formation designed to redress the economic scars left by decades of apartheid. New business opportunities arose even for small international marketers. In the USA, the National Minority Business Council in New York has developed a strategic programme for minority- and women-owned enterprises interested in establishing a beachhead in the South African market. The NMBC programme is matching up South African companies with American partners, developing a cooperative in South Africa to facilitate trade opportunities in the NMBC's absence and working with local small business assistance centres.[5]

Parties and Interest Groups.   Political parties are important factors of influence on a country-market's political environment because they channel public opinion into the formulation of government policies and laws. Even communist regimes, which traditionally installed a dominant political party and severely limited opposition to that party, used political polls to obtain information about the attitudes and concerns of members of society. Before opening its political system, for example, Hungary conducted 40 public opinion polls each year.

Knowledge as to which political parties exist in a country and how powerful they are is important to an international marketer since the role that foreign businesses are allowed to play in a given country-market is influenced by the philosophies of those parties. For example, the Greens, a rather small but vocal political party in Germany, have taken a strong stand on environmental issues. They work very hard to defeat any business activity that they believe will contribute to environmental pollution or destruction such as nuclear power, unnecessary road transportation and packaging, CO_2 emissions, or overfishing. Their long-term effect has proven to be quite important. Not only have they influenced German politics and law making by forcing the ruling parties to adopt most of the points brought onto the public agenda, but they have succeeded in spreading their influence through similar-minded political parties throughout Europe. The environment minister of the French government newly elected in 1997, for example, is the leader of the French 'Les Verts', and there is a pan-European green group in the European Parliament in Strasbourg.

Strong influences on a country's political decisions may also come from unions. In France or Germany, for example, unions have a significant influence on what is politically feasible or not. The Austrian political system is a special case. There, the Chamber of Workers and Employees, the Chamber of Commerce and the Chamber of Agriculture (workforce, companies and farmers are compulsory and paying members of these organizations) form what has been called a 'social partnership', a forum for discussion and political decisions which strongly influences the local government's decision making. As a positive consequence, the time lost due to strikes in Austria per year is counted in seconds (in 1996 there was no strike at all), compared to countries such as France, where unions and management act more as adversaries than as partners. This in turn leads to a situation where any significant negotiation between representatives of management and personnel is introduced by a strike warning. As a negative consequence of 'social partnership', any changes in government policies on regulations concerning Austria's economic environment are rather slow and taken in small steps.

Special interest groups may play a very important role in particular product-markets. Internationally organized environmentalists such as Greenpeace, for example, have not only exerted considerable pressure on companies such as Esso or Shell, but also on governments. As a reaction to strong campaigns against the clearing of thousands of square kilometres of tropical forests, in the early 1990s, various European governments, for example, considered bans or restrictions on imports of tropical wood. When the exporting countries threatened to retaliate by banning imports from those countries, most European governments withdrew their intended regulations. Environmentalists found other solutions. For example, they started cooperating with big Swedish firms, including AssiDoman and Stora, to develop timber 'certification' schemes. The idea behind certification schemes is to encourage consumers to buy products made from environmentally sound wood by giving such products a label or a stamp of approval. The Swedish firms, which together own about 40 per cent of the country's forests, are discussing what exactly they need to do to get their wood certified under the auspices of the Forest Stewardship Council, an international coalition of lobbyists and firms. In the UK, more than 60 big buyers of forest products, including B&Q, a do-it-yourself chain, and Tesco, a supermarket firm, have pledged not to buy uncertified wood products after 1999.[6]

Lobbyists also influence the international marketer's political environment; 3500 lobbyists for over 160 interest groups and countries are registered in Washington, DC, and it is estimated that perhaps twice that many are active. In Brussels, the headquarters of the European Union, about 4000 people are employed for lobbying purposes; 200 companies are directly represented, while others use about 100 law firms which try to influence EU regulations or about another 100 consultants. More than 30 countries or regions have their own representations. Together they spend around USD2.5 billion a year for lobbying purposes. The influence of lobbyists on European and US politics depends on the lobbyists' professionalism, the quality of their arguments, their knowledge about which person to contact for what purpose, and the number as well as the importance of the supporters they are able to mobilize.[7]

MAJOR POLITICAL OBJECTIVES

Depending on the people in power, their view of the world and whose interests they mainly follow, governments may have very different objectives. Some general objectives seem to be relevant for almost all governments, however. Those objectives include the maintenance of political sovereignty, the enhancement of national prestige and prosperity, national security, and the protection of cultural identity.

Political sovereignty. Like many other creatures, humans feel the need to manage and control a certain territory around them to assure their existence. Humans form states in order to manage and control a political territory and its economy. Maintaining the political sovereignty of those states has traditionally been a major goal of all governments. So-called 'nation-states' were formed. But because of expansion or splitting, changing borders, and the immigration or emigration of people, the term is misleading today.

Most nation-states have more than one nation inside their borders. The USA is a very impressive example. Despite long-term domination by its Anglo-Saxon population, there are many other nationalities present in the country, from Indian tribes to Africans, Hispanics and Asians, and all sorts of Europeans. But the great majority believe themselves to be part of one 'nation'. In other countries, such as China, Russia, Belgium and the UK, there is more than one nationality too, but they do not believe they belong to the same nation. Such perceived differences may lead to terrorism, such as in Spain, China and Turkey, or to outright warfare, such as in Chechnya or in former Yugoslavia. In total, close to 3500 groups of people describe themselves as a 'nation'. But there only are about 200 nation-states. This discrepancy has led experts to predict continued problems in terms of smaller groups of people, determined to apply the doctrine of self-determination to their own group – leading to considerable political instability throughout the next decades.[8]

Nationalistic feelings and their consequences have strong effects on the business of international marketers. In the USA, a marketer can count on the pride of most customers in being 'American'. In Bosnia, many international marketers that had invested there not only lost their capital, but – more importantly – their business partners and many customers.

Several recent trends, such as the increasing liberalization of world trade and the resulting globalization of an increasing number of industries, have worked against nationalism and have strongly decreased the ability of a country's government to control its own economy. But, even within the EU, political fragmentation occurs. The Danes, for example, first voted against the acceptance of the Maastricht treaty which should establish closer political integration. They only accepted the treaty after having achieved some exceptions which left more sovereignty with their government. The UK and Sweden did not voluntarily join monetary union ('Euroland') until 1999. Austria, Ireland and Sweden have maintained their status of political neutrality which means that they do not participate in the Western European Defence system, and the UK did not sign the Schengen Treaty which ties the internal security measures of members more closely together.

Governments are faced with a dilemma: to keep their country's industries internationally competitive or to help them develop faster they need to promote economic cooperation or even integration, but they do not wish to give up their political sovereignty. This dilemma results in a constantly changing political environment which may be detrimental to the business of international marketers.

National Prestige and Prosperity. The objective of governments to further or maintain their country's international prestige leads to results very similar to those of nationalism. In its more peaceful form, the struggle for national prestige often results in protecting or subsidizing national industries, with the consequence of distorted competition. For example, foreign companies complain about the Chinese government's tactics in cutting healthcare costs. The government maintains lists that define which drugs the state will pay for. If consumers want drugs not on the list, they must pay out of their own pocket. Many foreign drug-makers note that the lists contain few foreign products. They claim the lists are a disguised form of protectionism. Smith Kline Beecham, for example, in its factory in Tianjin produces thousands of Contac capsules every minute to feed what is already the largest market in the world for its cold medicine. Yet Contac was taken off the government reimbursement list in 1997, while Contac's main Chinese competitor, Black & White cold formula, remained on the list.[9]

A major objective of most governments is national prosperity, whether it be to increase the standard of living of the country's population or to increase the personal wealth of the members of the government and their families. Traditionally, a country's prosperity depended to a substantial degree on the availability of natural resources, such as iron, coal or water supplies. The example of Japan has shown, however, that even countries with a lack of such natural resources may prosper to an extent unimaginable some 70 years ago. The prosperity of modern industrialized countries which are economically interrelated depends on the international competitiveness of their industries.

The competitiveness of a country's industries partly depends on the level of local labour cost compared to other countries. Therefore, the issue of minimum social standards in global competition has become pre-eminent. Canada, France and the USA are major advocates of imposing minimum social standards on all 128 member states of WTO. They state that there is no fair global competition if child labour and the forced labour of prisoners are not banned and if minimum wages as well as freedom of association are not guaranteed. Industrially developing countries such as Indonesia, Malaysia and Singapore protest such claims as the latest attempt by highly industrialized economies to protect themselves against less expensive products and services.[10]

Competitiveness today is not only based on low labour cost. It is largely based on a country's infrastructure and the capabilities of its population. The capabilities a country's industries can rely on depends on the level of education and adaptability of the workforce as well as the level of available technologies. For that reason, US President Bill Clinton, when first elected, anounced his strong emphasis on further improving the educational system of the country. The Swedish government, after having turned around the national budget to result in no more deficits, substantially increased their spending for educational purposes in 1998. From an international competition point of view, such actions are overdue because in the mid-1990s a higher proportion of students in Asia were taking courses in applied sciences and engineering than in the USA. How much Asian governments try to add future technological superiority to the familiar ingredients of their recent economic success – education and adaptability – is shown in the Future Issues box.

National Security. To ensure national security, many countries not only build up armed forces, thereby creating large markets for weapon manufacturers, but many governments are also anxious to be able to acquire the weapons they need inside their own borders. For example, given shrinking defence budgets owing to the 'calamity of peace' and the need to reap economies of scale, Europe's defence industry has to consolidate. But for national security reasons, governments do not want to see technologies leave the country. Therefore, France's government, for example, decided that Thomson-CSF, Europe's number one in defence electronics, should be merged

FUTURE ISSUES BOX

The Asian Technological Offensive

THE AVAILABILITY OF LATEST TECHNOLOGIES WILL BE A significant factor of influence on a country's prosperity in the future. Therefore, updating their domestic industries has become a priority for many governments in Asia. The Chinese government, for example, has been particularly insistent that foreign companies must bring their technology with them. One of the companies it has leant on is Motorola, which opened a USD720 million computer-chip plant in north-eastern China. As Wu Jichuan, the Chinese telecommunications minister said: 'Motorola has earned quite a lot of money in the mobile telephone market in China. It's high time for them to transfer some technology.' Other high tech firms planning to manufacture in China will have to transfer their technology, too.

Taiwan's Hsinchu Park is an example of intelligent government intervention. It was set up in 1980 with the aim of luring back Taiwanese technologists from Silicon Valley. Companies were offered low rents, a five-year tax holiday and a promise (which the government kept) that they would be let alone. In 1996 the government broke even on the project's USD40 million-a-year running costs.

The Hsinchu companies employ 42,000 people, and spend around 5.5 per cent of their total sales on research and development (against a national average of 1 per cent). Productivity at the park's semiconductor factories is around 50 per cent higher than those at US chip makers (excluding Intel). The park's occupants include not only Acer but firms such as Taiwan Semiconductor Manufacturing Company, the world's biggest chip foundry, and Microelectronics Technology, a small firm which is a pioneer in satellite communication. A second park now being planned may focus on biotechnology and micromachinery.

Source: 'Bits and bytes', *The Economist*, 9 March 1996, p. 20.

with Dassault Electronique and the military telecommunications unit of Alcatel. Together they will reach total sales of about USD9 billion which is rather small compared to their US competitors such as Lockheed-Martin or Raytheon-Hughes.[11] The political sensitivities of defence prevent cross-border alliances which might be economically meaningful, such as a merger between British Aerospace (BAe) and Dassault. Combined, the two firms would be about the same size as McDonnell Douglas which merged with Boeing in 1997 to improve their competitive market position.[12]

Protection of Cultural Identity

Each society has its specific rules of conduct which are transmitted from one generation to the next by socialization. Changes of rules that occur over time lead to more or less conflict between generations or interest groups. But when members of a society perceive that changes of behavioural norms come from outside, resistance is usually strongest. The example of resistance against fast food restaurants by some religious groups in India has shown how sensitive governments react to such 'foreign attacks on the cultural identity of their people.'

Such reactions are not limited to countries that are experiencing economic development. During the GATT negotiations of the Uruguay Round,

STRATEGY BOX

Central

European Media

CENTRAL EUROPEAN MEDIA, A HOLDING COMPANY FOR 11 Eastern European television stations bought its first TV licenses in 1993, in Prague and Berlin. Central European Media then added licenses in Hungary, Romania and Slovenia, in each case partnering with local entrepreneurs. In 1995 and 1996 the company bought licenses in the Slovak Republic, Ukraine, Poland and Germany.

Nova, the Czech TV station, launched in 1994, earned USD44 million in station operating income in 1996 on revenues of USD108 million. Such success did not come from the fact that Central European Media has the entire market to themselves. But they correctly sensed that the local regulators wanted their television to retain a local flavor, and not just provide new outlets for a Western media combine's old shows. At Central Media's Nova station in Prague, only a third of the programming is accounted for by made-in-Hollywood shows. Another 20 per cent or so of the programming comes from Europe, Canada and Australia. This leaves 49 per cent of Nova's airtime open for local shows, most of which Nova produces in its own studios. Pro TV in Romania, another of Central European Media's subsidiaries, produces between 40 and 50 per cent of its own local programs.

Pro TV claims a 50 per cent share in the 200 Romanian towns where it broadcasts. Nova has 65 per cent of the Prague market. Overall, Nova's local programs have about a third more viewers than foreign shows. As a consequence, multinational clients such as Unilever, IBM and Ford which spend approximately USD10 million a year on advertising in the Czech Republic, place most of that budget for ads on Nova.

Source: Gubernick, L. (1997), 'Chip off the old block,' *Forbes*, 24 February p. 103f.

European countries strongly resisted attempts by the USA to open up the markets for entertainment products entirely. Because of the dominance of US producers, they feared too much of an influence on the culture of their societies. A total 'Americanization' of life is definitely not wanted by most European governments, with the French leading the pack.

International marketers must be careful, therefore, to know exactly how far they can go, for example, in standardizing goods and services, distribution activities, and – most importantly – market communication. The Strategy box gives an example of how sensitive treatment of local needs to maintain certain constitutent parts of cultural identity can contribute to the business success of an international marketer.

INTERNATIONAL TRADE POLICY

The prevailing political interests in a country-market and the major political objectives of the governing forces determine the policies of government. The international trade policy of a country's government is a set of laws and rules that regulate the flow of goods and services across a country's borders. This policy provides a framework for exports, imports and foreign investment and therefore needs to be more closely analysed by the international marketer.

Export/Import Policy

All countries control exports and imports to some degree, providing both barriers to trade and support for certain domestically as well as foreign produced goods and services.

Export/Import Assistance.   One way to encourage trade between two countries is to use political relations as a means to establish contacts between companies from both countries. The German Economy Ministry, for example, brought the leaders of 125 medium-sized Chinese companies to Bonn to meet with German counterparts.

Another way to stimulate and assist exports is to provide **financial assistance** either directly or indirectly. The People's Insurance Co. of China (PICC), for example, is the country's agency responsible for the export credit insurance sector. PICC's 43 subsidiaries nationwide offer comprehensive export credit insurance and guarantees, export documentation insurance, and foreign investment insurance.[13] German Hermes Bank provides long-term low interest rate loans ('soft loans') to companies bidding for projects in industrially developing countries. Without such loans, many projects would not be financially viable, either for the customers or for the suppliers. The US Export-Import Bank (Eximbank) provides financial support to US exporters which allows those exporters to charge competitive prices. The Japanese approach of identifying key industries and then developing an export policy for those industries has proven particularly effective. The Japanese External Trade Organization (JETRO) has been so successful in implementing an agressive export promotion policy that the Japanese government has asked it to help marketers in other countries increase their exports to Japan.

Governments may also support international marketing of their industries by **refunding domestic taxes** to exporters. This policy is often found in countries which rely heavily on exports. Commonly, value added taxes on supplies are refunded to domestic producers, giving them an advantage over competitors from countries with sales taxes that are not refunded. Another commonly rebated tax is the import duty on items such as component parts for machinery intended for re-exportation. The US government applies lower tax rates to profits generated through exports by permitting the creation of foreign sales companies (FSCs). These are corporations that are not located in a US customs zone. An FSC is allowed to export products and pay little or no income tax on those sales, thereby increasing its profits or price competitiveness considerably.

Sometimes governments support imports of particular goods or services. The EU and Japan as well as the USA have import-support programmes that offer **tariff preferences** for selected products from industrially less developed countries, in order to stimulate their economies. Normally, when these products are viewed as fully competitive, they no longer qualify for import support and the tariff structure is changed. In India, a company that exports at least 80 per cent of its products is considered an 'Export only unit' (EOU). Such EOUs are allowed to import raw materials without paying tariffs. In addition, all goods purchased in India by such companies are exempt from taxes during the first eight to ten years of the company's existence. In the first five years after their establishment, EOUs do not pay taxes on profits left in India. Profits transferred outside the country are subject to a 20 per cent tax.[14]

Trade Barriers. Barriers to trade include tariffs, non-tariff barriers and trade embargoes or sanctions. **Tariffs** have traditionally been used as barriers to international trade. They either protect domestic industries by raising prices to non-competitive levels or compensate for subsidies by governments to their exporters. In the last decade of the twentieth century, international trade liberalization has led to a significant reduction of tariff barriers. But they still exist. The USA, for example, has especially demanded market-opening measures from Europe and Japan in various fields such as telecommunications, entertainment or agricultural products. Japan for its part has responded positively in some cases, such as the total abolition of import tariffs related to automobiles, while the USA itself still imposes a small import duty on passenger cars and a 25 per cent duty on commercial-use cars, one of the highest in the world.[15]

Non-tariff barriers to international trade are government laws, regulations, policies or practices that protect domestic producers from foreign competition. Because trade liberalization has progressed through GATT (WTO) and international economic cooperation agreements, governments are using non-tariff barriers to protect some of their countries' industries which they think are unable to endure free international competition. Table 4.1 lists some of the most popular non-tariff barriers applied.

Sometimes international marketers are confronted with an unpredictable manner in which a country's tariff administration classifies its products. Such **arbitrary product classification** may strongly affect the tariff status of the export product. In India, for example, international investors are officially supposed to pay a 20 per cent import duty on equipment. But because of imprecise legal regulations, in reality, the tariff ends up being not 20 per cent but whatever the customs inspector wants it to be on the day the firm's products arrive.[16]

Import quotas are quantitative restrictions on imports that may be expressed as individual units imported or as a total value of imports. Such quotas are commonly imposed on an annual basis. Austria, for example, imposed import quotas on cement from the Czech Republic and Slovakia, decreasing over the years. The reason given was that unrestricted low-priced imports from those countries would destroy the Austrian cement industry. It needed some time for restructuring, in particular because competition was 'unfair' considering that the Czech and Slovakian firms did not have to obey the same cost-driving regulations concerning environmental protection as their Austrian counterparts. One effect of such quotas is that international marketers try to make their deals during the first months of each year, as long as the quota is not yet met and all imports cease. Promotion, inventory and financing have to be managed accordingly. Another effect is retaliation by the affected country's government. They also impose quotas on certain products until the first mover steps back from its errected barriers.

Import licence requirements may exist in the form of restrictions on the number of foreign companies allowed to enter a country-market or without limitation on the number of firms but with the obligation to apply for an import licence for each business contract. Owing to bureaucratic delays, it may take years to obtain the right to import. For example, Dornier, the

Table 4.1 POPULAR NON-TARIFF BARRIERS TO INTERNATIONAL TRADE

NON-TARIFF BARRIERS TO INTERNATIONAL TRADE

Arbitrary product classification
Import quotas
Import licence requirements
Export licence requirements
Discriminatory government procurement contracts
Port-of-entry requirements
Local content requirements

Governments are very creative when it comes to the invention or virtuous use of non-tariff barriers to protect their countries' industries from international competition. This list contains some of the most popular non-tariff barriers in international trade.

German manufacturer of weaving machines, had to prove that no producer in India could make the same kind of machine in order to receive an import licence. To circumvent this restriction, which would have forced the company to disclose its technological know-how in a country where intellectual property rights are not well protected, Dornier decided to enter into a joint venture with an Indian producer.

In service industries, government permission may be needed to operate in a country-market. For example, Econet, a Zimbabwe-based telecommunications firm in which Telecel International, a US firm, had a 40 per cent stake, was all ready to start operations in 1996. It had built a base station and switching centre in Harare, the capital of Zimbabwe; it had USD3 million of mobile phones sitting in warehouses or containers; and 5000 subscribers had already signed up. But Zimbabwe's government did not stop trying to prevent them from operating. Econet had already won two court cases: the first eliminated the government's claim to a monopoly on all telecoms; the second upheld Econet's claim to be able to install a cellular network under the constitutional right to freedom of expression. Not content, President Mugabe issued a proclamation in February 1996 making it illegal for anybody to operate a cellular network without state permission. Econet's foreign contractors, fearing imprisonment, have stopped working; Telecel International has withdrawn its stake.

Most goods need no licence to be exported from their country of production. But exports of some products that might affect national security or are in limited supply are controlled. For example, exports of products and technologies related to nuclear power are restricted because of concern about the proliferation of nuclear weapons. For such sensitive goods, or goods exported to politically sensitive countries, a validated, written **export licence** must be obtained after appropriate governmental agencies, such as the Departments of Commerce and Defense in the USA, have been consulted. Such policies allow suppliers from other countries that do not prohibit such trade to gain contracts they would not have obtained otherwise. For example, after the war against Iraq, the Iranian government wanted to finish construction of two nuclear power plants that German suppliers had begun building before the war started. When neither Western industrialized countries nor Japan were ready to allow any of their firms to bid for the contract because of fears that the Iranians could use the radiant material of those power stations for military purposes, the Russian nuclear power industry stepped in and finished the plants.

Another non-tariff barrier that is popular among governments and public administrations is **discriminatory government procurement contracts**, that is, discrimination against foreign suppliers in bidding for government contracts. Such a policy reflects the desire to spend public funds in the domestic economy. In industrialized countries, the large volume of public expenditures makes the economic impact of such barriers to international suppliers significant. For example, 'Buy America' rules oblige the US Defense Department to purchase many kinds of defence equipment at home. Even when a foreign weapon is chosen, it must be made in the USA. In the EU, discrimination against suppliers from other EU member states is illegal. Another example of such illegal discrimination would be the use of bidding deadlines that are too short to be met by suppliers from another country.

Sometimes imports to a country are only allowed when using a specific harbour or airport or a specific customs office. In most cases, such **port-of-entry requirements** are accompanied by **taxes or levies** that are placed on the use of those facilities. The official purpose of such regulations has traditionally been to finance the development of transportation infrastructure and to streamline bureaucratic infrastructure for specific customs purposes. However, the taxes often endure well past the time necessary to offset the original capital cost, are often higher than operating costs would indicate, and centralized customs activities are located in places where international marketers have logistical disadvantages. The French government, for example, some time before the EU made such actions impossible, centralized all customs activities concerning the import of consumer electronics at Poitiers, a city in the middle of France well away from any port or border of the country.

Finally, governments may impose **local content requirements** on international marketers wanting to sell their products in the local market. Such requirements are typically expressed as a certain percentage of a product's total value added that must be produced in the host country to get an import licence or to avoid high tariffs. For example, the Thai government requires local content of 60 per cent for pickup trucks and 54 per cent for passenger cars. Tenders for the construction of industrial plants or for big infrastructure projects in industrially developing countries, as another example, generally contain such local content clauses. They are intended to force some technology transfer, to provide some degree of domestic employment, and to improve the country's balance of payments position. Local content requirements may be fulfilled, for example, by the local acquisition of component parts, the use of local construction services, or local product assembly. But because local suppliers in many cases may be less reliable than suppliers in the international marketer's home market, it may be necessary to bring those suppliers to the new market as part of the total operation. For example, 70 out of 107 suppliers of Japan's Honda in Thailand are joint venture operations with Japanese companies.[17]

Investment Policy

A government can either support or deter foreign investment. A country's investment policy consists of all general rules that govern legislation concerning domestic as well as foreign participation in the equity or ownership of businesses and other organizations of that country. All products that need a great deal of customer participation in their production process, such as most services, cannot be exported, that is, produced in one country and consumed or used in another country. A hotel, a telecommunications network or a retailing outlet, for example, must be located where their customers want to use them. They are therefore more concerned about the investment policies of governments in the potential country-markets than about those governments' international trade policies.

A government's policy towards investment reflects its market orientation. Each policy will be located between the two extremes of no private investment and only private investment. Consequently, international marketers assessing various country-markets for their attractiveness will need to consider the governments' policies concerning foreign direct investments, subsidies, take-overs, and general operating conditions.

Foreign Direct Investments.   Foreign direct investment occurs when a company invests in a subsidiary or joint venture with a partner firm in a foreign market. An example is Nissan's USD660 million investment in an automobile assembly plant in Smyrna, Tennessee. In contrast to financial investments in stocks, bonds, or funds deposited in a bank, which are generally left alone by the investor, foreign direct investment entails some degree of control by the investor.

This control by the foreign investor makes many governments nervous when the stakes become important. In the USA, for example, there is growing concern about the economic impact of foreign multinational corporations, such as Japanese auto makers or European food producers. In the case of Nissan's assembly plant in Tennessee, maintenance of the company's traditional supplier relationships has a dual impact. First, new jobs are created as Nissan's Japanese suppliers develop production facilities near the new plant to meet Nissan's 'just-in-time' delivery requirements. Second, US parts suppliers are excluded from these special arrangements, and a larger portion of automobile industry profits go to foreign investors. Some politicians claim that this pattern represents 'creeping colonialization'; others maintain that the jobs created by foreign investment are important to the economy.

In Europe very similar discussions concerning the heavy investments of US multinational firms took place in the early 1970s. But in the meantime, most of these multinational corporations have proven to behave as 'good citizens' not misusing their potential to the disadvantage of the host countries. In the 1990s there was even some competition among European countries to attract international partners for firms in need of financial and market restructuring and for foreign investors to improve the competitive position of the countries' industries. Foreign investments in the Eastern European countries have injected much-needed capital for improving the technological level of production facilities. Foreign investments also served to improve company and brand reputation and to establish greater credibility with customers and financiers.[18]

Problems may arise when radical shareholder-value-based decisions lead to the closing of subsidiaries without appropriate social plans for the personnel concerned. For example, the announcement of the shutdown of French Renault's Vilvord production plant in Belgium without prior negotiation of a social plan with personnel representatives not only provoked demonstrations in Paris but also a ruling of the European Court in Luxembourg declaring the Renault decision illegal.

Governments of industrially developing countries encourage foreign investment in an attempt to increase employment and domestic economic growth, but at the same time they are anxious to control the foreign investors' influence on the local economy. Malaysia, for example, allows only companies that export 50 per cent or more of their production to be up to 100 per cent foreign-owned. Vietnam, in a similar attempt, has licensed 14 foreign auto makers to compete for the market, after originally saying it would license only four. In Indonesia, Pertamina, the state-owned petroleum company, is an automatic partner in every oil and gas project under a system that calls for sharing production after developers of fields, such as Enron Development Corp. from the USA, have recovered their costs.[19]

One of the most effective deterrents to foreign investment in a country is the non-existence of clear regulations, too complicated or unstable regulations, and the very slow handling of bureaucratic work related to those regulations. For example, it took Houston-based Enron Corp. five years to be able to start building its USD2.5 billion liquified-natural-gas power plant in India. The company had to reverse a cancellation of its contract, secure approvals from three successive governments, and win 24 lawsuits.[20] In another example, US-based Amoco Corp. scrapped plans to invest USD1 billion in a methane-gas project because negotiations with the government dragged on too long. Though the project was approved by New Delhi in September 1994, it was still awaiting a key agreement on commercial terms in 1996. Among the pending matters, the company had demanded a clear legal title to the gas it extracted and assurance that the tax treatment would remain constant for the duration of the project. Lack of progress with the Coal Ministry prompted Amoco to give up the right to extract gas from a coal field in the eastern states of Bihar and West Bengal. Instead the company decided to explore methane fields in Australia, China, Poland and South Africa, where terms were completed faster.[21]

Subsidies.   Subsidies are payments made by local authorities (governments of states, provinces or cities) and regional institutions, such as the EU administration, to local and international firms in an attempt to improve either the competitive position of the firm or the attractiveness of a location to the investor. When governments subsidize local companies it is mainly to keep those firms in existence. The EU has forbidden any subsidies that lead to a distortion of competition in an industry. Nevertheless, member countries such as Italy, France, Greece and Spain have managed to keep their national airlines alive through subsidies. From 1991 to 1997, European governments spent USD5 milion per day keeping their national carriers' planes in the air.[22]

Governments offer subsidies to international marketers to attract their direct investments. Again, the EU has made subsidies that distort international competition illegal. Companies that have received such aid to their investment are forced to pay back the amount received. But there are various areas inside the EU – so-called E1 areas – which are considered economically less developed than the rest. In such areas, limited subsidies may be given to firms ready to invest. There may even be additional subsidies available from EU development budgets.

Where no direct subsidies are allowed, governments have found indirect ways to attract interesting international marketers. There is a kind of race among European governments as to which country is able to provide the most attractive taxation system to its own industries, but in particular to international investors. For some time Ireland was the champion, but other governments have managed to follow them closely. As a result, taxes on capital and capital revenue have steadily decreased in Europe over recent years.

A special case is so-called 'tax havens' such as the Bahamas, the Channel Islands, Liechtenstein and Monaco. Because they have low corporate tax rates, companies establish subsidiaries in such countries – they are sometimes no more than a 'letterbox' – and use transfer pricing to remit as much profit as they can to the low-tax-rate subsidiary. That is, they charge licensing and consultancy fees, for example, or they play the role of the international sales headquarters buying products at very low prices from the production subsidiaries of the firm. Of course, governments in the other countries that such companies are serving attempt to tax these funds.

Economically developing countries which do not possess enough free capital for direct payments subsidize foreign investments by offering tax breaks over substantial amounts of time, or the provision of energy and water at a subsidized rate. However, international marketers should keep in mind that capital invested and taxes are two important factors of influence on their market choice, but not the only ones to be considered.

Take-overs.   In opposition to subsidies to attract foreign investment, local governments sometimes take over foreign-owned firms. Such take-overs can take the form of confiscation, expropriation or domestication. Confiscation takes place when a company's assets are taken over without any compensation payment. In cases of expropriation, the government taking over the business operation offers some kind of compensation. In most cases, however, the compensation is too little, too late. Domestication may take the form of the forced sale of a dominant part of the firm to locals, the placement of local personnel in leading hierarchical positions, and/or the forced procurement of local supplies. Expropriation and domestication affect a firm very differently. With expropriation, the company suddenly loses all control over its assets. With domestication, the firm usually has enough time to manage the transfer of ownership or dominant influence in a systematic way.

Since competition has become increasingly global, most governments have understood that their countries' economic well-being at least partly depends on international investments. Because such investments will not take place under the continual threat of potential government take-overs, this kind of hostile intervention has become very rare. In some countries led by dictators and a small group of people in power that splits most of the country's wealth, the risk of take-overs may still exist. For example, in Zimbabwe the government has introduced legislation that no longer allows the ownership of land by companies. This means that agricultural firms with foreign capital majority ownership can no longer exist.

Operating Conditions.   Another important factor of influence on direct investment decisions is the operating conditions in a country-market. Governments have a significant influence on those conditions. For example, in mid-1995 Mercedes announced plans to produce minivans in China. Among the hitches apparently hindering Mercedes in realizing that USD1 billion plan is China's demand that production be split between factories in Guangzhou and Hainan Island, hundreds of kilometres away.[23] Before the economic crisis hit Southeast Asia, the minimum wage for an auto worker set by the Thai government was 10 000 baht a month, at that time about one-tenth the wage in

Japan. Engineers earned up to 15 000 baht a day. Benefits included family medical care, free bus transportation to and from work, a uniform, lunch, and 12 days of vacation.[24] Any potential foreign investor assessing the attractiveness of a country must gather such information to come up with a rational evaluation of given opportunities versus problems to be encountered.

Trade Sanctions

Besides the more long-term and stable political orientation expressed through laws and regulations, the international trade of and with a country is also influenced by much more spontaneous intergovernmental relations. They are often reactions to specific events which are difficult for the international marketer to anticipate. But they may have a significant impact on its business opportunities.

The USA, as the world's leading military and economic power, has in recent years increasingly used trade sanctions in an attempt to punish governments whose policies or actions the US government perceives to be hostile. For example, the shooting down by Cuban military forces of a private US airplane which had intruded into Cuba's territory led to the Helms-Burton act, designed to punish US as well as foreign companies 'trafficking' in property confiscated after the 1959 Cuban revolution. An action has to be initiated by aggrieved US individuals or companies. The D'Amato act, also signed in 1996, bans US and companies from other countries dealing with Iran (because the Iranian government allegedly supports international terrorist activities) and Libya (because the government is not ready to hand over two men suspected to be responsible for the bombing of a transatlantic flight). The act involves the US government: the president is required to impose at least two out of six sanctions on any company that invests more than USD40 million a year in the gas and petroleum industries of either Iran or Libya. Sanctions also apply to the export to Libya of goods or technology that would help Libyan aviation or the country's efforts to acquire weapons of mass destruction.

Potentially, the later legislation is more threatening to non-US companies because the investments are bigger: in 1995, France's Total signed a USD600 million deal to develop oil fields in Iran; Italy's Agip was planning a gas pipeline for Libya; and Spain's Repsol, Belgium's Petrofina, Austria's OMV and Germany's Veba all have business in one or both of the two countries.[25] As a result, Europeans and Japanese, who also depend very much on external sources of energy, were angered. They protested against the 'extraterritorial' measures at the World Trade Organization. And while most Arab governments have no affection at all for Iran or Libya, some are disturbed by the vehemence of the American campaign.

In addition, lately states and cities across the USA have started imposing sanctions on international trade and investments. According to the National Association of Manufacturers, in 1997, trade and investment with 35 countries that buy a fifth of the world's USD4 trillion annual exports were subject to US penalties of some sort. And the trend was accelerating. For example, Boston, Massachusetts joined a group of US cities – from Oakland, California, to Ann Arbor, Michigan – in imposing trade sanctions on companies trading with Myanmar in 1996. The measures ban or penalize bidding for public contracts.[26]

The question is whether such sanctions really do what their authors expect them to do. They surely drive most US companies out of the sanctioned country-markets. For example, US federal authorities charged equipment maker Case Corp. with violating US law by participating in the sale of excavators and other heavy construction machinery from Case's foreign affiliate in France for use in Libya's Great Man-Made River Project. This USD25 billion venture, begun in 1984, is the Libyan government's effort to pump some two million cubic metres of water daily from an aquifer beneath the Sahara Desert more than 1000 miles north to the Mediterranean coast. The network of underground pipes and reservoirs is an attempt to become more self-sufficient in food production and lessen Libya's reliance on imports. But under 1986 presidential orders, US citizens and companies are prohibited from performing 'any contract in support of industrial or other commercial or government projects in Libya.'[27] The withdrawal of Case Corp. and other US companies from the sanctioned country-markets results in business opportunities for other firms. Some companies are handed contracts on a plate while the offending government goes unpunished. For example, only one week after Bill Clinton had signed the D'Amato act, the Islamic Republic of Iran signed a deal, supposedly worth more than USD20 billion over 23 years, to sell natural gas to Turkey. The deal does not contravene the USA's new rules, the Turks can argue: it is not investment, merely trade.[28]

THE LEGAL ENVIRONMENT

When government policies are turned into formal rules and regulations, they are known as laws. The legal environment of a company is the set of laws and systems which enforce those laws, established by a society to govern its members' behaviour. When international marketers are assessing the political and legal viability of potential markets, it is important that they consider certain aspects of the legal environment relevant to their product-market. The generally most important considerations will be discussed in the following section.

International Business Law

There is no international business law in a formal sense. Traditionally, courts, laws and regulatory agencies have been national, not international, in scope. No agreed-upon regulations have existed that can be always applied to international business relations. Current laws vary considerably, sometimes in what seem to be quite silly ways. For example, it is illegal to send soap to Paraguay through the US mail. Even the terms under which parties to a contract can be released through an 'act of God' differ considerably in different countries. This distinction is important, because an 'act of God' normally releases a party from having to fulfil the terms of a contract. Thus, a labour strike might be viewed as an 'act of God' in some countries but not in others, where strikes are considered predictable and manageable.

There are some treaties and agreements among countries that provide frameworks and guidelines for business relations, but by and large the international marketer must work with different legal systems in different local markets. For example, in 1994, 22 banks ranging from Citibank of the USA to Barclays Bank of the UK and Rabobank of the Netherlands, took Kunnan Enterprise Ltd, the Taiwanese manufacturer of golf clubs and rackets, to bankruptcy court. Losses in 1994 were USD132 million, and the firm's liabilities exceeded assets. But one and a half years later, the owner and chairman of the company, Mr Kunnan Lo, was still in charge. Taiwanese law on the subject of who should run a company while creditors' claims are being heard is vague. The Securities and Exchange Commission argued for Mr Kunnan to be sidelined. But other voices emphasized his service to Taiwanese industry. The haggling and delays in Taiwan contrast with events in Hong Kong, where the banks initiated similar proceedings against Kunnan-related companies. The courts appointed an accounting firm to oversee their affairs while arguments were being heard.[29]

In view of the many differences, it is very important for a company that plans to internationalize its served markets to employ international legal counsel in making business decisions.[30] The Culture box gives an example of how cultural differences may influence the perception of proper conduct.

Legal Systems.   A country's legal system determines the rules that govern the conduct of business in that country as well as the norms and standards that goods and services have to fulfil. A major reason for differences among national legal systems is their legal heritage. Australia, Canada, New Zealand, the UK the USA and some other countries have legal systems based on **common law**, which is an outgrowth of English law. **Code law**, which is found in many countries with no Anglo-Saxon traditions, is based on Roman law. **Socialist law** and **Islamic law** are based on a different set of codes entirely. To further complicate matters, many countries have more than one set of laws. In code-law countries as well as in the USA, for example, laws may be commercial, civil or criminal. In most common-law countries, such distinctions are not made.

Under common law, precedent is critical in resolving any given issue. In reaching a decision, the court will examine existing laws and regulations, customary procedures, and previous cases dealing with similar issues. Under code law, in contrast, formal laws spell out precisely what constitutes proper behaviour, although sometimes some interpretation is required.

An example of the potential impact of these differences on international marketing can be seen in the case of rights to brand names and other intellectual property such as patents or publishing rights. Under common law, prior use is the most significant determinant in deciding who has the right to use a specific brand name. But under code law, whoever registers a brand name first controls the rights to it. Thus, in a code-law country, a company that uses a brand name first does not necessarily have the legal right to continue doing so. Anyone could register the same name. A company that wants to enter a market in a code-law country might have to purchase the rights to its 'own' brand name or even operate under a different brand name.

The legal system of socialist countries is based on a different view of society. In societies based on capitalism, each individual has the freedom to pursue his or her best interests, and legal regulations are made to indicate the rules of the game. The central principle underlying **socialist law**, in no matter what country, although it varies in the degree applied, is that the needs of the larger society dominate individual needs. For example, the idea of property varies from a strongly socialist country, for example North Korea, where no private ownership of the means of production and intellectual products is allowed, compared to a West European code-law country, for example Norway, where everybody may own capital goods and private intellectual property is protected.

CULTURE BOX

Flirting
with Danger

WHEN SWEDISH PHARMACEUTICAL COMPANY ASTRA AB learned about wide-ranging sexual harassment allegations against the chief executive of its US subsidiary, the company suspended him and two top-ranking managers. But Mitsubishi Motor Manufacturing of America Inc., faced with charges of pervasive sexual harassment by the US Equal Employment Opportunity Commission, has maintained that the agency is wrong and mounted a full-scale public-relations campaign to discredit complainers, even paying employees to picket the EEOC offices to protest the suit.

In strikingly similar circumstances, two companies operating in the US have reacted very differently to harassment charges, a perilous area in which laws and societal norms are rapidly changing – and exposing companies to more liability.

Both companies lacked a clear and strong written policy on harassment. They reflected a poor understanding of the legal, financial and public-relations liabilities involved in the issue. In the US Astra's three-paragraph policy was so brief that it failed to even define sexual harass-ment. While Mitsubishi's policy included an adequate definition and statement of management's philosophy, the policy suffered from a lack of discussion of social functions. What may have been the reasons?

A cultural gap is partly to blame. Neither Sweden nor Japan, for example, have laws that specifically define or prohibit sexual harassment, though victims can file charges under other laws. The relevant Swedish act passed in 1991. In Europe, women are beginnng to complain about harassment at work. But even the most outrageous acts do not bring settlements on a par with the US, largely because most European judges and juries do not grant the kind of huge awards for 'pain and suffering' seen in the US. In Japan, sexual harassment is still very much seen as a joke.

Still, those familiar with European countries point out that the dearth of specific laws proscribing sexual harassment does not mean that European women let the men walk all over them. It is less handwringing and more 'right-back-in-your-face, buddy'. The apparent difference stems in part from the fact that Europeans are far more reluctant than US Americans to go to court. Instead, Europeans tend to resolve such workplace issues through negotiations between trade unions and employers.

Source: Johannes, L., J.S. Lublin, B. Coleman and V. Reitman (1996), 'Flirting With Danger, Sex-Harassment Cases Trip Up Foreign Firms Operating in the US', *The Wall Street Journal Europe*, 10–11 May, pp. 1 and 6.

As the formerly communist and centrally controlled economies of Eastern Europe develop into full market economies, their socialist law systems which governed them for decades change too. A legal system is not quickly or easily changed, however. There are too many interdependent regulations to change, and law makers, courts and lawyers need to learn to think in different terms. For that reason, the Commission of the European Community has admonished the first Eastern European candidates, the Czech Republic, Hungary, Poland, Slovenia and Estonia, to work hard on the needed changes in their legal systems before they can become members of the community.

Islamic law, or Shariah ('God's rules'), is a form of code law. Its major

Exhibit 4.1 International Treaties and Conventions Dealing with Property Rights

Several international treaties and conventions address the problem of property rights. This table illustrates several of them.

Berne Convention

The Berne Convention created a union of nations in 1886 to protect literary and artistic works. Seventy-four nations are members of the union, including most European countries and some Asian, African and Latin American nations. The principal non-members are the United States, Russia and China.

The convention stipulates:

1. A work whose country of origin is in the union receives the same protection by other union members as is conferred on works of that country's nationals.
2. The enjoyment of protection in countries other than the country of origin is automatic and subject to no registration formalities.
3. The protection of an author's work does not rest upon whether it is protected in his home country.

The Berne Convention is administered by the World Intellectual Property Organization (WIPO) in Geneva, a specialized agency of the union.

Universal Copyright Convention (UCC)

The United Nations Education and Social Council (UNESCO) administers this major copyright convention, established in 1952. The purpose of the convention is to link countries with high levels of copyright protection, from the Berne Convention, with those of limited protection, as well as to secure the membership of the United States in an international copyright system. The UCC seeks to protect the rights of authors of literary, scientific and artistic works. UCC member nations are required to accord the same protection to foreign works as to their own.

International Convention for the Protection of Performers, Producers of Phonograms, and Broadcasting Organizations (Rome Convention)

This convention originated in 1964 and is jointly administrated by the International Labour Organization (ILO), UNESCO and WIPO. Only 23 nations have joined; Germany and the United Kingdom are its leading members. This convention, like the Berne and UCC conventions, requires the same protection for foreign as for national works. The convention seeks to protect performances, sound recordings, and broadcasts, but not films, which are protected by the Berne and UCC conventions.

Convention for the Protection of Producers of Phonograms against Unauthorized Duplication of their Phonograms (Geneva Convention)

Adopted by an international meeting in 1974 in Geneva, there are 36 member nations. Three important nations who signed this convention, but not the Rome Convention, are France, Japan and the United States. This convention seeks to limit record piracy, that is, duplicating records without permission. The convention requires that member nations protect sound-recording producers from other member nations against duplication and importation for distribution to the public. As with the Rome Convention, if the nation's domestic law prescribes formalities prior to protection, these are fulfilled if all authorized duplicates issued to the public bear the 'P' notice.

Convention Relating to the Distribution of Program-carrying Signals Transmitted by Satellite (Satellite Convention)

This convention was established at Brussels in 1974 and is administrated jointly by UNESCO and WIPO. Seven nations are members. The convention seeks to prevent satellite piracy or the transmission and distribution of 'poached signals' to unlicensed audiences. Member states are to prevent unauthorized distribution of a signal in their territory.

Multilateral Convention for Avoidance of Double Taxation of Copyright Royalties (Madrid Convention)

Established in 1979, only four states have signed this convention. It does not require compliance with certain minimum standards of protection; rather, it prescribes a model bilateral agreement for member nations to prevent double taxation.

Hague Agreement Concerning International Deposit of Industrial Rights

This convention enables an international application for design protection to be regarded as the equivalent of a national application. Membership is restricted to Paris Convention members. The agreement is effected by deposit of a sample registered at WIPO by a national of a member state. That deposit is then regarded by all member nations as if the formalities of the domestic laws of those nations have been met.

Paris Convention for Protection of Industrial Property

The basic principle is national treatment for patents and trademarks for all member nations. The principal advantage of the convention is that it allows persons who have sought protection (registration) in one member nation priority in another member nation for six months for trademarks and one year for patents.

Nice Agreement Concerning the International Classification of Goods and Services for the Registration of Marks

This provides a system of common classification of goods and services to use in the registration of trademarks. It does not bind member nations who may use it, or not, as they wish.

Trademark Registration Treaty

With only five members, this treaty provides for the international registration of trademarks.

Patent Co-operation Treaty (PCT)

This treaty is an agreement to provide for international cooperation in patent law and, especially, procedures to obtain patent protection. It was established in Washington, DC, in 1970 and has 32 members, including the United States, Russia, United Kingdom and France. It is administered by the WIPO.
Principal features include:

1. An application filed in one's national patent office will extend to as many PCT countries as the applicant may designate.
2. The application is researched and findings are sent to each designated national patent office.

The PCT thus facilitates examination of a patent in a national office, although it does not prescribe what each nation's substantive patent law should be.

International Patent Classification (Strasbourg Agreement)

This agreement was established in 1971 and has 27 member nations. It seeks to have a universal system of patent classifications and certificates. This is aimed not at the patent law of a nation, but to facilitate its administration.

Sources: Adapted from S. Ricketson (1984) *The Law of Intellectual Property*, Law Book Company; and J. Lahore (1977) *Intellectual Property Law in Australia*, Sydney: Butterworths.

distinguishing characteristic is that it is directly based on religious interpretations of the Koran and the Sunna. Even more than a code system, Islamic law governs all dimensions of human behaviour, and is extensively concerned with defining moral conduct. Pakistan, for example, introduced legislation in early 1991 that would make the Koran the supreme law, and bring all aspects of life, including social codes and civil liberties, under the law of Islam.

Two concepts in Islamic law directly affect international marketers, especially of financial services. They are based on the prohibition of gambling in the Koran. One is 'riba', which prohibits unearned profits. A common interpretation is that interest cannot be charged. Instead, 'fees' paid by a borrower are charged in order to compensate the lender for its services. The second concept is 'gharar', which prohibits unanticipated gain or profit. Thus contracts with organizations that operate under Islamic law must be very careful to spell out all outcomes and expectations.[31]

Agreements and Conventions. It would be easier, of course, if there were a standard legal system that applied to all countries. But for that purpose, governments would have to give up considerable political sovereignty. Nevertheless, faced with the reality of growing economic interdependence, many countries have signed multinational agreements and conventions to give some degree of consistency to the international legal environment. One of the great values of the EU, in fact, is the ongoing attempt to standardize laws and regulations among members. The European Commission has produced some hundreds of directives that have been more or less quickly transformed into national law by the member states' legislators, but which lead to a certain standardization of laws and regulations across the EU. To give a simple example, the EU has managed to put in place only one customs form for shipment among member countries, replacing the close to 60 forms a shipper used to have to fill out for the same trip.

Legal agreement among countries may be bilateral, such as the agreement between France and the USA that helps prevent double taxation of firms and personnel doing business in both countries. Or they may be part of a multilateral understanding like the Paris Convention, which established a patent-filing process that covers patent applications in 80 countries. If an application is filed in one member state, that company has priority over companies filing similar applications in all member countries for up to 12 months. Other multilateral conventions and agreements are illustrated in Exhibit 4.1.

Extraterritoriality. A particular aspect of a firm's international legal environment that can give rise to problems is the extraterritoriality of national law: the laws of the home country govern the operations of a company, including its subsidiaries or sales offices located in another country. Extraterritoriality creates a double legal standard. A practice that is legal in a host country may be illegal in the home country. To take just one example, in Hong Kong it is legal to discuss prices with a competitor; in the USA it is not. Thus, international marketers must be concerned not only about having to operate under more than one legal system but also with the fit between different systems.

The Court System. Just as there is no international business law, there is no international court system. The International Court of Justice, located in The Hague in the Netherlands, provides a forum in which countries can air their political grievances. And the European Court in Luxembourg applies uniform legal standards to all members of the EU. Member countries now follow the European Court's interpretations in applying national law. This court is thus functioning as a supreme court for the EU.

Such situations are unusual, however. More commonly, the problems caused by the lack of international business law are confounded by the lack of courts to hear international cases. Companies facing international legal action encounter difficulties similar to those faced by Union Carbide after the tragic chemical leak at its plant in Bhopal, India. The company had to defend itself against lawsuits related to the loss of over 2000 lives as a result of the accident. The plaintiffs preferred to bring these suits in US courts, where penalties and fines are much stiffer than in India.

Host-country courts often exhibit bias against foreign companies, particularly in countries where nationalism is running high or there is a history of exploitation by multinational companies. A company that loses a case in a host-country court has little recourse. About all it can do is attempt to influence intergovernmental relations in the hope of getting the ruling overturned. Only large firms with ample resources are in a position to exercise such influence.

Regulation of Competition

Deregulation of Markets.   Governments differ in the extent to which they regulate competition. Following the examples of the UK and the USA, all industrially developed countries have begun to deregulate their markets. That is, governments tend to decrease the number and specificity of regulations concerning competition. For example, in 1996, EU ministers agreed to open the electricity industry to competition – albeit only a little. The gas industry is next on the EU's agenda. The UK example, where big customers have been allowed to choose between competing gas suppliers for several years, indicates the consequences to be expected. British Gas, the former monopoly, has seen its share of the industrial and commercial gas market shrink to 35 per cent. British gas prices are among the lowest in Europe, whereas in Italy the monopoly SNAM posted 1995 earnings before tax of USD1.9 billion, or nearly 20 per cent of its annual sales.[32]

When governments are more or less forced to agree with international deregulation but do not accept its impact on local industries, they try to find loopholes in the deregulation agreements. For example, the deregulation of air travel in Europe as of April 1997 has given European airlines the opportunity to fly between any two cities in the European Union. But at Europe's major slot-controlled airports, governments can limit the number of slots to keep competition out. Airlines cannot buy and sell slots without approval. As a reaction, British Airways has acquired Paris-based TAT European Airlines and Air Liberté, largely for access to their slots at Orly airport.[33]

Examples from the telecommunications business show that large companies such as US-based AT&T, Germany's Deutsche Telecom and British Telecom are often better equipped to move quickly into recently deregulated markets. They have the resources needed to acquire smaller firms or business units of other firms in international markets or to set up joint ventures with local partners. Small and medium-sized companies may find international niche opportunities, or can successfully form a joint venture with an internationally operating partner.

Antitrust Controls.   Deregulation of markets only leads to increased competition if the new players in the industry are prevented from taking a dominant position that allows them to control the market. Antitrust commissions in the deregulating countries, therefore, are having a close look at every merger or acquisition that risks resulting in market dominance. One example that raised a lot of controversy is the merger between Boeing and McDonnel Douglas. The two companies together hold 70 per cent of the world market in commercial passenger planes, and through their access to US military contracts they have large funds for research and development. For that reason, the European Commission only accepted the merger when Boeing abandoned its exclusive supply contracts with major airlines and firmly promised not to force its suppliers away from delivering to other aircraft manufacturers.

In another case, Brazil's Administrative Council of Economic Defense, known as Cade, started investigating US-based Colgate-Palmolive's USD1 billion acquisition of the Brazilian Kolynos oral-care business after rival Procter & Gamble filed a complaint questioning whether Colgate should be allowed to dominate 79 per cent of Brazil's USD400 million toothpaste market. The approval of the deal came 20 months after the acquisition. But it included restrictions that required Colgate to make cumbersome changes. Cade said that Colgate, which had acquired Kolynos as a fast way to expand its business in the potentially lucrative Latin American market, must either stop selling toothpaste under the Kolynos brand in Brazil for four years, or license the Kolynos toothpaste trademark to another company for 20 years.[34]

Dumping.   Selling products in other country-markets below cost or below domestic prices, called dumping, can give rise to legal problems for an international marketer. Dumping is similar to predatory pricing, which has long been outlawed by US antitrust legislation. Both practices are aimed at capturing market share, injuring competitors, and in the long run giving the company a high degree of market control. Companies ranging from Japanese computer-chip manufacturers to US agricultural concerns have been charged with dumping products into other country-markets. The number of anti-dumping cases involving Chinese companies has soared in recent years, with the EU and the USA accounting for most of them. For example, in 1996 the EU accused about 30 Chinese companies of exporting unbleached fabric to Europe at below-market prices to gain market share.

It is not difficult to bring charges before a commission that hears dumping cases, such as the US Treasury Department, but it is often difficult to prove such charges. The definition of cost, such as marginal versus average cost, may be central to the case. Thus, accusations often focus on the difference between the price of the imported good and its price in the home market. Charging competitors with dumping can also serve as a means of gaining information about the structure of their added-value chain and product technology, or simply holding them off the market for some time. For the international marketer accused of dumping in such cases, the biggest problem is to prove that no dumping has taken place without disclosing too much information on new product technology.

Regulations Concerning the Marketing Mix

The most important part of a country's legal environment from an international marketer's point of view is legislation concerning the company's marketing mix. Each element of the marketing mix is subject to legal regulation. Some of the most important aspects are discussed in the following paragraphs.

Protection of Industrial Property Rights.   An important concern of every international marketer is the protection of industrial property rights, or corporate assets that have the potential to generate funds, such as brand names, trademarks, patents, copyright and technology. No uniform international legal code addresses this issue, although there are several multinational agreements in this area. The most important is the world trade pact agreed upon in 1993, setting up the WTO, which incorporates the trade-related aspects of intellectual property rights (the so-called Trips agreement), which extend to software, films, literature, trademarks and other expressions of creativity. This agreement makes disputes in this area subject to adjucation by the world trade body.

An important problem is **patent protection**. For example, US drug companies complain that they lose USD1 billion in yearly sales alone to Argentine copies. In 1996, Argentina's Congress which had been under heavy pressure from the US government, produced a bill to update its infamously weak patent laws dating from 1864. This bill, however, gives local producers five years' grace from royalty payments and ample scope to copy drugs still in the approval and testing stage.[35]

European unification has produced a new and improved system for **protecting trademarks** throughout the EU with a single application and registration. The application for a Community Trademark (CTM) must be drafted in one of the 11 EU languages plus a secondary language from one of the five official languages of the EU, English, French, German, Italian and Spanish. The fee to obtain a CTM from the Office for Harmonization in the Internal Market located in Alicante, Spain is about USD5000, assuming there is no opposition or significant complications in the process. One of the most significant advantages of the CTM lies in the 'leveraged use principle'. The proprietor of a CTM must prove use within five years of registration. However, the trademark proprietor can maintain rights throughout the EU by proving genuine use in just one member country. This allows staged introduction of their brand across the EU.[36]

Even improved international systems of trademark application and registration do not help to resolve the major international problem related to the protection of brand names and trademarks: **counterfeiting**, the intentional production or sale of a product under a brand name or trademark without the authorization of the holder of that name or trademark. Italy is the uncontested leader in European counterfeited product manufacturing and sales. An estimated 95 per cent of Bulgaria's CD production is illegal knock-offs for sale throughout Europe. In Asia, China and South Korea are the leading counterfeit countries. Despite strengthened Chinese efforts to close plants and smash stocks of fake compact discs since the country signed an intellectual property rights agreement with the USA in 1996, for example, CD piracy in China is soaring as manufacturing machines used to copy films, music and computer disks keep flooding in illegally, mostly from Europe via Hong Kong. According to one estimate, nearly 200 million illegal CDs are stamped out worldwide each year, almost 60 per cent of them from China. It is difficult to estimate total corporate losses due to counterfeiting, but the International Federation of the Phonographic Industry, for example, claimed annual losses to pirates of USD2.2 billion in 1996.[37]

Even when conventions and agreements exist, protection of industrial property rights is difficult and expensive. In addition to law enforcement actions, an option available to international marketers is retaliation. For example, Cartier of Paris made its retaliation against a Mexico City retailer that was selling other manufacturers' products under the Cartier name an international event. The company publicly gathered piles of faked Cartier watches and jewellery and Cartier's CEO personally gave the sign to a road roller which smashed them in front of invited international journalists. Because potential customers all over the world were informed of that event and became much more prudent in buying products bearing the Cartier label, counterfeiting of this trademark sharply decreased in the years following the event.

Product Liability.   Product liability is a producer's or intermediary's responsibility (independent of contractual obligations) for any personal damage or damage of a good (that is not the product itself) incurred by a person through a defective product. Legal systems vary considerably in their treatment of product liability. The strict liability laws found in the USA are often a source of surprise and alarm to international marketers planning to enter this market for the first time. For example, in 1990 Dr Gore paid USD40 750 for a new BMW which, he later discovered, had been damaged and repainted before he took delivery. Feeling cheated, Dr Gore sued BMW for the USD4000 reduction in his car's value, plus punitive damages based on the fact that BMW had sold 983 such 'refinished' cars in America over a ten-year period. An Alabama jury awarded Dr Gore his USD4000, along with a huge USD4 million award in punitive damages (later reduced to a USD2 million by the state's supreme court and finally rejected by the US Supreme Court).

Fearful of such lawsuits, companies whose products might be a target simply avoid the US market. For instance, Axminster Electronics, a small British firm whose devices help prevent cot death by monitoring a baby's breathing, does not sell in the USA because it cannot secure product-liability insurance. Manufacturers of small private aircraft have similar insurance problems. Research into medicines taken by people who are well, such as vaccines and contraceptives, has declined precipitously: after all, every drug company knows that, if a person subsequently gets ill, there is a good chance that a jury somewhere in the USA will blame the test drug, and levy a fine accordingly.[38]

Product-safety laws also vary from one country to another. When sales of the pesticide DDT were banned in the USA for safety reasons, for example, such sales continued to be legal in most industrially developing parts of the world. US manufacturers of DDT found themselves unable to sell the product in their own country, but they were able to exploit a ready export market – whatever ethical level such behaviour may express. Ironically, as US food imports increased, more contaminated produce was purchased in stores in the USA because of the relatively relaxed controls on pesticide use in food exporting countries.

Even similar product-use situations may be subject to different product-liability interpretations. Thus, theme-park rides that are considered safe in Queensland, Australia, are not subject to the same level of crowd control as similar rides in theme parks in Texas. By US standards, such rides may be dangerous. Eliminating the product-liability hazard in this case would require more equipment and personnel, which would increase costs and affect profits.

Mining Kids On-Line for Information

MR. JELLY IS AWFULLY SWEET TO KIDS ON-LINE. THE rotund mascot at candy maker Herman Goelitz Inc's World Wide Web site offers visitors free one-ounce samples of jelly beans – so long as they spill the beans about their name, address, gender, age and where they shop. Only in the fine-print disclaimer does Mr. Jelly Belly reveal what might be done with this personal data: '. . . anything you disclose to us is ours. That's right – ours. So we can do anything we want with the stuff you post. We can reproduce it, disclose it, transmit it, publish it, broadcast it and post it someplace else.'

As millions of kids go on-line, marketers are in hot pursuit. Eager to reach an enthusiastic audience more open to pitches than the typical adult buried in junk mail, companies often entertain children on-line with games and contests. But to play, children frequently are required to fill out questionnaires about themselves and their families and friends – valuable data to be sorted and stored in marketing databases.

That rattles many privacy advocates, who are pushing for new regulations. Critics say on-line come-ons aimed at kids are particularly insidious, and fret that the Internet could erupt into a frenzy of on-line infomercials toying with children's minds. They call for the same kinds of protections that now restrict television advertising geared to kids. But some experts question whether a raft of new legislation is the right answer, rather than simply extending current rules on fraudulent and deceptive practices to the on-line market.

On-line operators wish everyone would lighten up. Rob Muller, manager of marketing at Herman Goelitz, said the Jelly Belly legal disclaimer 'was intended to be somewhat tongue-in-cheek . . . to entertain, not intimidate.' He adds that the company has no intention of selling or renting out personal information on users, but was issuing a warning for Internet users at large.

Source: Sandberg, J. (1997), 'Marketers Mine Kids On-Line for Information, Alarmed Privacy Advocates Push for New Regulations', *The Wall Street Journal Europe*, 10 June, p. 12.

The EU Commission has created a bunch of common standards for various products, from kidney-dialysis machines to food colouring. However, when it comes to safety, the rules specifically allow countries to prohibit imports that threaten 'public security'. That has caused trouble for exporters inside and to the EU. Dormont Manufacturing Co., a US-based producer of hoses that hook up household appliances to gas outlets, for example, once sold those outlets freely throughout Europe. Since national safety specifications were written, by committees often dominated by domestic producers, the company needs individual approval in each country, because hoses are crucial to the safe operation of gas appliances. US trade officials estimate that at least USD300 million of the USD112 billion in US exports to Europe are goods that once needed no separate national approval but now require such approval from each country.[39]

Regulations of Advertising. Local legal regulation in international advertising may concern the use of media, comparative and other claims, advertisements for specific product categories, advertisements addressing children, and the use of language as well as agency–client relationships. For example, tobacco advertising is entirely banned in countries like Canada, China, Norway and New Zealand. In the USA the trend is to impose tighter tobacco advertising restriction, and the EU is considering a clampdown on tobacco advertising across the continent. Finland limits TV ads for fruit juices and mouthwash, while Belgium has forbidden spots for heating and insulation devices. Italy bans ads for diet products, daily newspapers and consumer magazines from state television. Greece requires car advertisers to mention emission levels.[40]

How important clear regulations may be to avoid abuse of potential customers is shown by the example (given in the Ethics box) of firms using the Internet to address children. On the other hand, the diversity of regulations from one country to another represents a major hurdle for international marketers in developing international campaigns. The difficulty of developing an advertisement that can be used across countries in view of existing restrictions is illustrated by the example of a TV spot for the launch of a new low-fat chocolate bar in Europe. The product was planned to be introduced in five countries, Belgium, Denmark, France, Germany and the UK, using the following claims: 'Does not make you gain weight', 'A treat after class that does not cut appetite', 'Contains only one-third of the calories of other chocolate bars'. The campaign could not get started because in Belgium dietary claims are not allowed in advertising. In Denmark, advertisements that make nutritional promises are forbidden. In France, advertising to children is illegal. In Germany, a comparison with other products is not allowed, and in the UK sweets may only be presented as snacks.

In view of such a multitude of different regulations, the EU Commission has made efforts to unify advertising regulations. As a result, in early 1996, for example, the EU Council of Ministers authorized comparative advertising, provided that certain conditions are met. Comparative advertising is legal for goods and services which are in fact comparable. The comparison must relate to one or more 'essential, pertinent, verifiable and representative characteristics', of which price is one. The text does not allow confusion over names, distinctive marks or brand names; it also bans 'knocking copy'. Because most EU countries have more restrictive laws, they will have to modify their own legislation.

In some countries there are constraining legal restrictions on agency–client relationships. South Korea, the second-largest advertising market in Asia, for example, has traditionally barred foreign agencies from the country. In response, agencies like Ogilvy & Mather have developed 'technical consultant' agreements with Korean agencies. These agreements enable the Korean agencies to serve their clients more fully. In the Ogilvy example, Korean agencies can offer global advertising support to their own clients. Such agreements also permit greater coordination of the advertising used in Korea with that used in the rest of Asia.

Restrictions of Sales-Promotions. The use of sales promotion tools may be constrained by the laws in some of the served country-markets. Laws against price discrimination may prevent the use of price-offs, for example. In the case of contests and sweepstakes, legal issues constitute the largest implementation problem. In the USA, for example, a sweepstake that requires proof of purchase is considered an illegal form of gambling. In Malaysia, contests are allowed, but they must involve games of skill and not of chance.

Taxes also affect the choice of sales promotion tools. For example, in Sweden liquor products are subject to high sales taxes which substantially raise the price to the consumer. A costly sales promotion item, such as a commemorative decanter, would not be feasible if it were to raise the price of an already expensive product beyond a level that consumers find acceptable.

Price Regulations.   At one time or another almost every country's government has engaged in some form of price control. In countries with highly inflationary economies it is common to find price controls on food and beverage products. Some countries, such as Ghana, control the manufacturer's profit margin, which has the effect of controlling the price paid by the consumer. South Korea forces international marketers, such as US-based Whirlpool, to label their products with the price at which they entered the country. That price does not include internal transportation costs, or the mark-ups of intermediaries. In the EU and the USA, antitrust laws limit international marketers' discretion in setting prices for intermediaries. Some countries, such as Germany and Norway, have fixed book prices, insisting that free competition, as in the UK, the Netherlands and Sweden, would drive many booksellers out of business and discourage investment in publishing less popular books. France prevents stores from selling goods at a loss. Retailers must charge their customers at least what they were invoiced by the supplier.[41] International marketer must make sure that they are informed about such country-market specifics before evaluating the attractiveness of doing business in a market.

Regulation of Distribution and Sales.   The legal environment affects the distribution channels available to international marketers. Door-to-door selling, for example, is prohibited in France. In Australia, a customer can send liquor anywhere in the country via a system similar to that used by florists in the Western industrialized countries, but in the USA most states do not allow the sale of liquor in that manner. Finland, Norway and Sweden traditionally restricted most alcoholic beverage sales to state-owned shops. Now that Sweden and Finland have joined the EU, they have had to drop state monopolies on the import and wholesale distribution of alcohol, and the retail monopoly may fall because it flouts European competition law.[42]

The legality of agreements between manufacturers and distributors can also differ considerably under different legal systems. For example, tying contracts specify that a retailer must buy all of a manufacturer's products in order to buy one particular product line. Although such contracts are illegal in the USA, in other countries they are not only legal but may signify the culturally desirable existence of a long-term relationship. Similarly, the establishment of exclusive territories for intermediaries is prohibited by antitrust laws in the USA. In contrast, it is an accepted practice in Europe and Latin America.

The US government has also stepped in with new rules to curb fraud in telephone selling. The Telemarketing Sales Rule requires telephone salespeople to tell consumers promptly that they are making a sales call, the nature of the products or services offered, and in the case of prize promotions, that no purchase is necessary to win. Market researchers are exempt from those rules.[43]

Regulations of Business Relations.   Legislation that deserves special attention by international marketers concerns the regulation of appropriate business relationships. What are considered corrupt practices may vary from one

Table 4.2 EXAMPLE OF A POTENTIAL LIST OF RISK EVALUATION CRITERIA

Political and economic risk is composed of many different dimensions. Depending on the product-market an international marketer has chosen to serve, appropriate criteria to assess the risk in different country-markets will vary. The table illustrates one potential listing of evaluation criteria.

1. Economic Factors
   1.1 Internal
   - ↔ Real GNP and real GNP growth
   - ↔ Annual growth rate in GNP per capita
   - ↔ Sectoral and employment trends
   - ↔ Inflation rate
   - ↔ Investment/GNP
   - ↔ Net government budget/GNP

   1.2 External
   - ↔ Foreign public debt/GNP
   - ↔ Debt–service ratio
   - ↔ IMF holdings of domestic currency as a percentage of growth
   - ↔ Current account/GNP
   - ↔ Average external debt
   - ↔ Leading export/total export
   - ↔ Balance of payments
   - ↔ Stability of currency convertibility
   - ↔ Remittance and repatriation regulations

2. Sociopolitical Factors
   2.1 Integration
   2.2 Capacity
   2.3 Social welfare system
3. Political and legal Factors
   3.1 General risks
   - ↔ Border conflicts
   - ↔ Alliance commitments or alliance shifts
   - ↔ Embargoes/international boycotts
   - ↔ Position of the host government vis-à-vis the company's home government
   - ↔ Civil war/(selective) terrorism
   - ↔ Stability of legal regulations

   3.2 Company-specific risks
   - ↔ Expropriation/domestication
   - ↔ Selected boycott
   - ↔ Operating restrictions
   - ↔ Special fees and taxes not levied on domestic firms
   - ↔ Restrictions on profit remittance

country-market to another. For example, the Foreign Corrupt Practices Act in the USA forbids bribery of foreign public officials, allows payment for services (known as 'grease', because it lubricates business transactions), and stipulates criminal penalties for violators. In other countries, where public administration personnel partly live on additional payments or gifts from their clients and where business relations are less functional than in North America, legislation concerning corrupt practices may be much more relaxed. Chapter 5 will elaborate on that issue.

'MANAGING' THE POLITICAL AND LEGAL ENVIRONMENT

Assessing Political Risk

A company operating internationally or a firm on its way to internationalization would prefer stable, friendly and predictable political and legal environments in the country-markets to be served. But this ideal is rarely found. So international marketers must develop a monitoring tool to be able to evaluate the degree of the company's exposure to political risk in all served and potential markets. The development of a list of risk assessment criteria may be a simple but effective way to go. In establishing the list the marketer will need to start from the definition of the company's business domain in the corporate policy statement. From there it may determine which of the factors discussed in the two preceding chapters – that is, factors concerning the state and potential development of the economic and political/legal environment of the company's product-market – are relevant for evaluating the firm's (potential) risk exposure. Table 4.2 gives an example of what such a list could look like.

In transforming such a list of risk evaluation criteria into a scoring model, the international marketer develops a company-specific tool for political risk assessment. A faster but perhaps less managerially relevant way to assess the political risk in country-markets served and under consideration is to buy risk assessment data from specialist consulting firms, such as the International Country Risk Guide (ICRG) published by Political Risk Services, IBC USA. Table 4.3, as an example, shows *Euromoney*'s assessment of which countries are the riskiest and those with the lowest risk.

Management Decisions

Having comparatively evaluated the risk involved with the political and legal environment of the potential and currently served country-markets, the management of an internationally operating firm will first have to decide which markets to avoid. The remaining markets can be ranked according to the risk they represent and decisions may be taken on how to handle the risk in the most attractive markets.

Basically an international marketer has two non-exclusive options for reducing the risk from its markets' political and legal environment. It may primarily rely on reducing the financial exposure of the firm by insuring the firm's activities against political risks, by minimizing fixed investments in the served country-markets, by raising local capital, or by producing only parts of the products' value added in one country. On the other hand, the international marketer may focus on the building and maintenance of strong relationships with the most important stakeholders in each country it serves. For that purpose the firm may cooperate with local investment partners; it may employ local executives, financially support public institutions and interests; or it may make its products an inevitable 'must' in the customers' eyes. All those possibilities will be further discussed in Parts III and IV of the book about an international marketer's basic strategic decisions and the building and sustaining of its international market position.

Table 4.3 The World Leaders in High and Low Political Risk

Political risk may be assessed in different ways. The following list gives the ranking of creditworthiness established semi-annually by *Euromoney*, one of the most well-known service organizations doing international risk analyses on an ongoing basis.

COUNTRY RISK RANKING 1996

RANK SEPT 96	MAR 96	CHANGE MAR TO SEPT		TOTAL	ECONOM PERFORM	POLITICAL RISK	DEBT INDICATORS	DEBT IN DEFAULT OR RESCHEDULED	CREDIT RATINGS	ACCESS TO BANK FINANCE	ACCESS TO SHORT-TERM FINANCE	ACCESS TO CAPITAL MARKETS	DISCOUNT ON FORFAITING
			WEIGHTING:	100.00	25.00	25.00	10.00	10.00	10.00	5.00	5.00	5.00	5.00
1	1	0	Luxembourg	99.51	25.00	24.51	10.00	10.00	10.00	5.00	5.00	5.00	5.00
2	2	0	Switzerland	98.84	23.84	25.00	10.00	10.00	10.00	5.00	5.00	5.00	5.00
3	5	2	United States	98.37	23.96	24.41	10.00	10.00	10.00	5.00	5.00	5.00	5.00
4	6	2	Netherlands	97.88	23.36	24.52	10.00	10.00	10.00	5.00	5.00	5.00	5.00
5	9	4	UK	96.14	22.17	23.97	10.00	10.00	10.00	5.00	5.00	5.00	5.00
6	10	4	France	95.74	21.42	24.33	10.00	10.00	10.00	5.00	5.00	5.00	5.00
7	3	−4	Singapore	95.66	24.48	21.50	10.00	10.00	9.69	5.00	5.00	5.00	5.00
8	7	−1	Germany	95.65	21.75	23.90	10.00	10.00	10.00	5.00	5.00	5.00	5.00
9	8	−1	Austria	95.18	21.69	23.48	10.00	10.00	10.00	5.00	5.00	5.00	5.00
10	11	1	Norway	94.97	24.14	21.53	10.00	10.00	9.79	5.00	5.00	4.50	5.00
172	170	−2	Somalia	14.97	4.09	0.00	0.00	10.00	0.00	0.00	0.88	0.00	0.00
173	173	0	Tajikistan	14.45	0.00	5.21	0.00	5.73	0.00	0.00	0.00	3.50	0.00
174	174	0	Cuba	11.50	3.71	3.03	0.00	0.00	0.00	0.00	1.76	3.00	0.00
175	177	2	Iraq	9.42	7.27	1.65	0.00	0.00	0.00	0.00	0.00	0.50	0.00
176	175	−1	Korea, North	5.39	1.87	2.64	0.00	0.00	0.00	0.00	0.88	0.00	0.00
177	176	−1	Surinam	4.78	0.00	4.78	0.00	0.00	0.00	0.00	0.00	0.00	0.00
178	178	0	Afghanistan	3.92	0.00	3.04	0.00	0.00	0.00	0.00	0.88	0.00	0.00

Source: Dobson, R. and C. Solomon (1996), 'Asia's economies start to slip', *Euromoney*, September, pp. 200–205.

Methodology:

The *Euromoney* country risk assessment uses nine categories that fall into three broad groups: analytical indicators, credit indicators and market indicators. The weighted scores are calculated as follows: the highest score in each category receives the full mark for the weighting; the lowest receives zero. In between, figures are calculated according to the formula: Final score = weighting ÷ (maximum score − minimum score) × (score − minimum score). The country risk ranking shows only the final scores after weighting.

The categories are:

↔ **Economic data** (25 per cent weighting). Taken from the *Euromoney* global economic projections 1996–1997. Each country scores the average of the evaluations for 1996 and 1997.

↔ **Political risk** (25 per cent). *Euromoney* polled risk analysts, risk insurance brokers and bank credit officers. They were asked to give each country a score of between zero and ten. A score of ten indicates no risk of non-payment; zero indicates that there is no chance of payments being made. Countries were scored in comparison both with each other and with previous years. Country risk was defined as the risk of non-payment or non-servicing of payment for goods or services, loans, trade-related finance and dividends, and the non-repatriation of capital. This category does not reflect the creditworthiness of individual counterparties in any country.

↔ **Debt indicators** (10 per cent). Scores are calculated using the following ratios from the *World Bank World Debt Tables 1995–96*: debt service to exports (A); current-account balance to GNP (B); external debt to GNP (c). Figures are the latest available, mostly for 1993. Scores are calculated by the formula: C+(A×2)−(B×10). The higher the score, the better. Because of the lack of consistent economic data for OECD and rich oil-producing countries, these score full points. Developing countries that do not report debt data to the World Bank score zero.

↔ **Debt in default or rescheduled** (10 per cent). A score of between zero and ten based on the amount of debt in default or that has been rescheduled over the past three years. Ten equals no non-payments; zero, all in default or rescheduled. Scores are based on the *World Bank World Debt Tables 1995–96* and *Euromoney* estimates for countries which do not report under the debtor reporting system (DRS).

↔ **Credit ratings** (10 per cent). The average of sovereign ratings from Moody's, Standard & Poor's and IBCA.

↔ **Access to bank finance** (5 per cent). Calculated from disbursements of private, long-term, unguaranteed loans as a per centage of GNP. OECD countries which do not report under the debtor reporting system score 5. Source: *World Bank World Debt Tables 1995–96*.

↔ **Access to short-term finance** (5 per cent). Scores are calculated taking into account coverage available from US Ex-Im Bank, NCM UK and ECGD and membership of OECD consensus groups.

↔ **Access to international bond and syndicated loan markets** (5 per cent). Reflects *Euromoney*'s analysis of how easily the country might tap the markets now, based largely on issues since January 1995. A score of five means no problem whatsoever; four, no problem on 95 per cent of occasions; three, usually no problem; two, possible (depending on conditions); one, just possible in some circumstances; zero, impossible.

↔ **Access to discount on forfaiting** (5 per cent). Reflects the average maximum tenor available and the forfaiting spread over riskless countries such as the USA, based on the average maximum tenor minus the spread. Countries for which forfaiting is not available score nothing. Data were supplied by Morgan Grenfell Trade Finance, West Merchant Bank, the London Forfaiting Company, Standard Bank and ING Capital.

Summary

Most companies are unable to influence the political and legal environment of their markets directly but their opportunities for successful business conduct largely depend on the structure and content of that environment. A marketer serving international markets or planning to do so, therefore, has to assess carefully the political and legal environments of the markets served or under consideration to draw the appropriate managerial consequences.

The first step in assessing the political and legal environments of country-markets is to determine which parts or characteristics of those environments are specifically relevant to the product-market(s) of the company. The generally most important factor is the stability of the served country-markets' political systems. The form of government has some impact on the extent of political stability in a country, but the two are not directly related. The power structure of the interest groups most strongly influencing local policies has a larger impact on political stability. Political parties channel public opinion into the formulation of government policies and laws. The role that foreign businesses are allowed to play in a given country-market are influenced by the philosophies of those parties. Strong influences on a country's political decisions may also come from unions, special interest groups and lobbyists.

Depending on the people in power, their view of the world and whose interests they mainly follow, governments may have very different objectives. Some general objectives relevant for most governments include the maintenance of political sovereignty, the enhancement of national prestige and prosperity, national security, and the protection of cultural identity. The prevailing political objectives of the governing forces in a country-market determine the policies of government.

The international trade policy of a country's government provides a framework for exports, imports and foreign investment and therefore needs to be closely analysed by the international marketer. All countries control exports and imports to some degree, providing both barriers to trade and supports for certain domestically as well as foreign-produced goods and services. One way to encourage trade between two countries is to use political relations as a means to establish contacts between companies from both countries. Another way to stimulate and assist exports is to provide financial assistance either directly or indirectly. Governments may also support the international marketing of their industries by refunding domestic taxes to exporters. Sometimes governments support imports of particular goods or services from industrially less developed countries through tariff preferences.

Barriers to trade include tariffs, non-tariff barriers and trade embargoes or sanctions. Tariffs have traditionally been used as barriers to international trade. International trade liberalization during the last decade of the twentieth century has led to a significant reduction of tariff barriers. Therefore, governments have been increasingly using non-tariff barriers to protect some of their countries' industries which they think are unable to sustain free international competition. A government may also support or deter international business through its investment policy, that is, the general rules governing legislation concerning domestic as well as foreign participation in the equity or ownership of businesses and other organizations of the country.

The legal environment of a company, that is, the set of laws and systems to enforce those laws established by a society to govern its members' behaviour, must also be assessed by the international marketer because it determines the political and legal viability of potential local product-markets. Generally important considerations are the existing kind of legal system, agreements and conventions the country's government has signed which are relevant for the company's product-market, and a country's competition regulation. Finally, legislation concerning the potential use of marketing tools needs to be closely analysed.

Having determined and analysed the current state of the relevant factors of influence from the political and legal environment, the marketer needs to anticipate their potential states of development at the planning horizon to evaluate the potential impact of the political and legal environment on the success of the firm. A comparison of the environments' impact in the served or considered country-markets will allow the international marketer to decide how to 'manage' those environments.

DISCUSSION QUESTIONS

1. Describe a current political trend in your home country that affects international marketers based in your country. What implications do you see?
2. Why is political stability so very important for international marketers? Find a recent example to underline your points.
3. How can the change of major political objectives in a country have an impact on the potential for success of an international marketer?
4. Take an example of a small company you know of and discuss how it can profit from the export support activities of your country's government, administration and related organizations.
5. What are the impacts of the absence of a body of international business law on an internationally operating firm? Find current examples for your points.
6. Why would some smaller companies opt for less deregulated and liberalized markets? Discuss the consequences they have to bear.
7. Why is dumping a controversial issue in international marketing? What can international marketers do about it?
8. What relationship do you see between antitrust controls and the deregulation of markets? Whose interests are involved? Discuss.
9. What can an international marketer do to protect its industrial property rights? Find examples from business newspapers.
10. Take an example of a company you know and develop a list of country risk evaluation criteria. Explain why you chose the criteria on your list.

ADDITIONAL READINGS

Baum, H. (ed.) (1997) *Japan: Economic Success and Legal System,* Berlin: Walter de Gruyter.

Brouthers, K.D. and G.J. Bamossy (1997) 'The Role of Key Stakeholders in International Joint Venture Negotiations: Case Studies from Eastern Europe', *Journal of International Business Studies*, 28 (2), 285–308.

Castro, J.O. De and K. Uhlenbruck (1997) 'Characteristics of Privatization: Evidence from Developed, Less-Developed, and Former Communist Countries', *Journal of International Business Studies*, 28 (1), 123–143.

Garten, J.E. (1997) 'Troubles Ahead in Emerging Markets,' *Harvard Business Review*, May–June, 38–50.

Read the daily issues of *The Wall Street Journal (Europe)*; or *The International Herald Tribune, Le Monde, Neue Zürcher Zeitung, Corriere de la Sierra;* or *The Economist.*

NOTES

[1] Kahn, J. (1996), 'Boeing's Chance at Sino-Korean Project Tangled in Area's Relations With US', *The Wall Street Journal*, 14 March, A11; and Goldsmith, Ch. (1996), 'China Will Buy 33 Airbus Jets As Part of Deals With France', *The Wall Street Journal Europe*, 11 April, p. 3.

[2] Borrus, A. and M. Collins (1995), 'What's keeping US Companies Out of Vietnam? The US', *Business Week*, 17 April, p. 21.

[3] Roberts, D. (1997), 'Where's that Pot of Gold', *Business Week*, February 3, pp. 54–59.

[4] Engardino, P.M. Shari and M. Clifford (1996), 'Tremors in Jakarta', *Business Week*, 12 August, 42–43; Rodier, A. (1998),'La chute de la maison "vingt pour cent"', Le Monde, 15 May, p. 4.

[5] Reynolds, R. (1995), 'South Africa: A trade haven?', *Black Enterprise*, 6 February

[6] 'Turning a new leaf', *The Economist*, 31 August 1996, p. 54.

[7] Metten A.(1993), 'Der Verhaltenskodex für Europa-Lobbyisten', *International Wirtschaft*, 17 June.

[8] Robinson, E. (1992), 'Experts Fear Rise in Bosnia-Type Ethnic Conflicts as Peoples Fight for Identity', *International Herald Tribune*, 20 August, p. 1.

[9] Roberts, D. (1997), 'Drugs: Plenty of Bitter Pills', *Business Week*, 3 February, pp. 58f.

[10] 'Streit um einheitliche Sozialnormen eskaliert', *Der Standard*, 11 December, 1996, p. 21.

[11] Haas, P. (1998),'Thomson: premier pas vers les regroupements européens', *Le Figaro économie*, 20 April, p. 3.

[12] 'Denationalise the armourers', *The Economist*, 2 March 1996, p. 17.

[13] Dai, X. (1996), 'PICC Expands Export Credit Insurance', *Beijing Review*, 25–31 March, p. 27.

[14] Ruff, C. (1996),'Hauptprobleme in Indien: Bürokratie, Zölle, Bestechung', *Der Standard*, 23–24 November, p. 31.

[15] Yoshida, N. (1994), 'Driving Downhill', *Japan Update*, October, p. 10f.

[16] 'You Have to be Pushy and Aggressive', *Business Week*, 24 February 1997, p. 56.

[17] Taylor, III. A. (1997), 'Danger: Rough Road Ahead', *Fortune*, 17 March, 114–118.

[18] Hooley, G. (1997), 'The Market Environment In Central and Eastern Europe', in *'The Effects of Privatisation and Foreign Direct Investment on the Marketing Approaches, Strategies, Implementation and Performance of Enterprises in Central and Eastern Europe,'* (G. Hooley, ed.), Final Report to European Commission under ACE94 Initiative.

[19] Richardson, M. (1996), 'Indonesia Moves Toward Gas-Power Plants', *International Herald Tribune*, 21 May, p. 17.

[20] 'You Have to be Pushy and Aggressive', *Business Week*, 24 February 1997, p. 56.

[21] Jordan, M. (1996), 'Amoco Withdraws From Gas Project In India, a Setback for the Government', *The Wall Street Journal*, 20 September, p. A11.

[22] Miller, K.L., H. Dawley *et al.* (1997), 'Flying Cheap in Europe', *Business Week*, 31 March, pp. 50f.

[23] Roberts, D. (1997), 'Where's that Pot of Gold?', *Business Week*, 3 February, 54–59.

[24] Taylor, III. A. (1997), 'Danger: Rough Road Ahead', *Fortune*, 17 March 17, 114–118.

[25] 'Total war', *The Economist*, 10 August 1996, p. 37.

[26] Magnusson, P. (1997), 'A Troubling Barrage of Trade Sanctions from All Across America', *Business Week*, 24 February, p. 59.

[27] Burton, Th.M. (1996), 'Case Corp. Is Charged With Violating US Law in Sale of Equipment to Libya', *The Wall Street Journal*, 22 April, p. A3.

[28] 'Is Iran the godfather?', *The Economist*, 17 August 1996, p. 33.

[29] Wong, J. (1996), 'Foreign Lenders Vexed by Taiwan Firm', *The Wall Street Journal*, 30 April, p. A10.

[30] Kim, W.Ch. and R.A. Mauborgne (1987), 'Cross-Cultural Strategies', *Journal of Business Strategy*, Spring, 33–35.

[31] Schaffer, R., B. Earle, and F. Agusti (1990), *International Business Law and Its Environment*, St. Paul, MN: West Publishing Company, p. 50.

[32] 'Countdown to explosion', *The Economist*, 21 September 1996, pp. 68f.

[33] Miller, K.L., H. Dawley, M. Trinephi and W. Echikson (1997), 'Flying Cheap in Europe', *Business Week*, 31 March, pp. 50f.

[34] Ono, Y. (1996), 'Colgate Purchase Gets Brazil's Blessing But With Restrictions on Brand Name', *The Wall Street Journal*, 20 September, p. A11.

[35] Friedland, J. (1996), 'Bristol-Myers Aims to Boost Patent Laws As Argentine Unit Sells Pirate Drugs', *The Wall Street Journal*, 23 September, p. A16.

[36] Retsky, M.L. (1996), 'Who needs the new community trademark?', *Marketing News*, 30 (12), June, 11.

[37] Greenberger, R.S. and C.S. Smith (1997), 'Double Trouble, CD Piracy Flourishes In China, and West Supplies Equipment', *The Wall Street Journal Europe*, 25–26 April, pp. 1 and 5.

[38] 'No pain, no gain', *The Economist*, 25 May 1996, p. 67; and 'It embarrasses them', *The Economist*, 30 March1966, p. 59.

[39] Aeppel, T. (1996), ' Europe's "Unity" Undoes a US Exporter', *The Wall Street Journal*, 1 April, p. B1.

[40] Murray, S. (1996), 'Double Vision, For Commercial TV In EU, Convergence Lags National Controls', *The Wall Street Journal Europe*, 7 May, pp. 1 and 9.

[41] Schuman, M. (1996), 'US Companies Crack South Korean Market', *The Wall Street Journal*, 11 September, p. A14; 'Read all about it', *The Economist*, 6 April 1996, pp. 69f.; and 'Not at any price', *The Economist*, 6 April 1996, p. 70.

[42] 'Temperate Nordic climes', *The Economist*, 10 August 1996, p. 38.

[43] 'Telemarketing', *ESOMAR newsbrief*, 4 (5), May 1996, p. 7.

CHAPTER **5**

THE CULTURAL
ENVIRONMENT

| INTERNATIONAL INCIDENT |

Give Me More

Social scientists agree that never before has a generation of so many Indians been rushing to make their way up and ready to pursue that goal. Today, India's middle class is about 200 million, a little more than 20 per cent of the entire population. Fifty years ago, when India became a sovereign state, only 10 million, or three per cent of the population could be regarded as middle class. The fast change in business and consumer behaviour only started in the early 1990s when India somewhat liberalized its international business relations.

Some of the new members of the middle class are millionaires below the age of 30. They started their businesses or took over and revamped existing firms at the end of the 1980s and in the early 1990s. Now they want to show off their success. Traditional Indian modesty is replaced by ostentatious consumption. Apartments, cars, leisure activities and vacation travel serve as indicators of wealth.

Asked about their models in life, the kids of the Indian success generation often mention the biggest US firms in their sector of industry. They are ready to work very hard to achieve their goals: 12 to 15 hours a day. Hard work, stress and job pressure are regarded as positive. To make money and to spend it are the most important activities of the 1990s. One of the dominant rules is: each one for him- or herself and against all others. Nothing is given, but everything may be achieved.

The dreamers and idealists, those who have fought for India's freedom and a better society, are gone or live without being noticed. 'Corruption! Immorality! Disaster!' say those who want to preserve traditional Indian culture. They consider the new consumption patterns as alien to Indian society. But a closer look into India's history and its famous stories reveals that rich Indians never were reluctant to pursue all kinds of pleasure. Now, economic wealth is only more widespread. More people can afford to enjoy consumption. Sociologists call them the 'Ego-Generation', suffering from the Give-Me-More syndrome. More success, more money, more pleasure, more sensuality.

Source: Voykowitsch, B. (1996) 'Leben auf der Überholspur,' *Der Standard*, Reportage, 3.

THE INFLUENCE OF CULTURE ON INTERNATIONAL MARKETING

Marketing managers are focusing on exchanges of more or less tangible products with business partners who are more or less personally involved in the exchange. The exchange may be a single transaction or take place as part of an ongoing relationship between the exchange partners. In any case, the initiator of the exchange has to know who its preferred exchange partners are.

A precise idea of what needs to be offered to them and how to make the exchange happen is critical for business success.

Understanding potential business partners and their open as well as latent expectations means understanding the reality in which they subjectively live. This personal view of the world determines the business partners' goals, decision making, and behaviour. People's subjective perceptions of reality depend on their cognitions and cognitive structures which they have acquired through experience during enculturation. Enculturation is the process by which individuals become a member of their culture. That is, they learn what a member of the group they belong to (or want to belong to) accepts as normal, necessary, reasonable and plausible facts, behaviour and actions, values, and social relations. As a result, both organizational buyer and consumer behaviour are strongly influenced by the cultural environment in which those persons have been raised.

A Definition of Culture

Culture may be defined as the standards of beliefs, perception, evaluation and behaviour shared by the members of a social group. Some authors even define culture as 'the collective programming of the minds' which distinguishes the members of one group of people from another.[1]

Markets, companies and exchange relations exist inside such cultural contexts. Culture affects people's tastes, preferences for colours, and attitudes towards product classes. For example, Dutch children often eat chocolate shavings on buttered bread for breakfast. Children in the USA frequently have fried eggs. Indian children may have a spicy hot sambal (a type of soup), and Malays have rice. All are culturally acceptable and appropriate within their culture, but seemingly strange in others. How exchange relations come to exist, how business partners communicate with each other, how they negotiate, perceive each other, or terminate business relations largely depends on the cultural environment. The Culture box gives an example that illustrates how strongly business behaviour is influenced by cultural factors.

The example also shows that a (potential) business partner's interpretation of the international marketer's behaviour depends on expectations of proper conduct which, in turn, depend on the cultural background of the business partner. For example, 'amae' is an important value of Japanese culture that stresses mutual goodwill, complaisance and kindness in personal relationships. Because of amae, Japanese managers tend to perceive detailed contracts, such as those to which US business people are accustomed, as signs of distrust.

Even business behaviour, down to details such as the proper way to present a business card, is determined by culture. North Americans and Europeans, for example, most often present a business card informally, between two fingers. They may turn the card over and take notes on the back. In Japan, a business card is an extension of the person – to be handled carefully and respectfully, with both hands. It is laid on the table and only put in one's pocket, or written on, after the meeting is over and the guest has gone.

In fact, all behaviour occurs within the framework of a culture. Thus, in order to adequately assess the impact of culture on its own business activities, any marketer must determine the specific role culture plays in the company's product-markets. Culture may influence business success via consumer culture, that is, the cultural factors determining consumer decision making and

CULTURE BOX

Confucian

Confusion

ROBERT ARONSON IS A US ENGINEER AND BUSINESS-man, owner of Revpower, based in Fort Lauderdale, Florida. In 1987 he signed a joint venture agreement with the Shanghai Far East Aero-Technology Import & Export Corp. to develop a battery factory. Revpower would provide the know how and distribute the product. The Chinese partner would organize the plant. In 1989 the Chinese imposed on Revpower a price hike of 40 per cent, purportedly because of higher utility costs. In reaction Aronson terminated the contract and started arbitration proceedings in Stockholm.

Aronson won a USD5 million award, which, with interest, came to USD8 million. But Aronson's award could be enforced for only six months, and the Chinese courts stalled recognition of it. After the US government applied diplomatic pressure on the Chinese to get on with it, the Shanghai Intermediate People's Court finally recognized the award. In 1996 Aronson discovered that most of the assets of his Chinese partner had been transferred elsewhere.

Aronson went home empty-handed, having learned too late about doing business in the world's hottest economy. The Chinese abhor litigation. Their traditional approach to resolving disputes has been through good faith negotiation. This, they believe, offers the obvious advantages of a disposition with neither side losing face. The Chinese aversion to litigation has its roots in the Confucian teaching of harmony in thought and conduct – people should conduct themselves by moral example, not legal compulsion.

Source: Zirin, J.D. (1997) 'Confucian confusion', *Forbes*, 24 February, p. 136.

behaviour, and through business culture, that is, all cultural factors influencing business behaviour. In international marketing the situation is further complicated because cultural differences among customer and stakeholder groups may lead to different perceptions and behaviour even in similar product-markets. Indeed, in the search for similar product-markets which exist across countries' boundaries, it is highly important that the international marketer understands well the cultural differences and similarities that exist.

Consumer Culture

Consumers have specific cognitions and cognitive structures based on their learning experiences. These cognitive systems make consumers perceive their environment, evaluate alternative sequences of behaviour, interpret actions of others, and behave in individual ways. But all humans are social individuals. That is, to survive they need social contacts with other humans (in particular in early childhood). As a consequence they gather in groups.

Much learning takes place in groups of people such as the family, peers, occupational or ethnic groups, and religious communities. Such social learning results in shared cognitions of the individuals belonging to a specific group. Cultures develop. For example, most of the basic values and norms of behaviour that individuals take for granted, that is, what they think is basically good or evil, what is desirable and what to avoid, are learned in the

Figure 5.1 LAYERS OF CONSUMER CULTURE

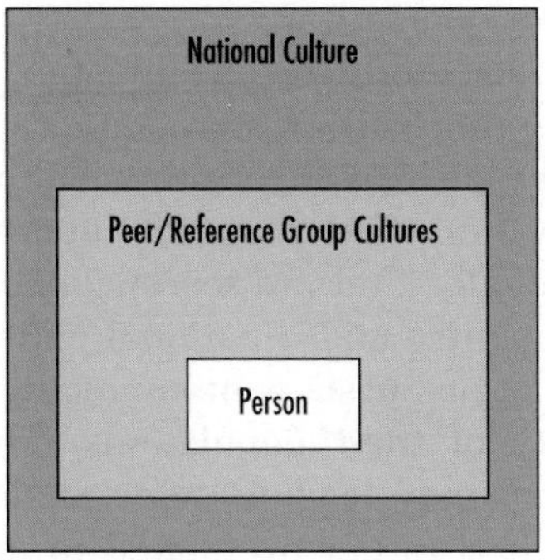

Consumer culture contains various layers: personal culture is part of reference group cultures which, in turn, are part of a national culture.

family during childhood. Some additional values and many of the norms and patterns of behaviour people follow during their lives are learned in groups of peers, that is, groups of people of the same age, sex, occupation, interests or religion. Aspiring to membership of groups that serve as references adds to this cultural learning (see Figure 5.1).

Groups of people with strongly shared cognitions may constitute subcultures in a society. In the USA, for example, there are numerous subcultures owing to the many different ethnic groups, religious denominations and regional societies that exist in the country. Each in its own way influences the conduct of business as well as consumer and buyer behaviour. For example, Campbell Soup sells different flavours of tomato soup depending upon the region of the country. Tomato soup sold in Montana is not quite as spicy as that sold in Texas.

Because of the many combinations of potential learning experiences, individual consumers show wide variations in beliefs and behaviour. But despite differences among individuals and cultures of groups constituting a society, they have some common values, norms and patterns of behaviour which indicate that they belong to a bigger cultural group that traditionally is called a nation. For example, a 20-year-old female university student from St. Louis, Missouri will have a unique blend of midwestern values, family ties, religious beliefs, and so forth, that combine to make her different from a male student of the same age who was raised in Turku, Finland. After graduation, each will get a job, and a layer of professional culture will be added to their cultural character. The female may work for Boatman's Bank in St. Louis, which is not highly active in international business compared to the Finnish graduate's employer, which may be Nokia Mobira Oy, the telecommunications firm which relies on international markets for over 90 per cent of sales. In addition, each has their unique values and patterns of behaviour shaped by the national culture in which they live. For example, US citizens tend to talk more often and more loudly than Finns.

National cultures. As described, there is a rich and complex diversity within national cultures. But a perspective on what is important within such cultures, and how a sizeable proportion of the population in a country behaves, is useful to international marketers in assessing the attractiveness of potential markets as well as in building marketing mixes which will appeal to customers belonging to a national culture.

When discussing national cultures, one must be careful to avoid two common traps. One is working with a stereotype, a conventional, usually oversimplified, and often negative view of other cultures; for example, 'the Japanese workaholics who think that they are superior than anybody else, cannot do anything individually, and are fervent machos.' The other is the unthinking equation of a country and a national culture. So-called 'nations' such as the USA, Iran, China or Russia contain a variety of national cultures owing to the heterogeneity of their populations. The fact that they live together in one big country may lead to some shared values, norms and patterns of behaviour, but it is rather overstated to talk about one national culture.

Keeping in mind those potential traps, general descriptions of what is important within a national culture may be useful to international marketers. For example, a general description of Australians might include that they typically avoid open displays of achievement. This is known as the 'tall poppy syndrome' (the tallest flower in the field is the first to get cut down). Australians have combined this reluctance to achieve, or at least to seem to over-achieve, with a strong support system for society. Further, they very much enjoy leisure time activities, travel extensively during longer vacations than average US citizens take, and are very active in outdoor sports such as tennis, sailing or swimming. They have been described as 'laid back' owing to this somewhat leisurely approach to life. The considerable Australian love of the outdoors, nature and exercise results in adults drinking substantial amounts of milk. It is drunk for lunch, as a snack, and in times when, for example, a soft drink is more likely the product of choice in Europe. Marketers have reacted by offering milk in many flavours, including chocolate, strawberry, mango and lime.

General descriptions of national cultures can be made more systematically in order to serve comparative purposes if they are based on an analytical framework. Perhaps the most well-known analytical framework for national cultures has been developed by the Dutch social scientist Geert Hofstede, based on research into the values and beliefs of 116 000 IBM employees from 66 countries. He empirically identified four dimensions of culture: individualism, power distance, uncertainty avoidance, and competitiveness (which he calls masculinity).[2]

Individualism is the degree to which individuals are integrated into groups. Individualism is high when the ties among individuals belonging to a social group are loose. Individuals are ready to start new relationships which are not very deeply entrenched, however. Highly individualistic countries like Australia, the USA or the UK find people responding to opportunities on a personal level. There is a strong belief that everybody is supposed to take care of himself, and an emphasis on individual achievement and initiative. In such cultures, goods and services helping to mark a consumer's difference compared to others should be well received.

When individualism is low, as in Venezuela, Japan or Norway, social relationships are characterized by strong ties. They take longer to be established, but are more enduring. In such more collectivist societies, cohesive in-groups exist in which the members protect each other. Norwegians consider it inappropriate, for example, to stand out in a crowd. There is a common belief that the unfortunate deserve sympathy. In such cultures an international marketer may want to understate market dominating positions. In exchange for protection by the group, all group members are expected to be absolutely loyal. Company personnel focus on team and organizational achievements, but are less inclined to cooperate across organizational borders.

Power distance relates to how members of a national culture view distribution of power; for example, how much less powerful members of a social group expect that power is distributed equally, how easy it is for people with different backgrounds to relate to each other, or how easy is upward social mobility. Power distance tends to be high for Latin, Asian and African societies. In India, for example, there is considerable difference between the status of people, and movement upward is difficult (even if the latest Indian president comes from the lowest caste, the 'untouchables'). Similar social norms are found in countries like Mexico and the Philippines. Austria, Denmark, Sweden and Finland are lower power distance societies, where upward mobility is much easier to achieve, and thus goods and services promising to support upward mobility are well received.

Uncertainty avoidance is the extent to which members of a culture feel comfortable or uncomfortable in unstructured situations. Unstructured situations are novel, surprising, and different from usual, and therefore unclear or unpredictable to individuals. Cultures dominated by uncertainty avoidance, such as Japan, Greece, Portugal or Belgium, tend to be highly regulated, having complex rules and regulations in terms of proper behaviour (such as safety and security regulations), and try to avoid risk taking. Low uncertainty avoidance cultures such as Hong Kong, Denmark, the UK, Ireland or Sweden operate in the opposite manner.

The **competitiveness** of a national culture is the extent to which individuals perceive social relations as a kind of competition (for all kinds of resources and rewards) as opposed to focusing on mutual benefits. Less competitive cultures, such as those existing in Scandinavia, the Netherlands or Thailand, tend to focus on solidarity. They are concerned with the social security of their members, attractive working conditions, and fairness. More competitive-oriented societies, such as Austria, Italy, Japan, Venezuela or Germany, tend to emphasize personal achievement, challenging tasks, performance and purposefulness.

Table 5.1 gives an overview of the ranks Hofstede found for European countries on these four dimensions of national culture. To these dimensions, a fifth dimension found in a 22-country study may be added: **time perspective**.[3] Time perspective is defined as the way members of a culture tend to approach decision making in consumer as well as business activities. They may have a dynamic, future-oriented mentality, including persistence, hard work, thrift and shame. At the opposite extreme, a culture may be characterized by a static mentality focused on the past and present, emphasizing reciprocation, 'face' and tradition. These values encourage keeping within well-known and well-accepted boundaries. In China, for example, saving 'face' is very important. Saving face involves preserving a person's dignity and social status whatever the person does. As a result, Western quality fashion designs are very successful with affluent Chinese consumers eager to wear a symbol of their status,[4] and Chinese managers tend to continue investing in product development even after serious questions about project viability arise.[5] National cultures such as those of Brazil, Hong Kong, Japan, South Korea and

---

Table 5.1 RANKS OF EUROPEAN COUNTRIES ON CULTURAL DIMENSIONS

In his international comparative study of national cultures, Hofstede found that cultures of European countries rank differently on the four detected dimensions.

COUNTRY	INDIVIDUALISM	POWER DISTANCE	UNCERTAINTY AVOIDANCE	COMPETITIVENESS (MASCULINITY)
Austria	18	53	24/25	2
Belgium	8	20	5/6	22
Denmark	9	51	51	50
Finland	17	46	31/32	47
France	10/11	15/16	10/15	35/36
Germany	15	42/44	29	9/10
Greece	30	27/28	1	18/19
Ireland	12	49	47/48	7/8
Italy	7	34	23	4/5
Netherlands	4/5	40	35	51
Norway	13	47/48	38	52
Portugal	33/35	24/25	2	45
Spain	20	31	10/15	37/38
Sweden	10/11	47/48	49/50	53
Switzerland	14	45	33	4/5
UK	3	42/44	47/48	9/10

Source: Adapted from Hofstede, G. (1991) *Cultures and Organizations*, New York: McGraw Hill.

Taiwan show strong future orientations. Canadian, Chinese, Pakistani and West African cultures tend to be more past and present oriented.

International Subcultures. For international marketers, it is important to understand their customers' personal values and accepted norms of behaviour in order to market to them properly. At the same time, marketers must search for groups with shared cognitions that result in shared views of the marketer's offerings and in similar product-related behaviour, to simplify their task. Such groups may even exist across country borders, either because the borders are not indicative of demarcations between ethnic groups or nations, or because international media, travel and education have led to the development of similar consumer subcultures (that is, groups of consumers characterized by shared values, common consumption preferences or habits).

For example, in Europe some trends have crossed country borders. Green awareness, interest in health and fitness, home orientation, creative use of leisure time and female careerism can be detected in all markets of Central and Western Europe at different levels and in different manifestations.[6] Exhibit 5.1 gives an example of how such trends on a global scale result in groups of consumers differing widely in their views and outlook which have a strong influence on their consumer behaviour.

As examples from sports-related, fashion, fast food and entertainment sectors show, international marketers themselves may be able to induce the creation of new consumer subcultures, such as Diesel jeans wearers, roller bladers (Roller Blade is a brand of Head), Burton snow boarders, Red Bull drinkers, Apple users, multimedia addicts, or fans of pop stars like U2, The Rolling Stones or Elvis Presley (even more than 20 years after his death).

Exhibit 5.1 COMMUNICATING WITH YOUNG ADULTS

According to a study by Research International Observer conducted in 34 countries, strong global trends in attitudes towards the media and the relationship young adults are seeking with brands can be identified. Four broad groups of young adults with widely differing views emerged in the study.

New Realists
↔ are found mainly in Northern Europe, the USA, Australia and white South Africa;
↔ are ambivalent towards TV, accepting its everyday role, but wary of its manipulative power;
↔ are resigned to the fact that they are never going to achieve the same level of affluence as their parents' generation;
↔ claim to be rejecting so-called '80s values in favor of the 'caring' '90s.

Enthusiastic Materialists
↔ are found in the world's emerging markets – India, Africa, China and Southeast Asia – as well as some of Europe's emerging markets, including Turkey and the Czech Republic;
↔ are enthusiastic consumers of media. There is also evidence that they are particularly interested in the press as they view the daily reading of a heavy-weight newspaper as important;
↔ set a lot of store by outward show and the material trappings of status.

Complacent Materialists
↔ are peculiar to Japan; these young people have been raised in favourable economic circumstances and seem oblivious to the tougher economic climate which now prevails;
↔ are very self-centered with little interest in others.

Swimmers Against the Tide
↔ are found in Latin America and parts of Southern Europe;
↔ aspire to the material trappings of success but are struggling to maintain '80s values in a '90s economic climate;
↔ feel impotent and forced to 'live to work' rather than 'work to live'.

Database: 160 in-depth focus groups with 20–35 year olds in 34 countries across Africa, Asia, Australasia, Europe, North America and Latin America, augmented by over 250 individual interviews among experts including marketers, advertisers, journalists and social scientists worldwide.

Source: 'Communicating with young adults', *ESOMAR newsbrief*, 4(4), April 1996, 21.

Members of such international subcultures do not need to meet and to know each other to develop shared cognitions. The brand they use, the personality they adore, or media reports about the common theme of interest are the centre of communication from where consumption-related norms and patterns of behaviour spread all over the world. Following those consumption patterns helps individual consumers to perceive themselves as members of a highly desirable group.

Caution must be taken, however, not to overemphasize the apparent similarities that an international subculture implies. Even within international subcultures, marketing adaptations may be necessary because national culture specificities do not entirely lose their influence. For example, advertising campaigns for international rock stars are still localized according to the media habits of concert goers. The international success of the film 'Babe', as another example, was partly due to the translation of the sound track into different local accents which gave the film additional interest.

Furthermore, in a backlash against trade liberalization and economic integration, nationalism is gaining popularity around the world. While the political and economic implications of this development have been discussed in Chapter 4, nationalism also brings increased support for local cultures, not necessarily national ones. In Spain, for example, this localization movement has resulted in the region of Catalonia, and speakers of Catalan, gaining such strength that Catalan was one of the four official languages, along with English, French and Spanish, at the 1992 Olympic Games in Barcelona. The 6 million people in Spain who use Catalan regularly, out of some 40 million Spanish citizens, must effectively be treated as a subculture of the national Spanish market.

Business Culture

Just as culture influences personal consumption patterns and buyer behaviour, it also largely determines accepted business behaviour. Not knowing the rules of the game puts any player at a disadvantage; not knowing the rules of the business game in a country-market means that a foreign competitor is at a disadvantage compared to local business.

Layers of Business Culture. As in consumer culture, there are different layers of business culture (see Figure 5.2). Internationally operating companies conduct their business and are managed inside **national cultures**, one of which traditionally dominates. In most cases this is the national culture of the headquarters' location. The national culture determines the values that influence corporate behaviour. But business conduct is also influenced by industry standards of behaviour which are more specific than national cultures, and, in regional or global industries, may extend across national cultures. In national cultures values prevail, whereas **industrial cultures** are mainly characterized by practices related to business conduct in the industry. For example, car manufacturers, independent of the location of their headquarters, follow certain (unwritten) rules of how to compete (or not to compete) against each other and when to announce and show new car models.

Each company is a social organization or group. As such, companies develop cultures specific to their organizations that are called organizational or **corporate cultures**. Those organizational cultures are embedded in the national and industrial cultures. That is, they are based on the values dominating the national culture and, in most cases, incorporate the norms of industry behaviour. In addition, an organizational culture contains rituals, heroes and symbols that make the firm unique (Figure 5.3). Rituals are common activities such as business meetings, initiation workshops for new entrants, or jubilees that serve the purpose of spreading shared norms of behaviour and conveying a feeling of belongingness. Heroes are profiles of ideal persons, alive or dead, in the history of the firm that serve the same purpose. So do symbols, such as a specific company language, its logo or possessions. Those symbols have meaning only for the people working for the company or having some kind of relationship with the firm.

The management of values shared by the members of a firm and the norms of behaviour accepted by the members of the organization becomes increasingly important with the extent of the company's internationalization.

Figure 5.2 LAYERS OF BUSINESS CULTURE

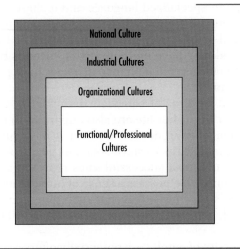

Business culture contains various layers: embedded in the national culture are industrial cultures, organizational cultures and functional/professional cultures.

Figure 5.3 MANIFESTATIONS OF ORGANIZATIONAL CULTURE

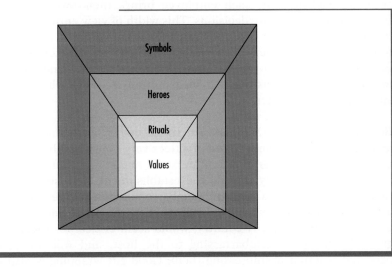

Based on values that characterize the national culture dominating the firm, a company's organizational culture contains rituals, heroes and symbols.

When people with increasingly diverse national culture backgrounds are hired by expanding firms, organizational culture can provide a common framework of how to do business. Employees of Atlanta, Georgia-based Delta Airlines, for example, know about the great importance of customer service to the company's success, whether they work in Tokyo, Berlin or Cincinnati. Organizational norms of behaviour even provide some assistance with highly controversial cross-national cultural problems such as ethics. The ethics code of Delta Airlines clearly indicates, for all employees of whatever nationality, what business conduct is undesirable.

Inside each business organization, people fulfil different functions. Because those functions require specific training which results in shared experiences, a common specialized language and a shared way of reasoning, membership in a functional group leads to the development of a functional or professional culture. For example, product managers of Procter & Gamble from all over the world may have more norms of business behaviour in common than a product manager and a finance manager in Copenhagen who also work for Procter & Gamble.

Values, norms and patterns of behaviour individually accepted by a person as guiding rules for his or her life are also important to international marketing managers when making decisions about who should perform which marketing task. For example, in Western societies people with a high need to achieve usually make the most successful sales representatives. Internationally active personnel must also possess a sense of humour and adventure, sensibility to differences, a readiness to accept such differences as different and not necessarily as bad, and an ability to relate to others, all of which will contribute to success.

The cultural diversity of employees potentially offers a strategic advantage to business firms. Asian marketing activities for US-based Procter & Gamble, for example, have traditionally been run for a considerable part through their office in Geneva, Switzerland. The employees there come from around the world, not just from Switzerland, the USA, or for that matter from Asia. Working in English, the only common language of all employees, in a French-speaking environment, each employee brings their own personal cultural background to corporate decisions. This width of view enriches decision making and leads to better decisions than, for example, if the same decision had to be made by managers from one national culture. Marketing decisions are more likely to capture the advantages of international standardization, while making necessary adjustments to local cultural issues which, if ignored, would spell marketing disaster.

Business Manners. Manners are social codes of conduct. Like personal manners, business manners and practices vary considerably from one culture to another. And like ignorance of personal manners, insufficient attention to business manners may impede the establishment of trusting business relations. For example, in China great embarrassment would result if one party to a business relationship failed to bring a gift for the other. Small gifts, not available or made in a nearby country, would seem critical for success. But large gifts will just prove embarrassing to the host, and will not produce the expected reaction of impressing them. Good gift wrapping is also especially important. And proper formalities should be observed. Giving the gift in private, and not expecting it to be opened in the presence of the giver, will avoid embarrassing both the guest and the host. Chinese consider opening gifts in front of the giver, as is custom in France, for example, as rude.

In Japan, floral arrangements have become the business gift of choice, partly as a response to Japanese executives travelling so much that they found it difficult to continue their traditional gift-giving habits.[7] But even the type of flower chosen may lead to difficulty, such as giving white chrysanthemums in Europe which are generally considered a bad omen because they are associated with funerals.

Exhibit 5.2 contains a selection of 'dos' and 'don'ts' for some European countries, seen from a US perspective. But knowledge concerning business

Exhibit 5.2 **PROTOCOL DOs AND DON'Ts**

When is the right time to act friendly? Or reserved? It is tough to know which stance to take without doing your homework first. Dorothy Manning of International Business Protocol suggests adhering to the *dos* and *don'ts* below when in the following countries.

Great Britain
DO hold your fork (tines pointed down) in the left hand and your knife in the right hand throughout the meal.
DO say please and thank you – often.
DO arrive promptly for dinner, 10 minutes late is acceptable, but 10 minutes early is not. And if invited to a British person's home for victuals, DO bring a gift for the lady of the house, but DON'T bring white lilies; they are a bad omen.
DO make appointments well in advance. The British are religious about keeping their calendars.
DO offer your 'mates' (friends) a cigarette when pulling one out for yourself. DON'T smoke until after the toast to Her Majesty's health.
DON'T ask personal questions. The British protect their privacy.
DON'T gossip about royalty. DON'T stare in public. DON'T wear striped ties lest they are copies of British regimentals.

France
DO be punctual for appointments. DO shake hands (a short, quick pump) when greeting, being introduced and leaving. Only close friends kiss cheeks.
DO address all women over 21 as *madame*, whether they are married or not.
DO dress more formally than in the US. Elegance is de rigueur.
DON'T expect to complete any work during the French two-hour lunch. DO ask your host to recommend something from the menu. DO keep your hands visible at all times. DO eat everything on your plate.
DON'T smoke before eating or between courses.
DON'T chew gum.
DON'T try to do serious business during *les vacances* (the vacation season from mid-July until the end of August).

Italy
DO write business correspondence in Italian for priority attention.
DO make appointments between 10 a.m. and 11 a.m., or after 3 p.m.
DO meet for a strictly social lunch or dinner and nightclubbing with Italian associates and spouses.
DO stand when an older person enters the room.
DO observe the *Passeggiata* – dress in your finest and stroll on the piazza between 6 p.m. and 8 p.m. to see and to be seen.
DON'T eat too much pasta, as it is not the main course.
DON'T get drunk. Drinking wine is a ritual; expect constant refills.
DON'T hand out business cards freely. Italians don't use them much.

Spain
DO write business correspondence in English, unless your Spanish is impeccable.
DO take business lunches at 2:30 p.m. and dinner at 9 p.m. or 10 p.m. Be prepared to dine until midnight, later if chatter flows.
DON'T feel offended when interrupted in conversation. Your host is not rude, but interested.
DON'T expect punctuality. Your appointments will arrive 20–30 minutes late.
DON'T make the American sign for 'okay' with the thumb and forefinger. In Spain, this is vulgar.
DON'T pay for a male colleague's lunch if you are a woman.
DON'T discuss bullfights.
DO talk about American lifestyle, sports and politics.

Greece
DO be prompt, but DON'T expect punctuality from your hosts.
DO distribute business cards freely so people will know how to spell your name.
DO eat appetizers with your fingers. DO eat a great deal.
DON'T be surprised or offended if the Greeks ask personal questions; it is a sign of interest.
DON'T expect to meet deadlines. A project takes as long as the Greeks feel is necessary.
DON'T discuss Turkey or Cyprus.
DON'T risk insult by waving with an open palm. To wave hello, raise the index finger while keeping the palm closed.
DON'T address people by formal or professional titles. The Greeks want to be closer than that.

Source: 'Protocol DOs and DON'Ts', *TWA Ambassador*, October 1990, p. 69.

manners goes beyond knowing how to handle gift giving or shaking hands, of course. It would include general training on how to behave in business contacts with partners from other cultures.

US business people, in particular, find themselves at a disadvantage in other business cultures, mainly because they have little (conscious) experience concerning other cultures or training for international appointments. In many ways this lack of cultural training is somewhat ironic, for in the USA great cultural diversity does exist. However, one dominant business culture glosses over such cultural diversity in the main. For example, the US tendency towards informality and 'getting right down to work' is considered inappropriate in most other cultures. Europeans find the American 'business breakfast' amusing, if not insulting. In fact, most Europeans think US managers' willingness to talk about business at breakfast, lunch or dinner to be a sign of someone who cares only about money, and does not care for his or her family. US business people, on the other hand, view their behaviour of paying attention to business at meals as representing their commitment towards their family – being so committed to providing for them that they will sacrifice their meal time, and talk about business.[8]

Business Negotiations. Business negotiation in Europe and North America is defined as the process in which two or more persons, as representatives of their organizations or organizational units, come together to discuss common, complementary and conflicting interests in order to achieve an agreement that will benefit each party. In Japanese, the most common term for negotiation is 'kosho' which implies fighting, conflict, verbal debate, and strategy.[9] Negotiation is something managers do constantly, usually in a familiar cultural setting and thus most often without thinking about how they are behaving. But, as the difference in the implied meaning of the term shows, culture shapes negotiation in much the same way it shapes all behaviour. For example, Russians traditionally negotiate by moving the discussion upwards through the organizational hierarchy. At each level the negotiator involved wants to gain a concession of some kind. Sellers who offer major concessions early in this process are likely to lose a lot of money, or may not make the sale at all. Exhibit 5.3 gives some examples of cultural differences in conflict handling, straightness, readiness to compromise, priority of organizational versus personal objectives, emotionality, formality, and relationship building.

Exhibit 5.3 CULTURAL DIFFERENCES IN BUSINESS NEGOTIATION BEHAVIOUR

Culture has an impact on conflict handling, readiness to compromise, goal orientation, predominance of organizational or individual objectives, emotionality, formality and importance of personal relations in business negotiations.

Conflict Handling
French, German and US negotiators prefer direct confrontation when conflicts of interest exist. In other cultures, such as the Japanese or Chinese cultures where it is important to let all negotiators keep 'face', conflictual negotiations are handled with respect and modesty. In the Middle East conflicts of interest are not subject to negotiations between business delegations. Conflicts are handled by middlemen who are fully trusted by both sides.

Readiness to Compromise
Readiness to compromise is perceived as a signal of democratic attitudes, of goodwill and 'fair play' in the USA. In many Latin American countries, making concessions to negotiation partners is positively valued as signalling honour, integrity and grandeur. In Russia, however, a concession is perceived as a weakness: to give in to a demand means losing control over one's own will and giving in to the will of the other.

Goal Directedness
Japanese prefer a negotiation style called 'haragei' where all aspects of a problem are discussed again and again in order to gain a 'holistic' view of the issue. North Americans, in contrast, prefer to 'come to the point' immediately, because they want to negotiate in an 'efficient' and 'systematic' way. This strive for efficiency is interpreted as pushiness by negotiators from other cultures. It also leads to starting negotiations at levels close to what the negotiators plan to achieve, whereas in countries such as Brazil or China as well as in Arab countries negotiators love to haggle and, therefore, start negotiations with exaggerated positions.

Organizational versus Individual Objectives
Western European, Japanese and US negotiators feel primarily obligated to reach their companies' objectives. In contrast, Indian negotiators tend to focus on the realization of their individual goals such as power, prestige or personal satisfaction.

Emotionality
Latin Americans and negotiators from countries around the Mediterranean Sea tend to show their emotions during negotiations. Brazilians talk at the same time and touch their negotiation partners. Arabs raise their voices. More harmony-oriented cultures, such as many Southeast Asians, prefer to keep respect and coolness. Chinese negotiators even allow for longer periods of absolute silence and wordless reasoning during negotiations. This is very difficult to accept for negotiators from Western industrialized countries who are used to a constant flow of discussion.

Formality
US negotiators are most characterized by informality and equality in human relations. Titles have no place in mutual addresses, and the negotiation partner is preferably called by his or her first name. This leads to misunderstandings on the part of Central European or Asian negotiators who are used to highly formal addresses with titles. They consider negotiation partners using their first names as wanting to express their personal closeness and not to be overly tough. In Japan the status of the interacting persons dictates the flow of negotiations. And in Arab cultures social interactions follow strict rules which have to be known to foreign negotiators who want to be successful.

Personal Trust
In countries were individualism dominates, such as in the UK, the Netherlands or the USA, personal trust does not play an important role for starting serious business negotiations. It is expected to develop during

negotiations. Sometimes close personal relationships are even considered as a barrier to achieving business goals. In contrast, personal relationships play a major role in highly collectivist countries, such as Brazil, Japan, Malaysia or Thailand. Personal trust is a precondition to serious business negotiations in countries such as China or Mexico where the legal system is not considered as an efficient or socially acceptable shelter against cheating.

Sources: Graham, J.L. and R.A. Herberger (1983) 'Negotiators abroad – don't shoot from the hip', *Harvard Business Review*, Vol. 61, July–August, 160–168; Herbig, P. and H.E. Kramer (1992),'Do's and Don'ts of Cross-Cultural Negotiations', *Industrial Marketing Management*, Vol. 21, 23–31; and Leung, K. and Wu, P. G. (1990) 'Dispute Processing: A Cross-Cultural Analysis', in R.W. Brislin (ed.), *Applied Cross-Cultural Psychology,* London: Sage Publications.

Within a culture there is a shared frame of reference as to what verbal and non-verbal cues during a negotiation process mean, and what they imply in doing business. In international negotiations the lack of such a common frame of reference may result in erroneous interpretations of meaning and mistaken reactions. For example, if a sales representative from San Francisco, California, notices that the people to whom she is trying to sell something in Dallas, Texas, do not smile at all during the sales presentation, the salesperson would probably interpret that behaviour as 'the potential customers are not happy; they won't buy.' The same non-verbal behaviour in another cultural environment, however, may have a very different meaning. Not smiling during a sales presentation can mean that those listening are paying serious attention to the salesperson's ideas. If the sales representative reacts there as she is likely to do in the USA, for example by telling a joke, the listeners may consider themselves insulted. International business negotiations, therefore, should be carefully prepared and planned. Chapter 16 will elaborate this issue in some more detail.

Business Relationships. Depending on the cultural background, managers tend to feel to different degrees the necessity of building and maintaining close relationships with stakeholders from the firm's operating environment, such as suppliers, intermediaries, customers, administrators or media, as well as with its personnel. The varying importance given to relationship building in different cultural environments is partly due to the importance of the **communication context** in those cultures. In some cultures messages are explicit; the spoken or written words carry most of the information. In other cultures, part of the information is contained in the verbal portion of a message, but the remainder is in the context, that is, the setting, atmosphere, the status and power of communicators, gestures, and other non-verbal communication. Thus, cultures can be ranked on a continuum from 'high-context' at one end to 'low-context' at the other.[10] Figure 5.4 ranks various national cultures from the standpoint of reliance on the communication context.

Managers from high-context cultures prefer doing business with people who are known and have a high status. To get to know new potential business partners, they use pre-negotiation or pre-transaction rituals, such as business visits by varying delegations, sight-seeing tours, or dinners including heavy drinking. Managers from high-context cultures have a lack of haste: time spent in building business relationships is not seen as diminishing efficiency. Infor-

---

Figure 5.4 'HIGH-CONTEXT' VS. 'LOW-CONTEXT' NATIONAL CULTURES

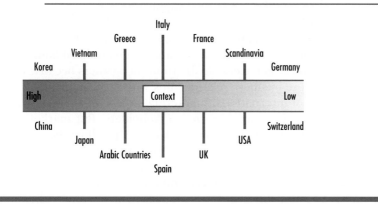

Depending on their reliance on cues from the situational setting, the characteristics of the interacting persons and all kinds of non-verbal cues for the interpretation of a verbal message, national cultures may be ranked on a continuum from 'low-context' to 'high-context' cultures.

---

mal, personal agreements are much more important than contractual, formal agreements.

Managers feel most comfortable in their own cultural environments. A particular approach that works very effectively at home, however, could turn into major problems abroad. For example, in Germany, Scandinavia and the USA, business negotiations may be started without having established a personal relationship beforehand. Negotiators rely on their competence and experience. The results of the negotiation process are laid down in detailed contracts. A personal relationship between business partners may develop over time when a one-time transactional exchange turns into repeated relational exchanges. Business people acquainted with such a culture may encounter major problems when they come to China, South Korea, Japan or Arabic countries for the first time. There, a certain level of personal trust needs to be established before meaningful business negotiations can be started. That is, personal relationship building comes before business negotiations. For that reason, negotiations between potential business partners who have not had previous contact are slow and ritual. On the other hand, specifying the results of the negotiation in an extensive contract does not seem very important.

Besides the importance of the communication context, the importance a culture attributes to family ties and friendship strongly influences building and maintaining business relationships. The Chinese, for example, are well known for their strong family ties in business. For instance, when a European marketer of spices wants to buy raw materials in Malaysia, it may first get in contact with a Chinese wholesaler in Singapore. Not content with the prices asked by the wholesaler, the procurement manager may travel to the plantations where the spices are harvested. A Chinese owns or at least runs them. When the manager has negotiated a contract at an acceptable price, shipment has to be arranged. And again, the manager encounters a Chinese entrepreneur. By the time the spices have arrived in Europe, they cost more than the wholesaler in Singapore would have charged. One thing has become evident: the entire chain of production and logistics, including intermediaries, is dominated by Chinese. But more importantly, they are either members of a single large family or very loyal friends. For the customer, it is often less expensive and time consuming to rely on their entire business network than to try, in vain, to establish their own supply chain.

Similar situations have been encountered by Western marketers entering the Japanese market. There, the distribution system traditionally not only contains many more layers than in Western industrialized countries, but it is also rather difficult to get access to distribution partners because of their long-term and very close business relationships with local suppliers.

The success of international marketing largely depends on the quality of relationships with the firm's external stakeholders. But marketing managers also need to make sure that internal relationships allow the implementation of strategies and actions. Companies in Western Europe trying to profit from the EU freedoms by expanding their business to neighbouring countries must be particularly concerned about cultural differences concerning the conduct of business, because differences in management abound. Adjustments may be required to become a successful marketer across the EU. German managers emphasize creativity, professional competence and coordination skills as key ingredients of organizational success. They tend to view the firm as a network of individuals who make appropriate decisions based on their professional competence and knowledge. UK managers favour interpersonal skills and the ability to influence others and negotiate effectively. They tend to view the firm as a network of relationships among individuals who get things done by influencing each other through communication and negotiating. French managers view the ability to organize and control as particularly critical. For them the firm is a pyramid of differential levels of power to be acquired or dealt with. Success depends on the ability to manage power relationships effectively and to 'work the system'. Italian managers, more than the rest, know how to maintain flexibility in bureaucratic structures.[11] When managers with such different views have to cooperate in one firm, considerable emphasis on personal relationship building may be needed to avoid major conflicts.

Business Ethics. Every culture, national, industry, organizational or professional, establishes a set of moral standards for business behaviour, that is, a code of business ethics. This set of standards influences all decisions and actions in a company, including, for example, what and how to manufacture (or not), what wages are appropriate to pay, how many hours personnel should work under what conditions, how to compete, and what communication guidelines to follow. Which actions are considered right or wrong, fair or unfair, in the conduct of business and which are particularly susceptible to ethical norms is heavily influenced by the culture in which they take place. For example, North American firms tend to emphasize ethical standards concerning internal issues, in particular fair treatment of personnel, whereas European companies tend to focus on ethical standards concerning the firm's relationships with its external stakeholders and the natural environment.

Perhaps the most common ethical issue faced by international marketers is how to handle corruption. Paying large or even small sums of money to administrators is considered unethical in many countries. Such behaviour is almost always illegal, unless it is considered as what US legislators term 'grease' or money which 'lubricates' decision making. The fine, and in many cases not clear distinction between bribery and grease shows how difficult it

can be for an internationally operating manager to meet differing ethical standards in a multicultural environment. Different cultures use different terms, such as 'baksheesh' in Arabic, 'mordida' in Mexico, 'chai' in East Africa, 'dash' in Nigeria, 'omaggi' in Italy, or 'on' in Japan, and give them different, culture-dependent meanings. For example, 'mordida' in Spanish literally means 'the bite' which is more of a 'gift' or a 'consideration'. The English word 'bribe' would translate as 'sobornar'.

In general, US criticism concerning bribery is met with the response that US managers have a very simplistic view of the world based exclusively on their culture. Other cultures view such activities as gifts, considerations among friends who need each other's support and help. The Ethics box goes into more detail concerning culture-specific views of corruption.

Some countries, such as India, are well known for 'requiring' small payments if customs officials are to allow goods to enter the country. While this may indeed be a bribe and illegal, the ethics of that country seem to allow it (at least to a certain extent). The company is then left with a problem: do they bribe the official, or do they wait for normal clearance and let their products sit in the customs warehouse for a considerably longer time?[12]

Fees and commissions paid to a firm's foreign representatives or to consultant firms for their services are a particular problem – when does the legal fee become a bribe? One reason for employing a foreign representative or consultant is to benefit from his or her contacts with decision makers, especially in a foreign administration. If the representative uses part of the fee to bribe administrators, there is little that the firm can do. For example, Munich-based Siemens, the Japanese firms Marubeni and Tomen, the UK's BICC and Italy's Pirelli have been barred from all public orders in Singapore until 2001 because of corruption accusations. The consultant Lee Peng Siong had paid bribes to Choy Hon Tim, vice-president of the state-owned utilities concern PUB, to obtain secret information concerning public projects. Siemens had used this consultant in a public power plant project, but they denied having paid any bribes.[13]

Ethics Box

What is Corruption?

THE WORD CORRUPTION COMES FROM THE LATIN VERB *rumpere* which means to 'break'. What is broken in the case of corruption is a moral or social norm of behaviour or, more often, administrative rules. To be broken, those administrative rules must be precisely formulated and transparent. A second element of the term corruption is that the administrator breaking the rules receives a favour in return for him/herself, the family, friends, his/her clan or party, or another social group. In addition, this favour in return must be seen as a direct 'quid pro quo' for a special act of breaking a rule. This simple description of corruption shows that there are many sources of problems with 'corrupt practices' in different cultural environments.

For example, in many countries legislation leaves tax allowances or granting import licences to the decision of the administrators. They are free to decide if an investment is 'essential' or the import of a good is 'necessary' for their country. The administrators are often the only authority to interpret the given cases. The greater the room for discretion, the greater the opportunity to use it for personal purposes. Seen from that point of view, the easiest way to avoid corruption is to establish precise and restrictive regulations for administrative decisions. But experience has shown that often it is exactly too many regulations that are the breeding ground for corruption because of the resulting lack of transparency.

When social relationships in a society tend to be close, it may be rather difficult to establish proof of a direct 'quid pro quo'. There are too many exchanges going on among the people belonging to the closely knit social network. Delayed compensations, such as a substantial gift when the daughter gets married, and indirect reciprocity – that is, the establishment of balance in an 'exchange' across a multiperson network – may inhibit the establishment of a provable corruption case. There do not even need to be direct contacts between the people involved. Social norms ensure that the administrative decision maker gets adequate recompensation in time.

And finally, social norms concerning reciprocation may be different from one culture to another. In an Indian village, for example, an attempt to establish an administration which works according to the (Western) dissociation principle that personal relationships are not allowed to make any difference in administrative decision making would collide with the highly accepted social norm that family and friends come first. People expect administrators to treat their family and friends in a preferential way even if such behaviour demands the breaking of administrative rules. A person refusing to act according to this dominant social norm would break that norm and be ousted. This may be one of the reasons why anti-corruption reforms in some industrially developing countries demanding personal distance were broken before they had really started.

Source: Tanzi, V. (1995) 'Korruption, Regierungsaktivitäten und Märkte', *Finanzierung & Entwicklung*, December, pp. 24f.

Corruption is, of course, not the only ethical issue involved when a company is engaged in international marketing activities. Other ethical issues, such as child labour, stealing of intellectual property, environmental protection or faked sales will be discussed throughout the book. Each chapter contains a special Ethics box discussing an issue related to the content of the particular chapter.

ANALYSING THE
CULTURAL ENVIRONMENT

Most managers, no matter where they are from, are culturally conditioned as to proper personal and business behaviour. But once cultural borders are crossed, the rules change to a set of unknown ones which are often difficult to understand. Confronted with other cultures, the secure knowledge of how to behave, how others behave, and how to market to them disappears. Therefore, an international marketer assessing the attractiveness and viability of country-markets needs to establish a list of cultural factors of influence that may influence the behaviour of potential customers in the firm's product-market(s). Based on that list, information can be gathered and used for a decision on which markets to consider further, how to adapt to the local culture or how to influence it.

Determination of Relevant Factors of Influence

To determine which parts of the considered country-markets' cultural environments have the most influence on the company's business, the international marketing manager needs to analyse its product-market(s). The definition of the firm's product-market contains three dimensions: it indicates which customers should be served, which benefits are to be provided to them, and which technologies are to be used for that purpose. Starting from those dimensions, the marketer may determine cultural factors of influence on each of the dimensions. Depending on cultural characteristics, the benefits may be more or less relevant in different countries, the applied technologies may have different meanings, and the target customer groups may be more or less substantive.

Self-Reference Criterion.   When searching for important factors of influence from the cultural environment, the international marketer must be careful not to fall into the trap of the self-reference criterion, that is, the unconscious application of one's own cultural experience and values to a market in another culture.[14] Consider the following example. A US marketing manager analysing the Egyptian market would find that elaborate sales contracts play a very minor role in that country. Applying the experience from the home market, the manager would evaluate doing business in that market as rather risky, because there is no 'reliable' system of legal contracts and courts for cases of litigation. In Egypt, however, giving one's word commits one to an agreement. This behaviour stems from the religious values of Islam, in which God holds people responsible for keeping their word. An Egyptian who has never done business with US salespeople before and has never heard or read about their business habits would be shocked by a request for a written contract. Such a request would be considered an insult to a Moslem's honour. Both the US and the Egyptian manager, unconsciously applying their own cultural experiences, would arrive at erroneous interpretations of the situation.

Application of the self-reference criterion to the analysis of cultural factors of influence can never be entirely excluded. Every individual interprets their environment based on former experiences. But, considering this as a given and the dangers of taking erroneous decisions, the international

"Well, I guess I'll have the ham and eggs."

marketer may take some precautions. One is to let a foreign TV team produce a video about the firm's product-market in its home country and show it to the managers analysing other country-markets. By recognizing what people from other cultures view as important characteristics of their product-market and how they interpret them, managers can learn what to look for when assessing foreign cultural environments. Establishing multicultural teams for the process of country-market assessment diminishes the danger of taking conclusions based on one cultural view. In addition, the use of more than one language in such a team may lead team members to new insights, because the use of different terms may evoke different meanings. If such a multicultural team gets the opportunity to scrutinize their judgements by doing some of their work in the countries under consideration, awareness of potentially incorrect interpretations of cultural influences will become even stronger.

List of Evaluation Criteria.   The final list of evaluation criteria for the cultural environments to be considered will be specific to the company and its product-market(s). There are some general factors, however, which in most cases will be relevant for international market success. Values and norms of behaviour, education, language, aesthetics and the social organization of a society will need to be considered by internationally operating companies. Education has already been discussed in Chapter 3. The potential impact of the other factors on international marketing is discussed in the following section.

Values and Norms

An important indicator of culture is the values shared by individuals within a given social group or society. A value is an enduring belief that a specific mode of conduct or end state of existence is personally or socially preferable to alternative modes of conduct or end states of existence. Values influence customers' perceptions. They underlie social norms, that is, accepted rules, standards and models of behaviour which direct the search for information and alternatives in a buying decision process, and influence consumption as well as usage behaviour. Therefore, an international marketer wanting to initiate and maintain exchange relations with specific customer groups needs to know the dominant values of its potential customers (relevant to the served product-market) in each of the country-markets under consideration.

Values potentially having an important impact on customer behaviour are based on religious beliefs, concern work, achievement and wealth, and are related to risk taking and change, as well as to consumption in general. These values will be discussed in the following paragraphs.

Religion.   The dominant religious values in a society determine many other values and norms of behaviour. Morality, etiquette, gender roles, and attitudes towards individual achievement and social change are all derived from religious values. Thus Confucianism in China, Shintoism in Japan, Islam in the Middle East, Africa and parts of Asia, Buddhism and Hinduism on the Indian subcontinent, and Judeo-Christianity in Western Europe, North and Latin America have a strong influence on norms of behaviour in those societies.

Religion may also help to boost international trade. For example, a good deal of the growth in international business of Utah, the US state located in the Rocky Mountains and known principally for its mountains, can be traced to the pervasive influence of the Mormon faith, formally known as the Church of Jesus Christ of Latter-day Saints. For more than a century, the Mormons have been sending their young overseas, mostly 19-year-old men dispatched for two-year stints in missions. In 1996, 41 000 Mormons were serving in 302 missions in 11 countries. Many of those young men, on their return, go into business, capitalizing on language skills and contacts developed over the years. For example, Evans & Sutherland Computer Corp. designs display systems for flight simulators. A cadre of former Mormon missionaries can speak Mandarin Chinese with the Taiwanese air force, give presentations in German to visitors from Germany, and speak Hebrew with Israeli customers. But the Mormon faith also has its drawbacks in international business. In many Asian societies, for example, drinking at night over dinner is critical to smooth business relationships. Mormons do not drink liquor. Nor do strict Mormons drink tea or coffee, because they are stimulants.[15]

Some conservative religious subcultures resist the quick introduction of new products. The Amish in the USA, for example, do not use electricity or motor vehicles in their everyday life, which is dominated by agriculture. Moslems and Jews shun pork; Hindus refuse to eat beef. But even in societies where active participation in organized religion is not high, the influence of religious values should not be underestimated in assessing the importance of this cultural element. The importance of success and achievement goals differs among countries depending on the extent to which their dominant religions value individual economic achievement. For instance, societies with a dominant protestant faith have traditionally been richer than others, partly due to the high value attributed to individual economic achievement which is considered a sign of having God's blessing. Islamic societies (with the exception of oil-rich countries), on the other hand, have traditionally been rather poor. This is partly due to the religious belief that wealth is to be used to satisfy basic needs in moderation. Thus, material richness does not entail higher status or merit. Many other patterns of behaviour, such as gift giving at certain times of the year, are based on religious beliefs. They must be understood by international marketers when evaluating the attractiveness of country-markets.

Work, Achievement and Wealth. Different cultures have different perspectives on work, achievement and wealth. For example, Asian followers of Confucianism do not make a clear-cut distinction between work and play like that contained in the Western ideas of 'weekend' and 'Sabbath'. Such differences are not only reflected in the values and norms of consumers, they also have an impact on how business is conducted.

A significant factor in a society's perspective on work is the historical importance of agriculture in that society. Countries that are known to have a strong work ethic and motivation to succeed may owe these values to an economy based on agriculture. In such societies hard work is less a moral issue than a prerequisite for survival. Even when its economy becomes less dependent on the production of crops, the society may continue to value hard work. This may be true of an entire society or a prominent minority group, such as the Indians in Uganda, who are noted for their achievements in distribution and commerce.

How long people work is only one measure of the value of work in a society, but it does provide a basis of comparison. For example, compared to Japan and the USA, but in particular compared to the newly industrialized and rapidly industrially developing countries of Southeast Asia, Western European countries have lower weekly and yearly working hours. Figure 5.5 shows the average working hours per year in some European countries compared to the USA and Japan. Over the years US business people have learned not to schedule major business trips to Europe during July, August or December, because their European partners or customers are likely to be on vacation during those months. *If It's Tuesday, It Must Be Belgium*, a film that pokes fun at US travellers in Europe, actually reflected the reality of short vacations for most North Americans (typically two weeks paid, compared to 4–6 weeks in most EU countries).

Inside the European Union there are significant differences in when people work. In 1995, one-half of employees in the European Union worked during the weekend. Sixty-two per cent of the British worked during evenings and at weekends, followed by Italians (57 per cent) and Irish (52 per cent). Work on Saturday is more usual, except in France, Germany and Spain where only about 10 per cent of the labour force work on Saturdays, but Sunday work is also common practice in Denmark, Belgium and the UK, where more than 35 per cent of employees say they work on Sundays (compared to about 5 per cent in France, Germany and Spain).[16]

Like other cultural elements, values concerning achievement and work change over time. The introductory example about changes in Indian society has shown how internationally operating firms, media and political liberalization together may be able to give rise to the development of a hard work-intensive consumption subculture in a traditionally contemplative cultural environment. As Table 5.2 shows, with increasing wealth, readiness to work hard and for long hours has declined in Japan. The same seems to be the case in South Korea where an attempt by government and business firms to diminish production costs by increasing working hours has led to violent mass

Figure 5.5 AVERAGE WORKING HOURS PER YEAR IN THE METAL INDUSTRY IN 1995

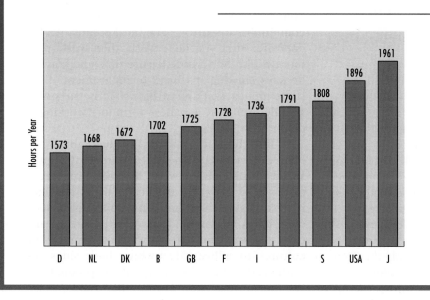

Japan and the USA have significantly longer working hours per year than most Western European countries.

Source: Baratta, M. (ed.) (1995) *Der Fischer Weltalmanach '96*, Frankfurt a.M.: Fischer Taschenbuch Verlag, p. 1043.

Table 5.2 WORK AND LEISURE PREFERENCES IN JAPAN

The Public Opinion Division of Nippon Hoso Kyokai has conducted a random survey on the attitudes of Japanese people every five years since 1973. The survey covers 5400 adult respondents, aged 16 and more.

Work ethics of Japanese have changed over two decades of steadily increasing wealth.

Question
Which of the options on work and leisure seems most desirable to you?
A: Devote all the energies to work to seek something to live for in it.
B: Devote a greater amount of energy to work, though enjoying leisure sometimes.
C: Divide energy equally between work and leisure
D: Enjoy leisure as much as possible by finishing work as quickly as possible.
E: Seek something to live for in leisure but not in work.

ANSWERS IN PER CENT

STATEMENT	1973	1978	1983	1988	1993
A	8	9	8	5	5
B	36	35	31	26	21
C	21	25	28	32	35
D	28	25	26	28	29
E	4	4	6	6	7

Source: 'Attitudes in Japan', *ESOMAR NewsBrief*, 3(2), February 1995, p. 20.

Future Issues Box

Clash Between Asian and Central European Work Ethics?

South Korean Daewoo bought 70 per cent of the Polish state owned car and component maker Fabryka Samochodow Osobowych (FSO) for USD1.1 billion in March 1996. In addition, Daewoo has acquired a smaller truck factory in southeast Poland for USD700 million, on top of a USD42 million complex making television sets, washing machines and circuit boards. Not only does the company hope to sell the EU the Tico, Nexia and Espero passenger-car models, they also see huge potential in selling auto parts and electronic components to producers in Western Europe.

Daewoo's expansion may be hurt by one problem: the differences in work ethics between South Korean managers and Polish personnel. "We Poles have priorities: family, friends, then work," says Mr. Wozniak the FSO Solidarity chief sitting in an office decorated with emblems of Solidarity's glorious days of striking and fighting communist authority. "For the Koreans, it's the opposite: First you have work, then work, then more work, then a little leisure time and family," he says shaking his head in amazement. "The trade unions won't allow *karoshi*," he says with a smile, using the Japanese term for "working to death".

"The biggest problem is mentality," he observes, voicing respectful amazement for the speed with which Daewoo Chairman Kim agreed to buy FSO. Now that the deal is done, Mr. Wozniak suggests, "they should use some Polish sociologists to understand us." Both Asians and Central Europeans agree it will take time for the cultures to adjust. Meanwhile, both sides see mutual advantage: Asian capital and products for European markets. Down the road, Asian investors also expect their ventures to increase Central Europeans' ability to buy their products.

Source: Michaels, D. (1996) 'To the East, Central Europe Enjoys A Surge in Investment From Top Asian Firms', *The Wall Street Journal Europe*, 13 June, pp. 1 and 9.

---

strikes. Nevertheless, the Future Issues box illustrates that work ethics in South Korea differ strongly from those in Central Europe, where it will be difficult to change a rather relaxed view concerning modern industrial work pressures which has developed over decades of centrally controlled company management.

Risk Taking and Change. A society's or a subculture's potential for change is strongly related to their members' flexibility. Flexibility, that is, the readiness to accept new, altered or different values and norms of behaviour, is heavily influenced by education that takes place largely through the family and in school. In tradition-oriented societies, family ties are very important. They tend to teach their children to do as their ancestors did, to be respectful of their parents' view of the world, and to accept the existing order. In such cultures, changes in values and patterns of behaviour take much time. An international marketer will be better off adapting its goods and services and how they are offered to the way traditionally accepted by customers in those cultures. Education in school may also have a strong impact on flexibility. Where the understanding of different reasoning patterns and value systems is emphasized, the chances that people are open to change are much better than in school systems where one view of the world – obviously the 'right' one – and the mastery of subjects through knowledge of concepts prevail.

The extent to which change is accepted in a culture affects the speed of product acceptance. Norms related to acceptance of change are often rooted in religious traditions, but they are influenced by the living conditions and material culture of a society. More economically advanced countries are usually characterized by greater acceptance of change than economically less developed countries. However, there are differences in the speed of adoption of new lifestyles and products within the group of most wealthy countries and their societies. For example, baby-boomers (that is, the generation now in their late 40s and early 50s) in Japan are a far less interesting target group than their peers in the USA. Unlike their American counterparts, there were few rebels. Largely content to absorb their parents' values, Japan's baby-boomers immersed themselves in their jobs. Growing up in a devastated post-war Japan, boomers did not always have a car. Therefore, they grew up aspiring to purchase a fancy sedan – and still do so. In contrast, the generation now in their 30s grew up expecting to have a car and treating it as an appliance. They, not the baby-boomers, are determining where the market is going – out of sedans and into minivans and sport-utility vehicles. They are the first demographic slice where more than 50 per cent of women even have a driver's licence, a key precursor to the two-car family.[17]

A useful approach to the analysis of consumers' and organizational buyers' readiness to change their consumption, buying or user habits may be to examine the elements that influence the acceptance of an innovative product within a culture. Table 5.3 lists product characteristics that influence the **diffusion of innovations** and indicates whether they encourage or inhibit them. Such information can help international marketers understand the likelihood of acceptance of or resistance to their products in a country-market under consideration.

The value of this approach can be seen in the example of marketing microwave ovens internationally. Microwaves sell well in all countries where the rate of women taking an active part in the official workforce is high. To many consumers in the USA and in western parts of Europe, the advantage of the product is easy to communicate: it saves time and does not demand that all family members eat at the same time. In countries where the buying decision makers do not usually do the cooking themselves, because they are mostly males or because they are affluent enough to afford a cook, such as in many Latin American countries, communicating the product's relative advantage compared to conventional cooking may be rather difficult. Sales of microwave ovens are likely to be lower, even among consumers in similar income groups. The international marketer will need to find other advantages of its product that are relevant to the local culture, perhaps prestige or energy savings.

For more affluent consumers, the financial risk of poor product performance is relatively lower than is true for low-income consumers. They may be more inclined to experiment with new offers from international marketers. But financial risk is not the only factor influencing customers' readiness to change. Europe's largest country, one of the most affluent countries in the world, Germany, had only 3 million Visa cardholders (Visa was the market share leader together with Eurocard) in 1996, compared with 30 million in the less affluent UK. Germans made only 1 per cent of their purchases with cards, compared with 18 per cent in the USA. Germans preferred to pay their bills

---

> **Table 5.3 Product Characteristics Affecting Product Diffusion**

Product characteristics can either encourage or inhibit the rate at which a product is adopted by a social group.		
	Relative advantage (encourages)	Degree of product superiority
	Trialability (encourages)	Degree to which the product can be tried at low financial, personal and social risk
	Ease of communications (encourages)	Degree to which relative advantage can be quickly and easily understood
	Compatibility (encourages)	Degree to which product use is consistent with current consumption patterns
	Complexity (inhibits)	Degree to which the customer finds the product difficult to understand

Source: Based on E.M. Rogers and F.F. Shoemaker (1971) *Communications of Innovations*, 2nd edn, New York: Free Press, pp. 22–23.

with debit cards, bank transfers and, most of all, cash. Even if the German card market takes off, the business might never be as profitable as in the USA. For one thing, German customers tend to pay their credit-card bills immediately rather than using the borrowing privileges. That means banks have to make their money almost exclusively on fees charged to merchants, instead of on interest paid by consumers.[18] Such behaviour may be associated with a deep-seated value that debts are an evil accompanied by all kinds of risks.

In analysing those risks potentially inhibiting international marketing success, the concept of **perceived risk**, which is cross-culturally valid, appears to be useful: when faced with a choice situation, both consumers and organizational buyers perceive varying levels of risk due to two factors. First, they may be uncertain whether the chosen object will meet their objectives. Second, they may be concerned about the consequences of the object's failure to meet those goals.[19] Depending on their goals and the potential consequences of failure, customers may perceive physical (harmful to health), functional (non-performance), psychological (negative effect on self-image), social (embarrassment in front of others), financial (loss of money), time (time wasted in product search), and environmental risk (consumption/use of the product causes harm to the environment). International marketers can employ the concept of perceived risk in understanding buyer and consumer behaviour in different cultural environments. However, they must be aware that the reduction of perceived risk can be achieved in different ways by customers across national cultures and subcultures. The Strategy box illustrates how international marketers may be confronted with perceived physical and environmental risk and what they can do about it.

Independent of the national culture, there are always some individuals who are more inclined to adopt new ways of thinking and behaving than others. For an international marketer assessing the attractiveness of various country-markets, it may be of interest, therefore, who the potential innovators are in the firm's product-market in a country, what purchase power they

STRATEGY BOX

Of greens and American beans

MONSANTO, A US CHEMICAL AND BIOTECHNOLOGY company, had difficulties persuading Europeans to buy its new, genetically engineered soyabeans. The company's beans are engineered to be resistant to Roundup, a herbicide that accounts for around half of Monsanto's operating profits, and which kills normal soyabeans.

US consumers have barely batted an eyelid at the product's introduction. In Europe environmentally and health conscious consumers have argued that the new soyabeans have not yet been properly tested and that the plant's genes could cause unforeseen problems in future. As a reaction, the German subsidiaries of both Nestlé and Unilever, the two European food giants, have said that they will not use genetically modified soyabeans in their main products. And a host of European food retailers have asked for the new beans to be kept apart from ordinary ones, so that consumers can choose whether or not to eat them.

Monsanto has said that this would be impractical and costly. But one of the few successful biotech foods in Europe is a genetically engineered tomato invented by Zeneca, a British firm. The tomato, which went on sale in early 1996, has captured 60 per cent of tomato-paste sales in big British supermarket chains – but only after an intensive campaign to make consumers aware of its safety and benefits. Moreover, consumers have been presented with a choice between the old and new-style tomato paste.

The conclusion from the two companies' experience is that it pays to spend plenty of time and energy educating consumers before introducing a largely new product. And second, that it is easier to introduce genetically engineered food when it is simple and cheap to distinguish it from unmodified products.

Source: 'Of greens and American beans', *The Economist*, 4 January 1997, p. 62.

represent, and how much influence they have on the behaviour of the remaining potential customers. A useful framework for such an analysis is the **product-adoption process**. It classifies potential customers into five categories: innovators, early adopters, early majority, late majority and laggards (see Figure 5.6). Customers may not belong to the same category for every product. Early adopters of the latest production equipment, even eager to cooperate with suppliers in the development of such equipment, may be much more reluctant to buy the latest office equipment or marketing consulting services, for example.

A major advantage of applying the product-adoption framework to cultural analysis is that it forces the marketer to consider the specific characteristics of potential buyers along with cultural influences on them. Early adopters tend to be relatively abstract in thinking and forward-looking in orientation. But early adopters are also influenced by their national culture, the subcultures they belong to, and the industry and company cultures. For that reason, an early adopter of steel-making equipment in South Korea will have different characteristics from an early adopter of the same product in Australia. Because those characteristics might make it difficult for an international marketer to open each market for its product or to introduce new

---

Figure 5.6 **PRODUCT-ADOPTER CATEGORIES**

Individual customers are differently inclined to buy new goods and services. Knowing the adopter categories in a company's local product-market, and their characteristics, helps the international marketer to assess the attractiveness of the country-market.

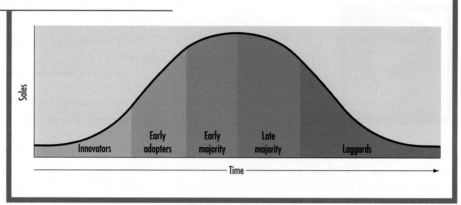

Source: E.M. Rogers (1995) *The Diffusion of Innovations*, 4th edn, New York: Free Press, p. 262. Reprinted with the permission of the Free Press, a Division of Simon & Schuster.

products there, the resulting assessment of market attractiveness will not be the same.

Consumption.   Basic values concerning the importance of material possessions (to 'have' something) versus ideal possessions (to 'be' something) strongly influence the consumption patterns in a country. In materialistic societies or subcultures, people express their self-image, their status and their success in life by the goods and services they buy and consume. For example, when the iron curtain between Western and Central Europe was broken down in the late 1980s, one of the first things East Germans, Hungarians, Poles and Czechs did was to spend their savings on new or second-hand Western cars. Nevertheless, in 1995, only 43 per cent of Polish households owned a car, while 96 per cent had a refrigerator which had become a standard for the entire population. Eighty-nine per cent of Poland's households owned a colour TV set, comparable with the number in the West. Nevertheless, 5 per cent planned to buy a new TV, amounting to 550 000 TV sets a year.[20] Table 5.4 provides some insight into what Central Europeans would have liked to own in 1995.

Pleasure seeking is positively valued in most affluent societies and in affluent subcultures of less industrially developed countries. Buying trips may be a means of entertainment for consumers. Consumers from the western parts of Germany, for example, are seeking pleasure when they buy fashion. In Europe, they are second only to Italian consumers in hedonism. A great part of their leisure time is taken up in finding clothes that fit them well and products that they enjoy. US consumers, in comparison, are traditionally looking more for comfort and simplification of everyday life. Time-saving goods and services are attractive to them. Many Germans plan their buying trips ahead, whereas US consumers tend to be more spontaneous. They buy when they are in the right mood.[21] Indian, Iranian or Tunisian consumers take planes for buying and leisure trips to big European and US cities. Business travellers to Tehran, for example, may encounter women boarding the plane wearing a chador (the black Persian dress for women covering the entire body, includ-

Table 5.4 CONSUMER ASPIRATIONS IN CENTRAL EUROPE				

| | COUNTRY | | | |
| | HUNGARY | CZECH REPUBLIC | SLOVAK REPUBLIC | POLAND |
PEOPLE WOULD LIKE TO:	%	%	%	%
have a fantastic car	47	55	53	54
spend holidays at the sea	50	49	47	41
travel by air overseas	44	50	47	41
have own house	36	38	37	36
have new beautiful furniture	36	31	28	32
have new household appliances	30	34	33	27
have new TV and music units	29	23	24	25
have fashionable clothes	28	40	45	26
have a weekend house	27	16	18	23
have a new bathroom	19	18	13	21
have a big new apartment	17	16	14	17
have a new kitchen	17	16	13	18

An IMAS-International study in Spring 1995 provided insight into what Central European consumers would like to own.

Question asked: 'Everybody has got his secret dreams and wishes. Assuming that money is no matter what, according to this list, would you like to have or do?'
Base: 6000 face-to-face interviews about 450 product and service areas with people aged 14 and more.
Source: 'East Facts', *ESOMAR NewsBrief*, 4(1), January 1996, p. 25.

ing their face), disappearing into the toilets, and coming back to their seats wearing the latest Western fashion clothing, before the plane has taken off from Tehran airport.

The most affluent parts of society in the EU countries are less concerned with material possessions; these have become a matter of course to them. Services have increasingly taken their place. A study conducted among affluent women in France, Germany and Italy, for example, showed that they are very interested in taking care of themselves by going to the hairdresser or a beauty parlour, playing sport, or going on a diet. Even more important to them is having time for themselves: going on vacation or away for the weekend, artistic activities, drawing or writing, meditation, yoga and psychotherapy, or simply doing nothing. There are differences between the various nationalities. French women leaders are more interested than other European women in culture, reading, writing and drawing. Italians like to buy more than other nationalities. German women consider that taking care of oneself equals doing nothing.[22]

With increasing wealth, consumers also become more concerned with health and nutrition issues. This concern creates numerous opportunities for international marketers. However, it should be kept in mind that different cultures define health differently, and these differences affect the types of products that can be marketed successfully in a given culture. For example, US consumers spend close to USD100 billion a year, or one-third of their total food-store expenditure, on low-calorie, low-cholesterol foods. This is considerably more, both in total and as a proportion of food purchases, than is spent on such products in any other country. Greeks, Italians and Spanish eat considerably more fruit and vegetables than other consumers in western industrialized countries, and have a significantly lower rate of heart attacks than the USA and Northern Europe.

Even consumption versus saving rates are influenced by culture. The US culture largely supports the 'pursuit of happiness' (guaranteed to every US citizen by the country's constitution), which – from a materialistic point of view emphasizing short-term orientation – means consumption. As a result, saving rates in the USA are three times smaller than in Japan, where longer-term orientation supports saving and self-sacrifice for the long-term good.

Communication

Differing values between the cultures of potential customers and the culture of the marketer are not the only source of many problems in international marketing. A second very important factor of influence on business success is the existence or non-existence of shared symbols. Symbols are abstract characters that represent ideas, feelings and other contents of communication. The message transmitted by a particular symbol or a combination of symbols, however, often changes from one national culture to another. For example, snakes symbolize danger in Sweden. In Korea they represent wisdom. A Korean company that uses a snake as its corporate symbol should expect some difficulty with its public image when entering the Swedish market.

Language. The most important symbols of human beings are their language. This language may use verbal, paraverbal and non-verbal expressions. In Korea, for example, there exists the concept of 'kibun' which is very important for interpersonal communication, but is unknown in Western cultures. 'Kibun' means something like 'feeling' or 'mood'. And Koreans know that they should interact in a way that addresses the 'kibun' of their partner if they want to build a relationship or keep it going.

Verbal expressions may be hard to translate into another language, because the cultural frames of reference are not compatible. The Spanish 'mañana' or the Arabic 'bukara', for example, are traditionally translated into the English word 'tomorrow'. But their real meaning is something like 'sometime in the future'. This difference in meaning may result in an important misunderstanding when it comes to carrying out projects 'in time' in countries speaking Spanish or Arabic. The Japanese 'hai', as another example, is literally translated into the English affirmative 'yes'. Its meaning, however, is more like 'yes, I have understood' than 'yes, I agree'. When negotiating with Japanese business partners, this slight difference may result in major misunderstandings concerning the progress of mutual consent.

Finally, identical non-verbal signs may have different meanings. For example, when potential business partners in Bulgaria shake their heads they mean 'yes', instead of 'no' as would be assumed by communication partners from Western Europe. The trouble is that Bulgarian managers who have experience of Western business partners might know about that difference and use shaking of the head in the sense of their Western counterparts. Reliance on that non-verbal communication, therefore, would be rather ambiguous.

Language is much more than a formal written and oral structure of symbols that permit communication. It is an essential element of culture. Understanding another language not only allows one to conduct business in that language but, perhaps more important, it also provides some insight into the social organization, the values, and the way of thinking of those who speak it. Even if a great number of business people in the world speak English to the extent that they can come to a deal, therefore, an international marketer should not rely on knowledge of English alone. There may be even some resistance to the 'English take-over'. The Academie Française is fighting the introduction of more and more English terms into the French language. English is not allowed to squeeze out Portuguese in Brazil, either. Sao Paulo's Abril media group, for example, started a commercial online service in Portuguese in 1996. In Japan, despite students studying English for eight years, many people think that personal computers are advanced enough to run good *kanji*-character programs easily.[23]

From the international marketer's perspective, a complicating factor related to language is that few countries are monolingual. In most countries several dialects are used, and in some countries several languages are spoken, often reflecting entirely different cultures or subcultures. Switzerland, for instance, has four major language groups: French, German, Italian and Romansch. And despite the fact that the people speaking those languages founded Switzerland some centuries ago, even today they represent clearly different national cultures. The dominant languages spoken in India are Hindi (about 30 per cent of the population) and English as the country's offical languages. Fourteen other languages, such as Bengali and Marathiare (both about 8 per cent of the population), are recognized across regions. Besides many others, such as Nepali or Mizo, that are recognized as official local languages, there are many not officially recognized languages. An international marketer who wants to reach more than the well-educated population of India, therefore, may be forced to communicate in many different languages.

But even a single language spoken in more than one country may have differences. Too often, business people in countries that share a language are not prepared for communication difficulties. For example, when a US participant in a business meeting suggests 'tabling a motion', the mover wants to postpone discussion; but UK participants will think that the person wants to begin discussion. In Australia, the suggestion of a US manager to have 'regular meetings' would lead to some surprise. North Americans use the term to mean normal, or acceptable: for example, 'regular coffee'. In Australia, the word is used in a different way. The closest Australian equivalent to 'regular guy', for example, would be 'mate'.

Paraverbal Communication. Paraverbal communication, that is, how speakers intonate their sentences and modulate their voices, is also culture specific. It leads to certain interpretations of the communication content or the communication situation. For example, the typical extent of pitch modulation of an 'educated speaker' in the UK is negatively loaded in other cultures. It is interpreted as a signal of the speaker's affectedness. In some African and Arab cultures, the volume of voice is used to regulate the sequence of speakers: the one who speaks loudest has the greatest chance of being listened to. In Europe, simultaneous loud speaking by a group of people is interpreted as an indicator of dispute. The personnel of international marketers need to be trained in the proper interpretation of such signals in order to be able to understand the meaning of communication in the cultures they want to do business in.

Map 5.1 Selected Major Language Groups of the World

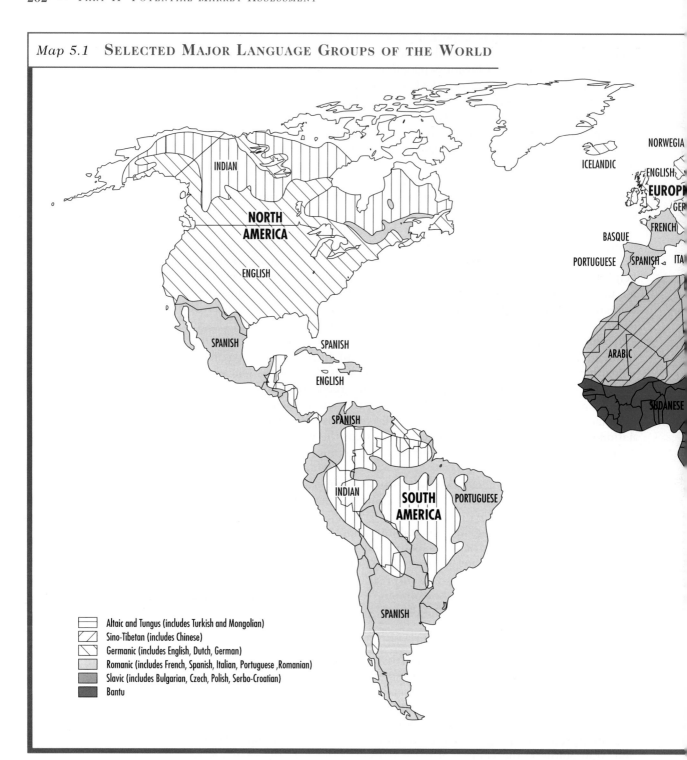

Legend:
- Altaic and Tungus (includes Turkish and Mongolian)
- Sino-Tibetan (includes Chinese)
- Germanic (includes English, Dutch, German)
- Romanic (includes French, Spanish, Italian, Portuguese ,Romanian)
- Slavic (includes Bulgarian, Czech, Polish, Serbo-Croatian)
- Bantu

The languages of the world are quite diverse. This map illustrates major language groups in the world, and shows how widely diverse a geographic area those languages cover. What it does not illustrate, however, is how concentrated those languages are. English, for example, is the first language of some 320 million people. Hindi (Indo-Aryan group), one of the major languages of northern India, is spoken by about the same number of people, but within a significantly smaller geographical area.

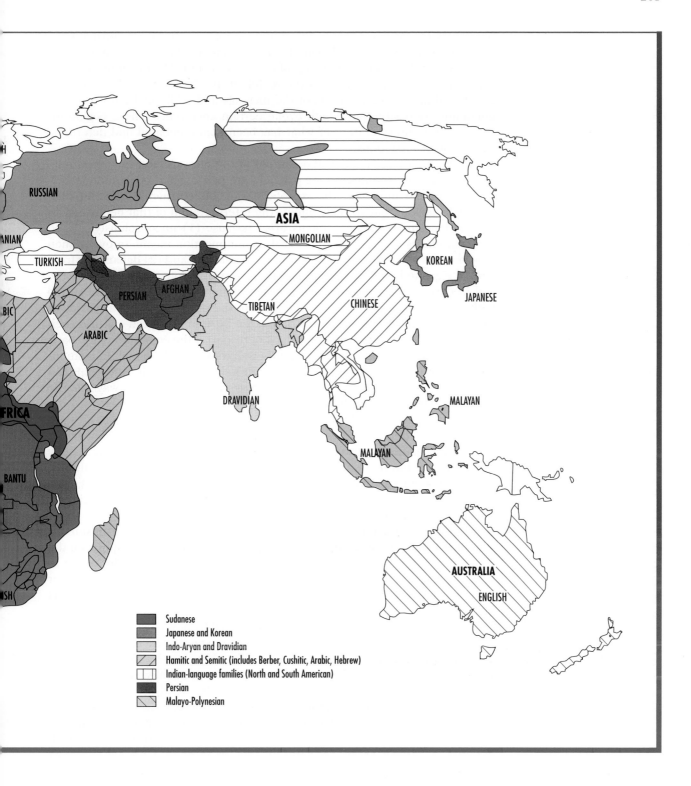

RUSSIAN

ASIA

MONGOLIAN

TURKISH

KOREAN

PERSIAN AFGHAN

JAPANESE

TIBETAN

CHINESE

ARABIC

DRAVIDIAN

MALAYAN

MALAYAN

AFRICA

BANTU

AUSTRALIA

ENGLISH

- Sudanese
- Japanese and Korean
- Indo-Aryan and Dravidian
- Hamitic and Semitic (includes Berber, Cushitic, Arabic, Hebrew)
- Indian-language families (North and South American)
- Persian
- Malayo-Polynesian

Non-verbal Communication.   Communication may be direct, during social interaction, or indirect through the use of media. Verbal communication rarely transmits the entire message of a communicator. The meaning of a message is produced in the mind of the recipient, partly due to verbal cues, but also based on non-verbal parts of the message and additional cues from the communication situation which evoke certain cognitions. Those cognitions serve for the interpretation of what has been communicated and determine the recipient's reactions.

In direct communication the content of the message and the social relationship between the interacting partners are part of what is communicated. Culture strongly influences the expectations of both partners concerning each other's behaviour and strongly affects the interpretation of that behaviour. In international marketing, problems arise because (1) unconsciously evoked expectations as well as the non-verbal communication means to evoke such expectations may differ from one culture to another; and (2) departures from what is expected as normal in a communication situation are attributed to the bad intention of the business partner. For example, a relaxed way of sitting with one lower leg crossed over the knee of the other leg is not a particular indicator of any specific social relation in the USA. In European cultures such a sitting position is interpreted as a lack of respect if the communication partners do not know each other sufficiently well to be socially equal. In communication with Arabs, showing the sole of one's shoe is an insult. And Thais feel insulted when communication partners cross their legs in such a way that the upper leg points in their direction.

Various types of non-verbal behaviour – also called silent languages[24] – are illustrated in Table 5.5. Each of these silent languages influences behaviour within a specific culture. The languages of time and space are highly important to international marketers. They vary widely across cultures. Indonesians, for example, show respect by arriving 'late' for a meeting. This once caused the president of a Dutch company some considerable difficulty. Expecting visiting Indonesian guests to be punctual (the Dutch way of showing respect), he was put off by the tardiness of his visitors. Similar misunderstandings can occur over the speed with which a meeting should approach the business topic or how long negotiations should take. For example, trying to force Japanese negotiators to reach an early decision is not only difficult but rude; it ignores the need of Japanese team members to reach a consensus before reacting to a proposal.

The concept of language of space is illustrated by how close to one another people stand or sit. Arabs, for instance, prefer to stand quite close to the person with whom they are speaking – uncomfortably close by North American standards. When a Canadian or US manager automatically steps back to a more comfortable distance, he or she inadvertently offends the Arab business partner. Similarly, in some cultures such as the Chinese, waiting in line means standing close together and jostling towards the front. UK managers, who come from a culture where one is expected to wait one's turn without crowding, may be driven crazy 'crowding in line' in front of a Shanghai airport check-in counter.

Context Relatedness.   The trap of using the self-reference criterion to interpret a communication or a situation is even more dangerous when confronted with non-verbal or paraverbal communication than with verbal communication. A manager travelling to another country expects differences in spoken

	Table 5.5 SILENT LANGUAGES	
Time	Appointments Deadlines Scheduling of people and events	Non-verbal communication accounts for a large amount of information received by a potential customer or a stakeholder. International marketers must take care to learn a culture's silent languages when conducting business in another country-market.
Space	Size of office Location of office Furnishings Conversation distance	
Things	Material possessions Interest in latest technology Personal connections versus material symbols of status, power and respect	
Friendship	Friends versus self as social insurance for times of stress and emergency	
Agreements	Rules of negotiations based on laws, moral practices, or informal customs	

Source: E.T. Hall (1960) 'The Silent Language in Overseas Business', *Harvard Business Review*, May–June, 87–96. Reprinted by permission of *Harvard Business Review*. Copyright © 1960 by the President and Fellows of Harvard College; all rights reserved.

language and even in some observable behaviour. Differences in silent language are much less obvious. Non-verbal communication is largely unconscious, but has a strong emotional impact. Much of the difficulty has to do with the extent to which communication partners rely on the context for determining the meaning of what is said or done. Business people from East Asian and Arabic countries, for example, derive much of what is meant to be said from the communication context. Confronted with business people from North America or the Germanic parts of Europe, who rely more directly on the spoken words themselves, emotional misunderstandings are commonplace.

But this problem may also arise in indirect communication. In cultures relying strongly on communication context, advertising campaigns are often highly visual and mood setting. How something is presented is as important, often more important, than specifically what is said. Japanese TV commercials, for instance, can be relatively informative with the inclusion of certain product information categories, such as packaging and performance. But they clearly avoid mentioning product benefits, guarantees and safety. Japanese marketers' media communications tend to be more intuitive, subjective, and human relations oriented, while marketers from Anglo-Saxon and Germanic cultures tend to be more logical, data and procedure oriented. Stressing company reputation is a more effective way to transfer the intended 'feelings' to customers in Japan than detailing specific product attributes and quality. Directly addressing why somebody should buy the product, as is common in much of Western advertising, would be perceived as an insult to the customer's intelligence concerning making a sound judgement. Japanese advertisers are also reluctant to use comparative advertising, which connotes a confrontational practice to denigrate competitors unfairly.[25]

Because of all the cited differences in communication, only intensive training may help internationally active marketing people to avoid major blunders in direct as well as indirect communication with potential customers. Such training must incorporate cultural self-awareness (making marketers aware that one's own thinking and behaviour are culture-bound), cross-cultural awareness (making them aware of culture-specific differences in the thinking and behaviour of others), as well as communication awareness (making them aware of the limits of mutual understanding in cross-cultural communication even after intensive training). The training should not be limited to knowledge transfer. To make it effective there must be important segments of practical experience training.

Internationally operating firms such as German-based chemical firms Bayer and Hoechst or French Merlin-Gerin, a producer of switching panels, for example, train their employees in nationally mixed seminars and workshops to let them directly experience the cultural differences in working style, delegation of responsibilities, communication and handling of time. For example, German managers perceive the French style of doing more than one thing at once as less serious. In contrast the French criticize their German counterparts for tending to stick to their plans even in unforeseen situations. French managers have a more paternalistic style of leadership than Germans who prefer a more team- and facts-oriented style. When French managers make presentations in a way in which brilliant formulations are as important as proper facts, German managers think that they take too long to say very little. But French managers feel they are being treated as beginners when their German colleagues go into details of facts and related background information.[26]

Aesthetics

Colours, forms, shapes, sounds – all that is considered attractive or unattractive in a given culture – constitute the aesthetics of a culture. They affect customers' responses to product, shop and office design as well as labelling and packaging, and they help define what communication is appropriate in a country-market. Therefore, the degree of potential product and communication standardization across country-markets is strongly influenced by the local customers' aesthetic preferences.

Those preferences and the meaning of aesthetic expressions may be very different. For example, when John Player, the English cigarette brand, was to be introduced in Hong Kong, Marlboro was the leading brand there at the time, and John Player was positioned to compete directly against it. One of John Player's distinctive brand characteristics was its black box with gold trim. At the time, black dresses were the leading fashion item in many markets, including Hong Kong. Player's advertising agency decided that the best time for the product launch would be the Chinese New Year. An extensive introductory campaign was designed and executed. Samples were distributed, coupons were provided, and an expensive advertising campaign was undertaken. The result was disastrous. Not only did the product not sell well, but people took the free sample packages to stores and traded them in for their usual brand. John Player had inadvertently violated the association of the colour black with bad luck and bad fortune. The timing of the launch made matters worse. At a time when people were in a happy, festive mood, they were especially sensitive to the negative connotations of the colour black. The fact that black was popular among fashion-conscious consumers did not help John Player in its appeal to the mass market. Fashions are temporary and change rapidly. Underlying aesthetic preferences are enduring and change very slowly. John Player's marketer mistook one for the other and paid the price – market failure.

But owing to the existence of subcultures, there are also internatonal product-markets in which very similar aesthetic preferences exist. Music, for instance, is particularly likely to have cross-cultural appeal. Jazz musicians like Wynton Marsalis tour the world; for a long time the rock group ABBA was one of Sweden's leading exports; and an Australian entrepreneur signed an exclusive contract to sell the recordings of Moscow-based Molodiya through-out the Asian Pacific Rim. The design of accessories such as Gucci bags, Etienne Aigner leather goods and Poiray jewellery, as well as the design of sporting goods such as Alfred Dunhill golf equipment, also seems to be attrac-tive to customers all around the world. In assessing the attractiveness of var-ious potential markets, the international marketer therefore has to consider carefully how the aesthetic features of its products may be received by the targeted customers.

Social Organization

Social organization provides the framework of a culture. It includes virtually every aspect of how people live together from day to day, the assignment of social tasks, and how and why people join together to meet their shared needs. Because the social organization of a society is so basic in terms of what con-sumers and organizational buyers are expected to do or not to do, information on social organization is extremely important to international marketers.

An example of this can be seen in the definition of what constitutes a household and how many households there are in a potential market. In the USA, for example, a 'typical' household is a nuclear family – one or two par-ents and their children. According to *Demographic Statistics 1995*, there are about 360 million Europeans living in about 140 million private households (average size is 2.6). About 70 per cent of the households are made up of families, two-thirds of which have children (average number of children per family is 1.8). In general, the Mediterranean countries – Greece, Italy, Portugal and Spain – have higher proportions of family households and fewer one-person households. Scandinavian countries are more likely to have more non-family households and more one-person households.[27] In Kenya, a typical household is an extended family – a nuclear family plus grandparents, aunts, uncles and cousins. Other aspects of social organization that are important to marketers are the roles people play within households and organizations, and the social groups to which they belong.

Social Roles. Through defining social roles, culture largely determines who influences, makes and carries out purchasing decisions, as well as who actu-ally uses goods and services. People's roles include their privileges and their responsibilities towards other people. Each one plays many roles in society – child, parent, sibling, student, worker, boss – and each of these roles causes needs and expectations potentially important to international marketers. For example, a woman playing the role of a mother may buy consumer products for her children, as a partner to her husband she may have the last word in the purchase of a family car, home furniture or household appliances, as a pro-curement manager in a firm she may be responsible for buying production raw materials and office equipment, and when inviting friends to go out for dinner she needs to decide what restaurant to go to.

The complexity of social organization and the stability of social roles and relationships are related to a society's level of technological and economic development. For example, in Zimbabwe women are almost excluded from participation in meaningful economic activities as owners or creators of wealth. Men have an entrenched absence of positive attitudes towards women and their capabilities. Women's status is reflected in the fact that a mere 5 per cent of Gross National Income accrues to the rural population, comprising 80 per cent of Zimbabwe's population – the majority of whom are women. In high-density urban areas women are no better off. Most of them work in cross-border trading, micro-manufacturing and vending. But the money they earn goes to supplement their husband's or family's income. They are unable to generate wealth for themselves. With an average take-home pay for urban dwellers of less than USD50 per month compared to the basic cost of living of more than USD65 per month, survival is the ultimate concern.[28] Where social roles are strictly defined on the basis of gender and change in social roles is taking place very slowly, if at all, the international marketer needs to under-stand those existing roles in order to predict buying and consumption behaviour.

In more economically advanced countries, social roles and relationships tend to be more ambiguous and dynamic. In the USA, for example, gender roles have been rapidly evolving towards more individualized and less pre-dictable forms. In Japan, where social norms based on Confucianism have long emphasized seniority among family members and the dominant role of the male, the level of well-being and happiness of the wife was considered sec-ond in importance to the well-being of other family members. In the work-place, female attractiveness was a highly appreciated trait. But Japanese women are increasingly dismissing the belief that women must remain at home and take care of the children. In the early 1990s the number of married working women in metropolitan areas for the first time exceeded that of mar-ried women working in the home.[29] The changing roles of women, in turn, are generating other types of change throughout society. For example, 70 per cent of American women of working age are employed outside the home and need services such as child care and household products that save time.

Social Groups. When people join together formally or informally to reach shared goals and to meet shared needs, they create social groups. People's behaviour in business situations is strongly affected by their previous experi-ences in such social groups: in the family, at school, and in different kinds of peer groups. In order to understand the behaviour of (potential) customers and stakeholders in another country, managers of internationally operating companies should therefore acquire some knowledge about families and social relationships in their target markets.

From a cultural point of view, the family is the most powerful social group in any society. Within the family children learn what is important, what to believe and how to behave, including what needs are socially acceptable and how to satisfy those needs in the marketplace. As the discussion of values has shown, variations in the process and outcome of enculturation inside the family from one culture to another can have significant impacts on international marketing.

As children grow up and go to kindergarten and school, they become members of peer groups which have an increasing influence on their view of the world and their behaviour. Such peer groups play the role of reference groups, that is, a number of related persons to whom an individual looks for guidance regarding behavioural norms. This guidance does not have to come from the group members themselves. They may follow the role model of a person highly attractive to them, such as a film or pop star; or they gather around the use of a certain brand which gives them the opportunity to differentiate their group from others and, simultaneously, to experience shared identity with the other consumers of the brand.

A person need not necessarily be a member of his or her reference groups. Reference groups may also be anticipatory (groups to which the person would like to belong) or dissociative (groups the person would not like to belong to). Reference groups are particularly important for international marketers in the case of products that are socially visible, unfamiliar to the buyer, or expensive.

'MANAGING' THE CULTURAL ENVIRONMENT

Having identified the most important factors of influence from the cultural environment on the firm's business and having analysed those factors, the international marketer is able to take decisions about how to react to the results of the analysis. On the one hand, less attractive markets will not be considered further. For example, marketers of industrial plants who cannot afford large time overruns in their projects because of capacity and capital resource restrictions may decide to put at the end of their list of attractiveness countries where respecting time limits is not part of the cultural heritage of customers and local stakeholders. On the other hand, in the more attractive markets, marketing management must decide to what extent adaptations to the given cultural specifics are needed.

Adapting to Cultural Differences

Marketing practices in a country are culturally dependent, and what works in one country-market does not necessarily work in another. Adaptation of the marketing mix is needed in many cases when the target customers belong to different cultural environments. Countries where women's major role is defined as homemaking, for example, are more often served by distribution systems that include bargaining. Arguing about the price of products requires that considerable time be spent shopping. Where women are more likely to have a career outside the household, time becomes more precious – a constraint on bargaining. In those cultures, fixed prices are more common.

Obviously, adjusting to cultural imperatives, such as language to ensure communication, is a must. But adjusting to other cultural elements which are not critical for success only adds expense and detracts from economies of scale and scope. Therefore, the international marketer must carefully analyse the cultural imperatives that exist in the served product- and country-markets and only adapt to those. Not only the application of marketing tools may need to be changed. Even the categories of thinking may be so essentially different from one society to another that the entire marketing approach may need to be adapted.

Marketing's Influence on Culture

Increasingly, international marketing managers must be aware that culture not only influences their decisions, but that their decisions and actions influence culture as well. International marketers act as agents of change within a culture. For example, most of rural Indonesia used to be beyond the reach of the cash economy. However, the situation is changing. Leading the way are women's toiletries and cosmetics. More than half of the women in the country's four most populous rural provinces use face powder, half use lipstick and body lotion, and a third use sanitary pads. Foods and beverages also have their attraction. More than half of the rural population buy candy and around a third purchase biscuits. Sixty per cent drink mineral water and about 40 per cent consume bottled soft drinks.[30]

After decades of buying poor-quality goods from state-run factories, Chinese consumers and private industrial buyers almost always prefer foreign-made goods and services when there is a choice. Capitalizing on that prejudice, an increasing number of companies have adopted foreign-sounding names or trademarks. But not everybody is content with such development. In 1996, a circular issued by the Communist Party and the city government of Guangzhou banned the registration of domestic company names and trademarks 'with the colour of colonial culture' that 'might harm the national interest and dignity' because they have no meaning but sound like foreign words. In the same year, the Vietnamese government launched a campaign against 'cultural poisons' that targeted English words used in advertising. Thousands of signboards were painted over as a result.[31]

Marketers conducting business across cultures should be clearly aware of the effect their activities have on local cultures and consider the rebounds such effects may have on their own business success. US-based multinational corporations, not only in East Asia, have sometimes been accused of 'cultural imperialism'. Taking advantage of the attractiveness of the American Way of Life to many customers all around the world, some companies, such as McDonald's, have been very successful. Others have encountered unexpected difficulties. For instance, in preparing the opening of Euro Disney (near Paris) in 1992, Euro Disney's first chairman proudly announced that his company would 'help change Europe's chemistry.' The French ridiculed the park as a 'cultural Chernobyl'. It took a series of adaptations such as renaming the park 'Disneyland Paris' and the addition of some special attractions to make the park profitable as of 1996 and the most frequented 'monument' of France in 1997.[32]

In the long run, as more country-markets are opened to international business, the rate of cultural change induced by international marketers will increase. As a result, more product-markets will become global. The further developed this globalization becomes the more standardization of business activities will be possible. The processes of cultural change and standardization reinforce each other. Thus, international marketers are contributing to the sharing of ideas, values and behaviour among cultures. At the same time, and as a reaction, local subcultures are becoming stronger. They open up business opportunities for local marketers, but also for international marketers that have enough flexibility to adapt to the local specifics.

SUMMARY

Culture, defined as the standards of beliefs, perception, evaluation and behaviour shared by the members of a social group, strongly influences the behaviour of organizational buyers as well as consumers. Consumers learn the most important values governing their behaviour during childhood in their families before they become members of peer groups and are attracted by reference groups from which they take additional standards of behaviour. Consumers participate in subcultures and they are members of national cultures.

Business people are also members of a national culture which strongly influences the basic values they share with others. In addition, they follow norms of behaviour which are part of the industrial culture to which their company belongs. Each company develops an organizational culture, that is, a set of behavioural norms specific to the firm. All those values and norms, potentially combined with a functional culture, influence the behaviour of potential business partners and stakeholders in international marketing.

Consumer culture and business culture both need to be thoroughly analysed by an international marketer in order to choose the most attractive markets and to determine the proper level of adaption of marketing activities in each of those markets. To reduce the amount of analyses to be conducted to a minimum, the international marketer must determine a list of cultural factors specific to its product-market(s) which are most important for business success.

Those factors may be specific values, may relate to verbal and non-verbal communication, education, aesthetics, or the social organization of society. They are used to evaluate the attractiveness of a country-market's cultural environment. Based on that evaluation, the potential country-markets may be ranked and the most attractive ones will be considered further. Later in the process of strategic international marketing, the acquired knowledge concerning the cultural environment of the company will be used to 'manage' this environment. Decisions will be taken as to what extent to adapt to cultural specifics and to what extent to try to influence the cultural environment through marketing measures. The tools an international marketer may apply in the analysis of country-markets and how the analytical process can be conducted in a rational as well as cost-efficient way will be discussed in the following chapters.

DISCUSSION QUESTIONS

1. Use examples to illustrate how the behaviour of consumers is influenced by different layers of culture.

2. What layers of business culture have the strongest impact on business people's behaviour? Support your points with some empirical evidence from the literature.

3. Find examples for international subcultures from

the business literature. How have they developed? How can they be used for international marketing purposes?

4. What role does the self-reference criterion play in international business ethics? Is there more than one set of ethical standards? Discuss.

5. Illustrate the difficulties in intercultural communication. What can an international marketer do about it?

6. What do differing work ethics have to do with international marketing? Give examples for the points you list.

7. Compare the role of women in your country to their role in another culture of your choice. How do the different roles affect women's behaviour as consumers and as business people?

8. Take an example of a firm you know and try to establish a list of cultural factors that this company would need to consider in assessing new country-markets to be served. Explain your choice of factors.

9. Take an example of a company from your home market and a foreign country-market where you have access to infomation about its cultural specifics. Based on that information, what adaptations of the company's marketing do you suggest?

10. Discuss the potential influences of marketing on culture. What are your conclusions concerning the impact of international marketing?

Additional Readings

Cavusgil, S.T. and P.N. Ghauri (1990) *Doing Business in Developing Countries*, Lincolnwood, Ill.: Routledge.

De Mente, B. (1994) *Chinese Etiquette and Ethics in Business*, 2nd edn, Linconwood, Ill.: NTC Business Books.

De Mente, B. (1993) *How to Do Business with the Japanese*, 2nd edn, Linconwood, Ill.: NTC Business Books.

Hall, E.T. (1990) *The Silent Language*, Doubleday: Anchor Books.

Herbig, P. and H.E. Kramer (1992) 'Do's and Dont's of Cross-Cultural Negotiations', *Industrial Marketing Management*, 287–298.

Kumar, V., J. Ganesh and R. Echambadi (1998) 'Cross-National Diffusion Research: What Do We Know and How Certain Are We?', *Journal of Product Innovation Management*, 15, 255–268.

Nakata, Ch. and K. Sivakumar (1996) 'National Culture and New Product Development: An Integrative Review', *Journal of Marketing*, January, 61–72.

Schlegelmilch, B.B. and D.C. Robertson (1995) 'The Influence of Country and Industry on Ethical Perceptions of Senior Executives in the US and Europe', *Journal of International Business Studies*, 859–881.

Terpstra, V. and K. David (1991) *The Cultural Environment of International Business*, 3rd edn, Cincinnati: South-Western.

Notes

[1] Hofstede, G. (1994) 'The Business of International Business is Culture', *International Business Review*, 3(1), 1–14.

[2] Hofstede, G. (1984) *Culture's Consequences: International Differences in Work-Related Values*, Beverly Hills, CA: Sage Publications.

[3] Bond, M.H. *et al.* (1987) 'Chinese Values and the Search for Culture-Free Dimensions of Culture', *Journal of Cross-Cultural Psychology*, 18 (June), 2, 143–164.

[4] Tomlinson, R. (1996) 'While Asian Women Buy . . . Americans Shun Fashion', *International Herald Tribune*, 16–17 March, p. 22.

[5] Nakata, Ch. and K. Sivakumar (1996) 'National Culture and New Product Development: An Integrative Review', *Journal of Marketing*, 60, January, 61–72.

[6] Lannon, J. (1996) 'Developing Brand Strategies Across Borders', in L. Caller (ed.), *Researching Brands*, Amsterdam: ESOMAR, pp. 43–60.

[7] Millar, H. (1991) 'The Protocol of the Flower', *Sky*, July, 84–88.

[8] Bates, K. (1992) 'Life Abroad: Culture Shock vs. Business Judgement', *International Herald Tribune*, 19–20 December, p. 13.

[9] March, R.M. (1988) *The Japanese Negotiator*, Tokyo: Kodansha International, p. 84.

[10] Hall, E.T. (1990) *The Silent Language*, Doubleday, NY: Anchor Books.

[11] Laurent, A. (1994) 'Managing Across Cultures and National Borders', in Hubert, T. (ed.), *Focus Cross-Cultural Management*, Brussels: European Forum for Management Development, pp. 5–7.

[12] Ruff, C. (1996) 'Hauptprobleme in Indien: Bürokratie, Zölle, Bestechung', Der Standard, 23–24 December, p. 31.

[13] 'Siemens auf der schwarzen Liste', *Der Standard*, 15 February 1996, p. 19.

[14] Lee, J.E. (1966) 'Cultural Analysis in Overseas Operations', Harvard Business Review, March–April, 106–114.

[15] Wysocki, B., Jr. (1996) 'Worldly Blessings, Utah's Economy Goes Global, Thanks in Part To Role of Missionaries', *The Wall Street Journal Europe*, 2 April, pp. 1 and 6.

[16] *Atypical working hours in the European Union*, Eurostat, London, 1995.

[17] Treece, J.B. (1996) 'Thirtysomethings dominate Japan's market direction', *Advertising Age*, 1 April, s18.

[18] Steinmetz, G. (1996) 'Germans Finally Open Their Wallets To Credit Cards but Aren't Hooked Yet', *The Wall Street Journal*, 9 April, p. A14.

[19] Verhage, B.J., U. Yavas and R.T. Green (1990) 'Perceived risk: A cross-cultural phenomenon?', *International Journal of Research in Marketing*, 7, 297–303.

[20] 'Durables in Polish households', *ESOMAR NewsBrief*, 4(4), April 1996, 20.

[21] Nelson, E. (1988) 'Der Konsument: Wohin geht er und was verlangt er?', *gdi impuls*, 4, 26–36.

[22] 'European women', *ESOMAR NewsBrief*, 4(4), April 1996, 20.

[23] Mandel, M.J., E. Hill, I. Katz and M. Johnston (1996) 'A World Wide Web for Tout Le Monde', *Business Week*, 1 April, p. 36.

[24] Hall, E.T. (1960) 'The Silent Language of Overseas Business', *Harvard Business Review*, May–June, 87–96.

[25] Lin, C.A. (1993) 'Cultural Differences in Message Strategies: A Comparison Between American and Japanese TV Commercials', *Journal of Advertising Research*, July/August, 40–47.

[26] Schulte, B. (1990) 'Wie Hund und Katze', *manager magazin*, Heft 9, September.

[27] 'Demographic Statistics 1995', London: Eurostat.

[28] 'The plight of African women', *The Mercantile Journal*, November 1995, 28.

[29] Henthorne, T.L., M.S. LaTour and T.W. Hudson (1997) 'Japanese couples' marital roles in stages of product purchase decision making', *International Marketing Review*, 14(1), 39–58.

[30] 'Rural Indonesia', *ESOMAR NewsBrief*, 4(4), April 1996, 20.

[31] Smith, C.S. (1996)', Guangzhou Bans Western-Sounding Company Names', *The Wall Street Journal*, 29 May, p. B3.

[32] Baverel, Ph. (1998) 'Disneyland Paris adoucit l'arrogance américaine', *Le Monde INITIATIVES*, 20 May, p. II.

INTERNATIONAL MARKETING INTELLIGENCE

INTERNATIONAL INCIDENT

New Products for Asia

Wolfgang Esser, head of international marketing research in BAYER AG's Self-Medication Business Group based in Leverkusen, Germany reports on a large scale marketing research project concerning the OTC (over the counter) market in the Asian countries of the Pacific rim:

The aim of our project was to identify the opportunities and risks for our business group's existing product range so that we would be able to take steps to create, where necessary from scratch, a product portfolio to suit the needs of the market. Our basic question was: what do we need to know in order to build up an OTC business in an unfamiliar country? Based on the maxim: 'We know nothing about Asia – and will proceed accordingly', we started the marketing research process by developing of a list of appropriate questions under the heading 'New products for Asia'. An interdisciplinary team held an initial brainstorming session to identify keywords which, following a check for redundancy, were transformed into a total of 300 questions. The questions were then sorted according to whether they were more likely to be answered successfully with primary or secondary marketing research methods.

A total of 16 Pacific rim countries underwent initial screening to establish priorities. The selection procedure resulted in three countries to be given priority. A more detailed analysis of each of the three selected countries was carried out and resulted in country-specific reports. At the same time we eliminated from our list around 100 questions which could be answered reliably and economically by desk research. New questions which arose as a result from the acquired knowledge were added to our list.

The remaining 200 questions made up the central element of the primary research briefing which we sent to several research agencies. The objectives were (1) to acquire intelligence of the markets, their prospects and risks as well as the factors which determine success or failure in these markets and (2) to acquire intelligence of the motives and needs, demand and purchasing and consumption behavior of consumers in the self-medication sector. It soon became clear that such an extensive list of questions coud not be handled by market research in the classical sense.

The alternative was a loose-leaf OTC manual for each country. As with a dictionary, our handbook revolves around 200 key questions which are operationalized as 750 subquestions. The loose-leaf format was chosen so that the manual could be updated and expanded. The dictionary-style structure suits the information needs of a variety of users and allows the responses for each country to be compared quickly.

The information was gathered from such different sources as laws, consumer surveys, retail sales statistics, or expert interviews. Furthermore, the research instruments varied from text analysis to group discussions and expert panels. In each of the three countries, 13 different target groups were surveyed using 17 different questionnaires.

The entire project was accompanied by a locally recruited panel of four experts per country representing medicine, pharmacy, marketing, and the health authorities. Each panel member checked the plausibility of the handbook and participated in a validation workshop where we confronted the

experts with the conclusions and scenarios which we had come up with using
the study results available at the time.

Source: Esser, W. (1995) 'From the "triad" to a "quadriga": a systematic qualitative marketing
research program for the Far East', *Marketing and Research Today*, 23(1), February,
20–24.

The International
Market Research Process

Lack of knowledge is a major barrier to successful decisions. In international
marketing the chance that management misses some knowledge necessary for
sound decision making is even higher than in domestic business. International
marketing intelligence is characterized by the fact that the firm is operating
or plans to do business within a number of different environments. To interpret their past and potential future development properly as a basis for
strategic and tactical decisions, the firm needs to establish an international
marketing information system that covers all important parts of those environments and the relationships among them. Data about the firm's external
environments – the economic, political-legal, cultural-social environments,
the product market, and the industry in which the firm operates – as well as
the firm's internal environment – the corporate policy, management systems,
resources and capabilities relevant to international marketing – have to be
systematically gathered and analysed. Their interpretation reveals valuable
information for international marketing decisions which has to be selectively
distributed to the decision makers in time. This chapter focuses on the planning and implementation of international marketing research processes (see
Figure 6.1). It discusses the adaptation of techniques successfully applied in
domestic marketing research to the more complex international environments and introduces some additional methods. Chapter 8 will discuss information needs concerning the internal environments of the firm and
conducting a comparative analysis of competitors.

International marketing research starts with the definition of its goals and
scope. From there, the information needed to answer the research questions
can be defined and its availability inside or outside the firm can be determined. Before research can be started, an effective, efficient and flexible data-
gathering procedure must be carefully planned, including what questions to
raise, when, and where to find the right information sources. In international
marketing research, only a particularly careful and culturally sensitive interpretation of findings can produce valuable information for decision makers.
The presentation of results has to be planned in terms of selected content,
amount of information, and timing in order to have an impact on management
decision making.

Figure 6.1 THE INTERNATIONAL MARKETING RESEARCH PROCESS: OVERVIEW

An international marketing research process must start with the definition of the research problem. Based on an assessment of information needs and availability, the international research project can be designed and conducted. To make the research findings useful for management purposes, they need to be carefully interpreted and presented to the target audience.

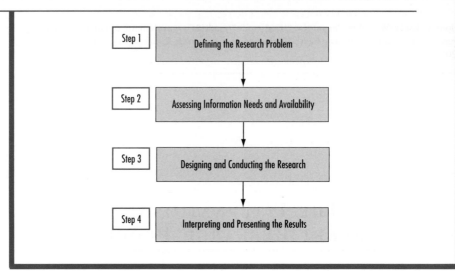

Step 1 — Defining the Research Problem

Step 2 — Assessing Information Needs and Availability

Step 3 — Designing and Conducting the Research

Step 4 — Interpreting and Presenting the Results

DEFINING THE
RESEARCH PROBLEM

Successful international marketing research requires a systematic and thorough approach. Lack of planning in this area can easily lead the company to the wrong markets or to make bad decisions about the right markets. Such mistakes can be costly and even cause managers not to pursue international opportunities.

One of the most serious, yet most common, mistakes made in international marketing is to begin studying a promising market without adequate planning. In one such case, an Austrian entrepreneur manufacturing plumbing fixtures read an American magazine on architecture and concluded that the USA might be a huge market for his products. The only problem, he thought, was to figure out how to sell them 'over there'. He decided to take a trip to the USA 'to study the market'. He departed without planning his research effort or identifying potential sources of information. After two weeks of travelling in the USA, struggling to find out where to go and to whom to talk, he had spent his entire marketing-research budget for two years without making a single valuable contact. After spending several nights in American hotels, the manufacturer was more convinced than ever that the USA represented a high-potential market for his products. But he had been able to gather only superficial information about potential customers, distribution channels, pricing, and the like. When he complained to a fellow member of a local business organization about the 'disappointing outcome' of his expensive and time-consuming trip, he learned to his surprise of the existence of Austrian trade delegations in four US cities. That resource alone would have provided better information free of charge than the entrepreneur was able to gather himself. His lack of planning had been costly indeed. Careful planning not only helps prevent research blunders but also ensures that better results are achieved within the firm's budget and time constraints.

Any planned international marketing research begins with the definition of the problem the firm is trying to solve. This is by far the most important step of the research process. The care and accuracy with which this step is carried out largely determines how useful the research results will be. Figure 6.2 presents the elements of this step.

A classic example of poor problem definition in international marketing research is a study concerning spaghetti consumption in different countries conducted by *Reader's Digest*. The study concluded (falsely) that West Germans eat more spaghetti than Italians. The researchers erred in measuring only the sales of packaged spaghetti. Italians buy much of their spaghetti in bulk, from local pasta shops, and they consume considerably more spaghetti (about 28 kilos per year) than West Germans (about 4.6 kilos a year). By defining the problem incorrectly, that is, as the need to measure sales of packaged spaghetti rather than total consumption of spaghetti, the researchers reached a false conclusion.[1]

As we can conclude from this example, management needs some preliminary information about international markets, such as the relevant decision makers, business habits or consumption patterns, to be able to define the research problem properly. Without such information, the problem will be treated as in the domestic market. To gather preliminary information about potential markets, the marketing researcher may read professional journals or talk with managers of other companies that serve the targeted market. Suppliers located in that market are another cheap source of valuable information.

It may also be helpful to visit major trade fairs or exhibits for the company's product in the market region to be researched. Major trade fairs include, for example, ISPO (for sporting goods) in Munich, Germany; the New York International Gift Fair; the International Fair in Frankfurt, Germany (the biggest fair in the world for consumer goods, with over 4400 participating firms from about 60 countries); and the Hanover Fair in Germany, which is the biggest fair in the world for industrial goods. They provide the marketing researcher with numerous opportunities to observe and talk with competitors, suppliers, distributors and customers; to gather brochures, catalogues, reports, reference lists and technical specifications; and to participate in cocktail parties and experts' talks and presentations. Information on trade fairs and exhibits can be obtained through local chambers of commerce and local embassies.

Effective problem definition may require the participation of the firm's decision makers as well as that of research specialists. The team approach has the added value of keeping key individuals informed and involved in solving the research problem and eventually using the findings.

To define the problem fully and accurately, the team must address not only the general content of the problem, but also specific elements. This has to be done in writing. A useful way to document the thinking involved in defining the problem is to develop a research brief or preliminary proposal to be submitted to management for approval. The research brief states the research problem, the objectives of the research (the benefits that will be realized), and the potential costs of making a decision without the information to be obtained from the research. The brief also defines the unit of analysis, the timing of the research, who will be responsible for the project, and a preliminary

Figure 6.2   THE INTERNATIONAL MARKETING RESEARCH PROCESS
STEP 1: DEFINING THE RESEARCH PROBLEM

The definition of an international marketing research problem contains a formulation of the research question and a definition of the unit of analysis, as well as basic information on project timing, organization and budget.

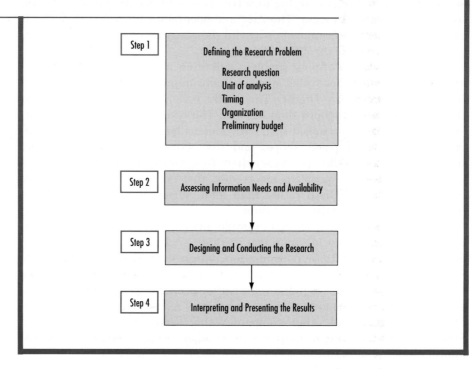

budget. This document serves as a framework for the research project and also provides a basis for deciding whether to proceed with the research.

The Research Question

The research problem should be defined as a research question. The information needed to answer each question varies with the type of question being asked. In international marketing, research findings are used to help make strategic as well as tactical marketing decisions.

Strategic Decisions.   Strategic decisions are mainly concerned with the allocation of scarce resources over more than one product- or country-market. They should ensure the overall success of the firm instead of local optimization. Market-development decisions concern where to invest, where to hold a competitive position, and where to retreat from. A small producer of highly specialized glass-treatment machinery, for example, may not have enough cash flow to finance research and development while maintaining a presence in every potential market. The market research questions that have to be answered are, for example: Which markets are more attractive than others? In what sequence should they be entered? What specific treatment do they need? How much emphasis should be put on the penetration of one of these markets before entering the next? Market-clustering decisions concern whether there is a chance to form clusters of similar product-markets, independent of national boundaries, that allow a standardization of the marketing mix or whether adaptation has to take place.

Finally, marketing research has to help the firm's management define how to position the firm itself or one of its business units or product lines in the international target markets. For example, a tour operator such as Waggon-Lits, based in Brussels, will not leave the decision of how to position the company and its product lines in each country to the local managers. Because the firm's customers may be in contact with a number of different offices, it is very important that they act uniformly. Market research will provide information about the strategies of local, regional and global competitors to help Waggon-Lits develop a competitive and consistent international market position.

The research question should reflect the nature of the marketing problem to be solved. If the problem is a strategic one, the question that the research attempts to answer must be framed in strategic terms, not as a tactical question. The Strategy box gives an example of a strategic research problem and its formulation as research questions by the Nissan Motor Company.

Tactical Decisions.   Tactical decisions relate to the marketing mix for a particular product-market or a special target segment. Marketing research can supply information concerning different expectations of various customer groups and their levels of satisfaction with existing products. Marketing research can also provide information on brand awareness and image, the usual terms of delivery and payment, the price of competing or substitute offers, appropriate outlets, and the availability and usage pattern of advertising media in each market.

For example, US-based Whirlpool Corporation, which after the acquisition of Philips' appliance business has become the largest appliance company in the world, regularly tests new products, interviewing people to determine their reaction to the product and brand; has set up simulated stores to see how people react to products and different messages from salespeople; sends mystery shoppers into a series of retail stores to find out exactly what the salespeople are saying and doing; conducts telephone interviews to measure brand awareness and brand image; and tracks progress using traditional financial data like sales, market share, and performance compared to budget and the previous year.[2]

Unit of Analysis

The unit of analysis is the smallest source of information that will be used to answer the research questions. For example, a research project that aims to compare total consumption patterns for fast food in Singapore, Thailand and South Korea will use the country as the unit of analysis. However, if the goal is to measure specific brand preferences within each country – for example, the preference between McDonald's, Kentucky Fried Chicken and local street kitchens – the unit of analysis will be the individual consumer.

Traditionally, the country has been the most common unit of analysis for international marketing research. The advantage of this approach lies in the fact that most information available on the environment (cultural, social, demographic, economic, legal and political) is organized by country. In addition, it is still common for the international sales force, the internal sales department, or the firm's subsidiaries to be organized according to national boundaries.

STRATEGY BOX

Global Marketing Research by the Nissan Motor Company Limited

THE NISSAN MOTOR COMPANY HAS PRODUCTION BASES located in 21 countries. For customers in these many nations to be fully satisfied with the performance of their cars, it is necessary to observe carefully and arrive at a full understanding of the customer from the very initial stages of product planning and strategy.

Nissan first started with exporting cars as designed for the Japanese market. Then they took factors related to the US and European markets into consideration, but designed mainly for the Japanese market. The resulting product matched none of the markets. As a consequence they installed the so-called 'lead country system'. Special attention was focused on the major tar-get markets and manufacturing vehicles to match the needs and requirements of those markets.

In the 4th phase Nissan is seeking to base its strategy on a global perspective. This global perspective is based on a strategic research effort that attempts to compare the perception and attitudes of car users in the Triad to identify the common and differing elements in these three areas. The research questions are phrased like, for example: 'Do Japanese, US, and European customers have the same values and the same demands regarding functions and performance of their cars?' 'If there are differences, what are the reasons for those differences?' They do not consider tactical elements such as, for example: How should the gear shift and the front lights look like to be equally attractive to the customers in the Triad countries?

Source: Hisatomi, T. (1991) 'Global marketing by the Nissan Motor Company Limited – A simultaneous market study of users' opinions and attitudes in Europe, USA and Japan', *Marketing and Research Today*, 19(1), February, 56–61.

Although this approach is convenient, it is not always effective. Its chief disadvantage is that data describing a whole country give an impression of homogeneity that may mask considerable diversity. Italy, for example, consists of the highly industrialized, wealthy north and the less developed, relatively poor, rural south. These two areas have differences in income distribution (although rich and poor people are found in both areas), marketing infrastructures, and, to a lesser extent, culture.

Research projects that use country data for purposes of comparison often fail to discover the best business opportunities. Such opportunities are more likely to be recognized if the unit of analysis is based on a product-market perspective. A product-market is composed of organizations or individuals. Units of analysis may be, for example, firms, buying centres, households or individuals. They face similar problems, seek similar benefits or display similar response patterns, but they do not necessarily share the same nationality. By starting with a product-market perspective, the marketer gains the advantage of being able to compare target segments regardless of size and geographic boundaries and to cluster them into homogeneous supranational markets.

The major disadvantage of using a product-market perspective to define the unit of analysis lies in subjective influences in defining product-market boundaries. The perspectives and ambitions of managers have a significant impact on the research design and findings. For example, if a manufacturer of downhill skis, such as French Rossignol, defines its market as wealthy, experienced skiers in the Rocky Mountains area of the USA who ski for fun, the research project to discover their purchasing behaviour will be very different from a project with a similar research problem, where the manufacturer defines its product-market as all the people in industrialized nations who like to spend their leisure time in winter doing outdoor sports. The impossibility of an objective definition of product-market boundaries should not discourage researchers from using that perspective, however. Marketing research could even help to find the most promising definition of the product-market to serve. It simply emphasizes the need to define clearly the problem underlying the research project.

Because the costs of data collection often rise as the size of the unit of analysis is reduced, it is important that researchers be clear about the level of detail needed. An easy trap to fall into, especially in an international context, is assuming that more information is needed, in more detail, than is really necessary. A practical way of choosing the unit of analysis may be to follow a stepwise procedure. This starts with an exact definition of the potential product-market to be served. Then the most attractive geographic areas are determined, and finally the adequate unit of analysis for the product-market in those areas is chosen. For example, a Dutch manufacturer of durable plastic pipes for use in building construction may want to explore international product-markets. But the firm may not be large enough to expand simultaneously from one country-market to all potential markets. To cope with such limitations, it should focus on product-markets for plastic construction supplies in a carefully selected geographic area, such as Scandinavia, and take a closer look at construction-supply wholesalers (as the unit of analysis) there.

Timing

Timing is an especially sensitive issue in the development of a research brief. Thorough international research projects often take more time than many firms believe they can afford. Alastaire Fairgrieve, Marketing Services Manager in the UK and co-Chairman of McDonald's Pan-European Research Group, for example, stated: 'We frequently move too quickly for tactical studies. Most of our research is used for strategic planning, helping us in our basic job of selling more hamburgers all over the world.'[3]

Before embarking on a full-scale research project, it is important to determine the latest possible date on which the results of the research could contribute to decision making. Similarly, it is important to determine the latest date on which one might begin the research process in order to produce results based on the most recent information available. These two factors obviously pose a dilemma. The marketing researcher will have to find a reasonable compromise that relies on thorough planning, paired with personal experience.

Organization

The assignment of responsibility for a research project depends not only on the specific problem to be explored but also on the size, resources and experience of the firm. Research for strategic purposes is usually conducted by members of the firm. The export manager, a marketing researcher or a business unit manager, for example, could take over the direction of the project. Small firms and those with little international experience may prefer to consult with experts outside the firm.

If a company plans to become active in a region where it has no experience and to assign a new manager to the region, the firm should assign the research responsibilities for this new market area to the chosen manager. Knowing that strategy, resource deployment and actions will be based on the findings of the research project, the manager will be much more motivated to produce reliable and relevant information than a marketing research specialist who is less involved.

In industrial marketing most of the international research for tactical decisions will also be done by members of the company. They have the technical expertise needed for research concerning their products, which is not usually available from external organizations. In addition, the number of distribution-channel members, potential customers and important competitors is rather restricted in many industrial product-markets. Little or no field organization is needed for data gathering, therefore.

In international marketing of consumer products and services, only a few companies have enough personnel and specialized knowledge to conduct marketing research projects for tactical purposes in an effective and efficient manner. They may be able to define the specifications for the research design. But in most cases they do not have a field organization to run interviews on an international level, or they are not familiar enough with local environments and languages to avoid misunderstandings and misinterpretations. They therefore rely on external marketing-research organizations. The choices they have, and related advantages and disadvantages, will be discussed later in this chapter.

Preliminary Budget

A tentative budget should be drawn up based on the research questions, a preliminary understanding of what information is needed and at what level of detail, and a consensus about timing, organization, and what the firm's management is willing and able to spend. This is only a preliminary budget. Assuming that the proposal goes forward and the project moves into the next stage, a more detailed budget and a full research design are developed to guide the remainder of the project.

Assessing Information Needs and Availability

A research brief is seldom specific enough to serve as a detailed research plan. But the defined research questions point to the second step of the research process: assessing information needs and availability (see Figure 6.3). This requires that the researchers define more clearly the dimensions of the research problem. The list of those dimensions allows researchers to find out what information is available inside the company and what information must be gathered from external sources. It also provides guidance for developing the research design and final budget.

Figure 6.3 **The International Marketing Research Process
Step 2: Assessing Information Needs and Availability**

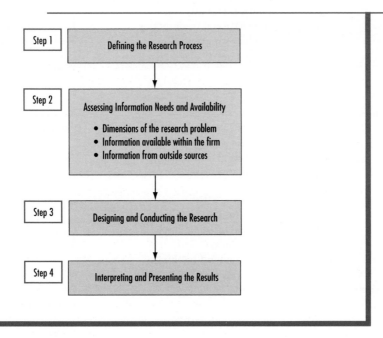

Step 1	Defining the Research Process
Step 2	Assessing Information Needs and Availability • Dimensions of the research problem • Information available within the firm • Information from outside sources
Step 3	Designing and Conducting the Research
Step 4	Interpreting and Presenting the Results

To assess information needs and availability, international marketers first need to specify the dimensions of the research problem. Then they can determine what information is available within the firm and what information has to be gathered from outside sources.

Dimensions of the Research Problem

In international marketing, the specific dimensions of a research problem depend on the research objectives, product-markets, geographic areas of interest and targeted market segments. Table 6.1 illustrates the dimensions of a research problem that were defined by a European manufacturer of eyeglass frames interested in entering the fast-developing South Korean market. Note that this outline only focuses on one country; other geographic areas might be included, and target segments within each would probably be identified. Different research dimensions for each segment may result. The researcher can use the list of dimensions as a checklist, which will be further refined during the research process. Its first use is to identify information available within the firm.

Information Available Within the Firm

Before looking elsewhere, the researcher should determine what data are available within the firm. The value and scope of such information vary with the firm's size, experience and policies. McDonald's, for example, considers itself an experience-based company with business units in different stages of development and a flat management structure in which managers can learn from each other by picking up the phone and discussing issues with people at all levels throughout the world.[4]

Statistics. Relevant information can often be derived from accounting records, especially sales and cost figures. The most valuable internal

Table 6.1		Dimensions for Assessing the South Korean Market for Eyeglass Frames	

Environment	Political/legal	Role of government
		Political stability
		International trade policy
		Trademark protection
			Restrictions on capital
			  flows
			Price regulations
			Restrictions on
			  ownership
			Regulation of
			  competition

	Cultural/social	Business ethics Negotiation customs Networks Resolution of disputes Social structure	Norms and values Attitudes towards foreign products Aesthetics Consumption patterns

	Economic	Growth of GNP
		Rate of inflation
		Balance of trade and
		  payments
		Currency and banking
			Population
			  development
			Communication systems
			Transportation systems

Product market	Structure	Potential Volume	Imports/exports Development
	Consumers	Buying power Buying and usage behaviour Product-specific physiological characteristics	Lifestyles Preferences
	Intermediaries	Number Reliability Margins expected	Size Buying habits
	Competition	Number Market shares Apparent strategies Product lines Price levels	Size Profitability Postitioning Distribution policy Promotion policy

statistical data for marketing purposes are summarized in Table 6.2. Internal statistics can help the marketing manager judge the effectiveness of various strategies and tactics. The eyeglass-frame manufacturer described earlier, for example, may examine data on orders, sales, and profits or losses for exports to other markets and conclude how large the market volume and market share would have to be in South Korea to be profitable. In order to overcome comparability problems caused by different rules of bookkeeping and cost accounting as well as tax legislation in various countries, firms operating in more than one legal environment must apply standardized systems that are used exclusively for internal purposes.

Table 6.2 INTERNAL STATISTICS FOR MARKETING RESEARCH

Order statistics
> Offers made
> Orders accepted (by delivery time)
> Cancellations of orders (including reasons why)
> Order structure (size of orders, costs per order, number and size of
> orders per customer and per salesperson)

Sales statistics

Sales (pieces, value)		Market segment
Average prices		Channel of distribution
Price cuts/bonuses	per	Sales area
Terms of payment		Product (line)
Promotion costs		Customer

Profit and loss statistics

Profit and loss structure		Order
(including absolute and	per	Product (line)
relative contributions to		Customer
gross margin)		Sales area
		Channel of distribution
		Market segment

Order, sales, and profit and loss statistics of a company may provide useful information for an international marketing researcher.

The increased use of scanning in retail outlets in highly industrialized countries has provided retailers and cooperating manufacturers of consumer goods with an extremely valuable internal source of information. It not only allows logistics and the variety of goods on offer to be optimized, it also provides information on issues such as price sensitivity, reactions to product presentations, and the purchasing patterns of customers.

Data Banks.   Some firms, in particular smaller ones and those whose interest in international marketing is relatively recent, may have internal data for only a limited market area. In more experienced and sophisticated firms with more complex information and control systems, up-to-date data banks may already exist. They will contain not only general information on market development, but also on customer, intermediary, supplier and competitor behaviour, based on reports from sales, maintenance and service people, procurement personnel, subsidiary managers, distributors or professional journals. Findings from other research projects that are relevant to the research problem at hand may also be available in the data bank.

Information from Outside Sources

Having gathered internal data, the researcher may need to obtain additional information from external sources. The question is how to obtain this information at a reasonable cost and in a timely manner. There are basically two ways of obtaining data from sources outside the firm: primary research and secondary research.

Secondary Data.   For reasons of cost, time, and problems in data collection, firms often attempt to satisfy their information needs by using secondary data. They gather and analyse data that have already been published by or are available from an existing source. Secondary data are most valuable in assessing the attractiveness of markets about which management has little knowledge. They are regularly used to identify country- or product-markets that merit in-depth consideration and to monitor changes in the international environment. Secondary data enable the researcher to roughly evaluate the risk associated with operating in a specific market, to determine the likely costs of alternative modes of operation and different marketing strategies, and to forecast the probable returns associated with operating in the market under study.

For example, Nielsen SRG, based in Hong Kong, has published a *Decision Book: China* which contains the results of a census of over one million retail outlets in China. It gives an overview of the country's retail structure, projected to 95 per cent of the population and half the geography of the People's Republic. The audit covers nearly 375 000 grocery shops and the distribution of a wide variety of consumer foods, penetration of 53 specific product categories by region, and shop facilities such as lighting, refrigeration and telephones.[5]

Secondary data provide information quickly and cheaply. But the researcher must be aware that in most cases they have been collected and analysed for purposes that differ from the firm's research objectives. Such data can be used to reduce the amount of information that must be newly obtained through studies initiated by the firm, thereby reducing the amount of time and money needed to complete the project. Most research problems can be addressed using secondary data, but require primary data for precision at the end of the research process.

Primary Data.   Primary data are new or as yet unpublished data collected and analysed by the firm. They provide specific and targeted information for a given research problem. Such data may come from customers, intermediaries, competitors, suppliers, or experts in a particular field. It is most useful during an in-depth analysis of product-markets, because it helps to identify the behaviour, needs, and benefits sought by customers in those markets. The feasibility and cost of obtaining primary data vary considerably with the product category and the geographic area.

For example, since their liberation from communism, the countries of Central Europe have seen rapid development of marketing research firms. AISA, as an example, privately founded in 1990, has offices in Prague (Czech Republic) and Bratislava (Slovakia). As one of its services to consumer goods companies, it provides media analysis data for both countries at prices below USD3000. In the Arabian countries of the Middle East there are excellent agencies with good qualitative researchers. However, most executive researchers are European expatriates who cannot conduct interviews in Arabic or attend Arab female groups. There are very few trained Arab female or male researchers who can take a research brief, conduct focus group interviews and debrief the client.[6]

DESIGNING AND
CONDUCTING THE RESEARCH

Figure 6.4 presents a two-step approach to research design and implementation, beginning with secondary research and following up where necessary with primary studies. The characteristics and difficulties of both steps in carrying out international marketing research will be discussed in the following.

Secondary Research

Secondary or desk research is the gathering and analysis of data that have already been published by or are available from existing sources. The cheapest sources of secondary data are census and other statistical reports published by government agencies, such as the US Department of Commerce or the European Commission in Brussels, and by specialized agencies such as trade associations, chambers of commerce, research institutes and banks.

Production Statistics.   Production statistics on product categories are available for all industrialized countries. Together with other statistics they help the marketing researcher to estimate market volume, the degree of saturation, and the level of local production. Production statistics are published with varying frequency, from monthly, as in Western industrialized nations, to every few years or not at all, as in some developing countries. In using production statistics for marketing research the marketer has to be careful, because:

1. *Not all production facilities are included in the statistics;* frequently, small firms are not included. If the industry the marketer is interested in is characterized by a multitude of small family businesses, as is the case with the European textile industry, production statistics would lead to erroneous conclusions.

2. *The way products are classified may vary from one country to another.* It is important, therefore, to study the product lists accompanying production statistics thoroughly or to ask for specific information at the office that publishes them.

3. *The product categories may contain a different number of products.* Smaller countries often use broader product categories than big ones. TV sets, for example, are in a category of their own in some countries, whereas in others they belong to the consumer electronics category.

4. *An industry may contain only a few producers, whose data are not published for competitive reasons.* For example, when an industry in an EU market is controlled by very few companies – such as aerospace and air traffic control industries – no production data are published, because they would provide too much information to foreign competitors.

5. *The value of the products in the statistics may have been calculated in different ways.* Some of the calculations contain only the production costs; others include sales or value-added taxes; and others consider market prices.

Figure 6.4 The International Marketing Research Process Step 3: Designing and Conducting the Research

International marketing researchers first try to gather the needed information from secondary sources. Primary research provides more specific information that cannot be gathered from those sources.

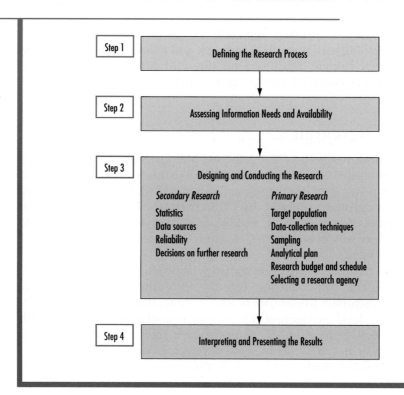

6. *The structure of the statistics may follow different international trade codes*, as shown in Table 6.3. The marketing researcher used to a particular domestic code may be misled.

Consumption Statistics.   Statistics on a country's consumption of consumer products are usually organized according to the major purpose of consumption or usage. For example, in the furniture category the statistics may be grouped into living room, bedroom, kitchen, and so on. Unfortunately, such statistics exist only for the highly industrialized nations.

Import-Export Statistics.   Import and export statistics contain data on the volume, value and destination of a country's imports and exports. They allow insights into the global flow of products and services. The major country-markets for a specific product, as well as the most competitive areas in a global product-market, can be determined. The statistics show the degree of saturation of demand through local versus non-domestic production. Therefore, they are the single most valuable source of information for a preliminary evaluation of a country's market attractiveness. But, as with production statistics, there are some problems with import and export statistics that a researcher should keep in mind:

> *Table 6.3*   **International Trade Codes for the Classification of Products**
>
> | | | |
> |---|---|---|
> | SIC | Standard International Classification (USA) | In international markets, products may be classified following different trade codes. |
> | SITC | Standard International Trade Classification (UNO) | |
> | BTN | Brussels Tariff Nomenclature | |
> | NIMEXE | Harmonized nomenclature of international trade of EU members | |

1. *Different product classification codes are used from one country to another.* In many countries not belonging to common markets such as EU or NAFTA, product classification codes are adapted to the customs classification applied by the national government. As a result the same product may be found in different classification groups from one country to another. A simple electrical motor may be counted in the categories of 'electrical motor' or 'drive unit for screens' depending on its application.

2. *Exports and imports are valued differently.* Exports are usually valued without international freight or insurance costs added at the export harbour, for example, whereas import figures usually contain those costs.

3. *The statistics are published at different intervals.* For example, companies such as EUROTAX publish figures on European car registrations indicating the obtained market share to car makers and dealers. As those customers are interested in short-term trends, EUROTAX publishes the statistics monthly. In other countries figures on car registrations published by official statistics agencies are only available once a year. They are not made available before the middle of the following year or even later. The data will therefore vary considerably in timeliness.

4. *The data are sometimes unreliable.* In researching small or economically less developed markets, the marketer may find the import data published by their administrations to be unreliable. The export statistics of the most developed industrialized nations generally provide more reliable information on imports in those markets.

Other Statistics.   Tax statistics for industrialized countries, in particular sales and value-added tax statistics, are organized by industry and product categories. They allow the assessment of the number and size of potential customers, intermediaries and competitors. Other statistics, such as construction, transportation and agricultural statistics, are not only of interest to marketers in these fields, but also provide information on a country's stage of industrial development, its general economic situation and its infrastructure.

Secondary Data Sources.   Embassies and consulates of country-markets potentially attractive to a firm provide access to a wide variety of references on business conditions and opportunities. Often a staff member, such as a commercial attaché, commercial officer or economic secretary, is available to provide specialized assistance. They have access to data banks, names of firms interested in business contacts, industry publications, address and telephone books, catalogues on industrial suppliers, and annual reports of potential customers. From these sources, information can be gathered on market conditions, potential intermediaries and competitors. Schedules of international promotion programmes are also available; they provide perspective on which industries are particularly important to the respective governments.

Valuable sources of information are public agencies such as patent offices or registration authorities. For US-based firms the US Department of Commerce's Global Market Surveys furnish detailed information on, for example, market shares, product use, repeat-purchase rates and competitive activities in key markets for selected products. For other countries, specialists known as country desks can provide the latest government import-export statistics for their country.

In the People's Republic of China a valuable source of information for foreign firms is the Economic Information Department (EID) of the computer centre of the Ministry of Foreign Trade and Economic Cooperation. Its market research section, for example, furnishes information on investment opportunities and cooperation partners. The China Trade and Commercial Service Co., another department, provides credit ratings of firms, and the Compass (China) International Information Service Co. manages a data bank of manufacturers and products and furnishes a directory of Industry and commerce.[7]

Some countries have governmental commercial delegations in the researcher's country of interest. Danish companies interested in doing business in Holland or Japan, for example, can contact the Dutch Trade Commission or JETRO (Japanese External Trade Organization) for valuable secondary information. These organizations, plus trade organizations sponsored by industries in the country of interest, also help companies to establish direct contacts with potential partners. In addition to government agencies, other organizations regularly compile and publish reports that are useful in international marketing research. Table 6.4 illustrates some of these sources.

Chambers of commerce and trade commissions regularly ask consultants to study particular markets. (Addresses of chambers of commerce and trade commissions can be found in address or telephone books.) Unfortunately, they usually concentrate on one country-market. An international product-market perspective is missing. When using industry reports from such sources, the marketing researcher must keep in mind that in many countries there is no obligation to belong to a trade commission. Therefore the data only cover the members of the organization.

A number of research institutes, such as the Institut für Weltwirtschaft of the University of Kiel and the Institut für Wirtschaftsforschung in Hamburg, Germany, regularly publish reports on global economic topics. Market research companies and information services, such as American Dun & Bradstreet or German Schimmelpfeng, offer purchasing-power maps, analyses of the economic structure of specific regions, reports on the development of an entire industry, and information concerning the financial reliability of potential customers and intermediaries. For example, the Dutch marketing research firm Inter/View, supported by Time Magazine and Consensus, a group of international advertising agencies, annually provides data on print media readership, TV viewing patterns, consumer buying habits and demographics based on a survey, called European Media & Marketing Survey, of more than 18 000 people in 17 European countries. Foreign-business departments in banks, insurance companies and forwarding agents provide informa-

Table 6.4 **SELECTED REPORTS PUBLISHED BY INTERNATIONAL ORGANIZATIONS**	

ORGANIZATION	PUBLICATION
United Nations	Statistical Yearbook, Yearbook of International Trade Statistics, Handbook of Industrial Statistics, Demographic Yearbook
United Nations International Development Organizations	Trade by Commodities
OECD	Country Reports
International Monetary Fund and EU	Analytical overviews of international trade
World Bank	World Tables, World Development Report

International organizations publish many reports that contain useful information for international marketing researchers.

tion on market risks, terms of payment, and transportation and insurance problems in different countries.

The fastest way to collect secondary data is through the Internet and electronic data banks. More than 3000 data banks are available for online use, and their number is growing steadily. Examples include

↔ COMEXT-EUROSTAT, a time series of import-export data from the European Community,

↔ BOS (Business Opportunities Services), a cooperation of the biggest European banks dedicated to the arrangement of international commercial exchanges,

↔ TED (Tenders Electronic Daily), which contains all tenders in EU member countries as well as tenders from the USA, Japan, Israel, Norway and Switzerland and those in other countries which are funded by the EU or the European Investment Bank,

↔ Euro-Select, containing funds of all European countries and the EU,

↔ EVIS (Environmental Information System), containing 2500 firms, 10 000 procedures, technologies and offers, and

↔ NIKKEI Economic, a source of economic statistics on Japan.

Approximately 75 per cent of the data banks are located in the USA, another 20 per cent are in Europe, and the remaining 5 per cent are in other parts of the world. Although most data banks charge fees for accessing the data, these costs are minimal compared to what a firm would have to spend to collect the information on its own. A carefully planned online search can reduce data-collection costs even further.

News agencies, broadcasting networks, and specialized publishers such as *Euromonitor* regularly publish data on industry structure, firms, brands, and sources of information. Trade journals contain information on market development, new products, and competitors. Newspapers like *The Wall Street Journal, The Economist, Frankfurter Allgemeine Zeitung, Neue Zürcher Zeitung, Asiaweek, Le Monde* and *Le Figaro* offer detailed analyses of environmental factors, specific features of country- and product-markets, and the latest news on suppliers, competitors and intermediaries. Public libraries often contain non-technical but nonetheless valuable sources, such as country yearbooks, economic atlases and tourist guidebooks.

Finally, personal contacts with international suppliers, domestic suppliers of complementary services or products, customers who have business experience in the market under consideration, or even competitors can be very helpful in the interpretation of information about environmental influences, specific business behaviours, consumption patterns, competitors and potential intermediaries. Contacts with companies with subsidiaries in the target country may provide similar information.

Reliability. To establish the comparability and usefulness of secondary data, the researcher must locate the original sources. In addition, the researcher must make sure that the data-collection and analysis procedures that were used in producing the secondary data meet the standards of the current project. In other words, using someone else's sloppily collected information will not save money and time; in the long run, the information will have to be collected again in a more effective manner.

Timeliness is another factor that must be considered. The data may be too old to be relevant for the current research problem. This would be the case, for example, when in 1997 a marketer interested in Austria finds census data gathered by the Statistisches Zentralamt (the national statistics agency) that is six years old, and an informative country report published by OECD that is five years old. The country's participation in the European Economic Area (EEA) since 1993 and its membership of the European Union as from January 1995 have produced changes in the legal and general economic environments, but in particular in the relevant product-market, in the meantime. New competitors have entered the scene, generating changes in price structures but also producing income effects through direct investments.[8]

Finally, the researcher should be aware that secondary data may not be fully comparable because

1. *The criteria used for grouping data into statistical categories are different.* For example, an area classified as urban in Japan has at least 50 000 inhabitants, whereas in Sweden and Norway the same term means an area with a population over 200.

2. *The categories in the statistics to be compared have been given different widths.* For example, occupational statistics in the USA use different age categories from the same statistics in Italy.

3. *The categories are defined too broadly.* For example, if a marketer of ball bearings for ski lifts wants to determine the market volume in France, production and import-export statistics won't help if the statistics only contain a category for all metal parts in ski-lift equipment.

4. *The data come from different units of analysis.* Two data sets about the projected markets for computer-paper forms in Switzerland and Spain, for example, would not be comparable if the first data set came from domestic manufacturers and the second from a survey of users.

To overcome some of these potential problems, ESOMAR, the association of European marketing researchers, has launched a working party on 'Harmonization of Demographics' which presented very promising results for Western

Europe. But convergence in the shape of published statistics is progressing rather slowly.

Decisions on Further Research.   After the firm has gathered and analysed secondary data, it must decide whether further research is necessary. It may turn out, for example, that the research problem has to be redefined in the light of newly gained insights. The marketing researcher may also use the data and the list of research issues to determine what additional information has to be gathered. Consider again the example of the European eyeglass-frame manufacturer. Based on secondary data, the firm may have decided that the South Korean market is attractive. But it may still need to know more about the lifestyles and preferences of South Korean consumers, as well as their attitudes towards foreign products. It may also want to find out more about potential intermediaries and the marketing strategies of competitors in the South Korean market. These kinds of information can seldom be obtained in any other way than through primary research.

The decision whether to go on to primary research or not will be based on estimates of how much research is still needed and what it will cost to obtain the desired information. If, for example, secondary data account for 75 per cent of the information needed by management at 10 per cent of the estimated research budget, the remaining 25 per cent of information may not be worth the additional expense required to obtain it. In most cases, however, management will not be able to avoid gathering information through primary research, in order to fine-tune the firm's marketing mix.

Primary Research

Primary or field research is the collection and analysis of new or as yet unpublished data. It promises the most specific and targeted information possible for a given research problem. But it is also costly and time consuming. Researchers used to studying domestic environments may face new problems. For example, statistical data for a reliable sampling frame may be missing. There may be the need to translate questionnaires into different languages. Moreover, in many parts of the world there are no service organizations to assist in the collection of data.

Because of such problems, careful planning of a primary research project for international markets is particularly important. Different types of research designs (exploratory for aid in problem definition and initial insights, descriptive for examining patterns of market behaviour, and causal for determining what stimulus leads to what behaviour) may be used to help answer the questions of market behaviour: what, when, by whom, and how much. The research plan must specify the objectives and scope of the study as well as what techniques will be used for data collection, analysis and interpretation. On the basis of this plan, a budget and schedule for carrying out the research can be established, and personal responsibilities for different parts of the project can be assigned (see Figure 6.4).

Target Population.   The appropriate target population for a research study depends on what management is trying to learn and what is likely to be the best source of this information. For example, researchers who want to learn about the attitudes and expectations of intermediaries who handle high-technology communications equipment will try to obtain data from wholesalers, retailers, and even independent sales representatives in that industry. The marketer of an expensive consumer product may try to get information directly from affluent consumers in a number of countries. A marketer of machine tools will be mostly interested in decision makers such as purchasing specialists, production managers, technical directors and top management.

Depending on culture-specific management structures and decision-making styles, the right choice of target population in industrial markets may be different from one country-market to another. In consumer product marketing, the relevant target population may also change from one country to another. In the USA and Western Europe, for example, family car purchases are strongly influenced by women and children. Therefore, they are part of the target population if consumer preferences for different cars are to be determined. In Saudi Arabia, religious guidelines and a patriarchal family structure do not permit the inclusion of women in the target population for research on car purchases.

Sometimes the firm may want to obtain information from more than one target population. For example, a vacation destination in Switzerland, such as St Moritz, will be interested in its image with both travel agents and travellers. The researcher will also have to decide if information on a topic has to be gathered in all potential markets and from all the potential partners, or if research findings from one area are representative for others. However, even if the budget is restricted and the markets under consideration seem to be similar, as would be the case for the Scandinavian markets, for example, researchers have to be careful in making generalizations. A Finn would not appreciate being classified as being similar to a Swede.

Data-Collection Techniques. Once researchers have determined the best potential sources of information, they must select the most appropriate method for collecting the data. The best data-collection technique is a function of what has to be found, who has to be contacted, the size of the sample, and how the members of the sample can be reached. There are basically three ways to get information from primary sources: (1) observation, (2) experiments and (3) surveys.

(1) Observation   Observation is a means of collecting information without asking questions. A French manufacturer of sun-roofs, for example, can hire an agency to observe the advertising campaigns of its three most important competitors in all of the EU markets. It can also gather information on potential intermediaries in the Italian market by observing the number of customers they have, their business behaviour, and their service capacity at the Ravenna trade fair.

The biggest advantage of observation is that it is not obtrusive. It is most appropriate when a behavioural sequence (e.g. information seeking, buying behaviour in stores or usage behaviour concerning a product) largely unknown to the decision makers in a company is to be explored; or when direct methods (experiments and surveys) might affect the way subjects behave or respond. Another advantage is less danger of researchers' imposing a cultural frame of reference on the units of analysis than there is with, for example, standardized questionnaires. The problem associated with observation, however, especially in an international context, is that the observer must understand what he or she is seeing well enough to interpret it.

A North American food-packaging expert scanning the European environment for new opportunities might notice that Dutch grocers stock milk in containers no larger than one litre. She might conclude that Dutch households do not consume enough milk to warrant the use of larger containers, such as the half-gallon and gallon jugs that are widespread in North America. However, upon seeing several shoppers purchase two litres at a time, she might conclude that there is a market for larger containers in the Netherlands. Neither of these conclusions would accurately reflect the milk consumption and shopping habits of Dutch families. Dutch consumers place a high value on freshness, shop every day (often by bicycle), and own small refrigerators. These factors combine to make one-litre cartons and bottles highly suitable for the Dutch market.

(2) **Experiments**   Experiments can be used to causally test the potential impact of a given marketing decision. A supplier of international travel tours, such as Germany-based TUI, might test a new arrangement with an airline carrier, such as Indonesia's Garuda Air, on a limited number of destinations, for example the flights from Frankfurt to Bali, to project how the target market will respond to the offer. A manufacturer of plants for burning toxic waste may build a plant at its own expense, to prove the promised benefits and to test the reactions of potential customers and environmentalist groups. Marketers of consumer products sometimes choose a smaller national market as a test arena for their products before they decide on entering a bigger market. A manufacturer of leather clothes in Istanbul, Turkey, for example, may choose Austria as a test market for its marketing strategy, before taking the risk to enter the much bigger German market.

Although in theory experimental techniques are applicable to all markets, in international marketing it is often difficult to control the experiment's reliability. Ideally, an international researcher has two experimental groups: one in which the experimental variable is manipulated while all other variables are held constant, and another in which no variables change at all. The researcher can then measure the impact of the experimental variable. Such conditions are even rarer in international research than in domestic test marketing. The difficulty is magnified when experiments are attempted in different cultures. Researchers may also confront technical problems. For example, it may be impossible for France-based Thomson Consumer Electronics to compare the effects of the same advertising approaches in France, Sweden and Greece because of media differences and the inability to control the behaviour of competitors.

In addition, the introduction of new products in international markets must be increasingly fast to be successful. When Philips introduced its new DCC music system, for example, they had to do it in all the Triad markets at once because Sony threatened to introduce their Mini-Disc system at the same time. There was no time left for extensive market testing. Consumer product tests have to be executed in parallel to the development of new products.

Even laboratory tests cannot rule out certain cultural elements. For example, cultural differences in attitudes towards authority affect perceptions of spokespeople in different countries. In India, a country where authorities play an important role, the behaviour of the person who conducts a test will have much more influence on the reactions of respondents than in Sweden which is characterized by low authority differences.

(3) **Surveys**   A third means of gathering primary data is to ask questions. Survey research is conducted for the purpose of gathering information that is difficult or impossible to collect in any other way, such as the attitudes and knowledge of respondents. How structured the survey should be depends on the amount of knowledge the researchers already have about the target population and the product-market under study. Basically, the less that is known, the more important it is to use an open-ended approach to data collection. Exploratory or pilot studies are very useful in identifying issues that can be addressed later in more structured surveys. Group interviews have become most popular for that purpose in Europe and the USA. The importance attributed to focus groups versus in-depth interviews differs widely across countries, however. For example, in the UK, Ireland, Italy, Denmark and Greece the emphasis is mainly on group discussions, whereas in-depth interviews account for a higher proportion of research turnover in Austria, the Netherlands and Germany.

On the other hand, when there is considerable knowledge about the research issues, a highly standardized and structured approach is more suitable. The marketing researcher can choose between verbal and visual surveys, or a combination of the two, depending on the research problem, the units of analysis, and the advantages and disadvantages of each technique.

Mail surveys can be effectively used in many industrial marketing-research projects. The costs of administering a mail survey appear to be low on a per-unit basis. But, in addition to problems that are well known from domestic surveys (such as varying levels of literacy), in an international context there are additional limitations on this approach. Motivation to respond may be even lower than in the domestic market, and mail surveys may suffer from inadequate or unreliable postal services. In some African countries, for example, mail delivery is so unreliable that mail surveys are useless. In India, the postal service claims to deliver mail anywhere in the country within two days, but recipients may not be able to read the questionnaire because of language differences – there are 15 major languages in India!

Telephone surveys, like mail surveys, can be used effectively in international industrial marketing research and sometimes in consumer research. Almost all firms have telephones, and relevant respondents can be identified by means of a few preliminary questions. Multiregional studies can be conducted from a single location, saving time and money and increasing the response rate, because of the higher motivation to respond to international telephone calls. The main drawback of telephone surveys in industrial marketing research is the anonymity of the interviewer. Respondents may be concerned about revealing information that competitors could use, or reluctant to respond fully because of work pressures. As a result, only a limited amount of information may be obtained.

Compared to the USA where telephone surveys are popular, European marketing researchers are on average less inclined to use this method of gathering primary data (13 per cent of total research expenditures in 1994). In the Scandinavian countries (Norway 32 per cent and Sweden 25 per cent) the proportion of telephone interviewing is particularly high.[9] Limited ownership of private telephones in many other areas of the world, such as China, Indonesia, Thailand or the Philippines, restricts the feasibility of telephone surveys for consumer research, except among the most affluent consumer groups (see Table 6.5).[10] But also in Greece and Ireland, telephone interviews only accounted for 4 per cent of total research expenditures in 1994.

Table 6.5 TELEPHONE RESEARCH IN ASIA

COUNTRY	HOUSEHOLD PENETRATION		POSSIBILITIES FOR TELEPHONE INTERVIEWS	
	NATIONAL %	URBAN %	CONSUMER	BUSINESS-TO-BUSINESS
Hong Kong	98	NA	yes	yes
Singapore	97	NA	yes	yes
Australia	95	98	yes	yes
New Zealand	95	97	yes	yes
Japan	95	97	limited	limited
Taiwan	95	97	limited	limited
Korea	84	90	no	limited
Malaysia	54	70	no	limited
Thailand	9	37	no	no
India	5	15	no	no
Philippines	5	10	no	no
Indonesia	2	18	no	no
Vietnam	1	2	no	no
China	2	10	no	no

Data produced by SRG Nielsen indicate the possibilities and limitations of conducting telephone research in Asian countries.

Source: 'Telephone research in Asia', ESOMAR NewsBrief, No. 2, February 1996, 21.

Moreover, in many cultural contexts, such as Latin America, there is a strong reluctance to respond to strangers and respondents may be unaccustomed to lengthy telephone conversations.

Computer-aided surveys may be useful in conducting specialized research on consumer behaviour. This approach is limited to urban areas in highly developed countries where people are familiar with keypads or keyboards and video screens. Automated interviews, in which respondents answer questions posed on the computer screen, produce lower error rates and fewer biases than other survey techniques. Visual aids make them easy to use, and the computer can register the response time of interviewees as well as the responses themselves.

Personal interviewing is the most expensive survey method, but it is also the most cost-effective. This is because high response rates, a flexible interview situation, and the ability to address complex issues in face-to-face studies all result in higher-quality data. In Europe face-to-face interviews clearly account for the majority of survey expenditures (25 per cent in 1994)[11] but their share is decreasing.

In areas where postal services are poor, illiteracy rates are high and telephones are not available, personal interviews are mandatory. However, in some cultures interviewers may encounter suspicion. For example, in Latin America they may be perceived as tax inspectors. In Russia people are concerned that interviewers might cooperate with burglars because they ask questions about possession of consumer goods. Thus, care must be taken in the selection of interviewers. The social class and language of the interviewer and the target group should be matched.

Most survey research is done ad hoc, but continuous research has won an important share of national and international research budgets. In Europe, for example, continuous research accounts for 47 per cent of total expenditures. The importance of panel research is substantial (nearly two-thirds of the total expenditure on continuous research in Europe in 1994) and increasing. As a reaction, European competitors SOFRES from France and Germany-based GfK have joined forces with the US market research agency NPD to launch a Europe–North American mail panel service, utilizing the partners' existing consumer panels. The merged panel will consist of NPD's 350 000 households in the USA and Canada, GfK UK's Home Audit rolling sample of 25 000 and 6000 Home Trak panel, GfK Germany's 30 000 panel and SOFRES' 86 000 households across France, Italy and Spain.[12] Omnibus studies tend to play only a secondary role (7 per cent of total expenditure in Europe in 1994), but as Figure 6.5 shows, there also exist regular international omnibus services in Asia and Oceania.

In survey research, ethics play an increasingly important role. Because there are so many researchers with greatly varying self-interests concerning the results of their work and their usage, respondents have become increasingly sceptical. There is a growing trend for legislative restrictions on the publication and even on the conduct of surveys. Restrictions have recently been proposed in Greece and Ireland, for example, and legislation has been enacted in countries like France, Italy, Portugal and Spain. As a reaction, professional associations of marketing researchers such as ESOMAR have developed and published guidelines on the proper conduct of surveys. The Ethics box contains parts of a code that sets out the basic principles which must guide the actions of those who carry out or use marketing research.

Validity and Comparability. The greatest challenge in conducting survey research in an international context is to obtain valid, comparable and reliable data. The Culture box describes some of the problems that can occur even when doing international comparative marketing research in neighbouring countries. Researchers must check the validity of each variable measured in the different geographical areas. That is, they must make sure that the survey instrument really measures what it is intended to measure.

One way to improve the validity of a research design is to use triangulation. If marketing researchers can afford to apply at least two data-collection techniques which are as different as possible and, therefore, contain different sources of error, they can make sure that similarities or differences in the gathered data are not due to the research design, rather than market differences. For example, to assess the purchasing behaviour of consumers in a street market in Hong Kong, a researcher may use open-ended interviews, observation by video cameras and analysis of ethnographic documents. Only if the outcomes of the three data-collection techniques converge should results be interpreted.

Even if validity is assured, comparability or equivalency of findings is a concern. When comparing product-markets in dissimilar countries in order to find opportunities to standardize parts of the marketing mix, comparability of the data has to be assured. Comparability should be established for the research process as well as for content. For example, the questions used in data collection and interviewees' responses to these questions must have the same meaning in the markets to be compared. And the respondents must interpret the questions and their own responses in the same way.

Figure 6.5 INRABUS ASIA

Source: INRABUS ASIA advertisement in *Marketing and Research Today*, March 1992, 57.

INRABUS ASIA
Your Gateway to Asia/Pacific Markets

What is INRABUS ASIA?
It's the first, quality Omnibus survey operating across Asia/Pacific, giving you:
* *Simultaneous access* to major markets
* Information gathered *in a way most appropriate for each culture*
* Analysed *to a common format*

Where?
Countries covered (sample sizes in brackets) are:

India (2000)	Hong Kong (600)
Thailand (2000)	Korea (1000)
Malaysia (3000)	Japan (1000)
Singapore (2000)	Hawaii (400)
Indonesia (1800)	New Zealand (2000)
Philippines (2000)	Australia (1200)
Continental U.S.A (2000) can be included	

When?
Every country in Feb/March, May/June, and Nov/Dec: *most countries* in August/Sept; *some countries* monthly or more often.

How do I contact INRABUS ASIA?
Choose your own Contact Point for bookings or more information from:
1   The INRA associate in your own country.
2   The INRA EUROPE Co-ordination Office,
     Brussels, Belgium, Jean Quatresooz.
     Phone (32-2) 772-4444; Fax (32-2) 772-4079
3   The INRASIA PACIFIC Co-ordination Centre,
     Australia, Mike Larbalastier.
     Phone (61-2) 449-5804; Fax (61-2) 988-4022
4   INRA Worldwide, Mamaroneck, NY, USA
     Jean Henry / Tom Miller
     Phone (914) 698-0800; Fax (914) 698-0485
5   The INRA associate in the particular Asia/Pacific
     market or markets you are interested in.

INRABUS ASIA
a service of INRASIA PACIFIC LIMITED

ETHICS BOX

The ICC/ESOMAR International Code of Marketing and Social Research Practice

1. MARKETING RESEARCH MUST ALWAYS BE CARRIED out objectively and in accordance with established scientific principles.

2. Marketing research must always conform to the national and international legislation which applies in those countries involved in a given research project.

3. Respondents' cooperation in a marketing research project is entirely voluntary at all stages. They must not be misled when being asked for their cooperation.

4. Respondents' anonymity must be strictly preserved at all times. If the Respondent on request from the Researcher has given permission for data to be passed on in a form which allows that Respondent to be personally identified:

   a) the Respondent must first have been told to whom the information will be supplied and the purposes for which it will be used, and also

   b) the Researcher must ensure that the information will not be used for any non-research purpose and that the recipient of the information has agreed to conform to the requirements of this code.

5. The Researcher must take all reasonable precautions to ensure that Respondents are in no way directly harmed or adversely affected as a result of their participation in a marketing research project.

6. The Researcher must take special care when interviewing children and young people. The informed consent of the parent or responsible adult must first be obtained for interviews with children.

7. Respondents must be told either at the beginning or end of the interview if observation techniques or recording equipment is being used, except where these are used in a public place. If a Respondent so wishes, the record or relevant section of it must be destroyed or deleted. Respondents' anonymity must not be infringed by the use of such methods.

8. Respondents must be enabled to check without difficulty the identity and bona fides of the Researcher.

9. Researchers must not, whether knowingly or negligently, act in any way which could bring discredit on the marketing research profession or lead to a loss of public confidence in it.

10. Researchers must not make false claims about their skills and experience or about those of their organization.

11. Researchers must not unjustifiably criticize or disparage other Researchers.

12. Researchers must always strive to design research which is cost-efficient and of adequate quality, and then to carry this out to the specifications agreed with the Client.

13. Researchers must ensure the security of all research records in their possession.

14. Researchers must not knowingly allow the dissemination of conclusions from a marketing research project which are not adequately supported by the data. They must always be prepared to make available the technical information necessary to assess the validity of any published findings.

15. When acting in their capacity as Researchers the latter must not undertake any non-research activities, for example database marketing involving data about individuals which will be used for direct marketing and promotional activities. Any such non-research activities must always be clearly separated and differentiated from any organization which carries out marketing research and the conduct of any marketing research activity.

16. These rights and responsibilities will normally be governed by a written Contract between the Researcher and the Client. The parties may amend the provisions of Rules 19–23 below if they have agreed to this in writing beforehand; but the other requirements of this Code may not be

altered in this way. Marketing research must also always be conducted according to the principles of fair competition, as generally understood and accepted.

17. The Researcher must inform the Client if the work to be carried out for that Client is to be combined or syndicated in the same project with work for other Clients but must not disclose the identity of such Clients.

18. The Researcher must inform the Client as soon as possible in advance when any part of the work for that Client is to be subcontracted outside the Researcher's own organization (including the use of any outside consultants). On request the Client must be told the identity of any such subcontractor.

19. The Client does not have the right, without prior agreement between the parties involved, to exclusive use of the Researcher's services or those of his organization, whether in whole or in part. In carrying out work for different Clients, however, the Researcher must endeavour to avoid possible clashes of interest between the services provided to those Clients.

20. The following Records remain the property of the Client and must not be disclosed by the Researcher to any third party without the Client's permission:

    a) marketing research briefs, specifications and other information provided by the Client

    b) the research data and findings from a marketing research project (except in the case of syndicated or multi-client projects or services where the same data are available to more than one Client).

    The Client has however no right to know the names or addresses of Respondents unless the latter's explicit permission for this has first been obtained by the Researcher (this particular requirement cannot be altered under Rule 16).

21. Unless it is specifically agreed to the contrary, the following Records remain the property of the Researcher:

    a) marketing research proposals and cost quotations (unless these have been paid for by the Client). They must not be disclosed by the Client to any third party, other than to a consultant working

for the Client on that project (with the exception of any consultant working also for a competitor of the Researcher). In particular, they must not be used by the Client to influence research proposals or cost quotations from other Researchers.

    b) the contents of a report in the case of syndicated and/or multi-client projects or services where the same data are available to more than one Client and where it is clearly understood that the resulting reports are available for general purchase or subscription. The Client may not disclose the findings of such research to any third party (other than to his own consultants and advisors for use in connection with his business) without the permission of the Researcher.

    c) all other research Records prepared by the Researcher (with the exception in the case of non-syndicated projects of the report to the Client, and also the research design and questionnaire where the costs of developing these are covered by the charges paid by the Client).

22. The Researcher must conform to currently agreed professional practice relating to the keeping of such Records for an appropriate period of time after the end of the project. On request the Researcher must supply the Client with duplicate copies of such Records provided that such duplicates do not breach anonymity and confidentiality requirements (Rule 4); that the request is made within the agreed time limit for keeping the Records; and that the Client pays the reasonable costs of providing the duplicates.

23. The Researcher must not disclose the identity of the Client (provided there is no legal obligation to do so), or any confidential information about the latter's business, to any third party without the Client's permission.

24. The Researcher must on request allow the Client to arrange for checks on the quality of fieldwork and data preparation provided that the Client pays any additional costs involved in this. Any such checks must conform to the requirements of Rule 4.

25. The Researcher must provide the Client with all appropriate technical details of any

research project carried out for that Client.

26. When reporting on the results of a marketing research project the Researcher must make a clear distinction between the findings as such, the Researcher's interpretation of these and any recommendations based on them.

27. Where any of the findings of a research project are published by the Client the latter has a responsibility to ensure that these are not misleading. The Researcher must be consulted and agree in advance the form and content of publication, and must take action to correct any misleading statements about the research and its findings.

28. Researchers must not allow their names to be used in connection with any research project as an assurance that the latter has been carried out in conformity with this Code unless they are confident that the project has in all respects met the Code's requirements.

29. Researchers must ensure that Clients are aware of the existence of this Code and of the need to comply with its requirements.

If, for example, a survey on radio listening behaviour in Belgium using the same method for radio audience measurement shows that the Flemish-speaking Belgian spends 219 minutes with radio on an average day but the French-speaking Belgian only 113 minutes, the finding may be due to real differences in behaviour but also to different reactions to the measurement instrument. Even a similar difference in Switzerland (the German-Swiss listen for 170 minutes but the French-Swiss for 113 minutes) does not allow us to conclude that there is a cultural difference in radio listening behaviour due to the French culture. The different cultural background may simply lead to different interpretations of the questions or the responses. We would need an observation of overt listening behaviour to validate the results.

The problem of potential miscommunication between researcher and respondent is particularly prominent in international marketing research. On the one hand, the data-collection form has to be translated into other languages and dialects in a way that exactly transmits the intended content. This may be difficult with new technical terms, which may not even exist in the other language. Even if the translation is perfect, the researcher may find that respondents in the countries under consideration have different levels of education. For example, in Vietnam the use of scales is particularly sensitive, as only very easily understandable scales can be used, and each questionnaire has to be very carefully tested several times to ensure that the questions are fully understood by everyone.[13]

For the respondents in one country it may be appropriate to formulate a question in an abstract, verbal manner. But for the respondents in another country the same question may have to be communicated through visual means. There may be culturally based differences in the meaning of a question that lead to incomparable responses between people from different countries. The content, phrasing and presentation of the question may result in different responses (for example, 'to be outstanding' means 'not to stand out' in China).

To obtain comparable results, it may be necessary to use different approaches in different areas. The most important thing is to ensure the proper equivalency of the survey instruments used in each culture. That may lead the researcher to abandon the spurious security of having the same

CULTURE BOX

Cultural Problems
with
Survey Instruments

WHEN YOUNG & RUBICAM DEVELOPED A MEASUREMENT tool to define lifestyle segments across all member countries of the EU they encountered the following problems:

↔ Influences of Language Differences
When translated from one language to the other sometimes questions underwent a subtle, but significant shift of emphasis even though the intention was to make them exactly equivalent. For example, the English statement: 'There are times when it is right to disobey the law' got another nuance when it was translated to the French statement: 'Il y a des fois où désobéir aux lois est une bonne chose'. The French 'une bonne chose' is far less strict than the English notion of 'right'.

↔ Ethnocentric Bias
Even when correctly translated, the same question meant different things in different cultures because people interpreted the meaning of terms and concepts, and gave answers, relative to the norms of the culture in which they exist. Some cultural differences were differences of fact. Agreement with the statement 'We drink more wine at home these days', for

example, clearly implied different things in the wine drinking country of Greece compared to the same response in the United Kingdom.

Other cultural differences were variations in generally accepted beliefs, or customs. Using the two statements 'Religion plays an important part in my life' and 'I go to Church very regularly', for example, to get some measure of how religious people are, produced incomparable results. In the UK 75 per cent of people claimed to be religious, because it is the socially acceptable thing to do, yet in reality it is not a religious country (less than 10 per cent of people regularly go to church). In Italy the situation was reversed. About 55 per cent of people regularly go to church, yet only about 30 per cent of people claim to be religious (going to church in Italy has a strong social function).

↔ Cultural Response Patterns
A third important influence of culture on responses to questions and statements Y&R encountered was national traits in the way people answer questions, even when they do have exactly equivalent meanings in every country. For example, Italians like extremes, and mark towards the ends of any semantic scale; Germans are more restrained, and mark towards the middle. Comparison of sample means between the two countries would lead to erronous conclusions.

Source: Williams, J. (1991) 'Constant questions or constant meanings? Assessing intercultural motivations in alcoholic drinks', *Marketing and Research Today*, 19(3), August, 173f.

---

questions and the same statistical analysis procedure in all geographic areas. What has to remain constant is the sociocultural significance of the questions used.[14] For example, energy-saving household behaviour may need to be measured in different ways in the USA and Norway. In the US, people who are highly motivated to save household energy may install insulating materials in the walls, floors and attics of their homes. But in Norway, where heating costs have traditionally been higher, homes may be insulated as a matter of course. There, a high level of energy-saving behaviour might be represented by the purchase of an energy-efficient heating system. Under such conditions, the use of a standardized data-collection form would result in astonishment or little understanding from respondents in one of the countries.

The marketing researcher must understand even slight cultural differences between countries and target groups. More than with domestic research, qualitative investigations to gain better insights into each culture and careful pre-testing of international data-collection methods is necessary. Statistical methods for dealing with comparability problems such as confirmatory factor analysis or latent structure analysis (for international comparison on the aggregate level) or equivalent standardization (for comparison on the individual level) are offered to marketing researchers.[15] However, they are still in the testing stage, and researchers should continue to seek expert opinions concerning the concept they are trying to measure in each nation.

Sampling

When the data-collection technique has been established, the researchers must decide how to go about selecting particular respondents for observation, experimentation or surveying. First, a sampling frame has to be established. Then a sample of appropriate size can be drawn by the use of a sampling technique which accounts for the given research problem and the reliability of the sampling frame.

Sampling Frame.   A sampling frame is a list from which elements of the target population can be identified. Researchers in Western industrial nations can choose from a variety of reliable sampling frames – mailing lists, telephone books, voter registration lists, motor vehicle registration lists, the International Business and Company Yearbook, and so forth. In many developing countries, however, there are few reliable sampling frames for either industrial or consumer target markets. Census data may not be available or recent enough to use. (India, for example, does not have an accurate count of its total population.) The reliability of the few lists that are available may be limited by such problems as unusual housing situations (such as people living on boats or out in the open), rapid changes in small-business ownership, and a high proportion of family-owned businesses. These problems not only make it difficult to compare markets but can actually prevent researchers from reaching sources of information. Under such conditions, different sampling techniques may be needed to obtain representative samples.

Sampling Techniques.   The method used to select potential respondents from a sampling frame is the sampling technique. With a reliable sampling frame, the researcher can choose a probability sample, in which each member of the population has a known chance of being drawn into the sample. When detailed sampling frames are not available, the marketing researcher may use a cluster sample. For example, the city of Bombay, India, might be divided into equal-sized units or neighbourhoods. A random sample of these units would then be drawn. Within these clusters, every member or every household would be included in the survey. But even with this techniques problems may arise. For most developing countries no reliable city maps are available. They are drawn by hand and nobody really knows how many people live in which neighbourhood.

Probability samples are more elegant from a theoretical point of view. The absence of a reliable sampling frame and other practical reasons, such as the educational level of respondents or simply their reachability, often lead international marketing researchers to draw a non-probability sample. A convenience sample allows the researcher to choose respondents who are readily available, such as people in a marketplace in Indonesia or production managers in Bolivian companies. Judgement samples are often used for industrial marketing research. With this technique the researcher chooses 'experts' or 'typical' representatives of a product- or country-market which allow fast and cost-efficient data collection at an acceptable level of reliability.

Because of their sensitivity to many sources of bias, such as high non-response rates, unreliable sampling frames and interviewer influences, the reliability of different sampling techniques varies with the market environments. It is not reasonable, therefore, to apply one standard technique independent of research areas and product-markets. An intelligent adaptation of the sampling technique to the specific circumstances encountered in the markets will greatly improve response rates, the quality of the data, and the price/benefit relationship of the research project.

Even large international companies, such as Cincinnati-based Procter & Gamble, which are well known for their high levels of process standardization, allow for different local standards of field work in countries such as China compared to Canada. Their main objective is to gather comparable data. Quantitative studies in highly industrialized markets are harmonized to a much higher extent than qualitative research which is mainly used in the initial stages of playing with an idea, to explore a development in an existing product category, or for understanding customer language.[16]

Sample Size. The quality of research results depends not only on the instrument used to collect data and the sampling technique employed, but also on the size of the sample. There are both technical and practical issues associated with sample size. Sample size is partly a function of the diversity in the population to be sampled. Samples with 50 units of analysis may be sufficiently large, when the statistical universe is quite homogeneous. In areas where the population to be surveyed is not well known, the degree of variability may be difficult to determine. For example, there are no census data for Ho Chi Minh City. To allow for possibly high variability among households, a larger sample would be required. In such instances, exploratory studies with small samples may help researchers gain a better understanding of the population to be studied.

On the practical side, since most research budgets are fixed, trade-offs must be made between the number of areas that can be studied, the size of the sample in each area, and the amount of data collected from each respondent. Even where larger samples are appropriate, their cost may be considerably reduced by using a multistage sampling technique. Such an approach was used by TRM, an Austrian manufacturer of cast-metal parts, when it studied the feasibility of enlarging its mould-construction department to serve all potential users of industrial moulds in Germany, Switzerland, Italy and Austria. In the first stage, a probability sample of potential customers was drawn from addresses provided by trade commissions. Telephone calls were used to find out which companies and which individuals within these companies should be included in the second stage. The individuals identified in this way were mailed questionnaires designed to gather additional information about potential customers. The responses to the questionnaires were used to

---

Table 6.6	WORLD TOP TEN MARKET RESEARCH COMPANIES		

Research agencies now provide a link around the world to help international firms on their marketing research processes.

Research company	Turnover in million USD 1994	Countries with office	Head office
D&B Marketing Information Services	2,388*	71	USA
Information Resources Inc.	400*	26	USA
GfK	251	25	Germany
Sofrès Group	193	7	France
Research International	183	46	UK
Video Research	142	1	Japan
Infratest/Burke	131	12	Germany
The Arbitron Co.	137*	1	USA
IPSOS Group	130	8	France

* Figures from 1995

Sources: ESOMAR, 'ESOMAR Annual market study on market statistics 1994', Amsterdam 1995, 27; Honomichl, J. (1996) 'Top 50 research revenue up 9.4% in '95', *Marketing News*, 30(12), June, H6.

identify a third sample of individuals who were interviewed personally, to get more details about how to approach new customers successfully.

Such a multistage sampling procedure keeps the costs of research lower than those associated with one-step projects. On the other hand, it takes more time to implement and the errors committed at each stage accumulate over the duration of the project. Unfortunately, there is no general recipe for how to draw perfect samples in international marketing research. The size and structure of research projects depend on the firm's information needs, the characteristics of the target market, and the research budget.

Equivalency of Samples.   If the market researcher wants to compare data from samples of different countries, the equivalency of the samples needs to be established. One way to find equivalent samples is to make them very broad to cover all potential influences of existing subcultures, that is, to draw representative samples of the entire target population. Another solution is to draw specific samples to represent similar subcultures in the geographical areas to compare (for example, Bolivian nurses compared to Argentinian nurses). In any case, inexperienced researchers will find it useful to rely on the services of international marketing research organizations, such as ESOMAR, or internationally operating marketing research firms (see Table 6.6) to find equivalent samples.

Analytical Plan

An important part of the research design is the plan for analysing the data. This involves determining which data are needed for which purpose, as well as which tools will be used in their analysis. For example, if the research is designed to find out how consumers in Canada and Mexico respond to one packaging design compared to another, the analysis plan must include a way to group and compare the responses of consumers to each design. Specifically, the plan has to specify if the researchers want to compare the average response of users of one design with the average response of users of the other design for each country, or if they want to identify groups of consumers in both countries for whom brand recognition is important. The statistical techniques to be used will depend on this decision. By answering these kinds of questions in the research design before data gathering has started, researchers ensure that information will be collected in an appropriate manner and that irrelevant and unnecessary (and therefore costly) information will not be sought. The tools used to analyse the data collected in international marketing research do not differ from those used in domestic research.

Research Budget and Schedule

The cost of each activity included in the project must be estimated. If the firm has a fixed research budget, the project must be designed to meet the constraints imposed by that budget. If the budget is based on the costs of the planned activities, the marketing researcher should compare these costs with the profit the company may lose if management makes poor decisions because of the lack of information.

Estimating a budget for international marketing research can be difficult. The costs of doing comparable studies vary in different countries, even in the same part of the world. As an example, Table 6.7 shows the price variation for a usage and attitude survey. Because of such variations, many marketing managers may prefer to establish the project budget in stages and review expenditures at the end of each stage. When this approach is used, the stages need to be outlined in the research brief.

Listing activities on which budgets are based also serves to help schedule the project and control its implementation. International marketing research projects are usually complex, taking place across many countries and using agencies that have a variety of skills and capabilities. In order to ensure that the job is done within the budget and on schedule, the activities list is used as a planning tool for these projects.

In order to control expenses and the efficiency of the firm's marketing-research activities, it is necessary to determine which unit within the company will bear the expense of the research. If the information is to be used to support strategic decision making, the costs may be assumed by top management or the appropriate business unit. If the firm is organized according to a category-management system or by region, the corresponding units may have to bear some of the cost of the study, especially if the findings are to be used in making tactical decisions. A marketing research unit that operates as a separate cost or profit centre that supports all of the firm's marketing research efforts may have its own budget.

Selecting a Research Agency

When considering hiring an outside organization to carry out a research project, management has three alternatives among which it may choose. These exist in all of the developed countries and in many developing ones. First, there are research agencies based in the geographic area of interest. They have expertise on the local environment, as well as the ability to cope with problems of language and concept translation. The difficulties associated

Table 6.7 Average Price Indices for a Quantitative Consumer Usage and Attitude Study

The price of a marketing research project can vary greatly depending on the country in which it is conducted. In the table the average price in Europe is indexed to 100, and each region or country is compared to that average.

Project 1: West European Average Price USD 36,265 = 100

WESTERN EUROPE		CENTRAL EUROPE		NORTH AMERICA	
16 country average	100	11 country average	40	2 country average	149
5 major markets	102	Slovenia	58	USA	173
Norway	143	Romania	47	Canada	125
Sweden	138	Others	41		
France	120	Slovakia	41	CENT./S. AMERICA	
Denmark	120	Poland	41	5 country average	84
Switzerland	117	Hungary	39	Brazil	124
Germany	113	Czech Republic	38	Argentina	109
UK	112	Lithuania	33	Others	62
Belgium	104	Bulgaria	25		
Ireland	101			AUSTRALIA/NZ	
Netherlands	89	EASTERN EUROPE		2 country average	128
Finland	87	2 country average	44	Australia	152
Italy	87	Russia	45		
Spain	79	Ukraine	43	PACIFIC RIM	
Austria	71			9 country average	85
Others	67	NEAR/MIDDLE EAST		Hong Kong	119
Greece	60	6 country average	72	Korea	88
Portugal	58	Others	74	Singapore	84
		Saudi Arabia	64	Others	80
TURKEY	44				
		JAPAN	175	ASIA	
				5 country average	32
		NORTH AFRICA		China	95
		2 country average	55	India	21
		Egypt	59	Others	15
		SOUTH AFRICA	73		

Source: ESOMAR, 'ESOMAR Prices study 1997', Amsterdam 1998, 6.

with using such agencies include finding reliable ones and coordinating their activities.

In Russia, for example, the main research suppliers based in Moscow are: AMER, CESSI, COMCON, GfK, MEMRB, MIC, MR Company, ROMIR, Russian Research, Validata and VCIOM. They conduct good quality quantitative research for mainly multinational clients (80 per cent in-home face-to-face interviews using random or quota sampling) in metropolitan areas. As Table 6.8 shows, even omnibus services exist. VCIOM, for example, was launched in 1988. It now has over 100 executive and administrative staff, 3000 interviewers, and a network of 32 regional offices spread over Russia and the 15 CIS countries.[17] But rural Russia, representing about 80 per cent of the country's population, is not well covered. Most agencies have limited experience in qualitative research applied to goods and services. They lack the needed infrastructure and know-how in interpretation of data. Business-to-business research is the least developed area.[18]

	Table 6.8 OMNIBUS SERVICES IN RUSSIA				
	ALL RUSSIA		EURO RUSSIA		
	SAMPLE	FREQUENCY	SAMPLE	FREQUENCY	
CESSI	1,000	11	1,000	6	The main omnibus
GfK	2,000	5	2,000	12	suppliers for the whole of
MIC	1,500	6	1,000	12	Russia and Euro Russia in
ROMIR	1,500	23	1,150	8	1995 were those indicated
VCIOM	2,400	12	1,950	6	in the table.

All face-to-face, in home. Sampling points all 100+.
Source: *ESOMAR NewsBrief*, Vol. 3, No. 11, December 1995, 9.

The second alternative is to select a research firm that specializes in the industry in question. Computer Technology Research Ltd, for example, is a UK market research firm specializing in studies such as the development of RISC technology or the spread of workstations, all concerning the computer industry. Such firms are more likely to understand the research issues related to that industry and may have experience in carrying out studies in many different parts of the world.

The needs of customers who do business on an international level have led some agencies to become international themselves. GfK Europe, for example, has 14 offices all over Europe, including the former Eastern bloc countries, which not only manage household panels but also realize a total volume of ad hoc research above USD120 million a year (for another example see Figure 6.6). Other research firms have signed multilateral cooperative agreements, thereby building worldwide chains of research agencies, such as US-based International Research Associates or EuroNet, a network of 18 individual research agencies working closely together in Europe and North America. Others have merged on a global level. For example, by merging, Dun & Bradstreet and A.C. Nielsen have formed the largest market research firm, called D&B Marketing Information Services, in the world.

Thus, a third option is to contract with a reliable internationally operating research agency or chain of cooperating agencies to manage the entire project. The customer deals with only one office, located in the home country.

Table 6.9 presents a checklist for evaluating market research agencies. But even with the help of outside experts, marketers may have difficulty carrying out primary research in some parts of the world. In developing countries in Asia and Africa there are relatively few market research organizations. In Southeast Asia the biggest weakness is the problem of 'too much, too quick'. Research tends to be seen as just another business, without the professional and ethical standards that set it apart in industrially more developed countries. Agencies may be technically weak and their staff needs further training. In addition, some governments, especially in China, Myanmar and Vietnam, see marketing research as threatening. This, plus Islam's attitude to family life, means permission for surveys is required in Indonesia and the government bans all surveys in the protracted run-up to elections.[19]

Figure 6.6 The Gallup Organization

The Gallup Organization.

Meet the future: not a 'network'—but a worldwide market and opinion research **company**.

Who is Gallup?
The Gallup Organization is:

- The world's oldest, best-known, and most respected survey research firm, founded over 60 years ago in Princeton, New Jersey, USA, by Dr. George Gallup.

- A worldwide company with direct subsidiaries in 23 nations. Gallup's international operations encompass nearly 60% of the world's population, and 70% of global economic activity.

- An employee-owned firm whose annual sales have risen twelvefold in the past eight years.

- 2,300 research professionals who, benefiting from a unified ownership structure, can provide clients comparable operating standards, products and services across national, cultural and linguistic borders.

- Extensive experience in marketing and management research, including customer satisfaction and loyalty measurement, employee attitude measurement, and brand and advertising research.

- The exclusive owner of the 'Gallup' and 'Gallup Poll' trademarks in dozens of major markets from Shanghai to Santiago.

Around the globe, Gallup is:

BRAZIL (São Paulo)
Princeton Pesquisa de Mercado Ltda.

CANADA (Toronto)
Gallup Canada, Inc.

CHILE (Santiago)
Gallup Chile Ltda.

CHINA (Beijing/Shanghai)
Gallup China Research, Ltd.

CENTRAL AMERICA
(Panama/San Jose)
The Gallup Organization (Panama),
w/CID S.A.

COLOMBIA (Bogota/Medellín)
Gallup Colombia, w/INVAMER Ltda.

DOMINICAN REPUBLIC
(Santo Domingo)
Gallup Republica Dominicana, S.A.

FRANCE (Paris)
Gallup France S.A.

GERMANY (Wiesbaden)
Gallup Gmbh.

HONG KONG (Hong Kong)
The Gallup Organization, Ltd.

HUNGARY (Budapest)
Gallup Hungary
(Magyar Gallup Intézet)

ICELAND (Reykjavik)
Gallup Iceland, Ltd.

INDIA (Bangalore/Bombay)
Gallup India PVT, Ltd.

JAPAN (Tokyo)
Gallup/JMAR, Inc.

LITHUANIA (Vilnius)
Baltic Surveys, Ltd.

MEXICO (Mexico City)
Gallup Mexico, S.A. de C.V.

POLAND (Warsaw)
The Gallup Organization, Warsaw

ROMANIA (Bucharest)
The Gallup Organization, Bucharest

SINGAPORE (Singapore)
The Gallup Organization
(Singapore) Pte. Ltd.

SPAIN (Madrid)
Gallup España Ltda.

TAIWAN (Taipei)
The Gallup Organization, Inc.

THAILAND (Bangkok)
The Gallup (Thailand) Company, Ltd.

UNITED KINGDOM
(New Malden/Weybridge)
The Gallup Organization, Ltd.

UNITED STATES OF AMERICA
(Princeton)
The Gallup Organization
World Headquarters
Tel. (01) 609 924-9600
Fax. (01) 609 924-0228

VENEZUELA (Caracas)
Gallup Venezuela, C.A.

The Gallup Organization
WORLD HEADQUARTERS
PRINCETON, NEW JERSEY, USA

Access our latest publicly released surveys
on the world wide web at: **www.gallup.com**

(Not associated in any way with 'Gallup International', a non-profit organization.)

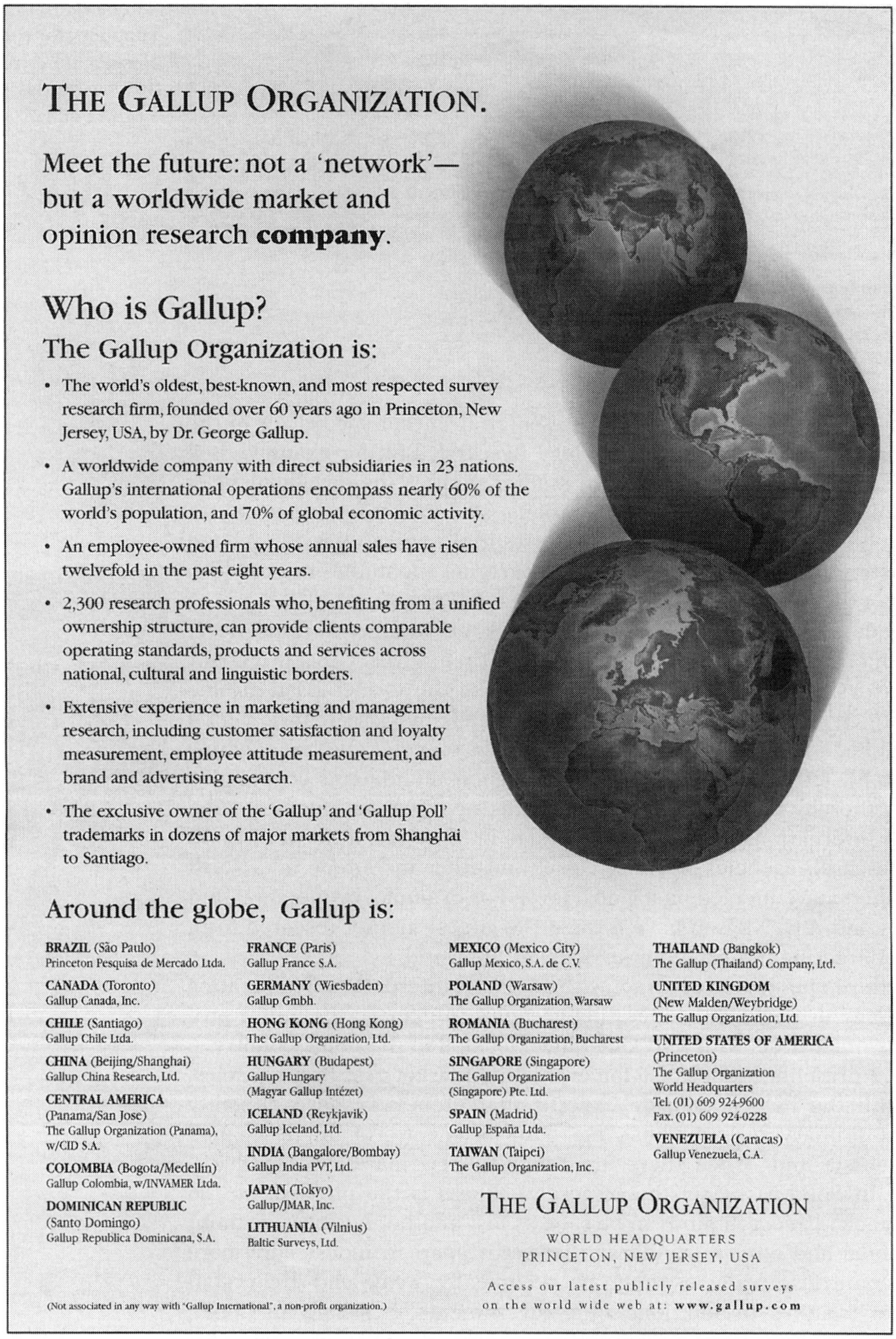

Source: Advertisement in *ESOMAR NewsBrief*, No. 6, June 1996, 12.

Table 6.9 Checklist: Selecting a Research Agency

1. Basic information about the agency
   a) How long has it been in business as a research company? Is market research its only (or at least its main) business, or is research just an element in a wider range of non-research activities such as marketing/management consultancy or direct marketing?
   b) If it belongs to another company or a group of companies, how independently does it operate?
   c) Is it part of any international research chain or association? If so, how close are the links?
   d) What clients has it worked for during the last 2 years or so, and on what types of project? Which ones does it work for regularly? (Although an agency is obviously restricted by confidentiality requirements in the information it can give, it will often be able to provide some general picture of its clientele and the type of work it carries out for them.)
   e) Are there any potential conflicts of interest which might need to be sorted out?
   f) How much practical experience does the agency have of tackling specific types of research problems or markets, or of using particular research methods?
   g) How firmly is it committed to following the accepted Codes of Professional Practice in marketing research – both ESOMAR and national Codes? What are its links with professional bodies in the field?
   h) Are its security/confidentiality procedures acceptable?

2. Information about the agency's staff
   a) What are the professional training, qualifications and experience of the agency's staff – both senior management and further down the organization?
   b) How experienced are they in dealing with marketing and other relevant non-research issues as distinct from research techniques as such?
   c) What specialist skills (psychologist, statisticans, etc) can the agency call on – either within the agency or on a regular basis from outside?
   d) Who would be responsible for looking after the client's own project(s)? Is it possible to meet them?
   e) Are there any potential problems of communication? In particular, do the key people (in client and agency) adequately understand a common language? If there are possible difficulties, how could they be dealt with effectively?

3. Information about the agency's facilities and operating procedures
   a) What procedures does the agency follow in setting up a research project? What form does a research proposal normally take?
   b) What kind of field organization does the agency use – its own or a separate supplier? Either way,
      ↔ how large and widespread is the interviewing force?
      ↔ are specialist interviewers available if required (e.g. for interviewing executives or professional people)?
      ↔ how are interviewers selected and trained?
      ↔ what briefing are they given on specific projects?
      ↔ how and to what extent are they supervised? What are the qualifications of the supervisors?
      ↔ what quality and accuracy checks are applied to the fieldwork?
      ↔ can the client see interviewers in action (in conformity with the ESOMAR Code requirements)?
      ↔ (if relevant) is the agency prepared to accept independent checks on the quality of the fieldwork?
   c) What types of sampling method does the agency customarily use?
   d) How does the agency handle its data processing (internally or subcontracted)? Either way,
      ↔ what editing, coding, data entry and processing procedures are used?
      ↔ what quality of staff are used and how are they supervised?
      ↔ what quality and accuracy checks are applied?
      ↔ can flexible and/or more sophisticated forms of analysis be provided when required?
      ↔ are checks of statistical significance routinely applied to the findings wherever relevant?
   e) What form of reporting does the agency normally use? Can it provide tabulation only/written summary of results/interpretation of the findings/recommendations for action, as required? Is it possible to see examples (allowing for possible confidentiality problems)?

(continued)

f) Does the agency give presentations of the findings, if required? If so, what form do these take? Are they charged for separately?

g) Does the agency offer any special research facilities (e.g. a telephone research installation, test room or laboratory, test shop, special testing equipment)?

h) Does the agency offer any special (proprietary research systems (e.g. for testing advertisements/packaging, market modelling or prediction)?

i) What are the agency's normal accounting and charging procedures? What billing systems does it normally follow?

j) What contractual and other legal arrangements are customary with the agency?

Note: not all of these questions will be relevant to every enquiry about an agency. Also, it will often be sensible in connection with a specific survey to go in greater depth into certain issues (e.g. the agency's sampling and interviewing approach on surveys among business).

Source: ESOMAR, 'Guidelines on Selecting a Research Agency', Doc.E.4, Amsterdam 1992, 4f.

In Latin American countries, consumer surveys are available only for urban areas. In addition, it may be difficult to establish a field research staff with enough training to produce reliable interviews. The cheapest and most effective way of getting information in such cases may be to design the research around secondary data and add interviews of carefully selected experts in the markets of interest. The marketer may visit each market to verify the interpretation of secondary data and the insights gained from expert interviews.

The Future Issues box gives examples that show the marketing research industry catching up fast in countries where strong industrialization trends exist. Such development can be expected in the most dynamic parts of East Asia as well as Latin America over the next decade. In India, for example, the marketing research industry is full of capable talent, is at least three times larger than it was ten years ago, and is enjoying an annual growth rate of 30 per cent.

Interpretation and Presentation of Results

Figure 6.7 illustrates the final stage of the international marketing research process. The data that have been collected and analysed must be interpreted and presented in a form that will help improve management decisions.

Interpretation

The interpretation of research results requires a healthy scepticism because of the potential for errors in data collection and analysis, especially when data have been collected under varying circumstances. For example, there may be substantial biases in the answers to attitude questions because of cultural differences. In some societies it is quite common to express one's opinion openly; in others, however, understatement is more common or people are reluctant to express their attitudes to strangers. If researchers want to com-

FUTURE ISSUES
BOX

Marketing Research in Fast Developing Countries

THE 1960S WAS THE MOST IMPORTANT DECADE IN THE history of market research in Hong Kong. Improved standards of living created a demand for higher quality products, which meant foreign products in those days. The international companies had a need for marketing research services, which gave rise to the formation of a few professional agencies.

Today the need to react speedily to market changes gave rise to continuous tracking services providing data on market share, consumption level, attitude shift, and other important barometers of the market. Hong Kong also experiences an upsurge in radio audience research as well as customer satisfaction research. For 1992, the total revenue of market research agencies in Hong Kong excluding revenue derived from research in China, was estimated at around USD24 million.

Hong Kong has still some way to catch up with industrially developed countries in the practice and application of marketing research. There is a need to educate more local companies

regarding its value. Nevertheless, it seems clear that after 30 years marketing research has been recognized as a respectable profession as well as an indispensable activity for corporations' sucess.

Due to NAFTA market research in Mexico is in a very favorable position. The penetration of foreign consumer goods in supermarkets is enormous, and this has forced companies established in Mexico to increase the number of research studies of every kind. The market size in 1993 was estimated as about USD65 million.

There is an ongoing dynamism in the Mexican research industry. Joint ventures have been agreed between marketing research agencies in Mexico and worldwide companies, especially the US. The Mexican company IMOP, for example, has joined Gallup, Gamma has joined Yankelovich, and G. de Villa has joined Burke International. The ten biggest research firms represent almost 85 per cent of total turnover in Mexico. But there is a boom in small companies (about 100 in 1993) and free-lancers.

In 1992, a Mexican Marketing and Opinion Research Agencies Association (AMAI) was created, and the first steps towards establishing harmonization of socio-economic demographic classifications have been taken.

Sources: Leung, A. (1993) 'The development of market research in Hong Kong', *ESOMAR NewsBrief*, No. 3, April, 15f; and Nadelsticher, A., 'Market research in Mexico,' *ESOMAR NewsBrief*, op. cit., 5.

pare the answers given to the same questions in two such different environments, they need to correct for biases due to the typical response styles of the respondents. This can be achieved by normalizing or standardizing the gathered data. In normalizing the data the researcher assumes that respondents of all countries use extreme scale values equally. Respondents in one country are, however, expected to be more positive about a construct than respondents in another country. Therefore only corrections for differences in mean are applied by setting each country's mean to zero, and expressing differences in terms of standard deviations. When the researcher has good reasons to assume that respondents from one culture are both more likely to give positive answers and to use more extreme values on the scales, these effects have to be removed before valid comparisons can be made. By setting the countries'

Figure 6.7 **THE INTERNATIONAL MARKETING RESEARCH PROCESS STEP 4: INTERPRETING AND PRESENTING THE RESULTS**

Findings of international marketing research projects need careful interpretation and well-prepared presentation to management decision makers.

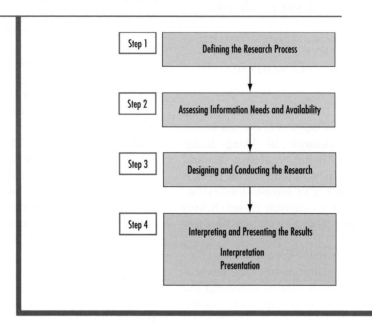

Step 1 — Defining the Research Process

Step 2 — Assessing Information Needs and Availability

Step 3 — Designing and Conducting the Research

Step 4 — Interpreting and Presenting the Results
Interpretation
Presentation

means to zero and standard deviations to 1, that is, by standardizing the data, comparability can be achieved.

The interpretation of data gathered on an international level demands a high level of cultural understanding. In international marketing research there is the constant danger of selective perception due to cultural biases, that is, a tendency to believe that other people perceive (or should perceive) things in the same way oneself does. Many Anglo-Americans are at the disadvantage that they have greater difficulty in recognizing that bias because they are only able to read or talk in one language. What is not said or published in English does not exist in 'their' world. This problem can derail an otherwise well-designed and well-executed research project. The probability of correctly interpreting data can be improved by ensuring that at least one person who interprets the data from a particular region is well acquainted with the culture and business customs of that region.

Presentation

The findings of a research project are a 'product' that, like any other product, deserves its own marketing strategy. The findings should be presented in a fashion that meets the needs of different 'customers' within the company. Because there are many different customers of research findings, with different degrees of technical and cultural expertise, it is almost always necessary to prepare both a written report and oral briefings.

The purpose of the research report is to explain to those who did not participate in the research exactly what problem was studied, how it was studied, what the results were, and how the researchers believe the results should be interpreted. The report should make a case for using the results of the research. The report should also be easy to understand. An extremely detailed and precise report is not best under all circumstances. Strategic and tactical decisions need different degrees of detail in information. Furthermore, high-level managers shy away from long reports. They prefer short summaries of the most important facts, backed by verbal and visual presentations where the managers can ask supplementary questions of special interest to them. On the other hand, product managers often need very detailed market information for their tactical decisions.

The shared commitment developed through a team approach to preparing the research brief can be reinforced through proper presentation of the findings. A preliminary presentation of the findings can be made to the team that helped generate the research brief. They can be asked for suggestions regarding revision or expansion of the findings. After the recommended changes have been made, the team may be willing to 'sponsor' the reporting of the research to the rest of the organization. This approach can result in a sense of shared ownership of the research. It can be especially important when the results of the research indicate a need for changes in the way the organization conducts business.

SUMMARY

Marketing research projects start with the definition of the research problem. While sometimes neglected, this is the most important step in the research process. The care and accuracy with which the research question is specified, the unit of analysis determined, the timing and organization of the project laid out, and a preliminary budget set up largely determines how useful the research results will be. Therefore, a written research brief containing all of these elements is prepared in a team of people concerned with the research problem and submitted to a decision maker for approval.

In the second stage of the research process, the research team must outline all the dimensions of the research problem. This outline is used to identify information that might be available within the firm and then to determine what information needs must be met from outside sources.

If external sources are needed, the researchers will first attempt to solve the research problem through the use of secondary data, which are inexpensive and often easy to obtain. If secondary research cannot provide enough information to solve the research problem, the firm may decide to carry out primary research. This will mostly be the case when precise data are needed for tactical decisions in an attractive market. Primary research starts with a definition of the target population. Then the most appropriate method for collecting the data has to be selected.

In most international research projects, some kind of sampling will have to take place. That is, the researchers will select a subset of the target population. With a reliable sampling frame, they can choose an appropriate probability sample. In its absence, convenience or judgement samples will have to be accepted. Such a sample will not necessarily be representative, but it may be more cost-effective than a probability sample.

To determine the final research budget, the cost of each activity included in the project must be estimated. The list of activities needed for budget estimation can also be used for preparing and monitoring the research schedule. If the firm has a fixed research budget, the project must be designed in such a way as to meet the constraints imposed by that budget.

In many cases the company may decide to hire a research agency to carry out the project. Research agencies may be based in the geographic area of interest, they may specialize in the industry in question, or they may be international agencies with branch offices or partners in all of the developed countries and in most developing ones.

The data that have been collected and analysed must be interpreted and presented in a way that is most useful to decision makers. When preparing the written report and oral presentation, researchers should keep in mind that the findings of a research project are a 'product' that should be 'packaged' and communicated in a fashion that meets the needs of different 'consumers' within the company.

Because of the multitude of information sources inside and outside the firm and the great variety of information available at many different levels of detail, international marketing research is best carried out in an integrated fashion embedded in a marketing information system. Chapter 10 will further elaborate on how to establish and manage such an international marketing information system.

DISCUSSION QUESTIONS

1. How does international marketing research differ from domestic marketing research?
2. How does the choice of the unit of analysis affect the results of marketing research?
3. 'An international marketing research project must have the latest in-depth market data to be of any value to a marketing decision maker.' Do you agree or disagree with this statement? Why?
4. How can information available within the firm help in an international marketing research project?
5. What are some of the problems associated with using secondary data in international marketing research?
6. When should primary research be conducted?
7. Why is it important to determine the target population before conducting primary research?
8. What special problems may be encountered in obtaining a sampling frame for international marketing research?
9. What types of agencies may be employed to conduct an international marketing research project? What trade-offs are associated with each type?
10. What is an international marketing information system?

ADDITIONAL READINGS

Diamantopoulos, A. and B.B. Schlegelmilch (1997) *Taking the Fear Out of Data Analysis – A Step-by-Step Approach*, London: The Dryden Press.

Marketing and Research Today, The Journal of the European Society for Opinion and Marketing Research, Amsterdam.

Souchon, A.L. and A. Diamantopoulos (1996) 'A Conceptual Framework of Export Marketing Information Use: Key Issues and Research Propositions', *Journal of International Marketing*, 4(3), 49–71.

Wierenga, B. and P. A.M. Oude Ophuis (1997) 'Marketing decision support systems: Adoption, use, and satisfaction', *International Journal of Research in Marketing*, 14, 275–290.

NOTES

[1] *ESOMAR NewsBrief*, No. 2, February 1996, p. 23.
[2] Vangelder, Ph. (1995) 'Global research: The Whirlpool strategy', *ESOMAR NewsBrief*, No. 3, March, pp. 20f.
[3] Vangelder, Ph. (1995) 'Marketing at McDonald's', *ESOMAR NewsBrief*, No. 6, June, 17.
[4] Vangelder, Ph. (1995) op. cit., 17.

[5] *ESOMAR NewsBrief*, No. 6, June 1995, 25.

[6] Pawle, J. (1994), 'Qualitative Research in the Middle East', *ESOMAR NewsBrief Supplement*, March, p. 8.

[7] Yue, Y. (1994) 'Effective Way to Avoid Investment Risks in China', *International Business Monthly*, 36f.

[8] Mühlbacher, H., M. Botschen and W. Bentelmayer (1997) 'The changing consumer in Austria', *International Journal of Research in Marketing*, 14(4), October, 309–319.

[9] ESOMAR (1995) 'ESOMAR Annual market study on market statistics 1994', Amsterdam, 20.

[10] Aldrige D. (1995) 'Research in Asia', *ESOMAR NewsBrief*, No. 10, November, 17.

[11] ESOMAR (1995) 'ESOMAR Annual market study on market statistics 1994', Amsterdam, p. 19.

[12] 'Companies', *ESOMAR NewsBrief*, No. 6, June 1996, 27.

[13] Standaert, J. (1993) 'Vietnam, a new frontier for market research in Asia', *ESOMAR NewsBrief*, No. 10, December, 22f.

[14] Grunert, S.C., K.G. Grunert, and K. Kristensen (1994) 'On a method for estimating the cross-cultural validity of measurement instruments: The case of measuring consumer values by the List of Values LOY', Working Papers in Marketing, No. 2, Odense Universitet, July.

[15] Van Herk, H. and Th.M.M. Verhallen (1995) 'Prerequisites for International Segmentation,' in M. Bergadaa (ed.), *Marketing Today and for the 21st Century*, Cergy-Pontoise: CERESSEC, pp. 2053–2057.

[16] Vangelder, Ph. (1995) 'P & G: the market research contribution', *ESOMAR NewsBrief*, No. 11, December, 14f.

[17] 'From Russia to learn', *ESOMAR NewsBrief*, No. 3, March 1994, 18f.

[18] 'Russia', *ESOMAR NewsBrief*, No. 11, December 1995, 9.

[19] Aldrige, D. (1995) op. cit., 17.

CHAPTER

7

POTENTIAL MARKET ASSESSMENT: DETERMINATION OF ATTRACTIVE MARKETS

LEARNING OBJECTIVES

After studying this chapter you will be able to:

↔

describe the different steps of an international market assessment procedure

↔

determine relevant criteria to assess the attractiveness of potential international markets

↔

assess the attractiveness of country-markets

↔

analyse the attractiveness of local product-markets

↔

help a company determine a short list of international markets to consider serving

CHAPTER OUTLINE

The process of potential market assessment

Assessment of country-markets

Potential assessment criteria
Assessment criteria concerning the macro-environment
Assessment criteria concerning the operating environment
Choice of market assessment criteria
Determination of attractive country-markets
Future market attractiveness
The most attractive markets

Summary

Hirschmann GmbH

Hirschmann GmbH is a German producer of special electrical plugs for industrial customers. It has developed its own technology, called Anspritztechnik, which is superior to the technology of competitors from East Asia, but more expensive to produce. The company is active in Germany, the Netherlands, France, Italy, Switzerland, Austria, Belgium, Spain, Canada and the USA.

Looking for additional attractive markets for products based on this new technology, Hirschmann GmbH first applied criteria specific to the firm's success in its product markets: the existence of a modern electrical infrastructure; a sufficient number of large, potential industrial customers; and a price level in the industry compatible with successful competition. These criteria led to a significant reduction in the number of potential markets. The company screened out all less developed countries in Africa, Asia and South America with an insufficient infrastructure, leaving South Africa in the pool of potential markets. The developing countries in the Far East and their highly industrialized neighbour, Japan, had to be ruled out as well, owing to low price levels in their product-markets.

The potential markets left after the first screening were reanalysed for political and legal restrictions. Because Hirschmann GmbH offers customer-specific solutions to electric-contact problems, it must be able to reach its customers directly. So all centrally controlled economies had to be screened out, even if they had a large number of potential industrial customers. Legal dimensions that were considered included prohibitions on importing finished goods; the respect given to patent rights; and whether funds could be freely transferred.

The application of these criteria to the screening process resulted in the following group of markets left for in-depth analysis: the Northern European countries (Sweden, Norway and Finland), Australia, Brazil and South Africa. Because economic indicators, such as per capita income, level of industrialization and number of large potential customers, as well as market openness, political stability and physical distance pointed in the direction of Sweden, Hirschmann GmbH chose this country as the most attractive market.

THE PROCESS OF POTENTIAL MARKET ASSESSMENT

To ensure an efficient and effective evaluation process, companies wanting to internationalize their business gradually should follow a progressive screening procedure. A series of logical steps systematically decreases the number of markets to be analysed in increasing detail (see Figure 7.1). The procedure is based on the firm's statement of corporate policy where it has determined its product-market(s). Product-markets will usually be distributed over a large number of country-markets. The assessment of those different geographic

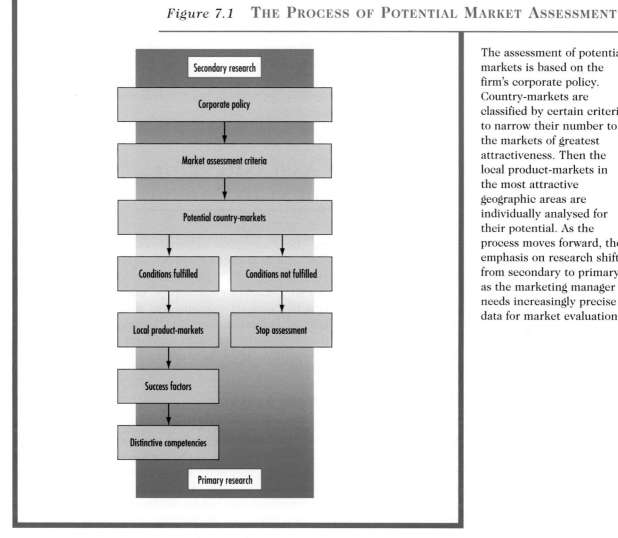

Figure 7.1 THE PROCESS OF POTENTIAL MARKET ASSESSMENT

The assessment of potential markets is based on the firm's corporate policy. Country-markets are classified by certain criteria to narrow their number to the markets of greatest attractiveness. Then the local product-markets in the most attractive geographic areas are individually analysed for their potential. As the process moves forward, the emphasis on research shifts from secondary to primary, as the marketing manager needs increasingly precise data for market evaluation.

parts of the product-market will quickly lead to a reduction of submarkets. Criteria relevant for the assessment of country-markets can be found in their macro-environment, for example geographic proximity, natural resources, the political/legal system, cultural and social characteristics, the level of economic development, and participation in cooperative agreements, as well as in the firm's operating environment, for example the number and purchasing power of potential customers, the availability of a skilled labour force, the kind and structure of available intermediaries, sources of local supply, and the intensity of local competition. They are chosen as market assessment criteria as far as they are relevant to the firm's business.

Country-markets which do not measure up to the standards imposed on the selected assessment criteria are not investigated further. Therefore, only a small number of remaining local parts of the global product-market will be assessed in detail. Problems, aspirations, and characteristics of potential customers as well as of other important stakeholders are assessed to determine the success factors in each attractive market (see Chapter 8). That is, management has to find out what resources and capabilities their firm must possess to be considered an attractive business partner. The final step in the process of market assessment is a comparison between the strengths and weaknesses of the firm and its major competitors related to the success factors (Chapter 8). This helps to draw up a list of distinctive competencies which provides important information for management in choosing the markets to serve and in determining the intended global as well as local strategic positions of the firm (see Chapters 9 and 10).

Assessment of Country-Markets

To systematically assess the geographic submarkets of the firm's global product-market, managers need to select assessment criteria that are relevant to the business of the firm (see Figure 7.2). The information gathered on these criteria is then compared in a market exclusion procedure to find a small number of currently attractive country-markets. For this group of markets, potential future changes in factors influencing their attractiveness are assessed. They will further reduce the number of attractive geographic areas in which the local product-markets are to be analysed in detail.

Potential Assessment Criteria

Sources of criteria to be used in screening potential country-markets are the macro-environment and the operating environment of the local product-markets. To keep the cost of information, and the time necessary for decision making, reasonably limited when assessing the attractiveness of country-markets, in a first step managers will choose only those characteristics of the macro- and operating environments that can be evaluated through secondary research and have an exclusive impact on the number of markets to be considered. For example, the different marketing strategies of local competitors will not be considered at this stage of the process, because gathering this information will demand some primary research. But the level of economic development, the quality of local infrastructure, the number of major competitors present in the market, the price level that can be reached, or the number of potential customers may be important criteria in assessing the attractiveness of country-markets and the information can easily be gathered from secondary sources. Primary sources of information are used only at later steps of the assessment process when the amount of needed data is reduced because the most attractive country-markets have already been determined and only a small number of remaining local product-markets have to be evaluated in detail.

Assessment Criteria Concerning the Macro-Environment

Criteria for the assessment of country-markets can be most easily found in their macro-environment. For the sake of speed and cost of decision making, therefore, managers tend to use the criteria discussed in the following.

Figure 7.2 ASSESSMENT OF COUNTRY-MARKETS

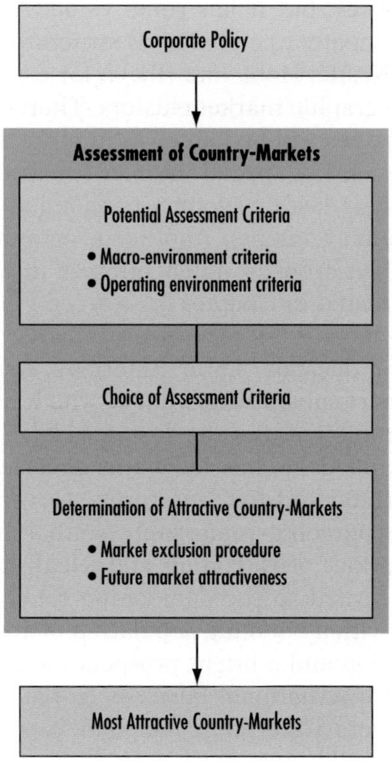

Geographic Proximity. The location of country-markets is often used as a basis for evaluation. Minimal physical distance most often results in low psychological distance which in turn leads to a perception of lower market-entry risk. Thus, a US firm may perceive the Mexican market as being less risky than the New Zealand market, even if this is not the case.

Classifying countries along geographic lines sometimes makes sense. For example, if the costs of transporting a product are high relative to production costs, the company may decide to export only to neighbouring countries; this helps to explain the high level of US–Canadian trade. However, a different market-entry technique, such as direct investment, may be appropriate for a more distant market and yield considerably higher long-term profits.

It is tempting to argue that markets located in the same geographic area are likely to share cultural traits and geographic conditions, and that they should therefore be grouped together as a potential target market. But geographic proximity does not guarantee that two target markets will be similar. To cite just one example, Austria, the Czech Republic and Hungary have a long history of similar cultural development. A closer examination of these countries, however, reveals that these nations differ considerably in social structure, economic conditions, language, infrastructure and natural resources. Therefore, treating them as a single target market would not result in a reliable evaluation of their potential or lead to the best marketing decisions.

Grouping countries according to geographic proximity is rarely enough for market assessment purposes, but it has some value. A geographic grouping makes it easier for the company to organize its structure and activities. Multinational companies like Nestlé, Mobil and HILTI, for example, structure their divisions according to geographic market clusters. Therefore, two groupings of countries or geographic zones will be looked at in more detail: Latin America and Southeast Asia. They are of special interest because of their supplies of critical raw materials, their fast-developing economies, and their changing political and economic environments. Another geographic area, Middle and Eastern Europe, which has aroused much interest in companies in recent years has already been treated in Chapter 3.

(1) Latin America.   For decades, Latin America's economic-development model was based on 'import substitution', under which imports were not just discouraged, but often prohibited. But the 'lost decade' of the 1980s, a decade of stagnation, inflation and debt, has led Latin America to discard its old model and look to free trade and free enterprise. Governments of the most important countries are pursuing remarkably similar free-market policies, including trade liberalization, privatization and fiscal discipline. In parallel, the subcontinent has returned to the democratic fold. Seen from that perspective, Latin America, with a booming population of 400 million, represents a fast-growing market region and a bright prospect for growth. US companies take the largest share of international business in Latin America. They are shipping capital goods, from Caterpillar Inc. bulldozers to IBM computers. Pizza Hut International would once have been seen as a Yankee assault on local cuisine, yet in 1995 it had 200 franchises from Chile to Mexico and aimed for 500, with 200 in Brazil alone.

Not all countries are moving at the same speed, however. Until 1994, **Mexico**, with a population of about 95 million, was the forerunner. Its economy grew at about 4 per cent a year. Electrotechnical, electronic and automotive products reached more than 40 per cent of total exports, 85 per cent of which went to the USA. Inflation had dropped from 160 per cent a year to less than 7 per cent in 1994. Tariffs were down to 20 per cent tops, and the government was selling state-owned companies. Even communication and transportation infrastructures were improving. But the end of 1994, following the presidential election, saw a heavy loss of confidence in the Mexican currency which lost about 50 per cent of its value against the dollar. The resulting substantial increase in prices of imported goods shocked Mexican industry. In two months, more than 250 000 people lost their jobs. A recovery programme containing price controls, completion of privatizations, tax increases, budget cuts, and a limitation of wage increases was established by the government. Since then, international financial aid has stabilized the country's economy. In 1997 the real growth rate of GDP was back at 7 per cent. Remaining problems are the country's dependence on crude oil income – 40 per cent of state income comes from taxes on the profit of state-owned Petroleos Mexicanos – and the large amount of bank credits (more than USD61 billion) given to companies without sufficient control of creditworthiness[1].

The average Mexican has only a sixth-grade education, and just 3 per cent of the people have college degrees. But if properly recruited, trained and motivated, Mexican workers can be as productive as their US counterparts.[2] An improvement of the education system, key to both competitiveness and population control, is under way. Top executives at Ford, Procter & Gamble, Thomson and Philips Electronics all rave about the quality of their workforces in Mexico. To what extent knowledge about cultural differences can influence the success of a foreign-owned firm in Mexico is described in the Culture box. Largely because demand is greater than supply, management salaries in Mexico are as high as or higher than in the USA. Average per capita income is only around USD3,700, not enough to support a mass market for most consumer products and services. But with increasing income the pent-up demand for quality goods and services in areas such as cars, cosmetics, computers, consultancy, canned goods, clothes and cellular phones will have to be satisfied.

Brazil is the most economically developed Latin American country, with an improving infrastructure and a rate of economic growth which reached 3.5 per cent in 1997. It has export-oriented automotive, metal and pulp industries. Aracruz Celulose, for example, is one of the world's most efficient pulp producers. But Brazil also exports many consumer goods; for example, it is the largest exporter of shoes to the USA. International tourism reached 8 per cent of GDP in 1995. The number of tourists visiting the country rose from fewer than 200 000 at the end of the 1980s to more than 2 million in the mid-1990s.

During the 1980s, Brazil was fanatically devoted to protectionism. For example, in 1989 Rogerio Marques ran a small computer-parts factory in Rio de Janeiro. He was sheltered from foreign competition by high tariffs, but importing parts was a bureaucratic nightmare. Since then, Brazil has opened up its industries, foreign companies are allowed to take shares in domestic companies, and many firms have been privatized. Marques landed the Radio Shack distributorship. He had two stores full of imports in 1992 and planned to have 75 by 1996. But then, in Spring 1995, owing to Brazilian consumers' demand for foreign goods which had been held back for years by hyperinflation (2800 per cent in 1993, 941 per cent in 1994) and suddenly became effective when Brazil's new and relatively stable currency, the real, was introduced in the middle of 1994, the country's trade balance reached a deficit of USD3 billion. To restore equilibrium Brazil's government established import taxes up to 70 per cent for 109 product categories such as cars, refrigerators and consumer electronics.

Despite those problems, the prospects of the country seem to be good. US and European companies have strongly invested in taking over Brazilian firms. Italy's food giant Parmalat, for example, has bought ten local brands which provide the company with higher total sales in Brazil than in their home market.[3] Car manufacturers have started a fierce battle for market share. They are attracted by free land, newly built infrastructure and tax exemptions. Paris-based Renault, as one of them, has decided to invest USD1 billion in a car assembly plant at Curitiba, near the borders of Argentina, Paraguay and Uruguay, Brazil's partners in the Mercosur free trade agreement. The investment will create 2000 jobs directly and another 15 000 to 20 000 indirectly. In 1999, 120 000 Renault Mégane vehicles are planned to be sold in Brazil, which at that time will have a total sales volume of up to 3 million cars per year.[4]

The country's biggest problem is its high percentage of impoverished people (approximately 60 per cent of the population of about 160 million). So far, the payoff from privatization and trade liberalization has gone to the higher income classes. Immediate costs are paid by the working and middle

CULTURE BOX

Culture

Clash

BUSINESS LIBERALIZATION NOT ONLY PROVIDES MULtiple opportunities to marketers, it also may lead to managerial problems when different cultures meet.

The culture clash between foreign managers and Mexican laborers has been most evident in the maquiladora programme. The problems in firms founded under that programme are rooted in the fact that the border plants generally fall under the control of US corporations' domestic divisions, rather than their international ones.

Less sensitive to the special problems of operating abroad, the domestic division chiefs usually select maquiladora managers based upon their skill in production rather than human relations.

The gulf between the Mexian workers and US managers results in a heavy turnover of both labor and management. It is 12 per cent for Mexicans, but American managers tend to burn out rapidly as well. To get anything done in Mexico, the manager has to be more of an instructor, teacher, or father figure than a boss. Ken Franklin, who manages assembly plants at Juarez's giant Bermudez Industrial Park, visits the production line every day at 6 a.m., to greet each worker individually. 'In Mexico everything is a personnel matter,' he says. 'But a lot of managers don't get it.'

Source: Moffett, M. (1992) 'Culture Shock', *The Wall Street Journal*, 24 September, p. R. 13.

classes: companies go out of business, and workers lose jobs as firms try to become more productive. The country may face tremendous social difficulties if people do not get their share of progress.

Argentina, with its large agricultural sector, is among the world's most competitive suppliers of grain and beef. To strangle hyperinflation (3100 per cent in 1989), it has quite successfully tied its currency, the austral, to the dollar (at an exchange rate of 1:1), backing all currency with hard reserves. Free convertibility was established. Remaining budget deficits were paid from privatization earnings. Inflation decreased below average European levels (1.5 per cent in 1997). Growth rates of GDP reached 7 per cent annually between 1991 and 1994. During that time foreign investment in Argentina went up to more than USD35 billion.[5]

A short recession at the end of 1994, caused by insecurities in the aftermath of the substantial devaluation of the Mexican peso, lead to fears that Argentina could fall back into the economic state of the 1980s. But 1996 brought a recovery. GDP growth went up to 8.5 per cent in 1997. Exports passed USD800 million. They are mainly due to a small number of big companies, such as the Techint group which holds interests in steel production, heavy machinery engineering and manufacturing, and energy business. Major problems of Argentina's economy are its high unemployment rate (16 per cent) and the insufficient international competitiveness of large parts of the economy – despite productivity gains of 30 per cent in only five years.[6]

Venezuela, a member of OPEC, has used its oil income to underwrite industrial development. **Chile**'s growth rate of 6.8 per cent from 1995 to 1999 will beat every country in East Asia except China. Chilean companies are the export stars of the subcontinent, shipping copper, lumber, fruit, and even software. Chilean firms are also finding lucrative niches. Fósforos Chilenos, a matchstick manufacturer, for example, sells millions of Popsicle sticks to the USA and is serving the Japanese chopstick market. As a result, Chile's per capita income was USD5,390, up 48 per cent from USD3,641 in 1994.

Together, these countries account for more than 90 per cent of Latin American exports of manufactured goods. Their growth in basic industries like steel, machinery, pulp and paper, gas, hydroelectric power and home appliances is based on imports of capital, machinery, materials and intermediate goods. They are attractive markets if governments can secure economic and social stability. The Future Issues box (see page 270) discusses some pros and cons of a free trade area tying together North and South America. Despite economic reforms, and while the broad move towards private enterprise is unlikely to be reversed, governments will still come and go, and rules can change. The inevitable ups and downs, while frustrating to European and US managers, have been a particular turnoff to the cautious Japanese. They are not as well represented as in other areas of the world, leaving important markets to their competitors.

(2) South East Asia. In the first half of the 1990s, Southeast Asia experienced the fastest economic growth in the world. Overall GDP growth in the Asian-Pacific region from Kazakhstan in the west to the Pacific island states in the east, excluding Japan, was 7.9 per cent in 1995 and stayed at that level in the following year. Forecasts were that by the year 2000 the economies of East Asia – spanning from Japan to Indonesia – would almost certainly equal the GNP of the USA and total about four-fifths of the European Community (Table 7.1). But in 1997 South East Asian countries were sharply hit by banking, currency and foreign-debt crises at the same time. Economists estimate that bank bailouts will cost taxpayers in Indonesia, Thailand and South Korea an amount equal to 20 per cent or more of one year's gross domestic product.

Table 7.1 COMPARISON OF SOUTH EAST ASIAN COUNTRIES

COUNTRY	POPULATION		ADULT LITERACY %	GNP PER CAPITA USD	PURCHASING PARITY PER CAPITA	GDP GROWTH RATE %	INFLATION %
	IN MILLIONS	URBAN %					
China	1,190	27	73	435	2.855	13.4	13
Hong Kong	6	95	88	18.500	19.446	5.5	8
India	899	26	52	310	1.198	4.2	9
Indonesia	190	31	82	645	2.891	6.7	10
Malaysia	19	55	80	3.680	–	8.5	4
Philippines	65	45	94	805	2.440	1.7	9.8
Taiwan	21	75	92	10.215	9.830	6.2	3.9
Thailand	69	24	93	1.905	5.665	7.4	4.8
Singapore	3	100	91	16.440	16.674	9.9	2.8
South Korea	44	76	96	7.250	8.694	5.5	6.4
Vietnam	71	20	90	230	1.263	7.9	6.1

(Database 1995)
Source: Merrill Lynch

One

America

Imagine: a free trade zone stretching from Port Barrow, Alaska, to Patagonia, tying all the nations of the Americas in a web of commerce and democracy. One America.

In the year 2005 such a free trade area will be reality if the Free Trade Area of the Americas (FTAA), which was envisioned in summer of 1995 at a meeting of the trade ministers of 34 North and South American countries, comes into existence. Until then, barriers to trade and investment are to be lifted. Free trade throughout the Americas, proponents argue, would channel investment and technology to Latin nations, radically restructuring their economies, and give US firms a head start in capturing business there. Gradually, free trade would lift millions from poverty.

In comparison, in the first quarter of 1995, bilateral trade between the USA and Europe reached USD61 billion, bilateral trade with Japan

exeeded USD46 billion, and trade between Latin America and the USA had a volume of USD48 billion. If Latin America grows, as expected, at an average of 4 per cent a year during the 1990s and continues trade liberalization, Latin imports will increase to USD170 billion annually by the year 2000. The USA could expect to supply USD70 billion of those imports. Until 2010 the USA plans to export more to Latin America than to Japan and Europe together. Optimists hope that through this trade expansion more than 2 million additional jobs will be created in the USA.

But opponents deride a hemispheric bloc as a pipe dream or, worse, a nightmare. They argue that NAFTA is already degrading blue-collar wages, health and environmental standards throughout North America because Mexico's wages are pitifully low and its environmental enforcement lax. A hemisphere-wide trade pact, giving US businesses a choice of poor countries in which to set up business duty-free, would depress standards even more. The result would be high unemployment rates in the USA and a lower standard of living.

Sources: Adapted from Davis, B. (1992) 'One America', *The Wall Street Journal*, 24 September, pp. R 1 and R 8; Gutfeld, R. (1992) 'Keeping it Green', *The Wall Street Journal*, 24 September 1992, p. R 9; and 'Grenzenloser Handel von Alaska bis nach Feuerland', *Der Standard*, 3 July 1995, p. 13.

Lost economic output could equal another 30 per cent of one year's GDP in Indonesia, less in Thailand and South Korea.[7]

Most nations in this area practise a brand of capitalism – even if it is called a 'socialist market economy' such as in the People's Republic of China – that combines industrial policy with freewheeling competition. In Singapore, for example, the government runs many industrial companies, including Singapore Technologies Group, which has more than USD1.5 billion in annual sales and has joint ventures with such companies as Xerox and Pratt & Whitney.

The six most dynamic economies beside China have been the newly industrialized countries (NICs) of East Asia which first included Hong Kong, Singapore, South Korea and Taiwan. Thailand and Malaysia started their development later but since then have gained much interest. Despite the financial crisis, the NICs remained highly competitive, export-oriented manufacturing countries. Their potential rates of economic growth are about 5 per cent a year. Low wages, long working hours and strong management have been the basic ingredients of their success. Political stability and market-oriented public policies have been top priorities. All of the NICs import technology and consumer products. South Korea, for example, was the fourth-largest importer of US farm products in the mid-1990s. But food products only reached a share of 4 per cent of total imports in 1994, whereas machinery and transportation imports accounted for 37 per cent.

The major problems of these countries are a lack of sound financial management, a lack of modern infrastructure and an increasing lack of a highly educated workforce. In its Asian Development outlook, for example, the Asian Development Bank states that Thailand and Malaysia are not producing the university graduates that their level of economic development suggests they need. The large inflow of foreign investment capital has built up inflationary pressures and was one of the reasons for the economic crash. The lack of a qualified workforce steadily increases production costs and demand for capital goods. In 1966, for example, wages for car workers in South Korea were higher than in northern Britain.

In reaction to this development, an increasing amount of manufacturing has been transferred to neighbouring countries with lower wages, such as Indonesia or Vietnam, to Latin America, or even back to parts of Europe. Samsung Electronics, Daewoo Electronics and Goldstar Co., the three most important companies of South Korea's electronics industry, for example, produced 15 per cent of their total export sales of USD11.3 billion in 1995 in 40 plants outside their home country. Samsung Electronics was present in 13 different countries. The dominating number of its assembly plants abroad was supplemented by a growing number of production facilities. In 1994, Daewoo planned to manufacture half of its total sales abroad at the turn of the century, up from 20 per cent in that year. Goldstar was building production plants in China, in other Southeast Asian countries, and in the NAFTA and EU areas. Thirty-five per cent of total export sales were planned to come from those plants in 2000.[8]

Upon closer examination, the so-called 'six tigers' just mentioned turn out to be quite different in basic economic structure. **South Korea** has become the 13th-largest industrial nation in the world. The country's economy is characterized by a few very large industrial conglomerates, called 'chaebols'. In 1995, five chaebols accounted for two-thirds of the country's GDP. They specialized in low-cost mass production, and had close links with the government. Problems arising from those links are described in the Strategy box.

The financial crisis of 1997 hit the country very hard. After 7.1 per cent growth in GDP in 1996 and 5.5 per cent in 1997, estimates for 1998 were that GDP would decrease by up to 5 per cent, the inflation rate would be above 10 per cent, and unemployment would surpass 7 per cent. Economic reforms were needed. To attract foreign capital, the government decided to privatize eight publicly owned companies in 1998, and to open up its own markets further. Until then, a marketer interested in doing business in South Korea must be aware that there are three different import categories. For luxury goods and products that compete directly with local production, the exporter needs a special import licence, which should be confirmed in the sales contract. For another group of products, import quotas exist. All other products can be brought into the country without restrictions.

Taiwan's economy is characterized by a host of small and medium-sized privately owned companies with highly skilled workers and a high level of technical expertise. The companies are extremely flexible in their response to

STRATEGY BOX

The War

Goes On

SOUTH KOREA'S GOVERNMENT OWNERSHIP IN COMPANIES leads to confrontation with chaebol strategies. One such argument concerned Hyundai, the biggest chaebol of all. They wanted to build a steel mill. The government had no legal way to stop Hyundai from going into steel making. But, nevertheless, they tried because government followed a policy of discouraging chaebols from diversifying into new businesses and Hyundai would have become a competitor to POSCO, the country's dominating steel maker, one-third of which is owned by the government.

In 1994 the government tried to ban Samsung, a USD60 billion conglomerate of more than three dozen firms employing 150 000 people in various industries ranging from shipbuilding, through semiconductors and washing machines, to petrochemicals and financial services, from moving into the car business. It reckoned that South Korea already had enough car makers. Samsung persisted and the government was forced to give the project its blessing at the end of the year.

Despite the grand plans the government unveiled for selling 58 state-owned firms by 1998, it acted slowly. By the end of 1995, it had sold only 15 firms, all of them small companies such as Korea Fertiliser and Chemicals. Another six minor firms, including Citizens' National Bank, had been partly privatised.

In 1996, many South Koreans were sceptical about the extent to which President Kim Young Sam intended to tame the chaebol, his country's mighty conglomerates. Although a number of chaebol leaders were being prosecuted for allegedly bribing a former president, nobody expected them to end up in prison. Some of them, however, reacted by seeking full autonomy from the government which constantly tried to interfere with the big companies' business strategies.

In the aftermath of the financial crisis of 1997, the new Korean government under President Kim Dae-jung made an attempt to force the chaebols into restructuring. With debts reaching 450 per cent of their capital, the conglomerates should be refocused on a limited number of commercial activities based on exact balance sheets. The government officially declared 55 companies, 20 of them belonging to the five biggest chaebols, to be liquidated or merged with others. Management tried to resist by calling for an 'indispensable minimum of discretion', but finally had to give in. Samsung sold its Heavy Industries division to Swedish Volvo for USD572 million. LG, the fourth-largest conglomerate, announced plans to gather USD6.5 billion for restructuring purposes by selling business activities outside their focus on chemistry and electronics. And Hyundai, the biggest conglomerate, announced that they would concentrate on five business areas: car manufacturing, chemistry, electronics, finance, and services.

Sources: Rodier, A. (1998) 'La Corée du Sud décapite ses canards boiteux', *Le Figaro économie*, 20/21 June, p. 34; 'Les "chaebols" se spécialisent', *Le Figaro économie*, 8 March 1998, p. III; 'The war goes on', *The Economist*, 2 March 1996, p. 62; 'Kurs auf die erste Wirtschafts-Liga', *Der Standard*, 22–23 July 1995, p. 15.

changes in customers' needs, but vulnerable to low-price competition from neighbouring developing countries. In spite of the high barriers against imports erected by its government to protect the domestic economy, Taiwan has become a viable market for high technology. The high surpluses in its trade balances, in particular with the USA, forced the Taiwanese government to open up its markets.

Compared to most of the neighbouring countries, Taiwan remained largely untouched by the financial crisis of 1997/98. The Taiwan dollar's (TWD) close link to the US dollar was given up during the financial turmoil. But, owing to the country's high currency reserves and very little external debts, the TWD stayed quite stable. Its devaluation was around 15 per cent. Industry production, external trade, inflation and unemployment rates did not show any alarming changes. Taiwan's companies continued to be important investors in the neighbouring People's Republic of China, Malaysia, Thailand, the Philippines and Vietnam.

In 1898 the UK leased the 'New Territories', most of today's **Hong Kong**, from China for 99 years. According to this contract Hong Kong was handed back to China in 1997. But the two were already economically linked before that. Since 1978 Hong Kong had invested more than USD80 billion in China. On the other hand, with more than USD16 billion of investment, China had become the biggest investor in Hong Kong, leading Japan and the USA. The former UK territory will remain a special region, keeping its economic, social, and great parts of the legal system as well as its autonomy for another 50 years. At present Hong Kong has the second-largest per capita income in East Asia, after Japan and before Singapore. It possesses the busiest container port in the world and represents a major manufacturing centre for watches, electronic consumer goods, toys, fashion fabrics, printing and design. With approximately 160 banks, it is the world's third-largest centre of financial transactions, behind New York and London; banking represents more than one-fifth of Hong Kong's GDP.

The financial crisis of its neighbours did not leave Hong Kong's economy untouched. Because the Hong Kong dollar is linked to the US dollar, the devaluation of the currencies of neighbouring states, which reached 20 to 70 per cent, made Hong Kong too expensive for tourists from those countries. At the same time, recession in Japan and the low value of the yen also decreased the inflow of wealthy Japanese tourists. Hotels, restaurants, shops and banks had a difficult time. GDP shrank in 1998, and unemployment increased to an unprecedented 5 per cent.[9]

Singapore, an island republic whose average citizens are as rich as Australians, has virtually no natural resources except for a deepwater harbour and three million industrious people. It has a strong shipbuilding industry and possesses the second-largest concentration of banking and financial institutions outside of the industrialized nations, after Hong Kong. These institutions actively attract foreign investment. By constantly upgrading the skills of its workforce, Singapore can staff highly automated factories for such companies as Motorola, Apple Computer and Sony. Motorola, for example, used its Singapore operation to design and produce a credit card-size telephone pager.

The **People's Republic of China** represents a special case. It is by far the most populated country in the world (1.2 billion), and it had a GNP of about USD435 per capita in 1995. Since economic reforms began in 1979, China's GDP has averaged growth rates of more than 8 per cent annually (13.4 per cent in 1995). China's volume of exports and imports doubled in 1992 (USD165 billion). Since 1990 foreign investments have increased by 33 per cent a year to reach USD45.3 billion in 1997, when accumulated foreign investments exceeded USD217 billion. In the same year, 145 000 companies with foreign capital – 63 per cent of which were joint ventures, the rest wholly foreign-owned subsidiaries – accounted for half of China's external trade

Map 7.1 SOUTH EAST ASIA

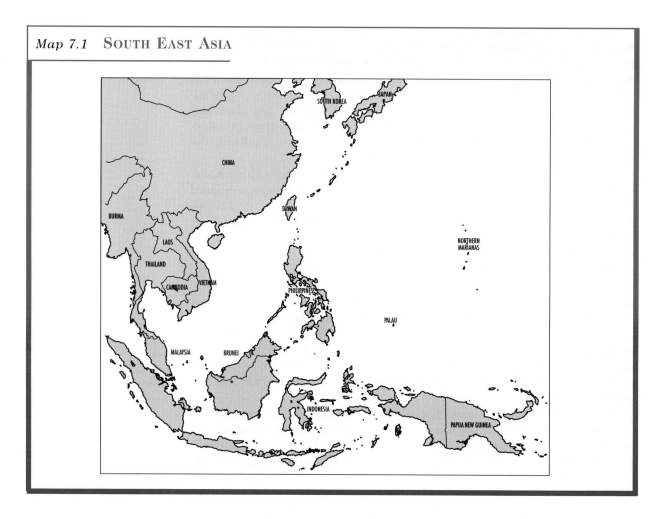

(against 5 per cent in 1988) and employed 10 per cent of China's active urban population.[10] Such economic success mainly resulted from two factors: economic liberalization, which allowed small private enterprise, and the set-up of so-called special industrial zones along the coastline, which were opened to foreign investors.

The biggest success stories in China are its small private businesses. Their share of industry production has grown eight times from 1985 to 1993, to reach 16 per cent in 1994. In the southern provinces (Guangdong, Fujian and Shanghai) where mainly light industry is located, the share of private industry is significantly higher compared to the more heavy industry-oriented north. Among the 150 000-plus private firms, there are more than 10 000 which possess over USD180,000 in capital. In addition, there exist more than 15 million private household businesses in the country, which also employ a large number of workers. Around 4000 Taiwanese firms have set up plants to make bicycles, handbags, sporting goods, and much else that can no longer be manufactured competitively in Taiwan. Taiwanese investors commit an estimated USD2.5 billion to the mainland every year.

A second reason for the fast economic development is the rising demand for consumer goods, in particular foreign brands. A growing number of joint ventures with foreign companies, such as the Volkswagen Santana plant in Shanghai, as well as wholly owned foreign investments profit from that demand. One of the biggest is Motorola's USD120 million pager, cellular phone and semiconductor plant in Tianjin. This pager plant is supposed to export 70 per cent of its production of 3000 units a week, but domestic demand would be strong enough to sell the entire production in China.

Another example is Mary Kay Cosmetics Inc. which opened its Shanghai office in Spring 1996, offering pink mobile phones as sales incentives and aiming to unseat Avon Corp. as the leading direct marketer in China's USD1.2 billion cosmetics market. Based on its factory in Hangzhou – a condition of getting a China business licence – and many well paid employees – 2600 'beauty consultants' are busy knocking on Shanghai doors – Mary Kay planned to quadruple its 1995 sales of USD2.4 million in the following year and to be represented throughout China within five to six years. However, legislation banning door-to-door selling threatened to stop Mary Kay's success story as of October 1998.

Guangdong Province, which borders Hong Kong, was the first to develop special economic zones. Today it is the most open, thriving economy in the People's Republic. It combines Taiwan's technology and financial power, Hong Kong's international marketing skills, and China's vast supplies of land, workers and ambition. With 6 per cent of China's population, already in 1992 Guangdong accounted for 21 per cent of the country's exports. Hong Kong companies employ some three million workers in 25 000 factories in Guangdong Province, more than triple the number of workers in Hong Kong itself. The annual per capita income has risen to USD1,500, compared to an average of below USD450 in the rest of the country. In Guangzhou, the provincial capital (known in the West as Canton), more than 85 per cent of households have refrigerators, and 90 per cent have TV sets. Nevertheless, labour costs in China are still among the lowest worldwide.

Some of the most urgent economic problems China has to resolve in order to further raise its level of economic development are the following:

1. Its notorious budget deficits, which, coupled with double-digit growth rates in the 1990s, triggered increased inflation rates and wiped out much of the improvement in the people's standard of living. An 'austerity programme' launched in 1993 decreased inflation from 24 per cent in 1994 to less than 2 per cent in 1997.

2. The consequences of ending the 'Iron Rice Bowl' policy of providing cradle-to-grave job security which, in combination with widening differences in living standards between urban and rural areas as well as between provinces in the south and others in the north and centre of China, could lead to social unrest. Chinese state-owned firms operate more like enormous feudal villages than modern corporations. It is not a simple matter of privatizing them, because they have to provide housing, recreation, hospitals, parks, and all manner of services, sometimes for hundreds of thousands of employees and their families. Hope for millions of Chinese workers and consumers comes from economic developments similar to the southern provinces in northern cities such as Dalian, Quingdao, Changchun and Tianjin, or Chonqing and Wohan in the centre.

3. The lack of efficiency of its state-run enterprises which still account for about half of the country's industrial output. In 1997, more than half of China's 305 000 state-owned enterprises, 118 000 of which work in industrial sectors, lost money. Losses reached 1.3 per cent of GDP,

endangering the country's banking system: 20 to 30 per cent of all credits given to companies will never be paid back. The government has presented a three-level plan to resolve that problem: About 1000 big conglomerates operating in so-called strategic sectors, such as defence, energy, high technology or infrastructure, will stay entirely state-owned. In big companies of no strategic importance and in middle-sized firms, the government will accept becoming one of the major shareholders among others. Small state-owned companies will be privatized. Since this plan was announced, a multitude of mergers and acquisitions – 3000 in 1997 – have taken place. On the other hand, during the same year 4500 firms declared bankruptcy, after 6200 in 1996.[11] Mergers and bankruptcies in Shanghai's textile industry, a pillar of industry for 100 years, threatened to put 50 000 workers out work.[12]

4. The insufficient infrastructure in most parts of the country.
5. The restricted convertibility of its currency, the yuan. The currency is partly convertible, but only for trade and tourism purposes.

But despite these problems and bureaucratic impediments, political uncertainties and cultural differences, China's market potential cannot be overlooked. Burmah Castrol, the marketer of the well-known Castrol lubricant brand, for example, in 1996 sold its fuel operations in the UK, Chile, Sweden and Turkey in order to invest in lubricants. An important project concerns the Chinese market. The company will set up a lubricant-blending plant in China with a local partner to establish itself firmly in the country which accounts for about an eighth of world lubricant demand. Burmah Castrol is aiming for 10 to 15 per cent of the Chinese market which it served only marginally in 1996.[13]

In addition, the government tries to make market entry as attractive as possible for foreign firms investing in the country. At the end of 1997, it restored duty and added-value tax exemptions on transportation, energy, natural resources, high technology and agricultural technology imported by foreign firms, and extended the privilege to local exporting companies. Further tax incentives are given to companies investing in inland provinces.

Natural Environment. Evaluating country-markets according to their natural environment, that is, climate, mineral resources, water supply or other resources, may help identify markets with differing attractiveness. In some industries, such as tourism, climate plays a major role in market assessment. In tropical areas, like Papua New Guinea, climatic conditions necessitate special treatment and storage techniques to ensure proper conditions of food and water supply for tourists. Mountainous areas, like the Andes, may lack adequate transportation infrastructures. And countries that are rich in natural resources like oil (Nigeria), productive farmland (Colombia) or iron ore (Australia) have a better chance of increasing the purchasing power of their citizens than do countries that lack such resources. Even so, using these criteria alone is not much more effective than using geographic proximity alone; the resulting rank order of attractive markets overlooks the complexities of business systems that largely determine market attractiveness.

Political and Legal Systems. Political and legal systems strongly affect whether a company can enter a national market, the risks associated with entering a market, and the conduct of business in a market. Therefore, a preliminary screening of countries according to their political and legal systems may be a useful way to assess the attractiveness of their markets.

A country's political system may be an important criterion for the assessment of market attractiveness when business opportunities depend on this system, the firm's business requires big investments, such as in the oil business, which may be jeopardized by political instability, or business is done directly with the political authorities of the country. Suppliers of military equipment, such as Oerlikon of Switzerland, Dassault of France or Sweden's Saab Scania, for example, rate the attractiveness of country-markets differently depending on their political system.

However, this approach presents several problems. The first is that the classification of a country's political system is sometimes very difficult. For example, how would you rank the levels of democracy in Slovakia, compared to Argentina, Thailand or Ukraine? Even if country-markets could be compared and grouped according to their similar political systems, those systems may generate quite different public policies. As a result, even in countries with relatively similar political systems and ideologies, economic conditions may differ significantly. For example, Cuba, North Korea, Vietnam and China have some political similarities, but their economic situations and the resulting business opportunities are quite different. Because of its centralized economy North Korea does not have any private firms, nor foreign investments from Western nations. Its people are starving. In contrast, Vietnam introduced 'doi moi' (= renewal) in 1986. At that time the country suffered from a very low GNP per capita which did not grow, a high inflation rate and unstable currency. Since then, it has opened three Export Processing Zones (in Ho Chi Min City, Hanoi and Da Nang); taxes on profits of companies with foreign capital owners are limited to 15 per cent; profits may be repatriated; foreigners are allowed to buy state-owned firms or to invest in wholly owned subsidiaries. A banking system is being developed. Small private enterprises flourish. They even offer branded consumer products such as Minolta, Milka and Honda in Hanoi where no official distribution channels for those products exist. In 1996, the per capita income in Vietnam did not exceed USD240, but the economy had been growing at rates around 9 per cent for three years (the US trade embargo was lifted in 1994), the inflation rate was down below 15 per cent, the currency was stable, foreign investments had reached a level of USD15 billion, and the country had become a member of ASEAN, the East Asian economic cooperation agreement.[14]

A country's legal system determines the rules that govern the conduct of business in that country as well as the norms and standards that products and services have to fulfil. Because there is no international business law system, international marketers must consider the consequences of different 'rules of the game' in various potential markets. How strongly such 'rules' may differ from what managers are accustomed to in the highly industrialized Western countries is illustrated in the Ethics box.

Country-markets may be rated according to whether their legal systems are based on common or code law. But even when two countries belong to the same group of law systems, they may have very different regulations governing business activities. New Zealand, for instance, regulates advertising much more strictly than the USA does. Thus, comparing the legal systems of country-markets in general terms will not provide the precise information necessary for a full assessment of opportunities in the attractiveness of those markets. On the other hand, norms and regulations specific to the business of

Ethics Box

The Short March
to Great Wealth

Between January 1992 and June 1994, 14,000 Russian companies were privatized. Seventy per cent of majority owners of those companies are insiders. Despite legislation limiting top management share of ownership to 9 per cent and attributing 56 per cent to personnel in the first wave of privatizations, top managers increased their shares very quickly. Personnel were pressed hard. Those who did not want to sell or tried to sell to outsiders were threatened with being fired. Transactions were only submitted for registration in the trade register when approved by top management. Later on, top management bought shares at (unofficial) auctions.

Particularly tight relations led to particularly exotic 'flowers'. In November 1995, Uneximbank, a banking house very close to Alexander Korschakow, head of security in Boris Yeltsin's staff, bought 38 per cent of Norilsk Nickel, the biggest producer of nickel in the world, which is a shareholder of Uneximbank. Appointed as auctioneer by the highest authorities, Uneximbank awarded Norilsk's shares to itself for a price only 100,000 dollars above the starting level of USD70,000 and less than 50 per cent below the highest offer.

The biggest coup was landed in the Russian energy sector, which represented about 17 per cent of GDP in 1995. Giant Gazprom, the Russian oil and gas monopoly, alone is estimated to be worth some hundreds of billions of dollars – a sum that makes General Motors look like a midget. Despite the fact that firms of such size are officially excluded from privatization programmes, 60 per cent of Gazprom's shares are owned by top managers, politicians, and former communist bankers. Viktor Tschernomyrdin, former CEO of Gazprom and then prime minister of Russia, is said to be the main owner. He denies it, but only a very few believe him, since his son has constructed a luxury home in a wood belonging to the firm.

Source: Adapted from Frydman, R., K. Murphy, and A. Rapaczynski (1996) 'Der kurze Marsch zu großen Reichtümern', *Der Standard*, 14 February, p. 17.

---

the firm, such as the prohibition of alcoholic beverages or of wholly foreign-owned subsidiaries, as well as the imposition of import licences, may quickly lead to the exclusion of a country-market from further analysis.

Cultural and Social Influences. The cultural and social environment of any country strongly influences customers' needs, tastes and expectations. The social organization of a society influences disposable income and purchasing processes. For example, who makes the decisions in the purchase of a family car? Do the children influence the choice of model, do Mom and Dad play an equal role, or does one family member dominate product choice? Education and living conditions influence product choices as well as the communication methods available to marketers. While many cultural and social characteristics play a role, here we will focus on those that are often used in the preliminary classification of markets: (1) language and (2) religion.

(1) Language. A nation's language (or languages) affects the way marketers communicate with customers and other important stakeholders in their market. The use of brochures, advertising, packaging, or training manuals, for example, is greatly simplified when the same language can be used in different country-markets.

There are some drawbacks to assessing the attractiveness of markets according to their dominant language, however. Grouping together countries in which the dominant language is derived from Latin, for example, would result in a heterogeneous set of markets including Argentina, France, Italy, Peru and Romania. Even sorting out the Spanish-speaking group, including countries like Mexico, Spain, Honduras and Venezuela, would result in a group of very dissimilar markets. Thus, although language must be considered in assessing country-markets (because the firm may have no potential to communicate effectively in this language), it cannot be used by itself as a basis for evaluating their attractiveness.

(2) Religion.   Religion is an important cultural element in most societies. Many kinds of behaviour, including buying behaviour, are based on religious beliefs. One might think that markets in which Christianity is the dominant religion differ significantly from markets in which Hinduism, Buddhism, Islam or Animism is dominant. Therefore, in some cases religion may represent an important criterion for determining the attractiveness of markets. For example, a New Zealand producer of lamb or a Central American producer of fruit juice might find markets highly attractive where other meat or alcoholic beverages are avoided for religious reasons, such as Saudi Arabia.

Yet a closer examination of countries with the same dominant religion reveals enormous differences between markets. In Bangladesh and India, Pakistan and Saudi Arabia, El Salvador and Italy, high percentages of the population belong to the same religion. But each market must be treated very differently, owing to other distinctions. Thus, like language, religion is an element that needs to be considered, but it is not by itself a viable criterion for evaluating the attractiveness of markets.

Level of Economic Development.   There are more than 185 nations in the world, and their levels of economic development range from very low to very high. Assessing market attractiveness on this basis results in groups of markets with comparable average purchasing power, demand for industrial products and development of infrastructure. Several approaches can be used in evaluating country-markets according to economic development.

(1) Gross National Product per Capita.   The simplest approach is to use gross national product (GNP) or gross domestic product (GDP) per capita as a basis for classification. This results in a rank order of 12 affluent countries, with per capita GDP over USD20,000, and at the other extreme, 12 countries that belong to the lowest-income category, with per capita GDP below USD220 (see Table 7.2).

Classifying markets on the basis of GNP or GDP alone, however, can be misleading. For example, oil- and gas-producing countries, such as Kuwait, or city-nations, such as Singapore, have very high national incomes and small populations. This results in a high per capita GNP figure (USD19,360 for Kuwait and 19,850 for Singapore in 1993), so these nations are in the same income group as Canada, Italy and the Netherlands.[15] However, their level of economic development is not directly comparable.

In addition, both GNP and GDP figures represent national per capita averages. Because of strong imbalances in the distribution of income and wealth, however, even in countries with low per capita income there may exist a group of potential customers with important disposable income. For example, **India**

Table 7.2 The Poorest and the Richest Countries in 1993

Country	GDP per capita 1993 in USD	Population (in millions, 1993)
Mozambique	90	15.1
Tanzania	90	28.0
Somalia	120	9.0
Sierra Leone	150	4.5
Bhutan	170	1.5
Vietnam	170	71.3
Burundi	180	6.0
Uganda	180	18.0
Nepal	190	20.8
Liberia	200	2.8
Malawi	200	10.5
Kambodia	200	9.7
The Netherlands	20,950	15.3
Belgium	21,650	10.0
France	22,490	57.5
Austria	23,510	7.9
Germany	23,560	81.3
Sweden	24,740	8.7
USA	24,740	257.8
Norway	25,970	4.3
Denmark	26,730	5.2
Japan	31,490	124.5
Luxemburg	34,320	0.4
Switzerland	35,760	7.0

(Base: GDP per Capita)
Source: Baratha, M. (ed.) (1995), 'Der Fischer Weltalmanach '96', Frankfurt a.M.: Fischer Taschen Buch Verlag, pp. 31–46.

(per capita GNP around USD300) has a middle class which consists of about 200 million people, growing at about 5 per cent a year, who have consumption expectations comparable to southern Europeans. One per cent of the population of approximately 850 million is very rich even by North American standards and lives in a small number of urbanized areas. This market might therefore be more attractive to a French producer of prestigious perfumes than, for example, Spain which has a significantly higher per capita income.

A similar statement holds true for industrial goods. In India, to continue the same example, the manufacturing sector is developing rapidly. In recent years Indian firms, such as Larsen & Toubro, an Indian multinational corporation with subsidiaries in the USA, Asia and Europe, have become increasingly competitive in such markets as machinery, computer software and railroad construction. Consequently, there is a growing market for industrial goods. The number of businesses where import licences are needed was greatly reduced, and foreign participation in Indian companies was fully liberalized. In 34 industries, such as metallurgy, telecommunications, or laboratory equipment, foreign joint venture partners are allowed to hold 51 per cent of shares. Infrastructure is a problem. The bigger firms, both foreign and

Indian, invariably have their own generators and dedicated satellite links, which allow them to bypass creaking telephones and power lines.[16] All this specific information, which strongly influences the attractiveness of the country's product-markets, is not provided through a simple evaluation using GNP data.

The size of population in a country may also play an important role. A marketer of convenience goods who only compares the per capita income of the Netherlands (app. USD21,000) and Mexico (app. USD4,000) may come to an erroneous conclusion about market potential. With a population of 81 million compared to 15 million in the Netherlands, Mexico might be the more attractive market.

(2) Complex Indicators.   Inconsistent data make it even more important not to rely on one single economic criterion to assess country-markets. More complex economic approaches can be used. Income measures can be combined with other characteristics of country-markets – such as social-class structure, national resources, environmental conditions, level of technological sophistication, existing infrastructure, level of education, and cultural and behavioural variables – to create a more realistic picture of the markets in question. This approach results in groups of countries ranging from highly economically developed to economically very undeveloped (LDCs = Less Developed Countries).

Although evaluating country-markets according to more complex economic indicators can be useful in the early stages of market assessment, the marketer must be aware of specific differences between markets that may be obscured by aggregate economic data. A firm that assesses developing countries as potential markets should keep in mind that there is a big difference between the well-educated and affluent members of a society and its workers, unemployed, and rural poor. Even if many urban dwellers in developing countries have the same low income as the rural population, there are significant differences between the consumption patterns of the two groups. Thus, differences in income, age and educational level within a population together with the environment they live in give rise to different lifestyles that must be taken into account in marketing consumer products or services to developing countries.

Another factor that has to be considered is the dynamics of economic development. By the mid-1990s, countries like Thailand, Malaysia and Indonesia had not yet achieved high per capita income or highly developed infrastructure. Yet their populations are not only numerous but also skilled and industrious. Low wage levels, relative political stability and industrialization programmes in these countries produced high economic growth rates until 1997. Economic development similar to that in their very successful neighbouring countries, Singapore and Taiwan, was started. As a result, these countries represent markets that should not only be considered as low cost production sites. In 1993, **Malaysia**, for example, had already reached a higher annual GNP per capita (USD3,150) than Turkey (USD2,970) or South Africa (USD2,980)[17] at growth rates of about 8 per cent a year. It is trying to move its economy from commodity exports to manufacturing. A large Matsushita plant near the airport of Kuala Lumpur, the capital, produces about one million colour TV sets a year for the Japanese market, for example. Yet Malaysia is running short of the skilled workers and managers needed to move up the technological ladder.

Indonesia, which is rich in natural resources but struggles to support its fast-growing population of 190 million, until 1997 hoped to increase its GNP per capita from USD740 in 1993 to above USD1,000 annually by 2000 – still only half the amount of Thailand's GNP per capita (which reached USD2,110 in 1993 at a real growth rate of about 12 per cent a year in the first half of the 1990s)[18]. Indonesia is the world's largest exporter of natural gas and a popular manufacturing site for foreign shoemakers, but also for the chemical and electronics industries. Thomson Consumer Electronics of France, for example, makes components in Indonesia that go into TV sets assembled in its highly automated plant in Singapore. Despite obvious problems with corruption and nepotism,[19] the Indonesian economy has grown at an average of about 7 per cent a year from 1989 to 1997. Owing to excessive credit growth, insupportable exchange rates and a pronounced drain of foreign-exchange reserves in relation to total money supply, a currency crisis broke out in 1997. It developed into a banking and debt crisis. As a consequence, Indonesia's economy will shrink about 5 per cent in 1998 at an inflation rate of about 44 per cent and it will take at least until the turn of the century to recover.

At first, the use of more complex economic indicators seems to result in useful classifications for purposes of market assessment. It might be assumed that the highly industrialized countries, for example, are a homogeneous target market for prestigious consumer durables, high-tech industrial products and expensive services. A closer look, however, reveals that such a classification is still oriented too much towards national averages. There may be some homogeneous product-markets, such as for designer boots or vinyl extruders, but what does such a classification of countries do for a marketer of ravioli or security services? High-income nations differ in a variety of ways. Sweden's social-class structure, for example, is very different from that of the USA (see Figure 7.3), while Japan is characterized by a system of economic cooperation that is unparalleled in either Sweden or the USA.

Other attempts to assess the attractiveness of country-markets based on their level of economic development lead to similar results. The group of nations that need technology transfer and open markets, rather than massive foreign aid, to further develop their economies, for example, includes countries such as Oman, Brazil, South Korea, Morocco and Taiwan. They are similar in certain respects of their economies, but goods desired by consumers in Oman are so different from those desired by consumers in Brazil or Taiwan that this grouping is of limited value to marketers of consumer goods. On the other hand, machinery and transport equipment, chemicals and cereals

---

Figure 7.3 Social Strata – USA and Sweden

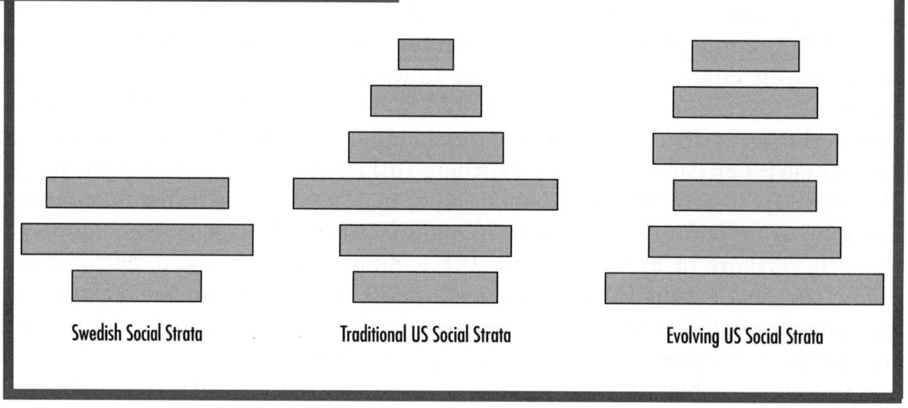

Sweden and the USA have traditionally had a similar social class distribution (although the USA has a lower class that is larger than its upper class). Due mainly to dual career households, the US distribution seems to be changing: upper and lower classes are increasing, while the middle class is shrinking.

Swedish Social Strata   Traditional US Social Strata   Evolving US Social Strata

needed in Morocco may not be very different from those needed in Ukraine, which depends heavily on foreign aid.

Cooperative Agreements. Independent of the product-market it serves, every company that assesses the attractiveness of country-markets must know whether the countries involved have signed cooperative agreements with others. Each type of economic cooperation has different effects on the conduct of business and the nature of competition. Therefore, it is important to devote some attention to economic agreements in evaluating the attractiveness of a potential market.

Economic cooperation can be expected to have the following effects on international marketing:

1. Larger markets, accompanied by opportunities for mass production, mass marketing, and more efficient use of resources. As a result, industries will become more and more dual, with a few major international competitors involved in most of the product-market segments at one end and small competitors focused on one segment (or a niche) at the other end. The publishing industry in Europe, for example, is already dual with a few international communication media groups (such as Pearson, Hachette and Bertelsmann) and smaller publishers, more or less specialized.

2. Higher income in those markets, which in turn stimulates internal trade and creates opportunities for external suppliers of industrial goods, consumer goods, and services. Even before the Mercosur free-trade area in Latin America with its population of about 227 million was founded in 1995, for example, trade among the four member countries – Argentina, Brazil, Paraguay and Uruguay (Bolivia and Chile only joined Mercosur in 1996) – was exploding. In 1997 the joint GDP of Mercosur members reached USD1,207.63 billion.[20] And companies are adapting quickly. BASF, the German chemicals giant, for example, had production facilities for the same products in most of those countries, because of closed borders. In reaction to the creation of Mercosur they reorganized production to avoid the duplication of products. But external suppliers also find increased business opportunities. From the initiation of the European Common Market 1992 programme in 1985 to the end of 1991, when the common market was not yet in place, the US–EC trade balance, for example, moved from a USD23 billion deficit in 1985 to a surplus of USD17 billion in 1991.

3. The possibility of direct investment, to avoid tariff and non-tariff barriers and to profit from the increase in internal trade. Extended tariff barriers may result if the members of a cooperative agreement abolish all tariffs among themselves, but keep tariffs for non-members. Such a decision would automatically give a cost advantage to companies located inside the 'tariff wall'. Non-tariff barriers include quota regulations and administrative hurdles. During the negotiations between the European Union (EU), Japan and the USA on the liberalization of international telecommunications markets, for example, the USA had to insist firmly on the abolishment of restrictions on foreign ownership of telecommunications infrastructure in Belgium, France and Spain.

4. An increase in the number of mergers, acquisitions and alliances initiated by firms inside as well as outside cooperative agreements. In

the wave of cross-border transactions following the creation of Mercosur, for example, Indufren, an Argentinian auto-parts maker, has sold half of its capital to two Brazilian companies, Cofap Cia. Fabricadora de Pecas and Freios Varga SA, so all three companies can gain better access to the other country's auto industry. In the European brewing industry, as another example, some competitors (Heineken, Kronenbourg, Carlsberg and Interbrew) have taken strong positions across Europe with the exception of the German market which is still highly fragmented. Australia-based Elders took over the UK Courage, and Budweiser acquired the Czech source of its name (the Czech Republic has signed an agreement of economic association to the EU). Such acquisitions help foreign firms ensure that they will have a local subsidiary that will allow their business to avoid the negative effects of cooperative legislation that might confront a 'pure' foreign firm. Such subsidiaries are also able to take advantage of subsidized research programmes within a cooperative agreement, which would not be available to the foreign firm on its own.

The various forms of economic cooperation among nations influence the environment in which international marketing takes place. The Future Issues box gives an impression of the opportunities that a free trade zone including all countries of North and Latin America would provide to international business. Whatever the specific arrangement, these agreements broaden the market and often unify conditions of market entry for companies based in non-member nations. This does not mean, however, that customer expectations, tastes or behaviour become unified. Even if international comparative studies on consumer lifestyles show a tendency to customer segments which exist across country borders,[21] the contextual situation varies considerably from one country to another, and therefore too may customer behaviour. This can lead to people in different countries doing the same thing for different reasons; but equally it can lead to people in different countries doing different things for the same reason. Despite increasing similarities inside economically cooperating regions, customer habits, norms and standards, infrastructure, the educational level of the labour force, and the level of salaries as well as taxes will stay different over a substantial amount of time. Closer economic cooperation mainly intensifies competition, allows companies to profit from regional cost and regulatory differences, and makes international business easier, but it does not allow companies to choose a country-market without closer examination of its specific environments.

Assessment Criteria Concerning the Operating Environment

Besides criteria concerning the macro-environment, an international marketer may use criteria concerning the operating environment of its business to assess the attractiveness of country-markets. To make the assessment process as fast and cost efficient as possible, criteria demanding secondary data will be preferred to criteria necessitating primary research.

Structure of the Operating Environment.   An important criterion for the assessment of a country-market's attractiveness may be the structure of the local operating environment of the firm. The company should know who, besides potential customers and competitors, are the major players in its product-market, what interests they have, and what influence they can exert on market processes. The marketer will find it easier to build customer relationships if the structure of customers, intermediaries and other buying decision influencers, such as media, consultants or administrators, in the country-market to be assessed is comparable to the structure in currently served markets.

Substance of Local Product-Market.   The substance of a local product-market is determined mainly by its size, that is, the number of customers, their purchasing power or investment expenses, their creditworthiness, and the rate of growth. A product market's size may be expressed in terms of sales, measured in some standard unit such as tons, or in terms of value (currency unit volume); the latter is referred to as market volume.

There are different ways to estimate the volume of a geographically defined product-market. If neither the number of customers nor their purchasing power can be determined from available statistics, total exports of similar products from the most important industrialized countries may provide a simple estimate of market volume. However, such an estimate does not account for exports from the country in question or for the activity of domestic competitors. Management can compare the size of industries in served country-markets to the approximate size of the same industries in a potential market. Relating those figures to the market share attained in served markets and expressing market share in terms of total sales leads to a rough estimate of the market volume in the potential market.

If the company is internationally active in business-to-business markets and management has some indications about the approximate size of customer industries in a potential market compared to served markets, it can estimate the volume of the potential market based on the company's market share achieved in served markets expressed as share of the firm's total sales (Table 7.3). For example, when a Luxembourg-based producer of small

---

Table 7.3   **ESTIMATION OF MARKET VOLUME BASED ON SALES AND MARKET SHARE IN OTHER MARKETS**

INDUSTRY	INDUSTRY SIZE AND FIRM'S COMPETITIVE POSITION IN SERVED MARKET	MARKET SHARE[1] IN %	TOTAL SALES[1]	INDUSTRY SIZE IN POTENTIAL MARKET	ESTIMATE OF PRODUCT-MARKET VOLUME
DIY tools	Small, strong position	40		3 × bigger?	
Pumps	Small, weak position	15		???	
Food	Big, strong position	60		7 × bigger?	
Chemical	Small, strong position	35		5 × bigger?	
Comments					

[1]In product-market related to served industry

Having some international experience, management can compare the size of industries in served country-markets to the approximate size of the same industries in a potential market. Relating those figures to the market share attained in served markets and expressing market share in terms of total sales leads to a rough estimate of the market volume in the potential market. The table contains an example of a supplier of small electrical engines.

electrical engines which is active in most EU markets wants to estimate the market volume for its products in Brazil but cannot get any reliable national statistic for this special product-market, management can proceed as follows. They take Portugal as a basis for comparison, because it is the industrially least developed of its served EU markets. First, they list the industries which are potential clients of their products, such as manufacturers of do-it-yourself tools, pumps, food, and chemical products. Then they evaluate the size of those industries and the competitive position of their company in the respective product-market segments. The firm's market shares in the different parts of the Portuguese product-market are then expressed as shares of total sales of small electrical engines in Portugal. Multiplying the result of a comparison of the size of relevant industries in Portugal and Brazil by those sales figures finally leads to an estimate of the probable size of the product-market in Brazil.

If more market data are available, more complex indicators can be used to estimate market volume. The volume of the market for disposable nappies, for example, can be estimated from the number of babies born per year, minus deaths, weighted by average household income. Although such a simple indicator does not take into consideration consumption behaviour or the activities of competitors, it will give the marketer a good estimate of the approximate size of the market.

To assess the substance of a local product-market, the marketer should also determine its rate of growth. This rate can be viewed as an indicator of the product's life-cycle stage. Early stages are associated with greater potential, growing market volume, and an improving return on investment. Later stages are characterized by stagnant or declining sales accompanied by low potential return on investment for new entrants to the market. For example, compact disc sales grew rapidly in Europe in the early 1990s. Many marketers were entering the market, their sales were rising rapidly, and their profits were increasing. But when market growth slows, as in CD markets at the end of the 1990s, marketers will be faced with lower profits as they increase promotion but lower prices in an attempt to keep sales active.

Besides the local product-market's existing growth rate, the company should consider potential additional sales that may be generated through its specific marketing mix. As shown by Figure 7.4, the potential of total sales in a market is never totally exhausted. The current volume of total sales achieved by the firm and its competitors may be increased through a stimulation of use (usage gap), an expansion or intensification of distribution (distribution gap), or an improvement of the product line (product line gap). By analysing the gaps in a country-market and their extent, the marketer can determine the firm's potential to expand the existing total sales volume in this market. Even such a rather complex approach to the estimation of market substance, however, will not reveal regional concentrations of potential customers, local customs regarding product use, and other special market characteristics.

Accessibility of Local Product-Market. Accessibility refers to the marketer's ability to reach the potential customers in a country-market effectively. To be successful, an international marketer must be able to reach the customers by means of communication and distribution. But individual customers can be more or less anonymous to the international marketer. Many international consumer markets are mass markets. Therefore, in consumer

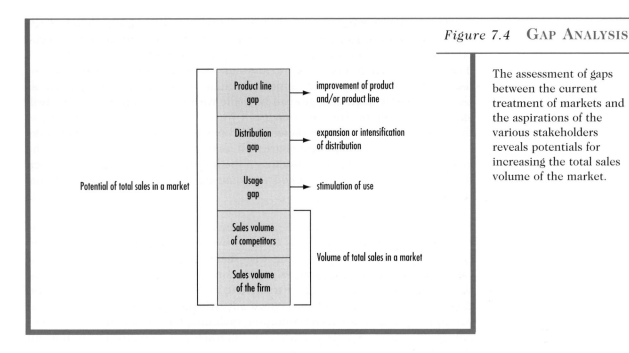

Figure 7.4 GAP ANALYSIS

The assessment of gaps between the current treatment of markets and the aspirations of the various stakeholders reveals potentials for increasing the total sales volume of the market.

markets, such as food products, consumer durables or entertainment, customers tend to be rather anonymous compared to business-to-business markets and government markets, unless the production of the consumer product needs participation by identified consumers, such as in international tourism or banking services. Consumer product-markets' attractiveness strongly depends on the availability of appropriate distribution channels and transportation as well as communication infrastructure.

Distribution Channels and Infrastructure. Accessibility is enhanced by adequate distribution channels and infrastructure as well as market communication media. If they do not exist, international marketers may have to invest considerably to enter a new country-market effectively. Some form of strategic partnership or direct investment may be necessary to gain access to local public administration/government markets. Inside the EU, public administrations are forced to call internationally for tenders and treat EU member firms equally, independent of their nationality. But 'buy national' tendencies persist. Even when a significant national presence is not necessary, an appropriate corporate presence is. Thus, Lockheed lobbied energetically to gain the support of influential politicians in Japan, a country that does not manufacture large aircraft. The danger in this area lies in identifying and maintaining the distinction between influence and bribery. Lockheed reportedly overstepped the line between the two, creating legal problems both for the company and for the Japanese prime minister, who was subsequently sentenced to a prison term.[22]

The existence, availability and negotiating power of intermediaries influence the attractiveness of any local product-market. A marketer needs to obtain information about available intermediaries, their organization, their capital equipment, their relatedness to competitors of the firm, the portion of the market they serve, their approach to doing business, their level of information, and the product range they cover.

The special conditions faced by marketers in LDCs have already been described. But even in highly industrialized countries there may be special problems to overcome. For example, in Japan it is highly unusual to transfer business from one intermediary to another. There, close inspection of potential intermediaries is more important than in other countries, such as Germany, where such changes can be made without a serious loss of goodwill and thus customers. The experiences of Western companies in Japan suggest that in most markets the marketer should pay attention to existing networks among producers and intermediaries. It may be very difficult to enter the market, even with a superior product, if the intermediaries necessary to reach the ultimate customer are linked to domestic firms or other international suppliers.

Legal Measures and Administrative Procedures. Legal measures such as restrictions on import licences or advertising can be effective barriers to entry in a market that would otherwise seem attractive to the company. For example, because of its enormous population and entrenched smoking habits, the Chinese market looks very attractive to every tobacco products marketer. However, legal restrictions on tobacco advertising – China has adopted total bans on all forms of tobacco promotion, including posters and magazine ads – reduce this attractiveness. They force marketers to creatively circumvent them. BAT, as an example, not only sponsors the great China bicycle race which allows it to be in all major media, but also endowed a chair at the China Europe International Business School in Shanghai in 1995.[23]

Relationships. Most business-to-business and government markets are not anonymous. Compared to consumer markets, in many international business markets there are a limited number of customers. For example, manufacturers of aeroplanes such as the Boeing 757 or Airbus 320 will find a nearly exhaustive list of potential customers in any listing of passenger airlines. Because of the higher transparency of international business-to business markets, it is very important for market success to develop and keep continual contacts with (potential) customers. When TSB, the large UK bank, planned to merge with Lloyds Bank, another UK bank, to create the UK's largest retail bank in terms of branches and customers, for example, it used US-based specialist JP Morgan to handle its negotiations with Lloyds. The decision to use JP Morgan was not based only on the firm's reputation in the merger and acquisition business, but was also due to the fact that TSB's chief executive, Peter Ellwood, had known the US bank's financial institutions M&A specialist, Terry Eccles, for two years before any talk of a merger with Lloyds bank arose.[24]

Close customer contacts are based on local presence. The attractiveness of local business-to-business and government markets may, therefore, strongly depend on the availability of suppliers and a labour force.

Suppliers. When evaluating potential suppliers of services, parts or systems, management should consider the size and number of such firms, the potentially available substitutions, the importance of the supplied service or good to their firm's product, the importance of their firm as a customer of the suppliers, and the threat of potential forward integration (when the supplier gains control of the next level of distribution, towards the customer) by the supplier. Like intermediaries, suppliers may be linked to certain competitors. Companies such as Ford, Honda and Volkswagen commonly sign long-range contracts with (or even hold equity shares in) their suppliers such as producers of metal sheets (for example, Thyssen, the largest supplier of this product category in Europe), electrical systems (for example, Germany's Bosch), climatization equipment (for example, Webasto, headquartered near Munich which operates worldwide). The suppliers conform strictly to the larger company's product specifications and profit from its technical and financial assistance.

Even in such cases, however, supply risks should be evaluated. If a manufacturer relies on just-in-time delivery of parts, disruptions of supply can be very expensive. Quality is also critical. Local suppliers in China, Indonesia or Vietnam, for example, may seem attractive because of the low wage rates in these countries. But they do not always have the skilled labour force necessary to deliver consistently high-quality parts for sophisticated products.

Labour Force. The number of potential employees seeking a job and, more importantly, their level of education and skill have a direct impact on a company's potential success in the market. So does the existence of strong labour unions. Many joint ventures in Eastern Europe, for example, have experienced serious trouble because of the lack of personnel with the management training expected in their Western counterparts. Cultural factors must also be considered. Western companies that have founded sales and service offices or subsidiaries in Japan, for example, have found to their great dismay that few Japanese like to work for foreign companies. And if they are ready to do so, they expect very high increases in salary.

Responsiveness of Local Product-Market. Responsiveness refers to whether potential customers and intermediaries in a market will react favourably to the company's offer. First estimates may be wrong in this respect. Shredded wheat has never become well accepted in the French market, for example, because it is too 'British', yet the very 'American' McDonald's, despite first guesses that such a style of eating, alien to French habits, would never be accepted by local customers, has become a big success in France.

To avoid the risk of guessing, it seems reasonable to determine first the most important factors that influence a market's responsiveness. However, such an analysis may require primary research that may be too expensive for many smaller firms at that stage of international marketing decision making. To get a low cost but reliable estimate of how responsive potential customers in a market might be to the company's offer, international marketing managers can evaluate existing direct or indirect contacts with customers from that market. Fasti, an Austria-based small firm manufacturing special machines to dehydrate plastic granulates, for example, when assessing the attractiveness of Far Eastern markets, analysed some business deals which had been solicited by customers from those markets. The firm also analysed how much business it did already in Far Eastern markets through indirect customer contacts, that is, via manufacturers of plastic extrusion machines located in Europe and the USA.

Other indicators of the responsiveness of a local market may be existing cultural or political prejudices which strongly influence the image of the international marketer's home country. In many European markets, for example, products manufactured in Germany, such as passenger cars or machinery, profit from a cultural prejudice that attributes particular technical skills and superior reliability to Germans.

The level and kind of a country-market's predominant international commercial relations may also be a good indicator of market responsiveness. If potential customers in a market are used to having business contacts with suppliers from the marketer's home country, it will be easier to approach them.

Intensity of Competition. Product-market attractiveness also depends on the intensity of competition in the market. Therefore, the major existing and potentially arising competitors, their number, market position, competitive strategy and expected reactions to the market entry of a new contender have to be determined. A competitor's reactions will depend on the new firm's strengths, weaknesses and strategy, as well as the competitor's view of the threat posed by the new firm. The impact of competitive reactions on the company's success will depend on their intensity and speed. The marketer, therefore, should analyse the predictable reactions of competitors to find out if entry to a potential market is attractive or not (see Chapter 8 for an intensive discussion).

Profitability. If a local product-market is substantial, accessible, and responsive to a marketer's product and the intensity of competition seems to be acceptable, the product-market has to be checked for its potential profitability. The estimated income generated by closing a deal effectively with an individual customer has to be compared with the estimated costs it would take to arrive at that point plus the costs of performance delivery. A product-market should not be considered attractive until this analysis has been finished with a positive outcome. Market dynamics have to be considered, however. Italy-based Generali, one of Europe's international insurance companies, for example, accepted substantial losses in Hungary from 1990 to 1994. But as one of the very few insurance companies which invested in this newly opened market, they achieved a comfortable market share position which allowed them to transfer the first earnings to headquarters in 1995.

Choice of Market Assessment Criteria

Product-Market Related Characteristics. In sum, each of the criteria from the macro- and operating environments that are commonly used to evaluate the attractiveness of potential country-markets may be partly useful for preliminary screening. But to be valuable for decision purposes, the assessment of potential country-markets must be based on criteria relevant to the product-market(s) the firm intends to serve (Figure 7.5). Political risk may be a relevant characteristic, for example, if the firm's business demands local investment to be run successfully. It may be rather irrelevant, however, if the company intends to sell products to customers who do not need any after-sales service. Which criteria are the most relevant will vary from one business to another. For a marketer of engineering services, for example, the technical norms to be followed in the country, the level of technology the country has reached, the existing infrastructure and the availability of a well-trained construction labour force may be of importance, whereas a firm from the fast food industry might consider factors such as disposable household income, the availability of reliable food suppliers, the level of urbanization, or habits concerning dining out.

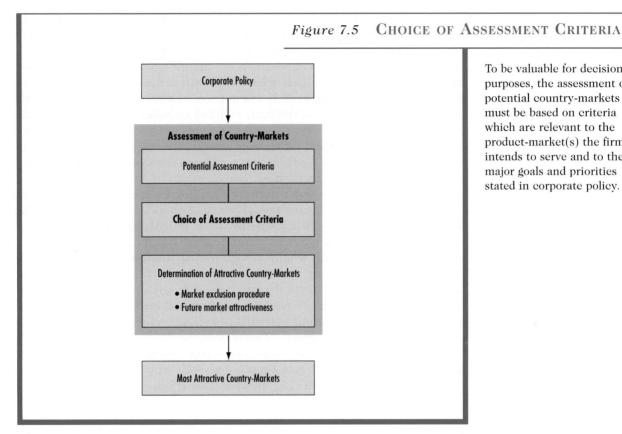

Figure 7.5 CHOICE OF ASSESSMENT CRITERIA

To be valuable for decision purposes, the assessment of potential country-markets must be based on criteria which are relevant to the product-market(s) the firm intends to serve and to the major goals and priorities stated in corporate policy.

Guideline. To choose meaningful assessment criteria for country-markets, managers need a guideline. Corporate objectives and priorities can be used to guide the decision of whether criteria are relevant for assessing the attractiveness of potential markets or not. For example, if a company seeks a high return on investment, it must select markets in which it can achieve a leadership position, in which demand is high in relation to supply, and in which customers have sufficient purchasing power. Therefore, the size of competitors present in the market, the ratio of market potential to market volume, and the economic wealth of potential customers will be relevant criteria for market attractiveness.

Companies that give a high priority to technological innovation tend to favour country-markets characterized by high levels of technological sophistication, such as Japan, where customers seek technical solutions that require significant research and development. Other companies prefer markets in which their level of applied technology fits the needs of the targeted customers. Thus, a Portuguese producer of hand scythes may not consider Denmark an attractive market but may be very interested in potential markets in sub-Saharan Africa. Relevant market assessment criteria in those cases might be the level of technological sophistication reached in a country, the quality of its infrastructure, or the availability and quality of higher education institutions.

Companies that rely on their global identity and the goodwill of inter-mediaries, customers and suppliers will look for markets in areas where their home country or company name has already earned a positive reputation. A Danish marketer of food products such as yoghurt, cheese, pork or bacon, for example, will focus on markets where Denmark is known as a country that manufactures high-quality food. It will not consider markets in which Danish products are avoided for ideological, political or religious reasons. In such cases, managers will find criteria such as volume of imports, amount of polit-ical influence on individual firms, legal restrictions concerning the product-market, or influence of religion on purchase decisions relevant for the assessment of market attractiveness.

Finally, the organization's priorities regarding independence or strategic cooperation may also influence the relevance of characteristics for the evalu-ation of country-markets. If a company, such as IBM, has special technical know-how over which it wants to maintain total control, it will not consider country-markets in which wholly foreign-owned subsidiaries are prohibited and joint ventures can only be started if the transfer of the entire production know-how is guaranteed, as is the case in some developing nations. On the other hand, a small company with limited financial resources might look for country-markets where strong potential cooperation partners are located who can help to speed up the process of increasing the share of the global product-market served by the firm. Therefore, both companies might find it useful to apply criteria such as legal regulations concerning activities of foreign firms or the importance of competitors in the country-market.

Determination of Attractive Country-Markets

Market Exclusion Procedure. As the assessment of country-markets pro-gresses, markets are classified by the chosen criteria to narrow their number to the markets of greatest attractiveness (Figure 7.6). The exclusion pro-cedure consists of either (1) a stepwise application of knock-out criteria or (2) a grouping of markets into homogeneous clusters and a subsequent ranking of the remaining markets through a scoring model.

(1) Stepwise Market Exclusion. In the first case the marketer applies eval-uation criteria which allow the immediate exclusion of country-markets if they do not reach a given standard. For example, a producer of cellular com-munication equipment, such as Sweden-based Ericsson, may exclude markets from further investigation if they lack the needed infrastructure. From the remaining markets, some may have technical norms (they use a specific com-munication technology) that the company is unable or does not want to fulfil. The reduced number of markets is further diminished when all country-markets are deleted where legal restrictions, such as state monopolies or the requirement of import licences, make market entry extremely difficult. Finally, the list of potential markets may become even shorter, if Ericsson's top management has set ethical standards which do not allow the serving of markets where dictatorships exist.

The major advantage of this market exclusion procedure is its simplicity and speed. The use of assessment criteria that lead directly to the elimination of a number of country-markets is appropriate, if the criteria are directly related to the corporate policy of the firm, such as ethical standards, or

---

Figure 7.6 **DETERMINATION OF ATTRACTIVE COUNTRY-MARKETS**

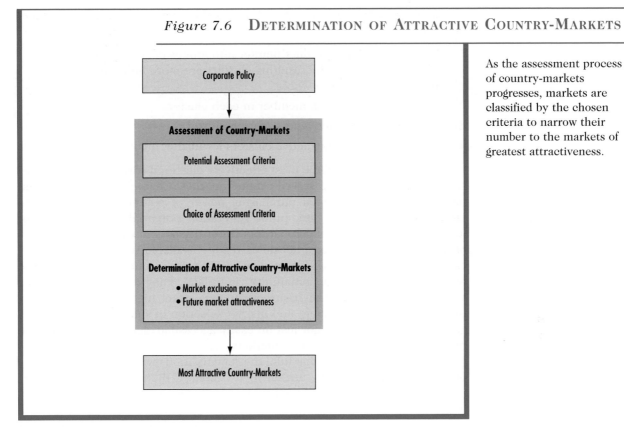

As the assessment process of country-markets progresses, markets are classified by the chosen criteria to narrow their number to the markets of greatest attractiveness.

---

represent constitutive features of the chosen product-market, such as the level of electrical supply infrastructure for a marketer of refrigerators.

There are several disadvantages to be considered, however. First, the application of knock-out criteria tends to support market assessment dependent on the firm's existing strengths and weaknesses. Even very promising markets will not be further considered if, currently, the firm does not possess the needed skills and resources to serve them successfully. For example, when a Belgian firm assesses the attractiveness of international markets in the field of sewage disposal, they may use 'existing customer relations' and 'available language skills' as part of the assessment criteria. The result may be a restricted choice of markets: the attractive US market will not be considered further, because the company does not have any relations with potential customers there, and all Spanish-speaking countries are ruled out because of lacking language skills. Such a procedure deprives a company of any perspective of strategic international development.

Second, the stepwise use of assessment criteria does not consider trade-offs between different market characteristics. For example, the quality of existing telecommunications and transportation infrastructure in the Czech Republic might not be up to the level of neighbouring Germany, but labour costs are only about 10 per cent. If both factors are of importance to a firm, such as a Japanese producer of textiles or a Korean manufacturer of cars considering implantation in Europe, it is important to use them simultaneously when comparing the attractiveness of the markets. Market clustering based on a set of assessment criteria is an appropriate solution.

(2) Market Clustering. The procedure used in market clustering consists of the following steps:

1. Splitting the global product-market into groups of geographic submarkets so that the resulting clusters are more homogeneous than the global market as a whole.
2. Describing the 'typical' member in each cluster.
3. Evaluating the attractiveness of each cluster.
4. Choosing the most attractive clusters for further analysis.

Country-markets will be most effectively clustered with criteria that consider the specifics of the served product-market. Characteristics often used include the product-related purchasing power of potential customers, the product-market growth rate, profit generation potential, transferability of funds, number and size of competitors (intensity of competition), availability of intermediaries, and local subsidies readily available to the company. For example, Japanese and US companies, such as Dell Computers, entered the markets of the European Community via Ireland. They did so because wages are relatively low and the Irish government offers high subsidies for new industrial plants. Assessment and market selection in such a case depend on strategic considerations, not just on easily accessible, general data about the macro environment of potential markets.

The country-markets that fulfil the set conditions will remain in the group of attractive markets to be further investigated. If the number of these markets is still too big to allow a quick and cost-efficient analysis of details, a scoring procedure can be used to rank the markets according to their relative attractiveness. Only for the best ranked markets will future opportunities and threats be estimated.

Future Market Attractiveness

In many instances, the decision to serve a country-market commits the firm's resources for a considerable amount of time. Therefore it should not be based on the current attractiveness of a market alone but should also consider potential changes in market attractiveness that arise from future developments.

For example, from 1989 to the present the countries in Eastern Europe have proven to be rather unstable markets. They first set out to become market economies, which was enthusiastically welcomed by many internationally operating firms convinced that they would find attractive new markets there. But from 1991 on, it became evident that those countries were encountering substantial economic problems in restructuring their economies, making some of the most optimistic forecasts obsolete. In 1993 compared to 1989, Poland's GDP was 86 per cent, Hungary's and the Czech Republic's GDP was 80 per cent, and in Russia GDP was only 61 per cent of 1989. But some of the countries, first Poland and Slovenia (1993), then the Czech Republic, Hungary and Slovakia (1994), recovered from the shock. Their economies started to grow. Others, such as most of the former parts of the USSR, however, had major difficulties in mastering their problems and have stayed in depression.[25] Forecasting techniques in such cases are either unreliable or have a very limited time horizon. To get a better estimate of potential developments in the macro-environments of a country-market and their impact on the product-market of the firm, a technique that is not based on forecasts should be used. Scenarios can fulfil this demand.

The scenario technique is a strategic planning technique. It uses systems analysis to identify the relationships between the essential dimensions of the macro-environment that influence the company and its operating environment. For a US manufacturer of electric power plants, for example, important dimensions of the UK macro-environment may be the political situation, technological development, legislation, existing infrastructure, and the development of the economy. Each of these dimensions must be specified by relevant factors of influence on the company's product-market. Relevant factors of technological development concerning the market of electrical power plants may be, for example, the development of anti-pollution equipment, security technology for atomic power stations, and the further development of photo voltaic technology.

The complexity of the firm's macro-environments, with all their interdependencies, is reduced to a matrix showing the degree to which the dimensions of the macro-environment (represented by the factors of influence) interact, that is, to what extent they actively influence the developments in the country-market's macro-environment or are influenced by other dimensions (Figure 7.7). For that pupose, the influence of each dimension on each other dimension is estimated on a scale from 0 (no influence at all) to 3 (very strong influence). When the lines of the matrix are summed, each sum expresses the influence of the respective dimension on all the others in the macro-environment. The sums of the columns stand for the potential of the rest of the macro-environment to influence the respective dimension.

The results of this analysis may be visualized by the use of a diagram such as the one shown in Figure 7.8. Autonomous dimensions are elements of the

---

Figure 7.7 **MATRIX OF INTERRELATIONSHIPS BETWEEN DIMENSIONS OF THE MACRO-ENVIRONMENT**

The matrix indicates the potential influence of each relevant dimension of a company's macro-environment on the other dimensions of this macro-environment.

Source: G.J.B. Probst and P. Gomez (1989), Vernetztes Denken, Unternehmen ganzheitlich führen, Wiesbaden: Gabler, p. 11.

POTENTIAL OF INFLUENCE on → of	A	B	C	D	E	Sum A (influence)
A						
B						
C						
D						
E						
Sum B (Influenceability)						

Figure 7.8 THE PATTERN OF INFLUENCES IN THE MACRO-ENVIRONMENT

Depending on its influence on the other dimensions of the macro-environment and on the extent to which it is influenced by those dimensions, each dimension of a company's macro-environment may be considered as autonomous, passive, reactive or critical.

A = Political Situation
B = Technological development
C = Legislation
D = Infrastructure
E = Economic development

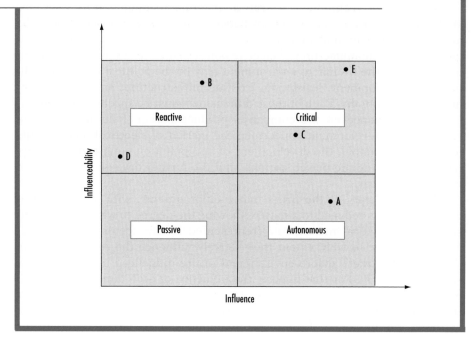

macro-environment which have a strong influence on the development of the other dimensions but are themselves hardly influenced by other dimensions of the macro-environment (see the political situation (A) in Figure 7.8). At the other extreme are passive dimensions which are strongly influenced by the other dimensions of the macro-environment, but have very little influence on the development of the macro-environment themselves. Critical dimensions (see the economic development (E) and legislation (C) in the example of Figure 7.8) have an above average influence on the rest of the macro-environment and are more strongly influenced by the other dimensions than the average. Reactive parts of the macro-environment are those dimensions that have no particular influence on the other dimensions but are influenced by them to an above average extent (see the technological development (B) and the existing infrastructure (D) in Figure 7.8). Such a diagram offers fruitful insights into which parts of a country-market's macro-environment – the critical and autonomous dimensions – are to be more closely watched than others.

When a time horizon is fixed for the analysis (one possibility would be to take the time needed to enter the market plus five years), potential future developments with respect to each factor of influence on each dimension of the macro-environment can be formulated. They describe the potential extreme states of development of the factors at the time horizon. For example, the development of photo voltaic technology may be completely stopped because of lack of commercializable results or, at the other extreme, may have reached a point where every household can produce the energy they need during the daytime. When the potential states of all factors of influence are analysed for their best logical fit, the two most highly consistent scenarios can be chosen which describe the two most different potential pictures of the macro-environment at the time horizon. The scenarios can be compared to the current situation and the country-market's attractiveness under each scenario can be assessed.

The scenario approach helps to avoid focusing too much on country-markets which are only attractive in the short run. The firm becomes alert to potential developments, such as changes in customers' basic values, countries' financial stability or the development of new technologies, that may have a strong impact on the attractiveness of a market.

The Most Attractive Markets

Having analysed the attractiveness of its product-market in various country-markets, marketing managers can rank the markets according to their attractiveness. To finally be able to decide which markets to serve, however, a comparison has to be made between the capabilities and resources a firm needs to be successful in those markets and the extent to which the company possesses those capabilities and resources compared to its major competitors. How to do such a comparison efficiently will be the subject of the next chapter.

SUMMARY

For a company that regards the entire world as a marketplace, there are many potential markets. In order to restrict the number of options to markets worth further investigation, the international marketer should go through a process of increasingly precise data collection and analysis. The process starts with a definition of the product-market in the company's corporate policy statement. From this definition, as well as from the company's objectives and priorities, criteria for market assessment can be derived. Focusing on characteristics of the economic, political and legal, as well as cultural and social, dimensions of the macro-environment which are relevant for the company's product-market, country-markets can be assessed and ranked according to their attractiveness.

This ranking of country-markets will also depend on their local product-markets' viability. The operating environment of the company in each potential country-market must be investigated. Customers are evaluated on the basis of substance, accessibility and responsiveness. Other important stakeholders, such as intermediaries, suppliers or the workforce, need to be considered. Together with the intensity of competition in the local product-market, they influence the potential profitability of serving a particular country-market. Scenarios of potential future developments in the macro-environment can help to evaluate potential changes of market attractiveness to be considered. The resulting rank order of most attractive country-markets serves as an input to the next step of the analysis: the determination of the international marketer's competitive position in those attractive markets.

Discussion Questions

1. What basic market exclusion procedures do you know? Describe their rationale and compare their pros and cons.

2. What sources of market assessment criteria can be used by a marketing manager? What are the differences between them?

3. Why is geographic proximity a market assessment criterion very popular with managers? Discuss its pros and cons, giving examples you have found in newspapers and magazines.

4. Compare the latest developments in Latin American markets to the information given in this chapter. What changes have occurred? Choose a company doing business in Latin America and discuss the impact of those changes on its business.

5. How does the level of economic development influence the attractiveness of a country-market? Find examples of companies to illustrate your points.

6. What information concerning the attractiveness of a local market can be derived from GNP (GDP) per capita figures? Illustrate your points by the use of examples you have found in newspapers and magazines.

7. Compare the latest developments in East Asian markets to the information given in this chapter. What changes have occurred? Choose a company doing business in East Asia and discuss the impact of those changes on its business.

8. Choose a product you are interested in and develop an estimate of the market potential and market volume of that product in a country in Europe, in Asia, in Latin America and in Africa. Indicate what sources of information you have used, what indicators you have applied, and the pros and cons of your approach.

9. Interview managers from three internationally operating firms about the criteria they use to assess the attractiveness of international markets. How does this compare to what you have read in this chapter?

10. Ask the same managers to describe the market assessment procedure used in their companies. Discuss your findings in the light of what you have read in this chapter.

Additional Readings

Bridgewater, S. (1995) 'Assessing the attractiveness of turbulent markets: the Ukrainian experience', *Journal of Marketing Management*, 11(8), November, 785–796.

Cole, S. (1992) *The Gulf States: a Business Handbook*, Cambridge, MA: Blackwell Publishers.

Tessun, F. (1998) 'Air Traffic – Quo Vadis? Scenarios for the next twenty years', *Marketing and Research Today*, November, 229–243.

Notes

[1] 'Finanzkrise kehrt aus Fernost wieder nach Mexiko zurück', *Der Standard*, 16 June 1998, p. 19.

[2] Millmanb, J. (1998) 'Mexico's "Maquiladoras" Are Flourishing', *The Wall Street Journal Europe*, 14 April, p. 4.

[3] Werner, Ch. (1997) '"Schlafender Riese" ganz munter', *Der Standard*, 2 January, p. 14.

[4] Guillermard, V. (1996) 'Renault au Brésil: le coup d'envoi', *Le Figaro économie*, 13 March, p. I; Guillermard, V. (1966) 'Le Mercosur, nouvel Eldorado de l'automobile', *Le Figaro economie*, 14 March, p. II.

[5] Raiffeisen Zentralbank (1996) 'Argentinien: Ein Land für Visionäre, aber auch für Investoren und Exporteure', *Auslandsdienst*, No. 71, April, p. 5.

[6] Herzlich, G. (1996) 'L'économie repart lentement après un an de récession', *Le Monde*, 25–26 February, p. 2.

[7] Goad, G.P. (1998) 'Asia Will Boom Again, but So Will Eastern Europe', *The Wall Street Journal Europe*, 6 May, pp. 1 and 10.

[8] 'Südkorea lagert Produktion aus', Der Standard, 18 October 1994, p. 19.

[9] Guyot, E. (1998) 'Hong Kong's Growth Slows Substantially As Asian Slump Hits Even the Healthiest', *The Wall Street Journal Europe*, 6 May, p. 4.

[10] Mamou, Y. (1998) 'Les investissements étrangers moteur de la croissance', *Le Monde Economie*, 5 May, p. III.

[11] Bobin, F. (1998) 'Chine: le grand bond en avant des privatisations', *Le Monde Economie*, 5 May, p. I f.

[12] 'Textile Woes Imperil Jobs In Shanghai', *The International Herald Tribune*, 14 March 1996, p. 3.

[13] 'Burmah Castro's Net Rises 18%', *The Wall Street Journal Europe*, 2 April 1996, p. 3.

[14] Raiffeisen Zentralbank (1996) 'Vietnam: Doi Moi, die vietnamesische Perestroika', *Auslandsdienst*, no. 71, April, p. 7.

[15] Baratta, M. (ed.) (1995) 'Der Fischer Weltalmanach '96', Fischer Taschenbuch Verlag: Frankfurt a.M., p. 42f.

[16] 'Bangalore bytes', *The Economist*, 23 March 1996, p. 67.

[17] Baratta, M. (ed.) (1995) *Der Fischer Weltalmanach '96*, Fischer Taschenbuch Verlag: Frankfurt a.M., p. 42f.

[18] Baratta, M. (ed.) (1995) *Der Fischer Weltalmanach '96*, Fischer Taschenbuch Verlag: Frankfurt a.M., p. 42f.

19 Rodier, A. (1998) 'La chute de la maison "vingt pour cent"', *Le Monde*, 15 May, p. 4.

20 Vangelder, Ph. (1998) 'Looking at Latin America', *ESOMAR NewsBrief*, Vol. 6, June, pp. 3–7.

21 Österreich Werbung (ed.) (1991) *Marketing 2000*, Wien: österr. Wirtschaftsverlag.

22 Tong, H.M. (1987) 'International Bribery: Cases Involving Pacific Rim Nations and Recommended Actions', Proceedings, Academy of International Business Conference, pp. 237–244.

23 'U.S. Legal Pressure Doesn't Cloud B.A.T.'s Outlook Overseas', *The Wall Street Journal Europe*, 2 April 1996, p. 6.

24 Eade, Ph. (1995) 'The ins and outs of target practice', *Euromoney*, November, 51–56.

25 'Österreichs Ost-Profiteure', *Der Standard*, 21 November 1994, p. 14; 'Osteuropa überwindet Rezession', *Der Standard*, 11–12 February 1995, p. 21.

CHAPTER 8

POTENTIAL MARKET ASSESSMENT: THE FIRM'S COMPETITIVE POSITION

LEARNING OBJECTIVES

After studying this chapter you will be able to

↔

assess a company's success factors in the most attractive international markets

↔

analyse major competitors' strengths and weaknesses concerning those success factors

↔

assess a company's potential to do business in the most attractive markets

↔

determine the distinctive competencies of the company

↔

explain the concept of competitive advantage

↔

distinguish different ways of determining competitive advantages

CHAPTER OUTLINE

Assessing potential success in international markets

Success factors in international marketing

General factors of influence on international marketing success
Determination of success factors

Competitor analysis

Structure of the competitive environment
Assessment of corporate policy
Assessment of corporate strategy
Assessment of management systems
Assessment of operations
Competitor information sources

Internal analysis

Corporate policy
Corporate strategy
Management systems
Operations

Determination of distinctive competencies

Profile of strengths and weaknesses
Comparison of profiles of strengths and weaknesses

Summary

INTERNATIONAL INCIDENT

Grohe Water Technology

With total sales of about USD750 million, German Grohe Water Technology is the market leader in Europe and among the world's top three fitting manufacturers, together with Masco from the USA and Japan's Toto. The company markets all kinds of fittings for residential and non-residential purposes, installation and flushing systems as well as water management systems. Grohe started its internationalization process by founding sales subsidiaries in Austria, France and Italy in the 1960s. A second wave of internationalization during the 1970s gave birth to sales subsidiaries in Belgium, Spain, the Netherlands, the UK and the USA. Until the mid-1990s, manufacturing sites were exclusively located in Germany. Since 1987 company sales have grown by an average of 10 per cent a year all over the industrialized world, resulting in tripled total sales in ten years.

Before Grohe's top management determined the firm's global strategy for the second half of the 1990s, they formed a special task force of marketing people and technicians to conduct a thorough analysis of the global USD8 billion product-market served by the firm and its most important competitors. Market analysis revealed an increasing concentration of retailers, a rising number of private labels, the emergence of new price-driven retail channels, increasing internationalization of key competitors, stagnant demand in core markets, and a polarization of demand. High-end and low-end product segments have been growing while the middle segment is virtually disappearing.

Competitors could be divided into two strategic groups following two basic strategies: (1) fitting specialists, such as Hansa, Kludi, Oras and Moen, and (2) all-in suppliers, offering everything for the bathroom, such as Ideal Standard, Roca, Masco, Kohler and Toto. Fitting specialists suffered from increasing density of competitors, a fragmented competitive structure, and rather narrow markets. All-in suppliers had to master very complex logistics problems which were not entirely counterbalanced by synergy effects. End users showed some resistance to the idea of getting everything from one supplier.

As a consequence, Grohe's top management decided to position the firm as a system supplier of sanitary technology. Because end users have a rather low involvement with the firm's products, Grohe concentrates on its relationships with planners and installation companies. Those customers are offered compatible product systems, access to new fields of technology, and an enhanced service level. Production sites were started in Canada, Thailand and Portugal. Companies possessing some additional know-how, have been acquired to further strengthen Grohe Water Technology's position as a system supplier. The product range was split into two groups under the brand names of GROHEtech (for the mass market) and GROHEart (for the high end). Annual pretax profits of around 12 per cent have shown that careful market assessment and a close examination of competitor strengths and weaknesses pay off.

ASSESSING POTENTIAL SUCCESS IN INTERNATIONAL MARKETS

To get a fairly unbiased picture of the attractiveness of potential country-markets, the firm needs to assess those markets independently from the perspective of its own resources and capabilities. When the most attractive country-markets have been defined, the company must determine whether it can serve them successfully. Potential success depends on the fit between the firm's capabilities and resources and the success factors in the markets. Success factors are the capabilities and resources that a company needs in a market to distinguish itself attractively from its competitors – seen from the potential customers' and most important stakeholders' point of view – and to be able to react to opportunities and threats from the market's macro-environment. Figure 8.1 provides an overview of the process that leads from the identification of the success factors in a potential market to the determination of the company's competitive advantages in that market. Competitive advantages are the result of a company's capabilities and resources that are demanded by a market and its macro-environment and that competitors cannot easily match, except at high cost and/or over an extended period.

First, the success factors in each potential market have to be determined. Then, an assessment of the firm's potential related to these factors compared to its competitors can be conducted. This process will lead to an understanding of the capabilities and resources that are crucial for success and that differentiate the company from its competitors. Management can use positive differences (= strengths) as distinctive competencies to build and sustain the firm's competitive advantages. It will work on negative differences (= weaknesses) to overcome their potential impact on the success of the firm. In this chapter the process of how to determine the success factors in a market, how to assess a firm's competitive position, and how to derive competitive advantages will be described and discussed in detail.

SUCCESS FACTORS IN INTERNATIONAL MARKETING

To determine its potential for success in a market, a company has to find out if it will be able to differentiate itself attractively from the major competitors at a profit. For that purpose, management must identify the current state of the firm's internal characteristics (see Table 8.1), evaluate them, and compare them to the characteristics of the major competitors.

General Factors of Influence on International Marketing Success

Figure 8.2 shows some general factors that influence a company's potential for international marketing success. First, international marketing success depends on how closely the skills of the company's personnel match the

Figure 8.1 DETERMINATION OF A FIRM'S COMPETITIVE POSITION

The competitive position of a firm in a market depends on its distinctive competencies, that is, on the strengths of the company compared to its major competitors. Distinctive competencies of a firm can be determined by a comparative analysis between the company and its major competitors. This analysis should concern the success factors, that is, capabilities and resources needed by a firm to be successful in a given market. Success factors can be derived from customers' and major stakeholders' expectations and aspirations as well as from present and future opportunities and threats in the environment of the market under consideration.

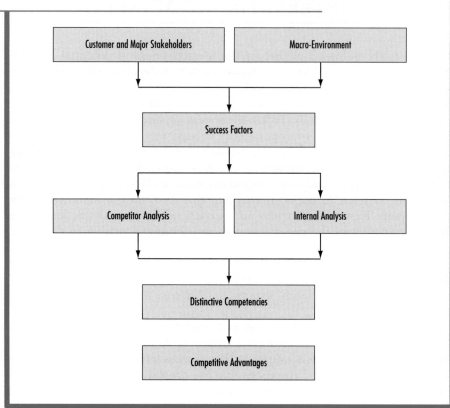

Figure 8.2 GENERAL FACTORS INFLUENCING A COMPANY'S POTENTIAL FOR INTERNATIONAL MARKETING SUCCESS

Capabilities of personnel and company resources contribute to a firm's potential for success in international marketing. If any of the factors are missing, the firm can hardly make up for them.

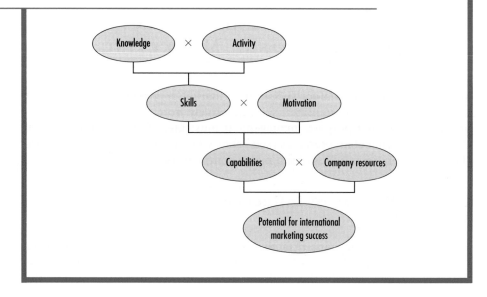

Table 8.1 UNITED STATES AND FOREIGN COMMERCIAL SERVICE
COMPUTERIZED EXPORT QUALIFIER PILOT PROGRAM

BUSINESS BACKGROUND

Before we get into an assessment of your company's international marketing potential, we need your answers to the following background questions.

Please respond to all of the questions. Circle the letter/number that corresponds to your response.

1. Which of the following best describes your product line?
   A. Product Manager
      (1) Components/Raw Materials
      (2) Industrial Products (equipment, machinery, instruments, etc.)
      (3) Commercial Products (office equipment, computers, furniture, etc.)
      (4) Consumer Products
      (5) Agricultural Goods
   B. Service Providers
      (1) Health Care
      (2) Education
      (3) Engineering
      (4) Consulting
      (5) Publishing/Printing
      (6) Computer
   C. Intermediaries
      (e.g. Export Trading Company, Export Marketing Company, etc.)
2. Approximately how long has your firm been in business?
   a. Less than 2 Years
   b. 2 to 5 Years
   c. 6 to 10 Years
   d. Over 10 Years
3. Approximately how many full time employees does your company have?
   a. Under 20
   b. 20 to 49
   c. 50 to 99
   d. 100 or Over
4. Approximately what were your gross sales last year?
   a. Under USD1 Million
   b. USD1 to USD5 Million
   c. USD6 to USD10 Million
   d. USD11 to USD20 Million
   e. Over USD20 Million
5. The growth rate of your company sales over the past 3 years has been:
   a. Less than Satisfactory (Did not take advantage of potential)
   b. Satsifactory (Moderate success)
   c. Very Satisfactory (Used full potential)
6. Which of the following best describes your sales & distribution activity?
   a. We have our own sales/distribution organization
   b. We do not have our own sales/distribution organization
7. Which of the following best describes your scope of marketing?
   a. We sell primarily to a few customers – locally
   b. We sell to a few customers – regionally or nationally
   c. We sell to a large customer base locally
   d. We sell to a large customer base regionally

(continued)

8. Currently, your senior management is likely to:
   a. Maximize profitability rather than sales growth
   b. Be moderately interested in sales growth
   c. Be highly interested in sales growth
9. Over the next 3 to 5 years, your management is likely to:
   a. Avoid new business ventures
   b. Cultivate new business opportunities selectively
   c. Develop new business opportunities aggressively
10. Which of the following best describes your firm?
    a. Currently not exporting
    b. Exporting by selling to middlemen in the US
    c. Exporting directly to foreign agents/distributors/customers
    d. Exporting through company-owner sales organization
    e. Exporting through subsidiary
11. Access to external funds for expansion purposes or working capital has:
    a. Not been a problem at all
    b. Been a moderate problem
    c. Been a serious problem
12. Your staff's knowledge of foreign cultures and business customs is:
    a. Adequate for most markets
    b. Adequate for selected markets
    c. Inadequate for any market
13. In terms of past exposure to international business, your staff has:
    a. No international transaction experience
    b. Limited international transaction experience
    c. Extensive international transaction experience
14. Members of your management:
    a. Are fluent in the language and culture of target market
    b. Have limited knowledge of language and culture of target market
    c. Have no knowledge of language of culture of target market
15. Resources for foreign market development can be freed:
    a. Without endangering home market position or long-term prospects
    b. Only at the risk of sacrificing domestic market position

Motivation for Going International

Companies follow a variety of objectives in pursuing international market opportunities. For each objective listed below, indicate how well it applies to YOUR company's desire to go international. Please be candid.

Please respond to all of the questions. Circle the letter/number that corresponds to your response.

1. Dispose of excess products/utilize excess production capacity.
   a. Strongly Agree
   b. Agree
   c. Unknown/Not Sure
   d. Disagree
   e. Strongly Disagree
2. Export by filling unsolicited orders only.
   a. Strongly Agree
   b. Agree
   c. Unknown/Not Sure
   d. Disagree
   e. Strongly Disagree

(continued)

3. Benefit solely by stabilizing seasonal market fluctuations.
   a. Strongly Agree
   b. Agree
   c. Unknown/Not Sure
   d. Disagree
   e. Strongly Disagree
4. Contribute to company's general long-term expansion.
   a. Strongly Agree
   b. Agree
   c. Unknown/Not Sure
   d. Disagree
   e. Strongly Disagree
5. Enhance firm's competitiveness by acquiring new markets.
   a. Strongly Agree
   b. Agree
   c. Unknown/Not Sure
   d. Disagree
   e. Strongly Disagree
6. Extend the valuable life cycle of existing products.
   a. Strongly Agree
   b. Agree
   c. Unknown/Not Sure
   d. Disagree
   e. Strongly Disagree
7. Supplement domestic sales with occasional export sales.
   a. Strongly Agree
   b. Agree
   c. Unknown/Not Sure
   d. Disagree
   e. Strongly Disagree
8. Reduce risks by selling to diverse markets.
   a. Strongly Agree
   b. Agree
   c. Unknown/Not Sure
   d. Disagree
   e. Strongly Disagree
9. Exploit the firm's unique technology and know-how
   a. Strongly Agree
   b. Agree
   c. Unknown/Not Sure
   d. Disagree
   e. Strongly Disagree
10. Improve overall return on investment.
   a. Strongly Agree
   b. Agree
   c. Unknown/Not Sure
   d. Disagree
   e. Strongly Disagree

TOP MANAGEMENT COMMITMENT

Senior management's viewpoint on international marketing can have a big effect on YOUR company's success rate. Please read the following statements and indicate to what extent each statement applies to your current management.

(continued)

Please respond to all of the questions. Circle the letter/number that corresponds to your response.

1. Top management has reservations about entering international markets.
    a. Strongly Agree
    b. Agree
    c. Unknown/Not Sure
    d. Disagree
    e. Strongly Disagree

2. Exporting will be limited to sales to middlemen in the US
    a. Strongly Agree
    b. Agree
    c. Unknown/Not Sure
    d. Disagree
    e. Strongly Disagree

3. Adequate funds will be set aside to develop foreign markets.
    a. Strongly Agree
    b. Agree
    c. Unknown/Not Sure
    d. Disagree
    e. Strongly Disagree

4. Management is willing to sacrifice profits for long-term sales during the start-up period.
    a. Strongly Agree
    b. Agree
    c. Unknown/Not Sure
    d. Disagree
    e. Strongly Disagree

5. Senior management will spend at least 10 % of their time for international expansion.
    a. Strongly Agree
    b. Agree
    c. Unknown/Not Sure
    d. Disagree
    e. Strongly Disagree

6. Foreign markets will be developed with a formal marketing plan.
    a. Strongly Agree
    b. Agree
    c. Unknown/Not Sure
    d. Disagree
    e. Strongly Disagree

7. Product is unique, differentiated, or represents advanced technology.
    a. Strongly Agree
    b. Agree
    c. Unknown/Not Sure
    d. Disagree
    e. Strongly Disagree

8. The production process is exclusive to your firm.
    a. Strongly Agree
    b. Agree
    c. Unknown/Not Sure
    d. Disagree
    e. Strongly Disagree

9. Company R & D level exceeds industry average.
    a. Strongly Agree
    b. Agree
    c. Unknown/Not Sure
    d. Disagree
    e. Strongly Disagree

(continued)

10. Price is competitive in the domestic market
    a.   Strongly Agree
    b.   Agree
    c.   Unknown/Not Sure
    d.   Disagree
    e.   Strongly Disagree
11. Product has sufficient advantages over competing products.
    a.   Strongly Agree
    b.   Agree
    c.   Unknown/Not Sure
    d.   Disagree
    e.   Strongly Disagree
12. No excessive inventory investment by distributors is needed.
    a.   Strongly Agree
    b.   Agree
    c.   Unknown/Not Sure
    d.   Disagree
    e.   Strongly Disagree
13. Product requires special US license to export.
    a.   Strongly Agree
    b.   Agree
    c.   Unknown/Not Sure
    d.   Disagree
    e.   Strongly Disagree
14. Product requires special storage (e.g., controlled temperature).
    a.   Strongly Agree
    b.   Agree
    c.   Unknown/Not Sure
    d.   Disagree
    e.   Strongly Disagree

expectations of customers and other important stakeholders in the market. A person's skills are a blend of superior knowledge and the ability to apply this knowledge appropriately. Managers and employees with distinctive skills such as production know-how, product development skills or extensive experience in relationship building may truly set a company apart from its competitors, who will have a hard time acquiring the skills at short notice.

Taitinger, a French producer of high quality champagne, for example, possesses a specific production know-how which has allowed it to be one of the most prominent brands in the world. Because the small number of the company's cellarers personally transmit their know-how from one generation to the next, the know-how specific to the brand does not leave the company, making it difficult for competitors to imitate their product quickly.

Superior skills are not enough for international marketing success. Company personnel must also be motivated to apply their skills internationally. Motivation of company personnel to adjust to new markets and their macro-environments is based on the dominating values and social norms that form the firm's corporate culture. An appropriate culture may be lacking, for example, if the compensation system does not reward foreign assignments, or worse, if it acts as a disincentive in terms of opportunities for promotion. That may be the case when managers returning from international assignments find that somebody else has taken their former position and they are offered an inappropriate position instead.

A firm's capabilities are the product of the skills of its personnel times their motivation to apply those skills in ways desired by top management. Capabilities include the interactions occurring inside the firm and between the firm's personnel and its stakeholders. If either personnel skills or motivation is insufficient, the resulting capabilities will not lead to the achievement of company goals.

But international marketing success depends on more than the company's capabilities. Success requires appropriate resources. Company resources that are of major importance for successful internationalization include financial, technological, production, information and organizational elements.

Overall, the internal factors that determine a company's potential for international marketing success can be described as the product of the company's resources times its capabilities. If the capabilities are not internationally oriented and up to competitive standards, or if the firm's resources are insufficient or inadequate, success is unlikely. Thus, when analysing a firm's potential for international marketing success, a manager must look at both. Capabilities and resources should be analysed in terms of the firm's corporate policy, corporate strategy, management systems, and operations.

However, any general analysis of a company's strengths and weaknesses includes two practical problems: the large number of potential characteristics to look at and the choice of criteria to evaluate them. Both problems can be resolved by first determining the success factors in the market. On the one hand, they indicate which characteristics of the firm and its major competitors should be analysed, and on the other the level of competence to be achieved on each of the important characteristics.

Determination of Success Factors

Core and Success Factors. When searching for the success factors in a market, a company has to make a clear distinction between success factors and core factors (Figure 8.3). Core factors are the capabilities and resources a company needs to be considered as a relevant supplier by the customers and other important stakeholders in this market, and to survive present and future threats from the macro-environment. A Brazilian producer of pharmaceuticals unable to provide the medical test information required in order to be accepted by the French medical administration will not be able to participate in that market, for example. Thus, the competitors in a market will usually not differ with regard to those capabilities and resources. To attract Scandinavian summer tourists, for example, an area must be able to guarantee sunshine. Italy, Greece and Tunisia, competing for those tourists, can satisfy the demand, but they do not differ from each other regarding that characteristic. The decision of Scandinavian customers on what country to choose for their summer vacation depends on other factors, the so-called success factors.

Success factors are the capabilities and resources that a company needs in a market to distinguish itself attractively from its competitors – seen from the potential customers' and most important stakeholders' point of view – and to be able to profit from present and future opportunities from the macroenvironment of this market. Business success will depend on how the firm scores on these factors compared to its major competitors.

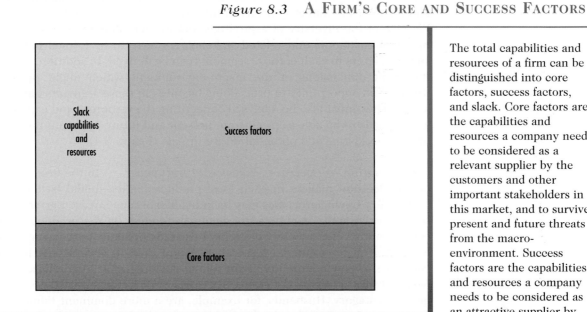

Figure 8.3 A FIRM'S CORE AND SUCCESS FACTORS

Source: Grunert, K.G. and Ch. Ellegaard (1993) 'The Concept of Key Success Factors: Theory and Method', in M.J. Baker (ed.), *Perspectives on Marketing Management*, vol. 3, Chichester: Wiley, pp. 245–274. Copyright John Wiley & Sons Limited. Reproduced with permission.

The total capabilities and resources of a firm can be distinguished into core factors, success factors, and slack. Core factors are the capabilities and resources a company needs to be considered as a relevant supplier by the customers and other important stakeholders in this market, and to survive present and future threats from the macro-environment. Success factors are the capabilities and resources a company needs to be considered as an attractive supplier by the customers and other important stakeholders in this market, and to be able to profit from present and future opportunities from the macro-environment of this market. All other capabilities and resources can be regarded as slack.

Ways to Determine Success Factors. When determining the success factors in attractive potential markets, some managers rely on their past experience. In the ever-changing environment of international markets, however, past experience is likely to be quickly outdated and it is dangerous to generalize from one country-market to another. French Gervais-Danone, for example, knows from its US experience that a big budget for national consumer advertising is very important for getting enough shelf space in supermarkets all over the country. But will that also be true in Japan? It may be much more important there to use networking skills, that is, to build up personal and maybe financial relationships, to obtain the desired shelf space.

Experienced consultants may have extensive knowledge based on work with numerous and diverse companies. Such individuals are in a relatively good position to determine general success factors for international marketing. However, because existing and potential expectations of customers and other important stakeholders vary in different product- and country-markets, attempts to define general success factors across markets have achieved high levels of attention but not much enduring success in international marketing.

The best way to determine the success factors in a potential market is to identify the expectations (concerning the satisfaction of needs) and aspirations (concerning the solution of problems) of the (potential) customers and stakeholders in the markets under consideration and to derive the capabilities and resources a company needs to fulfil those aspirations and expectations. Because of the diversity of aspirations and expectations in most cases, segments of customers and related stakeholders have to be formed before the success factors in each of those segments can be derived. In addition, the most important dimensions of the macro-environment which might present a threat or an opportunity to firms doing business in those segments have to be added. They must also be analysed concerning the resources and capabilities a firm needs to be able to profit from present and future opportunities and to overcome existing and potential future threats (Figure 8.4).

Determination of Decision Makers and Influencers. In the first step, the buying decision makers in each local product-market should be identified. Consumers' buying processes may be individual or may involve a group of persons, mostly family members or friends, depending on the product and the cultural norms of the society or group. In a study of family purchasing roles in Saudi Arabia, for example, researchers found that, in general, the husband continues to play a more dominant role in deciding what to purchase. But in Saudi Arabia, as in most nations, the roles vary by decision stages and by product category. Husbands, for example, are a more dominant influence on 'how much to spend', but husband and wives together are involved in 'when to buy'. Husbands exert more influence on the purchase of an automobile, while wives dominate decisions on women's clothing.[1] International marketers should be careful, however, not to project their gender prejudices or individual cultural experiences onto other cultures. More than half of all ties purchased in Germany and Austria, for example, are bought by women and a significant amount of women's underwear is bought by men. A careful analysis of the target consumers' buying behaviour seems to be advisable.

Organizational customers are frequently organized into multifunctional teams called 'buying centres'. For example, British Rover when purchasing a series of industrial robots for the production of a new car model would use a team approach in making the purchase decision. The team might include representatives from various functional areas, such as production, finance, engineering, maintenance and purchasing as well as a member of top management. Together they would weigh organizational objectives and the suppliers' potential contributions to achieving those objectives against the cost of the competing products.

How each individual member of the buying centre acts in the purchase decision process will depend on the role he or she plays inside the group (Figure 8.5). The possible roles involved in a buying centre include initiator, influencer, gatekeeper, decider, purchaser and user. In a smaller company the roles may be played by a single person or, at most, a few people. As the size of the organization and the price, complexity or importance of the buying decision increase, these roles are likely to be played by different individuals.

In addition to the organizational objectives and objectives related to the role each member of the buying centre plays, the personal objectives of the various members of the purchasing team are likely to affect the team's final decision. For example, the team member from production might prefer offers that have a short delivery time and fit the maintenance know-how of the firm's service crew. The procurement manager might prefer the least expensive offer because bonuses are dependent on capital spent, and the member of top management might focus on references provided by the competing suppliers.

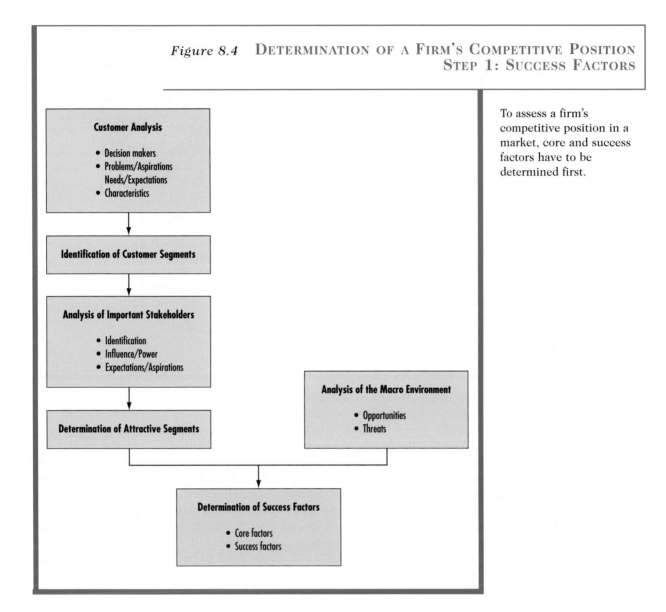

Figure 8.4 DETERMINATION OF A FIRM'S COMPETITIVE POSITION
STEP 1: SUCCESS FACTORS

To assess a firm's competitive position in a market, core and success factors have to be determined first.

There might also be a power struggle between some members of the group for personal reasons.

When serving globally active organizational customers, the problem of multiple roles and objectives may be complicated still further. In addition to having potentially different personal and corporate objectives, role players may come from different cultures or be located in different companies belonging to the firm. A marketer selling to Procter & Gamble's European headquarters, based in Geneva, Switzerland, may face a buying centre whose members are American, French, Irish and Taiwanese. Although the negotiations would be conducted in English, the cultural background of each member and specific career experiences in different parts of the firm would result in a complex matrix of roles, objectives and cultures very difficult for the international marketer to handle.

Figure 8.5 Business Customer Buying Centres

The multiperson-multifunctional purchasing situation that international business-to-business marketers face is characterized by the different objectives and roles that are involved as well as by the potentially different individual, cultural, corporate and national culture backgrounds of the buying centre's members.

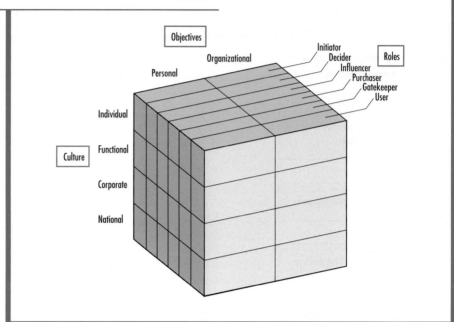

Customer Problems, Expectations and Aspirations. In the next step, needs and expectations of buying decision makers and important decision influencers that can be (at least partly) satisfied by the company have to be assessed. At this point the marketer should keep in mind that potential customers can only identify needs and expectations related to objects they know about. Innovative solutions to customer problems are rarely found from customer needs they describe themselves. Therefore, the analysis should focus on (potential) problems the customers need to be solved and on customer aspirations concerning potential problem solutions. For example, because of the rising environmental and personal health concerns of their customers, hairdressers in Denmark may need hair styling products with reduced negative impact on the environment and the condition of hair. They will only accept a new problem solution offered by French L'Oréal, however, if their customers are adequately informed about the improved features of the new product and if the price they have to pay stays roughly the same.

Customer Characteristics. The diversity of customer expectations and aspirations concerning highly attractive ways of solving their problems or providing certain benefits makes most international marketers group their potential customers in a country-market into more homogeneous segments. For that purpose, marketers may choose to segment their customers either by the benefits they are seeking or by characteristics that are relevant to the customers' market behaviour. For example, characteristics such as location in cities versus in villages, the occupational structure of their clients, the turnover of the shop, or the competitive differentiation of the firm (traditional vs. highly fashionable, cheap vs. sophisticated) can be relevant to the behaviour of hairdressers. Because benefit segmentation of customers demands more sophisticated primary research techniques to gather the data and, in addition, may result in segments which are difficult to reach, most marketers prefer to use customer characteristics for segmentation purposes. The choice of segmentation criteria is crucial for the homogeneity of the resulting segments in terms of similarity of expectations and aspirations which, in turn, strongly influences the quality of marketing decision making based on those segments.

Identification of Customer Segments. The gathered data are used for the identification of customer segments. In most cases the use of a hierarchy of segmentation criteria will be appropriate. The European customers of a French steel maker such as Sacilor, for example, might be segmented using the industry they belong to (automotive, durable consumer goods, machinery, construction), their annual consumption of steel, the quality standards they impose, and the intensity of customer service they require, in that order. Because there is no single best way of segmenting a universe of potential customers, alternative solutions should be considered.

Segmentation will result in a number of customer groups that are not equally attractive to serve. To reduce the amount of analytical work to be done further on, only the most attractive customer segments should be considered in the further steps of product-market analysis. But to arrive at a meaningful determination of the attractiveness of existing segments, the most important stakeholders in each of the segments need to be identified and analysed.

Analysis of Important Stakeholders. Important stakeholders, who most often include intermediaries, suppliers and the labour force, may have supportive or averse interests and more or less power to carry them through. Therefore, the attractiveness of a customer segment will be raised or diminished by the existence of such stakeholders. For example, a Swiss engineering firm which has developed a highly effective plant for the burning of industrial toxic waste may have identified the attractive-looking segment of chemical and pharmaceutical plants in Italy. The attractiveness of this segment is very much diminished, however, if green activists together with the media (via public administration) have the power to stop decision makers in the segment buying.

External decision influencers such as consultants or the clients of the potential customers have to be determined. The plastic raw material a manufacturer of car bumpers will buy, for example, is strongly influenced by the specifications of the car makers. Those specifications will be a co-production of procurement, quality assurance and marketing personnel of the manufacturer's clients. In public administration markets, the information search and supplier evaluation step often contains formal bidding requirements. Public agencies may be forced by law to accept the lowest bid that meets the particular set of specifications. International marketers who wish to compete in these markets must develop excellent relationships with the agents or consultants setting those specifications in order to be able to influence specification setting beforehand.

To identify the most influential stakeholders, an exhaustive list of all organizations, institutions and people who participate in the business, such as intermediaries, suppliers, potential workers and employees, special media, consultants, and others who have an interest in the business, such as administrators, legislators, environmentalists or unions, is drawn up. Then, in order to assess their power to influence the business system, a matrix such as the one used for the analysis of interrelatedness of macro-environmental dimensions (see Chapter 7) is developed. It shows the interrelationships between the members of the operating environment as well as the direction and strength of each relationship. For example, in a country such as France, unions may play a much greater role in the market for textiles than in Portugal or Greece, where their role may be more important than in Indonesia. By summing the lines and columns of the matrix, the positions of all stakeholders – from passive to autonomous – can be defined and the most important players identified.

Determining the Most Attractive Segments. For the evaluation of segments, a scoring procedure based on the assessment of segment substance (for example, volume and growth), accessibility (for example, entry barriers and intensity of competition), responsiveness (for example, urgency of need, innovativeness, and cultural prejudices), and profitability (for example, attainable margins, price sensitivity, and net present value of segment investments) may be applied. Because a scoring procedure uses a broader base of information and does not rely on estimations of future streams of income, in most cases the results of such a scoring procedure are more reliable than the calculation and comparison of net present values of investments in building and maintaining successful business relationships with the customers in each segment.

Deriving Core and Success Factors. The profile of expectations and aspirations varies from one attractive customer segment (including the most important stakeholders) to another. Therefore, the capabilities and resources needed to fulfil those expectations and aspirations will also vary. Table 8.2 shows a form which helps managers to go through a formal process of deriving core and success factors for each market segment.

First, managers need to list the customer group and most important stakeholders in the given market segment. They have specific aspirations and expectations concerning companies doing business in the market and the outcomes of their activities. Potential customers of Yves St Laurent in China, for example, expect their products to be easily distinguishable from ordinary clothes, to help express wealth and success, but also to be affordable (for them) and to have a certain level of fabric quality. Additionally, employees in shops selling Yves St Laurent products in China expect to be much better paid than sales personnel in shops selling Chinese products, to receive free housing, and to have secure jobs.

Such aspirations and expectations are not only listed on the form shown in Table 8.2, they are also distinguished into three categories: must-be, should-be and may-be. The first category contains all aspirations and expectations which 'must be' fulfilled at a pre-specified level for a company to be considered a relevant supplier. Nippon Cable, a Japanese manufacturer of lifts, for example, must guarantee the security of users and the availability of spare parts for 20 years after the end of construction in order to be considered a relevant supplier in China. Magna International, a Canada-based supplier of automotive parts and systems, has to deliver its products 'just in time' to French car factories, that is, at exactly pre-specified times, not earlier and not later, if they want to continue to do business with their customers. Because

Table 8.2 DETERMINATION OF CORE AND SUCCESS FACTORS IN A MARKET SEGMENT

STAKEHOLDERS	ASPIRATIONS AND EXPECTATIONS			IMPORTANCE WEIGHT	NEEDED CAPABILITIES AND RESOURCES	
	MUST-BE	SHOULD-BE	MAY-BE		CORE FACTORS	SUCCESS FACTORS
Customers	ISO 9001			5	Certificate	
		Simultaneous engineering		4		Team of technicians Know-how Online connections
	Just-in-time delivery			5	Production planning and control system	
		Flexible reaction to change in production needs		5		Warehouse at customer production site
			Amount and kind of products in stock	2		System of transportation Stock management system Relative cost position
		Personal treatment		3		Commitment of personnel to customers
	Pre-specified quality			5	R&D capabilities Quality assurance system	
Consultants		Latest level of information		4		Relationships with consultants
Public Administration	Adherence to pollution regulations			5	Quality assurance system R&D capabilities	

Depending on the level of pre-specification, aspirations and expectations of customers and other important stakeholders in a market segment are distinguished into three categories: must-be, should-be and may-be. Importance weights seen from the customer and stakeholder perspective can be given. Capabilities and resources a company needs to fulfil aspirations and expectations belonging to the 'must-be' category are core factors. Capabilities and resources needed to fulfil aspirations and expectations belonging to the 'should-be' and 'may-be' categories are success factors. Capabilities and resources needed to master present or future threats are core factors. Capabilties and resources allowing the company to profit from present or future opportunities are success factors.

the stakeholders have exact ideas of what to expect from a company, there is no potential for positive differentiation compared to other suppliers.

Aspirations and expectations belonging to the 'should-be' and 'may-be' categories may result in differentiation potential for the firm. The first category contains aspirations and expectations that stakeholders are aware of but without having pre-specified ideas concerning their fulfilment. For example, when American customers buy a car they expect the seller to provide some customer service. But Toyota, when introducing their Lexus model, had the opportunity to differentiate their offer from competitors by providing the customers with rental cars for free until delivery of the new car, bringing the new car to the customer's home, and programming the position of the driver's seat, mirrors and steering wheel to fit the sizes of all individual family members having a driver's licence.

Potential customers may not be consciously aware of 'may-be' aspirations and expectations. The company possesses the resources and capabilities to satisfy them, the customers have the related needs or interests, but they do not know about the potential solution. Such a situation occurs when a company plans to market a product or service which is an innovation to the customers or contains innovative features. Until some years ago, European consumers, for example, did not know of potential home delivery of dishes, except for handicapped people. For Domino's Pizza, the US-based home delivery specialist, when analysing success factors in Western Europe, this expectation belonged to the 'may-be' category. The company had the know-how but needed to make customers aware of this need satisfaction potential.

Having split the aspirations and expectations of customers and other important stakeholders into the three categories, the marketer may also want to attribute an importance weight (seen from the customer perspective) to each. Higher weights would point to greater importance for the firm to possess the capabilities and resources needed to satisfy the respective expectations.

In the next step the capabilities and resources that a company needs to fulfil the listed aspirations and expectations are derived. Capabilities and resources needed to satisfy expectations belonging to the 'must-be' category are classified as 'core factors'. The company must have them to be considered a relevant supplier. Magna International, for example, must have a production planning and control system as well as a distribution logistics system which allows them exact delivery to their clients in the automotive industry. The state of each control panel, for example, in the process from its order to the end of production and its position in the logistics chain to the customer must be traceable.

Capabilities and resources needed to satisfy aspirations and expectations from the 'should-be' and 'may-be' categories are success factors. They allow the company to be more or less attractive to the stakeholders in the market and to differentiate itself from major competitors. For example, to provide their Lexus customers in the USA with the extended services described above, Toyota needed to have a fleet of cars to rent (for free) to the customers for some time, to have a car seat supplier with the electronic and technical know-how to produce programmable seats, and to hire well-trained, highly motivated personnel in sufficient numbers to ensure home delivery of the new cars. Domino's Pizza needed a fleet of delivery vehicles at its disposal, pizza production sites fairly central to the location of potential customers, and personnel ready to deliver pizza quickly at any time of the day regardless of weather conditions.

The list of core factors in a market is completed by the capabilities and resources the firm needs to counter existing and potential threats stemming from important dimensions of the macro-environment. For example, if the political and economic situation in a country is not entirely stable, as in many Latin American countries, the company will need specific capabilities, such as establishing informal relationships with influential people, and resources, such as local management, to stay in business over time.

Additional success factors are based on existing as well as potential future opportunities from important dimensions of a market's macro-environment. If the population of a country is increasing significantly, as for example in India, and the per capita income is steadily growing, a success factor for a consumer products manufacturer such as Wilkinson, the UK globally established shaving products firm, might be to have a distribution system which tightly covers all urban areas where young and educated people live. For producers of tele-communications equipment, such as Sweden's Ericsson, the development of technical standards is of great importance. For them a success factor in a market such as India might be their ability to influence norm-setting bodies.

COMPETITOR ANALYSIS

To assess their firm's potential for success in the most attractive segments of highly attractive country-markets, management has to determine if the company possesses the needed core factors. If those basic capabilities and resources exist, the company's strengths and weaknesses related to the success factors in each market are then analysed. The result must be compared to the strengths and weaknesses of the firm's major competitors. For practical purposes, the assessment starts with competitor analysis to avoid too much of a biased perspective towards factors where the company has its strengths.

In analysing its major competitors, a firm seeks to find out how well its capabilities and resources fit the critical success factors in a market. To be able to complete such an evaluation, the marketer first has to determine the structure of its competitive environment, that is, the relevant competitors and their membership in strategic groups, as well as barriers to market exit. Then the marketer has to gather information concerning the most important competitors' corporate policy, their corporate strategy, the state of their managerial systems, and their operations (Figure 8.6).

Structure of the Competitive Environment

Relevant Competitors.   In order to analyse competition, the marketer has to decide on the definition of a relevant competitor. Competitors may vary depending on whether the product-market exists globally, regionally or locally. But a marketer should keep in mind that other companies in the same industry may define their markets differently. For example, a Norwegian marketer of cross-country skis may consider its business to be restricted to the Scandinavian countries, while a global competitor like Austria-based Fischer Ski defines its market as all country-markets where you can possibly do any cross-country skiing. In that case, the Norwegian marketer should expand its view of the relevant operating environment in order to cover all (potentially) relevant competitors.

The most important competitors will be firms that supply similar goods. Besides existing competitors, there may be a threat of new upcoming competitors. Important firms which have not served the market so far might consider doing so in the future. The marketer must therefore have a closer look at potential candidates and existing barriers to entry.

Figure 8.6 DETERMINATION OF A FIRM'S RELATIVE COMPETITIVE POSITION STEP 2: COMPETITOR ANALYSIS

Data concerning the level of success factors present in major competitors' organizations have to be gathered and analysed. They may concern the corporate policy, corporate strategy, management systems, and operations of the competitors. Results are summarized in a profile of each competitor's strengths and weaknesses.

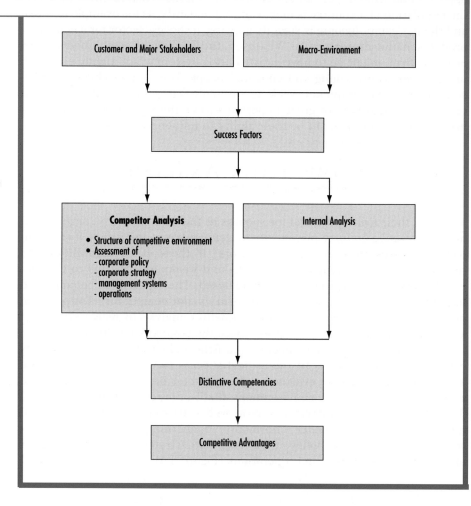

But relevant competitors may include not only domestic or international suppliers of similar goods. Marketers of substitute goods, that is, any organization supplying products or services that satisfy the same customer need, must be considered as potential competitors. From this broader perspective, for example, Red Bull, a stimulating drink made in Austria for young people who want to be 'cool', not only competes against Grolsch beer but may also compete against Chevignon shirts.

New competitors may arise from the development of a new technology. A marketer of fuel, such as Royal Dutch Shell, might see important competitors emerge when the production of electrical energy through photovoltaic is developed to be highly efficient. It may feel the need to follow the development of this technology closely and to consider companies working in that field as potential important competitors. But such competitors might also emerge from a change in customer behaviour. If an increasing number of people tend to avoid heating their homes during the cold time of the year by spending extended vacations in warmer regions of the world, Shell will be confronted with major competitors from the vacation services industry. Therefore, the determination of major competitors is not only a task that demands thorough analysis of the industry to which the firm belongs, but also a screening of the environment in search of potential substitute problem solutions that might become a threat to the firm.

Strategic Groups.   Not all existing suppliers of similar products or services in a country-market are automatically potential competitors of a firm that considers entering the market. There may exist strategic groups of competitors with differing relevance to the firm. A strategic group consists of companies relying on the same basic factors of competition. In the German car market, for example, Mercedes, BMW and Audi tend to base their competitive strategies on high quality combined with differentiation. They form one strategic group compared to the car makers from South Korea, Kia, Hyundai and Daiwoo, which form another strategic group relying mainly on cost/price leadership. The first group defends its position through intensive R&D, technological pioneering, and exclusive image; whereas the second group optimizes its cost position through high production volumes, rationalization, low wages and lean management.

The marketer has to find out what drives competition in the analysed country-market. Then the individual competitors that exist in the local product-market are described according to those factors. The companies are grouped on the basis of their specific competitive characteristics: the competitive strategy they have chosen (price, product/service differentiation, time, relationship building, or a mixture of those), where they allocate their resources (for example, R&D, production, marketing), and what else specifically characterizes them (such as degree of integration or diversification). Then the competitive structure in the strategic groups with the highest relevance for the firm can be analysed.

The competitive structure of a strategic group may be defined in terms of the number, size, relative market share, rate of growth and technical sophistication of firms in that group. The real number of competitors in a strategic group may be less important to a firm than the number of companies considered as relevant competitors by the customers in the market. To determine their names, the marketer may analyse the customers' evoked sets for the specific good, that is, try to find out the top-ranked suppliers in the minds of potential customers.

The size of the most important competitors can be estimated from such data as number of employees or annual sales volume. These numbers should be evaluated carefully, because they are influenced by the nature of the product or service and the production technology used. The number of people working for a shoe manufacturer in Brazil, for example, may be similar to the number working for a competitor in Italy. But this doesn't mean the companies are the same size, because different production technologies may be employed by the two firms. In many cases, therefore, it will be necessary to estimate competitors' production capacities.

The market shares of competing firms are a measure of their competitive strength. They indicate what portion of total sales volume in the product-market has been captured by each competitor. They may also be viewed as indicators of competitors' strategies. A large market share points towards cost leadership, whereas smaller shares may be a result of niche strategies, that is, the firm's focus on a selected part of the product-market. Such conclusions can be misleading, however, without knowledge of how stable the competitive situation is. Growth or decline in competitors' market shares must therefore be monitored.

Barriers to Market Exit. Barriers to leaving a market may result in an intensification of competitive action, because they prevent competitors from going out of business. Such barriers can be economic, technical, legal, social or emotional. If a government is interested in a firm, a national airline such as Italy's Alitalia, for example, may not be able to go out of business because the country's government finds ways to subsidize its heavy losses. Those subsidies allow the company to stay in fierce price competition with foreign competitors. Exit barriers such as this result in biased competition. Legal barriers to market exit may be, for example, high litigation such as in France, when agency agreements may have to be terminated. An example of a combination of economic, technical and emotional barriers can be cited from the US market. US industrial customers take a substantial time to trust foreign suppliers regarding their willingness to stay in the market and to ensure spare parts delivery. But when a foreign company's products are accepted, the company must be aware that it will be extremely hard for them to find a comeback to the market once they have left it. In the evaluation of potential markets, therefore, an international marketer must include such barriers.

Assessment of Corporate Policy

Corporate policy states the mission of the competitor and the business philosophy dominating its decisions and actions.

Corporate Mission. One important part of a competitor's corporate mission is the definition of its business domain. It limits the market considered as relevant, restricting the number of potential customers and (seemingly) relevant competitors. For example, if a competitor defines its product-market as sweatbands for European women who ski, the size of the market is different than if it is defined as sweatbands for European women involved in sports. Depending on this definition, the competitor will either not respond to the market entry of a new company with sweatbands for summer sports or take action to limit the success of the new entrant.

The major goals and priorities stated in the corporate mission influence the competitive strategy of a competitor as well as its organizational structure and its information, planning and leadership systems. A competitor striving to become a global player will tend to have a more complex organization than a local competitor, whereas competitors with a locally focused mission will defend their market niche more fervently than global competitors with many other markets to which they allocate their limited resources. Therefore, to assess the competitive position in a potential market, management needs some information about the major competitors' mission statements to be able to evaluate their potential reactions.

Business Philosophy. A competitor's reaction to a new contender is strongly influenced by the values shared by the dominant group in the organization. In most cases this is top management. In some countries,

STRATEGY BOX

The Corporate Policy of Asea Brown Boveri (ABB)

ASEA BROWN BOVERI AG IS THE RESULT OF A MERGER between Asea from Sweden and BBC from Switzerland. It represents an organization with 215 000 workers and employees in over 140 countries. With sales of more than USD30 billion the firm defines its business as a globally leading technology company in the fields of transportation and environmental protection technologies as well as electrotechnical equipment.

The business philosophy of ABB contains the following statements:

↔ We refuse hierarchies, centralism, and inflexibility. We try to combine the advantages of a big concern with those of a middle-sized firm to develop a dynamism that keeps us ahead of competition.

↔ It is allowed to make mistakes, as long as they are made fast, are quickly discovered and revised.

↔ We profit from the global interrelationship of firms with equal rights, following the basic rule: 'Think global, act local.'

↔ Communication is a production factor.

↔ We are fast, positively aggressive, and unconventional. Fantasy and creativity get their needed 'playground'.

↔ We are at home everywhere where we are active. We explicitly do not have any headquarters that run the company from any one country. To facilitate communication, our business language is English.

Source: G. Demling (1992) 'Vernetzte Kommunikation wird zum Erfolgsrezept', *absatzwirtschaft*, 5, p. 54.

including most EU nations, however, representatives of unions, financiers and government may belong to the group that dominates the company. The dominant group formally or informally develops a business philosophy, that is, rules on how relationships with internal and external exchange partners should be managed. Thus, aggressiveness against or cooperativeness towards competitors is somewhat predetermined.

Business philosophy affects decisions regarding resource allocation and competitive strategy. ABB, the Swedish-Swiss firm globally active in transportation technology, environmental protection and electrotechnical markets, for example, has defined a business philosophy that emphasizes flexibility, creativity and local good citizenship (see the Strategy box). As a consequence, the company represents a competitor with 1300 subsidiaries in more than 140 countries managed as profit centres with equal rights. Communication is regarded as a productive factor inside the company and in contact with its stakeholders. The firm attracts highly qualified personnel from all over the world who want to work in a creative environment. It is a technology leader in its product-markets.

Assessment of Corporate Strategy

The corporate strategy broadly defines the company's competitive posture, providing guidance regarding what it will do and imposing constraints by delineating what it will not do. It specifies the direction in which the company will develop in the future and outlines how the company will reach its goals and objectives. For example, a competitor such as Korea's Samsung in consumer electronics may have decided to become a cost leader. Other competitors have decided to be specialists in one or more market niches, such as Gucci, the Italian marketer of fashionable women accessories. Others strive to be technological leaders, such as Fuchs, a small German engineering firm in the field of electrical arch furnaces for steel production, or are content with being a 'me too' follower, such as Acer, the PC producer from Taiwan. Because such basic decisions strongly influence the behaviour of competitors, a firm must analyse their corporate strategy (or the strategy of the competing business unit).

Value Chain.   An important point of interest is the length of the value chain covered by the competitor, that is, how much of the entire production and marketing process from the procurement of raw materials to after-sales customer service is handled by the competitor. For example, when Mercedes, based in Stuttgart, Germany, developed a small car together with Swiss SMH's Swatch, they decided not to produce it themselves. Mercedes concentrated on the development, Swatch on the design and marketing of the car. Production in a plant located in France was delegated to Canada's Magna International.

Compared to US and European companies, which traditionally relied on the integration of more steps of the value chain, the big Japanese companies, such as Mitsubishi, tend to restrict their part of the value chain so that strategically leading firms cover the core of their business, that is, customer contact and core technology. The rest is provided by subcontractors focusing on either small parts of the entire process, such as just-in-time delivery of parts, or providing system solutions, like the development and production of all pollution equipment for a truck. Toyota, for example, only manufactures about 30 per cent of its cars' value itself. Competitors covering a shorter part of the value chain can develop an enhanced innovation potential from focusing on their specialities. They need fewer assets and profit from a smaller and more stable number of personnel, which is not only easier to manage but also represents a lower amount of relative fixed costs. For that reason, many companies in Europe and the USA went through intensive outsourcing programmes during the first half of the 1990s.

Configuration.   The configuration of the competitors' business needs to be checked next. Configuration means how concentrated the activities of the competitors are in specific countries or regions versus their spread across the world. A competitor may have concentrated the production of a part of its products in one place, such as General Motors which produces all its engines for the Corsa model in Spain. Such a concentrated approach increases the risk of political instability, strikes or delivery problems. But it profits from experience curve effects, lower wages, special skills of the available workforce, or lower taxes.

Other competitors may have located production and sales of their products at different places across the world, such as British-Dutch Unilever, one of the world's leading firms in grocery products, which has production and sales units in the Americas as well as in Europe and Asia. They may profit from their closeness to the customers and the local content of their products.

Depending on the success factors in a market, the configuration of a competitor's business will provide them with more strength or weakness.

Diversification.   Besides the length of the value chain covered by the competitor and the configuration of business, the degree of diversification, that is, the number of product-markets the competitor is serving, will influence its potential reaction to a new contender entering the market. Diversified competitors, such as the big Korean conglomerates Samsung or Daewoo, which produce everything from steel and semiconductors to cars and consumer electronics, can strategically transfer resources among their businesses. They are able to invest in a market to counter the entry of a new competitor even when the short-term economic situation does not allow more specialized competitors to spend their funds.

Internationalization.   In addition, each competitor is characterized by a degree of internationalization. More internationally active competitors might have the potential to react to a firm entering their 'home' market by expanding their coverage of the entrant's home market. Such 'cross subsidization' took place, for example, when Riva, the biggest Italian producer of high quality metal sheets, tried to increase its market share in the French and German automotive industries. German Thyssen and France's Sacilor fervently counter-attacked by saturating the Italian market with very low prices. Local competitors may apply what is called their 'local charm', a better knowledge of the local culture and strong personal ties in a closely knit network of mixed business and social relationships. The Spanish airline Air Iberia, as an example, is in a globalizing industry. It has a high local market share and is strongly entrenched in national business relationships. But other competitors, such as British Airways, have a higher return on investment, because their global shares are higher, allowing them to invest in new aircraft and higher-efficiency services networks.

If a competitor spreads available resources over too many product- and country-markets, it will suffer from 'underspending' in at least some of those markets and be easily attacked through a concentrated effort. That is one of the reasons why Allied Domecq, the UK producer of such well-known alcoholic beverage brands as Beefeater gin and Kahlua liquor, after having bought the Spanish and Mexican spirits group Pedro Domecq and a subsequent 15 per cent drop in sales in 1995, decided to reshape their business to focus on fewer brands and markets.[2]

If a competitor's resources are focused on too small a number of product- and country-markets, 'overspending' takes place. In such a case the competitor on the one hand does not use its entire capacity for international activities, but on the other hand will be able to spend slack resources in defence of its position in the served market. The Future Issues box gives an example of what a new entrant may expect in such a situation.

Competitive Behaviour.   Finally, the company must assess the competitive behaviour of the major players in the market. Some competitors seek confrontation, others are ready to cooperate where both parties can win. Microsoft, for example, attacks any competitor trying to do business in what it considers to be its market. Germany's chemical giant BASF and US-based DuPont, on the other hand, decided to cooperate in an equal share joint venture to produce and market materials for nylon manufacturing in Asia.

FUTURE ISSUES BOX

On Your Mark, Get Set – Phone!

THE BATTLE HAD BEGUN. WITH MEXICO'S LONG-distance telephone market set to open fully in 1997, competitors were taking aim at Teléfonos de México (Telmex). While the company had some serious flaws, its strong market position, dominance in local phone service and USD10 billion investment to create a modern digital network made it a formidable opponent.

At stake was a fast-growing telephone market. Even with Mexico's stagnant economy, local and long-distance volume was expected to grow from USD6 billion to close to USD9 billion by 1999. The question was how much share Telmex would lose to its new competition. Much depended on how Telmex dealt with its weaknesses: marketing and an abysmal image. Telmex had been slow to take its competitors seriously – though it was now bringing in new marketing managers, including a special corporate group. The company also was having trouble living down a reputation for dismal service before privatization in 1990. Telmex was now offering some hot new services, including Internet access, a high-speed data network, and video-conferencing.

Of Telmex' seven announced rivals, Avantel – the joint venture between US-based MCI Communications and Mexico's largest bank, Banamex – was the furthest along. The other main challenger, Alestra – originally a joint venture between AT&T and Mexican industrial conglomerate Alfa – got a big boost through its merger with a group that included Telefonica de España, Bancomer, Mexico's No. 2 bank and GTE. Other players were expected to go after niche markets. For instance, Iusacell, a leading cellular-telephone operator in which Bell Atlantic Corp. holds a 42 per cent stake, had a long-distance concession but was more interested in offering local service.

Telmex was expected to retain a near monopoly on local service for years. Although it was required to provide local access to long-distance providers starting in January 1997, Telmex was allowed to collect a fee on each call. The government protected the company's local rate subsidy by granting the carrier 58 per cent of the 39.5-cent-a-minute fee that Mexican carriers received from calls coming into Mexico. Competitors were entitled to receive as many minutes of these lucrative incoming calls as they send out. So they were likely to establish low international rates in Mexico.

Sources: Malkin, E. (1996) 'On Your Mark, Get Set – Phone!', *Business Week*, 6 May, p. 54; and Torres, C. (1996) 'New Phone Rules In Mexico to Allow Strong Competition', *The Wall Street Journal*, 29 April, p. A 18.

Although they are competitors in other markets, they decided to invest about USD750 million in what they intend to be a 'long-term engagement in the Asian nylon markets.'[3]

One competitor may be highly innovative, leading technological development in the industry. Others may rely on their ability to quickly follow any innovator with an improved version of the product. A third category of competitors may acquire smaller firms that have developed interesting problem solutions. AT&T, for example, having decided to dump its phone-making and computer businesses, bought shares of smaller firms in its move to become a global media company. To avoid civil engineering projects in wireless communication, it bought McCaw Cellular. Its acquisition of a 30 per cent share of DirecTv helped avoid having to launch their own satellites.[4]

Assessment of Management Systems

Management systems are the infrastructure of a competitor's operations needed to coordinate its function effectively and efficiently. When a competitor seeks to counter the market entry of the firm, it needs a flexible organizational structure, a planning system able to prepare the company to be competitve, an information system that ensures that the personnel involved have an adequate level of information, and a leadership system that motivates those people.

Organization. A firm's organization is characterized by its structure and the interactions that occur among the elements of this structure. The organizational structure of a competitor expresses the company's strategic emphasis and its priorities. In the early 1980s, for example, BP Oil focused on diversifying into related industries. It formalized its diversification projects as 'International Businesses' with the creation of a matrix organization embracing ten business streams and about 40 national associates around the world. At the beginning of the 1990s, BP Oil's focus changed to growth in share values and dividend performance. Consequently the organizational structure was simplified to become more efficient and flexible.[5]

Competitors that are organized around functions usually emphasize production. When distribution of products seems strategically important to the company, top management may structure the firm regionally. Liechtenstein-based HILTI, for example, has structured its worldwide operations in the fastening business along geographic lines. There are regional headquarters responsible for their business in the local markets. The growing importance of brand management to the success of many firms has led them to restructure their organizations around brands. For example, the French luxury brand group LVMH is organized along its brands such as Louis Vuitton, Guerlain, Moet-Hennessey or Christian Dior. Increased customer orientation leads competitors to organize around customer groups or around projects. Gore, the US firm which became famous owing to its Gore-tex, for example, has reorganized its entire company along project lines.

If the organizational structure of a competitor has many layers of hierarchy, it will have higher costs than 'lean' competitors with a flat structure. The lines of communication in the company will also be longer and as a consequence decision making is slower. The firm will react to changes in the market, such as the entrance of a new competitor, with a time lag. This is one of the reasons why most EU governments have taken such a long time to deregulate their telecommunications and air transportation markets. They do not want to see their national firms being overrun by foreign competitors which are more cost efficient and faster.

Interactions between elements of the organization are hard to assess from outside the company. But some hints, such as the existence or non-existence of training programmes, can be used as indicators. A competitor that conducts training programmes on an ongoing basis can adjust to new challenges much faster than competitors that lack such programmes. Plessey, a UK manufacturer of communications equipment, has installed a training unit to continually develop its sales force; it would have little difficulty in adding a special training session for salespeople to counter a new competitor. A competitor without any tradition of personnel training would find it more difficult to prepare its salespeople to deal with new competition.

Planning. A company's planning system consists of all the people formally involved in the organization of planning, the planning process itself, and the planning tools employed. Its major purposes are to define the right goals and objectives for all parts of the company; to develop strategies, policies and actions to achieve those goals and objectives; and to allocate the company's resources appropriately. If a competitor lacks a planning system, it might have difficulties in systematically matching success factors in any market. Its historical business would be based on the experience of influential managers or mere chance. On the other hand, if the formal planning system of a competitor becomes too complex and sophisticated, it leads to inflexibility in market behaviour. For example, if the local manager of a franchise firm in Japan, such as Kentucky Fried Chicken, has to contact headquarters for minor decisions concerning the size and outfit of stores as well as price actions to counter the market entry of a new competitor, such as Texas-based Churches Fried Chicken, decision making will take far too long to fend off the entrant effectively.

Information. How competitors gather, store and distribute information is crucial to their reaction to new contenders. A local competitor in Russia, for example, may not have any cost accounting system, and a rather bureaucratic and authoritarian information flow. When top management is confronted with a new entrant in their market, they might decide to slash prices in defence. By the time this decision is understood and executed by the firm's personnel, however, the new competitor may have won a foothold in the market.

The information system of a firm predominantly serves the purpose of coordination. The marketing manager completing a competitor analysis will therefore be interested in how the major competitors resolve the problem of coordinating all the activities in their organizations and the results of those decisions. At one extreme, decision making is decentralized and coordination is achieved through information flows between organizational subunits. Webasto, the German supplier of sun-roofs and air conditioning equipment for cars and buses, for example, has largely independent production plants in various countries near their customers' factories. To coordinate their activities in the fields of product development, marketing and personnel, the headquarters has initiated regular meetings of the local managers where they exchange information on successful and less successful operations and develop joint projects.

The other extreme is centralization of decision making and standardization of activities. Depending on the success factors in a market, some coordination mechanisms in between the two extremes will be more successful than others.

Leadership. Different cultures have different dominant styles of decision making. People in the Middle East, for example, assume that successful leaders impose their will on the firm. Managers in Thailand, Malaysia, Indonesia and the Philippines also favour an authoritarian style, whereas those in Singapore and Hong Kong are less authoritarian. The decision-making style of a competitor influences the company's potential success in an attractive market. Many successful US companies emphasize participative decision-making processes. But which decision-making style is effective will depend on the market enviroment.

For an international marketer it may also be important to know what incentive systems the competitors in a market use. Again, cultural differences may play a major role in which incentives are most acceptable. For example, a system of bonuses that rewards individual achievement may be appropriate for a Canadian sales force, but it may not be appropriate for salespeople based in Taiwan or Hong Kong. Asian employees tend to favour group rewards and recognition over rewards for individual behaviour. In Japan, job security is an important motivator. There, salespeople are more willing to perform when they are offered security than when they are offered a monetary bonus. In the Netherlands good interpersonal relations are a strong motivator, and employees disapprove of performance-oriented competition.

Assessment of Operations

Finally, the analysis of major competitors will focus on their capabilities and resources on the operative level. The procurement potential, the level of available product and process technology, marketing know-how and innovation behaviour, and financial resources as well as the skills and motivation of the personnel may contribute to a competitor's strengths and weaknesses in a market.

Procurement Potential. In general, companies with experience in international procurement are stronger competitors in international marketing. They have better chances of balancing currency exchange rate and price differences than their counterparts with only regional purchasing experience. A European firm that serves the US market will have much less trouble with a decreasing dollar value of the company's sales, for example, if it purchases substantial amounts of raw material, parts or systems in countries that belong to the dollar area, such as Southeast Asia, Latin America and the Middle East.

Technological Potential. To determine its competitive position concerning research and development capacities in an attractive market, the company needs to take an inventory of its major competitors' technological potential. This potential can be indirectly assessed through the number of patents, licenses or copyrights. But an increasing number of firms in industries with shortening innovation cycles, such as software production or mechanical engineering, no longer register patents because they fear signalling the latest developments to their competitors and giving them enough details to innovate around the patent. Therefore, in addition to patents, licenses and copyrights, it is worth taking a closer look at the competitors' product and process technology.

Product technology affects customers' perceptions of the relative benefits provided by a product compared to competitive offerings. When digital displays were introduced by the Japanese watch manufacturers Casio, the Hatori Group (Seiko) and Citizen, quickly followed by their Hong Kong competitors, Swiss analogue watches looked old fashioned. They risked being reduced to the very high priced and traditional segments of the world market. But ETA, today Switzerland's largest watch company and part of the SMH Group, developed a very light, thin, waterproof, shock resistant analogue watch powered by an inexpensive three-year battery with a face and strap made of durable colourful plastic. This stylish and attractive watch became a world success under the brand name Swatch.

The ability to produce and market Swatch was largely dependent upon a unique process technology developed at ETA. Process technology, that is, the kind of technology used in the production process of a good or service, has a strong impact on a company's capacity, production flexibility, cost structure and productivity (the cost per unit produced). Production capacity and flexibility influence a competitor's ability to adapt to changing market demands, as well as to react to the entry of a new firm in its market. High capacity results in lower costs per unit, but only when the capacity is filled. It needs high investments in production facilities which represent a barrier to exiting a market when it becomes less attractive. Therefore, a competitor with high production capacity will defend its market share with much energy and a tendency to lower prices.

The flexibility of a competitor's production system determines the speed with which it can make changes in the physical characteristics of a product or its package. Car manufacturers have made use of computer-aided manufacturing (CAM) to enable customers to 'compose' their own cars. But even greater flexibility is possible. On the one hand, computer-aided design (CAD) allows customers and manufacturers to design custom products jointly. On the other hand, the level of general qualification of workers is of major importance for production flexibility. Competitor analysis therefore also has to consider the potential of a qualified workforce available at all hierarchical levels.

High production flexibility opens the opportunity to adapt the output quickly to changes in the market. A highly flexible competitor, when confronted with a more competitive international marketer may choose to escape competition and a potential price war by altering its product lines. The production flexibility and cost structure of a competitor also determine the variations it can pursue in general marketing strategy. For example, when an auto maker like French Renault increases the number of robots in its plants, the cost per unit produced will decrease as long as robots are more productive than skilled workers. Fixed costs as a share of total costs will increase as variable costs decrease, because of the need for fewer workers. Renault would then be in a more advantageous competitive position. It could either lower the price of its cars, increase the margin for its dealers, or make higher profits, which could be reinvested to further increase productivity or develop the market.

Higher fixed costs can have major disadvantages. One is that the company needs a bigger market to be profitable. Therefore, the competitor is more vulnerable to negative economic developments in other parts of the world. Renault, for example, is vulnerable to economic stagnation in the USA and in Latin America. Additionally, the firm is faced with much higher barriers to leaving a market. In our example, if the car produced by robots is not successful, Renault will probably encounter a financial disaster.

Marketing Know-How. If local competitors are still developing their marketing know-how, as in the former socialist countries of Eastern Europe and in most LDCs, a firm from a highly industrialized country entering their markets will have an advantage. The reputation of internationally operating firms is often an additional strength. But it is not only marketing-mix skills that determine marketing success. In many cases building and maintaining relationships with intermediaries and final customers, and also with other important stakeholders in the market, is as important. Competitor analysis, therefore, must not only assess how traditional marketing operations are conducted, but must also include the search for and evaluation of existing formal and informal networks among companies and their stakeholders.

Such networks exist in every industry. Denmark, for example, has long been a European centre of the pork and bacon industry thanks to a network of pig farms, abattoirs and processing plants. In Vicenza, in northern Italy, the jewellery business is strongly related to a host of specialized services: banks used to the paperwork involved in handling precious metals, security services, gemmologists and others all helping to support the jewellers in a network. In the Veneto and Emilia Romagna regions of Italy, there is a network of designers and suppliers specializing in moto-cross machines which serves firms such as BMW.[6] And the Japanese economy is a formidable example of how firms can be interrelated with government agencies.

Financial Resources. The financial resources of the major competitors strongly influence their ability to react to a new firm entering the market and the way they will react. Financial resources can be internal or external funds available to the firm.

As a company becomes more international and invests in more subsidiaries around the world, the use and allocation of working capital (current assets minus current liabilities) becomes more complex. Internationally operating competitors can transfer funds internally through loans, equity capital, transfer-pricing mechanisms, or other financial transactions between subsidiaries. Thus they have considerable financial flexibility. This often results in a lower cost of funds, compared to a purely domestic competitor.

The ownership structure, that is, the number and quality of individuals or organizations holding equity in a competitor, also influences its behaviour in the market. In general, multiple ownership results in additional capital and a higher tolerance of risk. If a competitor is partially or totally owned by a government, it may have access to funds even in economically disastrous situations where private owners would not support the business as fully. Recent examples are the high amounts of capital spent by the French and Italian governments to keep their national airlines alive. If the competitor is part of a financial network of interrelated firms such as many Japanese companies, it may have advantages in building relationships with suppliers, intermediaries and final customers.

Commercial banks are still a major source of corporate funds. In analysing competitors' financial resources it is important to know that commercial banks operate quite differently in different countries. In Europe and Japan, they may underwrite security issues, and buy and sell bonds and equities on their own account. German banks, for example, have long dominated the corporate sector by acting simultaneously as creditors, supervisors and shareholders to many companies. They may not perform these activities in the USA, where these functions are performed by investment banks. When a commercial bank holds an equity position in one of its customers, the relationship between the bank and the customer will usually be more supportive.

An example is Deutsche Bank, Germany's largest bank, which took over a significant part of the shares of Cologne-based Kloeckner-Humboldt-Deutz in the wake of the collapse of the engineering group's trading house in 1988. The bank's involvement increased in 1995 when it again stepped in to help the group out of a crisis. In January 1995, Deutsche Bank agreed to write off about USD100 million of KHD's debt and joined other creditor banks to issue a

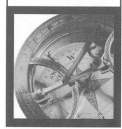

ETHICS BOX

The Wade System for Judging Sources of Information

Ethical

1. Published material and public documents such as court records.
2. Disclosures made by competitors' employees, and obtained without subterfuge.
3. Market surveys and consultants' reports.
4. Financial reports and brokers' research reports.
5. Trade fairs, exhibits and competitors' brochures.
6. Analysis of competitor's products.
7. Legitimate employment interviews with people who worked for competitor.

Arguably Unethical

8. Camouflaged questioning and 'drawing out' of competitor's employees at technical meeting.
9. Direct observation under secret conditions.
10. False job interviews with a competitor's employee (i.e., without real intent to hire).
11. Hiring a professional investigator to obtain a specific piece of information.
12. Hiring an employee away from the competitor to get specific know-how.

Illegal

13. Trespassing on a competitor's property.
14. Bribing a competitor's supplier or employee.
15. 'Planting' your agent on a competitor's payroll.
16. Eavesdropping on competitors (e.g., via wire-tapping).
17. Theft of drawings, samples, documents and similar property.
18. Blackmail and extortion.

* The numbers in the list are ranked in degree of ethicality of legality.

Source: Adapted from Wade (1965) by Murphy, P. E. and G.R. Laczniak (1992), 'Emerging Ethical Issues Facing Marketing Researches', *Marketing Research*, 4(2), 8.

USD130 million credit line, only to be confronted with a KHD announcement in Spring 1996 that previously undisclosed losses at KHD Humboldt Wedag AG, the plant-construction, refining and engineering subsidiary, could run as high as USD420 million. Acting as much as a partner as a creditor, the bank decided to put in another USD150 million in new capital.[7]

Skills and Motivation of Personnel. Competitor analysis in most cases is incomplete without an assessment of the major competitors' personnel. Personnel does not mean only top management. Acknowledging top management's importance to the development of a company and therefore to competitor analysis, highly skilled workers and employees can make a substantial contribution to market success. Take the example of Japanese competitors. Despite high labour costs they have gained an important share of many industrial and consumer markets, to a large degree because of the globally known 'Japanese quality'. This quality standard in turn can only be provided because of the well-trained and highly motivated workforce in the country.

Competitor Information Sources

The ways of obtaining information about major competitors range from the illegal activity of industrial espionage to the acceptable, and universal, practice of using salespeople to monitor competitors' public actions in the field (see the Ethics box). Management has to find the most efficient way of gathering the information needed for the evaluation of competitors' strengths and weaknesses in the specific market, without leaving the ethical path of research.

Some firms disassemble the products of their competitors, like for example Xerox with Canon copiers. Others enter joint ventures to obtain information on their competitors' manufacturing techniques, such as GM and Toyota, or set up an office in their major competitors' home country, as IBM did in Japan, to have current information on what competitors are doing there. Chapter 6 mentioned more examples of sources of information about competitors. Companies that have instituted formal intelligence programmes, such as Digital Equipment, Eastman Kodak and Gillette, have an advantage over others that do competitor research on an ad hoc basis.

INTERNAL ANALYSIS

When competitor analysis is completed, the next step is to add internal analysis data to allow a comparison of the extent to which the firm and its competitors possess the success factors needed in an attractive market segment. Internal analysis to assess the firm's competitive position follows by and large the same checklist of characteristics as competitor analysis (see Figure 8.7). Therefore, in the following section only some differences will be discussed in detail.

Corporate Policy

Corporate Mission. Internal analysis starts with an assessment of corporate policy and to what extent it is 'lived' by top management. The most important factor determining a company's potential for international marketing success is top management's ability and willingness to lead the firm in its international marketing effort. A study of small and medium-sized companies in Finland, Germany, Japan, South Korea and South Africa found that companies are significantly more successful in foreign markets (that is, they have much higher proportions of non-domestic sales) when their top managers have a global perspective.[8] These companies are even more successful than competitors that enjoy advantages in such areas as products, distribution systems and capital. If they are to have a global perspective, top managers should have experience with more than one culture. Such experience may come from family socialization, education, business experience or intercultural training.

For the company to be internationally competitive, top management must be committed to achieving and maintaining an international presence. Management must commit the firm to providing the necessary resources throughout the organization. For example, it must establish support facilities at headquarters such as a customer, intermediary and supplier data bank or a

Figure 8.7 **Determination of a Firm's Competitive Position Step 3: Internal Analysis**

Having analysed the relevant characteristics of the major competitors in the most attractive market segment, management can proceed to an assessment of the firm's capabilities and resources related to the success factors in those segments.

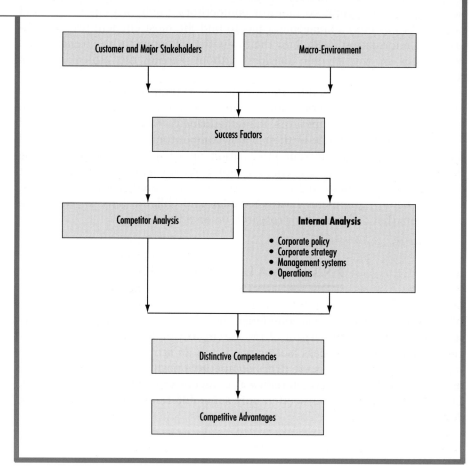

small staff for the analysis of potential acquisitions. Additional travel budgets are needed. And because it may take longer internationally than in the home market to achieve financial success, top management must take a long-range view of financial matters.

Business Philosophy. The company is best suited to international marketing when management, through communications as well as actions, sends clear, consistent signals regarding the priority of international business. Only by this means can the corporate culture become international in orientation. Corporate culture is the sum of values shared by the members of a company and the common rules of behaviour (social norms) they follow. That is, it represents a general frame of reference that the members of the firm use to interpret events and facts in the company's environments. Corporate culture results in observable behaviour among personnel, traditions, rituals, stories told about past events, and specialized language. High-tech firms such as Intel, the US producer of processors for PCs, for example, use a different vocabulary in their everyday work than do financial firms, such as Coopers & Lybrand. In an internationally oriented culture, internationalization of thinking and action is an important value for the members of the firm, and behavioural norms that further international business activities are positively reinforced.

From the perceptions of the firm's behaviour by its stakeholders, the company's identity develops. Every company has a unique identity, which is more or less formal or consciously managed. The specific identity of the firm influences its reputation and makes it easier or more difficult to enter new markets. Its adequateness for the market in question, therefore, has to be checked.

Corporate Strategy

As in competitor analysis, management must check the length of the firm's value chain, the configuration of business activities, the degree of diversification, the spread of international activities, and its traditional competitive behaviour. They are the result of existing capabilities and how resources have been allocated in the company so far.

In many companies resource allocation is based on experience or intuition. Sometimes it is based on partial analysis – for example, the sales volume of product lines during recent years. But allocation mechanisms such as 'first come, first served' or even 'they who shout the loudest get the most' can also be found. Since an internationally operating company faces a higher level of complexity than a domestic firm, it will encounter major problems with such approaches. Intuition allows the managers to recognize 'typical' situations, based on past experiences, and, in a stable environment, to draw the right conclusions in an extremely short time. If the business environment changes in a way not fully understood or not recognized by managers, however, the value of their experience is sharply diminished. A decision based on domestic experiences or on experiences obtained in another country-market may lead to satisfactory results, but if the manager ignores differences in the seemingly familiar environment, the quality of the decision over the long term is questionable.

Management Systems

In evaluating a firm's competitive position in an attractive market, managers must determine how well the existing management systems will fit the new realities: will they be able to cope with the new environments, what changes may occur without much managerial influence, and what changes will have to be strategically managed?

With internationalization increasing, a company's management systems have to be able to cope with greater complexity of environments and market interrelatedness. An information system, for example, may need to contain on-line connections with all of the warehouses to allow simultaneous stock management of products around the globe, thereby reducing the danger of stock-outs in one place and shelf-warmers in another. For example, Benetton Sports Systems, the Italian marketer of sporting goods, can tell at any time what products are in stock (and have been sold) by model and size in their warehouses. This information not only helps production planning, but also allows shipments between warehouses when different customer preferences lead to shortages in one area of the world, compared to an overstock in another.

Organization.   To assess how effective the development and implementation of a strategy can be, managers must take a look at their firm's organization. As described in the section on competitor analysis, the focus will be on structure, lines of communication, and degree of integration between functions.

Serving new international markets will place new pressures on the organization. Problems never before encountered must be resolved; a new environment must be mastered. If there is a lack of mutual support and understanding among different parts of the company, effective interaction will not be possible. Problems existing in domestic markets such as salespeople promising customers impossible delivery dates, procurement managers minimizing inventory levels at the cost of production interruptions, and production managers optimizing use of machinery without regard to delivery requirements must be resolved before the company attempts to operate internationally. If they are not, business will almost inevitably be lost to competitors where the decision-making and project work of interfunctional teams is part of daily routine.

Planning.   Without an adequate planning system it will be almost impossible for the company to develop lasting relationships with customers, intermediaries and other stakeholders in different country-markets, even though single business deals may be executed successfully. To fulfil the demands of international marketing, the firm's existing planning system should not be restricted to a simple budgeting system. Budget figures, even when they are based on careful planning of individual activities, do not reveal anything about underlying objectives or actions. If planning is highly budget-driven, centralized coordination is more difficult and synergy among different parts of the company is unlikely to occur (see Table 8.3). This negatively influences top management's ability to manage international marketing effectively.

The budget for the promotion campaign of an Italian winery such as Cav. G.B. Bertani, located in Verona, for the southeastern part of the USA, for example, may be simply projected from the Atlanta-based distributor's budget for last year plus an increase to account for inflation. But even if it is based on the distributor's action plans, the budget may not reflect the Italian winery's objective which has changed from gaining a foothold in the market to achieving a profit on each sale. Changing corporate objectives should alter promotion activities. A company with a planning system based on corporate objectives, basic assumptions concerning the development of international business environments, and clearly defined policies to be followed by local employees or business partners is better prepared to enter and be successful in international markets.

The organization of the planning process will also influence the firm's competitive position in the attractive markets. If plans exist only in the minds of top management, as is the case in many small and even medium-sized companies, marketing success will largely depend on chance. Because international marketing significantly increases the complexity of the entire business, companies which have established a formal planning procedure for their local business, with specific responsibilities for its execution assigned to members of the organization and set dates for the achievement of the different steps in the process, will be better off.

Information.   A company's potential for international marketing is greater when an effective information system for its domestic business is in place.

Table 8.3 **Problems of Companies that Rely Exclusively on a Budgeting System**

Lost opportunities for profit
Meaningless numbers in long-range plans
Unrealistic objectives
Lack of actionable market information
Interfunctional strife
Management frustration
Proliferation of products and markets
Wasted promotional expenditures
Pricing confusion
Growing vulnerability to environmental change
Loss of control over the business

While budgets are important planning devices, over-reliance on budget-driven planning means too much attention is paid to numbers, and not enough to the dynamics of international business.

Source: M.H.B. McDonald, (1982) 'International Marketing Planning', *European Journal of Marketing*, 16(2), 10.

The main purpose of gathering information is to help managers make better decisions. The marketer assessing the firm's competitive position in the attractive markets has to look at the way information is distributed in the company and how managers make use of it. For example, the internationalization of marketing will be hampered if customer information only exists in the minds of salespeople, because there is no system in place to summarize this information and then to distribute it to marketing, research and development, or production managers. In the complex environment of international markets, any attempt to develop a marketing strategy or to implement consistent product or communication policies will be impossible if the company's management cannot rely on timely and precise customer information from all markets.

Most companies have standardized processes such as quality control, cash management and managerial accounting which produce important internal management data. However, these processes may not be appropriate for the new potential markets. Financial accounting, for example, follows different rules in the USA than in Norway. Further, the systems may not be sophisticated enough to allow effective control of international activities. For example, the firm should be able to identify costs per customer, order and product, as well as costs per country- and product-market. Only if the company can determine its financial status and its profitability in any given market at any given time is it well equipped for international competition.

Another problem may arise if relevant information is available to the decision makers but they do not use it. Marketing managers, for example, may think that they know enough about the market without going through all the 'paper' on their desks. Research and development managers may believe they know the customers' problems better than the customers do and therefore ignore market information. If such conditions exist, the company's management will need to change their minds before potential markets can be successfully entered.

Leadership. When a company internationalizes its marketing efforts it will grow. Growth leads to chaos if management systems and personnel do not adapt to each stage of the firm's development. To assess the firm's potential for success, the marketer must check if the company's leaders have the skills to develop or continuously redesign the firm's systems and to manage the organizational learning process. That is, existing leadership processes have to be evaluated together with the personal characteristics of top management.

The dominant management style must be assessed. Relevant questions include: Is management able to motivate personnel to accept the additional stress of doing business in international markets? Will it be flexible enough to account for different norms of leadership behaviour in the societies where the company will have a workforce?

The best management style for leading a firm in international marketing depends to a large extent on the cultural background of personnel. Successful companies in the English-speaking and Scandinavian parts of industrialized nations tend to have a management style that stresses autonomy and entrepreneurship. Formal rules are kept to a minimum, and there is relatively little social distance between people at different levels of the hierarchy. For example, at IKEA, the international Swedish furniture retailer, nobody wears a tie and employees have the right to disregard the management structure when they feel it is necessary to do so. This management style, however, will work only when there is mutual respect among employees at all levels, responsibilities are accepted by each individual, and there is a high degree of trust between personnel and managers.

In other cultures the social and work background is very different. In the romanic countries of Europe, such as in France, Italy or Spain, managers and personnel have highly personalized hierarchical relationships dominated by authority and power. As examples of highly successful companies from these countries show, such as Michelin, the French dominator of the world tyres market, or Ferrero, the Italian candy company, such a different style of management must not make a firm less competitive in international markets.

Many publications have advocated the Japanese style of management as a recipe for global success. As the Culture box describes, there is much myth around Japanese leadership and it can be doubted that copying the Japanese management style would lead to the international success of firms headquartered in other parts of the world. But the success of Japanese companies shows that their management style is well suited to international marketing under social conditions found in Japan's society.

There is a strong relationship between a company's management style and its decision-making processes. When assessing the firm's competitive position, management should determine whether its decision-making processes are designed in a way that allows for timely and flexible responses to opportunities in new market environments. Business decisions are riskier and seem to be more complex in foreign markets. There is less information and it is less certain. In addition, the potential for conflict is increased. For example, in a European champagne-producing firm such as Veuve Cliquot, based in Reims, about to reinforce its business in the US market, the marketing manager may be enthusiastic about the market's size and growth potential. She will try to attract support from all of the firm's managers for serving this market. The national sales managers for France and Germany, the company's main markets so far, however, may worry about production-capacity restrictions. They

CULTURE BOX

The Myth of Japanese Management Style

JAPANESE MANAGEMENT STYLE IS HIGHLY VALUED IN many Western publications. Enthusiastic authors mention as its main elements: bottom-up decision processes involving all members of the company; goals, values and strategies made highly transparent to workers and employees to create motivation and identification; groups as the smallest functional unit, enhancing creativity, communication and responsibility; and a long-term strategically oriented human resource policy aiming for the generalist who has succeeded in many different functions.

In reality, the human resource policy of Japanese companies is based on the principle of seniority. Salary, advancement and fringe benefits predominantly depend on the age of a person. Japanese companies are extremely hierarchically oriented. Status symbols, such as titles and privileges, play a central role for Japanese managers. Collaborators are led in a much more authoritarian way than in Western companies.

People from more hierarchical levels are involved in decision-making processes, indeed, but they do not necessarily have any influence. German workers have more opportunities to effectively influence decisions taken in their companies than their Japanese colleagues. Working in groups has many advantages, but it also diminishes individual initiatives and risk taking. The high level of achievement is not so much due to a higher level of meaningfulness of work in Japanese companies as to a mixture of traditions, group pressures and financial coercion.

The undoubted advantage of Japanese management style is its long-term perspective in personal planning as well as personal development.

Source: Sonnenborn, H.-P. and M. Esser (1991) 'Japan II: Führen in einer fremden Welt – das Beispiel BMW', *HARVARDmanager*, 3, 109–115.

will tend to assure delivery to existing clients by evaluating the US market less optimistically.

Speedy and flexible decision-making processes are desirable. Simply making fast decisions in response to environmental stimuli does not result in immediate action, however. The decision must be implemented. If decisions are based on consensus, the individuals involved are more committed and generally the decisions can be implemented faster. The company's response to a new or changing environment will be more effective.

Decision effectiveness not only depends on consensus, but also on the technical quality of the decision, and the desired learning effect from decision making, that is, the development of technical and managerial skills of personnel. As comparative international studies have shown, there is no one best decision-making style. Processes ranging from highly autocratic to highly participative or democratic can be equally effective, depending on the particular decision situation. Successful managers fit the decision-making process to the situation at hand.

Because objectively similar situations will be subjectively perceived in varying ways across cultures, the problem of choosing an appropriate decision-making style is further complicated in international marketing.

Managers should be able to adapt the decision-making process not only to their own interpretation of the given situation but also to the perceptions of local personnel. What the US manager of a subsidiary in Indonesia perceives as overly authoritarian behaviour may be regarded as weak behaviour by the firm's employees. Similarly, what a German manager may regard as an emotionally based decision may be seen as a bureaucratically correct decision by Italian colleagues.

Operations

In order to assess the firm's competitive position in the most attractive foreign markets, management must determine the current state of its functions and their ability to design and carry out successful operations, that is, their ability to implement an international strategy effectively. In the section on competitor analysis we have already discussed some important factors that should be assessed. Therefore, in the following we will concentrate on some additional points which are particularly important for international marketing.

Marketing. The central question facing the company is whether its products or services can be sold in the most attractive potential markets. The firm's size, profitability and current market position are indicators of the resources it has available for investment in new markets, but they do not guarantee success. What is critical is the ability to develop relationships with customers and other important stakeholders such as intermediaries and a marketing mix which makes the firm's offerings the most attractive in the potential customers' minds.

Low costs are very important to be able to offer attractive prices. But low prices are not the only way for a firm to be successful in international markets. If the firm can clearly differentiate its products from those of competitors in a way that matches the needs of customers better than other product offerings, it can justify higher prices. In other words, marketing know-how can have a decisive impact on a company's competitive position when the product is equivalent in technical quality to competing products and production costs are higher. For example, perfumes can be produced in parts of the world where production costs are far less than in France. The technically testable quality of such perfumes is equal to the quality of French products. But nevertheless, French companies have acquired so much specific marketing know-how that their brands are successful competitors in the global perfume markets.

To get an accurate idea of a product's sales potential in a new market, managers must ask: What are the benefits our product provides to customers and are any substitutes available? Product technology affects customers' perceptions of the relative benefits provided by the product compared to competitive offerings. 'Too little' technology may result in problems for the marketer. For example, Hirsch Bracelets wanted to sell their leather watch straps to major watchmakers in Japan such as Citizen or the Hatori Group. The Austrian managers in research and development, as well as production, were convinced their product had the highest levels of tearing and perspiration resistance, as well as colour constancy and anti-allergy features, in the world. All of their European and American customers so far had been satisfied. But Japanese watchmakers required much higher technical specifications (already provided by the local suppliers of metal straps). For three years Hirsch's Japanese sales manager tried to convince potential Japanese customers that their specifications were exaggerated and had no practical value. During that time the firm did not sell one strap. Only when the company's management understood that its product had to meet customers' expectations, not vice versa, did sales start to grow.

But a company also needs to avoid putting 'too much' technology into the product. The most well-known PC makers such as Compaq or Hewlett-Packard face the problem that their PCs are too sophisticated, and as a consequence too expensive, for the great majority of potential customers looking for machines simply to play games or to use Internet services.

To assess the firm's potential for offering highly valued benefits to customers in the attractive markets, management can analyse the company's current operations by using of a modified version of the value chain already mentioned above. In this approach, a product or service is viewed as a bundle of related performances, and its production is viewed as a bundle of processes. The company splits its product or service into individual performances and processes, then determines what it does best or better than its competitors. For example, do the greatest strengths of a company operating in the style furniture market reside in its early determination of attractive market segments, its design true to the style, the production of reliable furniture, promotion, distribution, or customer service? Companies that concentrate on their core competencies, offering those parts of the value chain that they do best, can develop and defend a competitive advantage.

Selva, a Bolzano (Italy) based company in the high-style furniture business, for example, when analysing their core competencies concerning customer benefits in European markets, found that their strengths resided mainly in marketing activities, that is, defining international customer segments, designing attractively styled furniture, and promoting and distributing it. All production activities can usually be done better by firms specializing in certain processes. Zegna, another Italian firm marketing top-end menswear, is successful in doing the contrary. They manage most parts of the value chain, not only putting together their own clothes, at plants in Italy, Spain and Switzerland, but also spinning the yarn and weaving the cotton, cashmere and wool fabrics that go into garments. Zegna has established 30 own shops in top locations around the world, along with about 120 closely managed in-store boutiques. Zegna's core competency lies in the ability to manage the complexity of the value chain in a way that satisfies the expectations of an exclusive customer segment.[9]

Production processes, on the other hand, may involve a high level of expertise and may provide attractive customer benefits which give the firm a strong competitive position. Voest Alpine Industrial Services, an Austrian company, is one example. It has chosen to offer global training for managers and workers in new steel mills, or in mills with productivity problems that require additional training. The engineering, financing, management and maintenance parts of the value chain are done by other companies, which are better equipped to provide these services, but are pleased to find a partner who takes over the training function, which requires complex technical, cultural, educational and managerial know-how.

The rate of innovation and the speed of R&D processes may also be important in matching the success factors in a market. If, for example, Japanese competitors launch new car models every year and it takes them only three years to develop a new model, a car maker who wants to enter the Japanese home market successfully will have to find a way to come up to the customers' expectations created by the Japanese suppliers.

Production. The company's production must have enough capacity to properly handle orders expected from the new markets or must be able to find a way to outsource them to reliable suppliers. If additional investment in machinery, equipment or storage capacity is needed, the timing of market entry is affected. So, too, is the cost per unit produced – it may increase because of higher investment costs, but it may also decrease because of gains in productivity.

For service firms, capacity problems may arise through inability to acquire sufficiently skilled personnel in the numbers needed to ensure service quality or because of a lack of available locations. For example, the competitive position of gas distributing firms such as Netherlands-based Royal Dutch Shell or London-based BP in former communist countries of Central Europe very much depends on their ability to acquire the best locations for gas stations. Again, the competitive position in the attractive market can be endangered by delayed entry or personnel acquisition and training costs.

Before management decides to enter a new market it must make sure that the firm's production costs allow for competitive pricing. Low production costs may stem from low wages, low taxes or high productivity. Manufacturers from highly industrialized countries in Europe and North America encounter problems in this regard compared with producers from East Asia. For example, German employees only work 30 hours per week in real terms, and Swedish companies have to bear high taxes. Both have to emphasize substantial productivity improvements to stay competitive in global markets.

Finance. Without appropriate financial management, effective international marketing cannot occur. The company must have access to the funds needed to finance the increasing working capital or to invest in a promotion campaign in the potential markets. The most important aspect of financial management from the standpoint of international marketing is the degree to which top management is willing to make substantial investments that will not yield immediate return. Thus, Austrian Zumtobel staff AG, one of the three leading providers of light systems in the world, for example, decided to open sales offices in a number of promising markets, even though it would take up to five years for the investments to become profitable. To take such a long-term view the company must have healthy financial statements, a reasonable debt-to-equity ratio, sufficient cash flow, and consistent growth in revenues and profits.

International marketing places a greater strain on the firm's financial resources than domestic marketing does. For example, the government of Saudi Arabia charges a non-refundable fee or bond of up to USD 100,000 for the right to bid on certain large projects. The firm must either generate the necessary cash flow or be able to finance international activities from external sources. When the company's financial resources are limited, it must recognize that it cannot enter markets in which financing of activities via bank loans is impossible and cooperation with local business partners is not feasible. A company with a substantial cash flow can choose from a wider array of potential markets. It can afford to look at those markets as investments with different payoff periods and varying potential returns.

Personnel. Skilled personnel are a significant factor for a company's competitive position in international markets. Lack of personnel with the necessary language skills and cultural knowledge is often a major obstacle for small and medium-sized firms that wish to market their products in other parts of the world, even when the products are well suited to the potential markets. Many US and also European firms based in the major language areas (English, French, German) lack personnel with foreign-language skills. They tend to select markets in which they can communicate easily. This is one reason why, for example, Austria conducts about 40 per cent of its trade with neighbouring West Germany compared to about 4 per cent with France and 3 per cent with the UK, whereas Belgium, split into a French- and a Flemish-speaking part, conducts about 20 per cent of its trade with Germany compared to about 17 per cent with France and 15 per cent with the Netherlands. Although this approach is understandable from a practical point of view, it does not necessarily result in optimal market choices.

Another potential constraint is lack of experience in non-domestic markets, coupled with lack of knowledge about how to conduct business in those markets. Finding initial business contacts, closing a deal, and delivering the product or service may seem to be either insurmountable hurdles or, at the other extreme, without any difficulties, 'similar to the home market'. Both attitudes are dangerous.

Even when personnel with the necessary skills and experience are available to contact customers and close deals, the problems of providing training, technical assistance or maintenance services to customers may remain. Intermediaries are often unable to perform these tasks satisfactorily. If the firm does not have qualified personnel to perform these services, it will be forced to refrain from entering markets where the services are needed.

All of these problems could be overcome by adding new staff with appropriate skills or by engaging outside consultants. But most smaller companies are unwilling to invest in new personnel before they are assured of success in the new market; the risk seems too great. Consultants can help companies enter foreign markets and establish business contacts there, but the company will still lack skilled personnel to conduct business in the new markets on a regular basis.

The attitude of personnel towards the company's plans for serving new international markets is crucial to its competitive position. Training in language and cultural issues can be provided to those who need it. But the company must have enough people who are willing to undergo training if it is to take advantage of international opportunities. In Europe many employees, despite well-developed language skills, are unwilling to leave their own country for an extended period. They are reluctant to exchange a familiar environment for a strange one. Only high salaries can motivate them to spend some time in a foreign market. This attitude acts as a major constraint on companies' international activities.

If employees have marked prejudices concerning specific markets, or if they are not ready to cooperate with people from other regions, the company may have to refrain from entering such markets. An Indian company with mostly Hindu employees could be forced, for example, not to do any business with Islamic countries in order to avoid conflicts inside the company.

Figure 8.8 · Determination of a Firm's Competitive Position
Step 4: Distinctive Competencies

When the strengths and weaknesses of the firm concerning the success factors in a market have been assessed, their comparison to the strengths and weaknesses of major competitors leads to the determination of distinctive competencies.

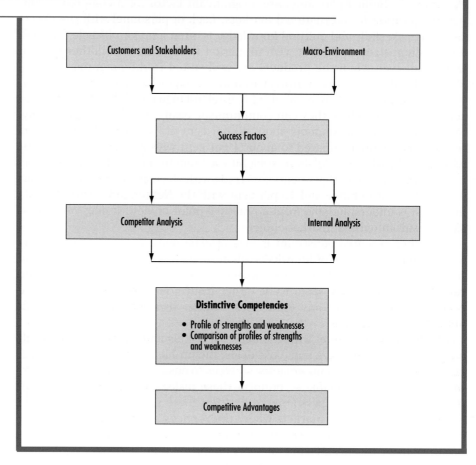

Determination of Distinctive Competencies

Having finished the assessment of the firm's characteristics related to the success factors in the most attractive potential markets, the marketer can establish profiles of the company's and its major competitors' strengths and weaknesses which can be compared to each other (see Figure 8.8).

Profile of Strengths and Weaknesses

A profile of strengths and weaknesses lists the success factors and indicates how well the existing capabilities and resources of a firm fit them. Figure 8.9 gives an example of a strengths and weaknesses profile of a competitor in the metallurgical engineering business in an LDC market. This profile

---

Figure 8.9 PROFILE OF A MAJOR COMPETITOR'S STRENGTHS AND WEAKNESSES

Competitor: Lurgi									Market: Angola

	Evaluation								
Success Factors	**Strength**								**Weakness**
References	1	②	3	4	5	6	7	8	9
Counterpurchase capability	1	2	3	4	5	6	7	⑧	9
Access to cheap loans	1	2	3	4	5	6	⑦	8	9
Relations to government	1	2	3	④	5	6	7	8	9
Training facilities	1	2	3	4	5	6	7	⑧	9
Project management experience	1	②	3	4	5	6	7	8	9
Mobility of personnel	1	2	③	4	5	6	7	8	9

The marketer must evaluate to what extent each of the major competitors possesses the success factors in a market segment.

reveals that the competitor can provide a number of references, has easy access to cheap loans, and enjoys high mobility of personnel. On the other hand, the counterpurchase capabilities which are important for market success and relations with government are less well developed. Importance weights for the different success factors may be derived from the form shown in Table 8.2. They provide additional information about the appropriateness of the structure of a competitor's and the company's capabilities and resources.

As Figure 8.10 shows, ideally the company's characteristics and the success factors in a market fit together perfectly (Case 1). For example, the Nigerian government may be interested in attracting communications-equipment industries, which would bring in new technologies, utilize local materials and allow Nigerians to move quickly into upper-level positions, at the same time that a US supplier who is able to provide those benefits seeks to market its know-how in the construction of turnkey plants for communications equipment in developing countries.

At times, however, a company's characteristics are not relevant to a particular market. For example, the sophisticated distribution know-how of a producer of frozen foods such as Eskimo-Iglo, a daughter firm of Unilever, may not be relevant in a market that lacks a sophisticated transportation and storage infrastructure, such as the Ukraine (Case 2). On the other hand, even if the Brazilian market for atomic power-generation plants appears to present a major opportunity for a French firm such as Electricité de France, EDF, the firm will not be able to respond to the opportunity if it lacks technical personnel who speak Portuguese which is a success factor in this market (Case 3). In short, a market opportunity cannot be translated into a specific business opportunity unless the company's characteristics match the most important success factors in the market. Where the match is strong, the company possesses a strength; where it is weak the company has a weakness or the firm's characteristic is not relevant to the market.

Figure 8.10 THE FIT BETWEEN A COMPANY'S CHARACTERISTICS AND THE SUCCESS FACTORS IN A MARKET SEGMENT

Before a company decides to pursue a market opportunity, it needs to determine whether it has the necessary company strengths to turn that opportunity into a viable business. The line that runs from the lower left to the upper right represents a match between company characteristics and success factors in the market.

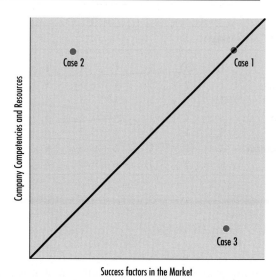

Case 1 A US turnkey plant supplier for communications equipment and the Nigerian government, which is interested in improving the country's communications infrastructure with locally manufactured equipment.

Case 2 A European producer of frozen foods with sophisticated distribution know-how and the Ukrainian market, which lacks a sufficiently reliable transportation and storage system.

Case 3 The Brazilian market for atomic power-generation equipment and a French manufacturer, which lacks technical personnel who speak Portuguese.

Comparison of Profiles of Strengths and Weaknesses

To possess certain strengths is not enough to be successful in international markets. If major competitors are equally able to match the same success factors, a distinction in the market becomes more difficult. Therefore, the profile of a company's strengths and weaknesses has to be compared with the profiles of its major competitors. Hopefully this will lead to a list of success factors which the firm matches better than its competitors. The capabilities and resources of the firm which allow this better match are called distinctive competencies. The marketer can rely on them in the development of a strategy. Apple Computer, for example, was well known for its superior know-how in the development of user-friendly computer surfaces. User-friendliness is a success factors in all markets where the personal computer is mainly used for visualization purposes. Apple has built its globally successful strategy on this distinctive competency.

SUMMARY

To assess its competitive position in the most attractive markets, a company must conduct a thorough analysis of its strengths and weaknesses compared to major competitors in those markets. To keep time and costs at the lowest potential level, the analysis will have to be focused on the success factors, that is, on only those resources and capabilities of a company which directly relate to the fulfilment of aspirations and expectations of customers and other important stakeholders in the most attractive segments of the most attractive country-markets.

First, the success factors in each market have to be determined. Depending on the specific market situation, they may be parts of corporate policy, corporate strategy, management systems, and operations of the firm and its major competitors. Then the resources and capabilities of those competitors related to the success factors must be assessed to determine their major strengths and weaknesses. Based on the following internal analysis, management can compare the strengths and weaknesses of the competitors with those of their firm. Competitors may be stronger or weaker on some of the success factors.

From the comparison a list of distinctive competencies of each of the major players per market segment emerges. It indicates the firm's competitive position, that is, its potential for success and failure. The existence of a distinctive competency does not automatically mean, however, that the company has an advantage over its major competitors. Distinctive competencies only result in competitive advantages if they can be transferred into unique customer benefits that the customers perceive as attractive and can be sustained over some period of time. The next chapter will discuss the basic decisions to be taken to build and sustain competitive advantages in a global business environment.

DISCUSSION QUESTIONS

1. What specific criteria can a manager use to determine whether a company has the potential to be a successful international marketer?
2. Discuss the usefulness of deriving success factors in a market from the aspirations and expectations of customers and major stakeholders as well as present and future opportunities and threats in a market.
3. Why is top management's commitment crucial to the firm's success in international marketing?
4. Describe the position in the value chain, the configuration, diversification and competitive behaviour of an internationally operating firm. Gather information from all sources available to you, and indicate what sources you have found.
5. How do the information system, planning, control and resource allocation affect a company's potential to succeed in the global marketplace?
6. What role does the company's ability to provide product-related services play in determining its potential for international marketing success?
7. What elements of research and development influence a firm's potential for success in global markets?
8. What role does the cost structure of production play in a company's ability to compete internationally?
9. 'Personnel aren't really important in determining whether we should go into a non-domestic market. After all, we can hire someone in that country.' Do you agree or disagree with this statement? Why?
10. Find an internationally operating firm and interview them about how they determine the company's competitive position in international markets.

Additional Readings

Barney, J. (1991) 'Firm Resources and Sustained Competitive Advantage', *Journal of Management*, 17(1), 99–120.

Day, G.S. and R. Wensley (1988) 'Assessing Advantage: A Framework for Diagnosing Competitive Superiority', *Journal of Marketing*, 52 (April), 1–20.

Chernatony, L. de, K. Daniels, and G. Johnson (1993) 'A Cognitive Perspective on Managers' Perceptions of Competition', *Journal of Marketing Management*, 9, 373–381.

Hunt, S.D. and R.M. Morgan (1995) 'The Comparative Advantage Theory of Competition', *Journal of Marketing*, 59 (April), 1–15.

Mahoney, J.T. (1995) 'The Management of Resources and the Resource of Management,' *Journal of Business Research,* 33, 91–101.

Prahalad, C.K. and G. Hamel (1990) 'The Core Competence of the Corporation', *Harvard Business Review*, May–June, 79–91.

Stalk, G., Ph. Evans and L.E. Shulman (1992) 'Competing on Capabilities: The New Rules of Corporate Strategy', *Harvard Business Review*, March–April, 57–69.

Notes

[1] Yavas, U., E. Babakus, and N. Delener (1991) 'Family Purchasing Roles in Saudi Arabia', Working paper.

[2] AP-Dow Jones News Service (1996) 'Allied Domecq Posts Fall in Profit on Lower Sales', *The Wall Street Journal Europe*, 15 May, p. 3.

[3] 'BASF, DuPont Plan Joint Venture in Asia To Manufacture Nylon', *The Wall Street Journal Europe*, 11 April 1996, p. 3.

[4] Kupfer, A. (1996) 'Why AT&T Is Taking a Flier on Satellite Television', *Fortune*, Vol. 133, 19 February, p. 26.

[5] Siddall, P., K. Willey, and J. Tavares (1992) 'Building a Transnational Organization for BP Oil', *Long Range Planning*, 25(1), 37–45.

[6] 'Single market, single-minded', *The Economist*, 4 May 1996, p. 64.

[7] Mitchener, B. and M. Marshall (1996) 'KHD Debacle Thrusts Supervisory Boards Back Into the Hot Seat', *The Wall Street Journal Europe*, 30 May, 30, pp. 1,7.

[8] Müller St. (1991) 'Die Psyche des Managers als Determinante des Exporterfolges: Eine kulturvergleichende Studie zur Auslandsorientierung von Managern aus 6 Ländern', Stuttgart: M&P Verlag.

[9] Rossant, J. (1996) 'Is That a Zegna You're Wearing?', *Business Week*, 4 March, pp. 84f.

Case Study
FASTI

When Harald Körber, director for development and production at FASTI – a manufacturer of peripheral equipment for plastics processing machinery, located in the heart of the Tyrolean Alps in Austria – drove home from his office on that evening in September 1997 he knew that he had just taken responsibility for a decision process which could be crucial for the future success of the company. During a top management meeting he had stressed the importance of East Asian markets to the further growth of the company. A great deal of global plastics and plastic products production was located in this part of the world. East Asian manufacturers not only produced the greatest share of qualitatively and technologically less sophisticated products, they also had started taking a growing share of high-tech-products. Processing PET, for example, demanded high quality drying of PET resin as well as complete drying of the production tools. For both, sophisticated drying and dehumidifying equipment was needed. Local presence in East Asian markets seemed to be of great importance to FASTI in its effort to become one of the major suppliers to extrusion blowing and injection moulding machinery manufacturers. Due to the latest information concerning the economic development of Japan and the NICs, some managers present at the meeting had expressed their doubts about the attractiveness of those markets. But the owners of the company had listened carefully to the ideas Harald Körber expressed and asked him to prepare a report until the next meeting. Now he drove through the beautiful landscape but his mind was absent, considering the development of the company and the latest news about potential East Asian markets.

Source: This case was prepared by Hans Muehlbacher, Professor of Business Administration at the Institut fuer Handel, Absatz und Marketing of Leopold-Franzens-Universitat Innsbruck, Austria.

The author would like to thank FASTI GmbH for the support of the project. Copyright © 1998, Hans Muehlbacher.

THE COMPANY

In 1991, Mr. Farrag and Mr. Stipsits founded a company for the development, production and sales of peripheral equipment for plastics processing machinery in the Austrian province of Vorarlberg. Abbreviating their names they called the company FASTI. Fast expansion caused a need for more space. In 1996, FASTI moved to Hopfgarten, a village in the Tyrolean Alps.

The World of Plastics Processing

The plastics industry has been continually growing during the last decade with high potential for further growth. To stay successful in this industry competitors need to become ever faster in improving the quality of their products as well as their production processes. Price competition in the global market and rising energy prices cause a race after diminishing energy needs in production.

The way from plastics resins to finished products is basically the same whether those products are bottles for Coke or gas tanks for Mitsubishi cars. The granules must be dried, that is humidity must be minimized and the material be brought to a processing temperature of 60 to 180 degrees Celsius. Then, the resin is knead to a viscous mass in an extruder (similar to a mincer). By this process the plastic is further heated. Depending on the finished product – hollow bodies, such as bottles or cans, or non-blowable forms, such as covers or screens – two different types of machinery are used for manufacturing them: injection moulding machinery or extrustion blowing machinery. In injection moulding the hot viscous plastic is pressed from the extruder through an appropriate mask into a water cooled die where the plastic solidifies into the final product. In extrusion blowing the hot viscous plastic mass is pressed from the extruder through a mask in a way to form a kind of tube. This hot tube is placed between two half moulds which form the negative of the intended final product's shape. The two half moulds are pressed against each other and cooled while compressed air pushes the hot plastic tube onto the mould. The plastic tube takes the form of the mould and stiffens in a few seconds. Then the two halves of the mould are taken away. The final product comes out.

Both technologies, injection moulding as well as extrusion blowing need a number of peripheral equipment in addition to the moulding and blowing machines. Such equipment contains driers to minimize the humidity of the resin, air conditioning equipment for drying the inside of the plastic machines, refrigerating equipment to improve the volume and quality of production, equipment for cold water production, and conveyor systems. FASTI has focused on the development of driers and chillers.

Product Lines

In 1997, 28 people at FASTI generated total sales of ATS 67 million (about USD5.5 million). Since its creation the company had experienced yearly sales growth rates of more than 45 per cent. The company's vision was to counteract the tremendous waste of energy in the traditional plastics industry by developing and marketing highly energy efficient and environmentally friendly peripheral equipment. FASTI's business domain was defined as to help plastic manufacturers improve the quality and increase the quantity of their products at reduced energy consumption by the application of advanced technology for granule drying, compressed air cooling, and energy efficient dry air production.

The company had four product lines:

↔ *MSP . . . Mould Sweat Protectors*   In warm and humid climate the cooled tools of injection moulding and extrusion blowing machines suffer from condensation. The sweat water creates spots on the products which diminish their quality or even make them unusable. Mould sweat protectors allow customers to ensure the best suited coolant temperature for production all over the year.

↔ *ERD . . . Economy Resin Driers*   Extrusion blowing machines produce hot air for blowing purposes. This dry air is used by a patented FASTI process for drying granules. In 1997, FASTI resin driers consumed up to 60 per cent less energy than conventional driers.

They were highly flexible and needed very little maintenance.

↔ *CAC . . . Compressed Air Chillers*
Compressed air chillers are important for extrusion blowers who want to increase the production capacity of their blowing machines. The normally hot compressed air used in blowing is replaced by chilled compressed air (−35 degrees centigrade). By this change in the production process the product is not only cooled from outside but also from inside, resulting in a greatly reduced production cycle time. Compressed air chillers generally pay off in 6 to 12 months.

↔ *AAC . . . Atmospheric Air Chillers*   In 1997, those special coolers were under development. Because of their controlled output temperature they allow foil manufacturers to increase production capacity of their machines and to simultaneously improve the quality of their products.

Objectives

FASTI's core strategy contained a decision to keep the work force at a minimum. Only activities important to total product quality and know how development were to be kept inside the firm. Consequently, FASTI had formed teams for product development, final product control, marketing and customer services. The marketing team contained a small number of sales people who cooperated with local representatives in Europe and the USA. The customer services team globally installed, started up, and maintained FASTI equipment. Production at the firm's premises in Hopfgarten exclusively focused on prototypes and small series. Larger scale production was outsourced to production partners in Austria and Germany.

FASTI planned to double total sales until 1999 at proportionally growing profits by intensifying cooperation with production partners, increasing the number of served customers, and by increasing market share through more intensive business relationships with attractive customers. Asia's share of total sales was expected to be 40 per cent at that time. Market expansion had to be financed through the company's cash flow. Therefore, a careful choice of new markets had to be made.

The Market

Customers

FASTI's operating environment contained three types of customers: manufacturers of plastics machinery, producers of plastic granules, and manufacturers of plastic products. Manufacturers of plastics machinery need peripheral equipment to be able to provide their own machines with dried granules, to keep them reliably working under varying climatic conditions, and to increase the production capacity of their machines (through coolers). Because of their potentially high order volumes FASTI considered producers of plastics machinery as their main customers. Those customers wanted to get the entire peripheral equipment for their machines from one supplier. The equipment had to be flexibly adapted to the size and capacity of the machines. It was not only expected to reach the given technical specifications (concerning drying, cooling or other effects) but also to be energy efficient and to be easily integrated into the blowing or moulding machines. Maximum expected delivery time was 8 weeks. Additionally, suppliers were expected to offer project specific terms of payment, perfect technical documentation, and a clean and reliable installation. The leading suppliers in the industry also offered equipment with a rather low level of maintenance service needs.

Producers of plastic resins need drying equipment to take off remaining humidity from their product in order to sell it to manufacturers of plastic products as predried high quality granules. They expect highly energy efficient drying processes, variable drying capacities, simple handling, little maintenance and delivery in a maximum of 10 weeks. Plastic products manufacturers use peripheral equipment for drying and conveying granules, for securing constant climatic conditions during production processes, and for increasing the production capacity of their machines. Equipment suppliers need to prove the potential increase in production capacity and final produce quality at decreasing costs. The equipment must be quickly adaptable to changing production runs. Plastic product manufacturers not only expect simple handling of the equipment supported by perfect technical documentation and a minimum need of maintenance, but also simple detection and removal of defects, direct support through a supplier hot-line, fast maintenance services and fast delivery of spar parts. Delivery time should not exceed 6 weeks.

Competitors

The global market of high technical quality peripheral equipment for plastics machinery has been dominated by some well established European competitors. The Asian market for granule dryers has been characterized by a great number of local manufacturers producing small equipment (up to 100 litres of granules) with little technical sophistication. This kind of equipment is well suited for standard applications, and is low priced because of low local wages. European suppliers have dominated the Asian market for drying equipment of more technically advanced plastics machinery.

Italy-based Piovan (with a workforce of about 250 people) had more than 20 years of experience in manufacturing drying containers. The fast expanding firm possessed long-term contracts with (European) plastics machinery manufacturers such as Husky. It was able to offer entire equipment systems (drying, cooling, conveying). With its modern manufacturing equipment, low production costs and high visibility in the market, Piovan was the best established competitor in the Asian resin drying market. If there were any relative weaknesses of that competitor it was the high energy consumption of their dryers and diminished flexibility due to increasing company size.

The products of another important competitor, Germany's Somos (with more than 100 people), were considered the Mercedes of drying equipment. The company's long-term experience in resin drying has been the basis for developing excellent equipment with highly attractive design. Modern production facilities and high customer awareness contributed to Somo's success. The price level of the products was according to their high level positioning. Relative weaknesses of the firm may have been the high energy consumption of their dryers as well as less flexibility to varying demands because of the company's size.

In 1997, FASTI's major competitors in the Asian plastics tool drying market were Piovan which had imitated FASTI's condensation drying principle, and Sweden-based Munters which applied adsorption drying technology. Munters was a well established manufacturer of a large line of attractively designed and fully developed dryers. Due to their technology Munters dryers were about 20 per cent less expensive than FASTI's, but they consumed significantly more energy and were more expensive in maintenance.

Cooling plastic products during the production process to increase the speed of production was a rather new technological solution. There existed no major competitor with a reliably working cooling system able to chill extrusion blown products with dry air at −35 centigrades. To increase production by up to 40 per cent applying that technology, specific know how in drying, cooling, aerodynamics and process engineering for plastic products were needed.

Austrian Eisbär and German Sulzer were the only competitors offering systems for improved extrusion of foils through adjusted cooling. Eisbär had a longstanding experience in manufacturing peripheral equipment for plastic foil production. Their products were characterized by operational ease, good documentation and highly constant air temperature under varying operational conditions. However, Eisbär's system was rather complex, expensive and voluminous. It was not easily adaptable to varying customer needs. Nevertheless the system was partially underdimensioned for the hot and humid climate in parts of Southeast Asia. Reliable air cooling could not be guaranteed in those regions of the world.

Sulzer was a well established manufacturer of peripheral equipment for plastic foil production, known for its short delivery time (2–3 weeks). The company produced equipment of similar size compared to FASTI's AAC products. However, the product line was relatively limited in number of products as well as potential applications (small volumes of cooling air, limited range of temperature). It contained only two small coolers with some technical problems concerning temperature regulation at different volumes of chilled air.

Distributors

An important stakeholder group were distributors, some of which had also taken over customer service responsibility. In Asian markets those distribution partners worked on commission. Because most globally important manufacturers of high quality plastics machinery were located in Europe and the US, distribution partners mainly served plastic granules producers and plastic products manufacturers. In parallel, they acted as representatives of other firms (but not of competitors of FASTI products).

Distributors expected to get attractive commission. Enquiries at the manufacturer's headquarters should be quickly answered and given dates of delivery should be exactly kept. Distributors wanted to get detailed sales and service documentation, fast technical support from the manufacturer, and continual training of their workforce.

Other Important Stakeholders

Beside customers, competitors, and distributors, FASTI had to consider a number of stakeholders who considerably influenced the company's potential success. In Asian markets systems suppliers and planners designed production systems, bought the needed plastics machinery and peripheral equipment, tested the system and supplied it to their customers. Because those planners played a highly influential role in the decision which suppliers were chosen, machinery and equipment manufacturers needed to carefully manage relationships with them. They must be able to provide provable specifications, informative documentation and planning support as well as attractive margins. Quick response to enquiries tended to be decisive for the establishment of a first contact and resulting orders.

FASTI's own suppliers were also of growing importance to the company's business. The fast increasing amount of outsourced production and the rising pressure of customers on shorter delivery time as well as punctuality made the suppliers' readiness for delivery and their delivery on time a major success factor. To simplify the task for the suppliers, FASTI needed to exactly specify their orders, to provide unequivocal construction plans and to give realistic delivery time instructions. Payment in time was an important incentive for FASTI's suppliers to keep their obligations.

Finally, banks and other financial institutions played an important role for FASTI in marketing to Asian customers. In those markets payment may be delayed up to six months. Therefore, a small equipment manufacturer like FASTI had to prefinance its substantial costs of development and production through external sources. Those financiers demanded securities or interesting rates of capital return based on a positive development of the company's value.

POTENTIAL EAST ASIAN MARKETS

Harald Körber planned to consider the most economically developed countries of East Asia, that is Japan, Singapore, South Korea and Taiwan, and – because of its enormous potential – The People's Republic of China (including Hong Kong), in his analysis of the most attractive markets for FASTI. Those countries all had a well developed plastics industry on the way to become global market share leaders.

Japan

In 1997, Japan – a country with 124 million inhabitants and one of the highest GDPs per capita in the world – experienced another year of economic difficulties in a row. The economy stagnated, at best. In the last years, the government had run high budget deficits which it tried to overcome by an increase of value added and other taxes. In reaction, consumers diminished their spending, investments decreased, unemployment rose. In the early 1990s, the banking system had become fragile because of high amounts of dubious credits. The financial crisis of some important economic partners in Southeast Asia led to additional problems for exporting firms. The country's currency, the Yen, had been decreasing in value and now could only be kept from plunging by concerted actions of the biggest industrialized nations' central banks. Forecasts of economic development were less than optimistic, reducing the stability of the country's well established political system.

Japanese customers are very demanding concerning product quality and delivery. To establish a durable customer relationship customer enquiries must be quickly answered, expectations meticulously satisfied, and after-sales-service must be absolutely reliable. Excellent infrastructure and tense networks of potential distribution and service partners exist. It might be difficult, however, to become accepted as part of such a network. Suppliers being able to fulfill customer expectations have a rather strong competitive position. Success in Japan is an important reference for entering other country-markets in East and Southeast Asia.

The demand for plastics machinery in 1998 was estimated to reach about 12 900 machines, 50 per cent of which were destined for customers in Japan. In the field of PET processing, the introduction of the new 350ml PET bottle was expected to significantly increase the demand for stretch-blowing machinery, for example. The yearly sales volume of blowing machinery for the Japanese home market was about 9 billion Yen (USD1 = 140 Yen). Cost reduction and environmental protection played an important role in plastics production processes.

Singapore

Singapore is a republic with about 2.9 million inhabitants, 78 per cent of which are Chinese, 14 per cent Malaysian, 7 per cent Indian and Pakistani. In 1997, there were about 350 000 foreigners living in the country which had a population tensity of 4.535 inhabitants per square kilometre. Singapore has one of the biggest deep harbours in the world (the second largest container port in the world) and one of the most important hubs in the area. It is widely known as a centre for conferences, trade exhibitions, and tourism. Singapore is an extremely busy place of international transit trade which is highly rated as a central point for doing business with the neighbouring ASEAN countries. Because firms based in Singapore have been very active in directly investing in those neighbouring countries (USD44.9 billion in 1996), Singapore also is an interesting base for market entry in ASEAN countries. The country is known for its more highly developed environmental consciousness compared to neighbouring countries in this region of the world.

Up to 1997, Singapore had recorded balance of payment and national budget surpluses, had gathered foreign currency reserves of about USD80 billion (7.3 months of import coverage), had one of the highest saving rates in the world (51 per cent of GNP), and a low inflation rate of around 2 per cent. In 1996, Singapore experienced a slight economic downturn because of the crisis in the global electronics industry (electronics production amounted to 50 per cent of Singapore's industrial output). The East Asian financial crisis starting in 1997 hit the country to a certain extent. The Singapore dollar experienced a devaluation of up to 26 per cent against the US dollar, but was revalued against the currencies of neighbouring countries. In addition, the forest fires in Indonesia which darkened the skies of Singapore for months reduced tourism income by estimated USD60 million. Nevertheless, the growth rate of GDP in 1997 was expected to reach nearly 8 per cent. For 1998, growth expectations of GDP were much lower, about 2.5 to 4 per cent. Although shrinking exports to neighbouring countries were expected to be offset by increased trade with the USA and the EU, the recession in Singapore's ASEAN partners was expected to hit the country's tourism as well as foreign demand. Loss of dubious credits, termination of projects, and the loss of customers going out of the market were forecast to end up with bankruptcy of firms based in Singapore.

In the first half of the 1990s, the country's plastics industry had been characterized by a substantial amount of plastics processing, in particular for the local electrical and electronics industry. There had been no important manufacturers of plastics machinery, but a number of plastics machinery importers. Their international sourcing had created fierce competition among potential suppliers. Importers substituted more expensive suppliers wherever they could. The market volume was below USD40 million. Singapore was the place where two important trade shows for the industry were planned to take place: 'Plastics Technology Asia '98' and 'AseanPlas Asia '99'.

South Korea

With is 46 millions inhabitants and a total volume of international trade representing about USD250 billion in 1996, Korea had reached the level of an industrialized nation. The country was the third largest supplier of semiconductors and the location of the fourth biggest automotive industry in the world. However, high international trade deficits and high external debts (about USD160 billion) made the country's economy sensitive to changes in currency value. When the financial crisis swept Southeast Asia in 1997, Korea's industry was terribly hit. Profits of the big industrial conglomerates shrank by up to 90 per cent. Eight of those conglomerates collapsed financially. Investments in production systems and machinery diminished by up to 40 per cent, depending on the industry. Due to rising interest rates, budget cuts, and price increases of imported goods, a further reduction of investments by the same percentage amount was forecast for 1998.

Because of Korea's strong dependence on imports of production technology, machinery

imports were relatively less affected (—20 per cent). They were expected to recover as soon as the economic reforms negotiated by the Korean government and the International Monetary Fund would begin to stabilize the country's economy. In 1997, the yearly market volume of plastics machinery was about USD75 million. It stagnated at that level because of the country's financial difficulties and the economic turmoil of most industries. Competition in Korea was limited in number and aggressiveness. None of the internationally leading suppliers of peripheral equipment dominated the market. Foreign direct investments had been made easier by the liberalization of the Korean capital market. But the extent to which foreign investors would take advantage from that opportunity was expected to depend on the Korean government's ability to stabilize the country's economy by disentangling politics, big industry, and banking.

Taiwan

Taiwan's GDP had grown by 5.4 per cent in 1996 and by 6.7 per cent in 1997. The country's GDP per capita reached an impressive level of USD12 838 in that year and further increased to USD13 233 in 1997. Inflation (0.9 per cent) and unemployment (2.7 per cent) rates were low compared to neighbouring countries. While those neighbours struggled with their financial crises or the negative impact of those crises on their economies, Taiwan stayed rather unimpacted. The country based its success on high foreign currency reserves (about USD90 billion), no external debts, and a democratic political system with strongly established legal control mechanisms.

Taiwan's industry production grew by 7 per cent in 1997. Taiwan-based firms had been very important investors in the People's Republic of China, in Vietnam, Malaysia, the Philippines and Thailand. They had established production facilities in those countries for exports to the USA and the EU. The Taiwanese headquarters partly delivered product components, but most importantly machinery and peripheral equipment. The currency devaluations in those countries helped Taiwanese companies increasing their export opportunities to the highly industrialized markets.

Taiwan's Plastics Industry Association contains more than 2000 members. They manufacture all kinds of plastic products from tubes, films, foils and sanitary products to containers, packaging material, household products and construction materials. In the years up to 1996 the industry's production volume averaged about USD11.8 billion per year.

In 1997, Taiwan counted about 100 producers of plastics machinery. Their average size of workforce was below 100. Those companies mainly manufactured injection moulding and extrusion blowing machinery at a quality standard below European competitors. Sales of injection moulding machinery totalled USD30 million in 1996. Sales of extrusion blowing machinery reached a total of USD10 million.

The People's Republic of China

In 1997, the People's Republic of China had about 1.5 billion inhabitants. With yearly growth rates of GDP around 10 per cent since 1979 and a rather stable political situation, the country was considered as the market of the future. The special economic zones in the South, the Shanghai area as well as the lower Yangtse river area had become world leading regions for the production of textiles, toys and other products of light industry. In the Shanghai area one per cent of China's population created five per cent of the country's GDP. The GDP per capita in greater Shanghai was by far the highest in the country. It was expected to reach about USD5000 in the year 2000. In 1997, three fifths of China's growth of GDP came from exports and foreign investment. In the Shanghai area 40 per cent of the local work force was active in firms with foreign capital.

Hong Kong had been taken back from the UK by the People's Republic in 1997. Despite some insecurities concerning the future political development Hong Kong's economic situation had not significantly changed. To the contrary, the now open access to the mainland had improved the region's position as a gate to the vast Chinese market. The economy grew by 5.7 per cent (GDP) in 1997. Inflation decreased to the same percentage. Hong Kong's well developed infrastructure was an attraction for foreign investors. The ongoing process of deplacing production capacities from Hong Kong to the main land had transformed Hong Kong's economy to become very much services focused (about 80 per cent).

Foreign investors with new technologies or processes were offered subsidies for investing in the New Territories. Among others, plastics pro-

ducers which cannot use multistory buildings as production facilities had invested there. With average growth rates of 11.5 per cent between 1984 and 1996 and a yearly market volume of more than USD100 million, the plastics industry was Hong Kong's eighth biggest employer in the manufacturing sector. Because of limited environmental consciousness and legislation less expensive technical solutions for drying and cooling problems in plastics production were favoured by many customers. Based on numerous skilled labour and a well developed infrastructure high-tech manufacturers found a promising potential for successful business in neighbouring markets. Firms considering sales and service offices of subsidiaries with some warehouse facilities were detracted by Hong Kong's high prices of land, office and dwelling space as well as high costs of living.

One of China's major economic problems was the deficit run by more than 50 per cent of the publicly owned enterprises. Bad management, unsellable products, and missing technology were major reasons for their failure. To resolve that problem government had decided to merge, sell, lease and transform such firms into stock corporations or to liquidate them. Until the end of 1997, 2980 firms with assets of about USD50 billion and a work force of 5.6 million were included in the reform project. However, the decision what firm should survive in what way or be liquidated was not taken by experienced managers, but by members of the ruling communist party. The transformation of publicly owned companies into stock corporations risked wasting savings of the population. In addition, unemployment levels which officially reached 10 per cent in the major cities but exceeded 40 per cent in certain regions of the country were a potentially destabilizing factor for the country.

The financial crises of China's neighbours was not without repercussions on the country's economy. Because of decreased values of competitors' currencies Chinese exports were expected to stagnate in 1998. Foreign investments had decreased by 25 per cent in 1997 and were forecast to further diminish by 33 per cent to a level of USD30 billion or less (because 80 per cent of foreign investments in China came from neighbouring countries). To revive foreign investments, government planned to allow taxfree imports of machinery and production systems as of 1998. Despite the government policy of import substitution, foreign suppliers of machinery and manufacturing systems which contributed to productivity gains and product quality improvement as well as suppliers of high quality means of production and of packaging machinery found excellent business opportunities.

The market volume of plastics machinery in China was estimated to be above USD200 million per year at a yearly growth rate of up to 10 per cent. Competition had started to enter the market. But because of the high yearly investments needed for market development only the most important global competitors were able to successfully establish themselves. Administrative barriers to entry had been largely diminished, but cultural barriers still represented a significant hurdle to foreign investors. To be successful in the long run a supplier to the Chinese market needed to establish a subsididary or to cooperate with Chinese partners in a joint venture. Another hurdle for any foreign supplier was the country's lack of appropriate infrastructure as soon as the more developed coastal areas were left. The low level of environmental consciousness started to change at a very slow pace. In Shanghai an academy for environmental protection was awarded USD6 billion (1 billion reserved for imports of foreign technology) to improve the very bad situation concerning air and water pollution as well as waste disposal.

BASIC STRATEGIC DECISIONS

T he preceding part of the book has shown how the attractiveness of international markets can be assessed and how a comparison with major competitors will help a company identify whether it can excel on any of the success factors in the most attractive markets. The firm will either be able to profit from distinctive competencies or can identify success factors it is missing which would prevent the company from successfully serving a market.

Based on this information, management now can assess existing strategic alternatives. Part III of this book describes the process of how to determine a global strategic position for the firm and how to base an international market-entry strategy on that decision.

As Chapter 9 will describe, management develops an international portfolio strategy, that is, it will choose the product- and country-markets to serve as well as select the technologies necessary to satisfy the existing and potential aspirations of cus-

tomers and stakeholders in those markets. Closely related to their choice of markets and technologies, management has to select the most promising competitive strategy – the way the firm will behave in the chosen markets. Choices range from a frontal attack on any competitor, to cooperative agreements that not only allow peaceful coexistence but also the exploitation of mutual strengths, achieving synergy. Microsoft, for example, frontally attacks any rival in its major product-markets, but cooperates with the most powerful marketers of PCs, such as IBM or Compaq, to increase the benefits to its customers. The competitive strategy also comprises decisions concerning the innovation behaviour of the firm as well as its policy concerning growth through mergers and acquisitions. Portfolio strategy, competitive strategy, and the following resource allocation decisions define the intended global strategic position that should help ensure the survival of the company.

Figure III.1 **BASIC STRATEGIC DECISIONS**

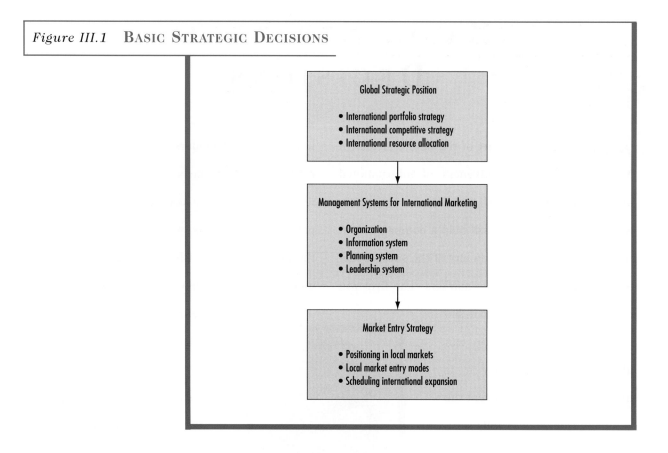

To ensure that the intended global strategic position is transformed into adequate international marketing plans and actions, a company needs management systems which support global business. Such systems can take different shapes, more or less well adapted to the business and internationalization level of a firm. How organization, information, planning and leadership must be shaped to enable the company to plan, implement, and evaluate its international marketing decisions will be discussed in Chapter 10.

When the intended global strategic position is determined and appropriate management systems are in place management must decide on how to position the company, a business unit or a product line in every local market it has selected. That is, it must fine tune the selection of customer group(s) to be served and the way it wants to attractively differentiate itself from the most important competitors. HILTI's global strategic position, for example, involves offering high-quality, high-priced fastening solutions employing the latest technology, to all construction businesses throughout the world. Nevertheless, positioning in individual country-markets has to be done in light of the existing customer segments and competition. The positioning process will be described in the first part of Chapter 11.

The intended global strategic position and the intended positions in the chosen country-markets determine the ways in which markets are entered. If international marketing is conducted only to reach operational goals such as boosting the total sales volume or taking up excess capacity, and control over local marketing activities is considered less important, low-risk market-entry alternatives will be favoured. Such low-risk entry modes, like indirect exporting or exporting via importers in each country-market, require a minimum of resources. If internationalization of business is a strategic objective and the company wants to keep its local positions under close control, it will take bolder steps, such as direct investment. IBM, for example, often prefers to invest directly abroad to maximize control over marketing activities linked to its name. Different market-entry modes and the decision process of how to enter new markets and in what sequence will be discussed in Chapter 11.

The basic strategic decisions described in the following chapters will be the base for all international marketing-mix decisions to be discussed in the last part of this book.

CHAPTER *9*

THE GLOBAL
STRATEGIC POSITION

International Incident

The Global Chip Payoff

Texas Instruments' high-speed telecommunications chip may look like any other semiconductor. But it's the product of a world's worth of effort. Conceived with engineers from Ericsson Telephone Co. in Sweden, it was designed in Nice with software tools the company developed in Houston. Today, the TCM9055 chip rolls off production lines in Japan and the USA, gets tested in Taiwan, and is wired into Ericsson line-cards that monitor phone systems in Sweden, the USA, Mexico and Australia.

'We're intent on using our geographic position as a competitive advantage', declares Th. J. Engibous, president of TI's semiconductor group. In fact, TI is the only other chipmaker besides Samsung Electronics Co. to increase global market share in the mid-1990s and to make respectable profits. Geographic balance and a broad range of chip products – aimed at everything from computers and telecom to autos and audio gear – protect the company if there is a sudden slowdown in European phone sales or American PCs. Additionally, countries such as Germany and Taiwan are offering companies big incentives to build locally. A regional base also gives chipmakers a valuable hedge against currency swings. And a local presence can win contracts from customers who are clamoring for a new species of customized chip that requires close collaboration to design.

In 1987, TI began swapping research with one of its toughest rivals, giant Hitachi Ltd. Collaboration helped TI keep up with a technological moving target. It launched a cost-sharing agreement on the production side, bringing its cost of capital well below that of the Japanese. Battered by an unprecedented four-year chip recession, TI broke with traditions and agreed to split the cost for a new plant in Avezzano, Italy, with the Italian government. Finding no ill effects, similar deals were completed with Taiwanese PC maker Acer, Japan's Kobe Steel, and a consortium in Singapore. In total, these alliances have saved TI more than USD1 billion in plant investment and have left it with an envied network of cutting-edge production plants. As part of a new joint-production company with Hitachi, a manufacturing plant was opened in Dallas in 1996.

Rivals begin to imitate TI's successful formula. Japan's Mitsubishi Electric Corp. and Oki Electric Industry Co. have partnerships to build plants in Taiwan. Samsung and Hyundai are building their first ventures outside Korea.

Source: Adapted from Burrows, P. (1995) 'The Global Chip Payoff', *Business Week*, 7 August, pp. 44–47.

Defining the Global Strategic Position

When a firm has completed its analyses of the external and internal environments, when the capabilities and resources were compared to the success

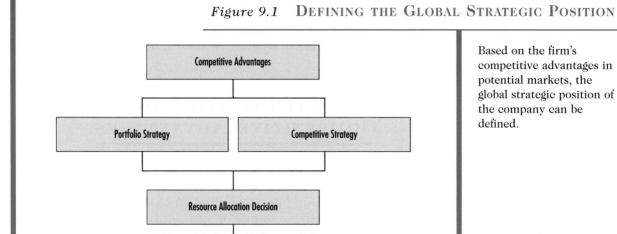

Figure 9.1 DEFINING THE GLOBAL STRATEGIC POSITION

Based on the firm's competitive advantages in potential markets, the global strategic position of the company can be defined.

factors in the most attractive markets, management has developed an overview of the company's market-related strengths and weaknesses. Their comparison with the major competitors' strengths and weaknesses reveals the distinctive competencies of the firm in each potential market. They are the sources of competitive advantages to be developed and sustained as foundations for success in the most attractive markets.

Based on distinctive competencies of the firm, management can decide what direction of development the firm should take and how this development should be achieved (corporate strategy). Those decisions are summarized in a written statement called the (intended) global strategic position of the company (see Figure 9.1). The statement must contain information on the firm's assigned mission, its portfolio strategy, that is, which kinds of customers the firm will serve in which regions of the world, and which benefits it will provide to those customers by the use of which technologies. And it must lay out the firm's competitive strategy, that is, a general guideline of how the company plans to behave in the served markets in order to achieve and maintain competitive advantage. Depending on its distinctive competencies, the firm can focus on building and sustaining competitive advantages by being more cost efficient or faster than competitors, provide differentiated benefits, establish closer relationships with customers and important stakeholders, or a combination of those. It can seek confrontation with competitors, or acquisition of firms having complementary competencies, but may also primarily look for opportunities to cooperate. It may strive to be an innovator or be a follower in new product and process development. Finally, having determined the markets to serve and the competitive behaviour in those markets, management must indicate how the limited resources available to the company are to be allocated across country- and product-markets in such a way as to ensure fulfilment of the set objectives.

Portfolio strategy, competitive strategy and resource allocation decisions together define the (intended) global strategic position of the company. Because marketing managers are most directly related to customers, intermediaries and competitors, they should play an important role in the decision process determining the global strategic position of the company.

Determination of Competitive Advantages

General Sources of Competitive Advantages

Depending on the degree of internationalization of its business, a company has access to different general sources of competitive advantage. A globally operating company may derive competitive advantages from qualities that are not available to firms with a regional or domestic focus, such as:

↔ Efficiencies of global scale and volume

↔ Transfer of experience, ideas and successful concepts

↔ Global reputation

↔ Transfer of resources between business units spread globally

↔ Exploitation of local advantages

↔ Ability to provide global services.

A global scale of business can lead to significant gains in production efficiency and sales volume that can be transformed into customer benefits. Global efficiencies of scale allowed Asian manufacturers of VCRs, for example, to make and sell their products at lower prices than was possible for US manufacturers serving only the regional market. As a consequence, US manufacturers no longer produce VCRs.

A global company is also able to transfer experience, ideas and successful concepts from one country-market to another. McDonald's country managers in Europe, for example, regularly meet to compare notes on products and promotional ideas, but also how to avoid waste, and to discuss whether such ideas might be appropriate in other markets. Faster knowledge transfer and learning result in superior customer benefits through lower prices and improved product and service features.

Moreover, global companies often have a stronger reputation than can be achieved by domestic companies. As travel and communication across national boundaries increase, this potential is likely to grow. To take the same example, McDonald's, which is active in many country-markets, enjoys a higher reputation for product quality in Australia than does the domestic Hungry Jack, an affiliate of Burger King, which was unable to use its better-known name in Australia because of legal registration problems.

Global companies can transfer resources between business units in different parts of the world. These resources may include personnel (such as experienced production managers), funds (global organizations usually have a lower capital cost than domestic firms), and superior market information. Firms such as Kraft-Jacobs-Suchard, the Swiss-based chocolate and coffee manufacturer belonging to Philip Morris, transfer their managers to operations where they need their specific know-how, for example in the growing markets of Eastern Europe, and profit from the capital transfer capacity of their company to respond quickly to market opportunities wherever they occur.

One might expect that global companies are less well situated than local firms to exploit local advantages, such as closeness to the market and working with distributors on a personal basis. However, domestic marketers, especially those located in small country-markets, are often underfinanced, lacking in well-qualified management, and not highly competitive in nature. The additional resources available to global marketers, coupled with a more professional marketing orientation, may make them better prepared to seek out and exploit local advantages.

Finally, global companies have the ability to provide global services. Increasingly, customers in industrial and consumer markets are looking for more complete products, including pre- and post-sale services. In particular, services that can be delivered through technology (such as international investment) may be performed more efficiently or more fully by global marketers. This is one of the reasons why former national telecommunications companies such as Deutsche Telekom seek strategic partnerships to improve their competitive position. They bought 25 per cent of P.T. Satelite Palapa Indonesia, jointly own 67 per cent of the Hungarian phone company, Matav, together with Ameritech, strongly based in its US Midwestern market, and share 20 per cent of American Sprint Corp. with France Telecom. In 1996 they were negotiating a 25 per cent share of Shinawatra International, a Thai telecommunications firm which has operations in Cambodia, Laos, the Philippines and India.[1]

Company-Specific Competitive Advantages

A company can identify its specific sources of competitive advantages by running through its list of distinctive competencies for the markets under consideration. For example, it may be critical for a French producer of steel construction parts who wants to start a joint venture in Russia to be able to establish firm relationships with members of the supply system, such as steel mills and transportation companies, in order to ensure timely distribution. If the firm has long-term experiences in building such relationships because of the company's involvement in Romania, it may possess a distinctive competency that can be transformed into a competitive advantage.

Distinctive competencies may become competitive advantages if the firm can successfully transform them into benefits for potential customers or relevant stakeholders. The distinctive competency of highly flexible low-cost production, for example, can only become a competitive advantage when it is transformable into low-priced customized products. Customers and stakeholders will have a high propensity to develop preferences and long-term relationships with the provider of such benefits if they are highly attractive to them. Competitive advantages are strongest when they are unique to the firm, that is, when they cannot be easily duplicated. The family ties of owners and managers of Taiwanese and Hong Kong-based companies with business people from the People's Republic of China, for example, give them a competitive advantage over US companies in obtaining joint-venture contracts with Chinese firms. A marketer should not overlook, however, the possibility that competitors might develop capabilities quite fast through acquisitions, mergers or cooperation. Finally, a competitive advantage only exists if the customers and stakeholders are ready to value the offered benefits by adequate exchange reactions, such as paying a good price or providing goodwill.

Sometimes a company does not have a particular distinctive competency. In such cases it must develop differences between itself and its competitors. Such differentiation may take the form of providing creative solutions to previously unsolved problems, applying new technologies, developing customer benefits that are not currently offered, or simply promoting or distributing in a new way. For example, Kodak developed a disposable camera with a wide-angle lens. Its rationale was that tourists often need a wide-angle lens while on vacation (to take a picture of the Colosseum in Rome or Niagara Falls, for example). While most people are not willing to invest in the cost of a wide-angle lens, they will do so if it is part of a low-cost camera that is disposed of when the film is developed.

Global Portfolio Strategy

Most companies have to take on new challenges and develop their portfolio of served markets if they want to survive in their competitive environment. However, no company will be able or willing to serve all potential markets. Firms have limited financial and personnel resources as well as basic guidelines of what business to make and what to leave for others. In the light of different attractiveness of country- as well as product-markets, and the distinctive competencies detected with respect to potential markets, management must decide whether to keep the status of the existing portfolio, increase the extent of the firm's international activity, or change the focus on particular markets (Figure 9.2). For example, lift makers like Finnish Kone have virtually no control over general demand for their products. When the construction industry is putting up new buildings it needs lifts; when it is not, as has been the case in North America and Europe in the mid-1990s, then demand disappears. Shrinking demand in one part of the world may be offset by rising demand in another. In the fast-developing markets of Asia, skyscrapers are sprouting up all over cities like Shanghai or Kuala Lumpur, each with a battery of lifts to be built by firms such as Kone. The lift makers react by shifting more of their resources to those new markets.

Decisions will be guided by the ground rules concerning the extent of internationalization laid down in the firm's corporate policy. If the major competitors are all active on a global scale, as is the case in the commercial aircraft, computer or watch industries, geographic market restriction may turn out to be fatal. On the other hand, in cases such as the furniture industry, where most business is local, the example of Sweden-based IKEA shows that a greater than average extent of internationalization can be very successful. They started internationalizing their business by supply agreements with factories in Eastern Europe and opening stores all over Western Europe and later on in the USA and Asia at a time when their competitors concentrated on local business opportunities.

Basic Strategic Options

In developing a portfolio strategy, the company can choose between four basic options: product-market penetration, geographic expansion, product-market development, and diversification (see Figure 9.3).

Figure 9.2 DEFINING THE GLOBAL STRATEGIC POSITION
STEP 1: PORTFOLIO STRATEGY

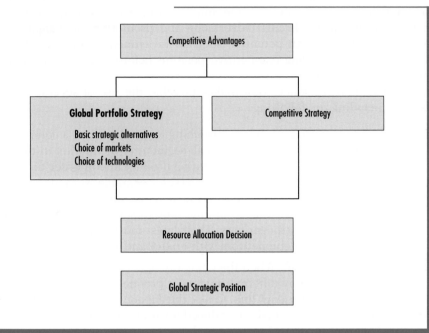

In defining the global strategic position of the firm, management first has to decide which markets to serve and which technologies to apply.

Figure 9.3 BASIC STRATEGIC PORTFOLIO OPTIONS

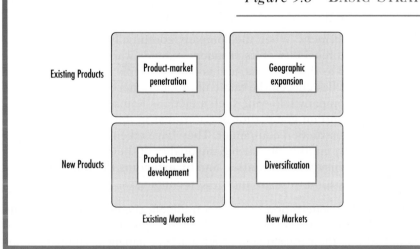

Basically a firm can be involved in an existing or a new market, with existing or new products.

Source: Adapted from Ansoff, H.I. (1957) 'Strategies for Diversification', *Harvard Business Review*, September–October, 113–124.

Product-Market Penetration. The highest degree of resource concentration occurs when the firm decides to penetrate a product-market in a limited number of country-markets that it already serves. This results in production and marketing experience curve effects, which permit the firm to lower prices and increase quality at the same time. The result is increasingly loyal customers.

Markets that are in an early stage of development require a greater investment of resources. When, for example, Eindhoven (Netherlands)-based Philips first introduced compact discs, a large budget was necessary to train sales personnel both within the company and in stores that would sell the new product, and to communicate the benefits of the new technology to customers through advertising and promotion campaigns. If the market has high growth potential, such an investment is justified, because it will establish a strong competitive position before other firms enter the market.

Product-market penetration makes possible the use of several different tactics, including the following:

1. *Product-line stretching*. When stretching its product line, a company which has successfully served a small segment of the market in the past gradually adds new items to the existing product line in order to reach a broader market. Japanese car producers, for example, started their market penetration in Europe with inexpensive, middle-sized cars. From there they first stretched their product line to small cars, then started offering bigger and stronger cars. Their latest move has been to challenge European competitors with luxury and sports car models.

2. *Product proliferation*. When the company opts for product proliferation, it introduces as many different models or product types as possible at each point in the product line. Casio, the Japanese calculator and watch manufacturer, for example, introduced a variety of hand calculators, with different functions, features and designs to cover the expectations of most customer segments in the product-market, from low-priced calculators for everyday purposes to highly sophisticated devices for special applications. The same tactic has been used by the company with watches in the lower priced ranges of the market.

3. *Product improvement*. When the company continually augments the capabilities and reliability of its products, extends warranties and services related to the products, and is quick to apply improved technologies, it has chosen the tactic of product improvement. An example of a company following such a tactic is Komatsu, the Japan-based most important competitor of Caterpillar in the market for earth-moving and construction equipment. They have taken a significant market share by continually raising the quality of their products, which allowed an extension of warranties, and by extending the range of their products' application through improved technologies.

Product-market penetration involves a trade-off: the more the firm limits the number of country-markets it serves, the more opportunities it gives competitors to build up their presence in other markets. Japanese companies, for instance, strengthened their competitive positions in Southeast Asia before entering the US market. They were not challenged in these markets by US competitors, who at that time focused their activities on European markets. In addition, too strong a focus on a product-market in a limited number of country-markets may reduce potential success. For example, although Ford Tractor operations had experienced varying profitability, cash flow and market share by product type (such as light versus heavy tractors), some of their greatest opportunities were due to wide potential profit variations across market areas.[2]

Geographic Expansion. Expanding operations to new geographic areas is most appropriate when the firm is relatively small and has developed an innovative product for which patents offer little protection or when the advantage of a firm's new product can be matched by competition in a fairly short time. For example, Austria-based Omicron, a very small firm specializing in electronic testing equipment, after having developed an innovative test set for protective relays, transducers and energy meters for electric utilities and industry, expanded globally in three years by cooperating with Germany's Siemens AG which let them use their distribution network. Geographic expansion is especially appropriate if the life cycles of the company's products in different markets are similar, as is often the case for industrial goods and consumer durables in developed economies, including the newly industrialized countries.

At the limit, a company is not even obliged to sell its innovative products in its current markets before entering new ones. If other markets are better suited to the new product, the firm should start there. For example, Matsushita, the Japanese consumer electronics giant, exported its colour TV sets to the USA five years before it introduced them at home; its managers did not believe that the Japanese market was ready for the new product.

Geographic expansion is also appropriate when important competitors are opening up new markets, or when opportunities in new markets will be available for only a short time. These characteristics are often found in high-tech industries like computer technology and advanced circuit technology. The speed with which new computer chips, for example, can be matched by competitors means that they are marketed globally as quickly as possible to take advantage of product superiority for as long as possible.

Geographic expansion also becomes necessary when intense price competition in slow-growing markets leads to diminishing profit margins. To achieve higher sales volume, the company introduces its products in markets where few product modifications are required. Eastman Kodak Co., for example, faced with strong competition from Japan's Fuji and Germany's Agfa-Gevaert in US, European and Japanese markets growing at very low speed, turned to China where 35mm film sales have quintupled since the early 1980s, to roughly 120 million rolls in 1995. Only one of the country's seven domestic makers, Lucky Film Corp., had a truly national brand in 1996. While just 12 per cent of China's 1.3 billion people owned a camera, picture taking is fast becoming as popular as it is in Japan. By the end of the decade, China is expected to overtake Japan, becoming the world's second-largest film market, behind the USA. But competition is unavoidable. With less than 30 per cent of the Chinese film market and an even smaller share of photographic paper in 1996, Kodak remains behind. Fuji leads in film and is fighting a price war with Agfa-Gevaert for that company's leading share of the photographic-paper market.[3]

Product-Market Development. Following the basic strategy of product-market development, a company allocates its resources to a limited number of country-markets and focuses its operations on the development of new product-markets in these areas. This approach is appropriate if the company is well established in its country-markets and lacks the motivation, ability or knowledge to adapt to a new environment. Product-market development is most appropriate when the served product-markets have matured and new product-markets are growing fast.

A 1996 survey, for example, found that one out of three small firms in Japan's consumer electronics industry which had delivered product parts to the big names, such as Sony or Hitachi, and were hit by those firms' exodus offshore, started developing new products. As another example, Japanese Hirata Technical used to make only car-body parts for Honda. Capitalizing on this business relationship and the specific local marketing know-how, the company has branched out into making parts for dry batteries.[4]

Diversification.   Diversification may be an attractive strategy when served markets stagnate and new product-markets in new geographic areas generate a high return on investment and have high growth potential. Körber/Hauni, the German top manufacturer of cigarette machines in the world, for example, was confronted with a stagnating market in the late 1980s when smoking became less popular and cigarette machines more efficient. While Körber/Hauni clearly defended its leadership in this market, it also entered into a quick and active diversification programme. The company founded Hauni Elektronik, which launched a breakthrough innovation in the field of oxygen production from normal air. E.C.H. Will, another result of diversification, established a world market share of 90 per cent for cut-size sheeters (machines that cut small papers for items such as passports and cheque books).[5]

There are two dangers associated with diversification, however. First, entering a new product-market in a new geographic area is risky, especially when it involves a technology that is new to the firm. The new business may have only few aspects in common with existing operations, so the firm may benefit very little from synergy. Second, even if the company is able to overcome this problem, competitors may choose a more focused portfolio strategy and dominate the markets in which the firm does not have the experience needed to develop strong competitive advantages. For example, it may seem attractive to Cathay Pacific, the Hong Kong-based airline, to invest in a hotel chain in Australia because tourism from the USA, Japan and Europe is increasing there and customers can be flown in on the company's jets. But Cathay Pacific may find itself confronted with US or European competitors specializing in global hotel management which possess long-established relationships with international tour operators and travel agencies. It may also be confronted with Australian competitors which are better entrenched in the intricacies of Australian regulations and have a stronger lobby when it comes to construction and operating permissions.

Choice of Markets

To decide which markets should be served, management must simultaneously examine the attractiveness of potential product- and country-markets and the firm's competitive position in the markets under consideration. On the one hand, management will try to focus the activities of the firm on the most attractive markets. On the other, it has to consider the firm's ability to build on or develop competitive advantages in those markets. Swiss-based Zurich Insurance Co., for example, has the priority of increasing earnings power by maintaining a consistent policy of focusing on selective growth. It is active in non-life and life insurance, reinsurance and asset management, benefiting from one of the industry's most global networks, an expanded position in the US market through acquisitions, a sharply focused approach to customers, and product innovation.[6] A potential method to simultaneously analyse the attractiveness of markets and the competitive position of the firm (its business units, product lines or products) in those markets is portfolio analysis.

International Portfolio Analysis.   Portfolio analysis provides an overview of how the firm has allocated its resources so far, what opportunities exist, and what threats have to be faced. For internationally operating companies, portfolio analysis is more complex than for a domestic business, because it must provide for additional units of analysis. It starts at the corporate level, where country- and product-markets, as well as available technologies, must be compared; proceeds to the business unit level, where for each of the units on the superior level of analysis the related customer segments and product lines can be analysed; then it goes down to the product-line level, where for each product line and customer segment the related portfolio of products can be assessed (see Figure 9.4).

For example, a firm such as Nike, the US marketer of sports footwear, will start a global portfolio analysis on the corporate level where it will not only compare different product-markets, like low-priced sports fashion for young consumers, footwear for fashion-conscious sports amateurs or expensive high-tech solutions for sports professionals, but must also consider the attractiveness of the country-markets it currently serves and compare its competitive position there to potential other markets. Figure 9.5 shows how a portfolio comparing country-markets with regard to market attractiveness and relative competitive position can be used in a defined product-market (for example, low-priced sports fashion for young consumers) to determine where the company has acted successfully, to seize opportunities in attractive areas and where it has allowed competitors to establish strong positions before it acquired appropriate market shares. By comparing the existing portfolio of country-markets to opportunities, management can determine whether the company is overcommitted in less attractive markets, leaving highly attractive markets untapped. In Figure 9.5 Belgium and Denmark represent attractive markets that need more attention compared to Canada.

In addition, the company can analyse different levels of technology (such as complete automation vs. hand assembly) used to produce its shoes. At the business unit level, customer segments, such as high school kids wanting to express their protest against parents, young single professionals wanting to work out on week-ends, or middle-aged women interrupting their time at home with their small children to perform some exercises in a spa, will be compared concerning their attractiveness and the firm's competitive position in each country-market or in a product-market. The portfolio position of product lines, like sporty leisure shoes or healthcare shoes for small children, can also be analysed per country- or product-market, or related to a certain production technology. And, of course, Nike will assess the product mix of every product line, such as running, walking or tennis shoes, as well as the product mix for each customer segment.

Market/Product Portfolios.   Besides the higher number of units of analysis compared by portfolio analysis, international firms have to consider more factors for the determination of their markets' and products' positions in the portfolio. Factors such as political and financial risk, transferability of funds, taxes and subsidies, or the potential for standardization influence the portfolio structure. They have to be introduced to the comparison to increase the

Figure 9.4 INTERRELATIONS OF PORTFOLIO CATEGORIES

Portfolio analysis can take place on different levels of a company: corporate, business unit and product line. On each level the analysis can focus on different units: product-markets, country-markets or technologies on the corporate level; customer segments and product lines on the business unit level; and products on the product-line level. Essentially, portfolio decisions taken on an upper level have an impact on the portfolio of the level below.

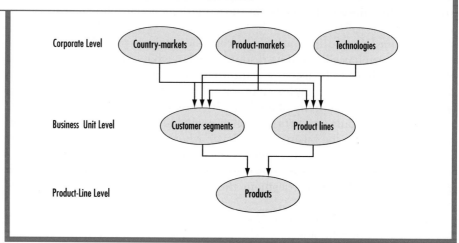

Figure 9.5 PORTFOLIO OF COUNTRY-MARKETS

Portfolio analysis can be used to determine market priorities. In this exhibit the firm has mapped the attractiveness of country-markets compared to the firm's competitive position. Thus France is its best market, but Denmark merits attention because it is large in size. However, the firm's competitive position in Denmark is only fair.

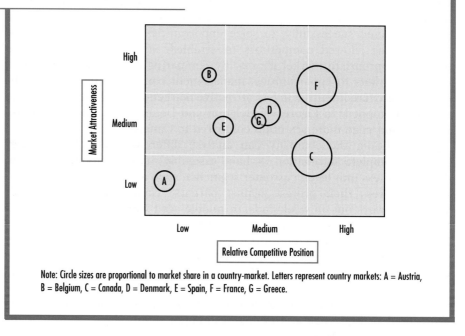

Note: Circle sizes are proportional to market share in a country-market. Letters represent country markets: A = Austria, B = Belgium, C = Canada, D = Denmark, E = Spain, F = France, G = Greece.

information level included in the analysis for decision purposes. A highly profitable market can be threatened by political unrest, religious upheavals, or restrictive laws concerning business. For example, trade between Ireland and Turkey, although profitable, may be less attractive owing to insecurities concerning Turkey's government and administrative barriers in the form of

Figure 9.6 POLITICAL RISK/PROFITABILITY PORTFOLIO OF COUNTRY-MARKETS

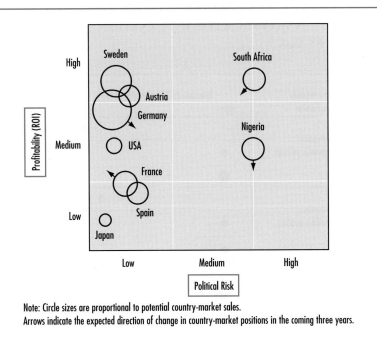

The profitability of a country-market can be mapped against an issue that affects the attractiveness of profitability – in this example, political risk.

Note: Circle sizes are proportional to potential country-market sales.
Arrows indicate the expected direction of change in country-market positions in the coming three years.

import restrictions. Such factors can be accounted for in the development of the scale which is used to measure attractiveness.[7] But they can also be explicitly considered in the way the portfolio is designed. Figure 9.6 shows an example of how portfolio analysis can compare profitability to political risk in various country-markets.

Possessing a balanced portfolio is of no help to the firm if the funds generated in one market or by one product (line) cannot be freely transferred to another. For example, if an agricultural products company such as Charoen Pokphand based in Bangkok has cash cows in the Philippines, Indonesia and China but is not allowed to transfer funds from there to its newly started business units in Eastern Europe, the international business strategy will be handicapped. To check this situation, the transferability of funds earned in different regions of the world can be introduced into the assessment (see Figure 9.7).

Technology portfolios. Markets, products and services are not only characterized by specific benefits provided to certain customer groups but also by the technologies applied to produce the intended benefits. An internationally operating firm, therefore, must decide which technologies to hold in its portfolio to contribute adequately to the resolution of their customers' problems. To take informed decisions, management can assess the attractiveness of each available technology for the product- and country-markets as well as customer segments and product lines under consideration and compare it to the firm's relative strengths in those fields of technology.

Figure 9.8 shows that the attractiveness of a technology is defined by its

Figure 9.7 PORTFOLIO COMBINING COUNTRY-MARKET ATTRACTIVENESS/ COMPETITIVE POSITION ANALYSIS WITH INTERNATIONAL TRANSFERABILITY OF FUNDS

Portfolio analysis is used in this figure to help the firm analyse the relationship between its product lines' position in a market attractiveness/competitive position portfolio and its ability to transfer funds, by major regions. In the given example most of the sales of 'stars' are in the NAFTA and EU, where the company can transfer funds. 'Cash cows' have their highest sales volume in the Pacific Rim where transferability of funds is restricted. But future growth of 'question marks' and further development of 'stars' depend on available funds. The firm faces severe funding limitations.

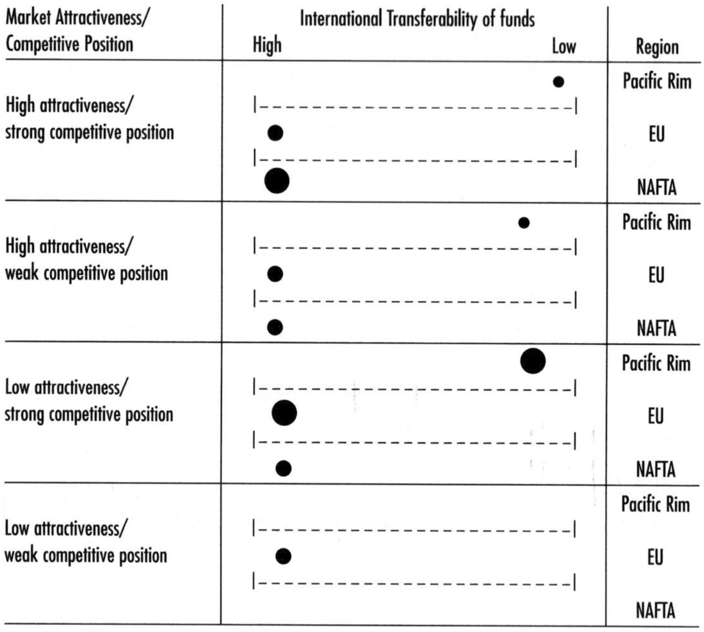

Market Attractiveness/ Competitive Position	International Transferability of funds		Region
	High	Low	
High attractiveness/ strong competitive position		●	Pacific Rim
	●		EU
	●		NAFTA
High attractiveness/ weak competitive position		●	Pacific Rim
	●		EU
	●		NAFTA
Low attractiveness/ strong competitive position		●	Pacific Rim
	●		EU
	●		NAFTA
Low attractiveness/ weak competitive position			Pacific Rim
	●		EU
			NAFTA

Note: Circle sizes are proportional to share of total sales.

Figure 9.8 FACTORS INFLUENCING THE ATTRACTIVENESS OF A TECHNOLOGY TO A FIRM

The attractiveness of a technology to a firm is determined by its potential to solve customer problems and its diffusion potential.

Source: Adapted from Specht, G. (1994) 'Portfolioansätze als Instrument zur Unterstützung strategischer Programmentscheidungen', in Corsten, H. (ed.), *Handbuch Produktionsmanagement*, Gabler: Wiebaden, p. 105.

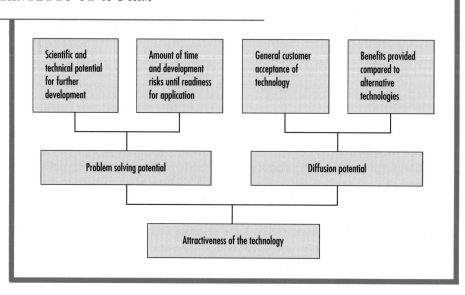

potential for customer problem solution and diffusion. The problem solution potential of a technology depends on its scientific and technical potential for further development as well as the amount of time and development risks until the technology is ready for application. Micro mechanics, for example, is a field of technology which not only has enormous potential for future application in toys but also in medicine, such as the treatment of effects from high levels of cholesterol. Japanese researchers have been working on its development for 20 years. They have made significant progress but no application with a strong economic impact has resulted so far.

A technology's diffusion potential is determined by its general customer acceptance and the benefits provided compared to alternative technologies. For example, microbiological cloning is a technology with great potential for further development. A company such as UK-based pharmaceutical manufacturer Glaxo that holds this technology in its portfolio, however, must be aware of the risks it takes concerning legal regulations or resistance from environmentalists in certain country-markets such as Germany.

The relative strength of the firm in a field of technology depends on the company's potential for differentiation from competitors and for implementation of the technology in the firm (see Figure 9.9). The potential of a company to differentiate itself from competitors in a field of technology is determined by the (technology-specific) know-how available to the firm relative to its competitors and the oportunity to become a technology leader in the field.

The potential for implementation depends on the fit of the technology into the existing competitive strategy of the firm and the availability of complementary technologies in the organization. For example, if a laser technology for cutting purposes fits the competitive strategy of being a technology leader in cutting problem solutions and the firm possesses the engineering know-how to construct the relevant machinery, the potential for successful implementation of this technology in the company is very good.

Choice of Markets and Technologies.   Based on market/product portfolios and the firm's technology portfolio, management can take decisions on which markets to serve with which products applying which technologies. The country-market portfolio will help to determine the geographic focus. Product-market, customer segment and product line portfolios assist in focusing the firm's expansion. The technology portfolio has to be considered in all of those decisions because it gives some information on the sustainability of competitive advantages in the delivery of superior products and services. When using the described portfolios for decision making however, managers should keep in mind that these techniques are useful for achieving some structured insights into a field of complex interdependencies but they do not provide them with rigid formula-based decisions.

Where the company possesses strong competitive positions in attractive country- or product-markets, technologies, customer segments and product lines, the global portfolio strategy should build on those strengths (Figure 9.10).

Where attractive opportunities exist but the company is in a relatively weak competitive position, the firm should either not (further) pursue those opportunities or invest a substantial part of its resources to overcome the weaknesses. Such investment may, for example, take the form of intensive reseach and development, or the search for a cooperation partner in distribution and logistics, but may also result in a take-over of a firm that possesses the missing competencies. The North American market for ski-lift equipment,

Figure 9.9   FACTORS INFLUENCING THE RELATIVE STRENGTH
OF A FIRM IN A FIELD OF TECHNOLOGY

The firm's relative strength in a field of technology is determined by its potential for differentiation and technology implementation.

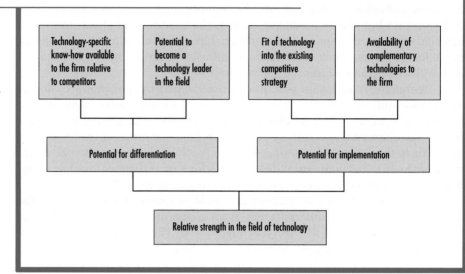

Source: Adapted from Specht, G. (1994) 'Portfolioansätze als Instrument zur Unterstützung strategischer Programmentscheidungen', in Corsten, H. (ed.), *Handbuch Produktionsmanagement*, Gabler: Wiebaden, p. 105.

Figure 9.10   MATCHING DISTINCTIVE COMPETENCIES WITH
MARKET ATTRACTIVENESS

A firm should build its portfolio on its competitive strengths in the most attractive product- and country-markets, technologies, customer segments and product lines.

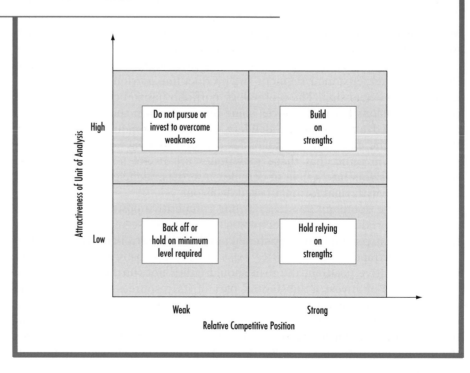

for example, may look promising to an Italian producer such as Leitner, but it should either refrain from investing money in this market if it finds that competitors are in a better cost position because they have production facilities in place, or undertake an intensive search to find a North American partner for a strategic alliance.

When a firm has distinctive strengths in a comparatively unattractive market, segment or product line, the strategy should be to hold the attained position, only investing as much of its resources as needed. If a Finnish chemical engineering company, such as Jacob Poeri, has long-lasting relationships with customers in the CIS, for example, it might decide to keep them alive to be prepared for potential orders but it will not do more than necessary to hold its position. On the other hand, if the company has weaknesses in serving a comparatively unattractive market, it will not pursue that market.

A company will be most successful in international marketing if it has a balanced mix of product- and country-markets, as well as technologies with different cash-flow positions and resource requirements, and when it serves an attractive mix of customer segments at different stages of product adoption with product lines that contain products at different stages of maturity. That is, the situation of the company is at its best when management can be sure that some parts of the firm's portfolio provide the resources needed by others for their positive development and when the choice of market and technology portfolios provides for a balance of business cycles in industries as well as regions of the world.

For example, Japan's Sony Corp. cannot count on its TV sets always selling well and being highly profitable. A portfolio of product lines would spread the market risk. If profits decline as its TVs move through the product life cycle, Sony will need new products to help maintain sales and cash flow. Thus over time, Sony developed hi-fi towers, the Walkman, the Watchman, compact discs and video cameras, investing in them in the expectation that future sales and profits of these products would be strong. Because investments needed to be in the forefront of technological development are substantial, Sony decided to serve only one broad product-market: consumer electronics. But again, to spread the risk of this decision and to profit from given opportunities, it developed a global portfolio of country-markets in which it serves different customer segments, such as teens buying their first stereo equipment mostly to play pop music or lovers of classical music who are ready to spend substantial amounts of money to own the best recordings and to enjoy perfect sound reproduction.

The Ethics box shows that management's choice of markets does not only depend on economic considerations concerning the attractiveness of markets, customer segments and product lines compared to the competitive position of the firm in those units of analysis. The personal interests of managers and general evaluations based on the values formulated in the corporate policy statement can play a decisive role.

COMPETITIVE STRATEGY

To be successful in implementing its portfolio strategy, the company must develop a way of attractively differentiating itself and its products and services from local, regional or global competitors. Management has to determine a

Levi's Global Sourcing Guidelines

CAN A COMPANY PRIDING ITSELF ON ENLIGHTENED attitudes towards employees at home turn its head when some of its foreign contractors abuse their workers? Should western companies justify paying near-starvation wages because that's what the market will bear?

While US- and European-owned factories in places like China, Indonesia and Thailand are often well run, some independent contractors and suppliers there and in other countries provide working conditions that are dismal even by Third World standards. At least that's what Levi Strauss found. The company, which in 1992 made about 50 per cent of its jeans and shirts overseas, investigated its 400 foreign contractors and has discovered that about 25 per cent of them treat their workers badly. According to Levi, its contractor in Bangladesh was routinely using child labour, for example. A contractor on the island of Saipan, a US territory near Guam, allegedly refused to pay employees back wages, often worked them 11 hours a day, seven days a week, and paid below the local minimum wage.

Levi not only terminated that contract. A company task force worked for three years on developing 'Global Sourcing Guidelines' for doing business abroad which reflect Levi's shared values. They contain 'Business Partner Terms of Engagement', among them: Suppliers must provide safe and healthy conditions that meet Levi's standards and must pay workers no less than prevailing local wages. Labour's work week is limited to 60 hours. Company inspectors make surprise visits to ensure contractors toe the line. The Bangladesh outfit has stopped using children.

The second part of the guidelines deals with country selection standards which focus on political or social instability, dangers to company employees, a country's impact on brand image, and human rights abuses. The company had suspended business dealings in Peru because it felt that employees were in danger from terrorist activity. When the danger subsided, Levi's lifted the suspension. Subcontracts in Myanmar and China were phased out because of flagrant human rights abuses.

Source: Dumaine, B (1992) 'Exporting Jobs and Ethics', *FORTUNE*, 5 October, p. 10; and Beaver, W. (1995) 'Levi's Is Leaving China', *Business Horizons*, March–April, pp. 35–40.

---

competitive strategy, that is, a guideline for its behaviour or actions in the market (see Figure 9.11). To be successful the competitive strategy must be based on competitive advantages that exist or can be built up and sustained for some time. Although specific to each company and market, such competitive advantages can be summarized into the four broad categories of cost leadership, superior value, time leadership and reliable relationships.

Depending on its basic values and resources, its market power compared to that of major competitors, and opportunities and threats in the external environments, the general market behaviour of a company can be more or less aggressive. It may emphasize confrontation with competitors or cooperation with partners. At first sight, confrontation seems to be the rule. Management should not overlook, however, the fact that market competition in most cases is not a zero-sum game. A firm cannot only win what it takes away from its competitors. In many cases sophisticated definitions of target customers and benefits provided to them allow the creation of 'new' product-markets.

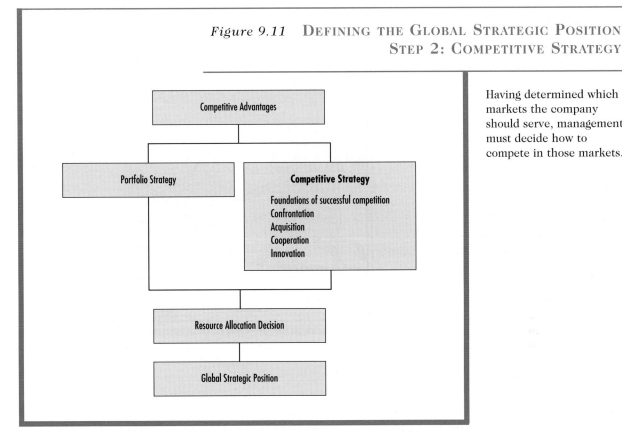

Figure 9.11 DEFINING THE GLOBAL STRATEGIC POSITION
STEP 2: COMPETITIVE STRATEGY

Having determined which markets the company should serve, management must decide how to compete in those markets.

For example, two-thirds of US households do not have PCs, with signs that home PC growth is levelling off. In 1996 only 8 per cent were on the Internet. In that year, Japanese Bandai Digital Entertainment, instead of seeking head-on confrontation with PC manufacturers, unveiled Pippin, a stripped-down Macintosh developed with Apple that looks like a videogame machine, offers Internet access and CD-ROM and plugs into a TV set. Bandai sells parents on Pippin's educational benefits accessible through the Net while pitching kids on games. Its price is closer to VCR than PC prices. The company has created its 'own new market'.[8]

Potential customers either do not perceive well-positioned companies and products as directly comparable to each other or they appreciate having a choice between various offers for different purposes. Direct confrontation can be avoided and all stakeholders in the market may subjectively profit.

Direct confrontation will also be successfully avoided when a company does not blindly imitate the way its competitors behave in a market but bases its actions on a thorough analysis of the business system and how customer value can best be created. By changing some 'rules of the game' the firm may establish a 'new' market with less competition. US-based PC makers Dell Computer and Gateway 2000, for example, have found that experienced business clients and knowledgeable consumers looking for the most cutting-edge PC models know what they want – and therefore, are ready to order hardware

"Vince! Just trample him!...He's drawing you into his kind of fight!"

over the phone. Both companies decided to build to order, rather than run up big inventories of various finished systems like most PC firms (35 for Dell versus 110 days for Compaq Computer). They created a mail-order market which in 1995 represented 15 per cent of total PC sales in the USA and nearly 30 per cent of total PC sales in the UK. Meanwhile Dell and Gateway are testing new concepts such as interactive kiosks, sales through the Internet, and showrooms in Paris and Frankfurt.[9]

The globalization of markets and the increasing speed of technological developments as well as international market introductions of new products forces even traditionally fervent competitors to enter strategic partnerships. For example, 'world cars' – designed, manufactured and marketed through cooperative agreements among car companies from many countries – are actually here. More than 25 major car and truck companies worldwide have joined together in over 300 strategic partnerships. The Ford Probe and the Mazda MX-6, for example, are made in the same plant. Peugeot and Fiat as well as Ford and Volkswagen have joint ventures where minivans are produced and sold under the brand names of each of the partners. Renault, Europe's fourth-largest producer of heavy trucks, cooperates with MAN, Germany's second-largest heavy truck maker, and in another business with General Motors to develop and market light commercial vehicles called panel vans.[10] Cooperation allows companies to enter more markets, faster, cheaper, and with a broader product line than if they tried it alone.

Because such behaviour largely depends on a firm's potential for innovation and acquisition, the competitive strategy must contain guidelines not only concerning confrontation and cooperation but also concerning product and process innovation as well as rules of acquisition behaviour.

Foundations of Successful Competition

A competitive strategy may rely on a bundle of special benefits. Californian Silicon Graphics, for example, sells mostly to companies that need to create complex three-dimensional images. Its machines, which animated the dinosaurs in *Jurassic Park*, dominate Hollywood's computer-graphics industry. The firm's 1996 bid for Cray Computers was an attempt to acquire the potential for providing even bigger customer benefits. The supercomputer firm builds some of the fastest computers in the world. Producing qualitatively superior three-dimensional graphics much faster than the competition would give Silicon Graphics a competitive advantage hard to beat.

A competitive strategy can also rely on technology. Picogiga, a French semiconductor manufacturer, for example, is the global market leader in gallium arsenide wafers used to make chips for cellular phones and digital TVs. Lernout & Hauspie, a Belgian speech-translation company, produces software that helps computers translate written text in one language to speech in another.

Finally, a competitive strategy can be based on a certain customer group. Dainichi Kiko, a Japanese robot manufacturer, for example, concentrates on close relationships with small customers that lack in-house robotized production system development capabilities. To be successful a company must have a competitive advantage in at least one of these dimensions. For example, Hong Kong's very successful apparel makers Toppy, Esprit and Theme all share something that Japanese apparel makers lack: cost competitiveness. Most of the clothes are made in China, and each of the three firms designs, produces and markets its wares itself. In Japan they are displayed near fashions from DKNY, Max Mara and Calvin Klein, but sell for half the price of the New York brands. They possess another plus that Europeans and Americans cannot match: a grasp of the fashion sense of Oriental women. Their colours are not overly bold, and the widespread use of materials like silk appeals to Asian customers.[11]

Successful competition, whether local, regional or global, can be based on cost leadership, superior customer value, time leadership, reliable relationships or a combination of these categories of competitive advantage. The best performers are likely to be driven by strategies that combine competitive advantages based on efficiency and on stakeholder orientation.[12]

Cost leadership.   A company striving for cost leadership does everything necessary to have the lowest costs per unit marketed and to pass this advantage on to their customers through low prices. Japan's three biggest semiconductor manufacturers, Hitachi, Mitsubishi Electrics and NEC, for example, poured billions of dollars into new factories in 1996, despite signs that the chip market was headed for a downturn. In earlier downturns, Japanese chip manufacturers had cut back on investments to protect profits. The result was a steady loss of market share to more aggressive Korean rivals, such as Samsung Electronics which by 1993 had taken the leading market share in memory chips from the Japanese, largely by investing heavily while the Japanese hesitated.

A manager who wants to base the company's competitive strategy on cost leadership must be aware that the costs a firm incurs largely depend on its production volume and the number of products (product lines) in its programme. Figure 9.12 shows that owing to economies of scale, an increase of

Figure 9.12 COST CURVES DEPENDING ON PRODUCTION VOLUME AND PROGRAMME SIZE

Increasing production volumes and decreasing programme size lead to reduced costs per unit.

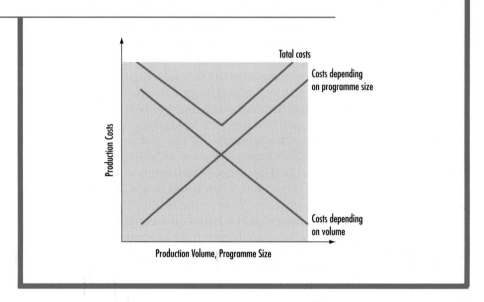

production volume of a single product leads to a decrease of costs per unit (doubling the volume may lead to cost decreases of 15–25 per cent). At the same time, any increase in the number of products produced and marketed increases the costs of inventory, storage, transportation and overhead. Experience shows, for example, that cutting the number of products by half increases productivity up to 30 per cent and decreases costs by around 17 per cent. This leads to a cost curve of the shape shown in Figure 9.12.

From there we can conclude that large, mass-producing firms such as IBM, Matsushita, Philips, Siemens or Alcatel can make maximum use of economies of scale and accumulated experience in all functional areas. Because of their broad range of products, however, they run the risk of lower productivity than smaller, more focused competitors. To achieve reductions of programme costs, the firms have to reduce the variety of their own production. They seek partnerships with more focused suppliers and cooperative ventures. In the automotive industry, for example, Japanese car producers buy 70 per cent of their products from suppliers they have close relations with, whereas in the early 1990s this share was only 40–50 per cent for European car producers and even less for car producers in the USA. Partnerships with suppliers and competitors permit a firm to maintain a large product programme at lower costs and provide access to technology and management expertise that would otherwise not be available.

Non-dominant firms, whether large or small, may cater to special market needs, concentrating their resources in a narrow field where they have a distinct competitive advantage. They can dominate the competition in the chosen market niche. Focusing on a small range of products allows them to market higher volumes and to produce at lower costs per unit. For example, Nutra Sweet, a low-calorie sweetener used in soft drinks such as Diet Coke and Diet Pepsi, and a business unit of large US-based Monsanto, was protected by patents in Europe until 1987 and in the USA until 1992. It used that time to march down the learning curve for making aspertame, the chemical name for the substance, giving it a significant cost advantage that could not be matched by any competitor when legal protection came to an end. Just prior to US patent expiry, both Coke and Pepsi signed new long-term contracts with Monsanto.

An example of a smaller company successfully focusing on a special market to gain economies of scale is Portugal's Corticeira Amorim which controls around a third of the country's cork-manufacturing. Amorim makes 70 per cent of the world's cork floorings, about 15 per cent of the world's wine corks (the world uses about 25 billion corks a year) and almost 95 per cent of the cork-based gaskets Portugal produces to seal engine joints. To further improve its cost position the company has been buying up cork distributors in almost 30 countries and has begun to distribute for smaller Portuguese producers.[13]

Superior Value.   A competitive strategy based on superior customer value uses the firm's potential for differentiation from competitors through higher attractiveness of core product characteristics or through additional services. Companies which are very close to their potential customers and other important stakeholders may offer a multitude of different product characteristics or an array of additional services targeted to special needs. Customer preference is not achieved through lower prices but through higher perceived value of the product. When Honda's motorcycle group had to fight an attack by Yamaha, for example, they introduced 113 new models in 18 months and offered new technical characteristics such as the V-Four engine, Anti-Drive (braking support) and Pro Link (rear wheel suspension). But additional value cannot only be produced by new product features concerning the function of a product. As the Future Issues box demonstrates, there are ample opportunities for the creation of superior value by adapting to new customer aspirations.

Time Leadership.   Time leadership is a way of competing successfully by being faster than competitors in every respect, from new product development through production to delivery. A series of examples of successful companies such as Benetton, Toyota and Motorola seems to indicate that in the most economically developed regions of the world, time leadership is the competitive advantage of manufacturers in the 1990s on which to build the most successful competitive strategies.

Benetton, for example, has online connections between its shops and a central logistics unit in Italy. This central unit is informed about stock movements and developments in demand wherever they occur. Because their knitwear is produced and stocked without being dyed, the greatest variety and quick response are ensured without uncontrollable risk. The products are dyed in the colours and numbers needed, and sent out by overnight delivery to the shops.

Toyota invented the so-called 'Toyota system' out of a need to make a greater variety of cars in small quantities and with the same manufacturing process. They used standardized materials, components and tools to minimize business complexity while optimizing product variety, compared with just-in-time delivery, total quality control, employee decision making on the factory floor and close supplier relations.[14]

FUTURE ISSUES BOX

Management's Responsibility for the Natural Environment

Some managers persistently perceive their responsibility as limited to the interests of the company's owners or shareholders. From that perspective all other interests of stakeholder groups are to be regarded as restrictions to the achievement of capital owner goals. Initiatives to protect the natural environment from abuse or destruction are no less than a threat to free enterprise. As recent examples demonstrate, successful managers and entrepreneurs of the future may take a very different perspective.

In an interview Anita Roddick, founder of the fast-growing Body Shop chain with more than 500 shops in 34 countries and an estimated private fortune of 22 million British pounds, said

the following: 'Money doesn't interest me. All Gordon (her husband) and I earn goes to a foundation. Our two daughters enthusiastically work on projects in the tropical rainforest and in Romania. They will not inherit a penny. I cannot sit still and wait until the world explodes with a big bang. And that's exactly what I preach to my employees: If you want to change something, don't talk, act! To be honest, who will think about a moisturizing cream all day long? Not me. And the Body Shop team does not either.

'With our employees you can talk not only about banana-shampoos but also about environmental protection problems. Of course, when we run a billboard campaign to protest against animal experiments in the cosmetics industry or when we offer soap bars that look like panda bears or blue whales together with brochures about endangered species, we offend some people. But that's worth it.

Source: Sturm, S. and Ph. Spencer (1991) 'Mit Haut und Haaren', *manager spezial*, September, p. 19.

Motorola's US production plant for cellular phones takes orders by computer connections with sales outlets and delivers the products in the following 48 hours. Such speed and flexibility were achieved by expanding just-in-time principles to the entire value chain. Tasks which were not needed to supply the intended customer benefit were eliminated. System response time was further reduced by doing things in parallel instead of sequentially. Work is done in small batches, eliminating idle or dead time wherever it existed.

To be faster than the competitors in any respect needs highly flexible production facilities with partly autonomous groups of workers, just-in-time delivery, short production runs, total quality management, fast and continuous product and process innovation (often) in close cooperation with suppliers and customers, in small steps and through multifunctional teams. Under such conditions a high diversity of products can be quickly and reliably delivered at a low cost compared to competitive offers.

But to be faster than competitors in only one aspect may also improve the competitive position for some time, in particular the position of smaller companies. Fortune Oil, a tiny Hong Kong company, for example, is trying to do what much larger oil companies have not yet managed to do: create a wide network of petrol stations in China. While urban Chinese are becoming used to paying a premium for branded consumer products, petrol is still just

gasoline to most people. Service stations are run by a patchwork of local operators, many with links to state-owned refineries. Fortune hopes to implant
itself before China opens its market wide to the big multinational competitors.
Partly by cultivating powerful connections, Fortune opened six stations in
1995 in the Pearl River Delta, one of China's richest areas, and is planning to
multiply its locations in the next three years.[15]

Reliable Relationships. The increased importance of time leadership
should not lead management to neglect the fourth basic dimension of competitive advantage: reliable relationships, that is, a network of positive personal and institutional relations with all the important stakeholders in the
relevant business system. Research on industrial business networks and on
service firms in highly industrialized regions of the world as well as experience
from Arab, Asian and African countries demonstrates how companies can
very successfully build their competitive strategies on personal as well as institutional relationships with important stakeholders (see Culture box).

Insurance companies, such as Swiss-based Basler Insurance, one of the
biggest insurance companies in Europe, for example, after having largely
improved their cost position by restructuring organizational processes which
also led to substantial gains in speed of new product development in reaction
to market needs, have discovered that the most important factor for long-term
success in their markets is the establishment and maintenance of close relationships with their customers. It is much less expensive to keep existing customers than to continuously build new customers. Because relationship
management strongly depends on personal contacts, the firm's customer contact personnel need permanent training. But they must also be highly motivated through having satisfying relationships with their company themselves.
In this respect, the standing of the firm in their local environment plays a
significant role.

IBM, for example, for a long time followed a policy of good local citizenship. On the French Riviera where they have located their European research
and development centre, the company sponsored the kindergarten, schools on
all levels, local festivals, concerts, and even the restoration of historical buildings. Such behaviour was not only attractive to IBM's highly trained international workforce who were assured of living in a culturally pleasant
environment where their children could have an excellent education, but also
to local administrators who in reaction largely facilitated the firm's business
in the region.

Non-dominant firms may formulate competitive relationship strategies on
a local basis, taking advantage of distinctive competencies in specific country-
markets. Such companies may rely on close contacts with formal commercial
and administrative stakeholders leading to government preferences for purchasing from specific suppliers. But they may also build on trusting personal
relationships with key local personalities such as 'market mammys' in West
Africa or 'bazaari' in Iran who can have strong influences on business deals in
developing economies. A number of small embroidery manufacturers located
in Austria's most western province of Vorarlberg, for example, have developed
substantial competitive advantage through cultivating their relationships with
local intermediaries and administrators, such as customs officers, in West
African countries. Developing and maintaining such contacts demands
specific knowledge of cultural and political conditions in a country and flexibility in responding to changes.

Relationship Building for Success in Third World Markets

WELL-PLACED LOCAL NOTABLES CAN PROVIDE CRITICAL assistance in early stages of a venture in developing markets. One influential phone call may lead to preferential treatment. One visit may assist in dissolution of a bottleneck. Such contacts may evolve into both mentors and allies, guiding newcomers through social or commercial minefields that could prove fatal if they were attempted on their own.

The term 'ally' means something different to non-U.S. residents than it does to most US citizens. In US corporate circles, business alliances are usually limited to specified commercial matters, rarely spilling over into private life. To Arabs, Africans, and Asians, however, the term suggests a blend of business colleague, lifelong friend, and younger brother – someone who will support their interests, in expectation of comparable favors within the future. The Chinese address participants in such special relationships with the phrase 'old friend'. West Africans say 'home boy', East Africans, 'elder (or younger) brother'. The terms define composite personal/professional alliances, wherein each side may ask favors but must also grant them.

Source: Fadiman, J.A. (1989) 'Should Smaller Firms Use Third World Methods to Enter Third World Markets: The Project Head as Point Man Overseas', *The Journal of Business and Industrial Marketing*, 4(1), Winter/Spring, 19.

Confrontation

A firm with local, regional and global competitors in its product-markets may choose among a variety of confrontation strategies. These include frontal attack, flanking, encirclement and bypassing.

Frontal attack. Frontal-attack strategies are appropriate for large companies or groups of cooperating firms with substantial resources and a significant competitive advantage in their product concept or its delivery. There are three types of frontal-attack strategy: limited, price based, and value based.

When the company limits its attack to a specific customer group and tries to win these customers away from the competition, it is applying a limited frontal-attack strategy. Anheuser Busch, the big US beer company, for example, might compete against Danish Carlsberg for exclusive supply contracts with top restaurants in major Italian cities. This strategy requires a great deal of attention to the specific needs of the targeted customers, in order to convince them of the superior benefits to be derived from the product and the related services.

A price-based frontal attack relies on product and service features that are similar to those of competitors, offered at a significantly lower price. This strategy was used in France by UK Cable and Wireless, US West and Germany's Veba, when they together launched the third mobile phone network on an initiative of their French partner Bouygues. Their prices offered for international calls to Belgium, Germany, the Netherlands and the UK were lower than the prices of existing competitors for calls using the normal earthbound phone network.[16] However, price-based attacks are risky. They work only when customers do not view price as indicative of quality and competitors are unable or unwilling to lower their prices further. The company must be willing to cross-subsidize its efforts or be a cost leader. In most cases price competition leads to a generally lowered price level in the market with no or not much advantage for the attacking firm.

A value-based frontal attack relies on product or service differentiation through characteristics other than price. The nature of the difference is determined by the company's distinctive competencies. The firm may use a competitive advantage in research and development, for example, to constantly improve its products. One such firm is the plastics division of US-based Allied Corporation, which starts with a rather simple, basic product – plastic granules – and adapts it for different applications of international customers such as manufacturers of yoghurt cups or car dashboards. In general, a value-based frontal attack can succeed only when customers and intermediaries in the distribution system perceive the firm's product as more attractive than competitors' offerings.

Flanking.   Flanking is a competitive strategy focusing on a specific, often just emerging segment of a larger product-market. It is chosen by companies that do not have the resources to attack established competitors head-on or that do not want to take the risk of spending the resources needed for a frontal attack. They use flanking to build a position that will permit direct competition in the other parts of the product-market later on.

With geographic flanking, the firm chooses geographic areas in which major competitors are weak or non-existent and offers products that are similar to those that competitors sell in comparable product-markets elsewhere. For example, in Mexico more than 95 per cent of all tortillas are produced and sold in little shops licensed by the government. These outlets are virtual monopolies in their neighbourhoods, with a captive market. In part, the reason is cultural: Mexicans like their staple fresh. But more importantly, Mexico subsidizes small tortilleras with low prices on corn flour, making it possible to sell corn tortillas for less than the real production cost. Thus, equipped with modern baking technology, Mexican Grupo Industrial Maseca has chosen the US market to launch their mass-produced, packaged tortillas, honing their marketing skills for the day when Mexico's tortilleras will no longer be subsidized.[17]

With segmented flanking, the firm enters a segment of a larger product-market that is not served by major competitors or in which customers are dissatisfied. When Honda entered the US market with its motorcycles, for example, it initially concentrated on small 'transportation' devices. Domestic firms such as Harley-Davidson continued to focus on larger sports motorcycles because they believed that the transportation market was very limited. Honda was able to gain market experience, establish its name, and generate local cash flow. Eventually, after consolidating their initial position, they started developing other market segments from this platform. Honda gradually introduced larger motorcycles that competed directly with local competitors' models.[18]

The success of segmented flanking depends on the company's ability to identify shifts in the market that will allow it to enter and develop a particular segment faster than potential competitors. The segment must be large enough to repay the effort. Both forms of flanking assume that competitors will not take notice of the firm's actions or see any reason to intervene in its chosen markets. Success can be achieved more easily when the entire product-market is growing or the potential size of the emerging market segment is unclear; under such conditions competitors do not fight for sales volume in a market niche, and dominant firms in the market do not consider the new entrant a major threat to their position.

Market Encirclement. With market encirclement, the firm tries to attack its major competitor in as many ways as possible. It offers product lines to customers in almost every segment of the entire product-market. The company applies product-line stretching and product proliferation simultaneously, as Japan's watchmaker Seiko has done in the watch market. They introduced a diversity of watch models (under varying brand names) in all existing price categories except the most expensive. Because the firm was able to satisfy all or most of the needs of potential customers in the given product category, intermediaries had less need to associate with other suppliers.

To be successful, encirclement requires that the firm spends large amounts of resources over a long period. It must gain sufficient market share to repay the large investment. Competitors should be unable or unwilling to invest similar large amounts of resources to defend their markets. This may not be the case if the firm encounters dominant competitors ready to defend their position.

Bypassing. Relatively small companies that are unable to confront major competitors in the international marketplace may choose a bypassing strategy. They can either satisfy customer needs in product-markets that are not served in a comparable manner by any competitor, or enter country-markets for existing products that no important competitor has yet served. In both cases the company needs adequate marketing experience and know-how.

In the first case, product bypassing, the firm may develop a new version of a traditional product or service, thereby opening up a new product-market with little competition. For example, the French tyre manufacturer Michelin first entered the US market with its radial tyre and focused on customers, such as fleet owners, who needed long-lasting tyres. At that time, Goodyear and other producers of bias-ply tyres established in the US market believed radials could damage their profitable replacement market. Therefore, they did not follow Michelin's move, but decided to ignore their new competitor's early efforts in an attempt to avoid giving radials a stamp of approval. The success of their French competitor forced them to follow later when they had already lost substantial parts of the market.

In the second case, geographic bypassing, the firm may concentrate on minor markets. Small firms that face strong competition in developed economies may seek opportunities in less developed countries. Although such markets may be difficult to enter, once established the firm may secure a quasi-exclusive position in the market. Thus, Merloni Refrigerators has signed a government procurement contract to meet the total need for refrigerators in a small, less developed country.

Innovation

When a company is confronted with global competitors, low-cost production, international sourcing and international marketing may not be sufficient for success. The firm's innovation behaviour becomes a major factor in formulating a global strategic position. Management must decide what role the company should play concerning innovation processes in its global product-markets in order to establish or sustain its competitive position. Such processes include product innovation as well as process innovation. Management must further decide whether it should be an early innovation leader or a follower in its industry. Related to this decision, a general rule must be formulated concerning the firm's intended rate of innovation; that is, how fast product and process innovations should follow each other and be transferred into changes in the company's offer to the market. All strategic decisions concerning the firm's innovation behaviour are influenced by management's attitude towards risk and the firm's resources, current market position, and orientation toward innovation.

Product and Process Innovation.   Product innovation involves developing new solutions to customer problems (for example, a new technology to produce irrigation water from sea water), making existing products more useful (such as developing portable VCRs which can assist in industrial selling), adding new services (for example, introducing banking by phone or on-line), or challenging the total product portfolio.

When production costs are high because of high labour costs (sometimes even lean production does not resolve the problem), a company that does not want to transfer production to low-wage countries may concentrate on product innovation for special international market segments. In doing so, it may have to give up large parts of the market, in particular if its products are priced too high for most customers. Wolford, the Austrian producer of high-quality tights, for example, has concentrated its innovation on high fashion and the production technology for seamless tights allowing it to concentrate production in Bregenz, a location where labour costs are eight to ten times higher than in the neighbouring Czech Republic. Wolford cannot compete with the prices of tights marketed by Sara Lee which are targeted to the mass market. The company focuses its activities on an up-scale market which is estimated to represent only 3 per cent of the total market. But in doing so, Wolford has gained a reputation as European fashion leader, growing faster than the industry average.

Companies located in countries with high labour costs may also find opportunities to grow in markets where a lower level of product technology (and, hence, a lower price) is better suited to customers' needs. For example, Dornier, a German manufacturer of weaving machines, found that its products were too sophisticated and expensive for most Latin American customers. It started a second-hand machinery market for those customers, adapting used machines which the company has to take back from customers who buy new equipment in highly technologically developed markets.

Even intensified product innovation may not protect the firm against situations in which high-tech, high-quality products become the industry standard. In such cases the company must turn to new product-markets, provide new customer benefits, or develop new technologies to regain a competitive advantage. An example of this approach is AT&T, the former only international US telephone company which, as a reaction to market deregulation and difficulties in differentiating its services from those of competitors in the telecommunications market, decided to compete in the multimedia market. Since then it has systematically acquired or started cooperation with firms having the appropriate know-how and the physical distribution systems needed.

In mature product-markets, where rates of real product innovation are low and cost pressures are high, process innovation, that is, changing the way processes such as production, new product development or product delivery are conducted, can be a significant means of gaining and sustaining competitive advantage. On the one hand, the costs of producing customer value can be reduced by restructuring procurement, production and distribution processes. On the other, the reorganization of processes can make them much faster and more flexible, adding value for the customers who get their products and services earlier or just in time.

In many cases, product and process innovation have to be pursued simultaneously. For example, the Smart car (co-developed by the Swiss watch holding SMH (Swatch) and Mercedes) which is only 2.5 metres long, contains new technical solutions in its realization and new distribution ideas in its launch.

Role in Innovation Process. Management must decide what role the firm should play concerning innovation processes in its product-markets. Basically there are two ways to behave: (1) to strive for innovation leadership or (2) to reach for attractive market positions as a late entrant.

(1) Innovation Leadership. Innovation leadership is not necessarily the same as pioneering. Pioneering firms are the first to introduce a new solution to a customer problem in the market. They have the opportunity to develop market know-how earlier than their competitors, enjoy customer loyalty, influence the direction of technological development, set industry standards, and experience high rates of market share growth leading to effective performance. But they also experience all the difficulties of introducing an innovation such as high development costs, quality problems, legal constraints, customers' misperceptions and intermediaries' reluctance concerning new products.

Early leadership is not so much characterized by being first to market but by some managerial factors which help a firm to profit from the opportunities of a pioneer and to reduce its disadvantages: a vision of the mass market, managerial persistence, financial commitment and relentless innovation. To be or to become an early leader in a new product category, a company must have managers who are able to envision the full potential of the new product. They need to develop the vision of a broad international mass market. Only the sales volume of such a market can provide the economies of scale and experience needed to overcome start-up problems such as high costs, limited features or missing distribution.

For example, Ampex pioneered the video recorder market in 1956 and was the leading supplier for several years. At USD50,000 each, initial recorder sales were limited. RCA and Toshiba, the only competitors, were way behind, so Ampex had almost a monopoly in sales and R&D. However, the company's managers did little to improve quality or lower costs; instead, they sought to reduce Ampex's dependence on video recorder sales, and pursued diversifications such as audio products and computer peripherals. In contrast, at JVC, Yuma Shiraishi, manager of video recorder development, asked his engineers to develop a machine that could sell for USD500, while using little tape and retaining high picture quality. It took JVC engineers 20 years to realize the goal. But when their efforts were successful in the mid-1970s, JVC's video sales went from USD2 million to almost 2 billion in the following 15 years.[19]

When deciding on what innovation behaviour guidelines to formulate for their company, management should be aware that most successful products are not the immediate result of technological breakthroughs but the fruit of small, incremental innovations in design, engineering, manufacturing and marketing over extended periods of time. They are only in existence because management maintained a commitment to the product over a long period of slow but continual progress. For example, it took VAI, one of the world's top three metallurgical engineering firms based in Austria, more than 12 years to develop COREX, a direct reduction technology for iron production which largely reduces the costs and environmental stress of the process, from the first technical solution to the point where customers around the world started to accept the new technology as a feasible alternative. In 1995 contracts were signed in Australia, India, Korea and South Africa, finally rewarding management for their persistence.

As the examples show, it can take significant time to overcome R&D as well as marketing odds of innovations. Therefore, the management of a company wanting to be an early innovation leader must be able and willing to commit substantial finances to last through this struggle. And it must be aware that innovation is an ongoing process of continual product and process improvement which will not take place in a large bureaucracy, when people are satisfied with their first success, or when management fears undermining current market success through the cannibalization of established products. IBM, for example, stymied its development of minicomputers and workstations to protect mainframe sales, even though competitors kept making inroads into the mainframe market. When they finally decided to put more energy into the development of this product category, they were slow to bring out new products because of their bureaucratic approval process.[20]

To maintain a leadership position, the company must continually develop and implement new technologies or acquire them through licensing, strategic partnerships or acquisitions. Japanese companies historically have bought the rights to use technologies that have been developed by companies in other advanced economies. They then improved the basic technology until they reached a level of experience and know-how that allowed them to take the lead in technology development.

(2) Late Entrant. A late entrant or follower may be able to avoid the mistakes made by the pioneer. It may also have lower research and development costs (in effect, lowering fixed costs) and may therefore be able to match the pioneer's low costs. But to be in a position to become market leader, to set standards and influence the development of the industry, the firm must hold a dominant position in a product category related to the new product-market, as for example Coca-Cola in the soft drinks market. Such a position allows it to leverage assets such as name recognition, an existing distribution network, production facilities or managerial expertise.

Royal Crown, for example, achieved great success when it expanded diet cola from the niche of people with special dietary needs and introduced it to the mass market in the 1960s. However, it was virtually powerless to prevent Coca-Cola from capturing market leadership within one year of its late market entry in 1982.[21] Merck, a producer of pharmaceutical products, also successfully pursues such a follower strategy. Operating in many different markets where it faces primarily local competition, it can use its global distribution network to quickly introduce the products, services or ideas of its more innovative, but localized, competitors in the markets where they are not present.

Rate of Innovation. For both product and process technology, the company's rate of innovation compared to the rate for the industry is of major concern. A company's rate of innovation is heavily influenced by traditions in the home market and the basic values of domestic customers, as well as the speed of innovation processes inside the company. German auto makers, for example, preferred not to change their models too often, not only in order to communicate an image of reliable quality and craftsmanship, but also to let their products develop a strong visual image in the minds of their relatively conservative customers. This strategy was of advantage in European markets. In the USA, in contrast, customers are interested in fast product changes and in East Asia they expect continual product improvement. There, the quality of a company's offerings is judged partly on the basis of the firm's rate of product innovation. Because there was no need for faster changes in their home markets, the European auto makers had developed lengthy innovation processes which in the 1980s took up to three times longer than those of their Japanese competitors and put them into a disadvantageous competitive position in the North American and Asian markets.

Owing to the different expectations of their customers, Japanese companies had learned to be much faster in new product development than their European (and US) competitors. The higher speed allowed them to swamp the markets with new products or product features. Such continual product innovation in small steps can lead to significant advantages over competitors. Japanese manufacturers of air conditioners, for example, after a few years of small but continual product innovation steps were seven to ten years ahead in product technology compared to their US competitors. But it can also lead to economic trouble as experienced by Mazda. The company had six models 15 years ago, selling about one million cars. In 1996, when Ford took over a majority stake in its shares, Mazda was offering 29 models but selling the same number of cars. The increased complexity of their range had dramatically decreased the firm's profits.

One way of overcoming the problem of different innovation rates expected by customers in different parts of the world is to split the world market into customer segments on the basis of innovation orientation and to develop different strategies for each segment. In many cases, however, this approach entails higher costs than selling to a unified market. Another way out is to offer customized flexibility in many different product features. Computer-aided production planning and production flexibility can enable customers to design individualized products. In the case of cars, for example, the customer can specify such features as colour, power, and 'options' such as sun-roof or air conditioning.

In general, an internationally operating firm should be able at least to meet the latest standard of technology in its field. To be able to compete successfully in global markets, the company may undertake any of the following steps:

↔ Monitor trade journals, patent and research reports and attend international conferences and seminars on relevant technological issues.

↔ Establish and maintain product as well as process innovation teams, supported by recognized organizational commitment, with a knowledgeable team leader and members from all relevant disciplines in the company who are rewarded for the success of the team work.

↔ Enter into agreements with research organizations that give the company access to recent research and the right to bring the resulting innovations to market.

↔ Hire specialized engineering firms.

↔ Engage in cooperative research projects with partners (such as lead users, intermediaries, suppliers, designers or competitors) that have complementary expertise.

↔ Acquire new technologies through licensing or acquisitions.

If a company cannot be among the innovation leaders in its industry, it does not necessarily lack international market potential, but it faces greater difficulty and must choose its target markets with more care. Most Latin American markets, for example, are not sufficiently technologically developed to use the latest generation of weaving machines. Workers lack the necessary skills, raw materials do not meet the specifications met by materials in highly industrialized markets, maintenance capabilities are lacking, and the machines are too expensive. As a result, there is a large market for simpler machines and second-hand equipment in Latin America, which can be provided by companies that are not among the technological leaders in the industry.

Acquisition

During the process of assessing potential international markets, management may find very attractive product- or country-markets that the company cannot serve adequately because of missing competencies or resources. Instead of leaving those markets to competitors which are in a better position or starting to build up the needed strengths, management may decide that the markets are of great importance to the firm and speed is the key to attain an attractive strategic position. In such a case, acquisition gives the company the opportunity to build a presence instantly. Germany's Robert Bosch GmbH, located in Stuttgart, the first company to offer ABS (anti-lock braking systems) for cars, for example, was confronted with the demand of its major car manufacturing clients to deliver entire product systems instead of only electronic parts to improve braking systems. It therefore acquired 24 brake-making factories in Europe, Latin America and the USA as well as shares of joint ventures in China, India and Korea from US-based Allied Signal Inc. With this acquisition Bosch became one of the four largest brake-making firms in the world, together with US competitors Teves and Kelsey-Hayes and the UK's Lucas.[22]

UK-based Unilever acquired Povltavské Tukové Závody in the Czech Republic to strengthen its operational base in the margarine and soap markets, which offered good growth opportunities in the early 1990s, and to have access to relationships between local business partners before competition takes away a significant share of the market.

The pressure to match global standards of efficiency and financial resources available to market and product development also contributes to an increasing number of mergers, particularly in Europe, where many firms in industries such as airlines, autos, banking and media have traditionally avoided international mergers and contented themselves instead with local markets. For example, French multimedia company Infogrames Entertainment and Ocean International Ltd, a similar privately held UK company whose catalogue of simulation, adventure and arcade software games is complementary to that of the French company, have announced their merger in a move that creates Europe's biggest entity in the fast-growing multimedia industry. The new firm, which is the world's fifth-largest in the multimedia sector, should possess the resources needed to compete with its global competitors.[23]

Other companies acquire (shares of) firms to reach a dominant market position. Japanese Softbank, for example, whose domestic business includes Japan's biggest computer software distributor and its leading publisher of PC magazines, seems to strive for as much control of the infrastructure of the PC market – from distribution to publications, information services and associated conferences – as possible. Since its listing on Japan's over-the-counter stock market in 1994, the firm has been obsessed with foreign investments. In 1995 alone it spent USD3 billion buying American high-tech companies mainly related to Internet activities (for example, 37 per cent of Yahoo! which provides a directory for the Internet, or 30 per cent of Unitech, a Californian software supplier that is developing software to offer Internet services in China).[24]

To be successful in acquiring other businesses, a company must constantly survey its markets for potential acquisition candidates, assess the attractiveness of the targets, the appropriate approach to initiating the acquisition and the steps necessary to integrate their business effectively into their own organization. Japanese-owned ICL, for example, has a special planning group called Acquisition Group which studies and evaluates targets on a global basis. Thomson Consumer Electronics of France, after a series of acquisitions of consumer electronics companies in Europe and the USA in the 1980s, has integrated all of these interests into a synergistic consumer electronics business.

How difficult such integration processes can be is best illustrated by the acquisition of a controlling interest of Ford Motor Co. in Mazda Motor Corp. in 1996. Mazda's new president, Mr Wallace, is a global executive, born in Scotland and raised in England, having served in six countries in 17 years and speaking English, Spanish and German, who is respected by his Japanese employees for listening to them and building close relationships. Nevertheless, American-style business practices clash with sacred Japanese big-business traditions, such as long-term employment, seniority-based promotions and institutionalized relationships with suppliers that value familiarity over price. Ford's men at Mazda have instituted previously unheard-of financial controls, reduced inventory and slashed exports to the USA rather than continuing to produce cars it would have to sell at a loss.[25]

Cooperation

Many small and medium-sized companies that wish to become international marketers possess the required technical know-how to offer attractive products and services, but lack the international experience or financial and personnel resources to confront their competitors in many markets simultaneously or to acquire businesses to reach the competitive advantages needed for success. In the USA, for example, about 250 mostly large com-

STRATEGY BOX

Abar Ipsen Industries Hunting for Growth in the Pacific Rim

Bensalem, Pennsylvania-based Abar Ipsen Industries is a producer of metal-strengthening furnaces whose domestic sales in the middle of the 1990s stagnated at USD 60 million-a-year because their traditional US customers were building fewer factories. The company looked for growth in China and other Pacific Rim countries, and thought they knew what they were getting into because they had sold furnaces in Japan for years.

But Abar Ipsen encountered a series of problems: thieves stole parts of their crates on the docks of Singapore. Electricity and water systems were lacking when the company's technicians arrived at a customer's plant in a remote province of China. At another Chinese site, the crate containing a furnace was soaked with rainwater and Abar Ipsen had to pay for the expensive repair. Moreover, the company went international without any technicians willing to live in foreign countries for extended periods. It ran up big bills ferrying technicians back and forth.

On its USD 10 million additional annual sales in Asia the company made no profit in 1995. But Abar Ipsen decided to stay the course. It is building a plant in Shanghai and turning to local technicians for help. Cooperation is seen as the key for future success.

Source: Bleakley, F.R. (1996) 'U.S. Firms See Gains of Cost-Cutting Over, Push to Lift Revenues', *The Wall Street Journal Europe*, 5–6 July, pp. 1 and 4.

panies account for 80 per cent of US exports. But there are at least 20 000 small and medium-sized firms which produce products that could boost their revenues by being offered internationally. The Strategy box describes such a firm and its experiences in going international.

When international business experience or financial or human resources are lacking, it is very difficult to enter international markets without co-operating with other companies that operate in these markets. Through cooperation, such as business clusters, supply agreements, original equipment manufacturing (OEM), licensing agreements, joint ventures and the use of strategic alliances even with competitors, the company can supplement its strengths with those of partners.

Aprilia, the fastest-growing motorbike company in Europe, based in Noale near Venice, and nearby Nordica, which has established itself as a world leader in ski boots, are European examples of firms using 'network' manufacturing in business clusters which allow even very small supplier firms to profit from internationalization. Neither Aprilia, taking on bigger rivals like Italy's Piaggio, France's Peugeot and Japan's Honda Motor, nor Nordica manufactures a single component. Instead, they work closely with hundreds of suppliers specializing in the production of parts where they can reach economies of scale and profit from experience. The firms' own resources go into design, assembly and international marketing.[26]

Energia, a Russian aerospace firm based in Kaliningrad, has established a joint venture with middle-sized German Kayser-Threde GmbH to secure access to sources of capital. The advanced technology equipment and industrial know-how of the Russian partner helped the German firm to become a major provider of remote sensing services to customers in Asia, Western Europe and North America.[27]

But big companies can also profit from cooperation. Japan's JVC, for example, in their global battle against Sony to make their video cassette recorder format, VHS, the market standard, entered a multitude of cooperation agreements. It licensed VHS to fellow Japanese manufacturers, supplied RCA of the USA with models carrying the RCA brand, and entered a manufacturing joint venture with Germany's Telefunken and the UK's Thorn-EMI-Ferguson. As a result, over 80 per cent of VCRs used in the world today are VHS machines.

Firms that want to gain access to markets in Asia, the Community of Independent States (CIS) and Latin America may have to establish cooperative agreements with local organizations. Hughes Rediffusion Simulation Ltd of the UK, for example, has joined Mikoyan Design Bureau, the Russian builder of MiG fighters, and GosNIIAS, a Russian avionics integration organization, to develop, co-manufacture and market training and simulation systems for Mikoyan military and civil aircraft.[28] Cable and satellite television-channel operator Flextech PLC, Britain's second-largest investor in multi-channel television, has signed a 50–50 partnership with Sumitomo Trading to launch a home-shopping service in Japan.[29] And Nike, the Oregon-based footwear company, entered into a manufacturing joint venture with Alpargatas SAIC, Argentina's largest shoe and textile company. The deal has given Alpargatas access to Nike's advanced shoe-making technology while Nike has got factory space and a ready-made sales force for the Argentine market. In late 1994, Nike gave the joint venture marketing rights to the big Brazilian market through 1999.[30]

Strategic partnerships or strategic alliances are a special type of cooperative behaviour. They involve two or more organizations, in which the combined strengths of the partners permit each to perform better in international markets. One or all partners contribute marketing knowledge and skills, production technology, manufacturing competency, and access to financial resources and distribution channels. Economies of scale and experience curve effects can be gained more quickly and efficiently through a strategic partnership than through the efforts of a single firm. The biggest airline in the world, British Airways (BA) and the second-biggest North American airline, American Airlines (AMR), for example, became partners by coordinating their passenger and freight business between Europe and the USA, code-sharing (joint flight numbers for computer reservation systems), and mutual acceptance of frequent flyer programmes as from April 1997. They will not only become one of the most powerful alliances in air transportation, sharing more than 28 per cent of the entire transatlantic business, but also significantly reduce costs through shared systems.[31]

The research and development investment needed to remain competitive on a global scale may be beyond the financial resources of a single organization, but become feasible through the establishment of a strategic partnership. St Petersburg-based Klimov, Korea's Hala group and the Korean Institute of Science and Technology, for example, have joined forces to develop a 1.5-megawatt ground-based electrical power and heating station. The technology developed by Klimov and the Russian Central Turbine and Boiler Institute has significantly contributed to lowering the R&D expenses of this project. The station designed by the Russian and Korean partners is expected to cost at least 30 per cent less to build than similar Western systems.[32]

For an increasing number of firms facing global competition the only way to remain independent is to enter strategic partnerships. This apparent contradiction is explained by the fact that, given global competition and the cost of resources, single organizations may not be able to generate enough cash flow to operate independently. Alliances make it possible to obtain resources and share experience with partners without acquiring or being acquired by others. Californian Oracle Corp. , for example, was joined by Apple Computer, IBM, Netscape Communications and Sun Microsystems for the development of an Internet device called NC that will combine the functions of today's telephones, televisions and computers in one simple unit at a price below USD1,000. The NC, the first recent effort by the computer industry to move away from software and electronics standards dictated by Microsoft and Intel Corps, may take many forms – from desktops to laptops to video phones, pagers and even conventional PCs.[33]

Strategic partnerships are not only feasible for large companies. Small and medium-sized firms that would like to take advantage of international market opportunities can also establish such partnerships. In strategic alliances between middle-sized firms, one partner may, for example, produce (part of) the product while the other sells it under its well-established brand name. Smaller firms can also run a sales office together, one bringing in its existing office facilities, the other an additional product line to be sold through the same distribution channels (improving the distribution of overheads across product lines).

As with any competitive strategy, there are risks associated with strategic partnerships. Often failure to foresee differences in corporate cultures may place the partnership at risk. Other problems occur when the partnership pushes one, if not both, of the new partners into areas in which it has no previous experience. Still another problem with establishing a strategic partnership is the cost of a one-way flow of technology. If guarantees are not established and strictly enforced, an organization might share technology only to find that it faces additional competition from its supposed partner.

Success in a strategic partnership occurs when each partner brings to the alliance a strength that the other partner lacks. The best partners might be those that do not have a dominant share of the market or are not even in the industry. US-based Corning Glass, for example, cooperates with over 14 different alliance partners in Europe, Asia and Latin America to learn of potential improvements in designing and manufacturing different glass and ceramic-based products, to penetrate new markets, and to share the risks of technical development. With Novartis of Switzerland, it focuses on medical diagnostics. The partnership with Siemens concentrates on fibre optics. The alliance with NGK Insulators of Japan produces ceramics for catalytic converters and pollution control equipment.[34]

The major problem is finding the right cooperation partner(s). For that purpose, interested firms should develop a profile of characteristics expected from an ideal cooperation partner, based on the intended global portfolio and the assessment of the firm's versus the competitors' distinctive competencies in the targeted markets. Based on the profile of characteristics sought, the company can either start a search process on its own or use foreign trade organizations or consultants to find the right partner(s).

Strategic partnerships must have shared and mutually understood objectives if they are to succeed. Partners that seek short-term profits will have problems with partners that are more concerned with long-term gains in market share. Similarly, organizations that are looking for marketing assistance may have difficulties with partners that prefer technical solutions. The cooperation partners must understand and trust each other. As the example of the partnership between KLM Royal Dutch Airlines, a European carrier with a tiny home market, and Northwest Airlines, a regional US player with great Pacific routes, impressively shows, there may be many advantages, such as allowing the merging of schedules, pricing and services – adding USD200 million annually to the carriers' combined revenue; nevertheless, a lack of trust can lead to fierce dispute. In 1996, after seven years of cooperation during which Northwest narrowly avoided bankruptcy thanks to USD250 million in loans arranged by KLM, Northwest's management claimed KLM was seeking 'creeping control' of their airline, whereas KLM charged that Northwest's management was only interested in quickly selling the company to the highest bidder.[35]

Other attributes of successful strategic partnerships include careful study of the market, sharing equity, respect for cultural differences, and maintaining a dialogue between the partners. The skills needed to ensure international competitiveness through strategic partnerships, therefore, are similar for small and big firms. One important skill is patience in negotiating with partners from different cultures. US executives, in particular, seem impatient with international standards. In the USA 'time is money', but in China, for example, 'time is eternity'.

In sum, strategic partnerships are both a response and a stimulus to globalization. Firms of any size should consider establishing such partnerships to enter markets, gain access to distribution systems, scarce resources and skills, maintain technological and manufacturing competency, monitor the activities of competitors, keep abreast of technological development, and gain economies of scale and experience curve effects, all of which serve to enhance a firm's international competitiveness.

RESOURCE ALLOCATION

When the management of the company has decided which markets should be served and how to compete in those markets, it has to determine how much of the firm's resources should be spent for what purpose (see Figure 9.13) and when. For that purpose it needs to compare the goals set for the company to the share of success each part of the intended portfolio will contribute if the intended competitive strategy works and how much resources the effective implementation of this strategy will need.

After all, the resource allocation decision boils down to an answer to how dispersed the firm's resources should be. As Figure 9.14 shows, at the corporate level management has to decide how much of the available resources should be spent on combinations of current and new country-markets, product-markets and technologies.

Scheduling the International Expansion

Underestimating the size and aspirations of new country-markets compared to the markets that have been served so far may result in too little resource

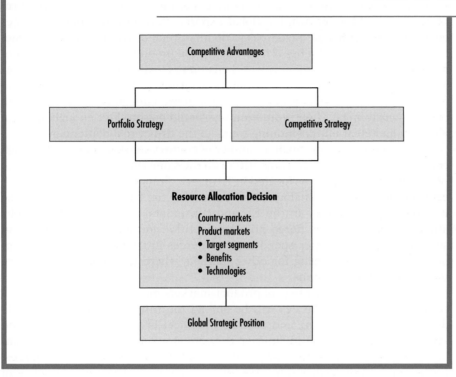

Figure 9.13 DETERMINING THE GLOBAL STRATEGIC POSITION STEP 3: RESOURCE ALLOCATION

Having determined how to compete in the chosen markets, management has to decide how much resources to spend for what purpose.

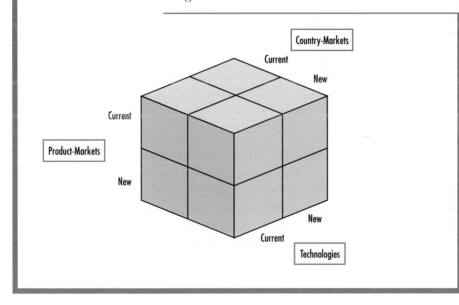

Figure 9.14 STRATEGIC OPTIONS FOR RESOURCE ALLOCATION

Management must decide how to allocate the firm's resources to country-markets, product-markets and technologies.

allocation. Thus, some European companies, such as Peugeot, have failed in the US market largely because of underspending. The government wanted Peugeot (at that time a state-owned company) to export to a market that would bring hard currency back to France. Because at the same time the firm planned to build a network for global exports, starting with France's former colonies, Peugeot had no resources to do more than distribute the cars its factory was already producing. Their budget for product development did not allow redesigning some models to US customers' expectations such as power windows and seats, air conditioning, or controls at familiar locations. The firm's dealer and service systems were not dense enough to seem reliable to potential customers. Their promotion budget did not produce enough national visibility and clear-cut positioning to make the firm a real contender.[36]

Overspending in too small a number of country-markets may lead to high competitive pressure when competitors do the same thing. For example, some producers of food products located in Denmark, France, Italy and Greece concentrate their international activities on serving the German market because it is the biggest country in the EU and consumers' purchasing power looks attractive. The result is fierce price competition for shelf space in German supermarkets. Companies spend their resources in trying to beat their competitors instead of looking for other markets where they could reach more profitable market positions.

Serving too broad a range of product-markets may lead to a loss of overall competency, since resources will be spread too thinly among research and development, engineering and customer service, or sales force training and support. On the other hand, limiting the company's activities to a small number of country- or product-markets may result in overspending of resources. For example, Friedrich Grohe AG, the Germany-based leading supplier of fittings in Europe, recognized that their focus on one product-market led to an overspending of resources in distribution, customer services and personnel development. To spread their resources over a broader range of markets, the company acquired DAL and AQUA, the leading brands in flushing systems and electronic water management in Germany, and introduced them in their international markets. The cost of the highly qualified global customer service organization was split between the three brands, procurement of materials was centralized, and a complete sanitary system could be offered to international intermediaries thus improving their market position.

Few companies can enter all potentially viable markets at once. Depending on their home market, the available resources, their experience with international business, and the nature of the business environment they face in the new markets, they will choose an appropriate form of expansion into the local markets: concentric expansion, platform expansion or focused expansion. This decision is strongly related to the timing of entry into the markets (Table 9.1).

Concentric Expansion. The firm's level of international experience is related to the degree of risk it is willing to accept in its process of internationalization. A firm that is entering its first foreign market is at the beginning of the international marketing experience curve. A firm that has been involved in foreign markets for years is usually willing to accept higher levels of risk, because it has progressed along the experience curve and is better able to manage risk. The Irish Jefferson Smurfit Group, a manufacturer of paper and packaging material, for example, has decided to apply what they call a

| Table 9.1 | SCHEDULING THE INTERNATIONAL EXPANSION |

SCHEDULING THE INTERNATIONAL EXPANSION

Form of expansion

↔ Concentric expansion

↔ Platform expansion

↔ Focused expansion

Timing

When taking strategic decisions on the allocation of scarce resources, decision makers have to fix a schedule for the international expansion of the firm.

'phased approach' to expansion in Asian markets. During 1995, the company made its first direct investment in Asia with privately owned Singapore-based New Toyo to form Smurfit Toyo, which makes folding cartons. Additionally, Smurfit formed a joint venture in China that bought a linerboard mill near Shanghai. Management is cautious, with the long-term aim of being an important player in the region. They want to become familiar with the served markets before making any major financial commitments.

Frequently a firm that is entering foreign markets for the first time uses a market that it perceives to be similar to its home market as a bridge, waiting until it has gained a comfortable level of international experience before entering a more dissimilar market. Danish companies, for example, often enter the UK market before moving into the US market. And US companies often enter the Canadian market before attempting to enter the UK and other European markets. Bridging is similar to a market roll-out campaign, in which the company uses its experience in a particular market segment to gain a competitive advantage in similar segments.

Many small companies successfully start their concentric expansion from a strong competitive position in their home market and enter neighbouring markets first, gradually expanding their marketing activities from those markets to their respective neighbours. A Norwegian firm, for example, might enter Sweden and Denmark before attempting to expand to Germany. (See Map 9.1.) Resources are allocated to well-defined product-markets. The company continually seeks to increase its penetration of the markets it is currently serving and gradually develops superior competitive advantages in those markets. Expansion is regarded as a long-term process.

The main problem with this approach is that neighbouring markets are not necessarily the most attractive ones. Moreover, competitors can gain a dominant position in other markets before the company reaches them. In addition, the firm may develop a false sense of security, underestimating the difficulties of entering neighbouring markets simply because they seem familiar.

Platform Expansion. In global product-markets of technologically advanced industries like computers, machine tools and consumer electronics, a company must quickly attain a sizeable share of the global market in order

Map 9.1   CONCENTRIC EXPANSION

A Norwegian firm following a concentric expansion schedule would probably move first into Sweden, Finland and Denmark before moving into Germany or the rest of Western Europe.

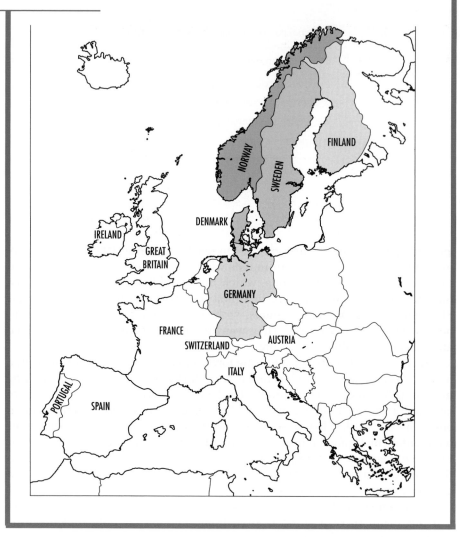

to remain competitive. Companies in such industries may choose a platform expansion strategy. This approach involves starting out simultaneously in the technologically advanced Triad markets and then expanding to other markets. Thus, IBM uses its US, Canadian, Japanese and EU markets as platforms from which it enters other markets in Latin America, Asia and Europe.

This strategy may seem to be appropriate only for large companies, but smaller firms can also use it, either by building a network of cooperative partners or by utilizing the services of a global trading house. A Canadian manufacturer of movable gas barbecues used a similar approach adapted to its company size. When the firm decided to enter the attractive German market, it also decided to expand from there to the neighbouring German-speaking markets (Austria, Switzerland, parts of Northern Italy), in order to take advantage of possible synergies.

Focused Expansion. Companies of any size operating in an industry in which physical distances are relatively unimportant (such as small consumer goods like shavers or large industrial products like ship cranes) may choose a focused expansion strategy. In this approach, starting from the product-market the company serves, the marketer examines the most promising country-markets, regardless of location, entering local markets according to their level of attractiveness.

Timing

A well-developed resource allocation strategy must be precisely timed for maximum success. It should include commitment to long-term goals. Bonduelle, the French producer of canned and deep frozen vegetables, for example, has the goal to be one of the major players in the markets of central and eastern Europe. The firm started expansion through exports to the Czech Republic in 1991, followed by Hungary a year later, and Poland in 1993. Slovakia and Russia were entered in 1994. After this period of commercial implantation, Bonduelle started local production to overcome the high costs of transportation and tariffs. They closed two production sites in Belgium and France, and following two years of leadership through management contracts, bought a factory in Hungary and another one in Poland.[37]

Part of timing is the decision on how long it may take before an investment in a new market becomes profitable. Management should not withdraw immediately if success cannot be achieved in a short time. International marketing, to a large extent, is a learning process. Only if a pre-specified reasonable amount of time has passed without success should management withdraw from a market.

Product-markets are characterized not only by specific benefits provided to certain customer groups but also by the technologies applied to produce the intended benefits. An internationally active firm, therefore, must decide how much resources to allocate to the development of new technologies compared to the maintenance of current technologies. Questions such as 'How much time and money should be spent on the development of a new product technology?' or 'Should current production facilities be expanded, or should new plants with newer equipment be built?' have to be answered. In 1992, when the enormous growth potential of the telecommunications industry became evident, for example, Finland's Nokia Mobira Oy decided to focus on telecommunications. They not only sold their computer division to the UK's ICL but also got rid of their other low-value-added commodity product businesses, including the original paper products group.[38]

GLOBAL STRATEGIC POSITION

At this point the global strategic position of the company can be formulated. Containing statements on what goals to achieve, which markets to serve, how to compete in the chosen markets and how much resources to spend for each purpose, the strategic position develops the firm's corporate policy to more detail. For example, in 1996 the global strategic position of OMV, the Austrian producer of oil, distributor of natural gas and manufacturer of petrochemicals headquartered in Vienna, stated that the firm in general wanted to achieve a critical size (relative market share) relative to the total volume of the markets it serves, to reduce business risks and to ensure independence. In particular the company planned to expand their gas business and to reduce costs in oil exploration and production as well as in petrochemicals. Concerning their portfolio of served country-markets, the firm took different decisions according to the product-markets. To achieve the set goals it formulated a competitive strategy based on superior customer value, reliable relationships, cooperation and outsourcing. In the gas market one of the major partners is Gazprom, the Russian oil and gas giant, and another is Italy's SNAM, with which a joint venture was founded in Bermuda to finance distribution. In research and development the company plans to intensify cooperation with a French partner, and it is searching for a partner for the exploration of crude oil fields and oil production. Activities that can be provided at lower costs by external suppliers were planned to be outsourced. The same rule was formulated for activities where the particular know-how of specialists which is not part of the firm's core competencies can be procured at no fixed costs.

The statement of global strategic position serves as the basic guideline for the following decisions in the company's functional areas. Because of their knowledge concerning (potential) customers, intermediaries and competitors in attractive markets as well as their skills concerning the comparative analysis of market conditions, marketing people should have had a strong impact on the development of the global strategic position. They will further build their market-entry decisions (see Chapter 11) and all the marketing-mix decisions (see Chapters 12–18) on that basic strategic guideline.

SUMMARY

An internationally operating company has to answer four basic questions: which markets to serve; how to compete in those markets; how much of its scarce resources to spend for what purpose; and how to establish and sustain competitive advantages. To answer the first question, management has to develop a global portfolio strategy, that is, a basic idea of which customer groups the firm will provide with which benefits by the use of which technologies and in which geographic areas of the world. For that purpose it will assess the attractiveness of potential markets and compare the specific resources and capabilities needed to serve them successfully with the distinctive competencies of the firm.

The most attractive markets in which the company has potential competitive advantages will be chosen and a strategy of how to compete in those markets will be developed. Management has to decide which distinctive competencies to rely on or to establish as foundations for successful competition. Four major categories have emerged in the past: cost leadership, superior value, time leadership and reliable relationships. Distinctive competencies are to be transformed into customer and stakeholder benefits which will be useful as advantages in confronting competitors.

In any case the innovation capacity of the company will have a significant influence on the competitive strategy it can choose. If the firm does not possess enough competitive advantages to be successful individually, cannot build such advantages fast enough, or perceives an opportunity to further increase existing competitive advantages, it might acquire other companies which have the missing or additional competencies. Lack of financial resources, the importance of flexibility, and potential partners' strive for independence lead an increasing number of internationally operating firms to cooperate with partners. Even for big companies, strategic alliances have become a must to ensure long-term success in global markets.

Global portfolio strategy and competitive strategy need resources for their implementation. Because a company's resources are never unlimited, management has to decide how much of these scarce resources to spend for what purpose and when. They have simultaneously to avoid the traps of underspending in too many served markets and overspending in too small a number of chosen markets.

Finally, the intended portfolio, the competitive strategy and the resource allocation decision result in the global strategic position the firm wants to achieve. Its formulation elaborates the corporate policy in more detail, containing statements on what goals to achieve, which markets to serve, how to compete in the chosen markets, and how much resources to spend for each purpose.

DISCUSSION QUESTIONS

1. What is the content of an internationally active firm's intended global strategic position? What is it needed for?
2. What are the basic steps in portfolio planning?
3. Why is global portfolio analysis more complex than domestic portfolio analysis? Give examples of a locally and an internationally operating company you have found reading a trade magazine.
4. What are the four basic strategic options that a firm may choose in managing its portfolio? What are the main advantages of each strategy?
5. What strategies are available to a firm that wishes to penetrate a current market further? Find recent examples in newspapers.
6. Find an example how a small company might follow a global niche strategy to survive when faced with larger global competitors offering lower prices.
7. When are confrontation strategies appropriate, and what factors determine which strategic option should be used?
8. What determines whether a firm should be an innovation leader or follower? What can make both decisions successful? Find recent examples in the literature.
9. How can management determine whether it should emphasize product or process innovation? Explain with the help of examples you found in business magazines.
10. Find examples of fairly recent acquisitions of an

internationally operating company and try to find out how their integration has worked. What factors led to successful integration versus conflicts?
11. What are the reasons for small companies compared to larger ones to enter strategic partnerships for international marketing? Find examples from your country.
12. Why is optimal resource allocation a difficult task for the management of an internationally operating firm?
13. Contact a company doing international business and ask them about their intended global strategic position. Do they have a written statement, or if not, why not? What are their goals in the markets they serve? What competitive strategy do they apply? How are resource allocation decisions made?

ADDITIONAL READINGS

Boettcher, R. and M.K. Welge (1996) 'Global Strategies of European Firms', *The International Executive*, 38(2), March–April, 185–216.

Brandenburger, A.M. and B.J. Nalebuff (1995) 'The Right Game: Use Game Theory to Shape Strategy', *Harvard Business Review*, July–August, 57–69.

Douglas, S.P. and C.S. Craig (1996) 'Global Portfolio Planning and Market Interconnectedness', *Journal of International Marketing*, 4(1), 93–110.

Gulati, R. (1995) 'Social Structure and Alliance Formation Patterns: A Longitudinal Analysis',

Administrative Science Quarterly, December, 619–652.

Hooley, G., J. Saunders, and N. Piercy (1998) '*Marketing Strategy and Competitive Positioning*', London: Prentice Hall International.

Khanna, T. and K. Palepu (1997) 'Why Focused Strategies May Be Wrong for Emerging Markets', *Harvard Business Review*, July–August, 41–51.

Simon, H. (1996) *Hidden Champions*, Boston: Harvard Business School Press.

Tellis, G.J. and P. N. Golder (1996) 'First to Market, First to Fail? Real Causes of Enduring Market Leadership', *Sloan Management Review*, Winter, 65–75.

Wright, P. , M. Kroll, B. Pray, and A. Lado (1995) 'Strategic Orientations, Competitive Advantage, and Business Performance', *Journal of Business Research*, 33, 143–151.

NOTES

[1] Keller, J.J. and G. Naik (1996) 'Phone Merger Presages Global Consolidation', *The Wall Street Journal Europe*, 3 April, p. 8 and 'Shinawatra Unit Is Mulling Tie With Deutsche Telekom', *The Wall Street Journal Europe*, 12–13 April 1996, p. 8.

[2] Marks, D. (1996) 'Smurfit Issues Cautious Outlook Despite a 32% Jump in Profit in '95', *The Wall Street Journal Europe*, 11 April, p. 3.

[3] Smith, C.S. (1996) 'Kodak, Fuji Face Off In Neutral Territory: China's Vast Market', *The Wall Street Journal*, 24 May, pp. A1, A6.

[4] 'Fabulous and fabless', *The Economist*, 29 March 1997, p. 69.

[5] Simon, H. (1992) 'Lessons from Germany's Midsize Giants', *Harvard Business Review*, March–April, 115–123.

[6] Studer M. (1996) 'Swiss Insurer Sees Extension of Profit Surge', *The Wall Street Journal Europe*, 30 May, p. 13.

[7] Harrell, G.D. and R.O. Kiefer (1993) op cit., p. 64.

[8] Johnson B. (1996) 'Will the Web win appeal world wide?', *Advertising Age*, 25 March, p. 36.

[9] Burrows, P. (1995) 'The Computer is in the Mail (Really)', *Business Week*, 23 January, pp. 44–45.

[10] Mitchener, B. (1996) 'Renault May Seek Tie-Ups, But It Rules Out a Merger', *The Wall Street Journal Europe*, 5–6 July, p. 3.

[11] Sakamaki, S. (1996) 'Asian Invasion', *Far Eastern Economic Review*, 2 May, p. 69.

[12] Wright, P., M. Kroll, P. Chan, and K. Hamel (1991) 'Strategic Profiles and Performance: An Empirical Test of Selected Key Propositions', *Journal of the Academy of Marketing Science*, 19 (Summer), 245–254.

[13] 'It grows on trees', *The Economist*, 4 May 1996, p. 64.

[14] Stalk, G.J. (1988) 'Time – The Next Source of Competitive Advantage', Harvard Business Review, July–August,

[15] Hagerty, B. (1996) 'Pumping Gas in China Gets Interesting', *The Wall Street Journal*, 1 May, p. A14.

[16] 'Bouygues lance son téléphone mobile', *Le Figaro économie*, 30 May 1996, p. I.

[17] Millman, J. (1996) 'Mexican Tortilla Firms Stage U.S. Bake-Off', *The Wall Street Journal*, 10 May, p. A6.

[18] Smith, C.G. (1995) 'How Newcomers Can Undermine Incumbents' Marketing Strengths', *Business Horizons*, September–October, pp. 61–68.

[19] Tellis, G.J. and P.N. Golder (1996) 'First to Market, First to Fail? Real Causes of Enduring Market Leadership', *Sloan Management Review*, Winter, 65–75.

[20] Tellis, G.J. and P.N. Golder (1996) op.cit.

[21] Tellis, G.J. and P.N. Golder (1996) op.cit.

[22] 'Bosch schließt zu den größten Bremsern auf', *Der Standard*, March 2–3 1996, p. 27.

[23] Pearson, D. (1996) 'Infogrames Plans Merger With U.K. Firm', *The Wall Street Journal Europe*, 12–13 April, p. 8.

[24] 'After the party', *The Economist*, 18 May 1996, pp. 65f.

[25] Reitman, V. (1996), 'Japan Is Aghast as Foreigner Takes the Wheel at Mazda', *The Wall Street Journal*, 15 April, p. A11.

[26] Rossant, J. (1996) 'Aprilia's Leader of the Pack', *Business Week*, 10 June, p. 16.

[27] Elenkov, D.S. (1995) 'Executive Insights: The Russian Aerospace Industry – Survey with Implications for American Firms in the Global Marketplace', *Journal of International Marketing*, 3(2), 71–81.

[28] Elenkov, D.S. (1995) op.cit.

[29] McIntosh, B. (1996) 'Flextech Aims to Profit From New Pacts', *The Wall Street Journal Europe*, 15 May, p. 4.

[30] Friedland, J. (1996) 'Reforms Reshape Argentine Shoe Maker', *The Wall Street Journal*, 24 April, p. A10.

[31] Nomani, A.Q. and S. Carey (1996) 'British Airways, American May Forge Strategic Alliance', *The Wall Street Journal Europe*, 20 May, p. 3.

[32] Elenkov, D.S. (1995) op.cit.

[33] 'Oracle's Net Device Advances', *International Herald Tribune*, 21 May, p. 13.

[34] Lei, D. and J.W. Slocum, Jr. (1992) 'Global Strategy, Competence-Building and Strategic Alliances', *California Management Review*, Fall, 81–97.

[35] Chandler, S. (1996) 'KLM and Northwest: Rumble in the Cockpit', *Business Week*, 11 March, p. 47.

[36] Archawski, J.-L. and F.W.Wolek (1995) 'The Long Farewell: Peugeot's Departure from the U.S. Market', *Business Horizons*, May–June, 39–46.

[37] Malet, de C. (1996) 'Bonduelle: à l'est, du nouveau', *Le Figaro économie*, 11 March, p. 11.

[38] Echikson, W. (1994) 'How to Win Markets Fast', *Fortune*, 30 May, p. 114.

CHAPTER 10

MANAGEMENT SYSTEMS FOR INTERNATIONAL MARKETING

INTERNATIONAL INCIDENT

Reinventing Unilever

Unilever, the British-Dutch food and home and personal care company, has changed its top management structure in the Fall of 1996. Reshaping Unilever was a complex task given the company's presence in dozens of product categories in over 90 countries and total annual sales of about USD48 billion.

The starting point was to establish which of Unilever's product categories actually benefited from the strategic direction and resources that headquarters could provide. Once categories that would benefit from corporate involvement such as laundry, personal wash, ice cream, or tea had been singled out, the roles, responsibilities and staffing levels required to oversee them were determined. This meant reviewing the roles currently carried out and assessing whether they might more effectively be played at the headquarters in London and Rotterdam or by operative Business Groups such as Food & Beverages Europe, Home & Personal Care North America, or South East Asia & Australasia. Two consumer categories (Foods and Home & Personal Care) and an industrial businesses director were established. They each have a group comprising resources in finance, research, personnel, and supply chain technology with category teams for the corporate categories.

In addition to developing worldwide strategies for their categories, the category teams act as custodians of what have been termed "Unilever brands"– brands that are present across several regional markets. Category teams also propose and monitor research program and assist the business groups by identifying best practice in specific areas. They maintain a continuous dialog with category "champions" in the business groups through networking and regular international meetings.

For Unilever brands, business groups which were developed from former Overseas Regional Management will be expected to follow clear guidelines worldwide. The business groups, however, enjoy greater flexibility when developing regional marketing mixes. The intention is that in the case of local and regional brands the center should step back, since individual companies have a clearer perception of local consumer needs.

A fundamental element of the new approach is the principle of an "annual contract" between the business groups and the Executive Committee. It embraces areas like strategy, investment, and human resources in addition to standard financial criteria. As the name suggests, the contract will be regarded as binding, and incorporates a two-way approach to ensure that both operational managers and headquarters fulfill their sides of the bargain. Business group presidents have been given the freedom to shape their own organizational structures, retaining the operating companies as Unilever's core building block.

Source: Fraser, I. (1996), 'Reshaping the business', *Unilever Magazine*, 2nd Issue, No. 100, 10–12.

THE ROLE OF MANAGEMENT SYSTEMS IN INTERNATIONAL MARKETING

A firm's statement of its intended global strategic position contains decisions on the markets to serve, how to compete successfully in those markets, and how much of its key resources to allocate to which markets and technologies. To implement those decisions, management needs to develop an international marketing plan. But to be able to develop such a plan and to realize both strategy and plan, management may need to adjust the resource configuration of the company. It has to rethink which activities are to be performed internally or externally and where those activities should be located. Recent years have seen a trend to globally distributed and locally specialized resources which are linked to each other by international flows of capital, knowledge, products and people within firms or within a network of closely related cooperating firms.

General Motors, for example, has established GM International Operations in Zurich, Switzerland, as its headquarters for all automotive operations outside the USA. Its 'Technisches Entwicklungszentrum' (Technical Development Centre), based in Rüsselsheim, Germany, the home-base of GM's global brand Opel, is a think tank that houses 8000 engineers developing platform concepts for cars, that is, globally standardized technological features on which different car models can be based. A factory located near Vienna, Austria, produces one million gear boxes, one million engines, and 300 000 cylinder heads a year which are delivered to assembly plants located in Asia, Europe, and the Americas.[1]

Puma, the German producer of sports equipment, with annual sales of nearly one billion dollars, as another example, is managed by a headquarters located in Herzogenaurach which employs 180 people. Shoes and textiles are produced by partner firms in 20 countries, and physically distributed and sold in more than 80 countries by other partners. Puma itself focuses on product development and marketing activities. By carefully changing the resource configuration of its business Puma has managed to turn a loss of about USD40 million in 1994 into a profit of USD20 million in 1995.[2]

Depending on the choice of markets to serve – in particular when management changes its perspective from an international to a global view of markets – and as a consequence of resource configuration decisions, the implementation of a firm's intended global strategic position may require changes in the company's coordination and control systems. Special roles may have to be allocated to organizational units. Linkages may have to be built between new or existing units. Embedded power structures may need to be broken down, and new mechanisms for managing dispersed activities may need to be established.

A company's formal coordination and control mechanisms are established through its management systems, that is, the firm's organization, its leadership, information and planning systems. They play a significant role in a company's struggle to attain and maintain its intended global position. For example, a company with an organizational structure that provides short lines of communication can more easily manage a diverse portfolio of product- and country-markets without losing control of operations. Management systems help build and sustain the competitive advantages on which the global strategic position is based.

Goals

For a firm to be successful in international marketing it needs to have three basic capabilities: it must be able to develop and maintain

↔ global-scale efficiency and competitiveness,

↔ local-level responsiveness and flexibility, and

↔ cross-market capacity to leverage learning on a company-wide basis.

It is part of management's basic responsibilities to shape the organization, leadership, information and planning systems of their firm in a way that will attain these goals. Marketing managers have a vital interest in how the management infrastructure functions, because they rely on this infrastructure in developing and implementing their marketing policies and actions. Therefore, they should participate in the decisions on how to shape the management systems.

Factors of Influence

To a certain extent, the shape of a firm's management systems is a consequence of its corporate policy. The business philosophy of IKEA, the Swedish furniture retailing giant, for example, contains two basic ideas: equality among employees and avoiding corporate bureaucracy. While this provides a positive climate for internal communication among employees at all levels, it also results in managers resisting formal planning and control systems.

Management systems are also strongly influenced by the firm's corporate strategy. For example, a global cost leadership strategy requires highly centralized control, but it may also require a planning system that permits flexible implementation of the basic strategy in local units. US-based Texas Instruments, for example, must centrally plan its global production to reduce costs to a minimum, but distribution channel decisions need to be adapted locally to sustain the cost leadership strategy.

The most successful internationally operating companies are characterized by management systems which match the specific requirements of their external environments, either through proper adaptation to external demands or superior business definition based on the existing management systems. If, for example, a marketer of branded consumer products such as French Lesieur, a manufacturer of cooking oils and fats, cleaning agents and other household products, is confronted with only a few powerful intermediaries, such as the UK's Marks & Spencer, Germany's Rewe or France-based Carrefour, who do business all over the EU, it might be well advised to install a key account management structure. On the other hand, a company that has a distinctive competency in its information system should choose product-markets where superior information is a success factor. For example, Italy's Benetton, which has a highly sophisticated high-speed information system, is well positioned in the fashion market where fast reactions to customer choices are a major source of success.

A good fit between environments and management systems helps to reduce the uncertainty inherent in international marketing. Uncertainty may stem from the complexity, variability or interrelationships of the environments in which the company operates.

The more complex the company's environments, the more diverse the structure of and processes in its management systems tend to be. If, for example, a US pizza-delivery firm such as Domino's Pizza decides to extend its business to East Asian and Latin American markets, the complexity of its environments will increase. To optimize its profits it will have to develop a planning system that takes into account national differences in taxation. Firms internationalizing their business tend to create increasingly specialized jobs, to narrow spans of control, and to lengthen chains of command. As the examples of globally operating companies such as British-Dutch Unilever show, however, reducing their organizational complexity is currently one of their most important goals to maintain competitiveness.

The greater the variability, that is, the rate of fluctuation in the firm's environments, the more flexible and adaptable an organization's management systems must be. Higher flexibility often requires a less formal ('lean') organizational structure and decentralized management processes with changing leadership. For example, Compaq Computer of Houston emphasizes multidisciplinary group decision making and minimizes hierarchical structures to better respond to the dynamics of the firm's environments.

Multiple interrelationships in a company's environment require management systems able to handle the complex power structure, interdependencies and information flows, as well as the diversity of aspirations in such an environment. Barriers to the diffusion of information inside the company have to be lowered. For example, information networks of varying people, regardless of their job title or grade, who have information or skills to contribute, may replace formal committees and boards. Process-oriented organizational structures such as those introduced by US-based Gore Corp. are able to bring together personnel from various functional areas of the firm whose contribution is needed to achieve the highest customer satisfaction all over the world.

ORGANIZATION

With the broadening of markets that occurs as a result of internationalization, a new corporate structure may become necessary. For example, a US insurance company preparing to serve the EU and Southeast Asian markets may find that a product-based structure (such as life, fire and liability policies), which may have worked very well domestically, will no longer be adequate. Instead, it may have to develop a new structure based on customer groups and regions in order to accommodate differences in lifestyle and, hence, insurance needs. Management has a range of organizational structures, each with its own strengths and weaknesses, to choose from.

International Marketing Manager

In small companies just starting to go international, organizational structure seems of minor concern, because one person or a few can handle all of the elements mentioned above. In most cases, however, international marketing responsibilities should not be given to someone whose main job lies in the domestic area. This person will rarely focus on the more complex and, in the beginning, often less rewarding job of starting an international business.

Small companies, therefore, are well advised to begin their internationalization process by hiring an international marketing manager. The appointment should be made before the company has analysed potential markets in detail and before marketing strategies, programmes and activities are decided on. The new manager should report directly to top management.

The international marketing manager should have administrative and management ability in addition to selling skills. She or he should be thoroughly familiar with the company's product, procedures and personnel. Specific markets may restrict the number of applicants who might be successful. For example, if the targeted markets are located in Southeast Asia or Arab countries, the manager will probably have to be male, because business partners in these areas are generally not prepared, or even willing, to deal with female business executives.

International Marketing Department

As the international business grows, the firm may first add an assistant to the international marketing manager. The assistant will gather, update and present information on specific markets and their relevant environments, help in executing decisions, organize international meetings and take over much of the administrative work.

From that nucleus an international marketing department may develop along with increasing business volume and complexity. Regional managers may be assigned specific geographical territories when the company has expanded its business to a range of different market areas. Regional managers call on distribution-channel members, introduce new products to them, and train their sales representatives and personnel. They monitor competitors and keep in touch with major customers and end users.

When the size of the company's international business grows further, sales offices, joint ventures or subsidiaries may be useful. At this point top management usually decides on one of the following two structural options.

National Subsidiary Structure

If national sales offices or subsidiaries report directly to top management, without intermediate levels such as the international marketing manager or regional managers involved, a national subsidiary structure exists. This structure is often referred to as a 'mother–daughter relationship'. Because this structure allows for direct influence by top managers, it is particularly popular with individually or family-owned and managed small and middle-sized European firms. Figure 10.1 shows the example of the organizational structure of Friedrich Grohe Group, the leading German firm in the European sanitary fittings market, as of 1996.

However, when an international business increases further in size, this form of organizational structure loses most of its attraction. Concentrating international issues in the hands of one or a few people results in an inefficient use of top management's time. And that concentration also leaves top management unable to attend properly to the vast amount of information necessary to maintain corporate growth.

Figure 10.1 NATIONAL SUBSIDIARY STRUCTURE OF FRIEDRICH GROHE GROUP

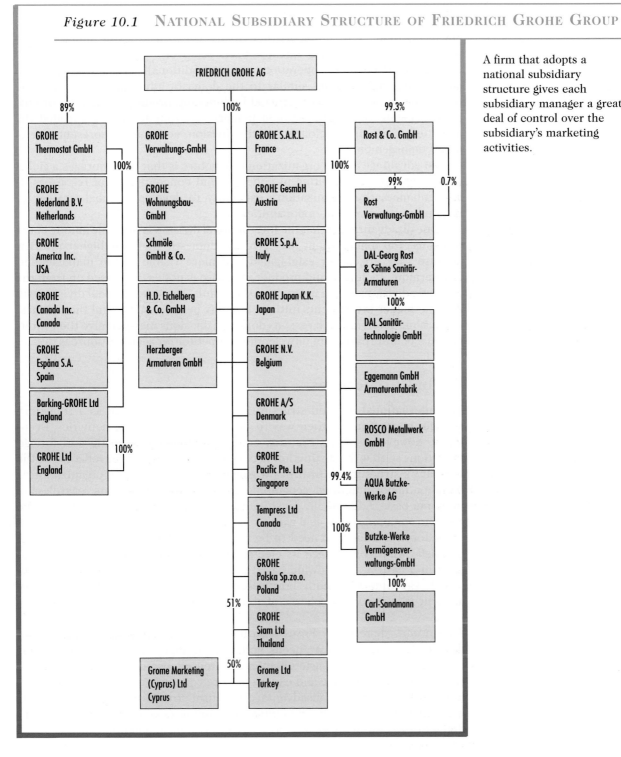

A firm that adopts a national subsidiary structure gives each subsidiary manager a great deal of control over the subsidiary's marketing activities.

International Division Structure

Owing to their huge home market, many US firms starting non-domestic marketing activities have already been relatively large. Therefore, their international business operations were traditionally organized through an international division, similar to the domestic divisions, with all of the operations in one division organized by function, product, geography or customers (Figure 10.2). The division manager coordinated and controlled the activities of the units belonging to the division, acting as a representative of upper management.

An advantage of this organizational structure is that it encourages a global view of operations, resulting in cohesion and concentration of resources. It also enhances the organization's capability to develop a global strategy to respond to international opportunities.

One disadvantage is that the international division is only one among many divisions. Top management may give the domestic divisions higher priority, because they are better established and more visible to top management. Furthermore, technical and product expertise is not easily passed on from the domestic divisions to the international division. The international division will demand higher investments initially but may be more successful than domestic divisions later; for both reasons domestic divisions may perceive their international counterpart as an unwelcome competitor for scarce resources.

Global Structures

The international division structure has proven to be useful as a transitory state for many firms on their way to globalization of business activities. Eventually, however, global structures emerge, equalizing domestic and foreign operations so that the distinction between the two is no longer reflected in the company's structure. A firm has a global structure when its organization is based on major functions, geographic areas or product-markets regardless of its home base. Additionally, customer-centered organizational units may be found in companies that deal with a restricted number of important customers or customer groups that need to be treated individually. For example, when Swedish-Swiss ABB merged its electric drives business with automation systems in 1993 on a worldwide basis, account manager positions were established. Customers in both businesses were pulp and paper mills. Every account manager was in charge of about 20 customers.[3]

Functional Structure. Firms with narrow, highly integrated product lines designed to satisfy similar needs across a number of country-markets (for example, producers of basic chemicals) often choose a functional structure (Figure 10.3). Knowledge and experience are concentrated, diminishing operating costs. The biggest disadvantage to a firm structured this way is that it will experience enormous difficulties in reacting flexibly to regional market differences as top management loses touch with local conditions.

Geographic-Area Structure. Where differences among country-markets make adapted operations necessary, a firm's activities may be grouped according to a geographic-area structure (Figure 10.4). Nestlé, the Vevey, Switzerland-based consumer products giant, for example, given its philosophy that 'all business is local', considers regional management very important.

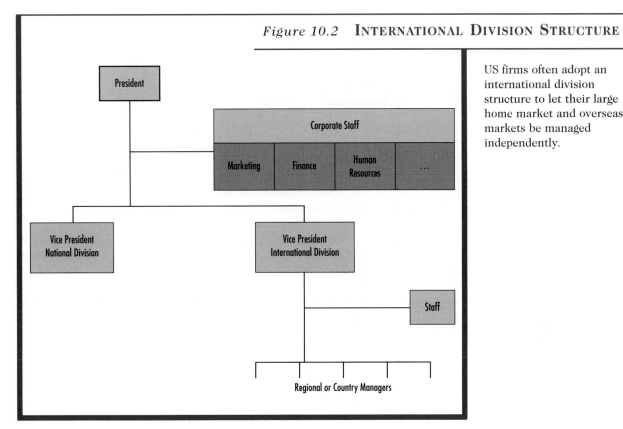

Figure 10.2 **INTERNATIONAL DIVISION STRUCTURE**

US firms often adopt an international division structure to let their large home market and overseas markets be managed independently.

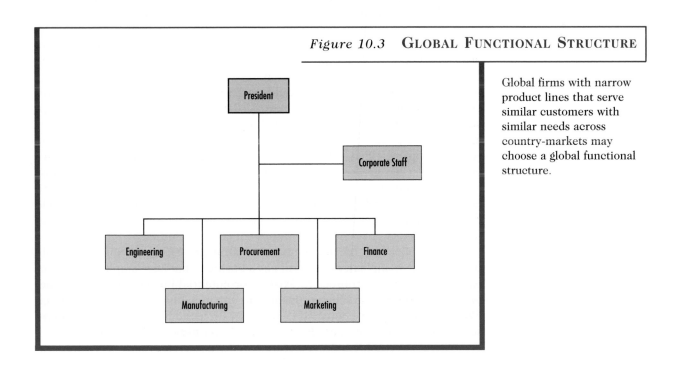

Figure 10.3 **GLOBAL FUNCTIONAL STRUCTURE**

Global firms with narrow product lines that serve similar customers with similar needs across country-markets may choose a global functional structure.

Figure 10.4 GEOGRAPHIC-AREA STRUCTURE

When a firm is faced with significant country-market differences, it may adopt this structure to gain manufacturing- and marketing-experience curve effects within geographic areas served by local units.

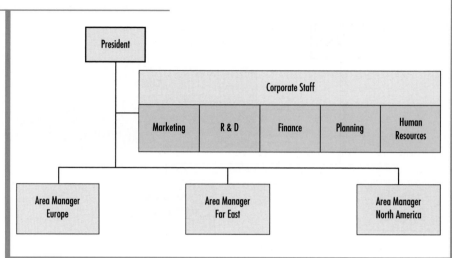

Regional units of an international company can be treated as strategic business units. A strategic business unit (SBU) is an organizational entity established along geographic lines (or according to product-markets, product lines, technologies, or a combination thereof). For example, a global cat food producer may establish SBUs based on geographic areas: the cat food market in Latin America, in the EU, the USA, and so forth. The resulting organizational units could be further split into local businesses and brands (for example, Whiskas in Brazil). Tasks and responsibilities are differentiated among business units. Business unit managers are given full responsibility. For managers to be able to bear that responsibility, SBUs must have strategic autonomy; that is, managers must be able to take decisions independently of decisions taken in other SBUs of the company. Furthermore, success and failure must be unequivocally attributable to individual SBUs.

Such autonomy, however, should exist without losing the advantages provided by synergy. These advantages can be illustrated by chopsticks. Each single chopstick is useful for pushing things, but together two chopsticks allow an individual to eat a meal. Thus with synergy, the whole is greater than the sum of its parts. That is, a company that properly manages multiple geographic SBUs has greater potential for success than the individual SBUs would otherwise generate. Information gathered in one SBU might help another to launch a new customer problem solution faster than its competitors. So would the development of a new technology in one SBU which may have an impact on new products or productivity improvements in another.

The application of the concept of strategic business units not only decreases the complexity of a company's business, but also simplifies the allocation of available resources to existing or potential business activities. Success can be directly attributed, leading to enhanced motivation of personnel. Flops and mistakes are detected faster and with less doubt, which allows more sensitive management of an internationally operating company.

With a geographic-area structure, products, services and related operations can be easily adapted to local conditions. The company can readily respond to consumer demands. Economies of scale are achieved within regions, but international product coordination is inhibited and functional efforts are duplicated, increasing costs overall. Perkin-Elmer, the Connecticut-based scientific instruments manufacturer, used to maintain divisions in the UK and Germany, for example. They went their separate ways on R&D, manufacturing and marketing. The concentration of functions at single locations that are best able to handle them delivered USD25 million to the bottom line in the first year after restructuring.[4]

Product-Division Structure. After Bonduelle, a French company head-quartered in Villeneuve d'Ascq specializing in canned and deep frozen vegetables, had gone through an expansion to middle and eastern Europe (Czech Republic, Hungary, Poland, Slovakia and Russia), the former geographically structured profit centres became dysfunctional. They were replaced by vertically organized divisions corresponding to Bonduelle's four strategically determined product-markets: canned vegetables for the mass market under Bonduelle-owned brands, canned vegetables under retail brands, canned vegetables for restaurants and other business clients, and deep frozen vegetables for the mass market. Each division is led by a vice-president responsible for all of Europe, supervising the local managers who, following a sacred rule of the company, are always locals from the country.[5]

When a company such as UK-based BOC Group which has three main divisions: gas, vacuum technology and health care, each split further into business units along product lines such as medical engineering systems or distribution-services,[6] is organized along its major product-markets and product lines, it has a product-division structure (Figure 10.5). Most often product responsibilities are centralized in corporate headquarters.

As the example of Unilever has shown, marketing strategies for the different products or product lines are developed, coordinated and partially implemented by the staff located in the headquarters. This centralization hastens the speed and reduces the complexity of the decision-making process. Problems are resolved in a general manner, and evaluation measures are decided on before regional or local units execute the adaptations required by their markets.

The product-division structure enables the development of specialized resources. It is most appropriate for a conglomerate that organizes its business activities along strategic business units, positively discouraging synergies between them. The role of the centre is allocating finance as a scarce resource and providing financial control. The Acer Group, a Taiwan-based personal-computer maker, components manufacturer and OEM supplier to firms such as Japan's Hitachi, for example, is divided up into different companies, each with its own top manager, personnel system and salary structure. Individual divisions do not have to buy from others within the group, and if they do, they pay market prices for goods and services. Mr Shih, Acer's founder, insists that he would not object if any division were to leave the group; he would simply require it to drop the Acer name. The headquarters, which is run by Mr Shih and employs 80 people, gets its revenues from dividends and from charging the divisions for its services.[7]

Firms that organize themselves along such independent SBU lines may encounter some difficulties in building critical mass to justify investments. SBU managers may be encouraged to establish networks of outsourcing and

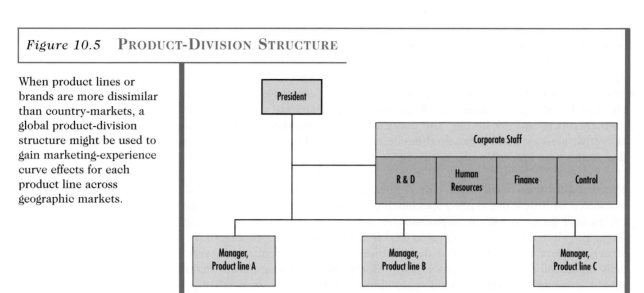

Figure 10.5 **PRODUCT-DIVISION STRUCTURE**

When product lines or brands are more dissimilar than country-markets, a global product-division structure might be used to gain marketing-experience curve effects for each product line across geographic markets.

joint technology development with external partners. For example, at United Technologies Corp., the US manufacturer of products such as Sikorsky helicopters, Pratt & Whitney jet engines and Carrier air conditioners, the different business units share several technologies, such as microelectronics, avionics, motion control and close-loop electrical designs. An excessive corporate focus on the autonomy of the SBUs, however, may be undermining each of these businesses' efforts to develop successful new products based on shared core competencies. Sikorsky developed a new generation of lightweight helicopters with a Korean partner, while Pratt & Whitney looked for foreign joint ventures to co-develop and co-produce a new generation of turbofan engines. Thus, the divisions of United Technologies have become open to predatory alliance partners willing to provide financing and markets in exchange for learning and technology transfer.[8]

Managers who are more intent on synergies may also organize their firms by product-markets, under conditions where the advantages of an internationally standardized marketing mix are higher than the advantages of adaptation to accommodate regional or local distinctions. Daimler-Chrysler, the German–US company most well known for its Mercedes brand but also active in the aviation and information technology industries, for example, is structured as product-divisions operating as business units. One of those, Deutsche Aerospace, is subdivided into the SBUs aviation, drives, space craft, and military systems. But they run the risk of insufficient linkages among divisions. To ensure the benefits from shared experience, resources, customers or economies of scale, corporate staff, such as the central research institutes and a technology group, must provide horizontal information in areas such as microelectronics, information technology, environmental protection or new materials. Other central units such as a strategic human resource management group, a controlling or a treasury unit contribute significantly to the formulation and authorization of strategic business unit plans.[9] Such staff can help individual divisions benefit from each others resources and capabilities. Danfoss, a Danish control components firm, as another example, has a network of central component, distribution and research entities all inter-related with its product divisions.[10]

To take advantage of the marketing know-how, creativity and skills in local units, extended information, planning and control systems seem to be needed. But they usually lead to sizeable overhead, and local units may struggle to maintain their independence. They tend to resist decisions made in the home office (the 'not invented here' syndrome). To overcome this prob-lem local business units can be assigned a status of 'centre of competency' as in the case of Nixdorf, a German computer company that belongs to Siemens. There, a local unit takes global responsibility for a specific application devel-oped on its premises. Other local units interested in the application commu-nicate directly with the centre of competency. A central staff that is organized according to customer groups coordinates the global activities. In a similar attempt to profit from global learning processes, keep overhead costs as low as possible and ensure the commitment of local units, ABB has located the product-line managers of its power-transmission business in different countries: the manager for switchgear is located in Sweden, the manager for power transformers in Germany, the manager for distribution transformers in Norway, and the manager for electric metering in the USA.[11]

Multidimensional Structure.   Each global structure has its own advantages and disadvantages. Management need not choose one or the other, however. The company needs competent functional management to accumulate specialized know-how and skills, as well as to transfer successful innovations throughout the company's international operations. It needs strong geo-graphic-area management, in many cases even further divided into specific customer group management, to detect, analyse and respond to the needs of different local markets. And it needs product-market management with world-wide product responsibilities to achieve the level of international efficiency and integration that is necessary to be an effective global competitor. A multidimensional structure, therefore, simultaneously meets the firm's needs for accumulated experience, market responsiveness and efficiency. Theoretically, the effectiveness of each management group is maintained, and each group is prevented from dominating the others.

The basic challenge is how best to coordinate functions, geographic areas, customer groups and product lines at each management level, and with the organization as a whole to achieve a balance between international integration and local adaptation of decisions and activities. One approach to resolving this problem is a matrix structure, where functional, area and product-market managers are on the same level in the firm's hierarchy. This forces them to cooperate with each other when making decisions. Dow Chemical is an example of a US company that has adopted a three-dimensional organiza-tional matrix combining six geographic areas, three major functions (research, manufacturing and marketing), and over 70 products.

Disadvantages of a matrix structure include increased cost, the difficulty of avoiding enduring conflicts, and the information overload with which cor-porate managers are confronted. In a globally operating firm, top management should be aware that it cannot directly influence a great number of important decisions. One of its major responsibilities is to identify and develop talented functional, area and product-market managers, and to balance the processes among them. They have to create an organizational framework in which decentralized processes can happen in the desired way and activities can be appropriately coordinated.

The development of a multidimensional organization structure does not necessarily imply that functional, area and product-market management must have the same level of influence on all basic decisions. The company can be regarded as an integrated network of interdependent central and local entities, each playing their specific and varying roles depending on the subject of interest. Influence can be determined by assigning responsibility for different sets of activities in the various business units. ABB, for example, has four hierarchical management levels (see Figure 10.6). Group Executive Management is the top level. Regional Segment/Business Area Management represents middle management while Local Company Management acts as the front-line management. Each front-line unit reports to a regional manager and to a worldwide business head. Finally, Profit Centre Management is in charge of the individual profit centres. Along one dimension the company is a 'distributed global network' where executives make decisions on product strategy and performance regardless of national borders. Along the second dimension, ABB is a collection of national companies, each serving its home market as effectively as possible.[12]

The roles of organizational units and their leaders must not be fixed. They should change when the relevant environments in which the firm is operating change. London-based BP Oil, for example, underwent a major change in organizational structure and roles of organizational units in the first half of the 1990s. Following the recommendations of the Project 1990 report, the BP Group head office, until then organized as a matrix embracing ten business groups and about 40 national associates, was reduced to focus increasingly on strategy, standards and policy. Four main international businesses now report to the head office: BP Exploration, BP Oil, BP Chemicals and BP Nutrition. The former large semi-operational centres of expertise have given way to focused networks of experts distributed around the globe. The four geographic divisions now have significantly greater autonomy to manage their affairs. The role of line managers has been strengthened and staff functions have clearer tasks and inputs. The 'ultimate network' which resulted from the project is the International Strategy Group. It is a forum for BP oil's most senior managers to share information, debate issues, commission studies, and develop consensus about the strategies and policies of the global business.[13]

New organization structures do not immediately replace former structures simply when decided by top management. The Strategy box describes the case of US Citibank's organizational development in Europe. It has been characterized by gradual adjustments in a transition process responding to external and internal opportunities and challenges as well as the personal strategic preferences of changing top managers.

Management should be aware that formal organizational structures are only one element in the struggle for efficient coordination. They might lose some of their importance in favour of project teams, information networks and informal processes happening inside the given structures. For example, during the time when Leif Johansson, now president of Electrolux, the Sweden-based marketer of electrical appliances, managed one of its divisions, the coordination of business strategy was ensured through teams that cut across the formal hierarchy. To protect the image and positioning of the Electrolux and Zanussi brands, Johansson set up a brand-coordination group for each. Group members came from the sales companies in key countries,

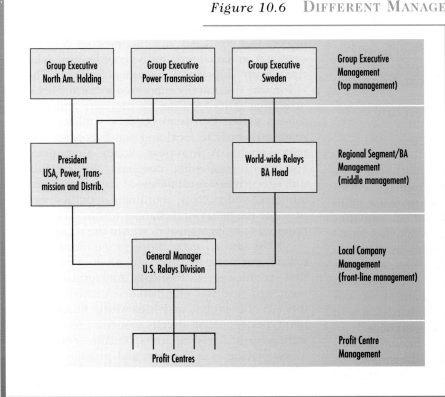

Figure 10.6 DIFFERENT MANAGEMENT LEVELS IN ABB

The worldwide operating company has four management levels. Local company managers report to both regional managers and business area managers. Product strategy and performance are governed regardless of national borders; local adaptation and close customer contacts are secured by national companies.

Source: Bartlett, C.A. and S. Ghoshal (1993) 'Beyond the M-Form: Toward a Managerial Theory of the Firm', *Strategic Management Journal*, 14, 27.

and the chairperson was a corporate marketing executive. Product-line boards were installed to oversee the various product strategies across Europe and to exploit any synergies.[14] Therefore, a marketing manager interested in implementing the firm's intended global strategic position effectively should also be involved in the shaping of the company's information, planning and leadership systems.

INFORMATION SYSTEM

International marketing requires a company-wide information system that significantly contributes to the coordination of activities. The importance of an information system to a company is comparable to the importance of the central nervous system to the human body. The central nervous system comprises a structure of cells, nerve tracts relating them, and processes taking place in and between them, to gather, process, evaluate and disseminate information in the body. In a similar way, a company's information system consists of a structure, such as data files, reports, analytical tools and PCs, a network relating those elements to each other, and information processes through which internal and external information is gathered, evaluated, processed and distributed among all of the decision makers in the company,

STRATEGY BOX

Citibank's Organizational Transition Process in Europe

CITIBANK HAS BEEN A PREMIER WORLDWIDE BANK throughout the 20th century. From the outset the bank operated through autonomous affiliates, which were responsible for all activities within each country and were evaluated based on local profitability. Citibank's geographic-based structure lasted until the 1980s, when the bank began to alter this structure in response to the changing structure of the financial services industry. A major focus of these changes was in its European corporate banking operations.

Citibank's initial response to mounting competitive and financial pressures in the early 1980s was largely within the context of its decentralized structure. Bank management sought to reestablish the profitability of its local affiliates by redefining its customer groups and launching new products. Because these initiatives failed to overcome deteriorating financial performance, in 1985, regional management developed a strategy targeting internationally active companies and financial institutions with sophisticated cross-border products. To implement this strategy, informal regional units were created focused on key products and customer groups. Typically an executive from a large affiliate was appointed to identify opportunities to build linkages across affiliates. However, these executives were given no authority over regional activities. The organization was still characterized by little cross-border dialogue among product, customer, and affiliate staff, reflecting the strong embedded power structure and culture of the traditional organization.

When new executives were appointed in 1988 a common vision for all corporate banking activities in Europe was created, referred to as 'The Unique European Bank'. It described the need for an internal partnership based on geography (preparing country plans, accessing local customers, providing local administrative support),

products (developing product expertise, preparing product strategies, defining product delivery systems), and customer units (coordinating relations with important customer groups). The vision was structurally supported by formal organizational units focusing on products and customers across European borders. Affiliate staff reported jointly to local and pan-European unit management. A European Policy Committee comprising geographic, customer, and product unit executives was established to review regional strategies and policies, coordinate activities, and promote the behavioral changes within each unit required to build teamwork within the region.

1990 saw an even more pronounced shift toward competition based on product-markets that extended across countries. Any formal European structure was eliminated. 53 activity centers (25 of them had activities within Europe) of four types, reporting directly to sector executives, were created: trading units, customer-contact units, placing (sales) units, and product units. The primary focus was to align activities across markets to coordinate locally based activities in line with cross-border market opportunities.

In 1992, again new executives were appointed who reestablished Europe as a formal regional organization, although it was comprised of interdependent activity centers. The strategy that emerged over the following two years was to move from being a large foreign bank in several markets to an international bank providing value-added cross-border financial services. Citibank concentrated product unit staff in London and Franfurt, gathering specialized resources and profiting from scale effects. Country managers became responsible for customer relationship management, marketing products developed in the centralized units, drawing on support services also from centralized facilities. Changes in roles were supported by the formation of cross-functional senior management committees and adjustments in information, planning, and leadership systems.

Source: Malnight, Th.W. (1996) 'The Transition from Decentralized to Network-Based MNC Structures: An Evolutionary Perspective', *Journal of International Business Studies*, First Quarter, 43–65. Reprinted by permission of *Journal of International Business Studies*.

as well as important stakeholders in the external environment. The major difference is that a company's information system consists of formal as well as informal structures and processes. The formal part of an information system is quite easy to manage compared to the informal part which is as important for successful decision making but less evident, in particular in companies comprising a variety of national cultures.

A company's information system has to keep the members of the company informed about relevant developments, such as new EU legislation on national quality standards or the signing of an agent's contract with a partner firm in Kuala Lumpur. It also has to inform the firm's stakeholders about all relevant company events, such as the introduction of a new product or the hiring of a new sales manager in the Mexican subsidiary.

Such an information system will be used to: (a) monitor the international macro- and operating environments; (b) help the firm make strategic decisions, such as decisions about market expansion or divestment; (c) monitor performance in different product-markets and geographical areas; (d) assess resource-allocation decisions and their impact on the company's overall success; (e) exchange and integrate experiences gained by different parts of the company; and (f) communicate information about the firm and its products, activities and achievements to relevant stakeholders. The information system must be able to gather relevant information from external and internal sources and adequately process, store, update and selectively disseminate that information. For that reason, a company's formal information system will contain a collection of data, tools and techniques based on the necessary software and computer hardware.

Organizing for Marketing Research

The way a firm organizes its research reflects its overall structure. Highly centralized companies are likely to centralize their marketing research, particularly strategic research activities. Procter & Gamble Europe, for example, has established a matrix organization of country-specific researchers and category research people. A planning manager in a specific country reports to the country research manager on research of local nature, which tends to be more trade-related or to do with the monitoring of the progress of an initiative after it has hit the market, and reports to the category research manager on research of an initiative-related nature – product tests or concept testing. Anything to do with sales volume forecasting has involvement from both. The market research function is centralized. All researchers in Europe, the Middle East and Africa report to the Market Research Manager for Europe located in Brussels.[15]

On the other hand, firms that decentralize management decision making, especially those that delegate tactical decision making to local organizations, are likely to have decentralized marketing research. For example, Kraft-Jacobs-Suchard has a Vice-President of Marketing Information in its head office in Zurich, but the responsibility for marketing research activities is in the autonomous business units which have their own way of structuring the research function. There are Category Research Directors for core products such as chocolate, coffee and cheese. But some market research managers, such as in Eastern Europe, have a geographical responsibility, because setting up an organization in that region is very different. The market research managers report to their business unit. Their recommendations and reports are monitored by the functional head, which is particularly valuable in subsidiaries where there is only one researcher.[16]

The advantages of decentralized marketing research are more intimate knowledge of markets, greater appreciation of differences among markets, and the potential for greater control over the implementation of research. French Groupe Danone, for example, has formed a network of research experts working for the marketing teams in different countries. The whole team, including research managers and executives, comprises only about 24 people spread over Europe, the USA, Hong Kong and New Zealand. Their role is to use their expert knowledge to help marketing managers take better decisions. Coordination and learning are achieved through international meetings where experiences are exchanged between marketing research personnel and international research agencies.[17]

Potential disadvantages include ineffective communication with the home company and lack of comparability of information gathered in different research projects. To overcome such difficulties, central coordination is useful to ensure agreement on research objectives. However, as in any other marketing activity, central coordination of research leads to higher costs and more delays.

A small firm is unlikely to have a formal marketing-research department. Usually only one or a few people are responsible for research and are part of another unit, perhaps the marketing department. For larger projects, therefore, such firms have to rely on outside agencies and experts. But even big consumer products companies, such as Groupe Danone, ranking third in Europe's food industry, concentrate their in-house marketing research activities on the key elements of research: at the beginning, helping marketing teams to move from the marketing problem to the market research problem; then helping them choose suitable suppliers for specific problems, to understand and choose the best proposals and help them work through the data gathering instrument; at the end, Danone's marketing research people have a very important role in understanding and interpreting the results.[18]

Whirlpool Europe, too, has established the principle of putting as much as possible out to research agencies, and letting marketing researchers function as enabling managers rather than as a data processing house. All of the companies mentioned here aim for a restricted number of external service suppliers who act as partners, are involved in the company, fulfil their processing and analytical standards, and can add value with their understanding.

Information Gathering

Any company gathers information in a more or less systematic way, whether the firm serves local or global markets. However, for an internationally operating company the information-gathering system must be more formalized.

For the gathered information to be relevant, the information requirements of different business units, management levels and stakeholders must be determined and satisfied. An overly general system of monitoring the firm's environments would not only be too expensive for most internationally active companies, but would also overburden the company's personnel with information requests. There is a widespread feeling among operating managers that the reporting required by headquarters is excessive and that reported information is only partially utilized. Many country managers view the home office as a place where uninformed people frame irrelevant, time-consuming questions. This is particularly so when highly standardized reporting procedures are uniformly applied to all organizational units independent of their stage of development or of their economic, cultural and regulatory environments.

For example, when St Louis-based Kentucky Fried Chicken founded a local sales subsidiary in Japan to learn about the different environment and to build up customer franchise in the new market, the local manager regarded it as bureaucratic nonsense when he had to report as extensively and in equal detail as his colleagues who were responsible for the mature US home market. Similarly, the local national managers of US Corning Glass Works had some difficulty in understanding why their headquarters insisted that they had to submit accounting information in English according to the American accounting system format, even though these procedures were not allowed in their countries and therefore useless to the subsidiaries.[19] Therefore, the formal information-gathering process must be highly selective and information dissemination must be regarded as useful for both local units and corporate headquarters.

At the same time, information gathering will have to be more flexible than is necessary when serving only local markets. Because of the greater environmental variety, a wider range of information-gathering techniques are needed. In the USA, for example, telephone surveys are a popular and viable marketing research technique. In other countries, however, they may not be legal, telephone service may be lacking, or people may simply refuse to answer questions over the telephone. Other techniques, such as personal interviews, may need to be used to gather information.

Managers of international businesses must also gather information from a much greater variety of potential sources. The best information concerning customer expectations, for example, may come from salespeople in the UK, agents in Saudi Arabia, consultants in Taiwan, suppliers in Spain, or a government agency in Japan. Management needs to apply considerable creativity concerning new information sources they are not familiar with, or that are of little importance in the domestic market. In order to find and select the best information sources, the relevant stakeholders in the company's international operating environment have to be known. Besides those important players, the most influential dimensions of the relevant macro-environment have to be specified. If nobody in the firm has any experience in this regard, it may be useful to hire a consultant to get started.

Because of the multitude of information sources and the great variety of information available at many different levels of detail, a marketing information system cannot fulfil those objectives when international marketing research is carried out on a study-by-study basis. Harmonization of procedures and methods applied wherever possible increases the efficiency and effectiveness of data collection and analysis.

Finally, a positive working environment within the firm is vital to successful international information gathering. Such an environment will not only ease feedback between managers and employees, but also encourage experienced employees to stay with the firm longer; the company benefits from increased experience curve effects. Such a positive working environment can be reinforced by taking local knowledge and requirements seriously. Central staff at Royal Dutch Shell in Rotterdam (the Netherlands), for example, try to understand the information-gathering approaches of locally operating companies and research firms to see if their approaches would be beneficial to follow more broadly. Although many information-gathering issues may be international ones, for example the launch of a new passenger car motor oil, ownership and implementation of information must be local. Shell, therefore, ensures that information gathering reflects local or cultural considerations as much as possible.[20]

Information Processing and Storage

Integration of data on different levels of decision making, for example for sales-people, product managers or business unit managers, increases their information value. A great part of formally available internal and external data that are routinely collected is usually consolidated in an object-oriented data bank, that is, an information system that stores and retrieves information by objects instead of relations. The potential manipulation of data at any level of aggregation makes the system totally responsive to the requirements of specific marketing decisions. For example, sales can be analysed by country, product or important customers across countries as well as by product sold to specific customers in selected countries. Such a system not only permits marketing managers to take well-informed decisions by tracking changes in the firm's marketing environments over time but also to avoid wasting budgets on information stored in other parts of the firm. The biggest problem is keeping the data bank updated. There need to be clear rules about which data are to be loaded by whom and when to make sure that stored information stays strategically and operationally relevant.

Besides formal information, there exists much informal knowledge and know-how in a company and in their business partners, for example intermediaries, suppliers or service firms. It is stored in the minds of the members of the organization as well as in shared values, assumptions and experiences. Routine behaviours that members of the firm do not consciously select each time a task arises are a typical example. They are strongly influenced by group, national and corporate cultures and can persist tenaciously even in the face of negative performance feedback. This becomes a problem particularly when a firm operates in a foreign cultural environment. When Japanese car makers, such as Toyota, first opened factories in the USA expatriate Japanese managers, for example, used long wooden sticks to tap American factory workers on the head to get their attention. This habit, perfectly acceptable in Japan, resulted in an escalating cycle of resentment and violence in a US factory before it was abandoned.[21]

Values, assumptions, experiences and rules of behaviour are passed on through special recruitment, training, role models, job rotation or stories and traditions. Mazda, for example, selected a group of 3500 American workers for its new Michigan plant from an applicant pool of 96 500 partly on the basis of performance in interpersonal dramas. During a ten- to 12-week training period new recruits were continually monitored as to their abilities to sustain new performance roles. The emphasis was on learning how to become part of an interactive, reciprocal team that performed according to a carefully written and rehearsed script.[22]

How important this 'soft' part of a firm's information system is to its international success is underlined by the fact that firms such as IBM, Procter & Gamble and Unilever have a policy of rotating managers through various jobs and moving them around the world, especially early in their careers.

Information Dissemination

Systematic distribution of relevant information to managers results in more coordinated decisions throughout the company. However, too much information is not only costly, but also reduces managers' interest in using available information. Therefore, new information should not be automatically distributed. It should be available to decision makers when they need it.

This objective is not always easy to fulfil. Because of local differences and changes in information requirements, central information managers rarely know the exact information needs of their colleagues in the firm's operating units spread across the world. In addition, managers in an internationally operating company are often located in several different time zones. Information distributed on paper can go astray during the dissemination process.

A PC network linked to a central database which gives managers of all levels and functions in the company access to information they need for their decisions can be of great help if the information is presented in a way easy to incorporate into the daily operation of the business and if adequate analytical tools which allow simple handling are installed. Expert systems that produce evaluations of decision alternatives under a range of operating environment scenarios can strongly expand the usefulness of information accessible to management. These systems stimulate the decision makers' thought processes, thus improving their decisions.

Daily operations can also be improved by computer networks. For example, by upgrading its global information system, Texas Instruments enabled engineers in Dallas to remotely operate giant testing machines at assembly plants in the Philippines that hunt for flaws deep within multimillion-circuit chips. With their new knowledge and support, the US-based engineers could actually reprogramme the computer-controlled production line by the time the morning shift arrived the next day in the Philippines. Special software lets operations managers distribute new orders to whichever factory needs the work at the moment. The result: with fewer delays Texas Instruments has improved on-time delivery from 77 per cent to 96 per cent in four years.[23]

Such examples should not give the impression, however, that integrated information systems are in widespread existence. The Future Issues box shows that even globally operating firms, such as Liechtenstein-based HILTI, which are well known for their elaborated management systems, have some homework left to do before they can use truly integrated information systems.

Even fully integrated and best managed information systems cannot ensure that managers will actively search for available information as a basis for their decisions. Therefore, information should flow to managers not only when they ask or search for it, but also when unforeseen events affect their area of responsibility. Computer technology permits a management-by-exception approach to information dissemination, which is particularly important for international organizations. Critical events have to be specified in a joint process involving managers and information-system specialists. Procedures for access to and distribution of information, and presentation formats for fast and easy communication, must be developed.

The personnel responsible for the information system in an internationally active firm must be able to communicate effectively across geographic, organizational, group and individual boundaries. They must be aware of contextual settings on both sides of each boundary. They therefore need

| FUTURE ISSUES BOX | *International Information Systems Integration at HILTI* |

To achieve HILTI's goal of full customer satisfaction in the market and also inside the company, employees must get the information needed for their decisions and actions in time and at a proper level of quality. Because the information system of Hilti Western Hemisphere until the first half of the 1990s was equipped with a big central processing unit and a multitude of varying software packages, sometimes it was a real challenge to access information generated in other parts of the firm. In 1991 HILTI started the Systems Integration Environment Project (SIE). In three years, the central data processing unit with its multiple layers should be replaced by a number of small but very powerful servers to entirely integrate the firm's computer system and improve its accessibility for all potential users. Simultaneously HILTI's reporting system should be unified.

Until 1995 the project was implemented in finance, production, personnel management, order handling, and procurement functions. Users were enabled to access the information needed for their work and to write their own reports. Redundant data were eliminated, report and order times were shortened, efficiency and productivity raised.

In its final stage the information system will be implemented in all parts of the global company. The biggest challenge left for the project team is the integration of information concerning HILTI's international marketing activities provided by the local operational units. Because of their varying requirements and information needs, standardization of data-gathering and processing procedures as well as information dissemination is difficult to master. The project team is confident of reaching the set goal at the end of this century by adapting the system specifically to the needs of each market area.

Source: 'Erste Phase des Projekts der Systemintegration abgeschlossen', *Hilti International*, November 1994, p. 27.

cross-cultural experience in addition to information-processing expertise. For example, consider the seemingly simple introduction of a new sales-order form in a global consumer-goods company. A form that serves the computer staff's needs may not be accepted by all the subsidiaries. Even if one country finds it useful, it may not reflect the sales approach used in another country. The personnel responsible for the information system should be regularly assigned to functional units in different countries to learn about their specific information needs.

Cross-cultural experience for information system managers may not be sufficient, however. It seems to be even more important that the potential users of a firm's information system adopt it as their system. When the top management of John Wiley & Sons, a mid-sized publisher of technical and scientific books headquartered in the USA, decided to adopt a common hardware and software platform for their international business, they chose to replace first the systems that supported their core business process: order processing, distribution, warehousing, publishing support, and fulfilment activities. The replacement process was started in Singapore, the location of the company's smallest office. The implementation team then took the Singapore system and transplanted it first to Australia, and then to the UK. When implementation was scheduled to start in the company's main market, the USA, both the business and technical (information systems) groups of employees initially resisted the concept. To overcome this resistance, eight representatives of the various user departments, from the manager level down, were invited to travel to the UK to see the system. Their UK business peers gave a system demonstration. After a week-long review in which the American guests could use the screens and see how easily modifications could be made, they decided to go with the new system. One business manager who initially resisted became so convinced of the new system's superiority that he volunteered to market it to his peers in the USA.[24]

PLANNING SYSTEM

Strategies and, in particular, marketing strategies are formulated on a number of levels, from corporate through business unit and product-line levels down to the product level. The further down in the planning hierarchy, the more operational the strategies become. An internationally operating firm, therefore, needs systems for strategic as well as operational planning.

Strategic planning involves the formulation of key goals and objectives for the entire company and its various business units. It includes the definition of basic strategies that determine the allocation of resources among markets, technologies, functional areas and other organizational entities. Operational planning encompasses detailed plans, procedures and budgets for organizational units based on the strategic decisions. Operational plans serve as a framework for day-to-day decision making, as well as controlling.

In general, top management has the primary responsibility for determining overall international business direction. It coordinates the strategies of all the business units worldwide. The responsibility for operational planning rests with the line managers of the organizational units. They are assisted in that task by planning and functional staff members at all levels. Irrespective of these fundamental responsibilities, the process by which (marketing) strategies are derived should involve interfunctional cooperation, qualitative as well as quantitative inputs, and a proactive perspective regarding the firm's external environment.

Centralized versus Adaptive Planning

Many of the planning problems that managers of internationally operating companies encounter revolve around the relationship between the company's home office and local units. Home offices play a range of roles in the planning processes of their non-domestic units. In some cases local units are completely free (unguided) in their planning efforts. In other cases the home office provides information on the global business environment, regional developments expected during the planning period, and the state of the industry. The London-based headquarters of Mobil Oil Europe, for example, provides its local European units with information on the development of the world oil market. The home office might also provide information about internal environments, such as new product introductions, price changes or public relations campaigns. This information then has to be incorporated into the local units' plans. Other companies go a step further and present their organizational units with a set of strategic goals to be attained and major action programmes to be implemented.

Top management's decision regarding the level of centralization versus adaptiveness of the planning process is expressed by the degree of standardization of planning procedures. Companies confronted with rapid technological change, worldwide sourcing or homogeneous markets tend to use centralized planning. Most companies operating internationally, however, have to achieve a balance between centralization and adaptation in their planning processes, to make effective and efficient use of all available managerial resources and to facilitate the implementation of plans.

Unfortunately, many existing company structures do not provide for direct information exchanges between their local units. This limits experience curve effects, which could be gained through a more global approach to international marketing. Local units could profit from the experience and information available from other units in their planning endeavours. They could, for example, compare the behaviour of competitors in different areas of the world (as does IBM in Japan and the USA), or they could gain from unifying their marketing efforts to the different subsidiaries of a global customer. The local subsidiaries of Hirsch, the Austrian watch strap manufacturer, supplying straps to the production plants of Seiko, the big Japanese watch company, in Germany, the USA and Japan, for example, follow a consistent policy with prices and business terms.

To overcome the problem of missing information due to the company's organizational structure, management can establish various forms of planning groups: (1) regular meetings, (2) international coordination groups or (3) planning forums.

Regular meetings. Regular meetings of local managers (product managers, market researchers, package designers, R&D specialists, production managers, or controllers) with their counterparts from other local units and from the home office improve integration and cooperation. Regular contact among managers helps ensure that informal and formal communication occurs and that good ideas, which allow a company to move down the experience curve to great advantage, are shared throughout the company.

Regular meetings for planning purposes must not be restricted to company personnel. Top-level Caterpillar managers, for example, meet annually with key people from the dealerships at regional conferences, where they discuss sales goals for each product line and what each party has to do to achieve them. In addition, all 186 dealers are periodically invited to a week-long conference in Peoria, Caterpillar's headquarters, for a comprehensive view of strategy, product plans and marketing policies.[25]

Annual conferences, strategy meetings and planning sessions are the backbone of relationships needed for international planning. What is most important for well-informed planning and for implementing planned actions, however, are the personal ties between company decision makers (and important stakeholders, such as intermediaries or suppliers) which develop at these meetings and the familiarity of people who depend on each other to ensure the company's success.

International Coordination Groups. International coordination groups, composed of delegates from the company's local units and its home office, are given responsibility for fulfilling specific tasks. Depending on the task, a strategic planning group, a communications group, an R&D group or a personnel group may be created. US-based Bristol-Myers, a manufacturer of consumer healthcare products, for example, created a group to assist in integrating a more global view with decision-making processes throughout the organization.

Planning Forums. The most effective way to give influence on strategy development to local entities is to create entirely new planning forums. Procter & Gamble's 'Eurobrand Teams', for example, are composed of business units that are assigned specific roles depending on their strategic importance to the company (market size, home market of major competitor, particularly quality-conscious customers, advanced technologies required) and their specific competencies (in terms of technology, production or marketing, for example). The company may distinguish between strategic leaders, contributors and implementors. Proctor & Gamble's Irish subsidiary, for example, is the strategic leader in Europe for the Dash brand, while Germany is Proctor & Gamble's strategic leader in Europe for Pampers. Both had proven to be particularly creative and successful with their respective brands in their home markets.[26]

Despite the fact that one country may dominate the strategic planning for a specific product (line), all other business units marketing the product should be involved in the planning process. Coordination in such teams is self-reinforcing, because cooperation helps all of the units to achieve their own interests.

Top management must consider the motivational as well as the strategic impact of assigning different business units different roles in the marketing planning process. It has to keep in mind that units that must continually implement strategies developed by other parts of the company will suffer from lower motivation to contribute innovative programmes to the company's success. Business units in strategically less important markets should, therefore, be assigned lead or contributing roles, even if only for less important products. Dutch Philips, for example, awarded its Taiwan subsidiary the lead role in the small-screen computer monitor business, enormously boosting the motivation of management and personnel in this subsidiary to do well in this field.[27]

Time Perspective

In many firms involved in international business, too much of the planning activity is focused on the operational instead of the strategic level. These companies primarily rely on financially oriented, short-term budgeting. Very often this perspective leads responsible managers to simply project current sales figures when preparing long-term plans. Such an approach does not provide for changes in competition, the market, and parts of the macro-environment. Nor does it result in information about potential sales that may be lost owing to suboptimal marketing efforts. For example, it doesn't indicate that a different distribution system would provide an increase in sales.

If such a short-term focus is additionally allowed to largely independent local units, financial problems for the company as a whole may result. For example, when Canadian auto-parts giant Magna International grew to 100 independently operating factories, managers piled on debt to grow. As a consequence of the resulting financial trouble, factory managers must now clear major spending with senior executives, who approve only projects that fit Magna's strategy to become the world leader in producing automotive systems, such as finished seats or outer body shells.[28]

Precision and Formalization

International marketers used to researching EU or US markets should keep in mind that there are many countries in the world where data on markets and environments are not comparable. If nationally effective planning procedures are forced on local business units outside those areas with no or only little modification, the plans often have to be based on rough estimates owing to lack of readily available, comparable data.

In countries with rapid industrial or social development, such as South Korea, Singapore and Brazil, it may be very difficult to come up with forecasts. The limited data that are available quickly become outdated. In much of the world, political and economic instability make accurate predictions practically impossible. If reliable data cannot be gathered, it may be better not to try to acquire enough information to develop a polished strategic or operational plan. It may be more reasonable to maintain the perspective that plans have to be adapted to new information, gathered on an ongoing basis.

But even in countries where precise data is available, a highly standardized planning procedure might produce negative results when it is forced on the organizational unit without considering its stage of development and local rules of behaviour. For example, after Gillette acquired French-owned Waterman Pen, it imposed the full repertoire of its bureaucratic procedures on its new affiliate. Francine Gomez, the President of Waterman, who had negotiated the friendly acquisition, was used to a French style of fast, intuitive decision making. She fought to preserve the continuation of Waterman routines and left the company when she saw that she could not win. Gillette lost the person responsible for the great success of the Waterman operation.[29]

Control

Planning involves setting goals and preparing coordinated actions of integrated functional units to reach them. What it means to a company to run out of control for some time is demonstrated by the example of Nokia Oy, the second-biggest mobile-phone maker in the world. In the first part of the 1990s it seemed that the company could do no wrong as its sales and earnings soared. Yet, in 1996, the firm posted heavy losses. There were signs that Nokia might have grown too fast in a market that was growing at 80 per cent a year. Fixed costs in Nokia's mobile-phone division grew 10 per cent faster than the business. The company missed the slowdown in the US market and failed to predict which of its products would be the most popular. The result has been shortages of some products, particularly in the firm's digital line, and gluts in others. And at the time when mobile-phone volumes at Nokia were growing by about 80 per cent, many of the firm's suppliers were unable to meet their quotas. That meant the company had to buy some of its parts, including microprocessors, on the spot market, where prices are higher. Other times, suppliers changed the specifications of their products, but the word never filtered back to the right people at Nokia; the result was faulty phones that had to be sent back to the manufacturer. As a consequence of all those problems, Nokia's top management vowed to revamp their information and planning systems, including internal control.[30]

Planning may serve as a means of organizational learning, if standards are set by which the implementation of plans and the achievement of set goals can be controlled. Any deviation from those standards can be analysed in terms of reasons why it happened and improvements become possible. To serve this purpose standards must be clearly defined, as well as understood and accepted by the personnel responsible for adherence to them.

Standards concerning the international marketing of a firm must relate to the goals set in corporate strategy. Such goals, for example an annual 10 per cent growth rate of sales, a shareholder value above the industry average, or to be one of the international innovation leaders, may be too general to serve as standards themselves. They need to be 'translated' into operational standards which cover all aspects of marketing relevant to the goals. For example, sales volume by product line, share of new products, market coverage, yield of participation in trade shows, or quality standards such as the percentage of orders fully delivered in 48 hours are potential effectiveness measures of goal attainment. Additionally, efficiency measures, such as cost per customer order or return on sales force expenditures, need to be formulated.

For managers to be held responsible for keeping to the levels set by the standards, the standards must be chosen in such a way that managers can affect the results. To assure high commitment from local managers, they should participate in the establishment of local standards. They will not only contribute their knowledge about the stage of local market development and adapted standards, but also about local cultures which lead to different reactions to similar standards. Management from headquarters will take care that the approved standards fit the company's information system and are challenging enough for all management levels. The Ethics box describes what may happen when headquarters is over-ambitious in setting challenging standards.

During the annual planning process, the exact levels of each standard as well as acceptable deviations are fixed in operating plans which are broken down by budgets. The most widely applied tools for monitoring actual performance against standards in internationally operating companies are reports, comparative analyses, meetings and audits. Depending on their formality and standardizability of contents, they vary in purpose, frequency and costs. A comparative analysis of distribution costs in different local business units, for example, can be centrally executed in a rather formal manner without much involvement of local management. When it comes to understanding differences found and taking appropriate action, a more personal approach in meetings will be necessary.

LEADERSHIP SYSTEM

People from different cultures live in different worlds of social reality. Different perceptions of social reality result in different processes of motivation, decision making, conflict resolution, personnel development and

Ethics Box

Blind Ambition

Bausch & Lomb is a Rochester, New York-based producer of optical equipment, eyeglass lenses, sun glasses, and contact lenses. The company's performance-oriented ethos delivered outstanding results for many years. By the early 1990s, the company's markets slowed and at the same time several acquisitions turned out to be less successful than expected. Nevertheless, Bausch & Lomb's top management maintained double-digit sales and earnings growth as all-important goals for the company. The resulting pressures on managers led to deviations from sound business practice or ethical behavior:

B&L's Hong Kong unit allegedly inflated revenues by faking sales of Ray-Ban sunglasses to real customers. Some of the glasses were allegedly then sold at cut-rate prices to gray-market dealers. B&L auditors discovered policy violations in 1995, and new local managers were appointed.

Under pressure to beat sales targets in 1993, contact lens managers in the US shipped products that doctors never ordered and booked them as sales. They threatened to cut off distributors unless they took on up to two years of unwanted inventories. These practices appear to violate acceptable accounting standards and have led to an SEC investigation. B&L blames the problems on overaggressive division executives.

By accepting cash payments and third-party checks, Lamex, a Latin American export unit in Miami, may have indirectly helped launder drug money from Latin America. Despite questions being raised at headquarters already at the end of the 1980s, nobody stopped the flow.

Source: Maremont, M., G. DeGeorge and J. Barnathan (1995) 'Blind Ambition', *Business Week*, 23 October, pp. 46–56.

---

organizational change. For example, in Japanese companies traditionally a decision will not be made until all the employees involved have had a chance to express their views and a solution is found that enables them not to be socially disregarded. In European firms, on the other hand, top management may decide to release personnel to increase productivity, without paying any attention to what it may mean to the working climate in their company because they regard shareholder value as more important (and it often increases when management takes 'downsizing' decisions).

National boundaries do not necessarily indicate distinct differences between leadership practices. Countries group together into clusters that share similar cultural values, and leadership practices are often similar within each cluster. For example, in Australia and the USA, identity is placed in the individual. There is a strong belief that everybody is supposed to take care of himself or herself, and an emphasis on individual achievement and initiative. Managers in both countries tend to reject interlocking group structures in favour of systems which focus on individual accomplishment and self-interest. On the other hand, the Culture box shows that important cultural differences may exist even between neighbouring countries such as the USA and Mexico that result in leadership problems having negative effects on the people and firms involved.

CULTURE BOX

Clash of Cultures

"IN MEXICO, EVERYTHING IS A PERSONAL MATTER," SAID Ken Franklin, who manages assembly plants at Ciudad Juarez's giant Bermudez Industrial Park just across the border of the USA. "But a lot of US managers don't get it." And Fernando Duenas, Federal Express's local manager who was born in Ecuador adds: "You are constantly fighting the mañana syndrome."

The culture clash between US managers and Mexican workers has been most evident in the maquiladora programme. The problems in maquiladoras are rooted in the fact that the border plants generally fall under the control of US corporations' domestic divisions, rather than their international ones. Less sensitive to the special problems of operating abroad, the domestic division chiefs usually selected maquiladora managers based upon their skill in production rather than human relations.

The gulf between the Mexicans and Americans at maquiladoras results in a heavy turnover of both labor and management. The turnover of Mexican workers is about 10 per cent a month. A less publicized problem has been the rapid burnout of American managers along the border. Even premium payments do not keep American managers in the border factories for a long time.

Source: Moffett, M. (1992) 'Culture Shock', *The Wall Street Journal*, 24 September, p. R13.

Managers of internationally operating companies must be willing, and motivated, to contribute to the determination of an attractive strategic position and to its implementation through international business activities. In order to do so, the firm's leadership system must invite them to carry out such programmes and to be inclined to undertake such tasks.

Leadership in a firm doing international business means having to develop and maintain a set of tools and processes that lead all members of the organization to strive for global-scale efficiency and competitiveness without becoming insensitive to demands of the local environments, and to be ready to learn from successful experiences of others in the organization, independent of their relatedness to a national culture, a functional area or a business unit.

Role Models

A positive motivation among employees can often be achieved through managers serving as role models. People learn much of their behaviour through imitation. If leaders consistently demonstrate behaviour that can be related to business and personal success, many of their employees will try to imitate them. For example, if a top manager such as Lou Gerstner, the CEO of Armonk, New York-based IBM, regularly visits customers to stay in close contact with the market, the firm's product managers and R&D managers will have to go regularly into the field, too.

Reinforcement

Performances that help the company achieve its goals should be rewarded through appropriate compensation packages and job assignments. The internationally operating firm faces the difficult task of developing a consistent performance-appraisal system and compensation system that can be accepted by all the personnel from a variety of cultures.

IBM, for example, striving to become the world leader in network-centric computing, a market estimated at USD1,000 billion in 1998, installed a system of feedback talks for all of their 215 000 people in 1995 which permitted them to access a data bank of 10 million different capabilities. The data bank can be used by managers to form successful project teams. If certain capabilities cannot be found inside the firm, management can hire new people. Because top management considers teams as extremely important if the company is to reach their ambitious goal, 30 per cent of the variable part of the income of people working for IBM has been made dependent on the collective results
of the teams they belong to.[31] How well this system will work depends on its acceptance by people from very different cultures who work for IBM.

US managers, for example, are used to one bonus per year and promotions based on achievement. Their Japanese counterparts receive bonuses at least twice a year, and whether they are promoted depends a great deal on their seniority and their capabilities in the long run. Japanese managers have budgeted amounts to spend on entertainment after work. German managers prefer fringe benefits like the use of a company car for non-business purposes. A company that is serving international markets with personnel from various cultural backgrounds must be ready and able to accommodate its incentive system to cultural differences without arousing conflicts in its different local units.

Human-Resource Development

Strategically meaningful and personally rewarding headquarters and non-domestic service assignments need to be supported by a human-resource development system that identifies and moves appropriate employees across business units or national borders. Poor human-resource planning may, for example, be the major reason for the high failure rate to be found among US business expatriates. That is, US managers often have to be recalled to headquarters or dismissed from the company because of their inability to perform effectively in a foreign country. Managerial inventories such as Unilever's, including detailed profiles of the best managers from all parts of the company, regardless of nationality, may help to lower such failure rates.

There exist widespread objections by managers and personnel to international transfers. Language deficiencies as well as limited mobility play a major role. In Southern Europe, for example, family ties are a strong reason against leaving a local job. In other parts of Europe they are less pronounced, but marketing managers and personnel who are transferred often feel that they risk being forgotten 'out there' in their new assignments. Clear career paths, based on a management-development plan, should exist to assure employees that they will not be forgotten or necessarily passed over for promotion.

Conflict Resolution

Conflicts in an international business are different from, and often greater than, conflicts in domestic firms. Not only do functional interest groups hold markedly different beliefs concerning the appropriateness of particular goals and strategies, but local managers may disagree with central staff concerning the strategic importance of business units, resource allocations among them, and the interpretation of market situations. Different meanings assigned to a company's actions are due not only to different interests but also to cultural differences.

Business units and local subsidiaries often feel they are undervalued by top management. Some European Black & Decker managers, for example, could not see that centrally directed highly standardized marketing was needed as a defence against Japanese competition, because their subsidiaries dominated the consumer power-tool markets in Europe. They resisted corporate strategic change, because they thought its impact was to threaten their individual power.

Conflicts may also arise between the company and its local stakeholders, such as governments, unions, special-interest groups or trade organizations. For example, when Continental, based in Hanover, Germany, one of Europe's leading tyre producers, decided to cut the profitable production of passenger car tyres in their Austrian Semperit AG factory by half and to transfer the latest technology production equipment to the neighbouring Czech Republic, where wage levels are only about one-eighth of those in Austria, they encountered strong resistance by local unions and government. Continental's top management was only interested in optimizing gains by improving the firm's geographic allocation of resources. The local interest groups saw the wilful destruction of a well-functioning factory to which government had given substantial subsidies a few years earlier to bring the level of productivity to the highest international standards.

The leadership system of an internationally operating firm must be able to cope with the entire range of potential conflicts. Table 10.1 contains various approaches to conflict management. Some managers aggravate conflicts by denying their existence. Others try to resolve conflicts by replacing employees or managers who resist direction, as was done in the Black & Decker case. Managers who perceive such replacements as losses of important management know-how or experience may seek to resolve or even avoid conflicts with improved information and greater participation by the people concerned.

Such managers should be aware that collective decisions tend to unfold in an incremental manner from processes of negotiation and compromise among participants living in different social realities and holding various self-interests. They often depend more on the partisan values and power of the interest groups involved in the process than on rational analysis. Thus, such decisions are easier to implement but they will not be of the highest potential quality.

There is no universal best conflict-resolution strategy. The best strategy for any given situation depends on both the objective features of the situation and the interpretations of different cultural and interest groups. Successful international marketing managers have to be able to apply the most appropriate conflict management technique specific to the situation to safeguard the long-term interests of the company.

Table 10.1 APPROACHES TO CONFLICT MANAGEMENT

Managers of internationally operating firms must choose an appropriate conflict management approach depending on the specific situation.

STRUCTURAL APPROACHES	PROCESS APPROACHES	MIXED APPROACHES
Common goals	De-escalation	Rules
Reward system	Confrontation	Liaison roles
Regrouping	Collaboration	Task forces/teams
Rotation		Integrator roles
Separation		

SHAPING THE INTERNATIONAL MANAGEMENT SYSTEMS

Managing Change

Because a company is a 'partly open' system, its management systems are subject to external influences as well as internal processes. Both lead to marginal but constant change in the management systems. That is, management systems – their structure and processes – continuously adapt to environmental developments in small steps. Such ongoing changes are not strategically managed, however, and therefore they do not automatically lead to an optimum result for the firm. If a misfit develops between management systems and the business environment because of important changes, such as occur when a company goes through different phases of internationalization, management intervention may become necessary. The firm may have to replace organizational structures, internalized policies and rules of behaviour with new ones.

For example, when Austrian Grass AG, one of the leading manufacturers of furniture fittings in the world, established a production company in the USA and sales subsidiaries in Canada, the UK, France and Italy, it found that centralized planning and control did not lead to the expected results. It therefore founded a holding company, which acts as a coordinating agency. As a result, the firm's information system became much more important. The existing leadership system also had to be adapted to the different motivations of managers and employees in the various countries.

Such a resocialization process is very difficult to manage. It requires a great amount of time, energy, skills and money. Also, management must be able to tolerate uncertainty and ambiguity, and must be willing to learn new attitudes and rules of behaviour. Developing and sustaining an appropriate corporate culture is especially hard when the growth of international business is fast. Robert Epstein, the founder of Sybase, a US-based company producing software for computer networking, personally spent six months working in the company's Paris sales offices for that reason.

The problems of managing organizational change are manifold under any circumstances. They are even more complex in a cross-cultural business environment. Communication, sources of change, the conceptual ability and participation of personnel, and management's involvement in and commitment to the change process all may differ from one business environment to another. Certain tools of organizational and personnel development may be difficult to apply because of labour union resistance, the general educational level, social structure or traditions in a society. For example, US articles on easing internal change frequently advise managers to include the personnel who will be affected by change in company planning, to reduce their resistance to the change. This advice may be appropriate for most organizations in the Western industrialized countries, but it may be of no value in parts of the world where more authoritarian processes are common.

Small and medium-sized companies that lack experience in non-domestic marketing are likely to find that they cannot globalize their business all at once. Rather, they must manage a continuous process of organizational change leading to a corporate culture that favours international marketing, changing management systems to accommodate the higher complexity of international business, and attracting or developing the needed number of skilled people.

Managers and employees must be systematically prepared for new tasks in a more complex world. For example, if they are not in the office or on the factory floor, US-based Motorola employees are at school. Each employee trains a minimum of 40 hours annually. Training and Education Center staff work directly with managers, tailoring the courses to their specific issues. The results are impressive. Productivity has risen 139 per cent in five years, and Motorola estimated that in 1994 it saved USD1.5 billion by reducing defects and making employees and processes more efficient.[32]

Training not only improves skills, but can also be used to encourage self-development of personnel as well as managers. The problem-solving and innovation potentials of all members of the company have to be developed. Supported by one of the most ambitious, well-funded employee training programmes in the USA (more than four times the national average), Motorola pushes employees to continually redefine themselves and how they do their job. Adaptability and flexibility in reasoning and action are part of the training programme. Leadership skills are improved. Typically, Japanese companies have more specialized training programmes to prepare managers for non-domestic assignments than do US and European firms. These programmes include language training, career training, field experience, and graduate programmes abroad. Japanese companies also enjoy a higher success rate of managers in non-domestic assignments.

It is rare that a smaller company has the resources to undertake personnel development on such a scale. It will need external consultants, coaches and training institutions to build up personnel for successful international marketing. But top management, no matter what the size of the firm, should be aware that lasting success in globalizing markets will not be possible without investments in personnel development.

Balancing the Firm's Management Systems

An internationally operating company that wants to reach the goals of global efficiency and competitiveness, flexibility and responsiveness to local market environments, as well as inter-unit organizational learning, must be able to control the firm's output, that is, the efficiency of organizational processes, as well as the behaviour of the firm's entities, that is, the effectiveness of ongoing processes. For that purpose it has to find a balance between centralization, standardization and socialization tendencies (see Figure 10.7). Centralization is best suited for output control. Standardization can be used for both output and behavioural control. For the latter the global marketer will be better off using socialization mechanisms, however. Behavioural control is less direct and less costly than output control, and it permits a longer time horizon.

Centralization.   Centralization means concentration of decision authority at the firm's head office and direct intervention in the operations of business units. Local units adapt corporate strategy to their domestic environment after receiving approval from headquarters. Control can be very specific and limited to the short term (for example, the annual budgeting systems, with monthly reporting, used by many US firms). It can be implemented vertically across the organizational structure, with the home office imposing identical roles, functions and responsibilities on all organizational elements at the same hierarchical level. Centralization leads to rather mechanistic decision procedures worldwide, equalizing the influence of business unit managers on the planning process, and using standardized criteria to evaluate performance.

Centralization becomes increasingly feasible as managers in the home office gain more global experience and as standardized procedures and rigid structures reduce the complexity of the operations for which they are responsible. In addition, improved transportation and communication allow easier evaluation and correction of performance of widely dispersed business units.

The major argument against centralization is that each organizational unit in the global company is itself a complex organization existing in a particular environment. If every decision or action must be cleared with a higher level, reaction time is slowed and resources are wasted. Control exerted through strict budgets generally requires a great deal of time for the process of coming to mutual agreement on the appropriate figures. Responsiveness to demands in the local environments is low. Similar treatment of local business units in different states of development might unnecessarily restrict the flexibility of those in the market entry stage, not give enough strategic guidance to those in their stage of growth, or not be interactive enough to allow for quick information sharing and transfer of successful innovations between local units in their stage of maturity.

Standardization.   Standardization is the formalization of tasks and decision procedures to be performed in different parts of the company to ensure similar performance processes and comparable results. Leadership, information, planning and control processes such as conflict resolution, quality control, new product development or managerial accounting are formally prescribed (usually in a manual), to be followed by all members of the organization. The more decentralized decision authority is in an internationally operating firm, the more top management will tend to standardize the processes by which its business units are managed. Philips, the Dutch electrical and electronics giant, for example, has an investment-project manual which helps assure top management that investment calculations for different projects are derived in the same manner and therefore can be compared to each other. The result are rather bureaucratic decision processes following identical rules without any tributes to the specifics of a decision situation.

Standardization helps to increase global-scale efficiency in a decentralized organization. Cross-market learning is difficult because the standardized

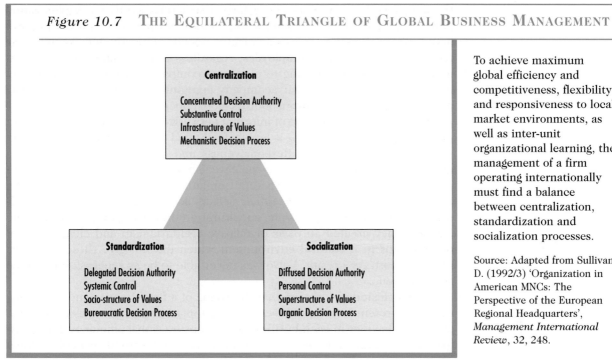

Figure 10.7 THE EQUILATERAL TRIANGLE OF GLOBAL BUSINESS MANAGEMENT

To achieve maximum global efficiency and competitiveness, flexibility and responsiveness to local market environments, as well as inter-unit organizational learning, the management of a firm operating internationally must find a balance between centralization, standardization and socialization processes.

Source: Adapted from Sullivan, D. (1992/3) 'Organization in American MNCs: The Perspective of the European Regional Headquarters', *Management International Review*, 32, 248.

rules hinder innovation. Flexible reaction to local demands is only possible as long as the decisions and actions fit into the given system of standards.

Socialization.   Socialization is the process of instilling and reinforcing basic values and behavioural norms in members of an organization in a way that leads to a common set of values and accepted rules of behaviour. If socialization is strong the employees of the company will act in a predictable manner consistent with the general goals of the firm, even if decision authority is spread out all over the globe.

Control is exerted on a personal behavioural level. It can be achieved through integration or enculturation. Integration is the building of a tight network of interrelationships among the elements (individuals or groups) of a social system. The stronger the integration of a firm's organizational units, the less output control is needed to ensure the implementation of strategies and plans. For example, when top management increases the flow of products, resources and information among local units, those units will recognize the need for coordinating their strategies, policies and actions. A car manufacturer, for example, may have a transmission factory in Hungary, an engine factory in Ireland, and assembly plants in Spain and Thailand. Because these units are dependent upon each other, they will recognize the need for integrating their activities. An organic decision process may emerge.

Enculturation takes place if top management succeeds in promoting company-wide understanding of, and commitment to, its basic values, goals and strategies. The superstructure of shared values and goals leads to informal agreement, information sharing and cooperation among all the parts of the company. Less emphasis on a formal structure, such as a sophisticated multidimensional matrix organization, and less formal control processes will be necessary. A major US-based consumer-goods company, for example, has chosen to train all of its employees, regardless of their national or cultural heritage, 'its way' (according to a defined company culture). The company believes this will improve intracompany communication and lead to similar management behaviour throughout its global operations.

Because of the multitude of informal networks resulting from socialization processes, inter-unit learning is largely facilitated. Global-scale efficiency may result but is not ensured. Responsiveness and flexibility to local specifics might be reduced. When Volvo, the Swedish automotive company, tried to replicate its successful Swedish retail organization in France, for example, they did everything to socialize their dealers according to the company's culture. Because of their own strong enculturation they overlooked, however, the fact that they created an oasis of relative egalitarianism and close personal relationships in a cultural environment which did not give those values as much support. As a result, Volvo was never able to be as successful in France as in Sweden.

In conclusion we can say that the shape of a firm's management systems should represent a compromise between top management's desire for predictable behaviour in each business unit to ensure global efficiency and cross-market learning, and the need for flexibility and responsiveness to local environments.

SUMMARY

The successful implementation of a firm's intended global strategic position as well as its marketing plans depends on the existence of an appropriate management infrastructure, that is, management systems that allow coordination of all the firm's activities. The shape of this infrastructure largely depends on the external environments relevant to the company's business as well as internal processes needed to achieve the goals of global-scale efficiency and competitiveness, local-level responsiveness and flexibility, and cross-unit capacity for organizational learning. Centralization, standardization and socialization processes need to be balanced in such a way as to define the structures and processes of the firm's organization and its information, planning and leaderhip systems, which allow it to come as near as possible to these partly contradictory goals.

Marketing managers are responsible for managing satisfactory relations with important stakeholders. Their potential success is directly related to their company's management systems. Marketing managers, therefore, should not only have a profound understanding of how management systems can be shaped and what consequences are to be expected. They should be directly involved in decision making concerning management structures and processes. They must be aware that the internationalization of their business not only demands careful strategic and operative decisions but also represents a major process of organizational change. This process has to be thoroughly managed to make international marketing a successful response to the globalization of the world's economy.

DISCUSSION QUESTIONS

1. Why should an international marketing manager care about the firm's management systems?
2. What are the basic goals to be achieved by shaping an internationally operating company's management systems?
3. How can different forms of organizational structures contribute to the implementation of a firm's intended global strategic position? What are their disadvantages?
4. How should an international information system of a company work to be accepted and used by management?
5. What potential conflicts between central and local management have to be considered to make an international planning system effective and efficient?
6. What factors need to be considered to make an international control system a well-accepted tool of motivation for managers in all parts of the company instead of a bureaucratic nightmare?
7. Find examples in business magazines that demonstrate the influence of a company's leadership system on the international success of the firm. What are your conclusions?
8. Why is an international marketer very much concerned with organizational change? What does that mean for you?

ADDITIONAL READINGS

Bartlett, C.A. and S. Ghoshal (1993) 'Beyond the M-Form: Toward a Managerial Theory of the Firm', *Strategic Management Journal*, 14, 27.

Gibson, C.B. (1995) 'An Investigation of Gender Differences in Leadership Across Four Countries', *Journal of International Business Studies*, 2nd. Quarter, 255–279.

Koopman, A. (1991) *Transcultural Management – How to Unlock Global Resources*, Cambridge, MA: Blackwell Publishers.

Malnight, Th.W. (1996) 'The Transition from Decentralized to Network-Based MNC Structures: An Evolutionary Perspective', *Journal of International Business Studies*, 27(1) 43–65.

Mead, R. (1994) *International Management, Cross-Cultural Dimensions*, Cambridge, MA: Blackwell Publishers.

NOTES

[1] Hertenberger, G. (1996) 'Das Milliarden-Vorhaben im Werk Aspern', *Der Standard*, 12 June, p. 23.

[2] Ulmer, M. (1996) 'Die virtuelle Fabrik am Bodensee', *trend*, 3, 130.

[3] Rajala, A., K. Möller, and M. Anttila (1995) 'From Marketing Departments to Lean Structures', Working Paper, Helsinki School of Business, p. 16.

[4] Jacob, R. (1992) 'Thriving in a Lame Economy', *Fortune*, 5 October, p. 5.

[5] Malet, de C. (1996) 'Bonduelle: à l'est, du nouveau', *Le Figaro économie*, 11 March, p. 11.

[6] Cocke, R. (1996) 'BOC Group Says Its Pretax Profit Rose 12% in Half', *The Wall Street Journal Europe*, 15 May, p. 3.

[7] 'Business in Asia Survey', *The Economist*, 9 March 1996, p. 23.

[8] Lei, D. and J.W. Slocum, Jr. (1992) 'Global Strategy, Competence-Building and Strategic Alliances', *California Management Review*, Fall, 81–97.

[9] Hanssen, R.A. and M. Remmel (1994) 'Strategische und operative Führung im Daimler-Benz-Konzern', in D. Hahn (ed.), *PuK-Controllingkonzepte*, 4th edn, pp. 849–955.

[10] Clarke, Ch.J. and K. Brennan (1992) 'Global Mobility – The Concept', *Long Range Planning*, 25(1), 75–78.

[11] Bartlett, Ch.A. and S. Ghoshal (1992) 'What is a Global Manager', *Harvard Business Review*, September–October, 127.

[12] Bartlett, C.A. and S. Ghoshal (1993) 'Beyond the M-Form: Toward a Managerial Theory of the Firm', *Strategic Management Journal*, 14, 23–46.

[13] Siddall, P., K. Willey, and J. Tavares (1992) 'Building a Transnational Organization for BP Oil', *Long Range Planning*, 25(1) 37–45.

[14] Bartlett, Ch.A. and S. Ghoshal (1992) 'What is a Global Manager', *Harvard Business Review*, September–October, 127.

[15] Vangelder, Ph. (1995) 'P & G: the market research contribution', *ESOMAR NewsBrief*, No. 11, December, 14f.

[16] Vangelder, Ph. (1995) 'The use of data', *ESOMAR NewsBrief*, No. 4, April, 20f.

[17] Lombard, E. (1996) 'Less is more: market research at Groupe Danone', *ESOMAR NewsBrief*, No. 6, June, 18f.

[18] Lombard, E. (1996) 'Less is more: market research at Groupe Danone', *ESOMAR NewsBrief*, No. 6, June, 18f.

[19] Kilduff, M. (1992) 'Performance and Interaction Routines in Multinational Corporations', *Journal of International Business Studies*, First Quarter, 134.

[20] Vangelder, Ph. (1996) 'Market research at Shell', *ESOMAR NewsBrief*, No. 1, January, 16f.

[21] Fucini, J.J. and S. Fucini (1990) 'Working for the Japanese: Inside Mazda's American Auto Plant', New York: Free Press, pp. 50–86.

[22] Ibid., 50–86.

[23] Burrows, P. L. Bernier, and P. Engardio (1995) 'The

Global Chip Payoff', *Business Week*, 7 August, 44–47.

24 Hofman, J.D. and J.F. Rockart (1994) 'Application Templates: Faster, Better, and Cheaper Systems', *Sloan Management Review*, Fall, 49–60.

25 Fites, D.V. (1996) 'Make Your Dealers Your Partners', *Harvard Business Review*, March–April, 84–95.

26 Bartlett, C.A. and S. Ghoshal (1986) 'Tap Your Subsidiaries for Global Reach', *Harvard Business Review*, November–December, 92.

27 Ibid., 92.

28 Symonds, W.C. and E. Frey (1995) 'Frank Stronach's Empower Steering', *Business Week*, May, pp. 43f.

29 Kilduff, M., op.cit., 135.

30 Pope, K. (1996) 'Troubles at Phone Giant Nokia Offer A Sobering Lesson on Runaway Growth', *The Wall Street Journal*, 12 March, p. A15.

31 Courage, S. (1996) 'IBM revient en force', *Capital*, No. 60, September, 42–46.

32 Flatow, P. (1996) 'Managing Change: Learning from Motorola', *Marketing News*, July, p. 9.

CHAPTER 11

THE MARKET-ENTRY
STRATEGY

| INTERNATIONAL INCIDENT |

In the Empire of the Tiger

At the end of September 1995 Hilti Asia Ltd (Hong Kong), the Southeast Asian Headquarters of Schaan, Liechtenstein-based HILTI AG, started production of drills, rawl plugs and installation devices in its new Chinese facility in the city of Zhanjiang. In little more than one year it had signed a joint-venture contract with minority investor Zhanjiang International Financial Building (Group), a subsidiary of the Bank of China, and had built the factory. The partner contributed its right to use the land and its excellent relations with local authorities which facilitated Hilti's start-up. Plans are to break even in 1997.

The major reason for this investment was not so much the tax privileges, which are limited to five years, nor the long working hours, which tend to become shortened from 45 to 40 hours per week, nor the rather low level of wages, which are at USD1.5 per hour but rapidly increasing. It was the promising Chinese market. Hilti runs an export distribution centre in Hong Kong and possesses distribution centres in Beijing, Shanghai and Guandong. But management considers China to become one of the firm's lead markets until the year 2000 which cannot be directly served without a production joint venture.

Major problems that have to be dealt with are the unreliability of electrical supply, the very low number of qualified personnel available, the high tendency of Chinese personnel once trained in Liechtenstein, Germany and the UK to leave the company when they have reached a level of technical competency which approaches European standards, and the cultural as well as language barriers for European employees sent to China as trainers for the local workforce. Nevertheless, the Chinese factory managed ISO 9001 certification in 1996 and plans to export 55 per cent of its production to neighbouring ASEAN countries.

Source: Winter, W. (1996) 'Im Zeichen des Tigers – Asien im Aufwind', *HILTI INTERNATIONAL*, 1, 8–13.

THE DEVELOPMENT OF A MARKET-ENTRY STRATEGY

Once the company's management has identified the markets to be served, has chosen a competitive strategy and has started to develop appropriate management systems for international marketing, it may decide how to conduct business in local or regional markets. It must develop an entry strategy (see Figure 11.1), that is, a unique position of the firm, the business unit, the product line or the product – depending on the size of the company's business – as well as an appropriate entry mode for each local market.

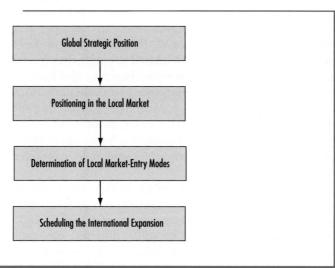

Figure 11.1 THE DEVELOPMENT OF A MARKET-ENTRY STRATEGY

A market-entry strategy consists of decisions concerning the positioning of the firm (product line or product) in the chosen local markets, the local market-entry modes, and the scheduling of the international expansion.

Entry into a new country-market is always a learning process during which a firm continually commits resources in smaller or larger steps to establish an intended position in the country-market. The intended position is determined through a strategic positioning process. In this process, management defines a company (product line or product)-specific set of benefits that is attractive to chosen target customers, is at least acceptable to important stakeholders in the market, and at the same time positively differentiates the firm (its product line or product) from competitors. If and how the intended position is reached not only depends on the company's actions but also on other stakeholders in the local operating environment, their interests, power and actions.

For example, none of the big companies in the film and photographic paper business paid much attention to China until George Fisher joined Kodak as its chairman and chief executive in 1993. As one of his top priorities he set out to conquer the Chinese market. Early on, Mr Fisher flew to Beijing to meet Chinese political leaders – officials Mr Fisher got to know as one of the first Western CEOs to visit the country after the suppression of Tiananmen Square demonstrations in 1989. Over tea he proposed to Chinese leaders that Kodak help restructure the industry. His aim was to tie up the country's film manufacturers and build a modern retail network in return for the market's dominant share. China responded by forming a high-level working group to study the matter. Kodak gathered a team of expatriates in Hong Kong. It grew from nine employees in 1994 to eight offices and nearly 300 employees, most of them sales representatives, by the end of 1996. At that time the firm was still in talks with the government, aimed at winning permission to become a domestic manufacturer and distributor. Mr Fisher's initiative brought China into focus, not only for Kodak, but for Fuji, too. Its Hong Kong agent moved immediately to grab market share ahead of Kodak. It wrested control of a distribution network from an independent chemical distributor and, in September 1994, began redecorating small developing and processing shops with green Fuji signs, in return for their commitment to buy Fuji products. By March 1996, 1650 shops were flying the Fuji flag.

The example shows how important it is for management to orient itself concerning the relevant stakeholders in the operating environment of the country-market to be entered. It must try to understand who are the important actors, how they are related to each other (technically, legally, socially and administratively), what roles they play and how powerful they are. Such information will allow management to evaluate various market-entry modes concerning their potential contribution to reaching the intended position in the country-market. A market-entry mode is the general way the company plans to enter a new country-market, for example through selling its goods to an importer or through direct investment in a production facility and a distribution system.

Sometimes choices of entry modes are relatively easy to make; for example, when the host government may grant market access only through joint ventures, as for many product categories in India. In other instances, however, the choice may be quite difficult, especially when the range of feasible options is extensive. When New Zealand-based growers of Chinese gooseberries were planning to enter the US market, for example, they did not want to shift production to the USA. However, Chinese gooseberries are fragile and must receive special handling as they move from the producer to the consumers. After carefully considering these and other factors, such as the size of the country, the available resources in personnel, capital and know-how as well as the state of the US distribution system, the growers chose to employ an import agent to direct the marketing of Chinese gooseberries in the USA. Among other things, the agent is credited with giving the fruit the more appealing name of kiwi.

Management must be aware that information concerning the relevant operating environment in a new country-market in most cases can only be superficial for an observer from outside, even one who uses highly sophisticated information-gathering tools. After entering the market in some way, more detailed information becomes available which may result in the need for an adaptation of the chosen market-entry mode. The amount of information available to the firm will depend on the degree of globalization of the product-market and the level of internationalization of the firm. Figure 11.2 shows that there are four typical situations with which a company seeking market-entry in a new country-market can be confronted.

An 'Early Starter' has no or just a few and unimportant relationships with business partners abroad. Because its product-market's level of globalization is low, other firms in the company's business environment are also very much focused on their country-markets. The level of information concerning new international markets directly or indirectly available to management is restricted. The firm must invest in information gathering which can take the form of preliminary market entry using a low-risk entry mode such as selling to an importer. For example, in the mid-1990s the European market for stove tiles was very much regional, mainly focused on Austria, Germany and Switzerland. When Sommerhuber, the Austrian market leader, decided to serve new international markets, it first had to invest in basic information-gathering activities such as focus groups with potential customers, semi-structured interviews with architects, designers and developers, and extensive talks with potential intermediaries as well as administrators, trade media representatives and financial institutions in the new country-markets.

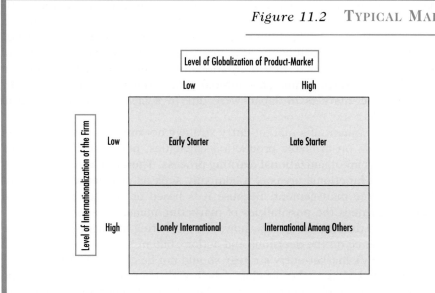

Figure 11.2 TYPICAL MARKET-ENTRY SITUATIONS

Depending on the level of globalization of its product-market and the extent of its own internationalization, a company seeking market entry in a new country-market can be confronted with four typical situations.

Source: Johanson, J. and L.G. Mattsson (1992) 'Network positions and strategic action – an analytical framework', in B. Axelsson and G. Easton, *Industrial Networks – A New View of Reality*, London: Routledge, pp. 205–217.

A 'Late Starter' is surrounded by suppliers, competitors and business customers which are internationally active or at least have indirect international marketing activities. The size of the firm largely determines how the market-entry process will proceed. Small firms will need to focus on entry modes which allow close relationships with customers in niche markets. Larger firms can buy market share through modes of entry which need substantial investment such as participation in or acquisition of local firms. Operating in the global product-market of motorcycles, for example, with international competitors such as Honda, Yamaha and BMW, the Hong Kong Ek Chor Investment Co., a Thai corporation, established a joint venture with Shanghai Automobiles Industry Co. for the production of component parts and motorcycles in China. In 1994, this joint venture accounted for about 10 per cent of the Chinese motorcycle market.[1]

When the company is an 'International Among Others' it has substantial international business experience in a global product-market. Its further expansion into new country-markets does not imply any significant changes in the strategy and competitive behaviour of the firm. Management can use the firm's position in other markets to leverage its entry into the new market. For example, Air Liquide, an internationally present French producer of industrial gas, has joined the globally active Japanese trading house Sumitomo in the creation of two production plants for industrial gas in Tianjin, in the north-east of China. The plants will produce oxygen, azote, hydrogen and argon for Toyota and Motorola factories to be built in the area – two companies with which business contacts existed already in other countries.[2]

A 'Lonely International' is a firm with highly international business activities in a rather locally structured product-market. It can use its position in and experience from other country-markets to facilitate entry into a new geographic market. Nevertheless, because the company is confronted with local customers, competitors and stakeholders who are not used to international suppliers, it will need to invest more time and capital in information gathering and relationship building than an 'International Among Others'. There may be traditions of business conduct or long-established close business relationships in the new market which make successful entry very difficult even for internationally experienced firms. Most of the problems foreign firms encountered when they first tried to enter various product-markets in Japan were due to a lack of understanding of such networks.

The development of a market-entry strategy not only depends on market factors but also on available production capacities, personnel and financial resources. It is an organizational learning process. Therefore it involves managers from all functional areas of a company such as production, finance or human resource management. Because it is based on market analyses and strongly influences the possibilities of marketing managers applying the different tools in the marketing mix, however, marketing managers should have a major influence on the decisions and actions taken.

A company's market-entry strategy should not be confused with its distribution policy. It has to be developed before distribution decisions can be taken. The decision of kiwi growers from New Zealand to enter the US market through an import agent, for example, left to the importer the decision of how to distribute the fruits to the consumers in the USA. Unilever's decision to acquire the ice cream operations of the Hungarian state-owned dairy company VMTV, on the other hand, gave the company the opportunity to develop its national distribution system in the country. This chapter will focus on the development of a market-entry strategy. Distribution decisions based on that strategy will be discussed in Chapter 14.

In developing a market-entry strategy three rules can be followed:

↔ The naive rule, where only one potential entry mode is considered. For example, the management of a Danish manufacturer of furniture might follow the rule of doing all their international business through wholesalers in the local markets of the EU because their experiences with this mode of market entry were satisfactory when the firm exported its products to Germany for the first time. This rule greatly simplifies the task for the decision makers, but very often misses attractive opportunities and leads to inappropriate solutions.

↔ The pragmatic rule, where the company starts serving local markets with a low-cost entry mode, and if it is successful changes to a more complex and costly alternative. For example, because of a lack of financial resources as well as personnel with appropriate experience, most small and middle-sized consumer products companies in Europe and Asia decide first to export to wholesalers or agents in the neighbouring countries of their local market and from there enlarge their business horizon to the rest of the continent before they think of establishing sales subsidiaries. Others establish sales offices in the most attractive country-market of each continent and from there start expanding to the neighbouring countries, increasing investments step by step.[3] Only dominant firms can afford to enter many markets by directly investing in production sites.

The advantage of this rule is that it saves the time and cost of analyses and it takes low first-entry risks. Its biggest disadvantage is that the company might fail to identify other solutions with much higher potential for fast and lasting market success and it may encounter high costs for the change of market-entry mode.

↔ The strategic rule. The discussion of Figure 11.2 showed that there is no one best market-entry mode through which to internationalize a firm's marketing activities. Nor are there any logical steps to be followed from one market-entry mode to another in the course of increasing internationalization. The success of a chosen market-entry mode depends on the level of globalization of the firm's product-market and the level of internationalization the company has reached so far. Following the strategic rule of market-entry strategy development, decision makers therefore first try to identify feasible modes of market entry, then critically evaluate them through comparison against criteria significant for reaching the intended market position, and finally choose the solution which seems most appropriate. Despite the problem that information concerning a new business environment is always somewhat superficial, this rule has proven to lead to higher firm performance than the first two mentioned.[4] In the remainder of the chapter, therefore, we assume that this approach will be used in making market-entry strategy decisions.

POSITIONING IN LOCAL MARKETS

An important premise for a rational decision as to which mode to choose for market entry is the determination of the firm's intended position in the local markets (Figure 11.3). It starts at the intended global strategic position of the firm and develops a market position for each local business unit, product line or product, considering the specific conditions of the local markets.

The positioning process follows the steps outlined in Figure 11.4. It uses all the local market information gathered and analysed for the evaluation of potential markets (Chapter 7) as well as the distinctive competencies of the firm (Chapter 8) and adds more detailed information about the country-specific product-market where it is needed.

Selection of Target Customer Segments

Before management can select customer segments as target groups, the relative competitive position of the firm must be determined for each of the most attractive segments. As described in Chapter 8, for that purpose the marketer refers to the expectations and aspirations of the customer decision makers and most important stakeholders in each segment and transforms those aspirations and expectations into capabilities and resources needed by a firm to be successful in the market segment. Then the major competitors and the company are compared concerning those capabilities and resources to determine the firm's relative competitive position in each attractive segment. The combined assessment of segment attractiveness and relative competitive position (in that segment) leads to a more refined evaluation in a segment portfolio. It forms the basis for the choice of target segments.

Figure 11.3   THE DEVELOPMENT OF A MARKET-ENTRY STRATEGY
PART 1: POSITIONING IN LOCAL MARKETS

The development of a market-entry strategy starts with the positioning of the company in the local product-markets based on its intended global strategic position.

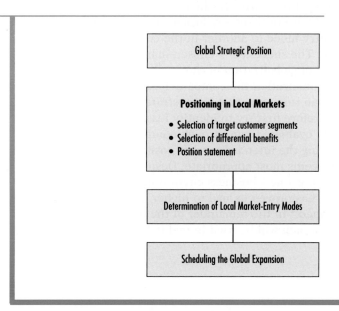

Selection of Differential Benefits

The attractiveness of target segments in a country-market and the firm's promising competitive position concerning the success factors in those segments are not enough to determine final segment choice. Management must make sure that the firm will be able to attractively differentiate itself or its offer from competitors in the eyes of customers. It has to analyse which customer and stakeholder aspirations the company should focus on and define the differential benefits that should be provided.

To make a careful choice, a congruency analysis between the aspirations of customers and important stakeholders in the potential target segments and the abilities of the company and its major competitors to satisfy them can be conducted. Table 11.1 shows a simplified example which would indicate to management that their firm could rely on better references and low price as differential benefits in the target segment considered. However, to be a successful competitor the firm would have to improve its delivery time and training services.

Position Statement

The selection of target segments and differential benefits results in the formulation of a position statement. The position statement defines the market position of the firm (its product line or product) in a local market. It describes the selected target customers and the most important stakeholders and indicates the differential benefits provided to those customers and stakeholders. For example, in the US market Porsche is positioned as a brand of

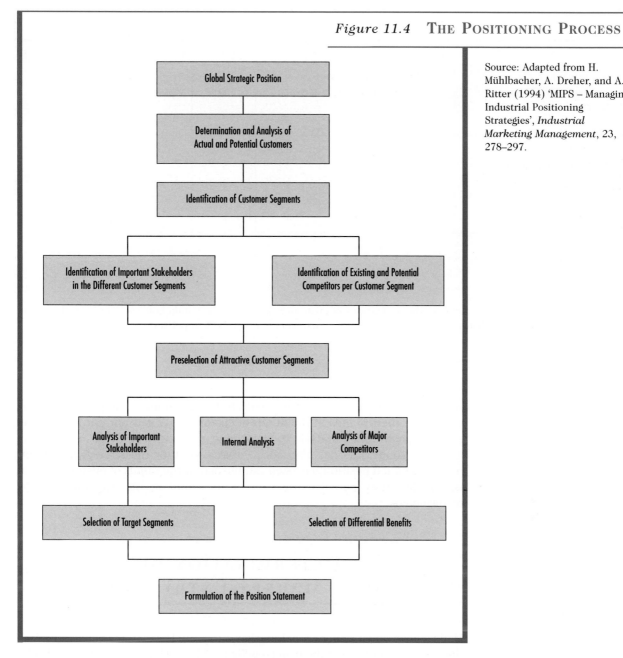

Figure 11.4 THE POSITIONING PROCESS

Source: Adapted from H. Mühlbacher, A. Dreher, and A. Ritter (1994) 'MIPS – Managing Industrial Positioning Strategies', *Industrial Marketing Management*, 23, 278–297.

sophisticated, well-engineered status symbols for high-income, sporty people, providing prestige to buyers and substantial margins to its intermediaries. Hyundai, in contrast, is positioned as a supplier of affordable, dependable individual transportation for people who look for bargains. In other words, positioning chooses a bundle of benefits that is attractive to certain customers (and related stakeholders) in a target market and distinguishes the product or company from its competitors.

Such a strategic choice of customers to serve and benefits to provide should not be confounded with positioning analysis – a tool of marketing

Table 11.1 CONGRUENCY ANALYSIS

ASPIRATIONS OF CUSTOMER SEGMENTS AND IMPORTANT STAKEHOLDERS	IMPORTANCE OF ASPIRATIONS TO CUSTOMER SEGMENTS[a]			DISTINCTIVE COMPETENCIES[b] OF		
				FIRM	COMPETITOR	COMPETITOR
	1	2	3		1	2
References	5	3	3	4	3	2
Innovative technology	3	5	3	5	3	5
Low price	5	2	2	5	4	3
Short delivery time	3	3	5	2	5	3
Training of staff	2	5	4	1	4	2

[a] 1 . . . .unimportant
3 . . . .important
5 . . . .very important

[b] 1 . . . .very weak
3 . . . .average
5 . . . .very strong

Congruency analysis helps to compare the aspirations of customers and important stakeholders in each of the most attractive segments to the distinctive competencies of the firm versus its major competitors.

research. Firms use positioning analysis to determine their position or the position of their brands in the minds of customers. A new entrant in a market can use positioning analysis to determine the positions of its competitors and after some time has elapsed, to assess whether the strategically determined intended position has been established in the minds of customers, that is, whether they perceive the firm or its brand in the way intended by management.

DETERMINATION OF LOCAL MARKET-ENTRY MODES

Management must choose local market-entry modes that are consistent with the intended position of the firm (see Figure 11.5). They have to make a trade-off between the degree of risk the firm assumes with a certain entry option and the control it can exert over the entire value chain from production to the delivery of the product to the final customer.

As the company becomes more involved in marketing and production in a country-market, control but also risk increases. More involvement means that the company can directly influence the marketing mix for its products. But simultaneously resource involvement increases, raising the level of risk (see Figure 11.6). For example, to support its market position in the USA, Porsche has founded a subsidiary, Porsche US, to coordinate dealer selection, advertising campaigns, special events, pricing, and post-sale services. Because of its high-level positioning, Porsche must maintain maximum control over

Figure 11.5 THE DEVELOPMENT OF A MARKET-ENTRY STRATEGY STEP 2: DETERMINATION OF LOCAL ENTRY MODES

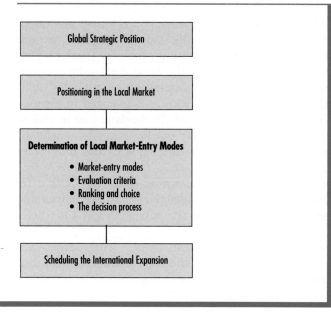

Depending on the intended positioning of the firm in the local product-markets, the appropriate entry modes can be determined.

Figure 11.6 ALTERNATIVE MARKET-ENTRY MODES: INVOLVEMENT, RISK AND CONTROL

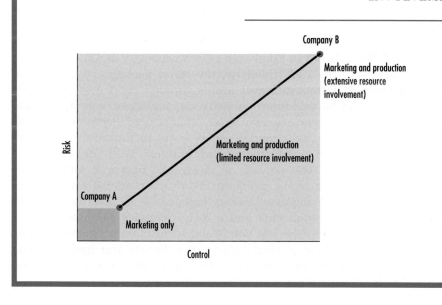

As the company becomes more involved in marketing and production in another country, the risk and control of the organization increase. For example, Company A is involved in marketing only – its risk and control are low. Company B, involved in marketing and production with extensive capital, has assumed higher risks to gain greater control in the local market.

marketing activities and therefore must use a market-entry mode that entails a relatively high degree of risk and a high level of management involvement.

Market-Entry Modes

When Timberland Company, a US-based marketer of outdoor shoes, was deciding how to enter the Japanese market, it considered options ranging from using a Japanese trading company (thereby passing along some risk but also losing control over the local marketing activities) to operating its own retail stores (thereby maintaining a great deal of control but also significantly increasing the level of risk). As illustrated in Figure 11.7, the many market-entry options among which Timberland had to choose can be classified along two dimensions: whether market-entry is sought directly or indirectly and whether they involve marketing activities only or both marketing and production in the host market.

In the following the whole range of options, from casual exporting to establishing a foreign subsidiary, and the advantages and disadvantages of each are discussed from the perspective of a marketing manager.

Indirect Entry, Marketing Only. The market-entry mode that offers the lowest level of risk and the least market control to an expanding firm is indirect entry involving marketing activities only. There are several variations on this approach:

Casual Exporting. For example, Professional Training Systems, based in Atlanta, Georgia, a company specializing in the production of video-discs, receives an unsolicited order from a customer in Spain and responds to the request on a one-time basis, it is engaging in casual exporting. However, just as risk is minimized in this approach, so too is opportunity. If the exporting firm does not follow up the contact with a sustained marketing effort, it is unlikely to gain future sales.

Catalogue, Telephone and Computer Sales. Catalogue and telephone sales may be pursued on either a casual or a continuing basis. In either case, risk is limited to the costs of producing the catalogues and distributing them in foreign markets or to the cost of the telephone calls. Consumer goods are increasingly frequently sold in this way. For example, a specialist in Scottish foods based in Edinburgh uses a catalogue to sell products to up-scale markets in the USA. Similarly, the travel packages of a Japanese firm are offered to European travel agents through catalogues. But even industrial goods can be sold internationally via catalogues or by telephone. Balzers AG and Wild Leitz AG, two Swiss producers of electronic measuring and guiding devices, sell standard spare parts to European customers through catalogues and conduct standard business with long-time customers by telephone. The spread of electronic networks will further increase the importance of the computer as an international sales device. La Rose Noire, a Hong Kong-based bakery founded by an Austrian food and beverage manager, a French chef and a Swiss patissier, for example, not only sell their desserts to the top hotels and to restaurant chains in Hong Kong but also offer their products internationally via the Internet.[5] The Future Issues box gives an example of the increasing importance of the Internet for the international marketing of services.

Figure 11.7 MARKET-ENTRY MODES

	Indirect Entry	Direct Entry
Marketing only	Casual exporting Catalogue and telephone sales Export management companies Export trading companies	Import houses Wholesale or retail purchasing groups Public trading agencies Foreign sales representatives or branch offices
Marketing and Production — Limited capital	Licensing Franchising Production or management contracts	
Marketing and Production — Extensive capital		Joint ventures Direct foreign investment

Market-entry modes can be classified according to whether they require indirect or direct involvement on the part of the firm, and whether they involve marketing activities only or both marketing and production. Note that a direct entry strategy for marketing and production has to involve extensive capital, while indirect market entry never involves extensive capital.

Consultation

and Offers

via Internet

ELECTRONIC CONTACTS WITH POTENTIAL INTER-national customers become increasingly feasible not only in business-to-business but also in consumer markets through the rising spread of Internet connections in the households of industrially developed countries.

Buying insurance will soon become easier and more transparent with software called JIBS established for the Internet which allows consultation by customers and offerings via the World Wide Web. Having chosen the respective page, potential customers are presented with a form on which they are supposed to enter personal data such as age, professional status, income and marital status. Activation of a 'calculate' button lets potential customers receive various offers of insurance packages most appropriate for their personal situation. For example, with texts such as 'You need a leisure time accident insurance because you are thirty years old, practice some risky sports, and have two small children to take care of', the programme explains to its users why a certain insurance package is recommended to them. The potential customers can simulate variations with different levels of coverage and insurance content, receiving their prices in a few seconds.

Insurance companies interested in this kind of international market-entry mode can develop a company-specific communication interface for their potential clients.

Source: Fischer-Wickenburg, V. (1996) 'Beratung und Offert im Internet', *Der Standard*, 14/15 August, p. 19.

Export management company. Export management companies function like external export departments. They assume most or all of the company's risk of market entry. Often such companies perform all the services necessary to sell the exporter's product in a foreign market. A popular arrangement is for the export management company to buy the product from the manufacturer; however, some companies perform an agency role and do not take title to the goods. Export management companies vary in other ways, too. They handle different product lines, and the completeness of the service provided varies. Regardless of these differences, they are all located in the same country as the producing firm and provide a relatively risk-free means of entering foreign markets. The manufacturer, however, does not have any access to foreign market information. It is not able to react flexibly to changes in market demand or to innovate based on knowledge about customer problems.

Trading company. A trading company is one that not only buys products or acts as an export agent but also imports, invests, manufactures, or engages in countertrading (the trading of goods for other goods, instead of money). Trading companies may operate in several national markets and handle a variety of products, or they may specialize in a single industry or product-market. For example, the Shanghai Lan Sheng Corp., housed in the new Foreign Trade Cypress Building in Shanghai, is one of the ten largest foreign exchange-earning enterprises in China. The firm imports whatever raw materials and production equipment for manufacturing balls, bags, sportswear and sports shoes are not available in the country, runs sports shoes factories in the Pudong New Area and in Shenzhen, and produces golf balls. It is also active in hotels and shipping. Shanghai Lan Sheng works as an export agent for 300 factories and 80 cooperative and joint-venture businesses in six Chinese provinces. It markets Chinese products – partly under well-known brands such as US Wilson for golf balls and Japanese Ace for bags – in 134 countries.[6]

Perhaps the best-known trading companies are the sogo shosha of Japan. Their worldwide operations, combined with an information network that provides market knowledge and links to capital resources throughout the world, make them major trading organizations in a number of markets. In recent years sogo shosha have reached beyond their traditional functions and become involved in direct global investment (see Chapter 14).

Export group. An export group is a cluster of manufacturers with similar production programmes or complementary product lines that cooperate to enter international markets. The cooperating firms stay legally and economically independent, but transfer all or most of their export activities to a central export unit which does business either in the name of the individual manufacturers or on its own account. We have already seen examples of very successful export groups such as the small firms with complementary product lines grouped around international marketers like Aprilia, Nordica or Selva, all located in Northern Italy, who do the international marketing of their production partners on their own account.

The advantage of such a cooperation agreement is the significant reduction of costs and risks that small companies with no international experience have to bear and the much improved market information flow compared to other forms of indirect exports. Problems occur in export groups with similar production programmes when bigger orders have to be split between members of the group who are potential competitors or when group members start following different basic strategies. For example, the Stubaitaler Werkzeug Genossenschaft, a cooperative of small, independent producers of metal tools from drills through pliers and chisels to highly sophisticated equipment for mountain climbing located in the Austrian Alps, got into trouble when some of their members decided to specialize in high-quality special-purpose tools at high prices while others preferred to stick to their traditionally produced product lines which can only be sold at low prices. Such differences in opinion about the most successful competitive strategy and the fear of another group member getting too much business are the main reasons why most export groups do not last for a very long time.

Direct Entry, Marketing Only.   Direct entry involving only marketing occurs when the firm becomes directly involved in marketing its products in the host market. In general, this approach represents a stronger commitment to global markets than indirect approaches do. It also entails greater risk for the firm, because it requires that more corporate resources be invested outside the home country. But the results are often well worth the risk. In the following, the common direct-entry modes for marketing purposes in industrialized countries will be discussed. The Culture box gives an example of how complicated things can become in industrially less developed countries.

Export Department.   Expansion into international markets often begins with hiring an export manager or the establishment of an export department. This is not actually a form of market entry; rather, it is an internal response to the need or desire to move into new country-markets or regions. Located within the home organization, the export department is responsible for international sales and possibly shipping, advertising, credit evaluation, and other activities related to operating in foreign markets. As described in the preceding chapter, export departments are organized either by geographic area (such as Northern Europe, Eastern Europe and East Asia) or product lines (such as steel constructions, casting products, construction material, and molding products).

Their chief disadvantage is their domestic base; despite the fact that employees of export departments may regularly visit their foreign customers, it is hard for them to maintain close enough contacts to react quickly enough or obtain enough information about trends in international markets.

Import House.   Perhaps the simplest form of direct, marketing-only entry is selling to an import house. An import house, based in the host country, provides marketing services through which products are sold either to intermediaries or directly to the final customers. The exporter needs only to sell its products to the import house. Philip Morris sells its cigarettes to Mitsui, for example, and R.J. Reynolds to Mitsubishi, both using import houses to serve the Japanese market. Until recently, General Motors sold its vehicles in Japan through a large importer, Yanase & Co., that also stocks several other imported brands. Because control over local marketing activities passes to the import house, the exporter loses the ability to determine how its products are marketed in the host country. But this loss of control is offset by a lower level of business risk.

For example, until 1995 conventional marketing wisdom held that big US

Culture Box

'Sponsors' in Saudi Arabia

A 'SPONSOR' IN SAUDI ARABIA IS ANY SAUDI PERSON OR firm that entertains business or private relationships with a foreigner or foreign company. The Saudi term for sponsor is 'kafil' which means guarantor. It stems from the legal regulation that any foreigner who wants to get permission to stay in the country has to name a Saudi citizen who guarantees that the person will leave the county after finishing his task.

The relationship between the Saudi and the foreigner can take various forms. The sponsor may be the person who invited the foreigner to business talks. He can be an agent, an employer, or a joint venture partner. But he may also be a person that lends his name to a foreign company interested in doing business in the name of the sponsor.

Thus, the term sponsor is very popular but not precisely defined. A marketer getting in contact with a potential 'sponsor' is therefore well advised to clarify carefully the legal relationship hidden behind the term before entering into a contract. The term should not be used for specifying the function of a business partner in Saudi Arabia at all.

Source: Ehlert, D. (1992) 'Der Sponsor und andere rechtliche Möglichkeiten einer Kooperation in Saudi-Arabien', *Internationale Wirtschaft*, 7 May, 8.

---

appliances would not suit Japanese consumers' tastes or fit into their small kitchens. As a consequence, most US appliance makers such as Benton Harbor, Michigan-based Whirlpool Corp. have largely ignored the average Japanese consumer, selling their products as niche-market luxury items through Japanese importers. Those importers sold them in low volumes to customers such as developers of high-priced condominiums. But conventional assumptions were dashed in 1995 when Kojima, a large discount store, created a surprise success out of General Electric's big refrigerators by selling them at prices that sharply undercut Japanese-made models. Now Whirlpool wants to do the same. It accepted the increased risk and set up a branch office in Tokyo to reach the potential of selling in Japanese mass markets.

A special case of import houses are public trading agencies in centrally controlled markets. For example, firms offering consumer and industrial products to the North Korean market have to sell their products to a state trading company. The agency, not the ultimate buyer, is the customer of the exporter. It distributes the product to the (state-owned) retail outlets or to industrial users. The advantage is that the exporter only has to deal with one business partner organization which is easily identified. If a close relationship can be built with the decision makers in the state trading company, sales are secured for a substantial period of time. The great disadvantage of this kind of business is that the exporting firm does not have any contact with the final customers. If the administrators in the state trading company for whatever reason do not like the arrangement, no sales can be made even if the products offered would exactly fit the needs of the final customers.

Wholesaler.   In a similar manner, the sale may be made to a wholesaler, independent distributor or retail purchasing group in the served country-market. Normally, such business partners serve a number of retail outlets within the host country or a specific industry.

For example, Whirlpool has started marketing refrigerators, microwave ovens and clothes washers through Daiichi Corp., a big Hiroshima-based discount retailer with 300 stores in Japan, three stores in Taipei and a dominating share in Brashs, an Australian retailer with 130 stores. Supplying the retailing organization directly from Whirlpool's factories, the firm is able to sell its appliances for as little as half the price of comparable Japanese models.[7]

Compared to a wholesaler, a distributor normally carries fewer product lines and therefore focuses more of its interests and resources on the products of the manufacturer. For example, Liechtenstein-based Ivoclar, a world-leading producer of products for dentists and dental laboratories, sells its products through wholesalers and mail order firms specializing in dental products. To improve the information level of customers about their products, they have additional local representatives who do not sell products but counsel (potential) clients concerning the benefits derived from the product.

Agent (Sales Representative).   One way management can improve the company's ability to react to market trends while maintaining a relatively low level of risk is to use foreign sales representatives. They are not employees of the home organization; rather they are independent sales agents working on a commission basis. Dodwell, for example, represents Brinton carpets, Christie's contemporary prints and Mars pet food, as well as Pitney-Bowes office machinery in Japan. They may focus only on selling or act as a total foreign sales department for the home organization.

A well-run system of sales representatives can provide the foundation for a successful long-term export programme. Japan's Fuji Photo Film Co., for example, depends largely on exclusive independent agents in Asia, including such family-owned businesses as China-Hong Kong Photo Holding. While Fuji provides promotional support – picking up the tab on some advertising, for example – expanding the business is left to the local agents.

The potential disadvantage is shown in the example of Dodwell cited above: a sales representative may represent more than one firm or one product line and, therefore, may not focus appropriately on the development of market share for products that are harder to sell or that provide less sales margin.

Representation Office.   The simplest form of actual market presence for an exporter is achieved through a representation office. It does not have an individual legal status, is not allowed to do direct sales, and is not taxed. The person representing the firm in the local market has to make contact with potential customers and other important stakeholders, maintain existing relationships, gather market information and disseminate it to people in the home base for whom it might be relevant.

In comparison to all other modes of market-entry discussed so far, a company opening representation offices has much closer contacts with the local market, its needs and developments. The major disadvantage of representation offices comes from the fact that one person is rarely able to hold equally good contacts with all potential customers if the company sells to different product-markets. A representative for a Swedish manufacturer of pre-fabricated homes in Switzerland might find it difficult, for example, to simultaneously build up relationships with architects, developers, decision makers of construction firms, and private customers. For complex technological products such as mechanical equipment or engineering, the representative may not be able to go into enough detail to gather all relevant information for the home company or to negotiate with potential customers.

Branch Office. When a representation office is staffed with more personnel (normally employees of the home organization) to cover the local market more intensively and when the unit is officially registered, it becomes a branch office. If it is even organized as a formal unit according to the legislation of the host country it is called a sales subsidiary. In Italy, for example, sales subsidiaries most often take the form of Società per Azioni (SpA) or Società a responsabilità limitata (Srl.).

One advantage of this option is that in addition to performing the relationship building, maintaining, and information function, branch office staff may perform other marketing activities, such as sales, customer service, warehousing, or even joint product development with customers. They also participate in the home organization's planning of its international marketing efforts and are much easier for the home organization to lead than independent sales representatives. Friedrich Grohe, the European leader in sanitary fittings, for example, established branch offices in Poland and in Singapore in 1995. Grohe Polska, located in Warsaw, has a training facility where Polish plumbers are supported through technical and management seminars. Grohe Pacific in Singapore has announced a design award recognizing modern design and environmental protection which has created much interest in the Pacific region.

The greatest disadvantage is the high fixed cost of sales subsidiaries. The Strategy box gives an example of a company which has taken the very popular way of starting their international activities with sales representatives or a branch office and, as the market grows and the company gains experience, establishing more extensive operations in the host market.

Indirect Entry, Marketing and Production. There are three indirect market-entry techniques that involve production with limited capital involvement: licensing, franchising, and production or management contracts. For organizations that want to establish a market presence rapidly with limited capital risk, licensing and franchising are especially popular.

Licensing. Industrial property rights, including rights to technology, patents, processes and trademarks (registered brand names), may be licensed to an organization in the host market. Ralph Lauren, for example, has a licensing agreement with Seibu to open the Japanese market. A marketer that wants to serve a bigger number of country-markets simultaneously, but does not have enough resources to build up the required production and marketing capacities, may pass on its technological know-how to partners in those markets. An example is the arrangement of San Miguel, a Philippine beer brewer, with Mt Everest Breweries of Nepal to produce and market San Miguel beer in Nepal.[8]

A firm that is focused on services like the Disney Company may license a trademark, say, Mickey Mouse, to several companies in foreign markets,

Cerberus

SWISS-BASED CERBERUS AG, THE WORLD MARKET leader in fire detection installations, is a good example of how market-entry modes may be changed depending on the stage of the product-market life cycle.

The company started in 1941 with an innovative idea of how to automatically detect fire in its early stages. Extraordinary growth over many years led to a monopoly position in the market for nearly 20 years. Because of their restricted financial resources, the young entrepreneurs first decided to focus their installation business on Switzerland. Then, they entered France through a joint venture with Guinard. As the rest of the world quickly recognized the importance of the invention, licensing agreements and sales representative contracts were signed with firms such as Siemens (for Germany, the Netherlands and Austria), Ericsson (for Scandinavia), Sielte (for Italy), Thorn-EMI (for the UK), Nohmi Bosai (for Japan), and Baker Industries (for the USA). Cerberus became the world leader in the production of early warning detectors.

When semiconductors were developed in the early 1960s Cerberus quickly changed to this new technology, but it could not prevent the rise of competitors from Japan and the USA. Growth rates declined in the 1970s. The contractual agreements with the different partners increasingly became drags on the further development of the firm because they prevented Cerberus from direct contacts with their final customers.

In 1982 Cerberus decided to serve the product-market for fire security installations on a global scale. To be able to offer all the services needed for successful business, existing contracts had to be cancelled and wholly owned subsidiaries to be installed. Wherever possible, the business organizations of previous partners were acquired, as for example in Scandinavia. In the USA the licensing partner was taken over, and in Italy and the UK new subsidiaries were founded.

At the end of 1990 Cerberus had 15 subsidiaries with 80 branch offices. Sixty-one per cent of its employees worked outside of Switzerland.

Source: Hug, L. (1991) 'Globale Marktentwicklung am Beispiel Cerberus', in *Management Zeitschrift*, 60(2) 45–48.

---

thereby permitting the production and marketing of Mickey Mouse products in those markets as long as they observe certain rules of behaviour and pay a licence fee or otherwise compensate their partners.

Licensing allows companies with small capital resources to exploit competitive advantages if they are either legally protected or difficult to imitate quickly at short notice. In addition, companies with little international experience can profit from their local partners' marketing know-how. Licensing may also be regarded as a source of additional profits if spin-off technologies are not to be used by the firm itself or if the company is not interested in international business.

The capital risk associated with licensing is relatively low. At the same time, however, the profit potential of this market-entry mode is lower compared to alternatives with more intensive involvement in the local markets. Moreover, the home organization must retain some measure of control to ensure that quality standards are maintained and the corporate or brand image remains positive. If later inconveniencies are to be avoided, the object and content of the licensing agreement should be precisely specified in the contract. The danger that a licence partner improves the licensed technology and becomes a major competitor cannot be excluded.

Franchising.   The reasons for franchising are similar to those for licensing – the organization wants to enter a foreign market quickly with a limited degree of risk and a minimum of capital involvement. Whereas licensing may embrace all forms of industrial property, franchising, in contrast, is usually limited to the use of trademarks and the associated marketing strategy. In addition, the franchisees get counselling and help in the management of their business. They can profit from the experiences of all other franchise partners. Because the trademark has a high degree of market awareness and the marketing strategy has proven to be successful, access to capital is facilitated.

The franchiser may either sign individual contracts with a number of partners per country-market or prefer a master franchise, that is, a single contract with a general franchisee in a country-market or region who, in turn, sells franchises in that market. St Louis-based Kentucky Fried Chicken, for example, has more than 400 franchised outlets in Japan, not more than ten of which are owned by a single partner. Ziebart TidyCar based in Troy, Michigan has established an automotive aftermarket business specializing in products and services for detailing, accessories and protection. Using master franchisees who took over the organization and control of sub-franchise relationships in their country, the company is present in 41 countries all over the world.

The major attraction of franchising as a market-entry mode is due to the combination of the advantages of an internationally operating firm and small privately owned businesses. An advantage of franchising compared to licensing is that it strikes a balance between adapting the marketing mix to local conditions and maintaining a high level of international standardization. Stefanel, the Italian fashion franchiser, for example, delivers its products to all partners, controls the appearance of shops, and runs internationally standardized advertising campaigns. The franchisees deliver useful market information to the Italian partner and run sales promotion campaigns that are specifically tailored to their local environments. The franchising organization tends to be more directly involved in the development and control of the marketing mix, while the franchisee is more involved in the execution of that strategy in the host market.

Franchising permits rapid market expansion with relatively little capital risk (the franchisee invests some of its own capital). But because the franchisee is directly involved in running the business, franchising offers less control by the home organization than would be possible if it owned the foreign organization. Indeed, sometimes control must be reclaimed by the home organization. For example, McDonald's has had a stormy relationship with some of its franchisees in France, owing to concerns about the maintenance of corporate standards. On the other hand, franchising has allowed McDonald's to expand rapidly and profitably. Of the firm's 1995 USD29.9 billion in worldwide sales, restaurants outside the USA accounted for 47 per cent of sales and for 54 per cent of McDonald's USD2.6 billion operating profit.[9]

Many successful examples, from restaurants, such as Ponderosa Steakhouse, hotels, such as Ibis or Scandic Crown, employment and travel agencies, computer or language training, such as New Horizons Computer Learning Centers or Berlitz, to cleaning services or print shops, such as Alpha-

Graphics, have proven that franchising allows rapid expansion of the served market as well as of international customer awareness if the provided benefit is accepted by the targeted customer segments across countries and the competitive advantage can be sustained against imitators because of its perceived uniqueness.[10] Before choosing this market-entry mode the firm's decision-makers should check the legal situation in the local markets. Otherwise, antitrust legislation and product-liability regulations could lead to negative surprises.

Production Contract.   Another mode of indirect market entry for production and marketing purposes is to sign production contracts with partners in the host countries. They do not pay any fee, but get paid for their performance. For example, a machine tool manufacturer entering the Indian market may decide to sign a production contract with an assembly plant in the country to overcome some of the problems due to import licences. In many cases the production partner only receives the minimum know-how needed to accomplish its job. A German marketer of women's fashion such as Jil Sander, only transmits its patterns to the production contractor in Thailand and delivers the fabrics to be used. Nevertheless it cannot make sure that very quickly similar designs manufactured in other Far Eastern production facilities will not appear on the European and US markets.

Japanese companies often seek closer cooperation with partners in production contracts. Such cooperation may range from information about the latest production technologies to the joint development of production know-how. Strategic partnerships may result. In any case the firm operating internationally markets the products itself.

Management Contract.   A management contract allows the firm to be involved in the management of an enterprise in a foreign market. Such contracts are sometimes entered into as a result of the expropriation of a company or industry by the host-country government. The former investors in the enterprise may be asked to continue to manage the business after it has been nationalized, and in this way they may recover some of their losses. Simultaneously they train national managers until they are able to take over.

Increasingly, companies are actively seeking management contracts in foreign markets. Energy corporations like Aramco, for example, provide technology, skills and experience to countries in the Middle East that have oil fields but lack the management capacity to develop them. Hotel management firms sign contracts with countries such as China or Russia that want to develop their tourism industry faster than they can manage on their own.

Engineering and construction contracts in economically less developed countries often include a management contract that stipulates that the leader of the consortium or the general entrepreneur will continue to manage the operation for a certain period at a specified fee. Such contracts are called turnkey contracts. The plant is built, started up and run at the risk of the constructor. For the time specified, he also takes care of the training of workers and employees as well as the maintenance of the plant.

Direct Entry, Marketing and Production.   For financially strong companies that want to keep control over their international activities and consider the markets to be served as sufficiently attractive to justify the capital risk, direct investment alternatives seem to be the market-entry modes to choose from.

The company may either make venture capital available to an innovative partner in the local market, establish a new firm together with a local or international partner, participate in or acquire a firm in the market to serve, or start up a subsidiary.

Venture Capital. If a company on its way to internationalization detects an innovative firm working on promising developments in the international markets it wants to enter, it might decide to offer venture capital to this firm. Innovations are risky; and firms working on such high-risk projects normally find it difficult to attract a sufficient amount of capital from traditional sources such as banks or stock markets. Making such an investment gives the funding corporation a 'window' on the market; it keeps itself informed on research and development through its links to innovative firms, yet avoids full commitment to those firms and their local product-market, thereby reducing overall risk.

Joint Venture. As capital involvement increases, the level of risk and the need for control by the home firm also increase. Yet many companies are still willing to share control in order to share or diversify risk. One frequently used market-entry mode that shares both risk and control is the joint venture. A partnership between home- and host- or third-country firms is formed, usually resulting in the creation of a new firm.

For example, Moscow McDonald's is a Russian-Canadian joint venture. The three restaurants operating in Moscow in 1995 have served more than 80 million customers since the first restaurant opened in January 1990. Because obtaining quality inputs on a timely basis is very difficult in Russia, the joint venture comprises a farm to raise cows for beef and grow potatoes for French fries. The company also invested USD45 million to build McComplex, a state-of-the-art food processing plant located in the Solntsevo region of Moscow. This plant runs a meat production line, a potato processing plant, a garnish line, and bakery, pie and liquid products lines, and houses a quality control laboratory and a distribution centre.[11]

There are also cases where, because of legal restrictions, the internationally operating firm only takes shares in its partner in the market to enter. For example, Deutsche Telekom, the German phone company, which considered the UK market key to its aspirations to become a global player and did not see other ways to enter the market, considered buying the UK's Cable & Wireless. Because of possible UK government objections to a foreign company taking over the sensitive international-communications services that Cable & Wireless handled for the UK, Deutsche Telekom only launched a bid for part of the firm. Earlier, in a partnership with France Telecom, Deutsche Telekom had bought a 20 per cent stake in Sprint, the third-largest US long-distance company.[12]

A joint venture often combines the market knowledge and skills of the host-country firm with the production or technical skills of the firm that wants to enter the market. For example, Nissan Motor Co. holds a minority stake in a joint venture with Thai die-maker Sammitra Motor Group, the Chinese-government-affiliated China International Trust & Investment, and the Zhengzhou truck factory planning to build 50 000 pickup trucks a year in China's Henan province by the end of the 1990s.[13] This sort of technology transfer is at the heart of many joint ventures involving production. Host-country partners in a joint venture usually bring other critical resources to the partnership, such as low labour costs, access to scarce natural resources and important stakeholders in the business system, or the avoidance of negative national prejudices.

Joint ventures are not only sought by firms that want to enter less economically developed markets. Global giants, like Matsushita Electrical Industrial Co. of Japan and Siemens AG of Germany, also join forces. They have completed a USD52 million joint venture to produce electronic parts in Germany, Austria, France and Spain. And other companies seek ways to reduce their production costs, for example the French Pierre Cardin company which manufactures large parts of its fashion outfits in a joint venture in India.

The desirability of joint ventures is often tempered by factors in the macro-environment, especially the legal and political environment. In Vietnam, for example, the process of establishing and managing a joint venture is still so unregulated that would-be partners must weigh the potential advantages against the effort and risk associated with the endeavour. In most middle European countries like Hungary, Poland or the Czech Republic, legislation concerning the establishment and management of joint ventures (including taxation issues) is developed to a point where risks for foreign investors are reduced to the level of normal business risks in market economies.

The selection of an appropriate partner is critical to the success of a joint venture. If the partners do not understand each other well, and have not jointly analysed the feasibility of the project, coordinated their goals, and regulated foreign currency issues and management responsibilities, the venture may be a disaster. In one such case an American firm entered into a joint venture with an Asian company. They planned a large, simultaneously run promotional effort that never materialized because each company assumed that the other would coordinate and pay for all promotional activities. The venture was eventually terminated. On the other hand, a carefully chosen partner can significantly contribute to the success of a joint venture. Austria-based Lenzing AG, the world's biggest producer of viscose fibres, for example, entered a joint venture with an Indian partner to construct and manage a plant in Indonesia. Its success is based not only on the technical know-how of the Austrian firm but to a substantial extent on the capability of the Indian partner to lead the Indonesian workforce sensitively.

Acquisition. The acquisition of a firm in the market to enter speeds up the entry process. It provides an opportunity to serve the targeted customer segments much faster and more efficiently than through the other entry modes discussed so far. Along with the firm itself, the buyer also acquires its experience and its network of existing relationships with customers, intermediaries and other important stakeholders. For example, faced with auto makers increasingly bent on global expansion which prefer to have suppliers that keep up with them rather than seek local suppliers in new markets themselves, US and European parts suppliers, including General Motors' Delphi Automotive Systems, are turning to international acquisitions to keep up with their customers.

Multinational corporations often prefer acquisitions to other market-entry modes because they help to gain access to new skills or technologies quickly, to move along the experience curve more quickly, and to establish a strong position in a new country- or regional market. South Korea's Daewoo, for example, wanted to buy the French Lotus Group. It was fended off amid fears that Daewoo would scare off other auto makers that work closely with Lotus's design studio.[14]

Ethics Box

Weihai Toush on Pollution

Shandong Province's Weihai High-Tech Industrial Development Zone is particularly attractive to foreign high-tech businesses. Five high-tech industrial groups with 225 projects were functioning in the zone in 1996. They specialize in electronic information, biomedical engineering, electromechanical products, new materials, and energy. But such development areas also attract businesses which in their home countries have difficulties in maintaining production facilities because of dangerous environmental pollution.

Early in 1996, an American businessman hoping to establish a high-tech firm in Shandong Province's Weihai High-Tech Industrial Development Zone with an investment of USD 7.6 million was rejected because his products contained radiation.

Similar rejections have taken place involving more than 10 projects and 2.2 billion yuan during the past five years. For example, an enterprise with 20,000 employees which wanted to invest 100,000 yuan in 1994 to move into the Industrial Development Zone was also rejected because its projected production procedures would have produced unacceptable high levels of pollutants. As a result, Weihai's environment, which because of its clear natural environment is particularly well suited for manufacturing electronic products, is being protected.

Source: 'Weihai Toush On Pollution', *Beijing Review*, 25–31 March 1996, p. 27.

Acquisitions are a mode of market entry focusing on the fast expansion of market share. In the period between 1988 and 1992, when the formation of the European Union was decided and before it came into existence, US-based companies bought 516 European firms at a value of USD17.5 billion, most of them in England, Germany and France. During the same period Japanese companies bought 204 European firms for USD12.5 billion.[15] In 1995, 32 per cent of all foreign investments in the Czech Republic were spent on acquisitions and the trend was growing.[16] The decision makers should not overlook, however, the fact that different corporate as well as national cultures may lead to conflicts in management that can potentially use up the time lead achieved through acquisition. Acquisition candidates, therefore, should be evaluated not only concerning their economic attractiveness and positions in the local business network, but also concerning their quality of management systems and the values and norms dominating their management behaviour.

Subsidiary. Establishing a wholly owned subsidiary for production and marketing purposes usually means hiring host-country workers and employees. Cultural differences will inevitably lead to leadership problems which can never be completely resolved. At first, US managers, for example, impress European superiors with their 'efficiency'; French employees, for their part, initially have problems dealing with the 'efficiency' of their German superiors; or American women may consider as sexual harassment what their Japanese superiors view as normal male behaviour.

On the other hand, examples like Japanese car factories in the USA or US production plants in China show that intensive training and appropriate focus on the development of corporate culture can do a lot to ensure the quality standards of the headquarters. General Motors' gear box factory near Vienna and Sony's compact disc production facility near Salzburg, both in Austria, even provide examples that show that the quality and output expectations of the investors can be surpassed by foreign subsidiaries. This may be one of the reasons why the most successful middle-sized German companies prefer founding subsidiaries to the acquisition of existing companies.

IBM in Japan, Nestlé in Australia, Toyota in the USA and Pfizer in Ireland are but a few large companies that have decided to take this approach. They did not only accept taking a higher capital risk compared to other market-entry modes (minority shares taken by investors from the local markets can diminish that risk). They may also be subject to protectionist policies and more backlash than either domestic companies or joint ventures. Large-scale foreign investment is controversial in most countries. Restrictive laws governing such investment are becoming increasingly common in developed countries, as well as in developing ones. The Ethics box describes a situation where such restrictions are defensible because investors try to escape restrictive environmental laws in their home countries.

On the other hand, there are more and more countries, such as in Eastern Europe or the industrially fast-developing nations in Southeast Asia, which actively solicit direct investments. Such investments allow a company to show potential customers and other stakeholders that they are serious about their commitment and are determined to stay. For example, German auto makers have spent nearly USD1 billion building up dealer, supply and service-support networks in Japan. When BMW entered the Japanese market, its initial investment was several times higher than the amount required to run what was then a very small operation. The company used the heavy investment as a selling point to dealers, banks and potential customers. Today BMW has its own highly visible and prestigious building in Tokyo, a symbol of its continued commitment. Volkswagen Audi Nippon completed a USD320 million import facility in a deepwater port which includes an inspection centre, a parts warehouse and a training centre. Mercedes has spent USD355 million since entering Japan in 1981. As a result, each of the German 'big three' now sells about 30 000 cars a year in Japan.[17]

Evaluation Criteria

The criteria on which a firm bases its decisions about market-entry modes may be classified into five categories: issues specific to the firm, characteristics of the served product-market, product considerations, conditions of the local business environment, and macro-environments. As with the various market-entry modes, there are several evaluation criteria within each of these categories (see Table 11.2); all applicable criteria should be applied in a specific case.

Issues Specific to the Firm.   The company goals formulated in its corporate mission statement strongly influence the firm's decisions concerning market-entry modes. A company that has formulated as one of its corporate goals to 'be number one or two in every market' it serves would probably choose a direct market-entry mode. To achieve and hold a market leader position, it

Table 11.2 EVALUATION CRITERIA FOR MARKET-ENTRY MODES

Each criterion influences the attractiveness of alternative market-entry options, and all should be considered for inclusion in a market-specific catalogue of evaluation criteria.

CRITERIA	ELEMENTS
Issues specific to the firm	Corporate mission Competitive strategy Personal resources Financial resources Acceptable capital risk
Characteristics of the served product-market	Level of influence Availability of information Market resistance Control of resources Market volume Product-market life cycle
Product considerations	Level of customer service Product usage
Conditions of local business environment	Competition Distribution channels
Macro-environments	Geographic distance Capital risk Currency risks Level of technological development Infrastructure Political situation Legal restrictions Trade restrictions Cultural environment

usually needs to tightly control the marketing of its products in the served markets. High sales or market-share objectives demand a major presence in the market. As the example of IBM shows, in such situations the company is likely to establish a joint venture or a subsidiary. At the very least, a corporate sales office is required.

Firms that view international sales as an 'extra' and only pursue follower positions in their non-domestic markets, on the other hand, are more likely to select an indirect market-entry mode. Also, a firm that wants to test a market or start a long-term sales-growth trend can use an exporting approach or appoint sales representatives. When the firm has become familiar with the market and wishes to increase its control, it can move towards higher-risk forms of market entry, like direct foreign investment. Garrett Automotive, for example, originally entered the Japanese market as a US-owned sales and warehouse operation. Following a plan calling for slow, careful growth, the company developed its Japanese operation into a wholly owned plant (direct production with capital involvement).

The firm's competitive strategy in many cases excludes some market-entry modes and favours a number of others. It may even dictate certain entry modes. Nestlé, with 98 per cent of its sales outside its home market of Switzerland, has a philosophy of decentralization of responsibility. It therefore markets global brands like Quik, Nescafé and Carnation through autonomous subsidiaries in major markets.

Small firms often define their competitive strategy in terms of their home market. In the USA most of them lack an export orientation. This means that they also lack the ability to respond to international opportunities. At most, they might engage in indirect market-entry modes, such as casual exporting. Because their home market is so restricted, many small companies in Switzerland, on the other hand, believe that their survival depends on regular exporting; they therefore tend to choose direct market-entry modes.

Other companies define their international competitive strategy in terms of marketing only. They want to have their production concentrated 'at home' and tend to see a 'natural' development of their market-entry modes from exports (to import houses, wholesalers or distributors) to direct-entry modes such as sales subsidiaries. Such companies refer to the pragmatic rule of choice between alternative market-entry modes. They do not even consider immediate direct entry into a new market to build a strong market position quickly; nor do they assess entry modes for marketing and production to overcome entry barriers or to improve their competitive cost position.

The firm's personnel resources also affect its preferred market-entry modes. Management personnel that have worked on an international business level for years can choose entry alternatives associated with higher risks. They are experienced and therefore better able to manage the risk of more direct market-entry modes. Without properly trained and internationally experienced personnel, however, an organization is well advised to avoid high-risk, high-control entry modes. If the firm's management resources are fully occupied by the current business and additional capacities cannot be built up fast enough, entry modes that demand only a little management involvement are to be preferred.

Well-managed small companies often have only the number of highly qualified personal they need to be successful in their domestic market. But even without slack personnel resources they may still be successful in foreign markets. Some indirect market-entry modes, such as using a trading company or signing a licensing contract, but also simple kinds of direct entry, such as selling to an importer, allow the company to use external personnel with the necessary skills and experience.

For many small and middle-sized firms, the amount of capital involved in the choice of a market-entry alternative is crucial. Even very dynamic entrepreneurs cannot seriously overdraw the financial resources of their companies. Indirect market entry with less capital needing to be spent for the internationalization of the firm will seem more attractive to them. Small companies may find that the only way to enter a major market, such as the USA, that requires extensive marketing support (in the USA, supporting a national consumer brand costs USD25–35 million a year) is to sell through an export group or a trading company. The export group or trading company may be able to bundle together several products that may be profitably sold as a group. Or the home organization may wish to sell to an import house or a purchasing group which performs similar services in the market to be entered.

The degree of capital risk that a company is willing to accept is largely determined by corporate strategy. Together with the amount of capital required to finance market entry, it is often central to the market-entry decision. Franchising is popular, for example, because it allows a company to expand quickly and to share capital risk with firms in the local markets. The global expansion undertaken by companies like McDonald's and Pizza Hut but also Hertz and Novotel would not be possible if the home organization had to provide all the necessary capital.

Even bigger companies that are well equipped with financial resources or have access to external capital will tend to choose cooperative forms of direct market entry, such as joint ventures, when the business environment is not entirely stable or entry requires expensive marketing campaigns, strong local networking, or large capital spending for plant and equipment.

Characteristics of the Served Product-Market. The most important characteristic of a product-market to be entered is the level of influence on intermediaries and customers a firm needs to have in order to market its product or service successfully. If the company wishes to influence customers directly and is unable to do so from its home base, direct-entry modes are called for. ETA, the Swiss manufacturer of Swatch, for example, after some unsuccessful trials with local sales representatives, recognized that mass marketing its watches to target customers in the USA and Europe was impossible without securing some direct influence on the local marketing activities, such as choice of outlets or market communication activities. Thus, top management decided to open sales subsidiaries in all major markets.

Because of its close link to market influence and control, the availability of information is an important factor in market-entry decisions. When in-depth market information is needed for local success but is difficult to obtain, the most attractive alternative is a direct, marketing-only entry mode, or it may be a direct marketing and production entry mode with capital involvement. In both of these cases a local partner is needed, either because it possesses the required information or because it is better able to gather the information than a foreign organization would be. For example, a Canadian manufacturer of maple syrup planning to enter the Malaysian market would be well advised to form a joint venture with a Malaysian partner. Food preferences are quite different in Malaysia than in Canada, and a local partner could provide the information necessary for successful product adaptation. At the same time, because market information is not as readily available in Malaysia as in Canada, a local partner may be the only viable source of the needed information.

The greater the market's resistance to a product, the greater the need for a market-entry mode that gives the organization direct control over local marketing activities. Microwave ovens, for example, met with fairly strong resistance in Puerto Rico and the UK, owing to cooking habits and social norms that were not consistent with the benefits offered by the marketers of the product. Microwave-oven manufacturers must undertake appropriate marketing efforts to carefully reposition the product. To make sure that marketing tools were properly applied in the local markets, the manufacturers had to choose direct market-entry modes. If the product is likely to diffuse rapidly through the market, the decision makers can opt for an entry alternative that leaves great parts of market control to the intermediary in the host-market.

The need to control the flow of resources also influences market-entry decisions. A company that needs to be vertically integrated from raw materials through to distribution to be competitive should probably use a direct marketing and production entry mode. Foreign copper companies in Chile, for example, want to control copper mining, extraction and processing into a semi-finished product. They therefore invest directly in mining, melting and processing activities.

Market volume can also influence the choice of market-entry mode. In large markets, especially those with strong growth rates, direct investment is more easily justified than in small markets with low or stagnating growth rates. One of the reasons US and Japanese companies have made major investments in Europe is that the EU represents an even larger market than the USA. Before the economic integration provided by the EU, national markets in Europe were mostly entered by less financially risky methods, such as exporting.

Some products can find high-volume markets outside the Triad markets. The macro-environments of those markets, in many cases, are less attractive, however. They suggest entry modes that minimize capital risk. For example, in Chad, an African nation where per capita income is about USD210 per year, foreign firms generally prefer to export their products or sell them to wholesale or retail purchasing groups rather than establish subsidiaries there. In their view, the level of economic activity in Chad is too low and the political environment too unstable to justify direct investment. International marketers should not forget, however, that more direct involvement in such markets might encourage a process of development, improve the market situation, and strengthen their own position in the country.

Just as the marketing mix changes at each phase of the product life cycle, attractive market-entry modes also change depending on the phase of the local product-market life cycle. For product-markets in the early (introductory) phase of the life cycle, indirect market-entry techniques are often preferred. But if the local product-market is highly attractive it may be wiser to invest directly in the early stages, gain product and brand awareness, and thereby gain market share quickly while raising barriers to entry by competitors. Japanese and Korean firms, in particular, employ this approach with great success.

High-growth product-markets often require direct market-entry approaches because in such cases the firm usually wants to manage and control the local marketing of its product as closely as possible. Companies planning to enter a local product-market in the mature phase of its life cycle will have to choose an alternative which, on the one hand, ensures the firm's intended competitive position and, on the other hand, generates the expected cash flow to be spent in markets in earlier stages of their life cycle.

Companies already present in a market often change their entry mode over the product-market life cycle. The Strategy box gives an example of the Swiss company Cerberus which has followed such a stepwise change. In the mature phase of the market they tend to extend the direct approach followed during the growth phase, so that the product will maintain its market position and profit margin for as long as possible. During the decline phase of the product-market, the firm may switch back to an indirect approach, decreasing the costs as sales fall, if it plans to slowly draw back from the market.

Product Considerations. The characteristics of a product influence not only the speed of its diffusion in a new market, but also the choice of market-entry mode. The greater the level of customer service needed to support a product, both before and after the sale, the more the preferred market-entry alternative will be one that entails direct capital involvement or allows significant influence on the behaviour of the local business partners. The chosen entry mode must enable the home organization to control the quality of services provided by their own employees or those of their local partners.

Japan's Daimaru department store chain, for example, entered the Australian market through direct foreign investment. The company is convinced that its high levels of customer service, especially its packaging and wrapping of products, give it a competitive edge that can only be sustained through direct control and may even force other Australian department stores to change their approach.

Caterpillar, the Peoria, Illinois-based manufacturer of machines and diesel engines, is an example of a company which is committed to worldwide service excellence but chose to enter most markets without capital involvement. They closely cooperate with 186 independent dealers around the world who are long-established members of their communities and therefore have close ties to local customers and stakeholders. They advise customers on the selection and application of a product, financing, insurance, operator training, maintenance and repair, and help in deciding when it makes economic sense to replace a machine. Through extensive training and involvement of dealers in product design and delivery, service and field support, and the management of replacement-part inventories, Caterpillar has managed to develop a common understanding of what it takes to provide superior customer service.[18]

Product usage affects the degree of control needed in particular markets. Industrial goods normally make entry modes involving direct marketing or production (often with capital involvement) more desirable than consumer goods. But also an advertising agency, for example, that wishes to serve major global corporations must be directly involved in the markets its clients seek to reach. For example, London-based Saatchi & Saatchi Advertising has undertaken a series of multinational joint ventures and acquisitions in an effort to offer efficient and effective advertising to corporate clients throughout the world.

Conditions of the Local Operating Environment. The conditions of the local operating environment not only influence the attractiveness of a market but also the choice of market-entry mode.

Management must assess the competitive situation in broad terms – size, intensity, relative market share, rate of growth, interweaving with other stakeholders in the operating environment and technological sophistication, to name a few examples. Each of these aspects of competition affects market entry in different ways. For example, foreign companies entering the car market in the USA face intense competition. In this situation it is more effective to 'buy' market share through affiliation with a firm that is already in the market than to enter the market alone and build market share slowly. Mazda used this approach when it affiliated with Ford to get better access to the US market.

Existing distribution channels as well as the level of interrelationships of their members and the company's distribution objectives strongly influence the attractiveness of different market-entry modes. For example, when the distribution system is complex and its members have long-lasting personal ties as well as mutual capital involvement, as is the case in Japan, local partnerships seem to be a good choice. Direct investment in distribution systems may be necessary when marketing objectives cannot be met using existing distribution systems. For instance, in the case of a local market where food products usually pass through several levels of wholesalers and retailers before reaching consumers, it might be appropriate for a firm that wants to market perishable products to invest in a new distribution channel. Also, when a firm wants to lower distribution costs it might establish a more efficient channel.

When entering a market in which the distribution system is sophisticated and accepts new entrants easily, as is the case in Hong Kong, an indirect entry technique may be used. A Dutch company that exports UHT milk (which is processed at very high temperatures, so that it does not need to be refrigerated before the container is opened) to Hong Kong, for example, has achieved a substantial market share by selling to two supermarket chains that together control some 70 per cent of the market.

Macro-Environment. Characteristics of the macro-environment affect the final selection of a market-entry mode by eliminating some options and making others more viable. Besides the geographic distance of the local market, evaluation criteria from the macro-environment are economic, technical, political, legal and cultural factors.

The geographic distance between the home market of a firm and its country target market can affect the market-entry decision. Most managers tend to choose indirect market-entry modes for distant markets because they perceive increasing risks with increasing distance. But this is mainly an emotional reaction due to the psychologic distance to such 'foreign' markets. A Finland-based company, such as Polar Electro Oy, a producer of measurement devices for physical training purposes, entering the New Zealand market would probably use some low-risk direct market-entry mode, such as a wholesaler or a sales representative. Given the distance between the two countries, some 8000 miles, such a decision would pass most control (including market information sources) to the host-country organization. A branch office, such as Polar Electro Germany, on the other hand, would ensure direct contact with local customers and facilitate contacts with importers in neighbouring countries such as Leuenberger Medizin Technik in Switzerland.

Recently the impact of distance has been reduced by advances in telecommunications. Phone calls, telexes, fax messages and online computer information are conveyed as easily between Scandinavia and New Zealand as they are within either country. Nevertheless, distance still creates a gap in face-to-face communication which cannot be fully overcome by videoconferences. If personal contacts are crucial for market success, the choice of market-entry mode should consider that fact independent of geographic distance.

Even highly capitalized firms will tend to choose less risky market-entry modes when the capital risk involved with direct entry alternatives exceeds a pre-specified limit. In countries with unstable economic or political environments, most companies prefer joint ventures to wholly owned subsidiaries. This was proven after the fall of the iron curtain in Central Europe where most international involvement in the early 1990s was through joint ventures. The share of more direct forms of capital investment grew in the mid-1990s when the economic and political stability of countries such as the Czech Republic, Hungary and Poland seemed to be assured.

Currency risks, such as quick changes in the value of currencies, decrease the attractiveness of direct marketing and production entry modes. For example, a profit margin of 10 per cent of gross sales can be eliminated by a more than 15 per cent currency devaluation in the host-country, as took place in Italy in 1992 compared to most other European currencies. Profit would be increased, of course, if the exchange rate were to shift the other way. Market entry by means of direct production permits the firm to avoid the impact of rapid changes in exchange rates through reinvesting profits and improving the long-term performance of the company.

The level of technological development in a market also influences the selection of a market-entry mode. When entering a technologically sophisticated market like Sweden, an inventor of a new crank mechanism for bicycles may be able to transfer its technology directly into the market. This might be done without capital involvement, through a licensing arrangement between the inventor and a Swedish firm. In a market with a lower level of technological sophistication, direct marketing-only alternatives or even indirect marketing-only entry modes may seem preferable because appropriate use of the technology in local production might possibly not be ensured. In Argentina, for example, a sales representative or an import house might be used for the same new product.

Some technologically less developed countries, however, impose the creation of joint ventures with local firms. The goal is to improve the technical know-how of host-country managers and personnel as well as to get hold of the latest machinery. Only if the product is very complex and cannot be ordered at any other supplier, as in the case of a Cray Computer, might the host country allow the company to export to its market. This approach is used by China, which is trying to upgrade its technology.

A nation's infrastructure can act as either a resource or a constraint in the evaluation process of market-entry alternatives. A French vacation company such as Club Méditerranée, developing a vacation resort in Sierra Leone, will have to use a market-entry mode that entails capital involvement. It will probably need to build roads to transport tourists to the vacation site. It may also have to build its own electrical power plant and house its employees. But when entering the Portuguese market the same company could use an indirect technique, because the infrastructure there is more highly developed.

The political situation in a market to enter influences both the choice and the success of a market-entry mode. Whereas companies that wanted to do business in the Soviet Union had a rather restricted range of choices to enter the market (either selling to public trading agencies or establishing joint ventures with one of those agencies), they have a much broader set of choices now to enter product-markets in Russia. Positive political relations between two nations, such as those between Australia and the UK, permit a free decision among market-entry alternatives.

Legal restrictions on the choice of market-entry mode may be motivated by economic concerns (public or private), as when a host country requires local firm participation in business conducted by a foreign company like in Saudi Arabia, or government participation in specific businesses, such as in weapon deals. Legislation may restrict foreign investment for market entry. US advertising agencies, for example, have been denied any role other than non-equity affiliation in Korea. In countries with publicly owned companies, those firms often hold exclusive rights for the production and distribution of certain products or services. This is one of the reasons why the denationalization of major industries, as occurred in the UK, Hungary and the Czech Republic in recent years, has drawn so much interest from foreign investors.

Trade restrictions control or limit trade within a nation or between that nation and others. India, for example, has very tight restrictions on imports of automobiles, including low import quotas and a high tariff on each vehicle, as well as on most industrial goods. Exports to this country are very much complicated by the procedures governing the receipt of an import licence. The exporter must prove that no Indian competitor exists that could provide similar products. The government introduced this rule to induce as many potential exporters as possible to transfer their technology to India by entering the market through joint ventures with Indian partners.

When trade restrictions are eased, a wider array of market-entry options is available. Since 1985 when trade restrictions were eased in Japan, for example, foreign firms no longer have to submit products that meet their own safety tests to the Japanese testing bureau. As a result, foreign companies can enter Japanese markets more quickly than before.

Sometimes high trade restrictions in an otherwise attractive market make direct foreign investment the most appropriate entry technique. In the USA, for example, increased protectionism, coupled with the devalued dollar and a sizeable market, have resulted in increased direct foreign investment by Asian and European manufacturers.

As the discussion of cultural influences on international marketing has shown, the local success of an internationally operating company can strongly depend on its capability to adjust to the cultural environment. If a Caribbean fruit producer usually negotiates with purchasing agents of powerful retail organizations and relies on those organizations for marketing its products to the target customers in EU markets, it may encounter difficulties when trying to enter east Asian markets the same way. There, most food products are sold by small retailers in open markets. The market-entry mode must be adapted to the cultural environment of each local or at least regional market.

A society that is characterized by a high level of ethnocentrism is probably best entered through a management contract, licensing, or a joint venture. In contrast, Japanese electronic firms entering the USA are probably better off maintaining their home-country identity. Because American consumers believe that Japanese manufacturers produce higher-quality products, a market-entry mode that keeps the Japanese name visible probably makes the most sense.

The Decision Process

An attempt to assess the attractiveness of each existing market-entry mode for each country-market to be served would not only require masses of information which would be hard to acquire but would also consume considerable management time. The resulting high costs and the loss of time would a priori decrease the competitiveness of the firm. A less extensive approach to choosing an adequate market-entry mode which leads to satisfactory results is to

↔ establish a set of 'knock-out' criteria which have to be satisfied by an entry mode in order to be feasible;

↔ reduce the great number of alternatives to a small set of feasible entry modes;

↔ critically evaluate those and rank them into an order from which the best placed entry mode that can be implemented in the existing macro-environment will be chosen.

The establishment of k.o.-criteria for local market-entry modes is tightly related to the corporate policy and the competitive strategy of the firm. It starts with an assessment of the corporate mission and the stated rules of behaviour. If the company wants to minimize its financial risks, for example, market-entry modes that entail high capital involvement, such as establishing a subsidiary with production and marketing, would be excluded. 'Needed capital equipment' becomes a k.o.-criterion in the pre-selection of entry options. If the company strives to gain the highest degree of control over market information flows and the marketing of its products to the final customers, criteria such as 'Access to market information' and 'Influence on local markets' will have significant influence in the pre-selection process.

All market-entry options that survive this first reduction step will then be checked according to criteria related to the competitive strategy of the firm, which contains statements concerning the fundamentals the firm plans to compete on, the major benefits to be provided to the customers, and the competitive behaviour of the company. From there, important criteria for the selection of market-entry modes can be deduced. For example, if cooperation with potential competitors is not allowed, all entry alternatives that rely on such cooperation, for example licensing or joint ventures, are to be excluded from further investigation.

The small set of feasible entry modes quickly determined by this approach then undergoes a critical evaluation through comparison against criteria related to the intended local market position. Factors such as the needed control over resources, the market resistance to be expected, the existing market volume, or the capacity to secure a high level of customer service may play a prominent role in the evaluation process. Table 11.3 gives an example of how the evaluation process can be formalized.

After listing the most important factors of influence on the implementation of the local market position, the decision makers can grade the remaining entry modes considered as feasible on a scale that might range from 1 to 5. The entry options are then ranked according to the number of points they are assigned. To keep the evaluation procedure understandable and verifiable for other managers in the firm, a comment column should be used to indicate why the scale points were attributed as given. The result is a rank order of theoretically feasible market-entry modes according to their potential contribution to the intended local position of the firm (its product line or product).

Once this ranking is established, the remaining short list of entry options is assessed for the implementation potential of each mode in the existing macro-environment of the local market, that is, for example, the political or legal situation in the market. The procedure starts with the entry mode ranked first. If this most preferable option cannot be chosen because of unresolvable problems in the macro-environment, such as missing infrastructure or too high currency risks, the next ranked option is assessed until a market-entry mode is identified which not only comes up to the standards of corporate policy and global strategic position, but also to the intended local position and the demands of the local macro-environment.

In the decision process described above, analytical work is reduced to a realistic volume without leaving the decision to the gut feelings of management or taking it on the basis of 'successful traditions'. Management does not make a final decision until all available information on the effects of potential market-entry modes has been considered. In effect, this approach forces

---

Table 11.3 EVALUATION OF FEASIBLE MARKET-ENTRY MODES

EVALUATION CRITERIA	FEASIBLE ENTRY MODES				COMMENTS
	BRANCH OFFICE	SALES SUBSIDIARY	FRANCHISING	JOINT VENTURE	
Needed personnel resources	4	3	5	2	
Needed capital equipment	4	3	5	1	
Influence on local market	3	4	2	5	
Access to market information	3	4	3	5	
Level of customer service	2	4	4	5	
Intensity of competition	1	2	3	4	
Market volume	5	3	4	1	
Capital risk	4	2	5	1	
Distribution system	2	2	4	5	
Trade restrictions	3	4	5	5	
Total points	31	31	40	34	

Scale: 1 = very bad
      3 = satisfactory
      5 = very good

When the decision makers have established a short list of feasible market-entry modes, they can evaluate the remaining options by comparison against evaluation criteria relevant for the intended local position of the firm.

---

management to re-evaluate criteria and options continually from different perspectives. Each local market-entry analysis might, therefore, result in a different entry-mode decision even if the intended position in the markets is the same.

SUMMARY

Before the firm can enter the product-markets in the geographic areas determined in its portfolio strategy, it must develop a market-entry strategy. The first step to attain this goal is to define its intended market position (or the position of its product line or product to be introduced) in all the local markets to be served. The positioning process consists of determining the specific customer segments to be served and making the company or its product distinct and important to those customers and related stakeholders. A company positions itself relative to competitors, always bearing in mind its basic corporate policy and intended global strategic position.

Management must select market-entry modes that are consistent with the firm's desired position in the markets to be served. Market-entry options range from casual exporting to direct foreign investment. Each option entails a different combination of risks and market control, and each market under consideration may require a different market-entry mode.

Market-entry options can be classified along two dimensions: whether they are direct or indirect approaches and whether they involve only marketing or both marketing and production. Each market-entry mode involves trade-offs between market control and degree of risk. The approach that offers the lowest level of risk and the least market control is indirect entry involving marketing activities only. The firm achieves the closest control over its markets through direct entry for marketing and production purposes. Because of the high capital involvement linked to this entry mode, however, the resulting risk may be substantial.

Because of the great number of market-entry modes theoretically available, decision makers have to reduce that number quickly to a manageable amount before a detailed assessment procedure can start. For that purpose, criteria such as the goals formulated in the corporate mission and the competitive strategy as well as personnel and financial resources are used. The remaining market-entry modes are critically evaluated for their fit with the intended position of the firm in the local market. Characteristics of the served product-market, the product, and the industry are considered for that purpose. The result is a ranking of feasible market-entry options.

Criteria that should be considered when finally deciding which market-entry mode to choose come from the macro-environments of the local markets. For many decision makers, the geographic distance of a market plays an important role in their evaluation process. Economic considerations, such as limited buying power of customers, may require entry modes that minimize capital risk. The political situation can influence both the choice and the success of a market-entry mode. Legal restrictions play an especially important role in market-entry decisions. And trade restrictions may be so severe that firms are prevented from entering the market at all. Cultural conditions, such as a high level of ethnocentrism, the existing infrastructure, the level of technological development in the market and the available distribution system also affect the choice of market-entry mode.

When the entry modes for all the local markets to be served have been determined, the firm has to develop a schedule for its international expansion. The sequence of market entries and its timing have to be fixed. The now developed market-entry strategy allows the company to implement the strategic decisions through the application of the marketing mix to be discussed in the following chapters.

Discussion Questions

1. What trade-offs are involved in selecting a direct market-entry mode over an indirect one?
2. What trade-offs are involved in deciding to enter a market with marketing activities only or to enter it with marketing and production activities?
3. Explain how the legal, cultural or economic environment might affect market-entry decisions.
4. Explain how the nature of a local business environment influences market-entry decisions.
5. What characteristics of a firm have important implications for market-entry decisions? Why?
6. How does the nature of the product affect market-entry decisions? Find examples from business magazines.
7. Find examples in the press of conditions under which a firm might find it necessary to produce a product in a foreign market. When is this approach desirable, if not required?

8. What conditions favour direct foreign investment as a market-entry strategy? Why?

9. What are the pros and cons of establishing a joint venture? Find an example of a successful and a less succesful joint venture and indicate the reasons why they have developed more or less successfully.

10. How does the existing infrastructure in a market influence the choice of a market-entry mode?

ADDITIONAL READINGS

Andersen, O. (1997) 'Internationalization and Market Entry Mode: A Review of Theories and Conceptual Frameworks', *Management International Review*, Special Issue 2, 27–65.

Andersson, U., J. Johanson and J.-E. Vahlne (1997) 'Organic Acquisitions in the Internationalization Process of the Business Firm', *Management International Review*, Special Issue 2, 67–83.

Johanson, J. and L.G. Mattsson (1992) 'Network positions and strategic action – an analytical framework', in B. Axelsson and G. Easton, *Industrial Networks – A New View of Reality*, London: Routledge, pp. 205–217.

Kotabe, M., A. Sahay, and P. S. Aulakh (1996) 'Emerging Role of Technology Licensing in the Development of Global Product Strategy: Conceptual Framework and Research Propositions,' *Journal of Marketing*, 60 (January), 73–88.

Leonidu, L.C. and C.S. Katsikeas (1996) 'The Export Development Process: An Integrative Review of Empirical Models', *Journal of International Business Studies*, 27(3), 517–551.

Trommsdorff, V., M. Binsack, M. Drüner, U. Koppelt (1995) *'Erfolgreich kooperieren in Osteuropa'*, Köln: Dt. Wirtschaftsdienst.

Tse, D.K., Y. Pan and K.Y. Au (1997) 'How MNCs Choose Entry Modes and Form Alliances: The China Experience', *Journal of International Business Studies*, 28(4), 779–805.

Vanhonacker, W. (1997) 'Entering China: An Unconventional Approach', *Harvard Business Review*, March–April, 130–140.

Welch, D.E. and L.S. Welch (1996) 'The Internationalization Process and Networks: A Strategic Management Perspective', *Journal of International Marketing*, 4(3) 11–28.

Woodside, A.G. and R.E. Pitts (eds) (1996) *Creating and Managing International Joint Ventures*, Westport, CN: Quorum Books.

NOTES

1. Qian, Y. (1994) 'Shanghai-Ek Chor Motorcycle Co., Ltd. – An Outstanding Sino-Foreign Joint Venture', *China's Foreign Trade*, September, 23.

2. 'L'Air Liquide se renforce en Chine', *Le Figaro économie*, January 1996, p. VI.

3. Hildebrandt, L. and Ch. Weiss (1990) 'Entry Strategies in Newly Industrialising Countries – The Case of German Companies', in *Advanced Research in Marketing*, Vol. 1 (H. Mühlbacher and Ch. Jochum, eds), Proceedings of the EMAC Annual Conference, Innsbruck, pp. 565f.

4. Jones, R.E., L.W. Jacobs, and W.v. Spijker (1992) 'Strategic Decision Processes in International Firms', *Management International Review*, 32(3), 219–236.

5. 'Im Namen der schwarzen Rose', *Der Standard*, 10/11 August 1996, p. 13.

6. Dong, F. (1994) 'Shanghai Lan Sheng Corp. – First Cinese Foreign Trade Company Listed on Shanghai Stock Exchange', *China's Foreign Trade*, September, 22.

7. Shirouzu, N. (1996) 'Whirlpool to Start Marketing Home Appliances in Japan', *The Wall Street Journal Europe*, 30 May, p. 5.

8. Czinkota, M.R. and J. Woronoff (1991) *'Unlocking Japan's Markets'*, Chicago, IL: Probus Publishing, pp. 150f.

9. 'Macworld', *The Economist*, 29 June 1996, p. 61.

10. 'International Franchising', *International Herald Tribune*, 8 March 1996, p. 18.

11. Fey, C.F. (1995) 'Success Strategies for Russian-Foreign Joint Ventures', *Business Horizons*, November–December, pp. 49–54.

12. Ascarelli, S. and R.L. Hudson (1996) 'Germany's Phone Giant Mulls Cable & Wireless Bid', *The Wall Street Journal*, 12 April, p. A10.

13. Reitman, V. (1996) 'Nissan Motor Gets Toehold in China Via Truck Venture', *The Wall Street Journal*, 9 April, p. A15.

14. 'GM Said to Be Considering Stake in Parts Supplier Valeo', *The Wall Street Journal Europe*, 10–11 May 1996, p. 3.

15. 'USA und Japan sichern ihre Position für den Binnenmarkt', *Der Standard*, 22 December 1992, p. 16.

16. 'Lockruf der Märkte im Osten', *Der Standard*, 29 August 1995, p. 19.

17. Updike, E.H. (1995) 'When in Japan, Do as the Germans Do', *Business Week*, 3 July, p. 19; and Simon, H. (1992) 'Lessons from Germany's Midsize Giants', *Harvard Business Review*, March–April, 115–119.

18. Fites, D.V. (1996) 'Make Your Dealers Your Partners', *Harvard Business Review*, March–April, 84–95.

Case Study

HIRSCH WATCH STRAPS
JAPAN

When Robert Hirsch left his father's office in late Fall of 1994 he knew that he had just taken over a major task: the responsibility for the firm's entire business in South East Asia. After having led the HIRSCH subsidiary in the United States and the company's worldwide OEM business with watch manufacturers, this new responsibility represented a big challenge to Robert, because the company had not done too well in South East Asian markets so far. HIRSCH Armbänder GmbH, headquartered in Klagenfurt, Austria, starting from a local business in 1945 had developed to be the world leading manufacturer of leather watch straps (the company called them 'bracelets'). Respectable market shares of up to 60 per cent in most EU markets had led top management to consider their company as the very best in product quality, service and delivery. But market penetration in the fast growing Asian markets did not follow. Robert knew that one of his first jobs was to more closely analyse the watch and watch bracelet markets of those countries and to develop a clear strategy of how to successfully expand the Hirsch business there. Japan, the second biggest market in the world and one of the most difficult to serve, would be his first target. Successful business in Japan would be a highly motivating signal to all those people in the company's headquarters who tended to quit that market.

THE COMPANY

In 1945, at the end of World War II, Hans Hirsch, a furrier who lived in Klagenfurt, in the South of Austria, bought remnants of leather from the shoe industry and started producing watch straps. He

Source: This case was prepared by Hans Mühlbacher, Chair of Business Administration at the Institut für Handel, Absatz und Marketing of Leopold-Franzens-University Innsbruck, Austria. The author would like to thank Hirsch Armbänder GmbH. for the support of the project.

cut them out of the remnants with a pocket knife. His spouse sewed the pieces together with her sewing machine. From that very first moment on, precise processing and highest product quality have been the guidelines for production. A few years later, Hans Hirsch invented the unique 'rembordering system', a seamless connection between the lower and upper leather of a watch strap for which he received patent rights. Rembordering largely improves the quality of wearing and the life of the strap. In 1949, the company which carried the name of its founder, had total sales of ATS 1 million (about USD85,000) generated by 25 people.

In 1957, today's president and CEO of the company, Hermann Hirsch, entered the firm and took over sales management responsibility. The company reached total sales of ATS 10 million in 1960. During the following decade HIRSCH became market leader in Austria. In 1967, Hermann Hirsch took over part of the company. He started exporting, first to neighboring Germany and Switzerland, then to Denmark and Norway. At that time a central part of the company's philosophy developed: 'All people working at HIRSCH must strive for outstanding performance to offer ideal conditions to retail customers for making profitable sales with watch bracelets.'

In 1975, Hermann Hirsch took a bank loan to buy the rest of the company from his father who wanted to retire. He started a period of fast growth and internationalization of the firm. Sales subsidiaries were founded on a global level: in Germany and Switzerland (1976), in the USA (1977), Canada (1979), Japan (1981), Belgium and the UK (1982), in Spain (1984), France and Sweden (1985) and in Hong Kong in 1989. Employment grew from 130 people in 1970, to 252 in 1983, 300 in 1985 and 500 in 1988, when the private firm was transformed into HIRSCH-Armbänder GmbH (HIRSCH Watchbracelets Co. Ltd.).

In 1990, the company proudly announced to have produced and sold 100 million watch bracelets since its beginnings in 1945. Production was concentrated in one factory located in Klagenfurt. 90 per cent of production was exported to more than 60 countries worldwide. Until 1994, total sales reached about ATS 650 million. HIRSCH had acquired the very small but prestigious Swiss watch bracelet manufacturer Frischknecht who produced watch bracelets by hand and delivered them to the most prestigious watch manufacturers in Switzerland. To stay price competitive, HIRSCH had also started a joint venture with a production partner in Hong Kong and planned direct production investment in India. The major objectives of the company were to create a global watch bracelet culture and to be the main supplier for watch bracelets to customers worldwide under the precondition of making a profit.

To reach those objectives product lines had been expanded to contain various materials from leather, to metal and synthetics. HIRSCH followed a three brand policy. The three brands were HIRSCH, Marcco and Frischknecht. HIRSCH Armbänder GmbH was the development and logistics centre for all three brands. All products were directly distributed to retail outlets (in the so-called refill business) and to OEM customers (watch manufacturers) through distribution centres located in Klagenfurt, Austria, Dulliken, Switzerland (for Frischknecht), West Caldwell, USA and Hong Kong.

The Refill Business

Each brand had a specified retail distribution network overlapping the other brands' distribution network only in defined areas. The local sales subsidiaries and distribution partners were responsible for local distribution and coordination of sales and market communication activities.

Marcco was positioned as a lifestyle oriented fashion bracelet for all young consumers who shop in supermarkets and discount stores and want to buy watch bracelets at reasonably low prices. Marcco products were distributed through department stores, supermarkets, D-level jewellers and watchmakers, discounters as well as through all other shops selling watches, such as electronics stores, photostores, and catalogue showrooms. The product line contained leather straps in fashion colours, a small but deep range of department store oriented metal bracelets in gold colour, bicolour or steel, and straps made out of synthetic materials fitting well selling fashion watches. The retail price of Marcco started at USD2.85 and went up to a top price of USD23.30.

HIRSCH was positioned as a lifestyle oriented classical accessory with high functional quality based on technological leadership, targeted to consumers who want to wear a branded high quality product chosen from the best available assortment. Typical products were no allergy, waterproof, diamond calf, or classic certified croco. The HIRSCH product line contained three product groups: Classic, an assortment of about 1500 leather bracelets (including all lengths and sizes); Solo, a restricted number of synthetic straps fitting on well selling sport watches; and Bijou, containing nickelfree well selling metal bracelets. HIRSCH bracelets were distributed through A, B and C jewellers and watchmakers, fine department stores, duty free and watch repair stores. Retail prices reached from USD8.75 to USD73.

Frischknecht was exclusively sold through A and Top A jewellers and watchmakers. The brand was positioned as handmade, exclusive, service-oriented, of high aesthetical quality, made in Switzerland. It was targeted to consumers who like luxury products and associate a high value with Swiss handmade products. Frischknecht bracelets were only made of a small range of selected extremely soft kinds of leather, such as croco, lizard, shark, or ostrich. Once a year a high image product was introduced in a limited and numbered edition. Products were offered in elegant wooden presentation trays. Retail prices ranged from USD28.5 to USD115.

FRISCHKNECHT

The OEM Business

HIRSCH Armbänder GmbH not only served retailers through its local sales subsidiaries and distribution partners. The company was also strongly involved in direct supplies to customers from the watch making industry, such as Citizen (Germany), Omega or Swatch. Most of those customers were located in Switzerland, the USA, Germany, Japan and Hong Kong. They were offered the three branded product lines for their watches. Marcco straps were directly shipped from their production site near Hong Kong, Frischknecht bracelets were delivered from the distribution centre in Dulliken, Switzerland and HIRSCH bracelets from the production site in Klagenfurt, Austria. The company also offered to deliver specially developed products without brand names upon customer requests. The most important objective was to get as many watches as possible designed with leather straps.

HIRSCH JAPAN CO. LTD.

HIRSCH Japan Co. Ltd. was founded in 1981. The strategic aim at that time was to become a major supplier for watch bracelets in the Japanese retail market and to establish official supplier contracts with the four major watch manufacturers in Japan: Seiko, Citizen, Ricoh and Orient.

Refill Business

To more easily enter the Japanese retail distribution network and to profit from existing business relations the firm entered a cooperation with Nihon Siber Hegner (NSH). But due to a lack of preceding market and process analysis the partnership did not meet the expectations of either partner. Following substantial start up losses of about 150 million yen (about USD1.25 milion), the retail business was at least covering its direct costs and

was partially contributing to the overheads of the reponsible division inside Nihon Siber Hegner. Nevertheless, the company gave up their position of importer in 1989 and of distributor in 1991. Further losses of about 40 million Yen were produced when Nihon Siber Hegner wrote off their HIRSCH stock.

HIRSCH installed Mr. M. Ohyama as CEO of their Japanese business. Mr. Ohyama was an excellent administrator who did stock control, bookkeeping, reporting, purchase and product quality control, order management, EDP programming, translations and sales management all by himself. M. Ohyama managed to decrease expenses by 18 per cent in 1992. He reduced inventory by 6 million Yen during 1993. As a result, inventory turnover improved from 39.7 months to 36.3 months. But M. Ohyama had no retail experience. Based on very strict standards concerning the retailers' prestige, liquidity, behaviour, and demand for special terms of payment, he reduced the number of served retail customers from nearly 300 to 143 (out of a total of about 1500 potential and qualified retail customers). In 1993, 90 per cent of HIRSCH Japan's total retail sales of 82.8 million Yen were made with 75 customers (see Exhibits 1 and 2). There were 8 customers in Tokyo, 6 in Osaka, and 4 in Fukuoka with monthly sales of more than 100 000 Yen. The company employed 6 sales representatives who cost each 4 to 5 million Yen per year, plus an additional 1 to 2 million Yen per year for travelling and entertainment. Average direct sales costs in the consumer goods sector in Japan reached from 10 to 15 per cent.

Exhibit 1	Ranking List of Retailers

Percentage of Total Sales 1993	Number of Retailers
10	1
50	20
60	28
70	40
80	55
90	75
100	143

Exhibit 2   HIRSCH Japan Retail Sales in 1993

Sales Office	No. of Reps	No. of Custms	80% of Sales	Pieces per Month	Sales per Month (Yen)	Change (1992)
Tokyo	2	45	16	853	2.1 million	+ 3.1%
Osaka	3	55	20	1111	3.0 million	+ 15.3%
Fukuoka	1	43	19	726	1.9 million	− 15.4%
Total	6	143	55	2690	6.9 mio	+ 1.5%

Increasing HIRSCH's market share at each of the served retailers had been an uphill struggle in the highly competitive Japanese environment. M. Ohyama estimated HIRSCH's market share at its top 55 retail customers to be about 7 per cent. At some retailers, such as Isseido in the Tokyo area or the leading customer in the Osaka area, HIRSCH reached shares of above 25 per cent. But at no retailer had HIRSCH gained the leading position or the position of single supplier as the company did in many European countries. Until 1994, HIRSCH had not reached the goal of operating profitably in the Japanese retail market.

OEM Business

The OEM business had been the primary reason for the foundation of the HIRSCH subsidiary in 1981. As the only foreign based supplier HIRSCH Japan had established official supplier contracts with all important OEM customers in Japan until 1993. But the OEM business so far had been characterized by low margins and low predictability. Due to the loss of the NSH/SMH Omega contract OEM sales fell to 40.6 million Yen (−31.8 per cent) in 1993. HIRSCH had failed to become one of the major suppliers to the watch manufacturers.

Business Development in 1994

Overloaded with operative actions, M. Ohyama had no time to develop a marketing plan. For 1994, he decided to focus the company's activities on the retail sector in order to gain market share at each of the served retailers. No efforts were made to win new customers. Retail sales grew nicely in the Tokyo area (+11.0 per cent) and the Osaka area

(+10.1 per cent) during the first half of 1994. In Fukuoka, however, HIRSCH had to face another setback (−19 per cent). Overall net sales in the first half of the year increased by 1.6 per cent. Return merchandise by retailers came down from 11.1 per cent to 8 per cent. Public prices were strongly decreasing compared to 1993. For example, in Osaka the price level decreased by 11 per cent.

In 1994, the OEM business hit the bottom. In the first half of the year sales decreased by 90.4 per cent compared to the first half of 1993. No one at HIRSCH Japan Co Ltd. concentrated on the OEM business anymore. Since one of the Tokyo sales representatives quit the company the remaining person took care of all Tokyo retail business and the possible OEM business.

THE JAPANESE MARKET

To improve the existing information base for decision making, Hermann Hirsch had commissioned a study of the Japanese watch and watch strap markets by M. Pedergnana, a Tokyo-based Austrian consultant with ample experience in Japanese markets. The report of M. Perdergnana contained the following information.

Japan and Its Present Problems

The Japanese economy has been growing at high rates during the 1980s. At the beginning of the 1990s, the ever-expanding economy started to slow down, due to internal problems (the burst of the speculative bubble-economy) and external reasons (such as the recession in major export markets). In 1994, both the breadth and depth of the recession in Japan have become impressive. Consumption has decreased (saving ratios have increased despite lower disposable income) and the level of manufacturing output has dropped to the level of the mid-1980s. One indicator of the recession are department store sales: As of December 1993, they have fallen for 22 consecutive months by an average of 5–6 per cent on a year-to-year basis. Even though the Bank of Japan has decreased the official discount rate to a record low of 1.75 per cent, this and other economic stimuli have shown only limited results. There are far more dramatic problems ahead in the Japanese economy:

↔ stagnation of the domestic economy (growth rates of GNP until 1997 are estimated to reach 0–2 per cent);

↔ increasing unemployment (yet still lower than throughout Europe);

↔ aging of the population at a high rate (demographic and social security problems);

↔ relatively unstable political system (Japan is experiencing the first coalition government in its history and has seen its Prime Minister step down after only 8 months in office);

↔ outside pressure to open its domestic markets;

↔ readjustment of extremely high prices of stocks and real estate (and decrease in the amount of bad debts);

↔ further internationalization of Japanese corporations (what is good for Japanese corporations is no longer necessarily good for Japan).

Although there are many reasons to be pessimistic about the Japanese economy, the situation is by no means desperate. The fundamentals of a healthy economy, including superior technological prowess, a high standard of education, industrious workers and high rates of savings and investment have not disappeared.

Japan's Watch Market

Japan is the second largest watch market in the world. In the pre-bubble economy, watch sales had grown from 60 million watches per year in 1986 (a retail-based sales volume of 140 000 million Yen) to a peak of almost 80 million watches in 1990 (value-wise the peak was reached in 1991 with total retail sales of 470 000 million Yen). In 1993, the total volume of the Japanese watch market was estimated to be between 40 and 55 million watches with an ex factory-value of 120 000–160 000 million Yen (on shipment basis). On retail basis, watch sales were about 300 000 to 450 000 million Yen. The average retail price was below 10 000 Yen. The renewal rate of 'one watch every three years per citizen' in Japan is the world's fastest, followed by the USA (3.5 years).

Sales projections for 1993 had been very pessimistic. But despite the difficulties in the economic environment Citizen was able to increase its sales by 4 per cent value-wise and by 10 per cent quantity-wise. There still seems to be some market potential in the high-volume medium-price range. According to insiders, even Rolex has increased its sales quantity-wise by about 6 per cent, but saw their total sales value decreasing by 3 per cent in 1993.

Japan's watch imports have continuously increased since the early 1980s to 57 100 million Yen in 1988. Then they saw a sudden increase to 94 800 million Yen in 1989 and peaked at 127 800 million Yen in 1990. Two years later, the value of all imported watches had decreased to 107 900 million Yen and further decreased slightly to 102 500 million Yen in 1993. Quantity-wise, the watch imports decreased from 45.6 million watches in 1988 to 30.6 million watches in 1990 and remained at that level until 1992. An all-time record of 47.1 million watches were imported in 1993, an increase of 43 per cent in 12 months. Cheap imports from Hong Kong and Korea have fallen rapidly, while imports of (moderately) expensive watches from Switzerland have been on the rise. Swiss watch imports increased from 2 million pieces in 1992 to 3.1 million pieces in 1993 (at an import value of 69 900 million Yen). This growth stemmed from a strong growth of low-priced watches (Swatch), whereas imports of middle- and upper-range watches stagnated or declined. Most negatively affected were watches made of precious metal (−30 per cent).

More than half of the watch retail business takes place in department and specialty stores and about one third with traditional retailers concentrating on medium- and low-priced product segments. The restructuring in this retailer segment led to a huge drop out during the past 20 years: in 1970, there were still some 47 000 retailers with watch and jewellery corners/sections; by 1990, only 12 000 had survived. Many of them tended to be family-owned, family-operated and hardly profitable. This restructuring process continued in the 1990s at the retailer level as well as at the wholesaler level.

There are about 1500 watch specialty retailers (sometimes including jewellery) which sell high-quality import watches (for example, Omega, Longines, Rado, Rolex). For example, there are 500 who are official Rolex retailers in direct business contact with Rolex (Japan) KK. Other retailers buy Rolexes through different distribution channels (for example, other retailers or parallel importers) and lack the company's support in sales, after-sales and market communication activities. Out of the 1500 watch specialty retailers, less than 10 per cent sell HIRSCH watch bracelets (among others).

Japan's Watch Bracelet Market

The Japanese watch bracelets market came into existence in the 1960s with wrist watches becoming increasingly popular. Since then, the retail market has grown rapidly to a size of 5 to 8 million pieces per year, estimated by Mr. Ohyama (Exhibit 3). Following this estimate, with a total sales volume of about 17 500 million Yen per year the watch bracelets retail market would amount to about 3 per cent of the total Japanese watch market. In 1994, sales in Japan's watch bracelet business have not yet turned into overall stagnation. Sales in units are expected to still go up, but mainly in the high-volume market segment with moderate unit prices. Despite the highest watch renewal rate in the world, Japan has not yet become a market for widespread watch bracelets exchange.

Watch bracelets have several unique characteristics as retail products in Japan:

1. Production costs (incl. raw materials) account for only 10 to 15 per cent of the public price. The greatest part of costs comes from shipment and delivery, sales representatives (incl. traveling and entertainment), administrative services and promotion.

2. Retail margins account for most of the public price (50–70 per cent); as in the watch business, they are lower for top-quality products such as HIRSCH bracelets than for products on the lower end of the market scale. Retail margins for watch bracelets are nowhere as low as in the case of refill bracelets for Rolex, Omega and Longines (around 10–20 per cent).

3. Consumers still buy more expensive bracelets in department stores. Very few timepiece and jewellery retailers have a reasonable selling volume of high-quality leather and metal bracelets. A small, but increasingly important role is being played by mass merchandisers and supermarkets. Wholesale direct outlets and mail order play a negligible role.

4. Tight salary and bonus payments have led consumers to be more price-conscious. But there is a consumer segment for upscale bracelets which can be reached with sound selling advice.

5. Consumers choose bracelets for their functionality rather than for prestige or as a means for expressing personal tastes. Factual demand is still a lot higher than fashion-oriented demand.

6. There is an enormous variety of bracelets, that is many product types in a large number of materials, colours and sizes produced in relatively small quantities. From the sales list of HIRSCH Japan 1993, we can learn that the strongest demand is in ostrichgrain and crocograin (that is, less expensive imitations of real ostrich and croco). These two categories account for more than 20 per cent of sales. The next strongest demand is for rainbow, camelgrain and lizard. Japanese consumers tend to move away from traditional colours. Customer preferences become more diversified. As a consequence, the market for HIRSCH Japan shifts slowly but continuously from its traditional focus on volume sales to any retailers toward a more unique pattern of high-quality, high-service, and wide-variety geared to each individual retailer.

7. Watch bracelet purchases tend to be based on comparison shopping, where consumers often literally look at a huge number of different items (branded and no-names) side by side. At Isseido in Meguro-ku, Tokyo, for example, there are 2000 to 3000 bracelets on display at first sight.

Exhibit 3   Estimated Leather Watch Bracelets Retail Market in Japan 1993

Segment	Public Price Range	Average	Pieces Per Year	Sales Volume
Top (A)	40,000–15,500 Yen	17,500 Yen	0.03 million	500 million Yen
Medium (B)	15,000– 4,100 Yen	5,800 Yen	0.35 million	2,000 million Yen
Low (C)	4,000– 1,500 Yen	2,500 Yen	6.00 million	15,000 million Yen
Total	40,000– 1,500 Yen			17,500 million Yen

Source: Estimates by M. Ohyama, HIRSCH Japan

8. The large number of bracelets available, combined with the relative infrequency of purchase, means that customers tend not to develop cumulative knowledge about watch bracelets. They do not know any brand names. There is no brand recognition. French-spelled brands stand for being fashion-oriented. HIRSCH is not known, even by insiders.

9. The customer service by sales clerks is weak. Selling pressure and aggressive behaviour are uncommon. Sales people still try to sell original watch bracelets first of all. When changing, for example to a HIRSCH bracelet, they tend to put the original buckle on the new bracelet. Japanese sales people can sell high-quality watches nicely, but they are not able or willing to sell watch bracelets the same way. It needs not just patience but long and intensive training and coaching. Sales skills and sales efficiency are in general pretty low, not just at HIRSCH Japan.

10. It is very difficult to find skilled floor managers and sales people in Japan and to train them for a watch bracelet culture. Leather bracelets have a difficult social standing in Japan's class-oriented society. It is very common that sales people do not like to work with leather material or with watch bracelets at all. Lack of social status of the product as well as the company makes it difficult to hire good sales representatives. For HIRSCH Japan, the aspect of being a foreign-owned subsidiary is a further drawback.

11. Wholesalers and retailers have an unusually high level of stock in Japan. As sales slow down, they will certainly try to run down their stock as well. Yet established brands with a concept of style and reliability prevail over newcomers. Retailers are currently reevaluating their inventory concerning profitability and return on investment.

12. Metal bracelets have been more popular than leather bracelets due to the social stigmatization of the leather industry. In the 1980s, this started to change structurally, especially among the young population who like leather bags, leather accessories, leather jackets etc.

13. Department stores want to fill a public need as some sort of a social service organization. They want to project themselves as institutions who serve the public in its interest. This is the reason why, for example, Seibu Shibuya is rather different from Seibu Ikebukuro, just one mile away. The department stores' raison d'être is to be profitable by pleasing the full range of customers and suppliers. They do not want to have enemies. As a consequence, they might push HIRSCH's competitor Jean Rousseau with a special sale in March, then HIRSCH one month later, and another competitor two months later.

14. A majority of specialty retailers is yet just not interested in selling watch bracelets. Their interest lies in watch and clock selling. Because straps are important parts of the watches those retailers carry some in their stores, but consider them a necessary side product.

The Japanese watch bracelet market (watch manufacturers and timepiece retailers) is only partly captured by domestic suppliers. Imports are important, but available figures only allow rough estimates. Total imports of watch bracelets to Japan (including retail, OEM, and transfers from, for example, subsidiaries of Citizen and Seiko located in Hong Kong and Thailand to their Japanese headquarters) seem to have been decreasing in quantity and value since 1991 (Exhibit 4). In 1993, about 510 tons of watch bracelets were imported for a value of 5,445 million Yen of which about 18.5 tons were leather (n.e.s.) watch bracelets valued at 696 million Yen. This is an increase of 29 per cent in quantity and 8.4 per cent in value compared to 1992.

A closer look at leather watch bracelets' imports with the international tariff code 9113.90-190 (Exhibit 5) shows that imports from Thailand seem to stagnate quantity-wise, whereas imports from Hong Kong increased rapidly. If the import value is considered an indicator for quality among non-European imports, it can be concluded that watch bracelets from Thailand are of superior quality compared to the shipments from Hong Kong. European exports have lost market share. In 1993, their combined share of total imports was less than 10 per cent quantity-wise. In particular, French and Italian competitors have lost share, while German and Swiss competitors have gained market share since 1991. Value-wise the share of all European exports exceeded 30 per cent in 1993. But it was down from far above 40 per cent in 1991. Austria (HIRSCH) lost significant market share in the growing import market of leather watch bracelets. Value-wise, HIRSCH's market share decreased from 9.1 per cent in 1991 to 3.4 per cent in 1993. Quantity-wise, HIRSCH's volume share fell from 5.5 per cent (1991) to 2.2 per cent (1993).

Competition

The most important foreign competitors in the Japanese watch bracelet market are France-, Germany-, Italy- and Switzerland-based. French Camille Fournet has established a sales subsidiary which must be larger than HIRSCH Japan, selling boxes and other packaging material as well. In the bracelets sector the firm focuses on selling high-end croco bracelets. It is not known whether wholesalers participate in their distribution channels.

With their brand COBRA, the other French marketer – Jean Rousseau – have been targeting openly the HIRSCH customer segment since 1992. They entered the Japanese market through an importer by the name of Mimoza.

Dirschel from Germany use ROI Enterprises (one of Bear's wholesale arms) as a distribution channel. They have a rather small product range.

Japan's Bambi desperately wanted to have a European brand for their top leather bracelets. Elce from Italy provide them with their products. Elce is sold at lower prices than HIRSCH.

Golay & Guignard, based in Geneva, Switzerland, has established a sales subsidiary, but markets its products through a Japanese distributor. The firm's market share is hard to estimate. It seems to be almost negligible at the moment, but has started to grow. At Seibu Shibuya, for example, a wide range of G&G bracelets has been displayed in an exclusive pattern, with a Swiss cross and Japanese writing on the bracelets.

The most important domestic competitor so far has been Bambi, a Seiko-related supplier. Bambi has been getting increasingly aggressive with new selling units and new brands. They have their own 7 to 8 sales subsidiaries in Japan (Hokaido Bambi etc.) and use many wholesalers to be present all over the country. Bambi offers a 90–120-day promissory note payment to its customers, compared to HIRSCH's 'net 30 days in cash' term of sale. Bear Co. Ltd., another domestic competitor, is a wholesaler that markets many Hong Kong and Japan made cheap colourful straps. Maruman is a leather bracelet supplier. Hattori Seiko Co. Ltd., another wholesaler, is fading out as a watch bracelet marketer. Some other competitors are strong at some specific customers.

The distribution channels of each bracelet manufacturer tend to be complex. No one has access to the distribution channels of Seiko and Citizen. Consequently, not even domestic brands with strong manufacturer relations, such as Bambi, have a real competitive edge through watchmakers' distribution channels.

Up to 1991, HIRSCH's prices were far away from any domestic competitors. Prices were more than 200 per cent above those of domestic competitors and some 30 to 50 per cent above original watch brands' bracelets. For example, Bambi sold its Omega bracelets for 9,800 Yen when HIRSCH was offering a very similar looking bracelet for 15,000 Yen. As by 1993, all foreign competitors are

Exhibit 4 Imports of Watch Bracelets to Japan: 1991–1993 (in kg and million Yen)

TARIFF C.9113	QUANTITY 1993	QUANTITY 1992	QUANTITY 1991	VALUE 1993	VALUE 1992	VALUE 1991
10-010	304	13	212	9.5	7.9	46.8
10-020	475	490	1,146	310.1	341.6	951.7
20-010	25,287	47,189	46,462	544.8	942.4	1,005.5
20-020	448,985	558,266	579,732	3,590.1	4,440.6	4,845.3
90-110	9,298	10,408	6,813	202.5	268.5	181.8
90-190	18,542	14,369	14,124	695.8	641.7	657.5
90-210	1,419	3,091	4,957	10.1	23.5	30.4
90-220	7,052	8,354	7,795	82.4	84.7	65.3
Total	511,362	642,180	661,241	5,445.3	6,750.9	7,784.3

10-010: of silver or of platinum
10-020: other than of silver or of platinum
20-010: plated with precious metal
20-020: other than plated with precious metal

90-110: of leather or of composition leather
90-190: of leather or of composition leather, n.e.s.
90-210: composed of two or more materials
90-220: composed of two or more materials, n.e.s.

Source: M. Pedergnana, 1994 (JETRO).

Exhibit 5 Leather Watch Bracelet Imports to Japan: 1991–1993 (in kg and 1000 Yen)

TARIFF CODE 90-190	QUANTITY 1993	QUANTITY 1992	QUANTITY 1991	VALUE 1993	VALUE 1992	VALUE 1991
Austria	401	297	775	23,410	44,617	60,101
China	180	609	241	5,303	23,565	11,724
France	415	594	836	100,819	121,789	136,346
Germany	407	18	31	29,551	2,374	4,683
Hong Kong	10,347	6,061	4,804	252,871	142,567	109,757
Italy	66	285	268	7,979	21,099	18,979
Korea (South)	85	38	769	5,643	2,478	12,679
Pakistan	78	0	0	254	0	0
Philippines	15	3	0	236	205	0
Singapore	4	9	349	1,293	1,023	44,939
Spain	0	0	0	307	286	0
Switzerland	474	691	161	65,988	83,907	72,463
Thailand	5,888	5,681	5,683	190,601	190,385	174,943
USA	182	82	104	11,500	5,777	5,947
Total	18,542	14,369	14,124	695,755	641,702	657,523

Source: M. Pedergnana, 1994 (JETRO).

Exhibit 6   **Leather Watch Bracelet Prices in Japan 1993 (in 1,000 Yen)**

	HIRSCH JAPAN	FOREIGN COMPETITORS	DOMESTIC COMPETITORS
Babycroco	38–40	25–30	20–25
Croco	18–19	12–14	6–12
Ostrich	18	10–12	6–7
Teju	13–13.5	7–8	5–7
Shark	9.8	5.5–6	4–5
Lizard	8.5	6–6.5	3.5–4.5

Source: M. Ohyama, HIRSCH Japan, 1993.

---

established in the fast growing medium-priced segment, above domestic competitors, but also far below the HIRSCH price level. Exhibit 6 compares HIRSCH Japan's prices per product lines with its competitors in 1993.

THE DECISION PROBLEM

Robert Hirsch knew that he did not have much precise information concerning the Japanese bracelet market, but he was also aware that there was not much time left to improve the information level before taking basic decisions. Break-even had to be reached in short time or HIRSCH Japan was to be closed. The sales subsidiary so far had been considered as kind of a learning platform, but his father's patience had come close to an end. To ensure survival, Robert had to set up and implement a medium- to long-term marketing policy. Questions such as: How should the company be positioned in the Japanese watch bracelet market to reach the objective of becoming one of the major suppliers to retailers and OEM partners in the market; should it launch the Marcco brand at mass-merchandisers and/or the Frischknecht brand at top jewellers; should it concentrate on profitability in the retail sector or energetically improve its relationships with watch manufacturers; should the firm focus on increasing market share at served retailers, should it try to increase its retail customer basis, or should it look for a new distributor?

Case Study

HILTI CORPORATION
(A&B)

Lane Pennington put down the phone and gazed thoughtfully out his window across a forest of construction cranes to the Hong Kong harbour. As Hilti's regional manager for Asia, Pennington had ambitious growth objectives, but to achieve them – as he had just been reminded – he ceaselessly had to balance local needs and initiatives against the requirements of the head office for a continuing strong profit performance, and that in a manner consistent with Hilti's basic strategy.

As of the end of March 1996, Hilti Asia was running slightly below its target average net selling prices for the year. This was certainly not a crisis situation, but Lane knew that he would be expected to get the region's average up before too long. Lane also had to increase the average gross margin for Hilti Asia by 1.3 percentage points in 1996. He was reasonably sure that he could do this, but wanted to ensure that he achieved this objective with the least disruption to the operations of the eight country managers who reported to him.

HILTI CORPORATION

The Hilti company was founded in 1941 by Martin and Eugen Hilti in the Principality of Liechtenstein, which is nestled between Austria and the Eastern border of Switzerland. The first phase of development was as a supplier of machine parts for the textile and automotive industries. A second phase started with a breakthrough in the mid 1950s when a low velocity direct fastening tool was developed. Although not fully developed, this tool was recognized by the Hiltis as having great potential for the rebuilding of Europe. Patents were

Source: This case was prepared by Professor Peter Killing as a basis for class discussion rather than to illustrate either effective or ineffective handling of a business situation.

Copyright © 1997 by IMD – International Institute for Management Development, Lausanne, Switzerland. Not to be used or reproduced without written permission directly from IMD.

obtained and a product line centered on low velocity tools was created. (See Exhibit 1 for a selection of current products from Hilt's line of drills, anchoring and direct fastening systems.)

By 1960, Hilti had a major production facility in Liechtenstein and was well established in European markets. Martin Hilti's belief that 'market share is more important than factories' had led to a great emphasis on understanding and responding to customer needs. Recognizing that customers would value knowledgeable advice on how to best use Hilti tools, the company had established a direct sales force, rather than using distributors or dealers.

By the early 1990s, Hilti had augmented its original production facility by adding three plants in Germany, and others in France, the UK, USA, Austria, Sweden and Hungary. Sales had surpassed SFr2 billion, and profits had hit a record level of SFr173 million in 1993. Hilti shares were publicly traded, as non-voting participation shares, and the vast majority were owned by the Martin Hilti Trust.

In January 1994, Dr. Pius Baschera, age 44, became the first non-family member to take over the role of CEO of Hilti, as Michael Hilti, the son of Martin, became Chairman of the Board of Directors. He was taking the helm of a solidly profitably company with 11 600 employees, subsidiaries in forty countries, and more than SFr1 billion in the bank. (Financial information and a partial organization chart are presented in Exhibits 2 and 3.)

More than 6000 of Hilti's employees were salesmen. As one senior manager commented, 'That means as a company we are making 60 000 sales calls per day.' Approximately 60 per cent of company sales were in Europe, with Germany the largest single market, followed by the USA. However most of Hilti's markets in North America and Western Europe were mature, and the prospects for growth were greatest in the 'emerging markets' of Asia and Eastern Europe. 1995 was a year of celebration for Hilti's Korean managers, as their sales volume had grown by 28 per cent and they had made it on to Hilti's 'top 10' list, which ranked countries by size. Commenting on the Korean success, Michael Hilti stated, 'Victories in the East are

Exhibit 1   THE HILTI PRODUCT LINE

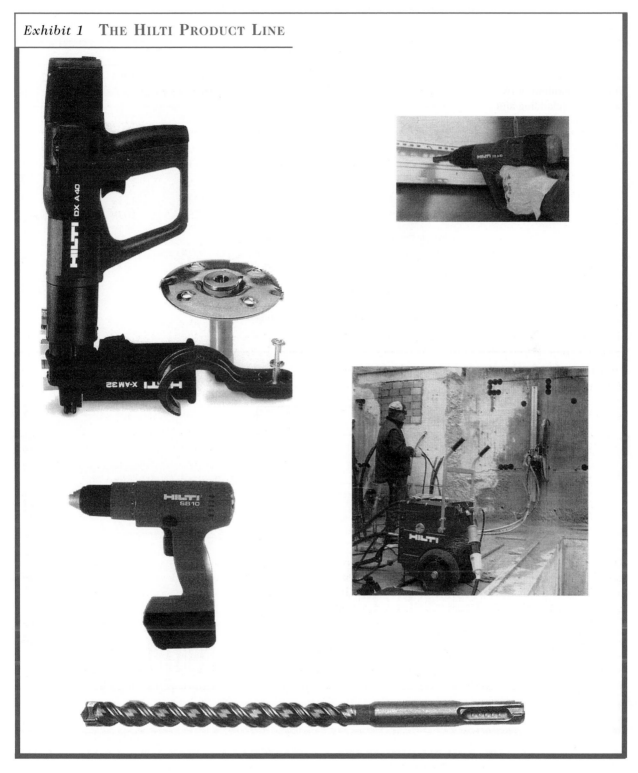

Sources: Top Left: 1994 Hilti Corporation Annual Report.
    Others: 1996 Hilti Corporation Catalogue 'Kompakt-Katalog Producte und Anwendungen'.

Exhibit 2   HILTI CORPORATION: SELECTED FINANCIAL INFORMATION

* 1995 net sales decreased by about SFr230 million due to divestment of two businesses (cladding and facade business and restoration business) that did not fit Strategy 2000.

	1995	1994	1993	1992
		(MILLIONS OF SWISS FRANCS)		
Net Sales	1983*	2237	2136	2076
Operating Profit	171	219	147	142
Net Profit	193	168	173	117
Return on Equity %	12.2	11.3	12.4	8.9
Total Equity	1633	1530	1439	1350
Total Liabilities	1138	1240	1114	991
Cash and Securities	1282	1254	1079	836
Stock Price				
High	1080	1085	930	467
Low	800	880	375	330

Source: Hilti Corporation Company Documents.

Exhibit 3   A PARTIAL ORGANIZATION CHART

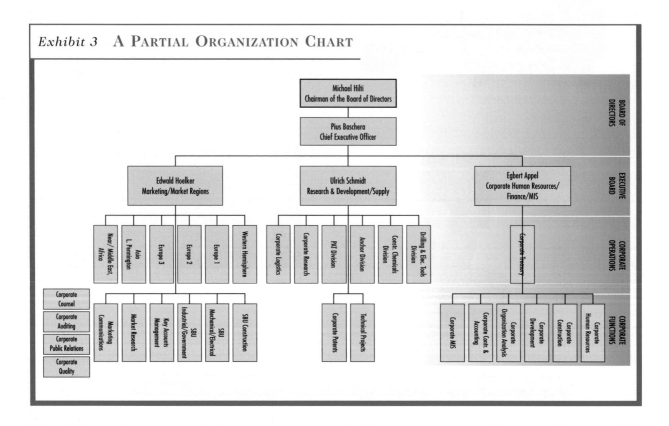

---

particularly important, because that is where the competitive battles of the future are going to take place. We must win in the East to defend our position in the West.'

Hilti employees were enthusiastic about their company. Hilti was widely seen as an excellent place to work, and morale was generally high at all levels of the company. A 1995 employee survey showed that more than 80 per cent of Hilti managers believed that the company was a pacesetter in the industry, and that there was a high level of vitality. Virtually all managers reported that they were expected to meet high levels of performance and were held accountable for end results. Among the few negative factors to come out of the survey was this: about 60 per cent of the 4000 employees surveyed felt that decisions were made too high up.

Michael Hilti commented on the situation facing the company in early 1996.

> Our target is double digit growth, and although we have been performing well, we are not achieving that. But as we push to increase our growth, we must not sacrifice profitability. We have seen too many companies pursuing profitless growth. We will not make that mistake – we want both growth and profitability.
>
> There are three keys to our future. First, we need a clear vision and strategy, which we have in our well established Strategy 2000. Second, we need inspiring leadership at all levels; we do not want managers who simply command and control. Third, we need an open, vital, competitive, high performance culture – rather like a sports team. We require high performance, and we reward it.

STRATEGY 2000

Hilti's 'Strategy 2000' was developed between 1986 and 1988 with the assistance of the Boston Consulting Group and the involvement of many senior Hilti managers. It was, in Baschera's words, a 'market driven' strategy, which emphasized serving the variety of customer needs the company faced.

There were two cornerstones to the strategy. First, the Hilti sales force in each country would be changed from its geographic focus (i.e. territories within the country) to a business segment focus. Each salesman would focus on one of three market segments: (1) construction customers, (2) mechanical and electrical installers or (3) industrial and government purchasers. In each major country organization, a senior manager was appointed to manage each segment, and was responsible for the profits generated in that segment.

Second, Strategy 2000 reaffirmed Hilti's strategy of selling directly to the end customer only via a company sales force. Further, each country would establish a central customer service operation which could be reached by telephone at all times, and a series of Hilti Centres, essentially small stores where Hilti customers could pick up commonly used fast moving Hilti products, such as drill bits. Through these three routes Hilti could service well both large and small customers.

The roll out of Strategy 2000 was gradual. Some countries adopted the segment concept more rapidly than others, but by 1995, the strategy was in place throughout the Hilti world. As the roll out progressed, modifications were made, the most significant of which was the creation of three strategic business unit (SBU) staff groups at the head office. The job of these groups was to encourage the transfer of successful innovations between their SBU units in various countries, to identify opportunities for segment-oriented line extensions, and to identify new business opportunities related to their SBU. These managers had no direct authority over country level employees, or product development personnel; they had to get their jobs done through persuasion.

HILTI'S COMPETITIVE EDGE

Almost without exception Hilti products were the highest quality and most expensive in each product category where the firm competed. Hilti salesmen spoke routinely of prices that were 30–40 per cent higher than those of the competition. They also knew from experience that such premiums could be justified, at least to sophisticated customers, not only by the enhanced durability and productivity of Hilti equipment but also by the high reliability in Hilti services. It was in demonstrating the superior value of Hilti products that the company's direct sales force proved its worth.

There was, however, a recognition that Hilti had not done well with small customers. In one major West European country, believed to be typical, Hilti's annual sales volume growth between 1993 and 1995 averaged 10 per cent to key accounts, 6 per cent to other large customers, but only 2 per cent to small and medium sized companies.

Baschera and his management team also recognized that competitors such as Bosch were working hard to close the quality gap. Bosch had, in fact, introduced a new product line in Germany in 1993 at a price which left some Hilti products selling at a 60 per cent premium. This proved difficult to sustain, and Hilti's share fell more than five percentage points in the segment. No amount of fine tuning could solve such a problem, and all eyes turned to Hilti's development department to design a less costly product that would nevertheless embody superior quality or features. This was a challenging but not impossible task, as in 1996 the German sales team had had major success in the marketplace with a newly developed Hilti drill selling at DM300. To that point, the least expensive drill in the Hilti line had sold for DM500.

Recognizing that time was an important source of competitive advantage, Hilti introduced a major 'time to money' program in 1994, with the help of an American consulting firm. By the end of 1995, the time from first conception of a new product to market introduction had been cut in half. Hilti planned to introduce 45 new or redesigned products in 1996.

In spite of the constant pressure on prices, Hilti had been able to slightly improve its profit margins during the 1991–1995 period through a reduction in manufacturing costs and carefully judged selective price increases. Thus, while sales had grown in the 1990s at an average of 6.6 per cent per year, Hilti's profit contribution had grown at 7.6 per cent per annum. It was not clear to what extent Hilti would be able to continue its policy of selective price increases, however, as large international customers increasingly wanted standard pricing and service from Hilti around the world. If prices were lower in a particular region, the best managed customers' firms were quite capable of adjusting their purchases accordingly.

Management also knew that the competitive battle was far from over, as firms like Bosch, Makita and Hitachi could achieve low manufacturing costs because of much higher volumes, made possible because they were in both the professional market and the 'do it yourself' consumer market, which Hilti had avoided. Bosch sold only through dealers, and in Germany, for example, might have had 20,000 dealers, whereas Hilti had 500 salesmen. At the other end of the scale were competitors like the German company Würth, which did not manufacture at all, but bought products from others

(including Bosch), added their own name, and sold at very low prices both through a direct sales force and Würth Centers. Würth's strategy seemed to be working, as the company had recorded annual growth rates of close to 20 per cent in the mid 1990s in Europe. Würth was in the process of entering and fully penetrating American and Asian markets.

THE HILTI CULTURE

Hilti senior managers believed that a key competitive advantage of the company was its culture of openness, flexibility, and shared commitment to common objectives. Pius Baschera explained:

> We know that with competitors like Bosch, Würth, and the Japanese, we will be hard pressed to maintain a conventional competitive advantage. They too will find ways to reduce their time to money cycle, lower costs, improve logistics, and so on. Our uniqueness, which they will have very great difficulty in copying – because you cannot buy it off the shelf or get it from a consultant – is our culture. We are fast, flexible, and constantly open to change. Our salesforce in the USA, for example, were using laptop computers as long as six years ago. We negotiated a joint venture and built a plant in China last year in record time. The American re-engineering consultants that we are using say that they have never seen such a 'change ready' company. As the employee survey shows, our managers see us as the pacesetters in our industry. We have to be.

Hilti's most recent annual report echoed many of Dr. Baschera's comments:

> For Hilti . . . global strategies are major factors for success. With this in mind, key positions in the group are managed at the corporate level. This permits the rapid implementation of a worldwide corporate policy. In the same way, a globally standardized corporate culture of innovation and entrepreneurial as well as individual development is consciously nurtured. Hilti employees share a great deal of responsibility. Common goals and values,

personal commitment, willingness to cooperate, openness, creativity, fairness and readiness to adapt are considered to be the basis for us to successfully shape our future.

Ebert Appel, the member of Hilti's executive board with responsibility for Human Resources, emphasized the role of training in establishing the Hilti culture.

It is not by accident that we have a strong shared culture in Hilti. We have standard training programs around the world which stress our basic values of self responsibility, commitment, freedom of choice, openness, and a willingness to take risks.

We also have a common belief that it is a manager's responsibility to develop his people. The executive board regularly visits the country organizations, spending a day with salesmen in the field, and at least a day with the country management team. As part of that session we review their people. Each employee is placed in one of five categories, depending on whether their competencies are under developed for the job they are in, just about right, or over developed. We insist that management pay particular attention to people on both ends of this scale, and indicate their plans to improve the situation. Managers must, for example, offer their best people – those in category five – more challenging jobs, even if they are in other Hilti units.

HILTI LEADERSHIP

Pius Baschera described the changing role of Hilti's Executive Board:

In the past two years, the four of us on the executive board have concentrated on improving operations in the countries, the SBU units at head office, and the support functions. These are areas that we know very well, and we have been able to add value to decisions about new products and the operation of major countries, for example. However, it is now time for us to become less involved in such purely operational issues.

We will focus instead on major projects

that cut across the whole firm. For example, the re-engineering project will impact how we run our factories, how we manage new product development, and how we manage the sales force. We also have a project underway which will result in a common logistics network across Europe. We cannot have each country managing its own inventories and transportation arrangements; it makes no sense. We promise 24 hour delivery to our customers, but we do not have a 100 per cent success rate in this. We think that this project can improve service and thus customer satisfaction and cut cost. Successful implementation of all of these projects is critical, and each executive board member is taking ownership of at least one.

All of this means that our country and region managers, among others, are going to have more freedom to run things as they see fit.

Egbert Appel added:

In the past, we have had tight central control in Hilti. We have been cost conscious and focused on the ratio of sales volume to expenses of each country organization. Headcount levels, for example, were managed from head office. Financial and growth targets were also set at head office, and accepted by the countries.

We want our country managers to become more courageous – to take risks, to be willing to make mistakes. We want growth initiatives to come from the country level. They need to find the high potential market areas and figure out how to penetrate them. We want them to tell us what is possible – to set challenging but not unrealistic goals – and then achieve them.

Pius Baschera continued:

Let me give an example. When we implemented Strategy 2000 in Hong Kong, we were coming into a country where our sales had been made predominately via dealers – not an unusual situation in Asian countries. Our first move was to stop selling through dealers and to significantly increase our direct sales force which, as it turned out, was not as effective as the dealers in selling to small customers. The net result was that sales fell by 10 per cent, at a time when we should have been growing by 20 per cent. The point is not so much that it happened, but that local management just did what they were told and did not tell us that this was a dumb idea – because the rule of Hilti was that as a local manager your job was to follow the corporate instructions.

We are working to change this attitude. But of course empowerment is a process that needs to be managed. You can't just say to the country managers that they can now do whatever they want within the framework of the strategy. We need to work out what makes sense.

Hilti in Asia

In 1995, Hilti had 8 company owned country operations in Asia,[1] the largest of which was Japan, representing 40 per cent of Hilti's Asian sales. Egbert Appel, who was president of the Japanese organization in 1989–1990, commented:

What we learned in Japan is that foreign markets are often not so different as people claim. Apparent differences can be more a question of perception than reality. What I mean is that a company like Hilti can do the same things that we do elsewhere, but say that they are different – or make a few small changes and emphasize them in the local market. For example, we were told emphatically that a direct selling organization would never work in Japan. Well, we proved that direct sales can work there very well indeed. The key is for our salesman to build a trusting relationship with the end customer on the jobsite. That's what we did, and that's why Japan has grown to its current position.

The more important point is that we will never survive if we just copy what other people are doing. We need to use our unique Hilti strengths and approach to doing business wherever we can.

In 1994, Hilti made its first 'bricks and mortar' investment in Asia when it created a 76 per cent owned joint venture in China to construct a manufacturing plant and create a direct sales organiza-

tion in that country. Ewald Hoelker, the member of the executive board with responsibility for all country operations, commented:

We spent a long time – about 15 months – deciding how to move into China, but once we were ready to go the elapsed time to complete the negotiations, build the plant and get to the point of having product available was a very short 18 months. That is probably some kind of record – certainly the Chinese partner did not think it was possible.

We had 33 Chinese managers and employees in Europe for between 2 and 6 months, learning to run the equipment that would be in their plant and to better understand our culture, philosophy and quality approaches. In fact, they finished by disassembling the equipment that they were working with and packing it into 122 forty foot containers for shipment to their new plant, where they reassembled it, and started it up beautifully. I was particularly happy that not one of those employees left Hilti, in spite of the fact that they were now very marketable, because of the training that we had given them.

The plant is producing a specially designed drill that is not quite the same quality as those we make in the rest of the world, but it makes a lot of sense for the Chinese markets, and is much cheaper to produce.

Historically, we have sold in China through dealers, and we are not going to change that overnight. But we are creating our own sales organization that currently accounts for about 5 per cent of sales. One of Lane's objectives is to increase that figure to 20 per cent. Of course, many of our customers in China will be the major Western construction companies, and they are used to our direct sales approach.

In 1994, Hilti also decided to move its Asian head office from Liechtenstein to Hong Kong. The relocation reflected the growing importance of the region, which represented approximately 15 per cent of Hilti sales in 1995. Lane Pennington's personal goal, which was not yet in any formal document, was that Asia would account for 25 per cent of Hilti's total sales and profits by the year 2000.

Lane commented on his 'mega growth' strategy.

> Instead of focusing on incremental growth and achieving plan, I want us to explore the full potential of what is possible here. If you exclude Japan, where we have recently experienced only limited growth, we grew at 25 per cent last year in Asia, and I think that we should target doubling that. Certainly there is a great willingness among our country managers.
>
> To achieve outstanding growth we are looking for what I call 'mega growth' opportunities. These include situations – which are not in our formal plans – where a price reduction on a particular product in a country will yield major volume benefits. Let's say we cut our price premium from 50 per cent above the market to 15–20 per cent, what could we realize as a volume gain? We did this recently with a product or two in a couple of countries, and tripled sales as a result! Additionally, our absolute gross margin doubles, but our relative gross margin slipped a few percent points. Now, of course, to maintain our average net selling price, and to get my average gross margin percentage up, both of which head office watches closely, we will have to make some carefully chosen price increases elsewhere.
>
> It looks like this in a strategy that is going to work, and my target is to find one mega growth opportunity per country per quarter.

As Lane looked to the future of the Asian region, he highlighted several other issues that Hilti had to deal with.

Dealer Related Issues

> In many Asian countries, we are using dealers, because it's the only way to reach very small customers, of which there are many. But it means lower prices and less control, and head office really doesn't like it very much, even though we limit dealers to our lower end products. And it's clear when you walk into a dealership that we are not very good at it. Bosch products will be on a nice display board – just the right size for the dealership. Our product will probably be in a glass case under lock and key. The customer will be told that our product is excellent, at a price of say 5500 units of local currency, but that the Bosch product is nearly as good at 3100. So they buy the Bosch product, and the dealer actually pockets more margin than he would have received selling ours, and earns points toward some contest or other. We don't have dealer programs like this.
>
> In small dealerships, you will see drill bits being sold one at a time to very small customers. The competition's bits are in individual sleeves hanging on hooks. Very convenient. Ours come in boxes of five from the Chinese plant, and don't hang up at all, so they are in a drawer, out of sight.
>
> In Asia, sales through dealers make up about 15 per cent of our total sales, and we need to get serious about doing a better job with them. It's going to require some up front investment.

Local Management

> Our country managers in Asia are extremely aggressive. In fact, we have had to reduce the objectives that four country managers wanted to put into their plans for 1996. They were just too optimistic, and we did not think it was a good idea to have them failing to make plan – the psychological impact can be huge.

Hilti's senior management team in Asia was led by Westerners. Lane Pennington and the manager in charge of China were American, and many of the most senior country managers were from Western Europe. Everyone agreed that local managers were needed; an active recruiting process was in place, which was scouring US universities for high potential Asian graduates. Other targets were large Western companies operating in Asia, and Asian companies operating in the West. Fourteen engineers and four SBU managers were needed in Japan alone. More SBU managers were needed for Korea.

There was no doubt in Lane's mind that the key to Hilti's medium and long term success in Asia would depend on the company's ability to recruit high quality local managers and manage them well. Lane commented:

> I think that our methods of compensating country managers are good, but should be improved. In Asia, country managers are paid

on five key targets: sales volume, operating profit, penetration of key market segments, development of their people, and particular issues specific to their situation. All managers receive some incentive compensation based on their performance – the formulas vary – in some countries the incentive portion is a maximum of 20 per cent of total compensation, while in others it can be as high as 40 per cent. I would prefer to standardize this.

As to recruitment, finding and attracting the right people will not be easy, but Hilti is a great place to work, if you like excitement and challenge. We will be able to get the best people.

NOTE

[1]Hilti had company owned operations in Japan, Korea, Hong Kong, China, Taiwan, Singapore, Australia and Malaysia.

Case Study
CEAC – CHINA

At the end of October 1995 the Board of Directors of CEAC held a meeting in Barcelona. With the company approaching its fiftieth anniversary, CEAC's directors were facing what could well be one of the most far-reaching decisions in the company's history: after almost two years of preliminary negotiations, they had to decide what action to take in China.

CEAC was an entirely Spanish, family-owned group of companies that had been founded in 1946 and was active in the closely related fields of vocational distance learning and publishing.

The Group had significant international experience. Starting in Argentina in 1964, it had achieved a presence in practically all Spanish-speaking countries. Subsequently, it had extended its activities, either directly or indirectly, to other countries such as Switzerland, Sweden, France and Portugal.

In the early 1990s – after the fall of Communism – CEAC had commenced activities in the Polish and Hungarian markets and had also begun exploring its possibilities in Romania and Russia.

In April 1994, Juan Antonio Martí Castro, Group Managing Director and founder of the FECEA[1] Foundation, had taken part in a trade mission to China organized by the said Foundation.

The task of organizing the contacts that the delegates were to make in China had been entrusted to Manuel Vallejo, a Spanish citizen with almost ten years' experience in China. At the end of 1993 he had joined Taxon, a company with permanent head offices in Beijing, to act as a commercial and business consultant in China.

Thanks to Manuel Vallejo's perseverance and dedication, after a number of tentative and unfruitful contacts, a possible Chinese partner for CEAC had eventually been found: New World Publishing Co., a company belonging to the State-run Foreign Language Publications Bureau. After several months' negotiations, they had hammered out the

financial and operational details of an agreement to set up a joint venture, which, curiously enough, would be formally set up as a consulting company: 'Beijing New World–CEAC Consulting Co. Ltd.'

By October 1995, the CEAC Group had invested around USD100,000 in trips, surveys and exploratory work for the project. But now, if CEAC's Board of Directors decided to go ahead and sign the agreement negotiated with New World Publishing Co., they would most likely have to invest a further USD300,000 at least.

Everyone present at the board meeting fully realized that the moment of truth had arrived and that if they approved the signing of the agreement with New World Publishing Co., they would be putting an end to the 'sounding out and exploration' stage and embarking upon a course that would involve far more substantial commitments of financial, human and technological resources. In fact, the decision could significantly influence the CEAC Group's strategic development in the 21st century.

BACKGROUND

The CEAC Group originated in 1945, when Juan Martí-Salavedra took the initiative of writing a course to prepare students for the entrance exam to the Architectural Technicians' Colleges of Barcelona and Madrid. These courses were advertised in the press and the material was mailed to the student's home address and paid for, lesson by lesson, on delivery.

Those first mimeographed lessons bore the words 'Centro de Estudios A.C.' on the cover, which quite simply meant Architectural Technicians by Mail ('Aparejadores por Correspondencia').

Martí-Salavedra secured the help of his brother-in-law, and subsequently that of José Menal Ramón, who was somewhat younger than Martí, had a degree in business administration and worked in a construction company. José Menal became Martí's chief collaborator and partner.[2]

They gradually developed other vocational

Source: Case of the Research Department at IESE. Prepared by Professor Lluís G. Renart and Francisco Parés, Lecturer. October 1996.

distance learning courses. At first, these new courses were all on subjects connected with the building industry ('Draftsman', 'Reinforced Concrete Technician', 'Surveyor', etc.). Later on, they started offering sold-by-mail courses for other professions, such as machinist ('Milling Machine Operator', 'Lathe Operator', etc.) and automobile repairman.

The procedure for developing courses in each new speciality was the same as for the building sector: they first produced a general course (e.g. 'Automobile Repairs'). If this was a success, they would write other more highly specialized courses on the same subject (e.g. 'Automobile Electrical Circuits', 'Automobile Mechanics', 'Bodywork', etc.). They later went on to offer distance learning courses on hobbies and artistic subjects, such as 'Drawing', 'Oil Painting' and 'Photography'.

Another significant development was the eventual separation of their two lines of business: producing and marketing vocational distance learning courses, on the one hand, and book and magazine publishing activities on the other. The latter were later consolidated in a new company: Grupo Editorial CEAC, S.A.

The growth of the company had been entirely self-financed.

'We have never taken bills to the bank for discount', declared Juan Martí-Salavedra proudly in 1995. 'We have confined ourselves to doing what we could finance out of our own resources, and if we could not finance something, we simply did not do it. This superbly sound financial position has always given us great peace of mind, and also liberty to experiment with new ideas and to embark upon entrepreneurial innovations and adventures, since if one of our new undertakings was unsuccessful, no damage was done. It was our own money, which we ourselves had generated and which, therefore, obviously did not have to be paid back to any financial institution.'

Selling Process for Distance Learning Courses in Spain, up to 1985

CEAC gradually developed distance learning courses in a number of different fields.[3] When CEAC first started up, students who signed up received one lesson a week by mail, paying cash on delivery (C.O.D.).

As early as 1955, the company management decided to offer – and, of course, subsequently honour – a total guarantee on their courses. Under this guarantee, students who had completed a course – and had done all the exercises – and were not fully satisfied, would be entitled to a full refund of the amount they had paid and, moreover, to keep all the teaching materials they had received.

The selling process for a specific course began with advertisements in newspapers and magazines, or direct mail compaigns targeted at certain segments of potential customers, which were defined according to demographic criteria or the content of the course (see Exhibit 1 for two adverts published at the end of 1995).

Potential students sent CEAC a request for further information, using the coupon from the advert or the coupon and prepaid envelope included in the direct mail piece.

CEAC immediately sent them a full-colour glossy brochure of several pages. The brochure emphasized the importance of the subject of the course for the student's career and gave a detailed description of the teaching programme, which was divided up into a number of chapters or teaching units. It also explained how the course would be carried out with the help of a teacher-tutor and gave CEAC's guarantee of a refund should the student not be fully satisfied at the end of the course. The brochure came with a registration form, which gave the price of each complete course.

If the potential students were persuaded, they would register by completing and signing the registration form, and mailing it to CEAC. A few days later, they would receive a letter from CEAC, congratulating them on their decision and enclosing the first lesson of the course, which was paid for on delivery. They would subsequently receive the rest of the course, lesson by lesson, paying for each one C.O.D., until the course had been completed.

From 1974 onward, still faithful to their guarantee, Juan Martí Salavedra and José Menal Ramón decided that students who enrolled on a course would receive all the relevant material in one go, immediately upon registration (all the teaching units, evaluation tests and other material), although they would continue to pay for it month by month, against a simple reimbursement card mailed to them.

Exhibit 1 CEAC ADVERTISEMENTS PUBLISHED IN SPAIN AT THE END OF 1995

COMPUTER SYSTEMS
- Introduction to computer systems
- Windows 3.1
- Windows 95
- Lotus 1-2-3 for Windows — NEW
- WP for Windows
- dBase for Windows
- Corel Draw
- Programmer-Analyst. Basic
- Master's in Office Automation DOS
- (Lotus 1-2-3, WP, DOS)

GEN. CULTURE
- School leaving certificate
- Childcare and pre-school education
- Psychology
- Entrance exams for Government Administration and Social Security auxiliary staff
- Study and speed reading techniques
- Guitar — NEW

DRAFTING
- General
- Mechanical
- Construction

ELECTRONICS
- Electronics and microelectronics
- Digital electronics — NEW

BUSINESS ADMINISTRATION
- Management and administration of small and medium-sized enterprises
- Taxation and tax consulting
- Accounting with updating services
- Financial and accounts management — NEW
- Analytical accounts management
- Balance sheet analysis and auditing
- Retail business management
- Marketing - Sales Director
- Professional salesperson

IMAGE
- Photography
- Video

BEAUTY CARE AND FASHION
- Tailoring/Dressmaking, with cassettes
- Hairdressing
- Beauty care (with and without videotapes)
- Fashion design

CONSTRUCTION
- Skilled bricklayer
- Construction technician

INSTALLATION TECHNICIANS
- Plumbing
- Electrical installer: General, home and industrial installations
- Electrical technician
- Gardening (with and without videotapes)
- Kitchen design technician
- Air conditioning/Heating
- Antenna installer
- Gas installer — NEW

AUTOMOBILES
- Automobile mechanic
- Motorbike mechanic
- Bodywork and painting
- Automobile electronics and electricity

CATERING
- Professional waiting — NEW

DRAWING, PAINTING AND DECORATION
- Humorous drawing
- Artistic drawing
- Oil painting
- Decoration

LANGUAGES
- English
- English with videotape
- French
- German — NEW

With CEAC, YOU can learn.

Automobile Mechanic Course

You will learn at home, at your own pace, without set hours or transport problems.
Your teacher can be reached by phone to answer your queries.
With all the necessary material for you to practise right from the very first day.
You will obtain your CEAC diploma that will vouch for your professional training and knowledge.

Under the CEAC guarantee, your money will be refunded if you are not satisfied after completing the course.

CEAC has 50 years' experience. More than a million and a half students have trained through CEAC.

902 102 103
24-hour information service
http: // www.ceac.com

APPLY FOR INFORMATION free, with no obligation
Fill in this coupon in block letters and send it to CEAC c/Aragón, 472 08013 Barcelona.
You may also request more information by phone (902 102 103) or by INTERNET (http:// www.ceac.com)

Please send me information on the Course on ....
Full Name ....
Address: Street name: ....
Nº................ Floor: .... Door Nº:.................. PostCode: ....
City: ....
Province: .... Tel: ....
Date of birth: .... Profession: ....

Ministry of Education and Science authorization nº 8039185 (Official Bulletin 3-6-83)

Exhibit 1 CONTINUED

COMPUTER SYSTEMS
- Introduction to data processing
- Windows 3.1
- Windows 95
- Lotus 1-2-3 for Windows NEW
- WP for Windows
- dBase for Windows
- Corel Draw
- DOS
- Programmer-Analyst. Basic

GEN. CULTURE
- School leaving certificate
- Childcare and pre-school education
- Psychology
- Entrance exams for Government Administration and Social Security auxiliary staff
- Study and speed reading techniques
- Guitar NEW

DRAFTING
- General
- Mechanical
- Construction

ELECTRONICS
- Electronics and microelectronics
- Digital electronics NEW

BUSINESS ADMINISTRATION
- Management and administration of small and medium-sized enterprises
- Taxation and tax consulting
- General Accounting
- Financial and accounts management
- Analytical accounts and budget control
- Balance sheet analysis and auditing NEW
- Retail business management
- Marketing
  Sales Director
- Professional salesperson

IMAGE
- Photography
- Video

BEAUTY CARE AND FASHION
- Tailoring/Dressmaking, with cassettes
- Hairdressing
- Beauty care (with and without videotapes)
- Fashion design

CONSTRUCTION
- Skilled bricklayer
- Construction technician

INSTALLATION TECHNICIANS
- Plumbing
- Electrical installer: General, home and industrial installations
- Electrical technician
- Gardening (with and without videotapes)
- Kitchen design technician
- Air conditioning/heating
- Antenna installer
- Gas installer NEW

AUTOMOBILES
- Automobile mechanic
- Motorbike mechanic
- Bodywork and painting
- Automobile electronics and electricity

CATERING
- Professional waiting NEW

DRAWING, PAINTING AND DECORATION
- Humorous drawing
- Oil painting
- Decoration

LANGUAGES
- English
- English with videotape
- French
- German NEW

With CEAC,  can learn.

Courses in Interior Decoration

You will learn at home, at your own pace, without set hours or transport problems.
Your teacher can be reached by phone to answer your queries.
With all the necessary material for you to practise right from the very first day.
You will obtain your CEAC diploma that will vouch for your professional training and knowledge.

Under the CEAC guarantee, your money will be refunded if you are not satisfied after completing the course.

CEAC has 50 years' experience. More than a million and a half students have trained through CEAC.

902 102 103
24-hour information service
http: // www.ceac.com

APPLY FOR INFORMATION free, with no obligation

Fill in this coupon in block letters and send it to CEAC c/Aragón, 472 08013 Barcelona.
You may also request more information by phone (902 102 103) or by INTERNET (http:// www.ceac.com)

Please send me information on the Course on ....
Full Name ....
Address: Street name: ....
Nº.................... Floor: .... Door Nº:.................... Post Code: ....
City: ....
Province: ....Tel: ....
Date of birth: .... Profession: ....

Ministry of Education and Science authorization nº 8039185 (Official Bulletin 3-6-83)

Should a potential student who had shown interest and received the brochure not register for the course, CEAC would send him/her up to seven reminder letters. It should be noted that at that time (1950s and 1960s) all contact with students was by mail.

INSTRUCTOR ATTENTION FOR ENROLLED STUDENTS

After the initial years, during which Juan Martí-Salavedra or José Menal personally attended to students' queries and corrected their exercises and exams, CEAC engaged an ever-expanding team of collaborators to handle these tasks. Eventually, CEAC created a Studies Department to cover two broad areas of responsibility: the development of new courses, and attention to and monitoring the enrolled students.

The monitoring was done by an ample staff of teacher-tutors, specialists in their respective subjects. These tutors were responsible for correcting tests and giving students guidance, both on the content of the course and on study methods and any difficulties that might arise during the learning period. The average length of a course was 15 months, the shortest being 6 months and the longest 36 months.

Each teacher-tutor was responsible for a certain number of students, whose progress he would monitor until the course was concluded, at which time they received the appropriate CEAC diploma.

INITIAL INTERNATIONAL ACTIVITIES

In the early 1960s, by which time the company was quite well consolidated in Spain, CEAC management began to think about ways of selling their courses in other Spanish-speaking countries. In 1964, with the help of the Ibero-American Education Office (OEI) and UNESCO, they started promoting the courses in various Latin American markets, starting with Argentina.

They decided to share the business with local partners, one in each country. These partners were called 'Licensees'.

CEAC gave its Licencees the benefit of the teaching and business experience it had acquired in distance learning, either by bringing the Licensee to Barcelona for training or by having Juan Martí-Salavedra do it 'on the spot'.

The courses were designed and printed in Barcelona. The Licensee would buy this material at cost, plus an 'industrial margin', and had one year in which to pay for it. The Licensee would then, at its own expense, take care of all marketing activities, as well as the support and monitoring of enrolled students. In addition to buying the courses from CEAC, the Licensee had to pay Barcelona a royalty of 10 per cent on sales, to be settled once the Licensee had received payment from its students.

CEAC had to deal with certain 'surmountable' problems, such as differences in terminology or in the words used for certain materials in the different Latin American countries. The real problem was finding Licensees who would put enough effort into the business and were capable of running it in a professional and responsible manner and were reliable as far as payments were concerned.

They also found that sudden, drastic devaluations of the local currency, or a scarcity of convertible currency, often led to situation where a Licensee was unable to pay its debts. However, in spite of these difficulties, CEAC at one time had up to 40 000 students enrolled with its Licensees in Latin America. As Martí-Salavedra admitted, 'on the whole, it was very profitable for CEAC'.

Outside of Spanish America, instead of negotiating and signing agreements with Licensees to sell the same courses as in Spain, CEAC opted to sell the translation and sales rights for its courses. This brought revenues from countries such as Switzerland, Sweden, France, Germany, Greece and Portugal. In these cases, a local firm would take on the job of translating, printing and selling the courses and monitoring students. The local firm would sell the courses together with its own courses – or courses acquired from other sources – under its own name on the domestic market, so that the students never actually saw the name CEAC or knew where the course came from. In some cases, CEAC reached an agreement to exchange courses. In this way, it also sold courses designed in other countries, duly translated and revised, in Spain and Spanish-speaking countries.

In the specific case of Portugal, an agreement was reached in 1965 with a local publishing company. The publisher would act as Licensee, although with certain special concessions, such as that CEAC would assist in translating its courses into Portuguese. The Portuguese Licensee set up a separate company called CETOP (Centro de Educación a Distancia de Portugal).

Juan Antonio Martí Castro Joins the Company

In 1974, Juan Antonio Martí Castro, the only son among Juan Martí Salavedra's five children, obtained his degree in Business Administration at ESADE. He joined the company after graduation and over the following ten years held posts of increasing responsibility in the different departments of the companies belonging to the Group, whose activities by then extended beyond vocational distance learning (with some complementary activities in the field of direct classroom teaching) to publishing, graphic arts and bookbinding.

In 1985 Juan Antonio Martí Castro was appointed Chief Executive Officer of the CEAC Group, taking the reins from his father, who, having reached the age of 65, stayed on as President of the Group.[4]

By 1989 the conversion rate of 'potential students' (those who had shown an interest in a specific course by replying to an advertisement or direct mail) into 'fully enrolled students' had fallen quite considerably, to reach a low of around 10 per cent, compared with 25–30 per cent in the past. As a consequence, the advertising and promotional costs per fully enrolled student increased significantly. At the same time, 'drop-out rates'[5] rose alarmingly.

In view of the situation, Juan Antonio Martí Castro took a number of decisions that radically changed the way CEAC conducted its marketing in Spain:

First of all, whereas previously the company had always promoted its courses through its own internal Advertising Department, they now started to use an outside advertising and direct marketing agency: Ogilvy & Mather Direct.

Secondly, and much more importantly, they started to build up a company sales force, which was gradually extended throughout Spain. This new sales force initiated a process of personal selling to potential students who answered the adverts or direct mail.

Under the new sales procedure, potential students who had responded to an advert or direct mail were visited in their homes by a 'cultural advisor' for CEAC, who personally gave them all the details of the course and encouraged them to sign up and enrol. If the customer was convinced, the 'cultural advisor' himself would hand over all the material for the course, and at the same time prepare the official payment documents. The payments documents took the legal form of a hire purchase agreement. Payment was no longer made through cards submitted each month for payment in cash through the Post Office but by means of a monthly direct charge to a designated bank account. The student him or herself, or a parent, would therefore authorize the necessary standing order for monthly payments until the total cost of the course had been paid. This new system of collecting payment through the bank was much more formal and reliable than the earlier arrangement by mail.

Lastly, the company went to great lengths to renew and update the range of courses it offered, in part by revising and updating the courses it planned to keep, in part by discarding certain courses altogether and replacing them with totally new ones.

Implementing a New Approach to International Activities

Although the Licensee in Portugal had set up CETOP as a separate subsidiary, the company still had the mentality more of a book publisher than of a distance learning company.

Consequently, in 1990 CEAC took an unprecedented decision in its international expansion: it purchased 100 per cent of CETOP and terminated its relationship with the Licensee. The name of the company was changed to CEAC-Portugal and 49.9 per cent of the new company was sold to another Portuguese publishing house (Plátano Editora), which was already working with CEAC in the field of publishing. From then on, CEAC-Spain took full responsibility for the management of the Portuguese firm and changed its operating policy: the subsidiary was to be an exact replica of the Barcelona head office, except that the courses would continue to be designed in Barcelona. But from now on the courses were to be translated, adapted and printed in Portugal. And, of course, all the marketing and everything to do with assisting and monitoring students was to be done there too.[6]

CEAC's management team then decided to adopt the Portuguese model as standard: from then on, no more Licensees would be appointed (although the existing ones would be kept).

This new way of operating meant setting up local subsidiaries in all new markets where CEAC planned to start selling its courses. CEAC-Spain would be the majority shareholder in these subsidiaries, but it was considered desirable to have a local partner as a minority shareholder in each country. As in Portugal, each local subsidiary would be an absolute replica of CEAC-Spain, except that all the courses would be designed in Barcelona.

This decision coincided in time with the fall of the Communist regimes in Central and Eastern Europe. Thanks to the experience it had acquired in Latin America and Portugal, CEAC was the first Western company in the field of vocational distance learning to start operations in these countries.

Poland

In January 1990, a small trade mission of Spanish businessmen led by Josep Antoni Durán i Lleida – head of Unió Democràtica de Catalunya, a Catalan political party – visited Poland and held a meeting with Lech Walesa while he was still leader of Solidarity.

After this initial contact, CEAC management entered into collaboration with Mercé Soley, a secretary at the Spanish Embassy, who had been living in Poland for over 20 years and was married to

a Polish citizen. Mercé Soley had set up an office offering services to Spanish companies.

In September 1990 they carried out the first, very tentative, market test, which consisted of placing advertisements in the press offering courses that had not yet been translated into Polish. It was soon discovered that there were hardly any requests for further information on vocational training courses. However, there was a lot of interest in the English Language course.

Consequently, after writing to the interested students to tell them that the course would be slightly delayed, within a month CEAC was established in Poland and was selling the English Language course. It was able to do this because the course it sold in Spain was not in fact a Spanish-English course but a progressive immersion course, written completely in English, so that it could be sold in Poland in virtually the same form.

What was intended to be just an initial market test, therefore, became the basis for setting up the new subsidiary in Warsaw.

CEAC invested some USD200 000 in the new subsidiary, including the subsequent translation of several courses into Polish. Initially, the subsidiary was managed by a Pole, a former high-ranking civil servant in the Polish Ministry of Education, who spoke Spanish. Unfortunately, after a period of successful growth in 1991 and 1992, sales levelled off in 1993 and began to fall in 1994. Accordingly, a new manager was appointed in 1995, a Spaniard, whose mission was to reorganize the company and set up – as in Spain – a team of 'cultural advisors', who would personally follow up all requests for information about courses, with a view to clinching more sales.

At the end of 1995, CEAC management felt that Poland was potentially a reasonably attractive market, although not the 'gold mine' they had originally thought. The market could perhaps stabilize at around 5000 enrolments per year. Nevertheless, it should be pointed out that, in view of the low purchasing power of Polish consumers, CEAC was selling at an average price of around 50 000 pesetas per course.

Hungary

Encouraged by the initial success in Poland, CEAC started to sell its courses in Hungary in 1991 and six courses were translated.

Unfortunately, after a promising start, the

business quickly came to a standstill and in 1995 the company decided to end its activities in Hungary.

Russia

In 1991–92, members of CEAC's management team contacted a State-run university that had some distance learning activities. However, the discussions were cut short after a strange dinner at which CEAC's managers felt it was being suggested that the project could not go ahead unless it had the 'protection' of certain unsavoury-looking individuals among the guests.

Romania

CEAC made contacts with a number of government institutions during 1994–95, but nothing came of them, so no courses were translated.

The CEAC Group in Spain at the End of 1995

The CEAC Group was expected to close the 1995 financial year with a total turnover (all the companies throughout the world) of approximately 13 billion pesetas. Of this figure, 10.5 billion pesetas came from sales in Spain and 2.5 billion from CEAC Group activities outside Spain.[7]

(a) Vocational Distance Training Activities

At the end of 1995, the CEAC Group was offering 58 different vocational distance learning courses. The total number of courses available was stable since whenever a new course was launched, one of the older courses was discontinued, in a process of constant renewal and updating.

The General Manager, Tomás Blay,[8] estimated that by the end of 1995, 25 000 new students would have enrolled. Since the courses lasted an average of 15 months, the CEAC Group would at any one time be training some 32 000 students in Spain. The record year for enrolments was 1991, with 41 000 new student registrations.

The average price of a course was around 125 000 pesetas. (Prices ranged from 75 000 pesetas for a course lasting 6 months to 175 000 pesetas for a 36-month course, which included audio-visual material and videotapes.) The student could choose between a number of different payment options.

Each pupil was assigned a tutor, who was an expert in his/her subject and an employee of the company. The tutor could be consulted at any time, in person, by telephone, by letter, by fax or on the Internet. The exercises that the pupil had to do at the end of each teaching unit were reviewed by a teacher-reviewer, who was not an employee of the company and who passed the reviewed exercises on to the tutor. The reviewers were normally specialists in their subject who worked in the relevant sector.

The whole process of following up and monitoring the progress of each student was highly computerized, so that if any student failed to send in his exercises on time, he was automatically sent a reminder note.

On finishing the course, students had to take a final exam, also by correspondence. If they passed the exam, they received the appropriate CEAC diploma, which, although not officialy recognized, was held in high regard by Spanish companies.

The profile of the students naturally varied according to the subject matter of the course. Overall, however, they were between 18 and 25 years old, of both sexes, of middle or lower-middle class families, and they tended – though not to any significant degree – to live in rural areas.

According to company management, the main *key success factors* in this vocational distance training activity in 1995 were the following:

(a) Juan Martí-Salavedra, Group President, insisted in 1995 that the company depended for its very existence, and always would depend, on the intrinsic quality of the courses, as well as on the quality of the constant monitoring, attention and support it gave to students.

Still sprightly at 75, Juan Martí-Salavedra's face lit up when he said, with total conviction:

'Our primary goal has to be prestige based on the quality of our courses and the service we give our students. Over and above any consideration of money and profit, we must ensure that people think of CEAC first and foremost as a centre of learning. The student must always come first. Internally, we have to operate as a company, with an organization chart, budgets, and all sorts of economic and financial calculations. But we would fail in our mission if our students did not receive more than they expect from us. We must ensure that the students feel they are getting more than their money's worth. We must be caring and encouraging and convey warm-hearted understanding.'

(b) Juan Antonio Martí Castro, Chief Executive Officer, agreed with his father; then, following the different steps in the business process, he said that the next key success factor was creativity in the advertising message. The advertisements in the press and those sent by mail had to generate enough serious requests for further information.

(c) The next key success factor, closely related to the previous one, was to accurately monitor the cost of a request for further information. CEAC had set up control systems and mechanisms that told them exactly how many requests for information had geen generated by each press advert or direct mail piece. Knowing the cost of each action in each medium, it was possible to calculate the 'yield' or cost in pesetas of each request for information they received.

With this information it was possible to continuously adjust and fine-tune a wide range of variables, such as the advertising message, the size of the reply coupon, whether a full-colour advert was more effective than a black-and-white one, the size of the press advert, etc.

(d) Ultimately, the most important thing was to effectively monitor and control the cost per new student enrolled. Juan Antonio Martí Castro emphasized that these two cost variables (the cost per request for information received and the cost per student enrolled) were not totally independent of each other, but were interrelated. For example, an advert for the guitar course published in the music magazine 'Super Pop', which was read by youngsters, might generate a large number of requests for further information, but few actual enrolments. At the other extreme, adverts for certain vocational courses, such as

the Tax and Fiscal Advisor course, which were inserted in more serious professional publications and targeted at a more adult audience, usually generated fewer requests for further information, but the rate of conversion into actual enrolments was higher. In summary, a whole range of variables was involved, such as the content of the course offered, the advertising medium, the average age of the readers, etc.

(e) Another key factor was the quality of the sales team, which CEAC called the 'network of cultural advisors'. At the end of 1995, CEAC had a strong team of sales representatives, who visited prospective students in their homes to explain the content of the course they had shown an interest in, the teaching method, methods of payment, and other details. They also filled in the enrolment forms.

The team covered the whole of Spain and was made up of a sales manager, 8 area managers, 23 assistant area managers and some 170 cultural advisors. The cultural advisors worked full-time for the company; however, they were not actually on the company payroll, but acted as mercantile agents. They worked entirely on commission and none of their expenses were covered by the company. In spite of this, the turnover rate was relatively low and 120 of the 170 could be considered to be working permanently for the company.

(f) The last key success factor was the payment default rate. In 1995, the company's internal accounts included a provision for unpaid debts of 11 per cent of the total gross value of the enrolment fees.

(g) As a result of the above-mentioned key success factors, the breakdown of the company's profit and loss account in Spain was as follows:

Gross sales	100% = average 125 000 pesetas per course
Cost of goods sold	6%
Marketing costs	22%
Sales force	20%
Personnel	10%
Bad debts	11%
Overheads	16%
Profits before tax	15%

Personnel expenses included the salaries of the tutors and the approximately 120 general administrative employees. Overheads included the variable compensation of the correctors of students' exercises and exams, together with depreciation and financial expenses.

(b) Book Publishing Activities: Grupo Editorial CEAC, S.A.

This company published books. There were several trademarks or registered publishing names within the Group, such as Ediciones CEAC, Timun Mas and Vidorama. Each of them specialized in publishing a particular kind of book: technical books, children's and fantasy books, art books, etc.

In 1995 the Group was publishing around 250 new books per year, with a turnover of approximately 1.8 billion pesetas.

(c) Other Business Activities

The CEAC Group held a substantial majority shareholding in Home English, S.A., a company that sold language courses by mail. In 1995 its turnover was expected to be around 3000 million pesetas.

It also had a majority shareholding in a company that sold women's underwear, using direct selling methods.

Another group company was in partnership with the Caixa d'Estalvis i Pensions de Barcelona, Spain's largest savings bank. It had a team of some 500 female sales personnel, working under an agency agreement, who carried out cross-selling activities to persuade customers of La Caixa to buy a wider range of financial products and services from the bank.

Finally, other companies belonging to the CEAC Group were involved in a variety of industrial activities, such as printing and bookbinding, plastic lamination of published materials, etc.

BRIEF BACKGROUND ON THE PEOPLE'S REPUBLIC OF CHINA

Economic reforms had begun in China in 1978, after the death of Mao Tse-tung. The first regula-

tions on foreign investment were issued in 1980. Step by step, foreign investment was authorized in the fields of oil prospecting and extraction, the hotel business, and light industry.

In 1990, after the Tiananmen Square incidents, the pace of foreign investment was to a certain extent frozen, to be resumed with great momentum after Deng Xiaoping's famous voyage and speech at Shenzhen in February 1992.

One of the main consequences was heavy investment in real estate and major infrastructure, and the first stirrings of activity on the stock exchanges. Even so, investment was still severely restricted in certain sectors, such as financial services (banking and insurance), the media (radio and television) and publishing. As in other countries, the defence and telecommunications industries were closed to foreign investment.

See Exhibit 2 for further information on China.

CEAC's ACTIVITIES IN CHINA

In January 1994, the FECEA foundation charged Manuel Vallejo with the task of organizing the visits to be made by the members of a trade mission that was due to visit China from 14 to 25 April of that year. Manuel Vallejo was a Spanish citizen with considerable international experience, particularly in China (see Exhibit 3 for a summary of his career up to 1994), where he had just become a partner in the consultancy Taxon.

Juan Antonio Martí Castro had known Manuel Vallejo for more than 25 years. They had both studied at ESADE, although with a difference of two years.

At the beginning of 1994, Martí Castro was fully aware that CEAC had achieved its highest sales peak in Spain back in 1991 and was now suffering from a certain inertia in sales. In 1993, as a result of what some called the 'post-Olympic shock', Spain's gross domestic product had fallen each quarter, and the country had entered the deepest and longest-lasting recession since the oil crisis of the 1970s.

Moreover, the company's attempts to penetrate new markets, such as Poland or Hungary, had not worked out.

Exhibit 2 Some Relevant Data About China

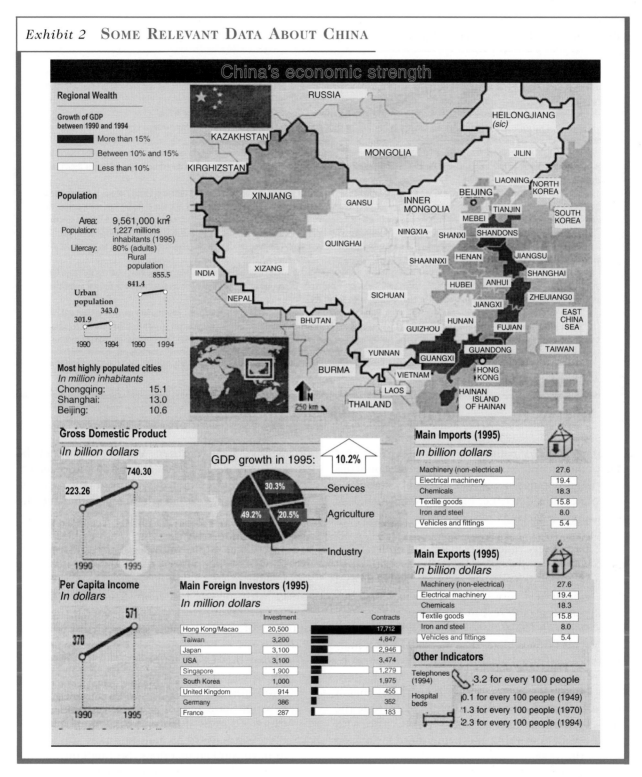

Source: *The Economist Intelligence Unit* and the *Financial Times, El País.*

Exhibit 3 SUMMARY OF MANUEL VALLEJO'S CAREER UP TO 1994

Manuel Vallejo was born in Barcelona in 1950. He graduated in Business Administration and obtained his MBA at ESADE in 1972. He later took a Law degree at the University of Barcelona in 1980. Between 1972 and 1980 he worked for several different companies in Barcelona (Agrolimen, Matutano, Fincas Anzizu and Banco de la Pequeña y Mediana Empresa).

In 1980 he joined the Nutrexpa Group as Assistant General Manager for the business in Ecuador and set up the branch office in Peru.

In 1984 he worked as a consultant in Peru with MAC and on behalf of the World Bank. And in 1986 he was in Venezuela, representing a Catalan investment group, in the area of aluminium smelting and recycling.

In 1987, right after Spain and Portugal joined the European Community, he participated in the Com/A470 competitive examination and was included in the reserve list as apt for level A5 in DGI of the European Community Commission. Until the end of 1988, whilst awaiting admission, he worked for the Economics and Enterprises Department of Barcelona City Hall.

In autumn 1988, the Nutrexpa Group offered him the post of resident General Manager in China, to start up a new joint venture in Tiajing that was to manufacture and launch their product, Cola Cao, on the Chinese market. Vallejo organized everything to do with installing the factory and personally took care of finding local raw materials, registering the trademark ('Gao La Gao'), creating the first television advertisements, appointing distributors, hiring personnel and organizing the accounting and financial structures.

The Cola Cao factory in China was officially inaugurated on 24 September 1990 by Juan Antonio Samaranch, the Chairman of the International Olympic Committee.

In April 1991, by which time the joint venture was producing, selling and generating income, Vallejo left for China for Nutrexpa-Poland to attend to the vicissitudes of Cola Cao and their new branch in that country until the end of 1991.

In 1992, he opened the branch offices of Agrolimen in Hong Kong and Canton, while living in Hong Kong and travelling regularly to Canton to supervise the Panyu Confectionery Co. Ltd., a joint venture that manufactured TA TA chewing gum, the leading brand on the Chinese market. He took care of power relationships with the local partners and of product and trademark falsification problems there. His contract concluded at the end of 1992.

During 1993, he gave lectures at the Fuqua School of Business, Duke University, and at Davidson College in the United States, based on his experience in China and Poland.

In mid-1993, Vallejo joined Taxon Consultants in Beijing as Senior Consultant. Taxon was founded by a Chinese businessman with an MBA from the CEMI school (a business school created under the auspices of the European Foundation for Management Development). He began carrying out surveys of the Chinese market for Spanish companies in a variety of industries (hospital equipment, wine, electronic components, motorbike spare parts, veterinary products, construction machinery, chemicals and pigments, etc.).

At the beginning of 1994, he was commissioned by the FECEA foundation to organize the trade mission that was to take place during the second half of April 1994.

Martí Castro came to the conclusion that CEAC should opt for entering developing countries with large populations, where it could establish a 'complete' subsidiary, i.e. one that was capable of operating just as CEAC did in Spain.

During Martí Castro's trip to China with the FECEA mission, Vallejo arranged for him to visit five State-run universities that already had a distance learning department or were active in that field, though in a very badly organized way. They all expressed an interest in exploring ways of collaborating with CEAC.

'My intuition told me that we would find a market there', affirmed Martí Castro. 'Our incursions into some of the countries of Central and Eastern Europe were not too successful, but I felt that it would at least be worth our while to try out the Chinese market; this was relatively easy to do, with Manolo Vallejo working and living there for a good part of the year.'

Therefore, in June 1994, after a few months' reflection, Martí Castro formally entrusted Vallejo with the task of carrying out studies and surveys of the potential market, and making contacts with a view to identifying, and possibly negotiating with, a prospective local partner. Vallejo would not be working exclusively for CEAC and would receive a fixed monthly retainer fee, plus a success fee, which would take the form of a small share in the capital of the hypothetical future CEAC subsidiary in China. The assignment was for an initial minimum period of fifteen months, renewable for a further length of time.

Vallejo started to work on the project in June 1994, with occasional help from his Chinese partner in Taxon. He was fully aware of the great difficulty of the undertaking:

I knew that CEAC had two main activities: vocational distance training and book publishing. Both of these fields were subject to strict State and ideological control in China. CEAC's Chinese partner would therefore have to be institutionally sound and to have good connections. So I patiently went about visiting a number of colleges and universities in Beijing and Tianjing. I soon came to the conclusion that the universities would never be suitable partners for CEAC, for at least two reasons: (a) because their standard response was that education in China could not be carried out by joint ventures, not could it be done for profit. At most there could be some kind of institutional collaboration under a non-commercial legal arrangement. And (b) because, naturally enough, the people I dealt with at the Chinese universities belonged to the academic world, not the business world. Some of them even disapproved of commercial activities . . .

Vallejo consequently decided to change his tactics and began to focus his efforts on the publishing world. But, once more, the contacts were unfruitful. One day he had dinner with a Colombian friend who worked as a translator and copy editor for the State-run firm New World Publishing Co., which belonged to the Foreign Language Publishing Group, formerly the International Publications Bureau of the Council of State. The Colombian friend very kindly offered to introduce Vallejo to some of the managers of New World Publishing Co.

The first contact was fruitless, because the person we visited had no interest whatsoever in our proposal. However, the second interview, held on the same day, was with a real gentleman, who spoke exquisite Spanish and who, as he later told me, had agreed to receive me purely for the pleasure of speaking Spanish for a while. His name was Zheng Mou Da, and he turned out to be a lucky find for our project.

Vallejo told Zheng Mou Da about CEAC and its activities in Spain and other countries. The first meeting was followed by a series of interviews – two or three a month between July and December 1994 – in which the two parties got to know each other better.

Gradually, as we slowly built up a relationship of trust, Zheng Mou Da told me that the Chinese government was putting pressure on them to find new business opportunities. A publishing operation for Taiwan, for example. They also realised that they needed to improve their business administration skills. Their interest in CEAC was completely centred on book publishing activities. He also felt comfortable talking to the representative of a small Spanish publishing company, which did not have the same approach as the large American and German publishing groups. Later, he confessed that they had turned down proposals for collaboration with other large Western publishing groups.

In October 1994, Zheng Mou Da gave Manuel Vallejo a draft that outlined a possible operating agreement between CEAC and New World Publishing Co. This draft had, in principle, been approved by Zheng Mou Da's superiors. Vallejo analyzed the document, added his own comments and sent it to Martí Castro.

In November 1994, CEAC's CEO, accompanied by Esteve Julià, manager of the International Division, went to Beijing, where they had several meetings with Zheng. This was a preliminary direct contact, basically just so they could get to know each other, since Vallejo had stressed how important it was in China first and foremost to establish good personal relationships. It soon became clear that an atmosphere of trust and understanding had built up between Zheng Mou Da and Juan Antonio Martí Castro. Among the various issues that were dealt with, Martí Castro came to the conclusion that the Chinese expected CEAC, should an agreement be reached, to appoint one of its experienced managers, one who had a thorough knowledge of the industry, to run the hypothetical future operation in China.

During these meetings, they also started to work out some of the details of a possible letter of intent.

Having made progress on both points, Martí Castro invited Zheng Mou Da to visit CEAC in Barcelona, along with some of his managers, so that they could see for themselves how the company worked. Their expenses in Spain would be paid by CEAC.

In January 1995, Zheng Mou Da visited Barcelona with two of his executives (future members of the Board of Directors of the hypothetical joint venture), where, with the help of an interpreter hired locally by CEAC, they were given a comprehensive presentation of the company's activities. They were also received by the President of the Catalan Parliament and had dinner with the Chinese Consul in Barcelona. Vallejo had recommended that CEAC show that it was well connected and had good contacts. Finally, CEAC invited the visitors, accompanied by Vallejo, on a trip to Madrid and Granada, once the Protocol of Intentions had been signed. This document specified the objectives of a joint venture to be formed by the two parties and the financial and other contributions to be made by each partner. It was stipulated that 70 per cent of the capital would be held by CEAC and 30 per cent by New World Publishing Co. All of this tallied with the framework mandate that had previously been approved by Zheng Mou Da's superiors.

The contract, articles of association and operating procedures for the new joint venture were negotiated by Manuel Vallejo in Beijing between February and June 1995. At the halfway point, in April, Vallejo came to Barcelona to analyze the way the plan was progressing with Martí Castro and his whole management team.

By 25 June 1995, Zheng Mou Da and Vallejo had completed their work, in that they had prepared drafts of all the documents needed to set up the new joint venture and start operations. Now it was up to New World Publishing Co. to obtain approval from the relevant Chinese authorities.

Meanwhile, on the strength of the Protocol of Intentions signed in Barcelona, CEAC had applied for an ECIP loan[9] from the European Community, which was to be approved in September 1995, for the amount of 250 000 ecus (approximately 41 million pesetas).

Finally, at the beginning of October 1995, Zheng Mou Da informed them that everything had been approved and that New World Publishing Co. agreed to the contents of the draft documents. It was now up to the CEAC Group's Board of Directors to ratify the project. Then, if both parties agreed, the new joint venture would be set up under the name: *Beijing New World CEAC Consulting Co. Ltd.*

This is all very well, but . . . who among the CEAC management team will be willing to go to China to set it all up?

This was a question that Martí Castro had been asking himself for some months. After signing the Protocol of Intentions in Barcelona in January 1995, it was becoming more and more crucial and urgent to find an answer.

Martí Castro was convinced that he would need to send a high-ranking CEAC manager to China to head the joint venture as Managing Director. This post could not easily be occupied by Manuel Vallejo – not because of any lack of personal ability but because his consulting firm, Taxon, had other

assignments to fulfil. Furthermore, although Vallejo had gradually become acquainted with the CEAC Group's business policy, he was far from having the intimate operational knowledge required to start up a subsidiary located so far away.

At the end of February 1995, Martí Castro was wondering whether he would have to resort to a head-hunting company to find a Managing Director for China from outside the CEAC group. However, one day, while he was discussing some details of the China project quite informally, over lunch, with a group of managers, it suddenly occurred to him to say, more as a joke than as a serious proposition: '. . . Well, if any of you wants to go to Beijing to be in charge of this project, speak up . . .'.

Among the managers having lunch with Martí Castro was Jesús Flores, Director of the Data Processing Department of all the companies within the CEAC Group.[10] He recalled that moment:

> I had made several trips to Portugal and had been to Poland a couple of times. Naturally, when the Chinese delegation led by Zheng Mou Da visited our company in Barcelona in January 1995, I had explained the Group's data processing systems to them. When Juan Antonio asked the question, I had to give an evasive answer at the time, but the truth is that, from that moment on, I started thinking about it. I saw it as a completely new challenge. After a few days of thinking it over to myself, I mentioned the idea at home. To my surprise, my wife Mireia agreed.

A few days later, Flores discussed the matter formally with Martí Castro, who thought it a marvellous idea. Thus, in April 1995, the 'China project' was assigned to Flores, once certain details had been settled, such as his acceptance of the assignment for a term of three years, which was the time it was expected to take to start up the new company in China.

In July, husband and wife spent a fortnight in Beijing to sort out everything to do with living there, especially housing and schools for their children. When they saw that these matters could be satisfactorily settled, their decision to go to China was confirmed, in spite of the fact that Mireia, who was an industrial engineer and PDD graduate from IESE, would have to leave a good job.

During the following months, Flores gradually devoted more of his time to the China project and handed over responsibilities to his replacement at the head of the Data Processing Department. 'During that time, I was in contact with Vallejo almost daily via the Internet.'

MARKET SURVEY CARRIED OUT BY OGILVY & MATHER

In October 1995, Ogilvy & Mather carried out a market survey by conducting a series of focus groups in Yantai (Shandong). The aim was to get to know the initial reaction of the market, that is, of the potential CEAC students in China. The participants in the focus groups were asked about their educational needs, their opinions on vocational distance training in general, their reactions to the type of courses that New World-CEAC Consulting Co. would be offering, both as regards content and as regards the system for monitoring students' progress by means of tutors, the exercises, the final exam, etc.

The opinions of about 50 participants were gathered. The following is a summary of the conclusions:

↔ The focus group participants did not consider what New World-CEAC was offering as distance training'. For them, 'distance training' was something quite different, with much lower quality materials and content, and without any real monitoring of students at all. Distance learning was seen as archaic, and as 'a poor relation' of the university, to the extent that the very words 'distance learning' made them nervous and tense. They said: 'Everything you have been showing us and telling us about is NOT distance training! It is something quite different, much better!' It was therefore decided that New World-CEAC would offer 'PERSONALIZED training' courses.

↔ The potential students expected to receive some sort of officially recognized certificate at the end of the course.

↔ Distance training, though of poorer quality, did exist in China in traditional subjects such as accounting, fashion design, English and medicine. However, there were no courses on subjects such as finance, marketing, automobile mechanics, air-conditioning systems or childcare.

↔ There was obviously a certain demand for courses – like the CEAC courses – that were not simply texts but a complete system for independent distance learning, taking the student through the material step by step, breaking it down into manageable chunks, highlighting the key features, so that '. . . pupils who are studying on their own do not feel that they are left to their own devices, given that they are accompanied by the text itself, the exercises and the teacher-tutor'.

↔ The participants in the focus groups were also asked about the price they would be prepared to pay for a course of this type. The conclusion was that they would be prepared to pay up to 100 yuan for each monthly lesson or teaching unit, i.e. about 1500 pesetas per month. This represented approximately 20 per cent of the average official wage of New World-CEAC's target market, which was around 500 yuan per month.

If it sold its courses at this price, New World-CEAC would obtain income equivalent to about 30 000 pesetas for a complete course (1500 pesetas per teaching unit × 20 monthly teaching units), whereas the average price of a course in Spain was around 125 000–130 000 pesetas. However, the economic effort made by the Chinese students would be relatively much greater, since the average CEAC client in Spain could pay for the whole course out of one month's wages, whereas in China they were willing to pay the equivalent of FOUR months' wages for a course!

This seemed to confirm the view expressed by Manuel Vallejo and the executives of Ogilvy & Mather that the average Chinese citizen earns little, but nevertheless has money to spend, perhaps partly from activities in the informal economy.

↔ Curiously, the participants were convinced that anything to do with education was a 'local issue'. They found it difficult to understand how anyone could possibly offer educational services from one city to another, or even across the whole country. They thought that

. . . 'a school in Beijing is designed to serve the citizens of Beijing'.

↔   Finally, contrary to what they had found in certain formerly Communist countries of Central and Eastern Europe, it became apparent that in China people were anxious to do things, to improve themselves, to build a better future, to make money.

Sales Forecasts and Quantification of the Project

In October 1995, using the information gathered by Manuel Vallejo and bearing in mind the results of the focus groups and CEAC's experience in Spain and Poland, Jesús Flores prepared forecasts of enrolments and sales (see Exhibit 4A).

Flores estimated that if the first adverts appeared in the press in September 1996, the company could expect around 1504 student enrolments in the last four months of that year. In 1997, the first fully year of operations, there would be 13 750 new enrolments, and 18 100 in 1998.

Flores then applied high drop-out rates. He assumed that only 45.7 per cent of those who enrolled on a course would actually complete it. For example, of the first 280 students to enrol in October 1996 (see Exhibit 4B), he assumed that a certain proportion would drop out each month, so that by May 1998 – after 20 months – only 128 students would buy and pay for lesson No. 20 and so complete the course.

Assuming gradually increasing selling prices and a gradually decreasing Yuan/Peseta exchange rate, Flores estimated that total revenues from students would be around 5.4 million pesetas in 1996 (3 months); 126.4 million in 1997; and 277.1 million in 1998. By the end of 1998, New World-CEAC would be enrolling 1540 new students per month. Taking into account the estimated 'drop-out rates', by December 1998 the company would be selling 16 000 lessons or teaching units per month to students who had enrolled during the previous 20 months.

Flores used these sales figures to prepare the projected profit and loss accounts for 1996, 1997 and 1998 (see Exhibit 5).

According to these projections, the new subsidiary would lose around 14.4 million pesetas in 1996, but would earn 26.4 million pesetas before tax in 1997, and 72.8 million in 1998. In theory, these profits were to be shared between the partners in proportion to the capital each one of them had put in, i.e. 70 per cent for CEAC and 30 per cent for New World Publishing Co. However, CEAC's management felt that, for many years to come, all profits should be ploughed back into the business.

The action plan specified that students would pay for their monthly lessons month by month. The lessons would be sent and paid for on delivery, or could be picked up and paid for in person at any of New World Publishing Co.'s 2300 retail bookshops. The new company would initially launch three courses, English Language, Marketing, and Accounting, with a view to extending this number to six during the first full year of operations.

The formal accounting procedures were as follows: CEAC-Spain would supply Beijing New World-CEAC Consulting Co. Ltd. with business and teaching expertise in exchange for a 6 per cent royalty on sales to students. New World Publishing Co., in cooperation with an adult education center, would take care of selling the courses and collecting payment. From these sales revenues it would deduct its translation, adaptation, printing, advertising and distribution expenses, as well as a commission for its services. The consulting company would then invoice New World Publishing Co. for the amount of this gross margin and from it deduct its own expenses (personnel, administration, communications, utilities, financing), plus the 6 per cent royalty on sales payable to CEAC-Spain. The remainder after tax, was the amount available, in theory, to self-finance the development of the joint venture or, even more theoretically, to be distributed to the partners in proportion to their shareholdings.

The accounting procedure was clearly rather complicated, since the idea was to specify and take into account the contributions and activities of each partner, allocating the costs incurred. There was a danger of disagreements in the future as to how it should be interpreted, but it seemed a workable system for publishing and selling CEAC's courses on the Chinese market, with royalties payable to the Spanish partner.

Exhibit 4A Forecasts Prepared by Jesús Flores in October 1995

1996

	January	February	March	April	May	June	July	August	September	October	November	December	Total
Print run (thousand units) of media used									8,000	8,000	8,000	8,000	32,000
Response rate from media adverts									0.04%	0.07%	0.09%	0.09%	0.07%
Number of requests for information									2,800	5,600	7,200	7,200	22,800
Conversion rate requests/enrolments									0%	5%	7%	10%	6.60%
Enrolments (new students)									0	280	504	720	1,504

1997

	January	February	March	April	May	June	July	August	September	October	November	December	Total
Print run (thousand units) of media used	10,000	10,000	10,000	11,500	11,500	11,500	11,500	11,500	13,000	13,000	13,000	13,000	139,500
Replies from media adverts	0.09%	0.09%	0.10%	0.10%	0.10%	0.10%	0.10%	0.10%	0.10%	0.10%	0.10%	0.10%	0.10%
Number of requests for information	9,000	9,000	10,000	11,500	11,500	11,500	11,500	11,500	13,000	13,000	13,000	13,000	137,500
Conversion rate requests/enrolments	10%	10%	10%	10%	10%	10%	10%	10%	10%	10%	10%	10%	10.00%
Enrolments (new students)	900	900	1,000	1,150	1,150	1,150	1,150	1,150	1,300	1,300	1,300	1,300	13,750

1998

	January	February	March	April	May	June	July	August	September	October	November	December	Total
Print run (thousand units) of media used	16,000	16,000	18,000	18,000	20,000	20,000	22,000	22,000	22,000	22,000	22,000	22,000	240,000
Response rate from media adverts	0.08%	0.08%	0.08%	0.08%	0.08%	0.08%	0.08%	0.07%	0.07%	0.07%	0.07%	0.07%	0.08%
Number of requests for information	12,800	12,800	14,400	14,400	16,000	16,000	17,600	15,400	15,400	15,400	15,400	15,400	181,000
Conversion rate requests/enrolments	10%	10%	10%	10%	10%	10%	10%	10%	10%	10%	10%	10%	10.00%
Enrolments (new students)	1,280	1,280	1,440	1,440	1,600	1,600	1,760	1,540	1,540	1,540	1,540	1,540	18,100

Forecasts prepared on the assumption that the new joint subsidiary in China would start selling vocational distance learning courses in September 1996

Exhibit 4B   **Forecasts of Revenue from Distance Training Courses in China**

1996 % OF DROP-OUTS/TOTAL ENROLMENTS

	%	JANUARY	FEBRUARY	MARCH	APRIL	MAY	JUNE	JULY	AUGUST	SEPTEMBER	OCTOBER	NOVEMBER	DECEMBER	TOTAL
Students enrolled														
Unit 1	3.44%									0	280	504	720	1,504
Unit 2	16.5%									0	270	487	695	1,452
Unit 3	8.25%										0	226	406	632
Unit 4	4.81%											0	207	207
Total		0	0	0	0	0	0	0	0	0	550	1,216	2,029	3,796
Amount in RMB		0	0	0	0	0	0	0	0	0	53,936	119,209	198,815	371,960
Amount in Pesetas		0	0	0	0	0	0	0	0	0	784,770	1,734,493	2,892,762	5,412,025

Retail price: 98RMB
1 RMB   = 14.55 ptas.

1997 % OF DROP-OUTS/TOTAL ENROLMENTS

	%	JANUARY	FEBRUARY	MARCH	APRIL	MAY	JUNE	JULY	AUGUST	SEPTEMBER	OCTOBER	NOVEMBER	DECEMBER	TOTAL
Number of students enrolled		900	900	1,000	1,150	1,150	1,150	1,150	1,150	1,300	1,300	1,300	1,300	13,750
Unit 1	3.44%	869	869	966	1,110	1,110	1,110	1,110	1,110	1,255	1,255	1,255	1,255	13,277
Unit 2	16.50%	581	726	726	806	927	927	927	927	927	1,048	1,048	1,048	10,619
Unit 3	8.25%	373	533	666	666	740	851	851	851	851	851	962	962	9,154
Unit 4	4.81%	197	355	507	634	634	704	810	810	810	810	810	915	7,995
Unit 5	6.87%	0	184	331	472	590	590	656	754	754	754	754	754	6,593
Unit 6	7.90%		0	169	304	435	544	544	604	695	695	695	695	5,378
Unit 7	2.06%			0	166	298	426	532	532	592	680	680	680	4,587
Unit 8	4.47%				0	158	285	407	509	509	565	650	650	3,732
Unit 9	2.75%					0	154	277	396	495	495	550	632	2,997
Unit 10	3.09%						0	149	268	383	479	479	533	2,292
Unit 11	0.35%							0	149	267	382	478	478	1,754
Unit 12	1.03%								0	147	265	378	473	1,263
Unit 13	1.72%									0	145	260	372	776
Unit 14	2.06%										0	142	255	396
Unit 15	1.72%											0	139	139
Unit 16	2.06%												0	0
Total		2,920	3,566	4,364	5,308	6,043	6,741	7,413	8,060	8,985	9,723	10,440	11,140	84,702
Amount in RMB		315,313	385,111	471,277	573,316	652,605	728,025	800,598	870,485	970,331	1,050,131	1,127,552	1,203,125	9,147,869
Amount in Pesetas		4,358,416	5,323,197	6,514,229	7,924,654	9,020,629	10,063,127	11,066,271	12,032,273	13,412,404	14,515,431	15,585,593	16,630,200	126,446,423

Retail price: 108 RMB
1 RMB   = 13.82 Ptas.

Forecasts of revenue prepared by Jesús Flores in October 1995

Exhibit 4B (continued)

1998	% OF DROP-OUTS/TOTAL ENROLMENTS	JANUARY	FEBRUARY	MARCH	APRIL	MAY	JUNE	JULY	AUGUST	SEPTEMBER	OCTOBER	NOVEMBER	DECEMBER	TOTAL
Number of students enrolled		1,280	1,280	1,440	1,440	1,600	1,600	1,760	1,540	1,540	1,540	1,540	1,540	18,100
Unit 1	3.44%	1,236	1,236	1,390	1,390	1,545	1,545	1,699	1,487	1,487	1,487	1,487	1,487	17,477
Unit 2	16.50%	1,048	1,032	1,032	1,161	1,161	1,290	1,290	1,419	1,242	1,242	1,242	1,242	14,400
Unit 3	8.25%	962	962	947	947	1,065	1,065	1,184	1,184	1,302	1,139	1,139	1,139	13,035
Unit 4	4.81%	915	915	915	901	901	1,014	1,014	1,127	1,127	1,239	1,084	1,084	12,239
Unit 5	6.87%	853	853	853	853	839	839	944	944	1,049	1,049	1,154	1,010	11,240
Unit 6	7.90%	695	785	785	785	785	773	773	757	870	966	966	1,063	10,117
Unit 7	2.06%	680	680	769	769	769	769	757	757	852	852	946	946	9,548
Unit 8	4.47%	650	650	650	735	735	735	735	723	723	814	814	904	8,867
Unit 9	2.75%	632	632	632	632	714	714	714	714	703	703	791	791	8,375
Unit 10	3.09%	612	612	612	612	612	692	692	692	692	682	682	767	7,962
Unit 11	0.35%	531	610	610	610	610	610	690	690	690	690	679	679	7,701
Unit 12	1.03%	473	525	604	604	604	604	604	683	683	683	683	672	7,422
Unit 13	1.72%	465	465	516	594	594	594	594	594	671	671	671	671	7,098
Unit 14	2.06%	364	455	455	506	581	581	581	581	581	657	657	657	6,659
Unit 15	1.72%	250	358	447	447	497	571	571	571	571	571	646	646	6,149
Unit 16	2.06%	136	245	350	438	438	487	560	560	560	560	560	633	5,525
Unit 17	3.09%	0	132	238	340	424	424	472	542	542	542	542	542	4,742
Unit 18	0.28%	0	0	132	237	339	423	423	470	541	541	541	541	4,188
Unit 19	1.50%	0	0	0	130	233	334	417	417	463	533	533	533	3,592
Unit 20	1.00%	0	0	0	0	128	231	330	413	413	459	527	527	3,029
Total		11,782	12,296	13,009	13,424	14,052	14,485	15,163	15,137	15,344	15,546	15,742	15,933	171,913
Amount in RMB		1,402,029	1,463,189	1,548,084	1,597,502	1,672,199	1,723,687	1,804,436	1,801,266	1,825,899	1,849,957	1,873,341	1,896,009	20,457,598
Amount in Pesetas		18,991,959	19,820,437	20,970,424	21,639,840	22,651,685	23,349,154	24,442,980	24,400,045	24,733,721	25,059,604	25,376,368	25,683,428	277,119,644

Retail price: 119RMB
1 RMB   =13.55 ptas.

Forecasts revenue prepared by Jesús Flores in October 1995

Exhibit 5 Projected profit and Loss Accounts in China for 1996, 1997 and 1998 (in thousands)

	1996			1997			1998		
	RMB	Ptas.	Percentage of sales	RMB	Ptas.	Percentage of sales	RMB	Ptas.	Percentage of sales
Gross sales	372	5,412		9,148	126,446		20,548	277,120	
Taxes (VAT, consumption)	43	623		1,052	14,547		2,354	31,881	
Net sales	329	4,789	100	8,095	111,899	100	18,104	245,239	100
Cost of goods sold	86	1,253	26.16	2,219	30,672	27.41	4,526	61,310	25.00
Distribution costs	6	84	1.75	145	2,003	1.79	324	4,390	1.79
Sales commission	11	159	3.33	270	3,726	3.33	603	8,166	3.33
Marketing expenses	320	4,656	97.21	1,473	20,355	18.19	3,174	42,995	17.53
Cost of reviewing students' exercises	3	38	0.80	132	1,824	1.63	295	3,997	1.63
Depreciation	35	507	10.59	100	1,376	1.23	208	2,820	1.15
Overheads (general expenses)	724	10,537	220.00	1,545	21,362	19.09	3,259	44,143	18.00
Office rental	70	1,019	21.27	140	1,935	1.73	280	3,793	1.55
Technology royalties	44	640	13.37	46	636	0.57	48	650	0.27
Profit before interest and tax	(969)	(14,104)	− 294.48	2,026	28,011	25.03	5,387	72,974	29.76
Interest	(25)	(364)	− 7.59	(115)	(1,590)	− 1.42	(15)	(203)	− 0.08
Profit before tax	(994)	(14,467)	− 302.07	1,911	26,422	23.61	5,372	72,771	29.67

Prepared by Jesús Flores in October 1995.

THE CEAC BOARD MEETING AT THE END OF OCTOBER 1995

In making their decision whether to sign the agreement with New World Publishing Co., the members of CEAC's Board of Directors[11] considered the following points in favour and against:

In favour

1. We have already invested around 100,000 dollars in the project. If we decide to back out now, this sum will have to be computed directly to losses.

2. Jesús Flores is willing to take charge of the project. It is very important that we have our man on the spot, managing the project.

3. We can also count on the continued collaboration of Manual Vallejo as a consultant and as a member of the Board of Directors of the joint venture. Vallejo can back Flores in any 'power relations' with the Chinese partners.

4. The ECIP loan has been approved by Brussels since September 1995. This means not only that CEAC-Spain will have to put up less capital of its own, but also – according to the rules governing ECIP loans – that if the project eventually fails, the entire loan will be written off.

5. Manuel Vallejo – who attended the meeting with a right to speak but not to vote – summed up his experience in the Chinese market: If you want to get into China, you have to do it gradually, step by step. There is an old Chinese proverb that says you must cross a river slowly, feeling the stones under your feet. It will be a process of trial and error. Although at the moment we are not too sure about the project, the important thing is to be there, to start doing business, to start gaining the confidence of our local partner and the Chinese authorities. They must see that we mean business, that we are loyal, cooperative partners. If we do that, we may find that opportunities start to emerge, sometimes even unexpectedly and in surprising ways.'

6. And, of course, for its sheer size the Chinese market is every entrepreneur's dream. More than 1.2 billion people, hungry for knowledge and for good-quality services. CEAC's vocational distance training courses would have practically no competition.

Against

Other members of CEAC's Board of Directors raised the following points against the project:

1. My first objection is a question of priorities. China is very far away and possibly more remote, culturally and politically, to us in Spain than any other country. Why don't we give priority to the Central and East European countries for the time being? Once we have consolidated our position there, I would be in favour of setting ourselves more ambitious goals. Going to China now seems like too great a leap. We should take a more gradual approach.

2. I don't like the substance of the agreement. We will be too dependent on our local partner. We are effectively placing ourselves in the hands of New World Publishing Co., since they are the ones who do the invoicing and collect payment from the students.

3. If we give our approval, we had better prepare ourselves to invest at least another 300 000 dollars in the project. And what is worse, if we start the project and it does not work, it could turn into a bottomless pit. The bigger our investment becomes, the more difficult it will be to abandon it if things do not work out.

4. We know practically nothing about the market or the way it might react. We hardly know what advertising media we would use, or what the cost per newly enrolled student might be. In fact, we do not even know whether the Chinese will be remotely interested in the courses we sell in Spain . . .

5. New World Publishing Co. is in the publishing business. We have an agreement with them to create a *consulting* company! As things stand, if we sign these documents, the only thing we would *really* be authorized to do in China would be to provide consultancy services in areas connected with publishing, such as photocomposition software and desktop

publishing. *Nowhere is it clearly stated that this new subsidiary can sell vocational distance learning courses, because it is legally FORBIDDEN for a joint venture with a foreign partner to carry out educational activities.* We have known for months that what little vocational distance training there is in China is run by State-owned universities, in other words, non-profit public corporations, which, naturally, do not have any foreign shareholders. It is impossible to guess how many years we might have to wait for a change in the laws, in a Communist country like China!

6. Furthermore, the market research carried out through the focus groups in Yantai clearly indicates that students will expect to receive a diploma or certificate on completing their studies. Not even New World Publishing Co. is authorized to issue such certificates – and it never will be authorized, because it does not belong to the Ministry of Education but to the Bureau of Publications. Our local partner is simply a publishing house, not a university or a school.

7. Manuel Vallejo warned: 'We are entering virgin territory, taking the first steps in an environment so far unexplored by foreign companies. We must maintain a presence, until the laws that govern this industry in China start to change . . . assuming they do eventually change, as we all expect. We must trust and rely on our local partner. They are institutionally powerful, and they seem to be ready to take active steps to ensure that we are allowed to operate, maybe under some exception to current legislation, or by finding some unexpected way around it. Of course, everything will be under the absolute control of the Chinese, to the extent that they will even censor the text of the courses we sell. All things considered, we do not know with any precision what our starting point is, and there is no guarantee that we will ever reach our target destination . . . and we have even less idea where all this might lead.'

Notes

[1] FECEA (Fundació Empresa Catalunya Europa Amèrica; Catalonia-Europe-America Business Foundation) was created in 1989 by a group of businessmen to promote the internationalization of Catalan enterprises, mainly through training activities and trade missions.

[2] The CEAC Group was still owned by the Martí and Menal families in 1996.

[3] The breakdown of students by subject groups in 1994 was as follows: Construction and Installation Technician (17.8 per cent of students enrolled in 1994), Electronics (5.6 per cent), Computer Systems (6.8 per cent), Automobile (5.3 per cent), Draftsman (2.7 per cent), Accounting and Business Administration (13.8 per cent), General Culture (21.7 per cent), Film and Photography (3.3 per cent), Beauty Care, Fashion and Tailoring/Dressmaking (8.7 per cent), and Languages (4.5 per cent). CEAC offered up to ten specific courses in each subject group.

[4] They still held the same posts in 1996.

[5] The drop-out rate was calculated by dividing the total number of students who dropped out, i.e. who did not pay all the monthly instalments for a particular course, by the total number of students registered on that course over a given period. The higher the drop-out rate, the heavier the loss for the company, as CEAC, in handing over all the course material on enrolment, effectively granted students credit, which they were supposed to repay month by month, using the reimbursement cards mailed to them.

[6] The Portuguese subsidiary was expected to achieve a turnover of some 2 billion escudos (equivalent to some 1.6 billion pesetas) in 1996.

[7] According to the 'Official Census of Spanish Exporters – 14th Edition', published in ICEX (Spanish Foreign Trade Institute), in 1993 CEAC, S.A. and Editorial CEAC, S.A. exported goods to the value of 58 and 159 million pesetas respectively, all under customs tariff 49.01 – 'Books, leaflets and similar printed matter, including loose sheets'.

[8] Tomás Blay was a lawyer and IESE MBA.

[9] The European Community Investment Partners (ECIP) Programme was set up in 1988 within the political framework of the European Community to foster cooperation with developing countries. It is a financial instrument that offers a number of 'facilities' or 'windows' to support the successive phases of such ventures:

identifying a business sector to invest in and a local business partner, carrying out a feasibility study, setting up a joint venture or expanding an existing joint venture, etc. Further information can be found in the book 'Politica communitaria de cooperación para el desarrollo', Instituto de Cooperación para el Desarrollo, Madrid, 1992, pp. 207–216.

[10] Flores was 36, married, with two children aged 4 and 6. He had graduated in Industrial Engineering in 1984. After working for 4 years in a computer services company, he had joined CEAC in 1989 as head of the Data Processing Department of Centro de Estudios CEAC, where he was responsible for a team of five. In 1991 he had been appointed Data Processing Director for all the CEAC Group companies, with a team of 18 people.

[11] The Board had four members: Juan Martí, José Menal, and their sons Juan Antonio Martí Castro and Guillermo Menal.

Case Study

BAD HOFGASTEIN

In August 1990, Karl-Heinz Muckhoff, managing director of the health resort in the town of Bad Hofgastein, talked to a committee meeting of the health resort and tourist board about his views on the state of tourism in the town. His comments are recorded below.

TOURISM IN BAD HOFGASTEIN – LOOKING BACK AND AHEAD

Based on the suggestion made by Director Peti in the last committee meeting, I should like to present a few points of information, and some of my thoughts arising from them, concerning tourism in Bad Hofgastein from my point of view as the manager of the health resort. Allow me first of all to thank Director Peti very warmly for his suggestion, as from experience we know that usually no time remains for discussion of certain areas in meetings, even though they are important, because points on the agenda which seem more topical have to be handled first. Nevertheless, it is doubtless all the more important to do some thinking about the present state of affairs in Bad Hofgastein.

Let me begin with a brief retrospective glance, most of which is statistical.

As we know, for many years Bad Hofgastein was number one in terms of overnight bookings in the statistics of comparable localities. However, our town has since been pushed into the background by Saalbach, Sölden and Zell am See (Table 11.1). While the number of overnight stays does not necessarily represent a generally valid criterion for the assessment of success – this number is only of marginal importance – much more important are the degree of utilized capacity and the turnover per

Source: Hans Mühlbacher and Hans Scharfetter,
University of Innsbruck, Austria

night dependent on the category of lodging. We still have to take note of the fact that for some 10 years now the number of bookings has ranged from sluggish to recessive.

The peak number of bookings was reached, as we know, in 1981, where the 1 382 032 bookings came close to hitting the 'sonic barrier' of 1.4 million. Parallel to this was the development in the degree of utilized capacity, which fell from the highest mark in 1980 from almost 50 per cent (49.9) to the lowest point thus far of 43.6 per cent in 1988 (Table 11.2, with the exception of 1968). Even though this figure is well above the average for Austrian tourist resort centres, it should still give us food for thought.

A division of the statistical figures into summer and winter bookings permits further conclusions to be reached. For example, in summer 1980, a total of 760 827 bookings was reached; in 1989, however, they dropped to 587 478. During the same period, the winter bookings rose from 622 358 to 694 407. This ought to show clearly that the real problem-child of our local tourist trade is not the winter season, but that of summer.

Since the summer season can be primarily identified with health resort orientated tourism, we have to find out here where the weak points are. So to stimulate summer bookings an analysis of the situation will be necessary, as was already touched on the last time in the discussion of 22 August 1990, when this problem was discussed and various assumptions were expressed rather candidly in the presence of Austrian TV and well-known print media.

The overassessment of the hysteria involving radon contamination, cost-curbing laws in Germany, the competition of exclusive travel destinations (for the same price!) and a number of other reasons were thrown into the discussion. One particular demand was upheld though, namely that it is absolutely necessary to update, modernize and extend what the health resort offers, on the one hand to stand up against the competition, and on the other to be able to appeal to new tourist groupings. For example, it was possible to refer to press reports about health resorts in the Black Forest

Table 11.1 AUSTRIAN TOURIST LOCALITIES ACCORDING TO BOOKINGS[1]

	LOCALITY	1988	1987	DIFFERENCE (%)
1	Wien	6 206 186	5 854 444	+6.0
2	Saalbach/Hinterglemm	1 890 286	1 905 567	−0.8
3	Mittelberg	1 650 605	1 615 281	+2.2
4	Salzburg	1 577 094	1 513 401	+4.2
5	Sölden	1 555 949	1 512 482	+2.9
6	Zell am See	1 377 359	1 367 437	+0.7
7	Bad Hofgastein	1 313 755	1 293 946	+1.5
8	Innsbruck	1 282 401	1 298 584	−1.3
9	Seefeld/Tirol	1 193 111	1 109 876	+7.5
10	Mayrhofen	1 134 741	1 079 887	+5.1
11	St Kanzian/Klop	1 119 156	1 045 303	+7.1
12	Villach	1 109 671	1 066 794	+4.0
13	Badgastein	1 041 958	1 087 687	−4.2
14	Bad Kleinkirchheim	1 003 000	944 467	+6.2
15	Hermagor/Press.	942 520	886 072	+6.4
16	Finkenstein/Kärnten	931 844	923 801	+0.9
17	Kitzbühel	929 702	975 489	−4.7
18	Kirchberg	906 295	934 108	−2.9
19	Lech und Zürs	899 957	872 601	+3.1
20	Ebena. Achensee	868 424	860 500	+0.9
21	Neustift/Stubai	843 672	803 724	+4.9
22	Wildschönau	802 537	801 088	+0.2

[1] The figures were taken from Booklet No. 930 of the Contributions to Austrain Statistics, *Der Fremdenverkehr in Österreich im Jahre 1988*. Listed are all localities with more than 800 000 overnight bookings in the tourist year 1987–88 (1 November 1987 to 31 October 1988).

A comparison with Bad Hofgastein is only partially possible because the listings of the other localities include not only the bookings in licensed hotels, boarding houses, private lodgings, camping areas and in other types of tourist accommodation (flats), but also those in youth hostels.

area in Germany having a similar problem. Bookings are sluggish there as well, the people there want to try new directions, and new considerations are being discussed.

The strategies that we want to implement are going to have to be worked out mutually between both the health resort and tourist board and the local economy. In particular, one point to think about is a reservation centre integrated into an international reservation system.

The extension of conference facilities, the creation of an incentive programme focusing on health and sports, the building of an 18-hole golf course, the introduction of health workshops, the founding of instructional facilities for physical and physiotherapy, and so forth, are a few ideas to bear in mind.

With the establishment of the Magic-Wellness-Programme, an important first step has been taken in this direction, one which has already begun primarily to affect the image of the town positively. The fact that conservative circles find it hard to get accustomed to this new policy has caused intensive discussions which, in the final analysis, has increased its acceptance. If you will allow me to quote from the statistics once again, then I would like to mention the month of July as an example of this year's summer season. An

Table 11.2   The Development of Tourism in Bad Hofgastein, 1965–89

Year	Total Overnight Bookings	Arrivals	Tourist Beds	Capacity Utilized (%)	Summer Bookings	Winter Bookings
1965	799 822	57 113	4546	48.2	542 666	257 165
1966	784 817	58 500	4709	45.7	524 053	260 764
1967	811 497	61 008	5099	43.6	510 443	301 054
1968	843 317	64 172	5415	42.7	525 666	317 651
1969	905 081	69 032	5489	45.2	559 870	345 211
1970	1 024 061	78 190	5471	51.3	622 732	401 329
1971	1 055 628	81 585	5376	53.8	649 376	406 252
1972	1 063 707	82 692	5706	51.1	664 434	399 273
1973	1 161 420	93 422	5783	55.0	731 462	429 958
1974	1 206 416	94 851	6038	54.7	717 467	488 949
1975	1 257 582	105 670	6528	52.8	739 736	517 846
1976	1 206 840	98 121	6808	48.6	694 249	512 591
1977	1 233 007	102 461	7239	46.7	702 654	530 353
1978	1 236 569	107 559	7390	45.8	696 219	540 350
1979	1 272 849	109 232	7555	46.2	738 549	534 300
1980	1 383 185	120 713	7599	49.9	760 827	622 358
1981	1 382 032	122 784	7710	49.1	735 746	646 286
1982	1 319 681	121 609	7791	46.4	676 660	643 021
1983	1 304 198	123 664	7841	45.5	671 777	632 421
1984	1 317 778	125 022	7910	45.6	674 541	643 207
1985	1 279 666	118 887	7979	44.6	652 860	626 806
1986	1 299 249	127 184	8037	44.3	624 726	674 523
1987	1 293 946	128 468	7963	44.5	625 272	668 674
1988	1 313 755	135 519	8248	43.6	619 348	694 407
1989	1 277 160	135 584	8011	43.7	587 478	689 682

analysis of the slight drop in bookings shows that it resulted primarily in the C and D categories of lessors of private rooms; at the same time, however, rises were registered in the A and B categories, with 4 and 4½ stars, respectively. Without wanting to make this slight drop seem harmless, it must be said that from an overall economic standpoint one must actually speak of a success. Nevertheless, it would be conceivable to take action to bring about improvements in those areas in which figures are recessive.

A glance at the statistical breakdown according to nations also gives rise to optimism (Table 11.3). The declining figures for German tourists are balanced by impressive increases from Italy, Great Britain, Sweden and Switzerland. This certainly ought to act as an adequate incentive to intensify advertising efforts for the summer season in these regions.

For a detailed discussion in a committee meeting with a short agenda we should allow for enough time to be really able to consider things thoroughly and to initiate any findings acceptable to all parties concerned. To make preparations for such a discussion, it is recommended that the necessary statistical documentaion be procured (Figures 11.1–11.6 and Table 11.4) from the administration of the health resort.

Table 11.3 Overnight Bookings According to the Country of Origin, 1986–9

	1986	1987			1988			1989		
	Total	Total	Summer	Winter	Total	Summer	Winter	Total	Summer	Winter
Australia	–	321	–	–	2 141	650	1 491	1 340	1 092	248
Belgium, Lux'mb'g	1 760	2 452	–	–	3 467	1 490	1 977	2 687	976	1 711
Germany	699 423	672 324	372 278	300 046	690 201	380 697	309 504	640 620	334 795	305 825
Finland	–	–	–	–	445	125	320	809	89	720
France, Monaco	2 259	2 365	–	–	1 711	1 023	688	2 167	1 365	802
Greece	133	319	–	–	643	–	643	413	106	307
Great Britain	3 769	3 429	1 680	1 749	6 999	1 312	5 687	11 232	2 252	8 980
Israel	8 523	10 144	9 767	377	7 878	7 335	543	9 575	9 460	115
Italy	2 327	2 552	1 650	902	4 420	1 752	2 668	7 191	3 490	3 701
Jugoslavia	1 365	2 271	–	–	1 845	106	1 739	1 611	16	1 595
Canada	1 653	1 045	–	–	–	–	–	–	–	–
Holland	8 740	8 074	2 405	5 669	7 282	2 219	5 063	10 901	1 560	9 341
Austria	571 395	541 106	214 783	326 323	535 796	205 523	330 271	529 785	207 599	322 186
Sweden	9 034	23 179	2 163	21 016	23 889	1 753	22 136	23 575	2 665	20 910
Switzerland	4 760	5 967	4 719	1 248	6 022	4 968	1 054	10 662	9 044	1 618
Hungary	–	280	–	–	1 624	229	1 395	2 431	292	2 139
USA	7 340	8 310	6 926	1 384	7 177	5 216	1 961	7 791	6 275	1 516
Other countries	6 768	8 763	–	–	12 215	4 950	7 267	–	–	–
Total	1 299 249	1 292 901	616 371	668 674	1 313 755	619 348	694 407	1 277 160	587 478	689 682

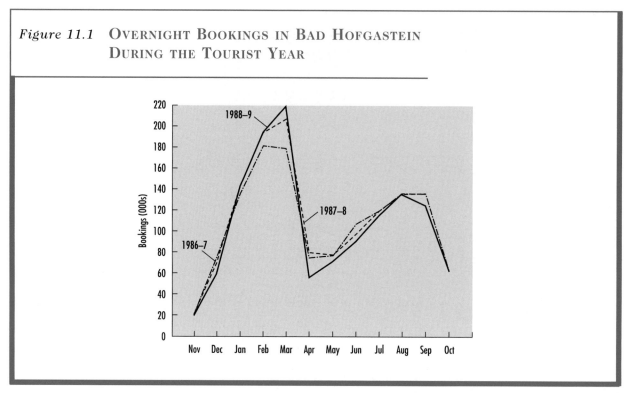

Figure 11.1 OVERNIGHT BOOKINGS IN BAD HOFGASTEIN DURING THE TOURIST YEAR

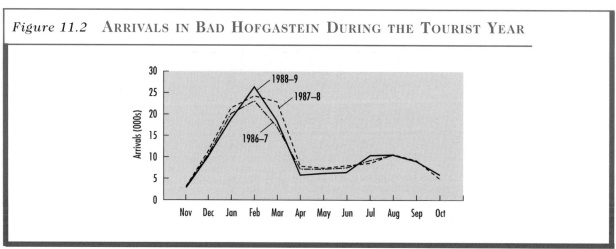

Figure 11.2 ARRIVALS IN BAD HOFGASTEIN DURING THE TOURIST YEAR

THE HISTORICAL DEVELOPMENT OF BAD HOFGASTEIN

Bad Hofgastein is the historical hub of the Gastein valley; it has been for centuries. The town is situated in the broadest and sunniest part of the valley, a significant trade route across the Alps since pre-Christian times.

In the Middle Ages, Hofgastein was the centre of gold and silver mining. It flourished a second time in the nineteenth century as a spa when it was granted the rights to the thermal water of the springs in Badgastein. The first thermal baths were administered in 1830. Fifty-four rooms were available for guests. This number was to increase during

Figure 11.3 OVERNIGHT BOOKINGS IN BAD HOFGASTEIN ACCORDING TO LODGING CATEGORIES (WINTER SEASON)

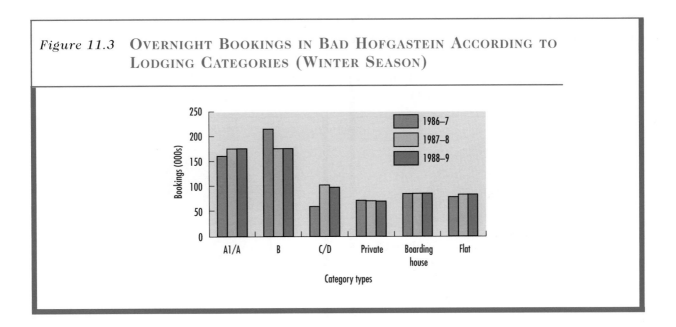

Figure 11.4 OVERNIGHT BOOKINGS IN BAD HOFGASTEIN ACCORDING TO LODGING CATEGORIES (SUMMER SEASON)

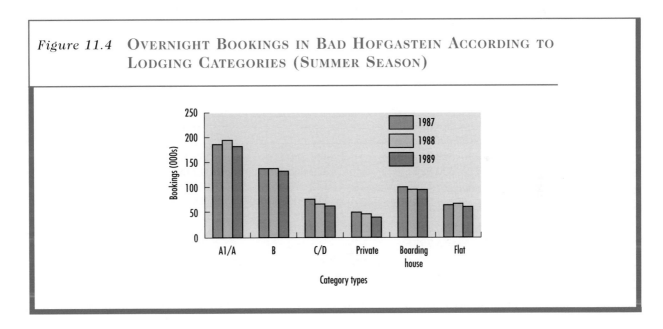

the next 50 years only from 158 to 198, up to the building of the Tauern railway. Following the opening of the railway in 1905, and until the outbreak of World War I, Hofgastein developed into a spa of the first order. The number of visitors reached its high point in 1914 with 5000, four times as many as in 1900. Within the same period, private construction increased the number of beds from 200 to 900.

The general economic decline in the post-war period had its effect on Bad Hofgastein as well. Nevertheless, on account of the increasing number of visitors over the years, 29 hotels and boarding houses were built and many establishments were renovated and modernized. The designation 'Bad Hofgastein' became effective in 1936.

Subsequent to a further complete collapse as the result of World War II, the town began once

Figure 11.5 Tourists' Reasons for Staying in Bad Hofgastein (Winter Season 1988–89)

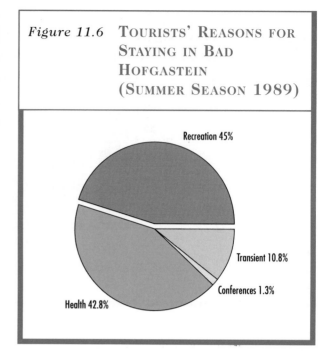

Winter sports 66%

Transient 8%

Conferences 2%

Health 12%

Recreation 12%

Figure 11.6 Tourists' Reasons for Staying in Bad Hofgastein (Summer Season 1989)

Recreation 45%

Transient 10.8%

Conferences 1.3%

Health 42.8%

Table 11.4 Overnight Bookings According to Lodging Categories, 1986–9

Category	1986[1]	1987	1988	1989
A1/A	349 741	347 560	369 186	358 938
B	320 925	352 663	312 098	306 739
C/D	78 329	132 279	169 263	158 788
Private rooms	124 692	118 606	115 647	109 614
Health Spa hotels	195 325	185 495	180 538	183 234
Flats	216 440	142 191	151 522	145 236
Others	13 797	15 152	15 501	14 611

[1]Owing to recategorization, from 1987 the licensed flats of category B and several establishments in category B had to be assigned to category C/D. For this reason the figures from the years 1986 and 1987 in the affected categories are not comparable.

again to make progress. Today, Bad Hofgastein is an internationally known and recognized health and winter sports resort. It has 135 licensed establishments offering accommodation, 65 of which have their own thermal baths; 275 lessors of private rooms; and 6 homes with medicinal facilities under the auspices of national insurance institutions.

EXCERPTS FROM THE 1989 ACTIVITY REPORT OF THE HEALTH RESORT AND TOURIST BOARD (HRTB) OF BAD HOFGASTEIN

Report of the Board of Directors

Since Director Muckhoff will be retiring in another one and a half years, after consultation with him it has been agreed that a suitable successor will take over at the end of 1990. A personnel agency has been commissioned to locate a suitable candidate. Various preliminary talks have already been carried out with potential candidates. It is assumed that a decision will be made by March of this year.

So-called 'regulars' talks' have been implemented to make sure our HRTB members are better informed. These talks are scheduled to take place from now on every three months within the circle of hotelkeepers and private room lessors. Newsletters have been sent out regularly by the board to a hitherto unknown extent. Telefaxes (networked with presently over 40 subscribers) will accelerate and improve the flow of information in future even more. And, of course, many personal talks between hotelkeepers (with lessors of private rooms) and the board of directors have contributed considerably, in our opinion, to the flow of information.

Even if a PR officer were hired, there would still be criticism about receiving too little information since, as we have found again and again, even written information (telefax) is read only partially or too superficially, or is passed on to the guests. In this regard, we are all going to have to find a satisfactory common solution once again.

The Gastein Valley Community of Interests (GVCI) has brought an info-brochure onto the market for the first time for the entire valley. An important prerequisite for this was an agreement between all the local HRT boards to no longer produce competitive brochures in their own localities. The deficit of the *Gastein Newsline* info-brochure and the *Gastein Journal*, as a result of this competition, was cut by ASch250,000 in the first year, which meant a strengthening of the GVCI budget. Moreover, further common measures were decided on, such as the 'Sun and Ski' campaign and a large

international symposium on radon in the coming year.

Mag. Gollnhuber has succeeded Fritz Zetting in the health resort administration, but has considerably changed duties. As the director in charge of health, sports and recreation, he has been given the task of developing a new philosophy and marketing strategy for the Gastein cure. The range of resort services tendered by Gastein are to be set up in that section of the market as 'vital' and 'healthy'. The terms 'sick' and 'old', like the word 'radon', are no longer marketable. It is a case now of getting the new marketing concept over as persistently as possible. To do this, it will be necessary to carry out additional market research and analysis. Mag. Gollnhuber will be presenting his concept to the public within the next few weeks. We shall inform you about this in later separate workshops.

In the past year, Bad Hofgastein had to put up with a drop in bookings. Even though the winter figures were almost equal (as compared with the year before), the summer season registered a decline. A primary reason for this was certainly the health reform becoming effective in Germany. Comparative figures from health resorts in Germany indicate that Bad Hofgastein came off relatively lightly with its 2.8 per cent deficit – in some German health resort areas the figures were around −40 per cent. Nevertheless, it should be mentioned that Austria on the whole registered growth in tourism during the summer. Consequently, it is certainly necessary to market all the other leisure-time activities just as strongly as our spa programme; hiking, mountaineering, holidays on a farm, bicycling, mountainbiking and so forth, just to mention a few. A particular area to concentrate on, though, from now on is golfing. This is developing very quickly into a very popular sport. At the present time, various European countries are experiencing growth rates of 100 per cent. There are signs that at some point in the future a new 18-hole course will be built in addition to the 9-hole course we already have. Along with Mayor Weber, a number of gentlemen in the local council have expressed interest in such a project, and efforts are already being made to work out satisfactory leasing contracts with the respective landowners.

A central room-reservation kiosk with two self-service terminals available around the clock will be erected in the next six months. The building of the new kiosk will cost about ASch500 000. The introduction of a sales-promotion company to investigate the possibilities of direct sale of bed quotas is being considered. Also, in future a central computer-assisted room-reservation system ('bed exchange') will be unavoidable. Estimates lead us to expect that by the year 2000 about 80 per cent of all tourist beds will be able to be booked within minutes in thousands of booking offices all over Europe. Since we are also receiving more short-holiday bookings, this step is becoming more and more important and urgent.

Report of the Health Resort Administration

Under the commission of the GVCI, Director Muckhoff has had opportunity to take part in the tourist exchanges in Berlin (ITB) and in Innsbruck (ATB). Besides this, he was represented at the tourist trade fair in Triest. As far as consumer fairs in 1989 were concerned, only participation in the 'Consumenta' in Nuremberg had been foreseen. An employee of the Palace Hotel represented the interests of Bad Hofgastein in the booth of the GVCI.

Two press trips were carried out in Germany, accomplishing a great number of editorial visits alongside press talks and conferences. These were first to Hamburg, Flensburg, Bremen, Oldenburg and Lübeck, then to Regensburg, Bonn, Cologne, Düsseldorf, Lippstadt and Nuremberg. Furthermore, under the auspices of the GVCI, Director Muckhoff handled the traditional press conferences in Linz and St Pölten. Among other things, in the course of these press trips numerous radio interviews were given.

Also worthy of mention is a press conference in Rome. On the way back from Rome one particular point of interest was a visit to Citta di Castello, which had expressed interest in a partnership with Bad Hofgastein. Here, exploratory talks took place.

Also, this sector of PR work covers the catering for numerous groups and individuals from the ranks of journalists, travel agency organizations, delegations of the ÖFVW and so forth which takes place right here in Bad Hofgastein. As usual, a great number of events were put on for the guests (Table 11.5).

In conclusion, I should like to express the hope that the earlier stagnation will not repeat itself in the 1990 summer season. I say this because although we can assume that German tourists will continue to avail themselves of our spa possibilities

in spite of the cost-curbing law, we could gain ground through the increase in tourists from other countries (primarily Italy!). In addition, because of the late Easter holidays, we can assume that with good snow conditions an improvement could again be achieved in winter too. Moreover, we must primarily hope that the new advertising policy is beginning to take effect and that, in consequence, new guests can be won for Bad Hofgastein from the right sort of clientele.

Report of the Committee for Leisure Time, Culture, Sports and Events

The artist craftsmen days, during which the first Austrian National Prize for handicraft design was awarded, and the exhibition and summer fete connected with it, have to be declared the high point of the 1989 summer season. As a result of their great public appeal, the responsible ministry has already agreed to these artist craftsmen days being held again in 1990.

Also worthy of mention are the organizational support and realization of various events during the summer months, for example the midsummer fete put on in the Alpenkurpark, numerous events focusing on customs (the *Gasteiner Hoagoscht*, folklore evenings, singing and dancing festivals) and social events in the sanitorium and congress centre (dance evenings, concerts, lectures). In the area of sports, the first *Marktlauf* (a footrace) of Bad Hofgastein as well as the Gamskogel-Rally were novelties for Bad Hofgastein.

A further success in the sports sector can be mentioned. The long-held wish of Bad Hofgastein for a high-altitude cross-country ski trail has been realized. The ski-touring and cross-country trail in the Anger valley was extended from 3.5 km to about 7 km with a budget of about ASch150 000. In the 1988–9 winter season the winter sports' section of the health resort administration managed over 40 ski-ing events, offered a weekly sports programme, and catered for a large number of journalists and press correspondents.

Report of the Committee for Advertising

In the 1988 activity report we announced that we had adopted a new advertising policy (Figure 11.7),

Table 11.5 EVENTS FOR GUESTS IN 1989

36 slide lectures (on travel, mountain climbing, adventure, Bad Gastein and the Gastein valley)
28 medical lectures (the Gastein cure, spinal column, arthrosis, the curative tunnel)
 5 other lectures (for example, astrology)
 8 classical concerts – serious (for example, Mozarteum-Quartett, Rosenau-Trio)
11 classical concerts – light (for example, operetta evenings, boys' choir, piano concerts)
13 other concerts (for example, Volga-Cossacks, choir singing, weekly concerts with soloists of the local
 Gastein orchestra)
20 folklore events (for example, evenings with traditional dancing and music, festivals of singers and
 musicians)
20 theatrical guest performances (for example, Scala theatre)
 5 guest performances by local folk theatre groups (for example, Tegernsee Folk Theatre)
87 dress balls
11 evenings with dancing (town orchestra)
33 special concerts by the town orchestra (for example, on the occasion of film and musical evenings,
 honouring of guests, concerts playing requests)
 4 medical congresses and conferences in the spa and congress centre

that we wanted to develop a series of new promotional material, a large-scale series of ads in the German media (Table 11.6), and that, above all, we wanted to create the most essential technical prerequisites for efficient work in the rooms of the health resort administration.

Hence the year 1989 was characterized by the intention to endorse the new advertising policy and to realize the strategic concept of the Kleiber-Wurm Agency in Munich. Owing to the extensive modification of the earlier policy there was naturally constant criticism and numerous justified discussions.

Both the graphic message and the 'Magic Moments' slogan are intended to convey an emphasis on emotional response, on the idea of experiencing a stimulating holiday, and on a youthful image. The overriding objective is to make Bad Hofgastein stand out through this completely different image and consequently to draw increased attention. With the catchy slogan, the attempt to support the new advertising concept both visually and verbally was successful.

Until now the advertising policy has consisted of the following:

(1) Posters (gratis for every firm).

(2) A shell folder (dispersion media, conceived for the printing of programmes, price listings, offers, and so on) accepted enthusiastically by the lessors of private rooms (Figure 11.8).

(3) Postcards, with different motifs from the new series of photographs. These cards were launched for the first time in a campaign in May in large German cities.

(4) The catalogue of firms and information (available from the health resort administration). The much discussed issue of its oversize has meanwhile been accepted by all branch offices of tourist advertising because of our intervention.

(5) Ads in print media and journals (Figure 11.9).

We are aware that we were and are in arrears with the image catalogue. The reason for this is that we have been trying to discuss all possible misgivings and conceptions; the result is that we are now on the fifth model for this product. What was primarily taken into consideration was the wish of several hoteliers to select realistic photographs. Also, a lot of effort has gone into finding text satisfying everyone. The catalogue is due to be completed shortly.

Furthermore, in the next few weeks, a 12-page summer flyer will be appearing which is like an illus-

---

Figure 11.7   STRATEGIC CONCEPT OF THE KLEIBER-WURM ADVERTISING
AGENCY FOR THE GASTEIN VALLEY IN 1988

Objectives	1	Make the Gastein valley popular as a holiday destination – image polishing.
	2	Introduce Gastein in the market as a brand name like BMW, Sony, IBM – creation of a premium brand.
	3	Fend off the competition.
Appeal groups	1	*General* Phases 1, 2 and 3 of the 4-phase consumer decision model.
	2	*Demographic* High-income middle to upper class with sophisticated aspirations.
	3	*Geographic* Germany, Switzerland, Italy, Austria; later France, the Benelux countries, Great Britain.
	4	*Psychologic* Persons interested in self-realization, luxury-orientated, quality living.
Conception	1	We create the happy moment between two people
	2	We appeal to the subconscious of our potential guests.
	3	We create messages aimed at the subconscious; dream behaviour instead of real behaviour.
	4	Message: Magic Moments. (English has a high appeal.)
	5	We communicate the word 'Gastein'; however, the term 'Gastein valley' is just as desirable.
	6	We do not prove anything in our advertising; it simply gives one's fantasy free rein.
	7	The addresses of the tourist offices are provided.
Design	1	Almost completely black-and-white shots are taken of the Magic Moments, with only two poeple in each shot.
	2	Surreal effects are attained with unnatural colours.
	3	Almost no text.
Media culture	1	We are betting on the following mix, which we envisage within a three-year schedule:
		Basic journal, Magic format, 4 languages, about 60 pages.
		Press ads in various countries – strong, big
		TV advertising in Germany, Switzerland and Austria
		Direct mailing
		Large-scale bill-posting in highly populated areas
		As required: radio advertising and sale of video tapes
	2	The principle of the media culture: 'less is more'.
Corporate identity	1	A consistent, visual design will be created; not, however, for reasons of formal conviction, but with regard to psychological learning effects.
Costs	1	A European budget of ASch10 million per year is targeted.
	2	The agency is paid on a fee basis.
Control	1	The money employed is an investment in future tourist structures and demand mentalities.
	2	A clear-cut instrument of control must be established which shows whether the set activities have been effective and efficient.

trated brochure for a locality, with a lot of information about the health resort. This flyer is to be distributed mainly at trade fairs, but is also an aid for those houses which have no brochure of their own. The same thing will be planned in due course for the 1990–1 winter season. For this, though, we still need a few winter shots which could not be taken last year because of the lack of snow.

Both the Gastein hiking map and local town map are presently being revised. An attractive listing of all lessors of private rooms is already at the suggestion stage. The new 'Info-Gastein' brochure, covering the activities and events in the Gastein valley, has been completed and is already in circulation.

In 1990 we are aiming at carrying on the new advertising policy and the above-mentioned activities, the extent of which will still have to be determined specifically in the current budget negotiations. The exact budgetary volume cannot be indicated at the moment, but it is planned to fix the appropriation for advertising if possible even higher than the ASch3 million for 1989 (see the 1990 budgetary plan of IAT Kleiber-Wurm in Appendix A).

Report of the Spa Committee

The activity of the health resort committee in 1989 consisted principally of discussions about new

Table 11.6 SCHEDULE SUGGESTION OF THE KLEIBER-WURM ADVERTISING AGENCY FOR 1989

PUBLICATION	CIRCULATION (000s)	FREQUENCY OF PUBLICATION	COST PER AD	COMMENTS
WAZ-Reisemagazin	1.351	Weekly	DM24 150 ASch169 100	Special travel and tourism supplements
WamS/Welt	0.553	Fri/Sat	DM22 200 ASch155 400	Combi: world of travel and modern travel
Die Zeit	0.535	Weekly	DM16 224 ASch113 600	Supraregional quality newspaper
Süddeutsche Zeitung	0.435	Daily	DM15 000 ASch105 000	Supraregional daily; travel supplement on Tue and Thu
FAZ	0.445	Daily	DM15 185 ASch106 300	Supraregional business newspaper
Sonntag Aktuell	0.923	Weekly	DM19 650 ASch137 600	Supraregional Sunday newspaper with a high circulation

We suggest insertion in supraregional German publications.
Size of ad 4 col × 250 mm high, 4 c; scheduling in spring and summer.

ways of disseminating information and the issuing of all-inclusive health resort prices. The suggestion was made to intensify the lectures held by spa physicians in various sanitoriums and to publish both informational posters and an explanatory handbook about the cure. The posters have already been supplied; the handbook is still in preparation.

The chairman (of the committee) held a number of talks with spa physicians, owners of establishments with spas, and the officials of the health resort administration in order to bring about optimal cooperation and coordination. As regards the issuing of all-inclusive price packages, we arrived at the opinion, after long discussions, that it would be very difficult to squeeze the classic course of medical treatment into a comparable, generally applicable flat charge. However, the need for short-term flat charges avoiding the term 'cure' (which should be used only for the three week version!) was affirmed.

Since the 1989 spa season was too brief, the decision was made to prepare the final procedure for 1990. In this context, contact was made with Prof. Dungl and Prof. Preiml in order to get suitable recommendations for the short-period stays of younger and financially sensitive or oriented guests. The result of this initiative was ultimately the involvement of Mr. Gollnhuber, whose main task was to work out attractive, modern and new kinds of all-inclusive packages in the area of cures and of sports to enliven summer tourism. In addition, the go-ahead was given to publish new information on the cure which would comply both with the latest changes and with the new advertising policy.

Report of the Committee for Transport and Environment

The town passed the resolution to introduce a city bus service at the beginning of summer 1990. Through the increase of the visitor's tax as of 20 December 1989 (50 per cent of the additional proceeds are to be used for the bus service), and the collaboration of the town, the spa administration

Figure 11.8 Shell Folder

and the local cable-car company, the financing of this project is secured. In the event that the bus service cannot be undertaken in the summer as scheduled, the proceeds foreseen for this from the visitor's tax will be deposited in a separate account and earmarked specifically for the city bus service.

Report of the Director for Sports and Recreation

My personal objective is to offer guests in beautiful Bad Hofgastein more in the way of recreation and activities. To realize this, it is absolutely necessary to develop a concept acceptable to the entire population of the town.

Since October of last year I have endeavoured to get ideas and opinions from local institutions and establishments offering lodgings in order to offer guests more activities. Health plays an important role in this regard. On account of the changing values in today's society, this particular aspect has become even more important than before. For this reason the Gastein cure needs to have a new image breathed into it. The magic phrase here is 'active recuperation' (getting well actively). The 'leisure-time fitness sports' area will be running in a test phase in the summer of 1990. Essential talks involving personnel, infrastructure and financing are already underway.

The advertising activities for 'Magic Moments Watches' and 'Magic Moments Ski Suits' have caught on very well. A large part of the financing of the ski suits was sponsored by the Hypobank. The special programmes conceived as all-inclusive price packages for 'Wedeln in December' and 'Ski-active in January' could not be carried out because of the lack of snow. The generous support of the hoteliers in Bad Hofgastein, of the cable car company and of the spa administration have made it possible to organize the 1990 guest ski races more attractively. The winners will be invited to a 'Guest Ski Race of the Best' on the 21 and 22 of April 1990 in Bad Hofgastein. The top three men and women can expect super prizes.

APPENDIX A
ADVERTISING BUDGET OF
BAD HOFGASTEIN FOR THE YEAR 1990

Radio Advertising

Bad Hofgastein   17 January 1990/pe
1990

30 Sec spot
Private stations in southern Germany
Time: April–June 1990
     7–8 a.m., 5–7 p.m.

Kombi III plus
Reach: 1 million/programme
Heilbronn, Mannheim, Karlsruhe,
Stuttgart, Reutlingen, Baden-Baden
10 × 30 sec   ASch140 000 (= DM20 000)

Antenne Bayern
Reach: 3 million/programme
Bavaria, parts of Hessen and Baden-
Wurtemberg, Austria and Switzerland
10 × 30 sec   ASch102 900 (= DM14 700)

30 sec spot
Local stations ORF
Time: April–June 1990
     7–8 a.m., 5–7 p.m.

Local radio Vienna
10 × 30 sec   ASch39 600 (= DM5700)

Local radio Salzburg
10 × 30 sec   ASch31 350 (= DM4500)

Note: In choosing the German stations we assumed that the age of the target group for summer holidays is above average. Well-known city stations, for example Radio Xanadu in Munich, have a much younger audience which does not belong to the group of potential summer holiday guests.

TV Advertising

Bad Hofgastein   17 January 1990/pe
1990

30 sec spots
Private stations in Germany supraregional

Time: April–June 1991
  6–8 p.m.

RTL plus
Reach: 19 million
1 spot of 30 sec   app. ASch70 000 (=DM10 000)

SAT 1
Reach: 23 million
1 spot of 30 sec   app. ASch45 000 (=DM6600)

Note: This listing only gives an approximation of the size of costs of private TV advertising. The stations were chosen not only on the basis of target group aspects but also because of cost reasons. The suggested scheduling time for the year 1991 would also be April to June because summer should be advertised more heavily in the coming year.

Print Advertising

Bad Hofgastein
1990   17 January 1990/pe

1/1 page, four colours
Magazines with predominantly female readers
Time: April–June 1990

Title and country	Circulation	Cost for 1 ad (ASch/DM)	
Germany			
Cosmopolitan	430 000	228 900	(32 700)
Madame	115 000	147 000	(21 000)
Vogue	115 400	196 000	(28 000)
Vital	387 700	140 000	(20 000)
Sports	138 000	136 500	(19 500)
Intermediate total	1 186 100	848 400	(121 200)
Italy			
Cosmopolitan	204 000	122 500	(17 500)
Total		970 900	(138 700)

Rebates are not taken into account.
Price changes may occur.

Large-scale Posters

Bad Hofgastein
1990   17 January 1990/pe

18/1 sheets (252 × 356 cm)
Billboards in big German cities
Time: April–June 1990
  First decade (10–11 days)
  Quota: 1 : 6000

		ASch	DM
Hamburg	271 BB	238 000	(34 000)
Hannover	88 BB	66 500	(9500)
Bremen	91 BB	66 500	(9500)
Dortmund	100 BB	70 000	(10 000)
Düsseldorf	91 BB	67 900	(9700)
Duisburg	91 BB	63 000	(9000)

Essen	106 BB	73 500	(10 500)
Cologne	160 BB	115 500	(16 500)
Frankfurt	103 BB	74 900	(10 700)
Stuttgart	96 BB	77 000	(11 000)
Munich	215 BB	178 500	(25 500)
Berlin	312 BB	224 700	(32 100)
Total Germany	1 730 BB	1 316 000	(188 000)

18/1 sheets
Billboards in big cities of Austria
Time April–June 1990
    1 month

Vienna	100 BB	97 200	(13 900)
Linz	25 BB	27 000	(3900)
Salzburg	15 BB	18 000	(2600)
Graz	30 BB	35 000	(5000)
Klagenfurt	10 BB	11 500	(1700)
Innsbruck	15 BB	18 000	(2500)
Total Austria	195 BB	206 800	(29 600)

Note: This list indicates how much should be spent as a minimum in each country. Due to the restricted budget a choice will have to be taken.

Media Recommendation

Bad Hofgastein
1990   17 January 1990/pe

In view of the restricted budget available we suggest advertising in only a part of Germany and Austria this year. In our selection we concentrate on southern Germany, the state of Salzburg and Vienna as the capital and biggest city in Austria.

1. Radio Advertising

		ASch	DM
Budget:		210 000	(30 000)
Antenne Bayern			
15 × 30 sec spots		154 350	(22 050)
Radio Vienna			
15 × 30 sec spots		59 400	(8 500)
Total		213 750	(30 500)

2. Print Advertising
In magazines as suggested.

3. Large-scale Posters

Budget:		420 000	(60 000)
Germany			
Frankfurt	103 BB	74 900	(10 700)
Stuttgart	96 BB	77 000	(11 000)
Munich	215 BB	178 500	(25 500)
	414 BB	330 400	(47 200)
Austria			
Vienna	100 BB	97 200	(13 900)
Total	514 BB	427 600	(61 100)

Budget

Bad Hofgastein
Overview 1990

17 January 1990/pe

01. Image Catalogue
Circulation: 50 000

		ATS	DM
Remaining production cost	ATS720 000		
+20 per cent added value tax	ATS144 000	864 000	(= 123 500)

02. Flyer summer
Circulation: 30 000

Lay out and production	ATS220 000		
+20 per cent avt	ATS44 000	264 000	(= 37 700)

03. Flyer Winter
Circulation: 30 000

Lay out and production	ATS220 000		
+20 per cent avt	ATS44 000	264 000	(= 37 700)

04. Postcards
5 motives

Lay out and production	ATS50 000		
+20 per cent avt	ATS10 000	60 000	(= 8600)

05. Fee IAT

	ATS	DM
	200 000	(= 28 600)
Intermediate total	1 652 000	(= 236 100)

06. Radio Spot
Length: 30 sec

Concept and production	ATS28 000		
Scheduling costs	ATS210 000	238 000	(= 34 000)

07. TV Spot
Length: 30 sec

Concept and production	ATS210 000	210 000	(= 30 000)

08. Ads
Magazines in Germany and Italy
1/1 page 4c

Lay out and production	ATS75 000		
Scheduling costs	ATS1 000 000	1 075 000	(= 153 500)

09. Large-scale Posters
18/1 sheets (252 × 356 cm)

Lay out and production	ATS200 000		
Scheduling costs	ATS420 000	620 000	(= 88 500)
Preliminary total (incl. avt)		3 795 000	(= 542 100)

APPENDIX B

Cross-cultural consumer lifestyle research in 13 countries of Europe had revealed 16 different types of consumers to be found in all the countries. Figure B.1 gives an overview of close lifestyle types. They are characterized by more or less of an inclination towards valuables versus values and towards movement (change) versus settlement.

Based on this typology and data on the holiday travel behaviour of the various lifestyle types, a typology of holiday consumers was established. It contains the five types of consumers shown in Figure B.2.

1 Prudent Recreation-Seekers

This market segment includes the following lifestyle types: prudent, defence, vigilante and olivadados. They are older than average and married; most of them no longer have children at home. They are workers, craftsmen or employees, sometimes retired. Women are mostly housewives. They have rarely finished higher education and have low to middle incomes. They seek stability and moral order. Change frightens them. they are innovation averse.

Motivation

Holidays must be recreation. Even if they leave their normal envirnoment they prefer to stick with their habits. Recreation means rediscovering nature. Travel should lead to one place that has not to be left during the holiday. For short trips they like to visit attractions and amusement parks. Sometimes they visit large museums.

Behaviour

Most of them rarely have travelled elsewhere in Europe: They are not inclined to travel within the next two years, but often dream of travel in the future. Their holiday travel normally is limited to the home country and tends to be directed to the same place because of habits or attachment.

They generally look for maximum predictability and structure, therefore they are the major target group for organized travel ('all-inclusive').

Preferred leisure activities

Staying at home, relaxing, watching TV or browsing through a magazine are their preferred activities. They are fairly focused on their individual universe and prefer their home as the place to spend leisure time.

Some of them are addicted do-it-yourselfers or love to play games. They practise very little or no sports (except some football), but love to watch sports on television. They either do not take pictures at all or only take pictures as souvenirs (during holidays or special events). Their photographic equipment is rather basic.

Consumption outlook

Member of this lifestyle type believe that they will have to reduce or at least stabilize their spending for travel and holiday purposes in the future. They plan to reduce the amount of money spent on leisure-time activities during the year; eating-out, theatre, cinema, books, discs or magazines.

2 Traditional Culture-Consumers

This segment contains the following lifestyle types: moralist, gentry and strict. They are of average age or higher, between 45 and 65 years old; married with children who have left their family home. They are higher level employees, entrepreneurs or self-employed (gentry, strict), employees (moralist) or retired with higher incomes. They live in homes in the countryside or in attractive suburbs. They are conservative opinion leaders tending to conform with traditional norms and values.

Motivation

This group of consumers prefers peaceful holidays focused on discovery and culture. They choose a place to discover without much moving around. They look for natural monuments, beautiful landscapes and historical sites to get to know more about a new region or country.

For short trips they love to visit European capitals to see historical sites or a famous museum. But they also leave home to 'get out into the country' or to do something for their health. Generally speaking, they are striving for individual peace, well-being and personal enrichment.

Behaviour

They take short holidays of one or two weeks at most, mainly during summer, but also in spring or autumn. They also love to take short holidays of one or two days in low season. They have gained certain travel experience in Europe and know a couple of countries.

In future they may want to take short holidays to learn more about their own country, make short trips to close destinations or even stay in their home town. At the same time, they are attracted by specific targets for their longer holidays. They have rarely travelled to places outside of Europe and do not plan long-distance trips.

Transport

This is a target group for organized bus travel (particularly for short trips). They quite often use public transport and would opt for the modern and progressive railroad transport. They are the most demanding airline traveller.

Organization

They prefer to choose, decide and book themselves, but for short trips they also like to take all kinds of organized package offers.

Figure B.1 THE EURO-CONSUMERS

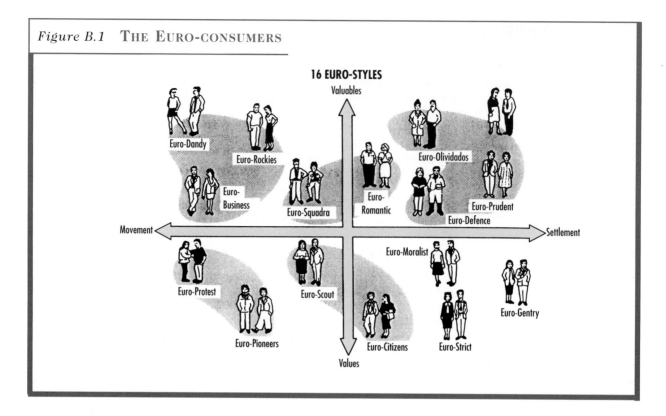

Source: IHA-News, 3/1989.

Preferred leisure activities

For this group of consumers, leisure activities are a source of individual enrichment. They often are indoor-orientated (like to read or to browse through a magazine) and are art lovers.

They tap TV information to preserve important events, love to take a walk (particularly the moralists), but rarely practise any sports (they watch it on TV). They do not take many photographs.

Consumption outlook

Most members of this segment – just like the average European – plan to increase their spending for trips and holidays in the future.

3 Pretentious Experience-Seekers

This segment includes the following lifestyle types: business, protest, pioneers, scout and citizens. This group consists of mainly young or middle-aged urban consumers (singles or young couples with children) with university degrees, working in middle or higher management positions or in private practice and enjoying high incomes.

They are realists trying to achieve a certain quality of life in a rather egocentric manner, but want to be part of a society in which a great number of people can enjoy leisure time and holidays. They are hedonistic consumers, focused on leisure and entertainment, always looking for innovations, and interested in high-tech products and sports achievements.

Motivation

These consumers are addicted tourists who have a variety of different expectations and motives. They love mobile, active holidays, and a rich menu of entertainments but as well as the cultural discovery of a country they also look to laze around on a sunny beach.

They love to travel in other countries to discover new landscapes, new views and different cultures. They want to see 'a little bit everywhere', watch, change their holiday destinations and have sports activities during their holidays.

This group is the most interested in long-distance travel. They love taking some days off during low season to visit a European capital or a famous museum or to participate in a music, theatre or film festival. They want to discover the Europe of the future and would take every

Figure B.2 **TYPOLOGY OF HOLIDAY CONSUMERS**

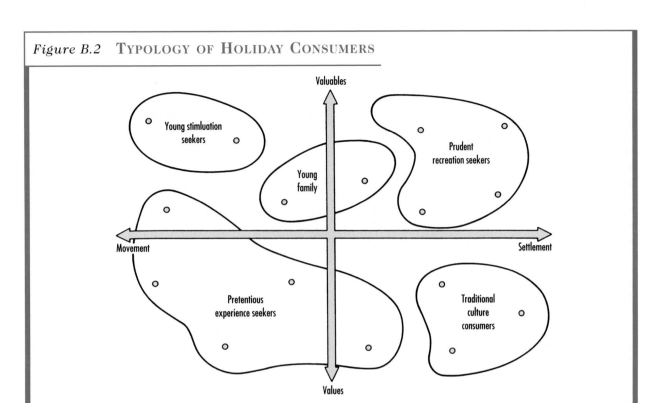

Adapted from Österreich Werbung (Hrsg); Marketing 2000, Wien; Österreichischer Wirtschaftsverlag 1991.)

opportunity to travel through a neighbouring country.

Behaviour

These travel consumers know most European countries and a couple of others outside Europe. They have much longer holidays than the average European; they take their holidays in several parts during summer and spread all over the year.

Transport

In general, they prefer taking their cars; that gives them most autonomy or independence, particularly when they have arrived at their destination. but they are also the best customers for business and long-distance air travel.

Organization

This is a group of rather autonomous customers, not much attracted by organized forms of travel. Reservations are made with the help of travel agencies. Club atmosphere is appreciated. But, most of all, holiday travel is planned individually, in particular when it takes place during low season.

Preferred leisure activities

Leisure orientation dominates the year: going out, meeting with friends, going to the theatre, to a concert, to see a film or to dine out. All sorts of sports activities are in. But they also love to read, hear music or do some artistic work. They watch little TV, carfully choosing the programme, but they see hi-fi and video use as valuable leisure activities. This segment also covers the highest share of amateur photographers, owning quite professional equipment and taking pictures most regularly.

Consumption outlook

This group is a major target for tourism. Many of its members plan to increase their spending for travel and holiday purposes. They also want to spend increasing amounts on leisure activities.

4 The Young Stimulation-Seekers

This segment includes the following life-style types: rockies and dandy. Both belong to the young urban population, often unmarried, students, workers or employees with middle to lower incomes. They live in flats, small houses or bedsits in the cities or in suburbs.

Motivation

Sun, beach and sea are the major ingredients for their holiday. To take a holiday means to enjoy privileged moments of leisure and relaxation.

The most important things are to enjoy life and to make a profit: take part in everything somehow, practise some sports activities and enjoy inactivity. Get away from the usual environment to increase the opportunities for happiness and relaxation. These consumers like to discover nature and new places, they enjoy attractions, amusement parks, new experiences and so far unknown activities, as well as entertaining sports. Dandies also are attracted by European capitals. They love to buy things there they cannot find at home. They often fancy trips throughout Europe but also to destinations further aways (such as the USA or the Caribbean).

Behaviour

They have not travelled much outside of their own country, but nevertheless they know some countries in Europe. Dandies also travel abroad to learn a language or to improve language skills. For that purpose they take their entire holiday allocation, mostly during summer. Some of them take weekend trips at any season. Because they have only limited resources, they mainly travel in their own country. But they are ready to take every opportunity to go on a long-distance trip.

Transport

They travel mainly by car, but they also take planes. From a good airline they expect: prices affordable for everybody; good organization; maintaining the flight schedule, and the possiblity of changing flight arrangements or cancelling.

Organization

They often rely on travel agents for the organization of their holiday, or they improvise as soon as they have arrived at their holiday destination. For short trips during the year, they prefer to travel without much planning and to look for accommodation at their destination.

Preferred leisure activities

During the year this group of people wants to live a good life. The most important thing is amusement: having a drink, going out with friends or practising some sports. Dandies, in particular, own the most sports equipment. they love to listen to music and to watch sports events on TV. Everything innovative attracts them. They are interested in hi-fi and video.

Rockies also see handicrafts and do-it-youself as acceptable leisure activity. They own simple photographic equipment and take pictures for fun.

Consumption outlook

Like most Europeans, Rockies want to increase their spending for travel and holidays. Dandies have clear plans of how to spend more and more for that purpose.

5 The Young Family

This segment of European holiday travel consumers includes the following lifestyle types: romantic and squadra. They are married couples of age 25 to 44, with children. They live in flats or small houses, mainly in suburbs or in small towns. Women are housewives or employees. Men are craftsmen, employees or workers with average income. These people search for stability and a certain quality of life.

The well-being of the family and the education of their children are of major importance to them. They strive to maintain their homes and to live pleasantly and safely. At the moment they consider spending much less than average for travel and holiday purposes; in fact, they spend significantly below average. There are many different leisure activities they spend their money on: books, CDs, tapes, going out to the threatre, a concert, the cinema and restaurant – but they have to make economies in all of them.

Motivation

During their main holiday time, above all, they want to rest and relax. The ideal formula reads: sun, beach, sea.

They practise lazing around, moving only very little after arriving at their holiday destination, and try to relax together with their family. Short trips during the year are made to get out in the country, to rest and to discover nature. Attractions and amusement parks attract them, too. It is most important to them to leave their usual environment without losing their anchor point and without changing their way of life.

They have not been to many countries so far. In general, they take rather short holidays and they do not have elaborate plans on where to travel during the next two years. Long-distance trips outside Europe do not mean much to them. For short trips they mainly stay in their own country because it is cheaper.

Transport

These consumers generally go on holiday by car. Because they do not have much experience with flights, their aspirations concerning an ideal airline are rather limited. Prices are very important to them, in particular special fares for families with children.

Organization

They highly value organized trips and all kinds of 'all-inclusive' packages for greater ease in travelling with their families. Romantics also choose private rooms for accommodation.

Table B.1 DISTRIBUTION OF CONSUMER LIFESTYLE TYPES OVER EUROPE

CONSUMER TYPE	NUMBER PER COUNTRY COMPARED TO EUROPEAN AVERAGE												
	A	D	CH	NL	B	GB	D	S	N	I	F	E	GR
Dandy	O	+	O	–	O	O	O	O	O	O	O	O	O
Business	O	O	O	–	O	O	O	O	O	O	–	–	+
Rockies	–	–	O	+	+	+	–	–	+	–	–	–	–
Squadra	–	–	–	–	–	O	O	–	–	+	O	+	O
Olividados	O	O	–	O	O	–	+	O	–	–	+	–	O
Romantic	+	+	O	–	–	+	O	+	O	O	–	O	–
Defence	–	–	–	–	–	+	+	O	–	+	O	O	+
Vigilante	O	O	O	+	O	O	O	–	–	O	O	+	–
Prudent	+	+	+	O	+	O	O	O	O	O	O	O	–
Protest	O	O	O	O	O	O	O	O	O	O	O	O	+
Pioneers	+	+	O	O	O	–	+	+	O	–	O	O	+
Scout	–	–	O	–	O	–	–	–	–	+	+	+	O
Citizen	O	O	O	O	+	–	O	–	O	+	+	+	+
Moralist	+	+	+	–	O	–	O	–	–	–	O	–	–
Gentry	O	–	O	O	O	O	+	+	+	–	O	+	–
Strict	+	O	+	+	+	+	–	O	O	–	–	+	–

+ = above average   O = average   – = below average
A = Austria   GB = Great Britain   I = Italy
D = Germany   D = Denmark   F = France
CH = Switzerland   S = Sweden   E = Spain
NL = Holland   N = Norway   GR = Greece
B = Belgium

Adapted from: Österreich Werbung (Hrsg.): Marketing 2000, Wien: Österreichischer Wirtschaftsverlag 1991.

Preferred leisure activities

These people are intensive TV consumers. They love to play with their children, play games or meet with friends. They generally practise very little sport (with the exception of the romantics who try to stay in good physical condition by practising aerobics or dance). But they love to watch sports events on TV. They are interested in video and hi-fi, only seldom taking pictures during holidays and at big family events.

Distribution of Lifestyle Types over Europe

The 16 lifestyle types are not equally distributed all over Europe. Table B.1 shows their distribution per country compared to the European average.

BUILDING AND SUSTAINING THE GLOBAL POSITION

Decisions concerning international marketing are taken on all levels of a company's management hierarchy. In this hierarchy of decisions, upper-level decisions constitute frameworks for decisions and actions on lower levels. Lower-level decisions and actions influence the conditions of a company's internal and operating environments which are to be considered in upper-level decision making. Depending on the size and extent of a company's internationalization, the decisions guiding the firm will be executed by different levels of management or by only a small group of company leaders. Top management's corporate policy and the basic strategic decisions concerning the markets to serve internationally, the competitive strategy to apply and how to allocate the firm's resources across businesses, functions and time constitute the general framework for lower-level decisions and actions to make the company reach the intended global strategic position (see Figure IV.1). The strategic

positioning of each business and its adaptation to local market needs as well as the market-entry modes and timing together constitute the strategic framework for managers who are responsible either for business processes, such as international brand or quality management, or for single business functions, such as advertising, database management, or warehousing. These managers have to develop functional or process-related policies, that is, another set of guidelines, indicating the room to manoeuvre for managers making operational plans and translating them into actions. In any case, the interrelatedness of different decision levels will have to be taken into account to ease implementation processes.

Marketing policies, plans and actions will have an important impact on a company's ability to build and sustain its intended global position. The central part of any company's marketing activities is the development and maintenance of an offer of goods and services which are attractive to

Figure IV.1   THE INTERRELATED HIERARCHY OF DECISION LEVELS IN INTERNATIONAL MARKETING

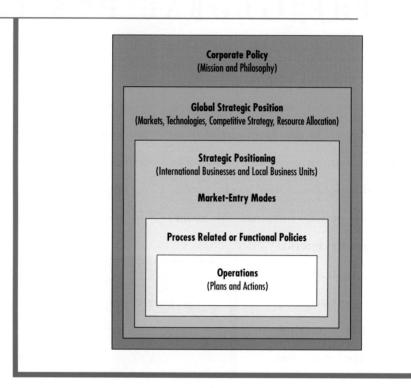

customers and important stakeholders. In most cases material (good) and immaterial (service) parts of the total product delivered are so strongly inter-related that they have to be managed together. Chapters 12 and 13 will show that international management of total products (goods and services) is even more demanding than in local business.

International distribution, marketing logistics and sales management are the subjects of Chapters 14, 15 and 16. They focus on how to ensure that the company's offer is made by a high-quality sales force so that market exchange can occur and customers' orders are executed in the right place at the right time. The international distribution and sales process not only demands attention to the choice and management of distribution channels fitting the intended local market position (Chapter 14). The firm must also manage the physical movement of goods and the local provision of services (Chapter 15) as well as the behaviour of salespeople which strongly influences the quality perception of customers concerning the company's offer (Chapter 16). Personal relationships between people working for the supplier and customers may exert a strong influence on the customers' perceptions of a total product's attractiveness. They have such a prominent place in many customers' evaluations of an offer that they have to be considered part of it. Relationship building and maintenance as part of international sales management are often central to successful international marketing.

As one might expect, communication between a company and its various stakeholders in an international environment has many hazards for the unwary marketer. Culture, legal regulations or the level of economic development have a major impact on what is suitable in international market communication and what is doomed to fail. Even familiar market communication techniques or media vary considerably across country-markets. Chapter 17 discusses the need for a communication policy to integrate the various communication activities of an internationally operating firm. Opportunities for pursuing a highly standardized approach to international market communication are analysed and contrasted with necessities for local adaptation.

Chapter 18 focuses on an important concern for international marketers: how to set prices and negotiate terms of payment that will help to make the company's offers even more attractive to potential customers and provide the firm with sufficient profit. Here again, international marketers face a wider set of issues than domestic marketers. They have to consider a whole range of additional risks which can be covered in various ways but at different costs; and they may be confronted with customers who are very much attracted by the company's offer but have no money to pay for it. Countertrade is discussed as a means to resolve such problems.

To apply all available marketing tools in an effective and efficient manner allowing the intended global strategic position to be reached, an international marketing plan has to be established. Chapter 19 presents the content of such a plan, and discusses the problems related to the development of the plan as well as methods to resolve those problems. Financial and managerial accounting issues to be considered for a presentation of the international marketing plan to top management or to financial institutions are also covered.

CHAPTER 12

INTERNATIONAL PRODUCT AND SERVICES MANAGEMENT: PRODUCT POLICY DECISIONS

INTERNATIONAL INCIDENT

Bongrain: Adapting the Product to Local Tastes

Bongrain, the French cheese giant, markets its unchanged French products internationally wherever they are accepted by customers. These products are liked by cheese consumers independent of their location. For example, soft cheeses such as Saint-Agur which is parsley flavoured and easily spread are well accepted all over Europe. Hard cheeses, Gouda, Manchego or Emmenthal style, which can be cut and adapted as snacks are also widely popular with European consumers. As a consequence, Bongrain has launched its Fol Epi brand, a very successful variation of Emmenthal.

But this standardized approach is not successful everywhere. Cheddar cheese is not popular outside the Anglo-Saxon part of the world. In Europe local differences in tastes which can be attributed to 52 culturally different regions, not always corresponding with country borders, are still very strong. In France cheese is served at the end of a meal, a unique use pattern when compared to most cultures. In Italy it is served after the salad course. In other countries, such as Germany or Holland, cheese is served for breakfast, as an appetizer or snack. In the USA it is more popular in salads and sandwiches. In China and Japan, eating cheese is not a common custom. International acceptance of local specialities is slow. As a consequence, Bongrain produces Mozzarella in Italy and Stilton in the UK.

Dairy products are generally positioned inside a 'triangle' which has its 'points', pleasure, healthiness and practicality. But the 'centre of gravity' changes from one country to another. Anglo-Saxons prefer practicality and healthiness (food is fuel). Germans put more emphasis on practicality and hygiene. Latins are more pleasure seekers. Bongrain's local subsidiaries, therefore, adapt the products to local preferences. They may propose different flavourings: Saint Moret has a flavour of chorizo in Spain where it is called San Millan, and Tartare got a flavour of paprika in Hungary. Saint-Albray has eight petals in Germany versus six in other countries. The core-product itself is hard to adapt. For quality reasons the balance of the recipe has to be respected. Taste can obviously be adapted to customer expectation, by small changes in ingredients, by selling the cheese at an earlier point in its ripening time, and by taking it back from the points of sale earlier (at a less ripe stage).

Source: 'Bongrain: la culture, plus fort que le marketing', *L'Entreprise*, No. 127, April 1996, p. 36.

INTERNATIONAL PRODUCT DECISIONS

The core of the marketing mix is the bundle of benefits offered by the company to the potential customers via its product. To satisfy the customers those benefits must be attractive and fulfil the customers' expectations. The other elements of the marketing mix – price, distribution and market communication – must be carefully managed as well, but they cannot compensate for a product that does not come up to the customers' desires. Therefore, positioning decisions are at the heart of product management: potential customers have to be carefully chosen. Product features as well as processes that are part of the product have to be selected in a way that ensures attractive differentiation recognized by those customers, in comparison to benefits offered by competitors' products.

When a company decides to go international, it must decide whether its products and product lines can be kept unchanged, or if they must be changed and to what degree. For example, if a Swedish producer of wooden windows and doors wants to enter the UK market, it has to find out if its products come up to the expectations of local customers, if the products need to be adapted, or if UK customers might be ready to change their expectations because of greater benefits provided by the Swedish products. Changes may be needed not only in the core-product itself. Customer expectations concerning customer service, warranties, packaging, width and depth of the product line, or brand image may be different in the UK compared to Sweden. The international marketer has to assess the amount of change needed to modify the existing product, or if it is necessary to develop new products. The marketer may have to create added features and will manage symbolic features, such as the brand, in a way to offer the most attractive bundle of benefits to customers in all served country-markets.

To be able to take the described decisions in an effective way, international marketers must first make sure they know exactly who are the customers or decision makers to be targeted. That is, the international marketer needs to know its customers closely before taking product management decisions. Chapter 7 has shown how secondary data about potential customers may be used for the assessment of various country-markets' attractiveness. Chapter 8 discussed the use of more detailed primary customer information for the purpose of segmenting a firm's product-market in the most attractive country-markets, and to determine the company's distinctive competencies in each of the most attractive market segments. In a general way the firm's customers have been determined by the intended global strategic position (Chapter 9) which defined the product-markets to be served. The positioning statement of the responsible business unit specifies the target customers (Chapter 11). But if the company is large, its business units will be responsible for more than one product. Therefore, target customers for each of the products may need to be specified before any marketing-mix decisions can be taken. The discussion in this chapter is based on the previously taken decisions and the data gathered for the purpose of taking them. It will focus on how international marketers react to different environments and product-related customer behaviour by standardizing part of their total products, adapting or even individualizing them (Figure 12.1).

The chapter starts with an overview of what may be the major driving forces of customers concerning an international marketer's product category, what the customers do with the product, and how their buying process is structured. Gathering that information, the marketer has to assess what constitutes its product seen from the customers' point of view. For that purpose a view of the product as a bundle of processes in which customers are more or less integrated, and as a bundle of material and immaterial results created by these processes, has proven to be useful. This view does not result in clearly

Figure 12.1 INTERNATIONAL PRODUCT AND SERVICES MANAGEMENT

The international product manager must know how similar or different potential customers are in the markets to serve. This information helps to determine the appropriate levels of integrability and immateriality of the firm's products. An international product policy has to be developed. This product policy serves as a guideline for decisions concerning the firm's product portfolio, its brands, and the management of the total product.

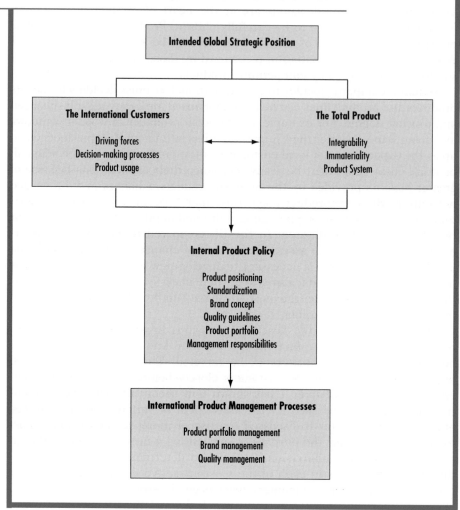

distinguishing between goods and services because every good has immaterial features, such as product information, and to a certain extent involves customers in its development, production or delivery process. But this view of the 'total product' opens an integrative perspective on how to market all kinds of products internationally.

In the following, an international product policy is to be developed. A firm's product policy statement contains guidelines for all product management processes to be conducted, that is, for product positioning, the intended level of standardization, branding, quality standards and product portfolio management. The product policy also determines the distribution of responsibilities among managers and management teams concerning those processes. Chapter 13 will focus on the specifics of international product management processes.

International Customers

Driving Forces

When searching for the major driving forces of customer behaviour in international markets, a basic differentiation has to be made between consumers, businesses and public administrations or governments as customers of the firm. The primary distinguishing characteristic of business customers compared to consumers is that they purchase products for the purpose of creating other products. Whether the product is a typewriter, mainframe computer, maintenance service or software, all business products will be used in the production or offering of some other product. The core-product itself may be identical to a consumer product. A PC, for example, may be purchased as either a consumer good (to be used by the final customer) or a business product (to be used in an office). What differs are the additional features and the processes that create the value for the customer. A consumer might, for example, wish to get the PC at a very low price with some basic software for free and regular updates. A business customer might be more interested in the PC's fit into the existing network and its ergonomic quality.

Like consumers, organizational customers – procurement managers in companies or agents in public administrations – buy to gain certain benefits. But for a professional buyer the benefit sought is less personal. It is mainly a solution to a business (or administrative) problem – a way to achieve a business (political) objective, such as improving productivity on the shop floor, lowering costs by purchasing less expensive supplies, or acquiring new technology to produce a superior product. Business demand is ultimately derived from consumer demand for particular products. As a consequence, it tends to fluctuate more widely than the demand for consumer products. For example, auto makers like Ford use forecasts of consumer demand for cars in making decisions regarding their own purchases. If Ford and its competitors all forecast a long-term increase in the demand for cars, they will all want to buy the needed products at the same time. This will cause demand for transfer equipment, steel, tyres, glass, brake systems, and so forth to increase sharply. On the other hand, if all the major auto makers forecast a decrease in consumer demand for automobiles, they will cut back on their purchases of raw materials, parts and systems. This will sharply decrease the demand for automobile-related business products.

Purchasing agents and buying teams in business firms are judged by the extent to which their decisions contribute to the accomplishment of the company's objectives. Although there are some differences among business buyers in different locations, the fact that all corporations need to remain competitive and profitable creates fairly similar product evaluation criteria among business buyers throughout the world, such as performance capabilities, reliable delivery, availability and price.

Decision-Making Process

Because business and public administration customers take their purchase decisions to fulfil organizational purposes, the decision-making process tends to be more formalized than a consumer buying process. While the buying process may vary for different products, organizations and cultures, the steps illustrated in Figure 12.2 are common to many business and government buying decisions. The buyer first recognizes a need, then determines product specifications, then searches for information and evaluates suppliers, and finally generates a purchase order. Feedback occurs through performance evaluation.

For a routine purchase, such as office supplies, need recognition may occur when someone notices that supplies are running low. In the case of a more capital-intensive product, such as a more powerful PC system, the need may become apparent when staff members recognize that they cannot get adequate marketing information using the existing system.

Consumers are more or less involved with the product they buy and with the purchasing process, depending on their perceived importance and the risk involved. The international marketer, therefore, must evaluate the necessity and the firm's capability to adapt the presentation of the product and the processes personally involving the consumers. For example, the National Basketball Association of the USA shows kids in Asia how to play the game, especially in countries such as China where television penetration is not as deep as for example in South Korea. In China, the NBA, in cooperation with Nike Inc., the international marketer of sports shoes based in the USA, has revamped basketball courts in major cities, using remilled shoes to create a spongy playing surface. The partners are also working on shooting competitions and clinics where teenagers can learn to play the game.[1]

Business and government customers are generally at least highly involved with the purchasing process. They are ready to search for and process more information than the average consumer. But they also need more personal interaction to be gained and retained as customers. Therefore, Deutsche Morgan Grenfell, the London-based investment-banking arm of Germany's Deutsche Bank AG, is investing high amounts of capital in the reorganization of its Asia-Pacific operations. Besides expanding its Tokyo workforce, the bank made new appointments at the regional head office in Singapore, and will have new equity operations in India, Sri Lanka and Vietnam.[2] Additionally, governments or public administrations may be strongly interested not only in the product to purchase but in technology transfer or in countertrade opportunities (see Chapter 18). In such cases, the marketer will need the capability to structure its offer accordingly.

Product Usage

An in-depth knowledge of what consumers use a product for may be extremely helpful in designing the customer value creation process. For example, Scott Wallace, the owner of Wallace Theater Corp. which has 101 multiplex cinema screens in Hawaii, Nevada and California, opened a multiscreen cinema on Tutuila Island in American Samoa in 1995. He is convinced that his competition is the church. But consumers are not allowed to eat in church. At Nu'uuli Place Cinema they are offered local favourites like Mochi Crunch, a rice cracker, and dried squid chunks as well as nachos, popcorn and soda. Revenues in 1995 were USD1.5 million and operating margins slightly above 40 per cent.[3]

In most cases consumers buy products for their own use or for the use of a family member. Organizational buyers mostly buy for others. Their emotional participation in the buying process, therefore, is less pronounced or at least different because it is derived from organizational objectives.

Figure 12.2 ORGANIZATIONAL BUYING DECISION MODEL

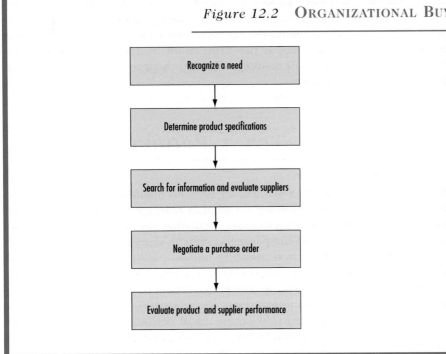

The organizational buying decision process is complex and varies each time. But most authorities agree that the basic steps illustrated in this diagram describe that decision process.

Source: Cravens, D.W. and R.B. Woodruff (1986) *Marketing*, Reading, Mass: Addison-Wesley, p. 163. For an examination of the generalizability of a similar model across the United States and Europe, see Woodside, A.G. and E.J. Wilson (1985) 'Supplier Choice Strategies in Industrialized Nations', *International Marketing Review*, Winter, 75–79. Reprinted by permission of Addison Wesley Longman Ltd.

Governments and public administrations make their purchases in fields such as defence and public protection, infrastructure, health care, education and tourism to fulfil their public mission. Purchases for their own use are also derived from that mission. Business customers use a product for the production of their company's own product. Raw materials, parts and systems, machinery, maintenance, computer or consulting services are needed for general management, research and development, production or marketing processes. Depending on the importance of a product for the core competence of the business customer, the international marketer will either be able to take over responsibility for entire parts of the customer's value-added chain or may need to closely follow the exact specifications of the customer in order to stay in business. For example, an industrial services firm taking over all maintenance activities for the equipment of electric generator manufacturers may have full responsibility but also the freedom to do the job its way, whereas a supplier of preformed steel sheets for car-making customers will have to deliver exactly according to technical and logistical specifications.

Compared to marketers selling to business firms or public administrations, international consumer product marketers particularly have to watch the individual meanings of their products. The meaning of a product to its buyers or users may be based on its functionality, but also on the personal joy the possession of the product can provide, the personal relationships and social belongingness it can help to express, and the product's ability to represent the identity of the customer. Each customer constructs the meaning of a product in a situation-specific way depending on personal experiences, social relations, and situational circumstances which seem relevant at the moment. That is, the variety of potential meanings of a marketer's product in international markets is caused by more than different cultural environments. It is also a result of varying individual product perceptions in different situations. Therefore, the marketer must carefully assess the potential meanings of its product if the firm wants to actively shape its value creation processes and their results, and target them to individuals or specific consumer benefit segments.

The Total Product

A product can be a good, a service, an idea, an organization, a person, or a combination of those, depending on what is marketed to the potential customers. In any case a product is more than what the customer can touch or see. For example, in China the pager has seen an unexpected market success. At the end of 1995, there were some 14 million paging subscribers in China. Resourceful Chinese use the pager not as an accessory to the phone, but as a sort of primitive substitute for it. The conventional phone system has a penetration rate of some three to four lines for every 100 Chinese, meaning that even if you find a phone, the other party might not be in a position to receive your call. Only the well-heeled business person can surmount this annoyance with a costly cellular phone. So native genius stepped into the breach. Chinese paging subscribers spontaneously devised a method of carrying code books, allowing them to interpret numeric messages flashed on their pagers: 75416, for example, might mean sell gravel at 6,500 yuan a ton or bring home a cabbage for dinner. Today's pagers have alphanumeric displays that read out short bursts of Chinese characters, eliminating the need for number codes. They also come in stylish packages, priced so that a moderately successful worker can afford one: from about USD120 for a basic model to USD220 for one with a Chinese character readout.[4]

As the example shows, from the customer perspective a product consists of a bundle of tangible (the pager) and intangible (ability to communicate, prestige) results which are created by processes that more or less integrate the customer. In the case of the pager, its production process is neither visible nor able to be influenced by the customers (it could be, for example, if the customers were allowed to compose their individual pagers from a menu of options concerning colour, design, and display features). To create the expected customer value of the pager, however, the development of a code of communication strongly integrates the customers in a process that is needed to allow the use of their pagers as a kind of telephone. Consequently, a product can be conceived as a bundle of processes and a bundle of results stemming from these processes through which value is created for a customer.

The customer of a product may be more or less integrated in the value creation process. For example, to get their hair styled, consumers all over the world must be present during the production process and must leave their hair to the skill of the hairdresser whether its 'shop' is a sidewalk in the streets of Xian, China or a fine boutique in Milan, Italy, whereas the production process of a kitchen machine by French SEP does not involve future customers at all. They are only indirectly integrated in the value creation process through consumer research during the design stage and become directly involved at the very end of the marketing process, when they buy the machine at a retailer.

The product as a bundle of results stemming from its value creation process can have more or less tangible attributes. A vacation in a New Zealand ski resort, for example, contains elements such as the slopes, the hotel room, and the food in the restaurants. All of them can be physically experienced. At the same time the total vacation product also consists of intangible elements such as the friendliness of service personnel, the waiting time at the lifts, or the kind of 'people around'.

Level of Customer Integration

The chain of activities by which a company creates value for its customers can be conceived as a series of processes that the firm conducts more or less autonomously. From the creation of a product idea through product development, production and sales, however, there is always some minimum integration of the customer in this value-added process. All products, consumer and business/government goods as well as all kinds of services, can be positioned on a continuum ranging from highly integrative to highly autonomous according to their added-value processes (see Figure 12.3). Depending on the kind of interaction with the customer, where in the process customers are integrated, how often, and to what level of intensity, international product management decisions will differ.

The integration of the customer can take the form of personnel involvement, for example, when a specialist at Ochsner Hospital in New Orleans, Louisiana transplants a kidney to a Brazilian customer. But customer integration can also take place by the contribution of an object, such as a PC in the case of Otten, an Austrian producer of printed textiles, when using the hotline of its international production software provider. In other instances customers provide a right or some information to the value-creation process. For example, when the Boston Consulting Group gets an order to develop a new organizational structure for Basler Versicherungen, one of the biggest internationally operating Swiss insurance companies, the outcome of their work highly depends on the information provided by the company's personnel.

If the supplier and customer of a product need to have direct contact to produce customer value, the product is bound to a certain location. Such products cannot be traded and therefore cannot be exported. Internationalization of business in such cases can only be achieved through international multiplication of self-operated or foreign-operated production sites. On the other hand, if the contact between marketer and customer may be time and space-wise decoupled via some intermediary (for example, a retailer) or media (such as a computer), the product can be traded and exported. Banking services, for example, which for most of their history were bound to the location of a bank and its outlets, could only be internationalized by opening up subsidiaries or cooperating closely with local banks. Since then, electronic banking has made banking services independent of specific locations, and therefore exportable.

For some products, direct customer contact is limited to the initial phase of product development and production or to the last phase of the customer value creation process. But customer integration may occur in any phase. For instance, when Danish customers of sailing yachts provide the engineers of a Norwegian shipyard with particular information concerning their expected

---

Figure 12.3 THE PRODUCT AS A BUNDLE OF PROCESSES AND RESULTS

Each total product consists of processes which are needed to create customer value and of results which are the outcome of those processes. The total product must be differently managed depending on how much the customer is integrated in the value creation processes and to what extent the results of those processes are material or immaterial.

Source: Adapted from Engelhardt, W.H., M. Kleinaltenkamp, and M. Reckenfelderbäumer (1993) 'Leistungsbündel als Absatzobjekte', *zfbf*, 45(5), 417.

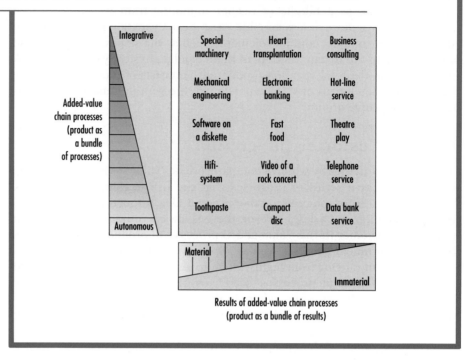

---

use of the ships – for example, winning an international race versus entertaining customers on a cruise – those customers take part in the development process of their product. The procurement manager of a food production company, such as US-based Kraft Foods, who specifies the material to be used in the production of plastic trays, participates in the purchasing process of the supplier. The UK buyer of a Motorola portable cellular phone who indicates the colour of the phone and the specific features expected when ordering the phone via the Internet is partly integrated in Motorola's production process. A French customer of Sweden's furniture giant IKEA is integrated in the company's marketing process when she describes the family's living room, the family size, structure, and living habits to the salesperson, picks up the bought furniture, transports it to her home and sets it up there. Even for consumer products produced and marketed to a global mass market, such as Sensodyne toothpaste or Pampers nappies, for which autonomous processes dominate the customer value creation, at least some communication has to take place in the final phase between the customer and sales personnel or a computer.

The parts of the value creation process which take place in the presence of the customers are above their line of visibility. They strongly influence the customers' perception of product quality and their satisfaction with the product. The invisible remainder of the process is locally independent. It can be performed wherever is best for the supplier, if the parts or elements of the total product produced in a distant location can be physically or virtually transferred to the place of consumption or use. For example, for the consumer of a pizza delivery service, the order-taking process via the phone and the end of the delivery process are above the line of visibility. Where the pizza is made and how it is transported to the customer is up to the producer as long as the delivery time is short enough and the pizza looks nice and tastes good.

Products need to be managed differently depending on their interaction intensity between customers and the supplier. The higher the interaction intensity, the more customer satisfaction with the product and customer retention will depend on how interactions take place. It becomes increasingly important for the firm to manage its customer interaction processes; but it also becomes increasingly difficult because social relations are hard to control. In international marketing the firm may try socialization, that is constant training in and compliance with strong company rules of behaviour overlaying personal rules of behaviour. Companies such as Kentucky Fried Chicken or McDonald's have successfully trained their personnel to ensure a certain standard of customer interaction independent of the location of the store. But even these companies, with rather strong internal rules of behaviour, have to leave some freedom for customizing those rules to requirements of local cultures. KFC in Japan, for example, adapts how customers are greeted to Japanese customs, including bowing to the customer after the sale to show the company's appreciation for the purchase.

Material and Immaterial Results

The result of a firm's value creation process is a product. Such a product can be more or less immaterial (Figure 12.3). Even a physical product, such as a Compaq computer, has immaterial features, for example its ease of use or its brand name which stands for a certain reliability. Services, such as transpacific air travel offered by Korean Air, have a much higher degree of immateriality. In this example, they also have some material features associated with them, for example the size of the seats, the number of rows, and the quality of food served during the flight. But there need not be any material results of a company's value creation process. Telephone service provided by a company such as France Telecom, for example, or a show by the US-based Harlem Globetrotters basketball team, do not have any material features provided to customers.

For international product management, it is critical to remember that customers may be attracted to a product by both material and immaterial features. Customers do not evaluate and choose just a good (a physical product) or a service. They buy a bundle of benefits which they expect to enjoy through the consumption or use of the total product, that is, the combination of material and immaterial features offered by a provider. Coca-Cola, for example, is more than just a soft drink. In several languages, 'Coke is It'. This slogan recognizes that coke is not only a physical good but also offers refreshment, enjoyment, entertainment, and represents the 'American Way of Life', all of which are immaterial features but are part of the total product.

Customers of an international advertising agency such as US-based Grey Advertising expect the agency to do more than produce international and local campaigns which reach their objectives. They also value personal contacts with a known partner in different parts of the world and the standard application of tools they have experience with. In addition, the name of the agency and its country of origin as well as special references may evoke positive associations in the managers who decide which partner to choose for market communication purposes.

Products conceived as combinations of material and immaterial results of a firm's customer value creation process are not limited to goods or services.

Ideas (which are immaterial only), people and organizations can also be marketed internationally. For example, social issues such as population control can be marketed in an attempt to change people's ideas about family-planning practices. To increase the attractiveness of population control measures, for example, in many cases material incentives were added to the idea, such as portable radios for people willing to accept surgery. Politicians, such as several candidates for the General Secretary of the United Nations from African countries in 1996, were internationally marketed by their governments, but also by interested foreign governments. When social organizations such as UNICEF or the Red Cross use marketing techniques for international fund raising, the organizations themselves often are the products 'sold'. But in any case, seen from the customer perspective, the offered product consists of a bundle of benefits which can be gained from the product's material and immaterial features.

The Product System

Products are bundles of more or less integrative customer value creation processes and bundles of more or less immaterial results of such processes. Both processes and results interactively influence the benefits customers derive from the total product. The total product can therefore be conceived as a system which contains elements as described in Figure 12.4.

Elements constituting a total product are the core-product, additional features expected by the potential customers, features added by the marketer to increase the total product's attractivity, and symbolic features. The core-product is the starting point of a potential market transaction. In certain cases it might be sufficient to provide the core-product. For example, when a well-informed person searches for an overview of potential forms of capital investment offered by an international bank, he or she may be satisfied with the information provided by the bank's homepage on the Internet. In most cases, however, the potential customers expect more than the core-product to regard an offer as relevant. The investor might, for example, firmly expect to be personally informed about the choices offered.

Potential customers tend to have different expectations depending on their knowledge of and experience with existing offers. Consequently, in international marketing the features expected by potential customers from different country-markets vary in composition and importance. Internorm, Europe's second-largest manufacturer of doors and windows based in Austria, for example, found expectations of Spanish customers concerning technical standards such as cold and noise resistance as well as workmanship to be very different from its German and Austrian customers. The reasons for those differences in expectations are not only due to the climatic conditions of the countries and the varying style of living; they are also a result of the existing product offers consumers are acquainted with in their own markets.

The international marketer must decide how important it is to adapt the firm's product to the existing expectations in the served markets. The need for adaptation will depend on the customers' willingness to trade off some expected features for unexpected 'added' features (see Figure 12.4). When introducing its Lexus model in the USA, Toyota, for example, offered its potential customers a car looking very much like a Mercedes but not providing the same prestige. Toyota not only counteracted this lack with a lower price, they also offered two weeks of trials, and offered to deliver the ordered car to the home of the customers and to programme the electronically

---

Figure 12.4 THE TOTAL PRODUCT SYSTEM

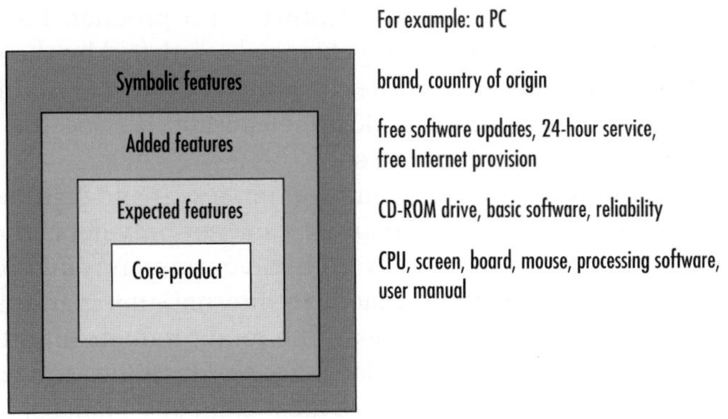

For example: a PC

Symbolic features — brand, country of origin

Added features — free software updates, 24-hour service, free Internet provision

Expected features — CD-ROM drive, basic software, reliability

Core-product — CPU, screen, board, mouse, processing software, user manual

A total product consists of the core-product, additional features expected by the potential customers, added features and symbolic features the supplier can provide to increase the total product's attractiveness, and the processes leading to those features.

---

adaptable driver's seat for various family members in advance. All those were added features not expected by but very welcome to the American customers. On the other hand, when Internorm, the Austrian window producer, tried to convince its potential Spanish customers that higher technical standards and resulting energy savings – also not expected by the customers – would justify a higher price for windows and doors, they failed.

International marketers increasingly offer product features added to the features expected by customers in a local market to differentiate their products attractively from existing competitors. Ermenildo Zegna, the Italian menswear maker, for example, offers clients who buy a Zegna suit an 'idea card' that entitles them to all sorts of privileges: once a year for a two-year period, the suit will be cleaned and, if needed, repaired; should the suit be stolen or lost, the company will replace it at 50 per cent off and the client is entitled to a 50 per cent discount on his son's first Zegna suit.[5]

When the potential customers are rather affluent relative to the price of a product or when they perceive the offered products as being largely similar, emotional attraction becomes more important in their buying decision. The symbolic features of a product can be decisive. Car buyers all over the world, for example, will always watch the price category and will expect certain additional services. But when the decision regarding a price category has been taken, very often symbolic features such as the brand, country of origin, status symbol, or the signal of belonging to a specific social group become important. Why would anybody buy a Ferrari despite its high price if it were not for the emotional benefit of the product?

INTERNATIONAL PRODUCT POLICY

International product managers must be aware that their customers may be attracted by different features at all levels of the product system as well as by the processes that create those features. Depending on cultural preferences, the specifics of the local environment, and competitive offers, the potential customers of a product may not only have varying expectations but may also derive different benefits from the same processes and features, or the same benefits from different processes and features of a product. For example, a Vietnamese owner of a Honda motorcycle may be satisfied by the opportunity to buy petrol bottled in the back corner of a hut. A UK owner of the same bike may expect his petrol station to tank up, clean and service the motorcycle while he is buying a soft drink in the shop.

Because the importance and meaning of processes and features constituting a product from the customers' point of view not only depend on personal predispositions but also on influences from the customers' environments, the variety of product management decisions in international marketing tends to be much broader than in local business. The total products of internationally operating firms must be adaptable to local needs. Flexibility and variety, however, strongly contrast with the desire of most company managers to keep the complexity of their product features and processes low. To avoid unnecessary complexity and resulting cost, an international product policy has to be developed (Figure 12.5). It is based on the intended global strategic position of the firm and a detailed analysis of potential international customers' driving forces, decision making and total product usage. The international product policy provides guidelines for all product management processes to be conducted – product positioning, intended degree of product standardization, branding and quality standards, and product portfolio management. The product policy also determines the distribution of responsibilities among managers and management teams concerning those processes.

Product Positioning

A company's international product positioning defines the global differentiation of its products from their major competitors. That is, the central benefit of each product is to be determined independently of the country-markets to be served. For polaroid cameras the central benefit could be, for example, the instant delivery of the picture; for Cartier watches it could be the image transferred to the customer wearing the product. The local target group(s) and the adaptations needed to produce the central benefit do not need to be defined. Even the brand name used locally may be up to the local managers. The UK's Unilever, for example, marketed a product which was variously called Kuschelweich in Germany, Snuggles in the USA, Huggy in Australia, Coccolino in Italy and Cajoline in France. But the primarily emotional benefits offered were the same everywhere: security, trust, softness and affection.[6] Because of the rising mobility of customers in many countries, such a formulation of product positioning has proven to be more useful than a detailed definition of product features accompanied by total freedom of communicative differentiation. Customers becoming aware of strongly changed presentations of 'their' product from one country to another do not appreciate such differences.

To provide the central benefit defined in the product positioning statement to individual customers in various country-markets, adaptation of product features or of processes which result in those features may be needed. Not only are the cultural, economic and legal environments of served country-markets different, but individual customer expectations and needs vary continuously depending on given circumstances. Such differences have made

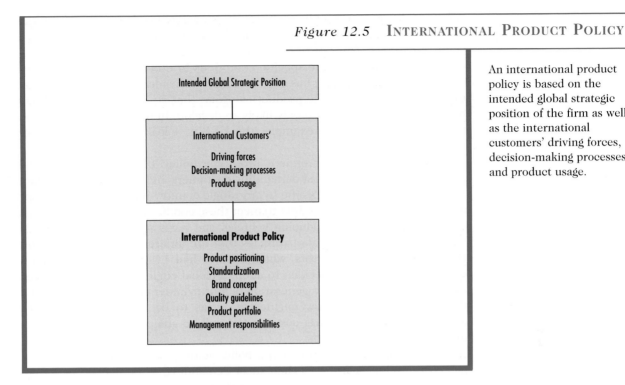

Figure 12.5   INTERNATIONAL PRODUCT POLICY

An international product policy is based on the intended global strategic position of the firm as well as the international customers' driving forces, decision-making processes and product usage.

many companies adapt their product positioning to local market characteristics. Nestlé, for example, uses the brand name Bolino to offer its instant soups to young French singles as a snack. In Germany they call the product Maggi 5 Minuten Terrine and position it as nutritious and balanced food for 30 to 40 year olds. And in Switzerland the same product is marketed under the brand name Quick Lunch as a fast meal young people can enjoy with their mothers' consent.[7] However, any change in existing processes or the design of a product has an effect on its costs. In many cases the costs of a product increase with the number and diversity of adaptations to local or even individual particularities. Therefore, the international product manager must define guidelines to what extent the firm's products should be standardized, locally adapted, or even individualized.

Standardization.   To gain a clear competitive advantage, a company operating internationally must develop products that are more attractive to customers than those of their competitors and can be provided for lower costs. Economies of scale in production and marketing can bring down the price of mass-produced products so much that many customers are willing to forgo their individuality and settle for standardized products. Thus, Japan's Honda was able to market a small motorcycle to a worldwide market, including the Americas, the EU and the fast-developing economies of East Asia, that appealed to the basic need for transportation at a much lower price than local competitors. In the USA, for example, Honda took share away from Harley-Davidson, which had followed a purely domestic strategy.

Basically, international marketers have three ways to standardize their products: product extension, the premium prototype approach, and a global common denominator policy.[8] Product extension involves the use of the product presentation developed for a single country-market in all other served country-markets. This policy can be justified if the reason for it is not ethnocentric or ignorance of the specific conditions in other markets. It is a suitable policy if management has good reasons to consider the reference market to be a lead-market for the product category, that is, a market which shows how demand in other markets is likely to develop. In the field of information technology products, for example, the USA is a lead-market for all other countries in the world.

When choosing the premium prototype policy of standardization, the marketer identifies the most demanding customers and conditions of product use – which may not be specific to any single country-market – and develops an appropriate standard product to meet these conditions. For example, in its effort to cut costs by producing vehicles and parts for markets worldwide instead of making an array of vehicles that are different for each continent, Detroit-based General Motors, which in 1995 had 12 different types of four-cylinder engines alone, decided to adopt a global engine policy. GM invested USD1.3 billion to develop a generation of four-cylinder engines for use around the world.[9] This will allow engineering costs to be reduced dramatically, driving a hard line on parts costs as GM will be able to deal with a smaller number of suppliers.

The major problem with such a policy is that many customers may not need the product features of their most demanding peers or may live in environments with lower quality and performance standards. They may be unwilling to pay for a level of performance that seems exaggerated to them. As a consequence the cost savings from standardization may be eaten up by the lower margins.

The goal of a global common denominator policy is to define an international product-market which contains customers that can be served with a standardized product. Such standardization is possible as long as functional benefits dominate the customers' perceptions, or the product is similarly used across cultural environments. Examples of product categories where functional benefits dominate in most customer segments are PCs, software, camcorders, calculators, and suitcases. SAP, based in Walldorf, Germany, for example, which has a market share of one-third of all business administration computer programmes sold worldwide, leading Dutch Baan and US firms such as Oracle, SSA and Peoplesoft, sells standard software packages. Their implementation necessitates the adaptation of the customer firms to the features of the product.[10] The Culture box gives an example of a consumer product for which a common denominator policy seems applicable.

A global common denominator policy may also work for customer segments containing a large share of highly mobile early adopters who have experienced a product in one country, want to be able to use it in others, and present the product to other customers as highly attractive. This, for instance, may have been the reason for the early success of Club Méditerranée, the French vacation resort company. They started with highly standardized resorts in various parts of the globe which attracted highly mobile consumers who looked for an enjoyable but predictable vacation environment in a variety of destinations.

Finally, for some products such as pop music, ethnic food or fashion clothes, adaptation would be counterproductive. As the Strategy box shows, their major benefit stems from the non-adaptedness of the product. The

CULTURE BOX

Citibank Blitzes Asia

FROM BOMBAY TO JAKARTA, TAIPEI TO SEOUL, Bangkok to Manila, plastic is proliferating in Asia at a terrific pace. Outlets accepting Visa cards increased by 700,000, to 3.6 million in the two years to 1995.

Citibank identified a global consumer who behaves quite similarly wherever he is: They dine out, go to concerts and movies, take vacations, and buy consumer durables and clothing. Even though they may not all be Westernized, they all have Western spending habits. But not the Western default habits: Citibank's loss rate on cards in Asia is just half of the 4 per cent industry norm in the USA.

There is a status and prestige in holding plastic. Plastic is a payment instrument, but it is also increasingly a lifestyle product. A typical Citibank credit card ad, airing on television in Singapore, features a young Asian couple traveling to Paris, Spain, and New Orleans, staying in elegant hotels, driving fancy cars, sipping champagne and eating sumptuous dinners. Few of Citibank's real-life customers fit the image, but they evidently like to identify with it. In Asia, getting a Citibank card is like gaining admission to a club.

Source: Tanzer, A. (1996) 'Citibank blitzes Asia', *Forbes*, 6 May, p. 44.

marketer should not overlook, however, the fact that even for such products some adaptation may be well accepted by local customers. Mexican restaurants in the USA or in Europe, for example, are better off serving their food not exactly the way it would be served in the home country.

Adaptation. Product standardization does not work everywhere. For example, when Snapple, the US new-age beverage, was introduced in Japan in 1994 without any adaptation to suit local tastes, thousands of stores stocked peach-flavoured iced tea, pink lemonade and other Snapple variations. But by the end of 1995 Snapple sales had fallen to 120 000 bottles a month from a monthly 2.4 million bottles a year earlier. In January 1996 Quaker Oats, the US-based owner of the brand, stopped shipping Snapple drinks to Japan. It had become clear that Japanese consumers loathe some of the very traits that made Snapple popular, at least for a time, in the USA: the cloudy appearance of the teas, the sweet fruit-juice flavourings – and all that *stuff* floating in the bottles.[11]

Even the most careful determination of the global product-market to serve and the choice of a well-defined customer segment often does not necessarily avoid product adaptation to local customer needs and the demands of the macro-environment. For example, Procter & Gamble's Vidal Sassoon shampoos and conditioners contain a single fragrance worldwide, with variations only in the amount: less in Japan, where subtle scents are preferred, and more in Europe. Packages of Ariel detergent look the same all over Eastern Europe, but they are printed in 14 languages, from Latvian to Lithuanian.[12]

Chapter 2 discussed various factors of influence on the need for

STRATEGY BOX

Tea

for Taro

CARON COOPER OPENED HER FIRST TEA SHOP IN TOKYO in 1994 to sell the English tea ceremony in Japan. In partnership with Beazer, a British construction company, she modelled the shop on the one that Ms Cooper already had been running in Nettleton Shrub, a cosy English village in Wiltshire: cobbled floors, old oak beams, red-and-white checked table cloths, lace wherever possible. The tea was supplied by a venerable firm with the finest Raj pedigree. The jam was made from Ms Cooper's own recipe. The scones were made from special flour shipped from England because Japanese flour is too "heavy".

Ms Cooper knew her market. Her seven-bedroom hotel put up 1,200 Japanese tourists visiting Bath a year. Ms Cooper's book on Wiltshire had sold 12,000 copies in Japan.

Surely Japan's Ministry of Agriculture and Fisheries had blocked Ms Cooper's plans to import clotted cream, calling it a health hazard. But without the stuff, insisted Ms Cooper, a real British cream tea was impossible. Happily there was a way around this obstacle. Jersey cows, the only sort whose milk is good enough for clotted cream, roam Japan's northern island of Hokkaido. So far nobody on the island knew the trick of making clotted cream. But with the help of Britain's Department of Trade and Industry, Ms Cooper found an expert clotter to teach Hokkaido's farmers.

Source: Adapted from 'Tea for Taro', *The Economist*, 3 April 1993, p. 72.

---

adaptation coming from the product-market's macro- and business environments and the internal environment of the firm as well as the product itself. For example, the basic concentrate of Orangina, a French soft drink, is produced in a factory in the South of France, from where it is exported all over Europe. The soft drink is distributed in all markets using the same strategy: it is first sold in coffee shops before it is presented to consumers in supermarkets. All over Europe the logo, the recipe and the price are the same. But the positioning of the brand needed some adaptations. Whereas in France the product is a French soft drink for young adults, it has become an international brand for 13 to 18 year olds in other countries. And different sensitivity to environmental concerns forced Orangina to be sold in glass deposit bottles or recyclable plastic bottles in Northern Europe, whereas in the southern parts of the continent non-recyclable bottles can be used.[13] As the examples of Microsoft's MS-DOS and Sony's VHS video standard have shown, however, a company operating globally may be able to set its own standards in a product category which is fairly new and has yet to develop norms. In the European Union the 'home-country rule' is applied. That is, (with some exceptions) imports from member countries cannot be forbidden as long as the product meets the norms of the country of origin.

For the international marketer to enjoy many of the benefits of product standardization and, at the same time, respond to the adaptation demands of local markets, product modification can be applied. A modified product is one where the impact of the changes made in the product's features has a relatively minor influence on the firm's cost situation and marketing efficiency.

Basically, there are two product modification policies to choose from: modular modification and the core-product approach.[14]

An international marketer who opts for a **modular modification policy** has to develop a standard range of product components usable worldwide which can be assembled in a variety of configurations. Such components can be physical products but also immaterial features and processes. Efficiency is likely to be greatest when the physical components are mass-produced at single locations, immaterial features and processes are highly standardized, and the number of variants of each is strictly limited. For example, Benton Harbor, US-based Whirlpool Corporation mass-produces the physical components of its high-end European Bauknecht brand products, uses pan-European advertising to assure its standardized positioning, but modifies trade marketing activities around promotion and merchandising, and the day-to-day pricing activities with trade partners.[15]

A **core-product policy** of international product adaptation requires the design of a standard core-product which can be locally adapted by adding different features or processes. For example, US-based Massey-Fergusson can develop a standard tractor for agricultural use which is designed to operate under various climatic and topographic conditions, and which additionally can be equipped with special components adapting the standard product to its specific use. Budget, the US-based international rental car company, as another example, can use the same basic operations system all over the world, specifically adapting the kinds of cars offered to local customers.

Individualization. Both product standardization and product adaptation policies are based on the idea that strategically determined global product-markets can be split into well-defined customer segments which in turn can be served with internationally standardized or locally adapted products. However, increasing global competition has made it difficult for many companies located in highly industrialized countries to rely on cost leadership to sell internationally standardized products at a competitive price. Such companies may be forced to improve their competitive market position by increasing the value their products on offer to customers. For the individual customer, most added value comes from an increase in the personal benefits derived from a product. But even products carefully adapted to local conditions represent an average that is offered to the 'average' customer of the selected market segment. As a result, there is a gap between the company's offering and what each customer expects. When the pressure of competition increases, the international marketer must try to close this gap.

International product individualization seems to be a potential solution. That is, the marketer needs to treat every single customer as his or her own market segment with specific requirements that must be fulfilled. To do this, the international marketer will first have to determine the points of common uniqueness, that is, to find out where the potential customers generally differ in their needs, expected benefits, usage or consumption behaviour. To get a complete picture, the product features have to be considered as well as all processes creating customer value. From this analysis the marketer can decide which features and processes to individualize and at which stage in the value creation process – during product design, production, delivery or use – to provide the greatest customer value at the lowest possible cost.

Individualization can be achieved in one of the following four ways: adaptive, cosmetic, autonomous or collaborative.[16] When customers want a product to perform in different ways on different occasions, the company may choose an **adaptive individualization policy**. That is, the company offers one standard product that is designed in a way that allows users to alter it themselves. For example, software applications have the built-in technical potential to be adapted to the needs of individual customers by the customers themselves. Car seats, fashion watches or home shopping services may accommodate different users having different needs at different times. Customers independently derive their own individual value from the standard product because it allows multiple permutations changing the product's functionality and/or its emotional value.

Because it is the product itself, rather than the supplier, that interacts with the customer, adaptive individualization is readily applicable in international marketing. For example, America Online, the US online provider that entered a joint venture with Germany's Bertelsmann to set up a Europeanized version of their service, gives its global subscribers the ability to create their own stock portfolios that list only the particular equities and funds they wish to track. In addition, it automatically delivers information from financial publications on the investments in the customers' portfolio, saving them considerable time in searching for information.

When customers in an international product-market use a product the same way but differ in the benefits they expect, as for example the worldwide users of Swatch products, the marketer may choose a **policy of cosmetic individualization**. That is, the company offers a standard core-product with a certain number of expected features which delivers the functional (basic) benefit, such as indicating the time or giving the ability to phone. Added as well as symbolic product features and the processes creating them are individualized to provide emotional value. For example, Hertz Corp., the world-leading rental car company based in the USA, uses standard rental cars in its #1 Club Gold Programme. But customers belonging to the programme bypass the line at the counter, get shuttle service to the car park, find their name displayed on a screen that directs them to the location of their car, find the trunk of the car open for their luggage, and the heater or air conditioner turned on when the weather demands it.[17]

Efforts to individualize products cosmetically with large shares of tangible features and autonomous value creation processes will focus near or at the end of the value creation chain. For example, the name of the client may be added to a clock face, or a strap chosen by the customer may be mounted to give the watch a personal note. On the other hand, when a product is highly integrative and most of its features are immaterial, those processes that involve customers and can make a positive difference from the customers' point of view will be individualized. For example, a bank operating internationally, such as Utrecht (the Netherlands)-based Rabobank International which focuses on corporate, investment and private banking in 80 offices in more than 30 countries in Europe, the Americas and Asia/Australia, will have largely standardized back office procedures but may design its offices and train its customer contact personnel so that they treat their customers according to their individual expectations.[18]

When its customers' needs are well known to or at least identifiable by a company and when the customers do not want to bother with the product because it does not seem important enough to them, the international marketer may decide to choose a **policy of autonomous individualization**. Companies such as the Franco-UK Sema Group or US-based Electronic Data

Systems, both specialists in computer services, for example, take over all hard and software installation, integration and maintenance activities of their industrial customers. The customers – in the case of Sema they are mainly cellular operators in Europe and Asia – outsource their computer systems activities because they are not part of their core competency. The marketers take over the responsibility of keeping the systems running at a specified level of availability.

The marketer observes the customers' behaviour over time without direct information-gathering interactions. The product is individualized according to the determined preference structure and usage behaviour of each customer within a standard package. The customer may not even be aware of the individualization. For example, the consumption behaviour of customers of Ritz-Carlton hotels is observed during each stay. The information is stored in a database, and service is tailored to each customer on the next visit.

When customers have to take one-time decisions based on difficult trade-offs between product features, such as comfort for elegance or flexibility for functionality, and when the decisions seem important enough to the customers to exert some effort, the international marketer may decide to apply a **policy of collaborative individualization**. In this case supplier and customer together determine the features of the total product. The marketer helps the customers to articulate their expectations concerning the product and their problems with known offers. Together they identify the precise offering that fulfils the customer's needs. For example, Chicago-based International Components Corporation, the world-leading manufacturer of (battery) chargers, collaborates with its customers in 13 countries in all parts of the globe. In most cases customers approach the company with their product and ask ICC for advice on how to charge it. The company then designs and produces the charger for that product, with a prototype typically available for testing within a few weeks.[19]

Such collaborative individualization has been the rule in most international contractual businesses such as mechanical or software engineering, legal services or business consulting. A special example is employment services provided by temp agencies. International agencies, such as Netherlands-based Randstad or the merger of Switzerland's Adia and France's Ecco which has created Europe's top employment-service company, are able to offer international clients an exclusive contract to provide them with the number of qualified personnel they need in all their operating units.

In international consumer product marketing, collaborative individualization has not found many supporters so far. Most mass marketers have tried to increase the customer value of their products by adding new features or improving existing processes. As a consequence and owing to the great variability of individual needs in international markets, product portfolios have become more and more complex, and therefore more difficult and expensive to manage. In addition, large assortments of unsold products have piled up in stock or expensive largely unused service capacity has been built up because of erroneous forecasts of exactly which products will be needed in which countries and at what time.

By collaboratively individualizing its products, a company replaces back-end adaptations to local needs and circumstances with front-end specifications on how the most attractive product for the individual customer should be designed. No inventories of finished products are waiting to find customers. Raw materials or component parts are stocked to be able to react quickly to individual customer demand. Customer contact personnel is trained to inter-act sensitively with clients who have strongly differing demands. For example, Paris Miki, a Japanese eyewear retailer that owns the largest number of eye-wear stores in the world, has developed the Mikissimes Design System. The system first takes a digital picture of each customer's face and analyses its characteristics as well as a set of customer statements concerning the kind of look he or she desires. Then it recommends a distinctive lens size and shape and displays the lenses on the digital image of the consumer's face. The con-sumer and the optician next jointly adjust the shape and size of the lenses until the customer is pleased with the look. In similar fashion, consumers select the nose bridge, hinges and arms. Then they receive a photo-quality picture of themselves with the proposed eyeglasses. Finally, the eyeglasses are produced in one hour.[20]

Collaborative individualization can also take place in the production and delivery stages of a product, for example when customers specify where, when and how the ordered products should be delivered. This is the case in just-in-time contracts between car makers such as Italy's Fiat and its suppliers, but also in grocery home delivery services where customers can not only order the products they need but may also indicate when they want them to be delivered.

Brand Concept

A basic product management decision for every company is whether to actively brand their products or not. For an internationally operating com-pany, independent of the kind of customers it serves, the branding of their products may be of great importance. Brands can be conceived as the mean-ing of products to their customers, that is, their cognitive and affective struc-tures concerning those products and their use. Independent of the supplier's decision to actively brand its products or not, customers will develop specific product meanings. If a marketer can manage its customer contacts in a way that successfully builds up an attractive meaning of its products to those cus-tomers, however, selling the products will be greatly facilitated.

International vs. Local Brands. Globally active companies, such as Accor, the French leading hotel group in the Asia-Pacific market (Novotel, Ibis, Mercure), American Express, the US credit card and travel service company, or Lego, the Danish producer of toys, often decide to create global or at least continental brands. That is, they use the same product-related cues, such as the trademark or design of the product, in all of their served country-markets in an attempt to make their (potential) customers perceive a specific meaning of the product. For a brand to be global it must be sold in most, ideally all, con-tinents. Its essential positioning has to be consistent across the world, result-ing in universal recognition as the same brand. To achieve that goal, brand name, design, packaging, distribution and advertising must create the neces-sary signals for recognition and acceptance, even if most parts of the product-related marketing activities are locally different. The higher the level of standardization, the bigger the decrease in fixed costs per unit and learning effects. But they require the existence of a global product-market. That is, there must be customer segments in each of the served country-markets which are quite similar concerning their product-related needs or at least do not have contradictory needs.

The lack of such homogeneous international product-markets may be one of the reasons why, despite the economic advantages of an international or even global brand, a market study by Nielsen showed that in 1995 the number of totally Europeanized brands – which have the same brand name, the same ingredients or functions, the same packaging, price level and communication – was rather limited. Only 14 of the 100 biggest brands: Barilla, Coca-Cola, Danone (cheese and desserts), Fanta, Jacobs, Langnese (ice cream), Milka, Nescafé, Pampers, Parmigiano Reggiano, Pedigree, Persil, Pepsi and Whiskas were Europeanized.[21] In addition, the long tradition of thinking in terms of national markets as well as cultural differences between managers may have contributed to that finding. Table 12.1 shows that there are brand policy differences between managers from different countries.

But the process of internationalization or even globalization of brands is on its way. For example, Avon Products, the world's biggest direct-sales cosmetics maker active in 125 countries and taking about 650 million orders for USD4.5 billion-worth of beauty products a year, increasingly focuses on a number of global brands it can sell the world over. By 1996, it had created six lines, including Far Away perfumes and Anew skin-care products, with two more set to be launched by 1997. Global brands in this year generated USD725 million in sales, that is, 27 per cent of Avon's cosmetics, fragrance and toiletries revenues. Plans are that by the year 2000 that proportion will rise to 60 per cent. By increasingly globalizing its brands, Avon has been able to improve quality and reduce the number of suppliers, cutting costs by USD35 million a year. This and other economies, such as uniform ingredients and packaging, mean that gross profit margins on Avon's global brands are up to four percentage points higher than those of its other lines. And just as global brands such as 'No. 5' have boosted Chanel's worldwide brand recognition, Avon is globalizing its new brands to raise its profile around the world.[22]

Most internationalizing companies are aware of the difficulties related to the international establishment and maintenance of a brand. South Korean firms such as L. G. Electronics Inc., for example, acquire foreign brands which give the company instant name recognition. Acquiring established brands often is a less risky policy because the great majority of new brand names fail to catch on with consumers. This was a major reason behind L. G. Electronics Inc.'s decision to buy a controling stake in Zenith Electronics Corp., the US manufacturer of TV sets.[23] Similar objectives lay behind Sara Lee's takeover of brands such as Delial (sun protection), Natreen (sweetener), Satina (body care), and Quenty forty (cosmetics) from Bayer, the German chemical giant.[24] But such a policy inevitably leads to a portfolio of many different local brands in maybe the same product categories. Companies having acquired various local brands, therefore, try to initiate a process of brand globalization by making their visual identities converge, before they change anything else.

Brand Purpose.   A brand may serve customers as a means of orientation among a great variety of potential choices. McKinsey, for example, for many managers is a brand name with a clear profile of processes and expected results. It stands out from a very large number of offers in the international consultancy market. Brands ease customers' choice processes because they reduce the amount of information to be searched, retrieved and processed to make a 'good' decision. Brand names such as Hennessy cognac, Compaq computers or Marriott hotels evoke a bundle of associations in potential customers who may not need to search for further information. But because all

Table 12.1	The Brand Internationalization Policy in Different Countries		
Location of Headquarters	We leave it open to local managers to decide	We push homogenization and standardization	No response
Germany	4.5%	95.5%	–
UK	5.3%	94.7%	–
Japan	–	85.7%	14.3%
Switzerland	20.0%	80.0%	–
USA	5.7%	77.2%	17.1%
France	24.0%	69.0%	7.0%
Italy	30.0%	60.0%	10.0%

Depending on the location of a firm's headquarters, the tendency of their managers to push the internationalization of their brands varies.

Source: Euro-RSCG/J.-N. Kapferer in: 'Adapter ou standardiser?', L'Entreprise, No. 127, April 1996, p. 35.

customers have different experiences and varying social relations, and live in diverse environments – particularly when the marketer serves an international product-market – brand management must consider such differences. Hennessey cognac, for example, is presented as a cocktail drink in North America to win young American customers whereas in most European countries it is a drink to be taken after a good meal.

The meaning of a brand also allows a customer to identify with it or to use it as a means of self-projection. Rolex, Porsche, Ungaro or even Miele are examples of brands which customers all over the world use for such purposes. The international product manager must determine what purpose its brand should mainly fulfil: to be a signal of orientation in a mass market or a symbol helping to project the customer's self. Any mixes are possible but bear some inherent dangers. For example, French Guerlain has launched a Petit Guerlain for babies, Givenchy attracts adolescents with Fleur d'Interdit, and other luxury brand marketers such as Paris-based Christian Lacroix have tried to enlarge their product portfolios to increase their potential markets. The risk is becoming a brand like many others, seeing the margins shrinking and the life cycle shortened.

To avoid such developments, companies like Dior, the inventor of brand licensing based in Paris, have reintegrated most of the activities covering their brand name. Hermès, Cartier, Louis Vuitton and Chanel have even bought many manufacturers of their products. And Hermès sells all of its 20 000 products, except perfumes and table wear, in its 145 Hermès shops which are designed by the same architect to increase the presence of Hermès's brand identity.[25] International marketers with brands that have a strong symbolic meaning need highly centralized brand management.

Brand Manuals.   In order to keep local brand adaptations in a certain range that is needed to create similar meanings in different country-markets, companies operating internationally develop brand manuals. Such manuals specify which parts of brand appearance have to be standardized across country-markets, as for example the logo or the colour and shape of the package, and which parts are open to local adaptation, for example the visual and verbal creation of a certain meaning. Brand manuals may also contain guidelines concerning brand extensions or ingredient branding activities. That is, they indicate what kinds of products may be launched under a certain brand name, or they specify the type of customers who may be allowed to use the name of the supplier as part of their own communication campaign and the conditions of the brand's use.

In companies with a long-standing tradition of local autonomy, the process of developing and implementing brand management guidelines can take a while. For example, it took Germany's Henkel AG five years to develop and implement its first international 'Manual of Packaging-Design and Brand Identification'. Other companies prefer to give their local subsidiaries more freedom of action. US-based Colgate could, for example, define its Colgate brand as a global brand to be introduced first in all international markets as the 'flagship' of the company. Around this leading brand, local managers could introduce local brands with differentiated customer benefits to address specific customer segments.

Conflict Handling. A brand policy statement should also contain a guideline on how to handle potential conflicts between manufacturers and retailers. The struggle between manufacturers and retailers for international markets and remaining margins tends to extend to product areas which have been largely dominated by manufacturer brands, so far. On the one hand, for example, manufacturers and designers of well-known fashion brands are increasingly opening their own chains of retailing shops. On the other hand, after two decades on the defensive, during which consumers of fashion have taken the signature of a famous designer as the ultimate guarantee and names like Armani, Dior, Yves Saint Laurent and Gucci convinced customers they were making wise buying decisions, clothing retailers are now attempting to recapture consumer confidence. In most of the highly industrialized countries, designer labels are rapidly giving way to retailing labels. In 1995, for example, Quadro, a knitwear firm in Italy's Tuscany, manufactured more than 600 000 pieces of knitwear for stores in the USA, about one-third of which went to The Limited chain. By themselves, house brands or private labels are nothing new in fashion retailing. What is new is that products identified with the retailer rather than the designer are now being positioned at the high end of the market. Most retailers in the past used own labels to fill the middle of their line. Because of the high degree of specialization involved, the process is most advanced in the accessories field. High-end men's silk ties are a typical example. Men's suits are another area. Italy's two biggest textiles groups, GFT and Marzotto, are both very active in private-label men's clothing.[26] Marketing managers of both international manufacturing and retailing companies will have to define their policies of what course of action to take in such an environment.

Big retailers like to use established brands of manufacturers' products as low-price customer attraction devices. For example, UK supermarket chain Tesco PLC began selling Levi's jeans at cut-rate prices in Spring 1997. Levi, the San Francisco-based clothing giant, does not want its fashion icon sold in locations like grocery stores, which do not meet its criteria for retail outlets. It prefers authorized dealers, such as department stores and approved retail outlets, where staff are specially trained to sell a wide range of 'genuine' Levi apparel and there is the 'optimum service presentation' to match the brand's image. Tesco is not part of those distribution channels. Levi refused to supply Tesco with jeans. Undeterred, Tesco located a consignment of 45 000 pairs of men's jeans from what it described as an official supplier in Mexico. It put them on sale in 128 of its supermarkets at USD49 each, compared with USD85 at an official Levi's store in London. In an official statement Levi insisted that the company does not dictate retail prices. If Tesco changed its retail environment the supermarket chain could be supplied.[27] To be prepared for such events, the international marketer has to formulate a guideline on how to manage the relationship with such retailers.

Quality Guidelines

Superior product quality based on the higher attraction of processes involving customers, the superior material features of the total product or the uniqueness of its immaterial features is a major platform for international marketing success. This is particularly true in country-markets where local suppliers have not invested in the quality of their products. For example, the success of Japanese department stores in countries such as Australia may be partly due to the more intense efforts of their managers and personnel to deliver superior customer service.

Product Reliability. In general, increasing global competition has resulted in a continual increase in expected quality standards. One major factor constituting quality from many customers' points of view is the reliability of a product. But, depending on the level of immateriality and integrativeness of a product, it is more or less difficult for a customer to assess beforehand if a given product will perform as expected. When the product has mainly material features and its processes involve the customer to a high degree, such as custom-made special weaving machines for Italian La Perla, a producer of high quality women's swimsuits and underwear, the customer can first search for the most appropriate supplier and then control the production and delivery process. However, the customer must believe the supplier concerning its service, spare parts delivery, and availability.

Products with mainly material features but highly autonomous processes of production and delivery, such as kitchen appliances, furniture or compact discs, let the customers evaluate their tangible features before purchase. But customers must believe the supplier concerning the product's reliability. When the product is characterized by mainly immaterial features and highly integrative processes, such as most business consulting activities, the customer must first rely on signals provided by the supplier, such as references or the reputation of their personnel, to take the purchase decision, but can influence the production and delivery process of the product. For products that involve highly autonomous processes and have largely immaterial features, such as international telephone services, the customer must exclusively rely on the promised performance of the product. Signals, such as reputation, warranties or the friendliness of personnel, are the only means of quality assessment.

Business and government customers all over the world want to be sure that the purchased products make the intended contribution to their own customer value creation process. Consumers want to buy safe products which perform in the expected way. Consequently, the international marketer will have to define its product's quality standards for the processes and features that are accessible to the customers. They may be integral parts of the product or peripheral cues used as indicators of product quality. For example, Robert Kuok, one of Asia's richest overseas-Chinese tycoons and the owner of the Shangri-La luxury hotel chain that runs hotels in China, the Philippines, Indonesia and Fijii, is said to have once lectured his hotel managers on what sort of fruit they should have in the rooms.[28]

Because the quality expectations and quality perceptions of customers may vary in an international context, the international marketer needs to analyse closely what influences those expectations and perceptions. On the basis of that analysis, quality standards can be formulated that should be followed throughout the company. Such a guideline may read as follows: 'The quality of our products concerning the processes and features central to the intended customer benefit has to be oriented at the highest standard demanded across all served country-markets.' For a marketer of watch straps this might mean, for example, that the level of perspiration and tearing resistance of its products would have to fulfil the standards expected by its Japanese watch-making customers. But the variety in the colour and design of the straps would have to fulfil different expectations of consumers in Italy and France, and the quality of delivery service and after-sales services would be oriented according to German standards.

If a company has a total quality management programme, the development, formulation and control of product quality standards will be part of that programme. For example, when US-based Motorola started semiconductor assembly in China, they trained their personnel intensively in the concepts of 'Total Customer Satisfaction' and 'Six Sigma' (that is, fewer than four defects per million units). Within six months, Chinese line operators had achieved Six Sigma output quality.

To assure business and administrative customers of the purchased product's contribution to their customer value creation process, quality certification has become the rule in many product-markets. International norms, such as European ISO 9000, define quality as the controlled compliance with exactly defined company-specific and documented processes of customer value creation. They force the supplier to rethink its processes starting from the customer benefit and to document all processes related to the firm's products. Customers of certified companies are assured that their suppliers conform to the stated processes. In case of problems with the performance of a purchased product, the source of the defect can be found by analysing the related documentation. International marketing managers either have to make manuals developed inside the firm during a quality certification process part of the international product policy statement or they need to formulate a policy of which quality certification – if any – to go for.

Because not all marketers are similarly aware of the importance of product reliability, product liability legislation has been introduced in all highly industrialized countries to protect consumers from unsafe products. Product liability is the responsibility of a product's supplier or intermediary to cover damage to the life, health or property of a customer or a third person that are caused by the performance of the product during consumption or use. Fines in such cases may reach a level many times over the total annual sales of the company involved. Because product liability legislation is not as severe in some countries as in others, the international marketer has to determine which country's legislation to take as the level to use as an international standard and if certain countries' standards cannot be met, which country-markets to avoid serving.

Business Sustainability.   With customers' increasing environmental consciousness and the decreasing reserves of natural resources, the sustainability of a firm's business may become part of its international quality standards. Sony, the Japanese manufacturer of consumer electronics, for example, has a guideline that calls for developing TV sets in a way that makes them last for 40 years. In order to keep those products attractive to customers despite technical progress, new technologies are to be loaded into the TV sets from disk. Rank Xerox in Holland has set a goal of reaching a reutilization rate of 80 per cent for its products. This rate has been reached by developing a highly modular product design where parts with longer life cycles than others can be reused.[29] For the UK's Unilever, environmentally sound and sustainable products have such importance that they have published Environmental Reports. The first contains a policy statement which can be found in the Ethics box.

Product Portfolio

The international product policy of a firm should contain guidelines concerning its product portfolio. Because the age structure of a company's products influences its long-term success, there may be a statement concerning the desired share of new products. For example, 3M, the St Paul and Austin, USA-based specialist for all kinds of coating and sticking, stated that 30 per cent of its annual sales volume must come from products not older than four years. In addition, they formulated the rule that 70 per cent of 'new products' must be more than simple replacements of existing products. As a consequence they registered 600 patents in 1996 and made USD1.5 billion – that is, slightly above 10 per cent of their annual sales – with 'first year' products.

The complexity of the company's portfolio is another important factor of influence on the long-term success of the firm. The international marketer has to develop a guideline concerning the appropriate level of complexity and the central elements which bring synergy to the product portfolio. Companies such as Procter & Gamble, in an attempt to reduce costs and improve customer service, have developed clear guidelines to reduce their international portfolio's complexity. Other firms such as the UK's Virgin, in their focus on expansion, do exactly the contrary. The company has not only taken on British Airways and survived, it also introduced its Virgin Megastores – large record, film, book and multimedia stores – all over Europe and in the USA. The company is selling consumer products such as Virgin vodka and cola which is a great success in the UK. There are a variety of properties under the Virgin name, but they all have the same essence. They are about innovation and value for money, and there is always an element of fun. Because the attributes migrate across the product categories as well as across country-market borders, there is marketing synergy in Virgin's portfolio.[30]

But too much creativity and an unrestricted range of fields of innovation in most cases diminishes an international marketer's financial success. The Future Issues box gives an example of what may happen when a company does not have any guideline for product innovation or only a guideline defined in very broad terms.

ETHICS BOX

Unilever

Environment

Report:

The Policy

"UNILEVER IS COMMITTED TO MEETING THE NEEDS OF customers and consumers in an environmentally sound and sustainable manner, through continuous improvement in environmental performance in all our activities.

We ensure that our products and operations are safe for the environment, while we seek to build environmental performance into our innovation strategy.

We aim to reduce waste, conserve energy, examine reuse and recycling throughout our business and exercise the same concern for the environment wherever we operate.

Our policy reflects our commitment to the International Chamber of Commerce Business Charter for Sustainable Development. It reflects our emphasis on those issues outlined in the Charter which we regard as current priorities.

We also fully support the principles for environmental protection set out in the OECD Guidelines for Transnational Companies, and will contribute to meeting the increasing number of international conventions on environmental protection."

Source: Glaskin, M. (1996) 'Catalyst for Action', *Unilever Magazine*, 2nd Issue, No. 100, pp. 16–18.

FUTURE ISSUES BOX

A Killer Commute,

Nasty Gamma Rays,

But What a View!

JAPANESE COMPANIES ARE FAMOUS FOR LONG-TERM thinking. They have larger research budgets than most western competitors, shareholders who have a longer term perspective, and a characteristic reluctance to stop any new product research project that does not turn out immediate results.

Like other big Japanese builders, Shimizu Construction Corp., a big builder of Japanese suburbs, has a division for moon-based-construction research. Dr. Kanamori, Shimizu's concrete specialist, has spent two years pulverizing simulated moon rocks from Mount Fuji to make simulated "moon cement" – a raw material his employer will need for the condominiums it hopes to build on the moon. Along with the condos, Shimizu's moon lab is considering plans for lunar tennis courts and golf courses. And it has designed a four-storey egg-shaped dwelling that would inflate as a massive auger drills it through the lunar surface. The company spent USD3 million for lunar projects in 1997.

American scientists discovered there may be ice on the moon, which would be a very good thing for Hiroshi Kanamori's cement project. Moon cement will require moon water, of course, so any ice up there could come in handy. Shimizu put about USD200 000 and six years into helping the tiny Houston company Carbotek Development Laboratories Inc. build a machine that squeezes oxygen out of moon rocks, oxygen being one of the two ingredients of water. Separating the second ingredient, hydrogen, from Earth water can be done, says Dr. Kanamori.

Mastering the moon is just the beginning for Japan's construction companies who try to give a new sheen to their old "dirt-and-wood business", as Japanese call construction.

Source: Steiner, R. (1997) 'A Killer Commute, Nasty Gamma Rays, But What a View!', *The Wall Street Journal Europe*, 3 April, pp. 1 and 7.

Management Responsibilities

International product management is a complex task involving various functions inside the company as well as outside partners. To produce the best quality from the customers' point of view, all processes needed for the creation of customer value must be closely coordinated and optimized with the intended customer benefit. The marketer has to develop guidelines as to which processes should – in general – take place where in the company and who is responsible, which processes are to be outsourced, and which kinds of external partners are needed to cooperate.

Depending on the driving forces of product innovation, research and development activities may be largely centralized, such as in the case of 3M, or the marketer may encourage locally operating business units to drive their own innovation. 3M's product innovation, for example, mainly focuses on the development of specific technologies and their application to the solution of as many customer problems as possible. Therefore they have centralized most of their R&D activities in their headquarters in St. Paul, Minnesota and in Austin, Texas. Unilever, a quarter of a century ago, when its South African Elida Gibbs subsidiary developed Impulse, was essentially focusing on local marketing know-how. Before the launch of Impulse, the body spray or deo-perfume product category did not exist. Elida Gibbs South Africa recognized a gap in the local market for a refreshing daywear spray, created for use all over the body. The product concept proved transferable to other countries. Today Impulse continues to be highly profitable in more than 40 markets, including the UK, Germany, France, Argentina, Brazil and Australia.[31]

With the globalization of many markets and increasing competition, it has become more important to develop products for a greater number of country-markets or even a global product-market at once. Market-driven companies such as Procter & Gamble tend to involve multifunctional teams of people from the most important and the most interested local units in their new product development processes (see Chapter 10). When Ford Motor Company developed its 'global car', marketed in North America as the Contour sedan, the executives of the auto maker adopted video-conferencing and CAD/CAM technologies to create a car that would incorporate its best engineering, design and marketing talent worldwide while also bringing to bear a vision of how a single car design could appeal at once to all major world markets. Rather than creating national product teams or convening elaborate design summits, Ford established a virtual work team to develop the car. In the virtual world, the product development team could transcend the limitations of time and space that characterize management in the physical world. They built and tested prototypes in a simulated computer environment and shared the designs and data with colleagues, 24 hours a day, around the world.[32]

Other companies such as W.L. Gore Inc., the US fibre products firm which has many small operating units all over the highly industrialized and fast-industrializing parts of the world, leave much of their product management activities to the initiative and dedication of local 'champions'. That is, managers who develop a new product project, regardless of position or function, are encouraged to go and get a budget from their 'leader', may build a team of people from all international parts of the firm who are needed for and interested in the project, and take responsibility for its success. If the project is successful, a new operating unit may be constituted which manages the new product internationally.

International brand building and management have proven to be particularly successful when senior managers make it part of their personal responsibilities and strategic plans. Examples are the Body Shop's founder and CEO, Anita Roddick, Peter Brabeck, the CEO of Nestlé who was the champion for the Buitoni brand when he was Nestlé's executive vice president for global foods, or Fritz Humer, the CEO of Wolford. Such persons not only have the ability, authority and incentive to ensure that the intended brand identity is being delivered consistently across the firm's active and passive communication activities, but they personally represent the brand. This personal attachment makes it easier for all people inside and outside the company who are involved in the implementation of brand-related activities to develop a common understanding of the brand's meaning. This common understanding, in turn, is the condition for creating a strong, clear and rich brand identity.

Some processes of product management may be outsourced to specialized firms which hold highly specific resources and have acquired in-depth know-how that even a firm operating internationally could hardly build up economically itself. The Frauenhofer Institutes in Germany, for example, take over basic but also applied research projects from international marketers. Graz, Austria-based AVL is the leading developer of car engines in the world. Most new engines of car makers from all over the world are at least partly developed by this company. Other specialized product management activities, such as searching for an internationally acceptable and protectable brand name, may also be outsourced. The marketer will have to state in its product policy which product management processes or activities are considered as central to the firm's competency and therefore must be kept inside the company.

Because customers evaluate the attractiveness of the total product, all processes creating customer value have to be coordinated. For that purpose, close cooperation with selected suppliers, intermediaries and customers may be required. However, cooperation does not automatically lead to improved use of pooled skills and resources. It has to be built on trusting relationships that need to be developed and maintained. Cooperation can also imply a drain of information and know-how to competitors. Therefore, the international marketer may wish to specify in its product policy statement how to choose suppliers, intermediaries and customers with whom to build a network.

SUMMARY

The core of the marketing mix is the bundle of benefits offered by the company to the potential customers via its product. From the customers' point of view, the total product offered by a firm is the bundle of processes the customer can experience and the outcomes of those processes for the customer. Together they create value for the customer. Processes to develop, produce and deliver a total product can be more or less integrative. The outcomes can have various levels of immateriality. The international marketer must integratively manage all parts of the customer value creation chain.

Each marketer needs to know its customers before taking product management decisions. That is, it must first make sure it knows exactly who are the customers or decision makers to be targeted, their major driving forces concerning the given kind of product, what those customers do with the product, and how their buying process is structured. Then the marketer has to assess what constitutes its total product seen from the customers' point of view. In international marketing, the processes and features expected by potential customers from different country-markets may vary in composition and importance. So do the meanings customers attach to a product.

Because the importance and meaning of processes and features constituting a total product from the customers' point of view not only depend on personal predispositions but also on influences from the customers' environments, the variety of product management decisions in international marketing tends to be much broader than in local business. The total products of firms operating internationally must be adaptable to local needs. Flexibility and variety, however, strongly contrast with the desire of most company managers to keep the complexity of their product features and processes low. To avoid unnecessary complexity and the resulting costs, an international product policy has to be developed. It is based on the intended global strategic position of the firm and provides guidelines for all product management processes to be conducted: product positioning, brand management, quality management and product portfolio management. The product policy also determines the distribution of responsibilities among managers and management teams concerning those processes. It is the basis for operative product management decisions, to be discussed in the following chapter.

Discussion Questions

1. Explain why a company operating internationally needs a policy governing its international product management.
2. Search for examples of total consumer products which fit the extremes of Figure 12.3. How will the international product policy decisions differ for those products?
4. How can a company decide the extent of standardization of its products and which standardization policy to choose?
5. Find examples of successful international consumer product individualization and compare them to successful consumer product adaptations. What are the reasons for success?
6. Explain the need for an international branding policy.
7. Find examples of international companies that have gone through quality certification processes. How do they differ in their organizational processes compared to firms which do not have any quality certification?
8. What consequences can be expected from the existence of international product portfolio guidelines?
9. Describe different ways of structuring international product development responsibilities and discuss their impact on the product innovations to be expected.

Additional Readings

Clark, T., D. Rajaratnam and T. Smith (1996) 'Toward a Theory of International Services: Marketing Intangibles in a World of Nations', *Journal of International Marketing*, 4(2) 9–28.

Davis, J. (1993) *Greening business. Managing for a sustainable development*, Oxford: Basil Blackwell.

Kutschker, M. and A. Mößlang (1996) 'Kooperationen als Mittel der Internalisierung von Dienstleistungsunternehmen', *DBW*, 56(3) 319–337.

Yavas, U. (1998) 'The bases of power in international channels', *International Marketing Review*, 15(2) 140–150.

Notes

1 Warner, F. (1996) 'Basketball Thrills Koreans, as NBA Dribbles Into Asia', *The Wall Street Journal*, 17 May 17, p. B9.
2 Curtin, M. (1996) 'Deutsche Morgan Grenfell Aims at

Major Growth in Asia', *The Wall Street Journal Europe*, 2 April, p. 22.

[3] La Franco, R. (1996) 'Narcotic betel nut on your popcorn?', *Forbes*, 3 June, p. 41.

[4] 'The Pager Race', *Fortune*, 27 May 1996, p. 120.

[5] Loyer, M. (1996) 'Luxury Companies Focus on Services', *International Herald Tribune*, 16–17 March, p. 20.

[6] Riesenbeck, H. and A. Freeling (1991) 'How Global are Global Brands?', *The McKinsey Quarterly*, 4, 3–18.

[7] 'Adapter ou standardiser?', *L'Entreprise*, No. 127, April 1996, p. 41.

[8] Walters, P.G.P. and B. Toyne (1989) 'Product Modification and Standardization in International Markets: Strategic Options and Facilitating Policies', *Columbia Journal of World Business*, Winter, 37–44.

[9] Blumenstein, R. (1996) 'GM to Develop Engine Family For Models Around the World', *The Wall Street Journal Europe*, 15 May, p. 5.

[10] Haas, P. (1996) 'SAP: réussite allemande dans le logiciel', *Le Figaro économie*, 11 March, 8.

[11] Shirouzu, N. (1996) 'Snapple in Japan: How a Splash Dried Up', *The Wall Street Journal*, 15 April, p. B1.

[12] Schiller, Z., G. Burns, and K. Lowry (1996) 'Make it simple', *Business Week*, 9 September, 96–104.

[13] 'Orangina: la petite bouteille ronde secoue toute l'Europe', *L'Entreprise*, No. 127, April 1996, p. 38.

[14] Walters, P.G.P. and B. Toyne (1989) op.cit.

[15] Ronkainen, I.A. and I.Menezes (1996) 'Implementing global marketing strategy', *International Marketing Review*, 13(3), 56–63.

[16] Gilmore, J.. and B.J. Pine II (1997) 'The Four Faces of Mass Customization', *Harvard Business Review*, January–February, 91–101.

[17] op. cit., 98f.

[18] AP-Dow Jones News Service (1996) 'Rabobank Aims to Double International Activities', *The Wall Street Journal Europe*, 9 July, p. 8.

[19] Fisher, L. (1997) 'Charged Up and Ready to Roll', Accountancy – International Edition, February, 30f.

[20] Gilmore, J. and B.J. Pine II (1997) op. cit., 92f.

[21] 'Adapter ou standardiser?', *L'Entreprise*, No. 127, April 1996, p. 33.

[22] 'Scents and sensibility', *The Economist*, 13 July 1996, pp. 57f.

[23] 'Brand names in Korea', *ESOMAR Newsbrief*, No. 10, November 1995, 11.

[24] Luger, F. (1996) 'Sara-Lee-Tochter schluckt Santora', *Der Standard*, 27 December, p. 19.

[25] 'Elargir la gamme en respectant la marque', *Enjeux*, October 1996, p. 122.

[26] Hansen, J. (1996) 'Retailers Push Own Labels', *International Herald Tribune*, 16–17 March, p. 23.

[27] 'Jeans Are the Rage At U.K. Supermarket, But Levi Is Distressed', *The Wall Street Journal Europe*, 2 April 1997, p. 10.

[28] 'Room Service', *The Economist*, 1 June 1996, pp. 62f.

[29] Steiger, U. (1996) 'Wie man aus Altem Neues macht', *Neue Zürcher Zeitung*, 30 September, pp. 29f.

[30] Miller, C. (1996) 'The British invasion', *Marketing News*, 30(12), 3 June, pp. 1 and 10.

[31] 'A lasting romance', *Unilever Magazine*, 2nd issue 1996, pp. 14f.

[32] Rayport, J.F. and J.J. Sviokla (1995) 'Exploiting the Virtual Value Chain', *Harvard Business Review*, November–December, 75–85.

CHAPTER 13

INTERNATIONAL TOTAL PRODUCT MANAGEMENT: PRODUCT MANAGEMENT PROCESSES

INTERNATIONAL INCIDENT

CK:ONE

CK:ONE, the shared fragrance for men and women from Calvin Klein Cosmetics, a business belonging to Britain's Unilver, is a bestseller from Tucson to Tokyo, Madrid to Montreal, and Singapore to Sydney. Launched in the US and Canada in the fall of 1994, within the first year it tripled its projected sales target. Rolled out a year later across 32 countries in Europe, Central and South America, Asia and Australia, it again took the market by storm. Within three months, CK:ONE exeeded its European sales target by 30 per cent. In 1995 it was the number one fragrance for men and women in the UK and the third largest-selling fragrance in Europe behind Chanel No 5 and Lancôme's Trésor.

From the moment of its inception, CK:ONE took a fresh route. Managers within the Calvin Klein Cosmetics business recognized for 'Generation X', the young and style-conscious market of 17 to 24-year-olds, values were shifting and rules were changing. This generation had an openness to new ideas that had not been seen for years. For them, boundaries between race, sex and age were diminishing. Their focus was on exposing similarities between people, not highlighting differences. Members of Generation X are supposed not only to accept others for what they are, but also to accept themselves.

This was what CK:ONE's emotional appeal would be all about: a celebration of individuals who share a common attitude. The concept of a shared fragrance builds cleverly on this idea. The product name, CK:ONE, melds together the concept of individuality, the sense of being at one with the world and the newness of the product range. The full CK:ONE range consists of eau de toilette, skin moisturiser, body massage, body wash, soap, deodorant, fragrance candle, talc, hair gel, and shampoo/conditioner. The packaging for CK:ONE avoided the opulent excess packaging of cosmetics products. In keeping with the values of the brand, it is simple, stylish and honest. The products appear in recyclable glass or aluminium containers. The fragrance and soap are packed in cartons made from 100 per cent recycled paper.

The success of CK:ONE extends much further than simple sales statistics. It has opened up a new, shared category within the fragrance market, introduced a younger audience to prestige fragrances, and encouraged a new type of shopping habit for fragrance – buying for yourself rather than for others.

Source: Thomas, H. (1996) 'Look no rules', *Unilever Magazine*, Second issue, No. 100, pp. 13–15.

PRODUCT MANAGEMENT PROCESSES

An international product policy provides the company with a framework of guidelines in which to operate. The general directions given indicate the goals to be achieved by day-to-day operations as well as the limits of decisions and actions to be respected by central as well as local units.

The most important processes in international product management are related to product portfolio management, quality management and brand management. All three cover more than one functional area of the firm, requiring the interfunctional integration of various subprocesses to achieve their goals.

Product portfolio management has multiple goals. Primarily its goal is to supply the markets served by the company with a stream of constantly renewed products which are attractive to customers. The products must also be competitive compared to other suppliers' products; and they must be priced to allow the company to make attractive profits as well as to stay financially sound. The goal of quality management is to keep customer satisfaction with the company's products at the highest levels in order to have as many loyal customers as possible and to win their positive references to other potential customers. Brand management tries to achieve and maintain a consistent meaning of the company's products to customers which positively differentiates them from competitors' products and simplifies customers' decision-making processes in a way profitable to the firm.

PRODUCT PORTFOLIO MANAGEMENT

The most important process of international product management is to develop and maintain a competitive combination of products – a product portfolio – to be offered in the served product-markets. That is, customers in those markets consider it as at least as attractive as offers from competitors and the cash flow generated by the given combination of products assures the long-term success of the firm. Development and maintenance of a successful product portfolio requires answering the following questions:

↔ Which existing products of the company may be marketed internationally? Which products should not be offered internationally?

↔ How can the products to be marketed internationally be bundled into an attractive offer for the different local or regional markets served?

↔ What additional products are needed to increase the local or regional attractiveness of the existing product portfolio? Should they be developed or procured from suppliers?

↔ When should which products be introduced in which country-market? When should products offered in international markets be eliminated?

↔ How much of the limited resources of time, capital and capabilities are to be invested in which parts of the product portfolio?

The Product Life Cycle

For the development and maintenance of an international product portfolio, the marketer needs to consider the international life cycles of the product categories concerned, which were discussed in Chapter 1. But the individual products constituting the portfolio will also be in different stages of their life cycle, and those stages may vary across the served country-markets. The duration of life cycles will be different across products and so will the duration of their various stages. The shape of the total sales curve will not always follow its theoretically supposed form of an S. And, because of the increasing globalization of many product-markets, the difference between the stages of a product's life cycle across country-markets tends to decrease. Nevertheless, the marketer will need to monitor the development of its products in their international markets and consider adequate reactions.

Stages. Because of the high costs of introducing a product in more than one country-market simultaneously, or lack of production capacities or personnel capabilities, a company may decide to enter country-markets step by step. As a consequence, an internationally marketed product may be in different stages of its life cycle across the various served country-markets. For example, the strategy of New York-based Morgan Stanley, ranking third in worldwide underwriting and first in US and international mergers and acquisitions in 1995, has a strategy to build for the long term in a focused, gradual and cost-conscious manner. The firm opens an office only when a specific US business unit, such as asset management or commodity trading, agrees to pay for its start-up. Other businesses are then added gradually. As a result, the company's products are in different stages of their life cycle from Beijing to Bombay to Johannesburg to Geneva to Sao Paulo.[1]

Such regional differences in the stage of a product's life cycle may also be due to factors which cannot be influenced by the marketer, such as legal regulations, technical norms or customers' receptiveness to innovation. One example is the market for temporary work in Europe. In 1996, the services of temporary work agencies were illegal in Italy and Greece, while in Germany they faced tough regulatory restrictions. The UK, France and the Netherlands stood out as more liberal country-markets for temporary labour. But as politicians worried about Europe's continued failure to create new jobs even in periods of economic growth, many governments started reconsidering old labour-market tenets and progressively lifting the legal obstacles. As part of a pact to create more jobs, for example, Belgium's labour union, employer and government representatives agreed to stimulate the use of temporary work.[2]

If the aspiration levels of local customers are in various stages of development, the customers are differently inclined to accept products from other countries, or if the degree of mobility in the various local societies varies, different stages of a product's life cycle in those markets will result. Colourful fashion watch straps, for example, have been an essential part of French, Italian and German jewellers' stock for many years. They are in a much more advanced stage of their life cycle in those countries compared to the USA where most customers prefer black or brown watch straps, or in most Asian countries where metal straps are common.

In any case, differences in the stage of a product's life cycle across country-markets have an impact on the marketing mix to be applied locally and on the resources deployed. Insufficient adaptation of a product to local preferences or norms unnecessarily increases the duration of a product's introduction stage. Kentucky Fried Chicken, for example, took a couple of years before it entered the growth stage in the Japanese market. This was not so much due to the customers' need to learn a new consumption habit. Fast food stores existed in Japan long before Kentucky Fried Chicken was founded in the USA. But the company initially tried to introduce its unchanged model of an American fast food restaurant and its menu to Japan rather than making necessary adaptations to local tastes.

Duration.   Product life cycles are usually longer for industrial products than for consumer products, especially for construction equipment, component parts, raw materials and maintenance services. Fads and fashion changes, which tend to shorten product life cycles, are less common for industrial products than for most consumer products. Also, the higher levels of investment required for many industrial goods necessitate a longer product life cycle, so that the firm can recover the costs of research and development. Nevertheless, in international business there is a general trend towards a shortening of product life cycles. One reason is the sharp increase in global competition which forces companies to innovate constantly. New or improved products are introduced quickly, in order to stay attractive in the minds of potential customers. Research and development processes are speeded up as companies try to apply their innovations simultaneously in as many products as possible. In addition, to stay cost competitive in globalizing product-markets, the production processes of total products are continually shortened and global sourcing tries to minimize procurement expenditures. This, in return, again increases the pressure for innovations on the suppliers' side.

In addition to more intense competition, the number and level of environmental protection regulations have been increasing during the past decade, at least in the most highly industrialized countries. As a result, new or at least improved products which meet the revised environmental norms had to be developed quickly. As a result, the duration of the original life cycle was shortened.

Finally, some of the shortening of product life cycles is due to managers' errors with regard to the positioning of their products. For example, when a marketer of products which are considered attractive by their customers succumbs to the pressure on prices and terms of sale of its intermediaries to grow faster than the competition, or to keep market shares in the short run, the life cycles of those products are shortened because those decisions place negative pressure on their gross margins. As a result, the need for constant innovation or product changes is growing.

Therefore, product innovation is the most important process in international portfolio management. But it has to be based on a careful consideration of how well the company does and will do with its existing products, which ones need to be renewed and which resources may be spent for what purpose. This is the task of the international product portfolio analysis and determination process.

International Product Portfolio

The product portfolio of an international marketer contains a certain number of product lines which are in turn characterized by an additional number of product variations. To optimize a company's international product portfolio, the marketer has to determine how many product lines should be offered internationally and with how many variations. But it is not only the width and depth of an international marketer's product portfolio that strongly influences the firm's success. The right balance of the portfolio may be as important from a long-term perspective. The management of both will be discussed in the following.

Width and Depth of the Portfolio.   The more different product lines a company offers to its customers in a market, the broader its product portfolio is.

In most cases a broad product portfolio attracts a higher number of customers than a deep product portfolio by offering various versions of what is basically the same total product. A French marketer of winter sports equipment, such as Rossignol, for example, which serves the New Zealand market with alpine skis, cross-country skis, ski poles, ski boots and ski clothes, has a broader range of customers than a US marketer of snow boards, such as Burton, which at least initially served the market only with an assortment of boards for different purposes. The Future Issues box gives an example of how new information technologies may allow an international marketer to increase its customer base considerably by increasing the width of its product portfolio.

However, the number of potential customers is not directly related to the financial success of a firm. A marketer specializing in a small number of product lines but providing a great variation of versions may better satisfy the specific needs of an international customer group or may be able to cater specifically to different customer groups in or across countries. For example, Queensland Uniform Foods sells over 20 flavours of milk in Australia. Lime-flavoured milk appeals more to children, while coffee-flavoured milk appeals mostly to adults. The company gains considerable production economies from producing many versions of milk, since the marginal costs of changing flavours are insignificant. A deep product portfolio, therefore, may ease the positioning of an international marketer in its customers' minds and keep the costs of entering a new market at an acceptable level.

In taking the decision on how broad and deep the company's international product portfolio is going to be, the marketer should keep in mind that the major goal is to provide an attractive customer benefit and to lay the groundwork for the creation of a specific meaning of the firm's offer in the customers' minds. From this point of view, product lines and individual product variations may be analysed according to their contribution to those goals. Some products that are needed in one country will not be of importance in another. Others which may be needed in a new country-market to make the portfolio attractive to local customers may be added by procurement from external sources. For example, when US-based MCA Inc. decided to invest in its first international venture, a USD1.6 billion theme park in Osaka, Japan, it carefully investigated what kind of entertainment products Japanese customers want to buy. In that country, where Disney enjoys an almost religious reverence among consumers who spend about USD4 billion a year on its consumer products and make Tokyo Disneyland the most popular theme park in the world, it was particularly important to combine the right products in a portfolio of attractions which would be able to differentiate attractively itself from Disney. Osaka offered the right combination of space, location and government enthusiasm. In 1996, the city was working with MCA on plans for Universal City Osaka, a 1200-acre urban redevelopment project featuring resorts, shopping, office space and housing.[3]

Balance of the Portfolio.   In managing the firm's product portfolio, an international marketer must have a mixture of products in different stages of their life cycle. Compared to a local company, the portfolio management of an internationally active firm is complicated by the fact that an international balance of the portfolio has to be achieved. There always needs to be a sufficiently large number of products (in potentially different country-markets) which provide enough cash flow to finance either the development and launch of new or improved products in existing markets or the launch of

Delivering Value to the Customer in the 'Market Space'

UNITED SERVICES AUTOMOBILE ASSOCIATION IS AN early example of what may globally happen on a much larger scale when companies start fully using the distribution opportunities offered by new information technologies.

USAA began as an insurance company. Over time, it has used its information systems – installed to automate its core business, insurance sales and underwriting – to capture significant amounts of information about customers, both individually and in aggregate. USAA integrated information about customers and distributed it throughout the company so that employees are ready to provide products, services, and advice anytime a customer contacts the company. Having made this investment, USAA found that among other things it could prepare customer risk profiles and customize policies. Managers invented business lines targeted to specific customers' needs, such as insurance for boat owners.

But the company also used its growing expertise with information to create new value for customers in ways that had little or nothing to do with insurance. For example, it designed financing packages for purchasing boats. In fact, USAA now offers a wide range of financial products as well as shopping for everything from jewelry to cars. When a customer calls in with a theft claim, the company can offer to send a check or to replace the stolen item. By aggregating demand statistics and likely loss ratios, USAA has become a smart buyer for its loyal customer base, getting discount prices through high-volume purchases and passing some or all of the savings along to the customer. Today USAA is one of the largest direct merchandisers in the USA.

Although USAA's "product line" is eclectic, it represents a logical, cost-effective, and profitable progression of new business ventures, all of which are underwritten by the information about customers. Management of that information has become USAA's central activity. Through clever integration of the available customer information the company creates new value for customers by serving a broader set of their needs.

Source: Rayport, J.F. and J.J. Sviokla (1995) 'Exploiting the Virtual Value Chain', *Harvard Business Review*, November–December, 80–81. Reprinted by permission of *Harvard Business Review*. Copyright © 1995 by the President and Fellows of Harvard College, all rights reserved.

existing products in new country-markets. In fast-growing and globalizing industries, both alternatives will need to be financed.

Which products to introduce where and when, and which products to delete from the portfolio must be decided. In addition, the international marketer must determine how much resources to spend on each product, in each of the served or intended country-markets. The goal is to constantly increase the success of the firm or at least to keep it at a level which allows all important stakeholders of the firm to be satisfied. For this purpose all products in the portfolio have to be compared across all country-markets concerning their existing and potential contribution to the company's success. Portfolio analysis as described in Chapter 9 has proven to be a useful tool for such comparisons.

Figure 13.1 shows a potential result of the comparison of a firm's entire

Figure 13.1   COMPARISON OF A COMPANY'S PRODUCTS ACROSS COUNTRY-MARKETS

A company operating internationally may compare the position of its products across markets along two dimensions: the attractiveness of the served product-markets and the relative strength of each product compared to its major competitors.

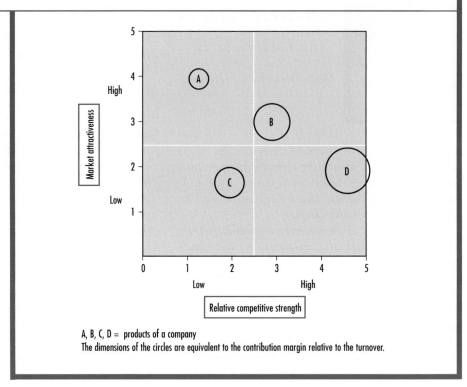

A, B, C, D = products of a company
The dimensions of the circles are equivalent to the contribution margin relative to the turnover.

products across all country-markets from the use of portfolio analysis. The company's products are evaluated according to two essential criteria. The attractiveness of served product-markets (on the vertical axis) consists of factors of influence such as market growth, intensity of competition, relative market size, or achievable margins. The estimation of the products' relative competitive positions (depicted on the horizontal axis) is based on factors such as relative market share, relative cost and quality position, or relative position concerning customer services. That is, the horizontal axis contains factors which express the extent to which the products' features fit with the expectations and aspirations of their product-markets relative to the competition. Which factors should be used to best describe the attractiveness of served international product-markets and the relative international competitive position of the company's products will depend upon the business the company is in and must be individually determined by the marketer.

When assessing the relative competitive position of the firm's products, the marketer must not only consider the known products of the most important competitors, but also products which presently do not exist but are known to be under development or could be developed inside the planning horizon. A product's contribution to total profit or cash flow, its share of total sales volume or its contribution per sales ratio can be depicted by the size of the circles in the graphic.

Figure 13.2 shows the results of a portfolio analysis in which the competitive positions of one product have been compared across served country-

Figure 13.2 Comparison of Competitive Positions of Product A Across Served Country-Markets

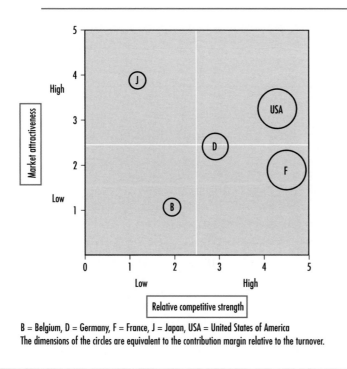

B = Belgium, D = Germany, F = France, J = Japan, USA = United States of America
The dimensions of the circles are equivalent to the contribution margin relative to the turnover.

An international marketer may be interested in a comparison of the competitive position of one of its products in each of the differently attractive country-markets served.

markets. One might conclude from this picture that the Japanese market is rather attractive for the product. But the company has not yet been able to develop a sufficiently strong competitive position to take a profit from the attractiveness of this market. If a realistic way of improving this position could be found, the resources needed might be transferred from the German and French markets. But before such a decision is made, the information from both portfolio analyses needs to be linked. Only a total comparison of the competitive positions of all products across all served country-markets allows a meaningful decision concerning resource allocation.

Table 13.1 shows how such an information link can be achieved by portfolio analysis. The vertical axis contains the four quadrants of Figure 13.1. Inside each quadrant are the served country-markets. Horizontally, the competitive position of each product is indicated for each country-market. In general, a product with a weak competitive position in a relatively unattractive market (for example, product A in Belgium) represents a drain on the entire company. It might seem plausible to keep a product in a more attractive country-market which at the moment needs more resources than it can provide, such as product A in Japan. But products which are not profitable and which do not expect future improvement, for example by outsourcing the production, are to be eliminated. Careful management of a smaller number of products generally allows positive effects of coordination and concentration on a company's profits.

Table 13.1 Comparison of Competitive Positions of a Company's Products Across Served Country-Markets

In combining information concerning the position of the firm's products in the served country-markets and their position in the respective international product-markets, management may establish a useful basis for resource allocation decisions.

Position of product in overall comparison	Position of product in country-market				
	?	Star	Cash Cow	Dog	Country
?				A	Belgium
	A				Germany
			A		France
	A				Japan
		A			USA
Star			B		Belgium
		B			Germany
	B				France
	B				Japan
		B			USA
Cash Cow		D			Belgium
			D		Germany
				D	France
		D			Japan
			D		USA
Dog			C		Belgium
				C	Germany
			C		France
		C			Japan
				C	USA

Source: Business Week, May 1 1989, p. 20.

International Product Innovation

To maintain a balanced international product portfolio, new products have to be continually developed and, together with variations of existing products, introduced to the markets in a planned way. In international marketing a product can be 'new' in different ways. On the one hand, it can be a real innovation for its global product-market. Real innovations are seldom globally successful. This may be due to the varying innovativeness of customers. For example, German consumers are known to be considerably slower in adopting innovations than US consumers. But lack of success may also be due to a lack of corporate information necessary to properly guide adapted product development and market entry.

On the other hand, a 'new' product may only be new for a specific country-market. Often a company has been successfully marketing a product in some markets before it introduces it in other markets. For example, Georgia Coffee, a non-carbonated soft drink that has a taste of coffee, was introduced by Coca-Cola into the Australian market after having been successfully marketed in Japan for years. Finally, a product may only be new to the company itself. In this case most companies find it difficult to establish themselves in markets they do not know well, with products with which they do not have much experience.

New Product Ideas.   To launch a single new product in international markets successfully, several new product ideas are needed. These ideas may be developed with a domestic market perspective, with several different country-markets in mind, for global product-markets with planned modifications for different regions, or from a global standardization perspective. Only one in seven product concepts is a winner. That is, 46 per cent of the resources firms spend for product development purposes result in losing products. Fifty per cent of new products fail at launch. But research has shown that product ideas generated with an international market in mind are generally more successful than product ideas developed for a domestic market only.[4]

To generate a sufficient number of new product ideas, a company may use internal and external sources (see Figure 13.3). New product ideas may be of a variety of types, including the development of a new technology, a new application of an existing technology, new solutions for existing customer problems, or new product features.

An international marketer has access to a greater number and diversity of sources of ideas for new products than a locally operating competitor. For example, the marketer may count on the experiences of salespeople, application engineers, and maintenance and customer service personnel operating in various cultural environments with different levels of economic and technological development and different regulatory environments. Different expectations and aspirations of customers, suppliers, intermediaries, consultants and inventors located in the country-markets served by the firm can be transformed into new product ideas not available to local competitors. Highly successful products of such local competitors may even be exploited for new product launches in other markets. As the Ethics box shows, however, there are some limits to be kept in mind in imitating competitors' products and in developing new products based on their ideas.

Because of the great variety of potential sources of new product ideas, the international marketer will have to choose the most valuable ones. Not every served market is equally important to the company. Liechtenstein-based HILTI AG, for example, despite its worldwide activities, considers Germany as its lead market for drilling and fixing devices, because the technological level of products needed to be successful in this market is very high compared to most other country-markets, including Japan and the USA. Many international services providers, such as CompuServe, America's and Europe's biggest online service with about 2.5 million customers in the USA and about 200 000 in Europe in 1995, consider the US market as their lead market. Product ideas coming from those markets receive special attention.

The danger of such focus is twofold: the marketer might not pay attention to real innovative ideas coming from 'minor' markets or might overstandardize its new products. Online services provide such an example. The EU has a slightly larger population than the USA. Nevertheless, in the mid-1990s the EU's online market was rather small: about 17 per cent of households had personal computers (versus 37 per cent in the USA); just 1.6 per cent used online services (versus 14 per cent in the USA). Fragmentation of product usage and taste made the market even smaller: a survey of 10 000 people conducted by Inteco, a research firm, showed that in France, 91 per cent of PC owners used

Figure 13.3 SOURCES FOR NEW PRODUCT IDEAS IN INTERNATIONAL MARKETING

New product ideas may come from sources internal or external to the firm.

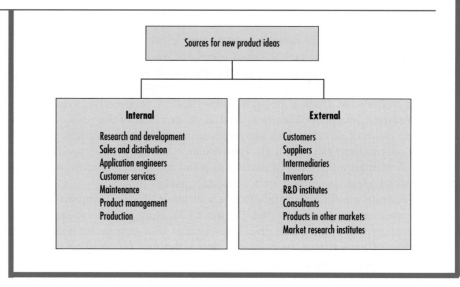

Internal	External
Research and development	Customers
Sales and distribution	Suppliers
Application engineers	Intermediaries
Customer services	Inventors
Maintenance	R&D institutes
Product management	Consultants
Production	Products in other markets
	Market research institutes

ETHICS BOX

Spying, Stealing, Copying

IN A TALE REMINISCENT OF A JOHN LE CARRÉ SPY novel, a unit of Corange Ltd. of Bermuda in June 1996 sued US-based Johnson & Johnson, accusing the medical giant of secretly infiltrating company meetings, stealing confidential documents and pilfering a secret prototype.

The unit, Boehringer Mannheim Corp. in Indiana, is a rival of J&J in the highly competitive business of making glucose monitors for diabetics. According to the suit, from 1992 to 1994 executives at J&J's LifeScan unit directed workers to surreptitiously attend several Boehringer sales meetings at hotels around the world. The executives, according to the suit, even established awards for J&J employees who did the best spying, including the "Inspector Clouseau Award" and the "Columbo Award".

At a Boehringer meeting in Istanbul, Turkey,

a J&J spy allegedly found out about a secret prototype for a new glucose monitor. When LifeScan executives then "challenged" workers to obtain a copy of the prototype, a J&J worker in Germany "illegally obtained" a model and shipped it back to the US, the suit charged.

The suit was more surprising because Boehringer admitted two of its people did a little spying of their own – but it insisted it was nothing on the scale of what it was alleging J&J did. Boehringer said once one of its employees, acting on his own, impersonated a doctor while talking to J&J officials at a trade show; on another occasion, a worker took home J&J documents he found in a waiting room.

In a statement J&J admitted that an internal investigation found that both companies had engaged in unspecified "improper activities" and expressed "regret" that its employees had been involved in such activities. But J&J maintained that its lifeScan unit did not gain any competitive advantage from "information improperly obtained."

Source: Langreth, R. (1996) 'Rival's Suit Accuses J&J Unit Of Spying, Stealing Papers', *The Wall Street Journal Europe*, 21–22 June, p. 4.

their machines to play games; 38 per cent admitted to working with them. In Germany, in contrast, 48 per cent said they played games, and 62 per cent worked. In the UK the top ten television shows were mostly dramas or comedies; in Italy the top ten were almost entirely football (soccer) broadcasts. In Italy the television is often in the kitchen; in Germany it is in the family room.[5] No wonder that firms such as CompuServe or America Online regard the US market as their lead market for innovations. But the European diversity also challenges the 'department store' model of online services which attempts to supply all the information potential customers might want, as it seems to fit with US customers' expectations. European diversity leads product developers to take a 'shopping mall' approach to online services. Microsoft, for example, establishes networks to open doors to information sources – not the content of those sources itself. IBM's infoMarket also provides access to various databases on the Internet and elsewhere.[6] In other words, the international marketer should not automatically consider its biggest market as the lead market for product innovation ideas. Depending on the served product-market, criteria other than size may be more important.

In a similar manner, persons, companies or institutions as sources of new product ideas are not all of similar value to the marketer. Ideas coming from 'lead actors', that is, persons or organizations which may be considered as more innovative or more sensitive concerning the firm's product categories, should be followed more closely. For example, a business-to-business marketer may arrange an international meeting of such lead actors in its product category. They are invited to attend presentations about the latest developments in areas relevant to their own business. In addition, they are asked to participate in special workshops where they can identify and discuss problems to be resolved by a supplier in order to help its customers improve their future market performance. Valuable information concerning the development of new products or the improvement of existing products can be derived from such workshops. In a simpler fashion, for example, a UK clay company asks all its international customers coming to tour their mine to participate in a 30-minute brainstorming session about problems to be resolved in order to increase their own customers' level of satisfaction.

The most sophisticated, demanding and fast-moving customers adopt new products first. Less sophisticated customers follow their lead after some months. Marketers able to cultivate relationships with lead actors in their industry can therefore pick up new product ideas faster and create a waterfall effect. Moreover, if such lead actors are potential customers, they often agree to 'sponsor' their selected partner, meaning that they agree to participate in product development and guarantee a certain sales volume at product launch. For example, Shinko, a Japanese semiconductor packaging manufacturer, used Intel, the world's leading MPU chip producer, as a sponsor company. By working closely with Intel, Shinko was able to meet Intel's packaging design requirements for various chip forms, and became its supplier of choice. When customers such as IBM and Texas Instruments adopted similar technology to Intel's, Shinko was able to provide them with leading-edge materials. As a result, Shinko increased sales from USD68 million in 1980 to USD726 million in 1994.[7]

To profit fully from the potentially greater flow of new product ideas in an internationally operating firm, this flow must be carefully organized. Organizational units at different locations led by entrepreneurial people may further local initiatives and diminish central adminstrative barriers to innovation. To avoid cultural one-sidedness and tunnel vision, such units may be supported by internationally staffed teams of people from all functional areas concerned which evaluate new product ideas and try to choose the best. At Exxon Corp.'s Polymers Group, for example, the choice of ideas to be considered more closely is based on an investigation of eight key areas: strategic fit, market attractiveness (existence of need, substantive market), technical feasibility (including manufacturing), supply/entry options, competitive advantage (better quality as defined by the customers and/or reduced customer costs, solves customers' problems with competitive products, unique and highly visible benefits), legal/regulatory issues, financial attractiveness, and a solid launch plan.

Product Development. An assessment process of a new product idea that produces a positive outcome results in a product definition, that is, a definition of the new product's intended target market and competitive differentiation as well as a list of required features and specifications that the new product needs in order to deliver the intended customer benefits. Based on such a new product definition, a development project can be started. In this stage of the product innovation process, an international marketer again has to resolve some specific problems. The product development process needs to be organized in a way that will facilitate the process itself. Further, the product to be developed has to be continually checked for its potential market success. Its design has to be adapted to the specific needs of the international markets. And the introduction of the new product in the markets has to be prepared.

The product definition states the goal posts of product development. Accordingly, development activities are assigned to the members of a cross-functional development team. Under the leadership of a project manager, the team members concurrently work on their assignments. Continuous feedback among the team members who are empowered to take decisions allows the development process to be stopped when insurmountable obstacles of a technical, financial or marketing nature arise.

Product development can be conducted at the company's headquarters such as in the case of 3M, based in Minnesota. This company runs 45 production plants in 42 countries. It has 30 technology platforms, that is, technological competency centres, and 25 worldwide product divisions. But all product ideas coming from the firm's various local sales organizations are centrally gathered, evaluated and, if considered relevant, introduced into the product development process. The only exception is electronics. Because 3M had a hard time finding electronics specialists willing to go to St Paul, Minnesota, they centralized all innovation processes for this domain in Austin, Texas. The innovation success of 3M (placed 31st in total sales and 19th in profits in the list of Fortune 500 firms in 1995) and other examples from the computer and pharmaceutical industries, such as Basel, Switzerland-based Novartis which has centralized all its antibiotics development in one location, illustrate that centralization of product development works well in technologically driven product-markets.

In customer-driven product-markets, it might be better to anticipate potential conflicts arising from country-market-specific differences in a multinational product development team. Procter & Gamble, for example, has had positive experiences with its 'Euro Brand Teams' when developing new products for the European market. Nestlé might have prevented the dismal start for Twin, a powdered blend of milk and soya milk, in Asia by listening more carefully to local management. Twin, invented in Brazil and Switzerland, is made in Indonesia and Mexico with locally grown soya beans and milk, and is sold regionally. The development of soya milk was strongly pushed by the Swiss headquarters, not only because it is more available and more stable than cow's milk in Asian and South American climates, but also because the company's president, at that time Mr Maucher, was intent on fashioning products for those regions from native ingredients. What was overlooked, however, is that Asians consider soya beans to be an inferior product.[8]

The pressure to cut project costs and sharply reduce time to market for new products, that is, the cycle time from the product idea to the launch of the product, has led many companies to downsize their central product development groups. Motorola Inc., for example, in its effort to reduce product development cycle time by a factor of ten in just two years, assigned the design of their products to where they are made, to the operating units. For certain parts of product development, such as design, independent design consultants, such as US-based Product Genesis, are increasingly assuming the former role of internal staff. They offer everything from research and engineering to producing pilot products.[9]

The assessment of a new product idea's potential for success completed in the first stage of the innovation process will be further discussed during product development. For that purpose, milestones are defined at which the project's market, financial and production viability are checked. Some firms operating internationally have formed new project review teams comprising senior management which meet regularly to review those projects ready to move on to the next stage. At 3M, for example, a 'European Management Committee' decides which new product projects should be further pursued. But while idea assessment may be performed based on checklists, in the product development phase the evaluation process is often based on scoring models. Because the new product and its potential are known with increasing precision, five-point scales can be used where at least the extremes and the median are quantitatively anchored or defined by verbal descriptions. New product projects are cancelled when the summed scores do not reach a pre-specified level. In the case of a positive result, the next step can be started.

Product Testing.   An important stage in every product innovation process is the development of a prototype, a working model or a sample of the product which can be tested. Tests can be conducted in laboratories, but preferably are conducted at the sites of cooperating business or administrative customers or in consumer test markets. Highly intangible and integrative products may be tested through trial demonstrations at company-owned locations. Lego, the Danish toy manufacturer, for example, opened a Legoland theme park prototype at its headquarters in Billund in 1968 which served as a testing ground before massive international expansion was decided upon in the early 1990s. The company plans to open 15 theme parks in the USA, southern parts of Europe, and in Asia by 2050. In this endeavour Lego will encounter competitors such as Japan's Sega Enterprises which first opened two test centres called Joypolises in their home market before they opened Segaworld, a vast video-game arcade, in London in 1996, followed by another one in Sydney which is supposed to be followed by dozens of others around the globe.[10]

Test markets for consumer products deliver information about customer reactions and enable managers to identify appropriate adaptations of the marketing mix before product launch. In international marketing the problem of determining representative test markets is even harder to resolve than in domestic business. For this reason, firms operating internationally frequently use the most representative test market they can find. The Netherlands and Belgium, for example, are often used as test markets for Europe. They cannot be considered representative of the entire EU. But experience has shown that the results from a test in those markets provide information that is useful for marketing purposes in Western Europe in general and are more than worth the cost of the test.

For industrial products, international market tests are difficult to establish. Because of the significant level of concentration in many of those markets, a market test would be equal to a product launch. Nevertheless, before introducing the product on an international level, the business-to-business marketer should let a small group of closely cooperating customers try the product, at least in the lead market. If there are improvements to be made, they can be carried out without losing the trust of potentially dissatisfied international customers. If the product works as expected, the customers who tested them may be used as references.

Quality Management

Customer Satisfaction

A great number of studies conducted in various parts of the world convincingly show that customer satisfaction with the total product of a firm is an important factor of influence on the long-term success of a company.[11] Because customers' satisfaction is strongly related to their perception of a product's quality, quality management is a central process of international product management. Customers may experience attractive product quality based on superior tangible features of the product (for example, the longest battery life of all the portable phones on the market), uniqueness of the interaction experience with the supplier (for example, the feeling of being treated like a family member in a small vacation hotel in the Italian Alps), or based on purely symbolic features of the product (for example, the ability to express a certain personal identity by wearing a Ferragamo skirt).

All product portfolio management processes must be managed in such a way as to achieve customers' satisfaction with the total product. As Figure 13.4 shows, customer satisfaction is based on an interaction between customers' expectations concerning the product and their experience with the product. Expectations are influenced by direct as well as indirect (word-of-mouth) experiences with the product and market communication by the supplier and its competitors. Product experience is based on the material and immaterial features the marketer provides with its total product, but in the end depends on the degree of fulfilment of customer expectations concerning the product. That is, a product's quality is defined by its customers.

Marketers have two ways of influencing their customers' quality perceptions: on the one hand, they may ensure a certain level of performance on each of the material and immaterial features important to the customers (quality assurance); on the other, they may shape customers' product-related

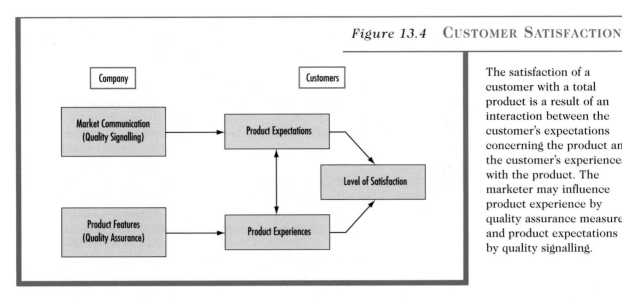

Figure 13.4 CUSTOMER SATISFACTION

The satisfaction of a customer with a total product is a result of an interaction between the customer's expectations concerning the product and the customer's experiences with the product. The marketer may influence product experience by quality assurance measures and product expectations by quality signalling.

expectations through market communication (quality signalling). Both will be used by an international marketer to be successful.

Because quality perceptions are subjective, they may vary among groups of customers in a country-market as well as among different country-markets. As a consequence, the quality assurance and quality signalling processes of a local company and a company operating internationally are basically the same as far as their objectives and their contents are concerned but in international markets some additional opportunities and threats may occur.

Quality Assurance

Quality assurance is an ongoing process that runs in parallel with the production of the total product. Depending on the share of material versus immaterial features constituting the product as well as on the level of integrativeness of the total product, quality assurance processes will focus more on material or immaterial aspects of the creation of customer value.

Material Features. Quality assurance processes start with the development of a product. The number of potential failures can be significantly reduced in advance by an improvement in construction quality. Webasto AG, the German world leader in car sun-roofs, as an example from the industrial goods sector, has found that 70 per cent of product costs are determined during the product design and construction phase. They have therefore introduced FMEA (Failure Mode and Effect Analysis) in all of their product development processes. Potential failures are identified and analysed beforehand in dialogue with major suppliers and customers. The probability of failure occurrence, failure detection, and the resulting costs of such failures are determined. The FMEA team works on the following questions: What is the potential problem? Why does it occur? What can be done to avoid it? What do we do? What has been done? With what effect? What are the consequences? Products with high FMEA scores are reconstructed to avoid all potential failures right from the beginning. Suppliers are obliged to do the same. And the company cooperates closely with the car makers it supplies during the start-up phase of the use of one of their products in the car makers' assembly line.

In parallel to product development, the quality of potential suppliers' products needed for the production of the total product is assessed. In international business it may not be sufficient to specify the features of those supplies exactly in written contracts. Some marketers must first train their suppliers' personnel to increase their level of product-related know-how. A smaller number of suppliers – not more than two per product category supplied – allows the development of long-term relationships which make such investments economically reasonable. For example, when an international hotel chain such as Marriott Hotels enters a formerly centrally controlled economy, such as Ukraine, it might find itself forced to develop a network of suppliers of all the goods needed to serve their international customers in the way they expect. Because neither the existing distribution facilities nor the local product quality and reliability come up to the standards of the company, it will have to choose its supplier carefully, train them accordingly, and make them long-term partners in order to be successful.

Computer online connections between a company and its suppliers may even allow the quality of the supplies to be checked during their production process. For example, when a truck manufacturer such as Sweden's Scania needs a new tube system for an innovative truck model, the company might not only closely specify its needs to a tube supplier, but may also use its online connection to this supplier to develop the mould jointly as well as monitor the quality control measures in the prototype's production process.

The next step in quality assurance is to assure the required efficiency and performance of production. Simplification of production processes by reducing parts and tolerances has strongly increased the (technical) quality of many consumer and business-to-business products. Reduction of parts can be achieved by standardization of product components or processes which are a black box to customers. Hertz, the world number one in car rentals, for example, has analysed its processes with regard to their visibility to customers and their effect on the perceived quality of the product. All processes invisible to customers have been simplified and standardized in accordance with the expected customer benefit.[12]

Reduction of tolerances is led by the goal of 'zero default'. In the car industry, for example, PPM (parts per million) is a major quality criterion on which suppliers are measured. It expresses the share of defective parts delivered in a total of one million parts. In 1997 the ppm level accepted by the most important car makers was 0.1 per cent. To achieve such a level of technical quality, constructive and organizational measures alone are not sufficient. The company personnel must understand that it is in their own best interest to reach the goal of zero default, and they must be allowed to act as they see fit in their area. If they get increased control over 'their' part of the total product's production process, they will be more strongly motivated to continually improve the processes for which they feel responsible. Vertical (instead of functional) team structures help to increase the understanding of mutual dependence of personnel in the process of creating customer value.

Immaterial Features. Quality assurance of the total product is not only achieved through measures concerning the production process of its material elements. Immaterial features of the total product have as much influence on customer satisfaction and therefore also have to be included in total quality management processes. One part of a total product's production process which contains mainly immaterial elements – at least from the customer's perspective – and strongly influences the perceived quality of the product is its distribution. Delayed delivery of industrial products, non-availability of consumer products, or negative experiences in personal contacts with the marketer's or its intermediaries' staff may lead to the superior material quality of a product becoming of secondary importance.

In comparison to a locally active firm, the international marketer has to bear the disadvantage that usually the distribution of its products not only needs to cover much broader areas but also involves a higher number of personnel as well as intermediaries who have a variety of cultural backgrounds. That is, the number of potential sources of imperfections is multiplied. Only close cooperation and alignment with the members of the firm's distribution channels can help in assuring appropriate quality. Chapter 14 will further elaborate on this point.

Products which are largely dominated by immaterial elements and are highly integrative, such as many services, are particularly difficult for the marketer to assure quality. Because their production and consumption take place simultaneously, each product is to a certain extent unique. Consistent perceptions of high quality by customers are difficult to achieve. Because a customer's subjective experience with a product is influenced by the environmental setting in which the contact between customer and supplier takes place, a high degree of standardization of this environment contributes to customers having similar quality experiences over time. This is particularly important in international services industries such as restaurants and hotels, but also for the consistent management of customer experiences with global brands. Louis Vuitton customers from Japan, for example, would be very surprised when travelling to Paris if they found a Louis Vuitton shop there that looked completely different from the stores in their home country. At the least the main visual cues should stimulate a perception of sameness.

Another key to consistent quality experiences by customers are the processes which add up to the total product. There are basically two ways for international marketers to assure the quality of their products via process management. One is to map the entire customer value creation process related to a product, distinguish phases where the customers are directly involved in the production process from those which are invisible to them, and then divide the entire production process into a sequence of small process units which can be more readily standardized. Each member of personnel directly or indirectly involved in the customer value creation process assumes responsibility for one or more of those process units. At McDonald's, for example, each staff member plays a predetermined and highly specialized role which is part of the customer service delivery process. Each role can be specifically trained. Such a strict functional division of labour reduces the complexity of each staff member's duty which, together with the training provided for the narrowly defined job, leads to a reduction of variance in the service provided to the customer, independent of the location of the McDonald's restaurant.

The second way to assure the quality of highly intangible and integrative products is to tailor each individual product as much as possible to the specific expectations of the customer. Instead of offering predetermined bus tours all over Europe, an international tour operator might, for example, only provide the bus and a special consultancy service for customers who want to plan the route and related programmes themselves or in cooperation with the tour operator. Such individualization of the product allows increasing customer satisfaction by providing custom-made quality levels of service.

Many highly integrative and immaterial products, such as international consultancy or banking, demand high levels of professional as well as social competency from their providers. In addition, if the service provided so far has fully satisfied their customers, demand might grow faster than the capacities of qualified personnel available to the marketer. Company growth has to be brought into line with quality assurance needs. For example, when Madrid-based Banco Santander, in turning to Latin America as the source of future growth, increases its retail bank business in Chile and Puerto Rico and sets up a sizeable investment banking operation in Argentina, it might not be able to sufficiently staff retail bank operations in Peru and a financial services unit in Chile with personnel trained in-house. The capability of the firm to follow its intended path of international growth may depend on the number of appropriately qualified personnel it can hire and train in the company-specific ways of doing business. If there are not enough candidates available, the choice of partners (franchisees, licensees, joint venture, strategic or merger partners) or the choice of adequate acquisition objects becomes a critical element of quality assurance. In the case of Banco Santander, for example, they bought two Peruvian retail banks and a controlling interest in Banco Osorno & La Union SA.[13] The success of the company will only be maintained if the personnel of the acquired firms have a similar view of quality and its level to be provided to customers.

In a similar manner, when global industries grow at a fast pace, such as tourism and travel which is expected to produce USDD7.2 trillion of gross output over the next decade (business travel is expected to increase by more than 50 per cent, and capital investment by nearly 70 per cent), firms participating in those industries may see themselves forced to grow accordingly.[14] A global hotel company such as US-based Doubletree, which operates in an industry that represents more than USD11.2 billion of total sales, on its fast track to expansion cannot hire and train enough qualified personnel to provide its customers internationally with the reliable and consistent service they expect. To keep growing internationally, the company might be forced to acquire other firms, such as the Renaissance Hotel group, or to enter partnerships with former competitors.[15] In such cases, the international marketer can contribute its know-how, its management techniques and its planning and control system to the newly acquired unit. But the quality of service experienced by customers will largely depend on the qualifications of the acquired personnel and the personnel development activities set by the marketer.

Because of the increased complexity of customer value creation processes for companies operating internationally, quality assurance may appear to be more difficult in such firms. Beside considering cultural influences on work discipline, adhering to rules, the importance of precision, or friendliness to customers, the international marketer has to develop a programme which creates awareness of the importance of the highest quality for the success of the firm and, therefore, for the job security of personnel throughout the international firm. The distribution of colourful brochures containing leading ideas, norms and rules will not be sufficient to achieve such awareness.

Ongoing organizational and personnel development activities based on an understanding of individuals as exchange partners will be needed.

Quality Signalling

Depending on a product's level of immateriality, it is more or less difficult for a potential customer to evaluate the product before taking a purchasing decision. Highly material products can be visually or physically tested. The customer may at least partially experience the benefits those products provide. By contrast, when a product's level of immateriality is high, customers need other cues to assess its attractiveness. They will look for material or immaterial signals informing them about the quality of the product. Such signals may come from the environment in which the product is offered and consumed, from the people offering the product, from warranties given by the supplier concerning the functionality of the product, from references provided by other customers, from the country of origin of the product, its local content, or the general reputation of the product's supplier.

Location and Physical Outfit.   The location in which a product is offered or consumed has an important influence on customers' perception of its potential quality. A Swiss Rado watch offered in a street market in Hong Kong would be considered a fake and could only be sold at a very reduced price, whereas a simple lentil salad with onions served in a five-star restaurant on the Caribbean island of St Barthelemy is considered by some customers as a real treat worth USD100. That is, when customers are insecure about the quality of a product they look for external cues to help them develop appropriate expectations. One such signal is location. Rue St Honoré in Paris, for example, is known for its concentration of haute couture shops. New designer brands from Italy, Japan or the UK, even from product categories other than fashion, try to establish themselves with a reference shop in this street.

Companies internationally offering legal, financial, business or communication consultancy services may furnish their offices in a way that allows customers to visually experience the quality level of their work. For example, an Austrian information systems consultant firm specializing in CIM software for textile factories buys fabric from their (potential) customers. Well-known fashion designers transform it into fashionable outfits for the firm's personnel. When visiting a customer or receiving a customer at their premises, staff members wear the appropriate clothing, signalling to those customers how much they are willing to focus on their business.

International marketers have to be careful, however, because symbols may have different meanings in different cultural environments. North American customers, for example, partly evaluate the reliability of a potential business partner by the size of their office, whereas in the Netherlands office size is not very important.

Warranties.   Warranties are well suited to signalling a marketer's confidence in the functionality of its products. For example, Duo Vac, a Canadian producer of central vacuum cleaning systems, offers a 30-year warranty to its international customers and adds a satisfaction guarantee (customers have six months to declare if and why they are not satisfied with the product and will get their money back). This strongly signals how highly customers should rate the quality of its product. Similarly, Laytron-Intralox, a New Orleans,

USA-based producer of plastic conveyor belts for food products, guarantees that a newly installed system will be operational on the date specified in the contract or else it will forgo any payment. Such warranties strongly contribute to the attractiveness of the offered products even to customers who were not familiar with that company before considering a purchase from it.

Warranties are particularly important where customers cannot check the quality of a product before buying it. For example, if a sender of a parcel has no experience of express mail services, such as US-based UPS (United Parcel Service) or Federal Express, he or she may hesitate to use such a service. It is more expensive than normal postal services, and who knows if it will really do what it promises. But if one of the service providers offers a warranty that the parcel will be at the given address within 48 hours or the customer gets his or her money back, the credibility of the offer will be greatly increased.

In international marketing the potential for standardized offers of warranties is limited by differences in the legal systems of the served country-markets. Local competitive practices and the level of technology with which customers in a country-market are familiar also influence the firm's ability to offer similar warranties across markets. But locally adapted warranties may be powerful tools to signal the product quality customers may expect before they buy the product. Yet, international marketers must not commit their organization to a level of performance that is not realistic. Sometimes it may be necessary to delegate warranty performance to partners in a host market, owing to legal or cultural constraints. Too often, however, such delegation runs the risk of reduced customer satisfaction since those partners may not give the products, repairs or customers' complaints the level of service that the company would provide.

References. Where warranties cannot be given for legal or technical reasons, references might take over their role in diminishing potential customers' perceived risk in buying a product. The number and quality of early references may strongly influence the competitive market position of suppliers in a product-market. In international metallurgical engineering, for example, references from properly functioning plants are so important for market success that marketers fight hard to be first with a reference when a new technology is introduced to the market. They even go as far as 'buying' a reference, that is, they are ready to lose substantial amounts of money on their first project which implements a new technology on the premises of a well-known customer.

Personal references are important in many consumer and industrial services. For example, when a European personnel manager needs to decide which employment-service company to choose for the provision of well-qualified temporary workers, he or she may limit discussions by relying on the big players, such as Adida-Ecco, a merger of Switzerland's Adida SA and France's Ecco SA, Manpower, the biggest US firm with headquarters in Brussels from where it coordinates its international expansion, Randstad Holding NV of the Netherlands, or France-based BIS SA.[16] But to ease the business of comparison and to reduce the remaining risk, the manager may partly rely on the experiences of colleagues. Their references are highly informative about the quality of service to expect from the suppliers.

Country of Origin. For a customer who has no experience with a product category or is not involved enough to actively consider more complex information, the country of origin may represent an important cue to the quality of a product, in addition to brand name and price. The origin of the product has symbolic value. It arouses specific characteristics attributed to the country. For example, in 1997 the 150 biggest companies in Scotland and in particular the country's 50 biggest producers of food products joined forces to launch a 'Made in Scotland' campaign in the EU and the USA. Most of the participating companies, such as The Caledonian Brewery which employs only 30 people but won the title of 'British Brewery of the Year' in 1996, would have been too small to establish their brands in those markets themselves. But by exploiting the image of their home country they were able to increase their international market coverage considerably.[17]

Customers' associations with a country contain cognitive elements, such as the level of technical or design competence attributed to the country, and affective elements, such as the friendliness of people experienced during a vacation in the country or the prestige that can be gained from possessing a product 'Made in . . . ', as well as normative elements, such as 'You should not buy a product from a country where human rights are constantly violated'. Some countries are attributed with high quality levels concerning specific product categories. Switzerland, for example, is 'known' for its watches, the UK for its pop music, France for its luxury products, Italy for its fashion design, Germany for its machinery, Japan for its consumer electronics, and the USA for its consultants and convenience services. Many such country-related associations have been developed during customers' socialization process. They help consumers as well as business customers to simplify their information-gathering process needed to make a subjectively reasonable decision.

The international marketer should be aware that the characteristics attributed to a country and its products may differ. Shared history, such as in the case of Austria, the Czech Republic, Croatia, Hungary, Slovakia and Slovenia, or shared language, such as in France and parts of Belgium and Switzerland, may lead to mutual images which are different from those existing in other countries. Characteristics attributed to countries may also change over time. For example, for a long time European customers perceived products from Japan as cheap imitations of qualitatively much better products from Western highly industrialized countries. Because of Japan's superiority in some areas of technology and management, its products today are associated with high precision, reliable quality and competitive prices.

Country-of-origin-related associations can become an essential part of the meaning of a brand and its attractiveness to potential customers. For example, Barilla, the Italian pasta manufacturer, has managed to use its Italian origin to achieve a high-end image in most European markets which it does not have in the home market. German craftsmanship is a constitutive part of brand perceptions concerning Mercedes. Both McDonald's and Coca-Cola are strongly related to the 'American Way of Life', and brands such as Gucci or Armani evoke Italian design competency in the minds of their customers. Studies have found that country-of-origin information has stronger effects in less industrially developed countries compared to highly industrialized 'Western' countries.[18] According to a survey by South China Marketing Research-Research International based on face-to-face interviews in Shanghai, Guangzhou and Beijing conducted in 1995, for example, eight out of ten Chinese urban consumers believed that products made in the West were likely to be of higher quality than comparable products produced in China, and over 75 per cent thought that Western products would be more durable than similar items made in China. Seven out of ten Chinese thought that Western goods were better value for money than their locally produced equivalents.[19]

Some products may only be marketed on the basis of their specific cultural background. It is precisely the difference in culture that makes them desirable. When Japanese consumers go to eat a piece of chicken at a Kentucky Fried Chicken restaurant in Osaka, for example, they may be buying a bit of the American way of life. Without its specifically American image, this service would just be another way to eat chicken in a whole range of Japanese restaurants. On the other hand, customers in Europe and the USA do not care much about the production sites of their Nike shoes, the Pampers nappies they buy, or the Goodyear tyres they use. In those cases other connotations of the brand are strong enough to determine its meaning to customers.

A special problem may arise when the perceived origin of the brand and the country in which the production site is situated are not consistent in customers' minds. Such hybrid products may not be bought because customers perceive increased uncertainty concerning product quality. Figure 13.5 contains a sequence of questions an international marketer should answer before deciding to produce its products in a country which has an image that is different from its brand's perceived origin.

Local Content. Ethnocentric customers are highly interested in the supposed country of origin of a product or at least the home base of the product's supplier. Products produced in their own country are more highly valued than those produced abroad. Ethnocentric customers in the USA, for example, when asked to evaluate different brands of cars, clearly rate US brands higher than their international competitors. A significantly higher share of French consumers perceive products manufactured in their home country to be superior compared to the evaluations of consumers from other EU member countries.

The return of more nationalistic feelings has led marketers in countries such as Australia, Austria, France, Japan and the USA to make customers explicitly aware of the country of origin of their products. For example, in the USA a not very successful campaign, 'Crafted with Pride in the USA', was launched as a reaction to the notoriously negative balance of trade. In Austria, local food producers, when confronted with overwhelming competition from other EU member countries, started a campaign featuring the country as the 'food speciality shop' of Europe.

When facing such a situation, a marketer from another country wishing to be successful has several choices. It may choose to become a local supplier through licensing, franchising, joint ventures or the establishment of a subsidiary, or it must try hard to convince customers through outstanding references, proven better quality, extended warranties, prestigious intermediaries, or significantly lower prices. For example, many of the Korean marketers, such as Samsung or Kia, which had the same country-of-origin problems as their early Japanese counterparts, have chosen the low-price way to win customers in Europe and the USA.

Another potential reaction to customers' ethnocentricity may be to increase the share of locally provided parts of the total product. Unilever, for example, uses locally available oils for the production of their margarine. By doing so they also increase the goodwill of local politicians and stakeholders in public administra-

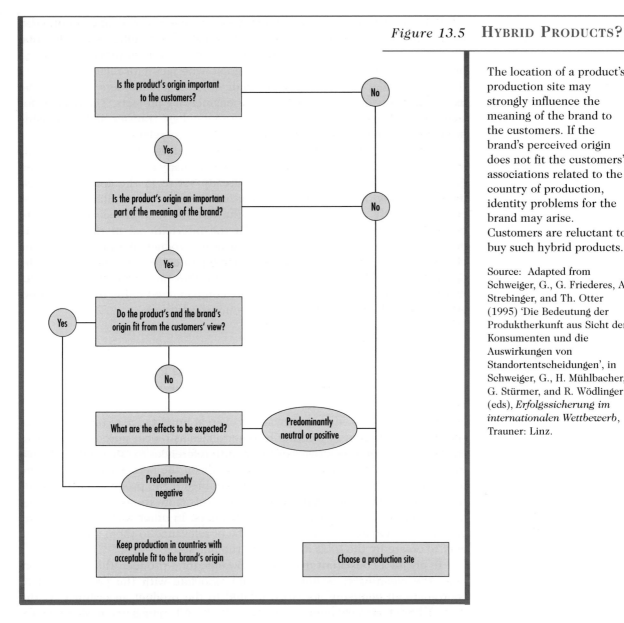

Figure 13.5 **HYBRID PRODUCTS?**

The location of a product's production site may strongly influence the meaning of the brand to the customers. If the brand's perceived origin does not fit the customers' associations related to the country of production, identity problems for the brand may arise. Customers are reluctant to buy such hybrid products.

Source: Adapted from Schweiger, G., G. Friederes, A. Strebinger, and Th. Otter (1995) 'Die Bedeutung der Produktherkunft aus Sicht der Konsumenten und die Auswirkungen von Standortentscheidungen', in Schweiger, G., H. Mühlbacher, G. Stürmer, and R. Wödlinger (eds), *Erfolgssicherung im internationalen Wettbewerb*, Trauner: Linz.

tion. A more important local content of a product may do more than increase the attractiveness of the marketer's offer. The marketer may also profit from low-priced local supplies, circumvent import restrictions, take advantage of country-specific know-how, and develop local business relationships.

But the international marketer should also be aware that local content diminishes its autonomy. Engineering companies, for example, are often faced with the demand of their international customers that a certain amount of the product's total added value must be produced in the customer's home country. Fulfilment of such a demand leads to additional problems in the organization of the work flow as well as quality assurance problems. It might be difficult to find an appropriate local partner and to meet deadlines set in the contract.

Potential customers may demand a certain amount of local content, such as 10 to 40 per cent of the total product's value, or a specific part of the total product to be produced locally. For example, it is common in Saudi Arabia to prescribe the use of 'sponsors', local people who facilitate relations between the international marketer and its Saudi Arabian stakeholders. In Libya the use of local consultants is obligatory for engineering projects. The reasons for such demands range from forcing some technology transfer and decreasing hard currency payments, to using existing business relations.

In choosing local cooperation partners, mainly information problems arise. Searching on the spot is too expensive for many companies. Information gathering from cooperation partners already active in the country-market, banks, chambers of commerce, commercial attachés or consultants is in most cases less costly and time consuming. But the information received needs to be double-checked for its reliability. If the international marketer has the opportunity to transfer the local content of its product to a firm that can be closely controlled because of capital ownership or contractual agreements, the optimal share of local content may become rather important. The closer elements of the total product are to the core competencies of the marketer, however, the less they are suited for local content purposes.

Brand Management

For most companies customer loyalty is of great importance to their long-term success, independent of whether it materializes as repeat purchases, as positive references, or as positive word-of-mouth references to other potential customers. Customer loyalty very much depends on the perceived quality of the total product. But it can be more easily attained if the product has a consistent market appearance that arouses high levels of awareness, is easily recognizable and positively valued by the customers. In other words, the meaning customers attribute to a product must be of relevance to them and should be easy to create by the tools available to the marketer.

To create a consistent market appearance for a product, that is, to determine the meaning(s) customers should associate with the product and to coordinate all company activities related to the product accordingly, is the goal of brand management. Consequently, brand management significantly contributes to the success or failure of an internationally operating company. The global appeal of the McDonald's brand means, for example, that in many established markets the company may be able to achieve the predominance it boasts in its US home market. In 1996, for instance, about 5 per cent of Australians ate at McDonald's every day, not far behind the 7 per cent of Americans who do so. And the scale of the global Mac attack based on its well-established brand is impressive. The company, which in 1996 had 18 700 McDonald's outlets serving 33 million people every day, planned to open up to 3200 new restaurants both in 1997 and in the following year. About two-thirds of them were planned to be outside North America.[20]

How important it is to manage a firm's international brand appearance consistently is further illustrated by the example of US-based PepsiCo Inc. Its top management found that their overseas sales grew at the same percentage rate as their arch rival Coca-Cola's, but Coke outsold Pepsi abroad nearly 3 to 1 and earned more than 80 per cent of its profits abroad, compared with Pepsi's 30 per cent. An in-depth analysis of the reasons showed that overseas, some Pepsi billboards were more than 20 years old, and the brand's market appearance was less than inconsistent: a grocery store in Hamburg used red stripes, a bodega in Guatemala used 1970s lettering, and a Shanghai restaurant dispayed a mainly white Pepsi sign. A hodgepodge of commercials featured a variety of spokespeople, ranging from cartoons and babies to doddering butlers. Worse yet, consumers said the cola tasted different in different countries. During visits to stores in Europe, one striking thing became apparent: Coca-Cola's red logo dominated the shelves, all but obliterating Pepsi. So, after studying the success of Pepsi Max, its popular overseas diet drink that comes in a blue can, Pepsi devised a drastic change called Project Blue: a globally standardized new market appearance with an electric blue as the dominating colour.[21]

Some product categories, such as commodities, seem rather alien to branding for many international marketers. Success stories such as Outspan Oranges, Cichita Bananas, Intel microchips or Gore-Tex and Lycra fibres have proven the contrary. If a business-to-business supplier has a technological advantage over its competitors which can be directly translated into a benefit for the customers of its customer, an international brand may be established. Ingredient branding may even improve the attractiveness of a consumer product to customers all over the world. For example, PCs are more easily sold when the buyers know that the product has an 'Intel inside'. Sports textiles that have a little booklet attached explaining how Gore-Tex has been used to make the product water resistent without keeping perspiration inside are more attractive to many consumers. In addition, such branding decreases the dependence of the former commodity supplier on its direct customer.

Choice of Brand Name

The meaning of a product to its potential customers is characterized by what they associate with the brand and how they value those associations. Such associations may be based on experience, the supplier's communication, or on personal references. Their value depends on what the customers have learned to be good or bad as well as more or less important during their socialization in the local culture, in the different organizations to which they belong, and in reference groups relevant to them.

An essential part of a brand's presentation to the market is its name. If the marketer decides to endow its product with a brand name or to use its company's name as a brand, the brand becomes part of the total product. Therefore, the choice of the brand name and its communicative loading with specific meanings is of particular importance. In this choice international marketers are faced with additional problems, compared to their locally operating counterparts.

If a company entering a new country-market keeps its current brand name unchanged without checking its potential, problems with the pronunciation of the brand name may occur. For example, most German-speaking customers of Worcester Sauce have difficulties in pronouncing its name properly. The meaning of the brand name in another language may even have negative effects on sales. The name of Soupline, a French detergent, for example, would be inappropriate for markets where English is the dominant language, because

– pronounced in English – the brand would be loaded with meanings that are detrimental to the sales of a detergent.

To avoid problems with pronunciation or the resulting meaning of a brand name, the international marketer may either decide to use different brand names in each country-market or language area or try to find a name which can be used throughout its entire international product-market. The Strategy box describes how Nestlé, a very prominent example, implements the first alternative.

The example of Nestlé shows that a company can be very successful by developing local or regional brands. They may even be focused on a part of a multicultural country-market, such as the most southern parts of the United States which are populated by many Spanish-speaking consumers. Local brands are particularly advisable where more differences than similarities exist between country-markets in the benefits provided by a product. Regional brands make sense where cultural similarities among neighbouring markets exist, the same language can be used in brand communication, the same media are used by the customers across borders, and there is intensive cross-border traffic.

Because communication channels are becoming increasingly international, however, an increasing number of firms wants to take advantage of standardizing their brands. They therefore seek brand names that can be used internationally. A good name must sound appropriate in the languages of the country-markets to be served and spark associations that are both pleasant and express the meaning of the product or its most important benefit. A good name also has to stand out and have an emotional impact. Most international marketers prefer to choose brand names which automatically evoke certain associations in customers' minds. Otherwise, artificial or technical names must get their meanings attached through costly communication campaigns. Car makers, for example, increasingly choose real names over the numbers and letters that long marked their models. Perhaps the most revolutionary step in that direction was taken by French Renault when they stopped numbering their models in the manner of R-4 and R-5, and launched the Twingo, the Clio, the Mégane and the Safrane.

To find an internationally usable name that meets their needs, international marketers may use the services of professional name-finding agencies such as Nomen, a Paris-based agency which also has subsidiaries in the UK, Spain and Italy, and reports annual billings of USD3.2 million. Nomen has created names such as Chamaris and Caf'Conc for Delacre SA, the French biscuit-making unit of US-based Campbell Soup, Lift Serum for cosmetics maker Chanel, Eurocity for a group of European train operators and Bi-bop, an inexpensive mobile-phone system by France Telecom. For an elaborately designed stereo system by Japanese electronics maker Sony, Nomen sought ideas from painters, rock musicians, actors and marketing experts who came up with some 2000 names. The company then checked for ideas in encyclopaedias on opera, film and theatre. Special computer programmes scanned the words for possible variations. As a next step, Nomen checked online data banks for overlaps with existing brand names across the globe before presenting a list of ten names to the client. The whole process took two months and ended with the name Scenario.[22]

How difficult it may be for an international marketer to find an appropriate brand name that is usable across different cultures is illustrated by the Culture box. If brand name and company name are the same, which is often the case for business-to-business goods but also for many services companies, such difficulties may even be increased. The company cannot easily change

STRATEGY BOX

Nestlé's Brand Building Machine

NESTLÉ REPRESENTS A THUMPING REJECTION OF THE one-world, one-brand school of marketing. The company prefers brands to be local and people regional; only technology goes global. Call it the Roman Empire school of marketing: Colonize as much territory as fast as you can, adapting to native conditions, and then work at holding off the advancing competitors.

Nestlé has poured nearly USD 18 billion into aquisitions as over the past decade and now owns nearly 8000 different brands worldwide. Of those 8000 brands, only 750 are registered in more than one country, and only 80 are registered in ten.

In the industrially developing world, Nestlé grows by manipulating ingredients, or processing technology for local conditions, and then putting the appropriate brand name on the resulting product. Sometimes that is a well known one like Nescafé coffee; generally a local one works fine – for instance Bear Brand condensed milk in Asia. In new markets Nestlé alights with a mere handful of labels, selected from a basket of 11 strategic brand groups. The idea is to keep complexity low, limit risks, and concentrate the attack. Then the company can allocate marketing budgets into just two or three brands per country to gain big market shares.

Nestlé is the market leader for instant coffee in Australia (71%), France (67%), Japan (74%). In powdered milk Nestlé holds a market share of 66 per cent in the Philippines. Already the largest branded food company in Mexico where it holds 85 per cent of the instant coffee market, in Brazil where its market share of powdered milk reaches 58 per cent, in Chile where Nestlé has 73 per cent of the cookie market and 70 per cent of soups and sauces, and Thailand, Nestlé is on its way to becoming the leader in Vietnam and China as well.

Source: Rapoport, C. (1994) 'Nestlé's Brand Building Machine', *Fortune*, 19 September, pp. 147–156.

its name. If the problem is caused by difficulties in pronouncing the name, as for example Bazar de l'Hôtel de Ville for English-speaking tourists coming to Paris, a simplification or abbreviation of the name can be helpful. In the case of the Parisian department store, the three initials BHV were used.

Besides pronunciation and semantic problems which have to be resolved in international brand management, existing brand awareness needs to be considered. If a brand name has already reached a certain level of awareness in its served markets and evokes meanings that increase the product's attractiveness to existing customers, it would not be reasonable to change the name just to standardize branding across country-markets. For example, the Austrian cheese manufacturer Rupp had successfully launched the brand Pumuckl for their children's product line in Germany. There, children as well as buying parents knew the figure from a TV series of the same name and liked it. When the firm got ready to launch the same product line in Italy and the UK, they could not use the same name because in those countries consumers would not only have had difficulties pronouncing the name but did not know the TV series. On the other hand, changing the very successful name in Germany to allow internationally standardized brand communication would have destroyed the brand equity built up in the German market.

Culture Box

The Challenge of Finding International Brand Names

A Volkswagen named Diago would never sell in Britain. Rolls-Royce's Silver Mist model is called Silver Shadow in Germany. And Citroen's Evasion model was launched as Vicinity in Britain in the Fall of 1995.

Why? Mist in Germany means manure, or rubbish. Evasion makes Frenchmen think of freedom and adventure, while English speakers think only of tax evasion. And Diago reminds Britons of Argentinian soccer star Diego Maradonna, an unpopular person in England after a controversial goal in the 1986 World Soccer Championship that evicted England from the tournament. By discovering the name's negative connotation before the launch, Germany's Volkswagen AG saved a costly flop. The car was eventually baptized 'Vento'.

Gone seem the days when corporate executives picked product names at random – such as Germany's Gottlieb Daimler, who named his flagship car Mercedes, after the daughter of a client in Argentina. Professional namefinders also smile when thinking of the origins of Sweden's Ikea AB, which was named after furniture maker Ingvar Kamprad from Elmtaryd in the province of Algunazyd. With some ten million brand names around the world and fierce competition among an ever-growing number of new products, companies increasingly ask for professional help from name-finding agencies in developing distinctive product names. Nevertheless, problems remain. Reebok International Ltd., for example, was embarrassed to learn that the designation of its women's running shoe, 'Incubus', is the name of a mythical demon who preyed on sleeping women. And Nike Inc., another leading athletic supplies manufacturer, was accused of wanting to insult Muslims because the logo on their new shoes which was meant to look like flames resembled the word 'Allah' in the Arabic script.

A good name is particularly important for products consumers identify with, such as cars. Flop stories abound. Japan's Mitsubishi Motors Corp. had to rename its Pajero model in Spanish-speaking countries because the term describes the process of masturbation. Toyota Motor Corp.'s MR2 model dropped the number from its name in France because the combination sounds like a French swearword. And Italy's Lancia, a unit of Turin-based Fiat SpA, posted slow sales of its Dedra model in Britain partly because the name sounds like the word dead to British ears.

Sources: Abu-Nasr, D. (1997) 'Muslims want apology from Nike for "insult"', *The International Herald Tribune*, 10 April, p. 12; and Rohwedder, C. (1996) 'Name of Nomen's Game Is Crafting Brand Monikers', *The Wall Street Journal Europe*, 10 April, p. 4.

Brand Protection

Developing new international brands demands careful consideration of potential brand names. In addition, the chosen name or trademark must also be protectable. Trademarks may be graphic signs, that is, words, names of persons, pictures or slogans, as well as the design and packaging of a product which can be used to differentiate goods and services of one supplier from another. Figure 13.6 shows one of the oldest international trademarks and its development over the last 270 years.

The loss of a trademark may have devastating effects on the sales and profits of a firm. If the Coca-Cola Company, for example, lost its trademark,

Figure 13.6 **The Trademark of the Staatliche Porzellan-Manufaktur Meissen**

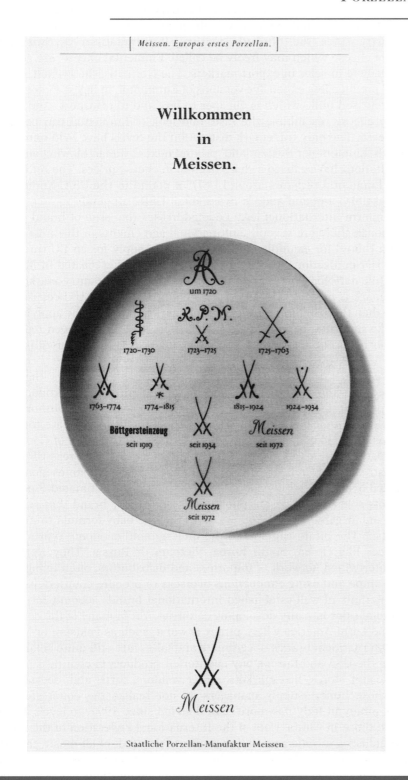

In 1723 the porcelain factory of Meissen, Germany, which was the first to produce fine porcelain outside China, chose two crossed swords as their trademark. Since then the trademark has been kept largely unchanged. It has only been adapted to the graphic taste of the time.

any soft-drink maker could bottle a sweet, brown carbonated beverage under the Coca-Cola name. The effect the loss of a brand name can have is illustrated by Swiss Emmenthal cheese. Cheese is Switzerland's oldest export product, and it remains the top agricultural export. The Emmental Valley, situated along the Emme River, has been the heart of Switzerland's cheese-making industry since the fifteenth century. But imitations of Swiss-made Emmental cheese which may freely be called 'Emmental cheese' are generating a large hole in sales in export markets. The Germans, the French and the Dutch all produce less expensive versions of Emmental, in bigger factories and with pasteurized milk, which is cheaper to buy and to transport. And, in the USA, any cheese resembling the taste and look of Emmental can be called Swiss cheese. The only trademark distinction the Swiss have held onto is the label, with 'Emmentaler Switzerland' printed next to a man blowing an alpenhorn. Imitations have caused a sharp decline in cheese prices. The retail price of Swiss Emmental registers around USD5 a pound in the USA, Netherlands Emmental USD3 a pound and US Swiss about USD2 a pound.[23]

No uniform international legal code addresses the issue of brand protection, although there are several multinational agreements in this area. In the European Union, for example, any company can apply for an EU trademark from the Harmonization Agency for the Common Market located in Alicante, Spain. While national brands are only protected in their country-markets, the EU trademark is protected in all member countries of the EU. Because there are more than three million registered trademarks in the EU, the applying firm must make sure that its requested trademark has not already been registered by another firm. The registration procedure takes at least four months.[24]

Counterfeiting. A major problem for international marketers that have established well-known brands is counterfeiting, the intentional production or sale of a product under a brand name or trademark without the authorization of the holder of that name or trademark. It is difficult to estimate total corporate losses due to counterfeiting. The International Chamber of Commerce has calculated such losses at over USD10 billion a year,[25] whereas US federal and industry surveys indicate that annual losses of US companies alone have quadrupled over the past decade to USD200 billion. An estimated 5 per cent of products sold worldwide are phony, and almost any brand that sells well becomes unfair game, from Windows 95 to Similac baby formula to ACDelco auto parts.[26] The pirate captains of the underground economy typically hail from places like China, South Korea, Vietnam or Russia. They work as a loosely intertwined network of importers and distributors, often living in the USA or Europe and using connections overseas to procure counterfeits.

Counterfeits of well-established international brands account for half or more of total sales in many developing countries. Yet in many of the countries of Asia and Latin America where piracy is worst, such as Pakistan or Mexico, sales of international brands – legitimate and fake – are still quite small. Consumers in the USA and Europe buy counterfeit products in countless places – small discount stores, flea markets, street vendors' carts, and, occasionally, chains whose honest supply managers do not realize the counterfeit. For example, piracy in Italy has more than doubled since 1992, to levels comparable with those in China. Data of the International Federation of the Phonographic Industry, a trade association, indicate that half of all music cassettes and about one-third of the compact discs sold in Italy are either illegal copies, unauthorized bootleg recordings or out-and-out counterfeits.[27] Covert retailing is on the rise, such as Tupperware-like parties for phony Rolex watches, Louis Vuitton bags or Porsche design eyeglasses. The USA, which buys 30 per cent of all the world's annual USD41.8 billion sales of recorded music, accounts for 13 per cent of pirated sales value. Americans have the questionable distinction of spending more on pirated music than any other country apart from Russia.[28]

Counterfeiting causes not only the direct loss of sales but also long-term losses that may be even more serious. For example, counterfeit products are usually of inferior quality, and some such products may even be harmful to their users. Textiles, such as counterfeit Lacoste T-shirts, but also Carreira glasses or Dunhill leather goods are often counterfeited by the use of substances which are not tolerated by the skin. Consumers wearing such fakes may break out in a rash or get allergies. Even worse, in 1995, the US Federal Aviation Administration grounded 6000 piston-powered aircraft to check for bogus crankshaft bolts that could cause crashes.[29] When such items cease to function properly or cause injury or other problems for their users, the negative image is transferred to the brand which was used in an unauthorized manner.

As a reaction, some companies join forces to fight brand piracy more effectively. For example, in 1995 Adidas, Replay, Windsurfing Chiemsee, MCM, Chipie and BAD & BAD formed an association to fight product piracy, VPM, in Munich, Germany. They exchange know-how on the installation of security mechanisms such as changing the details of product design or construction and information concerning distribution channel members suspected of participating in the counterfeiting network. The Business Software Alliance, representing a group of US software firms, has launched a scheme offering rewards to employees who tip them off about firms using illegal software. As a result, for example, Roman Financial Press, Hong Kong's biggest publishing group, paid the BSA USD54,000 for using unauthorized Microsoft and Adobe software.[30] Other companies engage private detectives, such as Professional Investigating & Consulting Agency, based in Columbus, Ohio to investigate cases of counterfeiting.

Packaging

How a company or a product appears to its potential customers in a market is not only influenced by the brand name, the logo or the country of origin. The packaging of products may contribute strongly to their meanings in the minds of potential customers. Because the package is often the last point at which the marketer has a chance to influence the customer's purchasing decision, it can play a powerful role in promoting the product. Both product delivery and product communication are strongly influenced by elements of the local environments of served country-markets. Therefore, packaging deserves particular attention in international marketing. Legal regulations, existing or non-existing infrastructure as well as social and cultural specifics need to be considered. Because infrastructure mainly influences the physical distribution of a product, its impact on packaging will be dicussed in Chapter 15. The following section will concentrate on the potential impact of legal regulations and social as well as cultural elements on packaging.

Legal Regulations. The international marketer has to consider local legal regulations concerning the packaging material to use, the design of the package, and the kind and amount of information to put on it. In Australia, Aim toothpaste, after spending USD5 million on a promotional campaign, had to change its package because it was ruled to be too similar to that of a competitor. The number and intensity of legal regulations concerning the reusability of packages and their recycling potential, has been increasing significantly in the European Union.

Many countries have different regulations concerning how product ingredients are to be listed and the manner in which promotional material is presented on labels. Cigarette labels, for example, have to include statements ranging from Japan's rather mild warning, 'Don't smoke too much', to Oman's much stronger statement, 'Smoking is a major cause of cancer, lung disease, and diseases of the heart and arteries'.

Regulations on ingredient listing are not automatically less demanding in countries with a lower level of industrial development. In Saudi Arabia, for example, there is a nomenclature for food products to be respected in addition to the list of ingredients, the net filling weight, name and address of the producer, production and latest consumption date to be indicated on the package. The entire information has to be given in Arabic as well as English.

The differences in legal regulations make it particularly difficult for an international marketer to standardize packaging across country-markets. Venezuela, for example, prescribes the indication of prices on the package, whereas in Chile this practice is illegal, as is recommending retail prices to intermediaries.

Cultural Elements.   Because packages are the visual surface of a product that customers first come into contact with, they may strongly influence the product's meaning to the customers. For new perfumes or cigarettes to be launched internationally, for example, changing the package colour or style may affect sales more than changing the product's name. For highly intangible products, such as legal or cosmetics consulting and restaurant services, the appearance of the location where the service takes place as well as the look of the service providers may serve the purpose of a package: to create a certain meaning of the product to the customer.

Like any perception of meanings, customer reactions to packaging are highly subject to influence by cultural specifics. The design of the package must fit the customers' expectations in size, style, material and colour. Packages that are the wrong colour, such as a black cigarette package in Hong Kong – black is a bad-luck colour there – or the wrong size, such as a 2-litre soft-drink bottle in the Netherlands – 2-litre bottles are too large for most Dutch refrigerators – can have a negative influence on sales. So can the number of products contained in one package. A US manufacturer of golf balls, for example, which exported its products to Japan, packaged the balls in groups of four. However, when the Japanese word for four is said aloud, it sounds like the word for death. Products grouped in fours, therefore, do not sell well in Japan.

Visuals on packages may also strongly influence local customers' acceptance of a product. An experiment measuring consumers' reactions to packaging in Hong Kong and the USA, for example, found that the reactions of female consumers to floral designs on soap packages differed considerably. Consumers in Hong Kong tended to give such designs a low value, whereas Americans associated the same designs with feminine products of neutral value.[31]

Socio-economic Factors. Socio-economic factors, such as the available family income or family size, may also influence the packaging decisions of international marketers. Multiple packs, which are designed to increase sales because of added convenience, for example, are affected by those factors. US-based Warner-Lambert offers its chewing gums in two-packs to Latin American consumers because of their rather low disposable income, compared to 12-packs in the USA where household income is significantly higher. Owing to different family sizes, Pillsbury offers its products in the USA mainly in packages for two people, whereas their packages sold in less industrially developed markets contain servings for six to eight people.

Even the level of education of the customers targeted in a country-market may have an influence on the packaging of a product. Kenya, Malaysia and Singapore, for example, have introduced standard sizes for cans, bottles and other food packages to avoid consumer confusion owing to a variety of different sizes and to facilitate price comparisons.

Standardisation. International standardization of packaging provides significant sources of cost reduction, such as reduced production, printing, storage and handling costs, as well as increased speed and quality of physical distribution. For that reason, Bonduelle, the French producer of canned and frozen vegetables, which traditionally had different packaging from one country to another, decided to create the same visual identity for its entire product range all across its 18 European country-markets: on packages dominated by a yellow background the name of the company, which is also the brand name, is printed in green below an orange arch which is meant to express the well-being derived from consuming the product.[32]

Multilingual labels, standardized content declarations, internationally used trademarks, or fit with Euro-pallets have been used by many companies for the purpose of cost reduction. But full packaging standardization across country-markets can only be achieved when the expectations of customers and intermediaries in those markets are not contradictory, when the highest levels of expectations concerning the package's functions can be fulfilled in each market, when cultural differences do not lead to undesirable effects on the product meaning created by the standardized package, and when cost limits can be respected.

For example, standardization of toothpaste packaging across Europe is hampered by the fact that German-speaking customers are increasingly demanding non-packaged products. They want to avoid waste of natural resources and environmental pollution through packaging material. On the other hand, important shares of customers in the southern and eastern parts of Europe still value expensive-looking 'modern' packages, because for those consumers they indicate progress. Both expectations can hardly be satisfied with one standardized packaging concept.

Consistency of International Brand Management

Table 13.2 contains the names of the 14 best-selling brands in Europe in 1995. From the years of their first appearance on the market one can conclude that consistent brand management not only strongly contributes to short-term success but also to the longevity of international brands.

What customers associate with a brand is not directly influenced by the brand itself. It is based on the individual and collective experiences customers

Table 13.2 The Top 14 Brands in Europe 1995

According to a study by Nielsen, the top selling brands of consumer products in 14 European countries in 1995 are international brands, most with a high degree of standardization. None of them is less than 15 years old, showing that well-managed brands are not subject to short-term life-cycle curves.

Brand	Product Category	Sales Volume in Billion USD	Year of Market Launch
1. Coca-Cola	Soft drink	3.59	1886
2. Ariel	Detergent	1.45	1968
3. Pampers	Nappies	1.36	–
4. Barilla	Pastas	1.105	1877
5. Jacobs	Coffee	1.07	1895
6. Nescafé	Coffee	.94	1938
7. Danone	Yoghurt	.82	1919
8. Whiskas	Pet food	.79	1959
9. Pedigree	Pet food	.59	1963
10. Langnese	Ice cream	.57	1935
11. Persil	Detergent	.555	1907
12. Fanta	Soft drink	.55	1958
13. Pepsi Cola	Soft drink	.525	1898
14. Milka	Chocolate	.505	1892

Source: 'Top 100 Marken in Europa', Werbung & Print, December 1995, p. 9.

have when they come into contact with the total product and its communication. A lasting cognitive structure can only develop in customers' minds when their brand-related experiences are consistent over time.

To manage a brand consistently on an international level, the marketer must first make sure that all members of the company, as well as intermediaries who take decisions and act in situations that may influence the meaning of the brand to the customers, fully understand the intended 'identity' of the brand and are highly motivated to support that meaning. The top management of Rodenstock, the Munich-based manufacturer of optical products, for example, has developed a description of its brand's most important characteristics. Those characteristics should mark the identity of the brand as perceived by the firm's customers. To make this perception possible, managers from all international parts of the company as well as employees and workers are informed about their brand's identity, and are invited to workshops where they can discuss their potential contribution to achieving this identity and what coordinated actions need to be set in motion to ensure consistency of their customers' brand-related experiences across country-markets.

The establishment and consistent management of a brand need perseverance. Strong Japanese brands, such as Sony, Toyota or Canon, have taken years to develop their global position. It also needs patience. Both the use of pricing tools and continual changes in market communication to increase market shares rapidly have proven to be detrimental to a brand's lasting success. Companies which, for personnel or financial reasons, are not able to ensure a high level of continuity in their brand-related decisions and actions across countries are well advised not to try establishing an international brand.

Impact on the Marketing Mix

The product is the key element of the marketing mix. It must provide an attractive benefit to the customer if the entire marketing mix is to be successful. The greater this benefit to the customer and the higher the perceived quality of the product compared to its competitors, the more freedom the marketer has in setting prices. But prices (and customer benefits) are also influenced by the costs of a product. Therefore, the international marketer needs to take care of those costs from the very beginning of the product development process, through the production of the product, to its eventual recycling. Because of their lower sales volume, products exclusively conceived for domestic markets are often less price competitive than their internationally conceived counterparts. By influencing product innovation processes in such a way as to have an international marketing perspective, the marketer can influence the span of manoeuvre for pricing decisions.

Quality management decisions and brand management have an impact on the choice of distribution channels as well as the management of business and personal relationships with intermediaries. The closer the company is to its customers, the better the control over the customer contact personnel and direct customer communication. If available channel members in a country-market provide little or no personal selling, the brand must be quickly recognizable. Packaging has to take over an important part of market communication.

Communication and distribution mix in the various country-markets served must be managed carefully in order to avoid negative surprises for mobile customers who find 'their' brands differently positioned in other countries. At least the core of a brand's positioning must remain the same across country-markets. Local adaptations to different tastes as well as technical and social norms and varying added features to increase the local attractiveness of a brand must not endanger the internationally shared central meanings of the brand.

The potential for internationally standardized market communication is directly affected by product management. Local brands generally require localized communication, leading to higher budget needs. When the product concept can be easily captured in a symbol, such as Mickey Mouse or the Michelin Man, which makes visual sense in multiple cultures, communication standardization is eased.

Summary

The most important processes in international product management are related to product portfolio management, quality management and brand management. The goal of product portfolio management is to supply the markets with a stream of constantly renewed products which are attractive to customers, competitive compared to other suppliers' products and allow the company to make attractive profits as well as to stay financially sound. To achieve this goal, international product management has to develop and maintain a balanced combination of products, a product portfolio.

To optimize a company's international product portfolio, the marketer has to determine how many product lines should be offered internationally and with how many variations. To keep an international product portfolio balanced, new products have to be continually developed and introduced to the markets in a planned way together with variations of existing products. Each successful launch of a new product in international markets needs several new product ideas to start with. Compared to a locally operating competitor, an international marketer has access to a greater number and diversity of sources of ideas for new products. The international marketer will have to determine the most valuable sources. Ideas coming from lead markets and lead actors in those markets will be the most preferred.

Product development needs to be organized in a way that eases the development process. In addition, the product to be developed has to be continually checked for its potential market success. Its design has to be adapted to the specific needs of the international markets. And the introduction of the new product in the various markets has to be prepared in time.

The goal of quality management is to keep customer satisfaction with the company's products at the highest levels in order to have as many loyal customers as possible and to win their positive references to other potential customers. Marketers basically have two ways of influencing their customers' quality perceptions: they may use quality assurance to ascertain a given level of performance on each of the material and immaterial features important to the customers and they may shape the customers' product-related expectations through quality signalling. Both will be chosen by an international marketer to be successful.

Brand management tries to achieve and maintain a consistent meaning of the company's products to customers which positively differentiates them from competitors' products and simplifies customers' decision-making processes. An essential part of a brand's presentation to the market is its name. Therefore, the choice of the brand name and its communicative loading with specific meanings is of particular importance. But developing new international brands does not only demand careful consideration of potential brand names; the chosen name or trademark must also be protectable. The loss of a trademark or a brand may have devastating effects on the sales and profits of a firm.

A major problem for international marketers that have established well-known brands is counterfeiting. Counterfeiting causes not only the direct loss of sales but also long-term losses that may be even more serious. For example, counterfeit products are usually of inferior quality, and some such products may even be harmful to their users.

The packaging of products may strongly contribute to their meanings in the minds of potential customers because packaging is the visual surface of a product that customers first get in contact with. Customer reactions to packaging are highly subject to influence by cultural specifics. The design of the package must fit customers' expectations in size, style, material and colour. In addition, the international marketer has to consider local legal regulations concerning the packaging material to use, the design of the package, and the kind and amount of information to put on it. Full packaging standardization across country-markets will only be possible when the expectations of customers and intermediaries in those markets are not contradictory, when the highest levels of expectations concerning the package's functions can be fulfilled in each market, when cultural differences do not lead to undesirable effects on the product meaning created by the standardized package, and when legal regulations as well as cost limits can be respected.

DISCUSSION QUESTIONS

1. Try to find a product category where an international product life cycle exists. Prepare a demonstration of your data and some explanations of why this phenomenon exists.
2. Take a case you are familiar with and develop an international product portfolio for the company. What suggestions do you make?
3. How does the product innovation process in an internationally operating firm differ from the product innovation process in a firm with a domestic business focus?
4. Why is quality assurance particularly difficult for an international service provider? Gather some information concerning an example substantiating your points.
5. What inherent dangers do you see in quality signalling? Find examples of successful and less successful quality signalling attempts.
6. How may country-of-origin effects be used in international brand management? Find some recent examples and report on their level of success.
7. What are the differences concerning brand protection between the USA, the EU, and an Asian or Latin American country of your choice? What consequences would you draw as a brand manager?
8. Would you buy a counterfeited product? Discuss your reasons why.
9. In what respects may the packaging of a product influence its meaning to the customers? What would you as an international brand manager do to avoid major packaging mistakes?
10. Why is the consistency of international brand management decisions so very important? Find an example where a lack of consistency led to problems for a firm.

ADDITIONAL READINGS

Ballantyne, D., M. Christopher, and A. Payne (1995) 'Improving the Quality of Services Marketing: Service (Re)design is the Critical Link', *Journal of Marketing Management*, 11, 7–24.

Caller, L.(ed.) (1996) *'Researching Brands'*, ESOMAR New Monograph Series, Vol. 3, Amsterdam.

Herstatt, C. and E. v. Hippel (1992) 'From Experience: Developing New Product Concepts via the Lead User Method: A Case Study in a "Low-Tech" Field', *Journal of Product Innovation Management*, 9, 213–221.

Jain, S.C. (1996) 'Problems of International Protection of Intellectual Property Rights', *Journal of International Marketing*, 4(1) 9–32.

Llosa, S. (1997) 'L'analyse de la contribution des éléments du service à la satisfaction: Un modèle tétraclasse', *Décisions Marketing*, No. 10, Janvier–Avril, 81–88.

McCracken, G. (1988) *Culture and Consumption: New Approaches to the Symbolic Character of Consumer Goods and Activities*, Bloomington: Indiana University Press.

Nebenzahl, I.D., E.D. Jaffe, and S.I. Lampert (1997) 'Towards a Theory of Country Image Effect on Product Evaluation', *Management International Review*, 37(1), 27–49.

Steenkamp, J.-B.(1990) 'Conceptual Model of the Quality Perception Process', *Journal of Business Research*, 21(4), December, 309–333.

NOTES

[1] Nathans Spiro, L., S. Moshavi, M. Shari, I. Katz, H. Dawley, G. Smith and D. Lindorff (1996) 'Global Gamble – Morgan Stanley is charging into the Third World. Will it get burned?', *Business Week*, 12 February, pp. 63–70.

[2] Du Bois, M. (1996) 'Off the Dole, Europe Sees Market In Temporary Workers Profit From Jobs Crisis', *The Wall Street Journal Europe*, 10–11 May, pp. 1 and 8.

[3] Iritani, E. (1996) 'MCA Challenges Mickey', *International Herald Tribune*, 23 May, p. 15.

[4] Cooper, B. (1994) *Winning at New Products: Accelerating the Process from Idea to Launch*, 2nd. edn, Reading, MA: Addison-Wesley.

[5] Browning, J. (1995) 'Europeans On-Line', *Scientific American*, May, p. 35.

[6] Sager, I. (1996) 'IBM's Tollbooth for the I-Way', *Business Week*, 13 May, pp. 58f.

[7] Davis, R.J. and S. Ueyama (1996) 'Developing customers before products', *The McKinsey Quarterly*, No. 3, 72–83.

[8] Rapoport, C. (1994) 'Nestlé's Brand Building Machine', *Fortune*, 19 September, pp. 147–156.

[9] Nussbaum, B. (1995) 'Is In-house Design on the Way Out?', *Business Week*, 25 September, p. 54.

[10] 'Sega's sonic hedge', *The Economist*, 14 September, 1996, p. 69.

[11] Ballantyne, D., M. Christopher, and A. Payne (1995) 'Improving the Quality of Services Marketing: Service (Re)design is the Critical Link', *Journal of Marketing Management*, 11, 7–24.

[12] Gilmore, J.H. and B.J. Pine II (1997) 'The Four Faces of Mass Customization', *Harvard Business Review*, January–February, 91–101.

[13] Friedland, J. and C. Vitzthum (1996) 'Santander Says It Plans to Buy Stake in Osorno', *The Wall Street Journal Europe*, 12–13 April, p. 9.

[14] Harper, T. (1996) 'Industry Geared to Luxury and No-Frills Travel', *International Herald Tribune*, 9–10 March, p. 17.

[15] 'Die Hotel-Imperien weiten weltweit ihre Grenzen aus', *Der Standard*, 2 January, 1997, p. 15.

[16] Du Bois, M. (1996) op. cit.

[17] Gachet, G. (1997) 'Le tir groupé des producteurs écossais', *Le Figaro économie*, 15 April, p. X.

[18] Verlegh, W.J. and J.-B.E.M. Steenkamp (1997) 'Country-of-origin effects: A meta-analytic review', *Marketing: Progress, Prospects, Perspectives* (D. Arnott *et al.*, eds), Warwick Business School, pp. 2136–2140.

[19] 'Consumer optimism in urban China', *ESOMAR newsbrief*, 4, (1) January 1996, 23.

[20] 'Macworld', *The Economist*, 29 June 1996, p. 61f.

[21] Frank, R. (1996) 'Seeing Red Abroad, Pepsi Rolls Out a New Blue Can', *The Wall Street Journal*, 2 April, pp. B1 and B6.

[22] Rohwedder, C. (1996) 'Name of Nomen's Game Is Crafting Brand Monikers', *The Wall Street Journal Europe*, 10 April, p. 4.

[23] Calian, S. (1996) 'Swiss Cheese Now Is A Mature Market In Switzerland', *The Wall Street Journal*, 4 March, pp. 1 and 6.

[24] 'Modell Coca-Cola? – Eine einzige Handelsmarke für 350 Millionen Verbraucher', *EUR-OP NEWS*, No. 4, Winter 1995, 9.

[25] Rohrhofer, B. (1995) 'Unternehmen verfolgen Piraten ihrer Marken', *OÖ Nachrichten*, 7 August, p. 9.

[26] Stipp, D. (1996) 'Farewell, My Logo', *Fortune*, 27 May, pp. 128–140.

[27] Hansen, J. (1996) 'Live, and Pirated, From Italy', *International Herald Tribune*, 16–17 March, p. 11.

[28] 'Stolen melodies', *The Economist*, 11 May, 1996, p. 64.

[29] op. cit.

[30] 'Bazaar software', *The Economist*, March 1997, pp. 77f.

[31] Knutsen, J., S. Thrasher, and Y. Kathawala (1998) 'The Impact of Culture Upon Package Perception: An Experiment in Hong Kong and the United States', *International Journal of Management*, June, 117–124.

[32] Malet, C. (1996) 'Bonduelle: à l'est, du nouveau', *Le Figaro économie*, 11 March, p. 11.

CHAPTER
14

INTERNATIONAL DISTRIBUTION MANAGEMENT

INTERNATIONAL INCIDENT

Make Your Dealers Your Partners

A decade ago, many observers predicted that Caterpillar, headquartered in Peoria, Illinois, would join the long list of US corporations that had fallen to the Japanese. They focused particularly on the rivalry between Caterpillar and Komatsu. With Komatsu boasting cost advantages of as much as 40 per cent in some product lines and excellent products, observers accepted as a foregone conclusion that Komatsu would fulfill its vow to 'encircle Cat' and become the dominant producer in the construction and mining equipment industry. Like many predictions, this one fell short. Despite determined efforts by Komatsu, Hitachi, Kobelco, and other competitors, Caterpillar's share of the world market in 1995 was the highest in the company's history. And after suffering heavy losses in five of 11 years from 1982 through 1992, Caterpillar has rebounded financially with record profits and a return on equity in the mid to high thirties.

Several factors played a part. They include the high value of Caterpillar's brand name; the excellent quality of products; the high resale value of the machines; a reorganization that made the company leaner and more responsive to customer needs; big investments in manufacturing productivity; faster new product development processes; and the weakening of the dollar relative to the yen. But the biggest reason for Caterpillar's success has been its system of distribution and product support and the close customer relationships it fosters.

The final customer knows that there is a company called Caterpillar. But the dealer creates the image of the firm. Caterpillar's 186 selected dealers tend to be prominent business leaders in their markets who are deeply involved in community activities. Their reputation and long-term relationships are important because selling Caterpillar's products is a personal business.

Caterpillar helps its dealers finance purchases by customers. It supports dealers in inventory management and control, logistics, equipment management, and maintenance programs. Dealers are involved in programs dealing with product quality, cost reduction, and manufacturing issues. The company also publishes a huge volume of technical material each year and underwrites technical training and support for dealers' personnel.

Caterpillar's top management is convinced that the relationship between a company and its dealers is much more important than the contractual agreements or the techniques and tactics that make the relationship work on the surface. Mutual trust, continuity and consistency in policies, constant communication, uniform performance standards and equal consideration of dealers while recognizing that they are independent and unique in many ways helps the firm to present one face to its customers around the world.

Source: Fites, D.V. (1996) 'Make Your Dealers Your Partners', *Harvard Business Review*, March–April, 84–95.

INTERNATIONAL
DISTRIBUTION DECISIONS

Every company must manage distribution, or the flow of products to final customers. In some cases distribution is relatively straightforward. Before the Gulf war, a brewery in Iraq put bottles filled with beer into cases, placed the cases on pallets, and transported them from the end of the production line to the fence surrounding the company's property. There, customers were waiting impatiently to purchase the product. They climbed to the top of the fence, where the cases were lifted up to them and the price was paid. The firm's distribution system consisted of a forklift and its driver.

The example may seem strange to readers who are familiar with distribution in highly developed countries, but it clearly shows that any company's distribution system has two major components: (a) distribution channels, that is, the people, organizations or institutions by which goods or services are offered to the customers, including agents, dealers, wholesalers and retailers, and (b) the means of physical distribution, that is, the tools and facilities, including the related information, used by people and organizations to bridge the physical distance between the company and its customers.

An international distribution system shares many characteristics with a domestic one. Both, for example, must make the product available to potential customers, help inform them about product benefits, manage distribution partner relationships, and be suited to the company's intended strategic position. However, designing an international distribution system is more complicated because it must take into account different geographic areas, the varying expectations of distribution partners, differences in competitive structure, and the dimensions of the macro-environment, such as legal regulations, culture-specific buying habits or the level of economic development, relevant to the company's business. This chapter addresses such factors and others that help determine the best distribution system for goods and services for an international marketing effort.

For the purpose of determining the best distribution system, management has to examine different types of systems and assess the advantages and disadvantages they offer. It will use various customer and intermediary characteristics to compare alternative distribution channels available in the market. But channel selection is only part of international distribution management. To be successful, international marketers must carefully manage the relationships with the selected channel members. They need an appropriate organizational structure, as well as a bundle of tools for effective communication, motivation and control.

This chapter first discusses the need for an international distribution policy which is the guideline for the selection of a distribution system and of channel members described later. The importance of relationship management in international distribution channels is highlighted and some tools available to marketing managers are presented. Chapter 16 will focus on the structure of a company's own sales force, how to choose and train salespeople for international marketing, and will discuss important issues of how to manage an international sales force. The contribution of transportation, packaging, warehousing and storage to an appropriate level of international customer service will be the focus of Chapter 15.

INTERNATIONAL DISTRIBUTION POLICY

Many small and medium-sized companies are so overwhelmed by the complexity of international distribution that they simply conform to existing company procedures (which are likely to be inappropriate for international markets) or take advantage only of opportunities that arise by chance. Even multinational corporations often leave specific distribution decisions to their local offices. In both cases there is a clear need to establish an international distribution policy.

An international distribution policy is a general statement of goals that have to be attained by distribution decisions and of rules of behaviour which are to be met when implementing those decisions. A company's international distribution policy should reflect its basic strategic decisions. It should help to achieve the intended global market position by translating more general goals and objectives into a set of specific distribution guidelines. Those guidelines determine how the chosen market-entry alternative is to be executed. They indicate minimum and maximum levels of capital and personnel to be committed to achieving a desired level of coverage in each market. They contain pre-established goals regarding market share, sales volume and profit margins for each region, customer group and distribution channel, taking into account the desired level of company involvement in the distribution system, and the desirability of ownership of intermediaries.

The desirable level of market coverage has to be determined in light of the company's general competitive posture, its long-term market potential and expected return on investment, its financial strength, the positioning of strategic business units and products, and the geographic location of product-markets. For example, mass-production companies and manufacturers of speciality items need different levels of market coverage. The mass-production company wants intensive distribution, that is, to be represented in as many outlets as possible, because most customers will not be ready to shop for their products. Coca-Cola, BIC razors and Nescafé are examples of products that are distributed in this way. A producer of speciality items, on the other hand, may choose selective or exclusive distribution. Its customers are either brand loyal or ready to search for the product. Selective distribution may severely limit the number of partners in the distribution channel, cooperating only with channel partners that are well suited to the product's intended position in customers' minds. For example, Patek Philip, a Geneva, Switzerland-based producer of expensive watches, follows a policy of choosing a single renowned speciality shop in every major city to sell its products.

Guidelines concerning the level of the company's involvement in local distribution activities significantly affect the level of market control achieved by the company and the quality of marketing in the targeted areas. The international distribution policy has to ensure that the distribution system of the firm and how it is managed fits the image to be established through the firm's product, its price, and corporate communication. Dallas, Texas-based Mary Kay Cosmetics, for example, has a policy of selling directly to its customers through employees known as 'beauty consultants'. When they started business in China and Russia in 1995, they did not rely on the service quality of local retailing firms, but coordinated all of their marketing activities through their own people.[1]

ALTERNATIVE DISTRIBUTION SYSTEMS

In general, there are two ways to distribute goods: directly to the final customer or indirectly through a more complex system that employs intermediaries. Producers of industrial goods often sell directly to their customers, using an internal sales force to initiate and maintain business relationships. Most manufacturers of consumer goods, on the other hand, sell to wholesalers or large retailers, which may sell to other wholesalers and smaller retailers, which in turn sell to the final customer. In either case, distribution often becomes more complex when national boundaries are crossed. This section describes both direct (integrated) and indirect (independent or company-bound) distribution systems.

Integrated Distribution

In an integrated distribution system the company's own employees generate sales, administer orders and deliver products or services. The distribution system is integrated because employees, whatever their title or function within the company, are the agents of distribution. Several variables determine which members of a firm are most directly involved in generating sales: company size, size of potential market, level of customers' globalization, importance of customer services, the hierarchical level of purchase decision makers, the complexity of the product, and the available means of contact with customers.

Compared to large companies, in small internationally operating firms marketing and sales functions are less specifically assigned to certain people. Distribution activities, therefore, tend to be distributed across all levels of hierarchy. When the size of a local market is small, sales will mostly be generated by salespeople who often report to a regional sales manager. In larger markets, companies which prefer an integrated distribution system tend to establish more complex sales organizations. Liechtenstein's HILTI AG, for example, is dedicated to integrated distribution. Its global distribution system contains regional sales organizations such as Hilti Western Hemisphere, Hilti Latin America and Hilti Asia. In the USA, customer group oriented teams, each formed by a territory salesperson, an employee of the national Hilti centre and a member of the central customer service unit – both located in Tulsa, Oklahoma – contact and serve their customers. In China, about 100 HILTI salespeople sustained by regional distribution centres serve their local customers directly.[2]

The level of globalization of a firm's customers results in varying members of the firm being involved in business interactions. US-based Xerox, for example, has established a global key account management system. Each global account, that is, firms which require services in two or more countries, has the focused attention of a senior-level manager, whose responsibilities include working with foreign personnel to ensure delivery of products and services. Xerox also guarantees high-level management attention and support for its global accounts. Top management executives involved in the programme not only advise customers on Xerox's services, but also provide input into strategic decisions and participate in sales calls as necessary.[3]

Salespeople will handle the entire selling process if the complexity of the product is low and their customers are simply purchasing agents. The sales-people may report directly to the company's home office, but often visit customers in foreign markets; or they may operate out of subsidiaries or sales offices in different geographic areas. If the purchase decision maker is a powerful person, for example a category purchasing manager of Kmart, a large US retailing firm, yearly listing negotiations will be conducted by a high-level representative of the international marketer.

Sales of highly complex products or services, such as industrial plants or large consulting projects, usually involve higher-level members of the supplier organization. Most of the negotiation process is done by teams of functional specialists but final decision making or at least the signing of contracts is done by members of higher management. For example, when Italy-based Danieli SA offers large metallurgical engineering projects, such as the construction of a new continuous casting plant at the Magnitogorsk steel works in Russia, the specifications and terms of contracts are normally negotiated by specialists in sales, finance and technology, but the final negotiation and the signing of the contract are done by top management, because they involve important private capital owners, top managers, or high-level government(-related) customers in the purchasing organization.

Depending on the importance of customer services, such as planning or advice, and the available means of contact with customers in a market, marketers can also sell goods or services directly to the final customer through manufacturer-owned stores or showrooms, or by means of mail-order, telephone or electronic markets. A system of stores owned by the manufacturer is a type of distribution channel that is usually available only to financially strong companies. Less well-capitalized firms can choose franchising, as described in Chapter 11 (see also Table 14.1). This approach may also be used when all other distribution channels are blocked or when the company's marketing strategy is based on direct contact with the final customer.

Mail-order selling is a distribution system that is becoming increasingly important in international marketing. A number of specialized companies, such as Great Universal Stores, headquartered in England, operate internationally. US Dell Computer Corp., which gets 30 per cent of its sales in Europe, and Gateway 2000 Inc., which is active in Asia and Latin America and entered Europe in 1994, dominate the mail-order business for PCs. Mail-order is the preferred method for the best PC customers – experienced business clients and knowledgeable consumers looking for the most cutting-edge (and inexpensive) models. Dell and Gateway, rather than run up big inventories of finished systems, can build to order and therefore have lower costs. By selling direct, they can afford to undercut the prices of big brands, which need to leave a 4 to 10 per cent profit for dealers.[4] Manufacturers of high-tech industrial products sometimes also use the mail-order approach. For example, Wild-Leitz, a Swiss-based company specializing in opto-electronics, sends catalogues to customers to sell standard products and spare parts.

Telephone selling can be used in various ways. Sales clerks or call centres may use the telephone to establish and maintain contact with customers who are never contacted personally. Potential customers may be called to generate leads for the field sales force. Or existing customers may be called to sell products, promote new services and collect information.

Electronic markets exist for both consumer and industrial goods and services in the most developed economies. The Future Issues box gives an example of how electronic media will allow companies to virtually extend

Table 14.1 TYPES OF INTERMEDIARIES

Representatives establish and maintain relationships with prospective and existing customers in a specified geographic area on behalf of the principal. Representatives do not take physical possession of the product, do not arrange for its shipping or handling, and do not take any credit, market or exchange risk. A representative does arrange sales between the manufacturer and buyers. The representative must pass all legal documents to the principal for approval and cannot sign them on behalf of the principal. In a continuing relationship the representative may handle only the principal's product lines and complementary lines of other firms. Compensation is in the form of commission.

Brokers and factors are independent agents. They can legally bind the principal to a contract and expose it to risk without taking any risk themselves. **Brokers** are independent individuals or organizations that bring together prospective buyers and sellers to facilitate sales. They often deal in commodities and food products, handling large volumes of merchandise. Normally this is not a continuing relationship and exclusivity is not expected. **Factors**, many of which are banks, perform all normal brokerage functions plus financing. They may finance goods at various stages of the value-added chain. Factors serve to relieve both the seller and buyer of credit risk. The non-continuous relationship between the principal and the factor is also non-exclusive; that is, a factor can serve other sellers as well. Brokers and factors are paid a fee by the seller for services provided.

Distributors have a formalized, continuing relationship with the manufacturer, with exclusive sales rights for a specified geographic area. Distributors take title to (buy) the products they sell to other merchants (wholesalers or retailers) or to industrial customers. Close cooperation between the manufacturer and distributor gives the principal more control over prices, promotional activities, inventory and service policies than it has when it sells products to a wholesaler.

Dealers have the same function as retailers. But, in addition, they have the same type of continuing relationship with suppliers that distributors have. The major difference between dealers and distributors is that dealers sell the principal's goods directly to final customers. Sometimes the principal holds an equity share in the dealer's business. In such situations the principal has considerable control over the relationship and the dealer provides the principal with a great deal of market information. In most cases dealers have exclusive selling rights for the manufacturer's products in a specified area and the principal is the dealer's only supplier. Most automobile manufacturers use dealers as their intermediaries. Dealers are also common in the marketing of industrial goods.

Franchising is a special kind of dealership agreement that is well suited to companies with innovative products and fully developed marketing strategies, but insufficient capital to implement those strategies. A franchisee is an individual or organization that is granted the right to conduct business under the franchiser's trade name. The franchiser assists the franchisee in locating, equipping and designing the business premises. In most cases franchisees must closely follow the terms of contractual agreements regarding how business is to be conducted. The franchiser is paid a fee or royalties as compensation for fulfilling such functions as management assistance and training and global marketing. *(continued)*

Table 14.1 (continued)

International franchising has become increasingly popular in a number of industries in which standardized services or brand names are especially important to customers. Fashion franchises like Benetton, Rodier, Champion and Escada are found in most developed countries. Fast-food franchises, like McDonald's, Kentucky Fried Chicken, Wienerwald and Wimpy's, and hotel franchises, like Novotel, Holiday Inn and the Hilton, are also found throughout the world.

Importers fulfil the same functions as distributors but generally do not have exclusive territorial rights. They may be either wholesalers or retailers, and they may handle the products of many suppliers, sometimes even competing product lines. As a result, the principal has limited control.

Distributors, dealers and importers do not receive direct compensation; their profit is the margin between the buying and selling prices of the products they carry, minus their costs. The margins or discounts offered to merchants vary greatly from one country to another. They depend on the level of competition in a given market, the level of service offered by the intermediary, geographic distance, sales volume, purchasing power, efficiency and tradition.

product and service offers to customers. Computer-based systems provide customers with product offers and information, service, and billing with the help of a video screen and a printer. For example, US-based Digital Equipment Corporation has a World Wide Web site that allows prospective customers to use a personal computer to contact sales representatives, search for products and services, review the specifications of DEC equipment, and actually take a DEC machine for a 'test drive'.

A public system, Minitel in France, is an interactive information service that allows users to request product or company information from a central data bank, which contains information supplied by participating companies and institutions, and to order products or services. Even with the increasing array of 'facilitating technology' already in place, it still appears, however, that the majority of European customers are not actively seeking further opportunities to shop from home. They essentially see electronic markets as supplements to the shops.[5] Teleshopping, popular in the USA, is also not a major sales outlet in Europe. US teleshopping giant QVC Inc. started a joint venture with British Sky Broadcasting in 1993. Success has been moderate. Sweden's TV-Shop, a subsidiary of AB Kinnevik, offered in 15 European countries, has demonstrated only moderate success also. With 1995 sales of USD100 million, TV-Shop is nonetheless the largest European teleshopping company. In France, the two providers, Club Teleachat and Teleachat, together generated sales of only USD20 million in the same year.[6]

The China Internet Company, backed by the Xinhua News Agency, has developed a network of Internet sites for 40 industrial cities in China. On this network, users can find multimedia documents that describe a wide range of products, from toys to towels to auto parts. The China Internet Company also provides a catalogue of Chinese laws pertaining to trade and export, a

FUTURE ISSUES
BOX

Distribution via the 'Marketspace'

THE TRADITIONAL PRODUCT OF A MAJOR RECORD LABEL such as US-based Geffen is a package of pre-recorded music captured on an audiocassette or compact disc. It is sold via retail outlets such as record stores or special departments of department stores. Increasingly, new competitors for Geffen's business are emerging in the market-space, a virtual world of information provided by electronic media. For example, groups such as the Internet Underground Music Archive (IUMA) are posting digital audio tracks from unknown artists on the network. Today's technology allows musicians to record and edit material inexpensively themselves, and to distribute and promote it over networks such as the World Wide Web or commercial on-line services. They also can test consumers' reactions to their recorded performances, and distribute their products entirely in the marketspace.

Bringing music to market can sometimes be done faster, better, and less expensively in the marketspace. Hence the challenge for Geffen. The company has a site on the World Wide Web devoted to the label's bands and uses it to distribute digital audio and video samples and to provide information about the bands' tours. The Web page has not only become Geffen's showroom, but also a potential retail channel.

To truly exploit the existing opportunities Geffen might go further, utilizing the digital information captured during a band's practice sessions by inviting fans to sit in the studio on the Internet. They might also allow fans to listen as engineers edit the material or to electronically download interviews with the band's members before they are distributed more widely. Electronic media present opportunities to develop new relationships with customers at very low cost – for example, a customer not interested in a new compact disc by the Rolling Stones may nevertheless pay to sit in on a chat session with them in the Internet's Voodoo Lounge.

Source: Rayport, J.F. and J.J. Sviokla (1995) 'Exploiting the Virtual Value Chain', *Harvard Business Review*, November–December, 75–85.

translation service, and news. Because China does not have an adequate physical infrastructure for information about exports, they hope to create a virtual platform first.[7]

Independent and Company-Bound Distribution

Independent distribution systems are not directly controlled by the organization. The company uses intermediaries to establish contact with the final customers. Companies that use intermediaries but largely control them are said to have company-bound distribution systems. In domestic as well as international marketing, there are basically two types of intermediaries: agents and merchants.

Agents (in domestic marketing they are often called manufacturers' representatives) fully represent the company (also called the principal) in a particular market. They operate in the name of the principal, but they do not take title to the products being distributed, nor do they bear any economic risks.

Merchants, in contrast, do take title to the goods, which they buy, handle and sell on their own account. In domestic marketing, they are commonly referred to as distributors or wholesalers. Through merchants' activities, time, place, finance and service utilities are added to the product bundle. A more complete discussion of the types of intermediaries that international marketers use is provided in Table 14.1. In most cases the intermediaries in a distribution channel are a mixture of the types described.

Integrated versus Independent Distribution

The following conditions favour an integrated distribution system:

↔ Specialized product or product use knowledge

↔ A high level of service requirements

↔ A highly differentiated product

↔ A product closely related to the company's core business

↔ A strong need to control local marketing practices

↔ A lack of potential cooperation partners

↔ Lower costs and margins

For example, with complex products such as IBM mainframe computers, marketing success depends on specialized product or application knowledge. With automobile marketers, a high level of service is necessary, especially after the sale. Speciality steels are examples of products that are highly differentiated from competitors' products, or unique. In each of these cases, the firm is likely to select an integrated distribution system, because only company employees may be able to acquire the know-how that is necessary to serve customers adequately, and only employees can ensure close enough contact with customers and aggressive sales support when the product is very important to the company's core business.

An integrated distribution system facilitates corporate control and motivation of system members. A member who is a company employee can readily monitor distribution activities and use the authority of the company to influence the behaviour of distribution personnel. For an integrated distribution system to be successful, the company must know what customers expect in terms of delivery time, product modifications, personal contact, and the like. Then it must ensure that it hires personnel who are willing and able to meet those expectations.

In some regions of the world it may be impossible to find appropriate distribution partners or individuals and firms who are willing to cooperate. In such cases the marketer will be forced to choose an integrated distribution system. This may also be the case where the existing distribution channels and facilities are so expensive that they would not allow the company to serve the market at a competitive price level.

An integrated distribution system has drawbacks as well as advantages. Legal restrictions on foreign investment may prevent marketers from using such a system. But the major disadvantage of integrated distribution is its potential high cost. Sales managers, salespeople and physical distribution staff must be hired and trained. The sales organization is likely to lose money during the first few years in a new market, because sales volume will not be sufficient to cover overhead costs. For these reasons, most companies that are expanding into foreign markets at least initially choose a company-bound or independent distribution system.

Also, when a company competes in a mature product category, direct competition by similar products is likely to be strong. Low costs and prices are crucial to success. In such a situation most companies use non-integrated distribution. As examples from Japan show, however, company-bound distribution systems can be highly successful because they ensure more influence on the marketing behaviour of intermediaries. Hitachi KK, with its sales volume of about USD35 billion making it one of the biggest firms within the electrical and electronics industry of the world, for example, holds 59 per cent of shares of Hitachi Sales KK. Hitachi Sales KK, which has 3500 employees, is responsible for the communication policy, catalogue production, and the management and control of a very great number of wholesalers on three hierarchical levels. The wholesalers are basically financed by the central firm (Hitachi KK) which in a number of cases holds small quantities of their shares. Hitachi KK does not hold any inventory of finished goods. These are delivered to the wholesalers immediately after production. The principal wholesalers might be forced to sell Hitachi products exclusively. Wholesalers on the third level are allowed to sell other branded products to cover their costs.[8]

The tendency to choose independent distribution partners is reinforced by sociocultural differences between domestic and non-domestic markets. Such a choice may be reasonable, because transferring title to an independent channel member also transfers risk. From the customer's perspective, however, the choice of an independent distribution system may be entirely wrong.

The use of independent distributors reduces the company's opportunities to become familiar with the specific characteristics of the new market, thereby limiting its ability to offer a product that meets the market's needs. Independent distributors may also be a problem because they have considerable freedom to establish local marketing policies. Moreover, independent distributors' loyalty to the manufacturer is likely to be limited, because they may carry a wide range of products, from different manufacturers, and they will favour naturally those products that yield the greatest sales and profits. To overcome these problems, some firms only work with distributors who will focus exclusively on their product lines. This can only be done, however, if the product line is broad enough to generate sufficient sales volume for the distributor, and the profit margins are attractive.

In general, companies tend to develop an international distribution system that reflects their domestic choice. For example, Tissot, a Swiss marketer of watches, may wish to follow a strategy of appealing to a mass market interested in high quality, using as many jewellery stores – which are numerous in Switzerland – as possible supplied from a central warehouse located at the site of the company. Often a similar distribution system does not exist in another national market, however. In such situations management must determine whether a different distribution channel can be used without departing radically from the overall corporate strategy. For example, an Italian manufacturer of high-fashion, high-priced women's shoes, such as Bruno Magli, considering a new market may find that there are not enough prestigious speciality shops in that market. To achieve sufficient market coverage, the company must look for other outlets. If appropriate alternatives cannot be found, the firm might decide not to enter the market, or it might enter it under a different brand name.

Companies that are successful in international markets generally rely on a mix of different, more or less integrated distribution channels. For example, Warner-Lambert, a US-based manufacturer of razors, chewing gum and pharmaceutical products, has succeeded in Japan by using distinct distribution channels for each set of product lines. When entering the market, razors and blades were sold through the Hatori trading organization, which in turn sold the firm's products through independent wholesalers that provided considerable service to retailers. When Warner-Lambert tried a similar channel for its chewing gum, it failed. Not satisfied with the wholesalers' efforts, the company bypassed them. This change made wholesalers angry and retailers suspicious about the company switching their distribution system. Warner-Lambert then successfully built up its own sales force to obtain orders from retailers and passed orders back to the wholesalers, resulting in a respectable share of the Japanese chewing gum market. In yet another product-market, Warner-Lambert has been manufacturing pharmaceuticals in Japan since 1960, and selling them with great success directly to large drug companies.[9]

INTERNATIONAL CHANNEL EVALUATION

Making the appropriate choice among the distribution channel options available in foreign markets requires an understanding of the ways in which each might contribute to the goals and objectives of the distribution policy. The marketer must consider a range of customer and intermediary characteristics from which to develop a set of selection criteria, a process that is discussed in this section.

Customer Characteristics

An evaluation of distribution methods for a particular region or country-market must consider the number of potential customers and their location, purchasing power and specific needs. For example, in analysing the US market, a European manufacturer of furniture fittings would find a considerable concentration of furniture manufacturers in North and South Carolina. It would therefore be likely to choose either an integrated distribution system with a sales office in the Carolinas or an intermediary that is familiar with the major customers and handles complementary product lines.

The purchasing habits of potential customers also affect distribution decisions. The main reason for these differences is variations in the cultural and economic environments. In Turkey, Saudi Arabia and most parts of India, for example, supermarkets are unpopular. Turkish consumers prefer fresh products that have just been harvested, while Saudis require that poultry and meat be slaughtered in accordance with the Islamic practice of Shariah. In India most people are unable to afford cars or refrigerators. They therefore need to shop at least once a day and buy very small quantities. The Culture box gives an impression of how such purchasing behaviour may change when changes occur in the cultural or economic environment of a country.

Danone yogurt is distributed differently in France and Hong Kong because of the different purchasing habits of customers in those countries. In France, Danone uses self-service discount stores, such as Auchan or Leclerc with spacious fresh-food areas and large assortments of general merchandise. These

CULTURE BOX

Malled?

COVERING MORE THAN 330 000 SQUARE METRES, Megamall in Manila is the largest shopping mall in Asia. Other enormous malls are opening across the Philippines. From Hong Kong to Jakarta, malls are the places where more and more Asians go – not just to shop, but to eat and be entertained. Asking where the money those customers spend comes from, there are two major factors: First, many Filipinos boost their disposable income by second and third jobs (paying no taxes) and second, the Philippines have the lowest savings rate in Asia.

In Asia, unlike North America, most malls are built in cities, not out of town. Most of the emerging middle classes are found in the cities. The income gap between town and country is particularly pronounced in the Philippines. Although official GNP per capita is only about USD 1,000, in metropolitan Manila the figure is around USD 2,500. Many of the people flocking through malls are only window shopping. Part of the appeal is that they are cool and air-conditioned.

In the USA a change in consumer buying habits seems to emerge. Youth between age 13 and 20 – 29 million people who have spent USD 63 billion in retail shops in 1995 – tend to increasingly turn their back on shopping malls and to prefer smaller specialty shops. Whereas in 1993 72 per cent of US-teenagers found it 'cool' to 'hang around' in shopping malls, in 1996 less than 50 per cent regarded shopping malls as 'hip'. This development may be partly due to restrictions on crowding and to increased surveillance by uniformed guards, but it is alarming to shopping mall owners because shopping habits of consumers are largely formed during their teenage years. Retail chains such as Tower Records, particularly focusing on young target groups, have already reacted to this new trend. They refuse to open shops in new shopping malls.

In Europe, speciality shops and speciality markets (having a bigger size) have regained some dynamics in their development. Also speciality discount stores are considered to have a bright future. But malls are still in with consumers. In Germany, for example, 72 shopping malls with a total of 1398 million square metres were under planning in 1996.

Sources: 'Malled', *The Economist*, 18 May 1996, pp. 69f.; and 'Einkaufszentren für US-Jugend "total uncool"', *Der Standard*, 15/16 May 1996, p. A3.

stores, which occupy as much as 250 000 square feet of space and have up to 100 checkout counters, serve French consumers as major outlets for dairy products when they do their weekly shopping. It would be impossible for Danone to rely on such outlets in Hong Kong, where 83 per cent of the home-makers shop once a day and buy most of their food in either a street market or an urban shopping mall.

Intermediary Characteristics

Functions. Any evaluation of potential distribution partners in a foreign market must be based on an analysis of the responsibilities, or functions, of both the distributing agents and the company itself. The same title may imply different responsibilities, depending on the location (see Table 14.2).

Table 14.2	FUNCTIONS POTENTIALLY PERFORMED BY MIDDLEMEN

Middlemen perform four basic functions. Each of the functions has subfunctions, which would still need to be performed even if the middlemen were eliminated from the distribution channel.

Physical handling of products
Importing the product
Arranging for customs clearance
Providing warehousing facilities
Maintaining a certain inventory level
Performing break-bulk operations
Adapting parts of the product to local needs
Assembling parts
Performing or overseeing delivery

Promotion, sales and service activities
Obtaining and maintaining a certain level of sales effort
Securing customer service levels
Providing existing customers

Management of business relationships
Building and holding good will of business-community members
Building and maintaining the necessary relationships with governmental agencies

Financing and risk taking
Providing foreign payment exchange
Financing the distribution process
Assuming certain business risks

Therefore, the marketer needs to find out what an intermediary's title actually means in each market.

It must be determined to what extent an intermediary can take over the physical handling of goods. This is especially important for companies with little or no international marketing experience. In addition, intermediaries can assist in promoting and selling the product, as well as providing services to local customers. As the example of Caterpillar's dealers has shown, intermediaries can help build and maintain the goodwill of government agencies and members of the local community. Finally, they often take over part of the financing and bear some of the risk of the distribution process.

Structure. The structure of a distribution channel is characterized by the number and types of intermediaries in the channel, the number of product lines carried, and the relationships among manufacturers, channel members and government agencies.

The number of levels and types of intermediaries define the length of a distribution channel. The longer the channel, the more expensive the company's products become to the final customers and the less the firm will be able to control or influence the sales contact with end customers. As a rule of thumb, the more economically developed a country, the shorter the distribution channels in that country. In the European Union, for example, there is a trend towards strong concentration of retailing. This trend is leading to a significant reduction in the number of wholesalers, to the dominance of some retail organizations in most Western European markets, and to the formation of voluntary chains of retailers sponsored by wholesalers, such as Intersport. Headquartered in Bern, Switzerland, Intersport is a voluntary chain of retailers of sporting goods from 16 countries including Canada, Japan and the

USA who have signed partnership contracts and hold shares in the cooperative. About 4200 points of sale made total sales of about USD4.8 billion in 1994.[10]

A similar trend towards the vertical integration of wholesaling functions is occurring in Japan: for fashion products in most cases there is only one level of wholesalers. As another Japanese example shows, however, a country's level of economic development is not the only factor that determines the length of distribution channels. The Japanese trade structure for food products is characterized by a multitude of very small retail shops ('Papa-Mama' stores in Japan account for more than 50 per cent of retail sales, compared to 3 per cent in the USA and 5 per cent in Western Europe) existing in parallel to very large supermarkets, chain stores and department stores. Up to five levels of wholesalers fill the gap between the manufacturers and the small retailers (see Figure 14.1). The first level, called Primary Wholesalers, is split into two groups: Direct Transaction Wholesalers deliver to the biggest department stores and supermarkets in the most populated areas. Principal Wholesalers split bulk goods into smaller units and deliver to Secondary Wholesalers who are located in the capitals of the provinces. They hold a gatekeeper function. That is, any manufacturer who wants to get its products widely distributed in Japan has to get accepted by Principal Wholesalers.

There are two types of Secondary Wholesalers: Intermediate Wholesalers deliver their products to third-level wholesalers, and Ultimate Wholesalers serve retail shops in their local area. Third-level wholesalers serve small local retailers and restaurants conveniently located for customers frequently purchasing small quantities of merchandise, or wholesalers of the next higher level. The ratio of wholesalers to retailers is four times higher in Japan than in the USA. This kind of distribution structure has proven resistant to change so far because high population density creates a shortage of storage space, which in turn requires low levels of inventory and frequent deliveries.

Japan's typical structure of a distribution system is even more complex than the structures in many industrially less developed countries. Distribution in the Philippines, for example, is characterized by a sort of wholesaler, called a bagsakan, to whom manufacturers sell their products or deliver them on a consignment basis. A bagsakan is usually a person that commands respect in the local area and has access to or possesses significant financial resources. The bagsakan does not deliver to the small retailers, called sari-sari stores, in its business area. It is the sari-sari store owners who pick up the merchandise on either cash or credit terms. Sari-sari stores are usually family owned and part of the private homes of their owners; thus, the average size of a store is two by four metres. Lumped together in this area are the display, stock, and a small workplace which also serves as an office. Transactions are undertaken through a wide window, with the customer staying outside the store.[11]

The width of a distribution channel is determined by the number of each type of intermediary in the channel. The larger the number of similar intermediaries in a market, the greater the width of the channel. High channel width should make it easier for a marketer to find distribution partners. In Europe the width of distribution channels is very different from one country to another. In Belgium, for example, a very small number of retailing organizations control the majority of total sales in most consumer goods whereas in Italy the concentration process in retailing has just begun.

Intermediaries carry different numbers and assortments of product lines. For example, the Japanese general trading houses, called sogo shosha, import

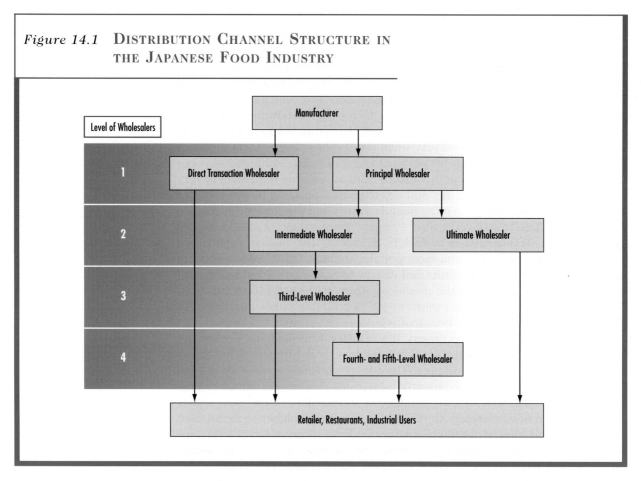

Figure 14.1 **Distribution Channel Structure in the Japanese Food Industry**

The structure of distribution channels in the Japanese food industry is characterized by a great number of hierarchical levels of wholesalers.

Source: Krause, A. (1992) '*Marken und Markenbildung in Japan*', München: GBI-Verlag, p. 140.

and export products ranging from consumer electronics to steel. They ensure supplies of raw materials and energy for their keiretsu ('family' of interrelated companies; see Figure 14.2) and sell all of its products. Sogo shoshas are also involved in services associated with those products, such as new product development or technology transfer, and in financing big retail outlets. In addition they have built up global information networks linking hundreds of sales offices (Mitsubishi Corp., for example, has 15 offices in the USA alone) 'on line' by the use of rented satellites. All members of the keiretsu and other firms which belong to the extended network may use those information services. Approximately 50 per cent of Japan's external trade is handled by the 12 biggest sogo shoshas. The five biggest among them, that is, Mitsubishi Corp., C. Itoh, Mitsui & Co., Sumitomo and Morutsoni, have sales volumes of about USD14 billion each. Sumitomo and Mitsubishi made annual profits of approximately USD1.6 billion in the early 1990s, the others half of that.

The international marketing manager should be aware that intermediaries handling broad product lines have to take resource allocation decisions. They

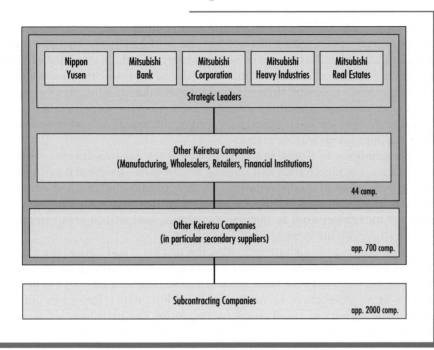

Figure 14.2 THE STRUCTURE OF A JAPANESE KEIRETSU

A keiretsu is a number of interrelated production companies, wholesalers and retailers grouped around a major bank and a general trading house. Mitsubishi is the world's biggest keiretsu with sales of more than USD270 billion and more than 550 000 personnel. The 'strategic leaders' hold shares in more than 1400 companies which themselves hold a multitude of shares in other companies.

Source: Sydow, J. (1991) 'Strategische Netzwerke in Japan', *zfbf*, 43(3), 242.

will put more energy into distributing the products of manufacturers with which they have long-established relationships or in which they hold a financial interest.

Networks. A company that seeks to establish a distribution channel in a new market must deal with an existing network of relationships. Because the network is already functioning with products, sellers and buyers, a variety of problems may arise. If, for example, the producer of a competitive product is related to the wholesalers or retailers, or owns the channels, entry is made more difficult. Typical examples of such networks are the Japanese 'keiretsu' such as Mitsui or Fuyo. These consist of a large number of production companies, wholesalers and retailers grouped around a big bank and a general trading house (sogo shosha) mutually holding each other's stock (see Figure 14.2).

Channel ownership by local competitors can be a major problem for new firms entering the market. For example, in Japan most of the wholesalers of household electrical appliances are owned by only four manufacturers. A similar situation exists for other products; in the 1980s approximately 70 per cent of all electronics retailers were tightly controlled by Matsushita, Hitachi and Toshiba, while the six largest producers of cosmetics controlled 70 per cent of all cosmetics retailers. Well-known examples are Shiseido Chain Stores or Kanebo Chain Stores. But changes have occurred since. Retailers have included new brands in their offering, and new distribution channels, such as party and door-to-door selling, have been developing.

Distribution channels may be blocked because competitors have well-established product lines and exclusive contracts with existing channel members. This is the case in some European beer markets, for example, where manufacturers sign up restaurants as clients for ten years, offering them large cash advances or financing part of their equipment. Distribution channels may also be quasi blocked because – like in Japan – local manufacturers finance their intermediaries' inventory, give them cumulative annual rebates, allow the return of all unsold products, and provide all sorts of aids from promotion material, through product and sales training, to sales personnel. Under such circumstances a foreign marketer who wants to enter the distribution system will have a hard time finding intermediaries willing to change their supplier on affordable terms.

For example, in Korea the chaebol appliance manufacturers – Samsung Electronics, LG Electronics and Daewoo Electronics – each have a proprietary network of mom-and-pop retailers. To get around the chaebol-dominated retail system, US-based Whirlpool joined with two South Korean companies that put its refrigerators in department stores, and with a small number of retailers specializing in imports.

Competitors may also have divided the market – and hence, the ability to control activity within the channel – among them by forming cartels. Powerful trade associations may have lobbied successfully to restrict channel alternatives or to close them to new entrants. Thus, many European countries protect the owners of small shops by regulating the placement of stores. In Sweden, for instance, town planners decide on the location of retail outlets, so that thinly populated areas, as well as elderly and handicapped customers, will be served. The Ethics box describes what can happen when no such protection for small retailers exists.

Finally, governments may control access to the channels, in order to control which goods are marketed. Or access may be allowed to one part of the channel, but effectively barred through regulation or practice from another level, which of course limits the channel's usefulness to the marketer. It is imperative, therefore, that the marketer understands the structure of the existing network.

A marketer faced with these kinds of obstacles can find ways to get around them. One possibility is to choose an innovative distribution channel. Franchising, mail-order and electronic markets are among the possible alternatives to traditional channels. By signing up franchise partners in Singapore, international retailers headquartered in the UK, such as Body Shop, Marks & Spencer and Habitat, have implanted themselves in Singapore, where personal and governmental relationships play an important role in business success. In the Philippines foreign retailers can only enter the market by skirting the rules. Makro, a Dutch retailer, for example, has formed a partnership with Ayala in order to operate a discount store as a club. The UK's Marks & Spencer has linked up with Rustan's, a local retailer, and in 1995 US-based J.C. Penney signed a franchise deal to open its first store in the Manila Megamall.[12]

The marketer can also look for ways to diversify channels. One way is to find distribution partners that want to broaden their product lines with complementary products. That was Sony's goal when it established its 'lifestyle shops' in Japan, for example. It is also possible to team up with other wholesalers or retailers that have been excluded from the distribution networks. In addition, new channels are always being created – speciality discount stores, for instance, or groups of hotels and restaurants – providing new distribution opportunities. It may also be possible to 'piggyback' into a new market by

ETHICS BOX

Supermarket Boom Threatens Small Retailers in Poland

THE OPENING OF FORMERLY CENTRALLY CONTROLLED economies to free market conditions and the entry of Western companies into those markets has improved the supply of goods to consumers who can afford them. Jobs have been created in more efficient companies. But the restructuring of the economy has cost many more jobs in inefficient firms. Now even largely privatized parts of Eastern European industries such as retailing encounter significant changes.

The expansion of supermarkets owned by companies from Western Europe threatens the existence of small private retailers in Poland. At the end of 1996 big retailers such as Germany's Rewe, Belgium's Globi, French Auchan, Docks de France, or Leclerc, as well as Norway's Rema 1000 had opened more than a total of 120 big supermarkets. At that time Poland counted 425 000 retail shops, 92 per cent of which had less than 50 square metres. There was one shop for 91 inhabitants.

No legal regulation provided any shelter to small retailers. Despite the fact that more than 90 per cent of trade in Poland was privatized, trade associations were just developing. For example, ZPHU, the biggest association in 1996, represented only 5 per cent of small retailers. They did not fight construction of new supermarkets in general, but claimed compliance with certain preconditions. One of them was fairness. Western supermarket chains should, for example, be forced to play by the same rules as in their home countries. Whereas opening hours were restricted in countries like France or Germany, partly to protect small retailers there, Poland did not have any such regulation. The small Polish retailers also protested against the preferential credit conditions offered by Polish banks to foreign companies.

Source: 'Supermarkt-Boom in Polen', *Der Standard*, 27/28 July 1996, p. 25.

---

using a distribution channel established by a friendly company. For example, to facilitate its entry into Asian markets, a Spanish manufacturer such as Majorica, which produces fashion products from industrially made pearls, uses the distribution channel, consisting of a number of wholesalers, jewellery stores, department stores, and tax free shops at airports, established by a cooperating manufacturer of crystal glass.

Other means of circumventing obstacles to market entry include offering higher margins to channel members than are offered by competitors, special bonuses, or other kinds of financial incentives. To build closer ties with their Korean retailers, New York-based Estee Lauder, one of the leading marketers of cosmetics in the USA, for example, invites local department store executives to New York City each year to meet with Estee Lauder management and visit major retailers. However, companies must be careful not to violate home country legislation, such as the Foreign Corrupt Practices Act in the USA, which prohibits specific types of payments that may facilitate business activity in international markets.

A company may also consider buying equity in an intermediary. In Japan, banks are used for this purpose, because they are closely linked with the large industry groups (keiretsu) through joint ownership and serving as board directors. With their assistance a foreign company can gain an equity share in a

Japanese intermediary; in most cases a 10 per cent share will enable the company to become part of an existing distribution network.

Power Relationships.   The distribution of power between producers and intermediaries varies from one country to another and from one product-market to another. For example, between 1963, when Carrefour's first hypermarket opened at Sainte Geneviéve des Bois near Paris, and the 1990s the French retailing landscape has seen what some observers call a 'commercial revolution'. The market share of small food retailers has dropped from 81 per cent in 1963 to about 27 per cent in 1995. Department stores and popular stores encountered great difficulty in maintaining their market shares. The activity level of traditional small retailers of textiles has decreased significantly. At the same time, 800 hypermarkets with a floor space of more than 5000 square metres achieved approximately 35 per cent of food sales and 20 per cent of other goods in 1995. When the 7000 supermarkets are added, big stores represent more than half the total of food retail sales. Home equipment and DIY retailing have seen the emergence of a new type of store: the specialized supermarket (some well-known names are Conforama, Darty, FNAC, Bricorama). Joint retailers became very important: Leclerc, an association of independent retailers, has a market share of about 6 per cent of retail sales. Such independent retailers run not only most of the supermarkets, but also 250 hypermarkets, that is, 31 per cent of the total. As a result, the concentration of retail purchasing power has dramatically increased. Most French retailers have joined purchasing organizations to improve their position when dealing with manufacturers. This is a reaction to the great concentration among the suppliers themselves: one flour supplier has more than 80 per cent market share. About 70 per cent of the cider market, 60 per cent of the market for instant chocolate powder, and more than 50 per cent of the pet food market are held by a single manufacturer. The top two French suppliers have more than 60 per cent of the market for cleaning chemicals, mineral waters and soft drinks, and more than 70 per cent of the market for goods for children, tins, oils, sugar, cereals and tea. Retail companies buy 30 per cent of their goods from the top ten manufacturers.

The power relationships between manufacturers and retailers in Japanese distribution channels depend on the degree of brand loyalty and the consumption rate of consumers. For example, TV sets have high brand loyalty and a low consumption rate. They fall into the category where major producers act as 'channel captains'. Where brand loyalty and the consumption rate are high, such as in the canned food or children's dresses markets, intermediaries have a dominant position. In other product-markets, such as calculators, bikes or shoes, consumption rate and brand loyalty are rather low. No single distribution channel exists and thus control of the channel is difficult for producers or intermediaries.

The balance of power in emerging economies is still very much in favour of the manufacturer. But concentration tendencies are beginning to take effect. In Mexico, for example, joint ventures between Wal-Mart and Cifra, Fleming Cos and Gigante, and Price/Costco and Comercial Mexicana are starting to concentrate retail power. Makro, a Dutch warehouse club operator, which opened its first store in Thailand in 1989, ran eight stores in this country in 1994 and had become the biggest customer of Nestlé. With seven stores in Taiwan, Makro reached sales of USD1 billion a year. The company also operates two stores in Malaysia, and opened stores in China and Korea in 1995.[13]

Power relationships affect a company's ability to control the implementation of marketing mix decisions at each level of the channel. In the UK, for example, the six largest retail companies represent 55 per cent of sales in their sector. Since a limited number of retailers effectively control access to retail outlets, they have enormous power over suppliers' strategies. Smaller suppliers who cannot afford large market communication budgets, for example, may have to give up their own brands and serve powerful retailers as OEM suppliers for their branded products. In the UK private label sales reached more than 37 per cent of all grocery sales in 1995.[14] Or marketers may have to provide special programmes and support fees before the retailer will agree to stock their product. Such funds would not, therefore, be available to spend on consumer advertising.

The creation of international purchasing units has further increased the power of retailers in the purchase relationship. For example, Deuro Buying AG regroups 14 European companies (such as German Metro, French Carrefour and Spanish Pryca) from ten different countries. Founded in 1990, it achieved total retail sales of about USD100 billion in 1993.[15] Electronic Partner – International, another example, is a cooperation of national retailing groups from nine different EU member countries. The Vianen, Netherlands-based purchasing unit regroups about 4400 retailers linked by partnership contracts and represents a procurement volume of about USD1.5 billion which is equal to a retail sales volume of about USD3.3 billion.[16]

SELECTION OF CHANNEL MEMBERS

The process of selecting distribution-channel members can be more or less actively governed by a company. Sometimes contacts take place by accident, such as during a flight when business people sit next to each other. A considerable number of firms try to find intermediaries in a new country-market by advertisements in a local newspaper or trade journal soliciting representation. Advertisements have the disadvantage that their response rate is generally low, and they often attract the weakest and most unreliable potential intermediaries. Other more active firms participate in a local exhibition and talk to potential intermediaries visiting their exhibits. The relatively low costs of such a search and selection procedure, in most cases, are by far offset by the opportunity cost of the internationally operating firm not knowing its final customers in the country-market and, therefore, not having market-related criteria on which to base the choice of distribution partner. In addition, the firm has only very little effective control over its distribution partner's marketing activities, resulting in a 'blind approach' concerning local adaptations.

In most cases, a company that wishes to enter a foreign market should take an active role in selecting intermediaries. Although contacts with intermediaries can arise from unsolicited orders or contacts at trade shows, the firm would be well advised to follow a series of systematic steps in investigating potential distribution partners (see Figure 14.3). First, the company has to develop a set of selection criteria based on its intended global strategic position, the intended local position, and the distribution policy. Then, following

---

Figure 14.3 SELECTION OF CHANNEL MEMBERS

The selection of channel members should be an active process following the steps shown.

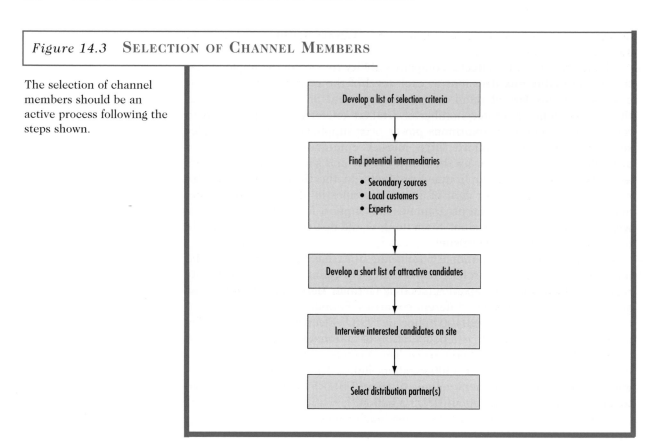

those criteria, it has to gather information on potential intermediaries. Such information can be obtained from secondary sources, local customers, and experts. Based on the available information, the number of potential channel members is reduced to a short list of attractive candidates by evaluating them against the selection criteria. Then the most attractive-looking candidates are asked whether they are interested in acting as intermediaries for the company. Those that express interest are interviewed, and the interviews are used as a basis for the selection of appropriate distribution partners. This active process for selecting channel members will be described in the following.

Selection Criteria

Ideally, an intermediary will resemble the most effective members of the company's existing distribution channels. The following criteria are useful in selecting channel members:

↔ Continuity of functions provided by channel member

↔ Adequate coverage of the market

↔ Control of activities within channel

↔ Compatibility between firm and channel member

↔ Capital required and costs to be covered

↔ Distance between firm and channel member

Because all businesses are not the same, each company will have to specify its individual selection criteria. No single candidate is likely to meet all of the firm's criteria. Therefore, the marketer will probably have to make trade-offs among the characteristics of various potential distribution partners.

Continuity of Functions. Depending on the customer needs, an intermediary will have to fulfil various functions. Storage facilities for products or spare parts help the marketer to reach the customer in time. For example, in order for a manufacturer of diesel engines for vessels to be globally competitive, it needs intermediaries in every big harbour who are able to keep in stock at least those spare parts which are most often needed. Extended stop-overs in a harbour because of missing spare parts would not be tolerated by shipping companies because of high quay charges.

In addition, a potential channel member who has access to appropriate transportation devices or who can provide local packaging facilities may be more attractive as a distribution partner. For example, a producer of frozen food, such as France's Bonduelle, needs local distribution partners which can provide a fleet of trucks equipped to transport their products.

Complementary products and the intermediary's ability to provide customer services based on product or product application knowledge may increase the attractiveness of the firm's offer to local customers. For example, if a Vietnamese producer of tableware made from bamboo is searching for intermediaries in Sweden, complementary products such as tablecloths carried by the potential channel member will strongly increase the attractiveness of the supplier's offerings to potential customers. The number of technically trained and experienced personnel available to an intermediary in Argentina, as another example, is crucial to the service level that a manufacturer of machinery, such as Japan's Komatsu, can provide to its local customers.

An intermediary's production facilities can increase the speed and flexibility of customer problem solution in a geographically distant market. For example, Douwe Egberts, the Dutch subsidiary of Chicago-based Sara Lee Corp., is one of the world's leading coffee roasters. To be better adapted to local customers' tastes, the firm produces its coffee for the Austrian market through Vienna-based Santora, an intermediary exclusively active in the restaurant business.

Finally, the potential channel member's market communication activity can help achieve awareness and build local preference for the marketer's product. For example, when a rather small producer of ceramic figures and decoration, such as Italian Thun which operates production sites in China but so far has concentrated its marketing activities on the EU markets, wants to penetrate parts of the NAFTA market, it will have to rely on market communication by its distribution partners to achieve some consumer awareness. Because of its size the company cannot afford the promotion activities needed.

Market Coverage and Control. What market coverage of a local intermediary is adequate to an internationally operating firm strongly depends on the chosen distribution policy. The size of a potential channel member's sales network – does it have sales personnel, sales reps or local sales offices and how many? does it provide access to a multilevel channel of local distribution? – as well as the intermediary's relations with potential customers are indicators of the market coverage the firm can attain by choosing this distribution partner. In Japan, for example, a company should gather information about the distribution network to which a potential channel member belongs. Because of the many levels of intermediaries and the close ties between certain members of a channel, choosing a specific partner can mean opening up a broad distribution system, but also losing the opportunity to get in touch with a whole range of customers.

Sales references help to assess the intermediary's relations. For example, if a distributor of electrical appliances in Spain has been serving Il Corte Ingles, the most well-known chain of department stores in the country, it can be considered as a competent partner. However, such references should not be taken only from the potential distribution partner itself. The marketer would be well advised to contact the given references and to counter-check the information received. Nevertheless, some understanding of the cultural background existing in a local market will be needed to interpret the content of references properly. For example, if a US supplier to a potential intermediary and some of its customers report that a particular firm is timely, financially reliable, and appropriately equipped with technical personnel, they probably mean something different from what a supplier and customer are trying to communicate when they say the same if they are located in Italy, India or Cameroon.

The importance of a potential channel member's control of local marketing activities increases with the supplier's need to influence final customer contacts. The relative size of an intermediary indicates the channel member's potential for control over activities within the channel. If the customers of the intermediary are much bigger in size than the intermediary itself, power relations will be negatively affected. For example, the Swiss producer of WC-Ente, a high-quality cleaning product for sanitary installations, distributes its products in Austria through a small firm, called Perolin. This firm is confronted with two chains of supermarkets which evenly split two-thirds of the entire market between them. As a result, control over local marketing activities tends to be difficult. The very strong position of the brand in consumers' minds is used by the retailers to attract customers through low prices, and even the strong brand identity cannot avoid yearly price negotiations becoming extremely difficult for the distributor.

But it is not only the intermediary's relations with its customers which are important. Depending on the company's product-market and the shape of the local macro-environment, relations with other stakeholders, such as media, unions, environmentalists or local politicians, may be important. For example, if a producer of genetically-manipulated products, such as US-based Monsanto, wants to distribute those products in an environmentally sensitive country such as Switzerland for the first time, it might be much easier to enter the market if the chosen distribution partner has strong relationships with local media and politicians. Otherwise, journalists communicating genetic-manipulation as a danger for consumers and their children would provoke resistance from environmentalists, forcing politicians to react in a negative way for the producer.

Compatibility.   The reputation of a potential channel member in its local market has to fit the intended positioning of the internationally operating firm or its product. The reputation largely depends on the person(s) representing the intermediary as well as on the positioning of the potential channel member's own product range or the product range it has represented so far. For example, when a company with high-prestige products, such as French Givenchy perfumes, searches for an intermediary in Indonesia, it will first need to find a firm which affluent consumers accept as competent for Givenchy's kind of luxury product. In addition, Givenchy will want to choose a firm owned or managed by a person whose reputation is compatible with its prestigious brand.

But compatibility also means the ability to communicate effectively and efficiently with the distribution partner. The company searching for an appropriate channel member will therefore evaluate the information technology available to the different candidates. Denmark's toy maker Lego, for example, might prefer a distributor in Sao Paulo, Brazil who is able to communicate in English, can be reached by e-mail 24 hours a day, and who uses an electronic data processing system compatible with the one used by the company.

Costs. Two kinds of costs are important in selecting a distribution channel: the capital costs of establishing the channel and the costs of maintaining it. The capital costs of establishing a channel depend on the size of potential partners and their financial standing. For example, when a Taiwanese bicycle manufacturer enters a distribution agreement with Wal-Mart in the USA its capital costs of establishing the channel will be significantly lower.

Maintenance costs include the direct costs of the firm's integrated distribution channels plus margins, markups, commissions, and other forms of compensation to channel members, whether integrated or independent. When a luxury sports car manufacturer such as Italy's Ferrari considers distribution in China, for example, it has to calculate the costs of a sales office as well as compensation for Chinese intermediaries. In addition, the costs of the management systems needed to manage the distribution channels have to be considered. These costs will vary over the life of a distribution relationship. In the beginning, travel costs for managers establishing the relationship through know-how and technology transfer may dominate. Later on, the costs of deepening the information links between the supplier and the local channel members may become more important.

Distance. The distance between a marketer and a potential channel member has five dimensions: geographic, social, cultural, technological and temporal. They must be bridged to develop a close working relationship. Geographic distance is the physical distance separating the two partners. From that distance point of view it might seem easier for a Singapore-based Chinese manufacturer to deal with a Malaysian intermediary than with a Chinese located in Hong Kong or in South Africa. An analysis of social and cultural distance may provide another picture.

Social distance stems from lack of familiarity with the partner's operating methods. Whereas managers of a Chinese manufacturer of dolls are accustomed to working with local distribution partners whose personnel work seven days a week, they may be highly surprised when confronted with Italian or French potential intermediaries which close down during August because of vacations. But social distance may also be more subtle. If a manufacturer such as Gore, the US-headquartered producer of chemical fibres for consumer and industrial textiles, mainly operating based on individual initiatives and responsibility, is confronted with potential channel members managing their businesses through orders and tight controls, social distance is large. Severe misunderstandings could be the consequence.

Such social distance is closely related to cultural distance which reflects differences in values, norms and behaviour. For example, a US service company, such as Citizen Bank, which is used to profit and income as primary motivators for business decisions, might have some difficulties in cooperating with Japanese business partners for whom loyalty may be the dominant motivator.

Technological distance is described in terms of the competitiveness, compatibility and quality of product lines currently carried by potential intermediaries, as well as differences in product experience and process technologies. When Coca-Cola Co. of the USA signs up Carlsberg, Denmark's biggest brewing group, as a distributor of Coca-Cola products in Sweden and Norway, for example, the technological distance is very small, because Carlsberg has already been acting as a distributor for Coca-Cola in Denmark for many years, through Carlsberg's soft-drink subsidiary Dadeko AS. On the other hand, when a ship-crane manufacturer, such as Austria-based Liebherr, searches for an intermediary who should be able to provide high-level service to international ship companies in Nigeria, the difference in the quality of product lines carried as well as in their way of handling the business may be considerable.

Temporal distance is measured by the length of time between placement of an order and delivery of the product. This time span will be influenced by the closeness of a potential intermediary to the customers. The number of layers of channel members as well as an intermediary's process technology will be crucial for temporal distance. For example, when a Norwegian producer of canned fish wants to distribute its products in the Netherlands, from a temporal distance point of view the Royal Ahold NV may seem to be an attractive channel partner. The company not only is one of Europe's best-performing retailers, but it also holds a 30 per cent market share with its flagship Albert Heijn supermarket chain and other stores, and, in particular, it has invested in sophisticated centralized logistics systems. Just four depots move all of the goods to more than 600 Dutch Ahold supermarkets.[17]

Finding Potential Intermediaries

Knowing which characteristics of potential intermediaries to consider, the management of the internationally operating company can start to search for potential channel members. Major sources of information about potential channel members in a local market are secondary information sources which in most instances are less costly, as well as local customers and experts in the firm's industry.

Secondary Information Sources.   The first step in searching for local intermediaries is to locate secondary sources of information. Management should investigate these sources before travelling to a country-market to gather first-hand information. Secondary sources of information about potential distribution-channel members are listed in Table 14.3.

Government agencies, such as registration authorities, will supply specific information for free or for a small fee. As an example, the relevant agencies of the US Department of Commerce are listed in Table 14.4.

Listings of industry members can be obtained from address services, from government sources, such as the US government's Foreign Traders Index, from international institutions, such as the European Union's Business

Table 14.3	SECONDARY SOURCES OF INFORMATION ON POTENTIAL DISTRIBUTION CHANNEL MEMBERS

Government agencies
Reports of international organizations
Trade organizations in the host country
National chamber of commerce
Home-country trade representatives in the host country
Banks and insurances
Related companies (carriers, forwarding agents, suppliers of complementary goods)
Own sales force, customers, suppliers, competitors
Annual reports of potential local customers
Industrial reports
Listings of industry members and address services
Industry or trade journals and magazines
Catalogues of exhibitions and trade fairs
Catalogues of industrial suppliers
Consultants

This table illustrates the information sources a company can consult when evaluating potential distribution-channel members.

Table 14.4	SERVICES OF THE US DEPARTMENT OF COMMERCE

NAME	SERVICES
New Product Information Service (NPIS)	Provides global publicity for new US products
Trade Opportunities Program (TOP)	Matches middlemen's interests indicated by the US company with product searches of non-domestic buyers
Foreign Traders Index (FTI)	Contains data on more than 150 000 potential middlemen, as well as final customers from 143 countries
Agent/Distributor Service (ADS)	Contacts up to six middlemen prospects in the countries designated by the firm and determines their interest in corresponding with the firm
World Traders Data Report (WTDR)	Provides general narrative reports on the reliability of the potential middlemen indicated by the firm, as well as a profile of their existing product line(s)

The US Department of Commerce provides many services for international marketers, for relatively small fees.

Cooperation Network (BC NET), the firm's national chamber of commerce, trade organizations in the host country, or the home country's trade representative in the host country. Listings can also be found in telephone directories (yellow-page section) and trade directories. Such directories are normally organized by geographical criteria and product categories. Very often they are incomplete and out of date, however, with new and small intermediaries missing.

Local industry or trade journals and magazines contain reports on potential intermediaries as well as on the structure of networks and power relationships in specific local industries. So do industrial reports. Catalogues of exhibitions and trade fairs can be used to look for intermediaries who are participating. Catalogues on industrial suppliers can supply relevant addresses. Annual reports of potential local customers may provide information concerning their current suppliers. The company's own sales force may have information on potential intermediaries gathered through personal contacts with personnel from those companies or from other suppliers. Finally, the firm can use specialized consultants to help them find the right local intermediaries.

Before entering into direct contact with any candidate, the marketer may obtain additional information on its business conduct and credit reliability from such sources as banks, insurers, and related companies like carriers or consultants.

Local Customers and Experts.   Using secondary information sources is the cheapest way to find potential intermediaries. But in most cases it does not provide enough detailed information about the available distribution partners in a market and how they are perceived by their customers to make a complete choice. Interviewing final customers in the target market, therefore, is a more expensive but very informative additional means of finding an appropriate channel partner. It helps to discover which distribution channels are preferred and why, and what the customers expect from their suppliers in terms of customer service level. The marketer may also learn the names of reputable intermediaries in this manner. If interviewing final customers seems to be too slow or too expensive, industry experts such as specialists from the chamber of commerce, specialized journalists or consultants can be used as information sources. They provide an overview of the industry structure, networks and power relationships, can give their interpretation of the success factors in local distribution, and can identify the most well-known potential intermediaries.

Developing a Short List of Candidates

Using the information gathered from secondary sources, potential local customers and industry experts, management can specify a list of candidates to examine in more detail. The marketer then sends selected candidates a letter inquiring about their interest in becoming a member of the company's distribution channel. The letter should contain an extensive description of the products to be carried, an explanation of the firm's general marketing policy and strategy, and a statement of its specific goals in the intermediary's market. The interested intermediary should be asked to describe the market from its point of view; the description should include major customers and competitors, an estimate of the firm's potential market share and sales volume within a specified period, and the marketing strategy and resources necessary to achieve those objectives.

The answers of the interested intermediaries are compared. The small number of potential channel member(s) which best fulfil(s) the expectations of the company are selected for on-site interviews. On-site visits are the best way to determine a potential partner's requirements and to start an effective working relationship.

Selection

Intermediaries used by competitors may seem to be the most attractive potential channel members at first. They are already familiar with the product and the market, and they have an established organization to deal with potential customers. However, there are risks associated with using intermediaries that are serving competitors. First, if an intermediary does not change its alliance, it may provide competitors with information about the firm's product line. Second, the intermediary may accept a new product line and maintain the competitor's line simply to drive the new line out of the market. And third, the intermediary may negotiate with a new competitor at any time. For these reasons, it may be safer to choose intermediaries that handle complementary products. They have an established organization and a history of contact with potential customers, together with the necessary technical proficiency and knowledge of the local market.

The Contract

In cases of conventional exports, the supplier and the channel member operate without contractual commitments. They act strictly as buyers and sellers, and bargain aggressively to establish trade terms for each transaction, each primarily motivated by its own profits and unconcerned about longer-term cooperation. The manufacturer frequently renegotiates its export arrangements, and the intermediary obtains products from a variety of suppliers to best adapt to its local business. Such a situation involves higher costs for a company that wants to do international business on a continual basis. It also handicaps an intermediary as it cannot profit from a secured flow of products with fixed quality and stable prices. In the past, many firms operating internationally stayed autonomous but coordinated their activities through informal, non-contractual agreements. Owing to ongoing business relations, manufacturer and intermediary understood each other's preferences, capabilities and expectations. Mutual trust allowed them to informally agree an allocation of functions which made their exchanges more efficient. Because of increasing global competition in recent years, suppliers and intermediaries are increasingly being forced to lower their costs further. As a consequence, intermediaries have tried to reduce their number of suppliers and manufacturers operating internationally have managed to obtain maximum operating economies as well as maximum foreign market impact. This can be achieved by carefully selecting international business partners and integrating activities on the basis of a formal contract for a longer period of time.

The contract drawn up must be reviewed in detail before being signed. Because of differences in legal regulations between different countries, the company wanting to formalize the partnership with a local intermediary should seek the advice of a legal specialist in the intermediary's market. For example, the contract-termination conditions, including 'just causes' of termination (such as deceit, fraud, damage to the other party's interests, or failure to comply with contractual obligations), must be spelled out carefully.

Even with explicit contract specifications, termination of a contract is time consuming, often expensive, and in some cases impossible. In Japan, for example, terminating a contract with a business partner means breaking a strong commitment; it can be very difficult to find another partner. In most European countries, termination, even with 'just cause', will cost the firm the equivalent of a year's commission as compensation for the intermediary's efforts to build market share. Thus, it is imperative that the marketer conduct an extremely thorough investigation before signing a contract with a distribution partner.

Even then, surprises may hit. In 1996, for example, Coca-Cola announced that it was teaming up with Cisneros Bottling Cos. to make and sell Coca-Cola products in Venezuela, ending a celebrated 40-year alliance between Cisneros and its major competitor PepsiCo Inc. Until then, Venezuela, the fourth-biggest soft-drink market in Latin America, had been one of PepsiCo's strongholds, with more than 40 per cent market share. PepsiCo, based in Purchase, New York, denounced the deal as illegal since Cisneros's exclusive contract with Pepsi ran to the year 2003. The company filed a petition with the Superintendent for the Promotion of Free Competition – similar to the Federal Trade Commission in the USA – charging that the partnership between Coca-Cola and the Cisneros Group violated antitrust laws, since it left Pepsi without a manufacturer or distributor. Coca-Cola maintained that the deal, boosting the company's market share from about 10 per cent to more than 50 per cent, was legal because the Pepsi–Cisneros contract allows for such a deal and because it was placing six of its plants, and a variety of trucks, vending machines, coolers and workers, in a trust for Pepsi to purchase.[18]

In some countries formal contracts do not have the same importance they do in other nations, particularly in the USA or in Europe. Most channel relationships in Japan, for example, do not involve legal contracts. But channel members there are known for working more closely together than counterparts in the USA who largely rely on legal contracts.

MANAGING CHANNEL RELATIONSHIPS

Careful management of relationships with intermediaries is critical to success in international marketing. Distribution can be viewed as an exchange system that incorporates many interdependent organizations, each with its own objectives. Only when the interactions satisfy the needs of all partners will the relationships between them remain stable and the marketing objectives of the internationally operating company be achieved. In order to manage its channel relationships in a way that keeps exchanges subjectively balanced, the responsible manager in the internationally operating company needs to analyse the expectations of its distribution partners and fulfil them to the extent that the company's own expectations concerning the relationships are fulfilled. Table 14.5 shows potential mutual expectations of both international marketer and local distribution partners.

The value of cooperation between a manufacturer and its intermediaries

Table 14.5 **Mutual Expectations of International Marketer and Local Distribution Partner**

EXPECTATIONS OF COMPANY	EXPECTATIONS OF DISTRIBUTION PARTNER
The **distribution partner** should ↔ have excellent relations with customers and other important stakeholders ↔ possess an effective and efficient sales and service organization ↔ provide storage facilities ↔ be able to offer added value to customers by delivering entire product systems ↔ implement the intended position in the market ↔ help to plan the local budget ↔ assist in planning and realizing projects ↔ watch competition and provide latest information on market developments ↔ deliver in time and corresponding to the order ↔ develop and execute market communication plans ↔ bear responsibility for local marketing activities	The **supplying partner** should ↔ agree on clear and understandable objectives ↔ be ready for joint marketing planning ↔ provide reliable marketing research data ↔ provide realistic gross margins ↔ have an excellent image ↔ possess latest know-how on the product and its application ↔ provide support through product information and training ↔ provide budgets for market communication ↔ have an efficient information system ↔ provide performance feedback ↔ be ready for joint visits to customers and joint realization of projects

To keep the relationship balanced and satisfactory for both sides, an international marketer needs to fulfil the expectations of its distribution partners to the extent that its own expectations become satisfied.

within a channel as perceived by the exchange partners is strongly influenced by the rate of change and the level of environmental complexity faced by the parties involved. The higher the uncertainty, the greater the need to gain information from channel partners and to perform some joint activities.[19] For example, in dynamically evolving markets, such as computer hardware and software markets, most intermediaries are interested in close relationships with major manufacturers providing them with technical, informational and marketing support.

When it is relatively easy for an intermediary to replace a supplier, the intermediary is unlikely to be motivated to form a tight relationship with the supplier. For example, when a procurement manager of Paris-based Printemps, a department store company, can cancel the listing of a no-name supplier of boys' underwear from Thailand and replace it by a cheaper supplier from Guatemala without facing any negative reaction from consumers, the buyer will not place high importance on cultivating that relationship. On the other hand, when the supplier is the technology leader in its market or possesses a strong brand image, such as US-based Motorola or Nokia from Finland in the portable cellular phone market, intermediaries will be interested in more intensive and potentially exclusive relationships.

The higher the contribution of its channel members to the satisfaction of customer expectations, the more the internationally operating company needs to be concerned about enhancing cooperation with its intermediaries.

Organizational structure, motivation, communication and control can help to manage the channel relationships.

Organization

The company must develop an appropriate organizational structure to manage channel relationships. These relationships can be quite complex; personal contacts between a supplier's and an intermediary's staff may span several levels of the organization and involve employees in the company's sales, service, design, manufacturing and quality-control departments. As an example, Figure 14.4 shows how Procter & Gamble in its distribution relationship with Wal-Mart has replaced the traditional transaction between a manufacturer's salesperson and an intermediary's buying agent by multifunctional integration between the retailing and supplying organizations. Teams of both partners representing all functional areas which are directly or indirectly involved in the business exchange work closely together to ensure maximum success for both sides. Channel relationships, therefore, represent a considerable investment of human resources in information exchange, negotiations, transfer of technical knowledge, and social bonding.

Because people tend to prefer social relations with partners from the same cultural environment, the company must take care not to allocate too great a share of organizational resources to domestic distribution partners at the expense of building satisfactory relationships with more distant ones. On the other hand, too much focus on difficult channel relationships might tie up organizational resources which are needed to keep the most cooperative intermediaries satisfied. To avoid those traps, firms confronted with intermediaries handling big shares of a country's or region's total sales volume tend to install key account managers who specifically handle the relationships with such major partners. In particular, when channel members become increasingly international themselves, they need to be treated the same in every country-market served. For example, when Rewe, the third-largest retailing organization in Germany and number six in the world, bought the biggest retailer in Austria, the Billa-Merkur Group, in 1996, all the firms which had supplied both retailers but with different prices and terms of sale experienced trouble. They not only had to accept the lower price for either served country but were forced to pay back the differential amount for the entire business year.

If a retailer operating internationally expects a supplier to take over the management of an entire product category, the manufacturer must be prepared for international product category management. That is, it needs the logistics and information systems to properly handle its own and the competitors' product lines in every outlet of the international intermediary. Similar things may happen to OEM suppliers in industrial businesses. For example, Stuttgart (Germany)-based Robert Bosch GmbH, a major producer of electrical and braking systems for cars, and the first company which offered ABS (anti-lock braking systems) for cars, was confronted with the demand of its major car manufacturing clients to deliver entire product systems instead of only electronic parts to improve braking systems. To be able to deliver those systems just in time at every site of a customer production plant in Asia, Europe, and North and Latin America, the company acquired 24 brake-making factories in Europe, Latin America and the USA as well as shares of joint ventures in China, India and Korea from US-based Allied Signal Inc.

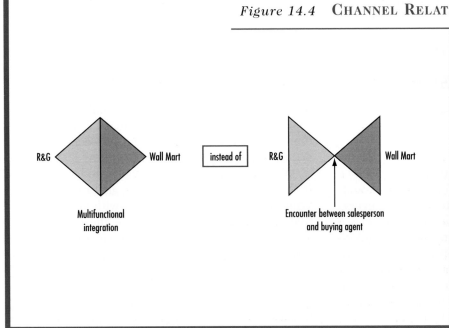

Figure 14.4 **CHANNEL RELATIONSHIP MANAGEMENT**

Procter & Gamble replaced the one-to-one encounter between a manufacturer's salesperson and an intermediary's buying agent as the traditional form of channel relationship in consumer goods industries by multifunctional integration between the retailing and supplying organizations. Teams from both partners representing all functional areas which are directly or indirectly involved in the business exchange work closely together to ensure maximum success for both sides.

Motivation

The intermediary must be able to make money by handling the product; otherwise it will have little interest in maintaining a relationship with the supplier. Higher margins, larger commissions or more advantageous credit terms have traditionally served as ways of motivating distribution partners. With increasing speed of new product introductions, however, keeping margins up becomes more and more difficult. Constant innovation compels manufacturers to sell quickly. As an individual PC ages, for example, its price can easily drop 30 per cent in six months. Consequently, the main complaint of computer retailers is that profit margins are low. In the USA and Japan, big retailers are pleased with gross margins above 10 per cent. UK margins are higher – around 16–17 per cent, but still below the 20 per cent or more typical for most other electrical goods, which in turn tend to have lower margins than other consumer goods.[20]

Keeping in mind that margins, commissions and credit terms are less important to channel members than the amount they derive from the selling process, an international marketer that does not want to sacrifice profits should offer the usual margin percentages and, at the same time, help intermediaries increase the turnover of products through the training of sales staff, the provision of sales consultants, intensive promotion and/or selling the product at a higher average price by providing a more attractive and better-positioned product line.

The Strategy box shows how assistance to intermediaries in the form of personnel training, technical assistance, special product displays, and advertising and sales promotion materials may increase the intermediary's selling effectiveness while boosting the company's sales. Some companies

STRATEGY BOX

We'll Provide the Shillelaghs

'GUINNESS IS GOOD FOR YOU,' WENT AN OLD British advertising slogan for the black-and-hearty Irish stout. Guinness stout is not to everyone's taste, but enough people love it that it is a perennial moneymaker for its owner, London-based Guinness Plc. The company gets about 45 per cent of its USD6 billion a year in revenues from brewing Guinness stout and other beers. Worldwide, sales of Guinness Brewing, Guinness Plc.'s beer arm, have climbed by over 5 per cent a year for the past few years.

The key to this strong performance in beer is the growing popularity of ersatz Irish pubs all over the world. These pubs try to create an atmosphere of conviviality and warm welcome for strangers; they feature Irish food and drink and Irish music. There are now some 800 of these Irish-themed pubs stretching from Italy and Germany to Hong Kong, South Africa and Moscow. The count is up from virtually none just five years ago.

Guinness does not own pubs. Better than tying up capital in bricks and mortar, Guinness gets what amounts to an override on every Irish pub, for the simple reason that no pub claiming Irish roots can fail to offer Guinness. Even rival brewers like Whitbread Plc. and Allied Domecq opening up Irish pubs, all sell Guinness.

When an entrepreneur wants to start an Irish-style pub, Guinness will be glad to help. It brings the entrepreneur together with an agency that will design the pub, provide the furniture and effects, and fit out the place right down to shillelaghs on the wall. Another agency will help the new pub's owner find Irish bar staff, arrange Irish music and provide food: recipes like Molly Malone's fish soup and roast stuffed pork loin Limerick style. The company's salespeople train bartenders to use a traditional pouring technique for Guinness. Encouraging the existing trend costs Guinness almost nothing, save the expense of a few contests (win an Irish pub in Ireland) or sponsoring cartoonists to draw patrons in an Irish pub. Guinness considers itself as the intellectual, not the financial pub owners.

Source: Banks, H. (1996) 'We'll provide the shillelaghs', *Forbes*, 8 April, pp. 68 and 72.

---

even provide sales personnel to assist retailers. In Japan, for example, many department store salespeople are paid by wholesalers rather than by the retailer. In Thailand, Nestlé created a new sales team, called the Red Hot Sales Force. Staffed with college graduates fluent in English, the team took over the job of building and maintaining relationships with managers of supermarkets and superstores. The team members routinely jet to Hong Kong, Australia or the staff training centre in Switzerland for instruction in the latest shelf-management techniques. They are supposed to train their customers, the supermarket managers. The hope is to establish solid relationships that will withstand the inevitable competition, when it arrives.[21]

Communication

International distribution channels require intensive communication to ensure that the activities of channel members conform to the company's global strategy. Communication efforts may be personal (visits or telephone calls) or impersonal (faxes, e-mails, or periodic corporate newsletters or magazines). Visits play an important role in reinforcing the personal bonds between distribution partners. So do personnel exchanges. These techniques may be used to resolve problems before they escalate and damage trust. For this reason, Honda USA's Japanese managers decided to spend up to 50 per cent of their working time visiting and talking with distributors and dealers in the USA. International and regional meetings can also be used for transmitting product information, planning, or simply exchanging experiences.

Caterpillar even goes one step further in their management of inter-mediary relationships. They actively help dealers keep the business in the family. When the principal of a privately held dealership is about 50 years old, the company offers seminars for the family on tax issues and succession plan-ning – both financial and management. These seminars are held two or three times during the principal's active working life to ensure that the next generation is ready. Caterpillar also holds conferences at its headquarters in Peoria, USA, for 15 to 25-year-old sons and daughters of dealership owners, aiming to introduce them to Caterpillar, to get them interested in the busi-ness, and to allow them to meet their peers. The company helps owners arrange jobs inside the Caterpillar organization for their children when they graduate from college, such as a parts salesperson for two years, then run the engine business, and next be put in charge of product support.[22]

Control

To control the activities of channel members and avoid conflict, the marketer must ensure that its corporate objectives are clearly communicated to inter-mediaries. Performance standards based on those objectives may include sales volume per product or product line within a specified period; inventory level; market share; and number of accounts per sales territory. For example, Wiberg, a globally operating producer of spices for meat production, based in Salzburg, Austria, uses the kind of portfolio analysis shown in Figure 14.5 to compare the performance of its international distribution partners and to communicate part of its distribution objectives. The analysis is based on two dimensions: the level of market penetration in a country-market (measured in terms of average sales per outlet) and the level of market coverage (measured in terms of the number of served outlets per 100 000 inhabitants). Inter-mediaries in countries located in the lower left quadrant must increase the number of outlets they serve as well as the average sales per outlet. Those located in the upper left quadrant have to increase the number of outlets, keeping the average sales per outlet at the existing level. Channel members who find their country in the lower right quadrant must increase the average sales per outlet, and those in the upper right field should basically maintain their level of achievement by sensitively dropping outlets with sales below average.

Attainment of the company's communication objectives is influenced by the promotional efforts of channel members. Those efforts, therefore, must be assessed from the standpoint of their contribution to the desired global cor-porate identity as well as their contribution to the intermediary's objectives. This assessment should be conducted jointly to avoid differences in interpre-tation. Visits and international meetings can serve such a control function without being obtrusive. Isao Makino, president of Toyota's US sales subsidiary

---

Figure 14.5 MARKET PENETRATION/MARKET COVERAGE-PORTFOLIO

By comparing the levels of market penetration and market coverage reached by its distributors, the international marketer can control part of the international channel members' goal achievement and can clearly communicate some of its objectives.

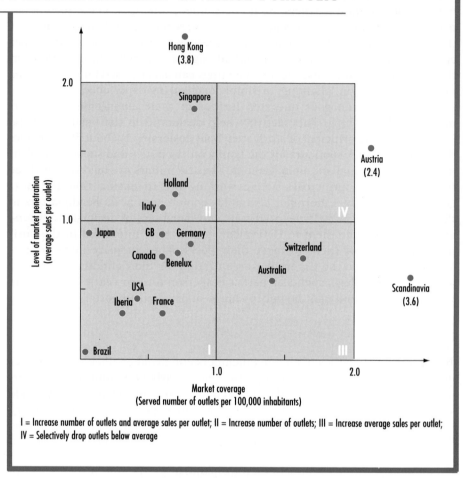

I = Increase number of outlets and average sales per outlet; II = Increase number of outlets; III = Increase average sales per outlet; IV = Selectively drop outlets below average

---

from 1975 to 1983 (a difficult period for the company), for example, visited every Toyota dealer in the USA at least once a year.

INFLUENCE ON THE MARKETING MIX

International distribution decisions influence product management. They strongly contribute to the value of a product provided to the customer. When a company cannot afford to establish an integrated distribution system and the level of technological sophistication of available distribution partners is relatively low, the firm may be forced to develop products that are easy to handle and with little demand for customer services. When the power of intermediaries is high and the resulting pressures on prices are considerable, new products will need to have lower costs of material, production and handling. Brands will not be properly established in a market where strong channel members cannot be found. And import agents will not provide the same level of service to final customers as company sales personnel.

Pricing is influenced by international distribution decisions. For example, longer distribution channels tend to result in higher prices. The 'quality' of a chosen channel strongly influences the market price charged. It is difficult, for example, to charge a premium price for products distributed through discount department stores. Finally, channel control and power relationships affect terms of payment. A firm selling to an integrated channel member can offer more liberal credit terms, because in most cases it is assuming less risk. A seller with a strong position in an independent channel can dictate more favourable terms of payment, such as payment in advance or an irrevocable letter of credit.

International distribution decisions also influence market communication. The potential for joint advertising and promotional activities depends largely on the nature of the channel members. In fact, marketers may use joint promotional activities to build stronger channel relationships. In addition, the 'quality' of the channel affects the image the marketer is able to convey through its promotional campaigns. It is difficult, for example, to convey a youthful, modern image via a channel dominated by small, old-fashioned, poorly decorated retail stores. Finally, the distribution channel affects the marketer's opportunities for personal contact and communication with customers. An important role of channels for industrial products and prestige consumer goods is to provide positive personal contact between the marketer and the customer. Thus, the impression conveyed by channel members is very important to the successful marketing of these products.

SUMMARY

Local distribution is a critical step in successful international marketing. If the product cannot be delivered to the market, sales will not occur regardless of the value of the product, the price charged, or the persuasiveness of promotion. Whether the channel is direct or indirect, the international marketing manager has a major challenge in making local channel decisions which result in a global distribution system that matches the firm's intended global strategic position and in managing relationships within its distribution system.

The manager must choose a channel that will reach customers effectively and efficiently and take their characteristics into account. The potential channel members themselves, the functions they perform, their structure, networking ability and power relations must be evaluated. Managers do so through the application of several selection criteria, including costs and the multiple types of distance (geographic, social, cultural, technological and temporal). Finding the best intermediaries requires an active search process, not dissimilar to the marketing research process as described in an earlier chapter. It starts out with secondary sources of information which are enriched by data from primary sources as soon as the amount of information to be gathered is restricted to a short list of seemingly attractive channel members.

Managing channel relationships across multiple nations and cultures can prove quite challenging to the international manager. The organizational structure of the company must provide for different power relations between the firm and its intermediaries as well as for different intensities of relationship management. Motivation of channel members does not depend only on the monetary reward they derive from being part of the company's distribution system. Assistance in the form of personnel training, technical help, advertising allowances and sales promotion materials may increase the intermediary's motivation for selling efforts. Communication and control systems must be established to enable all channel members to share information and understand how each member contributes to the entire distribution system's success.

Discussion Questions

1. Why is international distribution more difficult than domestic distribution, even if the functions performed by a channel of distribution are similar in both situations?
2. What are the advantages and disadvantages of using an integrated distribution system? What choice would you suggest under what conditions?
3. How do the characteristics of the final customers affect the evaluation of international channel options?
4. What influences the length of a distribution channel in a national market, and how does that impact international channel evaluation?
5. Why are intermediary networks of importance to the international marketer, and how should they be taken into consideration?
6. How does distance influence channel-member selection? What are your conclusions?
7. What are the advantages and risks to a marketer of discussing a possible partnership with an intermediary who already handles a competitor's product?
8. Describe the process of finalizing the relationship between a marketer and an intermediary. What environmental conditions will have to be considered?
9. What are the major elements in managing international channel relationships, and what potential problems must international marketing managers be prepared to overcome?

Additional Readings

Avlakh, P.S. and M. Kotabe (1997) 'Antecedents and Performance Implications of Channel Integration in Foreign Markets', *Journal of International Business Studies*, 28(1), 145–175.

Kim, K. and G.L. Frazier (1996) 'A typology of distribution channel systems: a contextual approach', *International Marketing Review*, 13(1), 19–32.

Pirog, St.F.III., P.A. Schneider and D.K.K. Lam (1997) 'Cohesiveness in Japanese distribution: a socio-cultural framework', *International Marketing Review*, 14(2), 124–134.

Yip, G.S. and T.L. Madsen (1996) 'Global Account management: the new frontier in relationship marketing', *International Marketing Review*, 13(3), 24–42.

Notes

[1] Bloomberg Business News (1996) 'China's Lighter Shade of Red', *International Herald Tribune*, 9–10 March, p. 12.

[2] 'Go for It', *Hilti International*, November 1994, pp. 25–31; and Winter, W. (1996) 'Im Zeichen des Tigers – Asien im Aufwind', *Hilti International*, January, pp. 8–12.

[3] Yip, G.S. and T.L. Madsen (1996) 'Global account management: the new frontier in relationship marketing', *International Marketing Review*, 13(3) 24–42.

[4] Burrows, P. (1995) 'The Computer is in the Mail (Really)', *Business Week*, 23 January 23, pp. 44–45.

[5] 'Do consumers want home shopping?', *ESOMAR newsbrief*, 3(6) June 1995, p. 23.

[6] Pentz, M. (1996) 'Teleshopping Gets a Tryout in Europe But Faces Cultural and Legal Barriers', *The Wall Street Journal*, 10 September, p. B5.

[7] Rayport, J.F. and J.J. Sviokla (1995) 'Exploiting the Virtual Value Chain', *Harvard Business Review*, November–December, 75–85.

[8] Schneidewind, D. (1991) 'Zur Struktur, Organisation und globalen Politik japanischer Keiretsu', *ZfbF* 43(3) 255–274.

[9] Corporate Performance', *Fortune*, 14 April 1986.

[10] ifo Institut für Wirtschaftsforschung, Munich 1994.

[11] Chen, K.-J. (1996) 'Philippines Informal Sector's Sari-sari Store: Nature, Management and Implications', *Working Paper*, National Open University, Taiwan.

[12] 'Malled', *The Economist*, 18 May 18 1996, pp. 69f.

13 Rapoport, C. (1994) 'Nestlé's Brand Building Machine', *Fortune*, 19 September, pp. 147–156.

14 'Private label sales', *ESOMAR NewsBrief*, 3(10) November 1995, p. 34.

15 M + M Eurodata, *EuroTrade* 1993.

16 ifo Institut für Wirtschaftsforschung, Munich 1994.

17 Du Bois, M. (1996) 'Dutch Grocer Moves Up U.S. Food Chain', *The Wall Street Journal*, 2 April, p. A10.

18 Frank, R. (1996) 'PepsiCo Asks Venezuela to Block Pact Between Its Ex-Bottler and Coca-Cola', *The Wall Street Journal*, 28 August; and Frank, R. (1996) 'Venezuelan Bottler Defects to Coca-Cola, Adding to Pepsi's Latin American Woes', *The Wall Street Journal*, 19 August, pp. A2 and A4.

19 Kim, K. and G.L.Frazier (1996) 'A typology of distribution channel systems: a contextual approach', *International Marketing Review*, 13(1) pp. 19–32.

20 'Too good to last', *The Economist*, 23 March 1996, pp. 61f.

21 Rapoport, C. (1994) 'Nestlé's Brand Building Machine', *Fortune*, 19 September, pp. 147–156.

22 Fites, D.V. (1996) 'Make Your Dealers Your Partners', *Harvard Business Review*, March–April, 84–95.

CHAPTER

15

INTERNATIONAL
MARKETING LOGISTICS

$$\boxed{\text{INTERNATIONAL INCIDENT}}$$

International Marketing Logistics Networks

The British warehousing specialist Tibbet & Britten has rented a 100 000 square metres warehouse in Hirschstetten, Austria as a product distribution centre to take over the responsibility for all warehousing activities of BauMax, the Austrian leader in DIY retailing.

Big retailing firms and consumer goods manufacturers increasingly tend to outsource the international physical distribution of their products to logistics specialists which organize the order disposition, transportation of products, warehousing and storage, and sometimes even packaging as well as recycling processes to serve their clients' customers at the quality level and time specified. Whereas manufacturers and retailers would have to establish their own international logistics organizations, those specialists can offer international logistics networks of cooperating partners, equipped with modern information management and product handling tools.

Their computer systems determine the optimal transportation routes. Specially designed packaging devices take into account the individual size, nature and perishability of the goods to be distributed. Highly automated warehouses reduce the fixed costs of manufacturers and retailers, in particular of companies with highly seasonal sales, such as sporting goods marketers for outdoor sports in most parts of the northern hemisphere.

Sources: 'Netzwerker der Logistik', *Lagerhaltung & Logistik*, 11 September 1996, p. A2; 'Schlaue Zauberformeln', *Lagerhaltung & Logistik*, 11 September 1996, p. A1.

INTERNATIONAL MARKETING LOGISTICS

Besides the establishment and maintainance of customer relationships, a firm's distribution system also exists for the physical distribution of its goods and services. A firm's decisions and actions concerning the physical distribution of its total products, including inventory management, warehousing, storage, shipping and receiving, and transportation as well as all associated information processes and documentation are called marketing logistics. In international marketing, logistics are increasingly recognized as an important source of potential competitive advantage. As the Future Issues box shows, logistics determine the level of customer service which is one of the elements of the marketing mix most difficult to imitate.

Factors such as rapid, punctual delivery and reliable supply with products and services of specified quality often outweigh competitive pricing in the international struggle for customers. To provide sustainable competitive advantage, all marketing logistics activities of an internationally operating company must be organized in a systematic way, based on a marketing logis-

FUTURE ISSUES
BOX

Making Global Connections at Caterpillar

IMAGINE THE FOLLOWING SCENARIO. A PART ON A Caterpillar machine operating at a copper mine in Chile begins to deteriorate. A district center that continuously monitors the health of all the Caterpillar machines in its area by remotely reading the sensors on each machine automatically spots a problem in the making and sends an electronic alert to the local dealer's field technician through his portable computer. The message tells him the identity and location of the machine and sends his computer the data that sparked the alert and its diagnosis. Then, with the aid of the computer, the technician validates the diagnosis and determines the service or repair required, the cost of labor and parts, and the risks of not performing the work.

The technician's computer also tells him exactly which parts and tools he will need to make the repair. Then, with a touch of a key, the technician ties into Caterpillar's worldwide information system, which links dealers, Caterpillar's parts-distribution facilities, Cat's and its suppliers' factories, and large customers' inventory system. He instantly determines the best sources of the parts and the times when each source can deliver them to the dealer's drop-off point.

Next, the technician sends a proposal to the customer by computer or phone, and the customer tells him the best time to carry out the repair. With a few more keystrokes, the technician orders the parts. The electronic order instantly goes to the factories or warehouses that can supply the parts in time. At the factory and warehouses, the message triggers the printing of an order ticket and perhaps automatically sets into motion an automated crane that retrieves the parts from a storage rack. Soon the parts are on their way to the dealer's pick-up site.

Within hours of the initial alert, the technician is repairing the machine. An interactive manual on his computer guides him, providing him with the latest best-practice procedures for carrying out the repair. The repair completed, the technician closes the work order, prints out an invoice, collects by credit card, and electronically updates the machine's history. That information is added to Caterpillar's database, which helps the company spot any common problems that a particular model might have and thereby continually improve its machines' designs.

Sound like science fiction? It isn't. Caterpillar hopes to have such a system capable of monitoring all its machines around the world within several years. Most of the pieces are already in place: the sensors in the machines; computers that diagnose problems and instruct technicians in how to make repairs; and the information system that ties together Caterpillar's factories, distribution centers, dealers, and large customers. The system links some 1,000 locations across 23 time zones and 160 countries.

Source: Prokesch, St.E. (1996), 'Making Global Connections at Caterpillar', *Harvard Business Review*, March–April, 88f.

tics policy and integrated with procurement as well as production logistics activities (see Figure 15.1). Efficient Consumer Response (ECR) systems, for example, which were first developed in the USA, coordinate the flow of goods among manufacturers, transporters, wholesalers and retailers with the help of data bank systems. Cash registers equipped with scanners not only recognize the products bought by a customer and add up the prices, they are also connected to a computer which controls stocks and launches repeat orders when

Figure 15.1 INTERNATIONAL MARKETING LOGISTICS DECISIONS

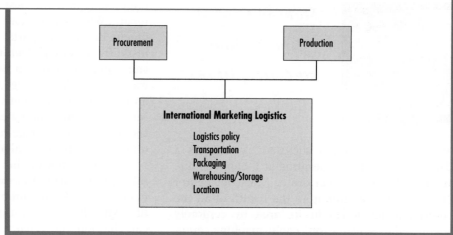

The international marketer first has to develop an international marketing logistics policy to coordinate the various people and organizations involved in the physical distribution process of the firm's products. Based on these guidelines, decisions concerning transportation, physical aspects of packaging, warehousing and storage can be taken. All marketing logistics decisions have to be coordinated with the company's procurement and production logistics decisions and actions.

stock falls below pre-specified levels. The manufacturer is connected to the same computer and knows at any time of the day how much of a product needs to be delivered to which retail outlet. Based on this information, production can be continually adapted and purchasing orders made. If the transportation unit is also linked to the information system, marketing logistics are efficiently integrated.

Such integration only makes sense if it is based on general objectives to be reached and basic rules that need to be respected by the parties involved. Therefore, in the following, the contents of an international marketing logistics policy will first be described. Then the operative decisions based on this policy concerning transportation, packaging, warehousing and storage as well as location will be discussed. The chapter will end with an overview of the terms of sale which express those decisions in the contract between a marketer and its customer and some hints concerning the mutual influences of marketing logistics and other marketing-mix decisions.

INTERNATIONAL MARKETING LOGISTICS POLICY

The physical distribution of a total product across a variety of international markets necessitates a great number of decisions and activities which in most cases are taken and executed by different people (maybe belonging to different organizations) specializing in certain functions and socialized in various cultural environments. To make sure that the objectives given by the intended global strategic position, the intended positioning of the business unit, and the positioning of the product are respected by those people, the international marketer or its logistics manager has to develop general guidelines indicating the objectives of marketing logistics and how these objectives should be achieved in general terms. That is, the policy statement indicates the level of customer service to achieve and the limits of decisions and actions allowed to reach the given objective. All operative decisions concerning customer service, transportation of goods, physical aspects of packaging, warehousing and storage, as well as the choice of locations have to respect those guidelines.

Level of Customer Service

The level of customer service in marketing logistics is generally measured as the percentage of properly delivered goods (the right goods at the quality level indicated in the sales contract) in a pre-specified period of time (or at a given point in time). German Würth, the biggest wholesaler of construction tools in Europe, for example, has defined the customer service goal of delivering 96 per cent of all orders to the customers' premises in 48 hours, exactly according to the customers' orders.

The level of customer service provided by an international marketer in non-domestic markets tends to be lower than that provided in its domestic market, because of factors like geographic distance, errors in transmitting and filling orders, inadequate packaging and preparation for shipment, transportation problems, and delays in clearing customs. In Japan, for example, the Japan Harbour Transportation Association controlls virtually all traffic by vessels. When a shipping company – foreign or domestic – needs to change a route, a vessel or a port of call, it has to ask the harbour association six weeks in advance. If the paperwork is not perfect, approval is delayed for a month.[1]

Time in transit can vary significantly from one country-market to another and from one shipment to the next because different carriers may be involved, multiple transfers of goods may be necessary, numerous national boundaries may have to be crossed, and the distribution channels used may be of different length. For example, in the USA about 56 per cent of the total sales in food products is made via independent wholesalers. That is, the logistics chain in the USA is longer than in Germany or the UK. The average time a food product needs to get from the producer to the consumer is about 100 days in the USA, compared to 50 days in Germany and 28 days in the UK.[2] Therefore, it may not be advisable for an international marketer to specify and maintain the same level of customer service in all markets.

In formulating its customer service policy, the international marketer should keep in mind that the quality of customer service is a subjective phenomenon. What is perceived as superior delivery service depends on customers' expectations. Any service level that is far higher than customers expect increases physical distribution costs without payoff. If the service level is below expectations, however, the perceived quality of the total product is lowered. Therefore, the company may specify a general service level in qualitative terms, for example to have the highest customer service level of the industry in each served country-market. Based on this general goal, the international logistics manager must adapt the company's physical distribution system to the local service requirements and the capabilities of the competitors in each market.

Integrated versus Independent Marketing Logistics

The physical distribution of a company's products can be executed through transportation devices, warehouses and storage capacities owned by the company (integrated marketing logistics) or through independent service providers (independent marketing logistics). Independent marketing logistics are not directly controlled by the marketer. Companies that use facilitating agencies but largely control them are said to have a company-bound marketing logistics system. There are basically two types of facilitating agencies to physically transfer the goods and services of a firm to the final customers: customhouse brokers and freight forwarders.

A customhouse broker serves as an agent for exporters and importers of goods, performing two essential functions: facilitating the movement of products through customs and handling the documentation accompanying international shipments. A freight forwarder provides a broader range of services, including coordination and assistance in all phases of shipment from the company's plant to its markets (see Table 15.1). Compared to the USA, Australia and the UK where big 'industrial' system carriers or contract distributors predominate, Germany has a great number of middle-sized freight forwarders. In Italy small transportation companies, called camionisti, characterize the market. The Strategy box describes the example of one of Europe's leading road transport and logistics service providers.

The extent to which companies use integrated physical distribution basically depends on the performance level achieved by service providers specializing in physical distribution compared to company-owned units and their relative costs. The benchmark is the service level expected by the firm's international customers which has at least to be achieved. If both alternatives, integrated as well as independent marketing logistics, are able to satisfy the customers' expectations, the cost of physical distribution should be minimized. Take the example of Germany's Liebherr, one of the leading ship- and harbour-crane producers in the world. They have to serve their customers around the world with spare parts in 48 hours. The company can only use external physical distribution partners where they are fast and reliable enough to fulfil this customer service target. In country-markets where such potential partners exist, the relative costs of each alternative will play a major role in the firm's decision.

The decision between integrated, company-bound and independent marketing logistics systems should be taken considering the more specific factors listed in Table 15.2.

Prices and Costs. Prices and costs will strongly influence the decision. An international physical distribution system may need large capital investment and a highly developed market information system to function properly. The difference between the maintainance costs of their own fleet of trucks and the transportation cost versus the price of the services of an international freight forwarder often leads companies to decide in favour of an independent physical distribution system. Because the reliability of the logistics chain heavily influences the level of service experienced by international customers, however, international marketers might tend to establish company-bound logistics systems through long-term cooperation contracts. Such contracts often give cost and price transparency to the marketer without the disadvantage of high fixed costs that characterizes integrated marketing logistics systems.

Table 15.1 SERVICES PROVIDED BY FREIGHT FORWARDERS

Preparation of export declarations required by the local government

Booking of cargo space

Transportation from the firm's premises to the indicated destination

Preparation and processing of airway bills and bills of lading

Preparation of consular documents in the language of the country to which the goods are shipped

Provision for certification of receipt of goods

Provision for warehouse storage

Provision for insurance upon request

Preparation of shipping documents and sending them to banks, shippers, or consignees as directed

The many activities required to ship a good from one nation to another are frequently provided by independent companies, known as freight forwarders. Without these independent companies, small and medium-sized businesses in particular would find it difficult (if not impossible) to be involved in global marketing.

Source: Stock, J. R. and D. M. Lambert (1983) 'Physical Distribution Management in International Marketing', International Marketing Review, Autumn 37f.

STRATEGY BOX

The Norbert Dentressangle Group

SOME EXPERTS CLAIM THAT GOODS TRANSPORT requirements in Europe could double by the year 2010. The Norbert Dentressangle Group, whose head office is located near Lyon in France, is one of the leaders in European road transport and logistics services. It has followed a sustained development policy over the last 20 years and today includes more than 60 branch offices all over Europe. The Group plays an active part in the whole process from delivering the raw materials to a factory to placing the finished product in its distribution channel. The company offers to European manufacturers a package comprising four services: the actual transportation as such, contract distribution, warehousing services and tailor-made logistics operations.

At the end of the seventies, the owner and CEO of the company, Norbert Dentressangle, chose to increasingly focus the firm's transport services policy on international business. In 1995 international services were responsible for 55 per cent of the Group's total sales. The international development policy tended to be based on geographical considerations, specializing the Group in transporting goods between Great Britain and the European continent. Because of this, the company became European leader in this field with a total of 120,000 Channel crossings in 1995. This geographically based policy then established the firm also along a north/south axis in Spain, Portugal, Italy and Benelux. Recently the Group is developing a further east/west axis through increasing its activities with Germany and opening up markets in Central European countries. The organization of tailor-made logistic operations is seen as the most promising line of development for the future since there is a growing tendency among European manufacturers to focus more on their core-business and to contract out their other activities, such as their logistics organization.

Source: 'Norbert DENTRESSANGLE "hits the road" to internationalization,' Groupe ESC Lyon, *Newsletter*, No. 17, June 1996, pp. 1f.

> *Table 15.2* FACTORS TO BE CONSIDERED IN THE CHOICE
> OF A PHYSICAL DISTRIBUTION SYSTEM

The choice of a physical distribution system depends on the prices and costs of available alternatives, as well as on how the level of physical distribution system development, the physical properties of the product to be distributed, the order size and frequency, and the movements of goods allow the set customer service level to be achieved.

Physical Properties
  Goods
  Packages
  Assortment
  Way of delivery

Order Size and Frequency
  by   sources
        product groups
        destinations

Movements of Goods
  Number of distribution levels
  Number of production sites and
  sales warehouses
  Transportation destinations

Prices and Costs
  Price transparency
  Price sensitivity
  Cost structure
  Cost variance

Level of System Development
  Quality
  Potential for rationalization
  Economies of scale and scope

Availability of Alternatives
  Potential for cooperation
  Need for differentiation
  Restrictions

Source: Rüppell, H.-B. (1992) 'Strukturen für eine europäische Di\stributionslogistik in der Konsumgüter-Wirtschaft', Betriebswirtschaftliche Forschung und Praxis, 3, 210f.

Level of Development. Beside prices and costs, the level of development of local physical distribution systems influences the 'make or buy' decision in international logistics. In country-markets where the level of physical distribution quality, in terms of delivery time or safety of goods, is low and there is a potential for rationalization or economies of scale and scope, integration of the physical distribution function might seem attractive. But if the existing means of physical distribution is very strange to the marketer, as for example in some areas of China where goods are delivered in carts drawn by animals or humans, it may be wiser to rely on experienced local logistical service providers.

Physical Properties. Physical properties, such as the kind of goods, the packaging needed, the selection to be presented to the customers, or the local means of delivery can make it impossible for an international marketer to establish its own logistics system. For example, a US exporter of machinery will not buy ships or aeroplanes to deliver its products to customers in the UK. Neither will it buy big containers to transport the product overseas, in order to keep the firm flexible concerning its transportation mode and to avoid unnecessary fixed costs. But the marketer may sign a contract with an express delivery service that guarantees 48-hour spare parts delivery to all destinations in Europe.

If the customers of an international marketer do not buy an individual product but a combination of this product with other products or services that are needed to reach the intended benefit, such as in the case of sanitary equipment, the manufacturer will also opt for independent or company-bound logistics. The same holds if the means of delivery of the product in a country-market is very different from what the marketer is used to. For example, in India most razor blades are not sold in big supermarkets such as in the EU or in the USA where deliveries can be made by trucks and in bigger loads, but in very small one-room shops that need low-quantity daily delivery because of a lack of storage space. An integrated logistics system would not make much sense under such circumstances.

Order size and frequency.   Order size and frequency by sources, product groups and destinations will also influence the choice of an integrated versus an independent logistics system. If a mechanical engineering firm that constructs big steel bridges all over the world wants to make sure that all the parts needed are on the construction site in time and without quality problems, it might decide to use a company-bound logistics systems. This would keep the fixed cost low, allow some price transparency concerning the physical distribution to the international marketer, and give the marketer the security of keeping the construction project on track.

Movement of Goods.   The movement of goods, that is, the number of levels of intermediaries in the local distribution channels, the number of production sites and sales warehouses to be serviced, and the number and spread of transportation destinations to be covered, are another bundle of factors to be considered. The more levels of intermediaries, sites and destinations, the greater the tendency to use independent logistics firms.

Taking all those factors into consideration, an international marketing logistics policy may need not to be overly rigid in defining the appropriate physical distribution structure. If the served country-markets differ widely in their means of total product delivery, the international logistics policy must allow flexible adaptation. In many cases, marketers operating internationally will choose a mixture of integrated and independent parts for their distribution system. Major retailing companies in Europe are an example: they tend to take over warehousing and storage as well as delivery from producers and to serve their retail outlets through distribution centres where goods of different suppliers are bundled. Handling as well as transportation costs are lowered because of fewer arrivals at the retail units. The central warehouses in the distribution centres hold little or no inventory. They act as transit terminals. This becomes possible because, based on local retail sales, the rhythm of orders is increased and goods are delivered in smaller amounts.

In parallel, more and more major retailers rely on 'outsourcing'. That is, they leave great parts of the handling of goods to 'distributors' or 'logistics specialists'. Distributors are often the main suppliers, called 'category managers', who look after the delivery of an entire product group, including products of competitors. Logistics specialists are mainly business units of big freight forwarders that take over the entire distribution function and add merchandising, financing (factoring), and other services such as mounting, finishing, or the addition of product usage information.

To allow adaptation and at the same time keep the international marketing logistics system of a company manageable, the minimum requirement for the formulation of a logistics policy is to establish a list of factors to be considered in taking local decisions and their importance. In addition, strategic or environmental considerations may be prescribed. If a company wants to differentiate itself from competitors through its distribution system, it can establish its own physical distribution network. Restrictions on investments in a country may then influence the decision in the direction of a company-bound marketing logistics system.

Choice of Logistics Partners

To ensure the intended level of customer service, an international marketer opting for an independent or a company-bound logistics system depends heavily on the availability and choice of qualified cooperation partners. The international marketing logistics policy of a firm, therefore, contains the profile of logistics partners to look for. Those partners must not only be reliable, but also need to be ready to participate in decreasing the total costs of logistics. An international marketer might establish a guideline that only logistics service providers willing to accept cost targets and an open book policy are to be considered as partners. Such partners are offered long-term contracts which allow them to build up their capacities and customer-specific capabilities without incalculable financial risk.

Marketing Logistics Management

Finally, the international marketing logistics policy also needs to contain some general guidelines concerning the roles to be fulfilled inside and outside the company, their coordination between central and local company units and the responsibilities for logistics planning, information and control. How important planning and control may be for a firm's international logistics is underlined by the fact that in 1990, because of unreliable freight organization, trucks in Europe were empty for two-thirds of the time they were on the road.

Because logistics can be considered as a horizontal function that concerns or is influenced by decisions from all parts of a company as well as from external partners, most marketing logistics decisions will be taken in cross-functional teams with members from central and local units as well as cooperating firms. Those teams may be led by an internal or external international marketing logistics manager or by varying members of the company depending on the field of experience particularly needed.

OPERATIVE MARKETING LOGISTICS DECISIONS

Based on the general guidelines given in the international marketing logistics policy, individual members of the firm can take operative decisions concerning customer service, transportation, packaging, warehousing and storage, as well as choice of locations. The decisions that need to be taken and the factors of influence that need to be considered will be described in the following.

Customer Service

The marketing logistics manager, working within the framework of the company's basic strategy, must be concerned with minimizing total marketing logistics costs, which in the first half of the 1990s reached a level of 5 to 15 per cent of net profits in European companies, while providing a satisfactory level of customer service. The level of customer service that a firm can attain is influenced by a broad range of factors from inside and outside the company. For example, while lower levels of inventory may reduce the cost of physical distribution by lowering the capital cost incurred, they may also entail the risk of providing less than satisfactory customer service. Raw materials, parts, or finished products missing from stock may greatly reduce the marketer's ability to react to customer orders in time.

The marketer must consider the entire logistics chain of the company in attempting to achieve the objectives set in the firm's marketing logistics policy. Close coordination between sales, procurement, production and physical distribution is needed to ensure a constant level of customer service at reduced cost. It is possible to reach a level of customer service in global product-markets that is as high as or even higher than the level maintained in domestic markets. The speed and precision of physical distribution can be augmented by the use of new transportation methods, improved packaging technology, advanced methods of preservation, warehouse merchandising, and direct delivery to the customers' premises, as well as by faster handling of orders through online information systems in a chain of cooperating firms.

For example, if an international manufacturer and its intermediaries are ready to participate in a real-time information system, POS-scanning data can be used to achieve just-in-time production and delivery, decreasing inventory level, transportation and handling. US-based Levi Strauss, for example, has developed an electronic data-interchange system called LeviLink. When a Levi garment is rung up by a cashier at a major retailer, the sales information can be sent electronically to the jeans maker. It uses the information to generate reorders, invoices or packing slips. The fast delivery based on orders diminishes the risk of wrong distribution of goods to warehouses and retailing outlets where the stock cannot be sold.

Telecomputing standards such as EDIFACT have been developed to enable communication between the different organizations involved. In Europe, a joint venture between France Telecom, Deutsche Bundespost Telekom, Digital Equipment and the Technology Management Group offers an information system called 'Euro-Log'. It contains modules for electronic data interchange between producers, wholesalers, retailers, banks and distribution facilitators, the door-to-door management of transport with various transportation modes, and a module for freight management.

There is one basic condition, however, to make such an informationally integrated marketing logistics system work: the company's logistics function has to be centralized, that is, the physical distribution responsibilities of national sales offices, subsidiaries or intermediaries must be limited to execution functions or even entirely deleted. The Switzerland-based Silver Crystal division of Austrian Swarovsky, for example, reduced the responsibilities of their sales offices to building and maintaining customer contacts. The physical distribution of crystal objects is handled out of a single distribution centre for each of Europe, North America and Southeast Asia.

In country-markets with complicated import regulations such as India, some manufacturers even establish local production plants in order to achieve a more predictable distribution schedule. Service delivery in global markets is also affected by local differences in available infrastructures. For example, an internationally operating bank such as London-based Barclays Bank must be aware that automatic teller machines are as popular in the USA as in Western

Europe but they are used to deliver many more kinds of banking services. In most parts of Europe the machines are limited to dispensing cash. And in most parts of Africa, such a distribution system for banking services does not exist.

Transportation

Based on the company's general policy decision to use either a company-owned, a company-bound or an independent physical distribution system, the international marketing logistics manager will have to make choices concerning the transportation of its products from the company's premises to the customers. There are different transportation modes available which are more or less suited to the marketer's product and the level of customer service to be achieved. The total costs and the reliability of those transportation modes will also have to be taken into account. In addition, international transportation of goods is not advisable without proper insurance. The logistics manager will have to consider the trade-off between insurance costs and the risk of losses. And finally, international transportation often involves extensive paperwork. Because of the specific know-how needed to provide the exact documents to cross borders and to minimize delivery and payment risks, in most cases the marketer will seek the services of an international freight forwarder.

Modes of Transportation. The most important mode of transportation in international marketing is by water. Table 15.3 presents an overview of the different types of water transportation available and the services provided. Water transport is advantageous when country-markets are characterized by extensive coastlines and heavily populated coastal regions. For example, about half of Australia's population is located in the crescent between Brisbane and Adelaide, which is readily accessible by ocean freight.

Water transportation requires an extensive transportation infrastructure to move goods from the ship to the customer. Port facilities in less industrially developed countries often lack the equipment to handle modern vessels. Even countries with large ports may have an inadequate internal transportation system, with the result that cargoes may remain on vessels or docks for weeks or even months before they can be transported to their final destinations.

Rail transportation is important in countries where roads are poor or railroad infrastructures are heavily subsidized by the government. All of southeastern Africa, for example, depends on a single railroad line leading from the coast of Mozambique to the mineral-rich inland countries. This line is so important to the economy of the area that the industrialized nations agreed to contribute significantly to the costs of its reconstruction after it was destroyed by rebels during a political coup.

Planned restrictions on truck shipping in the European Union – a result of pollution and noise (see the Ethics box) – have led to the development of mixed transportation modes using roll-on/roll-off railroad cars or special rail containers. The containers are loaded at the shipper's facilities, set on trucks going to the nearest rail terminal, and then loaded onto trains which go as near as possible to their destination. There they are picked up by other trucks to be transported to their final destination. Once the goods have been loaded into the containers, no other handling is required along the entire route.

Truck transportation can overcome the problems of inefficient or overloaded port facilities and the lack of adequate railroad lines. For example,

Table 15.3 TYPES OF WATER TRANSPORTATION AND SERVICES PROVIDED

Type of service	Scheduled services on regular routes		Charter services on individual routes	
Ship	Cargo liners	Container ships	Bulk carriers	Tramp vessels
Cargo	General cargo Ro/ro-cargo	Containers	Mass goods	Mass goods
Contract	Piece good freight contract		Volume freight contract	
	+ Booking	+ Service contract + Booking	+ Period/time charter	+ Trip charter + Consecutive trip charter + Period/time charter

Cargo liners carry general cargo over predetermined routes with scheduled times of departure and arrival.
Bulk carriers offer contractual services over extended periods of time or for individual trips.
Container ships transport containers of standard sizes on regular routes.
Tramp vessels are scheduled on demand on irregular routes.
Break-bulk ships are traditionally designed ships with their own cranes and cargo-handling equipment (particularly well suited for small ports in industrially less developed countries (LCDs))
Ro/Ro ships allow trucks to deposit their containers in the cargo space.
Lighter-aboard ships (LASH) store barges by crane and lower them at the point of destination.

Different types of goods use different types of water transportation.

Source: Adapted from Gray, H.P. (1982) 'International Transportation', in I. Walter and T. Murray, eds, Handbook of International Business, New York: John Wiley & Sons, pp. 11.3–11.18.

Swedish machinery and Austrian fruit juice are trucked to Saudi Arabia, where even the truck may be sold (because it is more economical than supporting an empty return trip) after having discharged its load. Because of the flexibility of truck transportation, this mode of transport is becoming increasingly popular in Europe. For example, each day more than 5000 trucks use the Brenner Autobahn (freeway) between Munich and the industrial centres of northern Italy.

Shipment by air reduces transportation time and the need to maintain a large inventory. In many cases air freight, despite its higher cost, is necessary for successful marketing. For example, Rosenbauer, a European marketer of fire engines, guarantees delivery of essential spare parts within 48 hours. Between 1983 and 1986 Porsche cars sold in the USA were shipped from Germany by air. Demand for the product was strong during those years, and profit margins were high enough to justify the use of this faster, though more expensive, means of transportation.

For air transportation to be efficient, good ground support services are vital. Such services tend to be more expensive than the services offered at truck terminals. In addition, in some regions theft and pilferage pose serious problems. The international marketer should ask an international carrier for advice before selecting this transportation mode.

ETHICS BOX

The Marketer's Responsibility for Environmental Protection

WITH CONSUMERS' GROWING AWARENESS OF ECO-logical problems in their environment two issues have become increasingly important in recent years: avoiding unnecessary traffic and retrodistribution.

In Europe there are about 2.7 million km of interlocal roads. The growth rate of roads built between 1980 and 1990 was 1.5 per cent compared to a growth in the number of cars and trucks of 25 per cent. Because of the increasing integration of EU markets and the opening of the formerly centrally controlled economies in Eastern Europe, the growth rate of road traffic has further increased. Forecasts are about 30 per cent until the year 2000. Railroad capacities for pan-European transport will not be sufficiently built up in time. The foreseeable traffic jam and the resulting CO_2 pollution which to a significant extent causes the warming of the hemisphere demand an optimization of vehicles, tours and loads on the part of responsible marketing logistics managers. If they are not willing to contribute voluntarily to the reduction of environmental pollution by their own means, they will be forced to adapt to external regulations coming from the EU administration.

In a similar way, manufacturers and retailers who are not willing to contribute to the reduction of package waste will be forced to take back, reuse or recycle an increasing amount of packaging material. In Europe, Germany and Switzerland have the most restrictive legislation in the field of packaging. Since 1 January 1993, transportation package material, boxes and containers, as well as sales package material must be reused or recycled. Even if other European countries so far have less restrictive legislation, international marketers are well advised to rethink their packaging and redistribution systems in advance.

Choosing Transportation Modes. To decide which transportation modes to use, the international marketer must evaluate the existing transportation infrastructures in the geographic areas it wishes to serve. These will differ from one country to another, as will the forms of transportation services available and their cost. For example, if a Romanian producer of asparagus wants to deliver 90 tonnes of its produce to Japanese customers, the logistics manager may decide to use the cheapest solution which is to transport the load to the Romanian port of Constantia by truck and from there to Yokohama by ship. Satellite-driven control of the cooling temperature in the trucks and the ship is able to ensure an undisturbed cold chain until the load's arrival in Japan. There, the length of existing channels of distribution might largely diminish the quality of the product before it arrives at the consumers. Another alternative would be to transport the asparagus by air from Bucharest via Paris to Tokyo. The problem is that there are only very few freight flights from the capital of Romania to Paris, and passenger flights can only take about 7 tonnes of goods (including the passenger's luggage). In addition, the cold chain could be interrupted during the time that the load is waiting in Paris. That leaves the marketer with the alternative of chartering two freight flights with a maximum load of 45 tonnes from Bucharest to Tokyo. But this would probably be the most expensive solution.

CULTURE BOX

Federal Express's Tracking Services

HOW MUCH THE LEVEL OF ADDITIONAL SERVICES needed to satisfy the expectations of customers in a country-market depends on cultural influences is illustrated by the example of Federal Express.

In the US where 'time is money' and many business transactions are based on distrust, the company allows individual customers with access to the Internet to track packages through the company's site on the World Wide Web. Customers can locate a package in transit by connecting on-line to the FedEx site and entering the airbill number. Customers can also request software from FedEx that allows them not only to track their parcels but also to view at any time the entire history of their transaction with FedEx. After the package has been delivered, they can even identify the name of the person who signed for it. Customers perceive this information as an additional value of the service.

Source: Rayport, J.F. and J.J. Sviokla (1995) 'Exploiting the Virtual Value Chain', *Harvard Business Review*, November–December, 75–85.

The choice between the basic transportation modes – surface, water and air – depends on the weight, size, form, volume and value of the products to be transported, the distance to be covered, the total cost, the acceptable transit time, the reliability (including loss and damage rates as well as punctuality) of the transportation mode, and the level of customer service required in a specific market. The final choice of the transportation service provider often depends on additional services offered by the suppliers (see the Culture box for an example).

The marketer should bear in mind that transportation costs may influence the competitiveness of its total product in a particular market, especially when the price per unit of weight is low (as in the case of many commodities). But for high-value products with high inventory-carrying costs, such as large computers, the total costs of distribution will be lower if a faster, though more expensive, mode of transportation like air freight is used.

Transit time and customer service level determine the amount of inventory required in the markets to which goods are being transported. For perishable and seasonal products, and especially for fashion goods, this can be a decisive factor in successful marketing. Fresh flowers exported to the USA from Colombia, Israel and the Netherlands, for example, are highly perishable and are therefore flown to wholesale markets in the USA each day.

The reliability of transportation affects the level of 'safety' inventory that must be maintained. It is especially important when marketing success depends on precise delivery dates and when a high unit price makes damage or loss very expensive. When transports of Western European products go to or through Russia, the first problem arises at the borders of Poland and Belarus. Border controls can take up to 48 hours, making precise delivery dates impossible. Then, in Russia the transport needs special guarding during the trip and overnight stops in specially prepared areas, if the marketer wants to make sure that its products arrive at their destination. Russia has largely taken over the infamous leadership in cargo theft from Italy. Companies such as Russian Mach have specialized in guarding transports in and through this country. Recently the Global Positioning System is being used to track the exact position of trucks and railroad cars by satellite.

The example of a lost German shipment to Georgia may illustrate the danger of theft that a marketer used to Western standards of transportation reliability has to face. When a railroad car full of technical products was shipped to Georgia, the load had to be reloaded onto another car at the border town of Brest, Belarus because of the larger gauge in the former Soviet Union. In the freight documents the local stationmaster certified the proper reloading as well as the sealing of the railroad car. When the car arrived in Georgia the unbroken seal was on, but the cargo had gone.

Documentation. The shipment of products in global markets is complicated by the need for extensive documentation. Besides the paperwork needed to document the goods transported, their origin and exact destination, and the details of their transaction, documents also serve the purpose of information and risk reduction for the parties involved. To serve the needs of simplification of administrative work and legal reliability of global business, the International Federation of Freightforwarding Organizations (FIATA) has developed standardized documents. These documents are particularly important for shipments using a combination of different transportation modes (multimodal transports) or for shipments of various goods in one load (collective load). The most frequently used documents are listed in Table 15.4. In addition to these documents, each transportation mode has its specific documents, such as the Sea Way Bill (SWB) or the Airway Bill (AWB).

An **export declaration** has to be filled out for statistical purposes of export administration agencies and for fiscal purposes such as the reimbursement of added value tax. The **commercial invoice** is a statement or a bill of the goods sold, describing the content of the transaction in detail. A **certificate of origin** is a document specifying the country where the product has mainly been manufactured. It is needed for specifying the applicable tariff. Country of origin legislation may be more or less rigid, however. For example, if an Italian manufacturer of decoration objects made from clay, such as Bolzano-based Thun, produces the raw objects in a factory in China and does some finishing in Italy, Italian laws allow a specification of origin as 'Made in Italy'.

Internationally used freight forwarders' documents are the **Forwarders Certificate of Receipt** (FCR), the **Forwarders Certificate of Transport** (FCT), and the negotiable **FIATA Combined Transport Bill of Lading** (FBL). The FCR is an international freight forwarder's take-over and shipment certificate in which the freight forwarder declares that it has taken over a good exactly specified in the document for shipment to a specified receiver or to the receiver's disposition. It serves the purpose of allowing the seller to be able to prove that it has handed over the goods. However, the buyer who receives the FCR from the freight forwarder cannot enforce the handing-over of the shipped goods. For this purpose the buyer needs an FBL.

In an FCT the freight forwarder certifies that it has taken over the load specified in the document for shipment and indicates its willingness to deliver the goods in accordance with the consignor's orders. By issuing this document the freight forwarder takes over the responsibility for the delivery of the goods to the holder of the FCT at their destination. The FCT is mainly used in cases

> *Table 15.4* **Most Frequently Required Documents in International Logistics**

Document	Purpose
Export declaration	A form serving the statistical purposes of export administration agencies
Commercial invoice	A statement or bill of the goods sold, describing the transaction in detail
Certificate of origin	A document specifying the exact origin of the product; needed for specifying the applicable tariff
Freightforwarders documents:	FCR = Forwarders Certificate of Receipt FCT = Forwarders Certificate of Transport FWR = FIATA Warehouse Receipt SDT = Shippers Declaration for the Transport of Dangerous Goods FBL = Negotiable FIATA Combined Transport Bill of Lading

Cross-border physical distribution frequently needs extensive documentation for statistical and tariff purposes but also to reduce the seller's and buyer's risks in the international transaction.

where the transportation risk remains with the seller until the physical handing-over of the goods to the customer. The seller can use the document to demand payment for the goods from the buyer via its bank.

The **FIATA Combined Transport** (FBL) is a transport document issued by the freight forwarder which is negotiable if the receiver is not specifically mentioned in the document and 'to order' appears instead. In this document the forwarder takes over the responsibility for the shipped good and its transportation. That is, the freight forwarder in its role as MTO (Multimodal Transport Operator) is responsible for all of the carriers used during shipment as well as the handing-over of the goods to the customer. A bill of lading should always contain a notification address in case the customer is not present at the point of destination indicated in the document.

In addition to these, export licences may be required for politically sensitive goods, such as electronic measurement devices. The marketer may also need to fill out a **Shippers Declaration for the Transport of Dangerous Goods** (SDT). This document enables the freight forwarder to identify the goods taken over, to take the needed measures in case of danger, and to clarify responsibilities in case of damage. A consular invoice may be necessary in the country of destination. And many LDCs require foreign-exchange licences (these enable the shipper to collect the price of the goods in hard currency) and import licences.

In the USA most of the documents required for international distribution are coordinated through the US Standard Master for International Trade, a master list of documents that improves the flow of international trade by having trading partners use the same documents. However, small and medium-sized companies should seek the assistance of a specialist if they do business in a number of countries or have a large number of items in their product lines. Not only must the necessary documents be filled out, but they must be processed accurately. Errors can cause delayed shipments, higher inventory costs, additional handling and shipping charges, customer dissatisfaction, and penalties and financial losses. In addition, customs procedures, restrictions and requirements differ from one country to another.

Insurance.   International transportation regulations, such as CMR (Convention Relative au Contrat de Transport International de Marchandises par Route) for road transportation or CIM (Convention Internationale Concernant le Transport des Marchandises par Chemin de Fer) for transportation by rail, contain rules concerning the range of liability, the compensation for loss, exceeding the time of delivery, and damage through intention or gross negligence. Because the amount of compensation stated in these regulations is rather limited, marketers in most cases will need to obtain additional insurance certificates if they have to cover the transportation risk. International insurance companies and freight forwarders will advise them on signing the appropriate contracts for their specific needs. For example, if the marketer ships its products by container to a harbour which is not deep enough to allow the landing of the container ship, the containers will need to be unloaded at sea onto smaller ships. An insurance contract against 'havarie grosse' would cover the risk of loss of the small ship (including its load) taking over the container.

Packaging

While it may seem that packaging's most important role is to help sell the product, packaging must play several roles and make many contributions if international marketing is to be successful. It must protect the product, should be easy to handle for intermediaries and customers, must be transportable at minimum cost and meet the legal requirements of the served country-markets, and should also support the company's logistics information system.

Protection.   In general, protection is even more necessary in international shipping than in most domestic markets. The US Carriage of Goods by Sea Act, for example, makes the shipper responsible for appropriate packaging to protect products from damage. The marketer, therefore, must pay special attention to handling characteristics in package design. The detrimental effects of insufficient packaging are illustrated by the example of a Western European manufacturer that sent four truckloads of plastic extruders to Iran, using the pallets (wooden platforms on which several extruders are loaded together) that are normally used in its domestic market. Shortly after the arrival of the merchandise, the marketer received a telex from the customer's bank stating that 90 per cent of the cargo was damaged or did not work. A group of service engineers sent to find out the cause discovered that the customer had neither a forklift nor a crane to use in unloading the trucks. The workers had simply pushed the pallets to the side of the truck and let them fall to the floor; thus the product on the pallet also fell on the floor; a way of unloading not accounted for in the construction of the plastic extruders.

For consumer goods, packaging also provides protection, a function that is often overshadowed by the promotion function. Still, protection may be essential for successful international marketing. For example, products destined for consumers in tropical areas need packages that withstand high temperatures combined with high levels of humidity. Goods destined for consumers in mountainous areas must be packaged carefully for transport over winding roads, and, in countries with less developed infrastructures, over rough terrain, sometimes even by pack train instead of trucks.

In international marketing the development of containers is playing a major role in fulfilling the protective function of packaging. Containers make it possible to keep the weight of the actual package relatively low. At the same time, the container protects the product against climatic influences, damage during transit, and pilferage. In some important markets of the world, however, packaging in containers is largely unknown. For example, IBM had to find out that shipping by rail in China is different from other parts of the world, where everything gets shipped in containers. In China, in many loading stations there are cargo handlers who virtually throw the cartons containing IBM PCs into trains. When Chinese customers complained to IBM that it was selling year-old machines as new, officials were puzzled. But finally, they identified the culprit: dust had seeped inside each carton despite two layers of plastic sheeting. Another layer ended the complaints.[3]

Freight Costs.   To keep freight costs down, the marketer must use transportation equipment and warehouses as efficiently as possible. This may also require adaptations in package design. For example, high stacks of products in containers or warehouses can be used only when the package is constructed so as to resist pressure.

Handling.   When the international marketer serves country-markets where its intermediaries or customers possess very different infrastructures to handle the product and its package, such as the highly automated central warehouses of big retail organizations in the UK compared to the multilevel distribution channels found in Japan and the small one-room retail outlets which have to be serviced on a daily basis in India, full packaging standardization will be impossible. In Japan, longer channels and smaller retailing outlets often require smaller packages. In India, many intermediaries and shippers handle products by hand, not by machine. Products that are packaged in too large or heavy a container will be difficult to move through the distribution channel. If the shipping containers are too large, the wholesaler will have no choice but to break them down for reshipment or storage, thereby increasing the risk of damage to the product. Retailers' needs too must be considered. Product packages must be of a suitable size and quantity to be manageable and financially affordable to the retailer. Finally, if consumers do not use cars for shopping, packaging must allow the transportation of the product across larger walking or biking distances.

The best-suited package size for all country-markets served can be approximated by developing packaging systems, that is, a combination of small to large packaging units which fit together. For example, when a Belgian manufacturer of chocolate pralines delivers its products to an importer in Toronto, the use of a container will ease transportation. Packaging the decorative retail boxes into cardbord boxes containing a greater number of retail packages will help the importer to split the entire shipment into smaller units easier to handle for the retailers. If the cardbord boxes may be stapled, they also ease the storage problem for the retailers. Consumers will be pleased by packages which are easy to open but can also be firmly closed to keep the chocolates fresh.

Support of Logistics Information System.   For logistics optimization purposes such as minimum inventory levels, shortest transportation routes, or avoidance of shelf-warmers, the product package must contain the information needed by the marketer and all other members of the distribution channel to clearly identify the product. For example, companies operating internationally in 80 different countries handle their international orders through an electronic data interchange system called 'Ecodex'. This kind of mailbox system allows the exchange of standardized data by consumer goods manufacturers, customers, freight forwarders and warehouse firms. Using special data strings of the communication system, which is called 'Eancom', orders may be set, changes in orders can be registered as well as any mistakes, the position of goods in the logistics chain may be determined, and inventory may be taken at any time. To make this system work, each package and each pallet transported must be equipped with a code which identifies the product, the amount delivered, its destination, the partners involved in production and physical distribution, and when the most recent changes to these data took place. This last information is of particular importance to the flexibility of the system in reacting to changing market conditions. Eancom is used by companies to handle a volume of about 377 000 products.[4]

Warehousing and Storage

A company can develop its own warehousing and storage facilities, or this function can be performed by the firm's intermediaries or by specialized companies. Products can be stored at different levels of the distribution channel – in a central or a number of regional distribution centres, at sales offices in various markets, with foreign freight forwarders, or with merchants. The marketer must decide how many warehouses to use, where to locate them, and how best to manage inventory. In international logistics these decisions are complicated by the highly complex interrelationships between production sites, warehouses, freight forwarders, carriers and levels of intermediaries. US-based Caterpillar, for example, maintains 22 parts facilities around the world, with more than 10 million square feet of warehouse storage. They service 480 000 line items (different part numbers), of which they stock 320 000. Caterpillar's and its suppliers' factories make the remaining 160 000 on demand. The firm ships 84 000 items per day, or about one per second every day of the year. In addition, the company's dealers, each of whom typically stocks between 40 000 and 50 000 line items, have made huge investments in parts inventories, warehouses, fleets of trucks, and sophisticated information technology.[5]

Number and Location of Warehouses.   In most industrialized countries, modern warehouse facilities are readily available. Specialists like Swiss-based Danzas offer customs brokerage, freight forwarding, insurance, packaging, labelling and transportation services, in addition to warehousing. Similar services are provided by specialist firms in the USA. In Japan, in contrast, there are few public warehouses, and demand for those that are available is high, resulting in high costs. In less developed countries, storage facilities are often limited or not available at all. The product may have to be stored in its package or container unprotected, in the open – a possibility that must be considered in designing the package.

Decisions about the number and location of warehouses are influenced by the intended level of customer service, the distribution of customers across the served market area, and the available infrastructure in a local market. The impact of the intended level of customer service is shown by the example of OSRAM GmbH, the number three producer of light bulbs in the world. In 1990 the company had 12 production locations and warehouses for finished goods in all 16 European countries served. To stay competitive OSRAM wanted to reduce costs by reducing its number of warehouses. But even in the light of European unification, the reduction of all warehouses to one centrally located distribution centre seemed impossible for one major reason: customer service at OSRAM is defined as proper delivery of ordered products in 48 hours. This could not be achieved for countries like Finland or Portugal from a warehouse in Central Europe, nor through a central logistics unit managing direct delivery from the production units to the customers. OSRAM decided to have three distribution centres acting as warehouses for related production facilities as well as distribution service centres for a region defined through service demands and not through national boundaries. Products not manufactured in the area of the distribution centre are directly delivered on order from the distribution centre carrying the product. Where the fixed 48-hour service level cannot be reached with this solution, regional distribution centres are added.[6]

A reduction in the number of warehouses reduces costs, but it does not necessarily reduce the level of customer service in parallel. For example, until 1993 Liechtenstein-based HILTI AG had individual warehouses for Hilti Western Hemisphere and Hilti Canada. Each warehouse was responsible for the planning, procurement, inventory management and physical distribution of the company's products to the network of smaller local distribution warehouses. Since 1994 the central warehouse of Hilti USA in Tulsa, Oklahoma, besides serving the US market, is the only supplier for the 21 distribution centres of Hilti Canada and Hilti Latin America, logistically managing about 98 per cent of all products sold to customers in those areas. This concentration of warehousing activities has not only led to a decrease in inventory, costs of freight, and storage space required as well as to a reduction in the number of suppliers, followed by a sharp rise in productivity, but it has also allowed the company to broaden the product range offered and to increase the availability of those products to Hilti's customers.[7]

Where major customers are concentrated in a certain area, such as the furniture industry in the Carolinas in the USA or the leather goods industry in northern Italy, suppliers to those industries will tend to build warehouses (or even production units) close to their customers. More and smaller local warehouses will be needed where the transportation infrastructure does not allow reliable delivery of mostly small amounts of products to customers or intermediaries. For example, the rather poor condition of the infrastructure in the mountainous areas of the Andes does not allow direct delivery to retailers from one central production unit.

Decisions about the location of warehouses may also be influenced by the availability of government subsidies, tax breaks or tariff protection. However, such advantages might be offset by controls on exports or imports, fluctuations in exchange rates, insufficient infrastructure, or restrictions on inventory levels due to government policies trying to control hoarding. Thus, the international logistics manager should look at the total picture before making a decision.

Free Trade Zones. Free trade zones (FTZs) offer interesting opportunities for international marketing logistics when decisions concerning the location of warehouses have to be taken. FTZs are special areas within a country to which companies may ship products for storage, bulk breaking, labelling, assembling, refining, repackaging, and the like without paying customs duties or taxes. For that reason, for example, a company that has so far delivered its tools and machine parts just in time to customers in the Arabian peninsula by air freight may decide to build or rent warehouse space in the FTZ of Dubai in the Arab Emirates. There it can store the products most often needed and may significantly reduce logistics costs by transporting those products to Dubai in containers by ship. Only when the products leave the FTZ to be sold elsewhere in the country do they become subject to local tariffs or taxes. The potential benefits derived from using FTZs are listed in Table 15.5.

There are about 380 free trade zones in the USA and about 150 more in another 50 countries such as Uruguay, Brazil, Colombia and Panama to name a few in Latin America. Usually, free trade zones are government owned and supervised by customs agents. They can take the form of real geographical zones, free ports, bonded warehouses, or areas restricted to a plant. For example, Italian Olivetti's typewriter plant in Pennsylvania has received the status of a free trade zone. The savings are interesting to the firm, because they can ship components to the factory, assemble them there, and sell the finished products in the NAFTA markets without paying the higher tariffs for semi-finished product imports.

Inventory Management. When it takes a long time to transport products from the company to its intermediaries or customers, and when delays during transportation are frequent, the company may have large quantities of products in transit at any given time. International marketers must keep more inventory 'in the pipeline' than domestic marketers generally do. As a result, more working capital is invested in inventory, capital costs are higher, and there are more accounts receivable. Inventory control is particularly important under such conditions.

As discussed earlier, international marketing logistics managers should consider centrally coordinated inventory management, in which a computer data bank is used to monitor the volume and value of products in transit or stocked in various warehouses. Because products are not sold at the same rate in every country-market, an item that is urgently needed in one place may not be selling in another. When computer monitoring is used, fashion products like knitwear or sunglasses, for example, can be shipped directly between two country-markets rather than indirectly via the location of the company's headquarters.

For products that must be delivered over larger distances at very short notice, inventory must be stocked at locations near the final customers if air transportation is too expensive. For products with longer order cycles, more centralized inventory stocks can be maintained or production may even follow orders. It is important, however, to consider the purchase patterns of final customers. Not only do the frequency and volume of purchases differ in different markets, but seasonal fluctuations and irregular demand (such as in the

Table 15.5 BENEFITS DERIVED FROM USING FREE TRADE ZONES

Decreased working capital
Exemption from paying duties on labour and overhead costs incurred in the FTZ
Lower insurance costs
Savings of duties on goods rejected, damaged or scrapped
Opportunity to stockpile products when quotas are filled or market conditions are suboptimal
Re-exportation without complicated paperwork

Products can be assembled, processed and stored in free trade zones. Companies using such an opportunity can profit from the benefits listed.

Source: 'Foreign Trade Zones: What's in It for the Shipper?', *Distribution*, March 1980, pp. 44–47.

fashion industry or for innovative products) complicate the task of the international logistics manager.

Inventory management may differ according to the extent of the company's control over the distribution channels in its various markets. Integrated channels may be fully stocked during periods of high inflation or unfavourable exchange rates, but independent channels will set their own policies. The latter can be influenced by discounts based on order size, order time and frequency, or other characteristics, depending on the firm's objectives. For example, a marketer may offer one free case of the product if the channel member orders ten. Or, if the buying firm changes from ordering every six months to every three months, the seller may reward that change with a lower price.

A centrally coordinated inventory management is also difficult to enforce when distribution channels are company-bound. A distributor's idea of an optimal inventory level is usually based on their market, sales level, and capital needs. The manufacturer will need an integrated information system that allows it to accumulate the sales volumes of all distributors for each product to optimize production runs and shipping activities. In order to balance the different points of view, the manufacturer needs to establish strong relationships with its distributors.

Location of Customer Contact Points

So far the discussion of international logistics decisions has focused on products dominated by tangible features that can be produced without much customer integration. Such products can be manufactured at a distance from their place of usage or consumpton. When the total product contains a high level of immaterial features and/or customers are strongly involved in the value creation process, an essential part of this process will need to be performed close to the customers' homes or premises.

For example, manufacturing elevators is a business without much customer involvement. Therefore, the location of a production site is not of great importance to customers. Five big elevator manufacturers can dominate the world market based on their economies of scale. In servicing elevators, customers are highly involved. Because stranded people are impatient, engineers must be based within half an hour of every elevator they maintain. As a consequence, a firm that can win service contracts in a small region around its location will be more profitable than one with contracts spread across a larger area. Small local firms can compete with the world's biggest. In such a case the international marketer has to consider the location of its points of customer contact as part of its marketing logistics system.

As Chapter 13 has discussed, the choice of location may have a very strong influence on the attractiveness and the meaning of the marketer's product to its customers. For example, for La Perla, the Bologna, Italy-based maker of fine lingerie, when it came to choosing a Paris location, the rue du Faubourg-Saint-Honoré was by far the most attractive because it is the most prestigious street in Paris. The Faubourg-Saint-Honoré area not only houses famous French names such as Hermès, Guy Laroche, Karl Lagerfeld, and Bernardaud, the oldest and most prestigious Limoges porcelain manufacturer. It has also attracted foreign designers and firms searching for the 'right' location for their boutiques and houses: Salvatore Ferragamo, Gianni Versace, Gucci and Sotheby's, to name only a few.[8]

Other service providers, such as McDonald's, do not look for prestigious locations. For them potential customer traffic is much more important. Therefore, closeness to public transport, recreation areas or shopping centres are highly attractive characteristics of potential locations for their restaurants. Sweden's furniture retailing giant Ikea, as another example, tends to choose locations outside of big cities. They need lots of space to show their products and provide parking lots for customers, and they need to be easily reachable by supply trucks as well as customers' private cars.

Each service provider operating internationally has to develop its own list of criteria that a potential location has to fulfil in order to be chosen. It will depend on the specifics of the service provided, the expectations of customers concerning the service, and the meaning of the service the provider intends to induce in customers' minds. Because all three factors are largely influenced by local cultures, many service firms will have to limit their headquarters' influence on location decisions to the establishment of general guidelines and business objectives to achieve.

Terms of Sale

The international delivery of goods or services has to be thoroughly negotiated and regulated in the contract of sale between the business partners. The contractual conditions of the sale are called the terms of sale. Today, sophisticated international marketers use terms of sale (and the related logistics costs) as a source of profit. Controlling more aspects of the physical distribution process can make the seller more competitive, because more than the price of the product can be manipulated. The Japanese and Australians, for example, typically try to purchase on an 'ex works' basis, that is, they are willing to take over the risk and the costs of the entire delivery process from the supplier's premises to their point of destination. This allows them to control all the costs themselves. In the position of the seller, they prefer to take over most of the responsibility and costs for the physical movement of goods until they arrive at the customer's premises.

Incoterms

Major difficulties in the negotiation of terms of sale may arise from a lack of knowledge about international logistics. Too often the business partners do not know much about the trade customs in the other country. Different interpretations of terms already agreed upon are a source of continuous trouble. Uncertainty about which country's laws will be applicable to the contract adds to the difficulties. To help avoid such problems, standard terms of sale have been developed in international trade over the years. These were precisely phrased by the International Chamber of Commerce which is located in Paris. Referred to as Incoterms (International Commercial Terms), their wide usage today is due to international acceptance of their interpretation of the terms of sale most often applied in international marketing. Following all industrialized countries of Europe, in 1980 the six most important US trade organizations (American Importers Association, US Chamber of Commerce, Council on International Banking, National Foreign Trade Council, National Committee on International Trade Documentation, US Council of the International Chamber of Commerce) suggested using the Incoterms instead of the American Foreign Trade Definitions (AFTD) applied until then.

In their latest revision, the Incoterms 1990 contain 13 types of trade terms.[9] They are listed in Table 15.6 in English, German, French and Italian, together with their abbreviations. The Incoterms regulate the forms of shipment (including destination), the location and point in time of loss and damage risk transfer from the supplier to the customer, as well as the repatriation of costs of shipment (including all additional costs such as for documents or insurance) between the business partners, and the obligations of the buyer and seller concerning the export, transit and import of the merchandise.

FAS, FOB, CFR, CIF, DES and DEQ are specifically formulated terms for transportation by ship. EXW, FCA, CPT, CIP, DAF, DDU and DDP are suitable for any transportation mode, including multimodal transportation. These Incoterms are discussed in the following.

Ex Works (EXW).   EXW signifies the term of sale most advantageous to the seller. It puts all the obligations of shipment, including documentation for export, transit and import, on the buyer. The buyer also bears the risk of merchandise damage or loss as soon as the goods leave the premises of the seller. However, when the seller and buyer agree on using EXW and the marketer – in an act of friendliness – helps the buyer to load the merchandise on the transportation vehicle, the marketer is fully responsible for any damage that might occur.

In considering which Incoterm is best to choose from the list of 13 terms, the international marketer should be aware that EXW may increase the 'perceived costs', including the psychological price the customer has to pay, to the point where they are greater than the 'perceived benefits'. In particular, internationally inexperienced customers located on other continents will not be ready to take over the burden of organizing the entire shipment on their own, even if they could rely on the help of international freight forwarders. A substantial number of business opportunities may be lost to competitors who choose terms of sale more convenient to customers.

Table 15.6	Abbreviations and Translations of Incoterms 1990			
INCOTERMS	ENGLISH	GERMAN	FRENCH	ITALIAN
EXW	Ex Works	Ab Werk	A l'Usine	Franco Fabrica
FCA	Free Carrier	Frei Frachtführer	Franco Transporteur	Franco Trasporto
FAS	Free Alongside Ship	Frei Längsseite Schiff	Franco Lelong Bord	Franco Sottobordo
FOB	Free on Board	Frei an Bord	Franco Bord	Franco a Bordo
CFR	Cost and Freight	Kosten und Fracht	Coûts et Fret	Costo e Nolo
CIF	Cost, Insurance, Freight	Kosten, Versiche-rung, Fracht	Coûts, Assurance, Fret	Costo, Assicurazione e Nolo
CPT	Carriage Paid To	Frachtfrei	Port Payé Jusqu'à	Porto Pagato
CIP	Carriage and Insurance Paid To	Frachtfrei versichert	Port Payé Assurance Comprise	Porto ed Assicurazione Pagato
DAF	Delivered At Frontier	Geliefert Grenze	Rendu Frontière	Reso Frontiera
DES	Delivered Ex Ship	Geliefert ab Schiff	Rendu Ex Ship	Reso Ex Ship
DEQ	Delivered Ex Quay	Geliefert ab Kai	Rendu A Quai	Reso Banchina
DDU	Delivered Duty Unpaid	Geliefert unverzollt	Rendu Droits Nonacquittés	Reso Nonsdoganato
DDP	Delivered Duty Paid	Geliefert verzollt	Rendu Droits Acquittés	Reso Sdoganato

Incoterms 1990, although standardized, have different translations, which the international marketer may need to know in order to manage the terms of sale. The listing of 13 Incoterms above ranks them according to the increasing obligations of the marketer concerning the delivery of its product.

Source: 'Incoterms 1990', ICC Publications No 460: ISBN 92.842.0087.3 (EF). Published in its official English version by the International Chamber of Commerce, Paris. Copyright © 1990 International Chamber of Commerce (ICC). Available from ICC Publishing S. A., 38 Cours Albert 1er, 75008 Paris, France.

Free Carrier (FCA). Using the term FCA, the contractual partners agree that the risk and the responsibility of covering the costs of shipment are to be covered by the buyer as soon as the merchandise has been handed over to the carrier at a specified location, at a specified point in time or during a given time period. The 'carrier' is the organization that either ships the goods specified in the sales contract or organizes their shipment (that is, a freight forwarder) through a third party. The seller has to provide merchandise ready for export. That is, the seller has to provide all documents and has to take care of all customs formalities needed to pass the border of its country. The costs of quality tests as well as volume checks needed for proper handing-over of the merchandise to the carrier are to be paid by the seller who is also responsible for packaging the goods in an appropriate way for the mode of transportation indicated by the buyer.

Carriage (and Insurance) Paid To (CPT/CIP). Under the term Carriage Paid To (CPT), the seller has to pay all the costs of packaging, shipment and documentation until the merchandise has reached the location at the time specified in the contract. The risk of merchandise damage or loss is transferred to the buyer when the goods are handed over to the first carrier. Again, the seller has to provide merchandise ready for export and has to inform the buyer about the handing-over of the goods to the carrier. The seller has to cover the costs of product tests and packaging needed for appropriate shipment.

When the conditions characterizing CPT are enlarged to include the seller's obligation to insure the merchandise (at a minimum coverage level) against damage and loss during shipment from the time when the goods are handed over to the first carrier until the merchandise is taken over by the customer at the destination specified in the sales contract, the term is called Carriage and Insurance Paid To (CIP).

Delivered At Frontier (DAF).   Compared to CPT, the seller using the term DAF additionally has to bear the risk of damage and loss of the merchandise until its arrival at the border location specified in the contract. Because the term does not say which border, the contract partners are well advised to specify exactly the location from where onwards the risk is to be borne by the buyer. In the interest of the marketer, the location should be the last possible before arriving at the border. If the place indicated in the contract is located across the border, the seller has to take care of all the customs formalities and pay the import duties. Concerning packaging, the marketer should note that it has to provide the kind of packaging appropriate for transportation after the customer has taken over the merchandise, if the marketer was informed about the transportation mode to be used by the customer before signing the contract.

Delivered Duty Unpaid (DDU).   DDU is a term newly added to the list of Incoterms in their 1990 version. It covers the need of marketers to have a term available that leaves all costs and risks to the seller until the merchandise has been handed over at the location in the buyer's country at the point in time or during the period specified in the sales contract, but which leaves all paperwork needed for import and the import duties to be dealt with by the customer. The customer also has to bear all costs and risks resulting from its failure to clear the merchandise for import in time.

Practical use of this term has shown how important it is to specify the exact location where the merchandise is to be handed over. It is not sufficient, for example, to indicate only the name of a town, such as Birmingham. A precise address will help to avoid problems between the contractual partners. So does a precise indication in the sales contract of who will have to pay added-value tax.

Because of the generally open borders inside the EU, this term is particularly suited for European marketers wanting to maximize the level of service to their international customers located in EU member countries. If there are any special documents needed for importing the merchandise or any dues to pay, the buyer, who knows the specifics of its national legal environment much better than the seller, is responsible for taking care of them.

Delivered Duty Paid (DDP).   DDP puts the entire burden of the costs and risks involved in the international shipment of goods on the seller. The merchandise must be delivered to the buyer's premises as stipulated in the sales contract. DDP is generally viewed as the least viable term. It requires considerable experience in international shipment on the part of the marketer, even when an international freight forwarder is used. In most cases, therefore, some other term of sale will be used by the business partners, leaving part of the obligations to the buyer.

Additions.   Even when the two parties to the contract agree on the Incoterm to use, care must be taken to make sure they are in complete agreement on the specifics. For that reason the following additions in the sales contract are advisable:

↔ It should be clearly specified how and where the handing over of the merchandise is to happen and who has to carry out the unloading procedure.

↔ The level and kind of insured risk should be clearly spelled out and be specified concerning its geographic and time coverage. Terms such as 'maximum insurance' are to be avoided.

↔ The exact modes of transport to be used should be listed.

↔ A 'force majeure' clause included in the sales contract is advisable as well as a time gliding clause, in particular when the marketer takes responsibility for customs clearance or delivery of the merchandise to a destination far from a habour in a country with a less developed transportation infrastructure.[10]

The UN Convention on International Sales

The marketer must be aware that in addition to the explicitly stated use of an Incoterm in a sales contract, the UN Convention on International Sales (CIS) is automatically applicable when both buyer and seller have their head-quarters in countries that have signed the convention. This convention, which since 1988 has been signed by more than 50 governments including most members of the EU, the members of NAFTA, Russia and Australia, regulates the signing of international sales contracts concerning goods as well as the resulting rights and obligations of the buyer and the seller.

IMPACT ON THE MARKETING MIX

Marketing logistics have major interrelationships with the other elements of the marketing mix. The length and diversity of international distribution channels influence the choice of transportation mode, the packaging of the product, and the number and location of warehouses. Inventory management has to consider the kind of distribution partners available in the local markets. On the other hand, if the firm's inventory management system, the transportation modes available or the packaging are more flexible, the international marketer has a broader range of distribution partners that can be serviced.

Market communication influences the product packaging. For example, mass-market customers engage in self-service at the point of purchase (such as a large supermarket). In such cases the package must convey a strong message to the customer. But the package must also be designed to protect the product on the store shelf, and to be easily handled and stored by inter-mediaries and customers. Some market communication ideas, therefore, might not be executable in international marketing.

Market communication, in particular public relations, is also influenced by marketing logistics. The way the company transports its products, how much it moves them around over long distances creating more or less traffic, or how it packages the products to be more or less harmful to the environment influences the opportunities of public relations managers to create attractive information concerning the firm's activities.

Product management is also influenced by international marketing logistics. In international business-to-business markets, for example, a short delivery time and accuracy increasingly become competitive necessities as part of the total product. Both strongly depend on marketing logistics. Warehouses close to important customers, inventory management based on online information systems, and close working relationships with international carriers are needed to fulfil customer service expectations. Product-line management also depends on the firm's logistics capabilities and resources. The faster and the more precise the information about products bought or staying in stock in different parts of the world, the more precise the offer of products that are attractive to the local customers can be.

Terms of sale may also be considered part of the total product. The more the marketer is able to relieve its customers of potential problems inherent in international delivery, the more attractive the total product may be. Moreover, terms of sale can make a difference in pricing. More sophisticated buyers and sellers want to control the transaction for as long as possible. If sellers can lower transportation costs, for example, they make additional profits by setting the price at the buyer's door. If the buyer sets the price at the seller's door, the buyer must pay freight, but in effect may have a lower total price if the buyer is able to lower transportation costs.

SUMMARY

Marketing logistics include a firm's decisions and actions concerning the physical distribution of its total products. In international marketing, logistics are increasingly recognized as an important source of potential competitive advantage. To provide sustainable competitive advantage, all marketing logistics activities must be organized in a systematic way, based on a marketing logistics policy and integrated with procurement as well as production logistics activities.

The firm's marketing logistics policy statement indicates the level of customer service to achieve and the limits of decisions and actions allowed to reach the given objective. It also contains a basic decision concerning the dependence or independence of the organizational units carrying out the physical distribution activities of the company. This decision will be based on considerations concerning prices and costs, the levels of logistics infrastructure development in the served country-markets, the physical properties of the merchandise, order size and frequency, and the needed movement of goods. If all those factors differ widely from one served country-market to another, the international logistics policy must allow flexible adaptation. In many cases internationally operating marketers will choose a mixture of integrated and independent parts for their physical distribution system.

The international marketing logistics policy of a firm further contains the profile of logistics partners to look for. Those partners must not only be reliable, but also need to be ready to participate in decreasing the total costs of logistics. Such partners are offered long-term contracts which allow them to build up their capacities and customer-specific capabilities without incalculable financial risk. Finally, the international marketing logistics policy also needs to contain some general guidelines concerning the roles to be fulfilled inside and outside the company, their coordination between central and local company units and the responsibilities for logistics planning, information and control.

All operative decisions concerning customer service, transportation of goods, physical aspects of packaging, warehousing and storage, as well as the choice of locations for direct customer contact have to respect the guidelines stated in the firm's logistics policy. The level of customer service provided by an international marketer in non-domestic markets tends to be lower than that provided in its domestic market, because of factors like geographic distance, errors in transmitting and filling orders, inadequate packaging and preparation for shipment, transportation problems, and delays in clearing customs. But in global product-markets a level of customer service can be reached that is as high as or even higher than the level maintained in domestic markets. The speed and precision of physical distribution can be augmented by the use of new transportation methods, improved packaging technology, advanced methods of preservation, warehouse merchandising, and direct delivery to the customers' premises, as well as by faster handling of orders through online information systems in a chain of cooperating firms.

To decide which transportation modes to use, the international marketer must evaluate the existing transportation infrastructures in the geographic areas it wishes to serve. These will differ from one country to another, as will the forms of transportation services available and their costs. The choice among transportation modes depends on the weight, size, form, volume and value of the products to be transported, the distance to be covered, the total cost, the acceptable transit time, the reliability of the transportation mode, and the level of customer service required in a specific market. The shipment of products in international markets is complicated by the need for extensive documentation. Besides the paperwork needed to document the goods transported, their origin and exact destination, and the details of their transaction, documents also serve the purpose of information and risk reduction for the parties involved.

Packaging, in addition to its promotional role, must be carefully considered in international marketing logistics. It must protect the product, should be easy to handle for intermediaries and customers, must be transportable at minimum cost and meet the legal requirements of the served country-markets. In addition, packages must be equipped in a way that supports the company's logistics information system.

An international marketer can build its own warehousing and storage facilities, or this function can be performed by the firm's intermediaries or by specialized companies. Products can be stored at different levels of international distribution channels. The marketer must decide how many warehouses to use, where to locate them, and how best to manage inventory. Evaluations of warehousing and storage alternatives are based on the need to be close to the market and to have minimum inventory and distribution costs while respecting the obligations coming from the legal and political environments.

When the total product contains a high level of immaterial features and customers are strongly involved in the value creation process, an essential part of this process will need to be performed close to the customers' homes or premises. In such cases the international marketer has to consider the location of its points of customer contact as part of its marketing logistics system. Each internationally operating service provider has to develop its own list of criteria that a potential location has to fulfil in order to be chosen. The criteria will depend on the specifics of the service provided, the expectations of customers concerning the service, and the meaning of the service the provider intends to induce in customers' minds.

Finally, an important part of the international delivery of goods or services which may have a strong influence on their attractiveness to customers or intermediaries is the terms of sale negotiated and regulated in the contract of sale between the business partners. They must be based on the marketing logistics capabilities of the firm. Sophisticated international marketers use terms of sale as a source of competitive advantage. On the other hand, different interpretations of terms agreed upon in the sales contract are a source of continuous trouble. To help avoid such problems, standard terms of sale, called Incoterms, and the UN Convention of International Sales have been developed. International marketers should know their specific content to be able to evaluate their impact on the customer and their own company.

DISCUSSION QUESTIONS

1. Contact a firm operating internationally and try to find out what policy they have established concerning their customer service level. What factors of influence did they consider?
2. Under what conditions would you suggest choosing an integrated marketing logistics system?
3. Try to find practical examples of mainly integrated, independent and company-bound marketing logistics systems. How do the companies using those systems differ in product-markets and country-markets served?
4. Discuss the factors that would lead a company operating internationally to centralize its marketing logistics versus factors that would lead to decentralization.
5. Find examples of firms operating internationally that are well known for their high level of customer service. What do they have in common?
6. Discuss the factors of influence on international transportation decisions.
7. Why is packaging so particularly important in international marketing? What problems need to be resolved?
8. How do warehousing and storage decisions relate to other parts of the marketing mix? Try to find illustrative examples.
9. Contact a firm operating internationally and find out what term(s) of sale they mainly use and why. What alternative(s) would you consider and why?
10. How is international marketing logistics interrelated with international channel management?

ADDITIONAL READINGS

Rayport, J.F. and J.J. Sviokla (1995) 'Exploiting the Virtual Value Chain', *Harvard Business Review*, November–December, 75–85.

Rüppell, H.-B. (1992) 'Strukturen für eine europäische Distributionslogistik in der Konsumgüter-Wirtschaft', *Betriebswirtschaftliche Forschung und Praxis*, 3, 210f.

NOTES

[1] 'Ports in a storm', *The Economist*, 8 March 1997, p. 77.
[2] Hallier, B. (1997) 'Wal Mart-Mythos führt zur falschen ECR-Positionierung', *Dynamik im Handel*, 4, 4–9.
[3] Hamilton, D.P. (1996) 'Untamed Frontier – PC Makers Find China Is a Chaotic Market Despite Its Potential', *The Wall Street Journal*, 8 April, pp. A1 and A9.
[4] 'Der Siegeszug der Elektronengehirne', *Lagerhaltung & Logistik*, 11 September 1996, p. A3.
[5] Fites, D.V. (1996) 'Make Your Dealers Your Partners', *Harvard Business Review*, March–April, 84–95.
[6] Schweichler, N. (1992) 'National Grenzen sind keine Logistikgrenzen – Auswirkungen der Euro-Logistik auf die Unternehmensstruktur', *BFuP*, 3, 231–233.
[7] 'Gesteigerte Effizienz durch Konsolidierung des

Vertriebs in Nordamerika', *Hilti International*, Nov. 1994, p. 32.

[8] McColl, P. (1996) 'For Paris Street, a New Lease on Life', *International Herald Tribune*, 16–17 March, p. 20.

[9] 'Incoterms 1990', International Chamber of Commerce, Publication No. 460, Paris 1990.

[10] 'Incoterms – oft falsch verwendet', *Internationale Wirtschaft*, No. 33, August 1996, pp. 1 and 6.

CHAPTER
16

INTERNATIONAL SALES MANAGEMENT

International Incident

Asia's Managers Think Differently

"There is very seldom a quick deal. Negotiating in Asia requires a lot of patience", says Gert Bergmann, the Secretary General of Volkswagen Asia Pacific Ltd in Hong Kong. Asia not only has booming markets but also different thinking and management philosophies that one has to consider.

The rapidly growing markets in Southeast Asia and China are a challenge for many companies from Europe and the USA; however, their managers have big difficulties in doing business in this region. Gert Bergmann has an explanation: "We emphasize the liberty of individuals, while Asians emphasize the group. What counts for them is team and common ground".

As a consequence, negotiations with Asian business partners take much longer because the members of a group first have to coordinate their opinions. "In Europe I would terminate comparable talks much earlier, considering them to be fruitless".

Source: Neumüller, H. (1995) 'Asiens Manager denken anders', OÖN, 12 August, p. XIII.

International Sales Management Decisions

Every company must manage its sales activities, or the establishment, development and maintenance of relationships with its direct customers. Depending on the decision on whether to distribute the company's products to the final customers directly or to use intermediaries for distribution, the direct customers of an international marketer may be final customers or intermediaries. In any case, the proper building and sustaining of relationships with customers is crucial to most international businesses' success.

Nevertheless, sales management has traditionally been a rather neglected area of international marketing. This is not only due to the fact that marketing and sales activities have been organized in different departments of the firm, and marketing managers perceived sales simply as part of market communication. There is also a widespread understanding that successful sales activities can be easily transferred from the home country of the company to other country-markets. However, even in the age of the 'global village', customer contact personnel have to consider that people interpret things based on their specific frame of reference which is strongly influenced by the cultural environment. As a consequence, any attempt to 'export' a certain way of thinking, feeling and acting rather than adapting to the different environment may lead to problems in building and maintaining business relationships.

Marketers also tend to neglect the fact that potential customers in other country-markets often need more information for their buying decision than customers in the home market. Communication problems, such as language barriers or different meanings of verbal and non-verbal language, which become salient in negotiation and buying behaviour, make potential customers feel uncomfortable, not knowing whether they have understood well enough to make the right buying decision. They may even consider some of the 'strange behaviour' as a clue to doubtful supplier reliability. Information offered by sales support material, such as leaflets or brochures which may be well accepted in the home market of the company, might be considered insufficient in other markets. Because international customers want to be convinced of the product and its supplier before they buy, intensive training of customer contact personnel may be needed, covering the product's features, benefits and proper application as well as intercultural communication experience.

In addition, companies doing only some international business tend to consider entering new country-markets as a side issue. Instead of appointing the most capable person to manage sales in a new market, top management intends to have 'somebody' handling that business besides other tasks. Such a perspective on international marketing leads to sometimes rather strange situations. For example, a company based in the UK may appoint three people to take care of sales to the 'continent' while a sales force of 12 people covers the UK market.

To emphasize the importance of sales management for international marketing success, the company first has to develop an international sales policy (see Figure 16.1). The sales policy is based on the company's intended global strategic position and the general market-entry strategy of the firm. It has to be closely coordinated with the company's distribution and market communication policies. The international sales policy is the guideline for decisions concerning personal selling, after-sales activities and the management of the firm's international sales force.

INTERNATIONAL SALES POLICY

To be successful in increasingly competitive global markets, international marketers should not leave their sales and after-sales activities to the discretion of the individual members of their sales force. Consistent building and maintenance of customer relationships across borders of country-markets need to be governed by a set of goals that have to be attained by sales management decisions and by basic rules of behaviour which must be obeyed when implementing those decisions in sales and sales-related activities. Such a set of goals and norms is called an international sales policy.

A company's international sales policy is part of its distribution policy. As such, it should help to achieve the intended global market position by translating more general goals and objectives from the global strategy of the firm into a set of specific sales guidelines. In addition, the company's international sales policy must consider the market-entry strategy of the firm. Depending on the company's decision on whether to enter new country-markets through import houses, wholesalers, independent agents or own sales personnel, or if market entry is to be achieved via joint ventures, acquisition or subsidiaries, different goals and norms of behaviour for sales management will result.

A company entering new country-markets through merchants can take

Figure 16.1 International Sales Management Decisions

Based on its intended global market position and the general market-entry strategy of the firm, the marketer develops an international sales policy that is closely coordinated with the company's distribution and market communication policies. The international sales policy serves as a guideline for decisions concerning personal selling, after-sales activities, and the management of the international sales force.

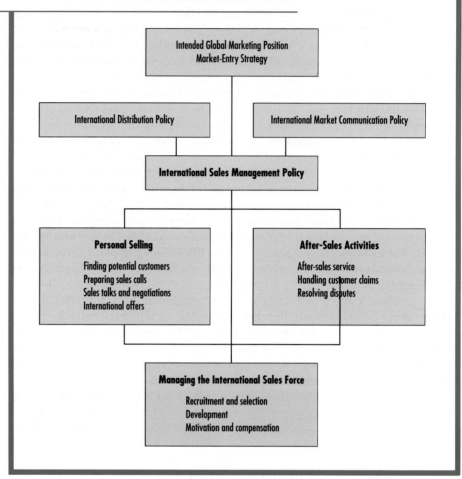

advantage of the lower costs, yet immediate availability, of an indirect sales source. The company sells its products directly to that organization, which then sells the products in the new market. Goals and rules of behaviour specified in the international sales policy in that case will mainly focus on the selection of and relationship management with those business partners.

An international marketer which decides to enter new markets through merchants or independent agents to keep the financial entry risk to a minimum, but plans to involve itself more intensively, for example through the creation of a joint venture or the establishment of a sales subsidiary, if the market proves to be profitable, will formulate a different international sales policy. French CFC, Compagnie Française des Convoyeurs, a manufacturer of conveyor systems for car makers, for example, hired and trained an agent when it first entered the German market. Knowing that German customers prefer to buy from German suppliers, they had followed an intensive screening procedure in the search for the agent. It was of great importance to them that the agent had the managerial skills to run a future subsidiary of the firm. When business activities had reached a sufficient level to cover the costs, the com-

ETHICS BOX

Cross-national Differences in Salespeoples' Ethics?

INTERNATIONALLY OPERATING COMPANIES BASED IN THE USA normally like to have one ethical code, which is applied in all situations, by all employees. However, there is concern among sales managers that when international expansion is ongoing, ethical complications may arise. Specifically, when marketers enter diverse country-markets, and use local sales personnel, this may cause a difficulty in terms of the established ethical policy.

One study researched salespeople's ethical views in the computer-related products and services industry in Japan, South Korea, and the US. For a variety of situations, each sales force representative was asked whether they considered it presented an ethical problem, whether their firm had a policy that addressed the issue, and whether the firm should have such a policy. As might be expected, sales personnel have very different views of what is ethical behavior, and whether their company should have policies regarding that behavior, on a country by country basis.

The results of the research indicate that when employing local personnel as part of a multinational sales force, sales managers need to evaluate ethical issues which may be found in the target country. Further, just transferring company policies regarding ethical behavior, does not seem to be useful or effective. On the other hand, automatically adapting to local customs regarding behavior does not work well either.

What may be useful is for the international marketer to develop, and clearly communicate throughout the organization, an overall principle which must be followed. For example, regarding whether governmental officials should ever be given 'fees' for services or not. For specific situations, however, ethical standards of a sales policy are more difficult to transfer to culturally and legally diverse country-markets.

Source: Based on Dubinsky, A.J. *et al.* (1991) 'A Cross-National Investigation of Industrial Salespeople's Ethical Considerations', *Journal of International Business Studies*, 22(4) 651–670.

pany decided to found a subsidiary in Germany. CFC's agent was appointed general manager of the new company.

Firms that want to be more involved in their international markets and gain greater control over the marketing processes there must establish and manage their own (direct) sales force. In such cases the firm's international sales policy specifies the minimum and maximum levels of capital and personnel to be committed to achieving a desired level of market coverage. Goals define the market share, sales volume and profit margins for each region, customer group and distribution channel as well as the expected return on sales. Rules of behaviour indicate how customer relations are to be managed, including after-sales activities such as the handling of customer claims. (The Ethics box discusses potential problems that may arise when a company wishes to establish a general code of ethics for all of its customer relations across different country-markets.)

Because of the substantial amount of personal communication with potential and current customers during most sales activities, the international sales policy of the company must be closely coordinated with the firm's market communication policy. Goals regarding the intended meaning or 'identity' of the company from the customers' and other important stakeholders' point of view and the position of the firm's products in the customers' minds have to be jointly determined. Rules of behaviour concerning the selection, training and motivation of sales personnel give general guidelines on how to contribute to the achievement of the firm's communication objectives through the proper management of the international sales force.

International Personal Selling

Personal selling is the most effective way to sell anything – any product in any market. This is true for local or international marketing, as the primary advantage of personal selling in either case is the same, its flexibility. If a potential customer objects to the product or conditions of sale, the salesperson can modify the message or the offer on the spot. The key to success in international personal selling is the matching of seller's product, knowledge and culture with the buyer's needs, knowledge and culture. That is, even more than within a specific country-market, international personal selling must be individualized – the 'fit' between seller and buyer must be fully understood and carefully managed.

But individualized communication costs money. On a per-contact basis, personal selling is more expensive than other sales techniques, such as catalogue sales, selling via the Internet, or simply through self-service in a supermarket. Imagine, for example, if Coca-Cola had to employ a door-to-door sales force in the worldwide country-markets in which they sell their products instead of using intermediaries. Therefore, finding and precisely selecting potential customers to whom to sell personally is of great importance to international marketers.

The use of personal selling to final customers is usually restricted to situations in which flexibility is required, and high per-contact costs can be justified. Marketers of capital goods such as computer systems or entire plants (which may cost millions of dollars) rely heavily on personal selling. So do marketers of most kinds of services which need to be tailored to individual customers to satisfy their expectations. In consumer goods markets, personal selling is used more selectively; it is used often, for example, in the sale of furniture and automobiles. In both cases, the customer's personal involvement with the product and the perceived risk incurred with the buying decision is relatively high for most customers. They expect to be personally informed and individually treated. Under similar conditions, personal selling for low-cost consumer goods, such as cosmetics, has also proven effective throughout North America, Europe and Asia as evidenced by the US-based Avon company and its sales forces of thousands of people.

When potential customers are defined, sales costs per successful business transaction can be further reduced by carefully preparing sales calls, sales talks and negotiations. A properly formulated international offer may also contribute to effective and efficient personal selling. In the following, these points will be further elaborated.

Finding Potential Customers

The fastest and least expensive way to determine potential customers is to use available internal sources. These may be the market knowledge of salespeople acquired through experience, and the creativity of company personnel acti-vated by special ways of reasoning. Enquiries by potential customers, invita-tions to tender, official authorities, such as Secretaries of Commerce, or private organizations, such as trade magazines or the yellow pages, which have been discussed in more detail in Chapter 6, may be further low-cost sources of information on potential customers.

Sales Force Experience. Marketers are often faced with the fact that mar-ket information, for example why customers prefer a certain brand or what they like when using a certain product, is 'stored' in the minds of salespeople serving a certain country-market but is not made available to their colleagues simply because no notes have been taken over the years. This knowledge, however, could be of considerable help in defining customers in newly served markets, because customers in a worldwide product-market may perceive fea-tures and benefits of a product or service in similar ways. Therefore, an in-depth investigation of what information has been collected over time by the company's salespeople is advisable. Table 16.1 suggests some worthwhile questions to ask. Depending on the stage of development of customer rela-tionships in the various served markets, such an internal inquiry will produce more or less abundant information.

The 'Pyramid of Acceptance'. Another important source of information about potential customers in new product- or country-markets is to observe the 'pyramid of acceptance' (Figure 16.2). Monitoring the development of many product-markets over time shows a recurrent phenomenon. At the beginning of their life cycles, innovative products are only accepted by a small group of pioneers, the market volume is small, and the price of the product is high. By the time the product is accepted by a substantial number of cus-tomers in the original market segment, it also finds more and more customers in other segments – with maybe different benefits, uses or applications. This development is accompanied by an increasing international market volume and by decreasing prices.

For example, originally the microprocessor was developed for the ambi-tious US Apollo project taking men to the moon for the first time. The quan-tities sold were low and the product was only accepted by a small group of experts. Considering the cost of developing the microprocessor and the low production quantities, the price had to be high. Today the microprocessor has reached households, being installed in video recorders, personal computers, fax and telephone equipment and microwave ovens as well as in toys for kids. Every modern automobile has more electronic and computing equipment installed than the Apollo space capsule.

This development is not limited to products: just-in-time systems origi-nated from the automobile industry and TQM from the aerospace industry. Other products and services have also followed the 'law' of the 'pyramid of acceptance'. Around-the-clock service, simpler use of products, lifetime guar-antees, increased consumer protection, ergonomic products, well-designed technical equipment – all the benefits people in industrially developed parts of the world are used to – started in a single industry. From there, over the years, they have penetrated many different product-markets through varying applications.

Analysing innovative ideas, technological problem solutions, or services from the point of view of the 'pyramid of acceptance' may be the key to new

Table 16.1 INFORMATION TO BE GATHERED FROM SALESPEOPLE

↔ Who are the company's best customers at present? ↔ What makes the company successful there?	
↔ How has the company identified and addressed new potential customers?	
↔ What are the buying habits of the current customers? Specify concerning: information gathering, search for and assessment of potential suppliers, preparation of an enquiry, people involved in negotiation, decision making, purchasing, . . .	
↔ What are individual expectations of customer groups as to product, supplier etc.?	
↔ What are the most important reasons why the company's offer has been accepted or refused by potential customers?	
↔ What are the customers' expectations as to distribution, pricing, logistics, services, . . . ?	
↔ What economic criteria have to be met by the company's product? (price/benefit, terms, after-sales service . . .)	
↔ What marketing strategies do the competitors apply, where do they come to limits and why?	
↔ What selling points, what offensive sales strategies could we derive from our competitors' weaknesses?	
↔ Which new competitors could enter the scene? (substitution products, link-up products . . .)	

Based on their market experience, salespeople have plenty of information that needs to be gathered, structured, carefully analysed, and played back to the sales force to help them do their job.

potential customers. It creates an opportunity for the international marketer to be a global pioneer in supplying a product or problem solution developed for a certain group of customers to other product- and country- markets.

Early Adopters. In each market there are potential customers who want to be the first to use a new product or service. But not all of these consumers or business organizations are accepted as opinion leaders by other potential customers. Early adopters that other potential customers use as role models who set trends in consumer markets or lead technological changes in industrial markets are of great importance to the international marketer. For example,

---

Figure 16.2   **The Pyramid of Acceptance**

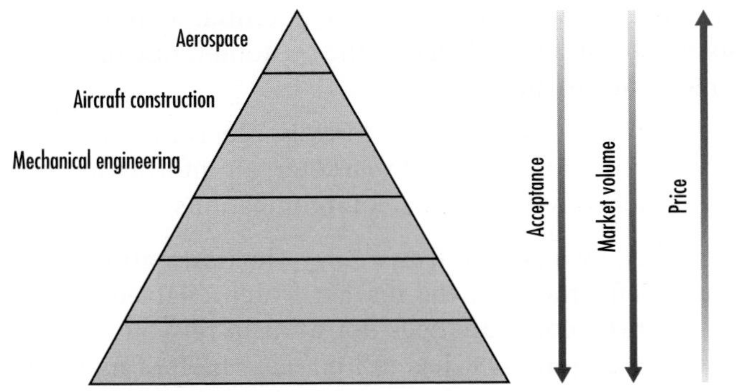

At the beginning of their life cycles, innovative technologies are only accepted by a small group of pioneers (in one industry), the market volume is small, and the price of the product is high. Over time, these parameters change dramatically.

Zurich-based Swissair is a very important customer for aircraft manufacturers. The company has one of the best maintenance and repair facilities and technical staff worldwide. Their acceptance of a new technology for aeroplanes makes convincing other airlines easier for an aircraft marketer.

The international marketer entering a market with an idea, good or service that is new to the market, therefore, has to find out at a very early stage which potential buyers are pioneers and accepted as trend-setters by other customers. Sales force experience from other product introductions may serve as a valuable source of information concerning such customers to be approached first.

Enquiries.   Quite a number of potential organizational customers take the initiative for a first contact in searching for a competent supplier that might help in solving a problem. The arrival of an enquiry by letter, phone, fax, e-mail, filled-in form, invitation to tender, or as a report from the responsible salesperson provokes a series of steps to be taken:

1. As a first step, the international marketer has to examine whether it is willing or able to quote. Many companies use checklists to allow quick examination of the feasibility and commercial attractiveness of the request. In the case of a negative result, the enquiring customer should be given an explanation of why the marketer has decided against making an offer, in order to prevent the prospective buyer from never sending an enquiry again. If the decision is positive, the marketer has either to prepare the offer immediately or to inform the potential customer of when to expect the offer.

2. Reservation of the necessary personnel capacity to prepare the offer and the preparation of a time schedule to respect the given time limits.

3. If the enquiry is not complete or could give rise to misunderstandings, the marketer must ask the potential customer for the missing data or a clarification. This can be done either directly or through the salesperson in charge. If the potential customer's request cannot be fulfilled in the way specified in the enquiry, the international marketer may either

prepare an approximate offer to keep a foot in the door and negotiate changes later, or ask the customer immediately whether an alternative will be accepted. Depending on the complexity of the customer's problem to be resolved, the number of potential technical solutions and the problem-specific knowledge of the customer, one or the other way may be more successful.

4. If the potential customer has never before received any detailed sales literature from the international marketer, an information package should be attached to one of the communications.

To be contacted by a potential customer, the international marketer obviously must have left 'traces' in the market which enabled the potential customer to find it. If the company does not want to rely on chance concerning potential customer enquiries, it has to find out which of its market activities attracted the potential customer's attention. Attention attractors may be, for example, previous product presentations, an advertisement in a trade magazine, participation in a fair or exhibition, presence in the yellow pages, a reference given by a satisfied customer, information provided by a commercial representative of the marketer's home country, suppliers producing complementary goods, data banks, or price agencies. By collecting information on which of its market activities has led to which kinds of enquiries, the international marketer can gather valuable evidence on how to deploy its resources.

Tenders. When it comes to bigger and therefore more expensive projects, both government and business customers invite potential suppliers to bid. Invitations are published by announcements in relevant newspapers or magazines, by e-mail, over the Internet or just by letter. In the European Union tenders for projects that pass a certain value and are launched by public adminstrations or by companies or institutions that are heavily influenced by government, for example in the sectors of water and energy supply, transportation or telecommunications, have to be published. TED (Tenders Electronic Daily) is the online version of 'Supplement S' of the official journal of the EU which contains such tenders (Table 16.2).

The number of potential suppliers invited may be limited. One reason may be, for example, that the local government does not want foreign companies to quote. Such restrictions are forbidden in the EU. Another reason may be that business customers want to limit their relationships to a manageable and efficient small group of long-term suppliers. Finally, when the project is rather voluminous, complex or difficult to handle, the customer may request potential suppliers to first pass a prequalification process. In such cases, the international marketer interested in bidding has to prove its ability to fulfil the kind of project at hand by presenting data concerning, for example, the financial status of the firm, references, engineering ability, machine tools or production capacity. Only if the marketer passes the prequalification is it put on the so-called 'long list' and invited to bid. Potential suppliers whose bids are accepted for their (technical) solution are put on a 'short list'. Marketers who get onto the short list are invited to negotiations.

Expert Interviews. Interviewing experts has proven to be a very efficient method for both gathering first-hand information about and acquiring potential customers. Experts may be decision makers of potential customer organizations, opinion leaders in the relevant industry or customer segment, or

Table 16.2 The European Union's TED – Tenders Electronic Daily-Database

Frequently Asked Questions about the Tenders Electronic Daily (TED) Database

What is TED?

TED (Tenders Electronic Daily) is a database with information on European calls for tender.

Which documents are published in TED?

Of course TED publishes calls for tenders, but also pre-information notes, contract awards and many more types of documents. The field TD ('type of document') in TED is used to specify the document type.

What is the 'CPV' code?

CPV, the 'Common Procurement Vocabulary', has been set up by GD XV of the European Commission. It contains more than 5000 product codes. It is used in TED to identify the relevant products.

Price up to 31 March 1996 inclusive:

↔ 60 Ecu per connect hour;
↔ 0,8 Ecu per document containing the TX or OT field (or both) includes output format 'ALL'.

Price as of 1 April 1996

↔ 30 Ecu per connect hour;
↔ 1 Ecu per document containing the TX or OT field (or both) – includes output format 'ALL'.
↔ 0,5 Ecu per document containing the AU or CO field (or both) – includes output format 'EXTRA'.

How can I connect to TED?

Access to TED is possible via National Gateways only. Please check on the gateway list if your country is on it.
↔ If yes: Please contact the gateway for access.
↔ If no: You can access TED either via one of the gateways or directly on *ECHO*.
If you have no online connection, you can use the TED Alert Service to obtain faxes with relevant tenders. For further information please contact your *TED alert agent*.

Which user documentation exists for TED?

Click *here* to download the TED user guide (85 pages).

Where can I find the Official Journal online?

The Official Journal is published in 3 series:
↔ *Official Journal L* legal matters;
↔ *Official Journal C* communications;
↔ Supplement S tenders
1. The content from the Official Journal L is used as input for the database *CELEX* offered via Eurobases.
2. The table of contents of the Official Journal C is available in the database *ABEL* offered via Eurobases.
3. The full text of the Supplement S is available in the database *TED* on ECHO.

Where do I find tenders which are not published in TED?

Publication of tenders is regulated by international, national and regional laws. The publication needs can vary considerably from one country to another. A good way could be to check with your nearest chamber of commerce or Euro Info Center.
Tender databases include:
↔ *French tenders:* BOAMP (Bulletin Officiel des Annonces des Marchés Publics), produced by Direction des Journaux Officiels, Paris. *On-line access: Direction des Journaux Officiels (fax +33–1–40 58 77 00).*
↔ *Spanish tenders:* CONPUB (Concursos Publicos), containing both national and regional invitations to tender, updated daily and taken from the official publication ('Boletin Official del Estado'). *On-line access: IMPI (fax +34–1–571 28 31).*
↔ *USA tenders:* CBD (Commerce Business Daily), on-line version of the printed official journal with the same name. *On-line access: Knight Ridder Information / Dialog (fax +44–1865–736 354).*
↔ *Indian tenders:* AKR Tenderbase. *On-line access: AKR Information (fax +91–11–331 26 01).*
↔ *International tenders (mostly third world):* SCAN-A-BID, on-line version of the 'Development Business' magazine published in the UN development forum. *On-line access: Knight Ridder Information / Data-Star (fax +44–71–930 25 81).*
↔ *International tenders (mostly third world):* 'BfAI-Auslandsausschreibungen', produced by the German Chamber of Foreign Trade. *On-line access: Genios (fax +49–211–88 71 520), GBI (fax +49–89–954 229), FIZ Technik (fax +49–69–4308 200).*
Tip: Check the I'M Guide database on ECHO for new databases on public procurement.

Source: European Union, Internet site – http://www2.echo.lu/echo/faqs/ted/en/ted.html

users of the product. With experts the international marketer can normally be quite sure of receiving information from somebody who is familiar with the product and its application or use. Such experts may be found by contacting the relevant industry associations in order to find out the names of key persons, searching for authors of relevant publications, or looking for people who maintain good public relations. Questions like 'Which changes does our product need to be accepted in your market?', 'Who are our competitors and how do they apply their marketing tools?' or 'How is the market volume shared between competitors?' will usually be answered without objection if the expert does not get the impression of being involved in a 'camouflaged' sales talk and enjoys talking with a person who has a high level of knowledge about the product and the relevant industry in the country-market.

Cooperation. An additional opportunity for international marketers to find new customers comes from the emphasis of economic communities like the EU or NAFTA on the support of small and medium-sized enterprises. The European Union, for example, has developed several programmes that are aimed at facilitating international cooperation between SMEs such as the Business Cooperation Network, Europartenariat, Interprise, and the Business Cooperation Office which are presented in the following.

The **Business Cooperation Network (BC-Net)** is a network of consultants and intermediaries such as Chambers of Commerce, Euro Info Centres and local authorities, created by the EU to help small and medium-sized companies find partners at regional, national, Community and international level. The local support organizations publicize the network to their clients, issue cooperation forms and administer the network at a local level. BC-Net is gradually opening up to include more and more non-member states worldwide. The network rapidly identifies potential partners in response to a specific offer of cooperation that may cover all sectors of activity, thus opening the way for all types of cooperation (financial, commercial, industrial and technological). Research is conducted confidentially to meet the needs of the enquirer. Table 16.3 contains more details concerning BC-Net.

Europartenariat is a bi-annual business meeting event whose purpose is to encourage regional development. It aims particularly at stimulating development of less favoured regions within the European Union, or those suffering from industrial decline, within the overall framework of the EU's regional policy. The programme encourages small and medium-sized enterprises within the Community to establish cooperative ventures with businesses from these areas by providing opportunities for face-to-face meetings over a two-day period. Participating firms pay only their travel and hotel expenses.

There are several stages involved in setting up a meeting event. First, the European Commission selects a Community host region requiring specific development action, based on requests from interested regions. Then the Commission chooses one or more organizers (such as Development Agencies). The organizers select 300 to 400 SMEs in the host region which meet specific criteria, such as size, record of participation in partnership projects, financial soundness, and ability to manage cross-border partnerships. A multilingual catalogue is produced two to three months before the event, detailing the selected SMEs and their projects. The event is promoted in all participating countries (including EFTA, Mediterranean countries and the countries of Central and Eastern Europe) through national advisors, the Business Cooperation Centre (BRE), Business Cooperation Network (BC-NET),

---

Table 16.3 **BC-NET**

DGXXIII at the European Commission
Business Co-operation Offers

The European Commission operates two different ways of helping businesses find new contacts in other member States: *BRE (Business Co-operation Office)* and BC-Net (Business Co-operation Network). Both use local support organisations such as Chambers of Commerce, Euro Info Centres, local authorities, professional organisations and consultants as intermediaries. These publicise the schemes to their clients, issue co-operation forms and administer the schemes at a local level. Both schemes are gradually opening up to include more and more non-member states world-wide, and can include co-operations of a commercial, technical or financial nature.

Fehler! Textmarke nicht definiert.**What is BC-NET?**

The Business Co-operation Network (BC-NET) is a *network of consultants* and intermediaries created by the European Union to *help SMEs* find partners at regional, national, Community and international level. The network rapidly identifies potential partners in response to a specific offer of cooperation that may cover all sectors of activity, thus opening the way for all types of cooperation (financial, commercial, industrial and technological). *Research* is conducted confidentially to meet the needs of your enterprise. The human dimension to the computer-based network, helps make BC-NET an effective partnership instrument from the outset.

Why use BC-NET?

When drawing up development strategies, all successful enterprises consider establishing partnerships – be they commercial, industrial, technological, financial, etc. – in order to consolidate their position and face international competition.

If you wish to:

- ↔ find a commercial distributor,
- ↔ reduce your costs by sharing logistic infrastructures or via joint purchasing, etc.,
- ↔ buy or sell patent licences,
- ↔ create, extend or be part of a franchise network,
- ↔ enter a new market,
- ↔ acquire or transfer a new technology,
- ↔ acquire a holding in another company,
- ↔ join forces with other companies to participate in calls for tender
- ↔ participate in Community programmeme

BC-NET: who are the consultants?

BC-NET consultants are private or public bodies specializing in business cooperation. They include consultancy firms, chambers of commerce and industry, professional organizations, law firms, banks, etc.

- ↔ They sign a contract with the European Commission that is renewable on a yearly basis
- ↔ They undertake to comply with a code of good practice which lays down the principles they should observed when handling a co-operation opportunity.

Some consultants run vast networks for the benefit of enterprises.

Services

Consultants offer a wide range of services to assist enterprises at every stage of the search for partners, depending on their nature, their objectives and the request of the enterprise. These are:

- ↔ analysis of your needs with a view to targeting the type of partnership sought;
- ↔ search for a potential partner via the network and other available means;
- ↔ assisting and advising you during the negotiations leading to the cooperation agreement.

Accustomed as they are to international contacts, they not only assist with technical, legal and administrative matters etc., but also help overcome the cultural and linguistic differences inherent in transnational cooperation.

Consultants can supplement the range of services offered by referring their clients to other members of the network according to the expertise required.

Costs

Ask your consultant for details of BC-NET charges, as these vary according to the type of request and the nature of the services offered.

How does BC-NET work?

There are several stages to the search for partners:

1. Preparatory phase

Once you have decided to look for a partner, you contact a BC-NET consultant, who helps you draw up a list of strong and weak points and produce an analysis of the enterprise's development potential in the light of your co-operation

---

Table 16.3 (continued)

---

objectives. If BC-NET can provide you with a suitable solution, the consultant draws up a co-operation profile outlining the type of co-operation required. He also drafts documents containing key information on your business.

2. **Comparing co-operation profiles and searching within the network**

Your co-operation profile is then forwarded to the BC-NET Central Unit, where a computer compares it with thousands of co-operation requests on file. Three criteria are used: type of co-operation, sector of activity and geographical area. Your consultant may also target dissemination of the co-operation profile using a Flash Profile. This is sent to BC-NET consultants working in the desired geographical areas. 'Flash Profiles' may be disseminated within the network, or dealt with on a broader basis depending on your needs. Finally, depending on the type of co-operation, your profile may be input into a database which can be directly accessed by all network consultants. Your consultant can also carry out active searches within the network.

3. **'Matching' requests and follow-up**

When a match for your co-operation request is detected, your consultant and that of your potential partner are immediately informed.

Your consultant processes the various matches by selecting those which best meet your needs, and informs you of the opportunities detected. He may then arrange a direct meeting between you enterprise and your potential partner.

4. **Assisting with negotiations**

The BC-NET consultant can help you with negotiations and contacts with a view to finalizing the co-operation agreement or referring you to other consultants, depending on the legal, fiscal and technical issues involved.

Given the complexity of certain co-operation agreements, personal assistance of this sort may be central to success.

What are the advantages of BC-NET?

↝ BC-NET is a **network of consultants specializing in assisting SMEs** and provides a permanent infrastructure for partnership development.

↝ The sheer scale of BC-NET makes it the **first European and international network** for partner search. Individual consultants thus have the backing of a large number of colleagues around the world.

↝ The system **targets co-operation proposals** according to sectors of activity, services, the type of co-operation sought and geographical location.

↝ Searches can be carried out in **strict confidence or openly**, in accordance with your wishes.

↝ The computing infrastructure makes for **rapid searching and matching**, and the daily scanning of thousands of offers allows the most suitable partner to be identified.

↝ Each consultant undertakes to provide a **quality service** in the area for which he is responsible.

How do I find a Consultant?

Via your nearest *Euro Info Centre*

Where can I get more information?

DG XXIII/B/2
BC-NET Secretariat
200 Rue de la Loi – AN80 6/24
B-1049 Brussels
Fax: +32–2–296.25.72

Source: European Union, Internet site – http://europa.eu.int/en/comm/dg23/bcnet/bc-net.htm

Euro Info Centres (EICs) and European Business and Innovation Centres (BICs). The national advisors accompany and assist firms during the two meeting days, which are organized around appointments requested and fixed in advance. The results of the meetings are monitored and assessed.[1]

The **INTERPRISE** programme is also a series of business meeting events. These are designed to support local, regional and national measures throughout the Community which aim to stimulate direct contact between business people in order to develop cooperation agreements between SMEs. Although the objectives and methodology of INTERPRISE are similar to those of the

Europartenariat programme, the scale is larger, involving industrial and developed regions as well as those eligible for assistance. Projects must include at least three regions of three member states but may extend to regions outside the Community.

INTERPRISE events bring together SMEs through personalized and pre-arranged meetings which give ample scope for discussion and negotiation. These will often concentrate on a particular theme or sector of industry, for example a medical INTERPRISE. Typical organizers of the events are chambers of commerce, development agencies, employers' federations, research, innovation and technical centres, consultants and Euro Info Centres.

Events must focus on cooperation between businesses, so export subsidy programmes do not qualify. It must be arranged by at least one body from each region taking part and the bodies involved must participate financially. Finally, the assistance of Directorate-General XXIII of the European Commission must be mentioned in any official document or publication.[2]

BRE (Business Cooperation Office) is an agency set up by the D-G XXIII of the European Commission in order to help SMEs located in the member states and many third countries which seek partners with a view to increasing competitiveness. The main characteristics of the BRE are: its wide dissemination of the cooperation requests and offers, its extensive geographical coverage, and the direct access for SMEs. These features enable the BRE to act as a catalyst to cooperation as well as a forum for dialogue between economic agents.

BRE procedures lean on a network of Correspondents who transmit and circulate offers and demands for cooperation at regional, national or international level. The tasks of the Correspondents involve promoting the instrument, assisting companies looking for partners, publicizing cooperation opportunities and participating in activities related to network animation. The Correspondents ensure the promotion of BRE in their region. They may set up seminars, use an existing publication, create a new one specifically dedicated to BRE, write press releases, keep in constant contact with enterprises in their region or any other measures to inform as many SMEs as possible.[3]

Preparing Sales Calls

Before making the first sales call in a country-market, the international salesperson has to do a lot of preparation. Proper preparation before contacting potential customers and starting negotiations should be viewed as a corporate investment (see the Strategy box). It strongly influences success or failure, yet insufficient attention is too often paid to doing this 'homework'. US Americans, for example, are trained early to 'think on their feet', to expect to be unprepared in effect, and to use their persuasive skills to succeed. This might be fairly well received in France where French managers are trained to 'operate by the seat of the pants'. However, in France, negotiators tend to be more formal, and do not go directly into the agenda at hand, but spend time getting to know the person first. In other cultures such as those found throughout Southeast Asia, thorough preparation is valued very highly. It would be their view that a lack of preparation is a strong signal that the potential partner does not view the business under discussion seriously.

General Preparation. Before any sales contacts with potential customers in a country-market which is new to the salesperson are made, it is highly

STRATEGY BOX

Planning an Effective and Efficient Business Trip

A BUSINESS TRIP SHOULD NOT BE CONSIDERED AS A single action but as part of a 'project', the individual steps of which need to be carefully managed to be effective and efficient.

Beginning with a 'Plan of action'
↔ Getting a general idea of all relevant aspects of the project
↔ Setting targets – defining all steps of the project to be taken
↔ Setting priorities
↔ Reserving capacities to fulfil the project
↔ Preparing a schedule

'You are the tip of the iceberg'
↔ Defining tasks
↔ Delegating as much as possible or out-sourcing

↔ Using systematically all help available

'Getting things under control'
↔ Controlling regularly the realization of the tasks, the schedule and the budget
↔ Keeping in mind all alternatives and thinking of changing the modus operandi when needed
↔ Preventing ill-considered steps or actions

'The business trip is the climax'
↔ Having all necessary sales tools and information on hand
↔ Taking advantage of all services offered in the customer's country
↔ Being prepared for spontaneous contacts

'Harvesting the fruits'
↔ Noting the results of the meetings and deriving the required actions to be taken
↔ Turning reactions into actions
↔ Preventing unproductive hours

Source: Kornberger, E. (1996) 'Effiziente Geschäftsreisen', *SWISSEXPORT*, September, 6f.

---

advisable for this person to review the cultural elements which might influence the establishment of a contact, a negotiation process, and the development of a relationship. When the salesperson contacts a prospective buyer for the first time, discusses a problem to solve, or negotiates a sales contract with an intermediary, the arguments put forward and the silent language used should be as close as possible to the cultural background of the customer. In addition, customers expect potential suppliers to be well informed about the specifics of their industry. First of all, therefore, salespeople who are appointed in a country-market that is new to them have to get accustomed to the specific characteristics of the economic, political, legal and cultural environments relevant to the company's business.

But the salesperson should not acquire only business-related information. Some knowledge on trivial things, like who is the president of the country, which party the prime minister belongs to, the names of the five biggest cities in the country, or milestones in the country's history, may be of great help during sales calls. Being well informed about a customer's home country is a sign of interest and politeness that is appreciated all over the world.

Customer Database.   To choose the most promising potential customers carefully and later, to manage the relationships with existing customers in a country-market, the international marketer will have to gather available information about existing and potential customers in a customer database. This database should at least contain basic customer data in forms, such as the one shown in Table 16.4.

Such a customer database may also serve as an important tool for the sales force when preparing their sales calls. As far as the business side of the contact is concerned, the salesperson can find all up-to-date figures of importance with regard to the customer, such as total sales, number of orders placed during the current year, or number and kind of maintenance contracts. Furthermore, information on whether there is still an enquiry not answered, how many offers are neither negotiated nor decided, what the issues of previous contacts were, or what has been promised but still not fulfilled by the marketer will be useful in preparing a sales call.

In international sales, language barriers and communication problems result in psychological distance between a prospective buyer and its supplier. The customer tends to perceive greater difficulty in getting in touch with a foreign supplier than with a supplier from the home market. The reliability of both the product and the salesperson, therefore, is even more important for success in international markets than in the home market of an internationally operating firm. To further a potential customer's perception of reliability, a salesperson should at least learn all the information that is available in the customer database by heart. But the salesperson should also try to learn more about the persons to contact than just their name and position – for example, marital status, hobbies, habits, preferences, sectors of interest, or peculiarities of their personality – without violating their privacy (which depends on the cultural background of the person). With this knowledge it is much easier to find the right words at a given moment, to prevent hurting people without knowing, and to build trust.

Planning Sales Calls.   In international sales, thorough planning and organizing of business trips and sales calls is of great importance. The cost per hour and per mile of travelling has to be kept as low as possible compared to the number of fruitful sales calls per day. Both the cost per hour and per mile and the number of fruitful sales calls per day are strongly influenced by the peculiarities of the country or sales region and of the potential customers located in those areas.

For example, high mountains as in Switzerland or Nepal, deserts as in many Arabic countries, vast areas with low population density as in Texas, a great number of lakes in extended woods as in Finland, or highly populated urban agglomerations like New York, Tokyo, Mexico City or Shanghai may represent conditions for business trips so far unexperienced by the salesperson. Climatic conditions, such as around −50° C in Siberian winters or monsoon rain seasons on the Indian subcontinent need to be considered in planning sales calls. The availability and reliability of the infrastructure, such as the conditions of roads in Romania, the availability (or lack) of reliable stationary and mobile telephone systems in parts of Africa and Latin America, the reliability of public transport in Pakistan, or the lack of copying facilities in Belarus will also influence the sales costs and number of successful calls in a planning period. Finally, bureaucratic hurdles such as the need for an invitation to enter Saudi Arabia, delays of more than a month in getting a visa for Vietnam

Table 16.4 **BASIC CUSTOMER DATA FORM**

BASIC DATA ON CUSTOMERS			
Name and address of the company			
Telephone / Fax / Telex / e-mail			
Legal form of company			
Year of foundation			
Owners			
CEO			
Most important decision makers			
Headquarters			
Branch offices, subsidiaries, chain stores			
Representatives			
Bank account(s)			
Can be addressed with the help of the following persons or companies			
Industry			
Main activities			
Product line (production and/or trade)			
Production sites and procedures			
Contact with other customers and/or influencers			
The customer's customers			
Existing suppliers			
Employees in			Number
	R & D		
	Sales		
	Production		
	Quality control		
	Administration		

Table 16.4 (continued)

	Logistics		
	Purchasing		
	Total		
Selling area in m²			
Equipment			
Total sales			
Realized sales with the customer in 19.. (per type of product)			
Planned sales with the customer in 19.. (per type of product)			
Financial status			
Accounts receivable			
Calendar/Appointments			

The basic customer data form contains basic information that salespeople should gather about potential customers and should have at hand about existing customers.

(while the salesperson's passport has to stay at the Vietnamese embassy), or complicated testing procedures before a sample of agricultural products may enter the USA, may cause extended waiting periods and additional costs if they are not properly considered in the planning of sales calls. Such peculiarities of the sales region concerning topography, climate, infrastructure and bureaucracy can be gathered from any informative country guide book.

Specifics of the customers in the sales area to be considered in planning sales calls are of equal or even higher importance. However, they are much more difficult to find out. First of all, it is not equally easy to get hold of customers all over the world. Some companies try to hold off salespeople by finding excuses, such as 'Mr Brown is in a meeting' or 'Ms Hancock is abroad' in the UK. Different time zones, such as in the USA or in Australia, may come as a surprise to salespeople used to working in a sales area with one time zone. Different weekends or holiday seasons such as in Islamic countries, and managers of potential customer firms in some cultures such as Argentina who do not keep their (written) word as to possible presentations, may mess up planned sales calls.

The length of discussions heavily influences the potential number of sales calls to be executed by one salesperson. For example, sales talks with Swiss procurement managers tend to be short and precise. In Germany many purchasing managers even predetermine the time they are prepared to reserve for negotiations with a salesperson, while their Tunisian counterparts prefer extended sales contacts which stay rather vague in their content. As Chapter 5 has discussed, punctuality may have different meanings depending on the cultural environment. But extended waiting times may result in higher sales costs per customer contact if they are not planned beforehand.

In addition, the size of the potential customers, the type of customer problem to be resolved, and the product experience or level of technological know-how of the customers may have an impact on the number of business trips needed, their extension and cost. For example, a salesperson responsible for internationally operating customers may have to present his or her product to a team of operations managers in a production plant near Hamburg, Germany, submit the offer to a European purchasing unit in Amsterdam, the Netherlands, and negotiate the contract in the customer's headquarters in Osaka, Japan. As another example, a salesperson wanting to sell successfully to the aerospace industry needs to develop excellent relationships with all the functional groups of the potential customer's organization in order to assure all of them that the supplier is able to master the high complexity of the customer's product and the high security standards of the customers' customers. Finally, selling a water treatment installation in Sweden may require much less explanation, provision of infrastructure and training than selling the same product in Uganda. Selling fashion items to Italian intermediaries may also be much less time consuming than selling them to purchasing agents of publicly held department stores in China.

Sales Manual. The most important tool for an international salesperson in preparing sales calls is the company's sales manual. Table 16.5 suggests the contents a sales manual should comprise. The first part of the manual serves to inform the potential customers about the company and its products. It lists information on the international marketer's business domain, size, capital structure, organization and employees potentially important to the customer. 'Product facts' describe the reasons why potential customers should consider the marketer's product. They offer an opportunity to identify with customers from the same or a closely related industry who have similar problems and needs. They also relate to the potential customers' experience with products that did not entirely come up to their expectations, and offer an improved solution. Brochures about individual products or product groups which preferably should be translated into the customers' language are accompanied by additional product descriptions and sample quotations. Sample quotations are offers of 'average' products. They should help potential customers to get a first impression of the marketer's capabilities.

The first part of the sales manual also contains a list of suppliers and a list of references. The list of suppliers contains the names of companies that have a reputation that is respected by the potential customers. It serves to demonstrate to the potential customers how carefully the materials used in manufacturing the marketer's products are selected. If the suppliers listed also offer their goods and services in the customers' country-market, the international marketer may gain additional trust from the prospective buyers.

The reference list is a very precious sales tool which should be handled with care. In the hands of competition it could be used efficiently to acquire new customers. Therefore, it is advisable to hand only part of the reference

Table 16.5	CONTENTS OF A SALES MANUAL

Information	Details
Presentation of the company	Legal form of company Year of foundation Main activities Owners Capital stock Bank account(s) Top management Headquarters Branch offices, subsidiaries Property, rented space Size of production and offices, storage capacity Number and education of employees (production, assembling, service, sales, quality insurance, purchasing, . . .) Equipment (machinery, test beds, . . .)
Organizational structure	Who is responsible for what regarding the customer?
Names and addresses of sales and service partners	Names, addresses, telephone and fax numbers of persons who can be reached around the clock
Product facts	Description of ↔ the shop, office, or plant of existing customers or of the production process of these customers ↔ the problems those customers wanted to be solved ↔ the previous – obviously not adequate – solutions to these problems ↔ the optimum solution offered and realized by the marketer ↔ spreading the news
Brochures	Translated into the language of the customers
(Technical) Descriptions	Additional information that is not mentioned in the brochure(s), such as dimensions, weight, maximum temperature, advice regarding transportation, storage, handling, maintenance, etc.
Sample quotations	
Reference list	
List of suppliers	
Spare parts (list / scheme)	
Introductory conditions	
Video films, slides, photos, diskettes, CD-ROMs	

Continued

Table 16.5 (continued)

Standards applied Certificates					
Operating instructions					
Articles					
Training programme					
List of arguments					
Competition comparison chart					
Proof					
(Technical) Questionnaire					
Price list					
Analysis of industries					
Customs tariff numbers (GATT)					
Payoff calculation					
Dictionary of technical terms					
Road map Zip code map					

The sales manual helps salespeople in preparing their sales calls and in negotiating with potential customers. It may also be used for the preparation of international offers.

list over to a potential customer, for example only reference customers in a certain sales area or in the potential customer's industry.

The second part of the sales manual helps the salesperson to prepare the sales call and provides potential customers with additional material to substantiate claims made during negotiations. Preparing a sales call means that the salesperson has to 'sense' any possible objections and to develop counter-arguments or alternatives in advance. In international sales where cultural differences between sales staff and potential customers come into play, the international marketer particularly has to make sure that its salespeople are well prepared to cope with objections from their potential customers. Basic preparation can be achieved by making salespeople analyse the industries belonging to their sales area. This can be done using information given in the sales manual about customer groups showing above-average results in country-markets served for some time. Salespeople may also analyse the reasons for the success of their most important competitors based on success criteria in established markets. And they may go through the training programme contained in the sales manual.

The sales manual also takes care of the fact that customers located in country-markets other than that of the international marketer's headquarters have more potential objections to the marketer and its products than to local suppliers. Some objections are related to weaknesses of the total product compared to its competitors. Therefore, the sales manual contains information on the standards applied in production, such as measures of environmental protection, and on certificates received, such as an ISO 9000 certificate. It may also contain articles from trade magazines or scientific reviews which describe the use or application of the marketer's products in a more neutral-sounding and therefore more reliable way. Operating instructions for technical products describe the product in more detail than any other sales literature. They provide clues as to outstanding features of the product.

But many customers' objections in international sales are based on emotional reactions rather than rational reasons, such as lack of confidence in a foreign company and its representatives, fear of new products that might not perform in the way they promise, a perceived lack of efficient communication with the supplier, possible misunderstandings when defining the product and its application, or a fear of lack of reliable after-sales service. For example, Imi-tech Fibres GmbH, an Austria-based member of the UK INSPEC GROUP selling fibres for technical applications such as high-temperature gas filtration, were surprised to learn from a market survey how much their local clients were influenced by the way the salespersons treated them rather than by the outstanding features of the product.

International salespersons have to anticipate such emotionally based objections from their potential customers. The sales manual supports them by providing lists of arguments to be used during sales calls. Experience has shown that quantified arguments are remembered much better by customers than just verbal ones. For example, a salesperson offering a machine tool should not only praise its high availability. Such verbal descriptions are too abstract to be well rembered by customers. Adding that the machine tool can be used productively by the customer for 94.8 per cent of the time and showing a record as proof of this claim makes high availability a feature of the product that is easily remembered.

The reputation of a salesperson and his or her reliability as perceived by a potential customer is strongly influenced by the salesperson's competence, that is, his or her ability to answer questions concerning the product and the offer without having to contact the back office for approval. Therefore, other important aids for the sales force in preparing a sales call are the price list, the list of spare parts and the introductory conditions contained in the sales manual. For example, when negotiating the terms of sale, the salesperson can choose between an extended guarantee, a price reduction, a test period, and a right of return which are contained in the standardized introductory conditions in the manual.

The sales manual may also contain support material to increase the potential customers' trust in the international marketer and its products. Video films, slides, photographs or CD-ROMs showing the marketer's manufacturing site and the application or use of its products increase their credibility. The international marketer may take advantage of the image of its country or of reputable customers. Attention needs to be given, however, to ensuring that the usage situation shown in the visual material is perceived by the potential customer as closely related to its own situation or to a very desirable state. CD-ROMs and diskettes may also offer questionnaires that customers can fill out in order to facilitate the preparation of inquiries. Through such questionnaires the customer can specify the problem to be resolved and the expectations to be fulfilled by the supplier without running the risk of forgetting important details. Language problems are less pronounced, experience with other products can be described, and the infrastructure available at the customer can be detailed.

Customs tariff numbers and a scheme for a payoff calculation are additional support materials to increase customer satisfaction with the sales call. Customs tariff numbers make it easier for the customer to do an import calculation for the entire product or parts of it. They help in avoiding import problems or paying too much customs taxes. A payoff calculation scheme enables a prospective buyer to fill in its own figures. As a consequence, the potential customer tends to trust the outcome of calculations highly.

Finally, the sales manual may support the preparation of sales calls by providing a dictionary of technical terms. Because dictionaries available in bookstores rarely contain the specific vocabulary needed for selling technical goods and services internationally, the international marketer is well advised to develop a collection of technical terms in several languages that the company's salespeople have learned during their discussions with customers and other relevant stakeholders in the markets served by the company. Such a dictionary assists other people in the company and interpreters in their translation jobs. A road map and a zip code map that facilitates finding addresses may round off the sales manual.

Sales Negotiations

After having carefully planned the sales calls, the salesperson may start contacting potential customers. Compared to sales communication in the home market, personal selling on an international scale requires that the salesperson pays attention to some special issues. The salesperson has to know and respect mostly unwritten rules of social behaviour when getting into personal contact with potential business partners. For example, it is important to know and respect the hierarchy of management in a potential customer firm in the UK and Japan. In Spain a salesperson should never try to make an appointment during 'la siesta', that is, between 1.30 p.m. and 3.30 p.m., and should never expect an invitation for dinner that will start before 10 o'clock in the evening. In Portugal business partners tend to expect a correctly dressed salesperson (men wearing suit and tie), while their Norwegian counterparts mostly prefer casual or sports clothing even at dinner.

Starting Negotiations. Sales negotiations are viewed and carried out differently from one culture to another. It is important to know how to start a sales talk and how to address negotiation partners. In German speaking parts of Switzerland, for example, where business people don't like to waste time, the salesperson must start talking business right away, whereas in Italy a very personal and rather long-lasting introduction is recommended. In Latin America too, one should never start negotiations right away as this is considered very impolite. Sales talks start with a 'chat' before getting into business matters. In Austria it is usual to address people by their surname and with their academic, business or honorary title, while in the USA addresses may vary, for example, from a very formal 'Good morning, Sir!' to 'Hello Mr Butler' and 'Hi, Frances!' (not forgetting the different formal forms of asking about the person's condition, even without any genuine interest in it).

But it is not only words that convey a message; body language plays an important role in communication. Shaking hands at any personal encounter of business or personal significance is typical in continental Western Europe. Inexperienced Europeans, therefore, consider the behaviour of Canadian and US business people, who shake hands only when meeting for the first time, as offensive. In many Islamic countries it is usual to embrace the – well-known! – business partner, while shaking hands with a woman in public would be considered as very insulting. Shaking hands and embracing are not the only gestures used when greeting people; kissing, bowing and many other forms are part of a nation's cultural heritage. In Thailand, for example, shaking hands could be interpreted as not respecting the country's culture and a lack of politeness, as a Thai greets by putting his palms together in front of his face. During talks with business partners and negotiations, additional things such as bearing, eye contact, or gestures need to be considered. For example, there is a big difference between a Finn and an Italian supporting an emotional discussion with hand gestures.

What to wear and how to greet may seem to be of minor importance compared to the business that has to be negotiated. But respecting or not respecting the individual rules of each culture in a country or region strongly influences the psychic distance between potential business partners, interpersonal attraction and the development of trust. Interested people may have learned much about cultural differences and the Do's and Don'ts from worldwide TV programmes, travelling, reading relevant literature and special training. However, knowing about differences is one thing, accepting and adapting to them is another. This is particularly true when it comes to manners. To be fully accepted in a foreign culture, a salesperson has to adapt to the manners of the host country, not just try to imitate them.

Bargaining. Bargaining is what most people think of when they think of negotiation – the 'give and take' of information and offers. Bargaining is viewed and carried out differently from one culture to another. Offers or expectations may be expressed in a non-verbal way, for example through the use of facial expressions. Even the very approach to negotiation, whether it is essentially a win–win exercise, or a win–lose one, is coloured by the business people's national culture. US Americans, in particular, seem to have difficulty in adapting to different bargaining methods. This may be because, despite the colourful mixtures of cultures in their home country they in generally have relatively little cross-cultural experience (that they are aware of) which prepares them for negotiation with someone with a different cultural background. Several successful Japanese business people have said, for example, that all they had to do to gain a price concession from a US salesperson was to remain silent. Sooner or later, the American would reduce the price just to break the silence.

Another issue is whether a sales technique that has been used effectively in one market will be effective in another. In their hurry to close a deal, US salespeople seem rude to many business partners from other parts of the world. They typically try to seek agreement on a point-by-point basis, assuming that there is already a basis for the overall agreement. Chinese negotiators, on the other hand, want to develop a complete understanding of the situation, developing an overall picture. That is, they are seeking to establish what the US salespeople have already assumed exists, a reason to negotiate. For that reason, even salespeople from southern parts of Europe, where chats and bargaining during sales negotiations may take a substantial amount of time, often underestimate the amount of time a contract negotiation will take in China.

Agreement between salesperson and customer may be difficult to reach. Each of them must be willing to give up something, to make a concession, in order to come to a business contract. Culture plays an important role in this phase as well. Open disagreement and using threats and warnings may work in some cultures. For example, Germans tend to disagree directly and openly; their ways of resolving disputes are also direct. In contrast, business people from Hong Kong would never disagree directly. They might even say 'yes' when what they mean is 'maybe' or 'I don't agree' in order to give 'face' to those with whom they negotiate. If agreement is reached the salesperson has to make sure that the degree and importance of what has been agreed upon is clearly understood by both parties. Otherwise, disagreement about the contract, sale, product, or even the words in the agreement itself will occur in the future.

Independent of the cultural environment of a sales negotiation process, there are some general rules which an internationally active salesperson should be aware of to be successful:

↔ During negotiations the salesperson needs to check constantly with the potential customer that there is a mutual understanding of the discussed issues. Language problems or the perceived obligation to let others save 'face' – the latter is true for many Asian business people – often make negotiation partners reluctant to ask questions. Salespeople's talk must be pertinent to make sure that most of what they are trying to communicate is understood and evokes the intended meaning.

↔ The salesperson must minimize monologues. Without listening to the potential customer's opinion, salespeople will never find out what this person really wants. When asked questions, the salesperson should answer in short, simple and only a few sentences. Otherwise the salesperson risks never being asked again, especially if negotiation takes place in the mother tongue of the salesperson and the business partner has to communicate in a foreign language.

↔ The salesperson must leave enough time for the potential business partners to take notes. The salesperson should not forget that after the meeting these notes are the basis for what the interested partners will convey to stakeholders inside and outside the company. The negotiation partners must be furnished with enough and sufficiently good arguments that they can 'sell' to those stakeholders. The benefits that the product provides to the potential customer and its stakeholders and the success story of the marketer in its field of competency are key factors in getting the order.

↔ The salesperson should not expect to negotiate a purchase contract at the very first meeting. The potential customer wants to have sufficient time to learn more about the international marketer, its products and the given references. Some more time is needed to check whether the arguments and statements of the salesperson are true. In addition, other people in the company have to be convinced of the advantages of accepting a new supplier. Sometimes, when potential customers are intermediaries, they may want to do some market research concerning the attractiveness of the potential supplier's products. In other cases, when the potential customers have closely regulated ties to their own customers, such as in the aircraft industry, they may even need to ask their own customers for approval of the new supplier or its product. Because of the time needed by potential clients to carry out all these things, salespeople must find ways of contacting prospective customers at regular intervals in order not to be 'forgotten'.

↔ Potential customers who are not familiar with the technology or the state of the art in a given industry must be 'trained' by the salesperson. Providing such customers with information or tools that enable them to evaluate suppliers and products in their particular field has proven to be of great help. Frequentis, a Vienna, Austria-based supplier of voice communication systems for air traffic control, for example, does business in a highly specialized product-market. Because most potential customers in this market are not able to follow technological development closely enough to systematically evaluate products offered by different potential suppliers, the company does its sales presentations in the form of a kind of training in order to let the customer know as much as possible about the equipment and its functioning before any decision is taken.

Structure of Sales Talks. Despite all the culturally based differences in business manners, there are some commonalities that salespersons have to respect independent of the country-market they serve. Most foreign marketers need to gradually overcome customers' prejudices, mistrust, or lack of confidence in the company and its products. Their salespeople, therefore, must indicate that they are genuinely interested in the customer's problem and in providing the expected customer benefits, but that they are also convinced of the product. They have to treat any objections by the customer carefully and must ask the customer for approval.

Consequently, a promising sales talk should start by introducing the salesperson and the company represented. Then the salesperson should thank the potential customer for their invitation and repeat or explain the reason for coming. In this phase the salesperson will also take the opportunity of presenting the objective(s) and the topics of the meeting. It may then be necessary to create problem awareness on the part of the customer. At that stage the salesperson will need to make customers talk about their current situation and to elicit their requirements and expectations concerning potential problem solutions. It is essential to agree upon the issues important to the customer. For that purpose and for the presentation of the benefits the company's product is able to provide, the salesperson may use the sales literature contained in the sales manual. Then the issues agreed upon are negotiated and the salesperson has to draw conclusions from this negotiation. To make sure that the business partner has a similar understanding of the meaning of these conclusions, further actions to be taken and the commitments on both sides need to be fixed. For example, the negotiation parties may agree upon sending documentation, organizing a test, preparing the offer, and negotiating with subcontractors. The salesperson finishes the sales talk by summing up what has been achieved.

The whole of the negotiation process, and the impact that culture may have upon that process, is summed up in the statement that 'without relationships, you have no deal'. Certainly, there are sales talks that will never lead to negotiations; and there are negotiations that will not be concluded with an agreement. But for international marketing to be successful over time, a salesperson must be aware that profit in business is dependent mainly on repeat business, in both the consumer and organizational markets. In most product-markets, relationships with customers must be established from a long-term perspective and must be maintained accordingly.

The International Offer

By presenting an offer the international marketer invites a potential customer to sign a sales contract. Because well-prepared offers may involve substantial costs, the marketer has to find out the purpose of its offer for the potential customer before quoting. An enquiry may have been placed to get an offer for budgeting purposes or a comparison of prices. The offer may serve as a part of a complete quotation by the potential customer for its own client, or it may encounter a real demand. When the decision to make an offer is taken, the offer may be made verbally or in writing. But both are equally binding. When preparing a written international offer the marketer has to consider which language to use, which legal regulations and local market usances to respect, which product specifications and applications and which terms of sale and delivery to offer, and for what period of validity the offer is binding. In addition, the structure of the offer may determine its attractiveness to the customer. After presenting the offer to the customer, the salesperson has to ensure an effective follow-up to close the contract.

Preparing the Offer.   The most convenient solution for the international marketer would be to execute all international correspondence in its own language. Many salespeople from English-speaking countries rely on their customers' ability to read and write their language. They do not consider how much more difficult it is for their customers to express themselves precisely in the way they would like, even if they seem to have mastered the foreign language.

The best solution for the customers would be to communicate in their language. This possibility is limited, however, by the availability of language skills in the internationally operating firm or of good translators if the language is not one of the most commonly used. Bad translations, particularly of technical and commercial terms, may lead to misunderstandings resulting in reduced attractiveness of the international marketer's offer or in disputes after the contract has been signed. Even professional translators should not be expected to know all the special terms included in the original. The dictionary of technical terms contained in the marketer's sales manual may provide valuable support for translators.

To prevent both an offer that does not conform to the norms and standards of the customer's country-market and possibly substantial fines for disregarding legal regulations, the international marketer must know the business usances, norms, standards and legal regulations relevant to its product-market before quoting. For example, electrical devices approved in the EU are not automatically approved in Switzerland; and many US customers interpret the delivery term 'FOB' (Free on Board) differently from the definition of the Incoterms (see Chapter 15).

In preparing an offer the international marketer must also consider that many prospective customers do not clearly define the product and its use when inviting potential suppliers to bid. Potential suppliers are assumed to know facts that are not mentioned in the enquiry. For example, when a Taiwanese investor sends enquiries about electrical blast furnaces to potential international suppliers, it is assumed that those suppliers have or will acquire additional information about facts such as the existing infrastructure at the construction site, the industrial standards and legal norms to be respected in the country, or the available lifting hoist. In such cases, the international marketer has two possibilities open to it. It may gather the additional information needed to make an offer that is reliable for the customer and minimizes the risk for the marketer, but at the same time its offer may be submitted too late when competitors have already gained an advantage by choosing the second possibility. This is to present an offer 'on the assumption that . . .'. By responding in this way the international marketer can react much faster, but it risks offering product features and services that the customers are not ready to pay for, or overlooking cost drivers that may lead to big difficulties in staying within the offered price. In choosing which way to jump, the international marketer must evaluate what is more important in the specific case: to get into close contact with the customer quickly and negotiate the details later on, or to make a complete offer to the customer that reduces the marketer's financial risk.

If a potential customer who has never had any contact with the international marketer before sends an enquiry that specifies the requested product in detail, the marketer can assume that those details stem from the potential customer's experience with competitors' products. In such a case the offer has to state clearly in which respects the product differs substantially from the specifications given in the enquiry. It must convince the potential customer that the product offers features which are at least equally or even better suited to fulfilling the customer's expectations and may provide additional benefits.

If an international enquiry specifies both the requested product and its use or the problem to be resolved by using the product, the marketer may be able to offer the product as specified by the customer and to present an alternative for the solution of the described problem that is more competitive than the product chosen by the potential customer. The international marketer should offer both, as the potential customer might have had good reasons, such as an existing stock of spare parts, tools, or specifically trained people, for specifying the product in the way it did. In any case, a personal check with the customer to clarify the situation is much more advisable than offering a supposedly 'better' solution that does not meet the customer's requirements.

When an enquiry or the attached terms of sale do not specify details such as the currency to be used, the place and terms of delivery or the terms of payment, the international marketer has to make the choice. There are two aspects to be considered. On the one hand, the marketer will want to suggest terms of sale which are in its favour – for example, payment in advance in the currency of the home country and delivery ex works (that is, the customer has to bear the cost and risk of international transportation). On the other hand, the marketer should not offer terms of delivery which complicate the business for the (potentially inexperienced) customer to the point of putting it off and offending the customer by signalling that the marketer does not trust its financial status. To take a satisfactory decision the international marketer might need to gather additional information about the potential customer and to consult external service providers such as banks and freight forwarders.

Offers may be binding or not binding. Offers that are not binding are rather rare in international business. They only occur when the marketer does not want to commit itself because it cannot entirely control the sequence of events, as in the case of late or non-delivery of substantial parts or services by subcontractors. However, the international marketer should state clearly why its offer is not binding. If the marketer does not declare an offer as 'not binding', the customer may claim the delivery of what has been offered. The customer may even sue the marketer if it cannot fulfil its commitment.

Structure of an International Offer.   Both the content and the format of an offer must attract the potential customer's attention. The offer is part of the international marketer's total product. Correct address, clear structure, faultless and pleasingly formatted text, and a transport-resistant envelope give the customer an impression of what to expect from the supplier. A clear structure facilitates the potential customer's task of reading, understanding, and comparing the offer with those of competitors. Because this is particularly important in international marketing where language problems may represent a significant obstacle, the structure of an international offer will be described in more detail in the following (see Table 16.6).

As with sales negotiations, the very first words count. They convey the first impression and should arouse the reader's interest. Referring to the enquiry or another reason for the offer indicates why the potential customer has received the offer. But it also is an occasion to thank the customer for having been considered in the bidding process or for the friendly reception of the salesperson.

When it is the marketer's first offer presented to the potential customer, both the company and the personnel serving the customer have to be introduced. Part one of an international marketer's sales manual as described above may serve as an information platform. By repeating the intended use of the product and by giving reasons for its purchase, the international marketer may communicate how well it has studied the customer's problem and its expectations.

The total product should be described considering its features and customer benefits. Depending on which type of product the international marketer is offering, a technical product description may consist of dimensions such as weight, material, function, technical data, mechanical or electrical input and output, information about required storage space or time, installation, maintenance, service, repair and spare parts, advice regarding environmental protection and safety, or packaging. The product description must be complete. It should not leave room for any misunderstandings which could increase the potential customer's doubts about buying from a non-domestic

Table 16.6 THE STRUCTURE OF AN INTERNATIONAL OFFER

Introduction
    Reason for the offer
    Introduction of the company and the personnel serving the customer
    Intended product use and reasons for purchasing the selected product
Total Product
    Description
    Quantity
    Shipment
    Packaging
    Guarantee
Price and Terms
    Price/Currency
    Terms of payment
    Taxes and customs duties
    Financial commitment
    Delivery time
Period of Validity
Reservation of Ownership
Order Cancellation Fee
Attachments

To be clear and easily understandable for the potential customer, an international offer should have the structure shown in this table.

marketer. Therefore, information on the amount of local production and how total quality is managed by the international marketer may round off the more product-oriented description.

Besides guarantees that the marketer has to offer based on legal regulations, there may also be voluntary guarantees aimed at strengthening the company's competitive position. When phrasing a guarantee clause, the marketer should make sure not to offer an 'unlimited' guarantee. For example, a special service guarantee for a new computer installation could be limited by a statement such as 'The guarantee ends 12 months after start-up of the new system, and at the latest 18 months after delivery'.

When indicating the price of its product in a certain currency, the international marketer should either use the name of the currency in the business language the partners have agreed upon or apply the internationally accepted abbreviations for currencies, such as CAD for the Canadian Dollar, SEK for the Swedish Crown or GBP for the British Pound Sterling. Many marketers will not be able to quote in their own currency. In such cases marketers should use a special clause in their offer, such as a fixed exchange rate, that protects them against exchange rate fluctuations.

Fulfilling an order may take a substantial amount of time. If wage increases or rising prices for supplies during that period may threaten the price calculation of the international marketer, a price escalator clause may be used. It normally links the indicated price of the offered product to national or international official indices which can be easily verified by the potential customer and may be certified by official bodies.

Who will have to pay which taxes and customs duties mainly depends on the terms of delivery that the international marketer is offering. In many international business relations, the financial commitment of the marketer strongly influences the attractiveness of its offer to the potential customer. By offering a mix of financial assistance through the company itself, a bank recommended by the marketer, and a state-owned institute that supports international business activities, the supplier may substantially raise its attractiveness.

In specifying delivery time, the international marketer should never state a date because it never knows when the prospective buyer will order. Usual wordings are, for example, 'four weeks after receiving the order' or 'prompt delivery after having received your down payment'. The marketer may also state the period of validity of its offer. If this period is not specified in an offer sent by letter, fax or telex, it generally ends after a period which consists of two elements: the delivery time of both the offer and the goods or services and the time the potential customer usually needs to evaluate the offer and make a decision. Verbal offers, given personally or by phone, must be accepted or refused immediately if not otherwise agreed.

A reservation of ownership serves to prevent the transfer of title to property when the product is handed over to the customer. Proper wording could be, for example, 'Our ownership will not pass before payment of the full purchase price'. Another safety measure for the supplier and the customer is to include a statement concerning an order cancellation fee in the offer. Such a statement informs the potential customer under what conditions, for example the payment of a certain percentage of the order value, a potential order that has been placed may be cancelled.

Finally, the international marketer may increase the attractiveness of its offer by attachments which appeal to all the senses of the prospective customer, such as photographs, videos, audio cassettes, diskettes, CD-ROMs or product samples. However, special care has to be taken that none of these attachments hurts the feelings of the persons involved in the purchasing decision process on the customer side for sexual, racial, religious, or other cultural reasons.

Follow-up. After the offer has been presented, the salesperson plays an important part in getting the customer's order. As soon as the salesperson can assume that the potential customer has had enough time to read and study the offer as well as to assess and compare it to offers from competitors, follow-up activities may be started. A personal discussion about how the customer evaluates the offer is better than a telephone call which, in turn, is better than a fax or an e-mail. The problem of international follow-up telephone calls is that talking to someone over the phone requires a much better knowledge of the communication partner's language than a face-to-face discussion where gestures, drawings or showing and pointing at something help to overcome communication problems. Table 16.7 contains some important questions to be answered as result of a follow-up with a potential customer.

If the customer wants to postpone its decision or the placing of the order, the salesperson has to find out the reason why, the date the customer might be contacted again and the possibilities of influencing the decision. If one of the competitors receives the order, the salesperson should gather information on who has received the order, which part of the company's offer did not meet the customer's expectations, and what can be done in the future to come closer to the potential customer's expectations.

Table 16.7 **Follow-up Questions**

↔ Has the prospective customer understood and appreciated all details of the offer?

↔ Are further explanations or even a revised offer required?

↔ Which parts of the offer have to be modified in order to improve the opportunity of receiving the order?

↔ Who are the competitors and what are their major arguments?

↔ When will the decision be made?

↔ Could a personal call from another company member contribute to the decision making by intensifying the salesperson's arguments?

↔ Is the prospective customer ready to accept the salesperson for negotiating a possible purchase contract? Who else may need to be involved?

During the follow-up of an offer, the salesperson should try to get answers to these questions from the potential customer.

After-Sales Activities

Besides personal selling, international sales management is also responsible for an international marketer's after-sales activities. Those activities encompass after-sales service, handling customer claims, and resolving disputes with customers.

After-Sales Service

After-sales service is frequently considered as technical service (installation, maintenance and repair) of the products sold. However, in order to ensure a long-lasting relationship with a satisfied customer, to be allowed to use the customer as a reference, and to encourage positive word-of-mouth the international marketer has to do more than simply service its products sold. The customer has to be kept satisfied with the product from its purchase to the end of its use or for as long as the customer keeps it in its product portfolio. For example, a software company not only has to install its product on the customer's computer (or provide easy installation advice) and to remove bugs from its software, but must also be continually accessible when problems arise, must regularly update the software, inform the customer about new developments which could be of relevance to its product, and may need to offer training for new users.

As a consequence of such extended demand, international after-sales service has first to check if customer orders have been fulfilled according to the contract and the expectations of the customers. Shipment may not have been complete, product quality may have been diminished during transportation, delivery time may have been overrun, or the customer might not have received all the necessary documents for proper product use, such as the operating manual. Secondly, the proper functioning of the product must be checked. For example, an international consulting firm specializing in producing productivity gains for their customers must offer some follow-up to check whether the changes implemented in the customers' processes have led to the promised results. Then, a system to ensure regular customer contact needs to be installed. Customers should not only hear from the company when they have a problem with one of its products.

Handling Customers' Claims

Even total quality management and excellent international after-sales service cannot entirely prevent customer complaints about a good delivered, a service rendered, or the way the customer was treated by the marketer's employees or its intermediaries. There are justified complaints and others where the customer is wrong. Most serious are customer complaints which are combined with a request either to remove the cause of the complaint or to compensate the customer financially for the damage. The international salesperson must be able to handle all cases properly. Certain steps need to be taken in order neither to annoy the customer further nor to commit the salesperson's own company inappropriately. The greater the cultural distance between the business partners, the more delicate the salesperson's task.

In general, the salesperson first needs to find out what exactly has happened and what has already been done to solve the problem. This analysis should indicate one or more possible reasons for the complaint. At this stage it is much more important to find out what caused the problem than who was responsible for it. Later, the measures to be taken can be decided, and, if it is an organizational customer, the key persons at the customer with whom the company should keep in touch identified. Finally, the question of how to prevent the problem happening again should be answered.

When discussing complaints or claims with a customer there is, of course, high tension between the two business partners. Because of increased emotionality, discussions tend to be less polite. If legal issues come into play, formalities become more important. In any case, intercultural differences play a major role. The salesperson must be closely familiar with the do's and don'ts of interpersonal communication in the customer's culture if insults are to be avoided. Any mishandling of such a situation will lead to even more trouble and to the loss of a customer who will probably broadcast what has happened to other existing and potential customers. On the other hand, if customer complaints are treated well, customer satisfaction may increase above the level reached before the cause of the complaint came to light.

Because sensitive handling of customer complaints is so very important for customer satisfaction and the international marketer's word-of-mouth reputation, patient, reliable and circumspect persons with intensive intercultural experience are needed to handle international claims. Complaint managers should also be extremely orderly as the activities to satisfy the customer have to be perfectly organized and realized. Discussions, decisions and actions should be carefully documented in order to have some proof concerning measures taken, when and by whom in a possible dispute later on.

Resolving Disputes

Even the best handling of customer complaints cannot entirely prevent disputes between an international marketer and its customers or other important stakeholders. Like negotiation practices, the processes for recognizing and resolving disputes also vary considerably among cultures. As Chapter 5 has

Table 16.8 INTERNATIONAL ARBITRATION RESOURCES

International Chamber of Commerce (ICC)
The International Chamber of Commerce counsels and arbitrates in Paris. It is controlled by an Administrative Commission constituted by one member of each country whose business organizations are affiliated with the ICC. The commission attempts to counsel a resolution to disputes after a hearing. If that fails, the matter is referred for arbitration to the Court of Arbitration, chosen by the parties and the ICC.

American Arbitration Association (AAA)
The American Arbitration Association enables foreign businesses to use arbitration in the United States and avoid the complex and costly US legal system. An arbitration may make an award that seems just and equitable under the AAA rules. The association appoints the arbitrator, giving consideration to the parties' preferences and objections.

Geneva Conventions on Arbitration
The Geneva Protocol (1923) provides that member nations recognize the validity of arbitration agreements made between parties who are under the jurisdiction of the member nations, irrespective of where the agreement was executed.

The Geneva Convention (1927) provides that member nations recognize as binding and enforce under the rules an arbitration award made under an agreement covered by the Geneva Protocol.

New York Convention
The New York Convention, created in 1958 by the United Nations Conference on International Arbitration, has no requirement of reciprocity. This means a member nation may apply the convention to awards made in the territory of another member nation, and not its own. However, each member nation must refer parties to a written arbitration agreement. Important member nations include the United States, Germany, France, Japan, United Kingdom, and Russia.

UNCITRAL Arbitration Rules
These rules were published by the United Nations Committee on International Trade Law in 1976. They are a model for international arbitration, but are not embodied in a convention.

Convention on Settlement of Investment Disputes
This convention provides for the formation of a Center for Settlement of Investment Disputes at the principal office of the Bank of Washington, to settle investment disputes between member nations.

International marketers may choose from several international arbitration resources when disputes need to be resolved.

Source: Adapted from A. Walton and M. Vitoria (1982) *Russell on Arbitration*, 20th edn, (London: Stevens E. Sons); and E. A. Marshall (1983) *The Law of Arbitration*, 3rd edn, (London: Sweet and Maxwell).

shown, different cultures have developed different methods and even different procedures for resolving disputes. Asians and Europeans are amazed at the American preference for resorting to the legal process, and for that matter having to rely on lawyers to be part of the negotiation team. They view going to court as an admission of failure, not as a method of resolving disputes. In more 'cooperative' societies, dispute resolution is achieved through discussion. If an impasse is reached, an arbitrator is called in to settle the dispute. Table 16.8 contains a list of resources for such arbitration processes.

Indeed, outside the USA arbitration is not only usual, but is the preferred method of resolving disputes that cannot be eliminated by negotiations. Courts in many countries tend to favour the local business partner's interests; and legal processes between a local customer and an internationally operating firm arouse public attention that tends to be mainly negative for the foreign company. Therefore, contrary to US habits, international marketers should avoid resolving disputes in court whenever possible.

Managing the International Sales Force

Personal selling is the most effective method of communicating with potential customers. But to ensure the efficiency needed for international success, the marketer has to recruit and select the best people for its specific purpose, and it has to develop its sales force, motivate them to reach ambitious goals and compensate them according to their performance.

Recruitment and Selection

Searching for capable sales personnel willing to cope with the challenge of international marketing is a demanding task. The international marketer may employ expatriate personnel, nationals from the country-markets to be served, or cosmopolitan employees.

Expatriates.   Expatriate personnel are employed by a firm in a country other than their home country. For example, an Italian citizen who works for Olivetti, the Turin-based maker of office equipment, in Spain is an expatriate. Expatriates have the advantage that they are well acquainted with the cultural specifics of the home base. If they have already worked for the company for some time they also know the peculiarities of corporate culture and the products to be sold. Because of this product and process expertise, expatriates are frequently used as salespeople for highly technical products.

But expatriates are expensive over the long term – they cost an average of 200 per cent over base salary. Additionally, they often have problems of personal adjustment in the new environment (see the Culture box). Foremost among these, and the ones over which management has the least control, are those that pertain to the employee's family. Spouses are often unhappy about moving to another country, partly due to limitations on their own career opportunities. Most countries issue a work permit to the firm's employee but make it considerably more difficult, if possible at all, for the employee's spouse to obtain a work permit. Children also worry about living in a foreign land. They must leave familiar surroundings and friends to attend a new school, sometimes in a foreign language. Music lessons, sports activities and other hobbies and interests that are important to them may be interrupted. In fact,

CULTURE BOX

Expatriate Salesforce: A Tough Life in the USA

MOST AMERICANS THINK, QUITE NATURALLY, OF EX-patriates as being Americans living abroad. But as foreign investment and business activity increases in the USA, so too do the number of foreign business people living there. They face the same basic problems adjusting to another culture that Americans do when going abroad.

Asian or European expatriates in the USA are isolated from the home culture and (usually) language. The expatriate's family has to adapt to new living conditions, schools and social systems. For example, one expatriate's wife was shocked when, alone one evening, she opened the door to her home to be confronted by people in face paint and strange clothing, celebrating Halloween. Of more serious concern to the approximately 200 000 Japanese business executives living in the USA is whether their children will get the education necessary to prepare them for the notoriously difficult entrance examinations at Japanese universities.

In general, employees' families are not pre-pared for foreign assignments as extensively as the employees themselves are, despite the fact that such training is good 'people policy' and makes strong economic sense. General Motors, for example, has found that spouses of expatriates have five times greater difficulties in getting accustomed to their new cultural environment than their partners; but the spouses' well-being is very important for the success of the international appointment. Many companies assume that a half-day seminar of general information will suffice to prepare families for foreign assignments. One four-hour seminar, which excluded children, claimed to prepare US families for a two-year assignment in Saudi Arabia. The Saudi religious environment and its implications for behaviour, including how executives' spouses could expect to be treated socially, were 'covered' in a 15-minute talk by an American national who had never been to Saudi Arabia or had any specific training in Saudi customs. In sharp contrast is a three-day course for NEC executives' wives. The course prepares them for the difficulties of living in the USA by offering some language training, information about social customs, and even tips on how to shop successfully in American supermarkets.

Source: Based on O'Reilly, B. (1988) 'Japan's Uneasy US Managers', *Fortune*, 25 April, pp. 10–14; and Stalling, B. (1995) 'Der teure Auslandseinsatz scheitert häufig an Integrationsproblemen', *Der Standard*, 25–26 March, p. 16.

US companies experience a higher overseas failure rate than European or Japanese ones. And one of the most important reasons for such failure is family pressures.

Some employees may refuse overseas assignments because of the fear, common among expatriates, that they will be forgotten if they stay away from the home office for several years. Relocation difficulties can represent a major problem to international marketers. When employees from Western Europe are assigned to industrially developing countries, for example, they are frequently provided with additional support for housing, domestic staff, cars, and special educational training for their children. Upon returning to their home country, they no longer receive this additional compensation package. Often the family and executive react negatively, sensing a loss of status. A further complication is that quite often, when given an international assignment, the employee has increased broader responsibility and authority. Returning to headquarters, usually with a narrower or less reasonable job, also causes dissatisfaction.

It may take substantial time for expatriate salespersons to become effective in country-markets foreign to them, and repatriation may cause additional problems. As a consequence, with world trade and the number of globally active companies increasing, the proportion of expatriate employees has declined. This switch away from expatriate personnel is due not only to their higher costs, but also to the increased availability of national personnel who are qualified for the job.

Nationals. Nationals are sales employees who are based in their home country. An Australian citizen who sells the construction services of Netherlands-based Hollandsche Beton Maatschappij in Australia is a national. There is a definite trend towards using nationals in international business. Many economically less developed countries are putting pressure on international marketers to employ nationals. Moreover, as educational systems and training opportunities improve, more qualified national personnel are becoming available.

Because of their lower total cost compared to expatriate sales forces, national sales forces are more attractive for organizational as well as consumer markets. The overwhelming argument in favour of nationals, however, is their superior understanding of the market and their ability to work within its cultural and social norms while pursuing the company's objectives.

Cosmopolitan. Cosmopolitan employees are citizens of one country who are employed by a company based in a second country and are working in a third country. A UK engineer who works in Indonesia for a business unit of Norwegian Statoil, for example, is a cosmopolitan. This type of employee is more often hired by large multinational firms than by a small company. One advantage of employing a cosmopolitan is similar to that of an expatriate – the availability of expertise or knowledge which is otherwise difficult to find. For example, when Patrick Choel, now president of LVMH's Parfums Christian Dior in Paris, was appointed chairman of UK Unilever's Chesebrough Pond's in the USA, the firm counted on his long-term experience as a manager on various levels of Unilever's business hierarchy in Greece, France, the UK and the USA.[4] Often, such cosmopolitans have a more strongly developed sense of cultural empathy than expatriates, owing to their tendency to remain a cosmopolitan employee throughout some considerable proportion of their career.

The increase in world trade as well as an increase in people's preference to live internationally has led to an increase in the availability and use of cosmopolitan employees. This trend has been reinforced by the development of educational programmes, such as master's degree programmes in international business studies offered by cooperating schools in Europe, North and Latin America and Asia. Such programmes are increasingly producing multilingual, cross-culturally trained, business-knowledgeable future business leaders.

Search Profile. For many years the leading criterion for selecting international sales personnel was the ability to speak the language practised in the company's headquarters. Thus, for example, US firms recruited Arab salespeople and sales managers by first screening them on the basis of their ability to speak English. Although communication between salespeople and management is essential, it is not clear that the ability to speak the company language is the best indicator of the employee's potential for long-term success, even though it may be the easiest standard to apply.

To undertake a more targeted search and to take a more meaningful decision concerning the applicant's qualification for the position to be filled, the marketer should define an ideal profile of the salesperson to be recruited. In most cases the salesperson has to be an excellent representative of the international marketer, an expert in solving the target customers' particular problems, a convincing advocate of the marketer's product who does not 'over'-commit the international marketer, and somebody who knows when to withdraw from a project, customer or market if spending additional resources risks not paying off.

Besides such general features, a search profile defines more precise criteria that candidates have to meet. Those criteria are based on the potential customers' and other important stakeholders' expectations and the needs of the international marketer. They may encompass features like the provision of references (people ready to give confidential information about the candidate), the person's knowledge about the product-market, or his or her readiness to move. Table 16.9 contains a more extensive list of salesperson characteristics to be potentially considered.

Readers following traditional ways of thinking may miss a criterion often applied by international marketers when searching for international salespeople: gender. As the Future Issues box tries to show, the importance of gender for success in most international markets has been continually decreasing and should become of minor importance in the future.

Finding qualified salespeople is sometimes a very troublesome task. Regardless of whether the international marketer has decided to use expatriate, national or cosmopolitan salespeople, the fastest and cheapest way to find the right person may be to look first to see if there is a person inside the company who matches the search profile, or if there is a person inside the company who comes close to the search profile and who can be further developed by training. If a salesperson has to be found outside the firm, the marketer can try to get help from its national chamber of commerce, the chamber of commerce of the country-market to be served, the company's suppliers, or suppliers producing complementary goods and their customers. Address services, consultants and head hunters also offer their services. The most effective way of finding salespeople for international marketing tasks is to ask existing or potential customers for relevant hints. That can be done during expert interviews. Sometimes even competitors are of help by not treating their sales personnel in the way they expect to be treated.

Development of Sales Personnel

Development programmes for international sales personnel generally consist of three elements: training, introduction to the market by a senior salesperson, and improvement of sales planning skills.

Training. To become effective as fast as possible, newly hired salespeople need to be trained about the company – its intended market position, structure, information system, market communication policy and actions. Even more important is intensive training concerning the product lines to be sold – their intended positioning in the customers' minds, their features, target

Table 16.9 **Potential Search Profile for International Sales Personnel**	

| An international marketer's search profile for international sales personnel could contain this criteria. | ↔ References
↔ Language skills (speaking/reading/writing)
↔ Experience as a salesperson (years, positions, size and kind of company, size of orders/projects)
↔ Knowledge about the product- and country-market(s)
↔ Knowledge about the product, its application or use
↔ Customers served so far/Relationships with important customers
↔ Relationships with other important stakeholders
↔ Capacity and motivation
↔ Additional skills (e.g. managing, repairing and servicing products, engineering, design, . . .)
↔ Place of residence/Readiness to move
↔ Availability of travelling means
↔ Availability of communication means |

customer-specific benefits in the country-market to be covered, their advantages (and weaknesses) compared to major competitors, and their proper application. In addition, salespeople have to be introduced to the sales planning procedures of the company – how to select and acquire potential customers, how to monitor market development, how to make sales forecasts and sales budgets, how to prepare sales calls and travel, and how to plan promotional activities. They also need adequate knowledge concerning the firm's order processing. These training programmes are traditionally covered by senior personnel or by internal trainers employed by the international marketer.

Most international marketers have realized that their international personnel at all levels need specialized training in how to perform effectively in a foreign environment. Nippon Electronic Corp. (NEC), a Japanese computer company, goes far beyond the norm. Its more than 160 courses help employees prepare for foreign assignments in a wide variety of ways, from polishing their language skills to familiarizing them with the business customs of other country-markets, and training them in negotiating skills.

External trainers are mostly used to improve the sales personnel's approach to customers and internal communication. External trainers are hired to cover subjects such as the continual improvement of the salespeople's skills in either the language(s) of the served country-market(s) or the company language, for the deepening of salespeople's sensibility to differences between the cultural environment of the company's headquarters and the country-market(s) they work in, to improve the salespeople's ability to recognize the buying habits of customers in selected country-markets, and to further raise their negotiation and other communication skills. International firms such as Swedish-Swiss ABB, US-based AT&T or Royal Dutch Shell provide their employees with intercultural sensitivity training through specialized companies like CIBS, before they send their personnel abroad.[5]

General Motors' automobile division, as another example, has established a worldwide training programme for all salespeople of the company and the firm's wholesalers. This programme is executed by the company-owned

FUTURE ISSUES BOX

Women in International Sales

AS MORE WOMEN HAVE AN ACTIVE INTERNATIONAL career, it would seem that one particular area is still less open to them – that of international sales. Only up to about 10 per cent of international sales positions are filled by women. What reasons exist for such a small proportion of sales personnel being women and what might the future hold? There seem to be four myths which are too commonly believed, which together result in few women being assigned to international sales positions.

The first myth is "Women Don't Have What It Takes." Male managers in many countries seem to believe that success in international sales needs a tough, aggressive approach to customers. Following this line of thought, "feminine traits" such as high empathy and sensitivity, understanding, and compassion, mean that women will be less successful in business. There is of course, no clear evidence that this is the case. To the contrary, it has been argued that such characteristics are highly useful for international assignments. In another culture, lack of empathy is more likely to lead to failure, than having empathy.

A second myth is "They Won't Go." (based on the prejudice that women are more family related and therefore, immobile). Again, this assumption is not verified by any research.

Indeed, there is some evidence that women are eager to grasp new business and career opportunities, including international assignments. Certainly, not all will want to do so, but the same is true for men. A study in the USA has shown that only 30 per cent of managers are eager for foreign duty and 60 per cent "would be willing" provided the combination of incentives was right.

Myth number 3 is "They won't be accepted." Too many male sales managers assume that attitudes of male customers toward women in other cultures will prevent women from being successful. Here, research indicates quite the contrary. Many countries have a tradition of women in leadership roles. And usually in those who don't, women (or men) may be seen as a representative of a company, not as a representative of their gender. In many cultures, the status of the expatriate or cosmopolitan sales person is first that of being a foreigner, then of gender. In all of these cases, assigning a female sales person does not necessarily increase the difficulty of the job being done well.

Finally, myth number 4, "It Won't Work." As discussed, failure rates of (mostly male) expatriates are quite high. But this is no evidence, and no necessary reason, that gender will increase these rates. Rather, training, support, and appropriate assignments will provide an opportunity for career enhancement, and success for women as easily as for men.

Sources: Milner, L.M., D.D. Fodness, and M. Speece (1992) 'Women in the Global Salesforce: A Call for Research', in *Enhancing Knowledge Development in Marketing*, Vol. 3, R.P. Leone and V. Kumar (eds), Chicago, IL: American Marketing Association, pp. 359–365; and Riley-Adams, R. (1993) 'Hands Across the Sea', *International Management*, 23–25 July/August.

Hughes International's Training Division, and is applied worldwide in the same way. It is typically product-market oriented, that is, there are only few minor concessions to local culture and behaviour. The programme has been carefully designed to fit as many differences as possible and was tested successfully in a train-the-trainer programme with participants coming from countries all over the world for a week.

More recently, 're-entry' training programmes have been established to deal with the problem of coming back to the home country. These difficulties are normally more severe for those who have been an expatriate for several years. An inability to readjust to the home culture also results in an increased number of cosmopolitans, employees and their families who have chosen to remain out of their home countries.

Introduction to the Market. Introducing new salespeople to a market by senior salespersons is probably the most efficient way of acquainting them with a new market, its rules and potential customers. The experience that a senior salesperson has collected over the years is very rarely written down for the next person to serve the market. Therefore, an excellent way of learning is by watching the senior salesperson doing things like making appointments, introducing him/herself to a new customer, arguing against objections, negotiating prices or closing contracts.

Besides that business-oriented introduction to the market, for expatriate salespersons and their families some support at a private level in getting established in the new environment has proven to be helpful. About 30 per cent of all international appointments fail because of lacking or insufficient preparation and introduction of employees and their families to their living conditions. Therefore, US-based computer maker Hewlett-Packard, for example, offers its designated expatriates and their families one or two 'preview trips' to the host country. Assistance in finding appropriate housing, financial support for removal costs, or paying tuition costs for schoolchildren are additional means of easing the introduction of expatriate salespeople to a new market.

Internal Networking. Well established personal relationships between sales people and people from other functions is important to avoid the controversy which often exists between procurement, production and finance managers on the one side and sales personnel on the other on how accurate the planning of sales figures can and should be. Salespeople do not always understand that without fairly precise figures from their side, procurement and production cannot plan their level of activity in such a way as to secure a sufficient flow of products to satisfy customer demand at lowest cost. Nor can finance plan the capital investments and liquidity needed to maximize the firm's success. On the other hand, people from those other functional areas tend to expect exaggeratedly precise sales forecasts. They do not consider that potential customers rarely guarantee that they will buy a certain quantity of products at a precise date in the future. In addition, in international marketing, country-markets are in different states of economic development and local product-markets differ in the stage of the life cycle they have reached. Therefore, in more mature markets it may be much easier to reach a high level of precision in sales forecasts, while markets in their early stages of development present substantial problems of accuracy.

For example, when Kentucky Fried Chicken first entered the Japanese market its business in the USA had already reached a much more mature stage of development. Sales figures could be forecast with high precision in the USA, whereas in Japan, sales forecasts were based on rough estimates of potential customer frequency and average amounts of money spent by those customers. Because of a lack of knowledge about probable market development and substantial uncertainty about their customers' purchasing behaviour, many salespeople are reluctant to present precise sales forecasts. They prefer to give 'between .. and ..' figures. But nevertheless, they count on the ready availability of the products their customers may need.

A very important part of sales personnel development, therefore, is to strengthen their personal relationships with people from other areas inside the company in order to increase mutual understanding. Training in how to do sales forecasts will not alone be sufficient to achieve the needed level of motivation of sales personnel.

Motivation and Compensation

Motivators. Understanding the role of the sales force in the organization, what motivates people, and the types of stress and concerns the sales force has are critical to managing it sucessfully. A comparison of studies from various country-markets with differing cultural environments reveals that the stress sales personnel report is largely similar. However, what motivates those people and how they should be rewarded may still be considerably different.

Motivating salespeople to do their best is one of the most challenging managerial tasks of the international marketer. Economic rewards, such as personal bonuses, are the most effective motivator in North America. But in Northern Europe, where personal income tax rates are substantially higher, non-economic motivators work better. In other, high-context cultures, economic rewards may not be as effective as social recognition. This is the case in many Asian nations, where sales achievement awards are more likely to be group oriented, and to be based on social acknowledgement of achievement, rather than economic incentives.

Even in US-based companies, high motivation of salespeople cannot be achieved just by offering a high salary and/or commission. Sales managers setting an example to their collaborators, appreciating their salespeople's work in the field, encouraging benchmarking between them, praising them for success and understanding their failures is a strong motivating factor in all Western countries. Caterpillar, for example, uses a variation of the socially visible award structure, an international working vacation, to motivate and train outstanding sales personnel. The best Caterpillar salesperson from each country is invited, together with his or her spouse, to Marbella, Spain, for a vacation combined with further training. This approach appears to be more effective overall than a straight economic reward as it combines an economic recognition (a free vacation including spouse) with public recognition of employee excellence.

Compensation. The same advantages and disadvantages of using salary versus commission, or some combination of the two, exist internationally as for domestic marketing. Generally, when selling is the individual's primary job, commissions are preferred. But when additional activities (such as gathering customer information or extensive post-sales service) are important, salaries and salary-plus-commission compensation are more popular. However, there are some markets where a commission-only approach is not useful. In highly collective societies (Asian or Arabic, for example) individual efforts and rewards (especially high commissions for the best sales representatives) may not be culturally appropriate. In other cultures, commissions may be interpreted as a signal that the firm is not committed to the employees and is prepared to get rid of them as soon as they fail to perform. So cultural norms should be considered when deciding how to pay sales representatives or branch office employees.

Salespeople may need to be compensated differently depending on their nationality. Central European companies, for example, tend to offer high bonuses to salespeople when they enter a new market. When most potential customers in the market have been reached, the bonuses are reduced. A US-based company might do exactly the opposite. US firms tend to perceive salespeople as entrepreneurs, as self-motivated achievers who want to have more security in the beginning but are interested in receiving larger bonuses after the firm has gained a share of the market.

International Sales Meetings. International sales meetings are conferences, usually held once a year, which assemble employed salespersons, agents and merchants cooperating with the firm, people from other functional areas of the company, such as production or finance, and sometimes guest speakers or a moderator from outside. Such international sales meetings may have various objectives, such as:

↔ Learning from reports on local successful problem solutions. Participants are invited to report on a subject of their choice. How has a problem been resolved or a target achieved (for example, restructuring the local logistics system to shorten delivery time, improving customer awareness of the company's superior quality, development of a new incentive and sales monitoring system to increase new product introduction endeavours)? Which of the planned and executed marketing activities were particularly successful, which have failed? What are the reasons? Lessons to be learned by the other participants in the meeting may be drawn in small workshop groups, and presented and discussed in the plenary.

↔ Comparison between sales units and intermediaries from all served country-markets. Relevant figures, like total sales per number of (potential) customers, share of newly acquired customers, number of sales calls per salesperson, market share, number of orders received per number of sales calls, average value per order, contribution margin per sale, fixed cost, deviation from the budget, number of failures – listed per product group and country-market – may be compared. In order to secure a fair comparison, the figures have to be weighted considering differences between sales areas, such as customers per square kilometre, market volume and potential, number and size of clients, development stage of the market and infrastructure of the country, price level, competitors, import restrictions, legal restrictions, etc. The 'winner of the tournament' then has to present their success story, motivating their colleagues to increase their sales efforts, too.

Austrian IFE AG, the world's leading producer of automatic doors for railroad passenger cars, for example, calls for a sales meeting every year, inviting the 'winner of the tournament' to present 'ten rules to achieve the salesperson's goal' explaining the recipe for success. IFE has found that such presentations showed much better results in motivating the sales force than any motivational speech given by the sales manager. Moreover, the participants immediately developed individual action plans for their country-markets from what they had learned.

↔ Presentation of new and/or improved products and internal processes to the salespeople and intermediaries. Many ideas for such new products or improvements of internal processes may have come from the served markets through salespeople and intermediaries. They enjoy seeing the impact of their feedback on the company. In addition, the sales force may be introduced to new technical solutions, new applications of a product, new designs, services or selling methods. As representatives of so many cultures are present at international sales meetings and many different languages may be spoken, misunderstandings may occur. It is advisable, therefore, to organize an unobtrusive test to see what messages the participants have got and what their conclusions from these messages are.

↔ Information concerning strategic and organizational issues. The headquarters management may want to present the results of market, competition and environmental monitoring. Scenarios about the future development of the firm's macro-environment as well as basic assumptions about the development of the firm's product-markets during the next planning period may be discussed. Participants may draw first conclusions for their sales budgeting. International sales meetings are also used to announce and discuss organizational changes in the company, to introduce new managers, and to present new acquisitions.

↔ Development of new ideas. Creative workshops may develop new functions and designs of the marketer's products, improved methods of selling, new applications, more efficient sales outlets, better selling arguments, improved service delivery, and internal actions to be taken to improve total quality, information flow or customer service.

Whatever objective an international sales meeting is specifically dedicated to, a properly organized meeting has a highly motivating effect on all participants. The marketer, therefore, has to select the venue, date and topics of the sales meeting very carefully. Sometimes it might be best to have a meeting at the headquarters, for example when a new product is presented; sometimes the meeting should take place at an intermediary to honour its special efforts; for creative purposes a resort hotel with seminar facilities might be best, and sometimes the location of an important fair may be the right spot. The right date may be before a fair, the end of the company's financial year, the launch of a new international communication campaign or a change in top management.

IMPACT ON THE MARKETING MIX

International sales management is closely related to distribution. Depending on whether the marketer has decided to use an integrated or an independent distribution system, salespeople have to find potential customers or intermediaries, make them clients of the company, and establish a relationship with them as business partners. Most of the activities of channel partner search, motivation and control described in Chapter 14 are based on contributions by the company's sales force.

Sales management is also closely related to international market communication. Personal selling may even be considered as one of an international marketer's market communication tools. Because personal communication has the strongest impact of all communication tools available to a marketer, the messages sent to potential and existing customers through personal contacts have to be closely coordinated with all of the company's other communication efforts. Based on an integrated communication policy, the members of the sales force need to be continually trained in how to behave and what to transmit to the customers. If the company's sales force, either willingly or unconsciously, transmits a message to the customers that does not fit with what the marketer tries to communicate through public relations, advertising, sales promotion and other activities, a great deal of the firm's communication budget may be lost and potential customers may be confused.

On the other hand, the international sales force may be used as an information source on what impact market communication activities have on the target customers. Because of their direct personal contact with the customers, salespeople can report on immediate customer reactions. This is particularly important for customer and intermediary sales promotion activities. But as the example of Shell, the Rotterdam-based British-Dutch oil and chemicals company showed when it wanted to sink its Brent Spar oil platform in the North Sea, direct personal feedback about the impact of communication measures is also extremely valuable in situations where a crisis hits the international marketer.

If price is defined as all the perceived contributions a customer has to make in a business exchange in order to get a desired product, personal selling significantly influences the customers' perception of that price. Customers' 'contributions' may start at the point where they are supposed to accept a salesperson they do not know or even dislike. But the price may also be lowered by close personal relationships between a purchasing manager and the marketer's salesperson. Trust in the business partner not only lowers perceived risks, but also allows purchase decisions to be made based on less search effort. Other suppliers need to be evaluated from time to time, to make sure that product quality and the price charged by the preferred supplier are at a competitive level. But a positively valued long-term relationship with a supplier diminishes the process costs of the customer. That is, successful relationship management by its salespeople has a significant positive influence on the attractiveness of an international marketer's offers.

Finally, sales management also has an impact on the customers' perception of a firm's total product. Depending on how well the international marketer's sales force treats customers in pre- and after-sales activities, and how much they serve customers as trustworthy consultants in the attempt to continually improve the customers' business, the total product of the marketer is more or less beneficial to its customers. On the other hand, the more complex or quickly changing the international marketer's product, the more training of the sales force is needed to make it an efficient and effective tool in gaining customer interest and trust.

Summary

Building and sustaining positive relationships with target customers is the major task of international sales management. To coordinate diverse sales activities across country-markets, the company has first to develop an international sales policy. The sales policy is the guideline for decisions concerning personal selling, after-sales activities and the management of the firm's international sales force.

Personal selling is the most effective way to sell anything – any product in any market. The key to success in international personal selling is matching the seller's product, knowledge and culture with the buyer's needs, knowledge and culture. That is, even more than within a specific country-market, international personal selling must be individualized – the 'fit' between seller and buyer must be fully understood and carefully managed. But individualized communication is expensive. Therefore, finding and precisely selecting potential customers to whom to sell personally, is of great importance to international marketers.

The fastest and least expensive way to determine potential customers is to use available internal sources. These may be the market experience of salespeople and the creativity of company personnel activated by special ways of analysing the market. Enquiries by potential customers, invitations to tender, official authorities or private information providers may be further low-cost sources of information on potential customers.

When potential customers are defined, sales costs per successful business transaction can be reduced by carefully preparing sales calls and sales negotiations. First, the cultural elements which might influence the establishment of a contact, the negotiation process, and the development of a relationship should be reviewed. A customer database containing available information about existing and potential customers and the company's sales manual which contains information concerning the company's products and the customer benefits they provide help the sales force in preparing their sales calls. Thorough planning and organization of business trips can keep the cost per hour and per mile of travelling at an acceptable level compared to the number of successful sales calls per day.

Sales negotiations are viewed and carried out differently from one culture to another. It is important to know how to start a sales talk, how to address negotiation partners properly, how to react in case of disagreement, and how to make sure that agreement has been reached. Some general rules of how to structure sales negotiations may be followed across country-markets.

A properly formulated international offer may strongly contribute to effective and efficient personal selling. By presenting a written or verbal offer the international marketer invites a potential customer to sign a sales contract. When preparing a written offer the marketer has to consider which language to use, which legal regulations and local market usances to respect, which product specifications and applications as well as which terms of sale and delivery to offer, and for what period of validity the offer is binding. In addition, the structure of the offer may determine its attractiveness to the customer. After presenting the offer to the customer, the salesperson has to ensure an effective follow-up to close the contract.

After the customer has taken its buying decision, an international marketer interested in repeat purchases has to keep the customer satisfied with the product from its purchase to the end of its use or for as long as the customer keeps it in its product portfolio. A series of after-sales activities, from checking if the customer's order has been properly executed to the professional handling of customer complaints and eventual disputes, are important tasks of international sales management.

Finally, to ensure the efficiency of personal selling needed for international success, sales management has to recruit and select the best people for its specific purpose, and it has to develop its sales force, motivate them to reach ambitious goals and compensate them according to their performance. Close cooperation with market communication as well as distribution and logistics management will help to keep the international marketer's activities focused on reaching the intended global strategic position.

Discussion Questions

1. How do the distribution policy, the communication policy and the sales policy of an international marketer relate to each other? Discuss.
2. What tools can a salesperson use to determine the most promising potential customers in a newly served country-market? Compare those tools by indicating their specific advantages.
3. What does a salesperson need to do in preparing his/her first sales calls in a newly served country-market?
4. Illustrate the influence of cultural differences on the potential difficulties at the beginning of sales talks. How can an internationally operating firm support its sales force in adequate preparation to avoid such problems?
5. Explain the reasons why sales negotiations should follow a certain structure independent of the cultural environment in which they take place.
6. Take an example of a company you are familiar with and describe how in your opinion an international offer by that company should be structured. Illustrate the points by giving examples.
7. What is the role of salespeople in the handling of international customer complaints? Compare with local complaint handling systems.
8. What can an international marketer do to find the best qualified salespeople for its country-markets? Take an example of a firm you are familiar with and discuss the pros and cons of different types of action.
9. Contact an internationally operating firm and interview them about their international sales force development activities. Compare with the information gathered by your colleagues. What are your conclusions?
10. What are the major issues of sales force compensation in general and how are they complicated in an international business environment? Find an example of a company operating internationally and bring it to class for discussion.

Additional Readings

Andaleeb, S.S. and S.F. Anwar (1996) 'Factors Influencing Customer Trust in Salespersons in a Developing Country', *Journal of International Marketing*, 4(4), 35–52.

Bergadaa, M. (1997) 'Révolution Vente', Paris.

Biong, H. and F. Selnes (1996) 'The Strategic Role of the Salesperson in Established Buyer–Seller Relationships', *Journal of Business-to-Business Marketing*, 3(3), 39–78.

Claycomb, V. and G.L. Frankwick (1997) 'The Dynamics of Buyers' Perceived Costs During the Relationship Development Process', *Journal of Business-to-Business Marketing*, 4(1), 1–37.

Dubinsky, A.J., M. Kotabe, Ch.V. Lim and W. Wagner (1997) 'The Impact of Values on Salespeople's Job Responses: A Cross-National Investigation', *Journal of Business Research*, 39(3), July, 195–208.

Harvey, M. (1997) ' Dual-Career Expatriates: Expectations, Adjustments and Satisfaction with International Relocation', *Journal of International Business Studies*, 28(3), 627–657.

Rao, A. and K. Hashimoto (1996) 'Intercultural Influence: A Study of Japanese Expatriate Managers in Canada', *Journal of International Business Studies*, 27(3), 443–465.

Winkler, J. (1989) '*Bargaining for Results*', London: William Heinemann Ltd.

Notes

[1] European Union, Internet site – http://europa.eu.int/en/comm/dg23/guide_en/europart.htm
[2] European Union, Internet site – http://europa.eu.int/en/comm/dg23/guide_en/interpri.htm
[3] European Union, Internet site – http://europa.eu.int/en/comm/dg23/bre/bre.htm
[4] 'Patrick Choel quitte Unilever pour les Parfums Christian Dior', *Le Figaro économie*, 8 March 1996, p. II.
[5] Stallinger, B. (1995) 'Der teure Auslandseinsatz scheitert häufig an Integrationsproblemen', *Der Standard*, 25–26 March, p. 16.

CHAPTER 17

INTERNATIONAL MARKET COMMUNICATION

INTERNATIONAL INCIDENT

Häagen-Dazs

British Grand Metropolitain launched Häagen-Dazs in Europe in 1989 despite an economic recession, a tired, stagnant category, and established competitors. Unilever, Nestlé, Mars, and a great number of small but strong local ice-cream manufacturers – such as Schöller in Germany, Mövenpick in Switzerland, and Sagit in Italy – advertised extensively, had high levels of name recognition, and controlled the limited freezer space in European super-markets. In countries such as the UK, strong private labels held more than 40 per cent of the take-home market. And in addition, Häagen-Dazs was launched at a price 30 to 40 per cent higher than its closest competitors. How did it succeed?

The conventional way to introduce a new product such as Häagen-Dazs is to lead with a major advertising effort. But Grand Met chose a different route. It first opened several ice-cream parlors in prominent, affluent locations with heavy foot traffic. The cafélike stores, deliberately designed to contrast with the more traditional, sterile ice-cream parlors common in the US, made a statement about Häagen-Dazs. Additional approaches were pursued to fuel word-of-mouth communications: branded freezers in food retail stores; sponsorship of cultural events; and a relatively low-budget print media campaign with the theme The Ultimate Experience in Personal Pleasure.

Linking the brand to arts sponsorship was a particularly savvy move. At one event, the Opera Factory's production of Don Giovanni in London, the ice cream was even incorporated into the show. When the Don called for sorbet, he received a container of Häagen-Dazs. A windfall of free publicity, begun and spread among target consumers.

Grand Met's brand building efforts in Europe were extremely successful. Häagen-Dazs brand awareness in the UK, for example, reached more than 50 per cent within a few months. European sales of the product went from USD10 million in 1990 to USD130 million in 1994. Today the brand commands one-third of the market for top-of-the-line ice cream even though it continues to charge a hefty premium over competitive brands.

Source: Joachimsthaler, E. and D.A. Aaker (1997) 'Building Brands Without Mass Media', *Harvard Business Review*, January–February, 39–50.

INTERNATIONAL MARKET COMMUNICATION

Visibility to potential customers and important stakeholders is very important for marketing success all over the world. People, wherever they live, tend to react positively to companies and products they know about, even if they have never had personal contact with them. Mere visibility can signal reliability, superior quality, and leadership. In the USA, for example, many consumers believe that nationally advertised products are better than only locally advertised competitors. When it comes to a buying decision, the products, brands and service-providing firms that come to the decision makers' minds first have the highest probability of being chosen. Therefore, communicating effectively with its potential and existing customers in the served markets is an extremely important task for every international marketer.

Visibility is important, but not enough. It can be accompanied by negative emotions because of unpleasant experiences or negative word of mouth. Visibility can also be achieved by competitors. In most international markets the marketer will encounter competitors' products that have been on the market for a substantial amount of time and with which customers have extended experience. To make those customers first try the new offer and then change to the new way of satisfying their needs, the international marketer will need to communicate additional benefits of its products to the customers. Therefore, attractive differentiation from competitive offers is a second major task of international market communication.

Potential customers are not the only audience to be addressed by a company's market communication. In every international market the company serves, there are other stakeholders who have an interest in or are concerned by what the company is doing and how it does it. Suppliers, intermediaries, capital owners, legal regulators and administrators, media, unions, or neighbours of the company's production sites all have their specific expectations concerning the company's activities. Depending on the level of satisfaction of those expectations, the local stakeholders will either promote the company, let it work, or use their power to counteract the international marketer's plans and activities. Effective communication with those stakeholders is of crucial importance to their reactions.

The international marketer basically has the same communication tools at its disposal as its local counterparts. However, public relations, advertising, sales promotion, sponsoring, and direct communication need additional international coordination. This chapter, therefore, will first focus on the need to develop general market communication objectives and guidelines for all parts of an internationally operating firm (Figure 17.1). The integration of all market communication activities – international and local – to achieve the intended global strategic position of the company, the intended position of its business units and products in the stakeholders' minds, will be an issue that runs through the entire chapter.

Based on an integrated international market communication concept, communication activities aimed at the various stakeholders that are important to the company's success in the served markets may be planned and executed. Because of its broad range of target audiences, the chapter will first discuss international public relations, before it focuses on advertising, sales promotion, sponsoring and some frequently used tools in international direct market communication. The most important direct communication tool used in the establishment and maintenance of personal relationships with all kinds of company stakeholders, traditionally known as 'personal selling', has already been discussed in Chapter 16.

Integrated Market Communication

The major objective of every marketer in its many different efforts to communicate with the various stakeholders of the company is to achieve the intended strategic position of the company, the intended position of its business units

Figure 17.1 INTERNATIONAL MARKET COMMUNICATION

The international marketer needs to develop an internationally integrated market communication concept as a basis for all communication activities aimed at various groups of stakeholders in different country-markets.

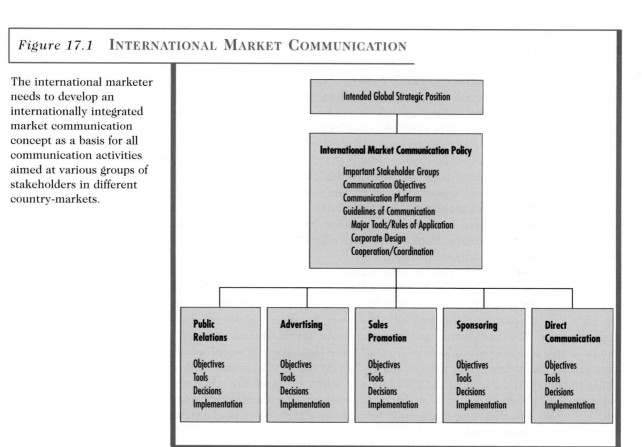

and its products in the stakeholders' minds. To reach that general objective the marketer needs to counteract the tendency to information overload of its target audiences, to ease their processes of recognition and learning, and to clearly differentiate the firm and its products from competitors while holding the costs of market communication activities as low as possible. Examples of internationally successful companies show that those goals can best be reached if all market communication activities are coordinated to achieve consistency. That is, any communicative efforts of the company should be consistent and supportive of its corporate, business unit or brand identity (see Strategy box).

For example, after some trial and error in the early phase of product launch, SMH, the Swiss marketer of Swatch watches, made sure that Swatch messages were driven by the core identity of the brand: a low-cost watch of excellent Swiss quality with a stylish, fun, youthful, provocative and joyful brand personality. For its launch in Germany, Japan and Spain, the company hung giant 165–metre 'watches' from city skyscrapers. In New York City, the company organized the Swatch Break-Dancing Championship. In London, it sponsored Andrew Logan's Alternative Miss World show, and in Paris, a street painting contest. Whatever the company did, the stakeholders immediately recognized that it had to do with Swatch.[1]

Market Communication Policy. To ensure consistency in all communicative activities of the firm, those activities need to be integrated. That is, based

Body Shop's

Self-consistency

THE BODY SHOP'S CORE BRAND IDENTITY IS IN ESSENCE its profits-with-a-principle philosophy. This philosophy sends a clear message to employees and customers alike. Consider how the company – in spite of the criticisms of its detractors – 'walks the walk' in terms of developing programmes reflecting the intended meaning of the brand. The company opposes testing on animals, helps less industrially developed economies through its Trade, Not Aid mission, contributes to rain forest preservation efforts, is active in women's issues, and sets an example for recycling. It participates in Save the Whales rallies, advocates for other endangered species, and supports the development of alternative energy sources.

These efforts are not ancillary to the Body Shop brand; they are the brand. And the vision carries right through the customers' in-store experience. Enter a Body Shop, and you are greeted by a clerk who not only wears a Body Shop T-shirt bearing a social message but also believes in the company's causes, values, and products. Displayed among the store's goods and tester samples are posters and colorful handouts (printed on recycled paper) that provide information about the products, about social causes the company supports, and about how customers can get involved in rallies, social-cause advocacy groups, and the like.

Compare the Body Shop's brand identity with those of its competitors. Most skin care and cosmetic lines are indistinguishable, focusing on similar product attributes and health-and-beauty promises. And their customers are not involved with even their favorite brands – except to make a transaction or to receive a broadcast-style advertising message. Clearly, the Body Shop has transformed the skin care and cosmetics experience into something more than it has ever been.

Source: Joachimsthaler, E. and D.A. Aacker (1997) 'Building Brands Without Mass Media', *Harvard Business Review*, January–February, 39–50.

on the intended global strategic position, the international marketer has to develop an international market communication policy. Such a policy development process starts with the determination of the firm's most important **stakeholder groups** in the product- and country-markets served. Then, for each of the stakeholder groups, **general communication objectives** can be fixed. They answer the question of what the company needs to achieve by communicating with each of the stakeholder groups in order to reach the intended position in their minds. For example, what should customers, intermediaries, suppliers, media and administrators perceive in order for the company to reach its intended position as the quality leader in its market?

The following development of an **international communication platform** is the centre-piece of an integrated communication policy. The communication platform defines the central message to be communicated to all stakeholders of the firm. For example, Avis, the US-based international rental car company, has chosen the central message 'We try harder', and EXXON uses the symbol of a tiger to visually represent its central message to the stakeholders. This central message needs to be refined into consistent core messages for each stakeholder group. For example, 'We try harder' may translate into the promise of complete international service for customers and excellent personal relations with media.

To coordinate the transfer of the core messages into a consistent choice of communication tools, the **major tools** the marketer wants to be applied in its international market communication also have to be determined. The choice will depend on the contribution each communication tool can make to reaching the stated objectives and how those tools can be used in a way that mutually increases the effects of others. For example, when Paris-based Cartier International, the marketer of prestigious jewellery and accessories, decides to sponsor an international artist, this artist could also be used in testimonial advertisements, and press and other media reports about the artist and his or her sponsored shows could be launched.

In addition, to ensure consistency of the firm's international communication activities, a guideline concerning **corporate design** has to be developed. It determines the logo, sign, colour(s), music, size and type of writing, layout of printed matter or even lighting to be used internationally. The example of the new Louis Vuitton North America headquarters in New York City shows that even a company's buildings can contribute to the communication of corporate identity. The building, planned by Christian de Portzamparc who won the Pritzker prize (the 'Nobel Prize of architecture') in 1994, expresses the extravagance of the firm, by using special materials, different fluorescent front lighting and a front that looks entirely different from the neighbouring buildings.

Finally, the international marketer has to specify some rules of cooperation and coordination concerning the implementation of market communication decisions. Those rules should help to overcome functional differences as well as the creative egoism of organizational subunits at different hierarchical levels, and help to prevent the dominance of short-term sales goals. The rules will also state to what extent and in what role external service providers such as advertising agencies are to be involved in the planning and execution of the communication activities.

Level of Market Communication Integration.   Not every international marketer needs a high level of integration of its market communication. The appropriate level of integration to be achieved depends on how important an internationally standardized identity is to the success of a company and its products. Total products with widespread international presence which are intended to have a similar identity across country-markets need the highest degree of integration of market communication. The management of global brands, such as Swatch, Windows, Hilton or Caterpillar, to cite a few examples, need to coordinate their various communication activities closely to achieve the intended position in their customers' and other important stakeholders' minds.

At the other extreme, a company operating internationally may market purely local products which do not have any external signs in common, such as the brand name, the logo or the package. Such products do not need any integration of their communication activities. In such cases, integration needs only arise from the goal of achieving the intended general position of the firm in the minds of customers and other important stakeholders. But even market communication for an entirely localized product may profit from some central coordination. When it comes to cross-market learning, for example, local managers may have an advantage over competitors if they are informed about successful communication activities in other local markets. The level of integration is restricted to fast and targeted transfer of information.

ETHICS BOX

Big Tobacco Takes the Biscuit

BY SCAVENGING THROUGH VARIOUS MEDICAL JOURNALS, Philip Morris, the world's largest cigarette company, has pulled together figures for the 'relative risk' of such apparently innocuous activities as eating pepper or drinking chlorinated water. In a series of advertisements Philip Morris trumpeted its findings in the European press, pointing out, for instance, that eating a biscuit a day raises the chance of coronary heart disease in women by 49 per cent; by contrast, living with a smoker (and breathing second-hand smoke) increases your risk of lung cancer by 19 per cent. Indeed, 'exposure to second-hand cigarette smoke' finishes well down the firm's list of everyday hazards.

There is nothing wrong with Philip Morris's figures. The 'biscuit risk' is based on a 1993 study by epidemiologists at Harvard University of the effects of hydrogenated oils; the 'second-hand smoke risk' is based on a study by the US Environmental Protection Agency. All Philip Morris (officially) wants to show is that increasing a very small risk by even 49 per cent still leaves it very small. Most epidemiologists treat increases in small risks of less than 100 per cent with scepticism, given the 'noise' of other poorly understood factors that affect disease.

France's biscuit makers see it differently. The Syndicat National de la Biscuiterie Française sued Philip Morris, claiming that the ads contravene France's laws against comparative advertising and against advertising cigarettes. A civil court in Paris took their side and banned the ads. Philip Morris will be fined USD 195,000 every time the ad appears in France. Company officials were said to be 'shocked' about the banning of a campaign which was conceived 'in the public interest'; and it appealed against the French decision. The question is, are not all these activities mounted to draw attention away from the really indisputable danger of cigarettes: first-hand smoke.

Source: 'Big tobacco takes the biscuit', *The Economist*, 29 June 1996, p. 62.

In any case, when it comes to the implementation of specific local communication activities, local managers or service providers will have to take responsibility. For any of the major communication tools discussed in the following section, therefore, the international marketer will have to decide how they should best be implemented. As a general rule, contradictory company and product communication as well as local communication activities that upset other local activities in neighbouring country-markets should be avoided; and the transfer of effective campaign designs to other markets should be encouraged.

PUBLIC RELATIONS

Public relations is the planned building and maintenance of communicative relations between a company and its stakeholders with the objective of establishing a positively valued identity of the company in those stakeholders' perceptions. A public relations manager designs and executes programmes which help earn and maintain stakeholders' understanding and acceptance of the company and its activities. The Ethics box contains an example of how difficult such an attempt may be. The ability to influence those stakeholders is very important in international marketing. Depending on the stakeholder group to be addressed, specific objectives will be defined and different public relations tools will be applied.

Investor Relations

Investor relations activities have the objective of establishing and maintaining the trust of (potential) investors in the way the company is led by its management. The more favourably the financial community views the company, the lower the interest rate the company may be charged when it borrows money to finance its international expansion, and the higher its stocks may be valued. This may be one of the reasons why top management of the USD21 billion delivery giant United Parcel Service of America Inc. (UPS) headquartered in Atlanta, Georgia is worried that the industry and freight customers around the world regard the company as a wallflower – while its flashy rival, Federal Express Corp., acts like the belle of the ball. UPS invests billions of dollars to build distribution systems in Europe and Asia where it does not have the kind of corporate identity enjoyed at home. But even in its home market UPS is no more than Big Brown to most customers. To remain competitive in an increasingly global business with very thin margins, the company needs recognition as the kind of dynamic, technologically nimble concern that customers now demand and the Wall Street financing required to satisfy them. As one of the company's leading managers puts it, however, 'until a few years ago, the requirements for being a public-relations person at UPS were how many ways you could say, "No comment"'. These days, UPS is talking. The company is opening up to journalists in a busy effort to build public profil. UPS began releasing quarterly earnings over a public business wire. In summer of 1996, the company agreed to a coming-out party at a hotel in suburban Chicago. Top UPS executives took public questions about the company's operations from financial analysts, investors and industry consultants. And also in 1996, UPS sponsored the Olympic Games in Atlanta.[2]

The tools most often used in international investor relations are financial reports, documentation concerning the company's strategy, product innovation and market achievements, site visits, and 'road shows' for financial analysts as well as major investors. With the global spread of the Internet, Web sites have gained in attractiveness.

Government Relations

A company's government relations activities should help to create and maintain a local regulatory and administrative environment that helps the firm to do business. The best basis for satisfactory relationships with local governments and administrations is the fulfilment of their rules and regulations. In addition, continual information on the latest technological standards as well as some technology transfer, investments in local infrastructure, donations or endowments may help to ease market entry as well as ongoing business. Microsoft, for example, learned that being a 'good citizen' can be very helpful for developing business in China. When it opened its Beijing office in 1992, the company

Picture 17.1 WOLFORD'S LADY SUPPORT AND FORMING RANGE

planned to use its Taiwan operations to supply a Mandarin-language version of Windows designed especially for the mainland's simplified characters. But the Electronics Industry Ministry resented the fact that Microsoft was relying on the mainland's rival for such sophisticated work. Bill Gates got a frosty reception in Beijing when he personally started the launch of P-Win, the Chinese version of Windows, in 1994. The Chinese electronics industry threatened to ban Chinese Windows, and President Jiang Zemin personally admonished Gates to spend more time in China and 'learn something from 5000 years of Chinese history'. In the meantime, Bill Gates not only took an extended vacation in China, but Microsoft has set up training institutes at the Chinese Academy of Social Sciences, three universities, and more than 70 centres. It employs 32 full-time Chinese instructors, trained in the USA, who teach computer architecture, networking and client–server applications. In addition, the company has become affiliated with Chinese researchers to develop technology in such areas as interactive television and Chinese handwriting and speech recognition. Windows is now officially 'endorsed' by the government.[3]

Not unlike many other relations, personal relationships built on some kind of trust may play a major role in government relations. Large internationally operating firms, therefore, hire lobbyists in the capitals of the most industrially developed countries or regions of the world such as Washington DC, Tokyo or Brussels, in order to help ensure favourable treatment in national or trade organization laws. In less democratically developed countries, members of the ruling establishment are paid for their roles as 'intermediaries' in making contacts or easing the negotiation of sales contracts.

Media Relations

Relations with print or electronic mass media, trade journals and magazines have the objective of keeping journalists directly informed about developments inside and 'around' the company and about its products, and by that means to indirectly inform members of the 'general public' who may be interested in that information but cannot be directly reached by the company. Media relations are mainly cultivated by personal contacts, press releases, press conferences and press events. Such relations generate 'free' exposure in the print and broadcast media, because the marketer does not pay for the media time or space. But obtaining the type of publicity expected requires careful preparation by staff or an outside agency, and that costs money. When entering a country-market for the first time, or when introducing a significantly different product into a market, a company may be able to generate considerable publicity. When the activity is less 'newsworthy', it is up to the public relations manager to make it interesting for the media.

For example, when Wolford, the Austrian tights manufacturer, introduced its new 'Support and Forming Range', ladies' tights and bodies which help women to have slimmer thighs and present their body more attractively, they saved at least an estimated USD500,000 of advertising budget by hiring Helmuth Newton, one of the most well-known photo artists in the world, to shoot ten pictures of models wearing those products (see Picture 17.1). The pictures were exclusively (for about 12 days) sent to one major medium per country in Western Europe, Hong Kong, Japan and the USA, together with a story of how those pictures were taken. The media reported cost free on two to six pages showing the pictures with the new products and the name of Wolford. This way, 8.4 million readers all over the world were exposed to the information. The pictures (including all rights for the entire world for five years) had cost the company no more than about USD300,000. At the end of the period, exclusive information and pictures were given to other media which were highly interested, and the same pictures were used for packages and displays.

Other ways to make company or product information 'newsworthy' are to 'wrap' them into special events for selected journalists or for a specifically defined group of target customers. For example, haute couture presentations employing world-famous models are regularly arranged by fashion houses such as French Christian Dior, Italian Ferrucio Ferragamo or US Donna Karan. Despite their regularity they are spectacular enough to attract journalists from all important fashion media as well as from television channels which report the shows globally. This publicity is very important for the marketers because their main sales do not come from haute couture. They all have prêt-à-porter product lines which are sold to the more affluent consumers all over the world, as well as perfume, accessories and other product lines which they sell either themselves or through licensing. But the image put across by the media reports about the haute couture presentations strongly influences those sales.

A problem with publicity is that because it is 'free', the international marketer loses some control over what is said about the company or product, how it is said, and where it is said. Thus, instead of having the ability to affect reach and frequency directly, a company is at the mercy of the media in terms of how much exposure it receives. Additionally, the media may edit the material in a manner which is not necessarily favourable towards the marketer or its products – 1995, for example, will stay a year that executives at Royal/Dutch Shell Group based, in Rotterdam and London, would like to forget. A bad slip in earnings was at least partly provoked by a media campaign in the spring that led to consumer boycotts of the firm's European retail outlets and forced Shell to back down on plans to dump its defunct Brent Spar drilling rig in the North Sea. In the autumn, Shell again got in the line of fire from activists backed by the media who wanted the company to get out of Nigeria following the execution of nine dissidents after what neutral observers called a sham trial. Shell found it difficult to claim the moral high ground in Nigeria. The company had to admit causing some environmental damage, and it had to concede that oil money rarely makes it back to needy communities. But because Nigeria accounts for about 14 per cent of Shell's crude-oil production and some USD130 million in operating earnings, Shell officials in major capitals around the world used all of their personal contacts to dissuade ministers from organizing an oil boycott. Shell also met with stock analysts, assuring them that the Nigerian operation's future was secure.[4]

For companies which have been seen as successfully dealing with crises provoked by events that the company in particular may consider outside its control, a clear crisis management plan is essential. Such a public relations plan should be in place and understood by all personnel concerned, before the crisis hits. For example, critical media who will share the public's reaction to the disaster must have been pre-identified. Preferably, the company will have established good working relationships with these media in advance. Secondly, key stakeholder groups will have been identified. There too, campaigns to regain trust and positive image will need to be undertaken. Speed of reaction is also critical. All of this depends, of course, upon a contingency plan which is fully developed, and shared.

Customer Relations

A company's relations with its customers and intermediaries are strongly influenced by personal contacts as well as by various types of non-personal market communication activities. The role of public relations is to prepare the ground for other communication tools by creating a generally positive perception of the company and its products. In an environment of credibility and trust, advertising messages have a greater chance of being effective and sales personnel have a greater chance of being listened to. For that purpose, business and research reports, customer magazines and brochures, direct mailings, telephone calls, documentary films, and teaching materials for schools can be used as media. More personal contacts may be established during site visits by customers or intermediaries. Reception and showrooms as well as events also serve the purpose of establishing personal contacts.

Personnel Relations

Personnel relations as part of a company's public relations have a twofold purpose. On the one hand, its activities should help to develop a kind of corporate identity in the minds of the company's personnel. People working for the international marketer should feel part of a social entity, different from others in a way that is attractive to them. On the other hand, personnel relations have an objective of projecting an attractive picture of the company, its products and activities to potential members of the workforce outside the firm. They should help to attract personnel with the level of qualification needed to ensure the future success of the firm.

In an internationally operating company, personnel relations may play a major role in the success of a company. A brochure that introduces new members of the organization to the corporate mission, the business domain and the major objectives of the firm in combination with some personal introduction to the most important 'rules of the game' given by a personal coach may help in socializing new entrants. An international company magazine, such as *Unilever Magazine* or *HILTI International*, can help to make employees all over the globe feel that they are part of an entity worth working for. Personal letters explaining extraordinary developments, such as new investments or the move of production units to other locations, as well as office outings, company ceremonies and financial participation in medical aid and retirement programmes, serve the purpose of increasing the attachment and identification of personnel with the company. So do company visits by family members of personnel.

Company presentations at schools and universities, participation in the financing of local infrastructure, such as kindergartens, ambulance services or housing, or financial involvement in local research or development programmes may help to attract the necessary personnel. Companies that directly invest in production sites in China, for example, may find it much easier to get qualified personnel in sufficient numbers when housing can be provided. Computer firms, such as IBM, have invested heavily in local university infrastructures to gain high visibility with students and to be interesting enough to attract the best job applicants.

The international marketer has to keep in mind, however, that the perception of such personnel relations activities by local groups of the company's existing and potential personnel is very much culture bound. A company ceremony which might be perfectly appropriate in the USA may be rejected as ridiculous in France and be disastrous for the local company's hierarchical structure in Pakistan. A company magazine, for example, has a very limited effect in a country were many of the workers in the factory are illiterate.

Implementing International Public Relations

A company's stakeholders may vary from one product- and country-market to another. So do those stakeholders' expectations concerning the company's behaviour and outcomes. Effective public relations activities, therefore, are mostly local in nature. They can be planned and executed in cooperation with local or international public relations agencies. In Europe, the trend of large internationally operating companies is to handle public relations themselves, with recourse to agencies mainly for back-up. At ABB, the Swiss-Swedish energy and construction giant, for example, the company's in-house public relations managers hire agencies with local market knowledge to ensure a better impact for each campaign.

International public relations agencies have followed their clients in the internationalization of business. For example, Shandwick, the world's largest independent public relations group, has 70 offices worldwide. Most of those offices, as well as those of the major international competitors, US-based Hill & Knowlton and Burson Marsteller, are concentrated in the more economically developed countries. In the EU, 80 per cent of existing public relations agencies are small to medium-sized, with fewer than 15 employees. Since 1992 cross-border associations of such smaller companies have multiplied. EuroPR, for example, is a network of nine agencies in the UK, Belgium, Denmark, Finland, France, Germany, Italy, Spain and Sweden. The constituent companies share a common expertise in information technology, and serve computer, software and communications clients.

Because the number of international media and the international mobility of many members of a company's local stakeholder groups are increasing, internationally operating firms need to coordinate their local public relations campaigns. A public relations policy must be developed that states some basic guidelines to be followed by local managers and agencies. In addition, the installation of a central public relations coordinator becomes increasingly important. This person has to initiate and lead the development process of an international public relations policy. Such a process would bring together managers responsible for public relations in the most important markets of the firm and local representatives of the public relations agency/network of agencies in those major markets to determine the guidelines to be followed throughout the firm and the major public relations tools to be used.

The public relations coordinator also has to ensure the consistency of local public relations activities, to stimulate the exchange of information and experience about successful campaigns throughout the company, and to coach local managers responsible for public relations through advice, feedback and training. Such a coordinator has to develop a company-wide monitoring system to compare the effectiveness and efficiency of public relations activities undertaken. And finally, this person is the company's public relations representative in a market communication team that ensures the consistency of the firm's market communications mix.

Advertising

Advertising is the paid communication of company messages through impersonal media. Like local marketers, an internationally operating firm uses advertising mainly to stimulate potential customers' interest in its products, to make those products reach an intended position in the (potential) customers' minds, and to continually remind the customers of the benefits to be gained by buying and using the product, thereby preparing the ground for positive buying decisions by the customers. Basically, an international marketer has to take the same kinds of decisions concerning its advertising activities as local competitors. An advertising policy must be developed, an advertising message and media chosen, and the message implemented in visual and/or verbal advertising copy.

When developing an international advertising campaign, the marketer, in addition, has to decide which parts of the campaign to standardize across country-markets and which parts to adapt locally. Besides influences from cultural differences, the availability of media in the targeted country-markets and legal restrictions on advertising in those markets need to be considered. The international marketer also has to decide how much of the advertising planning and execution should be done in-house, versus in cooperation with or entirely outsourced to one or more advertising agencies. Finally, the implementation of the planned advertising activities across all parts of the internationally operating company needs to be organized.

Standardization versus Adaptation

When deliberating the level of standardization of its international advertising campaigns, a marketer should not only look at the potential cost savings inherent in a high degree of standardization. The intended position of the product to be advertised in the target customers' minds and the psychological processes leading to that positioning must have a more prominent influence on the decision. Standardization may only concern the content of the advertising message, leaving advertising copy and media choice to local decision makers. But it may also concern the media used as well as the advertising copy.

Levels of Standardization. Depending on a product's intended position in the customers' minds and the target audience, the optimal level of standardization may range from complete standardization to complete localization. For example, Procter & Gamble used an entirely standardized campaign worldwide to advertise its Pringles potato chips (Figure 17.2). They used television as the medium and the ad – the rap-music theme, the young people dancing around, the tag line, 'Once you pop, you can't stop' – was the same all across the served country-markets.[5] Such a very high degree of standardization was possible because the target audience was rather young (and open to international, less local culture-specific appeals) and the positioning was independent of local preferences.

When Guerlain, a subsidiary of the French luxury products group LVMH, launched their new perfume 'Champs-Elysées', in an endeavour to increase the company's international visibility, they used almost as standardized an advertising approach. In a TV spot Sophie Marceau, a French movie star who

Picture 17.2 WONDERBRA ADS IN THE UK AND IN FRANCE

Figure 17.2 BLUEPRINT OF THE PRINGLES TV COMMERCIAL

has a strong attraction for Asian consumers, particularly Japanese, was shown on the globally known Parisian boulevard bearing the product's name. Only the language used in the sound track of the spot was adapted to the countries where the spot was aired. In this case the target group was not so young as to accept culturally 'foreign' appeals easily, but the message cues used were simple to interpret and attractive enough to be voluntarily accepted by the target audience.

At the other extreme, Nestlé, based in Vevey, Switzerland, used an entirely adapted advertising approach when introducing Nescafé to Thailand in 1987. Because selling a hot beverage in the tropics seemed to be the marketing equivalent of selling snow to Eskimos, the local managers decided to give up the traditional Western taste, aroma and stimulation message for advertising coffee on TV. Instead, the new ads played on the increasing urban stress, showing a man kicking a taxi door in frustration. The campaign promoted coffee as a way to relax from the pressures of the traffic, the office, and even romance. Within Nestlé, the switch caused a ruckus. The zone manager for Asia stalked out of a screening of the first TV ad of the campaign. But the local group still had authority for Thailand and held firm. Coffee sales in Thailand jumped from USD25 million in 1987 to USD100 million in 1994, when Nescafé held 80 per cent of the market.[6] An adaptation of the advertising message and copy was needed in this case, because the target audience as well as the intended meaning of the product to those customers was different compared to other parts of the world. The medium could be kept similar because it was

Figure 17.3 FRAMES OF REFERENCE INFLUENCING INTERNATIONAL
COMMUNICATION EFFECTIVENESS

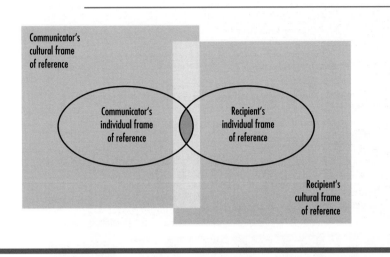

The communicator and the recipient both have their individual frames of reference for the interpretation of informational cues. In international communication those individual frames of references additionally are embedded in different cultural frames of reference. Effective communication can only occur if there are at least some common meanings concerning the communication object.

available in the country-market and reached the targeted audience.

In most cases the level of advertising standardization lies in between the two extremes. When the visual used in an ad transfers similar and acceptable meanings to the target audiences in the served markets and the media is appropriate in all markets to be served, only the text of the advertisement may need some adaptation. For example, Wonderbra ads (see Picture 17.2) all over Europe used the same series of visuals, but adapted tag lines. In the UK, for example, it read: 'Look me in the eyes and tell me that you love me', whereas in France it was: 'Regardez-moi dans les yeux . . . j'ai dit les yeux' (Look into my eyes . . . I said, into my eyes).

Adaptations of Advertising Copy.   Concerning the psychological processes involved in advertising communication, the international marketer must be aware that a communicator cannot directly transmit any message to its target audience. The communicator can only present informational cues selected in a way that will, hopefully, evoke the intended information in the minds of its target audience. The information itself is produced in the recipients' minds through interpretation of (selectively) received cues. What message the members of the target audience receive by interpreting the cues depends on the cognitions activated by the communicator. What cognitions are evoked depends on the recipients' individual frames of reference which have developed through socialization and individual experience. Effective communication requires that the communicator and the communicants share some common set of meanings concerning the communication object or at least that the communicator has enough knowledge about the cognitive structures of its target audience to be able to tailor its informational cues specifically (see Figure 17.3). If a shared set of meanings does not exist or cannot be

Picture 17.3   Billboards in the Streets of Ho Chi Min – City

established, the communicator will not be able to transmit its message to the target audience.

People who have been raised in the same cultural environment tend to have at least some common frame of reference. In international marketing the situation is further complicated by the fact that very often communicator and recipients have different cultural frames of reference. Because their interpretation is related to personal experiences and socialization, the meanings evoked by pictures are as culture specific as the meanings evoked by words. For example, DIM had great success when advertising their tights brand Diam in France showing a female torero encircled by male Minotaurs. French consumers – females and males alike – liked the perceived sexy touch of the message. But in Spain, the firm had to replace the ad in order not to offend Spanish machismo.[7] Therefore, the advertiser must find objects, persons and contexts by which the intended meanings may be evoked in the target customers' minds.

When the same meaning needs to be evoked in the minds of customers from different cultural backgrounds, an adaptation in visuals and text may be needed. For example, Reims-based Moet & Chandon wanted to make their target customers perceive their product as a piece of art comparable to a garment of a famous fashion house, in order to differentiate their champagne from a number of less prestigious brands also produced in the region of France called Champagne. For that purpose the company used print ads in the UK which compared their product with a classical garment. In France they also chose print ads but with a baroque garment for comparison, and in Italy they compared their product with a sensuous garment worn by a 'signora' (lady).[8]

An international marketer who wants to find out if the same visual and text cues may be used across all or a group of targeted cuntry-markets may want to check the correspondence of the meanings of those cues to the target audiences in the served markets. With the help of word association tests or in-depth interviews, the international marketer can determine the cognitions activated by an advertisement (or parts of it). The comparison of those cognitions across country-market target audiences allows an index of mutual relatedness to be calculated, that is, a measure of convergence among the audiences' cognitive structures. If the cognitions evoked by an ad in the target audiences across country-markets converge satisfactorily, a standardized use of the advertisement is feasible. If not, adaptations in text and/or visuals need to be made (see Culture box).

Media.　The possibility of implementing a more or less standardized advertising copy across country-markets also depends on the availability and cost of adequate local media. Media availability may be restricted in international markets. Whereas in some industrially less developed countries advertising in print media or television is limited to a very small number of available media, in higher industrially developed areas of the world legal restrictions, already discussed in Chapter 4, may reduce the number of media available to the marketer. In most countries of the EU, for example, there are limitations on the number and length of television commercials that may be broadcast on public television channels. On these channels commercials are normally broadcast in blocks between shows, not within the shows themselves. Only the development of private channels and satellite TV has begun to change that situation. In Australia only ads that have been produced in Australia or with Australian actors are accepted for airing on broadcast media. In South Africa telvision time must be purchased one year in advance.

Faced with the lack of media traditionally used in their home markets, international advertisers must try other options such as advertising in cinemas, in public transportation devices, on trucks and cabs or on billboards. Fuji

Full Steam Ahead for Diesel

Sumo wrestlers kissing. A row of chimpanzees giving the fascist salute. Inflatable naked dolls at a board meeting with a hugely obese CEO. Parents advised that 'teaching kids to kill helps them deal directly with reality'. When it comes to outrageous advertising, Italy's Renzo Rosso, the owner and CEO of Molvena-based Diesel, Europe's hottest marketer of blue jeans in the middle of the 1990s, wrote the book. From just USD 9 million in sales in 1985, Diesel increased its sales of jeans, sweat shirts, and T-shirts to USD 350 million in 1995, while profits reached USD 35 million.

European teens love the ads and the apparel, which is reminiscent of the 1960s and commands high prices: Jeans start at USD 89. Renzo Rosso wants to use the same formula to push up annual US sales from USD 15 million in 1995 to about USD 100 million by 1999. He plans to widen distribution by opening some 100 directly owned Diesel stores. In March 1996, the first Diesel megastore in the US, a cavernous two-story showcase replete with a coffee bar and full-time deejay, was inaugurated on New York's Lexington Avenue. The grand opening included miniskirted models dancing in the windows and an all-night party for 2,000 people.

Diesel's ad tactics could be a problem in the US, however. Its prankish campaigns have not always had the desired effect among politically correct or puritanical Americans. In 1993, the company had to withdraw from the US a series of satirical ads that applauded smoking and gun ownership with slogans such as: '145 cigarettes a day will give you that sexy cough and win you new friends.' Despite that lesson, Diesel is still running unorthodox advertising on MTV and in publications such as *Wired, Rolling Stone, Vibe, Details*, and the gay magazine *Out* which – from Renzo Rosso's point of view – reflect the essence of Diesel's irreverent youth culture.

Source: Sansoni, S. (1996) 'Full Steam Ahead for Diesel', *Business Week*, 29 April, p. 58.

Photo Film of Japan, for example, has replaced the blood-red billboards that once trumpeted the thoughts of Chairman Mao high above Shanghai's famous waterfront, the Bund, by its green logo. In Europe, bus tickets, supermarket till rolls and phone cards are used to advertise. Polygram Records has promoted new albums on the back of bus tickets in the UK. Joop! Jeans is one of the more visible companies using advertisements on and in taxi cabs in the EU. In Istanbul, Turkey, public buses are covered completely by an advertisement. Pepsi, Master Card and M&M/Mars, for example, have found this to be a very cost-effective way to reach large audiences;[9] and Calvin Klein Cosmetics's own in-house US advertising agency CRK, as a final example, has used buses, bus shelters, billboards, trams in Italy and the metro in Paris to launch its fragrance CK: ONE.

Sometimes the problem is too many media choices rather than too few. A country-wide advertising campaign using newspapers in India, for example, would require the purchase of space in about a hundred major papers. Because only the relatively wealthy, and well educated, buy newspapers in India, the marketer would not only face considerable problems of scheduling and possible overlap, but could still miss an important portion of the target audience.

Besides the lack of traditionally used media, another difficulty encountered in some country-markets is the inability to generate sufficient frequency (of advertising contacts). Frequency is, of course, important in making potential customers aware of the availability of the product, and what the product might do for them. Media in international markets vary considerably in their ability to contact the target audiences as often as the international marketer would like. Legal restrictions on buying advertising time or space, or on the total time and space which may be allocated to advertising, limit the number of times an advertiser may use specific media. However, compared to highly industrialized countries where customers are bombarded by hundreds of advertisements per day, audiences in other markets may not need such high frequency rates to still have effective advertising contacts. There, owing to the relatively low number of ads, the lower frequency might be at least partially offset by the increased likelihood that customers pay more attention to the ads.

Problems of frequency and reach may be overcome in markets where the targeted audiences have access to and use international media. For example, since media and telecommunications industries were deregulated in most Latin American countries, the pay TV market has grown very rapidly, given that there is considerable room for growth left in the cable TV market. Nearly 90 per cent of Latin American households had a TV set at the end of 1993, but only 16 per cent were hooked up to cable (Figure 17.4).

Table 17.1 shows the number of households possessing TV sets and radios in some of the major Asian markets.

The number and availability of international media for advertising purposes is increasing quickly. MTV, for example, reaches young target groups in more than 70 countries. MTV Latino has launched 40 new cable systems in Latin America, covering a total of more than 5 million homes across all countries in South America in 1995. CNN, as another example, reaches information-conscious customers in all parts of the world. It has decided to regionalize some of its news to become even more internationally attractive. For target audiences of industrial buyers and more highly educated consumers, newspapers and magazines providing international editions may be a potential choice. *The Wall Street Journal*, for example, publishes American, Asian and European editions; so do US-based magazines like *Newsweek*, *Reader's Digest* and the German *Wirtschaftswoche*.

If all the expected advertising media are available in a country, the international marketer must evaluate the cost/benefit ratio of advertising compared to other elements of the promotional mix. If costs are high compared to the overall market communication budget, then even if advertising would be the first tool to use from the company's market communication policy point of view, it may not be the best choice compared to other options.

International Advertising Implementation

The success of an international advertising campaign depends on more than the firm's ability to evoke the intended meanings in its customers' minds by choosing the right advertising copy and the appropriate media in accordance with the general market communication objectives of the firm; it also depends on the company's ability to properly organize the production and international insertion process of its advertisements. For that purpose the international marketer, on the one hand, needs to establish an internal group of qualified people willing to cooperate internationally, and on the other it has to manage its contacts with external service providers such as advertising agencies.

Figure 17.4 CABLE PENETRATION IN LATIN AMERICA

Latin America's pay TV market delivered by both cable and satellite is quickly expanding since the deregulation of the subcontinent's media and telecom industries took place. A bundle of new programmes, many produced by US broadcasters, is available as advertising support for international marketers.

Source: Kagan World Media, in *ESOMAR newsbrief*, No. 4, April 1995, 9.

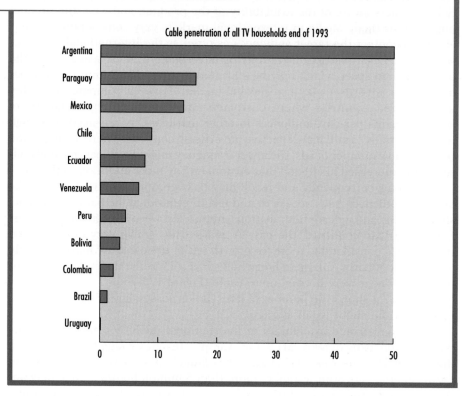

Cable penetration of all TV households end of 1993

Table 17.1 ELECTRONIC AUDIENCE IN ASIA

The number of TV households compared to radio households is growing fast in Asia.

	NUMBER OF TV HOUSEHOLDS IN MILLIONS	NUMBER OF RADIO HOUSEHOLDS IN MILLIONS
China	160	95
India	40	80
Indonesia (main cities)	11	13.6
Japan	43	43
Pakistan	6	20
Philippines	7.7	11.7
Thailand	11.9	8
South Korea	11.3	12.4

Source: Statesman's Year Book, World Almanac and Asia Pacific Market and MediaFact 1995; in ESOMAR newsbrief, No. 2, February 1996, 23.

For example, when US-based Whirlpool acquired the household appliances business of Philips, headquartered in the Netherlands, they were confronted with a situation where every country subsidiary or sales office had its own advertising agencies and did its own advertising development around individual markets. Whirlpool, in contrast, decided to be the first in the industry to develop a common advertising campaign across Europe. Initially they encountered a lot of resistance from the markets, each claiming to be different and needing local adaptation. To overcome these problems Whirlpool established an 'International Creative Council', which had members of the marketing or advertising people from the key European markets. That council worked directly with Publicis, the firm's advertising agency. The team members of the agency were also selected from their European network to represent the different country-markets. By gathering the key people and having the experts from the local markets involved, the development of the advertising campaign went smoothly and the campaign received immediate approval in all local units of the company.[10]

Increasingly, firms operating on an international level feel the necessity to coordinate their international advertising activities more closely. They are establishing the position of worldwide media director to coordinate international activities and to help solve problems like finding suffient funds for regional buys that cut across many countries' budgets. For example, US computer marketer Gateway 2000 hired a UK media buying specialist from the Carat media buying group as worldwide media director who is now responsible for Gateway's media investment in North America, Europe, Japan and Australia. In the first six months of his appointment, the new coordinator moved Gateway's European media buying account from Carat to London-based Optimedia, negotiated media for the company's launch in Japan and Australia, started a review of US media buying, negotiated global media buying deals with International Data Group and Ziff-Davis Publishing, and tested the use of newspaper ads in the UK and TV in the USA.[11]

Other international marketers consolidate their company's entire advertising account at one globally operating advertising agency. In 1994, for example, IBM's CEO, Louis Gerstner, initiated the firing of over 40 different agencies around the world and handed the entire USD400 to 500 million account over to one top-ten global agency, Ogilvy & Mather. The coordination requirements of agency clients which operate in increasingly global industries have led major advertising agencies to strengthen their international services. For that purpose, some agencies like BBDO have established a network of offices worldwide – BBDO has 54 – and assign personnel to serve each account exclusively. Young & Rubicam, like BBDO one of the world's top three agencies, has global managing directors and their teams who provide a corporate global perspective for each campaign. The managing director is responsible for all communications with the client. Other agencies like London-based Saatchi & Saatchi have either acquired local agencies (with sometimes questionable success) or established international networks of cooperating partners. London-based WPP Group is currently the world's largest network, consisting of a variety of agencies including Ogilvy & Mather, J. Walter Thompson and Scall, McCabe & Sloves, each of which also has their own set of subsidiaries. Table 17.2 lists the biggest groups of advertising agencies in the world.

Japan's advertising industry is dominated by two companies, Dentsu and Hakuhodo, which between them control most domestic billings and growing segments of the world's billings. Dentsu, which alone controls more than 20 per cent of the domestic advertising market, tends to buy blocks of space on TV channels and sell them to advertisers. The company covers every aspect of a client's needs with a 'total communications solution' package. Dentsu employs 34 000 people in Japan spread between dozens of national offices and 25 subsidiaries, which include film and video companies, theme parks and resort companies, real estate, property management and insurance. Hakuhodo employs 3500 people in 15 domestic branches and 17 more offices around the world.[12]

Agency–client relationships vary considerably in different country-markets. In many markets relationships with agencies are viewed as long-term personal ties, not simply as contracts that may be ended whenever the client or the agency is displeased. In the USA and Europe, it has been common to change agencies every few years. Some managers argue that such changes keep the level of creativity of their companies' advertising campaigns high. But McDonald's, for example, found that changing agencies in Brazil is not only difficult but can be harmful to the company's image. When the company switched to a new agency, its former agency generated a great deal of negative publicity, calling McDonald's 'paramilitary' and claiming that it had lost money because of the company's actions. In Japan, relationships once formed between a client and its agency are usually long-term. After years of working together, the agency becomes almost an integral part of the client company itself. With increasing single sourcing, that is, the concentration of the whole international advertising account in the hands of one single agency, and as a consequence of an increasing understanding that successful market communication needs an integration of all communication tools applied, the Japanese approach to building and maintaining long-term relationships with full service agencies as business partners has growing appeal for many international marketers.

Sales Promotion

Sales promotion is the catch-all term for short-term market communication decisions and activities that try to gain attention, stimulate interest, and provide motivation of (potential) customers, staff or intermediaries for a company and its products. All sales promotion activities have the general goal of stimulating sales. How important sales promotion activities have become in the past decade is illustrated by the fact that for many packaged consumer goods companies, sales promotion expenditures have passed advertising to become the largest single-cost item besides costs of production.

The variety of sales promotion activities of international marketers and the frequency with which they are offered have increased over time. Table 17.3 lists the sales promotion tools most commonly used in international marketing, their communication targets, specific objectives, and key issues to be considered in choosing among them.

Targets of Sales Promotion

Sales promotion activities may be directed at one or more of three types of target: customers, staff or intermediary.

Table 17.2 THE WORLD'S TOP TEN ADVERTISING AGENCY GROUPS

RANK	ADVERTISING GROUP	HEADQUARTERS	WORLDWIDE GROSS INCOME 1996	CAPITALIZED VOLUME 1996
1	WPP Group	London	3,419.9	24,740.5
2	Omnicom Group	New York	3,035.5	23,385.1
3	Interpublic Group of Cos.	New York	2,751.2	20,045.1
4	Dentsu Inc.	Tokyo	1,929.9	14,047.9
5	Young & Rubicam	New York	1,356.4	11,981.0
6	Cordiant	London	1,169.3	9,739.9
7	Grey Advertising	New York	987.8	6,629.4
8	Havas Advertising	Levallois-Perret	974.3	7,295.1
9	Hakuhodo	Tokyo	897.7	6,677.0
10	True North Communications	Chicago	889.5	7,040.9

The list above shows the top ten advertising groups of the world ranked according to their gross earnings worldwide in 1996.

Figures are in million USD.
Source: Ad Age's Agency Report.

Table 17.3 SALES PROMOTION TOOLS

TOOLS	TARGET GROUP	OBJECTIVE
Coupons	Customers	Stimulate trial or encourage repeat purchase
Price-offs	Customers	Encourage repeat purchase
Trade allowances	Intermediaries	Build distribution; increase orders
Samples	Customers; intermediaries; staff	Stimulate trial purchase; build distribution; increase orders
In, on and near packs	Customers	Increase attractiveness/perception of value packs
Self-liquidating premiums	Customers	Stimulate trial or encourage repeat purchase
Continuity premiums	Customers	Encourage repeat purchase
Bonus packs	Customers	Encourage repeat purchase
Contests and sweepstakes	Customers; staff; intermediaries	Stimulate trial purchase; increase orders
Displays	Customers; intermediaries	Attract attention; provide information
Training	Customers; staff; intermediaries	Provide information; improve sales capabilities
Events	Customers; staff; intermediaries	Attract attention; provide information
Trade shows and exhibitions	Customers; staff; intermediaries	Attract attention; provide information; build distribution; stimulate (trial) purchase
Product demonstrations	Customers; intermediaries	Attract attention; provide information; build distribution; stimulate (trial) purchase

The most often applied sales promotion tools in international marketing have different communication target groups and different objectives.

Customer promotions.   Sales promotion activities directed towards organizational buyers or consumers are called customer promotions. They may try to stimulate the marketer's total sales by reducing the price customers have to pay, by adding to the product's perceived value, or by increasing the attractiveness of the company's offers through some kind of information.

Direct price reductions for customers are achieved by the distribution and redemption of coupons or by price-offs. A coupon of Pantène, one of the Procter & Gamble hair-styling brands, for example, is aimed at consumers. Consumers respond differently to coupons, of course, depending upon culture, importance of the product, and level of income. North American consumers are the most frequent coupon users in the world. About 80 per cent of key grocery shoppers in Canadian households use coupons when shopping. In the USA, about 300 billion coupons are distributed to consumers each year. Consumers in Belgium and the UK are the EU's most active coupon users, while consumers in Italy and Spain are far more modest in couponing. They get their coupons mainly from in/on-pack promotions, whereas consumers in the UK clip most of their coupons from newspapers and magazines. In the USA, free-standing inserts in print media account for about 80 per cent of coupon distribution, while in-ad couponing represents the majority of all coupons distributed in Canada.[13]

Other customer promotion tools, such as bonus packs, free samples, in/on and near packs (coupons or additional products attached to or near the product), and premiums, all add value to a marketer's product. For example, the Albert Heijn grocery chain in the Netherlands distributes savings stamps based on the total amount of a customer's purchase. Contests and sweepstakes offer 'something for nothing', which has universal appeal. UK newspapers, for instance, 'give away' thousands of pounds daily in bingo and other contests that may be entered by readers.

Customer promotion may also be mainly used to provide information. For example, consumers may be targeted by displays used to draw attention to the marketer's product, to ease the handling of the product portfolio, and to improve product logistics. For example, Austria-based Hirsch Armbänder GmbH, the globally leading manufacturer of watch straps, uses a display developed by Mateo Thun, an Italian designer, to present its products to consumers in retail stores. Those free-standing displays not only attract the attention of consumers, they also present the entire product range to interested customers, serve the retailer as storage space, and automatically inform the shop manager about items running out of stock. Care must be taken by the international marketer that the displays it offers to retailers fit their stores and the sales volume handled. In small sari-sari stores in the Philippines, for example, a display that is well suited for Australian supermarkets may be larger than the entire store.

Sales promotion activities providing information may be particularly important in attracting potential customers' attention when introducing a new product. When a UK manufacturer of pharmaceuticals introduced a new cold remedy in the USA, for example, it used a promotional gift to attract the attention of medical doctors and to stay in their minds. The gift was a coffee mug with a drawing that showed a doctor and his patient. When hot coffee was poured into the mug the drawing changed. It showed the doctor giving an injection to the patient, an ugly bug trying to escape, and a text that read: 'Claforan kills bugs'. The sales promotion was a big success. Because the gift had a social value – the transformation of the drawing could be shown to others who did not possess the mug – the message was not only repeated to the members of the target group often enough to stay in their minds, but was also spread to many other people who learned about the existence of the new drug and its major effect.

Sales promotion tools that provide information are particularly important in internationally marketing technical products and services to organizational buyers. Product demonstrations during site visits to reference plants are an example of such customer promotion activities for organizational buyers. They allow the potential buyers to evaluate the product in action without risk. In addition, representatives of the potential buying organization get the opportunity to travel at no personal cost, a fact that may be an attractive added value for buyers from less industrially developed countries or less well capitalized organizations. For example, when a manufacturer of ultra-filtration devices, such as Sweden's Alfa Laval, invites agents from Bulgarian local administrations to visit an installation of the company's product in a customer's car painting plant near Paris, those agents will not only be able to see the Alfa Laval filters in action but might also enjoy an additional day in the capital of France.

Staff Promotions.   Staff promotion activities are designed to stimulate the marketer's own personnel or an external sales force. An international sales contest run by US-based Caterpillar, in which the most outstanding members of the distributors' sales force are rewarded by a trip to the headquarters in Peoria plus a subsequent 10–day vacation on a Caribbean island, is an example of a staff promotion. Issues which influence the international application of staff promotions are similar to those discussed in Chapter 16 for sales force motivation and compensation.

Intermediary promotions.   A company's activities having the purpose of increasing intermediaries' interest in buying and selling larger amounts of the marketer's products are called intermediary promotions. Because speciality retailers, mass merchandisers and buying cooperatives are becoming increasingly transnational in scope, intermediary promotions also have to become more international in design and coverage.

Internationally, intermediaries respond to promotions which have a positive impact on their profit. Therefore, trade allowances are the most common sales promotion tool used by manufacturers to target their retailers. They are especially effective in highly competitive markets or when no single manufacturer has a dominant share of the market. Consumer goods manufacturers should keep in mind, however, that increasing reliance on price promotions to boost short-term local sales results that might seem necessary in country-markets with powerful retail organizations tend to reduce brand profitability, to increase contradictory brand communication, and to dilute brand franchises with customers. In Europe many marketers of branded products complain about consumers' increasing price sensitivity and a tendency to buy exclusively at low (action) prices. In the Italian detergent market, for example, 80 per cent of sales occur as part of a special offer. German retailers report very similar consumer behaviour.[14] Many of the marketers concerned overlook the fact that they, together with their retailing partners, in an attempt to increase their sales volume and market share by the continual use of trade allowances and price-offs, have taught their customers to wait for special prices.

Objectives of Sales Promotion

Sales promotion activities may have the objective of informing the target audience about the company's activities and products. They may be undertaken to encourage trial purchases by potential customers or to stimulate repeat purchases. Finally, sales promotion also serves the purpose of building and enlarging distribution.

Information. Sales promotion activities aimed at potential customers or intermediaries may provide the latest information on company-related developments, such as going public, or on new products. Their interest is to capture attention and transfer the intended information. Some sales promotion activities have an openly stated goal of informing the target audience; for example, when about 90 managers from international computer and software companies, such as IBM, ICL, SAP and Unisys, meet with 135 managers from eastern European banks at an 'International Banking Forum' in the European Alps. Since the computer and software managers present their latest products and exchange computer application experiences, the information (and sales) purpose is predominant.

Other target groups, and in particular consumers who may be much less involved with a marketer's product, are not necessarily interested in a marketer's information. For them, sales promotion activities with an attention-getting purpose need to be predominantly entertaining. Events and theme parks have proven to be successful tools in that respect. For example, German Adidas has developed what it calls *urban culture programmes*. The programmes include participatory events across Europe such as a streetbal challenge and festival, and a track-and-field clinic. Events that draw respectable crowds of people include not only athletics but also fashion shows, music (including a hip-hop band) and other entertainment. Interested partners have joined Adidas in the events: major sports leagues, sports celebrities, other marketers targeting the same youth segment, and media services, which cover the events. They provide free publicity. The success of those sales promotion activities is striking. Adidas' decline in sales has been turned around into two-digit growth figures and market share gains in recent years, in spite of major media expenditures by competitors Nike and Reebok.[15]

The UK chocolate manufacturer Cadbury has developed a theme park called Cadbury World. Visitors can take a journey through the history of chocolate and the history of Cadbury complete with a museum, a restaurant, a partial tour of the packaging plant, and a 'chocolate event' store. They learn about the origin of cocoa and chocolate, the life of the Mayan and Aztec Indians, how chocolate reached Europe, and how John Cadbury's empire began and grew. Every year for the past three years, more than 450 000 people have visited the park and profited from hundreds of opportunities to sample the company's extensive line of chocolate products. The regional tourist board, hotel chains and the British Railways Board have publicized the park to promote their own services. And in 1996, Cadbury was named as the most admired company in the UK.[16]

Encouragement of Trial Purchases. Sales promotion activities are frequently designed to stimulate trial purchases. When other market communication measures, such as advertising, have captured a customer's attention, sales promotion can motivate the customer to try a product by reducing the perceived risk involved. This is the case when the customer is offered a free sample. For example, when Italian wine marketers from the Tuscany area offer free samples to Danish customers in supermarkets, they know that consumers are more likely to buy their wines. On the one hand, consumers have an opportunity to taste the wines before buying, and on the other, most consumers feel a certain obligation to reciprocate when they have accepted a free offer.

Stimulation of Repeat Purchases.   Other sales promotion activities are designed to convert trial users into regular users. Premium programmes, such as free airline miles invented by American Airlines in 1981, are an example. Mileage programmes, first started to give an incentive to airline customers to stay loyal, since 1994 increasingly include all manner of earth-bound goods and services. First, there were 'travel partners', such as hotels, car rentals and credit cards. Now carriers are selling miles to any company that wants to offer them as a sales incentive. Frequent-flier miles are available from lawn services, mortgage firms, investment houses, restaurants, furniture stores and moving companies. Even ABC, the American television network owned by Walt Disney Co., is studying ways to offer frequent-flier miles for watching TV shows. In 1995, American Airlines sold an estimated USD25 million in miles through 1000 companies buying its Aadvantage miles. In the UK British Airways launched an Air Miles 'club', through which members accumulate points from a variety of merchants, including Shell service stations, NatWest Bank Group credit cards, Wine Rack, P&O European Ferries, Hilton, Marriott and Hertz. Those points can be exchanged for free British Airways tickets, hotels, cruises, cinema tickets, and other awards.[17]

Building Distribution.   Sales promotion can also be designed to build distribution. For example, free samples are used to motivate the sales force and to induce intermediaries or final customers to increase orders. Trade shows and exhibitions are particularly important in international marketing for consumer and industrial goods, even if participation in such shows is increasingly expensive. Trade shows and exhibitions are used to build distribution by meeting potential intermediaries or licensing partners interested in cooperation and by securing the market presence needed to maintain successful relationships with business partners. Exhibitions, such as CeBIT in Hanover (Germany), the enormous annual European information technology exhibition with more than 6000 exhibitors from more than 60 countries located in 26 halls, most of them the size of aeroplane hangars, with more than 340 000 square metres of floor space and about three-quarters of a million visitors, allow the marketer to present and demonstrate its latest range of products, to announce new product launches and to cultivate its image. For that reason, not only industry giants such as Microsoft or Siemens are represented at this exhibition. Smaller firms, such as Taiwan's Advanced Scientific Corp. which in 1996 presented its multicoloured portable fax machines at CeBIT, are present as well as institutions or regions, such as the island of Mauritius which tries to attract investors for software production facilities.[18]

Participation in international exhibitions, such as Première Vision, the bi-annual get-together of about 850 European cloth manufacturers with fashion professionals from all over the world in Paris, is a must for all marketers that want to be present in their potential customers' minds. But presence is not enough. Each time the marketer has to have something new to present, something that attracts the interest of its customers and makes the company stand out from the crowd of exhibitors. To illustrate, companies such as Italian Botto or Belgian Ucco Sportswear specialize in high quality speciality cloth. At exhibitions the Italian firm continually presents new creations from wool, silk and cashmere combined with microfibres and Lycra. The Belgian firm concentrates on denim fabrics of the latest fashion and fantasy.

The number and importance of large trade shows and exhibits aimed at consumers has grown, too. The Consumer Electronics Shows, held in Chicago each year, for example, or the yearly Salon d'Automobile in Geneva, Switzerland successfully apply the ideas of industrial trade shows to consumer audiences. At the show, consumers have an opportunity to see and try new products; perhaps more important, manufacturers have an opportunity to observe consumer responses to new products and product lines. In addition, interest among magazine and newspaper writers in new products or upcoming new technologies can be aroused which in turn leads to publicity in their media.

Because of the rising costs of participation in exhibitions and trade shows in different parts of the world, the marketer needs to gather available information on the focus and size of the show, the kinds of visitors expected, other exhibitors present, and the space and locations available. In Arab countries participation during Ramadan should be avoided. Participation in exhibitions in the People's Republic of China which are arranged by Hong Kong firms but not officially supported by the government are usually expensive flops because of a lack of visitor interest.

Choice of Sales Promotion Tools

Several factors affect decisions about which sales promotion tool to use. Some of these factors are universal and must be taken into account regardless of the country-market in which the company is operating. Other factors are locally based and therefore have special significance for international marketers.

Fit With Market Communication Objectives. The first factor to be considered is the fit of a sales promotion tool with the general market communication objectives of the firm and the product. For example, when the Italian fashion house Giorgio Armani opens a new 'Emporio' store in Paris it may arrange a big event with some celebrities to draw a selected number of fashion magazine writers and potential affluent customers into the newly adapted building. But it will not use price-offs like big retailing chains such as French Auchan do when they open a new hypermarket on the outskirts of Paris. As the example shows, the sales promotion tools applied have to fit the communication targets and they need to be in line with other communication activities. Armani, for example, may use the opening of the new store to advertise in the most prestigious fashion magazines, such as *Vogue*. Auchan, in contrast, would send out flyers announcing super opening discounts and including coupons to all households in its market.

Level of Economic and Market Development. Depending on the level of economic development in a country-market, certain sales promotion tools can be applied more or less well. For example, coupons enjoy widespread use in most economically well-developed countries. In most economically less developed countries they are rarely used because of a lack of appropriate coupon distribution media and a lack of infrastructure for their redemption. In contrast, free samples and product demonstrations are by far the most widely applied tools of internationally operating firms in those countries.

The level of maturity a product-market has reached in different country-markets is another factor to be considered in the choice of sales promotion tools. Tools to promote customer trials may be more appropriate in markets where the product is new to the customers. For example, when pizza delivery services were introduced in European markets, the service providers used full-value couponing and cross-promotions with established products to make potential customers try their new service. In more mature markets, other sales promotion tools which put more emphasis on customer loyalty, such as customer loyalty premiums or membership of customer clubs, might be more effective.

Costs.   The cost considerations associated with a sales promotion campaign include, first, an estimate of the total cost of the campaign. Secondly, international marketers need to estimate what contribution the campaign will make towards reaching the given communication objectives and finally, towards increasing sales. For example, free samples are a much more costly means of attracting new customers than cents-off coupons. But when a product benefit, such as good taste, the perfect functioning of a weaving machine or the superior service in a new restaurant, is most easily communicated through trial use, the expense of samples may be necessary to make potential customers try the product.

Estimates of sales promotion costs in international marketing are complicated by the likelihood that the cost of the campaign, and contribution to sales, will vary market by market. For example, in the USA, where contests and sweepstakes are most popular, a contest costs about USD3 per thousand entrants, and sweepstakes cost about USD350 per thousand entrants. Despite the fact that payoffs or rewards are commonly many times higher than those found in Europe, Asia, Latin America or Africa, only about 20 per cent of the population generally sends in entries to contests or sweepstakes. As a general rule, the lower the average income of the target group, the lower the reward or prize has to be to stimulate interest.

Intermediary Capabilities.   The willingness and ability of distributors, wholesalers and retailers in various country-markets to accommodate the special requirements of sales promotion activities is another important issue. Price-off coupons or customer loyalty premiums, for example, must be handled and processed by retailers. Bonus packs and premiums may require flexibility in storage and shelf space so that oversized and oddly shaped products can be accommodated. Local distributors of machinery manufacturers must be ready to install sample machines at potential customers' sites and dismantle them in case of non-purchase. As was discussed in Chapter 14, intermediaries in different countries vary in their capabilities. In country-markets with a low literacy rate, for example, many retailers may not have the training or accounting skills necessary to keep track of coupon schemes. In countries where small store sizes predominate, such as in most Southeast Asian countries, the use of promotional tools that occupy store space or slow down checkout traffic is precluded.

Channel Power.   The importance of the members of a product's value-added chain relative to one another is also a factor to be considered in the choice of sales promotion tools. For example, when a manufacturer has a high degree of channel power because its products are in strong demand, trade allowances typically are not used. The distributor either buys from the manufacturer at the given price or not at all. When large intermediaries, such as Woolworth's in Australia, Ahold in the Netherlands, Carrefour in France, or Wal-Mart in the USA, have substantial channel power, they can demand large trade allowances and in-store consumer promotions from marketers with rather weak brands or threaten to buy from another manufacturer.

Norms.   The degree to which a sales promotion tool is consistent with or violates local legal, cultural or business norms is a factor to be considered carefully in each country-market. The potential influence of legal norms on the choice of sales promotion activities has already been discussed in Chapter 4. The influence of cultural norms may vary significantly among country-markets. Coupons, for example, are not widely used in Japan. Japanese consumers are still too embarrassed to be seen at a checkout redeeming them. Likewise, Danish Lego's 'Bunny Set' promotion – the toys plus a discounted premium offer, a storage case in the shape of a bunny – failed to impress its intended target of Japanese mothers, even though the same sales promotion had earlier proven very successful in the USA. Unlike their US counterparts, who thought the offering was a great bargain, the Japanese mothers considered the on-pack bunny as superfluous. They objected to the notion of being forced to waste money on unwanted products.[19]

Point-of-purchase displays work well in countries where self-service is the norm in the industry. But by placing the product within reach of the customer, such displays violate the service norms of small shopkeepers in many areas of the world. For example, in many countries coffee is still typically sold in small stores where the shopkeeper grinds the coffee beans. An introductory offer of a coffee mug with the purchase of ground coffee is likely to be resisted by retailers, if not by consumers. They would ignore such premiums.

Decision and Implementation.   In light of the differences in local conditions just described, companies operating internationally have traditionally treated sales promotion as a local affair. Local intermediaries or product, brand or sales managers have enjoyed great latitude in the formulation and implementation of sales promotion activities. However, because of the growing importance of sales promotion spending compared to other market communication activities such as media advertising, and the increasing realization of marketing managers that all market communication decisions and activities of an internationally operating firm need to be conceptually integrated, some thought needs to be given to the question of how sales promotion decisions and implementation responsibilities should be distributed in the company.

The objective of any solution for the distribution of sales promotion decision and implementation responsibilities in an internationally operating company should be to upgrade the performance of local market communication. The impact of sales promotion activities and their contribution to the achievement of the company's communication goals compared to their costs should be maximized. As the discussion of key issues to be considered when choosing sales promotion tools has shown, there are good reasons for leaving sales promotion activities primarily in the hands of local management. But some central coordination may help to improve local practices.

Table 17.4 contains a list of responsibilities a central sales promotion coordination unit or coordinator of an internationally operating firm could take. The central coordination unit would be responsible for leading the devel-

Table 17.4 THE ROLE OF AN INTERNATIONAL SALES PROMOTION COORDINATOR

The international sales promotion coordinator's role would be to:
↔ Lead the development process of guidelines for international sales promotion.
↔ Facilitate the information transfer about successful sales promotion campaigns.
↔ Encourage cross-fertilization of sales promotion ideas and practices among local managers.
↔ Develop and suggest training programmes on sales promotion planning, design and evaluation.
↔ Advise locally responsible managers on solutions to specific promotion problems.
↔ Develop standard systems for comparatively monitoring the effectiveness and efficiency of sales promotion activities and the performance of local managers.

An international sales promotion coordinator could play the role of a coach for the local managers who have to implement the international sales promotion policy of the firm.

Source: Adapted from Kashani, K. and J.A. Quelch (1990) 'Can Sales Promotion Go Global?', Business Horizons, May–June, pp. 37–43.

opment process of global sales promotion guidelines, expressing the main objectives to reach, the major tools to apply, and how to coordinate local sales promotion with other local market communication activities. The coordination unit would also have to facilitate information transfer about successful sales promotion campaigns among local managers and to encourage cross-fertilization of ideas and practices among the local market representatives. The coordinator would act as a coach in terms of suggesting training programmes and advising local managers on solutions to specific sales promotion problems. Finally, it would be the coordination unit's responsibility to develop standard systems for comparatively monitoring the effectiveness and efficiency of sales promotion activities and the performance of local managers.

Local or locally responsible managers still have to implement the company's sales promotion policy. Implementation means translating the international policy guidelines into country-market-specific objectives (for example, expand shelf space and increase trial purchases), into decisions concerning the tools to be used (for example, trade allowances and sampling), the products to be promoted, the timing and the specific terms of sales promotion activities (for example, which intermediaries should get what amount of allowances for what return). Implementation also means the execution of those decisions, such as the preparation of the sales force for their contacts with intermediaries or organizing the production of samples and their distribution to customers at the point of sale or at home.

SPONSORING AND DIRECT MARKET COMMUNICATION

Whatever country-markets an international marketer is serving, there are many different marketers trying to communicate with their potential customers – whether through advertising appeals in San Francisco or through personal communication in the souk of Marrakesh. To be noticed by its target audiences, an international marketer's communication needs to stand out from others in a positive manner. In highly industrialized economies, advertising appeals, personal selling and sales promotions have traditionally been used to communicate with customers. Advertising in particular, however, suffers from a commercial information overflow which confronts customers. This information overflow results in extremely small probabilities of a firm's commercial messages being recognized and, if recognized, attracting more than very short periods of attention. Faced with that problem, companies have invented new kinds of communication tools. The currently most important of those in international marketing are sponsoring and direct market communication. Other tools, such as infomercials on digital TV, interactive CD-ROMs and home pages on the Internet are in their infancy.

Sponsoring

Sponsoring can be defined as 'the provision of resources (e.g. money, people, equipment) by an organization directly to an event, cause or activity in exchange for a direct association (link) to the event, cause or activity. The providing organization can then engage in sponsorship-linked marketing to achieve their . . . objectives'.[20] Sponsored events may be sports events, such as the Olympic Games in 1996 sponsored by companies such as Coca-Cola, United Parcel Service and Hilton, or cultural events, such as Copenhagen being the cultural capital of Europe for one year sponsored by Danish Lego. Sponsored causes may be social or environmental, such as the construction of a new village for orphans and children from destabilized families by International SOS-Kinderdorf in Brazil, or a Greenpeace campaign against the deforestation of the Amazon river basin.

Until the 1980s most firms viewed sponsorship as an obligation to the community. Sponsoring had been placed close to charitable donations and public relations opportunities to be seen as a 'good citizen'. Since then, as traditional media have become more expensive, cluttered and overloaded with commercial messages, sponsoring has been increasingly viewed as a cost-effective promotion alternative. Sponsoring expenditures multiplied by about ten between 1985 and 1995 to reach more than USD6 billion in 1996.

Objectives. In many companies operating internationally, sponsoring is still understood as a way to achieve customer awareness; either directly through providing time and space for advertising messages (for example, when a brand name is shown on the perimeter board of an ice skating rink) or indirectly through media transmissions of events (for example, when the firm's logo on the headband of a ski jump celebrity is shown on television) or through reports about events in the media.

Besides customer awareness, sponsoring presents multiple opportunities to achieve awareness by other important stakeholders, such as media or administrators. But more importantly, sponsoring allows the meanings customers associate with the sponsors' name and with its products to be established, strengthened or changed. Just as customers associate celebrities with certain meanings, so too the events, causes and activities of sponsored organizations are associated with meanings.

For example, Hugo Boss, located in the provincial town of Metzingen in

Southern Germany, was founded in 1923. It was always a producer of high-quality clothing, but not many people knew about it. The company established its current image of exclusivity paired with high quality in large part through effective use of sponsorship. In the early 1970s, Hugo Boss sponsored Porsche in Formula One races to capitalize on Porsche's strong exclusive image and international presence. Since then, the company has sponsored international tennis, golf and ski competitions. It has funded exhibitions and artists, and it sponsored *Miami Vice* and *L.A.Law*, both of which featured Hugo Boss garments. The visibility and meanings transferred to the brand paid off quickly. Sales revenues increased tenfold during the 1980s from about USD65 million. Hugo Boss garments are sold in 57 countries. More than half its sales come from outside Germany, with 20 per cent generated outside Europe.[21]

Decision and Implementation. An international marketer interested in the transfer of meanings from a sponsored event or a cause to its company or its product must take care in choosing the most appropriate sponsoring object. That is, the marketer must check the type and characteristics of the event, cause or activity to be potentially sponsored, its similarity with the sponsoring object, the potential media attention to be attracted, and the involvement of customers with the sponsoring object as well as the firm's product.

The type of event, cause or activity considered for sponsoring must fit the image or meaning the sponsor wants to achieve in the minds of its customers and important stakeholders. For example, when Dominique Perrin, the CEO of Paris-based Cartier, decides to sponsor an exhibition of art works by César, he will not only consider how much he personally likes those exhibits, but also how well the meanings such an exhibition brings to the minds of the tens of thousands of international visitors fit the image that he wants to be transferred to the sponsor, Cartier. In addition, the number of visitors expected, whether they are among the target customers of the firm, and the news value of the event for the media will be considered in comparison to the cost of the sponsorship.

The similarity between the sponsor and the event or cause sponsored as perceived by the firm's customers may be based on the use of the sponsor's product during the sponsored event; for example, when Castrol sponsors a Formula One Grand Prix race, or when spectators of the 1998 soccer World Cup stay in rooms of an international hotel chain that sponsors the event. The perceived similarity may also be based on the relation between the image of the event and the image of the sponsor's product; for example, when Coca-Cola sponsored the Voodoo Lounge concert tour of the Rolling Stones around the world. Such similarity may be lacking, however, when Eastman Kodak of the USA replaces its major competitor, Japan's Fuji Photo Film, as sponsor of widely watched soccer matches in China.

Finally, the involvement of the sponsor's customers with the event or cause to be sponsored, that is, the personal importance they attach to the event or cause, and with the sponsor's product needs to be considered. If the involvement with the sponsoring object is high, such as for many social or environmental causes, but also for field hockey games in India, rugby in New Zealand or soccer in Columbia, the sponsor can count on a high level of attention from the target audience. If, in addition, the target audience's involvement with the sponsor or its product is rather low, the transfer of meaning from the sponsored event or cause to the sponsor might be easier.

FUTURE ISSUES
BOX

Marketing to the

Digital Consumer

THE RAPID DEVELOPMENT OF INTERACTIVE MEDIA HAS taken many marketers by surprise. Analyses of 95 *Fortune* 500 consumer marketing companies with product or service-related Web sites and of 603 major companies in Britain, France and Germany have revealed that most have started using the Internet and call it important to their international competitiveness. But at the same time most of the firms fall short of leveraging the full capabilities of interactive media. While most applications provide product information and feature basic e-mail capabilities, only a minority provide any sort of interactive content. Only very few Web sites make an effort to seriously collect information about their users, and fewer than 5 per cent provide an opportunity to allow user-to-user communications.

Most marketers still approach interactive media through the static, one-way, mass-market broadcast model of traditional media. The results of such an approach are uninspiring applications that fall short of the new media's potential. Marketers will have to learn how to create entirely new forms of interactions and transactions with customers. To do so they will need to accept a fundamental change in the traditional communication balance of power by giving the consumer more control over their relationship. In an interactive, two-way, addressable world, it is the customer – and not the marketer – who decides with whom to interact, what to interact about, and how to interact at all.

Marketers will need to build some of the more specialized skills that are emerging in interactive electronic communication, such as audience creation, that is attracting users to digital services, and intelligent agent development, the creation of value-added services based on the individual users' preferences. Finally, perhaps the biggest challenge for international marketers will be to manage the interdependences between their electronic market communication efforts and both the rest of the organization and existing outside partners, such as intermediaries.

Sources: Strassel, K.A. (1997) 'Wait-and-See: European Firms Are Treading Warily on the Internet', *The Wall Street Journal Europe*, 3 June, p. 12; and Kierzkowski, A., S. McQuade, R. Waitman and M. Zeisser (1996) 'Marketing to the Digital Consumer', *The McKinsey Quarterly*, No. 3, 5–21.

Direct Market Communication

In industrially developed economies, mass marketing has become increasingly difficult in recent years. More affluent consumers are less loyal, constantly looking for more attractive offers or lower prices. To respond appropriately to this development, the international marketer needs to have close contacts with its potential customers. A more direct market communication than the traditional contact via mass media is needed. Direct market communication might be a solution to the problem. Because the most important tool of direct communication, personal selling, has already been discussed in Chapter 16, the following section will focus on direct mailings and electronic direct communication.

Direct Mailings.   The traditional approach to direct market communication is direct mailings. The problems an international marketer may encounter in using direct mail and some solutions to those problems are illustrated by the example of Germany's Neckermann, one of Europe's leading catalogue businesses.

In conceiving its 1400-page catalogue of garments and home equipment for the German market, Neckermann bears in mind that some of those pages will be used for its French, Belgian and Dutch catalogues. In order to avoid too much of a bias in the direction of a local culture, accessories shown in the catalogue are limited. In addition, whenever possible, parts of the text are written in English to reduce adaptation costs. The models used to present the garments represent all types of people in the country-markets served. Nevertheless, some country-specific adaptations need to be made. First, the catalogue itself is differently positioned: in Germany as 'the intelligent buy', in the Netherlands as 'the thickest catalogue', and in France as 'the European catalogue'. The consumers in the served countries also wear different sizes; the Germans and Dutch are taller than the French. And some prices need to be changed: leather goods are used as rather low-priced attention attractors in Germany. In France they are considered as expensive. Finally, sales-promotion regulations vary between the countries. Samples and premiums are governed by very restrictive regulations in Germany compared to France.[22]

The applicability of direct mailing largely depends on high literacy rates in the served country-markets and dependable postal services. These requirements mean that direct mailing is not appropriate for a large number of markets. In some African countries, for example, it takes longer to send a letter to another city within the country than to send one from the capital overseas. India, on the other hand, boasts that a letter mailed in India will reach any destination in the country within three days. This means that international marketers should give serious consideration to sending direct mail to educated consumers in India.

Integrated Direct Market Communication. The key advantage of direct market communication is its ability to present (individualized) product offers to high-potential customers. Actually obtaining this advantage, however, depends on having access to a well-developed, targeted database. As the example of Nestlé's Casa Buitoni Club in the UK shows, such a database can be established by a creative campaign integrating various market communication tools. Nestlé's strategy was that Buitoni would become a helpful authority on Italian food – a brand and company to which consumers could turn for advice on the many varieties of pasta and their preparation. The first stage of the Buitoni direct marketing effort, which took place in 1992 and 1993, was designed to strengthen brand awareness and create a core database of consumers interested in getting involved in Italian cooking. Buitoni gave free recipe booklets to anyone who responded to its offers, which were made in the press and through teletext or direct-response television. Brand awareness was further improved by in-store sampling, sponsorship, a roadshow with many sampling activities, and public relations connected to the most popular running event in the UK. The integrated communications campaign resulted in a database of more than 200 000 consumers. In November 1993, the households in the database were invited to join the Casa Buitoni Club. Those responding received an Italian-lifestyle information pack and a full-colour quarterly newsletter (with articles about different Italian regions), pasta recipes and discount vouchers. Membership benefits also included a free-phone number for anyone wanting cooking advice or suggestions. In addition, there were the opportunity to sample new products, merchandise offered against proof of purchase, and suggestions on planning pasta feasts. The success of this direct marketing effort has influenced the marketing of Buitoni in other countries, for example Japan.[23]

Electronic Direct Communication. The rapid development of new electronic media has enlarged the international marketer's opportunities to enter into individual communication contact with its customers. Selling directly through television is an electronic option that originated in the USA and has expanded throughout Western Europe. Another option is electronic catalogues. France Telecom, for example, has established what is called the Teletel network. By the year 2000 there will be 6.5 million Minitel vidoetex terminals installed in French homes which not only serve as an electronic telephone directory but also display goods and services that can be ordered directly from the sellers by phone.

The direct communication media of the near future will be interactive, such as the Internet. By the year 2000, there will be an estimated 40 million 'digital' consumers expected to access interactive media at speeds five to 500 times faster than they can today. The Future Issues box provides some information on the current state of development and what needs to be done to successfully exploit the given opportunities in the future.

Interactive electronic media can dynamically deliver personalized two-way communication with identified users in real time. Procter & Gamble, the US No. 1 advertiser, for example, began advertising on the World Wide Web in April 1996, marking a major departure from TV and print advertising practice. Instead of compensating online companies, such as Yahoo!, for each consumer who sees a P & G ad, the company pays only when the online customer 'clicks' from that ad to one of Procter & Gamble's own Web sites. Thus the online provider only makes money if a customer who sees an advertisement promoting P & G's Sunny Delight juice drink, for example, moves on to its Sunny Delight Web site, which has a game with various prizes.[24]

The Internet can also be used for public relations purposes. For example, Parfums Fabergé, Paris, launched an Internet site in 1996 to accompany *The Shape of Things*, a four-part television programme it was sponsoring in the UK about design. The World Wide Web magazine, also entitled *The Shape of Things*, explored European design from various points of view. Although the site's principal aim was to provide an interesting and informative guide to European design, it also provided an obvious opportunity to build Fabergé's brand position – a passion for design – through overt linkage with contemporary design and style leaders.[25]

Beside information delivery and the opportunity to circumvent traditional intermediaries (discussed in Chapter 14), interactive electronic media allow the establishment of international customer relationships even for companies which would traditionally be restricted to doing only local business. For example, HotHotHot, a single-store retailer in Pasadena, California, which sells hot sauces, chilli mixes and other spicy food, created one of the World Wide Web's first commercial storefronts. Since the day the retailer's Web site became operational, HotHotHot has received daily orders, creating a steady revenue stream representing 20 per cent of total sales. What is more, the site drives store traffic, with online customers from all over the USA and Europe stopping by the store when they are in Pasadena, while communication costs on the Web site amount to only 5 per cent of online revenue.[26]

SUMMARY

The major objective of an international marketer in its many different efforts to communicate with the various stakeholders of the company in a multitude of country-markets is to achieve the intended strategic position of the company and its products in the stakeholders' minds. Examples of internationally successful companies show that this goal can best be reached if all market communication activities are coordinated in such a way that they are consistent and supportive of its corporate and brand identity. To ensure consistent market communication the international marketer has to develop a market communication policy. Policy development starts with the determination of the firm's most important stakeholder groups in the product- and country-markets served. For each of those stakeholder groups general communication objectives are fixed, and a communication platform is developed. The platform defines the central message to be communicated to all stakeholders of the firm. This central message then is refined into consistent core messages for each stakeholder group. To assure a local choice of communication tools appropriate for message transfer, the major tools the marketer wants to be applied in its international market communication also have to be determined. An additional guideline concerning corporate design defines the elements of all communication activities that have to be kept constant. Finally, the international marketer has to specify some rules of cooperation with external partners and rules of coordination among internal units for the implementation of market communication decisions.

Based on the international market communication policy, decisions concerning the integrated application of various communication tools can be taken. Public relations serve the planned building and maintenance of communicative relations between the company and its stakeholders with the objective of establishing a positively valued identity of the company in those stakeholders' perceptions.

International advertising is mainly used to stimulate potential customers' interest in the company's products, to make those products reach the intended position in the (potential) customers' minds, to continually remind the customers of the benefits to be gained by buying and using the product, and thereby preparing the ground for positive buying decisions by the customers. When developing an international advertising campaign, the marketer has to decide which parts of the campaign to standardize across country-markets and which parts to adapt locally. Besides influences from cultural differences, the availability of media in the targeted country-markets and legal restrictions on advertising in those markets need to be considered. The success of an international advertising campaign also depends on the company's ability to properly organize the production and international launching of its advertisements. For that purpose, an internal group of qualified people willing to cooperate across country-markets needs to be established and contacts with external service providers such as advertising agencies need to be managed.

Sales promotion is the catch-all term for short-term market communication decisions and activities that inform the target audience about the company's activities and products, encourage trial purchases by potential customers or stimulate repeat purchases, and help to build and enlarge distribution. Because sales promotion activities are basically local, the international marketer choosing the appropriate tools not only has to consider their fit with the general market communication objectives, but also the level of market development, the costs incurred, legal restrictions and intermediary capabilities as well as local cultural and business norms. For international coordination purposes the establishment of a central coordinator seems advisable.

As traditional media have become more expensive, cluttered and overloaded with commercial messages, sponsoring has increasingly become a costeffective alternative for international market communication. Besides customer awareness, sponsoring presents multiple opportunities to achieve awareness of other important stakeholders, such as media or administrators. But more importantly, sponsoring allows the meanings customers associate with the sponsor's name and with its products to be established, strengthened or changed. For that reason, the type of event, cause or activity considered for sponsoring must be carefully chosen to fit the image or meaning the sponsor wants to achieve with its customers and important stakeholders.

Finally, direct communication through electronic media is a market communication tool that is quickly increasing in importance. To stay internationally competitive, marketers will have to learn quickly how to use the entire communication potential of interactive electronic media creatively.

Discussion Questions

1. Discuss the need for internationally integrated market communication. Why is it that most international marketers are only at the beginning of such market communication integration?
2. What does it need for an international communicator to establish successful communication with the members of its audience?
3. Find an example of an event creating negative publicity for a firm operating internationally. How did the firm handle this situation? What do you suggest the firm should have done?
4. What needs to be checked and how, before an international marketer can decide to standardize its international advertising?
5. Why can companies with rather small international market communication budgets be as successful in communicating with their potential customers as much bigger companies with large advertising budgets? Find examples of what they have done.
6. Why are sales promotion activities mainly local? Find examples, and explain what an international marketer, nevertheless, can do to ensure their international coordination and their fit with the general market communication objectives of the firm.
7. Why can sponsoring be an attractive communication tool for international marketers? What does it need to make sponsoring internationally successful?

8. Compare examples of companies using new electronic media for direct communication with their potential customers and other stakeholders. How do their approaches differ? How internationally sensitive are they?
9. How would you suggest organizing the integrated market communication of a firm operating internationally and why?

Additional Readings

Harker, D. (1998) 'Achieving acceptable advertising: an analysis of advertising regulation in five countries', *International Marketing Review*, 15(2), 101–118.

Joachimsthaler, E. and D.A. Aacker (1997) 'Building Brands Without Mass Media', *Harvard Business Review*, January–February, 39–50.

Müller, W. (1996) 'Die Standardisierbarkeit internationaler Werbung: Kulturen verlangen Adaptionen', *Marketing-ZFP*, 3, 179–190.

'Integrated Marketing Communications' (1996) Special Issue: *Journal of Business Research*, 37(3), November.

Notes

[1] Joachimsthaler, E. and D.A. Aacker (1997) 'Building Brands Without Mass Media', *Harvard Business Review*, January–February, 39–50.

[2] Blackmon, D.A. (1996) 'UPS, Feeling Boxed In, Stages

Its Own Coming Out', *The Wall Street Journal*, 17 September, p. B4.

3 Engardio, P. and D. Roberts (1996) 'Microsoft's Long March', *Business Week*, 24 June, pp. 52–54.

4 Dawley, H. and P. Dwyer (1995) 'The Latest Shell Shock', *Business Week*, 27 November, p. 53.

5 Schiller, Z., G. Burns, and K.L. Miller (1996) 'Make It Simple', *Business Week*, 9 September, pp. 56–61.

6 Rapoport, C. (1994) 'Nestlé's Brand Building Machine', *Fortune*, 19 September, pp. 147–156.

7 op.cit.

8 'Comment les pubs se déclinent', *L'Entreprise*, No. 127, April 1996, p. 42.

9 Stewart-Allen, A.L. (1996) 'Creative new media in Europe here to stay?', *Marketing News*, 30(12), June, 15.

10 Ronkainen, I.A. and I. Menezes (1996) 'Implementing global marketing strategy, An interview with Whirpool Corporation', *International Marketing Review*, 13(3), 56–63.

11 Wentz, L. (1996) 'New power brokers hit world media scene', *Ad Age International*, 15 January.

12 'Adland Japan', *ESOMAR newsbrief*, 3(5), May 1995.

13 'Global coupon use up; Belgium tops in Europe', *Marketing News*, 25(16), August 1991, 5.

14 Diller, H. and I. Bukhari (1994) 'Pricing Conditions in the European Common Market', *European Management Journal*, 12(2), June, 163–170.

15 Joachimsthaler, E. and D.A. Aacker (1997) 'Building Brands Without Mass Media', *Harvard Business Review*, January–February, 39–50.

16 op. cit.

17 McCartney, S. (1996) 'Two Cents' Worth, Free Airline "Miles" Become a Potent Tool For Selling Everything', *The Wall Street Journal Europe*, 17 April pp. 1 and 6.

18 Hershey, J. (1996) 'CeBIT Is Big, Bold – And a Bit Too Much For Some Cybernauts', *The Wall Street Journal Europe*, 18 March, pp. 1 and 7.

19 Kashani, K. and J.A. Quelch (1990) 'Can Sales Promotion Go Global?', *Business Horizons*, May–June, pp. 37–43.

20 Lee, M-S., D.M. Sandler, and D. Shani (1997) 'Attitudinal constructs towards sponsorship, Scale development using three global sporting events', *International Marketing Review*, 14(3), 162.

21 Joachimsthaler, E. and D.A. Aacker (1997) 'Building Brands Without Mass Media', *Harvard Business Review*, January–February, 39–50.

22 'Un catalogue multinational . . . mais modulable', *L'Entreprise*, No. 127, April 1996, 43.

23 Joachimsthaler, E. and D.A. Aacker (1997) op. cit.

24 Schiller, Z. (1996) 'For More About Tide, Click Here', *Business Week*, 3 June 3, p. 33.

25 Glaskin, M. (1996) 'Making sense of the net', *Unilever Magazine*, First Issue, No. 99, pp. 22–26.

26 Kierzkowski, A., S. McQuade, R. Waitman and M. Zeisser (1996) 'Marketing to the Digital Consumer', *The McKinsey Quarterly*, No. 3, 5–21.

CHAPTER 18

INTERNATIONAL PRICING DECISIONS

LEARNING OBJECTIVES

After studying this chapter you will be able to:

↔

explain the complexity of pricing decisions in international business as compared to national sales

↔

explain the importance of an international pricing policy for the firm's sales activities

↔

distinguish the factors which influence the final price charged in a market

↔

explain their importance and impact on the price

↔

evaluate the risks to be considered and ways to reduce or cover them

↔

choose the method of payment best suited to a business deal

↔

discuss the pros and cons of countertrade

CHAPTER OUTLINE

International pricing decisions

International pricing policy

Standard pricing
Standard formula pricing
Pricing adaptation
Strategic pricing
Internal pricing

Factors of influence on price setting

Costs
The market
The macro-environment
Price escalation

Terms of payment

Factors affecting choice
Methods of payment

Managing financial risks

Choice of currency
Foreign currency account
Spot market
Selling foreign currency receivable
Foreign currency credit
Forward market
Foreign currency option
Guarantees
Insurance

Countertrade

Barter
Other forms of countertrade
Company and government motives
Concerns about countertrade
Countertrade opportunities

Impact on the marketing mix

INTERNATIONAL INCIDENT

Are International Prices Beyond Corporate Control?

The changing value of one currency versus the other is but one of the environmental issues which affect the setting of international prices. Generally, the exchange rate between currencies is seen as an uncontrollable variable, one which the organization must accept and one which they have little to no ability to influence. But recent changes in the US dollar to yen exchange rate, and the different ways Japanese and American carmakers seem to be reacting to those changes, may indicate that although the exchange rate cannot be directly managed, its impact upon international prices may be somewhat manageable.

Until the mid 1990s, US automakers enjoyed an average price advantage of USD 3,000 per car over Japanese models, thanks to the yen rising in value against the dollar (about 90 yen to the dollar), making Japanese exports more expensive in the US. But in the mid 1990s, that price advantage began rapidly evaporting, as the yen lost value against the dollar, rising to 115 to 130 against the dollar. Worse for US carmakers, North American consumers began to show an even greater interest in the affordability of new cars.

One challenge for US companies is that while the yen was very strong, Japanese firms designed lower cost-of-production cars, so they could be profitable at even 80 to 85 yen to the dollar. They also shifted more manufacturing to the US and Mexico, inside the NAFTA market. US automakers fought back by gaining in efficiency, even beginning to export more to Japan as the yen remained high and US companies gained in production efficiencies. Still, in 1997, Japanese car prices were cut by 1.1 per cent, while US companies increased their prices by 2.8 per cent. US companies lost even more sales to Japanese companies as a result. This loss is not only a result of the changes in the exchange rate, it is also partially a result of more investment by Japanese companies in design-efficient car models, increasing their spending on product development, and improving their processes in the value added chain.

Source: 'Detroit is Getting Sideswiped by the Yen', *Business Week*, 11 November 1996, p. 54.

INTERNATIONAL PRICING DECISIONS

Many marketers operating on an international level mention pricing when asked for the most difficult decision in their company's marketing mix. They attribute that difficulty to the increasing level of international competition from firms with different production costs, taxation systems, labour regulations or other business environments. Low growth in markets also contributes to the price-setting problem. So do different locations on the experience curve owing to the varying size of home markets.

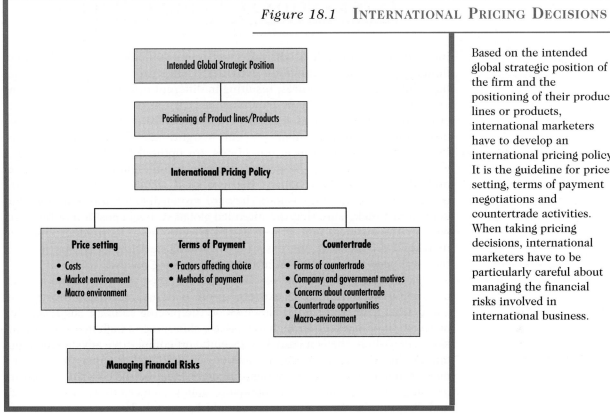

Figure 18.1 INTERNATIONAL PRICING DECISIONS

Based on the intended global strategic position of the firm and the positioning of their product lines or products, international marketers have to develop an international pricing policy. It is the guideline for price setting, terms of payment negotiations and countertrade activities. When taking pricing decisions, international marketers have to be particularly careful about managing the financial risks involved in international business.

When talking about prices most marketers think in terms of monetary returns. From a customer's perspective, however, the price of a good or service is the sum of all monetary and non-monetary assets the customer has to exchange (or 'spend') in order to obtain the good or service. As the balance of exchange discussed in Chapter 2 illustrated, customers may perceive that many 'costs' are associated with the product. Some of them cannot be influenced by the international marketer. Some are part of the product design; others are due to the distribution system the marketer has chosen or the positioning of the product offer.

But pricing decisions still need to be made, including the basic price of a product; the price structure of the entire product line; the system of rebates, discounts and refunds the firm will offer in exchange for specific actions; and the terms of payment under which a contract is entered (Figure 18.1). All international pricing decisions have to carefully consider and manage financial risks. Because of their importance in non-domestic marketing, this chapter gives special attention to non-monetary and partial monetary exchanges. Countertrade is of growing importance in a global business environment characterized by enhanced competition between industrialized and newly industrialized economies, as well as the hard currency shortages and huge trade imbalances of developing countries.

INTERNATIONAL PRICING POLICY

International pricing decisions are much more difficult to standardize than product decisions or promotion activities. Competitors in various countries have different cost structures, resulting in different prices. Taxes, duties, government regulations and political influences vary, as does the purchase power of the target markets. The distribution channels are of different lengths, and distribution-channel members expect margins specific to their markets. Prices set according to local conditions are optimal for the company as a whole, however, only if the pricing decision in one country does not affect profitability in another country. Because local managers tend to maximize goal achievement of the business they are responsible for, international marketers must make sure that the intended global strategic position of the company or the business unit as well as the positioning of its product lines and individual products are the basis for all pricing decisions. For that purpose they will need to formulate an international pricing policy.

The pricing policy should restate corporate objectives relevant to individual pricing decisions such as expected profit margins, returns on investment, and market shares. It should also include the pricing strategy, such as quick penetration of markets through low prices; skimming of high margins in market niches where the company has a significant competitive advantage; maintaining the competitive position in saturated markets; or concentrating on a market niche which requires a high-priced product versus covering the entire product category-market. The company policy concerning rebates, refunds and discounts given to customers should be stated. The terms of payment available to salespeople in their struggle to get orders, and to be used in specific markets, should also be indicated. These terms should be chosen according to company expectations, knowledge of the customers and the acceptable level of financial risk.

Standard Pricing

With a standard pricing policy, the marketer charges the same base price for a product in every country-market served. A company, for example, may set the price to wholesalers for its fountain pens at USD25 each in all markets. Either the customer has to pay for freight, insurance and duties directly, or the company adds a specific amount to the base price.

This is the simplest policy for a company to administer. The task of setting the product price according to the firm's position on the experience curve is also simplified. That is, the price can be set with reference to the company's projected unit costs. But standard pricing is also the least customer-oriented pricing policy, and it does not respond to competitive and environmental factors specific to each market. Products may end up overpriced, or even underpriced. Optimal positioning as well as maximum profitability are achieved only by chance.

Standard Formula Pricing

With standard formula pricing, the company calculates the price for a product following the same formula in all country-markets around the world. There are different ways to establish this formula.

Full-Cost Pricing. One formula is full-cost pricing. It consists of taking the full-cost price calculated for the product (production plus marketing, etc.) in the domestic market and adding the additional costs resulting from international transportation, taxes, tariffs, distribution and promotion. Often this alternative results in prices too high to be competitive in non-domestic markets.

Direct Cost Plus Contribution Margin. One option is to choose a direct-cost-plus-contribution-margin formula. The production cost of the product is taken as the basis and additional costs due to the non-domestic marketing process plus a desired profit margin are added. Because of the complexity of the international marketing process, however, additional indirect administrative and marketing costs may arise without being included in the formula. This method, therefore, may lead to prices that do not cover all the costs incurred by the company.

Relevant Cost. A differential formula or relevant cost formula is the most useful approach in standard formula pricing decisions. It includes all the incremental costs resulting from a non-domestic business opportunity that would not be incurred otherwise and adds them to the production cost. The manager then compares those costs with the additional revenues from the sale. If a suitable profit results, the price is set.

The biggest disadvantage of all these formulas is the resulting loss in company flexibility to react to differing or changing circumstances in the markets. A given strategic goal, such as high penetration of all served markets, may not be achieved owing to the non-flexible nature of the company's pricing policy.

Price Adaptation

Price adaptation as an international policy means that the prices of the company's products are determined in a decentralized manner, according to the local managers' analysis of the various markets. This policy allows extremely flexible reactions to market and competitive developments, but it has some major disadvantages.

First, local pricing increases the difficulty of developing a global strategic position. For example, a pen priced at USD15 (wholesale) in Italy but USD32 in Norway may represent two different market positions, one more prestigious than the other. Second, if the price differences between markets become too big there is a danger of parallel imports, or grey markets (basically, an import by an unauthorized party). When this occurs, channel members located in low-price markets not under the strict control of the firm may resell the product to market areas with significantly higher prices.

For example, the director of global marketing at the corporate headquarters of a US-based company selling prestigious high-priced liquor under the same established brand name in almost every country around the world received strong complaints from the head of the company's subsidiary in Japan about substantial quantities of the product that had entered the country through unauthorized channels. These imports were traced to the USA where they had been sold to a distributor at a highly competitive price. The distributor had sold some of the products to an exporter who shipped the liquor to Japan and made a profit by selling it to local wholesalers at prices below those charged by the liquor manufacturer's own Japanese subsidiary.

ETHICS BOX

Gray Markets

AS PARALLEL IMPORTING SPREADS, A GROWING number of nations will face the question: What does a trademark owner own? The answer to this question largely depends on ethical standards agreed upon in different societies.

The US Supreme Court affirmed the Customs Service in: (1) denying imports by a third party when US firms purchase US trademark rights from independent foreign firms; and (2) permitting entry when US firms register US trademarks for goods manufactured abroad by foreign partner firms, incorporated foreign subsidiaries, or unincorporated foreign divisions. The Court disapproved entry when a US trademark owner authorizes an independent foreign manufacturer to use the trademark abroad (Kmart Corp. v. Cartier, Inc. *et al.* (1988), 86 Supreme Court 495).

However, regulations on gray markets may vary considerably from country to country. In Hong Kong and Singapore there is a flood of parallel imports ranging from small ticket items, such as soap and batteries, to more expensive goods, such as watches and electronic equipment. Several sole agents have taken parallel importers to court, but so far the courts have ruled in favor of parallel importers, thus granting them a justifiable status.

A European Commission regulation mandates that auto manufacturers have to deliver a car to every citizen in any country of the EU. Also, each subsidiary of an automaker is required to back its warranty in every country regardless of where the car is purchased. Because this regulation has not led to a levelling of car prices, some car dealers in Europe specialize in offering 'Euro-cars', parallel imported from other European countries. The car buyer can order a car from a catalog for delivery in about three weeks.

Sources: Assmus, G. and C. Wiese (1995) 'How to Address the Gray Market Threat Using Price Coordination', *Sloan Management Review*, Spring, 31–41; and Palia, A.P. and Ch.F. Keown (1991) 'Combating Parallel Importing: Views of US Exporters to the Asia-Pacific Region', *International Marketing Review*, 8(1), 49.

Besides such parallel imports to served country-markets which may arise, price adaptation may also lead to reimports to the country where a product was manufactured if prices in the foreign market are significantly lower than in the home market. Henkel, an international marketer of adhesives headquartered in Germany, had such a problem with Belgian re-exporters because prices in Belgium were too low. Other examples such as Japanese 35 mm cameras imported from Hong Kong to Europe, and Kodak film, made in the USA, imported from Taiwan to Germany illustrate that lateral importation through unauthorized channels may take place.

Depending on the legal regulations in the countries involved, grey markets may be relatively easy to stop but also hard to rule out (see the Ethics box). In the EU countries, for example, Articles 85 and 86 of the Treaty of Rome forbid limitations of free trade between and among member states. EU Commission and EU Court rulings have established the legality of all kinds of grey imports. For example, the UK's Parker Pen paid a penalty of 700,000 ECU (about USD980,000) when it tried to prevent its German distributor, Herlitz, from exporting Parker pens to other European countries.

FUTURE ISSUES BOX

International Price Data Bases

IN THE EUROPEAN UNION THERE EXIST INTERNATIONAL price agencies which create markets of industrial and consumer products whenever price differentials between countries are large enough to support profitable operations. The basis of their success is a large database of price lists in a number of country-markets for every product-market they serve. Product specifications are backed up on CD-ROM so that customers' price, quality, and quantity requests can be answered instantly. The database is updated regularly – in most cases every week – by business partners in each country. Updates are made to the central computer via modem.

Direct customer access to such databases is the next logical step. In the future, every consumer or industrial buyer with a computer may have access to the prices of any number of product categories anywhere in the world, and will be able to buy directly from the least expensive source. A human intermediary will not be needed for the creation of international markets.

Source: Assmus, G. and C. Wiese (1995) 'How to Address the Gray Market Threat Using Price Coordination', *Sloan Management Review*, Spring, 31–41.

Distribution channels that are not at all consistent with the firm's strategic positioning can easily get certain products. Perfume, for example, that has been promoted as highly sophisticated and prestigious may suddenly be found in discount stores. The grey-market outlets profit from the marketing efforts of the company, but often they do not provide the same level of customer service as the approved intermediaries. Those intermediaries, of course, complain about the unexpected competition. Because customers do not draw a distinction between regular channels of distribution and grey markets, such a development is usually detrimental to the overall business of the company. The Future Issues box describes how internationally adapted prices have contributed to the creation of international price agencies for industrial and consumer products and what further developments marketers can expect through the spread of computer networks.

Strategies used to combat grey markets require suppliers to obtain accurate and timely information on their existence and magnitude. Data sources such as product serial numbers, warranty cards and factory rebate programmees need to be used. They increase costs but help to track the movement of the product to parallel importers and to assess the magnitude of the problem.

Strategies of a priori avoiding parallel imports are less costly than combating them after they have happened. Henkel, for example, learning from negative experience, has built a computer model, including cost factors, trade structures, physical distribution costs, and price differences regarded as acceptable, to calculate price differences ('price corridors') between European country-markets that will avoid parallel imports. In addition a 'European Management Team' including managers of subsidiaries in the most important European markets regularly discusses pricing policy issues.

Strategic Pricing

The absolute minimum of price standardization necessary to attain the intended global strategic position can be achieved through price lines (or price patterns) set by the home office. Price lines set the company's prices relative to competitors'. They are followed in each market, but regional or local management can accommodate local costs, customer-income levels, distribution margin requirements, and competition. Price lines also allow adaptation of prices to the changing market-saturation levels that accompany different stages in the product life cycle.

Price differentiation among country-markets can be achieved without hampering the company's overall pricing strategy. HILTI, Liechtenstein's specialist in fastening problems, for example, follows a global high-price strategy based on superior quality and direct distribution. Its products are more expensive than those of all competitors wherever they are sold. Nevertheless, HILTI's prices in Japan are only about 50 per cent of European prices over all its product lines, because of necessary adaptation to local price levels.

Strategic pricing requires central coordination of pricing decisions. The people responsible for local pricing decisions not only have to follow the price lines, but also report to company headquarters their decisions concerning specific prices. The specialists in the home office, having a general overview of the company's prices and the prices of relevant competitors, will then accept the suggested prices or negotiate with the local managers to come to a mutually acceptable solution. How difficult it may be to find a decision acceptable to all parties involved is illustrated by the variations of average prices in the European detergent market. The average price ratio of concentrated to powder detergents is about 60 per cent in Germany compared to 100 per cent in neighbouring Belgium. Product line pricing across markets would not be consistent with prevailing price structures. Too much adaptation would lead to grey markets.[1]

Internal Pricing

Goods, services, personnel, capital, rights and know-how are readily transferred across national boundaries between subsidiaries. As a consequence the company has to determine how it wants to be paid, where, and how much for its deliveries to non-domestic affiliates. It has to establish an internal pricing policy, also referred to as intracompany pricing or transfer pricing. In effect, guidelines have to be developed on how to set prices that transfer funds between different parts of the company and allocate resources to specific uses. The prices are not necessarily linked to the market value of the items transferred. The decision on what prices to charge has to take into account the firm's goals of maximizing and managing profits and of optimizing the development of the company as a whole, the subsidiaries' goals of successful development and earning recognition for their efforts, and headquarters' need to determine and compare the performance of its non-domestic business units. For example, if profit is transferred out of a subsidiary, the manager of that subsidiary should be evaluated on criteria other than just how much profit was generated.

Objectives. The company's tax payments can be lowered by using internal pricing to transfer profits from units in high-tax areas to low-tax areas.

Australian companies, for example, are said to move about USD2 billion a year to corporate links in low- or no-tax countries, like Singapore and Hong Kong. In Europe, companies locate a sales subsidiary that officially handles their entire international sales activities in a low-tax country such as Switzerland. That subsidiary purchases the products from the factory at cost and sells them at a profit to customers and affiliates around the world. Physically, the products never touch Swiss soil. They are shipped straight from the factory to the customers' premises.

Internal pricing can also be used to transfer profits from countries with foreign-exchange restrictions or other economic controls to the unit that is supposed to make profits. This transfer is made possible by charging higher prices than reflect their true cost of production for merchandise, royalty payments on licences, or payment for services delivered to the local subsidiary. Even if corporate tax rates are similar between parent and subsidiary countries, differences in tariff rates on the transferred goods are important in the determination of transfer prices. Machine parts, for example, might enjoy lower tariff rates than assembled machines.

Other uses of internal pricing include counteracting the influences of currency-exchange fluctuations, reducing the impact of inflation on the company's assets, subsidizing new subsidiaries while they build market share, and justifying high prices in one area of the world while making profits in another. For example, some oil companies have justified their high petrol prices in Europe by claiming they make very low profits, owing to high costs, in Europe. They purchase the petrol from their own European refineries, which also make low profits. The refineries, however, purchase crude oil from oil-transportation companies that are located in low-tax countries. Of course, the transportation companies, which make substantial profits, are also controlled by the oil companies.

The internal-pricing policy of a firm operating internationally must permit the achievement of corporate objectives while also allowing the company to live in peace with the local tax authorities. IBM, for example, is proud of being a good taxpayer in the countries where it does business.

Methods. Internal prices should be easy to determine. Basically there are two approaches to calculating internal prices. One is to calculate the market price of goods, services or know-how. This approach is well suited to adapting to, and accounting for, local market conditions. The internal price would be the local market price minus the margin necessary for the subsidiary to cover its costs and expected profit margin. The approach is easy to justify to government authorities. It also allows every affiliate to be organized as its own profit centre. But it raises the question of what costs to consider in the determination of the price. An international marketer introducing a product new to the local market may have difficulties in justifying the chosen internal price to government authorities.

For US-based companies, Section 482 of the Internal Revenue Code calls for the determination of arm's-length prices for internal pricing. This is the price that would have resulted from negotiations between independent business partners in a similar transaction. Only if this method cannot be applied, because no similar transfers have been made in an open market, can the company use another method to calculate the internal price. This code applies to all allocations of income between US parent companies and their foreign operations, as well as between US operations and their foreign parent companies.

Factors of
Influence on Price Setting

In certain cases the marketer has little influence on the price that can be obtained for a product. The mechanisms of supply and demand dictate the price for largely undifferentiated products (such as wheat, copper, coffee, cement, flour and crude oil) that are marketed in large quantities on international commodity exchanges. Also, when a government is the customer or the marketer is confronted with strongly restrictive government regulations, the company often has only one alternative: accept the price or lose the customer's business.

However, most manufactured products and many services offer the opportunity of price setting. The marketer analyses all relevant costs, the market environment, and relevant dimensions of the macro-environment such as economic conditions and governmental influences; sets the price based on these analyses; and then manages price escalation.

Costs

Costs determine the product's lower price limit. In the long run they have to be fully covered for the business to survive. In international pricing decisions, the same basic cost factors apply as in domestic pricing. There are some additional costs, however, that can strongly influence the minimum price of a product when sold in another country.

The costs of doing business, such as information gathering, travel expenses, and support of employees, are usually considerably higher in international than in domestic marketing. The longer the distribution channel, the higher the sum of margins and allowances added for middlemen will be (see Figure 18.2). Additional packaging and labelling, transportation and inventory-financing costs, as well as additional insurance against damage or loss, also increase the price. Regardless of whether they are absorbed by the company or passed on to the customer, taxes, tariffs and administrative fees (for documents, for example) add to international costs as well. Turnover taxes (in Japan and other countries) and value-added taxes (most popular in Europe) vary between 2 and 32 per cent.

The Market

Market factors that affect the prices of goods and services are customers, competitors, business groups, and the country-specific structure of distribution.

Customers. The attractiveness of a product to the target customers determines its real value, that is, the theoretical price ceiling in a given market. This price level will be decreased in many cases by the limited purchasing power of customers (especially in LDCs and developing economies in Eastern Europe, Latin America and Southeast Asia). When prices are negotiated between business partners (for example, marketers and government agencies), the final price also depends on their negotiation skills.

Competition. The prices of competitive products and customer satisfaction with those products strongly influence what customers are willing to pay for

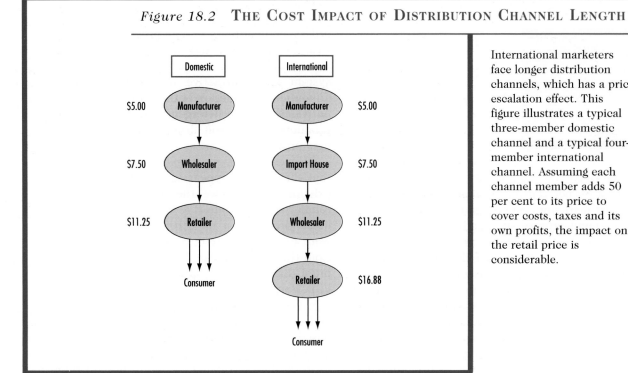

Figure 18.2 THE COST IMPACT OF DISTRIBUTION CHANNEL LENGTH

International marketers face longer distribution channels, which has a price escalation effect. This figure illustrates a typical three-member domestic channel and a typical four-member international channel. Assuming each channel member adds 50 per cent to its price to cover costs, taxes and its own profits, the impact on the retail price is considerable.

the international marketer's product. A company's price setting, therefore, is influenced by the competitive structure of local markets. In the ice-cream market of the European Union, for example, only one company – Eskimo, which belongs to Unilever – has achieved a significant presence in all member countries. In Germany, Italy, Belgium and the Netherlands, local firms play an important role. This means that Eskimo has to deal with varying competitors with different backgrounds and competitive advantages. In Germany, the main competitor has a strong position in the premium segment, whereas in Belgium the local prime contender has set prices in the low to medium range. Eskimo's international price setting has to take these country-specific con-stellations into account.[2]

Generally, competition has the tendency to lower prices, to a point that may become dangerous to the existence of the firm. Deregulation of the US air travel market, for example, has driven some well-known companies, such as Eastern Airlines or PanAm, out of business. Deregulation in Europe led to problems of existence for airlines such as Italy's Alitalia, Belgium's Sabena or French Air Inter. The example of Trans World Airlines' introduction of Comfort Class in 1993, however, shows that participation in price wars is not inevitable. Robert Cozzi, the US airline's senior vice president of marketing, proposed removing 5 to 40 seats per plane to give passengers more legroom. The move raised TWA's added value. The company soared to first place in customer satisfaction for long-haul flights. This was a win for TWA but also for other airlines. With fuller planes, TWA was not about to start a price war.[3]

Business Groups.   Companies may try to limit competition by forming one or more business groups. Industry associations, for example, gather informa-

STRATEGY BOX

The Battle: P & G Against Retailers

IN GERMANY THE 10 LARGEST RETAILERS CONTROL almost 80 per cent of the market and even the biggest marketers cannot ignore them. Retailers and manufacturers sit together at the end of every year to negotiate on product ranges (listings) and discounts for the following year. In this situation, a jungle of discount systems has emerged. Currently, there are at least 25 different types of discounts, for example for turnover increases, jubilees or mergers. These discounts mean that retailers can supply goods a little more cheaply than their competitors.

Because of the wide range of products and the variety of discounts, Procter & Gamble have enormous expenses. More than 100 people are responsible for handling and controlling the complicated order and discount system. They are among the first marketers to try to break it. In 1996, they began negotiations with retailers by announcing that they will cancel all discounts and replace them with a much simpler system of permanent low manufacturer prices. According to this system, discounts will be given based on the amount of goods ordered, continuity of orders, compatibility of data processing systems with those of P & G, and also on the ease of facilities to deliver the ordered goods. To make the system more attractive to retailers, P & G announced a reduction of the variety of its product range: 26% in detergents, 32% in baby care products, 30% in soft drinks, and 15% in body care products.

However, first reactions of retailers showed that they do not appear to want to give up the existing system. Rewe, the number one German retailer removed one P & G detergent from the listed products of its 2,100 Penny shops and were expected to remove more P & G brands from the listing. Edeka, hitherto having ordered more than USD 600 million worth of goods per year from P & G, said that it will stop ordering P & G's products. Although Procter & Gamble and a minority of retailers believe that the proposed system would be more effective, the future must show if the firm's brands are strong enough to force the big retailers to keep most of them listed. Experience in the US where P & G started the same attempt five years earlier, show that at first, retailers slowed purchases. But by 1996 the firm's overall volume market-share in the US had either held steady or increased for 38 months in a row.

Sources: Schöneberg, U. (1996) 'The battle: P & G against retailers', *ESOMAR newsbrief*, 4(1), January, 5; Schiller, Z., G. Burns and K.L. Miller (1996) 'Make it Simple', *Business Week*, 9 September, p. 58.

tion about market developments and transactions. They may represent their members in negotiations with governments or unions, as is the case in most European countries. Loose groups of competitors may agree on general rules of fair competition. Cartels may set prices (as OPEC tries to do), allocate market areas, establish sales volumes (as in the paper industry in some countries), or even constitute a selling unit that distributes profits to the members at the end of the year. The international marketer has to evaluate the market power of such groups and sometimes join them, when the legal regulations at home and in the local market are appropriate. When the chances of winning are high, some firms choose to fight them.

Distribution. The level of concentration in local distribution varies across countries. In the Netherlands, for example, the top two food retailers hold a higher market share than the top seven in Italy. As a result, the potential of international marketers to freely set their prices and to use various above-the-line discounts may differ considerably within similar retail formats (see the Strategy box).

But also the importance of retail organization types differs between country-markets. Watch distribution in Italy and Spain, for example, mainly relies on traditional retailers such as jewellers and watch stores. In Australia watches are sold by supermarkets and department stores. Such differences not only influence the channel costs to be considered in price setting but also the potential of an international marketer to set prices and freely determine terms of payment.

In addition, the degree of internationalization of intermediaries strongly affects a marketer's ability to achieve price differentiation. International retail chains or procurement groups may purchase in the country with the lowest price level or force their suppliers to charge the same (lowest) price in all served country-markets.

The Macro-Environment

Economic Conditions.   Of all the economic conditions, income distribution, growth rates, exchange rates and inflation have the strongest impacts on international pricing decisions. The income distribution of a country-market affects the prices at which different groups of customers can afford the company's products. Growth rates are an index of market maturity. In fast-growing, young product-markets pricing decisions are often made with the goal of keeping up with the pace or even winning a substantial market share before others. In more mature or stagnant markets, price competition may be fierce when local or regional competitors try to fend off new market entrants who set low prices to attract customers.

For example, in 1992, when Compaq Computer of Houston, Texas started selling desktop PCs in Japan for less than half of what local manufacturers had been asking, they started a price war. Fujitsu, Japan's biggest computer company, determined not to lose market share, reacted by selling PCs at a loss. It could easily make the loss up with profits from semiconductors and telecom gear. That stirred up market leader NEC Corp. which matched Fujitsu's price cuts, in some cases even undercutting them. As a consequence, Compaq, the world's leading PC vendor, boosted its market share in Japan by only 0.1 points in 1995, to a puny 3.8 per cent. CEO Pfeiffer reacted by de-emphasizing low-margin consumer sales and pursuing higher-margin business PC and server sales.[4]

The influence of exchange rates on prices is illustrated by fluctuations in the value of the US dollar in Germany in 1980–1988. The dollar was exchanged for DM 1.8 in 1980, went up to a value of more than DM 3 in 1984, but went down again to nearly DM 1.5 in 1988. This means that prices for US products headed for Germany first rose nearly 100 per cent, and then were cut in half in less than four years. Managing such fluctuations will be discussed in the section on methods of payment.

High inflation requires periodic price adjustments to cover rising costs. Because inflation rates are not the same in different country-markets, the international marketer is confronted with a sometimes complex puzzle of possible price changes and risks. If inflation is high in the country of production, the firm may not be able to adjust prices as necessary, and it may thus be forced to absorb increases in input prices. If inflation is high in the customer's country, the feasibility of increasing prices will depend on the reaction of customers, government controls, and the additional costs of changing price tags, reprogramming cash registers, and other activities related to price changes. If payment from a customer located in an inflationary market is expected to be delayed (which would lower the real price paid), the inflation rate should be considered in price negotiations.

Government.   Government activities and regulations also influence prices. The effects of exchange rate and balance-of-payment policies have already been discussed in Chapter 4. Governments may also impose price controls on specific products. These may be price floors, price ceilings, restrictions on price changes, or maximum or minimum profit margins. In some European nations, for example, retailers are forbidden to sell products below the price they paid for them, and standard-quality bread, milk, sugar and flour have regulated prices that retailers may not increase. In the early 1980s, all price changes were forbidden by the French government for a certain amount of time to support its struggle against inflation. More recently, for certain products the Norwegian government has set margins that may not be undercut by competitors.

Government subsidies can help lower prices to increase marketers' global competitiveness. Such subsidies often depend on the power of lobby groups and other non-economic developments. The US government, for example, is an ardent fighter against subsidies that decrease prices and distort competition in the iron and steel industries. But it heavily subsidizes farmers, allowing them to export grains at prices that cannot be matched by farmers in developing countries.

Frequently, exports of government-subsidized products are viewed in the importing country as dumping. In these situations, domestic competitors put pressure on their governments to impose a countervailing tariff to make the imported product equivalent in price to the domestically produced one.

Price Escalation

The result of all of these factors of influence may be price escalation. Table 18.1 contains an example of how the costs of an exported product, from manufacture to delivery to the first channel member, are calculated. Marketing costs and taxes in the local market have to be added to derive the final customer price. Considering all the additions to the domestic price 'ex works' (at the point of production), it is understandable that the consumer price for a Canada-manufactured product sold in Japan may be double the price charged in the domestic market.

In many cases, price-escalation effects will prohibit the marketer from successfully entering new country-markets. However, there are several approaches to counteract the problem, as is demonstrated by consumer products sold overseas at a lower price than the domestic price (such as Italian wine and shoes sold in the USA).

The firm may choose to enter markets that are in an early stage of the product's life cycle, and are therefore less resistant to higher prices. It may position the product (or product line) so that it does not directly compete with less expensive competitors. An innovative shortening of the distribution channel, without decreasing the level of customer service, may also reduce

> ### Table 18.1 AN EXAMPLE OF THE PRICE CALCULATION FOR AN EXPORTED PRODUCT

Production cost	USD10.00
+ Profit margin (10%)	1.00
Price 'ex works'	USD11.00
+ Transportation	.50
+ Transport insurance	.05
+ Freight-forwarding fee	.02
+ Handling costs	.02
Price 'FOR/FOT'	USD11.59
+ Cost of shipment to boarder	.20
+ Export support fee	.03
+ Export administration fees	.01
Price 'delivered at frontier'	USD11.83
+ Cost of shipment to port of departure	.05
Price 'freight carriage' (and insurance), port of departure	USD11.88
+ Port costs	.04
Price 'free on board', port of departure	USD11.92
+ Cost of documents	.01
+ Cost of bill of lading	.01
+ Sea freight	.15
Price 'C&F', port of destination	USD12.09
+ Freight insurance FPA (free particular average)	.06
Price 'cost, insurance, freight', port of destination	USD12.15
= Price 'ex ship', port of destination	
+ Port costs	.10
Price 'ex quai' (duties on buyer's account)	USD12.25
+ Import duties	1.10
Price 'ex quai', port of destination	USD13.35
+ Transportation costs	.70
+ Freight-forwarder costs	.25
+ Transportation insurance	.15
Price 'delivered, duty paid'	USD14.45

In order to export a product, many functions must be performed. Each, of course, must be paid for. This table illustrates how the price to the importer (the price 'delivered, duty paid') grows from the full cost of manufacturing.

costs. This is particularly important when a cumulative turnover tax has to be paid.

Product modifications, such as shipping components to be assembled in the target market, may change the tariff rate. Cars exported to Brazil, for example, once rated a lower tariff when the tyres were not mounted on them until after their arrival at the docks. The modification may also consist of replacing costly materials and features with less expensive ones, if the change does not negatively influence the value to the customer.

Assembly of components, production of parts, or production of the entire product either locally or in a third, low-wage country are other possible ways to counteract price escalation. Japanese car makers such as Toyota, Honda or Nissan have built factories in Ireland, the UK and the USA to be able to serve the EU and NAFTA markets at competitive prices. European companies, such as VA MCE, an Austrian supplier of mechanical engineering and industrial services, found it necessary to produce goods for the US market in Mexico.

A way to reduce the impact of higher prices on customer demand is to lease the product. This is a particularly attractive approach for international marketers of industrial goods, such as machine tools, transportation vehicles or industrial robots. It not only helps overcome the short-term negative effect of a high price, but may also help to lessen the problems of insufficient hard currency or the costs of product-maintenance personnel. In fact, the ability to lease, or to provide credit at low interest rates, is a significant marketing tool for today's international marketer.

A final solution is to lower the net price. This can be achieved by constantly increasing the company's productivity, then gaining economies of scale. But it can also be done for a short span of time by diminishing the profit margin. Or the firm can charge only part of the costs. Most or all of the product's R&D (research and development) costs, for example, can be charged to the home market. This approach has to be considered with prudence, however. It not only directly influences the company's profit margin (prices once lowered can seldom be substantially raised later), but may also lead to the filing of dumping charges by local competitors.

The final price for a product should not be set before the business partners negotiate the terms of sale and the terms of payment. The various terms of sale available to an international marketer and their consequences for business partners concerning costs and risks to be borne have been discussed in Chapter 15. The most frequently applied terms of payment in international marketing are discussed in the following section.

TERMS OF PAYMENT

Terms of payment are most often the result of a sales-negotiation process. They state the point in time and the circumstances of payment for the goods or services to be delivered.[5] Every marketer wants to get paid as quickly as possible and according to the invoice. Customers want to obtain the merchandise as ordered. A smooth process of exchange is in the interest of both parties, therefore. But many potential payment disputes can disturb the process, especially in international marketing.

Factors Affecting Choice

The most important determinant of payment terms is the financial risk anticipated by the business partners in the transactional process. Financial risk in international payment procedures may arise from various sources: business partner reliability, distance, the nature of the merchandise, political or social instability, fluctuating exchange rates, currency exchange restrictions, inflation and temporary financing.

Beside these sources of financial risk, the industry standards and degree of competition may affect the choice of terms of payment. Companies that are in a highly competitive industry (such as the telecommunications, PC or steel-making industries) or are mass marketers of consumer goods (such as Nestlé, Matsushita or Whirlpool) may have to accept a higher-risk payment form in order to offer a competitive pricing option to their customers. Other determinants of payment terms include the market strength and negotiation skills of each of the business partners, and the degree of the marketer's customer orientation.

Payment Risk. A lack of business-partner reliability results in payment risk. The level of trust and the strength of the relationship between the two business partners as well as the level of knowledge about the buyer's financial strength or weakness strongly influence the chosen term of payment. Sales subsidiaries normally get their merchandise on an open-account basis. But most Korean companies will not deliver anything to Colombian customers, for example, without having received an irrevocable letter of credit, owing to the higher risks.

Product Risk. Another source of financial risk is the distance between the business partners. Distance influences the duration and complication of shipment. It can also reduce the safety and quality of the product; that is, it results in a product risk for the customer. A Swiss wholesaler selling blue jeans manufactured in Thailand to an importer in Denmark, therefore, will not pay for the goods before his bank has received and approved the entire set of shipping documents agreed in the terms of payment.

The nature of the merchandise also influences the perception of financial risks. If Davidov, the Belgian marketer of cigars, purchases tobacco from Egypt, for example, it will not pay the invoiced amount before having inspected the quality of the merchandise. On the other hand, a Swedish supplier of fighter aircraft such as Saab Scania AB may not start to deliver Gripen fighters to The Republic of Congo before getting paid an advance of one-third of the entire contract's value.

Institutional Risk. Another source of financial risk is political or social instability in one or both of the partners' home countries. This results in institutional risk. For example, many companies in Hungary, Poland and Slovakia involved in business with the former Soviet Union not only lost essential orders but also their base of existence when the USSR was split up into a group of countries, such as Armenia, Azerbaijan, Belarus, Estonia, Kazakhstan, Latvia and Moldova to name just a few, with no convertible currencies.

Currency Risk. Currency risk arises from fluctuating exchange rates (=exchange-rate risk), which strongly affect the price of the merchandise and the potential profit, or from currency exchange restrictions. Exchange-rate risk arises from the need to conduct the international business transaction in at least one foreign currency. The terms of payment state a price in a particular currency. For example, an export from a US-based company to one in the UK might be billed at USD5,750, payable in 30 days upon receipt of the invoice. Thus the importer is assuming the exchange-rate risk. If the value of the US dollar increases after the price has been set, the UK importer will have to exchange more pounds for dollars, effectively raising the price of the imported product. Of course, if the price of the product is quoted in a foreign currency, the home-country organization bears the exchange-rate risk.

Associated with exchange-rate risk is the risk that the exchange of currencies might be restricted. A blocked currency means that the government does not allow any international transfer of domestic currencies. When selling consumer goods to Romania, for example, payment must be fixed in a foreign currency, mainly USD, DM (German marks) or CHF (Swiss francs). If the payment does not go directly from the customer to the local bank managing the supplier's foreign currency account and from there via the country's central bank to the marketer's bank in the home country, an even more complex cycle of bank transfers will be started. Because banks in most Eastern European countries have no direct relationships with each other, every transfer has to pass through the central bank. Each bank involved in the transfer charges some fee (mostly a percentage of the transferred sum), diminishing the final amount the marketer will find in his account.

Less severe than blocked currencies are currency licensing restrictions. These occur when all foreign-exchange transactions must be done through a central bank, or another agency, at the official (and fixed) rate. This system controls the sale or purchase of products by granting or denying a licence to sell or buy foreign currency. Taiwan, for example, requires all exporters and importers to buy currencies through its central bank. In Hungary and Poland licences for foreign-exchange transactions are no longer needed. But in most cases written documentation of the business deal is required before the national bank will become involved. This means that the handling of foreign-exchange transactions is rather time consuming, resulting in additional costs.

Multiple exchange rates also restrict currencies. In this case, products approved by the local administration are assigned currency exchange rates that facilitate sales by lowering their prices. Non-approved goods are in effect penalized by exchange rates that make their prices higher.

Import-deposit requirements influence the real exchange rate by requiring companies selling to a certain country to deposit a specific amount of money with the government or a domestic bank prior to the sale. Once the funds are deposited, a licence for foreign-currency transfer or permission to sell is granted. Many developing nations use this form of restriction, which effectively increases the amount of money lost while those inactive funds are held as the deposit.

Finally, national banks or administrative bodies may control the quantity of currency that is exchanged. For example, before 1990 tourists crossing the border from West Berlin to East Berlin had to exchange a specific amount of West German marks for East German marks. These marks could not be exchanged back when returning to West Berlin. Other countries may place a quota on the amount of foreign or local currency that may be brought into, or taken out of, the country. Countries with no freely convertible currencies, such as the People's Republic of China, do not allow their citizens to leave the country with more than the equivalent of a few hundred dollars, or less, in the domestic currency. Quantity control effectively influences the volume of products that can be traded, because it changes the price of the product and the costs of marketing support.

When exchange restrictions are lifted, sizeable adjustments in financial markets and trade flows may result. When Poland eliminated its convertibility restrictions, for example, trade flows with former COMECON partners decreased whereas markets for both consumer and industrial goods were opened to more international buyers and sellers.

All kinds of existing currency exchange restrictions will be considered when the terms of payment are specified in a sales contract. They mainly complicate the documentation needed before any monetary transaction takes place, or lead to commercial transactions with little or no financial settlement, so-called countertrade agreements.

Inflation Risk. Inflation directly affects the real buying power of the market and therefore constitutes another source of financial risk. While exchange-rate fluctuations are in theory supposed to exactly offset the inflation rate, inflation in fact may be greater or even less than the change in currency rates. Devaluation of a currency should increase exports, because export prices will be lower. But this may not occur if the change is overwhelmed by a high inflation rate.

For example, at the end of the 1980s Italy experienced an ongoing devaluation of the lira against the Dutch florin and other closely related European currencies. Simultaneously the difference in the inflation rates in Italy compared to the Netherlands and other more economically stable countries such as Austria, Germany and Switzerland were higher than the devaluation of the Italian currency. This caused exports to Italy to experience growing price advantages. The Italian government was forced to counteract that dangerous development for the country's industry. The national bank devaluated the lira overnight by about 25 per cent. As a result, exporters to Italy who had not sheltered their open lira accounts against devaluation encountered substantial losses.

The inflation risk also has a direct effect on international finance. Highly fluctuating inflation rates, for example, not only influence the price that must be set, but also the value of profits that are transferred back to the parent company. There are also certain asset-management decisions that must be made with respect to economies experiencing high inflation. For example, when the Brazilian economy was experiencing 1000 per cent inflation, Brazilian buyers tried to minimize accounts receivable and maximize accounts payable. This is because the value of the money used to settle accounts decreased daily. Thus prolonging payment meant that the buying company would pay in 'cheaper' (less valuable) money.

Interest-Rate Risk. Setting terms of payment also presents the company with an interest-rate risk. This risk exists when the inflow and outflow of a currency do not match, and temporary financing is required. This is true either domestically or internationally. An international cash manager has an opportunity to raise money from a wider set of sources than does a domestic manager. At the same time, funds owed internationally are also subject to changing interest rates. If two or more currencies are involved in the debt of a company and interest rates change, the internationally operating firm will be exposed to higher interest rate risks compared to a domestic one.

For example, a US-based seller of cattle to Japan and the UK may borrow to finance the costs of the sale and inventory, until an inflow of capital from the buyers occurs. A decision has to be made, including whether to be paid in dollars, yen or pounds sterling and in which country and currency the seller prefers to finance working capital. The loan is subject to interest-rate fluctuations. Depending on the fluctuation of interest to be paid or earned in the three countries, the profit of the cattle marketer can vary significantly.

Methods of Payment

The methods of payment not only regulate the way goods or services are to be exchanged, but they also represent a financial tool that can be used effectively in a competitive marketing programme. Figure 18.3 gives an overview of the parties potentially involved in international payment procedures and their relationships. In addition to the primary business partners, most often their banks will be involved. National regulations and international agreements also affect payment procedures and have to be followed. Third parties, for example

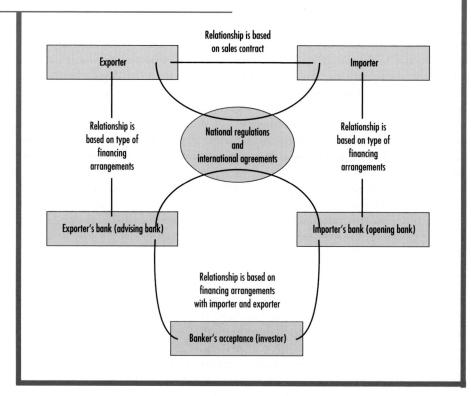

Figure 18.3 THE PARTIES INVOLVED IN AN
INTERNATIONAL PAYMENT PROCEDURE

To ensure that the exporter gets paid by the importer, various parties must be involved, and many activities must be completed.

Source: Eng, M. (1982) 'Trade Financing', in Walter, I. and T. Murray (eds.), *Handbook of International Business,* New York: John Wiley & Sons, p. 137. Reprinted by permission of John Wiley & Sons Inc.

investors who buy the financial arrangement (similar to the idea of factoring account receivables) or government-run export banks providing guarantees, may enter the picture. Depending upon the parties involved, and the factors that affect choice, the specific method of payment will be selected.

The methods of payment available to the international marketer range from high-credit, high-risk, customer-oriented methods to low-credit, low-risk, producer-oriented methods. These are discussed in the following section.

Consignment.   When a consignment contract exists, the marketer or consignor delivers the products to the customer but retains the title to them until the customer has sold them to a third party or has consumed/used them and paid the marketer. For example, Rhône Poulenc, a French marketer of special chemicals, may have a contract with a customer in Morocco under which the barrels containing the chemicals are stored at the customer's premises, but remain Rhône Poulenc's property until they enter the production process. The consignee is assured of having the needed volume of merchandise at each point in the production process and in many cases does not have to pay taxes or duties before using the products.

Efficient use of consignment requires that the marketer be able to control the volume of both the merchandise in stock and consigned merchandise. The

Open

Accounts

in Europe

THE TIME ALLOWED FOR PAYMENT AND THE RISK involved with open accounts in Europe differ from one country to another. Customers in countries with a Roman cultural background are significantly slower in paying their dues. In France, for example, the usual limits for payment are 90 days in the ice-cream market and 60 days for detergents compared to 30 days for both in the Netherlands. Italian customers have a reputation for being extremely slow in paying their open accounts. Ninety days are usually fixed limits, but payments may take twice as long.

Marketers from countries such as Germany or the USA who are used to shorter payment times and greater reliability of their customers concerning compliance with contractual facts tend to become very nervous and to threaten their customers with legal actions. Their Italian or French customers will not understand such impatience and change their suppliers if possible. International marketers who are aware of such cultural differences will gather precise information on the credit reliability of new customers, set their prices accordingly (to cover the higher costs for lost interest), and if they need to be refinanced more quickly, sell their accounts receivable to a bank.

major problem with consignment is that the marketer assumes part of the financing of the customer's inventory and absorbs a high credit risk.

Open Accounts. This is the payment method most often used in domestic marketing. It offers full credit terms to the customer. Because of the high risk involved in open accounts in international marketing, this alternative is mostly used between production and sales units of companies operating internationally or in cases where long-lasting, reliable business relationships exist.

In Western Europe many business deals have to be made on an open-account basis, because customers will not accept any other payment method. But as the Culture box shows, even in the European Union open accounts differ in the risk involved across countries. In such cases it is up to the marketer to gather precise information on the credit reliability of a new customer before signing a contract.

Payment Against Documents. An alternative method of payment that decreases the risk of the marketer is to make payment dependent on the presentation of documents specified in the sales contract. After shipping the goods to the customer, the marketer presents the documents to its bank. They prove that the goods were sent to the customer as specified in the contract. The bank, in turn, forwards the documents to the bank of the customer for collection of payment. This way the customer is guaranteed that the merchandise has been shipped as stated in the contract before it is paid for. The marketer gains security in that the documents are not handed over to the customer before the customer has agreed to pay for the merchandise.

In most cases, when payment against documents is chosen as the method of payment a draft is used. A draft for payment is an order written by a seller requesting the buyer to pay a specified amount of money at a specified time. Basically, there are three different kinds of drafts, which can be negotiated and included in the contract. On presentation of a sight draft the marketer has to be paid immediately. With a time draft, payment must be made within a specified time period, usually 30, 60, 90, 120 or 180 days. Deferred payment means that the marketer is paid by a specific date fixed in the contract.

Deferred payment may be negotiated when the merchandise has to pass government examination before it is allowed to enter the country, as is the case with food and drugs exported to the USA. If the marketer needs to be paid before the fixed time has elapsed, the draft can be sold in a financial market or to the customer's bank at a discount.

The two most popular forms of payment against documents are documents against payment (D/P), based on a sight draft, and documents against acceptance (D/A), based on a time draft. Upon receipt of payment from the customer, its bank proceeds as indicated by the marketer. The documents are handed over to the customer and the funds are remitted to the marketer's bank. This bank, in turn, makes them available to the firm. Costs incurred by the marketer for this method of payment are approximately 2 per cent of the sales volume.

Using this method of payment, the seller has no security guarantee to be paid even after having shipped the goods and presented the documents as specified in the contract. If the buyer refuses to pay, the supplier can only be sure of keeping ownership of the goods if the contract states specific documents, such as the bill of lading, that must be presented to get hold of the goods. Even then the situation is difficult for the marketer. The shipped goods have to be sold to another local client or repatriated. Because this is not only rather complicated but sometimes also expensive, the banks involved in the payment procedure should be given an address (of a reliable business partner or a freight forwarder) to be contacted in case of problems. Payment against documents, therefore, is only used as a method of payment when seller and buyer know each other as reliable partners and do not have any doubt concerning each other's willingness and ability to fulfil the contract.

Letter of Credit. A letter of credit (L/C) is a written obligation from a bank made at the request of the customer to honour a marketer's drafts or other demands for payment upon compliance with conditions specified in the document. Figure 18.4 depicts the entire process. For example, if a Canadian manufacturer of snowmobiles signs a contract with a Finnish customer requiring a letter of credit, the Finnish buyer will ask its bank to prepare a letter of credit in favour of the Canadian supplier. If that bank (the issuing bank) is ready to assume responsibility for payment, it will contact the marketer's bank in Canada. This bank (the advising bank) can either confirm the letter of credit or not, forwarding the letter of credit to the snowmobile manufacturer.

After receiving the letter of credit, the marketer should carefully review all the points listed in Table 18.2. If there are any discrepancies between the contents of the letter of credit and the sales contract, the marketer should ask the issuing bank and/or the customer for adjustment. It is important to do this before shipping the merchandise, because even an extremely small difference between the contents of the letter of credit and the shipment documents may result in refusal of payment by the issuing bank. For example, the Finnish bank may refuse to meet its obligations because one letter in one

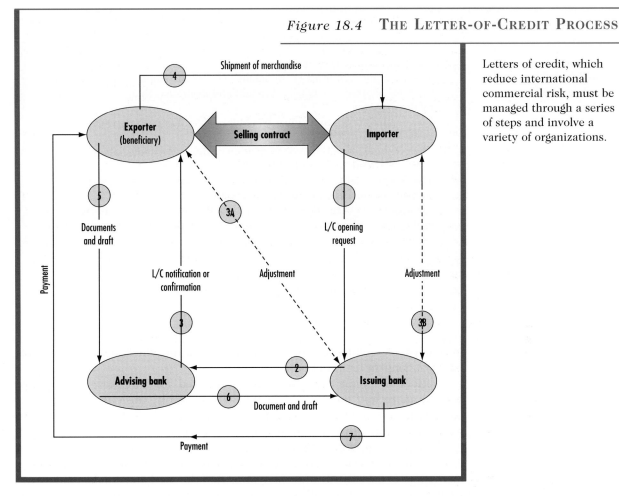

Figure 18.4 **THE LETTER-OF-CREDIT PROCESS**

Letters of credit, which reduce international commercial risk, must be managed through a series of steps and involve a variety of organizations.

word in the documents of the Canadian supplier is different from the letter of credit.

After shipping the merchandise, the Canadian marketer (the beneficiary) presents all the necessary documents and a draft to the advising Canadian bank. The bank reviews and forwards them to the issuing Finnish bank. This bank will closely examine the documents and the draft. If it confirms the information in the letter of credit, the marketer will be paid according to the type of draft, and the customer will receive title to the merchandise.

Depending on the decisions of the two banks involved, the letter of credit may take different forms. The issuing bank may irrevocably commit itself to pay the marketer's draft. If the bank keeps its freedom to amend or cancel the credit at any time, the letter of credit is revocable. In practice this form of letter of credit is not common, because it does not provide any security to the marketer and therefore does not justify the cost of the procedure.

Irrevocable letters of credit may be confirmed by the advising bank or not. If an irrevocable letter of credit is unconfirmed, the advising bank is not obliged to pay the draft. The advising bank will not confirm a letter of credit when the issuing bank (perhaps because of its political/economic environment) represents an unacceptable credit risk. Most banks located in

---

Table 18.2 POINTS TO REVIEW IN A LETTER OF CREDIT

A letter of credit must be reviewed in detail in order to avoid payment problems.

1. The name and address must be correct.
2. The credit amount must be sufficient to cover the shipment agreed on in the sales contract, especially if freight and insurance charges are to be paid by the exporter.
3. The required documents must be obtainable and in accordance with the sales contract.
4. The points of shipment and destination of the merchandise must be correctly stated.
5. The shipping date must allow sufficient time to dispatch the goods from the supplier's warehouse to the shipping point.
6. The expiration of the credit must allow sufficient time for the presentation of the draft and required documents at the banking office where the credit expires.
7. The description of the merchandise and any specifications must agree with the terms of sale.

---

industrialized countries issue lists of countries for which they are not prepared to confirm letters of credit.

Letters of credit must be closely checked for forgeries, which have become more and more sophisticated. For example, the only mistake in a faked letter of credit from Nigeria was that the trunk of the elephant in the bank logo pointed to the left instead of to the right.

Most marketers dealing with unknown customer banks will try to get a confirmed, irrevocable letter of credit. This is the most secure payment method, after cash in advance. It ensures that the marketer will be paid by the advising bank, provided all conditions stated in the letter of credit are met, even if the issuing bank will not honour the draft for any reason.

When goods are shipped to a customer on a continuing basis, a revolving letter of credit may be issued. In other words, the letter of credit applies to the sale of multiple shipments over an extended period of time.

Back-to-back letters of credit occur when an intermediary uses an irrevocable letter of credit to ask the advising bank to open a similar letter of credit in favour of the ultimate supplier of the merchandise. A small Swiss trading house may, for example, possess an irrevocable letter of credit for a shipment of electric generators, manufactured by General Electric in the USA, to Ethiopia. Because of the small size of the trading house, GE may not be prepared to do business without an irrevocable letter of credit from the trading house. The trader, therefore, may ask its bank to issue a letter of credit in favour of GE, offering the Ethiopian irrevocable letter of credit as security.

A special form of letters of credit used in raw materials delivery contracts with customers in East Asia and the CIS are the so-called 'red clause letters of credit'. They contain a special clause, printed in red, which allows the advising bank to transfer part or the entire cash equivalent before the documents claimed in the letter of credit are presented by the supplier. The payment in advance should give the supplier the working capital needed to fulfil its obligations. Any risk of non-delivery is borne by the customer, however.

The cost of a letter of credit can approach 3 per cent of the sales value shown in the invoice. Despite this high cost in comparison to an open account, the marketer will choose to rely on a letter of credit if the customer represents an unknown credit risk; if the foreign-exchange regulations of the customer's country do not allow simple, direct payments; or if transportation costs are high.

Payment in Advance. Payment in advance is the most attractive method of payment for the marketer, generating revenue before goods are shipped or services are provided. The customer bears all risks and, in effect, helps finance production of the goods or services. The payment can be made by the customer, its bank, or the marketer's bank at the time the order is placed with the marketer.

Full payment in advance is rarely encountered in international marketing. It may be used when the market position of the supplier is very strong and the customer's credit rating is unsatisfactory or unknown. For example, a company with a very strong brand, such as French Louis Vuitton, can ask its customers in industrializing countries, such as Indonesia, to pay for their orders in advance. And when China opened up its trading policy with Western nations, it offered payment in advance for training, by European specialists, of managers at industrial plants.

Partial payment in advance may be negotiated when the size of the order is so large that it overwhelms the supplier's financing capability. For example, customer-specific engineering and/or production involves enormous working capital. When the construction of a steel mill for the site of Ahwaz in southwestern Iran was negotiated between an Iranian delegation and Japanese as well as European engineering firms, the Iranians offered one-third of the project's anticipated dollar volume as payment in advance to indicate their willingness and ability to finance the huge project.

MANAGING FINANCIAL RISKS

Even the most elaborate methods of payment are not able to account for all the financial risks related to an international business contract. An organization engaged in international operations has several options available to help manage financial risk, including not engaging in international trade (hence no risk), and direct foreign investment (to avoid being considered a 'foreign' company). Before selecting one of these options, management should evaluate the risks and risk-management options in light of the existing global financial framework. Sources of funds and the organizations that regulate financial activity help determine the appropriate financial-management approach.

The exchange-rate risk can be assumed by the organization itself or it can be transferred to a third party in international financial markets, thus covering exchange-rate fluctuations. Markets that buy and sell currencies are made up of commercial banks, central banks, and some individuals and companies. In any case, the exchange risk must be borne by some organization in order for the exchange (sale) to occur.

Choice of Currency

One of the two business partners can avoid bearing exchange-rate risk through the choice of currency in the business contract. Doing business only in their own currency is an easy solution for companies located in world currency areas such as the US dollar, the German mark, the Japanese yen or the Swiss franc. If business is done with a subsidiary located outside such an area, however, the risk stays with the firm.

Foreign Currency Account

A company doing regular import and export business in a foreign currency can open a foreign currency account. A French textile company that buys raw materials from Bangladesh and semi-finished products from Malaysia and Vietnam, for example, and sells its branded products to the USA may do the entire business on a dollar basis. All the inflows and outflows of dollars accompanying the imports and exports are registered in a foreign currency account, thus covering most of the exchange-rate fluctuations.

Spot Market

If the company does only irregular business in a foreign currency or is not able to balance the flows of foreign currency, it can rely on the spot market to buy and sell major currencies (blocked currencies do not have a financial market, and financial markets for minor currencies are limited) for its immediate needs. While there are variations within the spot market, its basic usefulness to the company operating internationally lies in the ability to buy or sell foreign currencies at any time.

For example, a Mexican company importing products from Singapore could buy US dollars on the spot market, at the spot rate, when its bill becomes due (assuming the price is quoted in USD). But waiting until the bill becomes due means that the Mexican company is incurring a currency-exchange risk. If the dollar goes up against the peso between the date of sale and payment, the Mexicans must pay more for the product. If the dollar goes down against the peso, the Mexicans pay less.

Accurate prediction in any market, in particular one subject to political pressures and rapid changes, such as the currency-exchange market, is very difficult. For example, shortly before and during the Gulf war the value of the dollar went up because of general uncertainty about future world economic development; and some analysts forecast that it would stay up after the war because of war-induced economic recovery in the USA. The contrary was true: the US economy went into recession and the value of the dollar fell below DM 1.5 because German interest rates were significantly raised to attract foreign capital and to fight inflation due to the high financial needs for investment in former East Germany.

Most businesses do not wish to carry exchange-rate risk themselves, as speculation is not their primary business. They may either sell their receivables in foreign currency, take foreign currency credits, use forward markets, or buy foreign currency options to minimize a potential exchange-rate loss.

Selling Foreign Currency Receivables

Accounts receivable in foreign currency can be sold to a bank if the buyer has accepted a draft. Short-term receivables that are due in a certain period of time can be sold to factoring banks which credit the sellers in their own currency and take over payment as well as exchange-rate risks. The International Factors Group, for example, contains cooperating factoring banks from 27 countries, including the major OECD members but also Hong Kong, Hungary, Indonesia, Korea, Malaysia, the Philippines, Singapore, Thailand and Turkey. Long-term receivables might be handed over to a bank through a forfaiting contract. The seller is credited in its own currency (that is, the bank takes over the exchange-rate risk) but keeps the payment risk. In any case the bank will take a certain percentage of the invoiced amount as a discount to cover its costs and risks.

Foreign Currency Credit

To cover the firm's exchange-rate risk, management may take a credit of the same amount, period of validity and currency as a foreign account receivable. The credit is paid back when the buyer pays its dues. When an Indian producer of software sells its products to the UK and finances the working capital needed for that business through a pound sterling loan, it applies this risk minimization tool.

Forward Market

A forward, or future, market exists because there is uncertainty as to the future value or exchange rate of a particular currency. It is that uncertainty that prompts the buying and selling of currency-exchange risk. This process is usually referred to as hedging. For example, a Danish exporter of dairy products may sell DK (Danish crowns) 50,000 worth of yoghurt and butter to a buyer in Portugal. Assume the current exchange rate is DK1 = 26.5 escudos (the Portuguese currency unit). The terms of payment specify payment in escudos in 60 days. At the existing exchange rate, the Danish firm has a collectable in 60 days of 1.325 million escudos. At the time the agreement is signed, the exporter can sell that amount of escudos in the forward market for delivery in 60 days, in effect shifting the exchange-rate risk to the buying bank. If the 60-day forward rate is DK1 = PE26, the exporter will receive 1.3 million escudos. The 25,000 escudos difference is DK1,725 (=3.45 per cent) less than the DK50,000 value. But the exporter knows about this 'loss' in advance, and can adjust the price accordingly. Or the exporter may decide that a known DK1,725 loss is more acceptable than the risk of unknown loss or gain if it does not use the forward market (the bank can minimize its risk by simultaneously buying and selling foreign currencies).

Foreign Currency Option

Foreign currency credits and hedging are difficult to handle if the cash flow pattern resulting from different foreign accounts receivable is hard to be determined exactly. In such cases the internationally operating company can buy foreign currency options. That is, the firm buys the right to buy and sell foreign currency in a time span of generally three months. During this time the financial manager of the company can profit from exchange-rate fluctuations and limit the risk of losses.

Guarantees

A way to restrict financial risks other than exchange-rate fluctuations in international business is to use guarantees. Government-owned or government-directed organizations, such as Hermes and KFW in Germany, COFAS in France or Ex-Im Bank in the USA, provide financial packages designed to increase exports. Export financing is made available either through direct loans to importers or by making credit to importers more readily available. In 1996, the US Ex-Im Bank, for example, reported that its exposure in Southeast Asia amounted to USD14.2 billion, with USD3.4 billion in loans and loan guarantees tied up in China, ahead of Indonesia, the Philippines, India and Thailand.[6]

In addition, various types of guarantees that protect against different kinds of financial risks are available to exporters and importers through banks.

Bill-of-Lading Guarantees. These instruments ensure that the importer or receiver of merchandise will perform as stated in the documents signed by the importer. They cover the shipper against the demand of a third party when the shipper distributes merchandise to the receiver without getting the bill of lading at the same time.

Bid Bonds. Also called participation guarantees or tender guarantees, bid bonds guarantee the prospective buyer that the chosen bidding firm is willing and able to sign a contract according to the offer made.

Payment Guarantees. These ensure that the supplier will be paid as stated in the contract with the customer against presentation of the sales documents. Alfred Kärcher GmbH, a German producer of cleaning equipment for private and commercial purposes, for example, contacted one of its international banks to get a payment guarantee when it was signing an initial sales contract with a customer in Latin America. The country risk seemed acceptable and, according to available credit information, the customer was a prominent firm in its country. Nevertheless, Kärcher's treasurer considered the risk as unspecified. The company paid a premium for an insurance policy which allowed them not to have to give further securities to the provider.[7]

Insurance

Various types of international financial risks that are not due to exchange-rate fluctuations or cannot be covered by guarantees might be covered through insurance. Insurance is available from private agencies, governments and special organizations. Table 18.3 illustrates some of the insurance alternatives available from a US company, a UK company and a typical state scheme.

When private companies provide insurance, they offer the insurance against financial risks in specific countries as a product for sale. The contract value that may be insured, the percentage of the contract that is insurable, and the fees all vary according to the assessment of the risk involved. For example, an insurance policy for political risk in Hungary in 1992 was available at a rate of 1.0–2.5 per cent. The policy covered 90 per cent of the value

---

Table 18.3 COMPARISON OF RISK PROTECTION THROUGH INSURANCES

ITEM	AIG/CIGNA (USA)	UNDERWRITER LLOYD'S (UK)	TYPICAL STATE SCHEME (CENTRAL EUROPE)
Export embargo	Yes	Yes	Yes
Import embargo	Yes	Yes	Yes
Government-buyer non-payment	Yes	Yes	Yes
Exchange transfer	Yes	Yes	Yes
Failure of bank to honour ILC	Yes	No	Yes
Confiscation/Expropriation/Nationalization	Yes	Yes	Yes
Contract non-ratification	Yes	Yes	No
Private-buyer non-payment	Yes	No	Yes
Barter	Yes	Yes	No
Kidnap and ransom	AIG only	Yes	No

Although various agencies offer insurance against financial risks, their coverage varies considerably.

Source: J. Schwabe, Schwabe & Ley Ges.m.b.H., Vienna, Austria.

of the contract, with an upper limit of the contract of USD5 million. For Romania, the policy would have cost 5–6 per cent, been good for a lower per centage of the contract, and had a lower upper limit.

A special case is Exporters Insurance Inc., a Bermuda-based export insurance firm (founded by banks and large companies) with offices in Europe and the USA. They cover economic and political risks for up to ten years, insure uncovered parts of their clients' policies with public insurance agencies, and insure multi-sourced projects, that is, business deals where multiple firms from different countries cooperate in a way that does not fit the guidelines of national insurance agencies (too big a share of foreign business). The risk amounts insured are between USD300,000 and 10 million. Insurance premiums to be paid upfront are between 1 and 3.5 per cent a year. In addition, customers have to buy non-marketable interests in the insurance firm equivalent to 4 per cent of the insured dollar amount. When the contract is terminated, the customer gets back its investment with a return of about 3 per cent a year.[8]

State or federal agencies that provide insurance do so to support exports. The Ministry of International Trade and Industry (MITI) in Japan, for example, provides export insurance covering commercial and political risks in a manner similar to that of the FCIA in the USA. The Overseas Private Investment Corp. (OPIC), as another example, has a traditional role of being an insurer of last resort for US companies investing in overseas projects. In 1995, OPIC provided US firms investing in Asia with USD2 billion in political risk insurance, or 25 per cent of the total. Much of this support has been for power and telecommunications projects, with the rest going into transportation, banking and other sectors. Indonesia and the Philippines were the most intensely covered project destinations. The federal agency was not allowed to operate in China, Vietnam and Pakistan.[9]

COUNTERTRADE

Under certain circumstances, described in the following section, the customer may prefer countertrade. This has been defined as 'a commercial transaction in which provisions are made, in one or a series of related contracts, for payment by deliveries of goods and/or services in addition to, or in place of, financial settlement.'[10]

Countertrade has a long history in international trade. Manhattan Island, for example, was sold in such an agreement to settlers from Europe. Today some 20–30 per cent of international trade involves countertrade. Up to 1970, it was mainly COMECON and other centrally controlled economies, like Albania and Yugoslavia, that proposed countertrade agreements, usually to firms located in industrialized countries. The number of countries interested in countertrade has steadily expanded since then. Today, not only is east–west business characterized by countertrade, but also north–south business (between industrialized and developing countries) and a growing amount of south–south business (between LDCs).

For example, approximately 50 per cent of the trade between Eastern Europe and the developing countries is conducted through countertrade. Indonesia, the People's Republic of China and Malaysia are big countertrading nations. Thailand and India had high growth rates in countertrade in the early 1990s. Even highly industrialized economies (such as Australia, Austria, Belgium, Canada, the Netherlands, New Zealand, Norway, Sweden and the UK) have joined the ranks of countries that use countertrade arrangements for certain kinds of transactions.

In addition to trading companies that specialize in countertrade, many of the biggest companies in the world, such as General Electric or Coca-Cola, were involved in countertrade transactions in the 1990s. One of the most famous countertrade arrangements was signed between Pepsi Co. and the government of the former Soviet Union. Pepsi had been selling its products to the USSR for many years. Generally, it had exchanged soft drinks for vodka. But then, the Soviets proposed paying for the soft-drink syrup from Pepsi with obsolete submarines. They obviously profited from knowing that Pepsi did not want to lose the market. In fact, Pepsi made the deal. They did not turn the submarines into a chain of floating restaurants, but sold them for scrap.

Over the years many different forms of countertrade have developed. Barter is the exchange of goods or services without transfers of money in a short time frame, generally one year or less, formalized in one contract. All the other forms of countertrade are based on two or more separate contracts. They include full or partial monetary compensation, and the contracts are generally for periods longer than one year. Three different kinds of barter found in international business and three other forms of countertrade are discussed in the following sections.

Barter

In classic barter, both parties function as buyers and sellers in a mutual exchange of products with offsetting values. The exchanged products may be industrial goods, consumer goods, services or commodities. Bangladesh, for example, has classic-barter agreements with Eastern European countries, such as Bulgaria, and other LDCs, such as Pakistan. It trades agricultural commodities, textiles, hides and paper products for industrial equipment, machinery, chemicals, fertilizers, metals and medicines. Another example is the Malaysian-owned rubber trading company, Sime Darby, which exchanged cocoa beans delivered by Mexican tyre manufacturers for Malaysian rubber. Classic barter is relatively rare in international marketing.

Closed-end barter differs from classic barter in that one of the business partners already has a buyer at hand for the products to be traded before the contract is signed. Most often it will be the partner located in the more economically developed area. Closed-end barter very much diminishes the risk associated with barter.

Clearing-account barter is based on bilateral clearing agreements between governments. For years it was largely practised between CMEA members and LDCs. It is increasingly common between LDCs, but as Eastern European countries unblock their currencies, barter may become less popular for them.

Other Forms of Countertrade

Compensation Arrangements. Compensation is used for industrial projects which involve technology or capital transfer from industrialized to developing economies. When plant equipment or turnkey plants are sold to firms in those countries, their governments may sign the contract only if the suppliers are willing to take back the products manufactured by that equipment over an extended period of time (5–10 years) as part of the payment. For example, Dunbee-Combex-Marx, a UK toy manufacturer, and China agreed that the firm would furnish toy-making machinery and moulds to China in return for a 50 per cent cash down-payment and 50 per cent of the toys made in the Chinese factory. Such contracts are also called buyback arrangements.

Compensation arrangements help the international marketer to insure part of the firm's accounts receivable. Taking into account the costs of selling the products accepted as compensation (or the costs of an international trader who takes over the burden of selling them), the value of those products can be considered as insured payment. Compensation also allows the marketer to set a higher price in international tenders because the customer only needs to pay part of the entire project costs in hard currency. Varying compensation quotas can be used to differentiate the offer from competitors.

Counterpurchase. Counterpurchase is an indirect form of compensation trading. It is characterized by buying and selling agreements that are basically independent of each other. They are either partially or totally paid in cash or in bank credit. Counterpurchase is a form of countertrade, because the supplier in a business deal signs a second contract agreeing to buy products, defined within broad categories, from the customer within a period of time that ranges from 1 to 5 years.

When engineering companies want to do business with firms in Russia, for example, they often have to accept such buying contracts. Because of their lack of hard currencies, Russian firms can only buy Western technology if the sellers are ready to buy and market their products in exchange. The Western companies rely on the services of specialized trading houses to do that job for them.

A special case of counterpurchase is the establishment of evidence accounts. These usually occur when an exporter or a trading company in an industrialized country signs a counter-purchase contract with the government of a developing country. In an 'umbrella' trade agreement the two parties arrange that two-way trade between the firm – as well as other businesses designated by it – and firms in the developing country be partially or fully balanced over a specified period of time, typically 1 to 5 years. In one such deal, a trading company agreed to buy a large amount of crude oil from Iran at OPEC prices and use the country's bank credit stemming from that deal to pay Western companies, in hard currency, for their delivery of industrial as well as consumer products to customers in Iran.

Offsets.   Offsets are most common in sizeable weapon delivery contracts, the construction of big power stations, other public infrastructure projects and industrialization projects between a supplying firm (as general contractor) and a government. They usually combine domestic-content, co-production and technology-transfer requirements with long-term counterpurchase arrangements. The marketer is confronted with a (government) customer who is ready to sign a contract only if the marketer agrees to counterpurchase goods from the customer country, transfer technological know-how by producing components and equipment in the buyer's country, subcontract compatible components to local manufacturers, or meet other conditions.

In one such case, the Canadian government announced that in exchange for a USD2.3 billion purchase of McDonnell-Douglas F-18 fighter aircraft, Canadian firms would participate in the production of aircraft components; receive the necessary advanced manufacturing technologies; obtain expertise in solar energy, cryogenics, health care and processing of agricultural products; and receive market-development assistance for Canadian exports and tourism.[11]

Company and Government Motives

Government initiatives concerning countertrade vary. They range from incentives to the imposition of such agreements as a condition of doing business. Mexico has for some time imposed export-performance requirements on imports and investment. Brazil and Indonesia have imposed domestic-content requirements on imports and local industrial projects. EU nations are officially neutral concerning private companies' decisions, but most have created public services to advise firms or actively promote countertrade.

The reasons for the increase of countertrade in LDCs are found in the countries' economic-development difficulties. Many LDCs experience severe financial bottlenecks due to a combination of credit cuts, balance-of-payment problems, sluggish exports, and high debts with US, European and Japanese banks. These conditions have left most developing countries with few alternatives other than countertrade to acquire badly needed capital goods and services. As about 40 per cent of industrialized nations' trade is done with LDCs, this is of tremendous importance to firms from those nations.

A second major reason for countertrade agreements is the chronic shortage of hard currency in most firms of formerly centrally controlled economies and in LDCs. They need equipment and technology from highly industrialized markets to enhance their economic development and international competitiveness, but they lack economic resources. Countertrade is often the only way they can obtain those resources.

The lack of internationally competitive industrial skills is another reason some countries engage in countertrade. Most selling problems in LDCs occur because of their low level of familiarity with basic marketing activities. They do not have enough experience in building an international distribution system, packaging, design, promotion, and after-sale services. Many industrial exports from these countries are not due to active marketing by the manufacturer, but result from the purchasing activities of companies from developed countries. Those companies bring in product and process technology and management know-how, and they use the less-developed country's raw material and cheap labour, but they may not transfer much of their technology.

Another reason for countertrade is that it opens markets to products that would not be bought otherwise, because of existing global overcapacities or insufficient quality or promotion. Consumer goods from China, for example, might not have found their way to the US consumer without China's requirement that US companies accept countertrade items. Machinery from Romania would also probably not be sold to Western buyers without the imposition of countertrade agreements through the Romanian government or Romanian firms.

A fifth reason for countertrade is the restrictive production regulations of cartels, which have led to overcapacity in some countries' commodity production. The relatively low production quota for crude oil for OPEC members in the 1990s led some of them to use their overproduction in countertrade offers to industrialized countries at official OPEC prices. Nigeria, for example, trades crude oil with many nations in return for tyres, paper, gasoline, automobile parts and vegetable oil, among other products. Trading firms in highly industrialized countries accepted the prices as a means to open up the oil producers' markets to Western products.

Finally, there may also be political reasons for countertrade. Iran, for example, circumvented officially restricted relationships with some of the major Western countries by signing countertrade contracts with international trading houses for crude oil and chemicals in return for all kinds of industrial and even consumer goods. Those trading houses, not constrained by any similar political restrictions, were able to deliver the products from sources otherwise not officially available to Iran.

Concerns about Countertrade

Most companies located in Western industrialized economies have not entered the countertrade business with much enthusiasm. The major concerns are that the company may have no in-house use for the traded goods, or it may encounter difficulties in reselling them to third parties. This may be due to the type of compensating goods offered by the partners, or possibly their low quality. But it may also be due to a lack of sufficiently trained people in the companies. Coca-Cola, for example, in one of its first countertrade deals, found itself stuck with substandard Chinese honey that could not be sold for two years.

Another major concern expressed by Western companies is the uncertainty and complexity of a countertrade deal. Information from the countertrade partners regarding prices, product quality and proprietary issues may be hard to get. A firm dealing with an indebted country may find, for example, that banks and/or the IMF have prior claims on the goods offered as part of the countertrade agreement. Legal and contractual issues can be difficult to deal with.

There is the further problem of setting exchange ratios for the goods to be traded. Government instability, red tape and inefficiency add to the complications. Other concerns include increased costs, overpricing, negotiation problems, and the possibility of strengthening potential competitors.

Countertrade Opportunities

Despite these difficulties and constraints, countertrade can be regarded as a possible source of additional service for customers who have exchange problems, rather than as a burden. Countertrade can be a major competitive marketing tool vis-à-vis other firms that may not feel comfortable with such deals. It allows the firm to take advantage of local tariff laws that may be stricter for traditional imports than for countertrade goods. It can also be used to open markets and gain favourable recognition from local bureaucrats, an important asset later on.

General Electric, for example, has successfully used countertrade as a competitive tool, helping it to beat competition for business around the world. William Evonsky, GE's manager of advanced trade development, has reported that using barter helped GE save a deal the company had made to build turbine generators for nuclear-energy generation in Romania. When the country got into a cash-flow squeeze, GE agreed to accept USD75 million (one-half of the total contract) worth of Romanian industrial products, including railroad cars and ship containers. GE later won a second contract over competitors for nuclear-energy equipment worth USD165 million, in part due to its flexibility in accepting barter in the first contract.[12]

Traded consumer goods are sometimes difficult to sell, but specialized trading houses have proven to be very successful in finding customers. Countertrade is a way of developing a market despite credit difficulties, exchange problems and currency controls. It increases the company's sales volume, allows fuller use of the firm's productive capacity, and it may even provide a source of economically attractive inputs in the firm's production process.

IMPACT ON THE MARKETING MIX

International pricing decisions strongly interact with decisions concerning the company's product management, distribution, and promotional goals and efforts. The buyer may use the price of the product or service to judge its quality, its attractiveness to others and its general value. That is, in the absence of other cues, especially when the customer has little experience with the product, price will be used as an indicator of the product's technical and social reliability. Thus price may be a major communication tool for the international marketer.

Price can also be used to compete, through a better price–value relationship. When the product quality and design are at least as attractive as those of competitors, the price may nevertheless be set at a lower level to gain market entrance and penetration. The success of Japanese cameras, automobiles, motorcycles, and audio and video products in the USA and Europe is a striking example of the concerted use of such a strategy.

Price also interacts with distribution. High-fashion, high-prestige and high-quality products, which have correspondingly high prices, are not sold through discount outlets. Marketers of these products carefully choose the right distribution channels. On the other hand, if the existing distribution infrastructure in a country-market is complicated, with long distribution channels, the price will automatically be higher than in markets with short distribution channels. If a given price is essential for the company's market success, its management will try to establish control over the entire distribution process. The choice of distribution system will follow from this requirement.

SUMMARY

Proper pricing of goods and services is key to success in international marketing. Although a firm should have an international pricing policy, the actual price charged in the marketplace is influenced by many different factors, several of which the firm may influence in a limited way. Determination of that price – whether standard formula, price adaptation, or strategically set – must take these factors into account.

The major factors of influence include the cost of the good, which determines the lower price limit, and market demand, which sets the upper price limit. The final price usually lies between the two and depends upon the company's pricing policy, competition, structure and actions of local intermediaries, the general economic conditions, and regulations by the local governments.

In order to avoid direct price competition and to have a broader range of pricing alternatives, the international marketer must handle the terms of payment in a sophisticated manner. The methods of payment selected are affected by several factors: most importantly, the risks associated with the sale, the merchandise itself, and industrial and competitive practices. Alternative terms of payment must be chosen to make the firm's product more attractive to customers and to increase corporate profits.

Even the most sophisticated choice of terms of payment cannot avoid financial risks inherent in international marketing. Therefore, when taking pricing decisions, management has to consider which risks should be taken by the firm and which turned over to agencies, banks and insurance companies. The cost of such complex risk reduction actions have to be covered by price.

When economic or political factors inhibit the exchange of goods or services strictly for money, various forms of countertrade can be employed. Barter is normally a short-term, one-time, countertrade contract. Other forms of countertrade that are for longer periods of time, or multiple contracts such as buyback or counterpurchase, permit a more permanent relationship between buyer and seller without necessarily involving money. Companies usually engage in countertrade in order to enter markets that are otherwise blocked to them by governments that are trying to manage severe financial constraints. These deals are so important that no company operating internationally can afford to overlook countertrade in the future.

DISCUSSION QUESTIONS

1. Why is pricing probably the most difficult element in the international marketing mix to manage?
2. Which is the best international pricing policy for a corporation: standard, standard formula, price adaptation, or strategic pricing? Why?
3. 'Because a price is the market's perception of the product's value, costs really don't matter, especially in international marketing. Another less price-sensitive market can always be found'. Do you agree or disagree with that statement, and why?
4. How do government policies affect the international pricing decision?
5. Which of the terms of payment is of greatest advantage to the international marketer? Which results in the greatest risk being retained by the international marketer? Explain.
6. What factors affect the choice of terms of payment, and what is their effect?
7. When and why would you recommend that an international marketer use an open account as the method of payment?
8. What role does a letter of credit play in international marketing?
9. Will countertrade increase or decrease in importance in the future? Why?
10. Describe how pricing affects the other elements of the international marketing mix. Try to find examples from the trade press.

ADDITIONAL READINGS

Assmus, G. and C. Wiese (1995) 'How to Address the Gray Market Threat Using Price Coordination', *Sloan Management Review*, Spring, 31–41.

Dolan, R.J. (1995) 'How Do You Know When the Price Is Right?', *Harvard Business Review*, September–October, 174–183.

Paun, D.A. and A. Shoham (1996) 'Marketing Motives in International Countertrade: An Empirical Examination', *Journal of International Marketing*, 4(3), 29–47.

NOTES

[1] Assmus, G. and C. Wiese (1995) 'How to Address the Gray Market Threat Using Price Coordination', *Sloan Management Review*, Spring, 31–41.

[2] Diller, H. and I. Bukhari (1994) 'Pricing Conditions in the European Common Market', *European Management Journal*, 12(2), June, 163–170.

[3] Diller, H. and I. Bukhari (1994), op. cit.

[4] Brandenburger, A.M. and B.J. Nalebuff (1995) 'The Right Game: Use Game Theory to Shape Strategy', *Harvard Business Review*, July–August, 57–71.

[5] Brull, St.V. and G. McWilliams (1996) '"Fujitsu Shokku" Is Jolting American PC Makers', *Business Week*, 19 February, p. 50.

[6] This section is largely based on: Zahn, J.C.D., Eberding, E. and D. Ehrlich (1986) *'Zahlung und Zahlungssicherung im Aussenhandel'*, Berlin: Walter de Gruyter; and Marschner, H. (1989) 'Lieferungs- und Zahlungsbedingungen', in Macharzina, K. and M.K. Welge (eds), *Handwörterbuch Export und Internationale Unternehmung*, Stuttgart: C.E. Poeschel, pp. 1312–1322.

[7] Lachica, E. (1996) 'U.S. Ex-Im Bank May Fund Project in China', *The Wall Street Journal Europe*, 5–6 July, p. 5.

[8] Stephan, K.-G. (1994) 'Exportrisiken – Systematische Behandlung', *Treasury Log*, 5, 7.

[9] Scheibl, E. (1996) 'Bermuda-Nische', *Internationale Wirtschaft*, No. 22, June, 37.

[10] Lachica, E. (1996) 'U.S. Ex-Im Bank May Fund Project in China', *The Wall Street Journal Europe*, 5–6 July, p. 5.

[11] UN Economic Commission for Europe (1979) 'Countertrade Practices in the Region', *Trader*, 385, November.

[12] Verzariu, P. (1985) *'Countertrade, Barter, and Offsets: New Strategies for Profit in International Trade'*, New York: McGraw Hill, p. 44.

[13] Eason, H. (1985) 'Barter Boom', *Nation's Business*, March, p. 24.

CHAPTER 19

THE INTERNATIONAL
MARKETING PLAN

LEARNING OBJECTIVES

After studying this chapter you will be able to:

↔

summarize international marketing decisions in the form of a marketing plan

↔

explain the hierarchical structure of marketing decisions and plans

↔

illustrate the content and structure of an international marketing plan

↔

evaluate marketing and business plans

CHAPTER OUTLINE

The international business plan

Hierarchical levels of business plan development
Marketing's contributions to the business plan

International marketing strategy

International marketing plan

Audiences
Structure
Planning procedure

Summary

A Bumpy Ride

Michelin's roly-poly Bibendum, Goodyear's winged boot, Firestone's gothic script and Pirelli's bizarre, loopy 'p': few consumer industries can boast such a wealth of classic trademarks. In North America, which makes up about 40 per cent of the world market, wholesalers and retailers have been able to develop their own budget brands. In Europe, which accounts for about one third of world sales, the advent of budget tyres in the 1980s came as a shock to the established companies.

The main tyre makers in Europe had been pursuing a risky pricing policy. For decades, the industry had been convinced that it was worth making losses on tyres sold direct to car makers in order to guarantee profits in the retail market: drivers tend to replace their tyres with an identical set from the same maker. Tyre companies therefore compensated for larger losses on tyres sold to car makers by raising their margins on retail sales.

At the end of the 1980s Europe began to be targeted by obscure tyre makers from East Asia, such as Kumho and Hankook of South Korea, and by East European firms. Their tyres often sold at less than half the price of a premium brand. In Britain, the South Koreans alone have captured roughly 25 per cent of the market; in Germany the South Korean share is about 10 per cent. Because fixed costs in the tyre industry are high, and the largest firms had too much capacity, prices fell by more than 5–10 per cent a year at the end of the 1980s. That hurt still more after rubber prices began rising in 1994. Profits shrivelled or disappeared.

Not before the middle of the 1990s did the industry start recovering. Tyre makers have overhauled their business by redefining their strategic positions, revamping their management systems, improving productivity, and adapting their marketing-mix. For example, Italian Pirelli, present in Europe and Latin America, decided at the start of 1993 to concentrate on the world market for luxury and speed. The firm has worked hard since to become the supplier of tyres fitted in the factory on BMWs, Porsches and most fancy cars. The world's three biggest tyre makers, which each have a little under 20 per cent of the market, cannot afford to concentrate all their sales upmarket. Instead, they have developed second-tier and even third-tier brands. Michelin, for example, introduced its 'Classic' range of mid-priced tyres in 1994. In 1995 it signed a pact with Germany's Continental, part of which was an agreement to introduce Michelin's first budget tyre.

Continental, which had no fewer than nine brands in Europe, used to manage each brand separately. In 1994, the firm decided to organize itself by markets instead. Its brands now resemble a portfolio, with Continental and Uniroyal reserved for the top end, from which managers pick a tyre suitable for each segment of their market.

Cost cutting and increasing productivity was another important remedy: In 1990, only one per cent of Continental's tyres were made in Portugal and Slovakia, where labour costs are low. In 1996 that figure had increased to 25 per cent. In the same period, sales per employee had increased by more than a third. Between 1994 and 1996, Michelin decreased its stocks as a proportion of sales by 25 per cent. Its strict hierarchy was replaced by 21 decentralized business units, nine of them managing products and the rest providing services for the group.

All this has helped to halt the advance of new tyre companies. European tyre marketing has become a permanently lower-margin, cost-conscious, and more customer focused business.

Source: 'Tyres in Europe – A bumpy ride', *The Economist*, 17 February 1996, pp. 59f.

THE INTERNATIONAL BUSINESS PLAN

The description of the international marketing decision process given in the preceding chapters has illustrated the high complexity and interrelatedness of marketing analyses, decisions and actions in an international business environment. In addition to marketing specific considerations, a firm operating internationally needs to manage its financial and human resources as well as its production operations in a coordinated way to achieve its major objectives. The most important tool for the coordination of analyses, decisions and actions in an international environment is the development of an international business plan.

The business plan of a company presents the mission and philosophy driving the firm, a complete analysis of the business, its objectives, the markets in which it operates, the competition against which it must establish or sustain itself, and the problems which must be overcome in order for the objectives to be reached. The business plan contains the decisions made by managers on different levels of the organizational hierarchy and the activities planned to resolve the detected problems. It answers the questions why, what, how, when, where and who for each action during the planning period. As such, the business plan is a comprehensive operating manual which management will use to navigate their way to their objective.

This chapter will first discuss the contribution of marketing to the development of an international business plan. Then it will specifically deal with the establishment of an international marketing strategy, the development of an international marketing plan, and its potential audiences and structure as well as the necessary planning procedure for successful implementation.

Hierarchical Levels of Business Plan Development

At the corporate level, the basic task in developing an international business plan is to define or revise the corporate policy and to formalize it in a written statement. A corporate policy statement includes information about the company's mission and business philosophy. The mission states the rational for the existence of the organization. It defines its business domain, and the major objectives it hopes to achieve. The mission is the framework which guides the decisions and actions of all the members of the firm. The business philosophy formulates the rules of behaviour that are to be followed inside the company as well as in contacts with parties outside the company. It guides the manner in which relationships with different business partners and other groups of individuals affected by the company's activities are managed (Figure 19.1).

The corporate policy statement of a company operating internationally is generally defined by the people dominating the company. These may be the owners or top managers of the firm, but the dominant group may also contain representatives of other very important stakeholders, such as investors, creditors or the labour force. Managers of lower hierarchical levels may be invited to participate in the corporate policy development process in order to generate their commitment to its content.

Based on the corporate policy, a corporate strategy needs to be established which defines the scope, shape and structure of the firm. The formulation of a corporate strategy statement requires careful assessment of potential markets' attractiveness and the firm's distinctive competencies and potential competitive advantages. The statement of corporate strategy contains a definition of the company's portfolio of product- and country-markets to be served, the competitive strategy to be applied in those markets, and the international market-entry strategy of the firm.

If the portfolio of the company operating internationally contains more than one clearly defined product-market, the next step in developing an international business plan may be to formulate business unit strategies. A business unit strategy focuses on the achievement and maintenance of a strategic position in a specific product-market. It is basically developed in the same manner as the firm's corporate strategy. But its development is the responsibility of managers leading the individual business unit; and the decisions taken are based on a more detailed analysis of customers, competitors and other important stakeholders as well as the business unit's specific resources and skills for competing in specific market segments. Smaller companies or firms that focus on an international market niche may not need to distinguish between different business units. In such cases, they may step directly from the formulation of corporate strategy to the definition of their marketing strategy.

The marketing strategy serves the purpose of implementing the corporate or business unit strategy. Depending on the size of the firm's business, the marketing strategy is formulated by corporate or business unit managers specializing in the field of marketing. It contains the policies, that is, the objectives and basic guidelines which have to be respected by managers responsible for specific marketing decisions and actions, such as advertising, sales, product line management, or distribution. Similar to all other strategy statements of the firm, the marketing strategy tells those managers what they are expected to achieve and what courses of action are not appropriate management. The marketing strategy also defines the allocation of resources across the functional areas belonging to the domain of marketing management.

Finally, a marketing plan can be developed on the basis of the marketing strategy. In a firm operating internationally, which serves various country-markets, marketing plans will be developed for each of those markets. Those plans specify the objectives of local marketing management, showing how much the local units are able to contribute to the achievement of the overall objectives. The various marketing activities needed to reach the local objectives are presented in detail, and the budgets planned for each of the marketing tools and actions are given.

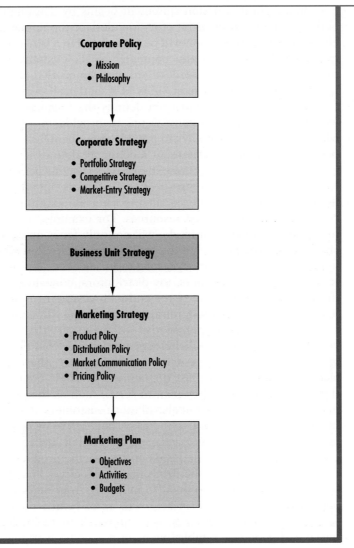

Figure 19.1 HIERARCHICAL LEVELS OF INTERNATIONAL BUSINESS PLAN DEVELOPMENT: FROM CORPORATE POLICY TO THE MARKETING PLAN

The work on an international business plan starts with the development of a corporate policy. Corporate strategy and business unit strategy are the bases for developing a marketing strategy which in turn, lays the groundwork for the marketing plan.

Marketing's Contributions to the Business Plan

As the discussion of the international marketing decision process in this book has shown, marketing orientation, marketing analyses and marketing techniques may contribute on all hierarchical levels to the development of a comprehensive international business plan.

Contributions to Corporate Policy. On the corporate level of business plan development, marketing managers may have an impact on the formulation of corporate policy. Marketing-oriented top managers or entrepreneurs will promote marketing orientation as the basic perspective from which to look at the company's business. Figure 19.2 shows which parts of corporate policy may be influenced by a marketing orientation, that is, by marketing's benefit, exchange and systems perspectives.

The corporate mission statement begins by defining the general purpose of the company – the vision of its founders or top managers. Based on a benefit perspective, this vision will be formulated in a way that expresses the central value provided by the company to its customers or to society. For example, Germany's Mercedes-Benz has stated that the firm wants to contribute significantly to the mobility of societies all over the world.

The mission statement then defines the business domain of the firm – which benefits the company wants to provide to which stakeholders and which technologies (or ways to provide those benefits) it will use for that purpose. Through such a statement a company defines its most attractive product-market(s) in general terms. Based on a systems perspective, the definition will include not only the prospective customers but all major stakeholders of the firm which need to be satisfied to a certain extent in order to provide the company with the needed resources. For example, a producer of electronic toys, such as Japan's Nintendo, will not only focus on children and their parents as their customers, but they will also be aware that other stakeholders are important for the company's long-term success. The expectations of electronic component suppliers, toy distributors, educators and media as well as the company's own labour force and its investors need to be satisfied at least to a level that makes them refrain from fighting Nintendo's interests.

Marketing's benefit perspective will make sure that the benefits to be provided to all important stakeholders are defined from the stakeholders' points of view. For example, the definition of Borealis', the Denmark-based manufacturer of plastics, business domain will not only contain a general description of the customers they plan to serve, such as the producers of packaging material and auto parts, but also of those customers' markets, such as the food industry and the automotive industry. Benefits to be provided to those stakeholders may be stated as 'packaging material at low cost, highly attractive to consumers, adapted to the needs of the specific product'.

The formulation of the firm's major objectives and their priorities in the corporate mission is also open to influence from marketing orientation. The objectives may include sales growth rate, return on sales, market share, acceptable level of risk exposure, approach to technology and innovation, image and goodwill, establishment of a specific working climate within the organization, or independence (see the Strategy box).

Depending on to what extent the authors of the corporate policy have adopted a systems perspective, the chosen objectives will focus on one stakeholder group's interests or cover the interests of a broader range of important stakeholders. The Ethics box may be the starting point for a discussion on what focusing on one stakeholder group's interests may do to a company's success in the long run.

Because objectives are not always consistent – a high sales growth rate goal may conflict with a goal restricting the use of foreign capital, for example – the mission statement should indicate which priorities are to be pursued. Here again, the level of systems perspective adopted by the authors of the corporate policy statement becomes important.

Finally, a marketing orientation will influence the basic values and norms the company wants its personnel to respect in their internal and external

Figure 19.2 THE IMPACT OF MARKETING ORIENTATION ON CORPORATE POLICY

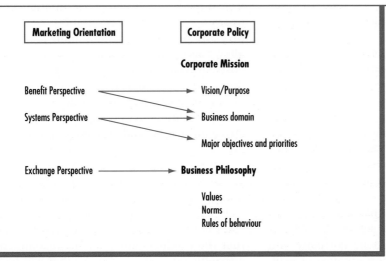

Marketing orientation's benefit, systems and exchange perspectives have an impact on the formulation of various parts of corporate strategy.

STRATEGY BOX

Hewlett-Packard's Corporate Objectives Revealed Over the World Wide Web

HEWLETT-PACKARD, based in Palo Alto, California, which has about 600 sales and support offices and distributorships worldwide belonging to 73 divisions in more than 120 countries, reveals its corporate objectives over the World Wide Web.

CORPORATE OBJECTIVES

The achievements of an organization are the result of the combined efforts of each individual in the organization working toward common objectives. These objectives should be realistic, should be clearly understood by everyone in the organization and should reflect the organization's basic character and personality.

PROFIT

To achieve sufficient profit to finance our company growth and to provide the resources we need to achieve our other corporate objectives.

The profit we generate from our operations is the ultimate source of the funds we need to prosper and grow. We measure our profitability not just as a return on sales but, increasingly important, as a return on the value of assets needed to produce our profits. These profitability measures, which will vary among our individual businesses, are absolutely essential indicators of our corporate performance over the long term. Only if we continue to meet our profit objectives can we achieve our other corporate objectives.

Our long-standing policy has been to reinvest most of our profits and to depend on this reinvestment, plus funds from employee stock purchases and other cash-flow items, to finance our growth. Effective asset management is essential to our ability to self-fund our growth. We will use debt from time to time as part of a prudent currency and tax-management program or to provide a source of financing for customers who prefer to lease (rather than buy) our products, but not as a basic instrument for financing growth.

Our rate of growth varies from year to year, reflecting changing economic conditions and varying demand for our products. To deal with these fluctuations, it is important we be consistently profitable. When our business grows slowly, our profits allow us to accumulate cash reserves for future investment. Conversely, during periods of rapid growth, we tend to draw down these reserves to supplement profit reinvestment.

Meeting our profit objective requires that each and every HP product and service is considered a good value by our customers, yet is priced to include an adequate profit. Maintaining this competitiveness in the marketplace also requires that we focus on businesses where we can make a contribution and that we perform our research and development, manufacturing, marketing, support and administrative functions as economically as possible.

Profit is not something that can be put off until tomorrow; it must be achieved today. It means that myriad jobs be done correctly and efficiently. The day-to-day performance of each individual adds to – or subtracts from – our profit. Profit is the responsibility of all.

CUSTOMERS

To provide products and services of the highest quality and the greatest possible value to our customers, thereby gaining and holding their respect and loyalty.

HP's view of its relationships with customers has been shaped by two basic beliefs. First, we believe the reason HP exists is to satisfy real customer needs. Second, we believe those needs can be fully satisfied only with the active participation and dedication of everyone in the company. We must listen attentively to our customers to understand and respond to their current needs and to anticipate their future needs.

The essence of customer satisfaction is a commitment to quality, a commitment that extends into every phase of our operations. Products must be designed to provide superior performance and long, safe, trouble-free service. We must work closely with suppliers to ensure that we receive high-quality materials, components and subassemblies at reasonable prices and with assurance of supply. Once in production, our products must be manufactured at a competitive cost and with superior workmanship. It's important that we choose our suppliers and production partners carefully to ensure they share our commitment to quality, safety and environmental protection.

Careful attention to quality not only enables us to meet or exceed customer expectations, but it also has a direct and substantial effect on our operating costs and profitability. Doing a job properly the first time, and doing it consistently, allows us to employ fewer assets, reduces our costs, and contributes significantly to higher productivity and profits. This applies to every aspect of our business, from research and development to order fulfillment and support. Each of us must strive for quality and efficiency in everything we do.

Providing innovative, reliable products and services is a key element in satisfying customer needs, but there are other important elements as well. HP offers many different products and services to a broad set of customers. It is imperative that the products and services recommended to a specific customer are those that will best fulfill the customer's overall, long-term needs. This requires that our field-sales and support people and our extensive network of dealers, resellers and other channel partners work closely with customers to determine the most appropriate, effective solutions to their needs. It requires, as well, that our products be readily available through our customers' preferred source, be easy to order and configure, and be supported with prompt, efficient services that will optimize their usefulness. When problems arise, we must respond in a way that demonstrates ownership and a desire to resolve matters quickly and effectively, thereby enhancing customer loyalty and trust.

Our fundamental goal is to build positive, long-term relationships with our customers, relationships characterized by mutual respect, by courtesy and integrity, by a helpful, effective response to customer needs and concerns, and by a strong commitment to providing products and services of the highest quality, value and usefulness.

FIELDS OF INTEREST

To participate in those fields of interest that build upon our technologies, competencies and customer interests, that offer opportunities for continuing growth, and that enable us to make a needed and profitable contribution.

Our company's growth has been generated by a strong commitment to research and development in electronics and computer technology. That growth has been accomplished by providing a rapid flow of new products and services to markets we already serve, and by expanding into new areas that build upon our existing technologies, competencies and customer interests. In addition, we've actively pursued emerging opportunities in related fields that our company is well-positioned to serve.

Our first products were electronic measuring instruments used primarily by engineers and scientists. In time, we extended our range of measurement expertise to serve the areas of medicine and chemical analysis. Recognizing our customers' needs to gather and use large quantities of measurement data, we developed a small family of computers which later evolved into a broad line of computer and computer-based products, including associated software, peripherals, support and services.

Today, HP is one of the world's foremost suppliers of measurement, computation and communication products and services. Our product offerings range from consumer products for home offices, small businesses and on-the-go professionals to precision instruments and extremely powerful computer systems for the most advanced applications. Service and support offerings also cover a broad spectrum, from world-class hardware maintenance and support to professional services, such as consulting and outsourcing.

We continue to invest heavily in research and development to strengthen our capabilities in measurement, computation and communication. Further, we've learned that combining and effectively applying our expertise in these three areas creates major new opportunities, both in our traditional markets as well as in important new fields, such as electronic commerce.

HP's basic purpose is to accelerate the advancement of knowledge and fundamentally improve the effectiveness of individuals and organizations. We provide products and services that help customers acquire, display, analyze, communicate, store and manage information. Customers' information needs may require a solution where HP must work in partnership with other companies to meet those needs. For that reason, our design goal is to provide highly functional, interactive hardware and software that can be integrated easily by HP, customers and other organizations.

Within its broad fields of interest, HP has ample opportunities to pursue a variety of businesses. In evaluating those opportunities, we favor those that link to or complement our existing technology and customer base or that build on an established competency (such as a strong presence in a key distribution channel). In addition, we evaluate those businesses on the basis of their profit potential, long-term stability, our ability to make a distinguishing contribution and achieve market leadership, and their likelihood of generating the cash flow needed to continue HP's tradition of self-financing.

GROWTH

To let our growth be limited only by our profits and our ability to develop and produce innovative products that satisfy real customer needs.

HP does not believe that large size is important for its own sake; however, for at least two basic reasons, continuous growth in sales and profits is essential for us to create shareholder value and achieve our other objectives.

We serve a dynamic and rapidly growing segment of our technological society. To remain static would be to lose ground. We cannot maintain a position of strength and leadership in our fields without sustained and profitable growth.

Growth is also important in order to attract and retain high-caliber people. These individuals will align their future only with a company that offers them considerable opportunity for personal progress. Opportunities are greater and more challenging in a growing company.

Increasing global competition and worldwide demand for technology products require that we establish ourselves successfully in every corner of the world. To compete effectively we must be close to our customers. We must also capitalize on our size and global presence to realize important economies of scale and to make best use of the broad array of skills and resources available to us.

OUR PEOPLE

To help HP people share in the company's success which they make possible; to provide them employment security based on performance; to create with them an injury-free, pleasant and inclusive work environment that values their diversity and recognizes individual contributions; and to help them gain a sense of satisfaction and accomplishment from their work.

We are proud of the people we have in our organization, their performance, and their attitude toward one another, their jobs and the company. The company has been built around the individual, the personal dignity of each and the recognition of personal contributions.

Relationships within the company depend upon a spirit of cooperation among individuals and groups, a commitment to teamwork, and an attitude of trust and understanding on the part of managers toward their people. These relationships will be good only if employees have faith in the motives and integrity of their peers, managers and the company itself.

On occasion, situations will arise where people have personal problems which temporarily affect their performance, and it is important that people in such circumstances be treated with understanding while the problems are being resolved.

HP selects and manages its businesses with a goal of providing long-term employment for its people and opportunities for personal growth and development. In return, HP people are expected to meet certain standards of performance on the job, to adjust to changes in assignments, schedules and the work environment when necessary, and to be willing to learn new skills and to apply them where most critically needed. This flexibility is particularly important in our industry where rapid technological change and intensifying worldwide competition compel us all to continually seek better ways to do our jobs.

Another objective of HP's personnel policies is to enable HP people to share in the company's success. This is reflected in a total compensation package, including pay and benefits, that places us among the leaders in our industry.

HP also places a high value on creating an inclusive environment that benefits from diversity at all levels, values individual differences and enables all HP people to develop and contribute to their full potential. HP actively supports or creates outreach programs that enrich the pool of diverse candidates available for hiring and promotion. By tapping the talents and ideas in such a diverse work force, the company can expand its base of knowledge, skills and understanding, become more responsive to customers' needs and strengthen our global competitiveness.

Advancement from within is based solely upon individual initiative, ability and demonstrated accomplishment. Since we promote from within whenever possible, managers at all levels must concern themselves with the proper development of their people. HP managers should anticipate customer and business trends, consider the impact on knowledge and skills needed in the future, and communicate these requirements to their employees in a timely way. They also should give them ample opportunity – through challenging work assignments and continuing programs of training and education – to broaden their capabilities and prepare themselves for more responsible jobs.

The physical well-being of our people has been another important concern of HP's since the company's founding. We believe all occupational injuries and illnesses are preventable and our ultimate goal is to eliminate them. We want people to enjoy their work at HP and to be proud of their accomplishments. This means we must make sure that each person receives the recognition he or she needs and deserves. In the final analysis, people at all levels determine the character and strength of our company.

MANAGEMENT

To foster initiative and creativity by allowing the individual great freedom of action in attaining well-defined objectives.

In discussing HP operating policies, we often refer to the concept of 'management by objective'. By this we mean that, insofar as possible, each individual at each level in the organization should make his or her own plans to achieve company objectives and goals. After receiving managerial approval, each individual should be given a wide degree of freedom to work within the limitations imposed by these plans, and by our general corporate policies. Finally, each person's performance should be judged on the basis of how well these individually established goals have been achieved.

The successful practice of 'management by objective' is a two-way street. Management must be sure that each individual understands the immediate objectives, as well as corporate goals and policies, and has the necessary training and tools to be successful. Thus a primary HP management responsibility is communication, coaching, constructive feedback and mutual understanding.

For their part, employees must take sufficient interest in their work to want to plan it, to propose new solutions to old problems, to take reasonable risks and exercise sound judgment in the performance of their jobs. 'Management by objective', as opposed to management by directive, offers opportunity for individual freedom and contribution; it also imposes an obligation for everyone to exercise initiative and enthusiasm.

In this atmosphere it is important to recognize that cooperation between individuals and coordinated efforts among operating units often are essential to our growth and success. Individual businesses must continuously seek the appropriate balance between focusing on their own needs and objectives and contributing to or drawing from the strength, size and reputation of the company as a whole. Our businesses are independent in many respects, but they're also part of a single company whose strength is derived from mutually helpful relationships among units that are closely linked through common technologies, customers, values, goals and objectives.

The dynamic nature of our business places an important responsibility on managers to create an environment that embraces change and helps employees manage the increasing demands of work with their other life activities. This requires a high degree of flexibility and a willingness to consider nontraditional approaches to getting the job done. At the same time, it is important for everyone to recognize there are some policies which must be established and maintained on a companywide basis. We welcome recommendations on these companywide policies from all levels, but we expect adherence to them at all times.

CITIZENSHIP

To honour our obligations to society by being an economic, intellectual and social asset to each nation and each community in which we operate.

All of us should strive to improve the world in which we live. As a corporation operating in many different communities throughout the world, we must make sure that each of these communities is better for our presence. This means identifying our interests with those of the community; it means applying the highest standards of honesty and integrity to all our relationships with individuals and groups; it means creating desirable jobs and generating exports and tax revenues; it means building attractive plants and offices of which the community can be proud; it means designing and providing products and services that are safe to use and can be manufactured, operated and disposed of in an environmentally responsible manner; it means contributing talent, time and financial support to worthwhile community projects.

Each community has its particular set of social problems. As citizens of the community, HP people can and should do whatever they reasonably can to improve it – either working as individuals or through such groups as charitable, educational, civic or religious institutions. In a broader sense, HP's 'community' also includes a number of business and professional organizations whose interests are closely identified with those of the company and its individual employees. These, too, are deserving of our support and participation. In all cases, managers should encourage HP people to fulfill their personal goals and aspirations in the community as well as attain their individual objectives within HP.

At a national and international level, it is essential that the company be a good corporate citizen of each country in which it operates. This means looking for creative ways to apply technology to societal problems and contributing HP products and support to philanthropic programmes that address immediate or long-term societal needs. Moreover, our employees, as individuals, should be encouraged to help find solutions to national or international problems by contributing their knowledge and talents. The betterment of our society is not a job to be left to a few; it is a responsibility to be shared by all.

At Hewlett-Packard, we have five underlying organizational values that guide us as we work toward our common objectives. They are part of the HP Way.

Source: http://www.hp.com/

ETHICS BOX

'Tobacco War' in Kenya and Tanzania

WHILE TOBACCO MARKETING IN EUROPE AND THE USA become more and more restricted, tobacco manufacturers, after having invested heavily in Asian markets, have discovered the African market as a promising business arena. In particular the countries south of the Sahara with 850 million potential smokers have become a new target.

In one of its 1997 issues, the medical journal *The Lancet* reported on a 'tobacco war' between British-American Tobacco and J.R. Reynolds in Kenya and Tanzania. Philip Morris, the third big player in the industry, was about to enter the market. Never before had the tobacco industry launched such a massive advertising campaign in Africa. In 1997, the year when the company agreed to pay millions of US dollars to partly compensate for damage their products have caused to the health of the country's population in the USA, J.R. Reynolds started the construction of a production plant in Dar-es-Salaam, the biggest city in Tanzania. The plant will produce about four billion cigarettes a year.

The question may be raised: Should managers do everything that is not explicitly forbidden to raise their shareholders' (and their personal) income? Is it ethically acceptable to pay millions of dollars for admitted damage to the health of the home country's population and in parallel to invest in the requirements for creating the same damage elsewhere?

Source: '"Tabak-Krieg" in Kenya und Tanzania', *Der Standard*, 13–14 September 1997, p. 4.

---

behaviour. The more an exchange perspective guides the formulation of business philosophy, the more the rules of behaviour will emphasize reciprocity, relationship building, trust and commitment in contrast to individual achievement, competition, exploitation or control.

Contributions to Corporate Strategy. An international competitive advantage can only be established and maintained if a distinctive competency of the firm meets customer or other important stakeholder expectations in specific country-markets. Careful analyses of expectations and aspirations in potential markets and competitors' strengths and weaknesses as compared to the company's skills and resources are needed to define the firm's intended global strategic position. The choice of market-entry modes and market-entry timing will depend on that position. As illustrated by Figure 19.3, marketing contributes an essential part of the capabilities needed to properly conduct the analyses that lay the groundwork for the development of corporate strategy.

After the product-market(s) to be served have been identified in general terms in the company's statement of corporate policy, the attractiveness of potential country-markets may be assessed. Their economic, cultural, political and legal environments as well as the specific operating environments of the local product-markets have to be carefully analysed to determine the most attractive markets. As Chapters 3–7 of this book have shown, marketing provides the necessary know-how to conduct those steps.

From the assessment of potential markets, the success factors in those markets – that is, the major skills and resources needed to be successful – are

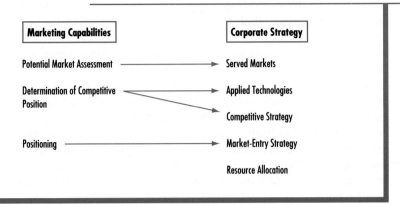

Figure 19.3 THE CONTRIBUTION OF MARKETING CAPABILITIES TO THE DEVELOPMENT OF CORPORATE STRATEGY

The marketing capabilities of a firm have a strong impact on its corporate strategy.

derived. They serve as the basis for a comparison between the firm's potential to serve the most attractive markets, and the related potential of its most important competitors. A comparison with major competitors will help the firm identify whether it can excel in any of the success factors, that is, whether it can identify a competitive advantage. Further, through such a comparison the firm can identify which, if any, success factor it is lacking which would prevent it from successfully serving a market. Chapter 8 has shown the essential role of marketing know-how in this stage of corporate strategy development.

Relying on the firm's existing and potential competitive advantages, that is, on distinctive competencies which can be transformed into customer benefits, management will assess strategic alternatives. It will develop an international portfolio strategy, the product- and country-markets to serve as well as the technologies necessary to satisfy the existing and potential aspirations of customers and stakeholders in those markets. Closely related to their choice of markets, management has to select the most promising competitive strategy – the way the firm will behave in the chosen markets. Choices range from a frontal attack on any competitor to cooperative agreements that not only allow peaceful coexistence but also the exploitation of mutual strengths, achieving synergy. The competitive strategy also includes decisions concerning the innovation behaviour of the firm as well as its policy concerning growth through mergers and acquisitions. Portfolio strategy, competitive strategy, and the subsequent resource allocation decisions define the intended global strategic position that should help ensure the survival of the company. Chapter 9 has shown how much marketing thought and capabilities may contribute to that definition.

The intended global strategic position determines the way and the speed in which country-markets are entered. If international marketing is conducted only to achieve operational goals such as boosting the total sales volume or using up excess capacity, and control over local marketing activities is considered less important, low-risk market-entry alternatives with a minimum of resources required, such as indirect exporting or exporting via importers in each country-market, will be favoured. If internationalization of business is a strategic objective and the company wants to keep its local positions under close control, it will take bolder steps, such as direct investment. Chapter 10 has shown that market-entry decisions are largely based on analyses conducted by marketing professionals and are strongly influenced by their market-related reasoning.

Contributions to Business Unit Strategies. Every company, whether operating internationally or only locally, will be positioned in the minds of its customers and other stakeholders. If it does not want that process to be entirely out of its control, the company has to contribute actively to the positioning process by addressing selected target audiences with cues that attractively differentiate the firm from its major competitors. To be more precise, the company must define an intended strategic position in every product-market it has selected. That is, it must select the customer group(s) to be served and the way it wants to differentiate itself attractively from the most important competitors.

In addition, business unit strategy statements must define the intended strategic position in every individual country-market to be served in the light of the locally existing customer segments, important stakeholders and major competitors. Local market-entry decisions will depend on that strategic objective. As a consequence, at the level of business unit strategy development, market segmentation and competitive differentiation dominate planning activities. Therefore, at this level a distinction between strategic planning and marketing planning may be rather difficult to make. It only becomes evident when, based on positioning and market-entry decisions, resource allocation decisions have to be made. There, financial considerations, the development and deployment of human resources, and operations management considerations, such as outsourcing decisions, alliances or location decisions, play a substantial part in the planning process.

Based on the intended strategic position in a product-market and considering the resource allocation decisions given in the same document, an international marketing strategy may be developed which, in turn, is the framework to be respected in developing a marketing plan. The following sections will focus on those parts of an international business plan.

INTERNATIONAL MARKETING STRATEGY

The strategic results of international business planning most influenced by marketing analyses and marketing thought are the intended global strategic position and the international market-entry strategy of the firm. Those decisions, in general, are valid for the longer term. They are part of an internationally operating company's general strategic plans. Those plans contain objectives that are relevant for all marketing decisions and actions of the firm, such as to be an early follower in all served product-markets or to first enter attractive country-markets with the help of distributors which may later be acquired if the market fulfils its promises.

The firm's strategic plans also serve as the basis for marketing policy decisions, such as branding, product line management or distribution channel decisions, which constitute some of the firm's mid-range policy statements. Those statements and the company's or business unit's objectives – as far as they concern marketing issues – constitute a major part of the firm's or business unit's international marketing strategy. In addition, the international marketing strategy contains a general overview of the served product market, its volume, structure, major players and expected development, which is called the 'basic assumptions'.

Chapters 12 to 18 of this book have each discussed the need for general guidelines in the different subareas of the marketing mix. An international product policy has to be formulated to avoid unnecessary complexity and resulting costs in a company faced with internationally varying customer perceptions of the importance and meaning of features and processes constituting its total product. Such a product policy provides a framework within which all product management processes of the firm are to be conducted. It lays down the general positioning for each product (line), the intended degree of product standardization, the intended meaning of brands and their market appearance, quality standards, and the firm's objectives and rules concerning product portfolio management.

The international distribution policy of the firm determines how its market-entry strategy is to be executed. It contains general objectives regarding market share, sales volume, profit margins and return on sales which may be specified by region, customer group and distribution channel, taking into account the desired level of company involvement in the distribution system and the desirability of ownership of intermediaries. Guidelines indicate minimum and maximum levels of capital and personnel to be committed to achieving the intended level of coverage in each market. They also specify general rules for the selection of intermediaries and customers as well as the management of relationships with those selected business partners. Other rules may concern the selection, training and motivation of sales personnel.

The international logistics policy of the firm determines the level of customer service to be achieved. It also determines whether an integrated or independent marketing logistics system is to be chosen, or specifies the conditions that determine when to favour which system. The logistics policy may also contain the profile of logistics partners to look for as well as some guidelines concerning roles in the distribution logistics chain that have to be fulfilled inside or outside the company, the coordination between central and local company units, and the responsibilities for logistics planning, information and control.

The international pricing policy restates corporate objectives relevant to individual pricing decisions, such as expected profit margins, return on sales, and market shares. It also includes the preferred pricing strategy, such as quick penetration of mass markets through low prices where the company has no defendable competitive advantage or skimming of high margins in market niches where the company has a significant competitive advantage. In order to make sales figures comparable across country-markets, the pricing policy may state how prices are to be calculated. The company or business unit policy concerning rebates, refunds and discounts given to customers is stated as well as the terms of payment available in specific markets to salespeople struggling for orders.

The international market communication policy of the firm aims to ensure consistency in all communicative activities across country-markets. General communication objectives for each of the important stakeholder groups are formulated. An international communication platform defines the central message to be communicated, which may be refined into consistent core messages for each stakeholder group. To coordinate the transfer of the core messages into a consistent choice of communication tools, the communication policy determines the major tools to be applied internationally. A guideline concerning corporate design determines the general formal appearance of every communicative activity of the firm. Finally, the international market communication policy should contain some rules concerning cooperation and coordination in implementing market communication decisions which help to avoid conflicts among organizational subunits at different hierarchical levels and regulate the role of external service providers in the planning and execution of communication activities.

The basic assumptions concerning the development of the product-market, the general marketing objectives of the firm or business unit and the marketing policies constitute the marketing strategy of the firm or business unit. The marketing strategy is the basis for more short-term operative considerations such as product development, advertising or pricing activities contained in what most companies call a marketing plan.

International Marketing Plan

The marketing plan is the core part of the operative level of an international business plan. It contains an overview of strategic decisions relevant to short-term marketing activities, such as the product- and country-markets to be served, the benefits to be provided to customers in those markets and how to achieve their satisfaction in a way that contrasts attractively with major competitors. The specific content of a marketing plan will vary depending on the company and the industry it is in. In developing the marketing plan the responsible managers have additionally to consider that varying audiences may be interested in the plan. Accordingly, the plan's content needs to be flexibly presented with differing focus.

The structure of marketing plans may be rather similar across industries and firms. In an internationally operating firm, marketing plans established by various operational units or close cooperation partners, such as distributors or franchisees, which are faced with different local environments, need to be comparable in order to allow the aggregation of data. The following sections will discuss how marketing plans may need to be adaptable to varying target audiences, the structure that local marketing plans should have to allow the aggregation of activities and data into an international marketing plan, and how the planning procedure should be organized to allow effective and efficient planning.

Audiences

The preparation of a marketing plan is an exercise which must cause marketing managers involved in whatever part of the planning procedure to examine their basic assumptions in the minutest detail since these must be justified to third parties. Hindsight is a quality that many marketing people have in abundance but a marketing plan is designed to eliminate the necessity of hindsight as much as possible. When preparing the international marketing plan, managers have to consider which target persons or groups they are addressing.

Internal audiences may be the chief executive officer or the board of directors who take the final decisions or the middle management and staff who need to be convinced of the plan's content to implement it properly. When evaluating a plan, controllers, accountants and finance managers usually look for a payback within a reasonable period. Although this may seem short-sighted, it must be recognized that financial personnel are risk averse, mostly because of external pressures. Other arguments are often needed to convince colleagues from the marketing, production or supply areas to switch to a new process, such as competitor and customer pressures that force quality improvement whithout raising prices, or increasing market share in parallel with increasing the firm's level of environmental protection. There may also be a works council, a supervisory board or an advisory board that may want to be informed about the marketing plan. Depending on their specific mission, they will be more or less interested in figures or details of particular activities.

External audiences for the marketing plan may be capital owners, creditors, private and institutional investors, and presumptive buyers of the company who are mainly interested in the return on and the risk of their investment. Shareholders, investors, venture capitalists and bankers want a marketing plan to contain all information needed by financial analysts to assess the financial consequences of the proposed decisions and planned actions. For them the marketing plan must demonstrate in a rigorous manner that the objectives set are reachable with actions that are commercially viable. Licensors and licensees, franchisees, potential joint venture and other cooperation partners, on the other hand, may focus more strongly on the capabilities of their (potential) partner. They are mainly interested in the firm's strengths and weaknesses compared to its major competitors, how the company plans to create or take advantage of market opportunities, and how it plans to fill detected gaps. Finally, national and international subsidizing councils as well as private and public national or international funding institutions may be mainly interested in a sound general concept that promises to provide public benefits.

In any case a marketing plan should be as short as possible, clearly structured, consistent and convincing. But some of the persons or groups that the marketing plan addresses may be more interested in figures, while others may focus on the served markets' potential and the marketing activities of the firm to take advantage of that potential. Still others may focus on how the marketing plan was developed (who participated in the process, what assumptions were made or how data were gathered), while another audience may just be interested in the outcomes of the process. In any case it is important to obtain agreement from all the parties involved as to the aims and objectives of the plan and to obtain commitment to its contents.

To be considered convincing by people with such differing preoccupations as the ones just described, an international marketing plan must have a flexible structure. It needs to comprise all required information. But it should allow the company to show in detail just those issues that the specific audience is mainly interested in. For that purpose the information needs to be presentable at different degrees of aggregation in each chapter.

Structure

Marketing plans are conceptualized differently in the literature. Even institutions like banks, funding organizations, or administrative authorities granting subsidies to firms presenting viable marketing plans, which should have a vital interest in well-structured, informative and plausible marketing plans, have differing requirements and standards concerning those plans.

One explanation for that finding may be that the businesses of companies preparing marketing plans vary greatly in their focus and extent. Small and only locally active firms have rather simply structured marketing plans compared to big and globally operating companies. The more product- and country-markets a company serves, the more individual marketing plans need to be coordinated and consolidated to produce one single marketing plan for the entire company.

In addition, the legal regulations regarding commercial and tax accounting differ from country to country, making a comparison between marketing plans of various origins rather difficult. However, for an internationally operating company to optimize the use of its skills and resources across product- and country-markets, marketing plans established by different oganizational units must be able to be equally interpreted. Differences in the meaning of the term 'plan' and in the structure of the plan's content have to be overcome for the purpose of making decisions comparable and planned actions based on those decisions acceptable to all persons involved in or concerned with their execution. For that purpose the following section will suggest a potential structure for local as well as consolidated marketing plans of a firm operating internationally which might be found in the company's international marketing planning manual.

Marketing Plans of Local Operating Units. Table 19.1 shows an example of the potential structure and content of a marketing plan to be developed by all local operating units of an international marketer serving consumer markets. Such operating units may be subsidiaries, sales offices or distribution partners in a country-market. But the structure suggested in Table 19.1 may also be used by sales managers of an exporting firm who need to prepare a marketing plan for the country-market or sales region for which they are responsible.

The plan starts with a short **preface**. In this introduction the author(s) of the plan state(s) the reason for presenting the marketing plan, the audience the plan is targeted to, the main assumptions the author(s) had to make (for example, the development of the inflation rate, getting an import licence in time, or finding a local supplier), the persons involved in preparing the plan (including a 'thank you' to all who cooperated), the time spent, and the decisions the author(s) are expecting.

Then the marketing plan summarizes the major results of the analyses undertaken and the conclusions drawn from those results in an **executive summary** taking no more than two pages. The executive summary is the most important part of the marketing plan because people reading the plan tend not to study the rest of the plan if the executive summary is not convincing. Most central decision makers in firms operating internationally suffer from continual information overload. They are not prepared to read more than two pages in order to find out the most important points of a message. As a consequence, marketing managers do not have much room for lengthy narration. Sentences

Table 19.1 POTENTIAL STRUCTURE AND CONTENT OF A LOCAL MARKETING PLAN

1. Introduction
2. Executive Summary
3. Actual Situation
    3.1 Internal Situation
        ↔ Strategic market position
        ↔ Objectives and levels of achievement
           (e.g. sales, profits, market shares, average prices by product lines,
           products, sales regions, customer (group)s)
        ↔ Marketing mix
        ↔ Organization and personnel
        ↔ Costs and financial status
    3.2 External Situation
        ↔ Macro-Environment
           (important dimensions, relevant factors of influence,
           development)
        ↔ Industry
           (e.g. sales potential, sales volume, structure, profitability;
           particular events and developments of significance)
        ↔ Intermediaries
           (e.g. structure, business behaviour, particular events and
           developments of significance)
        ↔ Customers
           (e.g. regional distribution, purchasing power, specific
           characteristics, purchasing behaviour, consumption behaviour,
           expectations, segments)
        ↔ Competitors
           (e.g. served customer segments, intended or existing
           differentiation, competitive strategy, market share, marketing
           mix, cost structure, financial structure, technical know-how,
           alliances)
        ↔ Other important stakeholders
           (e.g. media, legislators, trade unions, ecologists)
    3.3 Assessment of Internal and External Situation
        ↔ Strengths and weaknesses
        ↔ Opportunities and threats
        ↔ Gaps
4. Objectives
    4.1 Intended Strategic Position
        ↔ Target customer segments
        ↔ Differentiation from competitors
    4.2 Sales and Market Share Objectives
        (e.g. by existing customers, new customers, customer segments, sales
        area, product lines, products)
    4.3 Marketing Mix Objectives
    4.4 Financial Objectives
        (e.g. profit, free cash flow, return on sales, capital turnover)
5. Activity Plan
    5.1 Marketing Mix
        ↔ Product Management
        ↔ Distribution and Sales Management
        ↔ Pricing
        ↔ Market Communication
    5.2 Organization and Personnel

Following the introduction the most essential contents of a marketing plan are summarized. A description of the actual situation constitutes the basis for the formulation of objectives. The activity plan shows how those objectives are to be reached. The budget figures express the expenses for the planned activities and relate them to expected results.

Table 19.1   Continued

↔ Organization
   ↔ Personnel
      (e.g. personnel development measures, continuous improvement
      activities, lay-offs)
   5.3 Monitoring
      (e.g. marketing research, information system, controlling)
6. **Budgets**
   6.1 Product Management Budget
   6.2 Distribution and Sales Budget
   6.3 Market Communication Budget
   6.4 Personnel Budget
   6.5 Monitoring Budget

must be precise and self-explanatory, using an attractive style of writing. Furthermore, persuasive headlines are needed to gain and keep the audience's attention. They may be also very helpful when the statements made in the executive summary are presented to decision makers with the help of transparencies, slides, or a computer animation.

In the following material, readers interested in more detail may find information concerning the **actual situation** of the organizational unit as it developed over the past three to five years, as well as the development of the served market(s) during the same period. Set objectives and the degree of their achievement (for example, in terms of products sold in the market, their average price, the number of customers reached, sales per customer, or market share) are described, as well as the development of the firm's local strategic position, and the applied marketing mix (for example, activities set in trade advertising and related budgets, fairs and exhibitions attended, product launches, key account or merchandising activities, and terms of sale). Information concerning the local organizational structure and personnel development activities is given. The development of costs related to the activities undertaken, the local calculation of prices and the resulting price list are shown, together with the financial situation of the operating unit.

The description of the served market(s) may encompass an overview of the development of macro-environmental dimensions relevant to the international marketer's business, such as import regulations, inflation and currency exchange rates, the economic climate, improvements in infrastructure, or changes in values dominating the local society. Further, the marketing plan will describe the development of the local industry to which the company belongs. First, data on general development are presented, such as market volume compared to market potential, average price of products sold, shares of differently priced product lines, or the average profitability in the industry. Then, more specific information concerning intermediaries, customers and competitors is added. The structure of potential and served intermediaries, their relationships with major suppliers (share of company products sold compared to competitors' products), and their business behaviour may be of particular interest. Regional distribution, purchasing power, buying and consumption patterns, brand or supplier awareness as well as expectations of customers may be described and used to form customer segments. Major competitors are characterized by features such as their size (in sales, employees, market share and profitability), competitive behaviour, the strategic position they have reached, the marketing mix they apply, their cost structure, financial resources, relationships and alliances, or their market-specific know-how.

In addition to the description of past developments in the operating and macro-environments that makes the reader understand why the actual situation of the local unit is as has been indicated in the marketing plan, the foreseeable development of those environments (up to the planning horizon) is presented. In preparing that outlook for the future of the business, responsible managers will rely on the basic assumptions given by their company's marketing strategy. Short-term figures such as the development of sales, stock, accounts receivable or liquidity will be based partly on estimates stemming from field experience of staff and partly on forecasts using more or less sophisticated computer models. The central planning unit of US-based PC-marketer Gateway 2000, for example, provides its local marketing planning staff with a forecasting model that produces highly precise sales estimates for one-year planning periods.

An **assessment of internal and external developments** reveals the current strengths and weaknesses of the operational unit compared to its strengths and weaknesses at the planning horizon if marketing activities are carried on without change. It also highlights potential opportunities and threats stemming from the fit between the operational unit's current skills and resources and foreseeable developments in the macro-environment. Based on this assessment, gaps can be defined which need to be filled in order to make the operating unit contribute properly to the general marketing objectives stated in the company's or business unit's marketing strategy. For example, if the marketing strategy of a Japanese manufacturer of industrial transportation systems defines the objective of reaching at least a market share which places the firm in the first three ranks of suppliers in every served market, and its European subsidiary serving the automotive industry is in danger of slipping from rank four to rank five in its market, there is an evident need to fill this gap between general objectives and actual development with appropriate measures.

Because the general marketing objectives stated in the marketing strategy and the marketing objectives of the local unit in general do not totally fit in the short run, the **marketing objectives** of the unit are stated in the marketing plan. Most international marketers find it useful first to describe the local unit's intended strategic position, that is, the customer segments (ranked by priority) to be reached during the planning period and the differentiation from competitors to be achieved in those customers' minds. Then sales and market share objectives by existing and new customers, customer segments and regions may be indicated. They are more easily checked concerning their potential for realization if objectives concerning the marketing mix are added. For example, the objective of increasing market share in a specific customer segment may be supported by the objectives of launching an improved product, increasing distribution intensity, raising the attractiveness of terms of sale to intermediaries, and participating in special target group events. Finally, the organizational unit's financial objectives tell the audience what contribution local marketing managers expect to make to the overall profitability of the firm.

The following section of the marketing plan contains the **activities** to be implemented during the planning period in order to reach the set objectives and to monitor their success. In a marketing plan all marketing activities are described in detail. But organizational measures and personnel development needed to ensure marketing success are indicated as well as activities needed to monitor business development. Finally, the marketing plan presents the costs of the planned activities and compares them to expected revenues in detailed **budgets**.

To make sure that all managers and distributors of the company who regularly have to establish marketing plans employ the same structure and the same forms and definitions, the central marketing unit in the international marketer's headquarters may be well advised to develop an **international marketing planning manual**. Such a manual serves as a guideline for planners. It prescribes the general structure that all marketing plans have to follow. It contains the forms to be used, and ensures easy consolidation of data. This is important for the establishment of a company or business unit international marketing plan.

The Company or Business Unit International Marketing Plan. The marketing plans of local units must be consolidated to provide the information needed by senior management in order to agree or disagree with what has been planned. Basically, such a consolidated plan follows the same structure as the marketing plans of the subunits. But it provides information on an aggregated level; that is, activities are reported in less detail, and figures prevail.

As with the marketing plans of local units, the company or business unit international marketing plan starts with an **introduction** and an **executive summary**. Then the **actual situation** of the firm, seen primarily from a marketing perspective, is described. The description starts with an overview of internal preconditions and assumptions which underlie all marketing planning activities (see Table 19.2). First comes a statement of corporate policy and corporate strategy statements as far as they are relevant for marketing decisions and actions. Then the guidelines for the application of marketing tools stated in the marketing strategy are summarized.

An overview of the structure of the firm's or business unit's marketing organization shows the plan's audiences which functional marketing areas exist, where in the firm's hierarchy they are located and how they are coordinated by senior management. Regular teams and special task forces are described as to their purpose, size and participating members. The same is done for external cooperation partners such as market research agencies, market communication specialists, and new product development or logistics partners. A flow chart may inform the reader about the sequence of analyses and decisions, the participating organizational units and the timing of the international marketing decision process.

The description of the internal situation continues with the **marketing achievements** of the company or business unit during the reporting period (generally three years). It starts with a comparison of quantitative and qualitative marketing objectives as fixed in the reporting period with the results achieved in the same period. Those results are compared to the objectives stated for the planning period (for example, the coming three years). Then the range of products marketed by the company/business unit is described, indicating their specific features, their target groups, their applications, and major benefits provided to customers. An overview of existing customers is given. For the most important customers, their name, location, products purchased and sales are indicated. The other customers are grouped depending on their

Table 19.2 DESCRIPTION OF THE FIRM'S ACTUAL MARKETING SITUATION

I. Actual Situation

1. Corporate Policy and Strategies

    1.1 Corporate Policy
        Corporate Mission
        Corporate Philosophy

    1.2 Corporate Strategy
        Portfolio Strategy
        Competitive Strategy
        Market-entry Strategy

    1.3 Marketing Strategy
        Product Policy
        Distribution Policy
        Pricing Policy
        Market Communication Policy

2. Marketing Achievements

    2.1 Marketing Objectives and Results

Objectives	Results				Plan	
	1996	1997	1998	1999	2000	2001
1. Quantitative objectives (e.g. sales, market share, ROS, share of new products, customer retention rate, . . .)						
2. Qualitative objectives (e.g. reputation, awareness, customer satisfaction, lasting relationships, . . .)						

    2.2 Range of Products/Industries/Applications

Range of Products	Description	Features	Target groups Industries	Applications	Benefits

    2.3 Important Customers

Location	Name	Product	Sales 199

    2.4 Important Suppliers

Location	Name	Product	Value

The description of the actual marketing situation includes internal and external information needed to assess the relative strengths and weaknesses of the firm, as well as opportunities and threats it is facing from the macro-environment, and to determine strategic gaps to be filled by marketing actions.

Table 19.2 Continued

2.5 Other Important Stakeholders

Stakeholder group	Interests	Actions	Reactions

2.6 Major investments realized

Type	Purpose	Location	Value

3. **Development of External Environments**
   3.1 **Macro-environment**
       (e.g. political risk, currency exchange rates, legislation, liberalization, . . .)
   3.2 **Industry**
       (e.g. total sales volume, structure of supply, average prices, profit margin, emerging markets, technological innovation, . . .)
   3.3 **Customers**
       (e.g. structure of intermediaries, emerging intermediaries, customer segments, emerging expectations, . . .)
   3.4 **Competitors**
       (e.g. strategic groups, alliances, competitive strategy of major competitors, mergers/acquisitions, new product launches, . . .)
   3.5 **Other important stakeholders**
       (e.g. suppliers, investors, creditors, administrators, media, . . .)

4. **Situation Assessment**
   4.1 **Strengths and Weaknesses**
   4.2 **Opportunities and Threats**
   4.3 **Strategic Gaps**

purchasing volumes. If available, average contribution margins achieved per important customer or customer group, when provided, will further increase the level of information. A list of important suppliers and other important stakeholders, indicating their specific interests concerning the company's business as well as the actions set by the firm and the reactions of the stakeholders, further enriches the audience's picture of the actual situation. A description of major investments realized in the marketing area completes the marketing achievements section of the plan. It may contain information on special activities such as the construction of a new warehouse, the opening of new company-owned stores or the installation of a new marketing information system.

The description of the actual situation would not be complete without a presentation of the results of external analyses. The international marketing plan, therefore, contains a section that summarizes information concerning **developments of external environments** from the marketing plans of the local operating units. Important changes compared to earlier reporting periods and to assumptions that were taken for the actual reporting period are specifically highlighted.

As a conclusion from reported internal and external developments, in the next section of the plan a situation assessment is given. It determines the strengths and weaknesses of the company or business unit compared to its major competitors, focusing on the success factors in each of the served product-markets and in the major country-markets or regions. Together with the detected opportunities and threats from the international macro-environment of the business, those strengths and weaknesses provide the basis for an analysis of strategic gaps. The international marketing plan enumerates and illustrates the various areas in which the company needs to improve. For example, the setting of different transfer prices for distributors and sales offices may have led to price differences in final customer prices which may be considered an invitation for parallel imports. The lack of an efficient customer information system may have led to differing treatment of the subsidiaries of the same globally active customer, resulting in customer complaints and pressure on prices. A lack of total quality assurance may have caused the sending back of defective products, increasing costs and harming the firm's reputation. Those gaps must at least be partly filled by marketing activities.

The illustration of gaps found as a result of the actual situation analysis leads the audiences of the plan back to the objectives formulated for the planning period. The following section of the international marketing plan, entitled 'International Marketing Objectives and Budgets', particularly emphasizes sales forecasts for the planning period and budgets needed to realize those sales figures (see Table 19.3). It starts by reminding the audiences of the company's or business unit's intended global strategic position. This is the standard of comparison for all activities budgeted in the following. Any budgeted activity needs to make a contribution to reaching this standard.

Sales forecasts for each local product-market stored in a data bank allow fast and flexible computation of total sales forecasts for products, product lines, international product-markets, country-markets, regions, industries or international key accounts. As Table 19.3 illustrates, information can be sorted, filtered and combined according to the needs of the user. For example, the international sales forecast for a product-market can be determined by adding all sales forecasts for the local product-markets to be found in the marketing plans of the local operating units. The firm's forecast total sales are the result of adding up the forecasts for all different product-markets. Total sales in a country-market can be determined by adding up all sales forecasts for different product-markets in that geographic area. For liquidity planning purposes, a forecast of accounts receivable during the planning period is generated. It is based on the sales forecast and the customer's paying habits as far as they are known to the marketer.

The presentation of budget figures starts with a **general overview**. The total budget is given by types of costs, split into their variable and fixed parts. An overview of the expected order backlog and development of stock are added. Audiences interested in more details may switch directly to the presentation of product, marketing tool and marketing administration budgets. Product

---

Table 19.3 **INTERNATIONAL MARKETING OBJECTIVES AND BUDGETS**

---

1. **Intended Global Strategic Position**
    1.1 Target markets
        Product-markets
        Country-markets
        Customer segments
    1.2 Major benefits/Competitive differentiation
    1.3 Technologies

2. **Sales Forecast**
    2.1 Sales

Year	Product	Country	Rep	Industry	Number of customers	Number of orders	Units	Price per unit	Sales USD	Market share
1999	A	GB	I	Chemistry	12	14	91			
1999	B	GB	II	Steel works						
2000	D	A	III	Chemistry						
1999	B	F	IV	Food						
2000	E	USA	V	Food						
1999	C	NL	VI	Food						
2001										
2002										
......	......	......	......	......			......	......	......	

2.2 Accounts receivable

Product		1. Quarter 1999 USD	2. Quarter 1999 USD	3. Quarter 1999 USD	4. Quarter 1999 USD	1. Half-year 2000 USD	2. Half-year 2000 USD
A	accounts receivable						
	− payments						
	+ new accounts receivable						
	accounts receivable						
B	accounts receivable						
	− payments						
	+ new accounts receivable						
	accounts receivable						

Table 19.3 CONTINUED

Product		1. Quarter 1999 USD	2. Quarter 1999 USD	3. Quarter 1999 USD	4. Quarter 1999 USD	1. Half-year 2000 USD	2. Half-year 2000 USD
Total	accounts receivable						
	− payments						
	+ new accounts receivable						
	accounts receivable						

3. Budgets
3.1 Overview
Total Marketing Budget

Type of cost	Fixed costs in USD			Variable costs in USD		
	1998	1999	2000	1998	1999	2000
Total						

Order Backlog / Sales / Bookings

Product		1. Quarter 1998 USD	2. Quarter 1998 USD	3. Quarter 1998 USD	4. Quarter 1998 USD	1. Half-year 1999 USD	2. Half-year 1999 USD
A	order backlog						
	sales						
	bookings						
	order backlog						
B	order backlog						
	sales						
	bookings						
	order backlog						
Total	order backlog						
	sales						
	booking						
	order backlog						

Table 19.3 **CONTINUED**

Development of Stock

Product		1. Quarter 1998 USD	2. Quarter 1998 USD	3. Quarter 1998 USD	4. Quarter 1998 USD	1. Half-year 1999 USD	2. Half-year 1999 USD
A	stock						
	+						
	−						
	new stock						
B	stock						
	+						
	−						
	new stock						
Total	stock						
	+						
	−						
	new stock						

3.2 Product Budgets

Product A in all countries of the EU, NAFTA and Latin America					
Marketing Tool	Decision or action (examples)	Country	Fixed cost USD	Variable cost per ... in USD	Total cost USD
Product management	Brand (Registration and current cost per year)	EU		year	
	Patent (Registration and current cost per year)	EU		year	
	New product prototype testing	USA		year	
	Packaging (Design as fixed cost and price per unit)	EU NAFTA		unit	
	Packaging (Design as fixed cost and price per unit)	All countries		unit	
	Warranty	All countries		percentage of sales	
	Service free of charge	Latin America		percentage of sales	

Table 19.3 CONTINUED

Product A in all countries of the EU, NAFTA and Latin America					
Marketing Tool	Decision or action (examples)	Country	Fixed cost USD	Variable cost per ... in USD	Total cost USD
Distribution	Systems/Channels				
	Travelling expenses of sales staff	EU NAFTA		percentage of sales or by order	
	Travelling expenses of sales staff	Latin America		percentage of sales or by order	
	Representatives' commission	EU		percentage of sales	
	Representatives' commission	NAFTA		percentage of sales	
	Representatives' commission	Latin America		percentage of sales	
	Training of representatives	All countries			
	Equipment representatives	All countries			
	Sales meetings	All countries			
	Sales office (including rent, furniture, personnel, travelling, stationery, phone, . . .	USA			
	Logistics				
	Warehouse	USA			
	Warehouse	Spain			
	Storage fee	Sweden		percentage of sales	
	Transportation (if not considered elsewhere)	NAFTA			
	Transportation (if not considered elsewhere)	NAFTA			
	Transportation (if not considered elsewhere)	Latin America			
	Insurance (if not considered elsewhere)	NAFTA Latin America			

Table 19.3 CONTINUED

Product A in all countries of the EU, NAFTA and Latin America					
Marketing Tool	Decision or action (examples)	Country	Fixed cost USD	Variable cost per … in USD	Total cost USD
Pricing	Discounts/Rebates	EU		percentage of sales	
	Discounts/Rebates	NAFTA		percentage of sales	
	Discounts/Rebates	Latin America		percentage of sales	
	Action	USA			
	Transfer prices	NAFTA		percentage of sales	
	Average date of required payment	per country		percentage of sales	
	Del credere	per country		percentage of sales	
Market communication	Regional radio ad campaign	EU			
	Ads in trade magazines	USA Canada			
	Yellow pages	EU per country			
	Yellow pages	NAFTA per country			
	Image brochure	All countries			
	Video tape	All countries			
	Sales manual	per country			
	Press conferences	USA			
	Press conferences	Germany			
	Sales promotion activities	France			
	Direct mailing	USA			
	Fair	Italy			
	Fair	Brazil			
	Fair	Canada			
	Symposium	UK			
	Open house	EU USA			

Table 19.3 CONTINUED

3.2 Marketing Tool Budgets
        Product Management
        Distribution (inc. Logistics)
        Pricing
        Market Communication
3.3 Marketing Administration Budget
        Overheads
        Organizational Changes
        Investments/Divestments

Type	Purpose	Location	1998 USD	1999 USD	2000 USD	2001 USD
		Total				

4.0 Results

The objectives and budgets section of an international marketing plan should contain a summary of the intended global strategic position of the firm/business unit, sales forecasts, and budgets.

budgets contain all activities planned for a specific product or product line, indicating their fixed and variable costs and the country where those activities are set. The information needed to establish those budgets is again compiled from the marketing plans of the local operating units (see Figure 19.4).

The same information may be used to establish **budgets for each bundle of marketing tools**. In the international product management budget, for example, all activities concerning new product development, taking products off the market, finding brand names, registering patents or brands, warranties, and pre- and after-sales services across all served country-markets are aggregated to give consolidated figures for each category of activity.

The **marketing administration budget** contains all types of overheads, as well as special budgets needed for changes in marketing organization, such as project budgets for the improvement of the reporting system, the preparation of offers, order handling, or the reorganization of warehouses. A final subsection on special investments or divestments, such as the construction of a new warehouse or the outsourcing of logistics, informs senior decision makers about extraordinary expenses planned for the improvement of the firm's marketing effectiveness and efficiency.

Having presented the objectives to be reached, the activities planned and the costs of those activities, the international marketing planners need to add an estimation of **expected results** in order to convince senior decision makers and other interested audiences of how attractive it is to accept or follow their plan. Therefore, a section presenting forecast results based on the previously suggested actions concludes the international marketing plan. By comparing the results to be expected when extrapolating current marketing action with

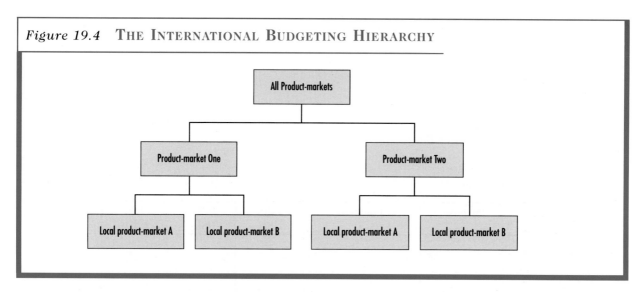

Figure 19.4 **The International Budgeting Hierarchy**

Based on the budgets of local operating units concerning marketing activities in their served product-markets, budgets for international product-markets may be established. Adding those budgets up leads to the total marketing budget of the firm operating internationally.

the results forecast for the suggested marketing plan, the impact of the plan can be most impressively demonstrated.

The most commonly used tools for that purpose are the pro forma profit and loss account (Table 19.4) and the pro forma balance sheet (Table 19.5).

In addition, the impact of the proposed marketing plan on the firm's or business unit's cash flow may be analysed (Table 19.6). The change in contribution margins of local product-markets, country-markets and international product-markets may also be forecast. Usually the contribution margin is first estimated for the local product-market. If the result is positive, that is, if the activities in this market contribute to covering the costs of the next higher level – the country-market – the estimation procedure continues. Similarly, the country-market has to contribute to covering the costs of managing the international product-market or business unit, and finally the latter has to contribute to covering the overheads of company management.

Finally, the impact of the proposed marketing plan on the break-even point of local and international product-markets as well as country-markets may be developed. Besides break-even point analysis, to get an impression of the risk involved in implementing the international marketing plan, a kind of sensitivity analysis of the suggested activities to major changes in the operating and macro-environment can be conducted. Instead of presenting just one single result, the planning team should develop two additional alternatives which consider significantly different developments of those environments. A more optimistic scenario may be considered as well as a more pesimistic one. When a company is facing economic or other difficulties, however, marketing planners may be well advised to probe the impact of two more negative scenarios, for example by simply reducing sales forecasts by 10 and 20 per cent. In fast-growing markets, on the other hand, it may make sense to develop alternative plans for market growth rates of 30 and 50 per cent. The important thing for the international marketer is to be intellectually prepared for

Table 19.4 PRO FORMA PROFIT AND LOSS ACCOUNT				
Income and Expenditures	USD*	USD**	USD*	USD**
	1998	1998	1999	1999
Sales income				
Cost of goods				
Gross profit				
Expenditure				
Administration				
Rent & rates				
Product management				
Distribution				
Pricing				
Market communication				
Overheads				
Depreciation				
Interest				
Total Expenditure				
PBIT (Profit before interest and tax)				
Taxation				
Profit after tax				
Gross % (Gross profit divided by Sales income)				
Total Expenditure % (Total Expenditure divided by Sales income)				
ROI % (Return on Investment)				
Gearing %				

*   Result when keeping the current modus operandi
** Result when implementing the marketing plan

The pro forma profit and loss account compares incomes and expenditures when the marketing modus operandi is kept unchanged with incomes and expenditures when the suggested marketing plan is implemented.

Source: Adapted from Office for Official Publications of the European Union – Directorate- General XIII (1994) 'Preparing a Technology Business Plan', Luxembourg.

alternative developments to what seems to be the most realistic assumption at the moment in time.

Planning Procedure

Responsibilities.   In general, marketing or sales managers of local operating units and distribution partners are responsible for preparing and presenting the marketing plans of their organizational units. If the international marketer relies on exports, the export market manager(s) will prepare the marketing

Table 19.5 **Pro Forma Balance Sheet**

	Assets and Liabilities	USD*	USD**	USD*	USD**
	Assets	1998	1998	1999	1999
A	Called-up share capital not paid				
B	Fixed assets				
I	Intangible assets				
	1. Development costs				
	2. Concessions, patents, licences, 3. Trademarks and similar rights and assets				
	4. Goodwill				
	5. Payments on account				
II	Tangible assets				
	1. Land and buildings				
	2. Plant and machinery				
	3. Fixtures, fittings, tools and equipment				
	4. Payments on account aid assets in course of construction				
III	Investments				
	1. Shares in group companies				
	2. Loans to group companies				
	3. Shares in related companies				
	4. Loans to related companies				
	5. Other investments other than loans				
	6. Other loans				
	7. Own shares				
C	Current assets				
I	Stocks				
	1. Raw materials and consumables				
	2. Work in progress				
	3. Finished goods and goods for resale				
	4. Payments on account				
II	Debtors				
	1. Trade debtors				
	2. Amounts owed by group companies				
	3. Amounts owed by related companies				
	4. Other debtors				
	5. Called-up share capital not paid				
	6. Prepayments and accrued income				
III	Investments				
	1. Shares in group companies				
	2. Own shares				
	3. Other investments				

| | | Table 19.5 CONTINUED |

	Assets and Liabilities	USD*	USD**	USD*	USD**
	Assets	1998	1998	1999	1999
IV	Cash at bank and in hand				
D	Prepayments and accrued income				
	Liabilities				
A	Capital and reserves				
I	Called-up share capital				
II	Share premium account				
III	Revaluation reserve				
IV	Other reserves				
	1. Capital redemption reserve				
	2. Reserve for own shares				
	3. Reserves provided for by the articles of association				
	4. Other reserves				
V	Profit and loss account				
B	Provisions for liabilities and charges				
	1. Pensions and similar obligations				
	2. Taxation, including deferred taxation				
	3. Other provisions				
C	Creditors				
	1. Debenture loans				
	2. Bank loans and overdrafts				
	3. Payments received on account				
	4. Trade creditors				
	5. Bills of exchange payable				
	6. Amounts owed to group companies				
	7. Amounts owed to related companies				
	8. Other creditors including taxation and social security				
	9. Accruals and deferred income				
D	Accruals and deferred income				

* Result when keeping the current modus operandi
** Result when implementing the marketing plan

The pro forma balance sheet compares assets and liabilities when the marketing modus operandi is kept unchanged with assets and liabilities when the suggested marketing plan is implemented.

Source: Adapted from Office for Official Publications of the European Union –
Directorate-General XIII (1994) 'Preparing a Technology Business Plan', Luxembourg.

Table 19.6 CASH-FLOW FORECAST

Cash Flows	USD*	USD**	USD*	USD**
	1998	1998	1999	1999
Cash inflows				
Sales				
Capital				
Loans				
Total inflow				
Cash outflows				
Machinery				
Raw material				
Labour				
Rent				
Rates				
Distribution-related expenditures				
Market communication				
General overheads				
Administration overheads				
Loan interest				
Total inflow				
Balance brought forward				
Balance carried forward				

* Result when keeping the current way of action
** Result when implementing the marketing plan

The cash-flow forecast compares cash flows when the marketing modus operandi is kept unchanged with cash flows when the suggested marketing plan is implemented.

Source: Adapted from Office for Official Publications of the European Union – Directorate-General XIII (1994) 'Preparing a Technology Business Plan', Luxembourg.

plans for each country-market or region. The top marketing executive in the company's headquarters is responsible for preparing and presenting the consolidated international marketing plan. The marketing planning unit in the company's headquarters may vary due to the firm's portfolio of product- and country-markets and its organizational structure. Because some companies manage by countries or regions, others by products or product lines and still others by customer groups, the major perspective of international marketing planning will vary with the organizational focus.

In establishing their plans, marketing managers will need help from other persons both inside and outside the company. For example, the salespeople of a country or region will plan their sales figures and distribution activities. The managers responsible for different tools of market communication will plan their events, advertising campaigns, sponsoring, or public relations activities. Production, controlling, personnel, procurement, logistics, research and development, or finance managers may contribute their information for pricing, personnel development or new product development decisions.

Planning Teams. Because of the complexity of the planning task which needs information input and know-how from all across the company's functional areas, interfunctional planning teams may help to ensure that all aspects of the planning task are appropriately considered. Under the leadership of the responsible marketing manager, at least in certain steps of the planning process (such as the establishment of the profit and loss account) or when preparing certain sections of the marketing plan (for example, the personnel development section), specialists from the functional areas concerned need to be involved. In addition to the know-how and information those people may provide to increase the quality of marketing planning, their participation in the planning process strongly contributes to its implementation. The Culture box gives an impression of the problems that may arise in intercultural planning teams, but also how much teamwork may contribute to improved planning results and the adherence of team members to the course of action decided upon.

As with any project carried out by a team, it is important to brief the participants in the planning process as to the basic requirements of the plan and to agree upon deadlines for the contributors. The team leader may go through the objectives and policies stated in the company's or business unit's marketing strategy. The basic assumptions concerning the development of the macro-environment and the industry may be discussed with the goal of creating some basic shared understanding of the major issues that need to be tackled, and the major objectives that should be reached. This technique, known as 'pre-briefing', takes some additional time to get planning activities started. But it has enormous benefits later on, resulting in fewer criticisms and internal politics which otherwise might sink a marketing plan at its first presentation.

Updates. Preparing the marketing plan starts where the strategic part of the international marketing decision process ends. The principal results of this decision process, for example which country-markets to serve with which kind of product through which market-entry mode, may be valid for some longer term. They represent the basis from which the more short-term-oriented marketing plan is developed. Because the activities contained in the marketing plan and the figures related to those activities are planned in great detail, they are subject to change. Consequently, at least a yearly update of the marketing plan is required. Planned activities and figures must be reviewed at least quarterly in the light of actual developments in all environments of the company. The Future Issues box gives an impression of how much advances in information technology will speed up the rhythm of plan reviews in the coming years. Any discrepancies between the original assumptions and the recorded development which result in performance figures that deviate from expectations must be accounted for and the assumptions modified if necessary.

Any revisions of marketing plans where inputs like sales, prices, costs or currency exchange rates may change should have a mid-range planning horizon. The horizon will vary with the company's business domain, but in most cases it is between two and five years. That is, activities and figures should not only be adjusted for the actual planning period which in most cases extends across one year from the time of the plan revision. Forecasts for the subsequent periods must also be adjusted in line with the revised assumptions. At

CULTURE BOX

Mercedes

Made in

Alabama

POSSESSING NOTHING BUT THE PROVERBIAL BLANK sheet of paper Andreas Renschler, CEO of the Alabama factory of Stuttgart, Germany-based Mercedes-Benz, set out to 'create' his factory in 1993. He very deliberately pieced together a team that included US executives with Detroit auto experience, along with a couple who had worked for Japanese transplants in North America. He drafted a perfectly balanced ticket: four Germans, four Americans at management's top tier. The plan was to plumb the assembled American automotive talent for fresh insights about how to run a factory. Those with Japanese transplant experience, he hoped, could provide point-ers on how a foreign automaker might best go about setting up shop in the US.

But the members of the management team hailed from very different manufacturing traditions and possessed vastly different ideas about how to do things. They all spoke different languages – GM-ese, Nissan-ese, Mercedes-ese, as it were. Questions such as how to configure the assembly line set off fierce debates. Progress would probably never have been possible had it not been for one of the headquarters' infrequent directives – a very rigid time frame that was in place from day one. Thus, the team had no choice but to fight until it came up with blueprints for a factory and plans for hiring a work force. Despite all the cultural differences, the Vance, Alabama factory has proven to be a success. The design, a sleek E-shape with interconnected shops, has turned out especially efficient.

Source: Martin, J. (1997) 'Mercedes: Made in Alabama', *Fortune*, 7 July, pp. 150–158.

least the central figures in the profit and loss account as well as in the pro forma balance sheet for the next two to five years need to be adjusted. This way the company and its subunits will have rolling marketing plans which are responsive to changes in the business environment.

SUMMARY

The primary objective in preparing an international business plan is to set out a convincing case to secure internal and external financing for the start-up, expansion or continuation of an international business. The business plan must demonstrate in a rigorous manner the commercial viability of the proposed actions. The plan should cover all aspects of the business: from the corporate mission, to the corporate strategy, business unit and functional area strategies, right down to functional area plans.

Marketing orientation and marketing analyses may have a significant impact on the formulation of corporate philosophy and corporate strategy. They influence the basic approach of a company's management to their business and lead their decision-making processes in a way that starts with the determination of attractive markets. The influence of marketing orientation and marketing technology leads market choice as well as competitive strategy decisions to be taken based on the skills and resources needed to serve the most attractive markets successfully.

FUTURE ISSUES
BOX

The Marketing Plan of the Next Decade

THE FAST DEVELOPMENT OF INFORMATION TECHNOLOGY will have a major impact on the development and update of future marketing plans.

The marketing plan of the future will probably be

↔ '**instant**': Inputs will be made at the customer's office and transferred immediately. All new data at the factory, like change in stock, price increase of a supplier etc. will be instantly considered by the system. This will offer an up-to-the-second information to all relevant people inside and outside the company at any given time.

↔ '**online**': All data will be collected, computed and saved at one location, that is the server or network of the marketer's company. As a consequence all relevant people have the same level of information and there is no time lag. Their notebooks will work as terminals.

↔ '**continually rolling**': All changes will be considered instantly. This way the marketing plan is kept permanently up-to-date and adapted to new facts, for instance changes of the macro-environment.

↔ '**independent of the location**': The next generation of mobile telephones will offer worldwide use of telephone networks across the globe directly via satellite, this way putting international marketers in the position of having access to their 'home' data bank day and night.

↔ '**standardized**': Software has been and will be developed that on the one hand, takes into account all features telecommunication systems and high-end hardware – like dictating directly into a machine – offer and on the other hand, uses standardized protocols for data transfer like the United Nations' EDIFACT.

↔ '**using more and more external data**': Data available in the World Wide Web concerning the macro-environment, industries, intermediaries, potential customers, competitors, and other important stakeholders may be automatically considered by the computer system by executing updating routines.

Sources: Negroponte, N. (1995) *Being Digital*, London: Coronet Books; and results of presentations and discussions at EUROPEAN FORUM ALPBACH, 1995 and 1996, Alpbach, Austria.

Marketing strategy and the marketing plan are the core parts of an international business plan. They encompass the results of analyses, decisions, guidelines and actions that are based on the basic strategic decisions of senior management and have been discussed in detail throughout this book.

Marketing plans should have a flexible structure comprising all required information, but a different degree of consolidation of each section depending on the audience to whom they are presented. In any case a marketing plan should be as short as possible, clearly structured, consistent and convincing.

The international marketing plan is usually based on the marketing plans of local operating units or managers who are responsible for certain international sales areas. All marketing plans should comprise a preface or introduction, an executive summary, a description of the actual position of the firm and the results from an analysis of the external environments relevant to the company's business. This analytical part of the plan concludes with the determination of the firm's relative marketing strengths and weaknesses, the opportunities and threats it is facing from being more or less well adapted to developments in the macro-environment, and strategic gaps that need to be filled in order to keep or make the company successful.

Based on that information, marketing planners have to specify the marketing objectives for the planning period. Those objectives will be derived from more general objectives stated in the corporate, business unit and marketing strategy statements. All marketing activities proposed in the following section of the plan have to contribute to reaching the set goals. The higher the level of plan aggregation, the more abstract the content of the plan becomes. That is, the marketing plans of locally responsible units describe all planned activities in some detail, whereas the company's or a business unit's international marketing plan mainly contains budget figures that reflect the planned activities.

To present the proposed marketing actions convincingly, the marketing plan needs finally to demonstrate how much better off the company will be when it implements the plan. For that purpose, result forecasts based on an unchanged modus operandi are compared to result estimates based on the assumption that the proposed marketing plan is implemented. Pro forma profit and loss statements, pro forma balance sheets, cash-flow projections, contribution margin estimates and break-even point analyses under both scenario's serve the purpose of comparison. An analysis of the sensitivity of those forecast results to changes in the assumed environment helps the final decision makers to get an impression of the risks involved in their decision.

What the real outcomes of international marketing strategies and plans will be, nobody can know exactly beforehand. The success of an international marketer will not only depend on the perfection of its analyses, the quality of the conclusions drawn, and the motivation of all the people involved in the implementation of the plans. The marketer will also need a substantial portion of luck to become and stay a major player in the international business arena.

DISCUSSION QUESTIONS

1. Why does the international marketing decision process have different hierarchical levels? Explain by using an example of a company you are familiar with.
2. Find an example of two corporate policies on the Internet and compare them concerning the visible influence of marketing orientation on their formulation.
3. To what extent does marketing influence the development of a corporate strategy? Find examples for the points you make.
4. Ask a local marketing or sales manager of a firm operating internationally to show you the table of contents of the marketing plan they have to prepare. How does it compare to what was discussed in this chapter?
5. What audiences may be interested in the international marketing plan of a firm? What are they particularly interested in?
6. How should international marketing planning

information be structured to be usable in a flexible manner for various audiences?
7. Describe the steps in the process of development of an international marketing plan. Who should be involved in the planning team and at what stage?

ADDITIONAL READINGS

Covin, J.G., D.P. Slevin, and R.L. Schultz (1997) 'Top Management Decision Sharing and Adherence to Plans', *Journal of Business Research,* 40, 21–36.

Schlegelmilch, B.B. and R. Sinkovics (1998) 'Viewpoint: marketing in the information age – can we plan for an unpredictable future?', *International Marketing Review,* 15(3) 162–170.

Varadarajan, P.R. and T. Clark (1994) 'Delineating the Scope of Corporate, Business, and Marketing Strategy', *Journal of Business Research* 31, 93–105.

Webster, F.E., Jr. (1992) 'The Changing Role of Marketing in the Corporation', *Journal of Marketing,* 56 (October), 1–17.

Case Study
UNITED COLORS OF BENETTON

It was October 1995. Luciano Benetton, chairman of Benetton Group S.p.A, prepared to address yet another audience of business leaders. This tall, smiling yet reserved man with very blue eyes and longish hair was the guest speaker at a dinner held by the Italian Chamber of Commerce for France in Paris. Over the past 40 years, Benetton had become famous for its technological advances and novel approach to retailing. By 1995, it had become one of the world's best-known brands, with 8000 shops world-wide, and a successful winning Formula One racing team (key financial data can be found in Exhibit 1). For most people, however, Benetton was synonymous with its communication strategy – one of the world's most visible and controversial, almost always provoking reactions of outrage or praise and, quite often, both.

Rather than advertising its products, Benetton used its communications budget to provoke debate on broad social issues such as racism, AIDS, war and poverty. A number of observers had criticised its 'use of social problems to sell knitwear'. Luciano knew that he would have to explain one more time why he spent Benetton's L115 billion[1] communication budget on 'penetrating the barriers of apathy', and that, inevitably, some of his audience would remain unconvinced.

THE FORMATIVE YEARS

Luciano Benetton was born in 1935 in Ponzano, a village in a depressed rural area near the northern Italian cities of Treviso and Venice. Like millions of Italians of his class and generation, his father, Leone, left Italy. In 1937 he emigrated to Ethiopia,

then an Italian colony, leaving behind his wife Rosa, Luciano, and three smaller children: Giuliana, Gilberto and Carlo. In Ethiopia, Leone was robbed of the small business he had managed to build and returned home poorer than when he had left. After his death in 1945, from malaria contracted in Ethiopia, the family eked out a living by doing odd jobs and selling, one by one, the small plots of land they owned.

Luciano's sister, Giuliana, joined a knitwear workshop when she was eleven years old. Luciano worked before and after school, selling soap door-to-door and carrying 30 kilos of newspapers to sell at Treviso train station before dawn. At 14, Luciano left school to work in a clothing store in Treviso, where he learned the rudiments of retailing:

> 'The Dellasiega shop was typical of Italy in those times. A long counter separated the sales assistant from the client and the goods were usually hidden away except for a few models in the shop window or on a hanger. The customer needed to have at least a vague idea of what she was looking for, and describe it to the sales assistant . . . Clothes were sold like medicine – by prescription only.'[2]

In provincial post-war Italy, clothes were still very much dictated by a person's occupation and social class. Traditional social structures were, however, beginning to break down, following the end of the war and the downfall of Mussolini. But despite a growing interest in leisure and sports, casual clothes were not available nor were there specific clothes for young people, who often wore hand-me-downs from their parents. During his long days at Dellasiega's shop, Luciano became convinced that there was a market for a youthful, casual range of clothing. In 1955 he and Giuliana set up their own workshop. He was 20 years old, she was eighteen. To buy a knitting machine, Luciano sold his concertina, while his brother Gilberto sacrificed his bicycle. Working in the evenings, Giuliana produced a collection of 20 knitted sweaters, helped by Gilberto, aged 14, and Carlo, aged 12. Rosa assembled and ironed the jumpers, and Luciano spent his

Source: This case was developed by Christian Pinson, Professor, and Vikas Tibrewala, Associate Professor at INSEAD, with the assistance of Francesca Gee. It is intended to be used as a basis for class discussion rather than to illustrate either effective or ineffective handling of an administrative situation. Copyright © 1996 INSEAD–CEDEP, Fontainebleau, France.

evenings cycling from door-to-door to sell them under the trademark *Très Jolie*. Luciano recalled:

> 'Our first collection featured very simple designs: high-neck, turtle-neck, V-neck, all in combed wool, English-style . . . but . . . we used pale blue, green or yellow wool, colours that nobody wore. We were the first to use them, and we realised that people were starved of colour, as if it had been rationed during the war.'

Six months later, Giuliana left her day-time job to concentrate on their family business. The following year she bought a second knitting machine and hired two girls aged eleven and twelve. In 1957 Luciano left Dellasiega's to devote himself full-time to *Très Jolie*. Gilberto joined in 1963 to look after the firm's finances. Luciano, aware that Italy lagged behind its competitors in terms of quality, visited knitwear plants in England and Scotland, and adapted some of their processes to improve his own products. The real breakthrough came when Luciano and Ado Montana, an impoverished dye specialist from Trieste, discovered a way to dye fully-assembled sweaters. Hitherto, knitwear had been produced using pre-dyed yarn as it was generally believed that the high temperatures necessary to dye wool would cause holes or severe shrinkage in the assembled garment. The new process enabled the Benettons to respond quickly to changes in fashion and customer demand.

THE YEARS OF GROWTH

Throughout the 1960s Italy experienced an unprecedented economic book, and the Benettons found themselves unable to keep up with demand. They obtained a bank loan to build a factory in Ponzano Veneto. The avant-garde plant, with luxuries such as landscaped grounds and air conditioning, resembled a spaceship set down in the fields near Ponzano, and was designed by Tobia and Afra Scarpa, a husband-and-wife team of inexperienced architecture students. As the firm continued to grow, the plant soon proved to be too small, even before it was finished.

In 1964 Luciano was approached by Piero Marchiorello, a penniless but enthusiastic 25-year-old from the small town of Belluno. Marchiorello wanted to open a shop that would sell only *Très Jolie* jumpers. At the time, the concept of a one-brand, one-product shop was unheard of in Italy. The small shop, called *My Market*, was inauspiciously located in a cul-de-sac in Belluno, which Luciano described as 'the worst site I had ever seen'. Marchiorella was more up-beat: 'Look on the bright side – if it works here, it can work anywhere!' The name *My Market* was chosen to evoke the swinging English fashion scene of the time, with open-air 'Carnaby Street'-type associations. The shop was an immediate success. As Marchiorella explained to Luciano: 'when clients enter, they stand frozen, as if they were drinking in the colours.'

The second *My Market* store opened in 1965 in Cortina d'Ampezzo, a trendy skiing resort and had no counter – a decision seen by Afra Scarpa as symbolising the removal of social barriers. 'Instead, there was a small table for the cash register, . . . all the [decorative] colour came from the clothes.' Realising that the name *Benetton* sounded 'English to the English, French to the French, and so on for Italians, Germans, Americans,' and was easy to pronounce in all languages, it was decided to label the knitwear with a logo featuring *Benetton* in white characters on a dark green background, and a stylised knot of yarn. As sales continued to grow, Luciano decided to expand into each new city by opening two or three shops rather than just one:

> 'It made more sense to compete with ourselves than with others. So we asked Scarpa to design several store interiors to appeal to different clients and varying local tastes. The *Mercerìa* design was classic in feel, oriented to the mothers of our *My Market* customers. *Tomato* was all glossy, chrome and ultra-modern. *Fantomax* had the feel of Art Nouveau and Swinging London.'[3]

Within four years, Benetton had 500 stores across Italy. In 1969 Benetton opened its first store abroad, in Paris's Latin Quarter. Profits grew from L800m in 1970 to L8 billion in 1979. But in Italy the *anni di piombo*, 'the lead years' of the 1970s, were marked by the onset of terrorism and frayed relations with trade unions. Luciano was himself the target of a kidnapping attempt, the violence of which haunted him for years. The Benettons decided to keep a low profile, as explained by Luciano:

> 'In Italy, even if in 1975 a thousand retailers sold our product exclusively, they did not know much about us. We remained invisible,

refused to grant interviews, kept financial information strictly to ourselves and never published an annual report. Because of our use of sub-contractors and the fact that many stores were called *Sisley*, *Tomato* or *Merceria* rather than Benetton, our real scale and scope remained unknown to the public.'

The 1980s saw a dramatic improvement in Italy's economic and political situation. In 1983 Benetton recruited Aldo Palmeri, a 36-year-old banker with a master's degree from the London School of Economics, to introduce modern management structures and methods to the family firm. Before this, Luciano had considered management education to be 'a luxury reserved for bureaucrats with nothing better to do'. Palmeri put in place a Board of Directors, an Executive Committee and a supporting management structure. He implemented a worldwide state-of-the-art information technology system. Senior managers with international experience were recruited and external consultants were brought in as needed. Benetton entered new markets such as the Soviet Union and eastern Europe, and acquired holdings in various other businesses. The creation of In Holding S.p.A. marked Benetton's foray into the financial services sector, enabling them to offer a comprehensive service to their partners.[4] In 1986 Benetton, which had recently published its first annual report, secured a listing on the Milan stock exchange. The stock was later listed on five exchanges world-wide: London, Frankfurt, New York, Toronto and Tokyo. The *New Yorker* remarked: 'It is worth remembering that Benetton, all but unknown in most places less than a decade ago, now owns one of the world's most recognised brand names, as familiar as Coca-Cola and Reebok.'[5]

THE BENETTON GROUP

In 1994, the textiles and clothing industry turned over US$250 billion in the European Union; it employed over 2.5 million people, produced a trading surplus of over US$2 billion, and was second only to the automotive sector in terms of value added in manufacturing.[6] Germany, France and Italy were the leading producers. Despite a recent surge in mergers and acquisitions the industry remained fragmented with over 100,000 producers

– the top 20% of whom accounted for about 80% of industry sales. Most clothes were bought in boutiques or department stores, although some variations existed across countries (see Exhibit 2).

Benetton Group S.p.A. was the world's biggest consumer of wool and Europe's largest clothing concern, with 1994 sales of L2,788 billion and net income of L210 billion. Its largest markets were Italy (34% of sales), Germany (12%), Japan (11%) and France (8%). 64 million items were sold worldwide in 1994, up 12.7% on 1993. Outside the EU, the increase was 36%. Aided by several devaluations of the lira, Benetton had cut prices by up to 40 per cent over the previous two years. Luciano was now the Group's chairman and main spokesman, Giuliana was in charge of design, and Gilberto and Carlo looked after finance and production, respectively.[7]

In 1995, the newspaper *Milano Finanza* listed the Benettons as the richest family in Italy. While clothes manufacturing remained the core of the family activities, they also, in 1989, began to acquire controlling stakes in a number of other companies. These businesses were regrouped as the family-owned Edizione Holding, chaired by Gilberto and with an aggregate turnover of nearly L10,000 billion in 1994 (see Exhibit 3)[8]. In addition to its range of clothing and accessories, Benetton licensed the manufacture of products such as sunglasses and spectacle frames, stationery, cosmetics, household linens, lingerie, watches, toys, steering wheels or knobs for gearshifts, golf equipment and luggage. These products, some of which are shown in Exhibit 4, provided net income of L9 billion in 1993. In 1995, Benetton was asked by Motorola to design and market a range of pagers. These colourful units, first launched in the UK, were intended to develop the youth market for pagers and were priced at £99, in competition with the Swatch pager, priced at £119. A joint-venture in Japan for the sale of designer condoms ('Benetton's smallest item of clothing') was expected to contribute $40m to turnover.

In 1995 Benetton had three main brands:

↔ United Colors of Benetton (clothing for men and women) which also included Blue Family (with an emphasis on denim) and Benetton Undercolors (underwear and beachwear): 60.8% of sales

↔ 012 United Colors of Benetton (clothing for children under 12) including Zerotondo (clothing and accessories for babies): 18.5% of sales

↔ Sisley (higher-fashion clothing): 11.8% of sales

Over two-thirds of their clothing was for women, who represented 80% of Benetton's shoppers. Fabrizio Servente, head of product development, commented:

'The "objective" target for the adult Benetton stores is the 18–24 year old, but of course there is no age ceiling. Our product takes into account quality and price. It's clean, international, with a lot of attention to design. It can be worn just as easily by Princess Diana and by her maid, or her maid's daughter . . . The way young people dress is becoming more and more "uniform", but there are differences from one region to another. Benetton must still be Italian in Italy, Brazilian in Brazil, Indian in India.'

Industry observers felt that Benetton had no clearly identifiable world-wide competitor. While Esprit, The Gap, Next, Stefanel, or Zara were often cited, it was generally agreed that they did not have the same geographical spread as Benetton. Servente's view was that Benetton had many competitors, and none:

'*The* Benetton competitor doesn't exist. On the other hand, we have plenty of local competitors. In Italy, it might be Stefanel. In France, Kookaï – although they target a different age group. In Britain, Next. In the US, Esprit. No [global] competitor can offer the same quality and cost as we can. A shop owner in Treviso may order jumpers in Hong Kong, and clearly he will be cheaper than us since he has lower fixed costs. If that is a competitor, then we have 10,000 of them. There are many that we keep an eye on, but not any one in particular.'

THE BENETTON SYSTEM

Benetton today operates through a complex system of over 500 sub-contractors and several joint ventures specialising in design, cutting, assembling, ironing or packaging, plus thousands of independent retail outlets. Benetton's success has been largely attributed to this ability to combine fashion with industry.

PRODUCTION

While the pressure to reduce costs had led a number of clothing firms to move their production to the developing world, Benetton, which operates factories world-wide, has kept over 80% of its production in Italy, a strategy made possible by its emphasis on automation and continuous modernisation.

The Castrette (Treviso) production centre currently covers an area of 190,000 square metres, including new twin facilities which are among the most advanced in the world producing cotton outerwear: shirts, jackets, skirts and jeans. They are Benetton's latest technological accomplishment. Afra and Tobia Scarpa employed a suspension technique hitherto used in naval architecture, to reduce the number of supporting pillars, allowing space to be organised according to production needs. A computerised system regulates humidity and lighting to limit energy waste and minimise colour distortions. The plants can produce 80 million items per year, with 800 staff. A fibre-optic communications network links the plants to Benetton's automated distribution centre nearby.

A computerised network provides the Group's central system in Ponzano with real-time data from retail points all over the world and interlinked retailing, production units and warehousing. The L42 billion distribution centre in Castrette is the length of a football pitch, with robots handling up to 30,000 boxes a day. On each box, a bar-coded label specifies the particular shop to which it is to be sent. The robots read the bar codes, sort the boxes and store them while a staff of five specialists monitor their movements on a computer. Benetton can produce and deliver garments anywhere in the world within 10 days of orders being taken.

All purchasing activities are centralised, since this is the main source of economies of scale in the clothing industry. From the beginning Benetton has used natural fibres – virgin wool and cotton. 'The Group can contemplate its own production of cotton and wool, with a complete cycle from sheep to sweater', said Carlo Benetton, the Group's production chief. Benetton owns a 3,600-hectare (8,900 acres) cotton farm in Texas and is the largest producer of wool in Patagonia, with ranches spread over 700,000 hectares. Although Benetton uses only 10% of the wool it produces, running these ranches enables it to understand and improve the technology of wool production, and to strengthen its negotiating power with suppliers.

Hundreds of sub-contractors perform knitting, assembly and most of the finishing (about 70% of the production process). They account for close to 30% of total manufacturing and distribution costs and often have less than 15 employees in order to save on social security costs. Most of them work exclusively for Benetton, which provides technical know-how, financial consulting and other services, and exerts strict quality control throughout production. A senior executive commented:

> '[They] provide our much-vaunted flexibility. With minimum investment, we can double production one season, then halve it the next season with no personnel or machinery costs to us.'

Strategic, capital-intensive and complex operations such as design, cutting and dyeing are performed internally. Every year, an international team of 200 stylists and designers prepare two world-wide collections and two re-assortment collections under Giuliana's supervision – a total of 4000 models. The designers are given contracts for a maximum of six seasons (three years) in order to encourage a constant flow of new ideas. Most of the production is assembled un-dyed, and colour decisions can then be made late in the production cycle. This process is slightly more expensive but it allows the company to produce 30% of its output at almost the last moment. Benetton uses the latest CAD-CAM (computer aided design and manufacturing) systems, allowing a new design to be created and moved into production in a matter of hours. A new software programme, developed by Benetton in collaboration with Japanese specialists, makes it possible to produce a seamless knitted sweater ('a concept which could revolutionise the industry') in half an hour.

RETAILING

Benetton's unique distribution philosophy was another important reason for its success. 'We didn't want to become directly involved in the selling side,' Luciano Benetton has said[9], 'so in the beginning it was friends with financial resources who moved into this part of the business'. By 1995, from over 8,000 retail outlets (see Exhibit 5), Benetton owned and operated fewer than 50 'flagship stores' in cities such as Milan, New York, Paris and Düsseldorf. The rest were owned by independent retailers who typically ran five or six outlets.

The company deals with these retailers through a network of 83 agents, controlled by seven area managers reporting to Benetton's commercial director. The agents, who are independent entrepreneurs, have exclusive rights over a territory; they select store owners, and receive a 4% commission on orders placed with them. They supervise operations in their territory, keep an eye on the market and offer guidance to store owners on product selection, merchandising and the location of new stores, making sure that Benetton's policies are respected. Another important responsibility of the agents is to find new retailers who 'fit' the Benetton culture. They are themselves encouraged to re-invest their earnings in new stores of their own.

Upon entering a new market, the site for a 'lead' store is selected, after which the agent tries to blanket the area with several other shops offering Benetton products (Milan alone has over 45 stores). Luciano Benetton commented:

> 'I discovered that, even if the brand was unknown, seeing three or four of our shops in one town would give a feeling of security equivalent to a good advertising campaign . . . We prefer small spaces . . . a very limited selection, in a store that's always crowded, if possible. We want a lot of people looking at the same thing, watching others buying clothes.'[10]

Some retailers have complained that Benetton was 'sticking too many stores together' or that 'the Benetton agent put us in the wrong location.' Shop owners have to sell Benetton products exclusively but they do not sign franchise agreements; neither do they have to pay Benetton a fee for use of its name or a royalty based on a percentage of sales or profits. Luciano Benetton explained:

> 'We selected them on the basis of personal knowledge and individual capability, rather than commercial experience . . . [Their] prior career was of no importance, but [they] had to have the right spirit . . . Many of them were friends, or friends of friends, we didn't ask them to give us a percentage of profits . . . Frankly, I was uncomfortable with the idea of American-style contracts.'[11]

In 1995, the retailers could choose from several store layouts designed by Scarpa, some of which are shown in Exhibit 6.[12] Benetton supplied point-of-sale advertising material; shops could advertise in the local press once the company had checked the advertisement. Prices were suggested by Benetton, mark-downs outside the sales periods had to be agreed with the agent. Stock control and cash flow management were major concerns for the retailers since Benetton produced to order six months ahead, did not take back unsold merchandise and required direct payment within 90 to 120 days of delivery. The importance of the end-of-season 'sales' periods, which accounted for up to 40% of total revenue, was growing. During these periods, the usual 120% mark-up could fall to zero, or even to a 10% loss.

Senior executives travelled constantly, visiting shops, talking to consumers and observing competitors. Luciano Benetton himself spent two weeks every month flying around the world in his private jet. An executive explained how new products and store concepts were tested:

> 'We don't do a lot of market studies. We find an entrepreneur who believes in the product and the brand, and who invests his own money. We give him all the support we can, and he opens a shop. If it works, we go for it.'

In recent years, Benetton had encouraged retailers to either upgrade existing stores to larger 'megastores' where the whole range was displayed, or start selling smaller, specialised collections.[13] Palmeri felt that this change posed a new challenge:

> 'Most people running today's stores are not ready to face a new strategy . . . They became very rich with the Benetton system. Others don't have the money to invest . . . Anybody can run a store of 50 square metres. It's a completely different thing to run a system of 10 superstores each with 1,000 square metres.'[14]

While international expansion had generally been successful, the USA proved to be a difficult market. Benetton opened its first store in New York in 1979 but had to wait till 1983 to see sales take off. Growth peaked in 1988 with a total of 700 stores, but by 1995 Benetton had only 150 stores[15] in the US.[16] However, the selling square footage had doubled over the preceding five years, due to the opening of megastores. Two strong markets were California

and the North East where, according to Luciano Benetton, 'consumers were more European'.

Industry observers attributed Benetton's US difficulties to a number of factors including high prices, increased competition from firms such as The Gap, The Limited and Land's End and a weak understanding of American customer service norms. For example, American consumers were frustrated that they could not return a Benetton product bought at one store to another, even in the same city. Further, Benetton's unique 'no written contract/no franchise' culture proved difficult to import and had led to several legal disputes. Other critics cited Benetton's policy of two collections a year versus that of The Gap which changed styles every four to six weeks. This was seen as hurting Benetton, especially among teenagers. An industry analyst commented, 'The trend is clearly going towards a much more continuous change of product and Benetton just has to learn that.' However, Luciano dismissed these concerns, insisting 'two collections a year is perfect.'[17]

Benetton's approach to international expansion is twofold: through its own independent agents or through local partners with whom it sets up a licence agreement and develops a joint venture for the local market. The Group hoped to be present in 'as many countries as competed in the Olympics'. In 1995, it had stores in unusual outposts such as Albania, Cuba and Libya, where it was 'the only store of its kind', according to Luciano. The Group was also targeting several other promising markets: China, where it planned to open 300 outlets by 1997 and where it saw a potential market of 120 million customers, India, with 80 million potential consumers, Latin America, with 70 million, Turkey with 60 million and Southeast Asia with 50 million. On 12 September 1995, a Benetton store was opened in Sarajevo, the besieged capital of war-torn Bosnia. Its manager, Vesna Kapidzic, commented, 'Anyone can open a store after the war. We think it is nice to open this store during the war.'[18]

BENETTON'S COMMUNICATION

Benetton's early advertisements were rather conventional, focusing on the product and stressing the quality of wool.

knitwear. The print and billboard campaign was distributed by J. Walter Thompson (JWT) in 14 countries.

The logo, a stylised knot of yarn and the word 'Benetton', were later united within a green rectangle with rounded corners. During the 1970s, the company reduced its advertising consistent with its decision to adopt a low profile in Italy. The first US advertising campaigns, handled by a small agency (Kathy Travis) stressed the European origins and international success of Benetton. 'Last year we made 8,041,753 sweaters ... sold through 1573 Benetton stores internationally.' These campaigns contributed less to Benetton's breakthrough in the US than the runaway success among students of a simple model (the rugby polo) and the awakening of Americans to fashion 'Made in Italy'.[19]

In 1982 Luciano Benetton met Oliviero Toscani, a well-known fashion and advertising photographer who lived in Tuscany and had studios in Paris and New York. His clients included, among others, Jesus Jeans, Valentino, Esprit, Club Med and Bata (see Exhibit 7). Toscani convinced Luciano that Benetton ought to promote itself as a lifestyle, not a clothing business. At Toscani's suggestion, Benetton retained Eldorado, a small Paris agency with which Toscani had often worked as a photographer.

ALL THE COLOURS IN THE WORLD

The first campaigns were conventional in style, stressing social status and conformism, and featuring groups of young people wearing Benetton clothing. The real departure came in 1984 with a new concept, 'All the Colours in the World'. This campaign showed groups of teenagers from different countries and ethnic groups dressed in colourful

The campaign was greeted with enthusiasm and Benetton received hundreds of letters of praise. But it prompted shocked reactions in South Africa, where the ads were carried only by magazines catering to the black community. A few letters, from England and the US reflected hysterical racism. 'Shame on you!' wrote one correspondent from Manchester in the north of England, 'You have mixed races that God wants to keep apart!'

UNITED COLORS OF BENETTON

In 1985, a UNESCO official visited the studio where Toscani was photographing a multi-racial group of children and exclaimed: 'This is fantastic, it's the United Colors here!' This became the new slogan: 'United Colors of Benetton'. The posters reconciled instantly recognisable 'enemies': a German and an Israeli, a Greek and a Turk, and an Argentinean and a Briton. Another poster showed two small black children bearing the US and Soviet flags.

The multi-racial message was made clearer still with the theme chosen for the 1986 and 1987 campaigns: 'the globe'. One ad showed a white adolescent dressed as an Hassidic Jew holding a moneybox full of dollar bills, next to a black teenager dressed as an American Indian. 'In the eyes of Eldorado's directors, all of them Jewish, the picture was humorous enough to make it clear that we were taking aim at the stereotype [of the money-grabbing Jew],' wrote Luciano Benetton.[20]

Benetton was flooded with protests, mostly from France and Italy. In New York, Jewish groups threatened to boycott Benetton shops. Benetton replaced the ad with a picture of a Palestinian and a Jew, which was also criticised.

Luciano commented:

'I was a bit discouraged, but I had learned a fundamental lesson. We had chosen to promote an image that touched very deep feelings, identities for which millions of people had fought and died. We had reached the limits and felt the responsibilities of commercial art. Everybody was now watching us, and even a small dose of ingenuity could hurt us and irritate others. I promised myself I would control our image even more rigorously.'[21]

The 1987 autumn/winter campaign, 'United Fashions of Benetton', showed models wearing Benetton clothes with accessories that evoked the great names in fashion. 'United Superstars of Benetton' was the slogan for the 1988 campaign, featuring pairs dressed up as Joan of Arc and Marilyn Mon-

roe, Leonardo da Vinci and Julius Caesar, or Adam and Eve – two-long haired teenagers dressed in denim.

A MESSAGE OF RACIAL EQUALITY

1989 marked a turning point in Benetton's communication activities. The company terminated its relationship with Eldorado.[22] 'From the beginning, Luciano Benetton wanted image to be an in-house product, so that it would reflect the company's soul,' Toscani explained later. United Colors Communication would soon handle all aspects of Benetton's communication including production and media buying. The entire process was managed by less than ten people; Toscani's visuals would be discussed by the advertising team, then shown to Luciano for final approval. This allowed Benetton to produce advertisements which cost about one-third of those of its competitors.[23] Benetton did not usually advertise on television because of the high costs but used print and outdoor media exentsively. It limited itself to two series of campaigns (Spring and Fall). Each campaign would typically last a couple of weeks, and consist of a small number of visuals shown in an increasing number of countries. By 1995, Benetton spent about 4% of turnover on communication, which included campaigns for United Colors of Benetton and Sisley, sports sponsorship, a quarterly magazine, *Colors*[24] and funding for its communications school, *Fabrica*.

This shift to in-house communications was accompanied by a radical change in approach. The 1989 ads no longer showed the product, didn't use a slogan and replaced the knot logo with a small green rectangle that was to become the company's trademark. Hard-hitting images began to deliver an unambiguously political message championing racial equality. One ad showing a black woman nursing a white baby generated controversy in South Africa and in the US, where it was seen as a throwback to the era of slavery. Benetton withdrew the ad in the US, explaining that 'the campaign is intended to promote equality, not friction.'

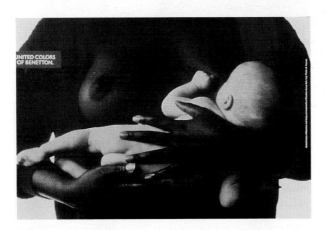

This became Benetton's most praised visual ever, winning awards in five European countries. Another ad, showing a black man and a white man handcuffed together, offended British blacks, who thought it showed a white policeman arresting a black. London Transport refused to show the poster in its network.

The 1990 campaign continued the theme, with softer images: the hand of a black child resting in a white man's hand; a white wolf and a black lamb; a small black child asleep amid white stuffed bears; the hand of a white relay runner passing a baton to a black team-mate.

Benetton's attempt to show two babies on their potties on a 770 square meter billboard opposite Milan's cathedral was banned by the city authorities and the Roman Catholic cardinal. That year, Benetton won its first advertising award in the USA.

SOCIAL ISSUES

By 1991 Benetton's campaigns, which now tackled issues beyond racism, were reaching audiences in more than 100 countries. A picture showing a military cemetery, released at the start of the Gulf war, was turned down by all but one newspaper, *Il Sole 24 Ore* in Italy.

An ad displaying brightly coloured condoms ('a call for social responsibility in the face of overpopulation and sexually transmitted disease') was intended to 'demystify condoms by displaying them in a playful and colourful way, like fashion items'.

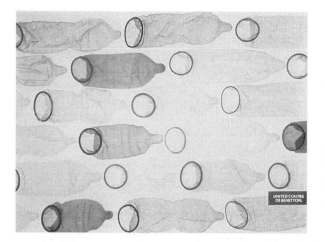

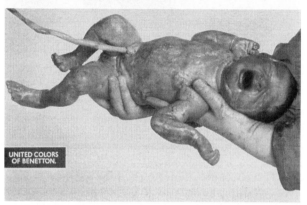

Simultaneously, condoms were distributed in Benetton's shops world-wide. Benetton also distributed HIV guides in the shanty towns of Rio 'because it was important that even people who could never buy a Benetton sweater should get the basic communication.'

Other ads included a white boy kissing a black girl, a group of Pinocchio puppets in different hues of wood, and a multi-ethnic trio of children playfully sticking out their tongues.

While this last ad won awards in Britain and Germany, it was withdrawn from display in Arabic countries, where it was considered offensive.

Later that year, Toscani chose to focus on: 'love, the underlying reason for all life'. The campaign featured, among others, a priest and a nun kissing; and Giusy, a screaming new-born baby with her umbilical cord still attached.

In the US, the Anti-Defamation League condemned the priest-and-nun ad for 'trivialising, mocking, profaning and offending religious values', and several magazines rejected it.

In France, the Bureau de Vérification de la Publicité (BVP), a self-regulating advertising body, recommended the removal of the priest-and-nun ad in the name of 'decency and self-discipline', whilst in England, it won the Eurobest Award. Others were also positive: Sister Barbara Becker Schroeder from Alzey, Germany wrote to Benetton: 'I feel the photo expresses great tenderness, security and peace . . . I would be grateful if you would let me have one or more posters, preferably in different sizes.'[25] In November 1991, Benetton won a court case initiated by AGRIF (L'Alliance générale contre le racisme et pour le respect de la famille française) where it was accepted that the nun and priest poster was not racist or anti-Christian.

In Britain, Benetton ignored a warning issued by the Advertising Standards Authority (ASA) concerning the Guisy ad and within days, the authority received some 800 complaints. The offending posters were withdrawn – and replaced with an ad showing an angelic blond-haired child next to a black child whose hair was styled to evoke horns, which the ASA also criticised.

In the USA, Giusy elicited some negative reactions but was accepted by *Parenting*, *Self* and

immigration, terrorism, violence, and political refugees. The use of real-life pictures showing, for example, a bombed car, Albanian refugees, a Mafia-style killing and a soldier holding a human bone provoked controversy around the world, despite Benetton's repeated claim that it was trying to prompt debate of serious social issues.

Vogue. It was rejected by *Child*, *Cosmopolitan*, and *Elle*. The posters were not displayed in Milan where the city officials complained of 'the excessive impact and vulgarity of the subject.' The local High Court ruled that 'the picture offended public order and general morality.' Giusy was also banned in France, Germany and Ireland, where the advertising space was donated to the Association for the Fight Against Cancer. These reactions surprised Benetton, as well as a number of others:

> 'We should ask ourselves the question of why such a natural, vital and basic image as that of a baby being born, offends the public. Every day we are confronted with pictures of death, often meaningless, and we put up with them in silence, or very nearly. Yet we are afraid to see an image of life.' (*L'Unita*, 10/9/91)

> 'Why must beer be drunk topless on the deck of a sailing boat and the smiling, happy mum always be half-naked as she swaddles the baby in a nappy like a scented pastry? Isn't all this rather ridiculous?' (*Il Giornale Nuovo*, 26/10/91)

According to Benetton, 'Once the period of rejection was over, the picture began to be understood and appreciated.' Giusy won an award from the Société Générale d'Affichage in Switzerland and Bologna's General Clinic asked for a copy to decorate its labour room.

THE REALITY CAMPAIGNS

In 1992, Benetton broke new ground with two series of news photographs on issues such as AIDS,

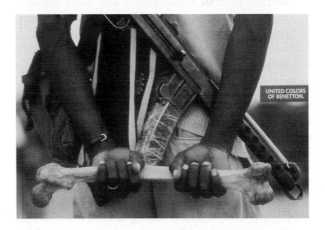

This claim was supported by Patrick Robert, a photographer with the Sygma agency, some of whose pictures had been used in the campaigns: '. . . the absence of an explanatory caption on my photographs [soldier with human bone, truck bulging with refugees] does not bother me . . . for me the objective of the campaign is reached . . . to draw the public's attention to these victims.'[26]

A picture showing David Kirby[27], an AIDS patient surrounded by his family on his deathbed, stirred particularly strong emotions.

In Britain, the ASA described the ad as 'obscene' and 'a despicable exploitation of a tragic situation' and asked magazines to reject it. Benetton donated the use of 500 paid UK poster sites to the charity *Trading*. Maggie Alderson, the editor of

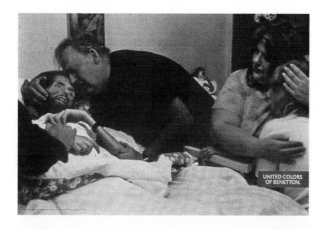

the UK edition of *Elle*, which ran a statement on two blank pages instead of the ad, commented:

> 'It is an incredibly moving image in the right context, but to use it as an advertisement for a fashion store selling jumpers is incredibly insulting. They have stepped out of the bounds of what is acceptable and what makes this so sickening is that they have touched up the photograph to make it look biblical because the AIDS victim resembles Jesus Christ.' (*The Guardian*, 24/1/92).

In France, the BVP took an unprecedented step: without even waiting for the ad to be printed, it threatened to exclude any publication that dared carry it. Only one publication ignored the ban: *Max*, a magazine for young people. Its editor, Nicolas Finet, commented, 'Our readers, those between 15 and 30 years old, are directly affected by this topic. This campaign is one way of approaching the AIDS problem whilst avoiding the socio-medical aspect. Our readers' letters have shown that we were not wrong' (quoted in the French advertising weekly *Stratégies*, 18/2/92). In Switzerland, *Schweizer Illustrierte* decided to accept the ad saying that it did not hurt mass sensitivity but 'wounded only one thing: the rules of the games according to which the message must be dull, stale even.'

Many organisations and advocacy groups for homosexuals charged Benetton with callous exploitation, saying it offered no information about prevention. However, some AIDS activists felt it gave the issue a higher public profile, an opinion which others shared:

> 'For the large majority of the population which thinks that AIDS is not their business,

Benetton's ads will be a slap in their face . . . and I am sure it will be more effective than every campaign to date by any public or private body.' (*L'Unita*, 25/1/92).

> 'The company estimates that between 500 million and one billion people have seen the AIDS image, far more than ever saw it when it came out in Life. A public that is reading fewer newspapers and believing fewer broadcasts might begin to swallow tiny doses of information between the ads for liqueur and lingerie.' (Vicky Goldbert in *The New York Times*, 3/5/92).

> 'The picture . . . has done more to soften people's heart on the AIDS issue than any other I have every seen. You can't look at that picture and hate a person with AIDS . . . As far as the comment that it was "touched up to look like Jesus Christ" . . . I know that at Pater Noster [hospital], several times, with several patients through the years, nurses have made the same comment, "he looks like Jesus"' (Barb Cordle, David Kirby's nurse in *Interview*, 4/92)..

The Economist (1/2/92) felt that the ads targeted the young and,

> 'what better means to appeal to them than by offending their elders . . . expect no repentance, or tamer ads, from Benetton unless its sales start to drop.'

Asked about the campaign's impact on sales, Peter Fressola, Director of Communications, Benetton Services New York, emphasised that individual ads were not geared to boost sales and that Benetton was aware that

> 'people are not going to look at an image of a burning car, and then make a best-seller out of our fuschia sweater.' (*The Wall Street Journal*, 28/5/92).

Reacting to the charges of exploitation, Benetton argued that the David Kirby visual increased awareness of the need for collective and personal solidarity with AIDS patients, created a media tribune for HIV organisations and others involved in the issue, and encouraged a debate on how best to communicate on AIDS.[28] They also stressed that David's family was in favor of the photo being used. In support of the ad, the Kirby family went on the record:

'It is what he would have wanted . . . We don't feel used. Rather it is we who are using Benetton. David is speaking louder now that he is dead than when he was alive.' (*Il Mattino*, 22/3/92).

The second 1992 campaign once more used hard-hitting news pictures: an oil-covered bird from the Gulf; an albino Zulu woman ostracised by other Zulus; a grime-smeared Salvadoran child carrying a white doll; pigs in a trash heap in Peru; children building a brick wall; KGB agents arresting a suspect; an empty electric chair in a US jail.

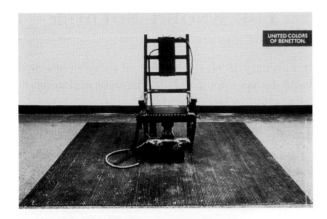

The *Financial Times* commented:

'Like its previous campaign, Benetton has again focused on the downbeat and the unhappy, this time selecting a set of apparent outcasts to sell its colourful jumpers.' (17/9/92)

THE CLOTHING REDISTRIBUTION PROJECT

The spring 1993 campaign showed Luciano Benetton, newly elected to the Italian Senate and named as Italy's leading entrepreneur, stark naked, modestly screened by a caption reading 'I want my clothes back'. A second ad followed: 'Empty your closets.'

People were invited to donate clothes of any brand at Benetton stores. The campaign, which ran in about 1000 magazines and 150 dailes, was widely welcomed: 'It is a clear break from Benetton's self-serious attitude of the past. It also marks the first time the company has engaged in direct action to support a cause.' (*The Wall Street Journal*, 27/1/93).[29]

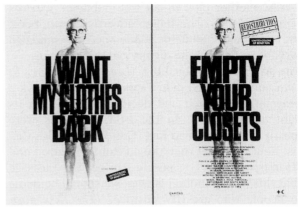

Some 460 tons of clothes were collected in 83 countries and re-distributed world-wide with the help of charities such as Caritas, the International Red Cross and the Red Crescent.

THE VENICE TRIPTYCH

In June 1993, Toscani exhibited a 400 square meter triptych at the Venice Biennial art show. A specially restored chapel housed the work, which showed 56 close-up photos of male and female genitals – blacks and whites, adults and children. Benetton added its logo and published the picture as an ad in *Libération*.

That day the newspaper sold an extra 40,000 copies. The BVP threatened to sue. Two days later, French men's underwear-maker Eminence published a double page in *Libération* showing as many (male) crotches with the same layout and the slogan: 'We like dressing them.'

THE HIV-POSITIVE CAMPAIGN

A near-unanimous outcry greeted the Fall 1993 campaign, which consisted of three stark photographs showing an arm, buttock and crotch, each branded with the words 'HIV Positive'.

Benetton explained that the pictures referred to the three main avenues for infection, as well as to the ostracism of AIDS victims. In Singapore, Danny Chow (President, ASA) dismissed the ads as 'easily another ploy to get free publicity' (*Straits Times*, 27/9/93). The Italian advertising watchdog, the Giurì della Pubblicità, condemned the campaign for 'not respecting the dignity of human beings.' The AIDS association LILA (*Lega Italiana per la Lota contro l'AIDS*) didn't approve of it but took a pragmatic approach and decided to use it in its fight against AIDS. In the USA, reactions were mostly negative. David Eng (Gay Men's Health Crisis, New York) felt that 'the ad can fuel hatred and disempowerment . . . people can get the message that this [i.e. branding] is what we should be doing to people who are HIV positive.' (*The New York Times*, 19/9/93). The *National Review* refused the ad without seeing it. The British ACET (AIDS Care Education and Training) demanded the ad's withdrawal.

The *Association Française de la Lutte contre le Sida* (AFLS), a French government-sponsored AIDS group, sued Benetton, for 'hijacking a humanitarian cause for commercial ends.' Four HIV sufferers joined in the lawsuit, with charges of 'humiliation' and 'debasement'. According to their lawyers, the brandings were an implicit call to discriminate against patients, and evoked the Nazi death camps.[30] A representative of AIDES, another French association, felt the ad could be misinterpreted: 'It is clearly stated that sodomy or intravenous drug abuse are the [major] causes of AIDS. . . . Such short cuts are misleading and stupid.' (*CB News*, 20/9/93).

The brother of one sufferer bought a full page ad in *Libération*, and published a picture of his brother's emaciated face with the caption: 'During the agony, the selling continues. For the attention of Luciano Benetton, from Olivier Besnard-Rousseau, AIDS sufferer, terminal phase.' There were increasingly strident calls to boycott the firm, including one from a former cabinet minister. Arcat Sida, a French AIDS support group headed by Pierre Bergé, CEO of Yves Saint Laurent, sponsored a poster showing a condom stuffed with bank notes next to a 'United Boycott' logo in Benetton's signature typeface and green colour. Stores were vandalised and sprayed with graffiti leading some store owners to complain that 'Mr Benetton listens to nobody.' (*Le Nouvel Observateur*, 20/12/93).

Luciano Benetton was himself surprised and hurt by the violence of these reactions. In the Group's defence, its long-standing commitment to the fight against AIDS and the extent of its actions were cited. On December 1, 1993 (World AIDS Day), Benetton in cooperation with the association Actup had a 22 metre pink condom placed over the obelisk in the Place de la Concorde in Paris. Other Benetton actions against AIDS are presented in Exhibit 8. In early 1994 Luciano received an award given by the President of South Korea in recognition of the consciousness-raising role played by the company.

THE KNOWN SOLDIER

In February 1994, a Benetton ad showing bloodied battle fatigues appeared on billboards and in newspapers across 110 countries.

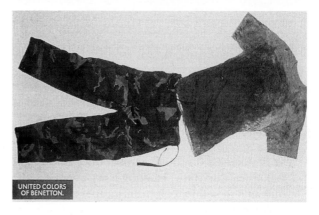

UNITED COLORS OF BENETTON.

The clothes had belonged to a Croatian soldier killed in Bosnia, as a caption in Serbo-Croat indicated:

> 'I, Gojko Gagro, father of the deceased Marinko Gagro, born in 1963 in the province of Citluk, would like that my son's name and all that remains of him be used in the name of peace against war.'

The advertisement was greeted by an immediate uproar. While it became an instant success in Sarajevo, where the *Oslobodenje* newspaper printed it, leading dailies such as the *Los Angeles Times*, *Le Monde*, and the *Frankfurter Allgemeine Zeitung* refused to carry it, and the Vatican denounced Benetton for 'image terrorism'. Reactions among the combatants and people in the war zones depended on whether Gagro was seen as a victim or an aggressor and whose cause the ad was perceived as helping. Indignation reached a climax in France, where the minister for human rights and humanitarian action urged consumers to stop buying Benetton clothes and to 'rip them off the backs of those who wear them.' Once again, several Benetton stores were vandalised, causing a growing sense of unease among some retailers.

The French advertising weekly *Stratégies* announced it would not write about Benetton's advertising as long as it remained in the same vein: 'Besides the disgust it causes, this [latest] ad raises the issue of the responsibility of advertisers. Can one do anything, use anything, to attract attention?' (25/2/94). Marina Galanti, Benetton's spokeswoman reacted to the outcry: '. . . If we were trying to sell T-shirts, there probably would not be a worse way of doing it. We are not that naïve. It's meant to question the notion of institutionalised violence and the role of advertising.' (*The Guardian*, 16/2/94). The autumn 1994 world-wide campaign featured in print media and billboards showed a mosaic of 1000 faces arranged to softly highlight the word AIDS at its centre. This campaign attracted little attention.

THE ALIENATION CAMPAIGN

The spring 1995 campaign featured two visuals based on the theme of 'alienation'. One showed lines of barbed wire, coming from a variety of troubled countries such as Bosnia, Lebanon and Israel as well as from private gardens.

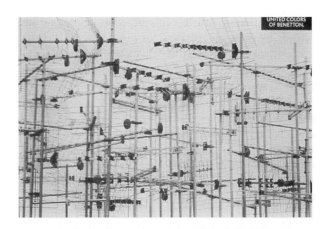

The other showed a jungle of TV antennae symbolising the 'invisible barriers erected by the overcrowding of video images, which not only affect interpersonal relationships, but also people's perception of reality.' Billed as 'an invitation to an open discussion on real and virtual prisons, on the mental and televisual dictatorships which restrict freedom', the campaign did not elicit strong reactions. Benetton denied that the ads reflected a softer, toned-down communications strategy.

Around the same time, Benetton's US retailers launched a campaign developed by Chiat/Day of New York, designed to appeal to more conservative audiences. The new US campaign focused on clothing and included TV spots as well as eight-page magazine inserts. Luciano explained that this initiative was not an alternative to their international campaign, but an additional support to its US store owners.

THE GERMAN LAWSUITS

The furore over the recent Benetton campaigns reached a peak in Germany. Here 12 retailers being sued by Benetton for non-payment[31] defended their case by accusing Benetton of provoking adverse reaction in consumers through their ads, with a consequent drop in sales. Benetton stated that '. . . total sales in Germany have remained stable in 1994 . . . 1992 was a record year . . . 8 million items were sold in 1993 and 1994 versus 4 million in 1985.' While the group of retailers claimed that the number of Benetton stores had dropped from 650 to 500, with 100 more dropouts expected, Benetton maintained that it had 613 stores in Germany in 1994 as opposed to 650 in 1993. Marina Galanti explained that, 'What we are talking about is a lawyer's trick to use a *cause célèbre* as a peg on which to hang every kind of grievance . . . these store owners may not like the ads, but the Frankfurt Museum of Modern Art has them on permanent exhibition.' (*The Independent*, 6/2/95).

Threats of legal action in France and other European countries had also been made. A body called The Benetton Retailers Interest Group had been formed to co-ordinate the various actions against Benetton. However, other retailers formed the 'Pro-Benetton' group in Germany to 'fight the discredit done to Benetton by the disgruntled retailers.'

In October 1995 Luciano indicated that all twelve cases had been won by Benetton and that 'the affair was now over'.[32] Financial analysts were generally optimistic about Benetton's prospects as they felt the markets had already discounted any possible negative impact due to the controversies. Salomon Brothers issued a 'Buy' recommendation on Benetton stock on 17 October 1995.

BENETTON'S COMMUNICATION PHILOSOPHY

Benetton argued that its communication philosophy was born out of a need to develop a distinctive image targeted at a global customer base and to make the most of its limited resources. The company claimed that 'various studies have shown . . . that consumers are as concerned by what a company stands for as they are about the price-value relationship of that company's products'. (*Financial Times*, 20/4/92). Further, the general feeling within Benetton was that the 8000 Benetton outlets in 120 countries constituted the best advertising for its products in the streets of the world's main cities. 'This is where we promote the products and the prices. Not in the ads.' (Luciano Benetton, *CB News*, 28/6/93). Benetton also explained that the sheer diversity of their product range made it impossible to design individual product campaigns for each market.

Benetton had received several major awards for its advertising campaigns (Exhibit 9) and some of its ads were displayed in museums world-wide. Even its critics acknowledged that 'it had achieved probably more visibility than any print campaign in world advertising history,' to quote Robin Wright, Chairman of the advertising agency WCRS (*Campaign* 25/3/94). Nonetheless, its communication approach had created a raging debate among advertisers:

'Advertising should sell happiness . . . this pair [Toscani and Benetton] have understood that society is adrift, and they have chosen the easy path: instead of extending a lifebuoy, they are pushing society's head down further under water, rubbing its nose in sex, in AIDS, in shit'. (Jacques Séguéla, Euro-RSCG, interviewed on *Antenne 2*, 16/9/93).

'Benetton's banal expressions of moral outrage were not bold, but transparent. Not courageous, but cowardly. Not socially responsible, but socially irresponsible – a cynical publicity gimmick contrived to horrify the many in order to sell pricey T-shirts to the few.' (Bob Garfield, *Advertising Age*, 27/3/95).

'[Toscani's] "advertising" is totally irrelevant to the products he is meant to be selling . . . You can put a four-letter word in a headline and it will certainly be noticed, but it doesn't mean I like you for it.' (Ced Vidler, Lintas Worldwide)[33]

'Benetton has restated a truth about successful advertising . . . that to create a distinctive "culture" around a brand is . . . often more important than a practical selling benefit.' (James Lowther, Saatchi & Saatchi)

'This is obviously a company with profound understanding of how advertising really works . . . Cynics say Benetton is using shock value to sell sweaters. Benetton counters they are doing important consciousness-raising. I would say both are right . . . They sell a little product. They do a little good. Most advertising does neither.' (Marty Cooke, Chiat/Day).

Toscani was extremely critical of traditional advertising and was seen as a maverick: [34]

'Advertisers have done a lot of social damage . . . using fake images and fake dreams to sell us their products, so that today if you are a girl you really are a nobody if you don't look like Isabella Rossellini . . . With the amount large multinationals spend on advertising they could make the best campaign in the world against drug abuse, for example.' (*Financial Times* 28/1/93)

'Advertising is the richest and most powerful form of communication in the world . . . Ad agencies are obsolete . . . They create a false reality and want people to believe in it. We show reality and we're criticised for it. Our advertising is a Rorschach test of what you bring to the image . . . Shocking violence in the news is normal. But when you take the same photo out of the news and put a Benetton logo on it, people pause and reflect . . . When they can't come to terms with it, they get mad at us . . . The more real a thing is, the less people want to see it.'[35]

'The advertising industry has corrupted society . . . One day there will be a Nuremberg trial of advertisers . . . I will sit on it, I will be the prosecution and the public.' (*The Independent*, 16/12/92).

'Today, kids get killed on the road because they have been convinced by the promise of happiness suggested by some car makers in their ads. But that doesn't stop them "selling whilst they're dying". Right now, I am exhibiting my posters on a 6,000 square metre surface in Brussels . . . 48,000 visitors have been to see these posters, already seen in the street. Next door, there is an exhibition of Flemish painters . . . they have had 3,200 visitors.' (*Jeunes à Paris*, January 1995).

Toscani saw himself not as an advertiser, but as a reporter–photographer.

'Benetton gives me the world's largest museum – the street, tens of thousands of posters in a hundred countries – every artist's dream . . . An artist must help change things . . . I want to show what people do not want to see . . . I am a modern illiterate. I don't read any books, almost never watch television, but I devour dozens of newspapers every day, dailies only, from all countries . . . Luciano is my patron, my Lorenzo de Medici.' (*Le Monde*, 17/2/95).

The company believed that their most controversial ads were considered scandalous not because of what they showed, but because of the Benetton signature. Claude Torracinta, a Swiss TV journalist

commented: '. . . twenty years ago, the picture of a child dying of hunger provoked a strong reaction . . . What Toscani is telling me . . . is that it has become banal to talk of the world's suffering [on TV news] . . . this does not affect people anymore. If you want to touch them, you need a *mise en scéne*, an escalation in the presentation.'[36]

In Benetton's mind, the images they used therefore had more impact than if they were featured by public or state organisations. Laura Pollini, Benetton's Image and Communications Director, stressed that their advertisements were intended to remain 'open' to all interpretations – including negative ones " another reason for not subjecting them to traditional advertising tests.[37] Pascal Sommariba explained: 'Ads are usually a totally closed text. What we thought was interesting was to have the text disappear totally . . . so that people had to write their own text . . . the pictures became rich through the interface with the public.'

Benetton itself never performed pre-launch tests nor analysed a campaign's impact. Toscani explained:

'Research? We try to do the very opposite . . . If you do research, you get yesterday's results. If they had done research 500 years ago, they would never have discovered America. They would have found out that the world is flat. You have to have the courage to make mistakes . . . Luciano didn't test the market for a taste in coloured sweaters.'

'The instructions I received didn't indicate selling as a target. Therefore I am free to create as I see fit.' (*Mainichi Shimbun*, 11/9/91)

'You see, Luciano owns the company. No company run by a manager would accept what I ask, they would say, . . . "We must know before if it will work." That way they get something mediocre.' (*The Times*, 26/1/93)

The visibility and uniqueness of Benetton's communications had prompted a number of advertising agencies and publishing and market research companies to conduct independent studies of their effectiveness, very often without Benetton's knowledge. These studies evaluated specific Benetton campaigns (Exhibits 10 and 11) together with the image of Benetton and other leading brands across a variety of countries (Exhibits 12 to 15).

OTHER COMMUNICATION ACTIVITIES

The Benettons have long been involved in sponsoring sports and the Benetton Treviso basketball and rugby teams and Sisley Volley are among Italy's top players in their respective national championships. In 1983, the company inaugurated the Palaverde complex, a venue for concerts, shows, cultural displays and sporting events. The 18-hectare Ghirada Sports Centre, built on the outskirts of Treviso in 1985, welcomes thousands of children every year to its gyms, basketball and volleyball courts, and rugby fields. The centre also includes a golf course and physical rehabilitation unit.

Luciano realised that Formula One Grand Prix racing attracted a world-wide audience and decided, in 1983, to sponsor the Tyrrell team at a cost of $6 million. In 1984, Benetton sponsored Alfa Romeo Euroracing, with mixed results. Benetton bought the Toleman team for L4 billion in 1985 and decided to compete directly under the *Benetton Formula* colours,

> 'All the characteristics of Grand Prix racing – speed, colour, internationality, excitement, plus the irresistible combination of high technology and the human factor – are a perfect expression of our corporate philosophy. This affiliation has been effective in creating an image for us in some countries before we had established a commercial presence.'[38]

Benetton Formula, with the German driver Michael Schumacher, won the Formula One World Championship in 1994 and 1995.

In 1992, Benetton launched *Colors*, a large-format magazine sold in five bilingual editions in over 100 countries and dedicated to racial integration. Its editor-in-chief is Toscani and the artistic editor is Tibor Kalman, an influential New York graphic designer. It rarely shies away from controversy, using, for example, computer imagery to show Queen Elizabeth II of the UK and Arnold Schwarzenegger with black skin, Pope John Paul II as an Asian or Ronald Reagan as an AIDS victim. *Colors*, which was initially distributed free in Benetton stores, has a print run of 400,000 and includes paid advertising for brands such as Kenwood, Philips and Alfa Romeo. MTV Europe is responsible for the sale of advertising space in *Colors*.

In 1993 Toscani set up *Inedito*, which he described as a 'fashion pictures production pool', in Paris. *Inedito* produced quality ready-made fashion magazine articles featuring 30% Benetton clothes and accessories and made them available to magazines world-wide. Each feature, complete with headlines, captions and full credits, is available in three languages.

In July 1995, 21 Investimenti, the investment arm of Edizione Holding, bought a local Milan TV station and renamed it *Sei Milano* (Milan 6).

And so, where next? *Fabrica*, another brainchild of Toscani, opened near Treviso in the autumn of 1995. This communications' research centre can host up to 50 promising young designers and artists from around the world. The institution is housed in a Palladian villa restructured by the Japanese architect Tadao Ando, the 1995 Pritzker prize winner. Luciano has said that 'It [*Fabrica*][39] will be a school without professors and textbooks. We want to see what creativity produces. Benetton's future communication will be *Fabrica*.'

NOTES

1   On 16 October 1995, US$ 1 = L1602.10
2   Quotes not otherwise attributed in this section and the next are from: Luciano Benetton and Andrea Lee, *Io e i miei fratelli*, Sperling e Kupfer Editori, 1990 (translated by the authors).
3   In 1996 there were still a few *Merceria* shops, and a very small number of shops called *Tomato* or *Fantomax*.
4   '. . . We quickly realised that finance was not for us. We came out of it in 1987, just before the crash, having made a few tens of billions of lire', Gilberto Benetton in *Les Echos*, 20–21 January 1994.
5   A. Lee, 'Profiles: Being Everywhere', *The New Yorker*, Nov. 10, 1986.
6   In 1994 European Union member countries were as follows: Belgium, Denmark, France, Germany, Ireland, Italy, Greece, Luxembourg, Netherlands, Portugal, Spain, United Kingdom. Austria, Finland and Sweden joined the EU on 1 January 1995.
7   Disagreements over the globalisation strategy led to Palmeri's amicable departure in 1990. He returned in 1992 to leave again in February 1995. He was replaced by Carlo Gilardi, a career banker.
8   Asked by the *Daily Telegraph* (27/2/95) about the link between clothing and these activities, Gilberto answered, 'There is no synergy with textiles but this group must grow and be developed.' He also

told *Libération* (9/3/95), 'Growth in our traditional areas had limits . . . We need to develop our heritage . . . we have many [14] children.'

9 *Io e i mei fratelli*

10 Luciano Benetton, 'Franchising: How Brand Power Works', in P. Stobart, ed., *Brand Power*, New York University Press, 1994.

11 *Io e i mei fratelli*

12 Full-scale models of these layouts can be seen on a mock 'Benetton Street' at Benetton's headquarters.

13 In March 1995, London-based Nota Bene, in collaboration with the UK's largest mail order company, Grand Universal Stores, secured exclusive rights to sell Benetton products through mail order in the UK.

14 W. Ketelhohn, 'An Interview with Aldo Palmeri of Benetton', *European Management Journal*, Sept. 1993.

15 In addition, Benetton had 271 'shops in stores' and concessions in the US.

16 In the same period, The Gap grew from 900 to 1400 stores.

17 'The Faded Colors of Benetton,' *Business Week*, International Edition, 10 April 1995.

18 'Bosnia: Store Opening Symbolises Sarajevo's Reawakening' *Los Angeles Times, 13 September 1995*.

19 Benetton's sales have always relied upon a few highly successful models. For example, in 1994, the crew-neck navy blue pullover accounted for 40% of the winter sales in France.

20 *Io e i mei Fratelli*

21 *Io e i mei Fratelli*

22 Two years later, Benetton fired JWT and set up United Colors Communication as a full-service agency.

23 *Financial World*, 17 September 1991, p. 41.

24 In 1993 spending amounted to 5.7% to finance the TV launch of Tribù, a line of scents and cosmetics. The complete Benetton fragrance business was restructured in 1995.

25 This is one of 100 letters (positive and negative) published at Benetton's initiative in P. Landi and L. Pollini, eds. *Cosa C'entra L'Aids Con i Maglioni?*, A. Mondadori Editore, 1993.

26 In *Benetton par Toscani*, Musée d'Art Contemporain, Lausanne, 1995.

27 The photographer Therese Frare won the World Photo Award for this picture.

28 Around this time, Benetton started advertising in gay magazines, which were generally ignored by major corporations.

29 Pascal Sommariba, Benetton's International Advertising Director, countered charges of a lack of charitable giving, saying: 'If a company makes 10% profits and takes 20% of it for charity, this is 2% of its turnover. If you take just 1/3rd of a communication budget of, say 5% of turnover, you are already there and it does not look like a charitable company, it is fairer.'

30 On 1 February 1995, a Paris court ruled against Benetton and awarded damages of about US$32,000. On 6 July 1995, a German court ruled that these pictures offended the dignity of HIV-infected people.

31 Ulfert Engels, the lawyer co-ordinating the 12 cases said: '. . . Our tactic was to get Benetton to sue, otherwise we would have had to fight in an Italian court and we prefer to fight in Germany.' *Marketing Week*, 3/2/95

32 'Germany: Benetton ends dispute with retailers'. *Handelsblat*, 12 October 1995

33 This and the next two quotes are from the article 'For and Against the Benetton Approach,' *Media International*, September 1993.

34 Nonetheless, he was considered 'a pillar of Benetton's success' by Ciro Tomagnini, analyst with Merill Lynch in London. Rumors of Toscani's resignation on 18 April 1994 caused a drop of almost 8% in Benetton's share price. (*The Wall Street Journal Europe*, 20/4/94)

35 In Tamotsu Yagi, '*United Colors of Benetton: A Global Vision*', Robundo, 1993.

36 Benetton par Toscani

37 I.G. Evans and S. Riyait ('Is the Message Being Received? Benetton Analysed,' *International Journal of Advertising*, 1993, 12, 291–301) recommended adding a text to aid the interpretation as some Benetton ads could yield different interpretations by different national or cultural groups.

38 Luciano Benetton 'Franchising: How Brand Power Works'.

39 In summer 1995, Benetton extended its use of Toscani's controversial images to its first global campaign for Benetton SportsSystem, the sports equipment subsidiary of Edizione.

Exhibit 1   Benetton Group SpA: Financial Highlights 1986–1995
(millions of lire[1])

	Italy	Other Europe	The Americas	Other Countries	Consolidated
1986 Revenues	388,872	470,530	173,322	19,558	1,089,983
Operating profits	99,680	86,160	16,180	4,030	206,050
Net income					113,029
Share price/MIB[2]					15,900/104.8
1987 Revenues	437,101	609,973	222,780	12,050	1,261,077
Operating profits	108,426	117,071	8,928	(2,526)	249,839
Net income					130,291
Share price/MIB					10,460/99.6
1988 Revenues	641,633	702,462	236,372	35,266	1,475,282
Operating profits	111,937	115,196	16,134	(2,361)	239,673
Net income					130,171
Share price/MIB					10,560/80.3
1989 Revenues	665,530	672,635	222,874	96,460	1,657,519
Operating profits	120,986	99,462	(637)	5,560	225,307
Net income					115,412
Share price/MIB					8,720/99.3
1990 Revenues	749,930	819,825	220,463	268,830	2,059,048
Operating profits	147,477	142,820	(8,265)	9,952	266,180
Net income					133,271
Share price/MIB					8,580/100.0
1991 Revenues	790,339	933,751	215,409	364,265	2,303,764
Operating profits	150,374	151,368	(12,255)	35,123	311,757
Net income					164,783
Share price/MIB					10,320/84.7
1992 Revenues	862,495	987,603	237,798	424,745	2,512,641
Operating profits	170,770	172,533	(12,029)	43,106	356,639
Net income					184,709
Share price/MIB					13,870/70.5
1993 Revenues	850,609	1,062,823	270,021	568,005	2,751,458
Operating profits	165,003	204,150	(22,418)	74,490	407,926
Net income					208,038
Share price/MIB					26,730/83.5
1994 Revenues	882,744	1,019,478	227,302	658,148	2,787,672
Operating profits	151,153	175,040	(19,318)	93,841	388,740
Net income					210,200
Share price/MIB					12,038/104.1

Note: Results for 1995: revenues of L 2,940 billion with net income of L 220 billion. Share price on 31.12.95: 18,890 lire

1 Exchange rate Lire/US$: 1986=1358; 1987=1169; 1988=1306; 1989=1271; 1990=1130; 1991=1151; 1992=1471; 1993=1704; 1994=1626
2 MIB=MIB Index, calculated by the Milan Stock Exchange and based on the average of all stocks traded on that exchange, 1990=100.
3 On 1 February 1994, Benetton had a capital issue of 10 million shares at L 26,500/share.

Exhibit 2 Clothes Buying Behavior in Europe, 1994 (A Time Magazine Study)

Methodology: questionnaire sent on 8 March 1994 to a panel of 5500 TIME magazine subscribers in 11 countries (500 per country)

"Where do you usually buy your clothes?"

| N = 2151 respondents | \multicolumn{14}{l}{COUNTRY} | | | | | | | | | | | | \multicolumn{2}{l}{SEX} | \multicolumn{5}{l}{AGE} |
	B	CH	D	DK	E	F	I	NL	P	S	UK	EUR	M	F	<25	25–34	35–44	45–54	55+
Boutiques	46	34	40	50	46	60	55	37	60	37	10	43	40	52	51	51	46	43	35
Department stores	34	52	56	50	57	43	38	40	36	46	68	47	48	46	44	43	52	46	47
Designer retail outlets	18	20	14	11	14	14	15	24	12	15	20	16	17	13	15	10	16	19	18
Catalogues/Direct mail	5	17	15	4	6	16	3	7	5	7	25	10	8	18	11	9	13	9	10
Tailor	2	3	4	2	2	1	2	1	4	1	3	2	3	–	2	–	–	2	5
All other	2	1	3	2	2	1	3	3	2	1	4	2	2	4	2	1	1	2	3
Can't say/it varies	17	16	15	13	12	12	9	20	17	19	10	15	14	17	14	19	14	12	15

"How important are each of the following factors and features when buying clothes"

| N = 2151 respondents | \multicolumn{12}{l}{COUNTRY} | | | | | | | | | | | \multicolumn{2}{l}{SEX} | \multicolumn{5}{l}{AGE} |
	B	CH	D	DK	E	F	I	NL	P	S	UK	EUR	M	F	<25	25–34	35–44	45–54	55+
Quality of material	8.34	8.47	8.29	8.13	8.31	8.11	8.70	8.36	8.60	8.30	8.17	8.34	8.29	8.52	8.21	8.23	8.23	8.36	8.52
Style	8.03	7.81	7.78	7.18	8.02	7.97	8.48	7.74	8.10	7.57	7.71	7.85	7.60	8.70	8.29	8.17	7.99	7.74	7.53
Cut	7.78	7.90	7.67	7.22	7.70	7.93	8.16	7.50	8.25	7.72	7.80	7.79	7.58	8.46	7.59	7.75	7.76	7.88	7.80
Colour	7.52	7.98	7.59	7.58	7.28	7.59	8.01	7.68	7.84	7.69	7.66	7.68	7.54	8.14	7.81	7.76	7.65	7.64	7.63
Price	7.11	6.87	6.97	6.73	7.30	7.20	7.35	7.05	7.38	6.28	7.36	7.06	6.94	7.47	7.02	7.34	7.18	6.87	6.97
Season	5.40	5.37	4.77	4.54	5.45	5.30	6.07	5.18	6.45	5.00	4.06	5.23	5.25	5.45	5.59	5.46	5.42	5.23	4.89
Partner's influence	5.43	4.33	5.10	4.78	4.47	5.04	4.88	5.98	4.43	4.90	4.84	4.93	5.17	3.83	4.63	4.96	4.97	4.95	4.92
Country of origin	2.85	3.13	2.99	2.99	3.23	3.73	3.68	3.17	3.63	3.47	3.09	3.27	3.38	2.92	3.41	3.05	3.23	3.33	3.34
Prestigious name	2.70	2.47	2.44	2.43	3.43	2.81	3.17	2.76	3.87	2.44	2.65	2.84	2.94	2.52	3.80	2.84	2.80	2.93	2.53
Loyalty to designer	2.57	2.37	2.09	1.94	3.23	2.63	2.98	2.64	3.33	2.24	2.00	2.55	2.65	2.20	3.14	2.63	2.33	2.58	2.49
Advertising	2.34	2.27	2.33	2.47	2.66	2.15	2.38	2.58	3.13	2.28	2.20	2.44	2.52	2.17	2.85	2.62	2.42	2.47	2.20

Average scores based on a scale of 1–10, where 1 = not at all important and 10 = extremely important

Code: Europe (EUR), Belgium (B), Switzerland (CH), Germany (D), Denmark (DK), Spain (E), France (F), Italy (I), Netherlands (NL), Portugal (P), Sweden (S), United Kingdom (UK)

Source: Images of Fashion and Fragrance 1994, Time Magazine Opinion Poll

Exhibit 3	Major Investments and Controlling Interests held by Edizione Holding

Benetton Group S.p.A	clothing, 71% owned, turnover L2788bn, net profit L210bn
Benetton Sportsystem	sporting equipment, 100% owned, turnover L1150bn, operating profit L31bn:
– Nordica	ski boots, 33% of total turnover
– Rollerblade	roller skates, 30%
– Prince	tennis rackets, 20%
– Kästle	skis, 9%
– Asolo	mountain boots, 4%
– Killer Loop	glasses and snow boards, 4%
GS-Euromercato	supermarkets, 60% owned[1], L4350bn turnover
Autogrill	highway restaurants, 60% owned[2], L1400bn turnover
21 Investimenti	partnership or minority interests in diversified sectors, 75% owned
United Optical	spectacle frames, 100% owned
Divarese	shoes, 85% owned, turnover L60bn, profit L230m
Verdesport	sporting activities, 100% owned
Edizione Property	commercial and non-industrial properties, including ranches in Patagonia and Texas, 100% owned
Minority Investments	1% of Banca Commerciale Italiana and others

Note: Data reflect the situation in March 1996. Edizione was itself 100% owned by the Benetton family

1 Partnership with Del Vecchio Group
2 Partnership with Mövenpick Group

Exhibit 4   MAJOR BENETTON ACCESSORIES AND LICENSED PRODUCTS

Exhibit 5   Number of Benetton Points-of-Sale, 1982–1994

Region	1982	1983	1984	1985	1986	1987	1988	1989	1990	1991	1992	1993	1994
Europe	1823	2180	2388	2708	3103	3646	3846	4007	4846	5378	5949	5881	5651
(Italy)	(1165)	(1227)	(1253)	(1279)	(1390)	(1470)	(1505)	(1601)	(1806)	(1969)	(2089)	(2044)	(2031)
The Americas	41	71	207	432	708	903	1225	1214	1187	1306	1075	1175	1144
(USA)	(32)	(66)	(190)	(400)	(640)	(n.a.)	(700)	(630)	(650)	(480)	(294)	(429)	(421)
Far East and others	53	45	49	62	85	99	412	651	1299	1204	1109	1458	1443
Total	1917	2296	2644	3202	4102	4995	5483	5872	7332	7888	8133	8514	8238

1 As of 1990, the figures include "shops-in-shop", corners and concessions.

Exhibit 6 **Major Benetton Store Layouts, 1995**

Mega Benetton	Area	>400 square metres
	Location	Main business and residential areas with good purchasing power
	Target	Young and very young, but not only
	Assortment	Most clothing lines and licensed products
Blue Family/Fil di Ferro	Area	>100 square metres
	Location	Main business zones and areas frequented by students with average purchasing power
	Target	Very young clientele
	Assortment	Blue Family line of clothing, accessories and licensed products
Benetton Uomo (Benetton for Men)	Area	>70 square metres
	Location	Main business zones and residential areas with good purchasing power
	Target	Youthful informal, classic informal
	Assortment	Benetton's men's line of clothing, accessories and licensed products
Benetton Donna (Benetton for Women)	Area	>150 square metres
	Location	Main business zones and residential areas with good purchasing power
	Target	Youthful informal, classic informal
	Assortment	Benetton's women's line of clothing, accessories and licensed products
O12	Area	>100 square metres
	Location	Main business zones and residential areas with good purchasing power
	Target	0 to 12 years of age
	Assortment	New-born and children's clothing, accessories and licensed products
Sisley	Area	>100 square metres
	Location	Main business zones and residential areas with above-average purchasing power
	Target	Sporty, outdoor and fashion-conscious lifestyles
	Assortment	Sisley line of clothing, accessories and licensed products

Exhibit 6 (cont'd) **Major Benetton Store Layouts, 1995**

Exhibit 7 **A Selection of non-Benetton Advertisements by Oliviero Toscani**

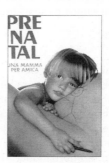

Exhibit 8 Some of Benetton's Actions Against Aids (1991–94)

1991

In parallel with Coloured Condoms ad, free condoms distributed in Benetton stores in Europe and USA. $50,000 donation to HIV/AIDS Education Fund high school educational programme in New York City

1992

Gigantic painted version of Coloured Condoms (26m × 26m) displayed in a Milan square. Donation made to the hospital to which David Kirby was admitted. Coloured Condoms posters displayed in Amsterdam during an international conference on AIDS. In South Africa, gigantic Coloured Condom posters hung outside five hospitals in Cape Town, Durban and Pretoria (at the Medical Research Council's request). Coloured Condoms used as part of national prevention campaign sponsored by AIDES organisation in France. Helped raise $600,000 for AIDS charities in USA.

1992–93

Produced and distributed guides to safe sex in collaboration with a number of associations: Gay Men's Health Crisis (USA); Lega Italiana per la Lotta Contro l'AIDS (Italy); Japanese Foundation for AIDS Prevention; Fundai (Argentina); Gapa (Brazil); Shine and The Guardian (Caribbean); Proyecto Alerta (Chile); Fundacion Amor (Colombia); Conasida (Mexico); Fundacion Marco Aguayo (Paraguay); FranSida and National AIDS Programme (Uruguay). In Germany, sponsored the first major AIDS fund-raising project in 100 night clubs (in collaboration with Deutsche AIDS Stiftungen); was one of two founding partners of the Deutsche AIDS Hilfe Communications Fund, created during an international AIDS conference in Berlin.

1993

200 HIV organisations worldwide were contacted to explore possible joint communication projects. In Brazil, organised a concert for the benefit of a hospital for children with AIDS in Latin America, special projects (fashion shows, musical and cultural events) were dedicated to AIDS. Sponsored the Films on Drugs Festival in Vienna, Austria. Sponsored the Gay Film Festival in Turin, Italy. In Portugal, donated outdoor advertising space to the HIV organisation Abraço. In France, supported survey on the sexual behaviour of young men with 20 Ans magazine. On Dec 1 (World AIDS day), a 22-metre pink condom was placed over the Obelisk on Place de la Concorde in Paris (in cooperation with the group Act Up). Also participated in a major national campaign to promote the use of condoms, in collaboration with AIDES, the national non-governmental organization. Was the first company to sign the UK Declaration of Rights for People with HIV and AIDS. Sponsored "Stopping AIDS Together', a fashion show to help raise funds for AIDS research and care in USA and Canada.

1994

An entire issue of Colors (N°7) was dedicated to AIDS (over 500,000 copies distributed worldwide). Sponsored "10th World AIDS Conference" in Yokohama, Japan and organised fund-raising operations. Sponsored Gay Film Festival in Turin and the Ripensare l'AIDS Convention in Bologna, Italy. Also donated T-shirts to the organisation SAMAN. In the UK, participated in the "Quilts of Love" demonstration and developed a pamphlet on AIDS prevention with various organisations (125,000 copies distributed). Co-produced one of ten award-winning films for the SIDATHON day in France. Organised distribution of free condoms during the Rio carnival in Brazil.

1995

In India, produced and distributed posters and leaflets on AIDS prevention.

Exhibit 9   Some Major National Awards recieved by Benetton

Year	Country
1984	**Netherlands** – Avenue Award
1985	**France** – Banque du l'Union Publicitaire **France** – Stratégies Grand Prix (Best Campaigns) and Awards in the Magazine, Out-door and Textiles/Clothing categories **Netherlands** – Avenue Award
1986	**Netherlands** – Avenue Award
1988	**Austria** – Kulturamt der Stadt Wien Award **Italy** – Confindustria Print Italia and Pubblicità Successo Awards **Netherlands** – Avenue Award **UK** – Eurobest Awards
1989	**Austria** – Kulturamt der Stadt Wien Award **Denmark** – Årets Guldkrone Award **France** – Stratégies Grand Prix (Out-door category) **Italy** – Finedit, IGP, Confindustria Print Italia Grand Prix Awards **Netherlands** – Avenue Award
1990	**Austria** – Kulturmt der Stadt Wien Awards **France** – Art Directors' Club of Europe Grand Prix **Italy** – Art Directors' Club Award (out-door category) and Confindustria Print Italia Award **Netherlands** – Avenue Award **UK** – Media and Marketing Europe Award **USA** – International Andy Award of Excellence
1991	**Austria** – Kulturamt der Stadt Wien Award **Finland** – Maximedia Special Award (outdoor category) **France** – Cannes International Golden Lion Award **Germany** – Art Directors' Club of Europe Award **Italy** – Art Directors' Club Award **Netherlands** – Avenue Award **Spain** – AEPE Award (out-door category) **Switzerland** – Société Générale d'Affichage Grand Prix **UK** – Epica and Eurobest Award **USA** – International Andy Award of Excellence (magazine and international retail category), Institute of Outdoor Advertising OBIE Award International Center for Photography (ICP) Jury Award
1992	**Europe** – FEPE (European Federation of Outdoor Advertising) Award (Best Poster for Italy) **France** – Cannes International Golden Lion (outdoor category) **Ireland** – Best Out-door Campaign Award **USA** – ICP Infinity Award, Institute of Outdoor Advertising's Fiftieth OBIE Award
1993	**Austria** – Kulturamt der Stadt Wien Award
1994	**Austria** – Kulturamt der Stadt Wien Award **France** – French Retailers Association's "Enseigne d'Or" Award **Japan** – Art Directors' Club of Japan Award **Turkey** – Kuzguncuk Lions Club Award **USA** – Art Directors' Club of New York Medal
1995	**Switzerland** – Swiss Federal Department of the Interior Award

---

Exhibit 10   **Ipsos Tests of Benetton Campaigns in France (billboards, Paris and suburbs), 1985–1995**

Date of Campaign: 1–20/3/85
Date of Test: 20/9/85
Cost[1]: 2,000,000 FF and 4,000,000 FF ($223,000 and $446,000)

	Recognition[2]	Attribution[3]	Confusion[4]	Liked	Disliked
Overall sample (N = 300)	57	29	3	73	23
18–34 year olds (N = 150)	63	36	3	73	21

Date of Campaign: 1989
Date of Test: 28/9 to 3/10/89
Cost: 2,396,000 FF ($375,543)

N = 301	Recognition	Attribution	Confusion	Liked	Disliked	Indifferent
Overall sample	75	64	2	79	20	1
Gender						
Men	75	60	3	77	23	1
Women	75	68	1	81	17	2
Age group						
18–24	81	77	1	83	16	1
25–34	81	76	1	83	15	3
35–55	69	53	3	75	25	–
Income group						
Higher	83	72	3	81	18	1
Medium	72	60	2	77	22	1
Lower	65	58	2	77	20	3
Ipsos standards[5]	43	18	–	60	35	5

Source: Ipsos Publicité, Paris, France

1 Estimated cost of the campaign in French Francs (US$). This refers only to billboards and does not include print.
2 Respondents were shown a folder containing several ads with the brand name blocked out. As they leafed through, they were asked which ads they remembered seeing. The recognition score is the % of respondents remembering having seen (at least one of) the ads listed
3 For each ad recognised, respondents were asked whether they remembered the name of the brand blocked out
4 Percentage of respondents who incorrectly identified the brand
5 Average score of all other billboard campaigns tested by Ipsos within the same industry and within similar budgets

Exhibit 10 (Cont'd)   **Tests of Benetton Campaigns in France (billboards, Paris and suburbs), 1985–1995**

Date of Campaign: 12/3 – 20/3/90
Date of Test: 22/3/90
Cost: 2,319,000 FF ($425,872)

N = 301	Recognition	Attribution	Confusion	Liked	Disliked	Indifferent
Overall sample	88	75	2	90	8	2
Gender						
Men	85	69	2	89	9	3
Women	91	81	1	91	8	1
Age group						
18–24	90	82	–	94	6	–
25–34	92	83	–	91	9	–
35–55	85	68	3	89	7	3
Income group						
Higher	91	81	2	92	6	2
Medium	89	74	2	90	9	1
Lower	81	67	–	86	11	3
Ipsos standards[5]	43	18	–	59	35	6

Date of Campaign: 3/9 – 16/9/90
Date of Test: 20–24/9/90
Cost: 2,001,000 FF ($367,473)

N = 301	Recognition	Attribution	Confusion	Liked	Disliked	Indifferent
Overall sample	83	72	2	88	10	2
Gender						
Men	81	68	3	88	9	3
Women	84	76	1	88	11	1
Age group						
18–24	94	90	1	95	5	–
25–34	91	85	2	90	9	1
35–55	75	58	2	94	6	–
Income group						
Higher	82	75	2	89	11	1
Medium	84	72	2	85	10	4
Lower	82	64	2	94	6	–
Ipsos standards[5]	43	18	–	59	35	6

Exhibit 10 (Cont'd)   **Tests of Benetton Campaigns in France (billboards, Paris and suburbs), 1985–1995**

Date of Campaign: 11/3 to 20/3/91
Date of Test: 21/3/91
Cost: 2,176,000 FF ($385,672)

N = 301	Recognition	Attribution	Confusion	Liked	Disliked	Indifferent
Overall sample	83	69	4	70	28	2
Gender						
Men	79	62	5	74	26	1
Women	87	77	2	67	30	3
Age group						
18–24	93	90	1	83	17	1
25–34	91	80	5	79	20	1
35–55	75	58	3	61	36	3
Income group						
Higher	87	75	5	74	25	1
Medium	78	67	1	66	31	3
Lower	84	63	6	69	27	3
Ipsos standards	43	18	–	59	35	6

Date of Campaign: 2/9 to 11/9/91
Date of Test: 19/9/91
Cost: 2,440,000 FF ($432,463)

N = 301	Recognition	Attribution	Confusion	Liked	Disliked	Indifferent
Overall sample	79	72	1	32	66	2
Gender						
Men	76	67	1	34	64	2
Women	83	77	–	30	69	1
Age group						
18–24	84	75	1	34	64	2
25–34	80	77	1	38	62	–
35–55	79	67	1	26	70	3
Income group						
Higher	80	71	–	44	56	1
Medium	82	78	1	23	75	3
Lower	75	63	2	27	71	2
Ipsos standards	43	18	–	59	35	6

Exhibit 10 (Cont'd) **Tests of Benetton Campaigns in France (billboards, Paris and suburbs), 1985–1995**

Date of Campaign: 2/9 to 11/9/91 and 14/10 to 21/10/91
Date of Test: 24/10/91
Cost: 2,440,000 FF ($432,463) and 1,097,000 FF ($194,431)

N = 193	Recognition	Attribution	Confusion	Liked	Disliked	Indifferent	Incites to buy[6]	Does not incite to buy
Overall sample	64	59	1	59	38	3	36	61
Gender								
Men	67	60	1	60	38	2	35	61
Women	60	58	–	58	39	3	38	60
Age group								
18–24	65	63	–	65	29	6	41	59
25–34	67	65	–	60	36	4	38	60
35–55	60	53	1	58	41	1	35	61
Income group								
Higher	67	63	1	56	43	1	41	55
Medium	60	53	–	66	30	4	36	60
Lower	66	62	–	48	48	3	21	79
Ipsos standards	43	18	–	59	35	6	–	–

Date of Campaign: 2/9 to 11/9/91 and 14/10 to 21/10/91
Date of Test: 24/10/91
Cost: 2,440,000 FF ($432,463) and 1,097,000 FF ($194,431)

N = 193	Recognition	Attribution	Confusion	Liked	Disliked	Indifferent	Incites to buy	Does not incite to buy
Overall sample	72	67	1	70	28	2	40	56
Gender								
Men	64	57	1	69	29	2	33	61
Women	80	78	–	71	28	1	48	51
Age group								
18–24	86	82	–	76	24	–	43	55
25–34	77	73	–	72	26	2	42	55
35–55	69	62	1	68	31	1	39	57
Income group								
Higher	67	66	1	64	34	1	38	56
Medium	73	69	–	74	25	1	47	52
Lower	79	69	–	76	21	3	31	66
Ipsos standards	43	18	–	59	35	6	–	–

6 The % of respondents who said that the campaign has created in them a positive or negative desire to buy the product. Ipsos reports the following standards for indication to buy: 27% positive "desire to buy" when ad liking is below 45%; 39% positive when liking is between 45% and 60%; 52% positive when liking is above 60%.

Exhibit 10 (Cont'd) **Tests of Benetton Campaigns in France (billboards, Paris and suburbs), 1985–1995**

Date of Campaign: 18/3 – 29/3/92
Date of Test: 2/4/92
Cost: 2,125,000 FF ($401,413)

N = 301	Recognition	Attribution	Confusion	Liked	Disliked	Indifferent	Incites to buy	Does not incite to buy
Overall sample	79	72	–	39	58	3	19	78
Gender								
Men	81	70	1	42	54	4	19	79
Women	78	74	–	36	61	3	18	76
Age group								
18–24	83	81	–	44	51	5	26	73
25–34	85	81	–	42	54	4	23	75
35–55	74	63	1	36	61	3	14	81
Income group								
Higher	76	71	1	37	61	2	16	79
Medium	82	74	–	37	59	4	19	78
Lower	80	71	–	45	50	5	23	76
Ipsos standards	43	18	–	59	35	6		

Date of Campaign: 22/9 to 29/9/92 and 19/10 to 26/10/92
Date of Test: 5/11/92
Cost: 2,000,000 and 2,527,000 FF ($377,800 and $477,350)

N = 301	Recognition	Attribution	Confusion	Liked	Disliked	Indifferent
Overall sample	77	73	1	42	54	4
Gender						
Men	77	73	1	52	42	6
Women	76	74	–	33	65	2
Age group						
18–24	84	83	–	44	55	1
25–34	84	82	–	42	56	2
35–55	70	65	1	42	52	6
Income group						
Higher	80	78	1	40	57	3
Medium	76	71	–	39	55	6
Lower	75	69	1	49	48	3
Ipsos standards	43	18	–	65	30	5

Exhibit 10 (Cont'd) **Tests of Benetton Campaigns in France (billboards, Paris and suburbs), 1985–1995**

Date of Campaign: 14/9 to 21/9/93
Date of Test: 23/9/93
Cost: 2,200,000 FF ($388,473)

N = 301	Recognition	Attribution	Confusion	Liked	Disliked	Indifferent
Overall sample	81	77	2	23	70	7
Gender						
Men	78	72	3	22	70	8
Women	85	81	1	24	70	6
Age group						
18–24	86	84	–	21	69	10
25–34	82	79	1	22	71	7
35–55	81	75	3	24	68	7
Income group						
Higher	86	85	1	20	75	6
Medium	82	75	4	25	68	7
Lower	69	60	–	28	62	10
Ipsos standards	44	21	–	61	31	8

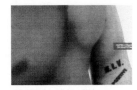 

Date of Campaign: 22/2 to 28/2/94
Date of Test: 3/3/1994
Cost: 1,754,000 FF ($315,900)

N = 302	Recognition	Attribution	Confusion	Liked	Disliked	Indifferent	Incites to buy	Does not incite to buy
Overall sample	60	55	1	27	71	2	14	86
Gender								
Men	63	56	1	28	71	1	14	86
Women	56	54	–	27	70	3	15	85
Age group								
18–34	66	64	–	28	72	1	14	86
35–55	54	46	1	27	70	3	15	85
Income group								
Higher	65	64	1	25	75	1	9	91
Medium	53	50	–	31	67	2	17	83
Lower	63	52	1	25	72	3	16	84
Ipsos standards	44	20	–	61	31	8		

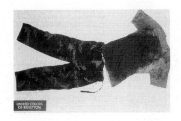

Exhibit 10 (Cont'd) **Tests of Benetton Campaigns in France (billboards, Paris and suburbs), 1985–1995**

Date of Campaign: 18/10 to 31/10/94
Date of Test: 3/11/94
Cost: 3,400,000 FF ($612,400)

N = 300	Recognition	Attribution	Confusion	Liked	Disliked	Indifferent
Overall sample	86	80	1	59	32	9
Gender						
Men	86	80	1	58	28	13
Women	86	81	2	60	35	5
Age group						
18–34	93	90	1	66	26	7
35–55	79	70	2	52	37	11
Income group						
Higher	87	81	1	61	29	10
Medium	86	80	2	58	35	6
Lower	84	79	–	57	29	14
Ipsos standards	44	20	–	61	31	8

Date of Campaign: 21/2 to 6/3/95
Date of Test: 9/3/95
Cost: 3,600,000 FF ($720,000)

N = 301	Recognition	Attribution	Confusion	Liked	Disliked	Indifferent
Overall sample	82	78	1	37	60	4
Gender						
Men	83	77	1	37	58	5
Women	81	79	–	36	62	2
Age group						
18–34	86	85	–	42	55	3
35–55	79	72	1	31	65	4
Income group						
Higher	80	75	2	35	62	3
Medium	84	83	–	38	59	3
Lower	82	74	–	35	58	7
Ipsos standards	47	23	–	63	30	7

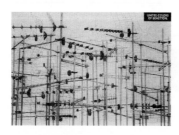
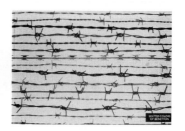

Exhibit 11   **Test of Benetton Billboard Campaign in Switzerland, 1991 (a société Génerale d'Affichage study)**

Campaign tested: "Giusy, the new-born baby" – Date of test: 9–12 August, 1991

Methodology: This SGA study tested the impact of 10 new outdoor advertising campaigns prior to their national launch in Switzerland. These campaigns were displayed in 2 metropolitan areas in greater Lausanne and Bern during a two-week period (29 July – 11 August, 1991) on 30 and 38 "B12" billboards respectively. The test campaigns included Benetton's "new-born baby" campaign as well as 9 other campaigns. The test occurred 7 weeks prior to the national launch in Switzerland of the "new-born baby" campaign. The 10 test campaigns a) had not appeared anywhere previously; b) were only displayed on "B12" billboards, and c) were the only campaigns run by these brands for 2 weeks prior to and after the test display period. The sample was representative of all persons aged 15 to 74 living in the greater Lausanne and Bern areas.

A. Unaided Recall[1]

LAUSANNE SAMPLE (N=401)		BERN SAMPLE (N=402)	
BRANDS	RECALL	BRANDS	RECALL
	%		%
1 Benetton[2]	18.0	1 Benetton[2]	33.8
2 Marlboro	7.5	2 Stop Aids	8.0
3 Stop Aids	5.7	3 SBB	3.5
4 Camel	4.7	4 Stimorol[2]	2.5
5 SBB	3.7	5 Migros	2.5
6 MacDonald's	3.0	6 Der Bund[2]	2.2
7 Clin d'oeil[2]	2.7	7 700th Anniversary	2.2
8 700th Anniversary	2.7	8 Circus Knie	2.0
9 AMAG/VW	2.7	9 Levi Jeans	1.7
10 Comptoir Suisse[2]	2.5	10 Marlboro	1.7

Source: 'Billboards B12', Société Générale d'Affichage (SGA), Switzerland, 1992 and Martial Pasquier 'Conscience et Comportement', Arbeitspapier Nr 21, Institut für Marketing und Unternehmungsführung, Universität Bern, 1994

Exhibit 11 (con't)

B. Recognition[3] and Company/Product Familiarity[4] for all 10 Test Campaigns

LAUSANNE SAMPLE (N=401)   BERN SAMPLE (N=402)

	RECOGNITION			RECOGNITION		
BRANDS	SEEN FOR SURE	PERHAPS	FAMILIARITY	SEEN FOR SURE	PERHAPS	FAMILIARITY
	%	%	%	%	%	%
Benetton	55.1	12.2	90.3	60.4	4.7	87.8
Heine	28.2	14.5	38.7	39.8	11.7	51.2
Providentia	20.7	18.0	70.1	27.1	9.7	57.2
Stimorol	34.9	23.4	91.8	45.3	10.4	92.0
Benetton	55.1	12.2	90.3	60.4	4.7	87.8
SGA	25.9	15.2	46.4	25.9	10.0	40.5
Clin d'oeil[5]	40.1	17.0	75.1			
Comptoir Suisse[5]	26.2	15.5	92.8			
L'Hebdo[5]	51.1	20.2	90.3			
Der Bund[5]				68.9	9.7	95.3
Wartman[5]				39.1	11.2	85.8

C. Variation of Benetton Total Recognition[6] by Sex and Age

	LAUSANNE SAMPLE (%)	BERN SAMPLE (%)
Men	65.0	60.1
Women	69.5	69.9
15–29	78.9	68.2
30–49	67.2	67.4
50–74	54.8	58.2

[1] Respondents were asked: "Can you spontaneously give examples of posters or billboards which you have seen during the last 2 weeks?"
[2] One of the 10 test campaigns.
[3] Respondents were asked: "Here are photos of billboards. Are there any among them which you remember having seen during the past two weeks? Please tell us which ones you have seen 'for sure', 'perhaps' or 'not at all'."
[4] Respondents were asked: "For each billboard, please say if the product or the company is familiar to you".
[5] Ad displayed only in French-speaking Lausanne or German-speaking Bern.
[6] Total recognition: "seen for sure" + "seen perhaps"

Exhibit 11 (con't)

D. Liking/Disliking[1] of Benetton Campaign

	LAUSANNE SAMPLE		BERN SAMPLE		REASONS FOR DISLIKING[2] (%)					
					LAUSANNE SAMPLE			BERN SAMPLE		
	DISLIKE	LIKE	DISLIKE	LIKE	A	B	C	A	B	C
	(%)	(%)	(%)	(%)						
Overall	58	15	62	12	23	39	54	32	44	38
Men	58	17	63	11	23	34	51	25	45	40
Women	59	15	64	12	23	43	57	37	42	35
15–29	52	24	55	14	19	33	51	32	44	39
30–49	59	15	68	12	26	37	56	37	49	32
50–74	65	9	68	10	18	44	56	27	39	41

[1] Respondents were asked to indicate whether they liked or disliked the ad using a 6-point scale (1 = does not like at all; 6 = likes a lot). Here, dislike scores correspond to 1–2 answers and like scores correspond to 4–6 answers

[2] People with a negative reaction were asked to select one or more of the following reasons for their dislike. A: use of the subject for commercial purposes; B: the image is shocking; C: the relationship between the subject and the brand

Exhibit 12   Awareness, Liking and Usage of Some Fashion Brands in Five European Countries, 1990 (A Euroka Project – Brigitte Magazine Germany)

Methodology: "omnibus" surveys in West Germany, France, Great Britain, Italy, Spain involving a random sample of 2,000 women, 14–64 years old, April–May 1990

CLOTHING BRANDS	GERMANY			FRANCE			G. BRITAIN			ITALY			SPAIN		
	AWARENESS %	LIKING %	USAGE %	AWARENESS %	LIKING %	USAGE %	AWARENESS %	LIKING %	USAGE %	AWARENESS %	LIKING %	USAGE %	AWARENESS %	LIKING %	USAGE %
Benetton	68	42	28	73	30	26	61	26	14	92	65	57	53	21	17
Armani	28	11	4	6	1	0	18	6	2	81	41	28	9	2	1
Esprit	73	46	33	3	1	1	20	4	1	8	2	1	6	0	0
Jil Sander	68	37	14	5	1	0	2	0	0	12	3	1	2	0	0
Triumph	91	60	53	49	6	8	43	10	6	31	10	10	30	7	12
Schiesser	93	64	56	2	0	0	2	0	0	3	1	1	2	0	0

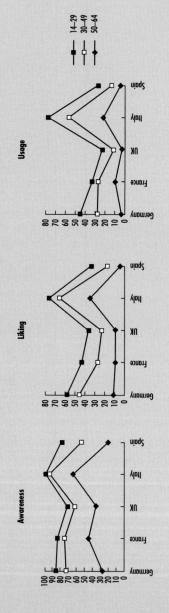

Benetton Awareness (Aided), Liking and Usage by Age Group

Exhibit 13 **Image of Benetton and some other clothing brands in France, 1994 (A Sofres Survey)**

BRANDS	AIDED AWARENESS[1]	EVOCATION[2]	PERCEIVED QUALITY[3]	CONVICTION[4]	REFUSAL[5]	INFLUENCE[6]	INFLUENCE RATIO[7]	USAGE[8]
Chanel	1000	969	782	863	250	226	476	1.11	130
Lacoste	1000	961	798	865	249	148	397	1.68	255
Benetton	1000	871	661	574	122	247	369	0.49	106
Chevignon	1000	814	607	582	106	252	358	0.42	80
Armani	1000	298	167	157	24	102	126	0.24	17
Boss	1000	263	145	148	24	95	119	0.25	16
Average 300 brands	825	591	539	168	223	391	0.75	254

Basis: Total population rescaled to 1000

Source: SOFRES, France. Data extracted from 'SOFRES Megabrand System 1994' database. The Megabrand system covers 300 international brands across a variety of goods and services with a representative national sample of 3000 French respondents.

1 Aided awareness: number of individuals who indicate that they "know the brand from amongst those presented, if only by name".
2 Number of individuals for whom this brand evokes "many things", "some things" or "a few things" (as opposed to "nothing").
3 Number of individuals for whom the brand is the "best available quality" or "better than others" as opposed to "inferior to others" or "worst quality available".
4 Number of individuals who state they "would definitely choose" this brand (as opposed to "probably", "probably not", "certainly not".
5 Number of individuals who state they "would *definitely not* choose this brand"
6 Number of individuals who are not indifferent to this brand (influence = conviction + refusal)
7 Influence ratio = conviction/refusal.
8 Number of individuals who use "almost only" this brand, or "more than any other", as opposed to "less than others" or "almost never".

Exhibit 14   **Images of some leading fashion companies in Europe, 1994 (A Time Magazine Study)**

Methodology: questionnaire sent on 18 March 1994 to a panel of 5500 TIME magazine subscribers in 11 countries (500 per country). Respondents were presented with a list of 40 fashion and/or fragrance houses and asked their perceptions of these companies. Only the top 10 fashion companies are shown in this exhibit.

"Overall familiarity with the company"

N = 2151 RESPONDENTS	COUNTRY	EUR %	B %	CH %	D %	DK %	E %	F %	I %	NL %	P %	S %	UK %
1 Benetton	I	80	84	83	87	64	87	87	89	69	90	67	69
2 Christian Dior	F	74	78	80	73	64	81	89	77	64	83	67	58
3 Lacoste	F	72	73	75	80	67	76	88	86	55	81	71	44
4 Burberry's	UK	72	70	73	61	79	85	74	73	62	76	72	65
5 Yves Saint Laurent	F	70	76	70	68	59	78	86	79	59	76	63	58
6 Chanel	F	68	65	71	61	59	66	88	80	63	82	55	63
7 Giorgio Armani	I	56	53	50	62	35	73	40	93	32	67	58	49
8 Hugo Boss	D	49	40	59	76	57	35	39	38	43	73	49	32
9 Karl Lagerfeld	F	47	46	48	67	46	39	60	33	43	47	55	36
10 Hermès	F	47	51	61	37	21	55	85	61	31	40	33	39

"Prestigious image"

N = 2151 RESPONDENTS	COUNTRY	EUR %	B %	CH %	D %	DK %	E %	F %	I %	NL %	P %	S %	UK %
1 Christian Dior	F	62	73	69	61	55	58	79	63	47	66	56	60
2 Yves Saint Laurent	F	56	66	64	49	43	61	75	59	38	63	55	50
3 Chanel	F	49	55	51	39	32	54	79	52	35	66	35	41
4 Giorgio Armani	I	46	50	36	53	26	63	28	73	24	56	42	52
5 Burberry's	UK	41	39	41	30	33	58	39	46	29	49	36	54
6 Karl Lagerfeld	F	38	49	40	57	29	30	48	17	31	40	39	36
7 Hermès	F	35	41	46	31	14	47	62	37	24	30	20	32
8 Lacoste	F	31	30	30	36	29	40	30	31	29	47	25	18
9 Calvin Klein	US	26	26	24	30	26	21	14	10	26	32	31	49
10 Nina Ricci	F	24	26	31	12	9	32	45	26	21	35	18	12
. . .													
15 Benetton	I	20	15	11	16	18	33	10	16	18	40	18	22

Code: Europe (EUR), Belgium (B), Switzerland (CH), Germany (D), Denmark (DK), Spain (E), France (F), Italy (I), Netherlands (NL), Portugal (P), Sweden (S), United Kingdom (UK)
Source: Images of Fashion and Fragrance 1994, Time Magazine Opinion Poll

Exhibit 14 (con't)

"Reputation for Quality"

N = 2151 RESPONDENTS	COUNTRY	EUR %	B %	CH %	D %	DK %	E %	F %	I %	NL %	P %	S %	UK %
1 Burberry's	UK	54	47	58	54	64	60	60	45	43	50	53	63
2 Lacoste	F	34	26	30	33	25	47	50	38	28	45	33	15
3 Hugo Boss	F	26	24	28	48	32	19	24	15	16	43	23	15
4 Aquascutum	UK	25	16	44	13	26	18	18	38	12	26	11	56
5 Chanel	F	24	23	28	17	17	29	37	23	24	30	16	20
6 Yves Saint Laurent	F	24	22	17	22	17	26	42	26	15	35	17	28
7 Giorgio Armani	I	23	16	17	23	13	29	21	44	13	31	23	25
8 Benetton	I	23	22	18	16	26	24	24	36	14	26	17	29
9 Christian Dior	F	23	18	21	17	17	33	34	27	16	27	13	26
10 Hermès	F	22	20	24	17	5	29	45	24	15	23	15	19

"Is more high fashion"

N = 2151 RESPONDENTS	COUNTRY	EUR %	B %	CH %	D %	DK %	E %	F %	I %	NL %	P %	S %	UK %
1 Christian Dior	F	42	41	46	38	34	42	61	38	41	40	32	48
2 Karl Lagerfeld	F	30	38	33	37	22	29	41	24	23	26	20	33
3 Giorgio Armani	I	30	36	30	36	18	42	21	42	14	28	28	30
4 Yves Saint Laurent	F	30	30	27	33	29	31	45	28	32	25	16	35
5 Calvin Klein	US	25	19	31	28	20	20	20	24	23	27	16	44
6 Chanel	F	21	25	22	16	16	25	37	30	22	22	9	22
7 Jean-Paul Gaultier	F	19	25	23	16	9	18	32	19	14	24	13	20
8 Kenzo	F	15	17	24	21	11	9	25	16	12	12	13	2
9 Benetton	I	15	11	16	25	16	13	9	12	11	11	15	27
10 Nina Ricci	F	11	10	9	7	3	17	23	14	3	15	9	6

"Caters for my style"

N = 2151 RESPONDENTS	COUNTRY	EUR %	B %	CH %	D %	DK %	E %	F %	I %	NL %	P %	S %	UK %
1 Burberry's	UK	17	9	19	17	15	22	16	15	18	20	11	25
2 Giorgio Armani	I	12	8	6	14	8	18	7	21	5	10	14	16
3 Lacoste	F	12	15	10	10	9	20	16	17	9	14	7	4
4 Hugo Boss	D	10	11	6	20	12	8	9	3	6	20	9	4
5 Ralph Lauren	US	9	7	11	9	9	10	5	10	8	11	8	12
6 Benetton	I	9	11	5	9	9	12	13	15	16	10	1	7
7 Yves Saint Laurent	F	8	5	5	6	4	11	14	7	5	9	8	10
8 Calvin Klein	US	6	3	4	5	8	9	4	4	8	9	3	12
9 Aquascutum	UK	6	3	11	5	4	2	3	7	4	9	1	15
10 Chanel	F	6	3	9	6	3	7	8	10	9	4	5	4

Exhibit 14 (con't)

"Would buy for day/work wear"

N = 2151 RESPONDENTS	COUNTRY	EUR %	B %	CH %	D %	DK %	E %	F %	I %	NL %	P %	S %	UK %
1 Benetton	I	38	35	40	45	30	37	44	58	33	44	24	24
2 Lacoste	F	27	31	37	28	23	37	40	29	11	34	18	13
3 Burberry's	UK	26	24	26	25	23	39	30	21	17	28	24	27
4 Hugo Boss	D	18	22	23	37	15	15	20	17	6	22	13	10
5 Ralph Lauren	US	16	11	16	15	12	22	15	17	13	22	11	16
6 Giorgio Armani	I	14	11	7	16	8	20	13	30	3	16	15	19
7 Daniel Hechter	F	13	17	15	29	8	10	37	9	2	7	9	3
8 Aquascutum	UK	12	7	21	9	10	8	9	18	5	13	2	27
9 Calvin Klein	US	12	11	11	15	10	11	7	8	15	14	6	19
10 Yves Saint Laurent	F	11	8	8	11	6	18	23	14	4	13	9	9

Code: Europe (EUR), Belgium (B), Switzerland (CH), Germany (D), Denmark (DK), Spain (E), France (F), Italy (I), Netherlands (NL), Portugal (P), Sweden (S), United Kingdom (UK)

Exhibit 15A **Overall Awareness and Use of Some Clothing Brands in 21 Countries, 1994 (A Young & Rubicam Brand Asset Valuator Study)**

	BENETTON		CHANEL		DIOR		ESPRIT		GAP		ARMANI		LACOSTE		YSL	
	AWARE[1]	USE[2]	AWARE	USE	AWARE	USE	AWARE	USE	AWARE	USE	AWARE	USE	AWARE	USE	AWARE	USE
Australia	59	2/81	93	4/84	94	11/73	87	7/63	12	1/93	43	2/95	74	4/65	82	16/76
Brazil	74	0/62	93	1/65	92	1/61	54	1/74	14	1/91	58	1/74	89	18/42	83	2/63
Canada	61	2/78	97	11/69	89	2/89	83	22/58	57	5/79	60	2/92	41	2/78	84	15/64
Czech Rep	69	1/77	92	3/38	91	6/36	32	1/45	23	1/70	22	0/47	51	1/57	37	2/44
France	91	8/53	98	16/64	98	14/65	21	1/96	25	2/91	37	3/91	97	24/30	99	19/58
Germany	71	8/51	80	5/66	83	3/70	68	8/54	19	1/79	44	4/72	66	4/54	63	2/71
Hungary	73	3/87	78	3/90	75	7/87	31	2/95	13	1/95	35	2/93	60	4/67	45	4/91
Italy	94	21/35	85	15/67	83	13/68	25	1/97	16	1/96	93	25/49	86	19/37	73	14/70
Japan	75	3/64	98	21/63	93	27/50	47	3/93	28	1/90	75	6/85	88	6/36	93	29/49
Mexico	54	3/81	51	1/93	42	4/86	30	0/98	9	0/98	20	1/97	29	6/85	34	5/88
Netherlands	74	1/53	93	10/70	86	5/73	66	3/41	11	0/10	36	3/31	78	2/54	78	6/64
P.R. China	19	2/95	15	1/97	23	1/98	7	0/99	11	0/99	7	0/100	9	0/99	13	1/98
Poland	40	0/81	69	2/50	58	4/52	13	0/59	9	0/76	31	2/57	27	1/70	32	2/55
Russia	17	0/99	53	4/91	67	4/91	5	1/99	11	1/98	22	1/98	22	0/93	12	1/98
S. Africa	25	3/88	29	3/91	49	13/72	56	3/89	25	1/89	12	1/97	29	2/86	22	5/88
Spain	73	9/48	85	6/69	86	7/65	28	1/79	12	2/77	55	5/72	87	18/36	59	7/66
Sweden	89	11/50	91	14/56	93	14/63	69	11/55	19	2/92	65	12/68	89	10/50	87	14/61
Switzerland	61	2/78	97	11/69	89	9/73	83	22/58	57	5/79	60	7/85	41	2/78	84	15/64
Thailand	55	3/18	51	3/25	64	5/37	14	1/6	37	2/12	23	0/12	49	6/20	39	2/17
UK	88	2/65	96	7/78	94	7/77	35	1/93	27	1/87	70	5/85	55	2/78	87	8/77
US	66	8/74	90	13/63	79	17/59	73	5/86	22	4/86	33	7/82	60	7/57	47	14/69

The data base consists of a survey of 30,000 consumers in 21 countries across 6,000 global and local brands and 120 product categories

Source: A Young & Rubicam Europe, Brand Asset Valuator Study, 1994.

[1] Awareness: respondents were asked to rate on a 7-point scale (1 = never heard of, 7 = extremely familiar) their "overall awareness of the brand as well as their understanding of what kind of product or service the brand represents". The figures correspond to the % of respondents answering 2 or above.

[2] First figure: % of respondents indicating that they "use or buy regularly/often"; 2nd figure: % of respondents indicating that they have "never used or bought".

Exhibit 15B	A Perceptual Map of Benetton, Esprit, The Gap and Lacoste in 21 Countries (A Young & Rubicam Europe, Brand Asset Valuator Survey)

<u>Method:</u> Correspondance analysis of respondents' ratings of the brand on 24 image attributes.

<u>How to read the map:</u> the further away a country is plotted from an attribute, the less the people in this country associate that attribute with the brand. Countries that are close to each other tend to have a similar perception of the brand. Two dimensional maps are presented. The % of variance explained by the third dimension is 13.1% for Benetton, 14.6% for Esprit, 12/9% for The Gap, 11.2% for Lacoste.

Benetton
% of variance explained: horizontal axis (factor 1): 39%, vertical axis (factor 2): 15.4%

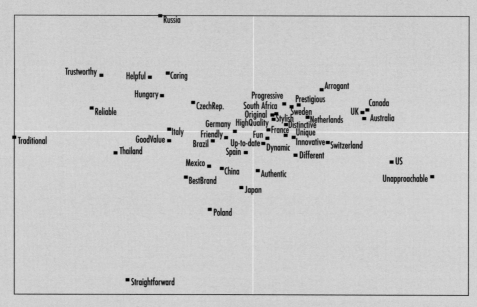

Esprit
% of variance explained: horizontal axis (factor 1): 20%, vertical axis (factor 2): 118%

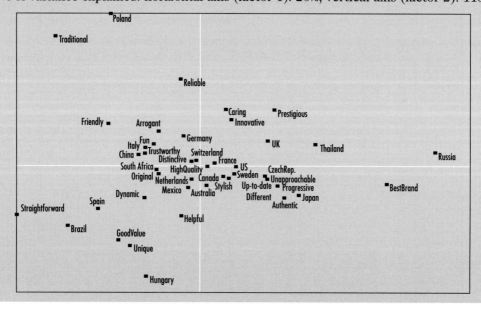

Exhibit 15B continued	A Perceptual Map of Benetton, Esprit, The Gap and Lacoste in 21 Countries (A Young & Rubicam Europe, Brand Asset Valuator Survey)

Benetton
% of variance explained: horizontal axis (factor 1): 39%, vertical axis (factor 2): 15.4%

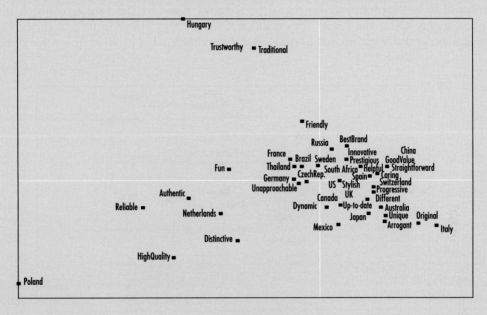

Esprit
% of variance explained: horizontal axis (factor 1): 20%, vertical axis (factor 2): 118%

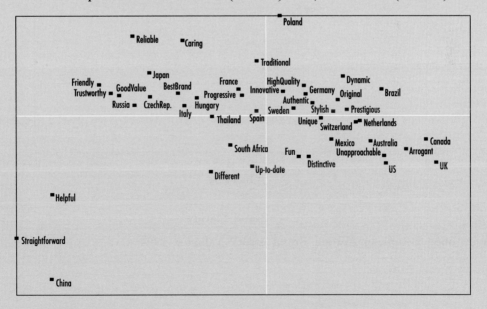

Source: Young & Rubicam Europe, Brand Asset™ Valuator, 1994

Exhibit 15C **The Benetton Brand Power Grid across 21 Countries**

<u>Methodology</u>: The Power Grid plots respondent's perceptions of a brand on two dimensions: Brand Vitality and Brand Stature. Brand Vitality is a combination of Differentiation and Relevance while Brand Stature combines Esteem and Familiarity. *Differentiation*: The extent to which the brand is perceived to be "Distinctive", "Unique" and "Different"; *Relevance*: The extent to which respondents perceive the brand to be "appropriate [for them] personally"; *Esteem*: The extent to which respondents "think or feel highly about the brand" or consider it to be "best brand in its category"; *Familiarity*: Overall awareness of the brand as well as understanding what kind of product or service the brand represents.

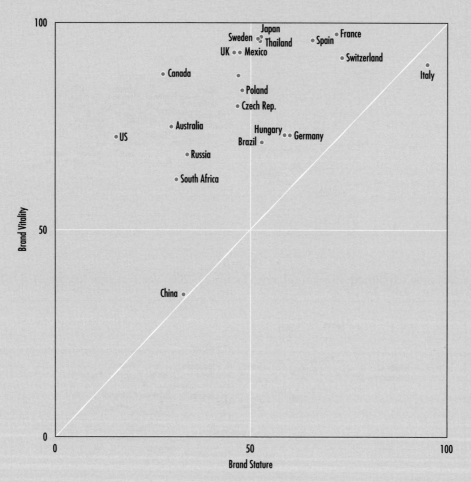

Brand Stature

<u>Source</u>: Young & Rubicam Europe, Brand Asset™ Valuator, 1994

Case Study

JAMES LLOYD

JAMES LLOYD

Mr. Walter has just taken the position of Sales Director at the Lloyd company a producer of luxury goods located in Great Britain. A quick analysis of the attractiveness of various markets and the results achieved in those markets by Lloyd, convinced Mr. Walter of the predominant need to develop the company's sales network in France. With this objective in mind, he asked a consulting firm to study Lloyd's competitive environment in France, the criteria to be used in choosing points of sale for a brand of luxury leather goods, and the different types of retailing options, from both a qualitative and a financial perspective. Mr. Walter's study brief included a description of Lloyd's development and business status in 1989.

I History of Lloyd

Birth and development

Lloyd was created in 1948 by James Lloyd, a British artisan from London, who had the inventive idea of creating golf bags using a special kind of leather he treated himself and which, after months of special treatment (the method used was kept a highly guarded secret), had the particular quality of being completely waterproof, stain-resistant and unusually soft.

His reputation on the golf circuit was quickly established and Lloyd became the most sought after craftsman in the golf world. In fact, Lloyd was the appointed supplier to the English Royal Court. He welcomed his clients, mostly members of the international jet set who came directly to his work-

This case was prepared by Frédéric Lorange under the supervision of Elyette Roux, Louis Vuitton-Moet Hennessy Professor of Marketing at ESSEC. It is the property of Elyette Roux for ESSEC and of LVMH for its own use.

The authors of the book would like to thank Professor Elyette Roux, and the LVMH group for allowing to include and reproduce the case in this book.

For confidentiality reasons some data have been disguised.

shop in London, where he hand-crafted their particular orders.

In 1954, he launched a new line of luggage (Club Line), with his expertise in the treatment and shaping of leather, Lloyd started combining together his specially treated leather with a new aesthetic look, still intended for an exceptional clientele. 1957 marked a turning point for the company Lloyd opened a boutique in London (New Bond Street). It carried a new line of matching handbags and small leather goods (Birdy Line), and began to offer its products in many different colors (red, green, blue, black). The leather was always treated in the same special way.

Sales took off at a rapid pace. Thus in 1964, Lloyd celebrated the opening of its second boutique in London (Knightsbridge). In 1965, the company opened a store in Milan. In 1967, Lloyd opened in New York and in 1969, opened its first store in Paris (Rue du Faubourg Saint-Honoré). In 1979, the company owned five stores in the most prestigious capitals of the world; the constant increase in demand could not be met; information about the products was mainly circulated by word-of-mouth, since no specific communication policy could have been defined; and finally, Lloyd held an exceptional image in the eyes of the public : a name synonymous of rarity, perfection, inaccessibility and aestheticism. A Sales Department was, therefore, created in 1979 which further stimulated the company's rapid growth.

In 1980, management set up a development policy for Lloyd, based on the following three main objectives:

↔ further internationalization and development of the sales network

↔ intensive and selective communication and advertising

↔ production control.

Further internationalization started in 1980 and consisted of two steps :

↔ Development of a sales network in South-East Asia, in particular Japan, which represented a huge potential market. The country had one of the highest saving rates in the world, Japanese tourism was beginning to take off, and Japanese were very attracted to European luxury goods and had proven to be fanatical golf lovers. Some even spent time on special practice areas fitted on the roof tops of their office buildings.

↔ Further develop the European market with the help of the cash generated by the massive success in the Asian market. Paris, New York, Milan, and London, where the number of points of sale kept growing, served as ideal showcases for Lloyd's international clientele.

This policy was very successful. Between 1980 and 1989, sales increased at a rate of 20 to 25 percent a year. In 1989, Lloyd was sold in 72 points of sales: 23 located in Japan, 18 in South East-Asia, 13 in Europe (7 in Great Britain, two in Paris, France, one in Geneva/Switzerland, two in Italy, and one in Germany), and 18 in the U.S.A.

In a majority of cases Lloyd had opted for a leased department or a corner rather than their own store, as they were a less costly alternative to company owned stores. In addition, those outlets were easier to find and to start because of readily available infrastructure and space in department stores. Table 1 shows the distribution of the total number of outlets split into corners, leased departments, and free standing stores in the major market areas in 1989.

In order to avoid a potential deterioration of Lloyd's image, due to the rapid growth of sales, an intensive communication policy had been implemented together with the development of the sales network. The main objectives of market communication were to highlight the brand's attributes: scarcity, perfection, and know-how. The policy was implemented along three main lines of direction:

↔ advertising in high profile magazines, based on themes dealing with art and nature

↔ sponsoring of prestigious events in the golf world (Golf Cup/Lloyd Trophy)

↔ patronage of master luthists (artists-artisans)

All this was done to help maintain Lloyd's exceptional image and the imagination and dream justifying the high prices of the products, while also helping to develop the sales network and the diversification towards other products: indeed, in 10 years' time, Lloyd was able to diversify its activities and enter into the production of golf umbrellas, plaids, scarves, ties, gloves, and belts, all of which were highly appreciated by consumers.

Production soon ran over the capacites available in the small Lloyd workshop in London, and was transferred to the outskirts of the city. In spite of this increase in the quantity of products produced per year during the eighties, the production itself remained unchanged: leather treatment and hand-assembly were still done the same way they had always been. At the same time however, in order to meet the growing demand and reduce production costs, some high technology procedures were installed. Lloyd was always referred to as a company specializing in "high-tech craftsmanship". In order to control the production process from the start to finish, and to insure the inherent quality of this process, no sub-contracting or licenses had been negotiated. The rare ones Lloyd had worked with in the past were rapidly bought out by the company. Today, Lloyd has full (100%) control of its production.

The Situation in 1989

In 1989, Lloyd commercializes three types of products:

Table 1 TYPES OF POINTS OF SALES BY AREA IN 1989

	JAPAN	SOUTH-EAST ASIA	EUROPE	USA	TOTAL
Free Standing Store (*)	7	12	11	2	32
Leased. Dpt. (*)	16	0	2	8	26
Corners (*)	0	6	0	8	14
TOTAL	23	18	13	18	72

(*) Definition of abbreviations and terms used in the Exhibit 1

↔ the timeless classics of the brand: the Putt and Birdy lines, which helped build the company's reputation.

↔ the fashion products: a new collection based on a central theme is launched on the market each year. In 1989, for example, Lloyd launches the Greenfield line).

↔ the diversification products : golf umbrellas, plaids, scarves, belts, gloves.

All the products feature the brand's logo, which is easily recognized because of its unique design: a golf ball embossed in the leather or on the fastener, belt buckles, etc.

Lloyd can be proud to have the image of one of the most prestigious brand names in the world. Lloyd's reputation is excellent when compared to its competitors. In England, for example, Lloyd's spontaneous notoriety is well above that of Gucci or Vuitton, and its sales are well ahead of its competitors', making Lloyd the unchallenged leader of the market (Table 2).

In the same manner, in spite of very few points of sale (only 2 in Paris), Lloyd enjoys excellent spontaneous brand awareness in France (Table 3). Lloyd's position among such international competition shows a high potential for the brand's development in countries where it is not well established yet.

Sales had increased by 20 to 25 per cent per year between 1980 and 1989. This increase was mainly due to the Japaneses' infatuation for the brand. Japanese had considerably increased their travelling abroad and related expenses (Table 4). At the end of the 1980s Japanese tourists spend the most per person when travelling (leading the Italian,

Table 2 RATES OF BRAND AWARENESS (UN-AIDED) OF THE SEVEN COMPETITOR BRANDS IN ENGLAND

	BRAND AWARENESS (UN-AIDED)		BRAND TRIAL	
	ITALY	GREAT BRITAIN	ITALY	GREAT BRITAIN
GUCCI	60%	39%	5%	21%
LLOYD	15%	62%	1%	25%
VUITTON	50%	43%	10%	13%
CARTIER	33%	35%	1%	9%
DIOR	22%	35%	1%	9%
HERMES	21%	28%	1%	14%
CHANEL	19%	29%	1%	8%

(Source: Panel January 1990)

Table 3 RATES OF BRAND AWARENESS (UN-AIDED) OF THE SEVEN COMPETITOR BRANDS IN FRANCE

	BRAND AWARENESS (UN-AIDED)	BRAND TRIAL
VUITTON	60%	7%
HERMES	52%	7%
CARTIER	23%	8%
LLOYD	7%	2%
DIOR	18%	3%
CELINE	12%	3%
CHANEL	11%	4%

(Source: Panel January 1990)

Table 4 NUMBER OF JAPANESE TRAVELLING AND EXPENSES ABROAD

YEAR	NUMBER OF PERSONS	AMOUNT SPENT ABROAD/PERSON IN USD
1980	3,909,000	
1985	4,948,000	970
1986	5,516,000 (+11%)	1,310 (+35%)
1987	6,829,000 (+24%)	1,580 (+21%)
1988	8,427,000 (+23%)	2,220 (+41%)
1989	9,663,000 (+15%)	2,330 (+5%)

(Source: JTB Report 1990)

---

the German, the French, the Swiss, and the American consumers). In 1989, their order of preferred destinations is the U.S.A., Korea, Hawaii, Hong Kong, Taiwan, Singapore, France, Germany, Guam, Thailand, Switzerland, Canada, Italy, and Great Britain. This also partially explains the great boom that Lloyd benefited from, when establishing itself massively in South East Asia. Japanese customers account for 59 per cent of Lloyd's total sales in 1989.

Table 5 shows Lloyd's total sales in 1989 broken down by geographical areas.

The company has acquired a certain financial stability, since net earnings of the company represent 13 per cent of total sales. The company now has the resources required to start the second phase of its international development: the penetration of the European market.

Customers in France

Although the original customers in England were mostly masculine, they have come to include an increasing number of women with the arrival of the fashion and diversification products. This is also true in France, where 60 per cent of customers in 1989 are women and only 40 per cent men. The market targeted is split into two groups. One group consists of those customers who buy different Lloyd products each year for the quality of their material and the finishing (8% of total sales in France). They are the opinion leaders. The other group of customers, representing 92% of total sales in France, buys the leading products of the brand as a symbol of social status. The population targeted in France is the A and A+ socio-economic categories, over 25 years old.

Only 20 per cent of Lloyd's customers in France are of French nationality. 30 per cent of sales are generated from Japanese tourists, another 30 per cent come from consumers of other European nationality, and 20 percent come from North American customers.

Table 5 BREAK DOWN OF LLOYD'S TOTAL SALES BY GEOGRAPHICAL AREAS IN 1989

GEOGRAPHICAL AREA	SHARE OF SALES
Japan	32%
South-East Asia	19%
Great Britain	16%
Europe	15% (4% in France)
USA	18%

Products of Competitors: Hermes

II The Study

The study of the consulting firm concerning the competitive environment in France, the criteria to be used in choosing points of sale for a brand of luxury leather goods, and the different types of retailing options revealed the following results.

Competition

In 1989, competitors in the French luxury leather goods market can be grouped along two dimensions, one is their history, age, origin, and control over production, the other one is the price of their products. Louis Vuitton, Hermès, Chanel, Cartier, and Loewe are comparable concerning the first dimension. Gucci and Lancel have a different background, no production of their own, but similar prices.

Hermès is the uncontested price leader in the market. Lloyd is positioned right between Cartier and Louis Vuitton. Table 6 shows a comparison of unit prices among competitors in France in 1989, the prices of Lancel hand-bags and small leather goods taken as the base line.

Table 6 COMPARISON OF UNIT PRICES AMONG LLOYD'S FIVE COMPETITORS IN FRANCE 1989

	HAND-BAGS	SMALL LEATHER GOODS	HAND-BAGS*	SMALL LEATHER GOODS
HERMES	479	802	7100	2800
CHANEL	302	372	4500	1300
CARTIER	212	287	3100	1005
LLOYD	205	243	3000	850
VUITTON	175	213	2600	745
DIOR	142	171	2100	600
LANCEL	100*	100	1500	350

(*) (BASE 100: LANCEL)

PRODUCTS OF COMPETITORS

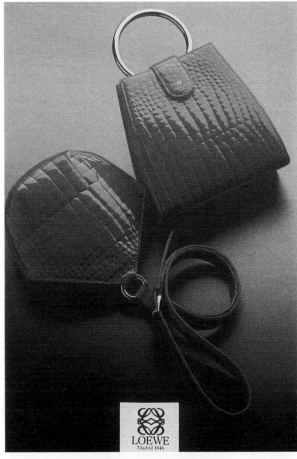

Products of Competitors: Louis Vuitton

A breakdown of total sales for this particular competitive environment is shown in Table 7. Provided that, in 1989, about 60 per cent of sales of luxury leather goods are realized in France, Italy, Japan, the UK, and the U.S.A. the figures do not take into account the sales in South East Asia and countries such as Germany or Switzerland.

The competitors' distribution was studied in two steps. First, the focus was on the number and type of points of sales in France (Table 8). At this stage, it was not possible to distinguish between company-owned stores and franchises of Hermès and Chanel. Due to the dynamism of the profession – new points of sale are frequently opened – as well as to the difficulty to count the points of sale other than stores and franchises, the figures indicated in Table 8 are only estimates.

Table 7 **BREAKDOWN OF LLOYD'S AND COMPETITORS' RETURN ON SALES (ROS) BY GEOGRAPHICAL REGION (1989)**

BRANDS	FRANCE		UK		ITALY		USA		JAPAN		TOTAL	
	ROS	%	ROS	%	ROS	%	ROS	%	ROS	%	ROS	%
HERMES	132	53%	10	4%	20	8%	47	19%	41	16%	250	100%
CHANEL	202	20%	65	6%	70	7%	405	40%	270	27%	1012	100%
CARTIER	49	14%	50	14%	70	19%	90	25%	102	28%	361	100%
LLOYD	39	5%*	155	22%	29	4%	174	25%	309	44%	705	100%
VUITTON	709	27%	75	3%	85	3%	479	18%	1248	48%	2596	100%
DIOR	118	33%	2	1%	4	1%	195	54%	41	11%	360	100%
LOEWE	9	11%	0	0%	0	0%	8	10%	67	80%	84	100%
LANCEL	417	81%	9	2%	20	4%	30	6%	36	7%	512	100%
GUCCI	37	5%	56	8%	223	30%	148	20%	269	37%	733	100%
TOTAL	1712	26%	296	4%	647	10%	1576	24%	2383	36%	6613	100%

* The difference between 4% (Table 5) and 5% (Table 7) is due to the fact that South East Asia is not taken into account.

Table 8 **DISTRIBUTION OF LLOYD'S MAJOR COMPETITORS IN FRANCE (1989 ESTIMATES)**

	FREE STANDING	FRANCHISE	CORNERS STORE	MULTIBRAND STORE	DUTY FREE	TOTAL
HERMES	<-------------19------------->		0	12	0	31
VUITTON	10	0	0	0	0	10
CHANEL	<-------------6------------->		3	0	0	9
CARTIER	13	10	0	1500	0	1523
LLOYD	2	0	0	0	0	2
DIOR	1	1	3	350	4	355
LOEWE	1	0	0	0	0	1
LANCEL	23	3	7	150	0	183

COMPETITORS' POINTS OF SALE

The second step of the distribution analysis concentrated on the distribution strategies of Lancel and Vuitton.

In 1989 Lancel used four types of retail outlets:

↔ own stores

↔ franchises

↔ multibrands

↔ duty free stores

This broad range of outlets illustrates Lancel's desire to reach the largest target market possible. But simultaneously, Lancel's desire to increase control of its distribution is expressed by the fact that the company bought back the shares in its distribution company in Japan. In 1989, Lancel controled 100 per cent of that subsidiary. The company's increasing selectivity in distribution also shows in a reduction of the number of franchises.

The choice of products offered is different depending on the type of retail outlet: in corners and multi-brand stores, one most often finds canvas luggage, which is lower priced than leather luggage and is less demanding concerning stocking and maintenance. The owners of corners and multi-brand stores buy those products from Lancel. Lancel's sales representatives visit the sales locations in order to provide them with a list of recommended retail prices andwith sales guidelines.

In contrast to Lancel, Louis Vuitton wants to have complete control over its distribution. Consequently, in France and the rest of the world, Louis Vuitton only retails through its own stores, corners or leased departments. This strategy aims at total price control, a coherent range of products, which is generally the same across all types of point of sale, as well as control over suppliers, sales force and displays on the point of sales.

Such a tight organization is quite costly in the short run and demands a highly efficient administration and reporting system (i.e. regular quantitative and qualitative reports from the sales network; turnover, stocks, promotions). Yet, this type of organization assures brand coherence on all levels, and has proven quite profitable in the long run.

Choice Criteria for setting up new stores
– The competition's location

Two brands of luxury leather goods were selected as examples for having well established points of sale throughout France: Vuitton and Hermès. Vuitton started setting up all over France in 1987, and thus, in 1989, is a good benchmark for Lloyd. Hermès has been already established throughout France and thus, can serve as a good indication of what can be achieved in a longer term.The list of points of sale of the two brands that existed in 1989 is given in Appendices 2 and 3.

Competitors' Points of Sale: Celine

Foreign tourism in France

Because 80 per cent of Lloyd's customers in Paris are foreign tourists it seems reasonable to use the number of foreign tourists as one of the selection criteria for sites where to set up shops. Appendix 4 shows a chart of the registered hotels visited by foreign tourists by region in 1987.

Selection criteria on the basis of French customers

French customers at a point of sale are composed of local and other customers of French nationality. Their shares have to be considered in the selection of a region and a particular town.

* Local component
In order to assess the opportunities a town can offer for a new point of sale in terms of local customers, many different elements have to be considered: given the targeted population category (A+/A), the following indications have been compiled and are presented in Appendix 5:

↔   total population of the city,

↔   number of commercial craftsmen, company directors, managers and higher educated professionals of the department the city belongs to,

↔   number of households with an income over 24,000 FF per month, in the department to which the city belongs,

↔   level of tennis facilities in the department,

↔   level of golf facilities in the department.

These indications are given for 10 cities (and thus 10 associated departments) divided into 2 groups: the in-land cities and the spa/seaside resorts. The chart also includes a map of France with the different levels of equipment and facilities for Tennis, Golf and indoor swimming pools for the different French departments (Appendix 6).

* National component
In order to choose the most favorable city in terms of customers from other areas of France, different indications have been compiled. Thus Appendix 4 gives French tourists' visits to registered hotels by region for 1987. In Appendix 7, one can find the number of visitors who attended fairs in 1985 and 1987 split by region. Finally, Appendices 8 and 9

show the number of visits and the number of days spent on vacation by French people by region in 1986, 1987, and 1988.

Geo-strategic criteria
Lastly, geo-strategic criteria can also be taken into consideration when choosing a town for a retail outlet. That is, political, economic, cultural, and geographical elements which could favorably influence and encourage Lloyd's sales. Appendix 10 gives the geo-strategic criteria for the following ten cities:

↔ Strasbourg	↔ Bordeaux
↔ Lyon	↔ Nice
↔ Marseilles	↔ Cannes
↔ Lille	↔ Deauville
↔ Toulouse	↔ Saint-Tropez

Analysis of different types of distribution networks in France

Qualitative analysis
To study the advantages and disadvantages of each type of distribution channel available for Lloyd's sales activities in France three types of retail outlets have been selected:

↔   short circuit:
– duty-free

↔   short contractual circuit:
– franchise
– agent (multi-brand)

↔   ultra-short circuit:
– corner
– leased department
– free standing stores (company owned stores)

In addition to the general advantages and disadvantages of the various distribution channels there are some strategic qualitative criteria that need to be taken into account. Those include the level of required in-store service, the image of the brand and the product that must be communicated to the customer, and finally the value of the product.

A special product, requiring a high standard of service, will preferably be sold either by specialized retailers, by retailers contract-bound to the producer, or by an ultra-short circuit. The more prestigious the brand image and the product, the more rigorous the selection and the control of the points of sale. It is up to the producer to establish a certain coherence between the sales circuit and the brand and product images without getting involved in legal battles as being accused of refusing to sell to a customer. The length of the circuit increases as the value of the product diminishes and vice versa. Indeed, the obstacle of a high price demands a very effective sales argument and a perfect level of service during the sale (the sales people must be completely impregnated with the culture of the company, thus often directly employed by them). Furthermore, a long circuit creates matching problems for the retailer, due to the high cost of stocks.

Simplified financial analysis of distribution networks

Lloyd usually uses three different approaches in calculating a point of sale's estimated turnover:

↔ The first approach consists of determining the size of the relevant local market for Lloyd, then calculating the size of the served target market, and finally weighing that market with an annual purchase rate per client. Since only people older than 25 years are used to buying leather goods, Lloyd considers 50 per cent of the population and 50 per cent of touristic attendances (French and foreign) of a total town market as potential customers of leather goods. From this relevant market, only 10 per cent are targeted. Lloyd's potential market share is estimated at 5 per cent. To estimate the average price of a potential sale, average prices of a Louis Vuitton sale (Appendix 3) are considered as base line and the price difference between Vuitton and Lloyd (Table 6) is taken into account. The purchase frequency of local customers is estimated to be 1/3 (one sale in three years). The purchase frequency of tourists is fixed at the same level, even if an actual tourist buys three times more than the local customers.

↔ The second approach consists of studying local competition: determining who are the main competitors, counting the number of buyers per day and store during a normal period, and finally, working out the price of an average sale based on the marked prices in the store and the type of articles bought by the customers. Based on those data, the turnover of a given store can be estimated.

Considering the price level of the brand as compared to major competitors and Lloyd's relative brand attractiveness a second turnover figure can be estimated (Appendix 3).

↔ A third approach consists of calculating turnover figures on the basis of standard profitability rates of the industry. Thus, an average sales outlet for luxury goods should meet the following levels:
  – Turnover/sales person = around 2 MFRF/year
  – Turnover/M2 = 80.000 FRF/year

By combining the three estimates, and by observing the principal of caution, Lloyd estimates and compares the potential turnover of points of sale in various locations.

To determine the potential profitability of its previous operations Lloyd has used the following ratio :

$$ROC = \frac{NR}{CE}$$

$$\Rightarrow ROC = \frac{NR}{TS} \times \frac{TS}{CE}$$

ROC = return on capital employed
NR = net result
TS = total sales
CE = capital employed

Net results have been calculated based on the following figures:

FIRST GROUP

↔ Duty-free:
Result = Gross margin – distribution costs (1% of total sales) Gross margin = 18%

↔ Multi-brand retailers:
The result is obtained the same way as for the Duty-free stores.

↔ Franchises:
Result = Gross margin + Royalties (3%–5% of unit turnover) – Participation in setting up, store arrangements, merchandising costs (generally 30 % of total costs) – Distribution costs.

> ## SECOND GROUP
>
> ↔ Corner:
> Result = Gross margin − distribution costs
>
> ↔ Leased department:
> Result = Unit margin − Rent Department Store (25 to 35% of turnover)
> – Salary of head sales woman (about 10.000 FRF per month + social charges)
> – Stock financing (3 months' worth of tax free turnover)
>
> The unit margin can be estimated to be between 40 and 60 percent, which corresponds to a multiplying coefficient between 1,7 and 2,3.
>
> ↔ Company owned store:
> Result = Unit margin
>   – Sales costs (1)
>   – Advertising costs (2)
>   – Administrative costs (3)
>   – Financial costs (4)

↔ (1) Sales costs: three main costs equal 75% of these:

- rent of the boutique: for 100m² of selling surface, one can estimate a yearly rate of 2,000 to 3,000 FRF/m².
- salary of sales people (their number depends on the size of the store): on average, a sales person costs 120,000 FRF per year + all social charges.
- yearly redemption : one can estimate a right to lease between 5,000 FRF to 10,000 FRF, plus standard computer equipment and some work on the store between 2,000 FRF and 3,000 FRF; the annual cost is between 650,000 and 1.100,000 FRF.

↔ (2) Advertising costs:
- they must not exceed 5% of turnover.

↔ (3) Administrative costs :
- they represent about 10% of turnover.

↔ (4) Financial costs :
- they must not exceed 7% of turnover, tax included.

Following a rule of thumb, a brand of luxury leather goods with total yearly sales up to 1 million FRF is best sold in a corner. If total sales reach 1 to 5 million FRF, a leased department is more appropriate; if total sales are above 5 million FRF, it is best to open a self-owned store.

Mr. Walter's Decision

Based on the information produced by the survey he has ordered, Mr. Walter needs to define his future actions. He wonders if he should pursue further development of the French market, and if yes, what channels and locations to choose in this highly competitive market. Special care will be needed to prepare the figures to convince top management of the financial soundness of the proposed decision.

APPENDIX 1
DEFINITION OF ABBREVIATIONS AND TERMS USED

Free Standing Store
Company owned store, ie. stores entirely owned by the manufacturer.
Average sales surface: 80 to 120 m².

Leased Department
A sales area rented to a specific brand by a department store, called a "shop-in-shop". In general, the area is laid out in the same way as a company owned store (same decoration and colour codes). The brand pays a royalty to the department store which takes into account the rental cost of the area in question, the amortization of material, etc. Stock management and wages of sales personnel are the brand's reponsibility
Average sales surface: 60 m²

Corner (or "counter")
A limited area inside the store where the brand has its own signalization. The brand sells its products to the department store wholesale. Stock as well as sales personnel are managed by the department store. As for a leased department, the sales area is often decorated according to the brand's usual appearance.
Average sales surface: 30 m².

APPENDIX 2
LIST OF HERMES POINTS OF SALES IN FRANCE

PARIS 75008
24, rue du Faubourg Saint-Honoré

PARIS 75015
Hôtel Hilton
18, avenue de Suffren

Airports:
ORLY SUD
ORLY OUEST
CHARLES DE GAULLES – ROISSY 1 (Ladies)
CHARLES DE GAULLES – ROISSY 1 (Men)

AIX-EN-PROVENCE 13100
23 bis, rue Thiers

AVIGNON 84000
18, rue Saint-Agricol

BIARRITZ 64200
Avenue Edouard VII

BEAULIEU-SUR-MER 06310
Hermès chez MADAM
Port de plaisance

BORDEAUX 33000
6, place Gambetta

CANNES 06400
17, La Croisette

DEAUVILLE 14800
Place du Casino

DIJON 21000
6, place Grangier

LILLE 59000
8, rue Grande-Chaussée

LYON 69002
95, rue du Président Henriot

MARSEILLE 13006
93D, rue Paradis

MEGEVE 74120
Hermès at JEAN D'ARBOIS
2, place de l'Eglise

METZ 57000
5, rue des Clercs

MONTPELLIER 34000
7, rue Jacques-Coeur

MULHOUSE 68100
6E, rue du Mittelbach

NANCY 54000
Hermès chez MISS LORENZO
21, rue Gambetta

NANTES 44000
2, rue Crébillon

NICE 06000
Aéroport international

Hermès chez MADAM
22, avenue Jean Médecin

Hermès chez MADAM
2, rue Paradis

PERPIGNAN 66000
Hermès chez ARINTA
17, rue de l'Argenterie

QUIMPER 29000
5, rue de la Halle

RENNES 35000
6, rue Lafayette

ROUEN 76000
5, rue du Change

SAINT-TROPEZ 83990
7, rue de la Ponche

STRASBOURG 67000
2, rue de la Mésange

TOULOUSE 31000
5, rue de la Pomme

TOURS 37000
Hermès chez KORRIGAN
9, rue des Halles

APPENDIX 3
LIST OF LOUIS VUITTON'S POINTS OF SALES IN FRANCE

TOWN	TYPE	SURFACE AREA (M²)	NB Customers /Days	Average price of sales
PARIS (Marceau)	M.P. (*)	NC (**)	NC	NC
PARIS (Montagne)	M.P.	NC	NC	NC
BORDEAUX	M.P.	80	15	1550
LYON	M.P.	110	22	1700
TOULOUSE	M.P.	70	13	1500
STRASBOURG	M.P.	80	12	1200
DEAUVILLE	M.P.	60	16	1400
NICE	M.P.	95	21	1500
CANNES	M.P.	95	20	1450
MONACO	M.P.	NC	NC	NC

(*) M.P.: Free standing store = Company owned store
(**) NC: Non comparable

APPENDIX 4
NUMBER OF NIGHTS SPENT IN CLASSIFIED HOTELS (1987)

	FRENCH (IN THOUSAND)		FOREIGN (IN THOUSAND)	
	ARRIVALS	NIGHTS	ARRIVALS	NIGHTS
Ile-de-France	5908	12010	5962	15509
Champagne-Ardenne	734	1072	424	509
Picardie	721	1060	311	421
Haute-Normandie	955	1602	229	399
Centre	1892	2661	911	1274
Basse-Normandie	1053	1868	328	514
Bourgogne	1789	2343	1133	1373
Nord-Pas-de-Calais	1293	2074	413	612
Lorraine	1300	2351	267	394
Alsace	1523	2761	759	1328
Franche-Comté	737	1316	187	245
Pays de la Loire	NC	NC	NC	NC
Bretagne	2817	4472	523	968
Poitou-Charentes	1015	2247	127	225
Aquitaine	3264	5474	517	896
Midi-Pyrénées	2855	6496	759	2137
Limousin	612	942	100	133
Rhône-Alpes	6159	13778	1706	3106
Auvergne	1207	2832	115	203
Languedoc-Roussillon	2531	4844	815	1397
Provence-Alpes-Côte d'Azur	4537	11571	2005	5274
Corse	137	390	150	533

Source: Direction de l'Industrie Touristique.

APPENDIX 5
SOCIO-ECONOMIC DATA (1989)

	TOWN POPULATION (IN THOUSANDS)	NUMBER OF HOUSEHOLDS IN THE DEPARTMENT WITH INCOMES ≥ 24000 FRS (IN THOUSANDS)	WEALTH INDEX NUMBER OF MANAGERS, LIBERAL PROF., AND ENTREPRENEURS IN THE DEPARTMENT (IN THOUSANDS)	DEPARTMENTAL FACILITIES	
				TENNIS COURSES	GOLF COURSES
Main towns					
LYON (69)	535	66.7	115.5	− −	+ +
MARSEILLE (13)	893	63.6	117.7	+ +	− +
LILLE (59)	194	69.2	134.9	+ +	−
STRASBOURG (67)	254	34.0	56.4	+	− −
BORDEAUX (33)	271	53.6	83.3	+ +	+ +
TOULOUSE (31)	380	38.0	68.9	+ +	− −
Sea resort					
NICE (06)	325	68.3	76.4	− −	+ +
CANNES (06)	68	68.3	76.4	− −	+ +
DEAUVILLE (14)	5	21.0	36.7	− +	− −
SAINT TROPEZ (83)	6	44.9	55.9	− +	−

Source: Proscop Média Data 1989.

France is split into a number of administrative areas called departments. The figures given in ( ) are the numbers of those departments; e.g. Nice belongs to department 06, Alpes Maritimes.

APPENDIX 6

DEPARTMENTAL FACILITIES IN TERMS OF GOLF COURSES, COVERED TENNIS COURTS AND COVERED SWIMMING POOLS (1989)

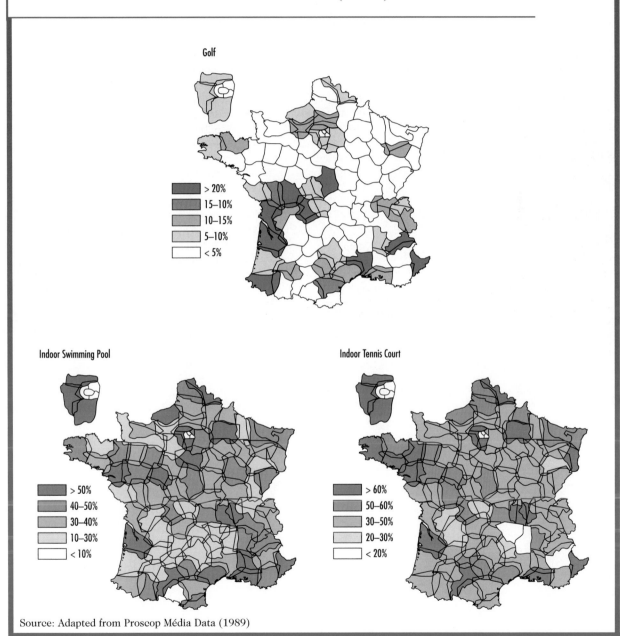

Golf

> 20%
15–10%
10–15%
5–10%
< 5%

Indoor Swimming Pool

> 50%
40–50%
30–40%
10–30%
< 10%

Indoor Tennis Court

> 60%
50–60%
30–50%
20–30%
< 20%

Source: Adapted from Proscop Média Data (1989)

Appendix 7
Fair Attendance by Region

Regions	1986	1987	1988
Ile-de-France	1 103 439	1 036 067	920 091
Champagne-Ardenne	310 405	230 932	332 862
Picardie	737 485	43 244	47 662
Haute-Normandie	180 693	154 768	146 522
Centre	93 130	99 629	97 606
Basse-Normandie	301 130	283 736	308 753
Bourgogne	419 923	389 691	363 311
Nord-Pas-de-Calais	364 132	317 784	397 072
Lorraine	352 100	381 284	368 607
Alsace	775 947	620 607	665 805
Franche-Comté	161 022	179 792	159 137
Pays de la Loire	562 988	596 723	630 133
Bretagne	515 638	534 013	447 766
Poitou-Charentes	390 266	346 370	368 665
Aquitaine	725 707	620 607	665 805
Midi-Pyrénées	443 451	440 768	400 877
Limousin	112 665	183 970	100 237
Rhône-Alpes	1 361 001	1 381 037	1 289 207
Auvergne	116 048	125 819	122 958
Languedoc-Roussillon	264 807	302 659	291 668
Provence-Alpes-Côte d'Azur	1 062 749	830 039	928 789
Corse	—	—	—
Total France	9 654 726	9 233 704	9 152 381
Number of Fairs	92	86	86

Source: Fédération des Foires et Salons de France.

APPENDIX 8
FRENCH SUMMER VACATION DESTINATIONS IN TERMS OF NUMBER OF FRENCH CUSTOMER ARRIVALS

		(UNIT: THOUSAND)	
REGIONS	1986	1987	1988
Ile-de-France	812	582	762
Champagne-Ardenne	289	289	266
Picardie	380	368	341
Haute-Normandie	449	338	526
Centre	759	690	653
Basse-Normandie	1057	1011	942
Bourgogne	430	645	639
Nord-Pas-de-Calais	549	754	686
Lorraine	584	429	545
Alsace	341	426	364
Franche-Comté	351	638	443
Pays de la Loire	2457	2422	2617
Bretagne	2564	2623	2519
Poitou-Charentes	1607	1682	1715
Aquitaine	2545	2783	2898
Midi-Pyrénées	1550	1875	1614
Limousin	423	496	507
Rhône-Alpes	2958	3137	3218
Auvergne	1238	970	1261
Languedoc-Roussillon	3794	3889	3945
Provence-Alpes-Côte d'Azur	4367	4780	4859
Corse	748	672	632
Total France	30 252	31 499	31 952
DOM-TOM*	99	73	150

Source: INSEE T.8.17.

* DOM-TOM is an abbreviation for French overseas departments

Appendix 9
French Customers' Summer Vacations in Terms of Number of Days

REGIONS	1986	(Unit: thousand) 1987	1988
Ile-de-France	10 225	6888	9890
Champagne-Ardenne	4430	3495	4248
Picardie	7443	5548	5193
Haute-Normandie	9297	6068	9149
Centre	11 757	10 004	10 827
Basse-Normandie	19 295	18 422	15 807
Bourgogne	9659	13 135	10 382
Nord-Pas-de-Calais	9902	10 667	11 610
Lorraine	8850	6310	8128
Alsace	5549	5200	4792
Franche-Comté	5232	9312	6648
Pays de la Loire	46 624	45 280	48 215
Bretagne	47 692	46 653	45 892
Poitou-Charentes	31 159	30 318	30 232
Aquitaine	44 430	48 945	50 140
Midi-Pyrénées	28 943	33 351	27 897
Limousin	7971	9566	8501
Rhône-Alpes	49 770	51 752	51 945
Auvergne	19 730	18 131	22 460
Languedoc-Roussillon	67 502	65 585	68 322
Provence-Alpes-Côte d'Azur	79 433	84 139	87 589
Corse	17 173	13 756	11 957
Total France	541 066	542 505	549 824
DOM-TOM*	4839	3104	4341

Source: INSEE T.8.17.

APPENDIX 10
GEOGRAPHIC-STRATEGIC CHARACTERISTICS OF 10 FRENCH TOWNS

Strasbourg:	– European Council – Germany proximity – Industrial center (chemical, agricultural production) – Harbour (Rhin)
Lyon:	– Connection Paris – South Region – Many events each year – Rhône Alpes Center – Winter Olympic Games (1992)
Marseille:	– Important harbour for French Trade – Important harbour for Travelers (Africa) – Industrial center
Lille:	– Benelux proximity
Bordeaux:	– Five important fairs per year – Attractive harbour: tropical products importations – Wine trade
Toulouse:	– Industrial center
Nice:	– Famous touristic station – Travel harbour – International airport – MIDTV events
Cannes:	– Famous touristic destination – Many cultural events (Festival du Cinéma, Midem)
Deauville:	– Famous touristic destination – Many events (Topcom, Festival du film américain)
Saint-Tropez:	– Famous touristic destination – 'Show-biz environment'

APPENDIX 11
OPERATING FORECAST

	AMOUNT	%
Net sales		100%
Cost of goods		
Gross margin		
Selling expenses		
Communication expenses		
Administrative expenses		
Total operating costs		
Operating income		
Financial costs		
Pretax income		
Taxes		
Total net income		

Case Study

VAN LEER PACKAGING WORLDWIDE: THE TOTAL ACCOUNT (A)

VAN LEER PACKAGING WORLDWIDE: THE TOTAL ACCOUNT

On June 21, 1995 at 12.34 Claude Hoareau, Business Unit Manager of Van Leer Steel Drums, a division of Van Leer France, received a copy of a message faxed from the Lubricants department at Groupe TOTAL to Van Leer's headquarters in the Netherlands. It read:

> "[We] are still very concerned by the proposed unit prices in France, and outside of France, which look rather high. Please investigate the possibility of further improvement. We would still like to continue our European relationship and do hope that you may be in a position to offer some improvements."

TOTAL was one of the largest French multinationals and the world's ninth oil company. A loss of the TOTAL account would be a serious blow to Hoareau and to Van Leer France. Hoareau had expected this account to supply 6% of expected sales in 1995.

The message was disheartening news for Hoareau, especially as he had spoken to TOTAL's buyer, Paul Laveissiere, earlier that morning and had faxed to Amstelveen,

> "As far as Van Leer France is concerned we are not in too bad a position. The final decision will be based on the proposal for Europe and not only for France. Laveissiere is totally unhappy with our last proposal, mainly due to the UK situation, aren't we interested in TOTAL UK?"

This case was written by David Weinstein, Professor of Marketing at INSEAD, with the assistance of Alain Debenedetti, Research Assistant. It is intended to be used as a basis for class discussion rather than to illustrate either effective or ineffective handling of an administrative situation.

Copyright © 1996 INSEAD, Fontainebleau, France.

The issue was also of great concern to Johan Ten Cate, Manager of International Accounts at Van Leer's corporate headquarters in the Netherlands. to whom the fax had been addressed. Ten Cate himself wondered whether a loss of TOTAL was not a symptom of the problem that Van Leer encountered in serving and retaining even larger global accounts. Some of these companies had already been in touch with him, "showing their teeth" and demanding significant global discounts and other benefits.

VAN LEER

Royal Packaging Industries Van Leer was founded in 1919 by Bernard Van Leer. From the outset, the company's capital belonged entirely to The Van Leer Foundation, a philanthropic association subject to Royal Dutch decree and legislation, funding special programs for socially and culturally impaired children. Van Leer began manufacturing steel drums in the Netherlands in 1925, launching into closure systems in 1927. By the 1930s the company was already the European leader for both of these products and by the 1940s it had established its presence in seven countries, across three continents.

In the '60s and '70s Van Leer expanded its product lines to flexible packaging, using paper and plastic materials, which facilitated the group's penetration into the consumer goods sector. The '80s marked a whole new expansion phase via a series of acquisitions, broadening Van Leer's scope of activities. In 1992, a new milestone was set in the company's mass consumer goods packaging with the acquisition from Unilever of 4P, its packaging subsidiary.

Van Leer's worldwide sales for 1994 reached NFL 3.958 billion (approximately $2.5 billion), a 3% growth from 1993. Profits soared that year to NFL 67 million. The company employed some 16,000 people across the globe, half of them in

Europe. Van Leer held 25% of the world's large steel drum sales that year. Exhibit 1 includes Van Leer's consolidated financial statements for 1994.

Products, Countries and Clients

In 1994, industrial packaging activities represented 46.3% of Van Leer's total sales, the main industrial end uses being industrial liquids such as chemicals and lubricants. Steel drum production accounted for 35% of Van Leer's global sales and for 74% of its industrial packaging division.

Steel drums being a very voluminous product, they were historically manufactured close to the clients' production sites. Van Leer's traditional approach to new international markets was dictated by a simple motto: "Wherever you need us, we go". Van Leer relied on its client relationships to set up factories abroad, giving it a foothold both in strong economies as well as in emerging markets. In 1994, a score of new contracts led Van Leer to set up operations in Russia, China and Costa Rica.

Van Leer was the only player in the steel drum industry to operate on such a worldwide scale, boasting a solid presence across five continents: 130 factories in 41 countries. In 1994, 57.9% of Van Leer's sales were in Europe, 22.5% in North America and Mexico, 7.9% in Australia and the Far East, 6.4% in Central and South America, and 5.3% in Africa.

Van Leer's client base was highly diversified. The company prided itself on being both a supplier for large multinational concerns, especially large chemical and oil giants, smaller multinationals and at the same time local family-owned businesses. Exhibit 2 presents some of the steel drum sales figures by major clients.

Organization

Van Leer's management genuinely reflected its international aspirations, with every executive board member being of a different nationality (see Exhibit 3). The company was organized in autonomous Strategic Business Units, some spanning product categories and others, geographical area (see Exhibit 4). Each business unit acted as a profit center with the objective of exploiting opportunities in its own area of responsibility. The business unit's performance was evaluated in this light, and financial rewards, in bonus and other payments, were granted accordingly. A manager's annual bonus could reach up to 30% of his or her annual income, some of it based on SBU performance and the rest on the BU performance. This structure had been designed to fit the international and diverse Van Leer markets.

The Steel Drum Market

The steel drum market developed in tandem with the oil extraction and refinery boom, since steel drums were the most practical way to transport and ship oil. The market was characterized by its numerous suppliers, primarily local companies serving local manufacturing sites using standard drums, but also companies developing highly specific products. The most frequently used drum was the 213 liter format, Van Leer having a market share of approximately 25% for this item.

In 1995, the steel drum market reached 150 million units sold worldwide. On the whole, the market was growing very slightly at a rate of approximately 1% a year. Nonetheless, there appeared to be significant growth disparities among regions. In Europe, which accounted for one third of the whole market, consumption had been decreasing at an annual rate of 1 to 2% since 1989. In the US, consumption had remained stable for the past ten years and no changes were anticipated. US consumption consistently accounted for 20–25% of worldwide consumption. The outlook for emerging markets such as China and Latin America was, however, optimistic.

The steel drum industry was unique in that it included both new and reconditioned drums. The cost of a reconditioned drum was about 70 to 80% of a new one, including collection, cleaning, repair and reassembly, and it could be reused several times.

The cost structure of a steel drum was as follows: steel – 50%, labor just under 10%, paint and lacquers – 9%, closures – 8%, transport – 6% and overhead and depreciation about 17%. Given the proportion of steel content, drum makers followed the price of steel vigilantly, attempting to pass on price increases to their customers through escalation clauses in drum supply contracts. Between the first quarter of 1994 and the final quarter of 1995 the price of steel shot up from $355 to $590 per ton.

Competition

In 1994, Van Leer was the only truly global steel drum manufacturer in the world. Competitors either stayed mainly within their territories or formed international alliances, in an effort to compete for multinational accounts. In Europe, Van Leer held a market share of 37% in 1995. One European competitor was Blagden, the British company holding 20% of the European market. While being second in new drums, Blagden led in reconditioned drums with a market share in Europe of 35%. Another major competitor in Europe was Gallay-Mauser, the Franco-German organization holding the No. 3 position in Europe, with 12% market share, and the No. 1 position in France and Germany.

Other types of containers were increasingly competing with steel drums, especially since the price of steel surpassed the $450 per ton threshold. At this level, steel drum manufacturers were no longer able to transfer the rising costs of steel to their clients. Hence, plastic and fiber packaging became viable substitutes for many applications. The result was that some steel drum manufacturers had to close down while the slightly more fortunate ones had to bite the bullet and increase productivity.

Customer Needs and Differentiation

The drum is a critical product for any chemical or oil company. It not only stores but also facilitates transportation of goods, especially since drums may use pallets for storage and transportation and may be rolled. With many customers going through reengineering and rationalization of their logistics, steel drum manufacturers were expecting pressure from their clients, in the form of demand for lower prices, better quality, as well as trying to shift the inventory of empty drums upstream.

Product differentiation in steel drums was difficult as the manufacturing process was widely accessible and easy to imitate. However some clients had specific needs of cleanliness, internal coatings of the drums, closure standards, external color and drum size mix, allowing price premiums. Traditionally, Van Leer managers had felt that their organization's global presence was a source of differentiation, assuring customers with standards of quality, service and responsiveness that local manufacturers could not match.

Van Leer's Strategy

Van Leer's management was sensitive to the following trends: global client companies were (1) transferring production to cheaper and emerging economies, (2) consolidating their purchasing into the hands of fewer suppliers in order to achieve price advantages, and (3) seeking to rationalize the range of their packaging material. According to Van Leer senior executives, these trends would result in both a lower demand for steel drums in parts of Europe and a smaller number of competitors. They felt that these pressures would require both an efficient cooperation among the business units of Van Leer on international contracts, and a review of the product range.

The position of Manager of International Accounts was created in October, 1994, as Van Leer's response to pressure by international accounts. Ten Cate, an executive with more than 30 years' experience in the company, was appointed to this position. Although Ten Cate did not have formal authority over local managers, he commanded extensive knowledge, experience, personal networking and respect inside the Van Leer organization, in the packaging industry and within the client base. Management expected his background, together with his personal sensitivity and negotiating skills, to enable Ten Cate to contribute to Van Leer's continued success with international accounts as their purchasing process evolved.

The TOTAL Account

Groupe TOTAL was the ninth largest oil concern in the world and one of the largest and most visible French companies. Its sales reached $27 billion in 1994. TOTAL was well established in a number of fields and its activities were quite diversified: oil and natural gas extraction, refinery and distribution, crude oil and oil derivatives, trading, production of chemical products such as resins, paints and inks and more. Established across five continents, TOTAL was still a growing empire, operating in 80 countries and boasting sound financial health and many years of experience in all its fields of activity.

TOTAL Lubricants was one of the company's profit centers. The division was broken down into three units: two departments devoted to selling automobile and insutrial lubricants and the third functioning as a cost center. The latter was called

FAL (Manufacturing Purchasing Logistics) and was "selling" the products and services that it sourced-in, at internal transfer prices, to the other two "selling" departments. The Purchasing department was in turn subdivided into three units: Packaging, Raw Materials and Special Materials.

In the final months of 1994, TOTAL went through a worldwide reengineering effort at the initiative of its president. Consolidating international purchasing was part of this scrutiny, through which the company expected to reduce the types of drums bought, thus standardizing and cutting costs. A senior executive at TOTAL commented:

> "We were hoping, through the consolidation, to also instill genuine collaboration between TOTAL and its suppliers, in the form of advice, assistance, technical information and perhaps deeper forms of collaboration, involving R & D."

Jean-Claude Delvallée, who managed Purchasing, embarked on the reengineering effort together with an internal TOTAL consultant, Michael Chouarain, who joined the Lubricants department temporarily for the duration of the reengineering project. Chouarain would participate, with Delvallée, in implementing purchasing strategy as well as in negotiating with major suppliers. Their message was that every supplier would have to: (1) offer goods on an international scale, (2) factor in TOTAL's international standards requirements, (3) keep track of sales volumes and negotiate globally via a single representative. A third purchasing manager, Hal Swinson, who represented TOTAL in North America, joined the two in the contact with global suppliers.

As in many international companies, globalizing purchasing activities was not an easy task. Globalization typically came after a competitive price had been reached locally, based on local competitive conditions and the establishment of personal relationships. In some cases global contracts would indeed obtain significant price reductions, beyond the ability of local organizations. However, market conditions in other markets could provide better local conditions that global purchasing could obtain. This phenomenon created resistance by some countries to comply with a global arrangement negotiated by headquarters. Commenting on this, a senior manager at TOTAL said:

> "We too have our problems of globalization. As local purchasing has an effect on local performance evaluation, we risk interfering with local relationships with suppliers. Clearly a manger would not like headquarters to impose prices and relationships on him or her, especially when these could potentially hurt local performance. Like all organizations, TOTAL will find the way to overcome this local resistance."

December 13, 1994

December 13, 1994 was the day it all started. A seemingly innocent letter arrived at Van Leer France signed by TOTAL's Delvallée. In it, he explained that TOTAL had decided to pursue a global purchasing policy for steel drums, for all its subsidiaries worldwide. Under this new approach, TOTAL announced that it would soon be contacting Van Leer to explore possibilities for "potential collaboration". The letter also said,

> "We also inform you that our Request For Quote [RFQ] which would have been applicable starting January 1995 is now frozen, and ask you to maintain current drum prices through March 31, 1995".

Hoareau, the Business Unit Manager of Steel Drums at Van Leer France, authorized his commercial director, to whom TOTAL's letter had been addressed, to issue the following response:

> "We thank you for associating our group with the globalizing of Groupe TOTAL's needs. We are clearly at your service and will cooperate fully with your analysis. Nevertheless you certainly know that our industry has been subject to the spectacular price hikes of steel [the price of steel rose by 15% in 1994]. That is why were were forced to readjust our prices starting January 1, 1995. We cannot endanger our operation's survival and regret that we are unable to satisfy your request for a price freeze. We ask that you consider the price we quoted in response to your recent RFQ as applicable starting January 1, 1995. We trust that you will understand our reasoning."

Meeting in Amstelveen

Ten Cate hosted the meeting with TOTAL at Van Leer's worldwide headquarters in Amstelveen on

January 13, 1995. Beforehand he had collected the necessary data pertaining to Van Leer's sales volume to TOTAL in different countries, as grounds for the discussion. The UK and France were clearly the two major European countries in TOTAL's steel drum purchasing. TOTAL was represented by Delvallée, Chouarain, and also by the American, Swinson. Hoareau came over from France to join the meeting.

Swinson, who was responsible for Purchasing in the US, was TOTAL's most active spokesperson. After having outlined the company's activities, he presented the highlights of the global steel drum purchasing plan, akin to the one already implemented in the United States. TOTAL was seeking to obtain (1) best prices at each location, based on the overall purchasing volume for the group, (2) all quoted prices would be firm for one year, with a multi-year proposal including cost escalation clauses for raw material starting only in the second year, (3) an annual rebate based on global purchasing levels, and (4) suppliers were asked to include information on their quality assurance and drum collecting facilities.

Later Ten Cate commented on this meeting,

"It was strange that the most active member of the three TOTAL executives was Swinson. Delvallée continued to act as the "old friend and elder statesman" sitting back and leaving Swinson the stage. Chouarain was totally silent and gave me the impression that he would rather not be there and was forced by someone to be present at this meeting."

Preparation of the Proposal

On January 17, 1995, following the meeting in Amstelveen, Ten Cate dispatched a message to all Van Leer subsidiaries, launching the preparation of his proposal to TOTAL. This note first contained a copy of TOTAL's presentation (see Exhibit 5) and TOTAL's European steel drums consumption plan for 1995:

Germany	45,000
Spain	17,000
France	458,000
Italy	23,000
UK	316,000
Sweden	13,000

Additionally, the note indicated that his proposal to TOTAL would include six European countries and establish a cumulative discount policy on all purchasing in Europe. Emphasizing the importance of this market for Van Leer, which meant 872,000 new drums per annum, Ten Cate instructed all the subsidiaries to contact their local TOTAL representatives for specifics on drum types and quantities they anticipated.

Ten Cate knew that TOTAL was having similar discussions with Van Leer's competitors. Van Leer's UK steel drum manager told him that (1) the relationship between Van Leer's management and TOTAL's in the UK was very strong, (2) Van Leer UK's price was competitive, and (3) Van Leer UK felt that TOTAL *in Paris* would not be able to "impose a supplier" on their UK subsidiary.

Based on his discussions with Van Leer subsidiaries, and on his knowledge of the market, Ten Cate was hoping that the competition would not offer more than comparable international discounts, while maintaining existing market prices.

Ten Cate was impressed by the attitude of Van Leer France to the situation. Hoareau took TOTAL's reengineering effort very seriously, especially in view of a new manager, Paul Laveissiere, designated to succeed Delvallée. Unlike the British, the French thought that this was not "business as usual" and the new purchasing team at TOTAL represented a real threat. Ten Cate had not met the new purchasing manager and relied on Hoareau for information and impressions.

Exhibit 1 Van Leer's Consolidated Financial Statements for 1993–1994

As at December 31, 1994 (after profit appropriation)

(NLG. 000)	1994		1993	
Assets employed:				
Tangible fixed assets				
Cost value	3,325,879		3,443,947	
Accumulated depreciation	(1,881,311)		(1,898,492)	
		1,444,568		1,545,455
Financial fixed assets				
Minority participations	4,360		1,117	
Loans	7,102		9,445	
		11,462		10,562
Total fixed assets		1,456,030		1,556,017
Current assets				
Stocks	534,256		508,867	
Debtors	717,320		668,125	
Cash and banks	39,588		49,715	
Total current assets	1,291,164		1,226,707	
Creditors	(714,169)		(645,072)	
Net working capital		576,995		581,635
Net capital employed		2,033,025		2,137,652
Financed by:				
Medium and long-term loans	662,331		400,201	
Banks	161,812		498,801	
Provisions for liabilities and charges		824,143		899,002
Unfunded pension liabilities and similar obligations	263,547		263,005	
Deferred taxes	139,438		140,791	
Sundry	141,528		152,759	
Capital and reserves		544,513		556,555
Shareholder's equity	502,464		514,958	
Third party interest in subsidiaries	161,905		167,137	
Total shareholder's funds		664,369		682,095
Financing capital		2,033,025		2,137,652

FOR THE YEAR ENDED DECEMBER 31, 1994
(NLG. 000)

	1994	1993
Net sales to third parties	3,957,640	3,844,497
Movement in stocks	15,327	(28,906)
Proceeds of production	3,972,967	3,815,591
Consumption direct materials	(1,798,180)	(1,638,026)
Value added	2,174,787	2,177,565
Operating costs	(1,968,712)	(1,979,966)
Gross operating result	206,075	197,599
Interest expenses	(63,840)	(75,927)
Foreign exchange results	(5,806)	4,518
Operating profit before taxation	136,429	126,190
Taxation on operating profit	(41,459)	(44,484)
Net operating profit	94,970	81,706
Net extraordinary expenses	(13,102)	(18,961)
Profit after taxation	81,868	62,745
Third party interest	(14,844)	(15,252)
Net income	67,024	47,493

Exhibit 2 **Steel Drum Sales by Selected Global Client in 1995 (in NFL '00,000s)**

	STEEL DRUMS EUROPE	NORTH AMERICA	SOUTH AMERICA	ASIA	AFRICA	AUSTRALIA	WORLDWIDE
Shell Oil/Chemical	36.20	1.00	1.00	7.00	4.10	0.60	49.90
ICI	31.60	4.50	—	0.50	0.70	3.90	41.20
Dow Chemical	13.60	6.50	0.60	9.00	—	0.30	30.00
Mobil	14.20	2.40	—	6.10	—	6.60	29.30
BASF	18.30	9.60	0.20	1.00	—	—	29.10
Dow Corning	2.20	18.90	—	—	—	—	21.10
Elf/Atochem	16.50	1.00	—	1.50	—	—	19.00
PPG	5.50	12.00	—	—	—	—	17.50
Burmah/Castrol	8.70	4.50	—	2.20	—	1.40	16.80
Esso/Exxon	13.40	—	0.40	1.90	—	0.30	16.00
DSM (Chemical & Resin)	15.30	—	—	—	—	—	15.30
Rhone Poulenc	13.30	0.60	0.40	—	—	0.30	14.60
AKZO/Nobel	12.70	1.30	0.20	0.30	—	—	14.50
BP	11.60	—	—	1.00	1.90	—	14.50
Texaco	4.10	—	6.60	3.80	—	—	14.50
Bayer	7.60	0.80	4.00	0.70	—	—	13.10
Witco	6.30	6.50	—	—	—	—	12.80
Rohm and Haas	5.00	7.30	0.40	—	—	—	12.70
Monsanto	2.30	7.30	0.20	—	0.40	—	10.20
Total Oil/Chem/Bostik	5.90	1.90	—	—	2.20	—	10.00
Hoechst	9.60	—	—	—	—	—	9.60
Union Carbide	2.70	2.90	—	0.90	0.60	—	7.10
Arco	1.80	—	—	5.20	—	—	7.00
IFF	5.50	1.20	0.20	—	—	—	6.90
Dupont	2.20	3.90	0.40	—	—	—	6.50
Cyanamid/Agrar	1.20	2.80	—	—	—	—	4.00
TOTAL	267.30	96.90	14.60	41.10	9.90	13.40	443.20

Exhibit 3 **Personal Backgrounds of Van Leer's Board Members**

Willem de Vlugt (b. 1942)

Chairman and CEO of Van Leer since 1992 and an executive board member since 1989. A Dutch national who joined Van Leer in 1968 and held executive positions in the US, France, Argentina and Brazil. Between 1977 and 1983, de Vlugt served in general management positions in the coatings divisions of Akzo Nobel, the Dutch chemicals group. He then returned to Van Leer, where, prior to joining the Executive Board, he served as president and CEO of Van Leer Containers, including the industrial container activities in the US.

André Saint-Denis (b. 1944)

CEO since 1992. A Canadian national who held several managerial positions at Air Canada, Alcan, Canadian and Kinburn Corp in both Canada and Switzerland. Prior to joining Van Leer in 1992, Mr Saint Denis served as vice-president finance and treasurer of Le Groupe Vidéotron Ltée in Montreal.

Francisco de Miguel (b. 1944)

Francisco de Miguel was appointed to the Executive Board in 1995 with a special brief for the industrial packaging activities of Van Leer. Mr de Miguel; a Spaniard, joined Van Leer in 1968 and held several position in Spain and Brazil. Prior to joining the Executive Board he was responsible for Van Leer's operations in Latin America.

Christian Betbeder (b. 1942)

A member for the Executive Board since 1995, Christian Betbeder was responsible for the development for the consumer packaging business. Prior to joining Van Leer in 1983, Mr Betbeder, a French national, served in various managerial positions in France. Before joining the board, Betbeder headed the strategic business in Flexibles, including Van Leer's activities in strength films, metallised products and industrial flexibles.

Exhibit 4   **Organization Structure Van Leer Group (Jan 95)**

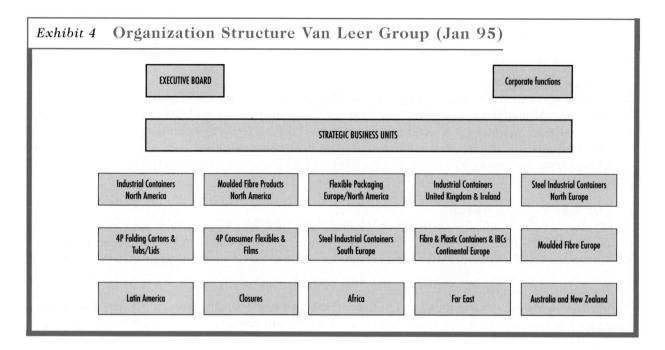

> ## *Exhibit 5*   Total Global Purchase Program Steel Drums

Elements of Proposal:

↔ Best prices at each location based on the total purchasing volume for the group.

↔ Purchasing data and names of local contracts provided for supplier to verify specifications, ordering patterns, etc.

↔ All prices to be quoted on a "delivered" basis.

↔ A multi-year proposal is encouraged, with price increases for raw material only in years two, three . . . .

↔ As an incentive to TOTAL, a yearly rebate proposal based on various purchase levels is encouraged.

↔ Along with the proposal, supplier is asked to include information on their:
  – Quality Assurance programs
  – Drum recovery and reconditioning program

TOTAL: Ranked 9th in the World

OVERALL RANKING

1. SHELL OIL	(NL/UK)
2. EXXON	(US)
3. MOBIL	(US)
4. BP	(UK)
5. CHEVRON	(US)
6. AMOCO	(US)
7. TEXACO	(US)
8. ELF	(FR)
9. TOTAL	(FR)
10. ARCO	(US)

(April 1994)

RANKING BY CRITERIA

Oil reserves	6th
Gas reserves	12th
Oil production	10th
Gas production	15th
Refining capacity	8th
Products sales	7th

* Excluding National Oil Companies from producing countries and ENI, PIW – December 1993

Case Study

VAN LEER PACKAGING WORLDWIDE: THE TOTAL ACCOUNT (B)

During February 1995, Ten Cate held discussions with the heads of the Van Leer country subsidiaries over a period of one month. He realized that competitive conditions and pricing strategies varied widely across Europe, with a significant contrast between the United Kingdom and France. While the British offered TOTAL the most competitive prices, the French were obtaining a premium. Moreover, managers in the two countries perceived the situation quite differently. France took TOTAL's move much more seriously than the British, who felt that the decision makers at TOTAL's UK subsidiary were very loyal to Van Leer, and much too independent to be imposed upon by Paris.

Ten Cate's conclusion was that Van Leer should retain the originally proposed 1995 local pricing to TOTAL. However a rebate on cumulative pan-European sales would be granted. Exhibit 1 includes a copy of the proposal, which Ten Cate sent at the end of February 1995. It included (1) an offer to dispatch a Van Leer representative who would participate in a task force exploring standardization of the drums (capacity, thickness, shape, internal and external coatings, paint, reconditioning, and the like), (2) the actual prices for each one of the 6 subsidiaries would remain the same until May 1st, 1995; and (3) a rebate on all annual purchases in Europe: 1% on purchases of 250,000 to 300,000 drums, 1.5% on purchases of 300,000 to 350,000 drums, and 2% beyond.

An Adjustment

TOTAL's reaction was slow to come. A possible explanation was that Delvallée was retiring after 15 years in his position and his successor, Paul Laveissiere, was studying the situation and taking his time to make a decision. Laveissiere, who was

This case was written by David Weinstein, Professor of Marketing at INSEAD, with the assistance of Alain Debenedetti, Research Assistant. It is intended to be used as a basis for class discussion rather than to illustrate either effective or ineffective handling of an administrative situation.

Copyright © 1996 INSEAD, Fontainebleau, France.

in his 50s, was appointed to the position of Purchasing Manager after many years at TOTAL in various sales and sales management positions.

In mid April 1995 Laveissiere invited Ten Cate and Hoareau to meet him at his office in the impressive Tour TOTAL at Paris La Defense. Ten Cate remembered,

> "Delvallée was still there and Laveissiere was very "sympathique" and professional. He challenged my proposal as I had expected. Chouarain, who also attended the meeting, continued his pattern of being rather passive. The active Swinson, who had been most aggressive at our first meeting, was not present. Moreover, the US market was not really discussed. To me, this fit with the views of my British colleagues. Hence we did not change our terms to TOTAL."

Hoareau was disappointed by the results of the meeting. His feelings that the negotiations had taken a bad turn were confirmed in a telephone conversation with Laveissiere after the Paris meeting. He faxed his impressions to Ten Cate (see Exhibit 2): (1) the proposed discount on the European level did not stand up to the competition; and (2) prices submitted by Van Leer UK were much too high and risked compromising the outcome of the negotiations. Hoareau concluded by asking Ten Cate to contact the British subsidiary and encourage them to reduce their price.

From this point onwards, the negotiations entered a new phase. Van Leer France took the initiative of the dialogue with Laveissiere and Chouarain. In a letter dated April 27, 1995 Hoareau wrote,

> "We suggest focusing our discussion on the French market, given its relative weight within your European operations. Clearly our action will have to fit into the European framework that you are seeking."

He proposed to help TOTAL develop a standardization plan and reduce the range of drums. Meanwhile, if 1995 sales to TOTAL exceeded 1994 results by at least 20,000 drums, Van Leer would grant an exceptional rebate of 1.75%. Prices would be re-negotiated only after the standardization project to account for any changes in the mix, which might have arisen in the interim.

In parallel, Ten Cate held additional discussions with his Van Leer UK colleagues. They convinced him that TOTAL UK would not walk away from a strong traditional relationship with Van Leer UK. He recalled:

> "The British position was that by bundling with other countries, they could only lose margins from this incident. TOTAL UK was not going to leave them in spite of any Paris pressure. Being evaluated on the basis of their local results, they were not motivated to either lower prices or even discuss the pan-European pricing with Van Leer France. The affair became de facto more and more French".

Ten Cate then sent a new price structure for the UK including only some marginal changes that Van Leer UK yielded.

The Final Proposal

Matters took a major turn in May when Hoareau briefed Ten Cate on the outcome of his telephone conversations with Delvallée. Even if the offer on France were accepted, TOTAL would remain very concerned about the rebate offered on the European level since it was much lower than the rebate the American subsidiary was offering. In fact Van Leer was no longer in the running. Neither in France, nor in the UK. Hoareau suggested setting the rebates at 1.25%, 1.5% and 2.25% respectively, instead of the initially suggested 1%, 1.5% and 2%. See Exhibit 3 for Hoareau's written note.

On June 14, 1995, Ten Cate wrote to the subsidiaries, following a visit to TOTAL two days earlier with Hoareau. The letter informed the countries of TOTAL's desires, requested their input and announced a revised structure of corporate rebates, which included changes in thresholds (see Exhibit 4). Van Leer UK did not change their prices in response to this appeal. Ten Cate then adopted

Hoareau's rebate suggestion and sent it to TOTAL (see Exhibit 5).

While Ten Cate's proposal was making its way to TOTAL, Hoareau discussed the situation with TOTAL's Chouarain. He reported to Ten Cate by fax:

> "I have mentioned to them what we intend to modify. Despite our efforts, Chouarain still seems to feel that Van Leer is not granting it the kind of attention it should, and does not seem determined enough to become TOTAL's No. 1 supplier. I disagree with his position entirely and hope that our most recent offer will reverse his perception."

TOTAL'S Response

One week later, on June 21, 1995, after a brief telephone conversation with Laveissiere, Hoareau informed Ten Cate that TOTAL was thoroughly disappointed by Van Leer's latest offer, mainly in light of Van Leer's pricing in the UK, and was wondering if Van Leer was genuinely interested in TOTAL. Laveissiere had also reminded him that the final decision would be based on an offer for the whole of Europe and not only for France.

That same day Laveissiere sent a fax to Ten Cate and Hoareau, responding to the June 14 offer. In it, he requested an additional decrease of the rebate threshold on global quantities. He also requested they look into the possibility of reducing unit prices both in France and other European countries.

Hoareau then wrote to TOTAL explaining that Van Leer could not reduce its prices any more, in spite of his personal appeals to Van Leer UK. At this point Ten Cate felt that it was time to leave the account in Van Leer France's hands and that he could not really contribute much to the discussions. He refused to believe the rumor that Gallay, the French competitor, had proposed a 5% rebate in France, and never felt for one second that Van Leer could lose the TOTAL account in the UK. As of the beginning of July, Hoareau was the only person maintaining direct contact with Laveissiere, who continued to voice his discontent.

Exhibit 1

Van Leer
Packaging Worldwide

Van Leer Nederland B.V
part of SBU Steel Industrial
Containers North Europe
Bergeeweg 6
Postbus 75
3633 ZV Vreeland
Holland

Telefoon   (029 43) 8911
Telefax Nr.   (029 43) 2441

<u>By Fax</u>
Mr. M. Chouarain
Total
24, Cours Michelet
Cedex 47
92069 Paris la Defense
FRANCE

Uw brief van Your letter of	Onze Ref. Our Ref. 95.075/JEtC/kh	Datum Date 27/2/1995

Onderwerp
Subject

Dear Mr. Chouarain,

We thank you for the recent inquiry for your total European 200 liter drum requirements, which have been studied and discussed with the various countries.

Taking into account the large range of different drum types and the very diversified oil and chemical products filled by your affiliates, we propose to start a packaging standardisation project for which we can delegate somebody from our national organisations as resource to participate jointly with Total members to working groups in order to define the possibilities of standardisation based on a corporate approach regarding:
– drum capacity
– drum thickness
– drum shape
– internal coating
– external paints and decorations
– replacement of reconditioned drums.

Attached please find for the relevant 6 European countries our tables with actual prices which are fixed till 1st May 1995.

In order to express our willingness to enlarge our mutual relationship all over Europe we offer you the following corporate rebate proposal:

Off-take number of large 200 ltr new steel drums in France, Germany, Italy, Spain, Sweden and the UK during 1 year:

250,000 – 300,000 pcs	1% rebate
300,000 – 350,000 pcs	1½%"
350,000 – 400,000 pcs	2% "

We hope to get your invitation for a next meeting in order to plan for the next steps to be made.

Kind regards

J.E. ten Cate

Exhibit 2

Van Leer France
Division Fûts métalliques
Chemin du Gord - B.P. 181
76120 Le Grand-Quevilly
Tel. 35 18 20 00 + Telex 770 073
Télécopieur 35 68 20 01

S.a.r.l. au capital de 30 000 000 francs
Siège Social: même adresse
RCS Rouen B 380 576 363
Siret 380 576 363 00010
APE 287 A

<u>*Mr. HOAREAU Fax nr is : 35 69 89 77*</u>

TELEFAX

TO: Mr. Ten CATE

FROM: C. HOAREAU

DATE: 25.04.95   NBRE DE PAGES: 1

REF.: CH/AH No 5184

<u>**RE: TOTAL**</u>

Following our meeting, I would like to express my concern on the present status of the negotiation.

Your offer for the European discount as mentioned in 2nd page of your offer does not seem to be very attractive to Total compared to other proposals from competition.

Selling price indicated by Van Leer U.K. are far to high as mentioned by Mr. Chouarain.

Van Leer France can do its utmost in order to make an attractive offer to maintain at least the present business with Total. But this offer will certainly not compensate the difference between global discount and British price.

Can you make some thoughts to the above and contact Van Leer U.K. to see if something can be done.

Thank you very much for your help.

Regards

C. HOAREAU

Exhibit 3

 **Van Leer**
Emballages Industriels

Van Leer France
Division Fûts métalliques
Chemin du Gord - B.P. 181
76120 Le Grand-Quevilly
Tel. 35 18 20 00 + Telex 770 073
Télècopieur 35 68 20 01

S.a.r.l. au capital de 30 000 000 francs
Siège Social: même adresse
RCS Rouen B 380 576 363
Siret 380 576 363 00010
APE 287 A

Mr. HOAREAU Fax nr is : 35 69 89 77

TELEFAX

TO: Mr. Ten CATE, Vreeland

FROM: C. HOAREAU

DATE: 17.05.95   NBRE DE PAGES: 1/2

REF.: CH/AH No 5222

RE: TOTAL

We discussed with Mr Delvallée over the phone.

The French proposal for France seems acceptable.

Mr Delvallée is still inquiring on the page "2" of your letter and the corporate rebate proposal.

This rebate is not in line with the one applied in the States and too low

In the States:

Up to 1 Million	US$	0	(5500 KF)
1M to 1,5 Million	US$	1%	(5500/7750 KF)
1,5M to 2 Million	US$	2%	(7750/11000 KF)
Over 2 Million	US$	3%	(11000 KF)

So I would propose as corporate rebate (in turnover)

1,5 ⇒ 20 000 KF	1,25%	150 000 Drums [⇒] 200 000 Drums	Average price 100 F
20 ⇒ 30 000 KF	1,50%	200 000 Drums [⇒] 300 000 Drums	
Over 30 000 KF	2,25%	Over 300 000 Drums	

This corporate rebate being paid on top of the local one.

On this basis, Van Leer France would pay to TOTAL

LOCAL REBATE	1,75%
CORPORATE REBATE	<u>1,25%</u>
TOTAL REBATE	**3,00%**

N.B. : Van Leer France turnover with Total in 1994 was 15 000 KF

According to Mr. Delvallée, Van Leer is not any longer in the race.

Gallay being the winner in France and Blagden in the U.K.

French decision will be taken next Friday.

URGENT contact with TOTAL has to take place today or tomorrow.

Regards.

C. HOAREAU

Exhibit 4

<table>
<tr><td rowspan="4">

Van Leer
Packaging Worldwide
</td><td rowspan="4">

FAX MESSAGE
</td><td>

Van Leer Nederland B.V.
Steel Containers
Bergseweg 6
3633 AK Vreeland

Tel. nr. 02943-8911
Fax nr. 02943-2441
</td></tr>
</table>

Company:	Your ref.:
Attn. : See distribution list	Our ref. : 95.212/JEtC/kh
From : J.E. ten Cate	No. of pages: 2 + attachment
Date : 14/6/1995	Fax no. :

Distribution list:

H.B. Bücker	Germany
C. Hoareau	France
L. Marthon	Sweden
J. Pereira	Spain
D. Pagnini	Italy
G. Redshaw	U.K.

Re: *Total Oil/Total Chemical*
     European Tender
     Visit report meeting in Paris 12/6/1995

Participants:

Total	M. Chouarain
	J.P. Laveissiere
	P.D. Wicks (UK)
Van Leer	C. Hoareau
	J.E. ten Cate

Following the various discussions which have taken place over the last months Total now wants to finalise a European contract for a period of 3 years starting 1/7/1995. We already made an original offer dated 27/2/1995 including prices fixed till 1/5/1995.

We have to answer the following questions to Total:

1) Are the prices mentioned in our offer of 27/2/1995 still valid per 1/7/1995?
   Can I have your adjustments please.
   In France the major supplier to Total has already given his original prices fixed till 1/10/95, however, based on the MEPS figures of March 1995.

2) How long can we offer fixed prices as from 1/7/95.

3) In connection with question 2): What price revision clause do we propose?

Also based on what has been proposed by the competition already in France, my suggestion is the following:
   1. Price revision raw materials on a quarterly basis with a raw material percentage of 70% and related to the MEPS of May 1995.
   2. Annual adjustment for other costs such as wages, transport, energy etc.

4) The following rebate schedules will be included in the contract:

   a) France
      1.75% annual rebate for all drums supplied to Total Lubricant and Chemical

   b) Corporate rebate:
      For the supply of new 200 l. steel drums to France, UK, Italy, Germany, Spain and Sweden:
      Annual turnover of:
      FF 12,000,000   -FF 20,000,000 1.25% of total turnover
      FF 20,000,001   -FF 30,000,000 1.5% of total turnover
      above FF 30,000,000   2.25% of total turnover
      (For your info: 1994 turnover was FF 19 min)

ACTION:
As Total asked us to mail our final offer this week, _I would like to have your comments on prices per 1/7 tomorrow (15/6)_.

Thanks and regards,

for J.E. ten Cate

Attachment

Exhibit 5

Van Leer Nederland B.V
part of SBU Steel Industrial
Containers North Europe
Bergeeweg 6
Postbus 75
3633 ZV Vreeland
Holland

Telefoon   (029 43) 8911
Telefax Nr.   (029 43) 2441

Mr. M. Chouarain
Mr. J.P. Laveisserie
Total
24, Cours Michelet
Cedex 47
92069 Paris la Defense
FRANCE

Uw brief van Your letter of	Onze Ref. Our Ref. 95.213/JEtC/kh	Datum Date 14/6/1995

Onderwerp
Subject

Dear Messrs. Chouarain and Laveissiere,

We thank you very much for the pleasant meeting we had on 12/6/1995 discussing a 3 year European drum supply contract starting as from 1/7/1995.

As agreed we provide you the following information:

1. <u>Drum prices per 1/7/1995</u>
   For France and Sweden, we are able to maintain the prices as offered with our letter 27/2/1995. Please find attached for Germany, UK, Spain and Italy our new prices valid as from 1/7/1995. All prices will be fixed until 1/10/1995.

2. <u>Price revision clause</u>
   As from 1/10/1995 prices can be adjusted every quarter in relation to raw material price development. The average content of raw materials in our prices is 70% which percentage will be related to the steel price development as published in the monthly MEPS bulletin. For France the basis will be MEPS March 1995.

   Price adjustments for the other cost elements as wages, transport, energy etc will be discussed on an annual basis as per 1st January.

3. <u>Rebate schedules</u>
   For **France** we offer you a 1.75% rebate for all 200 l. drums supplied to your lubricant and chemical division.

Corporate rebate
For the supply of 200 l. new steel drums to France, UK, Italy, Spain, Germay and Sweden we can offer you the following rebate schedule:

Annual turnover of:

FF 12,000,000	-FF 20,000,000	1.25% of total turnover
FF 20,000,001	-FF 30,000,000	1.5% of total turnover
above FF 30,000,000		2.25% of total turnover

We hope that the above mentioned conditions reflect the various discussions points and questions you brought up during our recent meeting.

We are looking forward to your reaction, and express the wish that both our companies will continue the existing european relationship.

Yours sincerely,

J.E. ten Cate

Attachment: 1

> ## Case Study
> # VAN LEER PACKAGING WORLDWIDE: THE TOTAL ACCOUNT (C)

In late October 1995 TOTAL informed Hoareau by telephone that Van Leer would no longer be their supplier in France but that it would remain their partial supplier in the UK. The contract signed between Gallay and TOTAL in France would therefore cover 80% of TOTAL's needs over a period of 3 years. However, Van Leer UK remained the main supplier to TOTAL in the UK. Hoareau's reaction was:

> "All through the negotiations I felt that the rigid position of my colleagues in the UK would eventually hurt us in France. We must

understand that Van Leer's prices in the UK were very competitive, while we sold at a premium. In addition to that, my UK counterpart's relationship with TOTAL UK is excellent. Their position was that a loss of an international contract was not threatening to them, while winning might hurt their profitability. Well, that is what happened. I did all I could but the UK did not budge. Not having Europe-wide authority I was the victim of Van Leer not being responsive to TOTAL's needs and global expectations."

Hoareau was now very concerned with how to remain a supplementary supplier of TOTAL, which would give Van Leer an opportunity to become their major supplier in the future. The implications of finding himself totally out of any relationship with this account would be devastating.

This case was written by David Weinstein, Professor of Marketing at INSEAD, with the assistance of Alain Debenedetti, Research Assistant. It is intended to be used as a basis for class discussion rather than to illustrate either effective or ineffective handling of an administrative situation.

Case Study

Van Leer Packaging Worldwide: The TOTAL Account (D)

Francisco De Miguel was appointed to the executive board as head of Van Leer's worldwide industrial packaging business during the time that the negotiation with TOTAL was in progress. He did not intervene in the TOTAL discussions and learned about the incident in France from Joareau, after the fact. De Miguel's reaction was:

> "For me, this was a red light. It was unacceptable. This confirmed to me the need for change in the structure and in our behavior. The account should have been treated differently . . .'"

A week after the loss of TOTAL France, De Miguel asked for an appointment with Laveissiere, whom he would visit together with Hoareau, the latter still being very disturbed by the incident.

In the meeting, which took place one week later, without Ten Cate, De Miguel explained to TOTAL's Lavissiere and Chouarain, in the most unequivocal terms, that the outcome of these negotiations was troubling Van Leer far more than they could imagine. He also emphasized that Van Leer embraced TOTAL's global approach and would like to be TOTAL's No. 1 supplier.

At the same meeting, De Miguel initiated a conversation on potential collaboration in the Far East, enabling him to demonstrate how serious the Van Leer Group was about pursuing a global relationship with TOTAL. It also afforded De Miguel the opportunity to emphasize the advantages of an international organization like Van Leer.

Hoareau felt encouraged as they left the meeting. There was still 20% of TOTAL France's steel drums to be had, and his impression was that De Miguel had improved Van Leer's chances of retaining the role of supplementary supplier in France. This would keep Van Leer France supplying the very important French organization and, eventually, provide an opportunity to regain its status as the major supplier. However, Hoareau felt that Van Leer should establish a different process of interfacing with international accounts in the future. He commented,

> "I was clearly handicapped and my decisions were only one piece in an international jigsaw puzzle. If we cannot work in harmony we shall suffer similar incidents in the future."

This case was written by David Weinstein, Professor of Marketing at INSEAD, with the assistance of Alain Debenedetti, Research Assistant. It is intended to be used as a basis for class discussion rather than to illustrate either effective or ineffective handling of an administrative situation.

Case Study

VAN LEER PACKAGING WORLDWIDE: THE TOTAL ACCOUNT (E)

In an interview with the case writers Laveissiere made the following statements:

> "A steel drum is, all told, a very banal product. There are quite a number of suppliers out there who meet the essential requirement standards in terms of quality, safety, supply and price. The fact that Van Leer is a multinational corporation did not give it a competitive advantage in this case. Moreover, they really did not think "multinational". They were not responsive to our pan-European needs, nor did they understand what we were trying to achieve here in this office. They were simply focusing on the French contract. They said that they were international, and they are, but could not come up with an acceptable international package."

> "This whole incident really left a bad taste in my mouth as this supplier never really understood my own point of view. However no contracts are forever and De Miguel's approach, along with the lessons I hope they will draw from the loss of the relationship with us, and I assume from those with similar customers, will probably push them to change."

> "It is a paradox that Van Leer France was the victim of the rigid behavior by Van Leer UK, who continues to sell as if nothing had happened. As you can see, we also have internal problems in implementing our globalization efforts. I lost this one case to the independence of my British colleagues, as Hoareau lost it to his. However, with better organization, more experience, and changing of the guards, we shall manage to have more global power over our subsidiaries, and bring value to TOTAL beyond what they can obtain locally. This does not only relate to prices. It has to do with innovating and pushing global suppliers to partner and innovate with us. We're learning and improving every day."

Case Study

CITIBANK

CITIBANK ARGENTINA

It was one of those quiet Buenos Aires afternoons when Carlos Noriega, Vice President, Citibank Argentina, returned from his favorite steak house *El Mirasol de la Recova*. He had to prepare a presentation to headquarters about Citibank's future strategy in Argentina's card business. While he was recovering from the 30 ounce T-bone steak he had ordered, he looked back at his achievements and reviewed his options for the future. Mr. Noriega was proud of his work in the last years. He had managed to successfully position Citibank as the number 1 foreign bank in Argentina. In the credit card business, Citibank was also the leader with a 12% share of the market. Moreover, Citibank was the only bank in Argentina that issued three different brands (Diners Club, Visa, MasterCard).

But despite all these success stories, Mr. Noriega wondered whether he could grow Citibank's overall card business at the same pace as in recent years. Customers would undoubtedly demand more sophisticated products, and strategies used in the past, like lower pricing, might not show the desired effects any more. Mr. Noriega reflected on Citibank's U.S. model, and wondered whether a 1:1 transfer of the U.S. marketing approach would be possible, considering Argentina's unique market situation. However, he was sure that he had to enlarge Citibank's portfolio of advanced products, like co-branded cards, which are used to deliver added value to the customer.

Mr. Noriega also had to take into consideration the competitive forces. He had heard from some

friends in the business about American Express's plans to extend its product portfolio in the Argentinean market. Besides the traditional charge card, two new products might be launched, the GRCC card and the Network card. Currently, American Express was trying to find partner banks for the distribution of these new products.

Mr. Noriega was informed that American Express already had a small test market with the GRCC cards. The card may appear self standing as an American Express brand, in which case American Express would presume the credit risk. It may also be co-branded with corporate partners or even be entered into partnerships with banks, in which case the financial institution would assume the business risk. The other American Express product in the pipeline, the Network Card, is always co-branded. The main difference to the GRCC card is that there is always a financial institution involved which assumes the credit risk. Mr. Noriega knew that these two new products were dependent on finding successful co-branding partners, and he wondered which steps he should take to block American Express's entry successfully.

Finally, Mr. Noriega wondered how he should balance his product portfolio. Should he maintain the current equilibrium in marketing expenses, or should he shift spending from bankcards (Visa, Mastercard) to Diners or vice versa?

CITIBANK: FULL SERVICE, WORLDWIDE

History

Citibank was established in 1812 as the City Bank of New York, with a starting capital of $2 million. In 1893, it became the largest bank in New York City, with $34.4 million in deposits and assets worth $38.9 million, and by 1894 Citibank was the largest bank in the U.S.

A significant characteristic of Citibank has

Source: This case was prepared by Professor Bodo B. Schlegelmilch, Chair of International Marketing and Management, and Mr. Kussai El-Chichalki, Case Writer and Graduate Research Assistant at the Wirtschaftsuniversität Wien. The authors would like to thank Citibank Argentina and the Thunderbird Graduate School of International Management for the support of this project.
Copyright © 1998, Bodo B. Schlegelmilch & Kussai El-Chichalki

been its innovations and first mover spirit in the banking scene. In the 1920s, the bank started its consumer banking business and was the first commercial bank to offer personal loans. In 1921, when national banks were permitted to open domestic branches for the first time, Citibank acquired its first domestic branches after merging with the Commercial Exchange Bank and the Second National Bank. In the same year, a Compound Interest Department was set up, paying three percent interest, compounded semi-annually on balances of $5 or more. And success followed soon: in 1922, 6,300 depositors with average balances of less than $300 had deposited a total of $2 million, and by 1929 there were 232,000 customers with $62 million on deposit. By the end of 1929, Citibank had 37 New York City branches with deposits of $305.3 million, and one in twenty New Yorkers was a Citibank customer.

Citibank was the first bank in New York City to offer consumers checking accounts with no minimum-balance requirement (1936), and the first commercial bank to offer unsecured personal loans. In 1955, the bank changed its name to The First City Bank of New York, which was shortened to First National City Bank in 1962, the year of its 150th anniversary. In 1976, the name was finally changed to today's Citibank.

In 1961, Citibank invented the Negotiable Certificate of Deposits, which allowed banks to compete against U.S. government securities, by paying a higher interest rate on funds deposited for a specific period. From 1979 on, Citibank has been the world's leading foreign exchange dealer.

In 1965, Citibank entered the credit card field, which today represents one of the bank's core businesses. In 1981, Citibank acquired Diners Club, and in 1993 Citibank became the largest credit- and charge-card issuer and servicer in the world. By1996, it had the largest number of credit cards in Asia, and Taiwan became the first country outside the U.S. with over 1 million credit cards.

In 1968, the First National City Corporation was founded as the bank's holding company. In 1974, the holding's name was changed to Citicorp, a signal that priority was given to its global businesses. In April 1998, the biggest merger ever to be effected was announced. It aligns the Travelers Group, which has a strong presence in the fields of insurance, asset management and investment banking, and Citicorp. The new group will use the name Citigroup, and it forms the world's biggest

financial services group, with assets of $700 billion, net revenues of $50 billion, and a stock value of $136 billion.

Citibank's goal is to provide its customers global access to all products and services offered, at any desired time. The bank sees its major strength in its depth of presence around the world. That gives it a wide range of growth opportunities and balance as well as diversity to its revenue stream: about 50% of earnings are attributable to Consumer banking, the other half being produced by Corporate banking.

International expansion

Citibank did not only rely on its strong homebase. It was the first U.S. bank to build a significant global presence. It usually enters a new market in the early stages of its economic development by providing basic services like cash management, short-term loans in local currency and trade finance. As the country's economy grows, new services such as project finance and securities custody, and clearing are added. If the market keeps growing, more sophisticated products such as bond underwriting and asset-backed securitization are introduced.

Citibank was the first major U.S. bank to establish a foreign department (1897), and it was a pioneer in the overseas business, opening offices in London and Shanghai in 1902 and in Buenos Aires in 1914. By the late 1930s, Citibank was present in 23 countries outside the U.S., forming the largest international bank.

In 1961, the First National City Overseas Investment Corporation was installed as the bank's holding company for non-U.S.-based subsidiaries and affiliates. This was the decisive step towards global coverage: in eight years Citibank expanded from 82 offices in 27 countries to 208 offices in 61 countries.

Citibank's swift reaction to new situations on international markets holds until today. In 1994, it opened the first fully foreign-owned commercial bank in Russia, and in 1995, it opened the first full-service branch in China, as well as branches in Vietnam and South Africa.

Technology

Citibank has always been very open to the use of new technologies to maintain its reputation as a customer friendly institute, that permanently creates new ways to facilitate banking services. In 1977, the first Citibank Banking Centers were formed, and Citibank was the first financial institution fully committed to the introduction of automated teller machines which were highly acclaimed by the public and gained them a multitude of new customers in the 1980s.

The continuous upgrading of technology is regarded as a strategic investment, which helps to improve customer service and effect higher cost control at the same time. Citibank tries to harmonize and modernize its technologies around the world to increase its responsiveness to the markets and the customers. That process also includes the consolidation of the worldwide systems. European customers' accounts are processed in the U.S., while retail banking customer inquiries for all of the U.S. are handled by a single service center in San Antonio, Texas.

In 1985 Direct Access was introduced in New York, linking personal computers in homes and offices with Citibank. Only one year later the first touch-screen automated teller machines came to the market, tested first in New York City and Hong Kong, and now used all over the world.

Today, Citibank represents one of the leading global banks engaged in providing full service to its customers. It has more than 3,400 locations worldwide and is expanding continuously. The rapid growth shown in the 1990s is mainly due to Citibank's concentration in underdeveloped markets and regions. Thus, Citibank has experienced a much higher return growth than many of its U.S. based competitors, for instance in the Asian market. Currently Citibank is present in 98 countries, of which 77 can be counted to the attractive but risky emerging markets. Citibank's goal is to build a truly global brand awareness which shall enable the bank to become the first financial institution being mentioned in line with Coca-Cola, McDonald's or Nike. One of the most important ways to reach this objective is by setting unique service standards worldwide which should help improve recognition substantially.

Credit cards: business facts

Beginnings

Credit cards are a widely used commodity in today's society, and considering their continuous boom and acceptance among customers, a future without them is difficult to imagine. The first credit card was launched in 1946 by the Flatbush National Bank of Brooklyn, New York. In 1950, the Diners Club card was born. It is the brainchild of Frank McNamara, who had a business lunch in New York, and made an arrangement with the restaurant to pay later. In 1951, already more than 40,000 people had the Diners Club card (the name derives from diner). In 1953, the first Diners cards have been issued internationally: in Great Britain, Canada, Cuba and in Mexico. In 1960, Diners Club was for the first time present on all five continents. Today, Diners Club has a network of about 4 million locations which accept the card.

Diners Club was to become known as the travel and entertainment card, focusing on dining and travel expenses. Other cards known as travel and entertainment (T&E) cards include American Express and Carte Blanche.

Inspired by the T&E cards success, several banks issued their own credit cards, also known as bank cards. They differed from T&E cards in that they were accepted at various types of merchants. The most successful cards became Visa (Bank of America) and MasterCard.

Mastercard

In the 1950s a network of U.S. banks was formed, depending on a franchise system, that had a single bank in each major city working with certain merchants that accepted the card as form of payment. In 1966, the Interbank Card Association (ICA) was established by one of these groups, which should later become MasterCard International. Unlike Visa, which started as the BankAmericard, ICA was not dominated by a single bank. In 1968, ICA initiated its global expansion by forming an alliance with the Mexican Banco Nacional. The same year, ICA entered a partnership with Eurocard, and the first Japanese members joined. The group was run by member committees, which established rules for authorization, clearing and settlement, and which were responsible for marketing and security issues.

The second internationalization wave followed in the 1980s, when MasterCard expanded into Asia and Latin America. In 1987, MasterCard entered as first payment card in China (which, by 1993, became the 2nd largest country in sales volume for MasterCard). In 1988, the first MasterCards were issued in the Soviet Union. Today, there are more than 30 MasterCard offices around the world including India, Thailand, Chile, South Korea and Taiwan.

Visa

In 1958, the Bank of America started its BankAmericard program. The card quickly became popular, and in the mid-1960s, the Bank of America began to license U.S. banks to issue its BankAmericard. Membership associations were created on an international scale, and in 1977, the name Visa was adopted as a global brand.

Today, Visa is controlled by the 20,700 member financial institutions, which own the association jointly. While each member distributes the cards at its own terms, the role of Visa International is to provide the systems to manage effectively the authorization and settlement of payments. Visa is accepted at 14 million locations, and the annual turnover of goods and services purchased with Visa accounts for $1 trillion.

Players in the card industry

The five key players in the credit card industry are the cardholder, the credit card issuer, the merchant, the acquiring bank and the flag institution. The organizations behind cards like Visa and MasterCard are flag organizations, i.e. companies that are owned by the cardholder's bank, yet are run by a separate board of directors. Their main source of income is the fee charged to the member banks. The roles of the flag organizations include licensing, patent and copyright protection, establishing regulations for card operations, creating national and international settlement and authorization systems, research and development of new products, as well as advertising and promotion of the flags.

The card issuer's role is to deal with the cardholders, namely to assign and manage the credit and to undertake the credit risk. The acquiring company is in charge of negotiating the acceptance of credit cards with retailers and to manage the relationship with the merchants once they have signed on. As in the case of Citibank, the card issuer and the acquiring bank may be the same institution.

The card issuer's revenues are the flow of three sources. First, interest income is received, which is determined by the annual percentage rate and the outstanding balance on a cardholder's account. The second income source is the interchange fee, paid

Table 1 THE FLAG ORGANIZATION'S DUTIES

WHAT THE FLAG ORGANIZATION DOES:	WHAT THE FLAG ORGANIZATION DOES NOT DO:
✓ Develop new products and services	✗ Distribute cards
✓ Establish industry norms and regulations regarding the use of its branded products	✗ Determine annual interest rates
✓ Establish procedures for the acceptance and settlement of all transactions	✗ Negotiate with businesses to accept the card
✓ Provide a network of communication to facilitate electronic authorization of card transactions and the subsequent clearing and settlement of charges	✗ Determine annual card fees
	✗ Decide the amount that the business must pay to access the organization's services

Table 2   THE ISSUER/ACQUIRING BANK'S DUTIES

WHAT THE ISSUER/ACQUIRER DOES:	WHAT THE ISSUER/ACQUIRER DOES NOT DO:
✓ Distribute cards	✗ Evolve new products and services
✓ Assign credit to cardholders	✗ Provide a network of communication
✓ Assume credit risk	✗ Define the industry norms and regulations
✓ Determine annual card fees and interest rates	✗ Manage the acceptance and settlement of all transactions
✓ Enlarge acceptance of credit cards with merchants	
✓ Manage relationship with merchants	
✓ Determine merchant discount rate	

by the acquiring bank to the issuer. Eventually, the issuer may charge penalties for violations of the cardholder agreement, such as late payments or exceeding credit limits.

The acquiring bank receives its revenues from the merchants. The main source is the merchant discount, which is a compensation for handling the purchases made on credit cards at the merchant's establishment. Another field of income is tapped from the rental of point of sale terminals.

Settlement & interchange

Interchange denotes the settlement of accounts and the flow of funds after the approval of a transaction. This system is internationally standardized and shall enable banks and financial institutions around the world to exchange information and transactions in a fixed and consistent manner. Examples for such systems are Banknet and Visanet. These authorization systems identify the standardized card number format, personal information on the cardholder, information on the issuing institution and details of benefits the card provides.

No financial service is offered for free, and for the interchange function, the charge is called inter-change fee. This fee shall compensate the cardholder's issuing bank for the time lag between the settlement to the merchant's bank and the definitive billing to the cardholder for his/her purchases. The interchange fee also comprises operating costs. The fee is reviewed by the flag companies like Visa and MasterCard, and adjusted if necessary.

The flag institutions' most important function is to provide a quick and efficient system that helps settle transactions between the acquiring bank and the issuing bank. This settlement of transactions generally follows a certain scheme: the card issuing bank charges the cardholder the full amount for purchases with the credit card. A percentage of the total payment, the interchange fee, is retained by the bank for its services and expenses. The funds (total payment minus interchange fee) are then moved over the interchange network to the acquiring bank. The acquiring bank keeps a percentage (merchant discount rate) of sales, and finally credits the merchant's account with the remainder.

To illustrate a typical transaction cycle, consider the situation where a cardholder makes a purchase of $100 on his/her credit card. The merchant then presents the $100 receipt to the acquiring bank. In return he receives approximately $97. Consequently, a merchant discount of $3 is withheld by the acquiring bank. This amount covers the bank's franchise payments to Visa or MasterCard, an interchange fee paid to the card issuer bank, and all its operating expenses. Finally, the card issuer bills the cardholder the full $100. Depending on the payment terms underlying the card, the cardholder has the choice of making full or partial payments (see Exhibit 1 for a graphical illustration).

In recent years, competition was reduced to offering better interest rates and annual fees. But since then terms have become more similar between issuers, forcing the players to seek new sources of differentiation. An obvious possibility is to include more services with the product, achieved namely through co-branding.

Business Trends

Co-branded cards

The co-branded card has been very popular in recent years. It is a cooperation between a financial institution and a company. The logos of all partners are shown on the front of the plastic card. Examples include the AAdvantage Visa Card and the GM MasterCard. What makes these cards so appealing to customers are various added benefits like bonus programs, preferential treatment, discounts or exclusive insurance packages.

The main benefit card issuers draw from co-branding is the opportunity to improve market share and customer loyalty. One of the toughest obstacles to overcome in the credit card business is customer turnover. Many customers constantly switch between companies in search of the lowest annual percentage rate and annual fee. While in the past much of the competition was based on who could offer the best terms, now that issuers offer very similar terms, the battleground has shifted from price towards added value. This leads companies to come up with new ways to attract and retain cardmembers. Co-branding is one of the most successful differentiation methods. Most of the benefits require the cardholder to charge a minimum amount before benefits are pocketed. Many realize that they are better off keeping cards for longer and using them more often to accumulate large amounts of benefits, because if they switched they would not be offered the best deals. This has the effect of increasing customer retention and volume charged per card. Customers also tend to accept higher annual percentage rates and/or annual fees than if they were not conferred these privileges.

In addition to the higher market share realized, partnerships and alliances are a popular way to share marketing costs. The setup and operational costs involved are split, and an enormous advantage can be attained through the combination of resources, services, products and especially through the bundling of the brand names and reputations of the partners. Furthermore, the companies gain access to each other's databases. That gives them insights to shopping habits and buyer behavior patterns of the partner's customers, which are a valuable base for tailoring new offers to specific segments.

Citibank was one of the first banks to offer a co-branded card. In 1986, they became a partner in the AAdvantage program, which is American Airlines' frequent flyer program. The cards resulting from this partnership are the Citibank MasterCard AAdvantage and the Citibank Visa AAdvantage card. It is probably easy to understand the formula that made the cooperation a big success: each dollar charged on the card is equal to one free mile in the AAdvantage program. Citibank was able to attract new customers, and undoubtedly the new card has led many customers to charge more than they otherwise might. Citibank also gained access to American Airlines' customer database, opening up an attractive target segment for the future.

American Airlines benefited in that they had entered a new and relatively inexpensive channel to promote their frequent flyer program. The agreement guaranteed American Airlines revenues on seats otherwise empty. Miles earned through the AAdvantage program could not be redeemed during peak flying seasons, such as Thanksgiving or the Christmas vacation. Being restricted to low demand flights, the AAdvantage program filled the airline's seats and pockets.

Another industry, in which co-branding agreements are used, is for instance the computer industry. Microsoft co-branded Hewlett-Packard's small-business PC, the Vectra 500, as well as Packard Bell's small-business systems (both co-branding agreements have since been dissolved).

Affinity Cards

Affinity cards underlie the same concept as co-branded cards. However, they differ in that they are joint card ventures between banks and non-profit organizations, such as Universities or Foundations. Often the cardholder is entitled to benefits such as free admission to the society's attractions and significant discounts on merchandise. Their popularity springs more from the need of declaring social commitment, or from the expression of a certain lifestyle, than from the pure run for advantages.

New Technologies

Latest advancements in microchip technology have made it possible to place small chips on plastic cards, allowing them to carry more information and perform simple functions. Smart cards, as these plastic cards with an embedded microprocessor chip are called, can effect various operations at the same time. In the near future, the cardholder will be able to do more with the credit card than just purchases. Such all-in-one cards can store any information, and may be used as personal ID, car key and bus ticket at the same time, reducing the number of cards that must be carried. Other possibilities may include the use of microchips for identification and security purposes, such as to access personal accounts or sensitive data via computer terminals. These universal cards, which can communicate with any thinkable device (such as ATMs, point of sales terminals, personal computers, mobile phones, telephones etc.), will one day be able to store fingerprints, pictures, medical information, insurance information, and even DNA information.

Technological progress will not only change the function of the credit card itself, but is also about to transform current business conditions. The network through which transactions are processed is one of the biggest barriers to potential entrants. This hurdle could quickly fall due to the increasing popularity of the Internet, which might become one of the preferred mediums for executing electronic transactions in the near future. However, the main obstacle for the diffusion of the Internet in the electronic marketplace is the security aspect. Therefore, a new technical standard for purchases made over open networks has been developed. This standard, called Secure Electronic Transaction (SET), has been created by Visa, MasterCard, Microsoft, IBM, Netscape and other leading technology companies. SET uses a combination of cryptographic techniques, digital certificates and digital signatures, that shall guarantee the authenticity of the parties involved in a card transaction over the Internet.

Card Business Argentina

Argentinian market

It seems that Argentina has mastered its way from a country shaken by persistent hyper-inflation and mismanagement in the 1980s to a more or less stable economy. Several reforms set off in the 1990s increased FDI substantially and recaptured the focus of the international business community's attention (see Exhibit 2). However, the whole region is still highly volatile and the Mexican Peso crisis as well as Brazil's prevailing economic constitution and conduct in MERCOSUR (see Exhibit 3) show that Argentina still reacts heavily to the other countries' performance.

The Argentinean market is served by 165 banks of which Citibank is the 5th largest bank in deposits, the 3rd largest private bank after Rio and Galicia, and the largest foreign institute (for a listing of the main players in Argentina's credit card industry see Exhibit 4). Citibank is present in 104 cities and it holds a market share of 5.15%, or 3.33% in Global Consumer Banking respectively. According to Young & Rubicam, Citibank is the clear market leader when it comes to the brand power of banks in Argentina.

Argentines seem to prefer more conservative forms of payment compared to U.S. Americans (see Exhibit 5). Cash dominates, being used for almost 4/5 of all transactions in Argentina, while checks are virtually unknown. Focusing on credit cards, the market is segmented by socio-economic criteria (see Exhibits 6 and 7). Currently, Citibank's primary target are the 895,000 ABC1 households, which are served by either T&E cards such as Diners Club and American Express, or by bank cards like Visa and MasterCard. While T&E cards are restricted to ABC1 households only, Visa and MasterCard are stretched further to the C2 segment. Citibank cautiously tries to penetrate the C2 level, and management has to take up the challenge of finding the golden path between a new lucrative opportunity and the risk of high write offs.

Less demanded are traveler checks and prepaid cards, which are mainly used for telephone. These products have to be paid fully before they can be used. In return they grant the customer some form of improved transaction assurance, otherwise not given. The traveler check's future might be that of a niche product considering its decreasing acceptance among customers. Prepaid cards, however, are in their initial phase and still have to prove their usefulness and positive reception.

Another product new to the Argentinean market are debit cards. They do not grant credit, but debit the customer's account at the time of purchase. Hence, they give the customer the comfort of paying without having to carry cash. In contrast to credit cards they are particularly employed for low value transactions.

Credit cards represent the most mature card product in the market. They fulfill the need of paying later by offering credit, and are commonly used for medium and high value transactions. Higher competition and more demanding customers force issuers to steadily offer new incentives. These may include the waiving of the card fee, which is becoming a more common standard among issuers, and run down to finding new attractions on the enrichment side. Recent developments were accompanied by increased marketing/promotion and sales expenses for the card issuers, and eroding merchant discount rates for the acquiring banks. As with any mature product, sub-segmentation may open up new business opportunities. In the case of credit cards, micro-segmentation has been achieved through co-branding and rewards programs. The difference between rewards and co-branding is that a rewards program does not imply that the logo and/or name of the partner has to appear on the card. The best example is Diners Club, that has a mileage rewards program without co-branding. While co-branding creates further possibilities to segment the market, there is a downside. Acting together with partners includes sharing profits, and the increase in billing volume achieved through co-branding is generally matched with dropping margins.

CITIBANK ARGENTINA

Current situation

Citibank Argentina follows the global strategy of offering the broadest product mix coupled with very innovative banking services. Supreme service to the customer is the centerpiece of Citibank's policies, and it actively uses its earned reputation and high-profile image for brand endorsement and leveraging. For Citibank, it is not only households but also merchants who are treated as customers, as seen with a service called one-stop-banking. At different times of the week, all receipts are collected and consolidated, and the merchant will be issued one check. With this kind of assistance, Citibank tries to improve merchant goodwill.

When looking at Citibank Argentina's credit card business, several strengths can be spotted. The very broad card offering (Classic/ Preferred/ Advantage/Corporate) puts the bank in the market pole position with a 12% share of cards and a 16% billing share (see Exhibit 8). The continuous introduction of innovative products like the photocard reinforces Citibank's image as a customer oriented institute. The photocard, which aims to minimize fraud by showing a photo of the cardholder on the front of the card, was originally started in the USA where it is used more as a marketing tool than as a safety against fraud. In Argentina, however, fraud is one of the central issues and thus the target is a 100% photocard coverage (compared to 15% in the U.S.A.).

One of Citibank's most valuable assets is the exclusive franchise of Diners Club in Argentina since the beginning of the 1980s. In addition to Diners Club, Citibank distributes Visa and Master-Card, thus being the only bank offering three different brands. This combination opens up several opportunities for Citibank. First, it can tie two global power brands, as in the case of Citibank/Visa and Citibank/MasterCard, to aggressively penetrate the market. Second, it can utilize Diners Club's prestige image to cover the high end customer segment.

Diners Club is Citibank's key product since no profits have to be shared with any franchiser as in the case of Visa and/or MasterCard. In the T&E sector, Diners Club shows a clear market leadership with 61% of all cards in force (see Exhibit 9). Between 1989 and 1993 Citibank followed the strategy of enriching Diners Club and attacking both bank cards and customers. They offered insurance products, published a magazine for members, and engaged highly in image advertising. Other innovations included the introduction of revolving credit (cardholders had for the first time the chance to pay the amount of their purchases in installments and automatically get new credit limit) and installment payment plans for high ticket items. Nevertheless, Diners Club shows a severe weakness: its image as an international card

Table 3	NUMBER OF CARDHOLDERS IN ARGENTINA AND WORLDWIDE	

	WORLDWIDE	ARGENTINA
Visa	560 million	1.9 million
MasterCard	399 million	1.9 million
AMEX	36 million	0.3 million
Diners Club	7 million	0.5 million

is decreasing, particularly because of the relatively low international coverage.

But the real highlight was the concept of cross sale between Diners Club and bank cards. Citibank tried to prevent losing market share to the other banks which were very successful with selling Visa and MasterCard. So they introduced the Citibank/MasterCard bank card, and triggered a concept totally new in the banking business: grow your key business by combining the rival product (MasterCard) with your own product (Diners Club). The point was that the package of Diners Club and MasterCard was lower priced than the combination of American Express and any bank card (see Exhibit 10 for an advertisement of September 1994 and Exhibit 11 for the UN MUNDO SIN LIMITES package). Citibank Argentina believed that the evolving trend was a customer, who did not really look for one specific brand but for a card that could meet all his/her needs.

As one manager expressed it:

> A household needs a minimum of two cards. Diners Club and a credit card for total coverage and high spending. The bank cards are weak in credibility and strong in retail coverage, while Diners is the opposite. You cannot go out and buy a 50,000 dollar diamond on a bank card - that's credibility.

The idea behind this was to position Citibank as the bank that offers the best combination of payment instruments (Diners Club plus bank card) to meet customers' needs in terms of credit flexibility, service coverage, image and globality. So Citibank tried to communicate to the customers that no one card can satisfy all of their needs. Instead, they should have a combination of cards that would give them all they needed at the lowest cost. Mr. Noriega was sure that the new concept of shifting the bank's emphasis from selling a product to servicing a household was the key to success:

While you fight for a household, you don't fight for a brand. Therefore, you give the customer a combination of products. And if you are successful in your communication, that results in the satisfaction of his total needs. In the U.S. the card business is one, and the bank business is another, and they don't talk to each other. They are looking at the old system which is fighting wars brand to brand, and we are following a different philosophy, because we are fighting for the household. The brand war is a losing war.

Key issues

Co-Branding

Should Citibank extend its co-branding program also to Diners Club? While Diners Club is positioned as an upscale card without further differentiation, Citibank tries to segment its bank cards through co-branding. Citibank's branding policy is to enter strategic alliances and to link their name only to the most attractive partners in order to block competitors successfully. In Argentina they entered partnerships with American Airlines, Renault and Telefónica. With already 60,000 cardholders, the Citibank/AAdvantage card is the bank's most successful alliance. Thus, co-branding fulfills two major objectives: a richer segmentation and the chance to block competitors. The major argument against co-branding is that profits have to be shared with your co-branding partner.

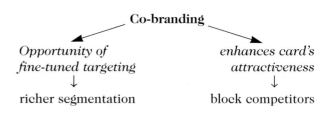

Payment Network

One of Citibank's major weaknesses in Argentina is related to their payment network. Compared to Citibank's only 42 bank branches, penetration of its main competitors is much deeper. And this difficulty does not remain static: Citibank faces the threat of a still growing branch network of its competitors. Citibank has tried to arrange distribution agreements with other banks or post offices. The problems arising from these cooperations are the huge gap in service culture (Citibank and post office), and the lack of continuity if the partner starts distributing cards on its own and becomes a competitor (Citibank and other banks). So Citibank attempts to solve the distribution challenge with electronic centers, spread all over the country. A barrier for success is the lack of confidence towards electronic banking services, as people have grown used to face to face communication.

New Segments

There is the opportunity of serving the C2 segment with Citibank credit cards. But considering probable target fallouts in Argentina's unstable economic environment, entering this segment could turn out to be more expensive later on.

Carlos Noriega thought:

> In the U.S. we are already in this C2 segment, we are actually lower than this C2 segment in the States. We have had all kinds of experiences in this segment in the States. However, it is not easy to transport these experiences to countries like Argentina or Brazil. We have to be incredibly sophisticated in the formula of risk and reward. No one else has suffered inflation rates of 1,000% yearly. The precarious political and economic situations we have are unprecedented. You have to realize what the middle class is suffering in terms of credit. You could not buy a house on credit. In order to buy a house they transported 50,000 dollars in a suitcase to the bank.

But he also had concerns that Citibank could miss a new chance:

> It is an opportunity to enter the C2 market. But if we are forced to enter the C2 market slowly, it will be difficult to change a customer to our card from a competitor.

Diners vs. Bank cards

Should Citibank Argentina try a major shift towards bank cards despite Diners Club's current success and its vital role in profit earnings? Mr. Noriega knew that the future belongs to the bank cards and in considering the worldwide decline of Diners Club he thought:

> What happened was that in 5-6 years Diners went from 230,000 plastics to 475,000. Nobody grew that big in the rest of the world. Now, going into the future, there is a major threat, because the brand is drying up. That's the bad part. The good part is that only 10% of our total volume is foreign volume. As long as there is a recession, that kind of protects you because people don't travel. If the economy gets better, the brand will suffer.

STRATEGIC ALTERNATIVES

Mr. Noriega took a piece of paper and briefly outlined the strategies he could pursue:

One possibility was to concentrate on bank cards, moving resources away from Diners Club. He was aware that this strategy would only work if the Argentinean economy grew. Because Citibank was the owner of Diners Club, any move towards bank cards implied more franchise fees and less profits. To keep the card business profitable, Citibank would have to increase the depth of market penetration, so that every household carried 3 to 4 different cards issued by Citibank instead of the current average of 1.7. The target would probably be 70% bank cards, 30% Diners Club business, the opposite of today's situation (70% Diners Club, 30% bank cards).

The second option would be more of the same. Mr. Noriega could extend his co-branding programs to Diners Club, but he could also enrich Diners Club in a second wave through rewards and mileage programs, and a merchandising catalog. In combination with more image advertising this could lead to a deeper cross sale between Diners Club and other Citibank products, ideally resulting in a healthier mix of profits.

A third option came to mind. Should he accelerate the death of Diners Club and shift all marketing expenses from Diners Club into bank cards? That was definitely the most radical way and it would work perfectly if the economy grew very fast in the next few years.

Mr. Noriega reviewed the other major issues. How should he solve the problem of the limited payment network? More electronic centers would underscore Citibank's image as modern, global player in the financial services industry. They could also give the bank a competitive advantage among the young target groups, who are very open towards new technologies. But what about the older population?

And finally the question of when to enter the C2 segment. Mr. Noriega knew that the other banks were preparing for entry as well. The "New Segments" argument was closely linked to the "Diners vs. Bank cards" issue: an entry into the C2 segment would be very attractive, if the economy grew. In that case he would use bank cards to attack the mass market, thus extending the bank cards' scope (and automatically achieving a new weight between Diners Club and the other brands).

Mr. Noriega went through his options again and again, and while the sun's power gradually faded away, he asked himself the crucial question. Should he scale down Diners Club's current position, leaving it as a cash cow, and gain new market share solely with bank cards? Or should Diners Club still play an active role, that of the local hero, who is strong in Argentina but has problems internationally? Mr. Noriega looked through the newspaper, and when studying the latest soccer results, a convincing comparison came into his mind: there are famous soccer teams, which cannot be beaten at home, but which have big troubles winning when they play abroad. But among these teams, has one ever finished the season as the cup winner?

Exhibit 1 **Typical Credit Card Purchase Transaction Cycle including a Co-Branded Company**

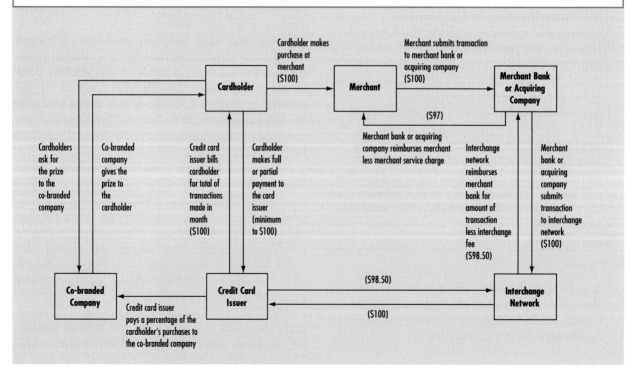

Exhibit 2 Argentina

In the last half of the 1980s Argentina suffered its longest period of stagnation this century. This economic performance was traceable to chronic public sector deficits and galloping inflation and each attempt to stabilize the economy did not only fail but ended in even more severe inflation. The Argentines, responding to the unstable economic environment, increasingly saved and invested abroad and by the end of the 1980s the Argentine state was insolvent and in crisis.

The recovery was initiated by the Law of Convertibility, introduced in 1991 by the economy minister, Domingo Cavallo. The plan fixed the peso against the dollar by guaranteeing a 1 to 1 convertibility, and established that any future printing of money should be determined by the level of dollar reserves. Thus, a limit was set to the public institutions' somehow institutionalized way of financing its deficit through inflation. The program was backed up by reforms which were directed towards establishing the central bank as a fully independent and effective monetary authority. Furthermore the government has undertaken difficult-to-reverse reforms in the legal framework, institutions, and policies.

The government has committed itself to privatization to reduce the budgetary burden and to make the firms more competitive. The administration has sold two television stations, the electric utility, the national telephone company, Aerolineas Argentinas, the defense industries, ports, reinsurance and the entire power sector.

Following an average economic growth rate of 7.7 % over 1991-94, the Argentine economy contracted in 1995, with an economic downturn of 4.4 % largely because of the Mexican economic crisis. The sharp recession caused an increase in unemployment and strained the performance of the financial system. The regional financial crisis was the first severe test of the Convertibility Plan. The government successfully resisted growing pressures to reverse the economy's liberalization. On the contrary, it decided to deepen this process and further accelerate economic adjustment.

The initial 1995 shock, generating a confidence crisis, was moderated by strong trade performance: a combination of good international commodity prices, the contracting domestic economy, the continuous real depreciation of the peso, and the fast pace of economic expansion in Brazil, resulted in a 32.3% nominal growth in exports. Consumer price inflation in 1995 was 1.6 %, the lowest in 51 years. In 1996, the economy has recovered slowly and unemployment still remains a persistent problem.

The government's central objective is to achieve strong long-term growth, while expanding employment and holding inflation to international levels. Recent developments in international financial markets have underlined Argentina's vulnerability to external shocks and the critical importance of enhancing its export performance. In the short term, economic prospects are for a cautious recovery. Following reforms of the financial markets, the labor market legislation, and the health insurance system, the Argentine economy could grow at a medium-term rate of 4 to 5 % and inflation should continue at or below international levels.

Source: World Bank & Economist Intelligence Unit (1996-1997)

Exhibit 3 Argentina & MERCOSUR

MERCOSUR (Mercado Común del Cono Sur) was founded in 1991 between Argentina, Brazil, Paraguay and Uruguay. These four countries have a combined population of 190 MM, and achieve almost 50% of South America's GDP. With a market of this size, MERCOSUR could have a significant impact on the economic growth rate of the four economies. The aim of this pact is to establish a full free trade area and to prepare for a common market. However, membership to other countries is open and the four member states have committed themselves to the establishment of a wider free trade area, the South American Free Trade Area. The aim here is to bring other South American countries into the agreement, and to increase internal free trade substantially within the next decade. The major problem this association faces is the instability of its member states' economies, whether it is either the incredibly high inflation rates until the beginning of the 1990s (Argentina), or the severe external debt (Brazil). A future success of MERCOSUR depends mainly on the sustained reforms of the two sleeping giants Argentina and Brazil. Since Argentina's trade in MERCOSUR is primarily with Brazil, which accounts for 20 percent of Argentina's trade, its prospects are closely tied to the stabilization of the Brazilian economy and resumption of lasting economic growth.

Exhibit 4 **Main Players in Argentina's Credit Card Business**

| (000 Cards) | BANK CARDS | | | | MARKET SHARE | | |
	MC	VISA	T&E	Local Brands	Total	Total Market	ABC1 Market
CITIBANK	267	12	476		755	12%	16.6%
PROVINCIA		450			450	7.1%	9.9%
AMEX			300		300	4.8%	6.6%
NACION	236				236	3.7%	5.2%
RIO		223			223	3.5%	4.9%
GALICIA		215			215	3.4%	4.7%
NAZ.DEL LAVORO	191				191	3%	4.2%
CREDITO ARGENTINO	76	116			192	3.1%	4.2%
FRANCES		172			172	2.7%	3.8%
QUILMES	76	66			142	2.3%	3.1%
LLOYDS	38	60			98	1.6%	2.1%
BOSTON		98			98	1.6%	2.1%
OTHER BANKS	1,022	453			1,475	23.4%	32.6%
OTHERS				1,753	1,753	27.8	
TOTAL	1,906	1,865	776	1,753	6,300	100%	100%

Exhibit 5 **Payment Tools Usage**

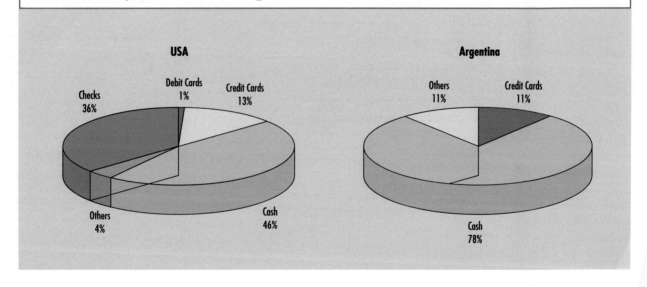

USA

- Checks 36%
- Debit Cards 1%
- Credit Cards 13%
- Others 4%
- Cash 46%

Argentina

- Others 11%
- Credit Cards 11%
- Cash 78%

Exhibit 6   Market Segments

Total Population	**34.3 MM (100%)**
Rural Population	4.46 MM (13%)
Urban Population	**29.84 MM (87%)**
Urban Households	**8.526 M**
ABC1 Households	*859 M*
% of Urban Population	10.5%
Considered Target Market C2	*1.117 M*
ABC1C2 Households	*2.01 M*

Exhibit 7   Socio Economic Segments

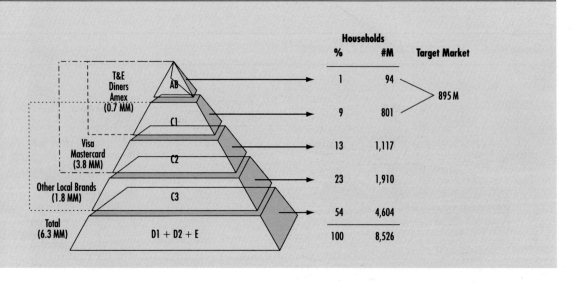